THE COMPLETE ENCYCLOPEDIA OF
ICE HOCKEY REVISED EDITION

The Heroes, Teams, Great Moments and Records of the National Hockey League
Plus the World Hockey Association

THE COMPLETE ENCYCLOPEDIA OF
ICE HOCKEY REVISED EDITION

The Heroes, Teams, Great Moments and Records of the National Hockey League Plus the World Hockey Association

EDITED BY
ZANDER HOLLANDER AND HAL BOCK

An Associated Features Inc. Book
Published by Prentice-Hall, Inc., Englewood Cliffs, N. J.

Credit for endpaper photos:

Front, Barton Silverman
Back, Scotty Kilpatrick

THE COMPLETE ENCYCLOPEDIA OF ICE HOCKEY (REVISED EDITION)
The Heroes, Teams, Great Moments and Records of the National Hockey League
Plus the World Hockey Association

Edited by Zander Hollander and Hal Bock

Prentice-Hall International, Inc., London
Prentice-Hall of Australia, Pty. Ltd., Sydney
Prentice-Hall of Canada, Ltd., Toronto
Prentice-Hall of India Private Ltd., New Delhi
Prentice-Hall of Japan, Inc., Tokyo

10   9   8   7   6   5   4   3   2   1

Library of Congress Catalog Card Number: 73-15019

Hollander, Zander and Bock, Hal
   The Complete Encyclopedia of Ice Hockey
Revised Edition
Englewood Cliffs, N. J.   Prentice-Hall, Inc.

ISBN 0-13-159913-5

To hockey's pioneers and peewees

FOREWORD

When the second Great Expansion of the National Hockey League, with six new teams, took place in the 1967–68 season—the first such expansion having occurred in 1925 and 1926—it marked the beginning of a completely new era in the development of the game.

It also served as a launching platform for a virtual explosion in the quantity of literature published about Hockey. It stimulated the writing of hundreds of articles about every facet of the sport and it inspired books about the history of the game in its first hundred years of evolution and of the outstanding players who have thrilled the ever-increasing hosts of spectators which it has attracted.

Now comes a new approach in *The Complete Encyclopedia of Ice Hockey* —edited by Zander Hollander of Associated Features, and the distinguished sports reporter, Hal Bock of Associated Press.

This is a truly remarkable combination of accurate historical information about the NHL from its inception assembled in chronological order; lively biographical data about many stars of the game both past and present, as well as leading officials; interesting incidents and anecdotes about the Stanley Cup; selections of Great Moments which produced intense thrills and concluding with all the current official individual and team records of the league.

The writing is superb, which, by the generous use of direct quotes, makes the events and the personalities both lively and exciting. The book is extensively illustrated with about two hundred photographs which add to its interest and authenticity.

This is a book for readers—and writers—and is one which will be an indispensable addition to the reference library of every hockey writer and commentator.

The Complete Encyclopedia of Ice Hockey is indeed a truly prestigious addition to the literature of the game.

Clarence S. Campbell
President
National Hockey League

ACKNOWLEDGMENTS

The researching, writing and editing of the *Encyclopedia* in its original edition, and in this revision, was not a two-man job. It could never have been done without the aid of a number of talented hockey experts and believers who deserve recognition for helping achieve the goal.

The editors thank Tim Moriaty of Long Island's *Newsday* for his writing of the chapters on THE PLAYERS and THE OFFICALS; Larry Fox of the New York *Daily News* for HOCKEY'S MOST MEMORABLE MOMENTS, and Ben Olan of The Associated Press for ALL-STAR GAMES and HALL OF FAME, and for his early inspiration in this project.

And we salute statistician Jerry Ahrens, who compiled the monumental ALL-TIME NHL PLAYER REGISTER for the first edition, and Art Friedman for updating it.

Others who helped make the *Encyclopedia* a reality include the National Hockey League's Clarence Campbell, Don Ruck, Ron Andrews, and Bob Casey; Maurice "Lefty" Reid, curator of the Hockey Hall of Fame; John Halligan of the New York Rangers, and the other publicity men of the National Hockey League and World Hockey Association; Bill Chadwick, announcer, ex-referee and member of hockey's Hall of Fame; Red Fisher of the Montreal *Star*; David Rosen, Richard Sherwin and Lee Stowbridge.

An encyclopedia depends in part on what has been written before—in newspapers, magazines, books. Among the books that proved helpful were: *The Trail of the Stanley Cup* by Charles L. Coleman; *50 Years of Hockey* by Bryan McFarlane; *The Stanley Cup* by Henry Roxborough; The Official NHL Guides, and the NCAA Hockey Guides.

INTRODUCTION

In the more than half century since the founding of the National Hockey League, hockey has grown from a simple game on the frozen lakes and ponds of Canada to one played on artificial ice in huge indoor arenas across the whole of North America. Today nearly 30 major league teams—the NHL plus the fledgling World Hockey Association—perform for stadium crowds that reach almost 20,000 and before additional millions on television.

On the amateur level the sport is part of the Olympic program, has its own world championship, and is played by increasing numbers of colleges, secondary schools and peewee teams.

As the slap shots of the shooters got faster, the reflexes of the defensemen and goalies quicker, and the response of the fans more ardent, it was obvious that the sport lacked a single, comprehensive work providing all the information a hockey devotee could want about his favorite game.

This then was our goal in *The Complete Encyclopedia of Ice Hockey*—to include not only the vital facts and figures, but the drama, the history, the heroics that have made the game so special to its growing army of fans.

The *Encyclopedia* covers every NHL season, including the climactic Stanley Cup playoffs and the All-Star Games, plus the WHA. We have profiled the careers of the sport's outstanding goalies, its best forwards and its greatest defensemen. These selections may provoke argument, but controversy, after all, is the lifeblood of any sport. We have tried to capture the excitement and significance of ten of hockey's most memorable moments. And we have cited the members of the Hockey Hall of Fame.

For those who love the sport as much for its voluminous statistics as for its violent action, we have compiled the all-time hockey records. These include not only the well-known feats of the Howes, the Orrs, the Hulls, the Espositos and the Richards, but the complete season and career records of every man who has ever worn the jersey of an NHL or WHA team—vital information on more than 2,000 players.

There is more to the complete picture of hockey than the NHL and WHA, and we have included material on the Olympic Games, world championships, collegians and hockey's minor leagues—another part of the ice.

Zander Hollander and Hal Bock

CONTENTS

THE COMPLETE ENCYCLOPEDIA OF

ICE HOCKEY REVISED EDITION

The Heroes, Teams, Great Moments and Records of the National Hockey League Plus the World Hockey Association

A Montreal Canadiens' practice session in 1914.

1 HOW IT ALL BEGAN 1917–1924

The family tree of the National Hockey League has its roots in the years around the turn of the century with branches spreading from the Eastern provinces of Quebec and Ontario clear across the vast prairie land of Canada to the west and British Columbia.

It is rich with legendary hockey names—Frank and Lester Patrick, Edouard "Newsy" Lalonde, Fred "Cyclone" Taylor, Frank Nighbor, Joe Malone—men who built the game from pastime to profession and nurtured it from the frozen ponds in small mining towns to packed big-city arenas.

Hockey began as a seven-man game with upright posts embedded in the ice for goals. There were no nets, no blue lines, no red lines and no face-off circles on the ice. But by the time the pioneers got through with it, the game closely resembled the sport we know today.

The Amateur Hockey Association of Canada and the Ontario Hockey Association were among the first organized hockey leagues in Canada. Players and teams freely shifted from league to league in those early years.

Finally, in 1910, there were two major leagues operating in competition with each other. The Canadian Hockey Association listed Ottawa, Quebec and three Montreal teams—the Shamrocks, the Nationals and All-Montreal. The National Hockey Association had teams in Cobalt, Haileybury, Renfrew and two in Montreal—the Wanderers and the Canadiens.

The bidding war for players was spirited. The Patrick brothers signed with Renfrew for $3,000 each and the same club lured Cyclone Taylor away from Ottawa and offered an Edmonton player $1,000 to come east for a single game.

Aware that the war would ruin them, the two leagues came to an understanding and merged into the single National Hockey Association, a seven-team league composed of Renfrew, Cobalt, Haileybury, Ottawa and three Montreal teams, the Shamrocks, the Wanderers and the Canadiens.

The Patrick brothers went west that year and organized their own league—the Pacific Coast Hockey Association with franchises in Vancouver, Victoria and New Westminster. The Patricks were veterans of the teamhopping in the East and started player raids of their own to lure established stars to their new league. Many, including Taylor, Lalonde and Nighbor, went west.

With top talent migrating to it, the Pacific Coast Hockey Association gained stature and eventually a series was started, pitting the PCHA and NHA champions against each other in a playoff for the Stanley Cup.

In 1912, the NHA introduced six-man hockey and added numbers to

1

players' jerseys. A year before, hockey's traditional two 30-minute periods had been switched to three periods of 20 minutes each. Slowly but surely, the sport was changing.

In 1913, the PCHA introduced blue lines, dividing the ice into three sections. It was the same year that, for the first time, assists as well as goals were credited to a player's scoring totals.

A year later, the NHA followed suit, crediting assists as well as goals. The Eastern circuit also allowed referees to start dropping the puck on face-offs instead of placing it between the two sticks, thus saving a lot of bruised knuckles.

And in the West, a referee named Mickey Ion, destined to become one of the greatest officials in the history of the game, began picking an All-Star team—a custom which added considerable interest to the game.

In 1914, Canada went to war and with the conflict came problems for hockey. Many players were called up to serve in the Army and some were given deferments conditional upon their not playing hockey.

Train schedules were disrupted causing cancellation of some games. The NHA clubs turned over the entire proceeds of their exhibition games to patriotic causes and a portion of the regular season income to the Red Cross.

By 1917, the NHA had evolved into a six-team circuit composed of the Montreal Wanderers, Montreal Canadiens, Ottawa, Toronto, Quebec and the Northern Fusiliers—an Army team representing the 228th Battalion of the Canadian Army.

When the 228th was ordered overseas, it was forced to withdraw from the league, leaving five teams and an unbalanced schedule. After considerable bickering, it was decided that Eddie Livingstone's Toronto team would also be dropped and its players redistributed.

There is some evidence that Livingstone was not the most popular man among his fellow owners and it was their desire to rid themselves of him that led to the creation of a new league—the National Hockey League.

1917–18

Tired of intra-league squabbling, much of which had centered around the Toronto franchise and its combative owner, Eddie Livingstone, NHA owners met in Montreal's Windsor Hotel on November 22, 1917 to settle their problems once and for all.

Their solution was a simple one. They simply created their own league and left Livingstone in the NHA all by himself. The new circuit would be called the National Hockey League, with franchises going to Ottawa, the Montreal Wanderers, Montreal Canadiens and Toronto, provided Livingstone was not included in that team's operation. Quebec was also granted a franchise, but chose not to play that first year and its players were

Vancouver's Fred "Cyclone" Taylor won the Pacific Coast Hockey League scoring
championship in 1917–18.   HOCKEY HALL OF FAME

divided among the other four teams in what turned out to be the NHL's first intra-league draft.

Major Frank Robinson, president of the NHA, bowed out and Frank Calder, secretary-treasurer of the NHA, was elected president of the new league. A 22-game schedule, running from December 19 through March 10, was adopted.

Joe Malone, Quebec's best player, wound up with the Canadiens and on opening night he scored five goals as Montreal whipped Ottawa 7–4. Malone, playing in only 20 games, won the first NHL scoring crown with 44 goals—a pace that has never been matched.

The Wanderers opened at home with a 10–9 victory over Toronto in a game that attracted only 700 fans. That was the only victory the Wanderers ever managed in the NHL. They dropped five straight games and then, on January 2, 1918, a $150,000 fire burned Westmount Arena to the ground, leaving them without a home rink.

The Canadiens, who had shared the Arena with the Wanderers, moved into the 3,250-seat Jubilee rink for the remainder of the season but the Wanderers dropped out of the league with owner Sam Lichtenhein apparently happy to be out of what had been a losing venture.

A major rule change was adopted during the NHL's first season that was to affect the art of goaltending forever. Until then, goalies had been forced to stand up to defend their nets and in 1914 a rule was added by the NHA imposing $2 fines on goalies who sprawled on the ice to make a save. Now the rule was changed and goalies were permitted to assume any position they wished.

If the rule helped, the statistics don't show it. The legendary Georges Vezina of the Canadiens led the league with 84 goals allowed in 21 games —a 4.0 average that is not very good by today's standards. In addition to Malone, the top shooters were Ottawa's Cy Denneny with 36 goals in 22 games, Reg Noble of Toronto with 28 in 20 and Newsy Lalonde of the Canadiens, who had 23 goals in 14 games.

Frank Calder was appointed president of the newly-formed National Hockey League.   HOCKEY HALL OF FAME

Joe Malone of the Canadiens was the first NHL scoring champion, with 44 goals in 20 games in 1917–18.   HOCKEY HALL OF FAME (TUROFSKY)

The Canadiens, first-half champions, and Toronto, winners of the second half, played off for the NHL title with Toronto taking the two-game, total-goals playoff, 10–7.

In the West, the Pacific Coast Association, cut back to three teams by the departure of Spokane, had a tight race almost all season. But Seattle finally finished two games in front of Vancouver and four up on Portland.

Vancouver's Cyclone Taylor led the league with 32 goals, including one game-winner against Seattle scored with his back to the goal. It was a routine play for Taylor, who boasted that he once scored a goal in the NHA by skating backwards through the whole Ottawa team.

In the two-game, total-goals playoff between the top two teams, Vancouver defeated Seattle three goals to two. The Millionaires traveled east to face Toronto for the Stanley Cup and split the first four games. Then the Arenas captured the deciding fifth game and the Cup, 2–1, as Corbett Denneny scored the winning goal.

1918–19

The demise of the Wanderers the year before had left the NHL with just three teams—the Montreal Canadiens, Toronto Arenas and Ottawa Senators. There was, though, a possibility that Quebec, which had not operated in 1917–18, might join the league for its second season.

President Frank Calder, reelected for a five-year term, drew up two schedules for the new season—one for a three-team league, one for a four-team league.

When Quebec's ownership failed to meet an NHL deadline for declaring its intentions, the league suspended the franchise and went with the three-team schedule. With the end of World War I, it was expected that many players would be returning from the Army. But few were discharged in time and when the season started, the teams had much the same personnel as the year before.

The NHL adopted several important rule changes including the adoption of the PCHA's blue line idea. This divided the ice surface into three zones with forward passing permitted in the 40-foot wide center area. Kicking the puck was also allowed and assists were added to regular season statistics. Penalty rules were reshuffled. A minor penalty would leave a team shorthanded for three minutes, a major penalty would cost five minutes and for a match penalty, no substitute would be allowed for the penalized player.

The 18-game regular season started on December 21 with Ottawa beating Montreal, 5–2. The Canadiens bounced back to lose only two more games and captured the first half championship. Ottawa, a so-so 5–5 in the first half, won seven of eight games and took the second half title.

Edouard "Newsy" Lalonde, player-manager of the Canadiens, won the scoring crown in 1918–19 with 21 goals.
HOCKEY HALL OF FAME (TUROFSKY)

Toronto, heavily favored after winning the Stanley Cup the year before, started in reverse, dropping six of its first seven games. The Arenas never righted themselves and finished in last place in both halves.

Newsy Lalonde, the Canadiens' fiery player-manager, won the scoring title with 21 goals and Ottawa's Clint Benedict was the top goalie with two shutouts and a 3.0 average in 18 games.

In the playoff between the Canadiens and Ottawa, Montreal dominated. Lalonde's team won the first three games, dropped the fourth and then wrapped up the series in the fifth game. The format had been changed from total goals in two games to a best-of-seven series.

In the PCHA, Portland's franchise was transferred to Victoria with Lester Patrick set as the team's playing manager. Lester's younger brother, Frank, was serving his sixth term as president of the league.

Seattle beat Vancouver in the opening game and held onto the league lead for six weeks before the defending champion Vancouver Millionaires took over. Vancouver won the regular season title by one game and Cyclone Taylor again was the scoring champ with 23 goals—one more than Seattle's Bernie Morris.

There was a celebrated fight between Cully Wilson of Seattle and Vancouver's mild-mannered Mickey MacKay in which Wilson's cross check broke MacKay's jaw. The incident cost Wilson a $50 fine, match penalty and eventual suspension from the league.

In the two-game, total-goals playoff, Seattle defeated Vancouver, 7–5, scoring six goals in the first game. That set up the Stanley Cup series against Montreal.

The NHL champion Canadiens dropped two of the first three games, played a scoreless tie in the fourth and then tied the series by winning the fifth. But the deciding sixth game was never played. The Canadiens' ranks had been shredded by the great influenza epidemic which covered the continent. Bad Joe Hall, a defenseman, was hospitalized, and four

The Canadiens' Joe Hall, a star defenseman, was a tragic victim of influenza in the spring of 1919. HOCKEY HALL OF FAME

others, including Newsy Lalonde, were confined to their hotel by the disease. The series was ended with no Cup winner—the only time in history that has happened. Hall never recovered. He died in a Seattle hospital.

1919–20

The player shuttle created between East and West when the Patrick brothers organized the Pacific Coast Hockey Association was in full swing.

Moving west from the NHL was a youngster used sparingly the year before by Toronto. But Jack Adams would one day be back and make his mark as a player, coach and executive in the National League.

Alf Skinner and Rusty Crawford also jumped to the PCHA while Cully Wilson, a rough, tough right wing, who was banned from the coast league for his overly aggressive play, showed up in the NHL with Toronto. His style stayed the same and he was the most penalized player in the league that season, spending 79 minutes sitting out infractions.

Toronto's management, disturbed over the team's disappointing performance the year before, undertook a rebuilding job. The first step was to change the club's nickname from the Arenas to the St. Patricks, perhaps in an attempt to attract the luck of the Irish.

The Quebec Bulldogs operated their franchise and reclaimed players who had been assigned to other teams for the NHL's first two seasons. The most dominant was Joe Malone, who had won the scoring title in the league's first year of operation and now returned to Quebec from the Montreal Canadiens.

Malone was the standout on what was a dismal Quebec team. On January 31 he went on a tear of seven goals in a single game against Toronto, setting an NHL record that still stands. He almost matched that performance a little more than one month later when he scored six times against Ottawa in the final game of the season.

Malone finished the season with 39 goals and nine assists for 48 points and his second scoring title in three years. But despite his brilliance, Quebec won only four games all year and finished last. Newsy Lalonde of the Canadiens gave Malone a run for the scoring title with 37 goals and six assists for 43 points.

Ottawa's Clint Benedict was the top goalie, posting a 2.7 goals against average and five shutouts for the 24-game season. No other netminder in the league recorded a single shutout that year.

With World War I over, Canadians began paying more attention to hockey and crowds began growing in size. On February 21, Ottawa's game at Toronto attracted 8,500—a record.

Ottawa won both halves of the NHL's split schedule, eliminating the need for the playoffs. The Senators would represent the NHL in the battle

Seattle's Frank Foyston won the PCHA scoring title in 1919–20.
HOCKEY HALL OF FAME (TUROFSKY)

for the Stanley Cup against either Seattle, the PCHA champion, or second-place Vancouver. Frank Foyston of Seattle had won the PCHA scoring crown and he led a 6–0 romp in the second game that gave Seattle the two-game, total-goals playoff over the Millionaires, 7–3.

Seattle traveled east to play Ottawa for the Cup but when it arrived, there was a problem. Seattle's red, white and green uniforms closely resembled Ottawa's red, white and black. The conflict was resolved when the Senators agreed to change to white sweaters.

Ottawa took the Cup in five games—the last two played on Toronto's artificial ice after hot weather turned Ottawa's natural surface to slush.

1920–21

Quebec's dismal showing the season before left the team's owners disenchanted and the Bulldogs faded from the NHL picture for the second and final time.

Percy Thompson of Hamilton, Ont., purchased the franchise for $5,000, moved the club to Hamilton and changed the nickname to the Tigers. It was obvious that the same players who had failed in Quebec would not do much better in Hamilton and an SOS was sent out to the other teams in the league, asking for player help.

The last time that had happened was in 1917, the NHL's first season, when the undermanned Montreal Wanderers appealed for help. The other clubs refused then and the result was Montreal's eventual drop-out from the league. It was perhaps with this in mind that the NHL responded favorably to Hamilton's plight.

Toronto contributed Goldie Prodgers, Joe Matte and Cecil "Babe" Dye, Montreal ticketed Bill Couture to the Tigers and Joe Malone led the leftovers from Quebec which included Eddie Carpenter, George Carey and Tom McCarthy.

The makeshift team stung the Canadiens with a 5–0 shutout in its home opener on December 22. Dye scored two goals and Toronto promptly reclaimed him from Hamilton and shipped Mickey Roach to take his place with the Tigers.

The move turned out to be a smart one because Dye scored more goals than any one in the league, finishing with 35. He had 37 total points, four less than Newsy Lalonde of the Canadiens, whose 33 goals and eight assists for 41 points led the league. It was Lalonde's second scoring title and both times he won because his assists gave him more total points than the leading goal scorer.

After the opening victory, Hamilton slipped badly and finished in the cellar for both halves of the season, managing only six victories in 24 games. Ottawa won the first-half title with an 8–2 record, three games better than Toronto's 5–5. But the Senators, saddled by a seven-game losing streak, slipped to third in the second half, behind both Toronto and the Canadiens.

Despite the second-half slump, Ottawa's Clint Benedict finished as the top goalie with a 3.1 goals against average and two shutouts. In the NHL playoffs against second half champ Toronto, Benedict and the Senators regained their touch. Ottawa shut out the St. Pats 5–0 in the opener and came back with a 2–0 whitewashing to sweep the series.

Vancouver won the PCHA title by one half game over Seattle—the difference being a 4–4 tie which Seattle played at Victoria on March 4, Moose Johnson night. Johnson, a veteran defenseman, was honored before the game and then the teams played through three overtimes before agreeing to end the game as a tie.

In the two-game playoff, Vancouver romped, outscoring Seattle, 13–2. The Millionaires then met Ottawa for the Stanley Cup. The opening game attracted a record 11,000 fans. The teams split the first four games and then Ottawa won the fifth match and the Cup, 2–1.

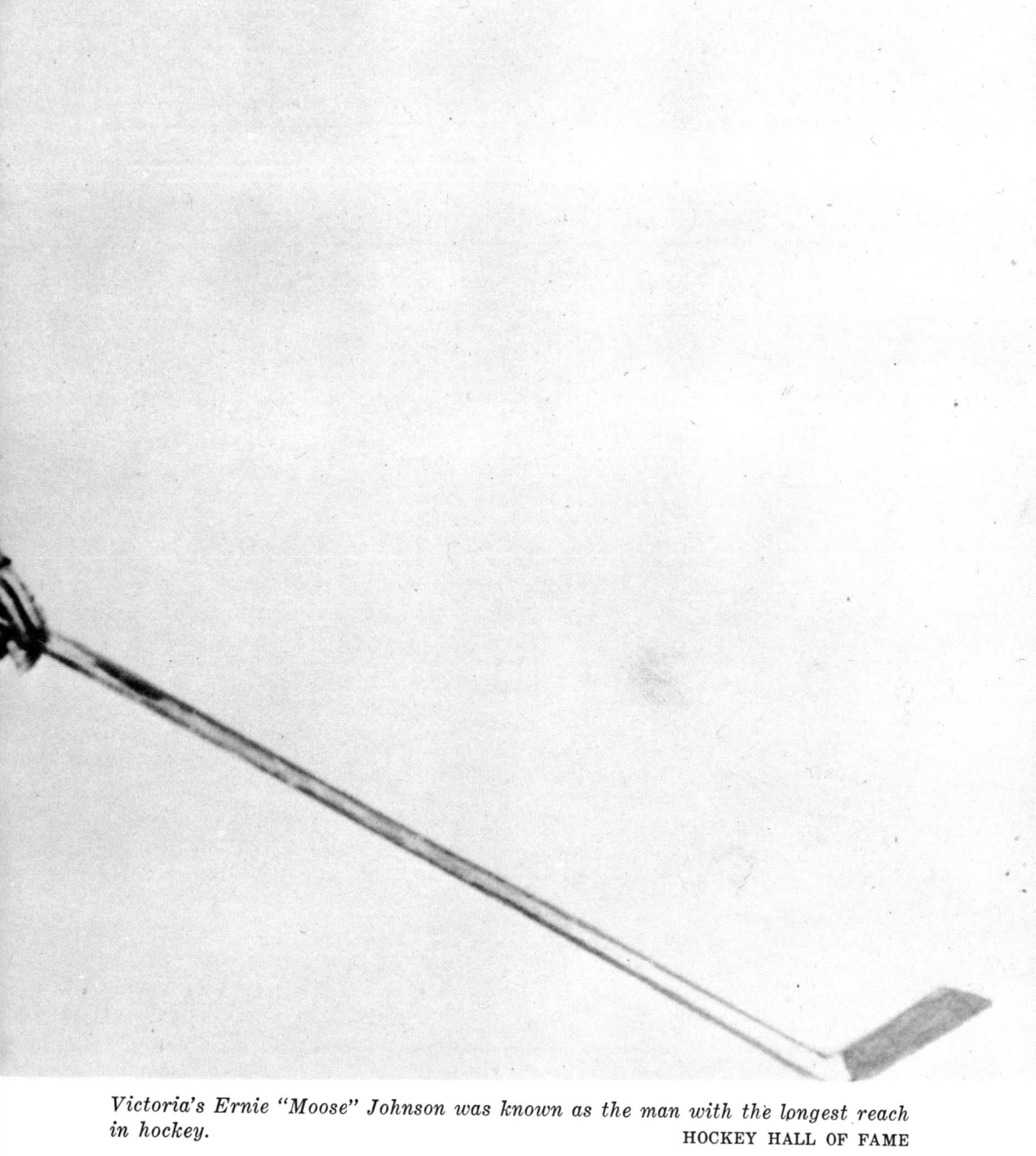

Victoria's Ernie "Moose" Johnson was known as the man with the longest reach in hockey.
HOCKEY HALL OF FAME

Odie Cleghorn (right) was a star forward on the Canadiens and his older brother, Sprague, played defense on the same team. HOCKEY HALL OF FAME (TUROFSKY)

1921–22

This was a year of major changes for hockey in both the East and the West. The NHL dropped the split schedule and its first and second-half champions, substituting instead a single schedule with playoffs between the top two teams. The PCHA introduced the penalty shot which was awarded to a player who was interfered with after breaking in alone on the goalie. There was a new league in the West and some new owners in the East.

George Kennedy, one of the founders of the NHL and owner of the Montreal club, died in 1921 and his widow sold the club to Joe Cattarinich and Leo Dandurand for $11,000—about $1,989,000 less than it would cost for a franchise 45 years later. Cattarinich and Dandurand were anxious to get Sprague Cleghorn, a defenseman who had starred for the Wanderers, back to Montreal and they accomplished this in a roundabout fashion.

The NHL, still trying to help the Hamilton club, devised the plan which eventually brought Cleghorn to the Canadiens. Players with the Wanderers when the club dissolved in 1918, said the NHL, became the property of the league. Cleghorn was one of these players and the NHL simply claimed him from Ottawa and assigned him to Hamilton. Provided with this windfall, the Tigers promptly offered Cleghorn to the Canadiens, who, they knew, were anxious to get him.

A neat package was arranged with Billy Couture and Cleghorn going to Montreal in exchange for Harry Mummery, Amos Arbour and Cully Wilson. It was the first major, multiple-player trade in the NHL.

The trade reunited Sprague Cleghorn with his brother, Odie, and the two ran wild one week in January. Each scored four goals on January 14 against Hamilton and they combined for six goals against Ottawa a few days later. Interestingly, this spree came shortly after Newsy Lalonde walked out on the team, claiming he couldn't get along with his new bosses. Frank Calder, president of the league, mediated the dispute and after missing four games, Lalonde returned. But his days in Montreal were numbered.

On February 1, Sprague Cleghorn almost wiped out the Ottawa team singlehandedly. He cut Eddie Gerard and Cy Denneny and charged Frank Nighbor. All three Ottawa players missed two games because of injuries and Cleghorn drew a match foul plus a $15 fine. Ottawa police tried to arrest him for assault in the wake of his one-man war.

Despite Cleghorn's rambunctious play, Montreal finished third behind Ottawa and Toronto. Harry "Punch" Broadbent of Ottawa established a record with at least one goal in 16 consecutive games and a total of 25 during the streak. He finished as the leading scorer with 32 goals and 46 points.

Toronto defeated Ottawa, 5–4, in the first game of the total goals playoff and then battled the Senators to a scoreless tie in the second to clinch the Stanley Cup berth.

Harry "Punch" Broadbent of Ottawa set an NHL record by scoring in 16 consecutive games in 1921–22.

HOCKEY HALL OF FAME

In the West, Jack Adams, playing center for Vancouver, led the PCHA in scoring with 25 goals. But Seattle, with Frank Foyston and Jim Riley scoring 16 goals each, finished in first place.

In Victoria, a combative goalie named Norm Fowler was thrown out of two games within 10 days for fighting and the team's manager, Lester Patrick, made his debut as a goalie.

Vancouver won the playoff with goalie Hugh Lehman turning in a pair of 1–0 shutouts over Seattle.

A new league, the Western Canada Hockey League, with clubs in Calgary, Edmonton, Saskatoon and Regina, had been formed and its players included Red Dutton, Bill Cook, and Dick Irvin. Regina finished second but knocked off pennant winner Edmonton in the playoff and challenged Vancouver for the right to represent the West in the Stanley Cup series against Toronto. Regina took the first game, 2–1, but Vancouver recovered with a 4–0 victory in the second game to clinch the playoff.

In the Stanley Cup series, Vancouver and Toronto split the first four games and then Babe Dye fired four goals, pacing a 5–1 St. Pat's victory that clinched the series and the Cup in the fifth contest.

1922–23

The split between Newsy Lalonde and Leo Dandurand could not be mended and eventually Montreal dealt its great star to Saskatoon of the new Western League. In return, the Canadiens received the rights to an

Aurel Joliat was a little man who figured in a big trade.   HOCKEY HALL OF FAME

amateur named Aurel Joliat, a slightly built left wing who belonged to Saskatoon but was playing with Iroquois Falls.

Joliat weighed about 140 pounds and was hardly an imposing looking athlete. The thought that Montreal had traded one of hockey's early greats for this little guy placed an extra burden on Joliat. But he was equal to it and was to develop into an outstanding NHL player.

In another trade, Montreal sent Bert Corbeau and Edmond Bouchard to Hamilton for Joe Malone, then in the twilight of his career. Vancouver swapped Jack Adams to Toronto for Corbett Denneny.

Joliat scored two goals in his first game for Montreal but Babe Dye had five for Toronto and the St. Pats beat the Canadiens, 7–2. It was the start of a fine season for Dye, who was to win the scoring title with 26 goals and 11 assists for 37 points.

Ottawa won the regular-season title, edging Montreal with Toronto finishing third. Clint Benedict again led the goalies with a 2.3 average and four shutouts in 24 games. It was the fifth straight year that he was the top goaltender.

Perhaps the most significant event of the season took place in Toronto's Mutual Street Arena in March of 1923. That was when a young man named Foster Hewitt, sitting in an airless glass booth erected in three seat spaces and talking into an upright telephone, broadcast radio's first hockey game.

It was the start of a new era for the sport.

In the playoffs, Ottawa blanked the Canadiens, 2–0, in the first game and won the Cup berth on the basis of total goals although it lost the second game, 2–1. Billy Couture and Sprague Cleghorn played viciously in the opener, injuring several Ottawa players with their sticks and elbows. Owner Leo Dandurand was so disturbed at the display that he suspended

Toronto's Babe Dye scored five goals in one game and won the 1922–23 scoring title.

HOCKEY HALL OF FAME (TUROFSKY)

both of them for the second game, without waiting for the league to act.

Lalonde flourished in the dual role of player-manager with Saskatoon and led the Western League in scoring with 29 goals in 26 games. But his team finished last, with Edmonton taking the regular season title as well as the two-game, total goals playoff over Regina.

The PCHA eliminated the position of rover and adopted six-man hockey which had been played in the East for some time. Victoria's Frank Fredrickson led the scorers with 41 goals in 30 games but Vancouver finished first and beat Victoria in the playoffs.

Ottawa, its ranks thinned by injuries, went west for the Stanley Cup playoffs and eliminated Vancouver in four games and then took Edmonton in two straight to clinch it. After watching the gritty show put on by the undermanned Senators, Frank Patrick, president of the PCHA, called them the greatest team he had ever seen.

1923–24

Until this year, hockey players had no individual trophy for which to compete. There was the scoring championship, of course, and the satisfaction of playing for the Stanley Cup winner for some, but no single award that a player could go after and call his own.

Ottawa's Frank Nighbor won the NHL's first Hart Trophy as the Most Valuable Player in 1923–24.

HOCKEY HALL OF FAME

This all changed in 1924 when Dr. David Hart, father of Cecil Hart, a manager-coach of the Montreal Canadiens, contributed a trophy to the league. The Hart Trophy was to be awarded to the Most Valuable Player in the league and the first one went to Frank Nighbor, Ottawa's smooth skating center.

Nighbor, whose poke check repeatedly relieved opponents of the puck, won the award by a single vote over Sprague Cleghorn, the Canadiens' boisterous defenseman.

It was ironic that Nighbor and Cleghorn were the top contestants for the first Hart Trophy. Their styles were a study in contrasts. Nighbor was a gentlemanly sort who rarely was involved in trouble on the ice while Cleghorn seemed to cause a ruckus wherever he went.

In fact, Sprague's rough play caused an NHL meeting at mid-season to consider his suspension. The Ottawa club claimed Cleghorn was trying to injure opponents deliberately, citing a spearing incident against Cy Denneny. The charges were rejected by the league and in Montreal's next game against Ottawa, Cleghorn charged Lionel Hitchman into the boards and earned a one-game suspension.

Ottawa's Denneny won the scoring crown with 22 goals despite a bizarre experience near the end of the season. The Ottawa club was on its way to Montreal for a game when the team train became snowbound. The

Cy Denneny of Ottawa fell down a well, but he climbed out and won the 1923–24 scoring crown.
HOCKEY HALL OF FAME (TUROFSKY)

Senators were stuck all night and Denneny, scrounging about for some food, somehow fell down a well. Luckily he emerged without injury. The game, of course, had to be postponed.

Georges Vezina of Montreal led the goalies with a 2.0 average and three shutouts, barely edging Clint Benedict. Ottawa took the regular-season title but Montreal beat the Senators in the total-goals playoff, 5–2, with a newcomer, Howie Morenz, starring.

In the PCHA, Seattle dropped eight straight games but came out of the slump and managed to win the regular-season crown. Mickey MacKay of Vancouver led the scorers with 23 goals and teammate Hugh Lehman was the top goalie with a 2.7 average for the 30-game season.

Calgary took the Western title and Bill Cook of Saskatoon was the scoring champ with 26 goals. Regina's Red McCusker had a 2.2 average, best among the goaltenders.

Vancouver eliminated Seattle in the PCHA playoff and Calgary ousted Regina in the Western series. Then Calgary earned a bye into the Stanley Cup finals by beating Vancouver in the three-game series before both teams came east to face Montreal.

The Canadiens whipped Vancouver 3–2 and 2–1 in the semifinals and then defeated Calgary for the Cup, winning 6–1 and 3–0.

II   THE YANKS ARE COMING 1924–1929

By 1924, the four-team National Hockey League had taken hold and fans were attracted to games in ever larger numbers. Hockey's popularity had grown to the point where NHL brass was seriously considering expansion into the United States. The Pacific Coast Hockey Association had been operating American franchises at Seattle and Portland successfully and there was reason to believe that a team in the Eastern U.S. would enjoy similar success.

There was no problem in finding a market for expanding the prospering league. Bids for franchises came from New York, Boston, Philadelphia and Pittsburgh. And Montreal interests were seeking a second team for that city. The league decided to move slowly on expansion, a policy that would continue for many years.

The groundwork for adding new teams was laid in 1924 when Thomas J. Duggan was granted options to operate two United States franchises. Duggan interested Boston sportsman Charles Adams and on October 12, 1924, final plans were made at Montreal's Windsor Hotel.

Adams would operate the Boston team with Art Ross, an NHL referee, chosen to manage the club. Donat Raymond and Thomas Strachan were granted a second Montreal franchise and New York would get a team for the 1926 season. The price for a new franchise was $15,000.

The league was clearly moving forward and the best proof of that was to look at the stars. Men like Newsy Lalonde and Joe Malone, who had come to the NHL as established players, were gone and in their place was a new breed—players like Aurel Joliat and Howie Morenz, who started their professional careers in the NHL and established themselves as first-line players in that league.

But with expansion came problems for the National Hockey League and its struggle to survive was to undergo a severe test in its very first year of international operation.

1924–25

With the addition of the new Boston team called the Bruins and the Montreal Maroons, the NHL also expanded its schedule, upping the total from 24 to 30 games. And this change was to cause a minor rebellion and a player strike late in the season.

Hamilton's Red Green, one of three players who scored five goals in a single game this season, was at the center of the squabble. The Tigers

Reg Noble, who later became a Hall of Famer, had to trade this Toronto St. Pats' uniform for a new Montreal Maroons' jersey.

HOCKEY HALL OF FAME (TUROFSKY)

had won the regular-season race and under a new playoff plan, the first-place finishers were to meet the winners of a series between the second- and third-place teams.

But Green, acting as a spokesman for the Hamilton players, pointed out that he had signed a two-year contract the season before which called for a 24-game schedule and that now he had already played 30 and was being asked to play even more for the same salary. Green and his teammates wanted $200 each to play against the winner of the semifinal series between Toronto and the Montreal Canadiens.

Frank Calder, the NHL president, refused to yield to the strikers and declared that the semifinal winner would represent the league in the Stanley Cup playoffs. On April 17, the NHL suspended the Hamilton players and fined them $200 each for their action.

The Maroons and Bruins assembled teams composed mostly of amateurs and old pros. Montreal came up with Clint Benedict and Harry Broadbent from Ottawa, Louis Berlinquette from Saskatoon and Reg Noble from Toronto, among others. Alf Skinner, Bernie Morris and Norm Fowler, all lured from the West, turned up with Boston.

The Bruins opened at home with a victory over the Maroons but then dropped 11 straight games. The Maroons inaugurated their new home, the Montreal Forum, by losing to their crosstown rivals, the Canadiens.

22

Toronto's Babe Dye won the scoring title with 38 goals and 44 points and Georges Vezina of the Canadiens was the top goalie with a 1.9 average and five shutouts. Billy Burch of Hamilton won the Hart Trophy as the league's MVP and a new award donated by Lady Byng, the wife of Canada's governor general, went to Frank Nighbor, the Hart winner the year before. The Lady Byng Trophy was awarded the player who best combined sportsmanship with effective play.

The Canadiens beat Toronto 3–2 and 2–0 in the playoffs and because of Hamilton's stand, Montreal advanced to the Stanley Cup finals against Victoria, which had joined the WCHL with Vancouver when Seattle bowed out of the PCHA, leaving that league with just two teams.

Victoria finished third behind Saskatoon and Calgary and knocked both clubs off in the WCHL playoffs, with Jack Walker starring. Victoria beat Montreal in the first two playoff games as Walker scored four goals. The Canadiens won the third game and then Walker set up two goals by Frank Fredrickson that gave the Westerners the fourth game and the Cup.

1925–26

The Hamilton club was sold to a New York group which paid $75,000 for the franchise. The team was renamed the Americans and rented a new sports palace, Madison Square Garden, for its home ice.

Albert "Battleship" Leduc, a Canadiens' defenseman, scored against the New York Americans on the opening night of a new Madison Square Garden in 1925.   HOCKEY HALL OF FAME (RICE)

The Amerks drew 17,000 fans on opening night in the Garden and big league hockey became an instant success in New York.

A seventh team was added to the circuit with Odie Cleghorn, the long-time Canadiens' star, named to the NHL Board of Governors to represent the new team, the Pittsburgh Pirates.

Cleghorn would also serve as playing-manager of the Pirates. The team, made up essentially of players from the United States Amateur League, fared remarkably well, with Cleghorn's rapid line changes always keeping fresh legs on the ice.

Pittsburgh spoiled the home opener of the Canadiens with a 1–0 victory and Montreal lost more than just a hockey game in that one. Midway through the game, the Canadiens' great goalie, Georges Vezina, collapsed on the ice from a high fever. Vezina, who had never missed a game in 15 years with the Canadiens, was suffering from tuberculosis and died four months later.

There were new stars around the league. Ottawa's Alex Connell had an amazing 15 shutouts and 1.2 goals against average in 36 games and the Maroons introduced Nels Stewart, who played both center and defense, and won the scoring title with 34 goals in his rookie season. Stewart also captured the Hart Trophy and Frank Nighbor took the Lady Byng Trophy for the second consecutive year.

Ottawa won the regular-season title with two of the league's newest teams, the Maroons and the Pirates, finishing second and third. Boston

Rookie Nels Stewart of the Montreal Maroons won the scoring championship and MVP trophy in 1925–26.

HOCKEY HALL OF FAME

was fourth and the New York Americans fifth, leaving the bottom two spots to Toronto and the Canadiens.

The Maroons eliminated Pittsburgh in the two-game, total-goals playoff, 6–4, and then whipped champion Ottawa as Clint Benedict shut out his ex-mates, 1–0, in the final game.

In the West, the troubles of the old PCHA seemed to spread to the WCHL. Regina's franchise was shifted to Portland and the name Canada was dropped from the league's title, making it the Western Hockey League.

Bill Cook of Saskatoon and Dick Irvin of Portland tied for the scoring lead with 31 goals apiece and a youngster named Eddie Shore made quite a name for himself on defense with Edmonton, which edged Saskatoon for the regular-season title. Third-place Victoria eliminated Saskatoon and Edmonton in the playoffs and advanced to the Stanley Cup finals against the Montreal Maroons.

Nels Stewart and Clint Benedict dominated the final series as the Maroons captured the Cup. Stewart scored six goals in four games and Benedict shut out the Westerners three times.

The 1926 series was to mark the last time any league other than the NHL competed for the Stanley Cup. The floundering WHL folded its tents. Its players drifted east to the still-expanding National League, which was getting ready to add three more American teams.

1926–27

Writers called this era the Golden Age of Sports, and the NHL was about to make itself a solid part of the scene which included baseball's Babe Ruth, tennis' Bill Tilden, football's Red Grange, boxing's Jack Dempsey and golf's Bobby Jones.

The success of the New York Americans at Madison Square Garden inspired the Garden owners to seek a franchise of their own, and they were awarded one. The team, called the Rangers, was one of three new clubs added to the NHL, the others being the Detroit Cougars and the Chicago Black Hawks. With the Western and Pacific Coast Leagues now defunct, there were plenty of players available.

The 10-team league was split into two divisions, the American and the Canadian. The four Canadian teams—Ottawa, Toronto, the Montreal Maroons and Montreal Canadiens and New York's Americans—composed the Canadian Division. The American Division listed the three new teams, the Rangers, Detroit and Chicago along with Pittsburgh and Boston.

The players came from professional as well as amateur ranks. A package deal was arranged with the Western loop in which whole rosters of players became available for a total of $25,000 per club.

Bill Cook and his brother Bun both wound up in New York where Conn Smythe was assembling the Rangers. Eddie Shore went to Boston, where

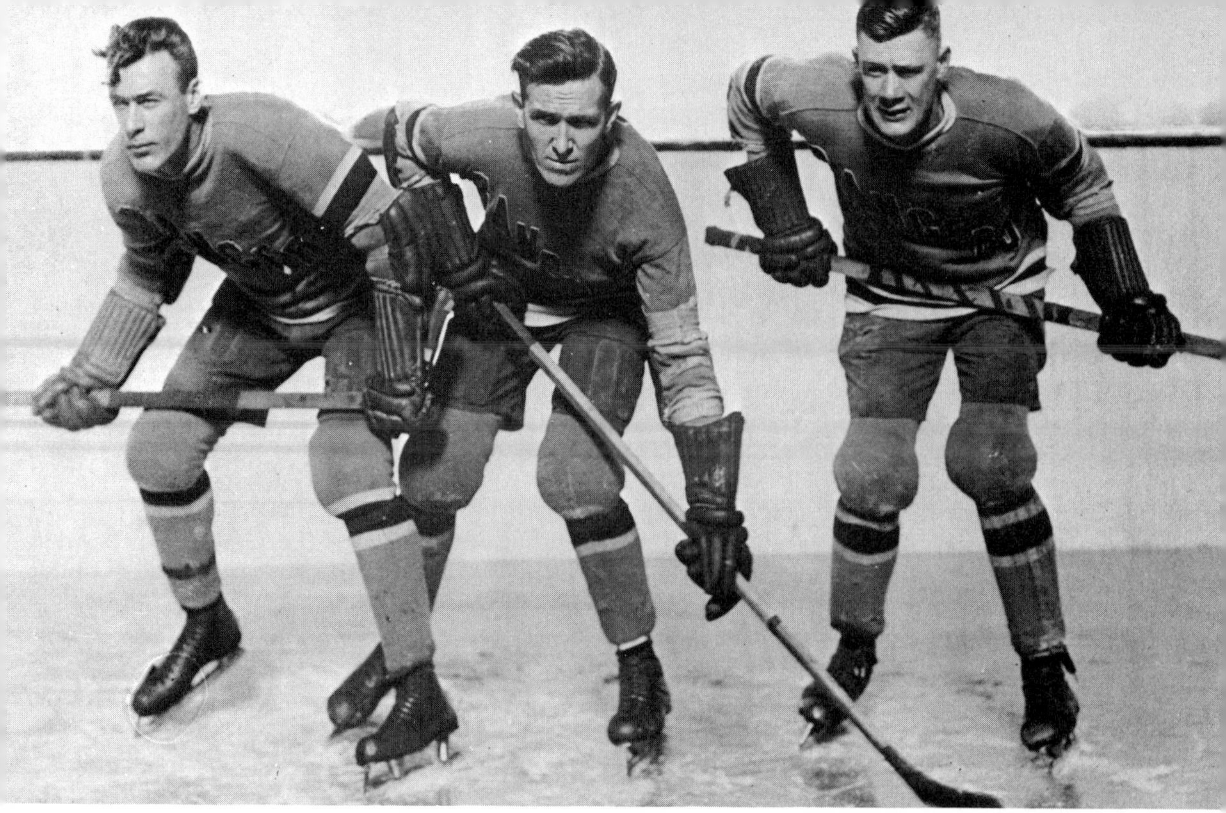

The great Ranger line: left to right, Bill Cook, Frank Boucher and Bun Cook.
HOCKEY HALL OF FAME

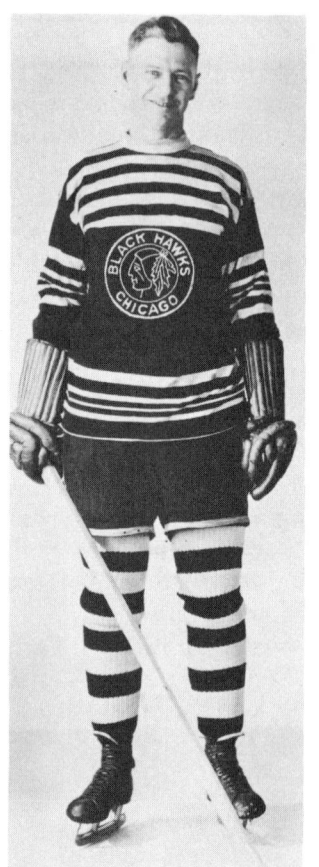

Duncan "Mickey" MacKay came from the west to join the Chicago Black Hawks.
HOCKEY HALL OF FAME

he would become perhaps the greatest defenseman in NHL history. Detroit came up with Frank Foyston and Frank Fredrickson while Dick Irvin and Mickey MacKay landed in Chicago.

Smythe had a falling out with the Garden management and was dismissed before the Rangers ever played a game. Lester Patrick was brought in from the West to run the New York team. Smythe went home to his native Toronto, determined to get even with the New York brass. The last-place St. Pats were in trouble and up for sale and Smythe raised $160,000 and made the deal. The club's name was changed to the Maple Leafs and flourished under Smythe's shrewd control.

In Montreal, the owners of the Canadiens donated a trophy to the league in the memory of Georges Vezina to be awarded annually to the goaltender on the team which was the lowest-scored-upon club in the league. George Hainsworth, Vezina's successor with the Canadiens, won the first one.

Howie Morenz took the Canadian Division scoring title with 32 points, including 25 goals. Bill Cook of the Rangers scored 33 goals and won the American Division scoring race with 37 points. Herb Gardiner of the Canadiens was named the MVP and Hart Trophy winner while Billy Burch of the New York Americans got the Lady Byng.

Ottawa won the Canadian Division and the Rangers took the American Division regular-season titles. Six teams qualified for the Stanley Cup playoffs with Ottawa and Boston reaching the finals and the Senators winning in four games.

1927–28

There have been many hexes in sports history but none so mysterious as the eerie Curse of Muldoon which shackled the Chicago Black Hawks for 40 years. It was in 1927 that Pete Muldoon administered it.

Muldoon had been brought in to coach the new Chicago team when the NHL added three franchises in 1926. The team had done moderately well, winning 19 games in a 44-game season, and finishing third to qualify for the playoffs. They were the highest scoring team in the league with 115 goals but also allowed more goals than anyone else, 116.

So Muldoon was understandably distressed when Hawks' owner Fred McLaughlin dismissed him at the start of the 1927–28 season. In fact, Muldoon was said to be so distressed, he placed his famed curse on McLaughlin and the Hawks. As comeuppance for his unjust dismissal, Muldoon told McLaughlin, Chicago would never win an NHL title.

Sour grapes one might say, but it's a fact that for 40 years the Hawks never did win the championship and only when they finally did make it four decades later was the Curse wiped out.

Muldoon's successors didn't do nearly as well with the Hawks as he had done in their first season. Barney Stanley and Hugh Lehman split the job and Chicago managed only seven victories all season, finishing a dismal last in the American Division race won by Boston. The Canadiens finished first in the Canadian Division.

The individual stars were Hart Trophy winner Howie Morenz, the scoring champ with 33 goals and 51 total points, and Frank Boucher of the Rangers, who led the American Division with 35 points and won the Lady Byng Trophy.

George Hainsworth again won the goalie's Vezina Trophy but the most outstanding goaltending job of all was turned in by Alex Connell of Ottawa, who set a record with six straight shutouts and 446 minutes, nine seconds of scoreless hockey. Connell became the center of contention the night Lester Patrick went in to play goal.

The Rangers had advanced to the Stanley Cup final by eliminating Pittsburgh and Boston while the Montreal Maroons knocked off Ottawa and the Canadiens. The Maroons won the first game of the finals, 2–0.

Early in the second period of the next game, Nels Stewart fired a shot that caught Ranger goalie Lorne Chabot in the eye. Chabot could not

Goalie Alex Connell of Ottawa turned in six consecutive shutouts, going 446 minutes, nine seconds, without allowing a goal.   HOCKEY HALL OF FAME

continue and Patrick asked Eddie Gerard, manager of the Maroons, for permission to use Ottawa's Connell, who was in the stands watching the game, as a replacement.

Gerard refused and when Patrick asked permission to use a minor leaguer who was in the stands, Gerard again refused. Patrick, seething, returned to the Ranger dressing room to tell his club what had happened.

"What do we do now?" he asked.

"How about you playing goal?" suggested Frank Boucher, half kidding, half serious.

Patrick, 44, had retired as a player several years earlier. But he mulled over Boucher's suggestion and said, "Okay, I'll do it."

The Rangers protected Lester like a piece of fine china. Patrick made 18 saves, allowed one goal and New York won the game in overtime.

After losing the next game, New York came back to win the final two games and the Stanley Cup.

1928–29

A rule designed to hypo hockey offenses was introduced in 1928, but instead it became the year of the goalie around the NHL. The new rule allowed forward passing in all three zones on the ice—that is the defensive zone, the area between blue lines, and the offensive zone. There was still no red line in the game and the ice was divided by only the two blue lines.

Previously, forward passing was allowed only in a team's defensive zone or center ice, but never in the offensive area. Eventually, the rule change would affect the game and open play up, but not this season.

In Montreal, little George Hainsworth almost obliterated the memory of the great Georges Vezina. In 44 games that season, goaltender Hainsworth recorded an incredible 22 shutouts.

Hainsworth allowed 43 goals all year—an average of less than one per game. The highest scoring team in the league was Boston, winner of the American Division race. The Bruins scored a total of 89 goals—a shade over two per game.

One of Hainsworth's shutouts came against Ottawa on December 22, 1928, a special date for Montreal and for hockey. It marked the first NHL broadcast of a Montreal game and started an era that brought hockey into the home regularly. Arthur Dupont, founder of radio station CJAD, handled the French broadcast and columnist Elmer Ferguson did the English.

"The hockey people of that era looked upon radio with a great deal of suspicion," recalls Dupont. "They feared that if stories of the games came into the home without cost, it would ruin the attendance. So we were

BOSTON BRUINS
WORLD CHAMPIONS
Stanley Cup Winners
AMERICAN DIVISION CHAMPIONS · PRINCE OF WALES TROPHY WINNERS
SEASON 1928-29

"DUTCH" KLEIN   BILL CARSON   GEO. OWEN   HARRY OLIVER   WIN GREEN, *trainer*   MYLES LANE   NORMAN "DUTCH" GAINOR   AUBREY "DIT" CLAPPER
PERCY GALBRAITH   EDDIE SHORE   "MICKEY" McKAY   ART ROSS, *mgr.*   FRED HITCHMAN   CY DENNENY   RALPH "COONEY" WEILAND
"TINY" THOMPSON

★ FINAL STANDING N.H.L., 1928-29
AMERICAN DIVISION

	P	W	L	D	Pts.	Goals For	Agst.
BOSTON	44	26	13	5	57	89	52
N.Y. RANGERS	44	21	13	10	52	72	65
DETROIT	44	19	16	9	47	72	63
PITTSBURGH	44	9	27	8	26	46	80
CHICAGO	44	7	29	8	22	33	85

·*Playoffs*·
N.H.L. CHAMPIONSHIP
SERIES "A"

MARCH 19 .. BOSTON 1, CANADIENS 0
MARCH 21 .. BOSTON 1, CANADIENS 0
MARCH 23 .. BOSTON 3, CANADIENS 2
SERIES "B" (2 GAMES - TOTAL GOALS)
MARCH 19 .. N.Y. RANGERS 0, N.Y. AMERICANS 0
MARCH 21 .. N.Y. RANGERS 1, N.Y. AMERICANS 0
SERIES "C" (2 GAMES - TOTAL GOALS)
MARCH 19 .. TORONTO 3, DETROIT 1
MARCH 21 .. TORONTO 4, DETROIT 1
SERIES "D" (2 OUT OF 3 GAMES)
MARCH 24 .. N.Y. RANGERS 1, TORONTO 0
MARCH 26 .. N.Y. RANGERS 2, TORONTO 1
STANLEY CUP (FINAL - 2 OUT OF 3 GAMES)
SERIES "E"
MARCH 28 .. BOSTON 2, N.Y. RANGERS 0
MARCH 29 .. BOSTON 2, N.Y. RANGERS 1

FINAL STANDING N.H.L., 1928-29 ★
CANADIAN DIVISION

	P	W	L	D	Pts.	Goals For	Agst.
CANADIENS	44	22	7	15	59	71	43
N.Y. AMERICANS	44	19	13	12	50	53	53
TORONTO	44	21	18	5	47	85	69
OTTAWA	44	14	17	13	41	54	67
MONTREAL	44	15	20	9	39	67	65

Charles F. Adams, PRESIDENT
Arthur H. Ross, VICE PRES. & GEN. MGR.

Ralph F. Burkard, TREASURER
Frank Ryan, PUBLICITY DIRECTOR

HOCKEY HALL OF FAME

limited to a brief description of the third period and afterwards a summary of the entire game."

As it developed, of course, broadcasts increased hockey interest and now the radio-television industry plays a major role in the sport.

With the goalies dominating play, Toronto's Ace Bailey captured the scoring crown with 32 points—22 of them on goals. Carson Cooper of Detroit was the top scorer in the American Division with 18 goals and 27 points.

Hainsworth, of course, won the Vezina Trophy, and another goalie, Roy Worters of the New York Americans, took the Hart. The Rangers' Frank Boucher won the Lady Byng.

A new playoff arrangement matched the first-place, second-place and third-place teams in each division against each other. The winners of the series between second-place teams and the series between the third-place finishers clashed in the semifinal with that winner advancing to the

Toronto's Ace Bailey took scoring honors in 1928–29.

HOCKEY HALL OF FAME (TUROFSKY)

Stanley Cup finals against the winner of the series between the two first-place clubs.

Toronto eliminated Detroit in two straight games and the Rangers knocked off the Americans in two straight. Then New York beat Toronto to advance to the finals against Boston, which had eliminated the Canadiens. The Bruins won the Cup in two games as rookie goalie Tiny Thompson turned in his third playoff shutout in five games. Thompson allowed three goals in the five games, a playoff goals-against average of 0.60.

III   A NEW WORLD OF OFFENSE 1929-1942

The NHL had taken a firm hold in the 1920s, expanding from four teams to 10 and emerging as the sport's universally recognized major league. But in the 30s, problems would arise. There was the American Depression and the shock waves traveled right through the Canadian sport which had franchises in five United States cities. And there was the complaint that hockey was too defensive a game...that the offenses were stymied.

Les Patrick, boss of the New York Rangers, agreed with the detractors to some extent.

"I believe in keeping the game wide open," said Patrick at the height of the debate over whether to remove all restrictions on forward passing. "Our followers are entitled to action...not for a few brief moments, but for three full 20-minute periods of a game.

"The open style of play calls for better stickhandling and speedier skating. What better system could the coaches and managers adopt to preserve and further popularize the fastest game in the world."

The NHL eventually went along with Patrick's ideas and, predictably, the game opened up considerably. The economic problems, however, caused several club shifts and a couple of franchise casualties.

But stickhandling and speed, the two qualities Patrick talked about, combined to give hockey a loyal core of fans that grew and grew, despite the Depression. The sport had its rough moments, it is true, but the game's brass, from NHL President Frank Calder on down, pulled it through the periods of crisis.

1929-30

It would take more than a Depression to stop Conn Smythe, who was determined to build the Toronto Maple Leafs into an NHL power, if for no other reason than to prove to Madison Square Garden's owners just how valuable a man they had lost when they fired him three years before.

Smythe needed a bigger arena for his club but raising the money to build one was a problem. So Smythe solved the financial question by turning to the trade unions and builders for help. As partial payment of wages, the workmen would receive stock in Maple Leaf Gardens.

The solution worked out beautifully for all parties. Smythe got his new arena and his shareholders had a part in what would become a highly successful sports and entertainment center.

Montreal Maroons' Clint Benedict: hockey's first masked goalie.

HOCKEY HALL OF FAME

Ralph "Cooney" Weiland of Boston led NHL scorers with 73 points in 1929–30.
HOCKEY HALL OF FAME

So the Maple Leafs spent their next-to-last season in the old Arena Gardens and it was less than a total success. They finished fourth in the Canadian Division even though they introduced a good-looking rookie named Charlie Conacher, who was destined for NHL stardom.

The new rules allowing passing in all three zones added scoring punch throughout the league and Boston's Cooney Weiland was the leading point-maker with 73, including 43 goals. The Bruins, with Weiland setting the pace, were the highest scoring team in the league and their goalie, Tiny Thompson, allowed the fewest goals. The combination gave Boston a fantastic 38 victories in 44 games including one record stretch of 14 straight victories. Naturally, the Bruins won the American Division title.

Hec Kilrea of Ottawa was the leading scorer in the Canadian Division with 58 points, three more than Nels Stewart of the Montreal Maroons, who won the Hart Trophy as MVP. Tiny Thompson broke George Hainsworth's three-year hold on the Vezina Trophy and Frank Boucher took the Lady Byng again.

While the Bruins won their division crown by 30 points, Ottawa and the two Montreal teams staged a three-way battle for Canadian Division honors. The Maroons and Canadiens both finished with 51 points and

35

Chicago's Johnny Gottselig chases the puck behind Maroons' net.   UPI

Ottawa had 50. The Maroons were recognized as the first-place team because they had more victories (23) than the Canadiens (21).

That was a break for the Canadiens because it meant the Maroons would have to face Boston's powerhouse in the opening Stanley Cup series. Sure enough, the Bruins eliminated the Maroons in four games while the Canadiens got past Chicago in the two-game, total-goals playoff. The Rangers eliminated Ottawa but then the Canadiens took the Rangers and stunned the Bruins, winning the Cup finale in two straight games.

Clint Benedict, the Maroons' great goalie, made hockey history by using the first face mask ever that season. It happened after Howie Morenz of the Canadiens had broken Benedict's nose with a shot. Benedict didn't stay with the protection, however, and it would be almost three decades before a goalie would try a mask again.

1930–31

The saga of how he financed Maple Leaf Gardens proved how determined Conn Smythe could be. In 1930, he decided that one of the things his Maple Leafs needed for improvement was a player of King Clancy's ability.

36

Smythe asked how much it would take to get Clancy away from Ottawa. A couple of players and cash...say about $35,000...he was told.

The players Smythe had. The cash was another story. He had most of his assets tied up in the construction of the Leafs' new home. But if $35,000 was what he needed to get Clancy, Smythe decided he'd come up with it.

He raised some capital from friends, giving himself a little room to maneuver. Then he bet the bundle on a longshot horse—his own Rare Jewel. Naturally, the horse won and Smythe had the price for Clancy.

Smythe's wheeling and dealing was typical of the problems of Depression-burdened owners. The Pittsburgh club was forced to move to Philadelphia because of poor attendance. The Pirates changed their name to the Quakers but were doomed anyway. They lasted just that season in Philadelphia.

In Detroit, the club changed its nickname from the Cougars to the Falcons in an effort to lift sagging interest. But with money in short supply, especially in the automobile capital, there was little left over to spend on watching hockey games.

Another step to inject interest around the league was the introduction of an All-Star team. The first squad selected was a study in immortals.

Roy Worters of the Amerks won the Vezina Trophy in 1930–31.

HOCKEY HALL OF FAME

Ebbie Goodfellow, later to be elected to the Hall of Fame, wears the new Detroit Falcon uniform. HOCKEY HALL OF FAME

Herb Drury was a center for the Quakers, who lasted only one year in Philadelphia. HOCKEY HALL OF FAME

The forward line included Howie Morenz of the Canadiens at center, his linemate Aurel Joliat at left wing and Bill Cook of the New York Rangers at right wing. The defensemen were Boston's Eddie Shore and King Clancy of Toronto. Charlie Gardiner of Chicago was picked as the goalie.

Morenz led the league in scoring with 28 goals and 51 points and won the Hart Trophy as the MVP. Frank Boucher took his fourth straight Lady Byng and Roy Worters of the New York Americans edged out Gardiner for the Vezina Trophy. Detroit's Ebbie Goodfellow led the American Division scorers with 48 points.

In the playoffs, division champs Boston and the Montreal Canadiens went five games before the Canadiens won. Three of the games went into overtime. Chicago eliminated Toronto and then whipped the Rangers, who had knocked off the Maroons.

In the final round, the Canadiens won their second straight Cup, coming from behind to beat the Black Hawks in the five-game playoffs.

Just as the Pittsburgh-Philadelphia franchise was in trouble in the American Division, the Canadian Division's Ottawa team had fallen on lean days. The Senators won just 10 games, finished in last place and requested and were granted a one-year leave of absence from the league.

1931–32

The departure of Ottawa and Philadelphia left the NHL with eight clubs, four in each division. The schedule was increased to 48 games per club, possibly in an effort to increase team income during the dreary Depression days.

But it was a gala night in Toronto on November 12 when Conn Smythe proudly unveiled his new Maple Leaf Gardens. A crowd of 13,542 packed the arena for the game between Toronto and Chicago. But the Black Hawks, who had never won a game in Toronto before, spoiled the party by upsetting the Leafs, 3–1.

The anger that burned within Smythe against New York and the Ranger organization could not be extinguished until he built the Leafs into a powerhouse. This was to be the year for him to get even, although it didn't start out that way. Toronto slumped into last place after one month and Smythe hired Dick Irvin to replace Art Duncan as coach. Irvin had been fired by Chicago the year before but when he took over the Leafs, they acted like a brand-new club.

Toronto soared from last to first place with Charlie Conacher, Harvey Jackson and Joe Primeau providing the fire-power. Jackson won the Canadian Division scoring title with 53 points, three more than Primeau. Conacher finished fourth with 48 and only Howie Morenz managed to squeeze his way between the Toronto trio with 49 points.

Joe Primeau of Toronto broke Frank Boucher's hold on the Lady Byng Trophy.
HOCKEY HALL OF FAME (TUROFSKY)

Morenz won his second straight Hart Trophy as the MVP while Primeau ended Frank Boucher's four-year domination of the Lady Byng award. Charlie Gardiner of Chicago won the Vezina again and was named the All-Star goalie for the second time.

Jackson, a left wing, and Morenz, a center, both made the All-Star team along with right wing Bill Cook of the New York Rangers, whose 34 goals and 48 points led American Division scorers. The defensemen selected were Boston's Eddie Shore and bald-headed Ching Johnson of the Rangers, who delighted in breaking up the rushes of Montreal's Aurel Joliat by sweeping the little guy's cap off his head.

Toronto finished second behind the Canadiens in the Canadian Division while the Rangers won the American Division crown. Now, if only the playoffs worked out properly, Smythe thought, he'd finally have a chance at his revenge.

After Chicago's Charlie Gardiner shut out Toronto in the first game, the Leafs exploded for a 6–1 victory to eliminate the Black Hawks on total goals. The Maroons beat Detroit in the other quarterfinal while, happily for Smythe, the Rangers advanced to the finals by eliminating the Canadiens.

Toronto got past the Maroons in the two-game, total-goals semifinal and now it was the Leafs and the Rangers for the Stanley Cup. Conacher,

40

Primeau, Hap Day and the other Leafs ran wild, beating the Rangers in three straight games and scoring six goals in each of them. The Stanley Cup was the ultimate ornament to adorn Smythe's new Maple Leafs Gardens. Conn's revenge was served!

1932–33

In an effort to tighten belts during the height of the Depression, NHL owners decided to put a ceiling of $70,000 on club payrolls with no single player to be paid more than $7,500. That represented a 10 percent slice for most teams and the players staged a small revolution over the move.

There were big-name holdouts all over the league including Frank Boucher of the Rangers, Reg Noble and Hap Emms of Detroit, the Canadiens' Aurel Joliat, Lorne Chabot of Toronto and Hooley Smith of the Montreal Maroons. President Frank Calder was given permission to suspend the dissidents but eventually all of the holdouts fell into line.

Seat prices were slashed too. The top price was $3 and fans could get into most arenas for as little as 50 cents.

Ottawa returned to the league after a one-year hiatus with Cy Denneny as its coach. Other great former players also turned up as coaches: Newsy Lalonde with the Canadiens and Jack Adams in Detroit where the team was about to adopt its third name, the Red Wings. In New York, Colonel John Hammond, who was instrumental in bringing hockey to Madison Square Garden, first with the Americans and then with the Rangers, resigned. As a result, coach Lester Patrick took on the added titles of general manager and vice president of the Rangers.

Before the season started, the Rangers sold goalie John Ross Roach to Detroit for $11,000. It was a worthwhile investment for the Cougars-Falcons-Red Wings. Roach was named the All-Star goalie on a team that included Bill Cook and Frank Boucher of the Rangers, and Baldy North-cott of the Montreal Maroons up front, and a defense of Boston's Eddie Shore and the Rangers' Ching Johnson.

Cook took the scoring title with 50 points, 28 of them goals. Boucher reclaimed the Lady Byng and Shore became the first fulltime defenseman to win the Hart Trophy. Boston's Tiny Thompson took the Vezina.

The Bruins and Detroit ended with identical records of 25–15–8 in the American Division with Boston recognized as the champion because the Bruins had scored more goals (124) than the Red Wings (111). Toronto took the Canadian Division race.

In the playoffs, the Maple Leafs eliminated the Bruins in five games. It was one of the most memorable playoff series as four of the games went into overtime and the final one lasted six extra periods.

Newsy Lalonde became coach of the Canadiens in 1932–33.

Detroit eliminated the Montreal Maroons and the Rangers ousted the Canadiens in the quarterfinals. Then New York finished Detroit off and went up against the bone-weary Leafs in the final series.

With Toronto softened up by the prolonged series against Boston, the Rangers had an easy time, winning in four games. The heroes were the Cook brothers, Bill and Bun, and their center, Frank Boucher, all of whom had been signed for New York by Toronto's boss, Conn Smythe.

1933-34

Eddie Shore was the epitome of a hockey bad man. He was a no-nonsense guy who was the scourge of the Bruins' blueline—the most feared defenseman in hockey. And in December, 1933, Shore was part of one of the most dramatic incidents in the game's history.

The Bruins were at home against Toronto, with the Maple Leafs leading, 1-0, when a pair of quick penalties left Toronto two men short. Dick Irvin sent defensemen King Clancy and Red Horner and forward Ace Bailey out to kill the time.

Bailey, a former scoring champ, was an excellent puck-carrier and stick-handler—just what the Leafs needed with the Bruins enjoying a two-man edge. He won a face-off and dodged Boston skaters, protecting the puck for a full minute before another face-off was called because Ace was not advancing the puck.

Bailey won the second face-off as well, again stickhandled for awhile and finally shot the puck into the Bruins' end, forcing Boston to retreat. Shore picked the rubber up and started up ice. Clancy met him and dumped him, regaining the puck for Toronto. As Shore slowly got up, he saw Bailey, still winded from his earlier one-man show, in front of him.

Eddie set sail for the Leaf star, caught him from behind and flipped him with his shoulder. Bailey hit the ice with a dull thud and lay motionless, seriously injured. When Shore grinned at Horner, skating to Bailey's aid, Red decked the Bruin defenseman with an uppercut.

Bailey hovered between life and death for several days with a severe head injury. He finally pulled through but never played hockey again. In February, Maple Leaf Gardens hosted a benefit game for Bailey between Toronto and a team of NHL All-Stars. The meeting at center ice between Bailey and Shore was shrouded in silence until the two embraced. That hug brought a thunderous roar from the crowd and eased the tension that had been building before the meeting.

"I know it was an accident," said Bailey, exonerating Shore.

Toronto's Kid Line—Harvey "Busher" Jackson, Joe Primeau, and Charlie Conacher—were challenging the Cooks and Frank Boucher of

Aurel Joliat of the Canadiens captured the Hart Trophy for 1933–34.
HOCKEY HALL OF FAME

Toronto fans stepped out to honor their King Clancy.
HOCKEY HALL OF FAME (TUROFSKY)

TO-NIGHT 8.30 "CLANCY NIGHT"

The King

The World's Best

MAPLE LEAF GARDENS   MARCH 17TH 1934

A New World of Offense   45

the Rangers as the top scoring line in the league. The Toronto unit finished
1-2-3 in scoring in the Canadian Division with Conacher leading the
league with 52 points including 32 goals, Primeau scoring 46 points and
Jackson 38. Boucher's 44 points led American Division scorers.

Conacher, Primeau and Boucher were named to the NHL All-Star team
along with defensemen King Clancy of Toronto and Lionel Conacher,
Charlie's brother, of Chicago, and Black Hawk goalie Charlie Gardiner.
Aurel Joliat of the Canadiens was the MVP and Boucher, as usual, won
the Lady Byng. The Vezina went to Chicago's Gardiner, who starred in
the playoffs and led the Hawks to the Stanley Cup.

Toronto finished first in the Canadian Division but lost in the playoffs
to Detroit, the American Division pennant winners. Chicago eliminated
the Canadiens and then the Montreal Maroons, who had finished off the
Rangers.

Chicago took the Stanley Cup from Detroit in four games. Two of them
went into double overtime with Gardiner shutting out the Red Wings in
the last one.

In the celebration that followed the victory, Chicago's Roger Jenkins
wheeled Gardiner through the city's Loop section in a wheelbarrow, never
dreaming his buddy would be dead from a brain hemorrhage a scant eight
weeks later.

1934–35

The Ottawa franchise, still floundering after two more last-place
finishes, was shifted to St. Louis where the team was christened the Eagles.
In a shift almost as momentous, the legendary Howie Morenz was dealt
to Chicago.

Morenz and Montreal had been synonymous and the great center never
acclimated himself to his new team. He finished the season with a mere
eight goals, far down in the American Division scoring list. Syd Howe,
who split the season between Detroit and St. Louis, led the American
Division scorers with 47 points while Charlie Conacher of Toronto and
his linemate, Busher Jackson, were 1-2 in Canadian Division scoring.
Conacher won the title with 57 points and Jackson finished second with 44.

The penalty shot, long a popular feature of Western League hockey, was
introduced in the NHL, which now had several Western figures in its
coaching ranks. There was Lester Patrick in New York, Dick Irvin in
Toronto, Jack Adams in Detroit and Lester's brother, Frank Patrick,
in Boston.

Scotty Bowman, purchased by Detroit along with Howe for $50,000
from St. Louis in mid-season, was the first player ever to score on a

Two standout defensemen, the Bruins' Dit Clapper and the Rangers' bald Ching Johnson, battle for the puck.   UPI

Alex Connell led the Montreal Maroons to the Stanley Cup in 1934–35.
HOCKEY HALL OF FAME (TUROFSKY)

penalty shot in the NHL. It came against Alex Connell, the Montreal Maroons' great goalie.

A couple of new names made their first appearances on the All-Star team. They were goalie Lorne Chabot, acquired by Chicago from Toronto to replace the deceased Gardiner, and defenseman Earl Seibert of the New York Rangers. Also chosen were Boston's Eddie Shore on defense and a forward line of Charlie Conacher and Busher Jackson from Toronto and Frank Boucher of the Rangers.

Chabot won the Vezina Trophy and Shore took the Hart Trophy. Frank Boucher won the Lady Byng for the seventh time in eight years and was awarded permanent possession of the trophy, which would, of course, be replaced by a new one.

Toronto, with the Conacher-Jackson-Joe Primeau "Kid Line" dominating the league, easily won the Canadian Division title while Boston squeezed past Chicago by one point to take the American Division.

Ranger Frank Boucher took permanent possession of the Lady Byng Trophy in 1934–35.   HOCKEY HALL OF FAME

In the playoffs, the Maple Leafs dropped the opener to Boston and then beat the Bruins three straight to advance to the Stanley Cup finals. Meanwhile, the Montreal Maroons eliminated Chicago on consecutive shutouts by Alex Connell and then knocked off the Rangers, who had topped the Canadiens.

In the final round, it was a matchup of two hot goalies—Connell of the Maroons and George Hainsworth of Toronto, who had allowed Boston just two goals in four games in the opening round. Connell proved to be hotter, giving up only four goals as the Maroons captured the Stanley Cup with three straight victories.

1935–36

The St. Louis franchise was dissolved only one year after being moved from Ottawa. This reduced the NHL to eight teams, four in each division. The Eagles' players were distributed to other clubs around the league and there were some good ones available. Boston probably came up with the best in Bill Cowley, who developed into a star.

Carl Voss, who had started in the league with the New York Rangers three seasons earlier, continued to move from club to club. Voss had already played with the New York Rangers, Detroit, Ottawa and St. Louis and that season moved on to the New York Americans after the Eagles folded. He would also play for the Montreal Maroons and Chicago Black Hawks before ending his career after six years in the NHL.

The Americans boasted the league's top scorer, second-year man Dave "Sweeney" Schriner, a left wing, who had 45 points including 19 goals. The leading scorer in the American Division was Detroit's Marty Barry, with 21 goals and a total of 40 points.

Schriner was named to the All-Star team along with Toronto's Charlie Conacher and Hooley Smith of the Montreal Maroons, Boston defensemen Eddie Shore and Babe Siebert and Tiny Thompson, the Bruins' goalie.

Thompson also won the Vezina Trophy and wrote his name in the record book as the first goalie to assist on a scoring play. It happened on a goal by defenseman Siebert, who scored after taking a pass from the goalie.

Eddie Shore won the Hart Trophy, his third MVP award in four years, while Chicago's Doc Romnes took the Lady Byng. The Black Hawks also had the league's hottest rookie, an American-born goalie named Mike Karakas, who stepped in when Lorne Chabot was injured and played so well that the Hawks sold Chabot to the Maroons. Chicago also dealt Howie Morenz to the Rangers, a move that still left the great center homesick for Montreal.

The Montreal Maroons won the Canadian Division race by two points over Toronto while Detroit had an easier time, taking the American Divi-

Boston's Tiny Thompson contributed an historic assist.   UPI

sion by six points over Boston. The opening game of the Stanley Cup playoffs between the Maroons and Red Wings was a memorable one.

The goalies, Detroit's Norm Smith and Lorne Chabot of the Maroons, played shutout hockey through the 60-minute regulation game and the scoreless tie lasted through five periods of overtime. Finally, with 3½ minutes remaining in the sixth extra period, Modere "Mud" Bruneteau put a shot past Chabot. The Arena clock read 2:25 A.M. and the goal ended 176 minutes, 30 seconds of futility. It remains the longest game ever played.

The Red Wings went on to win the next two games, eliminating the Maroons. Toronto ousted Boston and then downed the Americans, who

49

Eddie Shore of the Bruins was MVP in 1935–36.
HOCKEY HALL OF FAME (TUROFSKY)

had beaten Chicago. Then Detroit beat the Maple Leafs in the four-game finale to capture the Stanley Cup.

1936–37

It was a year for the great lines. Two immortal ones broke up and another one was reunited, but with a tragic outcome.

In New York, the famous Bill Cook-Frank Boucher-Bun Cook unit was finished when the Rangers sold Bun Cook to Boston. The trio had scored more than 1,000 points playing together for the Rangers ever since the team came into the league a decade earlier. In Toronto, Joe Primeau announced his retirement, breaking up the "Kid Line" he had comprised along with Charlie Conacher and Busher Jackson.

In Montreal, the Canadiens brought Howie Morenz back from his two years of exile in Chicago and New York and no one was happier about the move than the veteran center.

50

Reunited with his old linemates, Aurel Joliat and Johnny Gagnon, Morenz played inspired hockey. He had scored 20 points at mid-season when tragedy struck. Going into a corner after the puck, Morenz got his skates caught in a rut in the ice and snapped a bone in his leg.

The accident and his ability to overcome it weighed heavily on Morenz' mind as he lay in a Montreal hospital. Two months later, on March 8, his heart gave out and he died.

The funeral services were held at center ice in the Montreal Forum and 25,000 fans, many of them in tears, filed past his bier to pay their last respects to one of hockey's truly great stars.

The New York Americans, with owner Bill Dwyer in deep financial trouble, had their franchise taken over by the league. NHL President Frank Calder was to act as advisor to the club.

President Calder also introduced a trophy to be awarded annually to the league's top rookie. The first one went to Toronto's Syl Apps, a pole vaulter at the 1936 Berlin Olympics who turned pro with the Leafs after

The Hart Trophy went to the Canadiens'
Babe Siebert in 1936–37.
HOCKEY HALL OF FAME

Toronto's Syl Apps, a former Olympic pole vaulter, was Rookie of the Year in 1936–37. HOCKEY HALL OF FAME (ALEXANDRA STUDIO)

returning from the Games. Apps finished second in the Canadian Division scoring race with 45 points, one less than Sweeney Schriner of the New York Americans, who captured his second straight scoring crown. Detroit's Marty Barry led American Division scorers with 44 points.

The Red Wings dominated the All-Star team, gaining four of the six spots. Detroit's Larry Aurie was named at right wing, Marty Barry at center, Ebbie Goodfellow at one defense post and Norm Smith at goal. Toronto's Busher Jackson at left wing and defenseman Babe Siebert of the Montreal Canadiens were the only non-Red Wings named. Siebert won the Hart Trophy, Barry the Lady Byng and Smith the Vezina.

The Canadiens edged the Montreal Maroons for the Canadian Division title while Detroit won the American Division race. In the playoffs, the Red Wings beat the Canadiens in the first two games, then dropped two straight before winning the decisive fifth game.

The New York Rangers eliminated first Toronto and then the Maroons, who had beaten Boston. In the Stanley Cup finals Marty Barry and substitute goalie Earl Robertson helped the Red Wings come from behind with two straight victories to capture the five-game series.

1937–38

Clem Loughlin had set a longevity record by lasting three seasons in the revolving door for coaches operated by Chicago's boss, Major Fred McLaughlin. In 10 years, McLaughlin had employed an even dozen coaches—11 of them over the first seven seasons. When Loughlin was shown to the exit door in 1937, he was replaced by a baseball umpire and hockey referee named Bill Stewart, who would pilot Chicago to its first Stanley Cup.

A baseball umpire? Well, McLaughlin was like that, often depending for advice in running his hockey club on distinctly un-hockey types. Stewart, at least, did have some refereeing in his background.

In Boston, the Bruins assembled a new line destined for a long run of glory. Milt Schmidt was the center and his wingmen were Bobby Bauer and Woody Dumart—"The Kraut Line".

Lester Patrick, coach of the New York Rangers, brought up his son, Muzz, to join his brother, Lynn, and give the Rangers three Patricks. New York also added a rookie named Bryan Hextall who was to star during the war years and later see both his sons play in the NHL.

Toronto's Gordie Drillon won the scoring title with 52 points, 26 of them goals. Drillon was part of considerable confusion caused by the

Ranger Cecil Dillon shared an All-Star berth with Maple Leaf Gordie Drillon in 1937–38.   HOCKEY HALL OF FAME

similarity in name with another fine right wing, Cecil Dillon of the Rangers. In fact, both were selected to the All-Star team—the only time in history that two players were chosen for the same position on the first team.

The other All-Stars were left wing Paul Thompson of Chicago, who led American Division scorers with 44 points, Boston's Bill Cowley at center, defensemen Eddie Shore of the Bruins and Babe Siebert of the Montreal Canadiens and Boston's Tiny Thompson, Paul's brother, in goal.

Shore recaptured the MVP Hart Trophy—his fourth in six years— Drillon was the Lady Byng winner and Tiny Thompson took the Vezina for the fourth time. Chicago's Cully Dahlstrom won the Calder Trophy as the top rookie.

Toronto and Boston won the division championships and the Maple Leafs whipped the Bruins in three straight games to advance to the final round of the Stanley Cup playoffs. Meanwhile, in an intra-city showdown, the New York Americans eliminated the Rangers and reached the semi-finals against Chicago, which had come from behind to beat the Montreal Canadiens. The Black Hawks ousted the Americans and found themselves up against Toronto's powerhouse for the Stanley Cup.

Against Toronto, the Hawks were simply in over their heads. They had won just 14 of 48 games during the regular season and made the playoffs by only two points. Toronto, on the other hand, had won or tied 33 of their 48 games and had easily won the Canadian Division.

What was worse, Mike Karakas, Chicago's goalie, came up with an injured toe before the opening game. Coach Bill Stewart was not about to repeat Lester Patrick's feat of playing goal. Instead, he asked permission of the Leafs to use Dave Kerr, the Rangers' goalie. Conn Smythe refused and the Hawks wound up with Alfie Moore, a minor leaguer, in the nets, but not before Stewart and Smythe engaged in a brief jostling match outside the dressing room.

The Hawks won the opener, 3–1, and Moore thumbed his nose at the Leafs' bench. In the second game, with Moore ruled ineligible by NHL President Frank Calder, the Hawks came up with Paul Goodman, another minor leaguer who was fished out of a movie theater just two hours before the game began. He was beaten by the Leafs, 5–1, to even the series.

In the third game, Karakas returned and the Hawks won, 2–1, on Doc Romnes' goal with 4:05 left in the game. The Leafs argued that the shot had hit the post but were overruled by referee Clarence Campbell, a man who would play a different role in the NHL in later years.

The Hawks won the fourth game and the Cup, making Stewart the toast of Chicago—for about nine months.

In his rookie year, Frankie Brimsek of the Bruins totalled 10 shutouts.

1938–39

For years the Maroons were fighting a losing battle attracting fan support while the Canadiens enjoyed far more popularity in Montreal. Finally, the Maroons asked permission to shift to St. Louis. The league refused but did grant the franchise a one-year leave of absence to regroup its forces. But when they sold most of their players to other clubs, it became apparent that the Maroons were through for good.

The demise of the Maroons left seven teams still operating and they were grouped in a single division with six clubs qualifying for the rather crowded playoffs. Only Chicago, whose Bill Stewart was dismissed in mid-season and replaced by Paul Thompson, missed.

In Boston, manager Art Ross took a dramatic step. He sold goalie Tiny Thompson, a Bruins' favorite for a decade, to Detroit. The reason was

55

Ross' conviction that a youngster from Eveleth, Minn., was ready for the NHL. And Frank Brimsek really was ready.

Brimsek had played the Bruins' first two games while Thompson recovered from an eye ailment. Then Tiny returned and Brimsek was farmed out to Providence. But Thompson was 33 and Ross was anxious to create a spot for the good-looking rookie who had succeeded Chicago's Mike Karakas at Eveleth High School. On November 28, the deal was made, with the Bruins receiving $15,000 from the Red Wings. Brimsek returned two days later.

The Canadiens beat him 2–0 in his first game and then Brimsek produced three straight shutouts. His shutout streak extended to 231 minutes, 54 seconds, breaking Thompson's modern mark of 224:47.

After Brimsek's sensational streak was broken, he started another one. Three more shutouts—one against Thompson and the Red Wings—gave him six in seven games and another unbelievable streak of 220 minutes, 24 seconds of scoreless hockey.

Hector "Toe" Blake of the Canadiens won scoring and MVP honors in 1938–39.   HOCKEY HALL OF FAME

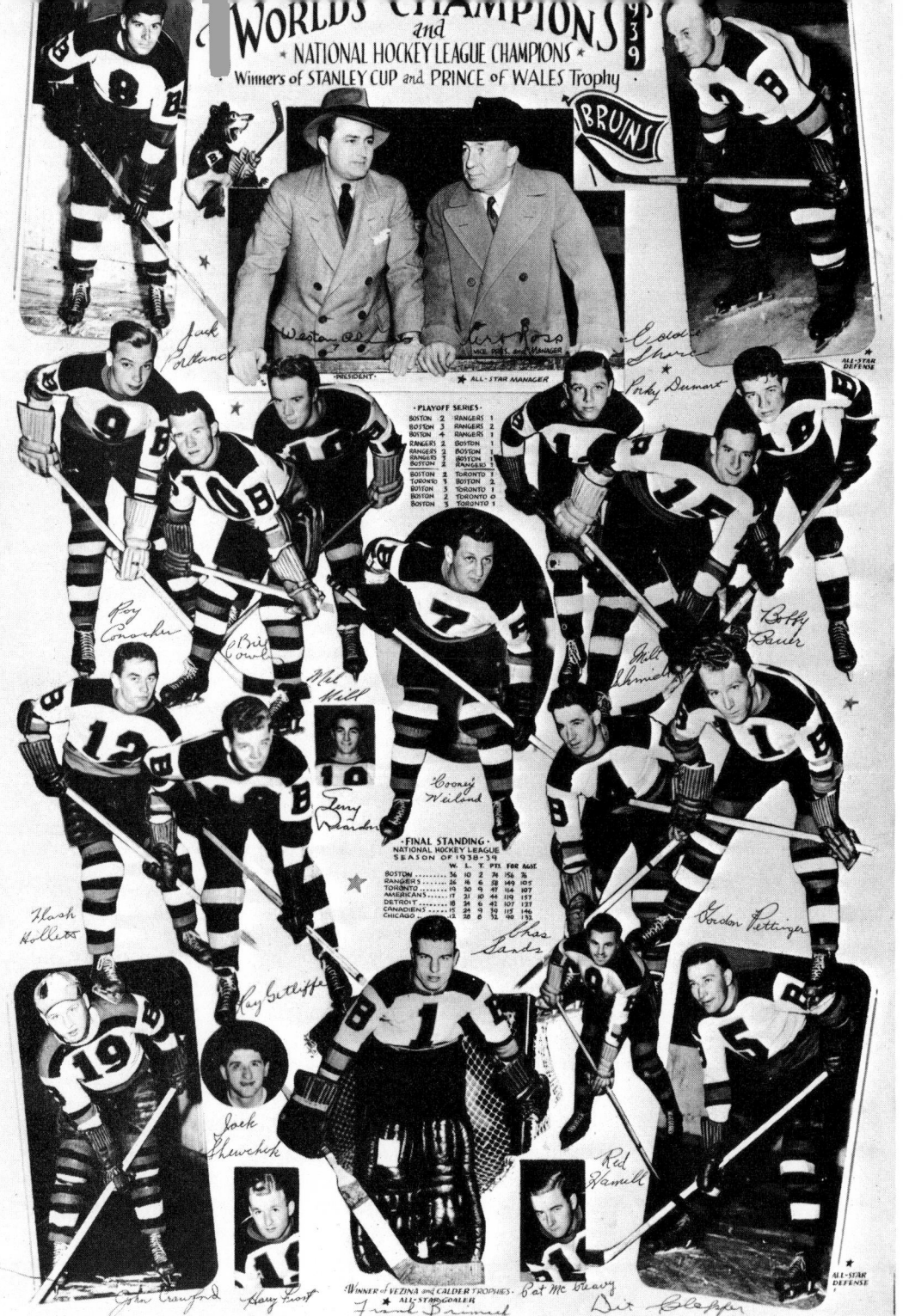

HOCKEY HALL OF FAME

The Boston fans, never easy to please, were unhappy to lose Thompson but Brimsek's fantastic debut made him an instant hero. He turned in 10 shutouts in 41 games, earning the Vezina Trophy as top goalie, the Calder Trophy as top rookie, a spot on the All-Star team and the nickname "Mr. Zero."

The other All-Stars were defensemen Eddie Shore and Dit Clapper of Boston, Toronto's center, Syl Apps, right wing Gordie Drillon of the Maple Leafs and left wing Hector "Toe" Blake of the Montreal Canadiens. Blake was the scoring champion with 47 points, including 24 goals, and captured the Hart Trophy while Clint Smith of the New York Rangers won the Lady Byng.

The Bruins won the regular-season title by 16 points over the Rangers and then the two clubs staged one of the most memorable playoff battles in history. Boston took the first three games—two of them on overtime goals by Mel Hill, an obscure 10-goal scorer during the regular season. Then the Rangers roared back to win three straight and tie the series. In the seventh game, Hill struck again, beating the Rangers eight minutes into the third overtime period and earning forever the nickname of "Sudden Death" Hill.

Toronto ripped through the New York Americans and Detroit, which had eliminated the Canadiens. In the finals, the Bruins whipped the Leafs in five games to claim their first Stanley Cup in a decade.

1939–40

The guns of Europe began firing before the 1939 hockey season got underway and before long the NHL would feel the manpower squeeze of world conflict. But, for the time being at least, the league's operations were not affected by the events overseas.

Ironically, the hottest line in the league was Boston's Milt Schmidt, Woody Dumart and Bobby Bauer, tabbed the "Kraut Line" because of their Germanic extractions. But the name proved a bit unpopular at this sensitive time so the "Kraut Line" was re-christened the "Kitchener Kids" because the trio all hailed from Kitchener, Ont.

Schmidt, the center, led the league in scoring with 52 points, 22 of them on goals. Dumart and Bauer tied for second with 43 points apiece.

The All-Star team had Schmidt at center, Bryan Hextall of the Rangers at right wing and Montreal's Toe Blake at left wing. The defensemen were Aubrey "Dit" Clapper of the Bruins and Detroit's Ebbie Goodfellow. Davey Kerr of the Rangers was the goalie.

Goodfellow won the Hart Trophy and Bobby Bauer the Lady Byng. Kerr won the Vezina and a 28-year-old Ranger rookie, Kilby MacDonald, took the Calder.

Woody Dumart was a wing on Boston's high-scoring Kraut Line.
HOCKEY HALL OF FAME

Davey Kerr of the Rangers took the Vezina Trophy and led the New Yorkers to the Stanley Cup in 1939–40.
HOCKEY HALL OF FAME

For the first time since they came into the league, the Bruins had to get along without the great Eddie Shore patrolling their blue line. Shore had become owner and manager of the minor league Springfield Indians and was available only for Boston's home games. The Bruins quickly tired of this arrangement and sold Eddie to the New York Americans. Shore finished the season with the Amerks and then retired to build the Springfield club into a hugely rewarding financial operation.

Even without Shore, the Bruins finished first in the regular-season race, again beating out the Rangers. But New York got revenge for the heartbreaking playoff loss of the year before by eliminating Boston in the Stanley Cup series, four games to two.

Toronto got by Chicago and Detroit eliminated the New York Americans in other playoff matchups. When the Maple Leafs and Red Wings met in the semifinals it turned into a little war. A 15-minute brawl marred the final game with every player on the ice and 17 who left the opposing benches joining in.

"The Wings are a bunch of hoodlums," declared the Toronto management. To which Jack Adams, manager of the Red Wings, replied, "We're just sorry we can't play the Leafs seven nights in a row."

In the Stanley Cup finale, the Rangers beat Toronto in six games, three of the New York victories coming in overtime. That wiped out the bad overtime memories Boston's "Sudden Death" Hill had left the year before.

1940–41

Dick Irvin left Toronto and moved into the coaching job at Montreal, hoping to rebuild the Canadiens, who had fallen on lean times. Irvin would do such a successful job that his teams of the early 1940s were hockey's most dynamic squads. And the reason for much of his success was a scouting job he did for the Canadiens shortly before becoming the club's coach. It was on that trip that he discovered a junior hockey player named Maurice Richard, who was destined to become one of the greatest scorers in hockey history.

Before the season started, Irvin predicted a fourth-place finish for Montreal—three notches higher than they had finished the year before. Asked his thoughts about the league's top rookie, he placed the name of his own Johnny Quilty in a sealed envelope.

Quilty made it but the Canadiens didn't. Montreal finished sixth but Quilty captured the Calder Trophy as the league's best rookie. Boston's Bill Cowley won the scoring title with 62 points—only 17 of them goals. Cowley also was the MVP and Bobby Bauer of the Bruins won his second straight Lady Byng. Turk Broda of Toronto won the Vezina, edging out

*MVP and scoring champ in 1940–41 was
Boston's Bill Cowley.*
HOCKEY HALL OF FAME

The Rangers and Maple Leafs scramble for the puck in December, 1940. CULVER

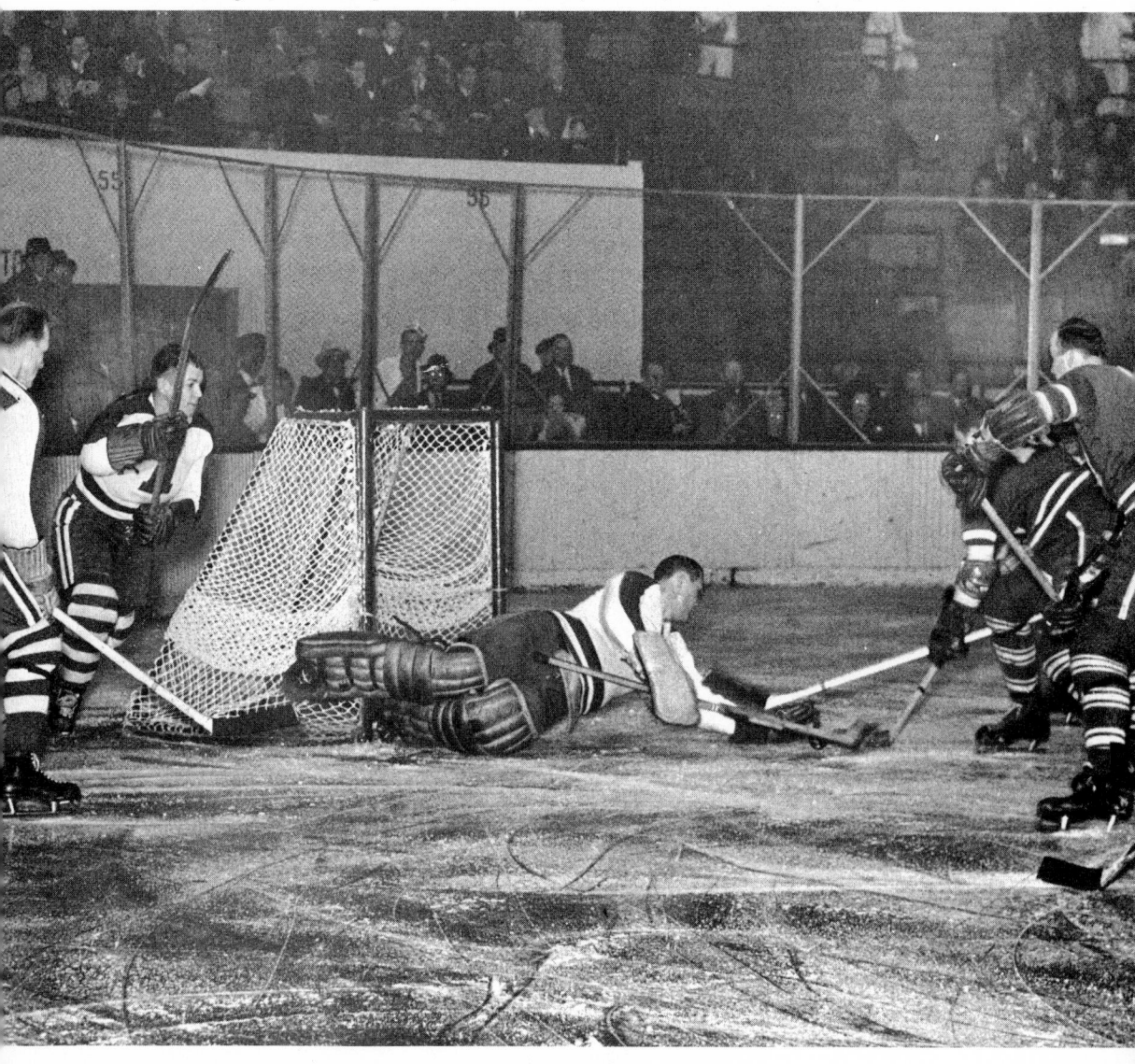

Detroit's Johnny Mowers on the final night of the season. It marked the first time a Maple Leaf had been the NHL's top goaltender.

The All-Star team had Broda in goal, Boston's Dit Clapper and Toronto's Wally Stanowski on defense, Cowley at center, Bryan Hextall of the Rangers and Sweeney Schriner, now with Toronto, on the wings.

The Bruins were the class of the league again and captured their fourth straight regular-season title. They set two records, going 15 games without a loss on the road over one stretch and 23 without a setback over another.

Boston finished five points in front of Toronto and knocked off the Maple Leafs in the opening round of the Stanley Cup playoffs. Detroit eliminated the Rangers and then Chicago, which had disposed of Montreal in the opening round.

In the Cup finals, the Bruins swept past the Red Wings in four straight games with Milt Schmidt and Eddie Wiseman, the player they had obtained from the Americans in the Eddie Shore deal the year before, starring.

War clouds had convinced players and executives around the league that it would not be long before the events in Europe and the Pacific would affect the NHL. Conn Smythe, owner of the Maple Leafs, advised all of his players to volunteer for military training and most of the club joined the Toronto Scottish Reserve. Other players around the league followed suit and before long many of them were trading shoulder pads and hockey sticks for field packs and rifles.

1941–42

The National Hockey League season was less than one month old in December, 1941, when suddenly, hockey didn't seem very important any more. It was on the morning of December 7 that Japanese bombs poured down on United States ships anchored in Pearl Harbor and plunged the U.S. into World War II.

On the night of December 7, the New York Rangers defeated Boston, 5–4, Chicago nipped the Americans, who had changed the designation of their franchise from New York to Brooklyn, 5–4, and Detroit edged Montreal, 3–2. But nobody cared about the results that night.

The next morning, many of the same fans who had packed hockey arenas the night before lined up at recruiting stations as America went to war. Hockey players, too, did their part.

Of the 14 players listed in the Ranger lineup the night of December 7, 10 eventually wound up in uniform. It was the same throughout the league as the service rolls swelled with top NHL talent. The names included Muzz and Lynn Patrick, Sid Abel, Boston's "Kraut Line" of Milt Schmidt, Woody Dumart and Bobby Bauer, Terry and Ken Reardon, Howie Meeker,

Black Jack Stewart, goalies Jim Henry and Chuck Rayner and scores of others.

But, as it had 25 years before when confronted by another world conflict, the NHL continued through World War II without a single interruption in its schedule.

On the day that Japan attacked Pearl Harbor, Bryan Hextall of the Rangers and Toronto's Gordie Drillon shared the NHL scoring lead. Hextall went on to capture the championship with 56 points, two points more than his teammate Lynn Patrick. Both Rangers made the All-Star team along with Toronto center Syl Apps, defensemen Tommy Anderson of the Brooklyn Americans and Earl Seibert of Chicago and goalie Frankie Brimsek of Boston.

Anderson won the Hart Trophy as MVP, Apps took the Lady Byng, Brimsek captured the Vezina Trophy and Grant Warwick of the Rangers was the Calder Trophy winner.

Red Dutton's troubled Americans weathered one of the longest holdouts in hockey history when Busher Jackson could not reach terms with the club. Finally, in desperation, Dutton shipped Jackson to Boston for $7,500 in January. Dutton also traded Lorne Carr to Toronto for four players. But nothing worked right for the Amerks. When they finished last and

Boston's Frank Brimsek battles the puck against the Rangers.   CULVER

their cross-town rivals, the Rangers, won the regular-season title, it marked the end of the Americans. They dropped out of the league at the conclusion of the season.

Toronto eliminated the first-place Rangers in the opening round of the playoffs while Detroit eliminated the Canadiens and then the Bruins, who had knocked out Chicago. That set up a final round meeting between the Red Wings and Maple Leafs—one of the most amazing series in Stanley Cup history.

Detroit stunned the favored Leafs by winning the first three games— two of them at Toronto. Billy Taylor of the Leafs kidded newsmen before the next game, saying, "Don't worry about us, we'll beat them four straight."

Few observers, except perhaps Taylor, were prepared for what followed. The Leafs shook up their lineup and with seldom-used Don Metz and Ernie Dickens supplying the spark, won the next four games and the Stanley Cup. It was Taylor who set up Sweeney Schriner's second goal of the game and the final one of the series in Toronto's 3–1 victory in the seventh game.

IV FROM A SOLID SIX...TO EXPANSION 1942—1973

With the exit of the Americans, the NHL was down to six teams—Detroit, Chicago, Montreal, New York, Boston and Toronto. This solid foundation would remain intact until the ambitious expansion program of the NHL's second half-century.

The war years would bring important changes to the NHL. Before the conflict was over, Frank Boucher, the creative center of the Rangers, who now coached the New York club, was to suggest the adoption of a red line at center ice to speed up the game. Overtime periods would be done away with in the interest of maintaining tight wartime travel schedules.

And Montreal's Maurice Richard emerged as the game's first truly super-scorer. The Rocket, as Richard became known, was to be the key man on one of the most devastating teams in hockey history—the Canadiens of the mid 1950s. They were so proficient that they forced a rule change to keep them from utterly dominating the sport.

In Detroit, a young man named Gordie Howe arrived on the scene with little advance notice and established himself as hockey's greatest scorer and its longevity king. It was Howe and Richard who ruled the game in the '50s along with the Canadiens and the Red Wings.

And then came the 1960s and Bobby Hull, the dynamic blond bomber of the Chicago Black Hawks, who epitomized hockey's next era of bigger, stronger, faster players.

The period would see the shifting of the league's administration from President Frank Calder, who had been head man since the NHL's inception in 1917, to Red Dutton and then to Clarence Campbell, the ex-referee, who would be at the helm when big-league hockey swung into its most successful era.

1942–43

Numerous NHL players and executives were in the service by the time the 1942 season began and early in the season a major rule change was enacted. Because of the tight train schedules during the war, NHL teams had to be precise about the length of games. Thus, they eliminated overtime.

Until then, when a game was tied at the end of three regulation periods, the teams played a 10-minute overtime period in an attempt to break the deadlock. Unlike Stanley Cup overtimes, the extra periods were not sudden death but lasted a full 10 minutes. Therefore, it was possible to have goals scored during overtime but for the game to still end in a tie.

Bloodied Jimmy Orlando of Detroit grasps referee King Clancy after a fight with Toronto's Gaye Stewart during the 1942–43 season. ALEXANDRA STUDIO

*Gaye Stewart of the Maple Leafs cap-
tured Rookie of the Year honors in
1942–43.* HOCKEY HALL OF FAME
(ALEXANDRA STUDIO)

Referee Bill Chadwick, a leading NHL official of the 1940s, believes
the elimination of the extra period was a good thing for hockey. "Overtimes benefitted the stronger teams," says Chadwick. "It gave them 10
more minutes to wear down weaker competition. If a weak club held a
stronger one to a tie for 60 minutes, it ought to be worth something."

With the Americans out of the league, the schedule was increased from
48 to 50 games. Red Dutton, the Amerks' head man, was disconsolate at
the demise of his club but he was to be back in hockey much faster than
he expected.

On his way to a meeting of the league's Board of Governors in Toronto
in January, President Frank Calder suffered a heart attack. Two weeks
later, the man who had been at the head of the league since its inception
in 1917, was dead. The Governors chose Dutton as president pro tem
with the understanding that Clarence Campbell, the man Calder had
chosen as his successor, would eventually take over.

Chicago's Bentley brothers, Doug and Max, battled Bill Cowley of
Boston for the scoring title. Doug Bentley finally won the crown with

*Chicago's Doug Bentley beat out his
brother Max and Boston's Bill Cowley
for the scoring championship in 1942–43.*
HOCKEY HALL OF FAME

73 points, including 33 goals. Cowley had 72 points and Max Bentley 70.

Cowley and Doug Bentley made the All-Star team along with Toronto's
Lorne Carr, Black Jack Stewart of Detroit and Earl Seibert of Chicago on
defense, and Johnny Mowers of Detroit in goal. Cowley also won the Hart
Trophy while Mowers took the Vezina. The Lady Byng went to Max
Bentley and Gaye Stewart of Toronto won the Calder.

In Montreal, the Canadiens introduced Maurice Richard, a young right
winger, who scored five goals in 16 games before a broken ankle put him
out of action.

Detroit won the regular-season title by four points over Boston while
Toronto finished third and the Canadiens made it to fourth place—
their highest finish in five seasons—and the final playoff spot in the
six-team league. The Red Wings eliminated the Maple Leafs and Boston
dropped the Canadiens in the Stanley Cup semifinals. Then, with Carl
Liscombe and Sid Abel starring, Detroit flashed past the Bruins in four
straight games to capture the Cup.

1943–44

The war had ravaged NHL rosters, leaving only youngsters, service
rejects or over-age veterans. The situation was so desperate that in New

York, coach Frank Boucher of the Rangers attempted a comeback at the age of 42. Boucher's return at center ice lasted 15 games and he averaged almost a point per game for hapless New York.

It was Boucher and Art Ross, Boston's manager, who pushed for, and eventually got, legislation introducing the center red line. The mid-ice divider was introduced at the start of the 1943 season in an effort to speed up the game. Boucher explained the reasoning behind it.

"My thought was that hockey had become a see-saw affair," said Boucher. "Defending teams were jammed in their own end for minutes because they couldn't pass their way out against the new five-man attack."

Before the red line was introduced, players could not pass the puck out of their defensive zone but had to carry it out themselves. This was difficult with five opposing skaters to weave through and Boucher suggested a solution.

"Why not allow teams to pass their way out of trouble, say up to mid-ice," he reasoned. "Use a red line to divide the ice. It would open the dam for the defending team and restore end-to-end play."

The idea was adopted and speeded up the game considerably.

Boston's Herbie Cain won the scoring race with 36 goals and 82 points but missed the first All-Star team. Chicago's Doug Bentley, Lorne Carr

Syd Howe of the Red Wings set an NHL record with six goals in one game.
HOCKEY HALL OF FAME

*Toronto's Babe Pratt was MVP in 1943
–44.*   HOCKEY HALL OF FAME

of Toronto and Bill Cowley of Boston were named to the All-Star forward line, with Toronto's Babe Pratt and Earl Seibert of Chicago on defense and Montreal's Bill Durnan in goal. Pratt was the Hart Trophy winner, Clint Smith of Chicago took the Lady Byng, Durnan won the Vezina and Toronto's Gus Bodnar captured the Calder.

And in Montreal, coach Dick Irvin assembled a new line. He used Elmer Lach, who spoke only English, at center; Toe Blake, fluent in French and English, on left wing, and young Maurice Richard, the darling of the French-Canadian fans, on the right side. The unit was tagged the Punch Line and produced 82 goals—32 of them by the fiery Richard.

With Durnan doing an outstanding job in goal and the Punch Line racing through the league, Montreal dropped just five games and won the regular-season championship by 15 points over Detroit. It was the start of a dynasty.

There were two notable goal-scoring feats. Detroit's Syd Howe blasted six goals in a 12–2 romp over the Rangers, setting a modern mark for most goals in a single game. And Toronto's Gus Bodnar, a rookie, set a

70

record for the fastest goal by a first-year man when he scored just 15 seconds after hitting the ice in his debut, also against the Rangers.

In the Stanley Cup playoffs, Richard really took off. The Rocket scored all five goals in the Canadiens' second game victory and Montreal finished off Toronto in the opening round before sweeping past Chicago in four straight games for the Cup. Richard set a Stanley Cup record with 12 goals in the nine playoff games.

1944–45

Maurice Richard's playoff explosion the year before set the stage for the Montreal star's greatest season. The Rocket zoomed through the NHL's 50-game schedule at an incredible goal-per-game pace, scoring a record 50 times. He had 15 goals in one nine-game stretch including five goals in

Ted Lindsay broke in with Red Wings in 1944–45.   HOCKEY HALL OF FAME

one game. Ten times during the season he scored two or more goals in a single game.

Richard was the first man to score 50 goals in a season and the only one ever to do it in a 50-game season. His accomplishment is often compared to the record he erased—Joe Malone's 44 goals in a 22-game season in 1917–18, the NHL's first year of operation. Malone's record was established in the era before forward passing; Richard's came in the modern era with the game much the same as it is today. Critics often pointed out that Richard's feat came against watered-down teams weakened by the war but the fact remains that the Rocket was the first man to hit the magic 50.

Richard's linemates also flourished from his record spree and the Punch Line finished 1-2-3 in scoring. Center Elmer Lach led all scorers with 80 points, Richard finished second with 73 points and left wing Toe Blake was third with 67.

Emil "Butch" Bouchard of Montreal was an All-Star defenseman.
HOCKEY HALL OF FAME (DAVID BIER)

The Canadiens dominated the league, winning the title again, this time by 13 points. Five Montreal players—Richard, Lach, Blake, defenseman Butch Bouchard and goalie Bill Durnan made the All-Star team with only Detroit defenseman Flash Hollett breaking the Canadiens' monopoly. Lach was the MVP, Chicago's Bill Mosienko won the Lady Byng Trophy, Durnan took the Vezina and Toronto's Frank McCool captured the Calder.

The Canadiens had lost only eight regular-season games in 1944–45 and a total of just 14 games (one in the playoffs) in two seasons while winning two straight league titles and the Stanley Cup. They were, quite naturally, favored to take the Cup again.

But Toronto stung Montreal with two quick victories in the opening round of the playoffs and eliminated the Canadiens in six games. Detroit wiped out a two-game Boston edge and whipped the Bruins in their semifinal series. That set up a final round between the Maple Leafs and Red Wings.

Detroit almost erased the memory of the embarrassing Cup loss to the Leafs three years earlier, when they had blown a three-game lead. This time, it was Toronto which won the first three games—all of them shutouts by rookie goalie Frank McCool.

Suddenly the Red Wings bounced back, just as the Leafs had done in 1942. Detroit won three straight games and it looked like history was about to repeat. But Toronto finally halted the storybook comeback by winning the seventh game on defenseman Babe Pratt's goal.

1945–46

With World War II drawing to a close, hockey players began returning to the sport. Players came back throughout the season, causing a constant shuffle of rosters throughout the NHL.

Many had lost the best hockey years of their lives while in service and found it difficult to make moves that once were second nature to them. Four years of war had robbed many of that vital extra measure of speed that separated the average players from the stars.

Some clubs, the Rangers among them, felt a sense of responsibility to the returnees and stuck with them until it became all too apparent that they just weren't able to keep up with the NHL pace anymore.

Chicago's Max Bentley got back in time to start the season with the Black Hawks and proved that his service years had not affected his hockey ability. Bentley won the scoring title with 31 goals and 61 points and earned the Hart Trophy as the league's MVP.

Bentley was picked as the All-Star center on a team that included Montreal's Maurice Richard at right wing, Gaye Stewart of Toronto at left wing, Montreal's Butch Bouchard and Boston's Jack Crawford on

Kraut Liners Milt Schmidt (left) and Woody Dumart (14) backcheck in front of the Boston net as the Bruins trounce the Rangers, 7–1. UPI

Boston's All-Star defenseman, John Crawford, wore this helmet to cover and protect his bald head.

HOCKEY HALL OF FAME
(ALEXANDRA STUDIO)

defense and Montreal goalie Bill Durnan, who won his third straight Vezina Trophy. The Lady Byng went to Montreal's Toe Blake and Edgar Laprade of the Rangers won the Calder Trophy as the NHL's best rookie.

Richard did not come close to the record goal-scoring pace he had maintained the year before, and finished with 27—less than three other players, including his linemate, Toe Blake.

Despite the Rocket's reduced output, the Canadiens won their third straight regular-season title, this time by five points over Boston. But they at least looked mortal, losing 17 games—just one less than they had dropped in combined regular-season and Stanley Cup play for the previous two years.

The NHL had a new look for the service returnees. In addition to the powerful Canadiens, who had been little more than also-rans when the war started, there was the red line and a new system of three officials— two linesmen as well as a referee—for every game. Goal lights were made mandatory.

In the playoffs, the Punch Line carried the Canadiens to their second Stanley Cup in three years. Blake and Richard had seven goals each and Elmer Lach added five and 12 assists as Montreal shredded Chicago in four games and Boston in five to clinch the Cup.

1946–47

Red Dutton had successfully steered the NHL through the war years and before the 1946–47 season announced his retirement. The new NHL president was Clarence Campbell, a former referee, a Rhodes scholar, a lieutenant colonel in the Canadian Army and on the legal staff at the Nuremberg Trials. All this was experience that would serve Campbell well at one time or another in the ensuing years.

In Montreal, Tommy Gorman announced his retirement as general manager of the Canadiens and his replacement was Frank Selke, who for many years had played a key role in Conn Smythe's Toronto operation. Selke's move to Montreal reunited him with another ex-Smythe employee, Canadiens' coach Dick Irvin.

Detroit introduced a slope-shouldered, rawboned right wing who would one day become hockey's top star. But Gordie Howe was just another rookie and his seven-goal season hardly portended greatness.

The league increased its schedule from 50 to 60 games and introduced a system of bonuses for All-Star selection and individual trophy winners. From then on, in addition to the honor of being selected, each player would get a $1,000 bonus from the league. In addition, the NHL boosted to $127,000 the regular-season and Stanley Cup playoff pools, making it more profitable than ever before for individuals and teams to do well.

Despite a faceful of ice, Toronto's Turk Broda stops this bid for a goal by Boston's Bep Guidolin.   WIDE WORLD

Clarence S. Campbell, a former referee, took over the presidency of the NHL in the fall of 1946.

NATIONAL HOCKEY LEAGUE

Montreal's power-laden Canadiens reaped most of the benefits from the NHL's new affluence. They won their fourth straight regular-season title and gained four of the six first team All-Star berths. Goalie Bill Durnan, defensemen Butch Bouchard and Kenny Reardon and right winger Maurice Richard were the Canadiens' All-Star selections. Milt Schmidt of Boston at center and Doug Bentley of Chicago at left wing completed the team.

Durnan won his fourth Vezina Trophy in a row—the first goalie to turn that trick. Richard took the Hart Trophy and Boston's Bobby Bauer was the Lady Byng winner. The Calder Trophy went to Toronto's Howie Meeker, who had been so badly wounded during the war that he was told he would never be able to play hockey again.

Chicago's Max Bentley won his second straight scoring title with 72 points—one more than Richard, who fired 45 goals. Interestingly, Richard earned the MVP designation in a season when he scored five goals less

Montreal's Ken Reardon was an All-Star defenseman. HOCKEY HALL OF FAME

The Toronto Maple Leafs: Stanley Cup winners in 1946–47.

than his record 50. The year he scored 50, the Rocket's linemate, Elmer Lach, was the MVP.

The Canadiens breezed past Boston in the five-game opening series of the Stanley Cup playoffs and then faced Toronto, which had knocked off Detroit in five games. The Canadiens won the opener of the final series, 6–0, prompting goalie Bill Durnan to scoff at the Leafs. "How did these guys get in the playoffs anyway?" needled Durnan. He soon found out.

Toronto bounced back with three straight victories that left Montreal on the brink of elimination. The Canadiens won the fifth game but the Leafs took game No. 6 and the Stanley Cup. It was in the midst of the final series that a high-sticking episode cost Richard a $250 fine and a one-game suspension by Campbell—the first of several scrapes involving the fiery Canadiens' star and the placid president of the league.

1947–48

The NHL pension plan was born in 1947, with contributions by both the players and the league. In an effort to build pension revenue, an annual

78

Toronto's Vic Lynn shudders as Montreal's Maurice Richard shatters a pane of protective glass at Maple Leaf Gardens.   ALEXANDRA STUDIO

All-Star game was initiated, pitting the previous season's All-Star squad against the winners of the Stanley Cup. The game was to be played just before the beginning of the regular season.

Toronto's Maple Leaf Gardens hosted the first All-Star affair and a crowd of 14,169 paid $25,865 to watch the All-Stars defeat Toronto, 4–3. Financially, the game was off to a good start. But the opening classic was marred when Bill Mosienko of Chicago fractured his left ankle.

The Maple Leafs were anxious to retain the Stanley Cup they had won the previous spring and Conn Smythe decided the best way to achieve that was to get Max Bentley into a Toronto uniform. That would not be easy since Bentley had won two straight scoring championships and, along with his brother Doug, provided Chicago with a very healthy gate attraction.

But the Black Hawks' farm system had not produced much in the way of NHL talent and Chicago was short of bodies. That gave Smythe the

Elmer Lach of Montreal was the 1947–48 scoring champion.

HOCKEY HALL OF FAME

Two great goalies: Montreal's Bill Durnan and Toronto's Turk Broda.
HOCKEY HALL OF FAME

opening he needed. The Maple Leaf boss assembled an attractive package of Gus Bodnar, Gaye Stewart, Bob Goldham, Bud Poile and Ernie Dickens which the Hawks could not turn down. Bentley and Cy Thomas went to the Leafs in the seven-player swap.

Smythe's bold move paid off. The Leafs soared to the top of the league and won the regular-season title as Bentley contributed 54 points, including 26 goals. The scoring title, however, went to Montreal's Elmer Lach, who had 31 goals and 61 points. The season marked the breakup of the Canadiens' potent Punch Line, on which Lach was the center. Toe Blake, the left wing, suffered a broken ankle in January, which ended his playing career.

A combination of circumstances, not the least of them injuries to Blake and others, dropped the Canadiens to fifth place and out of the playoffs.

Buddy O'Connor, traded by Montreal to New York before the season, won both the Hart and Lady Byng Trophies—the first player to capture both in the same season. Toronto's Turk Broda took the Vezina and Detroit's Jimmy McFadden was the Calder Trophy winner.

81

In Detroit, the Red Wings assembled a line of Sid Abel at center, Ted Lindsay on left wing and Gordie Howe on the right side and tabbed it the Production Line. And it produced handsomely with 63 goals—33 of them by Lindsay.

The league was rocked late in the season by a gambling scandal which led to lifetime suspensions for two players—Billy Taylor of the Rangers and Don Gallinger of Boston. President Clarence Campbell emphasized that no games had been fixed and that Gallinger and Taylor were punished for betting on games. A similar charge had resulted in a mid-season suspension for Babe Pratt two seasons earlier but Pratt was reinstated after missing nine games.

Detroit dominated the All-Star team with Ted Lindsay at left wing and Bill Quackenbush and Jack Stewart on defense. The other choices were goalie Turk Broda of Toronto and linemates Elmer Lach and Maurice Richard of Montreal.

While the Wings led in All-Star picks, it was the Maple Leafs who dominated the Stanley Cup playoffs. Toronto whipped Boston in five games and then clinched its second straight Cup by beating Detroit in four straight. In the final series, the Leafs held the Red Wings' vaunted Production Line to a single goal.

1948–49

When he first saw Sid Abel, Ted Lindsay and Gordie Howe on a line together, Jack Adams knew the Detroit trio would be something special. And he was right. Starting in 1948, the Production Line led the Red Wings to one of the most successful eras in NHL history—seven straight league titles.

Abel, Lindsay and Howe meshed together like precision gears and Adams, the genial Detroit general manager, marveled at the trio's uncanny anticipation. "They could score goals in their sleep," Adams once remarked. "They always seem to know where the play will develop."

Abel, the center, was the playmaker. Lindsay, at left wing, was a fierce checker and competitor who was deadly in the corners. And right winger Howe had a marvelous shot and could control the puck for what seemed like minutes on end.

Howe, only 21, was Adams' pet. The Detroit boss had almost lost the shy youngster in his first training camp when someone forgot to furnish the boy with a Red Wing jacket which Adams had promised him. When made aware of the problem, Adams produced the jacket in record time and Howe stayed with the Wings.

Injuries limited Howe to 40 games in 1948–49 and he scored just 12 goals. But Abel and Lindsay kept the Production Line output healthy with

Ranger Don Raleigh beats Canadien Bill Durnan from up close.   UPI

Roy Conacher, of the famous Canadian sporting family, was an All-Star left wing for Chicago.
HOCKEY HALL OF FAME
(ALEXANDRA STUDIO)

54 goals between them. Goalie Harry Lumley had a 2.42 goals against average and six shutouts as the Red Wings won the regular-season title by nine points over Boston. But the best goaltending job was turned in by Montreal's Bill Durnan, who won his fifth Vezina Trophy in six years with a 2.10 average and 10 shutouts. Durnan had four shutouts in a row over one stretch and established a modern record by not allowing a goal for 309 minutes, 21 seconds.

Roy Conacher of Chicago and teammate Doug Bentley staged an exciting battle for the scoring title, with Conacher finally winning it. He finished with 68 points, two more than Bentley.

Conacher was chosen as the left wing on the All-Star team with Maurice Richard of Montreal at right wing and Sid Abel of Detroit at center. Two Detroit defensemen, Jack Stewart and Bill Quackenbush, and Montreal's goalie, Durnan, completed the team. Despite his limited output, Gordie Howe made the second All-Star squad.

Abel won the Hart Trophy and Quackenbush became the first defenseman to take the Lady Byng. Penti Lund of the Rangers won the Calder Trophy.

In the playoffs, the Production Line riddled Montreal, scoring 12 of Detroit's 17 goals, eight of them by Howe. That put the Red Wings in the Stanley Cup finals against Toronto, which had beaten Boston in five games.

Turk Broda, the Leafs' great goalie, was more than a match for the Production Line. Broda allowed just five goals in four games and Sid Smith's hat trick in the second game set the tone as Toronto won the Cup in four straight.

The victory, marking the Leafs' second four-game sweep in two seasons, made them the first NHL team to take three straight Stanley Cups.

1949–50

Detroit's Production Line, with a healthy Gordie Howe rejoining Sid Abel and Ted Lindsay, tore through the league and finished 1-2-3 in the scoring race, matching the feat which Boston's Kraut Line, Montreal's Punch Line and Toronto's Kid Line had previously performed.

Lindsay won the scoring title with 78 points, Abel finished with 69 and Howe had 68. The trio combined for an amazing 215 points including 92 goals—35 of them by Howe.

Despite Howe's brilliant season, he had to settle for a second-team All-Star berth. For the second straight year the right wing spot on the first team went to Montreal's Maurice Richard, who scored 43 goals, the most in the league. The intense rivalry would continue through the early 1950s with the two men occupying the two All-Star berths eight times over a nine-year period.

In his last year in the NHL, goalie Frank Brimsek played for the Black Hawks and here he stops the Bruins' Red Sullivan.   WIDE WORLD

Throughout the league, fans argued the relative merits of the two right wingers and the extended debate created quite a feud between the Canadiens and Red Wings. Once, in a ruckus on the ice, Howe knocked Richard down. When the Rocket got up, Abel rubbed salt in the wound with a taunt. Richard wheeled and teed off on Abel, breaking his nose with a punch.

The other All-Stars in 1950 were Lindsay and Abel, defensemen Kenny Reardon of Montreal and Gus Mortson of Toronto and goaltender Bill Durnan of Montreal.

It was Durnan's sixth All-Star selection in seven seasons and he also captured his sixth Vezina Trophy. They were also his last, for he stunned Montreal by quitting in the midst of the Stanley Cup playoffs, saying that the pressure of big-league goaltending had simply become too much.

Two other goalies won individual awards that season. Chuck Rayner of the Rangers was the Hart winner and Jack Gelineau, a rookie who beat Frank Brimsek out of the Boston netminding job, took the Calder Trophy. The Lady Byng winner was Edgar Laprade of the Rangers.

Detroit finished first in the regular-season race and met Toronto in one Stanley Cup semifinal while the Rangers tangled with the Canadiens in the other. Going into the series, the Red Wings had dropped 11 straight playoff games to the Leafs and been eliminated three straight years by Toronto.

In the opening game of the series, a devastating injury almost cost Gordie Howe his life. Ted Kennedy sidestepped a Howe check and Gordie plunged face-first into the boards. He suffered a concussion, a broken nose, a fractured right cheekbone and a scratched eyeball.

The Wings, beaten 5–0 in that opener and deprived of their top scorer, gallantly bounced back and defeated the Maple Leafs in seven games. The Rangers hung three straight defeats on the Canadiens and then Bill Durnan went to Dick Irvin before the fourth game and asked that the Montreal coach use rookie Gerry McNeil in his place. McNeil won the fourth game but New York finished Montreal off in the fifth.

In the Stanley Cup finals, the Rangers led three games to two and were leading, 4–3, in the third period of the sixth game. But goals by Ted Lindsay and Sid Abel gave the Red Wings the game and tied the series. In the seventh game, Pete Babando's overtime goal sank New York and delivered the Stanley Cup to Detroit.

1950–51

Jack Adams was never a stand-pat general manager and although Detroit had won two straight titles, the Red Wings' boss shook them up before the 1950–51 season. He engineered a mammoth nine-player trade with Chicago—the biggest deal in NHL history.

Shuttled off to Chicago were forwards Al Dewsbury, Don Morrison and Pete Babando, defenseman Jack Stewart and goalie Harry Lumley. Babando's overtime goal had won the Stanley Cup for the Wings the season before, Stewart had made the first All-Star team three times and Lumley had turned in a 2.35 goals-against average the season before.

In return, Adams got defenseman Bob Goldham, forwards Gaye Stewart and Metro Prystai and goalie Jim Henry. Perhaps the main reason for making the trade was to give Terry Sawchuk a clear shot at the Red Wings' goalie job.

Sawchuk was not yet 21 when he became the Red Wings' regular goalie. The youngster did a spectacular job in his rookie season, with a 1.98 goals-against average and a league-leading 11 shutouts. He was the easy winner of the Calder Trophy and was named to the first All-Star team.

The other All-Stars included Detroit's Gordie Howe, who won the scoring championship with 88 points and scored 43 goals—one more than his right wing rival, Montreal's Maurice Richard. The other forwards were Howe's linemate, Ted Lindsay on left wing, and Boston's Milt Schmidt

Montreal's Maurice Richard checks New York's Edgar Laprade off the puck at the Canadien end of the rink in December, 1950. UPI

Maple Leafs (left to right) Sid Smith, Max Bentley and Bill Barilko celebrate an early playoff victory over Boston enroute to the Stanley Cup in 1950–51. UPI

at center. Red Kelly of Detroit and Bill Quackenbush of Boston were picked as the defensemen.

Schmidt won the Hart Trophy and Kelly took the Lady Byng, becoming the second Red Wing defenseman in three years to win the trophy for gentlemanly play. In spite of Sawchuk's incredible first-year statistics, he was not the Vezina Trophy winner. That honor went to Al Rollins, who split Toronto's netminding with veteran Turk Broda. Rollins played 40 games compared to Sawchuk's 70 and had a 1.75 goals-against average.

The Red Wings finished first with 44 victories and 13 ties, accumulating a record 101 points. But they were only six points up on Toronto, which won 41 games. It was a busy season for President Clarence Campbell. He slapped three-game suspensions and $300 fines each on Ted Lindsay of Detroit and Bill Ezinicki of Boston for a mid-season brawl. Gus Mortson of Toronto used his stick on Chicago's Adam Brown in March and it cost him a two-game suspension and $200 fine. Maurice Richard, still steaming over a game misconduct penalty he had drawn from referee Hugh McLean the night before, grabbed McLean in New York's Picadilly Hotel and as a result of the confrontation, Campbell fined the Rocket $500.

In the Stanley Cup opening round, the Canadiens were decided underdogs to the Red Wings. But Montreal won the first two games—both of them on overtime goals by Maurice Richard. Detroit squared the series by taking the next two but Montreal came right back and eliminated the Red Wings by winning the fifth and sixth games.

Toronto took Boston in five games and advanced to the finals against Montreal. The Maple Leafs and Canadiens set a record of sorts as all five games of their series went into overtime.

In the fifth game, Toronto was trailing, 2–1, in the final period when coach Joe Primeau yanked goalie Turk Broda to make room for an extra attacker. The maneuver paid off with Tod Sloan's game-tying goal with just 32 seconds remaining.

Less than three minutes into overtime, defenseman Bill Barilko won the game and the Cup for the Leafs with a goal. It was the last one he ever scored. Two months later, he was killed in a plane crash.

1951–52

Detroit won its fourth straight regular-season championship, but the most exciting moments of the season came on March 23 in a meaningless game between New York and Chicago. That was the night Bill Mosienko made hockey history.

The Rangers and Black Hawks were out of the race for a playoff berth when they met that night. New York was fifth and Chicago last. The Rangers, who had used Chuck Rayner and Emile Francis in goal during most of the season went with Lorne Anderson in this particular game.

Mosienko, one of Chicago's top scorers, was playing on a line with Gus Bodnar and George Gee. At 6:09 of the third period, Bodnar fed the puck to Mosienko and the right wing fired a goal. The puck was brought back for a face-off and at 6:20 the combination clicked again. Then another face-off and at 6:30 another goal by Mosienko. Three goals in 21 seconds earned him a spot in the record book for the quickest hat trick in NHL history.

In Detroit, the Red Wings were dreaming about the Stanley Cup. And it was no idle dream, either. The Wings had ripped through the regular season, rolling up 100 points—just one point under the record they had established the season before. They finished 22 points ahead of second-place Montreal.

Montreal defenseman Doug Harvey (2) breaks up a Boston rush.   UPI

Gordie Howe won his second straight scoring title with 86 points, the same number he had posted the year before. He scored 47 goals, making a serious run at Maurice Richard's record of 50. Howe was chosen MVP and named to the right wing spot on the All-Star team. The other All-Stars were Detroit's Ted Lindsay at left wing, Montreal's Elmer Lach at center, Red Kelly of Detroit and Doug Harvey of Montreal on defense and Detroit's Terry Sawchuk in goal.

Sawchuk took the Vezina Trophy with a 1.94 goals-against average and a league-leading 12 shutouts. Toronto's Sid Smith won the Lady Byng and Montreal's Bernie Geoffrion, nicknamed Boom Boom for his jet-powered slap shots, took the Calder Trophy as the top rookie.

Montreal battled through seven games before eliminating Boston in the Stanley Cup semifinals. The Canadiens took the deciding game when Maurice Richard skated through four Bruins and then fought off Bill Quackenbush, the last defender, before beating Jim Henry for the tie-breaking goal with four minutes to play. The significant thing about the goal is that Richard remembers very little about it. He had spent the second period of the game in the clinic at the Montreal Forum having six stitches put in his head after being belted by Leo Labine.

"I was dizzy and a few times when I got the puck I didn't know whether I was skating toward our goal or their goal," Richard recalls.

Richard's heroics got the Canadiens into the final round but the Rocket couldn't help against the Red Wing juggernaut. Howe and Ted Lindsay scored five goals between them and Sawchuk turned in his third and fourth shutouts of the playoffs as Detroit swept to the Stanley Cup in four straight games. In eight playoff games Sawchuk allowed only five goals—an incredible 0.62 goals-against average.

1952–53

Detroit's Production Line was broken up before the 1952–53 season when Sid Abel asked to be traded to Chicago. The Black Hawks wanted Abel as coach and Jack Adams, the Detroit general manager, did not stand in the way of his veteran center man.

Abel's replacement was Alex Delvecchio, who flourished playing between Gordie Howe and Ted Lindsay. He scored 59 points, including 43 assists. The switch in centers made little difference to right winger Howe and left winger Lindsay. They finished 1-2 in scoring for the second straight year with Gordie accumulating 95 points and making his most serious run at Maurice Richard's 50-goal record, finishing with 49. Lindsay had 71 points, including 32 goals.

The departure of Abel didn't seem to hurt the Red Wings, who won their fifth straight regular-season title, but it had a major effect on Chicago, the club Abel took over. Doubling as a player-coach, Abel piloted

Detroit's Terry Sawchuk has company in the cage, teammate Marcel Pronovost, as they hold off Boston's Milt Schmidt. UPI

the Black Hawks to a third-place tie with Boston for Chicago's first playoff berth in seven years.

The scoring crown was Howe's third straight and he became the first man in NHL history to put three together. Similarly, the Red Wings made NHL history with their fifth straight league title. Boston twice and Montreal once had strung four regular-season titles together, but no team had ever managed five.

Howe and Lindsay were named right wing and left wing on the first All-Star team for the third straight year. The other All-Stars were Boston

91

center Fleming Mackell, defensemen Red Kelly of Detroit and Doug Harvey of Montreal and goalie Terry Sawchuk of Detroit.

Howe won his second consecutive Hart Trophy as MVP, Kelly was the Lady Byng winner and Sawchuk, with a 1.90 average, won the Vezina. The Calder Trophy went to New York goalie Lorne "Gump" Worsley— the third goalie in four years to be honored as the NHL's top rookie.

Early in the season, Maurice Richard scored his 324th career goal, tying the NHL record held by another Montreal great, Nels Stewart. On November 8, he scored No. 325 to set the new standard. On the same night, Richard's center, Elmer Lach, scored the 200th goal of his career.

In the playoffs, the powerful Red Wings who had breezed to the Stanley Cup in eight straight games the year before, ruled as heavy favorites. They battered Boston, 7–0, in the opening game and looked like a sure thing to repeat as champions. But some clutch scoring by Ed Sandford and heroic goaltending by Sugar Jim Henry gave the Bruins a six-game first round victory over Detroit.

Chicago held a three to two edge in games against Montreal in the other semifinal when Gerry McNeil went to coach Dick Irvin of the Canadiens and suggested that he use Jacques Plante, a rookie, in goal. It was a repeat of Bill Durnan's action during the playoffs in 1950 when he had gone to Irvin and asked to be replaced by McNeil. Plante allowed the Black Hawks one goal in two games and the Canadiens advanced to the final round against Boston.

With Plante and McNeil dividing the netminding, Montreal whipped the Bruins in five games to capture the Stanley Cup.

1953–54

The Chicago Black Hawks slipped back into the NHL's cellar after their one-season move into the playoffs and established a record for futility in 1953–54. They managed only 12 victories and lost 51 times. Both are NHL records for 70-game seasons.

Ironically, the Black Hawks did achieve one important honor that season. Goalie Al Rollins was named the Most Valuable Player in the league. The award might very well have been for heroism in the face of a season-long barrage of enemy shots. Four of the 12 Chicago victories were shutouts by Rollins and the 242 goals allowed by the Black Hawks were the most in the league.

Even more ironic is the fact that Harry Lumley, whom Chicago had traded to Toronto for Rollins and three other players the year before, won the Vezina Trophy, a spot on the All-Star team and a line in the NHL record book with 13 shutouts, the most ever. But the MVP was Rollins.

Gordie Howe and the Detroit Red Wings again ruled the league. Howe won an unprecedented fourth straight scoring title with 81 points and

Montreal's Jacques Plante is on all fours after colliding with Detroit's Ted Lindsay (behind Jacques). Gordie Howe is behind the cage. WIDE WORLD

the Red Wings captured an unprecedented sixth consecutive regular-season championship.

Howe and his Detroit linemate, Ted Lindsay, made the first All-Star team for the fourth straight year. Montreal center Ken Mosdell, defensemen Doug Harvey of Montreal and Red Kelly of Detroit and Lumley, Toronto's goalie, completed the team. It was the third straight All-Star berth for Kelly and Harvey.

Kelly also won his third Lady Byng Trophy in four years and also captured a new award, the James Norris Trophy, as the league's top defenseman. The trophy was presented by the four children of the late former owner-president of the Detroit Red Wings. Camille Henry of New York took the Calder Trophy.

Detroit needed just five games to eliminate Toronto, and Montreal took Boston in four straight in the opening rounds of the Stanley Cup playoffs.

Then the Canadiens and Red Wings went at each other in the final round in a memorable series that stretched over seven games. The Red Wings, with Gordie Howe, Ted Lindsay and Alex Delvecchio starring, won three of the first four contests. Then Canadiens' coach Dick Irvin changed

93

Harry Lumley of Toronto won the Vezina Trophy in 1953–54.

HOCKEY HALL OF FAME (ALEXANDRA STUDIO)

goalies, recalling 31-year-old Gerry McNeil from the minors to replace Jacques Plante.

McNeil shut out the Red Wings in the fifth game, which Montreal won on an overtime goal by Ken Mosdell. Then he beat them, 4–1, to even the series at three games apiece.

The seventh game went into overtime tied at 1–1. With 4½ minutes gone in the extra period, Detroit's Tony Leswick lofted a shot toward McNeil. Doug Harvey, the Canadiens' superlative defenseman, lifted his glove to flick the puck away. Instead, it glanced off Harvey's glove over McNeil's shoulder and into the Montreal net, giving Detroit the Stanley Cup.

The Canadiens stormed off the ice instead of congratulating the Red Wings as custom dictated. "If I had shaken hands," stormed coach Dick Irvin, "I wouldn't have meant it. I refuse to be a hypocrite."

1954–55

Montreal was piecing together a powerful young team to make a run at Detroit's domination of the NHL. There was tall Jean Beliveau, the slick center from Quebec whom the Canadiens wanted so badly they purchased the rights to an entire amateur league to get him. There was flamboyant Boom Boom Geoffrion, a hard-shooting right winger. There was cool Doug Harvey, perhaps the finest defenseman in the league since Eddie Shore. There was colorful Jacques Plante in goal. And there was the Rocket— Maurice Richard.

The Rocket was always No. 1 with the Canadiens' fans. He was the heart of the club. The fiery Frenchman with the Gallic glare was long on talent and short on temper. It was the latter that got him in trouble, costing him the scoring title and leading to the riot of Ste. Catherine Street which rocked the hockey world in March, 1955.

Richard, Geoffrion and Beliveau were racing for the scoring title when the Rocket's temper sabotaged him. It was March 13 in Boston when Richard lost his poise, attacked Hal Laycoe of the Bruins with his stick and took a punch at linesman Cliff Thompson.

Clarence Campbell, the league president, was outraged by Richard's behavior and suspended the star for the final three games of the regular season as well as the entire playoffs. Campbell showed up at the Montreal Forum on March 17 to watch the Canadiens play Detroit in a battle for first place. When the president took his seat, he was greeted with some hooting as well as a shower of peanuts and programs. Then a tear gas bomb was thrown on the ice at about the same moment that a fan approached Campbell's box with hand extended as if to shake, and then whacked the president.

Outside the building, more trouble was brewing. As fans poured out of the besieged Forum, they turned into a mob, rumbling down Ste. Catherine Street, Montreal's main avenue, and looting stores.

The next day, Richard went on the radio to plead in French for calm. "I will take my punishment," he said, "and come back next year to help the club and the younger players to win the Stanley Cup."

The suspension left Richard with 74 points and Geoffrion edged past him with 75 to win the scoring crown. Beliveau finished third with 73. Richard was named to the All-Star team along with Beliveau at center and Sid Smith of Toronto at left wing. The defensemen, again, were Doug Harvey of Montreal and Red Kelly of Detroit with Toronto's Harry Lumley in goal.

Smith won the Lady Byng Trophy while Terry Sawchuk of Detroit took the Vezina with a league-leading 12 shutouts and a 1.94 average. It was the fifth straight season in which his goals-against average was less than

Montreal goalie Jacques Plante and teammate Butch Bouchard are down but not out as they block scoring attempt by Ranger Don Raleigh (7). UPI

Under general manager Jack Adams, one of the grand old men of hockey, Detroit won its seventh Stanley Cup in 1954–55. HOCKEY HALL OF FAME

two per game. The Norris Trophy went to Harvey, the Hart Trophy to Toronto's Ted Kennedy and the Calder to Ed Litzenberger of Chicago.

Detroit edged Montreal for the regular-season title, winning its seventh straight crown by just two points. In the Stanley Cup semifinals, the Red Wings whipped Toronto in four straight and the Canadiens needed five games to eliminate Boston.

In an effort to beat the Red Wings, Montreal coach Dick Irvin alternated his goalies, Jacques Plante and Charlie Hodge. But the Wings, winning all their games at home and none in Montreal, took the series and the Cup, four games to three, as Alex Delvecchio scored twice in the seventh game.

1955–56

There were important personnel changes around the league in 1955–56—both on the players' benches and behind them. After 14 seasons as coach of the Canadiens, Dick Irvin left Montreal and moved on to Chicago, where the challenge of rebuilding the Black Hawks seemed enormous. Irvin's replacement was Toe Blake, left wing on the old Punch Line. In New York, Phil Watson, always a firebrand, took over as coach, replacing Muzz Patrick, who in turn took over from Frank Boucher as the Rangers' general manager.

Detroit shook up its Stanley Cup champions and a series of trades left the Red Wings with only nine players from the squad that had captured the Cup the previous spring. In the biggest trade, Jack Adams swapped four players, including goalie Terry Sawchuk, to Boston for five Bruins. The Sawchuk deal was made because the Red Wing management felt that Terry's nerves were getting the best of him and also because Adams had a ready-made replacement in young Glenn Hall.

Adams also consummated an eight-player trade with Chicago as the Black Hawks feverishly tried to move out of the league's lower echelon. They didn't make it, but the Rangers did. New scoring punch from a group of recently-graduated junior players including Andy Bathgate, Dean Prentice and Ron Murphy, as well as a stiffened defense supplied by Bill Gadsby, Harry Howell and the fans' favorite, Louie Fontinato, vaulted New York to third place—their highest finish in 14 years.

Fontinato, a rookie, accumulated 202 minutes in penalties—spending the equivalent of more than 10 periods sitting out infractions. The New York fans loved his brawling and nicknamed him Louie the Leaper.

In Montreal, Blake added three rookies—Henri Richard, the younger brother of Maurice, defenseman Jean Guy Talbot, and forward Claude Provost. The Canadiens were clearly the class of the league and finished with 100 points, losing only 15 of their 70 games. Three of the top four

Jacques is nimble, Jacques is quick, Jacques leaps over the Toronto stick. Jacques, of course, is Montreal goalie Jacques Plante, and No. 9 is Maurice Richard.

ALEXANDRA STUDIO

scorers were Canadiens including the champion, Jean Beliveau, who had 47 goals among his 88 points.

Beliveau was named to the All-Star team along with teammates Maurice Richard, Doug Harvey and Jacques Plante. Beliveau and Richard were joined on the forward line by Detroit's Ted Lindsay while Bill Gadsby of New York won the other defense spot alongside Harvey and in front of goaltender Plante.

Plante won the Vezina Trophy with a 1.86 goals-against average, Harvey took the Norris Trophy and Beliveau was named MVP. Detroit's Earl "Dutch" Reibel won the Lady Byng while Glenn Hall, Sawchuk's replacement at Detroit, was the Calder Trophy winner.

Montreal finished off New York in five games and Detroit eliminated Toronto, also in five, in the opening rounds of the Stanley Cup playoffs. Then, with Beliveau, Bernie Geoffrion, Rocket Richard and Bert Olmstead supplying the firepower, Montreal beat Detroit in five games to win its first Stanley Cup in a decade.

1956–57

Montreal's powerhouse Canadiens became the scourge of the league with a collection of the finest shooters ever to occupy a single team's roster at the same time. Maurice Richard, Jean Beliveau, Boom Boom Geoffrion, Bert Olmstead, Dickie Moore and the others were all expert marksmen. And when coach Toe Blake assembled a power play to take advantage of an enemy penalty, the Canadiens' shooters could turn a game around.

Blake used Geoffrion and Harvey at the points on power plays because of their hard, accurate shots. Up front he would employ Richard at right wing, Beliveau at center and Moore or Olmstead at left wing. The effect was devastating. The Canadiens often would score two or three goals on a single penalty because at the time the rules required a penalized player to spend his full two minutes in the penalty box, regardless of how often the team with the manpower edge scored.

But the Canadiens made a travesty of the rule and eventually it had to be changed, specifically because of Montreal's proficiency. Starting in 1956–57, as soon as the team with the manpower edge scored, the penalized player was allowed to return to the ice and restore his team to full strength.

Detroit's assessment of Terry Sawchuk's nerves proved accurate when the ex-Red Wing goalie walked out on the Bruins in mid-season, saying he was ill. The Bruins put in a hurry-up call to Springfield of the American League and came up with Don Simmons to replace Sawchuk. Ironically, on the day he left Boston, Sawchuk was named to the All-Star team for the first half of the season. With Terry sitting out the second half, Glenn Hall, his replacement at Detroit, captured the final All-Star designation.

Canadien Henri Richard splits Ranger defensemen Lou Fontinato, on the ice, and Harry Howell in a 1956–57 encounter. HOCKEY HALL OF FAME

Montreal's Jean Beliveau zooms in on New York's Gump Worsley as Parker MacDonald tries to defend.   HOCKEY HALL OF FAME (DAVID BIER)

The other All-Stars were Detroit's Red Kelly and Montreal's Doug Harvey on defense, Jean Beliveau of Montreal at center and Detroit's Ted Lindsay and Gordie Howe on the wings.

Howe won his fifth scoring championship with 89 points, including 44 goals and also captured the Hart Trophy as MVP. The Lady Byng went to New York's Andy Hebenton, while Montreal's Jacques Plante took the Vezina, Larry Regan of Boston won the Calder and Doug Harvey of Montreal captured the Norris.

Detroit won its eighth regular-season crown in nine years, beating out the Canadiens by six points. But the Red Wings were upset by Boston's determined Bruins in the Stanley Cup semifinal series. Detroit bowed when Boston rallied for three goals in the third period to win the deciding seventh contest.

Montreal eliminated New York in five games with Boom Boom Geoffrion exploding for three goals in the third engagement. The Canadiens faced the Bruins for the Stanley Cup and Maurice Richard set the tone by exploding for four goals in the 5–1 opening-game victory. The Rocket

101

scored three times in the second period and Don Simmons, the victim of the assault, said simply, "It was humiliating." It took the Canadiens just five games to clinch the Cup.

1957–58

Two marvelously talented rookie left wings broke into the NHL in 1957–58. Toronto's Frank Mahovlich won the Calder Trophy as the top rookie, but it was Chicago's Bobby Hull who was to emerge as one of the game's most dynamic stars.

In Detroit, Jolly Jack Adams was again active in the player market. He took Terry Sawchuk back from the Bruins in exchange for Johnny Bucyk and made room for his returning goaltender by swapping Glenn Hall and Ted Lindsay to Chicago for four players. It was rumored that part of the reason Adams unloaded Lindsay was the veteran left wing's active participation in the formation of an NHL Players' Association.

It was the best of times and it was the worst of times for Montreal's Maurice Richard. On October 19, he scored his 500th regular-season goal, but less than one month later he collided with Toronto's Marc Reaume and his Achilles tendon was almost completely severed. For a time, it was feared that the 36-year-old Rocket's career might be over.

In February, the Canadiens again were jolted by an injury. This time it was Boom Boom Geoffrion, leading the league in goals at the time. The Boomer ran into teammate Andre Pronovost during a workout and ruptured a bowel. He was given the last rites of the Roman Catholic Church before major stomach surgery saved his life.

Despite the injuries, the Canadiens carried on and finished first, 19 points ahead of the surprising Rangers, who had uncovered a new scoring star in Andy Bathgate. Part of the reason for the Canadiens' success was left winger Dickie Moore, who played the last five weeks of the season with a cast on his right wrist but still won the scoring championship with 84 points as well as an All-Star berth.

Despite the Rocket's injury, there was a Richard on the All-Star team. Brother Henri, the Pocket Rocket, who finished second to Moore in scoring with 80 points, was picked as the center. Gordie Howe of Detroit was on right wing, with Bill Gadsby of New York and Doug Harvey of Montreal as the defensemen and Chicago's Glenn Hall in goal.

Howe won Most Valuable Player honors and Harvey took the Norris Trophy as the top defenseman for the fourth straight year. Camille Henry of the Rangers won the Lady Byng, Montreal's Jacques Plante, who had started using a mask in practice, was the Vezina winner and Toronto's Frank Mahovlich took the Calder. Mahovlich had 20 goals and 16 assists compared to Bobby Hull's 13 goals and 34 assists.

Dynamic Bobby Hull broke in with the Chicago Black Hawks in 1957–58.
SCOTTY KILPATRICK

Toronto's Frank Mahovlich beat out Chicago's Bobby Hull for Rookie of the Year honors in 1957–58.

HOCKEY HALL OF FAME (TUROFSKY)

Maurice Richard, who had missed 42 regular-season games after his injury and had scored only 15 goals all year, was the spark that drove the Canadiens to their third straight Stanley Cup. Montreal swept Detroit in four games with Richard's hat trick in the final contest, leading a last-period comeback that erased a two-goal deficit and gave the Canadiens a 4–3 victory.

Boston, which had eliminated New York in six games, was tied at two games apiece with Montreal when the Rocket's overtime goal in the fifth game put the Canadiens in the driver's seat. Montreal finished off Boston in the sixth game as Richard completed the 10 playoff games with 11 goals.

1958–59

Conn Smythe never was a very good loser and when his Toronto Maple Leafs slipped into the NHL cellar, he decided it was time for action. Smythe sought out George "Punch" Imlach, director of player personnel

104

for Boston, and offered him a front office spot with the Leafs. Imlach accepted, provided that the position was that of general manager. The Leafs had no one doing that particular job, so Smythe agreed.

A week after he was named general manager, Imlach decided that Billy Reay, Toronto's coach, wasn't doing a good enough job. Imlach went on a talent hunt and lured the best man available for the job—Punch Imlach.

The Maple Leafs had several new faces besides Imlach's. They had swapped Jim Morrison to Boston for defenseman Allan Stanley and signed another new defenseman in 21-year-old Carl Brewer. Bert Olmstead was acquired from Montreal and Imlach picked up a 33-year-old journeyman goalie, Johnny Bower, from Cleveland of the American League.

They all played a role in Toronto's helter-skelter stretch run to a playoff spot. With 20 games left to play, the Maple Leafs were in the cellar. On the final night of the regular season they won their fifth straight game while New York was losing its sixth in the last seven. As a result, Toronto sneaked into the fourth and final playoff spot, one point ahead of the embarrassed Rangers, who had to refund thousands of dollars worth of useless playoff tickets.

Montreal easily captured the regular-season title, beating Boston by 18 points. Detroit, meanwhile, had fallen on lean times and dipped all the way into the league basement despite a 32-goal season by Gordie Howe.

Referee Frank Udvari is about to whistle a penalty against Toronto in a game with Montreal.   HOCKEY HALL OF FAME (ROGER ST.-JEAN)

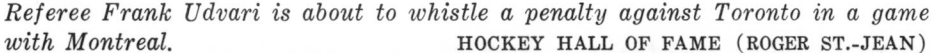

Montreal's Jean Beliveau breaks into a grin as his shot beats Toronto's Johnny Bower.   HOCKEY HALL OF FAME (DAVID BIER)

Dickie Moore of Montreal won his second straight scoring title with a record 96 points and earned the left wing spot on the All-Star team. Three other Canadiens also made the All-Stars, with Jacques Plante in goal, Jean Beliveau at center and Tom Johnson on defense. Johnson beat out teammate Doug Harvey, who missed the first team after seven straight selections. Right winger Andy Bathgate and defenseman Bill Gadsby of the Rangers completed the squad.

Bathgate won the Hart Trophy, Plante took his fourth straight Vezina and Johnson ended Harvey's four-year monopoly of the Norris Trophy. Montreal's Ralph Backstrom captured the Calder Trophy and Alex Delvecchio of Detroit was the Lady Byng winner.

Maurice Richard of Montreal missed 28 games with a fractured ankle and was virtually useless to the Canadiens in the playoffs. But his loss

106

made little difference to the Montreal powerhouse. The Canadiens eliminated Chicago in six games and ousted Toronto, which had eliminated Boston, in five games for an unprecedented fourth consecutive Stanley Cup.

1959–60

The pressures of modern hockey had taken their toll on goaltenders. There was Montreal's Bill Durnan, who retired prematurely because of nerves, Montreal's Gerry McNeil, another early retiree, and Terry Sawchuk, who left Boston in mid-season when he began seeing too much rubber. Montreal's Jacques Plante was determined not to let that happen to him.

Plante had been using a mask in practice for two years after fracturing first one and then the other cheekbone during workouts. Jacques had approached coach Toe Blake about wearing the mask during a game but Blake would not allow it.

Then, on November 1, 1959, a shot by New York's Andy Bathgate crunched into Plante's profile, inflicting a gash that took seven stitches.

When Plante subsequently emerged from the dressing room wearing a mask he looked like a creature from outer space. How could he follow the

Montreal's Maurice Richard (9) and Chicago's Elmer "Moose" Vasko fence for the puck.   UPI

puck through the mask's tiny eye slits? The answer was that Plante somehow saw it. That night, he beat the Rangers, 3–1, for Montreal's eighth straight game without a loss. The Canadiens tacked 10 more on to that streak as fans around the league flocked to see the masked marvel at work.

Plante captured his fifth consecutive Vezina Trophy, but the All-Star goalie berth went to Chicago's Glenn Hall. Chicago's Bobby Hull won the scoring race in an exciting battle with Boston's Bronco Horvath. Hull finished with 39 goals and 81 points—one point more than Horvath—and was the left wing on the All-Star team.

Gordie Howe of Detroit was the All-Star right wing with Montreal's Jean Beliveau at center. The defensemen were Marcel Pronovost of Detroit and Doug Harvey of Montreal. Howe won the Hart Trophy as MVP, Don McKenney of Boston was the Lady Byng winner, Harvey took the Norris and Chicago's Bill Hay, who centered for Hull, won the Calder.

The Canadiens won their third straight regular-season title, beating Toronto by 13 points. Then Montreal eliminated Chicago in four games in the opening round of the playoffs, with Plante turning in shutouts in the last two.

The Maple Leafs, perhaps inspired by a pile of $1,250 that coach Punch Imlach placed in the middle of the dressing room floor as a reminder of the difference between winning and losing, eliminated Detroit in six games.

But Montreal swept past Toronto in the finals in four straight games, to win the Stanley Cup in the minimum of eight games.

1960–61

An era came to an end in 1960 when Montreal's Maurice Richard retired. After 18 professional seasons and 544 goals, the Rocket was off the ice. But that didn't keep his name out of the hockey headlines.

That was because for the first time since 1953 when Gordie Howe scored 49 times, there was a genuine threat to the Rocket's record of 50 goals in a season. It would be more correct to say there were two threats, but Frank Mahovlich's early-season pace obscured Bernie Geoffrion's run at the Rocket's mark.

By mid-season, Mahovlich, Toronto's hard-skating left wing, had 37 goals and seemed a cinch to top 50. Geoffrion, on the other hand, missed six games with injuries and had only 29 goals going into the final six weeks of the season. And 14 of those had come over one 11-game stretch.

The defenses keyed on Mahovlich over those final weeks and Toronto's Big M finished with 48 goals. Geoffrion, a streaky player, hit another hot spell, exploding for 18 goals in 13 games and scoring his 50th of the season

Toronto's Dave Keon was Rookie of the Year in 1960–61.   KEN REGAN

in the Canadiens' 68th game—ironically against Mahovlich's team, the Maple Leafs.

Geoffrion did not score in either of the last two games of the regular season, but won the scoring title with his 50 goals and 45 assists for 95 points. He was the All-Star right wing with Toronto's Mahovlich at left wing and Jean Beliveau of Montreal at center. The defensemen were Doug Harvey of Montreal and Marcel Pronovost of Detroit with Toronto's Johnny Bower in goal.

Bower ended Jacques Plante's five-year hold on the Vezina Trophy while Geoffrion earned the Hart Trophy and Harvey won the Norris for the sixth time. Dave Keon of Toronto was the Calder winner and Red Kelly, switched from defense to center after being traded to Toronto, won his fourth Lady Byng.

The Canadiens captured their fourth straight regular-season championship, beating out Toronto by two points. And Montreal was favored to continue its string of five consecutive Stanley Cups when it opened the playoffs against third-place Chicago.

But the Black Hawks intimidated the Canadiens with some tough body work and got consecutive shutouts from goalie Glenn Hall in the fifth and sixth games to beat Montreal, four games to two. The turning point may have come in the third game, won in triple overtime by Chicago on Murray Balfour's goal. Montreal coach Toe Blake was so incensed at the officiating of Dalton McArthur that he rushed on the ice and took a swing at the referee. That sortie cost Toe $2,000.

Detroit knocked out Toronto in five games, setting up the final for the Stanley Cup between the third-place Black Hawks and fourth-place Red Wings. Unflattering remarks about the officiating cost coach Rudy Pilous and general manager Tommy Ivan of the Black Hawks $500 between them but the fines didn't hurt too much because Chicago took the Cup in six games.

1961–62

In August, the Hockey Hall of Fame erected on the Canadian National Exhibition grounds at Toronto, was officially opened. Built at a cost of $500,000, the hockey shrine honored 89 players, executives and referees from hockey's past.

But it was a player very much of the present who created the excitement, Chicago's blond bombshell, Bobby Hull. A scoring champion two years earlier at the age of 21, Hull boasted a slap shot clocked at better than 100 miles per hour.

Hull started his record run slowly and had only 16 goals after 40 games. But then, like Geoffrion had done the year before, when he tied Maurice

Rival players were awed by Beliveau's size and strength when he broke into the NHL. Bill Ezinicki, a vicious body-checker in his glory days with Toronto and Boston, remembers the first time he lined up Beliveau for one of his patented hip checks. "It was like running into the side of a big oak tree," Ezinicki recalls. "I bounced right off the guy and landed on the seat of my pants."

In those days, Beliveau had only one flaw in his makeup. His disposition was better suited to the priesthood than the savage atmosphere of the hockey rink. He was cross-checked, hooked and belted in every NHL rink. He didn't hit back because, he said, "I want to play hockey." He maintained that attitude until his third season with the Canadiens when he decided to retaliate. He wound up among the league's penalty leaders, a fact he wasn't proud of, but he also won the league's scoring title.

No longer did rival ruffians pick on Jean Beliveau. He had arrived— as a player and as a man—in the NHL. Other honors followed. In his first 18 years with the Canadiens he was named to the All-Star team ten times and twice won the Hart Trophy as the league's Most Valuable Player.

Toe Blake, Beliveau's coach for 13 years, summed up big Jean's value to the Canadiens this way: "In all the time he's been in hockey I've never heard anybody say a bad word against him. As a hockey player and a gentleman, Jean Beliveau is pretty hard to beat."

BILL COOK

No member of hockey's Hall of Fame got a later start in the big leagues than Bill Cook. He didn't reach the National Hockey League until he was 30, yet he went on to become the greatest right wing in the history of the New York Rangers.

Service in the first World War delayed Cook's arrival in pro hockey. A farm boy from Kingston, Ontario, he went overseas with a Canadian field artillery outfit in 1917 and saw action at Ypres, Vimy Ridge, the Somme and Flanders. When the armistice was signed a year later he joined a group of Canadians attached to the Royal Russian Army and fought the Bolsheviks near the Arctic Circle.

Cook returned to Canada in 1919, received his soldier's allotment of land in Saskatchewan and went to work transforming a wilderness of woods and scrub brush into good grain-bearing soil. He wasn't thinking then of resuming the hockey career he had quit as a junior. But farm life proved too dull for this war veteran and he returned to hockey in 1922, turning pro with Saskatoon of the Western League. He was then 26. Four years later, he joined the newly-formed New York Rangers.

Bill Cook

Playing on a line with his brother Bun and Frank Boucher, Cook developed into one of the league's top marksmen. In 11 seasons with the Rangers he scored 229 goals, a remarkable achievement in the years of short schedules. He twice led the NHL in scoring and was named to three straight All-Star teams, beginning with the first one in 1930.

Known as "Bad Bill" during his playing career, Cook knew how to use his stick as a weapon when the occasion so demanded. His most memorable brawl took place in a Stanley Cup playoff game against the Montreal Canadiens in 1935. His opponent that night was Nels Crutchfield, another tough hombre.

Here is Cook's version of the fight: "Crutchfield was interfering with me throughout the game and the referee wouldn't do anything about it. So I finally caught Crutchfield with the butt end of my stick. Then he hit me right on the bean with his stick. I don't remember much about what happened after that except I needed eight stitches on my head and I lost a lot of blood. When I came back in the third period I was still a little groggy."

But he wasn't too groggy to score the winning goal. Cook claimed that that was one of his biggest thrills along with the winning goal he scored against Toronto in 1933 to earn the Rangers their second Stanley Cup championship. He had also sparked the Rangers to their first Cup in 1928.

Cook turned to coaching upon his retirement in 1937. His first job was at Cleveland, where he took his last whirl as a player. When one of his men was injured by an opposing ruffian, Bill borrowed a uniform and skates and went on for one play. The ruffian wound up in a hospital.

Cook came back to New York as the Ranger coach in 1951, but lasted less than two seasons. He became disgusted when he discovered his players couldn't do the things Bill Cook used to do—like score goals and win fights. Even today, few can do both as well.

PHIL ESPOSITO

The first thing you notice about Phil Esposito is his determination. No matter what phase of hockey he's handling at the moment, Espo brings a fierce dedication to it. And that dedication has helped him develop from just another big, rather awkward-looking center into the most dramatic scorer in the game's history.

Born in Sault Ste. Marie, Ontario, Esposito grew up shooting pucks at his kid brother, Tony. "He was younger," explained Phil, "so he had to be the goalie." They would play the same roles years later in the NHL.

The Black Hawks sponsored the minor hockey program in Sault Ste. Marie, and in those days that was enough for an NHL club to gain the

Phil Esposito

ROBERT SHAVER

rights to the local hockey playing talent. That's how Phil filtered into the Chicago Black Hawks' system. His goaltending brother, Tony, originally escaped the Hawks' net by going to college, but Phil chose to pursue hockey through the traditional junior ranks and spent two years in the minors before being called up to Chicago midway through the 1963–64 season.

Three goals in 27 NHL games gave no clue to the kind of scoring that Esposito would one day produce. A bit clumsy on his skates, Phil's major asset was his strength and the Hawks used him to center superstar Bobby Hull. In the next three seasons, he scored 71 goals, many of them on rebounds of Hull bombs. Hull would unload and if the puck didn't hit the net, Espo was on the doorstep for the rebound. It takes size and strength to get into that area around the net called the slot, and to stay there. Esposito had both qualities going for him.

In 1967, the Hawks went shopping for a tough defenseman and asked Boston about Gilles Marotte. The talks expanded and finally on May 15, the deal was completed. Marotte, center Pit Martin and minor league goalie Jack Norris went to Chicago, with Esposito and two other forwards, Ken Hodge and Fred Stanfield, moving to the Bruins. Both teams remember the date well. Marotte and Norris departed the Black Hawks long ago while Hodge, Stanfield, and most of all, Esposito, reached star status with the Bruins.

In six years with Boston, Espo has won four scoring championships and finished second twice. He was the first man to go over 100 points in a single season and he passed the 50-goal plateau in three consecutive seasons through 1972–73—the only man other than Hull to accomplish that feat more than once. In 1970–71 he scored an all-time record 152 points. That total included a record 76 goals. In one unbelievable season, he scored five more goals than he had totaled in three years at Chicago!

Esposito entered the 1973–74 season with 398 career goals, 324 of them in the half dozen seasons with the Bruins, an average of 54 per season for Boston.

It is no coincidence that the Bruins ended a 29-year wait and won two Stanley Cups following the arrival of Esposito. The first Cup came in 1970 and en route to it, Boston eliminated Chicago in four games. The scoring star for Boston was Esposito and it was accomplished at the expense of his goaltending brother, Tony, who had wound up with the Hawks after graduating from Michigan Tech.

Phil has developed into an outstanding all-around performer. He is a workhorse, taking his regular turn, playing on power plays and killing penalties as well. He has been clocked on the ice for as much as five or six minutes at a time and plays between 25 and 30 minutes a game. He is a tower of strength for the Bruins.

Bernie Geoffrion　　　　　MADISON SQUARE GARDEN (DAVID BIER)

BERNIE "BOOM BOOM" GEOFFRION

There have been many National Hockey League stars who impressed coaches with their talents from the time they first entered organized hockey. Bernie "Boom Boom" Geoffrion was not one of them.

He still remembers a day back in 1945 when he was breaking in with a junior team in his native Montreal. "I was only 14," he recalls, "and this man (he was an assistant coach) takes my equipment and throws it out of the dressing room. He says to me, 'You will never make the National Hockey League. Go home.' This makes me mad. Wow. I am only a kid then and somebody tells me I cannot make the NHL. I think maybe I show that man something."

Fortunately for Geoffrion, he got another chance. And he did "show that man something" during a 16-year career in the NHL. He played right wing for the Canadiens for 14 seasons, retired in 1964 to coach Quebec City in the American League, and then returned to the NHL in 1966 to play two more years for the New York Rangers. He was coach of the Rangers for part of the 1968–69 season.

Perseverance and a blazing slap shot (it earned him the nickname Boom Boom) contributed to Geoffrion's emergence as one of the highest-scoring players in NHL history. He finished his playing career with 393 goals, ranking behind Gordie Howe, Maurice Richard, Bobby Hull and Jean Beliveau on the all-time scoring list.

Geoffrion never played minor league hockey, making the big jump from the junior ranks to the Canadiens in 1951. He arrived at a time when the territory he covered on right wing was "owned" by those perennial All-Stars, Richard and Howe. Their brilliance cut deeply into the number of individual awards that Geoffrion's talent normally would have brought him, but some of his achievements are his to keep for all time.

He became the second man to score 50 goals in one season, reaching that plateau in 1961. He won the league's scoring championship twice and was named winner of the Hart Trophy in 1961.

It was Geoffrion's slap shot, though, that earned him the most accolades. Its velocity struck fear into the hearts of all goalies. "He once hit my pads with a shot just under the knees," former netminder Al Rollins recalls. "It was so hard I thought my toes were paralyzed."

Geoffrion's career—and his life—almost was snuffed out in 1958 when he suffered a ruptured bowel in a practice session. He was rushed to a Montreal hospital for emergency surgery. His doctors later advised him to forget hockey—at least for the rest of the season.

Boom Boom Geoffrion ignored the advice. Six weeks later he returned to the Canadiens for a playoff series against Boston. In the sixth and final game, he scored the first goal, assisted on the second and scored the winner as Montreal won its third straight Stanley Cup.

A darkly handsome man with intense pride, Geoffrion once looked back on his junior days in Montreal and to the man who claimed he had no future in hockey and admitted, "I was never what you would call a good skater. I had to work hard to skate and to play...and to show that man he was wrong."

GORDIE HOWE

The dictionary defines durability as "the ability to withstand decay or wear." It is the word that best describes Gordie Howe and his fabulous career in the National Hockey League.

No player in the history of the NHL was more durable than this 6-foot, 205-pound right wing from the wheat fields of Saskatchewan in western Canada. He started his career with the Detroit Red Wings at the age of 18 in 1946; he finished it playing with the same team in 1971. In those 25 years of brilliant service he established league records for most games played (1,687), most goals (786), most assists (1,023), and most points (1,809).

Howe celebrated his 43rd birthday on the final night of the 1970–71 season. He wound up that campaign by scoring 23 goals, increasing his lifetime total to an incredible 786.

Hailed throughout the hockey world as a seemingly indestructible man of steel, Howe's career—and his life—were almost snuffed out in his third season with the Red Wings. He collided with Toronto's Ted Kennedy during a 1950 Stanley Cup playoff game, crashed head-on into the sideboards and suffered a severe brain injury. He hovered between life and death while surgeons operated to relieve pressure on his brain.

The injury left him with a slight facial tic; there are times when his dark eyes blink uncontrollably. His teammates called him "Blinky," and it was a mark of Howe's class that he never resented the nickname. He frequently startled newsmen with remarks like "Old Blinky was flying tonight" or "Did you see old Blinky miss that goal in the second period?"

Even in the twilight of his career, Howe remained an amazing athlete—the complete hockey player. He was big and tough and sometimes a little rough. He could still shoot with the best NHL marksmen; he could set up plays; he acted as the triggerman on power plays; he killed penalties. Only a troublesome arthritic wrist forced him to retire.

Jean Beliveau of the Montreal Canadiens claimed "Gordie Howe is the best hockey player I have ever seen." It is an interesting assessment from a man who once was a teammate of Maurice "Rocket" Richard. But even Richard admits "Howe was a better all-around player than I was."

Gordie Howe   BARTON SILVERMAN

Blessed with a powerful body, Howe would have made an ideal heavy-weight boxer. He had the sloping shoulders of a fighter, his neck thick and his muscular arms dangling loosely like the limbs of an oak tree. He had his share of fights on the ice, the most memorable taking place in 1959 when he tangled with Lou Fontinato of the New York Rangers. Fonti-nato's nose was broken, and his whole face needed considerable repairs.

Howe, though, was no troublemaker. He just kept rolling along, content to score goals and accumulate records and honors. He was named to the NHL's All-Star team 21 times in 25 seasons. He won the league's scoring title six times and was a six-time winner of the Hart Trophy as the league's MVP.

And he surprised the hockey world in the summer of 1973 when he de-cided to come out of retirement to join his two sons on the Houston Aeros in the World Hockey Association. He wouldn't last forever, but the old pro would give it a shot—for family and fortune.

BOBBY HULL

It starts from the instant he cradles the puck on the curved blade of his stick. One...two strides...and he's in full flight, skating and slamming his way across the neutral zone and into enemy territory. By this time a chorus of sound envelops the rink, rising into a long, drawn-out OOOHH! as this whirlwind on skates fires one of his patented slap shots.

The puck, traveling at more than 100 miles per hour, invariably winds up high in the net and Bobby Hull has scored another goal.

This scene has been enacted and re-enacted on an average of 40 times a season since Hull's arrival in the National Hockey League in 1957. In the years that followed, nobody has scored nearly as many goals or caused nearly as much excitement as this ruggedly-handsome, blond-haired muscle-man from the little Ontario town of Point Anne (pop. 1,000).

Hull was only 18 years old when he quit the junior ranks to turn pro with the Chicago Black Hawks. His great magnetism and goal-scoring ability turned a franchise which was losing money into the richest in the NHL. And as the Hawks grew in wealth, so did Bobby Hull. He became the league's first $100,000-a-year player when he signed a four-year, $400,000 contract at the start of the 1968–69 season. Other income from endorsements, several purebred cattle farms he owns and league awards and playoff money swelled his earnings that season to approximately $200,000.

In 1972, he accepted a $1,000,000 offer from the new World Hockey Association to play for the Winnipeg Jets. Despite missing 15 games because of court suits initiated by the NHL aimed at blocking his move to

Bobby Hull   KEN REGAN

the new league, Hull reached the 50-goal plateau for the sixth time in his career.

What makes Bobby Hull so great? Many things, really. He has combined some of the talents of his most famed predecessors—the speed of Howie Morenz, the goal-scoring instincts of Maurice Richard, the strength and control of Gordie Howe—into a blend of the perfect hockey player.

He is the fastest skater in hockey (28.3 mph with the puck, 29.7 mph without it) and by far the fastest shot: his slap shot has been clocked at 118.3 mph, nearly 35 mph above the league average. And then there are the Hull muscles.

Physiologists have called him "the perfect mesomorph." There is not an ounce of excess baggage on his 5–10, 195-pound frame. He has the solid legs of a fullback and his entire upper torso, including his biceps, chest and neck, are thicker than any heavyweight boxing champion since Rocky Marciano.

Hull totaled only 31 goals in his first two seasons with the Black Hawks, then developed the slap shot that has been the bane of all goalies ever since. He scored 50 goals in the 1961–62 season to equal a league record and progressively increased the mark. In 1968–69, he increased it to 58. In his first 15 NHL seasons, he totaled 604 goals, won the league scoring championship three times and played left wing on the NHL All-Star team 10 times.

Teammates and rival players still stand in awe of Bobby Hull. Boston's Phil Esposito claims: "Bobby's the best goal-scorer ever." Bernie "Boom Boom" Geoffrion, who perfected the slap shot while at Montreal, calls Hull's shot "the greatest...the hardest I ever saw."

The supreme compliment, though, came from Stan Mikita, the Black Hawks' star center. "To say that Bobby is a great hockey player is to labor the point," Mikita said. "He's all of that, of course. But the thing I admire about him is the way he handles people. He really enjoys signing autographs for fans. He's a genuine nice guy."

TED LINDSAY

No man on skates was ever too big or too tough for Ted Lindsay to challenge. He was small (5–8 and 160 pounds), but he always carried a big stick. And he used that stick—and his fists—to cut down some of the biggest, meanest men in the National Hockey League.

His tormentors called him "Scarface" or "Terrible Ted." Lindsay didn't mind. The scar tissue on his thin but rugged face represented his badge of courage. He stopped counting the stitches when they reached 400. And the nickname "Terrible" only applied to his reputation for getting into trouble because as a player he was magnificent.

Ted Lindsay   HOCKEY HALL OF FAME

Lindsay broke into the NHL in 1944, making the big jump from the junior ranks to the Detroit Red Wings at the age of 19. Playing left wing on Detroit's memorable "Production Line" with Gordie Howe and Sid Abel, Lindsay helped the Red Wings win eight league titles (including seven in a row) and four Stanley Cup championships in the late 1940s and early 50s.

A member of nine All-Star teams and the league's leading scorer in 1949–50, Lindsay retired in 1960 after 16 years of service, 13 with the Red Wings and the last three with the Chicago Black Hawks. He totaled 365 goals and 458 assists, a league high for left wings until Bobby Hull passed the goals figure in 1968.

Lindsay had established a partnership with another former Detroit player, Marty Pavelich, in a plastics firm late in his playing career. Now he was able to devote all his time to this prosperous business. But he missed the excitement of the brawling world of hockey.

After four years of retirement, he returned to the Red Wings as a player. He was 39 years old. Asked why he would risk possible injury by attempting a comeback at that age, Lindsay said, "It's certainly not the money. I'm well off. I just had this desire to wind up my career with the Red Wings."

The Red Wings—and their fans—welcomed Lindsay back with open arms. He launched his comeback against the Toronto Maple Leafs in Detroit's opening game of the 1964–65 season. A crowd of 14,323, largest ever to see a Detroit home opener, greeted the old battler and he responded by dealing out several vicious bodychecks to assorted Maple Leafs. Ted Lindsay was back, and soon the whole league knew it.

In a game at Montreal he drew a $25 fine for spearing Ted Harris, a rugged defenseman who towered seven inches over Lindsay and outweighed him by 40 pounds. Claude Larose, a Montreal youngster with a reputation for being reasonably talented with his fists, tried to even matters. Lindsay gripped his stick with both hands and slashed Larose across the legs. Larose, 17 years Lindsay's junior, hobbled away in pain.

Lindsay's comeback lasted only one season, but it was a season in which the Red Wings won their first league championship in eight years. They wouldn't have done it without old man Lindsay, who scored 14 goals and, coincidentally, was among the league leaders in penalties. Clarence Campbell, the president of the National Hockey League who had earlier scoffed at Lindsay's return, called it one of the most amazing comebacks in professional sports.

A year later, Ted Lindsay was inducted into the Hockey Hall of Fame.

HOWIE MORENZ

Babe Ruth and Bobby Jones, Bill Tilden and Jack Dempsey—these were

Howie Morenz   HOCKEY HALL OF FAME (RICE)

the men who dominated America's Golden Era of Sport in the Roaring Twenties. During that same period of bathtub gin and flappers and ragtime jazz, Canada had its own hero. He was Howie Morenz of the Montreal Canadiens, the greatest hockey player of his generation.

To the French-speaking fans of the Province of Quebec, Howie Morenz was *L'homme-eclair*. In English he was the same thing: the top man.

Morenz was a center for the Canadiens for 12 years and near the end of his career played with the Chicago Black Hawks and the New York Rangers. Once, in a 44-game season, he scored 40 goals—a remarkable achievement. He totaled 270 goals during his National Hockey League career and was among the first group of players admitted to the Hockey Hall of Fame in 1945.

A happy-go-lucky man with large, smiling eyes, a receding hairline and a heavy beard, Morenz was a typical sports hero of the 1920s. He was colorful and glamorous, hockey's fastest man on skates and a fiery competitor. Toe Blake, the most successful coach in the history of the Canadiens, was a rookie player with Montreal when Morenz was approaching the end of the line. He remembers Morenz: "He was an inspiration for all of us...a man with remarkable skills who laughed hard and played hard."

Dazzling speed and guile were Morenz's trademarks. A contemporary of his, Ott Heller of the Rangers, once remarked: "When Howie skates full speed, everyone else on the ice seems to be skating backward." Morenz's shot was equally impressive. Once he broke a goalie's nose with one of his bullet-like drives. Another time his shot caught a netminder square in the forehead, flipping him over on his back.

Although he never played at more than 165 pounds, Morenz bodychecked with the ferocity of a giant. He was so swift, so skillful and so fearless that the wildly nationalistic French-Canadians of Montreal were undisturbed when they discovered his secret sin: Howie Morenz was of German ancestry.

He was born in the Ontario village of Mitchell in 1902, moving with his family to Stratford, Ontario, at the age of 14. He attracted the attention of the Canadiens when he scored nine goals in an amateur game in Montreal in 1922. The following year he turned pro with the Canadiens for a $1,000 bonus and quickly earned the nickname of "The Stratford Streak."

Off the ice, Morenz's pace was just as fast. He sang and played the ukulele. He was a clothes horse; he changed his suits twice and sometimes three times a day. He wore spats. He was a charming and cosmopolitan young man living swiftly in the charming, cosmopolitan city of Montreal.

Then, suddenly, he was no longer quite so young. After 11 seasons with the Canadiens he was traded, first to Chicago in 1934 and then to the New York Americans the following year. In 1936, he was repurchased by the Canadiens. On the night of January 28, 1937, in the midst of a fine comeback, Morenz broke four bones in his left leg and ankle in a game against Chicago. Five weeks later, the bones were knitting well when he fell to the cold floor of a Montreal hospital. An embolism had stopped his heart.

Howie Morenz was dead at the age of 34. The funeral service was held at center ice in the Montreal Forum, where thousands of fans wept openly for "Le Grande Morenz."

MAURICE "ROCKET" RICHARD

Long after Maurice Richard retired in 1960, there were National Hockey League goalies who would sit around in locker rooms or coffee shops and recall what it was like to face the old Rocket from Montreal.

Glenn Hall, who was an All-Star netminder with Detroit and Chicago before winding up with the St. Louis Blues, has a rather unique memory of Richard. "What I remember most about the Rocket were his eyes," Hall says. "When he came flying toward you with the puck on his stick, his eyes were all lit up, flashing and gleaming like a pinball machine. It was terrifying."

Richard terrified goalies like Hall for 18 seasons, all with the Montreal Canadiens. He totaled 544 regular-season goals, a record until Gordie Howe wiped it out in 1963. He was the first to score 50 goals in one season (1944–45), and he is the only one to have reached that figure in a 50-game schedule.

There was nothing quite so dramatic as a Richard goal. He would run, not glide, down the ice, cut in from right wing as he neared the cage and then use either a forehand or backhand shot to fool rival goalies. That was another of Richard's great, unmatched talents. He was ambidextrous, a right wing with an unorthodox left hand shot.

"The Rocket did everything by instinct and with brute strength," said Frank Selke Sr., who was the Canadiens' general manager during Richard's record-breaking years. "He was the greatest opportunist the game has ever known."

Bill Chadwick, a former referee and a member of hockey's Hall of Fame, was another Richard admirer. "He was the greatest scorer I ever saw from the blue line in," Chadwick said. "And his strength was amazing. I saw him carry defensemen on his back right up to the goal mouth and score."

Richard learned the rudiments of the game as a teenager in Montreal's Lafontaine Park in the years preceding World War II. He was a prolific scorer in the city's Park League, but appeared too injury-prone to become a real star. He broke an ankle while playing amateur hockey, then fractured a wrist. He was finally promoted to the Canadiens in 1942, but was sidelined early by another broken ankle. "It looks as if we have a brittle-boned player on our hands," sighed Tommy Gorman, then the Canadiens' manager.

Gorman even considered releasing Richard, but the Rocket became stronger as he reached manhood, shook off his injuries and developed into a small bull on skates. He stood a shade under six feet and weighed 190 pounds at the height of his career. Many teams used two players to "shadow" the Rocket. He considered it a compliment. And when they got in his way, he would simply bowl them over and then glare at them with dark, menacing eyes.

He had a mean temper which got him into frequent scrapes with players and officials. His suspension by NHL president Clarence Campbell in 1955 for carving up a Boston player with his stick and punching a linesman precipitated a riot in the Montreal Forum.

All of Richard's transgressions, though, were forgotten when he was rushed into the Hockey Hall of Fame in 1961. This honor normally isn't bestowed on a player until at least the fifth year of his retirement. Maurice Richard had only been retired for nine months!

MILT SCHMIDT

He would glide behind the Boston net to pick up the puck and then start up ice. As he reached center ice he was under a full head of steam, his cowlick flying, his neck outthrust, his prominent nose sticking out like the prow of a ship. And he never had to look down at the puck, which he was shifting back and forth, left to right, right to left, on the end of his stick.

When he crossed the blue line and entered enemy territory he would skate around or barge through rival defensemen until he was close enough to the net to release his famed wrist shot. Then, bingo! The puck was in the cage and all Boston went wild.

This was Milt Schmidt in action, the kid from Kitchener, the center of the much-feared Kraut Line, who in 16 years as a player for the Bruins scored 229 goals and ranked among the most fiery competitors in the history of the National Hockey League.

One of his greatest admirers was Art Ross, who coached and managed the Bruins during Schmidt's big years. "Schmidt was the fastest playmaker of all time," Ross said. "By that I mean no player ever skated at full tilt the way he did and was still able to make the play."

It was Ross who scouted Schmidt and signed him to a Bruins' contract in 1935. Milt played one season of minor league hockey at Providence, then moved up to the Bruins and was reunited with two of his old school pals, Bobby Bauer and Woody Dumart. That was the beginning of the Kraut Line, so named because all three came from the Kitchener-Waterloo area of Ontario, which was predominantly German in origin.

With Schmidt as their center and leader, the Krauts led the Bruins to four straight NHL championships beginning in 1938. Boston also won two Stanley Cup titles during that same period.

Maurice Richard

Milt Schmidt

MADISON SQUARE GARDEN

Injuries frequently slowed Schmidt but never stopped him from playing. "That's the only trouble with Milt," Ross once said. "If he would not put so much of his heart and soul into his play, he wouldn't be injured so much."

In one Stanley Cup playoff series against Toronto, when both his knees were so banged up from repeated injuries that he couldn't bend them, he had his legs taped from the ankle to the thigh and then had himself lifted off the table and onto his skates.

Referees, normally impartial, were frequently amazed at Schmidt's courage. "Milt had more guts than any player I ever saw," said Bill Chadwick. Red Storey, another retired referee, said, "I'd take five Milt Schmidts, put my grandmother in the nets and we'd beat any team."

Schmidt was named to the NHL All-Star team four times and won the league's Most Valuable Player award in 1951 at the age of 33. He served as the Bruins' coach following his retirement as a player in 1955, then became the club's general manager.

He claimed he received his greatest thrill in 1952 when he scored the 250th goal of his career. It was Milt Schmidt Night at Boston Garden and Bauer came out of retirement for that one game to play alongside his old Kraut linemates. "That was a great night," Schmidt said. "The goal and the ovation we got from the fans...I'll never forget it."

Hockey fans—in Boston and everywhere—will never forget Milt Schmidt either.

THE DEFENDERS   Behind the Blue Line

FRANK "KING" CLANCY

The setting was Toronto's Maple Leaf Gardens just before the outbreak of World War II. The hometown Maple Leafs were involved in a rough game with Montreal, and referee Frank "King" Clancy was finding it difficult controlling the tempers of the players and the fans. When one rinkside customer went so far as to compare Clancy with the less personable end of a horse, the referee, always quick with a quip, bellowed, "If it wasn't for a horse you wouldn't have had me playing in this joint for six years."

It was a classic stopper. And Clancy, of course, was right. A horse did figure in his trade from Ottawa to Toronto in 1930. It developed this way: Conn Smythe, the owner of the Maple Leafs, made a hefty bet on a horse named Rare Jewel at longshot odds that year and collected $14,000. He used his winnings as a down payment to acquire Clancy from Ottawa. The total price was $35,000 and two players—a record hockey transaction in those days.

King Clancy   HOCKEY HALL OF FAME

Clancy was worth it, too, for he turned out to be a "rare jewel" for the Maple Leafs. He helped spark them to the Stanley Cup championship in his second year with the club and went on to lead them to two National Hockey League titles before retiring as a player in 1936.

In his 16 years as one of the NHL's greatest rushing defensemen (he spent his first 10 seasons with Ottawa), Clancy totaled 136 goals and assisted on 145. He was named to four All-Star teams, starting with the first one in 1930. Those are impressive credentials for a man who once was considered too puny to play hockey.

Clancy, born in Ottawa in 1902, entered the NHL as a 150-pound teenager. Most rival defensemen outweighed him by at least 30 pounds. But Clancy made up for his lack of heft with great speed and agility. And he never backed away from a brawl, although he admits he won only one fight, against Boston's Eddie Shore of all people. "I socked Eddie once as he was getting to his feet and skated like mad to the other end of the rink," he said.

Boston fans used to ride Clancy the most. He recalled one night when a Bostonian seated behind the Toronto bench needled him until he could stand it no longer. He turned to the fan and said, "You think you're pretty tough, buddy. Okay, stay around after the game and we'll see how tough you are."

Teammate Charlie Conacher overheard Clancy's challenge and grinned. "King, you'll be the next heavyweight champion of the world if you can handle that fan," Conacher said. "Didn't you recognize him? He's Jack Sharkey."

Clancy didn't keep his appointment with the champ.

The colorful Irishman with the dented nose and bellowing voice served as a coach both before and after his 11-year service as an NHL referee. His last coaching job was a three-year tenure with his beloved Maple Leafs (1954–56). He later was named an assistant to general manager-coach Punch Imlach of the Leafs.

"I'm sort of a good-will ambassador," he explained.

Hockey never had a better one than King Clancy.

DIT CLAPPER

There are various yardsticks by which a player can be measured for greatness in professional hockey. One is the number of goals he scores. Another is longevity. In both areas, Dit Clapper had few peers.

An even-tempered, six-foot, 200-pounder from Hastings, Ont., Clapper was the National Hockey League's first 20-year man. He played all those 20 years with the Boston Bruins, the first 10 as a right wing, the last 10 as a defenseman. He wound up his playing career in 1947 with 228 goals, a very respectable total for a man who drifted between two positions.

Dit Clapper

Clapper arrived in the NHL with the oddest nickname in hockey. His parents christened him Aubrey Victor and called him Vic. "I couldn't say Vic," Clapper once explained. "I'd lisp the name and it came out Dit. It stuck, sort of."

It was a name to stick in the minds of selectors for hockey's Hall of Fame. In 1947, Dit Clapper became the first active player to be named to the Hall. He had earned it. The late Bobby Bauer, one of Clapper's teammates on those great Boston clubs in the years preceding World War II, once hailed Dit as "the athlete's type of athlete. He was a big guy, but he used his heft to stop fights."

Clapper was a top-notch lacrosse player as a teen-ager, but he gave up that sport to play junior hockey in Toronto. He signed his first pro contract with the Bruins at the age of 19 in 1926, played half a season in the minors, then moved up to Boston in 1927.

Although a defenseman up to that time, Clapper was converted into a right wing by the Bruins and eventually wound up on Boston's "Dynamite Line" with Cooney Weiland and Dutch Gainor. In his second full season with Boston, the Bruins won the NHL championship and the Stanley Cup. The next year the Bruins repeated as NHL champions and Clapper enjoyed his greatest season, totaling 41 goals and 20 assists.

In 1937, Clapper returned to his old position on defense. He sparked the Bruins to four more league titles and two more Stanley Cup championships. These were Boston's glory years in the NHL. The Bruins had Frank Brimsek, the original "Mr. Zero," in goal, the famed "Kraut Line" of Bauer, Milt Schmidt and Woody Dumart to lead the attack, and good old Dit Clapper on defense.

Clapper was named to the first All-Star team in three successive years (1939–40–41). In 1942, he suffered a severed Achilles tendon in a game at Toronto. It was thought he would never play again, but he made a remarkable recovery and two years later was named to the All-Star team for the sixth time.

Boston fans will never forget Clapper's retirement ceremony on February 12, 1947. He stood at center ice in Boston Garden, wearing his familiar No. 5 jersey and looking as handsome as ever. Then, while a capacity crowd of 14,000 looked on approvingly, he received $7,500 in gifts. It was only part payment for all the thrills Dit Clapper had given his devoted followers for 20 glorious years.

DOUG HARVEY

Most hockey players are content to master only a few facets of the game. Doug Harvey literally controlled every part of it during his great years as a defenseman for the Montreal Canadiens.

Pacemaking is what set him apart from his contemporaries. He could slow down or speed up the tempo of most games with his extraordinary talents.

If the Canadiens wanted to kill time, Harvey would bring the puck up ice slowly, maneuvering his way past forechecking forwards until he reached the blue line. Then he would weave back and forth along the line, sliding soft passes to teammates and never becoming rattled.

If the Canadiens were trailing and attempting to beat the clock, it was Harvey who invariably led their fast-break up ice. And once the puck was in the enemy zone, he would station himself at the left point, waiting for a return pass and protecting against a possible breakaway by a rival player.

Harvey performed all these functions in a calm, almost lackadaisical fashion. He never seemed to fully extend himself, yet he was the unchallenged leader of the powerful Canadiens when they swept to an unprecedented five straight Stanley Cup championships from 1956 through 1960.

A native of Montreal, Harvey turned to hockey only after rejecting tempting offers from pro football and baseball scouts. It was the right choice—for him and for the Canadiens. During 13 seasons with Montreal he was named to the first NHL All-Star team nine times and once to the second team. He earned the Norris Trophy as the league's outstanding defenseman six times.

The only fault most experts found with Harvey was a minor one: he didn't shoot enough. (The most goals he scored in a season was nine.) He claimed he would rather finesse his way to within shooting range and set up a goal for a teammate than try one of his own slap shots. "I didn't have a bonus for goals," he once said, "so why not set up the guys who needed them?"

A hero to every youngster in Montreal, Harvey encountered trouble with the Canadiens' front office when he became involved with the organization of the NHL Players' Association. In 1961 he was traded to the New York Rangers and became their player-coach, leading the league's one-time patsies into the Stanley Cup playoffs for the first time in four years. During that same 1961–62 season he won his seventh Norris Trophy and once again was named to the All-Star team.

Harvey surrendered the coaching position after one season—he disliked the responsibility—but remained with the Rangers as a player for another 18 months. "When I was a coach, I couldn't be one of the boys," he said. "This way if I want a beer with them, I get a beer."

He then drifted to the minors, playing in Baltimore, St. Paul, Quebec City, Pittsburgh and Kansas City. He returned to the NHL with the St. Louis Blues during the 1968 Stanley Cup playoffs and, ironically, wound up against his old Montreal club in the final round.

Doug Harvey WIDE WORLD

Although he was then 45 years old, Harvey remained with St. Louis for the 1968–69 season as a defenseman and assistant coach. The next year he became defensive coach for Los Angeles.

RED HORNER

Conn Smythe, the patriarch of the Toronto Maple Leafs, coined a phrase that is often repeated by hockey coaches attempting to instill a little fight into their players. "If you can't lick 'em in the alley," Smythe maintained, "you can't lick 'em on the ice."

George Reginald "Red" Horner lived by this creed during 12 brawling years in the National Hockey League, all with Smythe's blue-and-white shirted Maple Leafs. A solid 190-pound defenseman with an openly aggressive style, Horner was a first-class alley fighter who developed into the most hated player in the NHL during the 1930s.

Whenever the Maple Leafs performed in Boston or Chicago, Montreal or Detroit or New York, the fans spent most of their time booing Red Horner. He was the "heavy" in the Toronto cast, the bad man with the flaming red hair and a temper to match who was always ready to fight at the drop of a hockey stick.

Toronto fans loved Horner for the same reason. They realized he didn't have the polished play-making style of a Charlie Conacher, a Busher Jackson or a Joe Primeau. But they knew he threw a scare into rival puck carriers, who were forced to carry their heads and sticks high whenever Red Horner was on the ice.

Horner launched his career with the Maple Leafs in typical fashion. In the third minute of his very first game with Toronto in 1928, he wound up in the penalty box for fighting. He went on to become the most penalized player of his generation.

He led the NHL in penalties for eight successive seasons, from 1933 to 1940. During the 1935–36 season, he was penalized a record 167 minutes in 43 games. That mark remained unchallenged until 1956 when Lou Fontinato of the New York Rangers accumulated 202 minutes in 70 games.

It was Horner's fighting spirit and determination that earned him his first berth on an organized hockey team in the mid-20s. A poor skater as a youngster, he had flunked his first tryout with a Toronto junior team. He then approached Frank Selke Sr., who was coaching another squad of juniors. "If you give me a chance, I think I can make your team," Horner told Selke.

Selke, who was to become one of the great figures in the executive branch of professional hockey, permitted Horner to work out with his team, then offered this advice to the youngster: "There are two things you must

Red Horner   HOCKEY HALL OF FAME

learn before you're a hockey player. First, improve your skating. Second, learn to break fast from the blue line."

Horner listened, then waited for the words which would tell him to come back another year. Selke patted him on the head and said, "But I sure like the way you keep trying, kid, so I'll put you on the team."

That was the beginning of Horner's career. He improved his skating and cultivated his reputation as a fighter and eventually earned admittance to the Hockey Hall of Fame. And waiting for him at the entrance to the Hall in 1965 was the man who gave him his start, Frank Selke Sr., the chairman of the selection committee.

CHING JOHNSON

More than a decade after his retirement as a player, Ching Johnson was serving as a linesman in a game in Washington, D.C., between the New York Rovers and the Washington Lions of the Eastern Hockey League. The game was spirited and Johnson was kept busy trying to keep up with the flow of action.

Suddenly, a Washington player slithered into the open in the New York zone. Johnson, fat and fifty, forgot himself. For that split-second, he wasn't an official any longer. He was the defenseman he once was with the New York Rangers and his goal was in danger. He cut over in front of the onrushing Washington forward and crunched him to the ice with a solid body check.

Johnson, the linesman, later apologized. "You know, I just can't explain it," he said. "Here was that guy racing for the goal and I just had to stop him. Why? Instinct, I guess. The old habit was too deep within me. I forgot where I was and what I was doing."

Something like this could happen only to Ching Johnson, a star for 11 years with the Rangers. He was one of the New York club's pioneer players, joining the team when it was organized in 1926 and staying on until 1937. His fearlessness, his one-man sorties on the opposition's net, were something to behold.

Year after year, he handled his duties on the Ranger defense even when his large body (he was a 210-pound six-footer) was racked with pain. But he ignored the skate cuts, the welts and the bruises while he went about his business of protecting the New York goal. His rugged face was creased by a permanent pixie-like grin. He smiled when he knocked people down and he smiled when he, himself, was sent sprawling to the ice.

The hockey "wars" Johnson engaged in were mild compared to his service with a Canadian Army trench mortar outfit in France in World War I. He was gassed at Passchandaelle, recovered and returned home to

Ching Johnson

Red Kelly

Winnipeg, where he launched his hockey career with a semi-pro team.

"I was a big, awkward kid then," he once recalled. "I couldn't skate very well. I looked like an elephant on skates. But after a while I started to get the hang of it."

Johnson moved from the semi-pros of Winnipeg to the old Central League. He was pushing 30 when he joined Bill and Bun Cook, Frank Boucher and Taffy Abel on that first Ranger team. "I told the Rangers I was 28 when I joined them," he said, "but I was almost two years older. That's why I demanded a three-year contract. I didn't think I could last any longer."

He lasted 12 years in New York, completing his NHL career by playing one season with the Americans in 1938. He bowed out with fine credentials —a member of two Stanley Cup championship teams and a four-time member of the league All-Stars. He was admitted into the Hockey Hall of Fame in 1958.

RED KELLY

The key lyrics in that old song, "Has Anybody Here Seen Kelly?" have always served to remind fans of the most versatile All-Star in the history of the National Hockey League. He is Leonard Patrick Kelly. And if he wasn't the Kelly mentioned in the song, he should have been, for "his hair is red and his eyes are blue and he is Irish through and through."

NHL fans first saw Red Kelly in 1947 when he joined the Detroit Red Wings as a pink-cheeked youth of 19, fresh from the junior ranks. A native of Toronto, he was ignored by the Maple Leafs when one of their scouts predicted he wasn't good enough to last 20 games in the NHL. It was a poor prediction. Kelly lasted 20 years.

Kelly spent the first 12½ years of his NHL career with Detroit. During that time the Red Wings won eight league championships and four Stanley Cup titles. Kelly was a defenseman then, the best rushing defenseman in the league. He was the first winner of the Norris Trophy, awarded annually to the league's outstanding defenseman, in 1954. He was named to the All-Star team six times and was a four-time winner of the Lady Byng (good sportsmanship) Trophy.

All these honors came Kelly's way while he was playing at Detroit. Then, late in the 1959–60 season, he returned home. The Maple Leafs, convinced that they had made a mistake in letting him get away the first time, talked the Red Wings into a trade after Kelly had balked at being peddled to the New York Rangers.

Kelly will never forget his first game in a Toronto uniform. "I was finally where I'd always wanted to be," he recalled later. "When the people stood up and clapped and cheered me I felt so tight I nearly burst."

Bobby Orr

The Maple Leafs, aware of Kelly's great playmaking ability, converted him into a center. He turned out to be just as valuable at his new position. In his first full season with Toronto, he propelled the previously disorganized Maple Leafs into the Stanley Cup finals, where they were finally stopped by the Chicago Black Hawks.

Toronto coach Punch Imlach called Kelly "my ace in the hole." The flaming redhead's greatest contribution to the Maple Leafs was the remarkable change he brought about in Frank Mahovlich, a brooding young man with great talent who increased his goal output from 18 to 48 the first season he played on a line with Kelly.

As a player, Kelly's style was so economical it almost looked lazy. He was a worker, though. He served two terms in the Canadian Parliament while playing for Toronto, but the extra duties as a parliamentarian didn't hamper his play. He scored 119 goals in 7½ seasons with the Maple Leafs, giving him a career total of 281, and he sipped champagne from the Stanley Cup four more times.

Following retirement as a player in 1967, Kelly became coach of the Los Angeles Kings. The Kings were a unanimous choice to finish last, but Kelly—then the only pilot in the NHL without previous coaching experience—led his team to second place in the West. He moved to Pittsburgh for 1969–70 and the Penguins finished second.

Red stayed as coach of the Penguins for the next 2½ seasons, piloting them to one more playoff berth before moving on to Toronto.

BOBBY ORR

He's the boy next door, the one with the winning smile and the cheery disposition. He's square-jawed and thick-necked and there isn't an ounce of fat on his five-foot, 11-inch body. His eyes are blue and his hair, which he has permitted to grow out of the crew-cut stage, is dirty blond. And he just might be the very best defenseman in the history of hockey.

He's Bobby Orr, who signed a record bonus contract with the Boston Bruins at the age of 18 in 1966 and four years later became the first defenseman in NHL history to win the scoring title when he led his club to the Stanley Cup.

Appropriately enough, it was Orr's overtime goal that won the fourth and final game of the playoff for the Bruins and brought them their first Stanley Cup in 29 years. It was his ninth goal and 20th point of the playoffs, both records. During the regular season, Bobby had made history with record-cracking totals of 33 goals, 87 assists and 120 points to win the scoring title.

The Stanley Cup triumph was Boston's first since 1941. "They say the Bruins started rebuilding that year," said Scotty Bowman, coach of the losing St. Louis Blues. "I don't believe that. I think they started rebuilding in 1948—the year Bobby Orr was born."

The Bruins discovered Orr in 1962 playing midget hockey in his home town of Parry Sound, Ont. He was only 14 but he had everything even then. Boston moved him into junior hockey at Oshawa, Ont. and in three years playing defense there, he averaged 33 goals per season, an amazing output.

It cost Boston $75,000 for a two-year agreement to get young Bobby's name on an NHL contract but it was the best investment the team ever made.

Orr won the Calder Trophy as Rookie of the Year in 1967. "Bobby was a star from the moment they played the National Anthem in his first NHL game," said Harry Sinden, Orr's first Boston coach and now a Bruin executive. Veteran Harry Howell won the Norris Trophy as the best defenseman that year and was delighted. "I'm glad I won it now," said Howell, then 36, "because it's going to belong to that Orr from now on."

So far, Howell's prediction has been perfect. Orr has won the Norris Trophy six straight years and in 1970 he became the first man in history to nail down four individual trophies in a single season. He took the Norris as top defenseman, the Art Ross Trophy for the scoring title, and the Hart Trophy as the Most Valuable Player as well as the Conn Smythe Trophy as MVP in the playoffs.

Orr repeated as playoff MVP in 1972 when he led the Bruins to the Stanley Cup championship again. He also won his third straight Hart Trophy as regular season MVP that year, becoming the first man in NHL history to win it more than two straight times.

"He's worth every penny they pay him," said Jean Beliveau of Montreal. "He does everything well. He is always there. He blocks the shot. He can skate. He can shoot. Is there anything else?"

Milt Schmidt, Boston's general manager, doesn't think so.

"He's the greatest player there's ever been," said Schmidt, "in the past or the present. And if anybody greater ever comes along in the future, I just hope the Good Lord lets me stick around to see him."

BRAD PARK

It is Brad Park's good fortune to be one of the most marvelously gifted defensemen ever to play in the National Hockey League. It was his bad fortune to arrive on the NHL scene shortly after Bobby Orr, who may be *the* most marvelously gifted defenseman ever to play in the NHL.

Had Park developed at any other time, he would stand head and shoulders above other blue line players. But, because of Orr, he must play second fiddle. "That's okay," laughs the good-natured, baby-faced Park. "I'm No. 2, so I try harder."

Brad Park

ROBERT SHAVER

Of course, being second best to Orr is no disgrace. And Park does for the Rangers just what Orr does for the Bruins. He is a rushing defender, who delights in lugging the puck out of his own end of the ice and leading the charge up ice. "Brad is like a fourth forward on our line," says Rod Gilbert.

Park has been plagued by a pair of gimpy knees and has missed huge hunks of three of his first five NHL seasons because of that problem. But in 1971–72, the one full season he played, Brad set Ranger records for a defenseman with 24 goals, 49 assists and 73 points. He became only the third defenseman in history to score 20 or more goals in a single season. The others were Flash Hollett of Detroit and, of course, Orr. Included in Park's big year were a pair of three-goal games, a rather unique trick for a defenseman.

Park is unquestionably one of the leaders of the Rangers. When New York traded for left winger Ted Irvine a couple of years ago, the new Ranger was introducing his teammates to his wife. Coming to Park, Irvine said, ". . . and this is Brad Park. We call him Baby Moses. He's going to lead us out of the wilderness."

Park grew up in the Toronto Maple Leafs' junior system and was drafted by the Rangers in June, 1966, when the Leafs, through an oversight, left him unprotected during an amateur selection round. King Clancy, a Toronto vice president and a great NHL defenseman himself, moans over the mistake. "I don't know how we ever let that boy get away," Clancy invariably says after watching Park perform.

Park was barely 20 years old when he showed up for his first NHL training camp. Little was expected from the young man but he came on so strong that he barely missed making the team. He was the last player cut before the season started and was sent out to the American League. But his minor league career lasted just 17 games. The Rangers couldn't wait for an excuse to recall him and they got it when veteran Harry Howell was injured. Park never saw the minors again.

Brad wrote his name in the NHL record book that season when he assisted on four Ranger goals in a game against Pittsburgh. Later that season, he scored his first NHL goal—the final one in a 9–0 romp against Boston. Delighted by the score, he leaped high in the air and landed, rather ingloriously, on his backside. "That's okay. That first goal was worth it," he said.

His offensive talent has enabled him to move among the Rangers' all-time leading blue line scorers. Only three defensemen—Howell, Bill Gadsby and teammate Jim Neilson, all of whom had much longer runs on Broadway than Park has enjoyed—are ahead of Brad in the all-time club point-making list.

Repeatedly selected to the first or second All-Star team despite his frequent injuries, Park has developed into one of the NHL's best defenders.

Not the very best, but No. 2's good enough for him, when you consider the kind of performer No. 1 is.

EDDIE SHORE

All the hockey greats—past and present—were gathered in a midtown New York restaurant for the annual Lester Patrick awards dinner in the spring of 1970. At a table near the rear of the dining room, the Patrick winner with the scarred features of a retired boxer was discussing hockey and how it had changed in recent years.

"The accent is on speed now," he said. "I guess it's better for the fans, but I liked it better in the old days. Then it was pretty much a 50–50 proposition. You socked the other guy and the other guy socked you."

The bald-headed man was Eddie Shore, who socked a lot of guys and caught a few socks in return during a brilliant 14-year career as the meanest defenseman in the National Hockey League.

Shore came out of Edmonton, Alberta, in 1929 to join the Boston Bruins. He infused them with a spirit and color which promptly lifted them from last place to second place in the NHL's American Division. Previously ignored by Bostonians, the Bruins also developed a loyal following—and all because of Shore. He was a drawing card wherever he went because of his free-swinging style, his cold and brutal attacks on rival players, and his brilliance on defense. He was the most applauded player of his time—and received the most boos, too.

Hammy Moore, who was the Boston trainer during Shore's heyday, once described Eddie's style of attack. "He was the only player I ever saw who had the whole arena standing every time he rushed down the ice," Moore said. "You see, when Shore carried the puck you were always sure something would happen. He would either end up bashing somebody, get into a fight or score a goal."

Shore totaled 108 NHL goals, a mighty respectable number for a defenseman, before retiring in 1940. He was named the league's Most Valuable Player four times and was voted to the All-Star team seven times.

But there are even more impressive statistics. He accumulated the astounding total of 978 stitches on his rugged body. He had his nose broken 14 times, his jaw shattered five times and he lost most of his teeth.

Shore's most celebrated fight occurred on December 12, 1933, in Toronto; it was one he always regretted. Red Horner of the Maple Leafs started it by slamming Shore into the boards. Shore picked himself up and went after Horner. He flew down the ice and, mistaking Ace Bailey for Horner, flattened Bailey with a vicious check.

Bailey's head struck the ice and he was taken to a hospital with a fractured skull. His life was saved by delicate brain surgery, but he was never able to play hockey again.

Eddie Shore   WIDE WORLD

The memory of that near-tragedy haunted Shore for many years. But he went on to play great defense for the Bruins and then the New York Americans before finally hanging up his skates and becoming owner of the Springfield Indians of the American Hockey League.

As a club owner, Shore remained a fighter. He fought with his players at contract time and with other owners in the committee rooms. Eddie Shore won most of those fights, too.

JACK STEWART

Jack Stewart did more to perfect the art of the teeth-rattling body check than any defenseman in the history of the National Hockey League.

There were bigger men in the league when Stewart was patrolling the back line for the Detroit Red Wings in the 1930s and 40s, but none hit with the shattering force of this 5–11, 185-pound wheat farmer from Pilot Mound, Manitoba.

The late Jack Adams, who coached Stewart during most of his 10 years with Detroit, was always impressed by his star defenseman's strength. "He was one of the strongest guys I've ever seen in a hockey uniform," Adams once remarked. "He worked hard on his farm all summer and that probably accounted for it."

Frank Boucher, the former coach and general manager of the New York Rangers, was another great Stewart admirer. "Jack played defense a lot like Ching Johnson, my old teammate," Boucher said. "He went all out in every game. And he was tough. Hockey was no tea party to Jack Stewart."

Stewart also was responsible for the development of other great Detroit defensemen both before and after World War II. Bill Quackenbush and Red Kelly attained stardom while paired with Stewart. "Jack did all the heavy work," said Lynn Patrick, the former coach of the Boston Bruins who claimed he received the hardest body checks of his career from Stewart. "He was always advising the other defensemen and if they made an error, Jack was there to back them up."

Hockey fans will always remember Stewart for his body checking, but he was a good blocking defenseman as well. He could clear the puck out of his zone quickly and rarely made a bad pass. He could also skate faster than most spectators realized, but they came to see him hit.

It was this penchant for flattening rival skaters that eventually produced a series of injuries and forced Stewart's retirement. After 10 great seasons at Detroit, during which he was named to five All-Star teams and was a member of two Stanley Cup championship teams, Stewart was traded to the Chicago Black Hawks in 1950.

Shortly after joining the Hawks, Stewart was sidelined with a slipped disc in his back. Surgery followed and it appeared then that the man known as "'Black Jack" had played his last game. But Stewart wasn't ready to

Jack Stewart

SCOTTY KILPATRICK

quit. He spent long hours of exercising, even while flat on his back in the hospital, and promised, "I'll be back, maybe next year."

He did come back the following season, but couldn't shake the injury jinx. In a game against the Rangers, Stewart suffered a fractured skull in a collision with teammate Clare Martin and New York's Edgar Laprade. That did it. Midway through the 1951–52 season, Black Jack Stewart retired.

Ebbie Goodfellow, the Black Hawks' coach, was saddened by Stewart's loss. "We're going to miss Jack," he said. "He was a great one." The selection committee of the Hockey Hall of Fame agreed when it voted Stewart into the Hall in 1964.

THE GOALIES   The Last Man

FRANKIE BRIMSEK

No player ever made a more spectacular debut in the National Hockey League than Frankie Brimsek, the frozen-faced "Mr. Zero" of the Boston Bruins.

In his first eight games as Boston's regular netminder in December of 1938 Brimsek turned in six shutouts, wiped out a league record for consecutive scoreless minutes, and helped the Boston citizenry forget the sadness that enveloped them when Tiny Thompson was sold to Detroit.

The Bruins elevated Brimsek from their Providence, R.I., farm club after Thompson, a great favorite with Boston fans, had been peddled to the Red Wings for $15,000. "I'll never forget my debut in Boston," Brimsek recalled. "Thompson was a popular guy and a great goalie. I could feel the coolness of the fans as soon as I joined the club. They were waiting for me to kick one."

Brimsek, though, turned that Boston coolness into hand-clapping warmth in less than a month. After losing to the Montreal Canadiens, 2–0, in his first game as Thompson's replacement, Brimsek posted three consecutive shutouts. He added three more shutouts in Boston's next four games and wiped out Thompson's scoreless record with 231 minutes and 54 seconds of flawless netminding.

The Bruins' followers now were ready to run Brimsek against old Jim Curley for mayor of Boston. Another factor that contributed to Brimsek's popularity—at least with fans in the United States—was his birthplace. He was born and raised in Eveleth, Minn., and thereby became an oddity in pro hockey—an American-born All-Star.

From Boston's Back Bay to the fish wharves of San Francisco, Brimsek was hailed as hockey's "Mr. Zero." He climaxed his first year with the

Frankie Brimsek   HOCKEY HALL OF FAME

Bruins by sparking them to the NHL title and the Stanley Cup championship. He won the Vezina Trophy as the league's most proficient goalie, the Calder (Rookie of the Year) Trophy and a berth on the NHL's first All-Star team.

The Bruins won two more NHL championships and another Stanley Cup behind Brimsek's nifty goaltending in the next three years. He entered the U.S. Coast Guard in 1943 and served two years aboard a patrol craft in the South Pacific. He returned to the Bruins from his World War II duty in 1945 and found it difficult to regain his old form in goal.

Brimsek reasoned that his years aboard ship had "tied up" his legs. "I was a little shaky when I got back," he admitted. "My legs and my nerves were shot."

After putting in four post-war seasons with Boston, Brimsek asked the Bruins to trade him to Chicago, where he would be closer to his Minnesota home, his family and business interests. The Bruins relented and traded him to the Black Hawks in 1949. He played one season for Chicago and then retired.

In 1966, the selection committee of the Hockey Hall of Fame remembered "Mr. Zero" and made him a member of that exclusive club.

WALTER "TURK" BRODA

Professional hockey can thank an anonymous school principal for launching the career of one of the outstanding clutch goaltenders of all time.

It all began for Walter "Turk" Broda when he was a chubby youngster in Brandon, Manitoba, where he was born on May 15, 1914. One day the principal at his public school announced he was organizing a hockey team. Young Broda, called "Turkey Egg" because of the freckles on his face, tried out for a defense position. It was a bad choice.

"I'm sorry," his principal said, "we have all the defensemen we need." Broda started to leave the ice. "Wait a minute," the principal said. "We need a goaltender, Walter. Get into the goal."

Turk Broda was a goaltender from that day. He started his pro career in the Detroit organization and landed with Toronto through sheer luck. Conn Smythe, the Toronto club owner, was seeking a replacement for Hall of Famer George Hainsworth in 1936 when he scouted a minor league playoff game between the Detroit Olympias and the Windsor (Ont.) Bulldogs.

Smythe had received glowing reports on the Windsor goalie, Earl Robertson. But when the Olympias trounced Windsor, 8–1, the Maple Leafs'

Turk Broda   WIDE WORLD

boss forgot all about Robertson. "I like the fellow tending goal for the other team," Smythe said. The other goalie was Broda.

Smythe wasted no time purchasing Broda from Detroit for $8,000. Early in the 1936–37 season, Turk replaced Hainsworth as the Maple Leafs' regular goalie. He held the job for 14 seasons, during which he helped Toronto win five Stanley Cup championships. He twice won the Vezina Trophy as the National Hockey League's top netminder and earned berths on three All-Star teams.

Broda was always at his best when the pressure was greatest, especially in playoff games. He played in 101 Stanley Cup games and allowed only 211 goals for an average of 2.08—both records. In the 1949 championship playoffs he gave up only four goals as the Maple Leafs swept Detroit in four straight games. In the 1951 playoffs he was again brilliant, allowing only nine goals in eight games.

A happy-go-lucky man of Polish extraction, Broda was inclined to be overweight, a condition which frequently aroused the ire of Smythe. Early in the 1949–50 season, when the Leafs failed to win in six games, Smythe called the chubby Broda into his office. "I'm not running a fat man's team," the owner said. "I'm taking you out of the nets and you're not coming back until you get down to 190 pounds." At the time Broda scaled almost 200.

The goalie knew Smythe wasn't kidding. He launched a crash diet. He turned his back on desserts. He went to a gym and was steamed, boiled and pounded. It was a Herculean effort for Broda, but he regained his job after missing only one game.

After retiring as a player in 1952, Broda turned to coaching. He was elected to the Hockey Hall of Fame in 1967.

BILL DURNAN

Bill Durnan's career as a National Hockey League goaltender was short in terms of service and sweet in terms of personal satisfaction.

He broke into the NHL in 1943 as a 29-year-old rookie with the Montreal Canadiens and, after seven brilliant seasons, was forced to quit the club in the middle of the 1950 Stanley Cup playoffs because of frayed nerves. But in that comparatively short time he established records which still stand.

During the 1948–49 season, Durnan set the league's modern record for the longest shutout sequence when he held the opposition scoreless for 309 minutes and 21 seconds. He was the first goalie to win the Vezina Trophy four consecutive years (1944 through 1947). Turk Broda of Toronto

Bill Durnan   HOCKEY HALL OF FAME

interrupted his string in 1948, but Durnan won the trophy for the next two years, giving him a record six in seven years.

Durnan's appearances on the league's All-Star first team matched his Vezina Trophy accomplishments. He made the squad as a rookie in 1944 and repeated each year except for 1948 when Broda again prevented him from fashioning a seven-year sweep.

Looking back on his career, Durnan once attributed his great success to the fact that he was ambidextrous.

"It was a tremendous asset and I owe that gift to Steve Faulkner, one of my coaches in a church league in Toronto when I was just a youngster," he said. "Steve showed me how to switch the stick from one hand to the other. It wasn't easy at first because I was so young and the stick seemed so heavy. But Steve kept after me and gradually the stick became lighter and I could switch it automatically."

This ability to use either hand to catch flying pucks or to bat them away with his stick was perfected by Durnan during a long career in the amateur ranks. By the time he finally turned pro with the Canadiens he was an accomplished netminder who rarely permitted a rebound in front of his cage.

In his rookie year with Montreal, Durnan gave up only 109 goals in 50 games. That was the same season (1943–44) that Maurice Richard scored his record 50 goals. Sparked by Durnan's netminding and Richard's scoring, the Canadiens lost only five of 50 games in winning the NHL pennant and then skated off with the Stanley Cup.

A big, friendly man who packed 200 pounds on his 6–2 frame, Durnan soon found that the pressures that eventually engulf every major league goalie were ruining his health. "It got so bad that I couldn't sleep on the night before a game," he said. "I couldn't even keep my meals down. I felt that nothing was worth that kind of agony."

Injuries—another occupational hazard of goalies—also bothered Durnan. Late in the 1949–50 season, he suffered a severely-gashed head from an opponent's skate. He recovered in time for the playoffs, but midway through a semifinal series against the New York Rangers he asked to be replaced in the nets.

Bill Durnan had played his last game. In a short span of seven years in the NHL he had accomplished great feats and won many awards. His most cherished came in 1964 when he was named to hockey's Hall of Fame.

CHARLIE GARDINER

Charlie "Chuck" Gardiner was one of a handful of European-born players to reach the National Hockey League. He was born in Edinburgh,

Charlie Gardiner   HOCKEY HALL OF FAME

Scotland, in 1904, emigrated to Canada as a child and learned his hockey in Winnipeg, Manitoba.

He was a goaltender from the start and advanced rapidly through the various minor leagues in his adopted city. His record as a teen-age goalie was not dazzling, but he demonstrated a sufficient amount of talent to attract the attention of the Winnipeg Maroons of the old Western League.

Gardiner turned professional with the Maroons in 1926. He was then 22 years old and quickly impressed major league scouts with his roving style of play. Other netminders in those days were content to remain in their cage but Gardiner would move out of his net and thereby cut down the shooting angle of rival attackers.

In later years, goalies like Chuck Rayner of the New York Rangers and Jacques Plante of the Montreal Canadiens perfected this art of rushing out to meet the enemy before he could strike. But it was Chuck Gardiner who first earned fame as a fearless rover.

After playing only one season with Winnipeg, Gardiner was signed by the Chicago Black Hawks. His reputation as the "Wandering Scotsman" had preceded him to the NHL and rival players predicted his reckless style would be his ruination in the majors.

Gardiner shrugged off warnings that if he didn't adopt a more conventional style of netminding he would find himself back in Winnipeg. He remained a wanderer with the Black Hawks and soon developed into the NHL's most outstanding and exciting goalie.

He won the Vezina Trophy twice, in 1932 and 1934. He made the league's first All-Star team in both of those years and was voted to the second team in 1933.

Despite Gardiner's brilliant work, the Black Hawks then were the perennial patsies in the American Division of the NHL. But all this changed in the 1934 Stanley Cup playoffs. The Black Hawks had finished second in their division during the regular season as Gardiner posted 10 shutouts and allowed only 83 goals in 48 games. Were they finally ready to win their first Cup? It was all up to the "Wandering Scotsman."

The Black Hawks won the first two games of the best-of-five final playoff series against Detroit. In the third game, Gardiner held the Red Wings scoreless until the final period when he suddenly weakened and gave up five goals. The Chicago fans stared in dismay at their goalie. No one knew that he was a sick man.

Shaken and fighting for strength, Gardiner insisted on playing in the fourth game two nights later. He grew weaker as the scoreless game wore on and went into one overtime and then another. Midway through the second overtime, teammate Mush March ended the agony for Gardiner. He scored the game's only goal and, finally, the Black Hawks ruled as world champions.

Eight weeks after his greatest triumph, Gardiner was rushed to a Winnipeg hospital. He was in a coma. On Wednesday, June 13, 1934, he

Glenn Hall

died. He was only 30, but Chuck Gardiner had already earned recognition as one of the greatest goalies of all time. And in 1945 he was elected to the Hall of Fame.

GLENN HALL

Glenn Hall once offered a terse explanation of what it is like to be a major league goaltender. "Playing goal is a winter of torture for me," he said. "I often look at those guys who can whistle and laugh before a game and shake my head. You'd think they didn't have a care in the world. Me? I'm plain miserable before every game."

Hall's main problem was a nervous stomach. Early in his career he used to become physically ill just sitting in the locker room waiting for a game to start. The attacks became less frequent as he grew older, but the butterflies were always there.

Despite these pre-game seizures of anxiety and nervousness, Hall once played 502 consecutive games in the National Hockey League. He launched the streak in his first full season in the league in 1955–56 when he played all 70 games with the Detroit Red Wings. He didn't miss a game with Detroit the following season, then moved on to Chicago, where he put in five additional 70-game campaigns before the string was finally snapped in November, 1962.

Hall was born and raised in Humboldt, Saskatchewan, a railway center, where he learned to tend goal on outdoor rinks. He turned pro with the old Indianapolis team in the American Hockey League in 1951, then put in three seasons with Edmonton of the Western League before moving up to the Red Wings. He was an immediate success with Detroit, winning the Calder Trophy as the NHL's top rookie in 1956.

After two seasons with the Red Wings, he was sent to the Black Hawks in the same celebrated six-player trade that put Hall of Famer Ted Lindsay in a Chicago uniform. During 10 years with the Black Hawks, Hall won the Vezina Trophy as the league's outstanding goalie three times and was named to the All-Star first team five times.

He reached his peak in the spring of 1961 when the Black Hawks won the Stanley Cup championship for the first time in 23 years. In the semi-finals against Montreal he was at his acrobatic best, holding the Canadiens scoreless for 135 minutes and 26 seconds at one stage of the series. And that Montreal team boasted such feared sharpshooters as Jean Beliveau, Bernie Geoffrion, Dickie Moore and Henri Richard.

At the end of each season, Hall would advise the Black Hawks that he was considering retiring, but the lure of a fatter contract would always prompt him to change his mind. Then, once the season had started, he would have further doubts. "Plenty of times I'm tempted to climb into my car and head for home," he confessed.

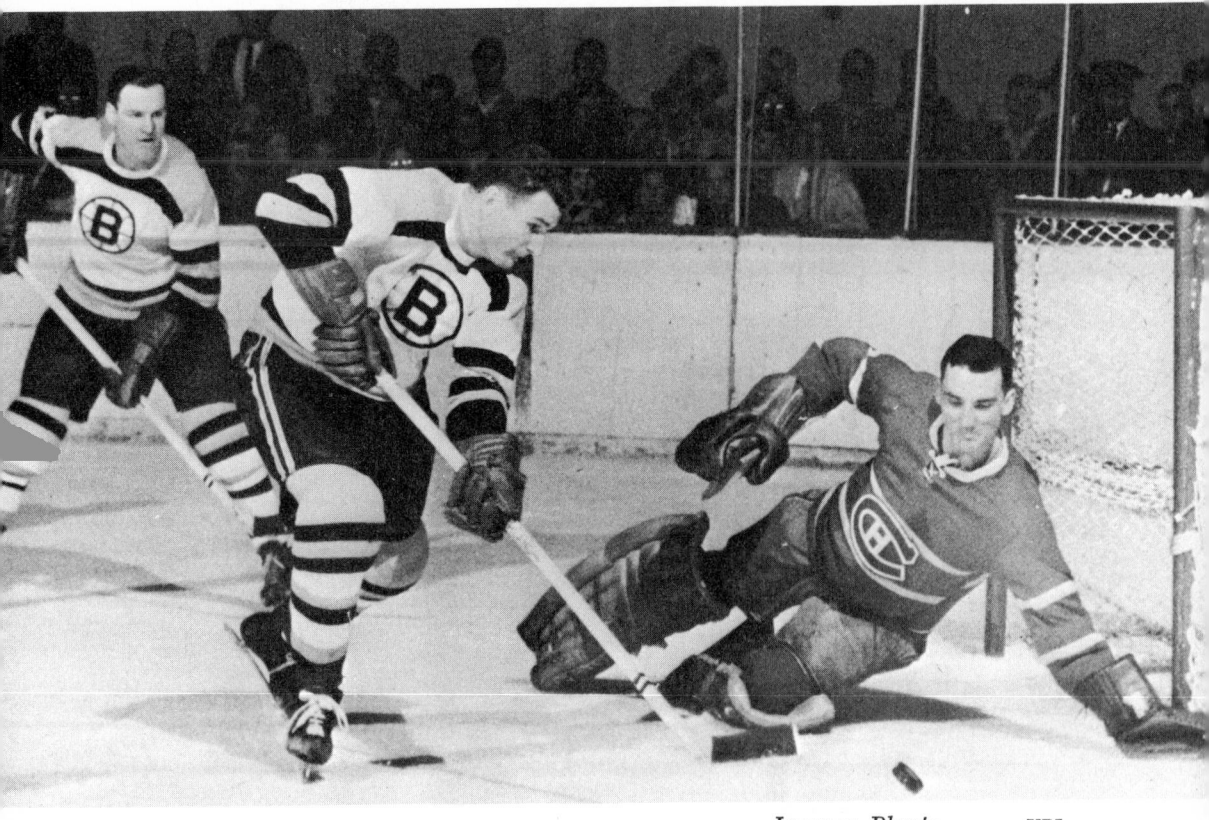

Jacques Plante UPI

When the St. Louis Blues plucked Hall from Chicago in hockey's first expansion draft in 1967, he was ready to quit again and become a gentleman farmer in Edmonton, Alberta. He was then 36 years old. However, the promise of the largest salary ever paid a goaltender—an estimated $45,000—encouraged him to leave his 160-acre farm for St. Louis.

Hall's great goaltending led the expansion club into the finals of the 1968 Stanley Cup playoffs against Montreal. The Blues were eliminated in four straight games, all of which were decided by one goal. But Hall won the Conn Smythe Trophy as the outstanding performer in the playoffs.

Then, in 1968–69 he teamed with Jacques Plante to win his third Vezina Trophy and 11th All-Star team berth in 14 NHL seasons.

JACQUES PLANTE

From a 50 cents per game goaltender with a factory team in Quebec to a $35,000-a-year All-Star in the National Hockey League was the road Jacques Plante traveled during a playing career that spanned more than two decades.

It all started back in Plante's home town of Shawinigan Falls, Quebec, when he was 15 years old. "I was playing goal for a factory team," he recalled. "We didn't get paid, so one day my father suggested that I ask the coach for some money. The coach agreed to give me 50 cents a game if I didn't tell any of the other players about it.

"Even 50 cents meant a lot to me in those days. I was the oldest of 11 children. We couldn't afford a radio...or luxuries of any kind. The only time we had soft drinks was at Christmas."

Plante went on from there to earn $85 a week as a netminder for Quebec City in a junior amateur league and turned pro with the Montreal Royals in the old Quebec Senior League at the age of 22 in 1951. He made his NHL debut the following season with the Montreal Canadiens in a Stanley Cup playoff game at Chicago.

That first game with the Canadiens is still stamped in Plante's memory. "I was so nervous I couldn't tie my skates," he said. But he shut out the Black Hawks, 3–0. Jacques Plante was on his way to becoming one of the highest salaried goalies in pro hockey.

He spent 10 glorious years with the Canadiens, helping them to five straight Stanley Cup championships (1956 through 1960). He won the Vezina Trophy as the league's top netminder a record-tying six times (five in a row) and was a member of the NHL All-Star team six times. In 1962, he became only the fourth goaltender in NHL history to win the Hart (Most Valuable Player) Trophy.

Terry Sawchuk   SCOTTY KILPATRICK

Plante's flair for the dramatic and his inventiveness also marked his career at Montreal. He became a roving goalie early in his career ("One of the amateur teams I played for was so bad I had to always chase the puck behind the cage"), and he perfected this art with the Canadiens.

He also will be remembered as the man who popularized the goalie mask in the NHL. It happened in a game against the New York Rangers on November 1, 1959. Struck in the face by an Andy Bathgate shot, he went to the dressing room, had the wound stitched, and then returned to the ice wearing a cream-colored plastic face mask. Before long most pro goalies adopted the mask as part of their equipment.

Plante was traded to New York in 1963, spent a year and a half with the Rangers and then retired to become a salesman with a Canadian brewery. In 1968, the St. Louis Blues offered him $35,000 to make a comeback. The lanky French-Canadian, who had started out playing for 50 cents a game and now was approaching his 40th birthday, couldn't resist the offer. He packed his pads and his mask and moved to St. Louis, where he shared the goaltending with another gaffer, 37-year-old Glenn Hall. And together, they won the Vezina Trophy and led the Blues to two consecutive West titles. Then he was sold to Toronto in 1970 and spent three seasons with the Maple Leafs. In March 1973, Boston, looking for playoff help, purchased the 44-year-old goalie from the Leafs.

TERRY SAWCHUK

Terry Sawchuk used to quote that old nursery rhyme which insisted "Sticks and stones may break my bones, but names will never harm me." Only in Sawchuk's case it was sticks and pucks which broke his bones. And the names that some people called him did hurt.

In more than two decades of professional hockey, Sawchuk overcame the following injuries and ailments to earn his place among hockey's top 10 goalies: a broken right arm that didn't heal properly and wound up inches shorter than his left arm, severed hand tendons, a fractured instep, infectious mononucleosis, punctured lungs, ruptured discs, bone chips in his elbows that required three operations, a ruptured appendix and innumerable cuts on his face and body, one of which almost cost him the sight in his right eye.

But the injury that hurt the most involved his pride. It happened in 1956 when he left the Boston Bruins in mid-season after his bout with mononucleosis. "Those Boston reporters called me everything in the book, including a quitter," he said. "It was so bad I threatened to sue four newspapers for libel. I didn't go through with it, though. I guess those guys have to make a living, too."

Tiny Thompson   HOCKEY HALL OF FAME

That's Terry Sawchuk—always quick to hate and always quick to forget.

He experienced his first pains of anguish when he was 10 years old back home in Winnipeg, Manitoba. His older brother, Mike, a goalie, developed a heart murmur and died. Terry inherited Mike's goalie pads and seven years later (1947) he broke into professional hockey as a fuzzy-cheeked netminder with Omaha of the old United States Hockey League. He won the league's rookie award that season, spent the next two years in the American Hockey League and then joined Detroit in 1950.

Sawchuk's unorthodox, gorilla-like crouch in the nets immediately captured the imagination of Detroit fans. It also helped him capture many awards. He won the Vezina Trophy, a prize awarded to the NHL's most proficient goaltender, three times and shared a fourth. His goals-against average was less than two per game in each of his first five seasons with Detroit.

The Red Wings traded Sawchuk to the Bruins in 1955, reacquired him two years later and then lost him to Toronto in the draft in 1964. He was picked up by Los Angeles in the 1967 expansion draft and a year later returned to Detroit, then went to New York for the 1969–70 season.

Hailed as the only NHL goalie to record more than 100 career shutouts, Sawchuk credited most of his success to his crouching style. "When I'm crouching low, I can keep better track of the puck through the players' legs on screen shots," he explained.

Ironically, this doughty figure who had survived many injuries on the ice died as a result of an off-the-ice accident in May, 1970.

CECIL "TINY" THOMPSON

When you think of stingy netminders you think of Cecil "Tiny" Thompson. Nobody was more frugal in doling out goals. Consider his record. Thompson completed 12 years in the National Hockey League with a miserly average of 2.28 goals allowed per game. His playoff record was even better: 2.00.

Thompson's hockey career was launched in Sandon, British Columbia, where he was born in 1905. Oddly, he disliked goaltending as a youngster. "I had to agree to be the goalie or the other kids wouldn't let me play," he recalled.

He also disliked the nickname Tiny. "But I had no choice in the matter," he said. "I used to play with older fellows when I was still a schoolboy, and alongside them I guess I looked tiny."

The nickname stuck, although he grew into a 5–10, 180-pounder by the time he broke into the NHL with the Boston Bruins in 1928. Boston won its first Stanley Cup championship that season, mainly through Thompson's brilliance in the net.

Boston fans thrilled to many Thompson performances in the years that followed, yet it is a measure of his class that he considers a losing game the finest he played in the NHL. It happened in the fifth and deciding game of a semifinal playoff series between Boston and Toronto on April 3, 1933.

Thompson and Lorne Chabot, the Maple Leafs' goalie, matched save for save through a scoreless regulation game. Neither budged through five overtime periods. During those eight 20-minute periods, Thompson handled 111 shots without a miscue. Finally, at 4:46 of the sixth overtime period, Ken Doraty and Andy Blair of Toronto teamed to end the marathon struggle.

Blair, who had been sent into the game primarily to shadow Boston's Eddie Shore, set up the winning play. He twice checked the Bruins' defenseman as he tried to break away. On Shore's third attempt, he batted the puck ahead of him—and right on Blair's stick.

In two long strides, Blair crossed the blueline into Boston territory. He sidestepped Shore and as the defenseman swung around to jab at the puck, Blair shot it ahead to Doraty, who was streaking for the Boston net. Doraty picked up the puck in full stride and whistled it past Thompson.

The game broke an NHL record for length of play, but it didn't break Thompson's heart. He was given a standing ovation when he left the ice. And when the awards were passed out that year he was awarded the Vezina Trophy as the league's top netminder for the second time.

During 10 seasons with the Bruins, Thompson won the Vezina four times, was named to the first All-Star team twice and made the second team on two other occasions. In 1938 he was sold to Detroit, where he played his final two seasons.

Sid Abel, who became Detroit's general manager after a great playing career with the Red Wings, remembers Thompson well. "I was just breaking in with the Wings when Tiny joined us from Boston," Abel said. "He was getting old and tired then, but you had to admire the guy. He always made the big play."

In 1959 Tiny Thompson's magnificent career record was recognized by hockey's Hall of Fame selectors and he was welcomed into the shrine.

GEORGES VEZINA

Goaltending, as Georges Vezina knew it in the first quarter of the century, was a different art than it is today. He played when a netminder was not permitted to sprawl on the ice to block shots. So Georges Vezina stood straight and tall in front of his net during a brilliant 15-year career with the Montreal Canadiens from 1910 to 1925.

Vezina was a product of the northlands of Quebec. He was born in 1887 in the lumber city of Chicoutimi on the Saguenay River. He was 23 years

Georges Vezina   HOCKEY HALL OF FAME (TUROFSKY)

old and playing goal for an amateur team in Chicoutimi when he first came to the attention of the Canadiens.

It was in February of 1910, when the Canadiens made an exhibition tour of the Province of Quebec. They were then kingpins of the National Association of Hockey, a forerunner of the National Hockey League. A game was arranged between Montreal's great pros and the Chicoutimi amateurs led by Vezina. However, the gangling, six-foot netminder didn't play like an amateur. He shut out the powerful Canadiens. In the fall of that same year, Vezina was playing for Montreal.

He went on to become one of Montreal's most valuable and loved players. With Vezina guarding the nets, the Canadiens won the NHA championship twice, the NHL championship three times and the Stanley Cup twice.

The most impressive part of Vezina's game was his coolness. In time, he became known throughout the NHL as the "Chicoutimi Cucumber." Even while the action swirled around him, he moved with a tireless, quiet dignity. In one historic game between Montreal and Ottawa, with the league championship awaiting the victor, the poker-faced Vezina turned back 78 of 79 shots.

He was also known as Montreal's "Silent Habitant," a man of few words who never complained. His whole life revolved around his large family (he was the father of 22 children), yet even those in his own household did not know he was fighting for his life when he played his last game on November 28, 1925.

The Canadiens' opponent in the old Mt. Royal Arena in Montreal that night was Pittsburgh. After a scoreless first period, Vezina left the ice bleeding from the mouth. He collapsed in the dressing room, returned for the start of the second period, then collapsed again and had to leave the game. Only then did his family and friends learn he had tuberculosis. Four months later, at the age of 39, he passed away.

The memory of Georges Vezina, the quiet man, is perpetuated in the trophy awarded each year to the NHL's outstanding goaltender. It is an impressive trophy—almost as impressive as the Hall of Famer it honors.

LORNE WORSLEY

A friend once asked Gump Worsley why he never wore a mask while tending goal in the slap shot world of the National Hockey League. The Gumper smiled one of his impish smiles and answered quickly, "My face is my mask."

Worsley was an enigma. He thought nothing of standing up bare-faced against the booming shots NHL players fired his way. But try and get him in an airplane and Worsley would break out in a cold sweat. The Gumper had an abiding distrust of air travel.

Gump Worsley   BARTON SILVERMAN

An unlikely looking athlete, the crew-cut, pint-sized goalie brought a perfect temperament to his job. He was cherubic, a happy-go-lucky soul who never let his nerve-wracking job get the best of him . . . until his team had to fly from one city to another. On the ice, he was cool as a cucumber. In an airplane, he was a bundle of nerves. Worsley's fear of flying dated back to his amateur hockey days when he was with the old New York Rovers. On a return flight from Milwaukee, one of the plane's engines caught fire and forced an emergency landing. The players survived but Worsley's psyche didn't. After that experience, the Gump suffered terribly every time he stepped into a plane. He would sit on the aisle, clench the armrests as tightly as he could and hang on for dear life. "It's the one time I don't talk," said Worsley. "I'm too scared to say anything."

Worsley was born in Montreal and grew up in a tough end of town where his buddies decided he looked like comic strip character Andy Gump and tagged him with that nickname. Gump was only 20 when he turned pro and two years later he found himself guarding goal for the otherwise defenseless New York Rangers.

Night after distressing night, Worsley would skate out to meet 40- and 50-shot onslaughts from other NHL teams. Once a newsman asked the New York goalie which team gave him the most trouble. Worsley never broke stride, answering quickly, "The Rangers."

New York's coach in those days was fiery Phil Watson. After one bad performance by his club, Watson started blasting his players publicly. He accused Worsley, a plump little soul, of having "a beer belly." Gump bristled at that crack. "He should know better than that," snapped the goalie. "He knows I only drink Scotch."

Worsley's career took an odd twist in 1963 when, after a decade in the shooting gallery at New York, he was traded to Montreal's defense-oriented Canadiens. After his experiences with the Rangers, this was a piece of cake for the Gumper. He subsequently shared two Vezina Trophies and helped the Canadiens to three Stanley Cups.

Early in the 1969 season, Worsley had a particularly rocky plane ride from Montreal to Chicago and quit on the spot, returning home via train. He was listed as voluntarily retired and was idle for much of the season. Then Minnesota obtained the rights to negotiate with the 40-year-old goalie and General Manager Wren Blair lured him back.

Playing like a rookie again, Worsley helped the North Stars into the playoffs for three straight years before retiring for keeps midway through the 1972–73 season. For keeps? Before the 1973–74 campaign was launched, a goaltender named Worsley announced his unretirement. He would return again for another whirl with the North Stars.

Ever since 1893, when Lord Stanley of Preston, the Earl of Derby and Governor-General of Canada, invested 10 pounds—about $48.67—in a squat, punch-bowl shaped trophy to symbolize amateur hockey supremacy, men have spent fortunes and lifetimes pursuing that elusive piece of silverware.

Its history is nearly as legendary and exciting as the game of hockey itself. At various times, Lord Stanley's Cup has been tossed in a graveyard, drop-kicked into a canal, dumped out of an automobile and stolen from its showcase. Each time, however, the Cup was rescued and it continues today as the oldest trophy in competition among athletes in North America.

Ironically, Lord Stanley never saw a Cup game. Shortly after one of his aides, Lord Kilcoursie, announced the Governor-General's intention of introducing a challenge cup symbolic of the amateur hockey championship of Canada, Lord Stanley returned to his native England. That's where he was on March 22, 1894, when the Ottawa Generals and Montreal Amateur Athletic Association met in the first Cup clash. For the record, Montreal won, 3–1, and the distinction of scoring the first Stanley Cup goal belongs to one Chauncey Kirby.

There is evidence that Lord Kilcoursie had more than a passing role in Lord Stanley's decision to initiate the Cup. Kilcoursie played hockey with Lord Stanley's sons and his deep interest in the sport soon spread to his boss.

Lord Stanley's guidelines for presenting the cup were simple enough. It was to go to the leading hockey club in Canada and the first recipient in 1893 was the Montreal A.A.A. When Lord Stanley left Canada to return to England, he designated two Ottawa sportsmen—Sheriff Sweetland and P.D. Ross—as trustees for the Cup, and they sifted through the various challenges from leagues all over Canada who wanted their chance to play for the trophy.

In those early days hockey was an amateur sport played by seven-man teams on outdoor rinks built for curling. Two portable poles, embedded in the ice with no net between them, constituted the goals, and goal judges stood behind these makeshift targets with no padding to protect themselves. Conditions were truly primitive and it was an appropriate setting for the most fantastic Cup challenge in history—that of Dawson City in 1905.

The Ottawa Silver Seven were the Cup holders from 1903 through 1906, successfully defending it against nine challenges from all parts of Canada. But none of the challengers could match the 1905 Yukon team's effort.

Colonel Joe Boyle, a wealthy Dawson City prospector, bankrolled the team's 23-day journey to Ottawa. The happy-go-lucky gold diggers traveled by dog sled, boat and train to cover the 4,400 miles. They made 46 miles by dogs the first day and 41 the second. Some of the players were forced to remove their boots because of blistered feet on the third day, with the temperature dropping 20 below zero.

The Montreal Shamrocks: Winner of the Stanley Cup in 1899.

HOCKEY HALL OF FAME (TUROFSKY)

They missed a boat connection at Skagway by two hours and had to wait five days at the docks before catching another boat from Seattle to Vancouver. Then they took a train on to Ottawa. They arrived in Ottawa, January 12, 1905, a day before the best-of-three series against the Silver Seven was to begin.

It was all for naught. The team that traveled the farthest to try for the Cup suffered the most lopsided elimination. The Klondikers lost the first game, 9–2, and the second and final game, 23–3. Frank McGee of Ottawa scored an unbelievable 14 goals in the second game rout—eight of them in a span of eight minutes, twenty seconds. What makes it truly unbelievable is that McGee was blind in one eye.

The year before the Klondike challenge, Ottawa had beaten off the Brandon Wheat Kings and the only notable thing about that challenge was the fact that Brandon goalie Doug Morrison incurred a penalty and was replaced in the nets by a teammate, Lester Patrick. A quarter of a century later, Patrick, then 44 and coach of the New York Rangers, would duplicate the feat and take over in goal during another Stanley Cup game.

The prestige of fielding a winning hockey team—possibly a Stanley Cup winner—was quite tantalizing to Canadian communities and the better players found themselves being offered fat contracts. Hockey's amateur posture was disappearing, and soon the Stanley Cup's would too.

By 1907 the Eastern Canadian Amateur Hockey Association had deleted the "Amateur" from its name. And in 1910 when the National Hockey Association—forerunner of the National Hockey League—came into existence, the Stanley Cup became the goal of professional hockey teams.

When Lester Patrick and his brother Frank moved west to organize the Pacific Coast Hockey League in 1913, a Stanley Cup series matching East and West was inaugurated. After the PCHL went out of business in 1927, the trophy became exclusively an NHL award.

Although there were no American teams in the NHL until 1924, it was seven years earlier that a U.S. team first captured the cherished Cup. In 1917, the Seattle Metropolitans, coached by Pete Muldoon, beat the Montreal Canadiens in the Cup series and transported the Cup below the border for the first time.

Through the years, the Cup has had varied adventures. It has been the most sought and at the same time most neglected trophy in sport.

Shortly after the turn of the century, following one of the Ottawa Silver Seven's several successful defenses, some members of the team were lugging the trophy back from a victory banquet. For kicks no doubt, it was suggested by one of the players that he could successfully boot the mug into Rideau Canal. And just to prove his point, he did.

The next day, when they realized what they had done, the Ottawa players rushed back to Rideau. Luckily, the canal had been frozen over, and there, slightly the worse for wear but still intact, sat the Stanley Cup.

Paddy Moran, a stand-up goalie, helped
the Quebec Bulldogs to the Stanley Cup
in 1912 and 1913.
        HOCKEY HALL OF FAME (TUROFSKY)

Russell "Barney" Stanley, no relation to
Lord Stanley, wears a Calgary Tigers
uniform here, but in 1915 he played for
the Vancouver Millionaires of the Pacific
Coast League, winner of the Stanley
Cup that year.   HOCKEY HALL OF FAME

Shortly after that, the Cup did a brief turn as a flower pot. That happened when the Montreal team gathered around the silver mug for a picture in a local photographer's studio. When the posing was over, the players left the studio, and the Cup as well.

The photographer's mother found the deserted silverware and, not knowing its significance, filled it with earth and planted geraniums. Eventually, the photographer discovered it and rescued Lord Stanley's Cup.

In 1924, the Montreal Canadiens were celebrating their Cup victory at a downtown hotel when it was suggested that the celebration be moved to owner Leo Dandurand's home. A group of players, the Cup in tow, started out driving for Dandurand's home when a tire blew out. In the course of changing the tire, the Cup somehow was removed from the car and placed on the sidewalk. When the repairs were completed, the celebrants took off for Dandurand's again.

It wasn't until the Canadiens reached their destination that they missed the Cup. They scurried back to the spot and, sure enough, sitting there undisturbed, waiting for them was the Cup.

Another time, an official of the Kenora Thistles stormed out of a meeting of hockey executives with the Cup under his arm. Angered over the refusal of his colleagues to authorize the use of two borrowed players during a Cup series, he was prepared to act drastically.

"Where are you going with the Cup?" he was asked. He replied quite simply: "I'm going to throw it in the Lake of Woods."

There are those who swear he would have, too, had compromise not been reached on the use of the two disputed players.

Once, during the Ottawa Silver Seven's Cup reign, one member of the team decided to cap off a celebration by taking the mug home with him to show to his mother. The idea wasn't terribly popular with his teammates and in the ensuing scuffle, the Cup was tossed over a cemetery fence.

In 1962, the Cup was on display in the lobby of the Chicago Stadium while the Black Hawks and Montreal Canadiens battled for it on the ice inside the arena. When Chicago took a commanding edge in the game, a Montreal fan left his seat. He went to the lobby, broke into the showcase, lifted out the Cup and was on his way out the door before he was stopped. He, too, had a simple explanation.

"I was taking it back to Montreal, where it belongs," he said.

Stanley Cup play is hockey's World Series. Through the years it has been packed with individual and team heroics that live on and even tend to expand as the years go by. The stories include some of hockey's most cherished lore.

• There was the 1919 series, the only time no decision was reached. The Montreal Canadiens had traveled west to play Seattle for the Cup and the teams split the first four games. But the great flu epidemic had riddled the ranks of the Montreal team, leaving five players bedridden. The series was halted because of the wave of illness and no Cup champion was declared. Joe Hall, one of the Canadiens' stars, never recovered and died in a Seattle hospital.

• There was the 1922 series, when Lester Patrick, boss of the Vancouver team, allowed crippled Toronto to use defenseman Eddie Gerard as an emergency replacement. Gerard starred in two straight Toronto victories that cost Vancouver the Cup. Six years later, Patrick, the New York Ranger coach, went to Gerard, then general manager of the Montreal Maroons, and asked permission to use a borrowed goaltender when regular Lorne Chabot was injured. Gerard refused and Patrick, at age 44, went in to play goal, won the game and the inspired Rangers went on to take the Cup.

• There was the 1936 series, when the longest game in hockey history was played. Modere Bruneteau, a rookie who had scored only two goals during the regular season for Detroit, broke the scoreless tie against the Montreal Maroons with the only goal of the night at 16:30 of the sixth overtime period, ending 176 minutes, 30 seconds of scoreless hockey.

• There was the 1939 series, when Mel "Sudden Death" Hill of Boston personally slew the Rangers. Hill, a Ranger reject, scored the winning overtime goal in three of the Bruins' four victories over New York that year.

• There was the 1942 series, when the Detroit Red Wings beat Toronto in the first three games and with their mouths watering for a taste of Stanley Cup champagne, went into an incredible collapse, losing four straight, the series and the Cup.

• There was the 1951 series, when Toronto beat Montreal in five games, all of them going into overtime. The winning goal in the final game was scored by defenseman Bill Barilko, who was in mid-air when his shot went in. It was the last goal he ever scored. A few months later, Barilko died in a plane wreck.

• There was the 1952 series, when Detroit swept through to the Stanley Cup in eight straight games and goalie Terry Sawchuk allowed a total of just five goals for an astounding 0.62 Stanley Cup average. Sawchuk's feat overshadowed Montreal's Maurice Richard, who emerged from a first aid room with six stitches holding his forehead together to score the Canadiens' winning goal against Boston in the semifinals.

• There was the 1964 series, when Toronto defenseman Bob Baun was carried off the ice on a stretcher during the sixth game against Detroit when his right leg crumpled under him. Baun demanded that the doctors pump some pain-killer into the leg and he skated out to score the winning, sudden-death goal. Only after the Leafs took game No. 7 and the Cup, did the defenseman consent to have X-rays taken. That's when they found a broken bone in his ankle.

Lord Stanley's original investment of $48.67 has obviously brought rich and assorted dividends.

STANLEY CUP WINNERS

Season	Champions	Manager	Coach
1892–93—Montreal A.A.A.		————	
1894–95—Montreal Victorias		————	Mike Grant*
1895–96—Winnipeg Victorias		————	
1896–97—Montreal Victorias		————	Mike Grant*
1897–98—Montreal Victorias		————	F. Richardson
1898–99—Montreal Shamrocks		————	H. J. Trihey*
1899–1900—Montreal Shamrocks		————	H. J. Trihey*
1900–01—Winnipeg Victorias		————	
1901–02—Montreal A.A.A.		————	R. R. Boon*
1902–03—Ottawa Silver Seven		————	A. T. Smith
1903–04—Ottawa Silver Seven		————	A. T. Smith
1904–05—Ottawa Silver Seven		————	A. T. Smith
1905–06—Montreal Wanderers		————	
1906–07—Kenora Thistles (January)	F. A. Hudson	Tommy Phillips*
1906–07—Montreal Wanderers (March)	R. R. Boon	Cecil Blachford
1907–08—Montreal Wanderers	R. R. Boon	Cecil Blachford
1908–09—Ottawa Senators	————	Bruce Stuart*
1909–10—Montreal Wanderers	R. R. Boon	Pud Glass*
1910–11—Ottawa Senators	————	Bruce Stuart*
1911–12—Quebec Bulldogs	M. J. Quinn	C. Nolan
**1912–13—Quebec Bulldogs	M. J. Quinn	Joe Marlowe*
1913–14—Toronto Blue Shirts	Jack Marshall	Scotty Davidson*
1914–15—Vancouver Millionaires	Frank Patrick	Frank Patrick
1915–16—Montreal Canadiens	George Kennedy	George Kennedy
1916–17—Seattle Metropolitans	Pete Muldoon	Pete Muldoon
1917–18—Toronto Arenas	Charlie Querrie	Dick Carroll
1918–19—a—No decision.		
1919–20—Ottawa Senators	Tommy Gorman	Pete Green
1920–21—Ottawa Senators	Tommy Gorman	Pete Green
1921–22—Toronto St. Pats	Charlie Querrie	Eddie Powers
1922–23—Ottawa Senators	Tommy Gorman	Pete Green
1923–24—Montreal Canadiens	Leo Dandurand	Leo Dandurand
1924–25—Victoria Cougars	Lester Patrick	Lester Patrick
1925–26—Montreal Maroons	Eddie Gerard	Eddie Gerard
1926–27—Ottawa Senators	Dave Gill	Dave Gill
1927–28—New York Rangers	Lester Patrick	Lester Patrick
1928–29—Boston Bruins	Art Ross	Cy Denneny
1929–30—Montreal Canadiens	Cecil Hart	Cecil Hart
1930–31—Montreal Canadiens	Cecil Hart	Cecil Hart
1931–32—Toronto Maple Leafs	Conn Smythe	Dick Irvin
1932–33—New York Rangers	Lester Patrick	Lester Patrick
1933–34—Chicago Black Hawks	Tommy Gorman	Tommy Gorman
1934–35—Montreal Maroons	Tommy Gorman	Tommy Gorman
1935–36—Detroit Red Wings	Jack Adams	Jack Adams
1936–37—Detroit Red Wings	Jack Adams	Jack Adams
1937–38—Chicago Black Hawks	Bill Stewart	Bill Stewart
1938–39—Boston Bruins	Art Ross	Art Ross

Season	Champions	Manager	Coach
1939–40	New York Rangers	Lester Patrick	Frank Boucher
1940–41	Boston Bruins	Art Ross	Cooney Weiland
1941–42	Toronto Maple Leafs	Conn Smythe	Hap Day
1942–43	Detroit Red Wings	Jack Adams	Jack Adams
1943–44	Montreal Canadiens	Tommy Gorman	Dick Irvin
1944–45	Toronto Maple Leafs	Conn Smythe	Hap Day
1945–46	Montreal Canadiens	Tommy Gorman	Dick Irvin
1946–47	Toronto Maple Leafs	Conn Smythe	Hap Day
1947–48	Toronto Maple Leafs	Conn Smythe	Hap Day
1948–49	Toronto Maple Leafs	Conn Smythe	Hap Day
1949–50	Detroit Red Wings	Jack Adams	Tommy Ivan
1950–51	Toronto Maple Leafs	Conn Smythe	Joe Primeau
1951–52	Detroit Red Wings	Jack Adams	Tommy Ivan
1952–53	Montreal Canadiens	Frank Selke	Dick Irvin
1953–54	Detroit Red Wings	Jack Adams	Tommy Ivan
1954–55	Detroit Red Wings	Jack Adams	Jimmy Skinner
1955–56	Montreal Canadiens	Frank Selke	Toe Blake
1956–57	Montreal Canadiens	Frank Selke	Toe Blake
1957–58	Montreal Canadiens	Frank Selke	Toe Blake
1958–59	Montreal Canadiens	Frank Selke	Toe Blake
1959–60	Montreal Canadiens	Frank Selke	Toe Blake
1960–61	Chicago Black Hawks	Tommy Ivan	Rudy Pilous
1961–62	Toronto Maple Leafs	Punch Imlach	Punch Imlach
1962–63	Toronto Maple Leafs	Punch Imlach	Punch Imlach
1963–64	Toronto Maple Leafs	Punch Imlach	Punch Imlach
1964–65	Montreal Canadiens	Sam Pollock	Toe Blake
1965–66	Montreal Canadiens	Sam Pollock	Toe Blake
1966–67	Toronto Maple Leafs	Punch Imlach	Punch Imlach
1967–68	Montreal Canadiens	Sam Pollock	Toe Blake
1968–69	Montreal Canadiens	Sam Pollock	Claude Ruel
1969–70	Boston Bruins	Milt Schmidt	Harry Sinden
1970–71	Montreal Canadiens	Sam Pollock	Al MacNeil
1971–72	Boston Bruins	Milt Schmidt	Tom Johnson
1972–73	Montreal Canadiens	Sam Pollock	Scotty Bowman

* In the early years the teams were frequently run by the Captain. *Indicates Captain. For other Stanley Cup material see annual Stanley Cup record and statistics book.

** Victoria defeated Quebec in challenge series. No official recognition.

a—In the spring of 1919 the Montreal Canadiens traveled to Seattle to meet Seattle, PCHL champions. After five games had been played—teams were tied at 2 wins each and 1 tie—the series was called off by the local Department of Health because of the influenza epidemic and the death from influenza of Joe Hall.

STANLEY CUP PLAYOFF RECORDS

(Editors' note: 1927 was the first year that the Stanley Cup was competed for exclusively by the National Hockey League. Until then, other leagues challenged for the Cup. The following records begin with that year.)

TEAM

MOST STANLEY CUP CHAMPIONSHIPS:

16—Montreal Canadiens

MOST FINAL SERIES APPEARANCES:

22—Montreal Canadiens

MOST YEARS IN PLAYOFFS:

43—Montreal Canadiens

MOST CONSECUTIVE STANLEY CUP CHAMPIONSHIPS:

5—Montreal Canadiens (1956–60)

MOST CONSECUTIVE FINAL SERIES APPEARANCES:

10—Montreal Canadiens (1951–60)

MOST CONSECUTIVE PLAYOFF APPEARANCES:

21—Montreal Canadiens (1949–69)

MOST GOALS, BOTH TEAMS, 4-GAME SERIES:

36—Boston Bruins, St. Louis Blues, 1972 semi-final. Boston won best-of-seven series 4–0, outscoring St. Louis 28–8.

MOST GOALS, ONE TEAM, 4-GAME SERIES

28—Boston Bruins, 1972 semi-final, outscoring St. Louis 28–8.

MOST GOALS, BOTH TEAMS, 5-GAME SERIES

35—Boston, Montreal, 1943 semi-final. Boston won best-of-seven series 4–1, outscoring Montreal 18–17.

MOST GOALS, ONE TEAM, 5-GAME SERIES:

24—Montreal, 1956 semi-final. Montreal defeated New York 4–1 in best-of-seven series, outscoring Rangers 24–9.

MOST GOALS, BOTH TEAMS, 6-GAME SERIES:

56—Montreal, Chicago, 1973 final. Canadiens won best-of-seven series 4–2, outscoring Chicago 33–23.

MOST GOALS, ONE TEAM, 6-GAME SERIES:

33—Montreal, 1973 final, outscoring Chicago 33–23.

MOST GOALS, BOTH TEAMS, 7-GAME SERIES:

54—Montreal, Boston, 1971 quarter-final. Montreal won best-of-seven series 4–3, outscoring Boston 28–26.

MOST GOALS, ONE TEAM, 7-GAME SERIES:

28—Montreal, 1971 quarter-final, outscoring Boston 28–26.

FEWEST GOALS, BOTH TEAMS, 4-GAME SERIES:

9—Toronto, Boston, 1935 semi-final. Toronto won best-of-five series 3–1, outscoring Boston 7–2.

FEWEST GOALS, ONE TEAM, 4-GAME SERIES:

2—Boston, 1935 semi-final. Outscored by Toronto 7–2.

Montreal, 1952 final. Outscored by Detroit 11–2.

FEWEST GOALS, BOTH TEAMS, 5-GAME SERIES:

11—New York Rangers, Montreal Maroons, 1928 final. Rangers won best-of-five series 3–2 although outscored by the Maroons 6–5.

FEWEST GOALS, ONE TEAM, 5-GAME SERIES:

5—New York Rangers, 1928 final. Outscored by Montreal Maroons 6–5.

FEWEST GOALS, BOTH TEAMS, 6-GAME SERIES:

22—Toronto, Boston, 1951 semi-final. Toronto defeated Boston 4–1 with one tie in best-of-seven series, outscoring Boston 17–5.

FEWEST GOALS, ONE TEAM, 6-GAME SERIES:

5—Boston, 1951 semi-final. Outscored by Toronto 17–5.

FEWEST GOALS, BOTH TEAMS, 7-GAME SERIES:

18—Toronto, Detroit, 1945 final. Toronto defeated Detroit 4–3 in best-of-seven series; teams tied in scoring 9–9.

FEWEST GOALS, ONE TEAM, 7-GAME SERIES:

9—Toronto, 1945 final. Scored nine goals against Detroit.

Detroit, 1945 final. Scored nine goals against Toronto.

MOST GOALS, BOTH TEAMS, ONE GAME:

15—Montreal-Chicago, 1973; Chicago 8, Montreal 7.

MOST GOALS, ONE TEAM, ONE GAME:

11—Montreal, 1944; Canadiens 11, Toronto 0.

MOST GOALS, BOTH TEAMS, ONE PERIOD:

8—Montreal-Chicago, 1973, in second period. Chicago scored five goals, Montreal three. Chicago won 8–7.

MOST GOALS, ONE TEAM, ONE PERIOD:

7—Montreal, 1944, in third period against Toronto while winning, 11–0.

LONGEST OVERTIME:

116 minutes, 30 seconds—Detroit-Montreal Maroons at Montreal, March 24–25, 1936. Detroit 1, Maroons 0. Mud Bruneteau scored, assisted by Hec Kilrea, at 16:30 of sixth overtime period, or after 176 minutes, 30 seconds from start of game, which ended at 2:25 A.M.

SHORTEST OVERTIME:

12 seconds—Chicago-Pittsburgh at Pittsburgh, April 9, 1972.

Chicago 6, Pittsburgh 5. Pit Martin scored winning goal.

MOST OVERTIME GAMES, FINAL SERIES:

5—Toronto-Montreal, 1951. Toronto defeated Canadiens 4–1 in best-of-seven series.

MOST OVERTIME GAMES, SEMI-FINAL SERIES:

4—Toronto-Boston, 1933. Toronto won best-of-five series 3–2.

Boston-New York Rangers in 1939. Boston won best-of-seven series 4–3.

St. Louis-Minnesota in 1968. St. Louis won best-of-seven series 4–3.

MOST OVERTIME GAMES, ONE PLAYOFF YEAR:

10—1968. Of 40 games played, 10 went into overtime: two in quarter-final as St. Louis and Philadelphia each won once, Minnesota once in quarter-final against Los Angeles, Montreal once in semi-final against Chicago, St. Louis three and Minnesota once in semi-final and Montreal twice in final against St. Louis.

FEWEST OVERTIME GAMES, ONE PLAYOFF YEAR:

0—1964. None of the 16 games played went into overtime, the only year since 1926 that no overtime was required in any playoff series.

MOST CONSECUTIVE PLAYOFF GAME VICTORIES:

11—Montreal. Streak began April 16, 1959 at Toronto with 3–2 victory in fourth game of final series, won by Canadians 4–1 and ended March 23, 1961 when Chicago defeated Canadiens 4–3 in second game of semi-finals.

MOST CONSECUTIVE VICTORIES, ONE PLAYOFF YEAR:

10—Boston, 1970. Boston defeated New York in last 2 games of best-of-seven quarter-final, Chicago 4–0 in best-of-seven semi-final and St. Louis 4–0 in best-of-seven final.

MOST SHUTOUTS, ONE PLAYOFF YEAR, ALL TEAMS:

8—1937. Of 17 games played, New York had four, Detroit three and Boston one.

FEWEST SHUTOUTS, ONE PLAYOFF YEAR, ALL TEAMS:

0—1959. Of 18 games played.

MOST SHUTOUTS, BOTH TEAMS, ONE SERIES:

5—1945 final. Toronto, Detroit. Toronto had three shutouts and Detroit two.

1950 semi-final. Toronto, Detroit. Toronto had three shutouts and Detroit two.

MOST PENALTIES, BOTH TEAMS—MOST PENALTIES IN MINUTES, BOTH TEAMS, ONE SERIES:

136 penalties—Montreal-Chicago, 1965 final. 375 minutes—Boston-New York, 1970 quarter-finals.

MOST PENALTIES, ONE TEAM—MOST PENALTIES IN MINUTES, ONE TEAM, ONE SERIES:

72 penalties—Montreal, 1965, final. 206 minutes—Boston, 1970 quarter-finals.

MOST PENALTIES, BOTH TEAMS—MOST PENALTIES IN MINUTES, BOTH TEAMS, ONE GAME:

38 penalties—Toronto-Boston, 1969, Boston-New York, 1970. 174 minutes—Boston-New York, 1970.

MOST PENALTIES, ONE TEAM—MOST PENALTIES IN MINUTES, ONE TEAM, ONE GAME:

20 penalties (93 minutes)—Boston, 1970, against New York.

MOST PENALTIES, BOTH TEAMS—MOST PENALTIES IN MINUTES, BOTH TEAMS, ONE PERIOD:

24 penalties (132 minutes)—Boston-New York, 1970. Boston received three minors, six majors, two misconducts and one game misconduct for 66 minutes. New York received three minors, six majors, two misconducts and one game misconduct for 66 minutes.

MOST PENALTIES, ONE TEAM—MOST PENALTIES IN MINUTES, ONE TEAM, ONE PERIOD:

12 penalties (66 minutes)—Montreal at Toronto, 1966, and Boston at New York, 1970.

FEWEST PENALTIES, BOTH TEAMS, ONE SERIES:

19—Detroit-Toronto, 1945 final. Detroit received ten minors and Toronto received nine minors.

FEWEST PENALTIES, ONE TEAM, ONE SERIES:

9—Toronto, 1945 final.

FASTEST TWO GOALS, BOTH TEAMS:

7 seconds—St. Louis-Minnesota, 1971. Craig Cameron of St. Louis scored at 2:42 of the second period, and Jude Drouin of Minnesota at 2:49.

FASTEST TWO GOALS, ONE TEAM:

5 seconds—Detroit 1965 against Chicago. Norm Ullman scored at 17:35 and 17:40 of second period.

FASTEST THREE GOALS, BOTH TEAMS:

38 seconds—Toronto-Montreal, 1965. Red Kelly of Toronto scored at 3:11 of first period, John Ferguson of Canadiens scored at 3:32 and Ron Ellis of Toronto scored at 3:49.

FASTEST THREE GOALS, ONE TEAM:

56 seconds—Montreal against Detroit, 1954. Dickie Moore scored at 15:03 of first period, Maurice Richard at 15:28 and again at 15:59.

FASTEST FOUR GOALS, BOTH TEAMS:

1 minute, 39 seconds—Toronto-Montreal, 1965. Dave Keon of Toronto scored at 2:10 of first period, Red Kelly of Toronto scored at 3:11, John Ferguson of Montreal scored at 3:32 and Ron Ellis of Toronto scored at 3:49.

FASTEST FOUR GOALS, ONE TEAM:

2 minutes, 35 seconds—Montreal against Toronto, 1944. Toe Blake scored at 7:58 of third period and again at 8:37, Maurice Richard scored at 9:17 and Ray Getliffe at 10:33.

FASTEST FIVE GOALS, BOTH TEAMS:

4 minutes, 19 seconds—Toronto-New York Rangers, 1932. Ace Bailey of Toronto scored at 15:07 of third period, Fred Cook of New York scored at 16:32, Bob Gracie of Toronto scored at 17:36 and Frank Boucher of New York scored at 18:26 and again at 19:26.

FASTEST FIVE GOALS, ONE TEAM:

3 minutes, 36 seconds—Montreal against Toronto, 1944. Toe Blake scored at 7:58 of third period and again at 8:37, Maurice Richard scored at 9:17, Ray Getliffe at 10:33 and Buddy O'Connor at 11:34.

INDIVIDUAL

MOST YEARS IN PLAYOFFS:
19—Red Kelly, Detroit and Toronto; Gordie Howe, Detroit.

MOST CONSECUTIVE YEARS IN PLAYOFFS:
16—Jean Beliveau, Montreal (1954–69).

MOST PLAYOFF GAMES:
168—Henri Richard, Montreal.

MOST POINTS IN PLAYOFFS:
176—Jean Beliveau, Montreal, 79 goals and 97 assists.

MOST GOALS IN PLAYOFFS:
82—Maurice Richard, Montreal.

MOST ASSISTS IN PLAYOFFS:
97—Jean Beliveau, Montreal.

MOST PENALTY MINUTES IN PLAYOFFS:
260—John Ferguson, Montreal.

MOST SHUTOUTS IN PLAYOFFS:
14—Jacques Plante, Montreal Canadiens, New York Rangers, St. Louis.

MOST PLAYOFF GAMES BY A GOALTENDER:
115—Glenn Hall, Detroit, Chicago, St. Louis.

MOST POINTS, ONE PLAYOFF YEAR:
27—Phil Esposito, Boston, 1970. Esposito scored 13 goals and 14 assists in 14 games against New York, Chicago and St. Louis.
—Frank Mahovlich, Montreal, 1971. Mahovlich score 14 goals and 13 assists in 20 games against Boston, Minnesota and Chicago.

MOST GOALS, ONE PLAYOFF YEAR:
15—Yvan Cournoyer, Montreal, 1973, in 17 games against Buffalo, Philadelphia and Chicago.

MOST ASSISTS, ONE PLAYOFF YEAR:
19—Bobby Orr, Boston, 1972, in 15 games against Toronto, St. Louis and New York.

MOST POINTS BY A DEFENSEMAN, ONE PLAYOFF YEAR:
24—Bobby Orr, Boston, 1972. Orr scored five goals and 19 assists in 15 games against Toronto, St. Louis and New York.

MOST GOALS BY A DEFENSEMAN, ONE PLAYOFF YEAR:
9—Bobby Orr, 1970, in 14 games against New York, Chicago and St. Louis.

MOST ASSISTS BY A DEFENSEMAN, ONE PLAYOFF YEAR:
19—Bobby Orr, Boston, 1972, in 15 games against Toronto, St. Louis and New York.

MOST POINTS BY ONE LINE, ONE PLAYOFF YEAR:
55—Dennis Hull, Pit Martin, Jim Pappin, Chicago, 1973, in 16 games against St. Louis, New York Rangers and Montreal. Hull had nine goals and 15 assists for 24 points; Martin 10 goals and six assists for 16 points; and Pappin eight goals and seven assists for 15 points.

MOST PENALTY MINUTES, ONE PLAYOFF YEAR:
80—John Ferguson, Montreal Canadiens, 1969, in 14 games against New York, Boston and St. Louis.

MOST POINTS IN FINAL SERIES:
12—Gordie Howe, Detroit, 1955. In seven games against Montreal, Howe scored five goals and seven assists. Yvan Cournoyer, Montreal, 1973. In six games against Chicago, Cournoyer scored six goals and six assists.

MOST GOALS IN FINAL SERIES:
7—Jean Beliveau, Montreal, 1956, in five games against Detroit.

MOST ASSISTS IN FINAL SERIES:
8—Bert Olmstead, Montreal, 1956, in five games against Detroit.

MOST POINTS IN SEMI-FINAL SERIES:
   14—Fleming Mackell, Boston, 1958. In six games against New York, Mackell scored four goals and 10 assists.

MOST GOALS IN SEMI-FINAL SERIES:
   8—Gordie Howe, Detroit, 1949, in seven games against Montreal.
      Jerry Toppazzini, Boston, 1958, in six games against New York.
      Bobby Hull, Chicago, 1963, in five games against Detroit.
      Bobby Hull, Chicago, 1965, in seven games against Detroit.

MOST ASSISTS, SEMI-FINAL SERIES:
   10—Fleming Mackell, Boston, 1958, in six games against New York.
      Stan Mikita, Chicago, 1962, in six games aganst Montreal.

MOST SHUTOUTS, ONE PLAYOFF YEAR:
   4—Clint Benedict, Montreal Maroons, 1928, in nine games against Ottawa, Canadiens and New York Rangers.
      Dave Kerr, New York Rangers, 1937, in nine games against Montreal Maroons and Detroit.
      Frank McCool, Toronto, 1945, in 13 games against Montreal and Detroit.
      Terry Sawchuk, Detroit, 1952, in eight games against Toronto and Montreal.

MOST CONSECUTIVE SHUTOUTS:
   3—Frank McCool, Toronto, in best-of-seven final, 1945, won by Toronto 4–3 against Detroit. McCool shut out Detroit 1–0, April 6, 2–0, April 8, and 1–0, April 12.

LONGEST SHUTOUT SEQUENCE:
   248 minutes, 32 seconds—Norm Smith, Detroit, 1936.

MOST POINTS, ONE GAME:
   6—Dickie Moore, Montreal, 1954, against Boston. Moore scored two goals, four assists.
      Phil Esposito, Boston, 1969, against Toronto. Esposito scored four goals, two assists.

MOST GOALS, ONE GAME:
   5—Maurice Richard, Montreal, 1944, against Toronto.

MOST ASSISTS, ONE GAME:
   5—Toe Blake, Montreal, 1944, against Toronto.
      Maurice Richard, Montreal, 1956, against New York.
      Bert Olmstead, Montreal, 1957, against New York.
      Don McKenney, Boston, 1958, against New York.
      Stan Mikita, Chicago, 1973, against St. Louis.

MOST POINTS BY A DEFENSEMAN, ONE GAME:
   5—Eddie Bush, Detroit, 1942, against Toronto. Bush scored one goal, four assists.

MOST PENALTIES, MOST PENALTY MINUTES, ONE GAME:
   8 penalties; 38 minutes—Forbes Kennedy, Toronto, 1969, against Boston.

MOST POINTS, ONE PERIOD:
   4—Maurice Richard, Montreal, 1945, against Toronto.
      Dickie Moore, Montreal, 1954, against Boston.

MOST GOALS, ONE PERIOD:
   3—Harvey Johnson, Toronto, 1932, against New York.
   —Maurice Richard, Montreal, 1944, against Toronto; 1945, against Toronto; 1957, against Boston.
   —Ted Lindsay, Detroit, 1955, against Montreal.
   —Red Berenson, St. Louis, 1969, against Los Angeles.
   —Jacques Lemaire, Montreal, 1971, against Minnesota.

MOST ASSISTS, ONE PERIOD:
   3—Shared by 20 players.

MOST PENALTIES, MOST PENALTY MINUTES, ONE PERIOD:
   6 penalties, 34 minutes—Forbes Kennedy, Toronto, 1969, against Boston.

FASTEST TWO GOALS:

    5 seconds—Norm Ullman, Detroit, 1965, against Chicago.

FASTEST GOAL FROM START OF GAME AND PERIOD:

    9 seconds—Gordie Howe, Detroit, 1954, against Toronto.
            Ken Wharram, Chicago, 1967, against Toronto.

FASTEST TWO GOALS FROM START OF GAME AND PERIOD:

    1 minute, 8 seconds—Dick Duff, Toronto, 1963, against Detroit.

MOST CONSECUTIVE GAMES WITH GOALS:

    8—Maurice Richard, Montreal, 1945 and 1951.

MOST GAME-WINNING GOALS:

    18—Maurice Richard, Montreal, in 15 years.

MOST OVERTIME GOALS:

    6—Maurice Richard, Montreal.

MOST OVERTIME GOALS, ONE PLAYOFF YEAR:

    3—Mel Hill, Boston, 1939, against New York Rangers.
        Maurice Richard, Montreal, 1951, against Detroit (two) and Toronto (one).

MOST OVERTIME GOALS, ONE PLAYOFF SERIES:

    3—Mel Hill, Boston, 1939, against New York Rangers.

MOST THREE-GOALS-OR-MORE GAMES:

    7—Maurice Richard, Montreal.

MOST THREE-GOAL GAMES, ONE PLAYOFF SERIES:

    2—Maurice Richard, Montreal, 1944, against Toronto.
    —Doug Bentley, Chicago, 1944, against Detroit.
    —Norm Ullman, Detroit, 1964, against Chicago.
    —Phil Esposito, Boston, 1970, against New York.

OFFICIALS' PLAYOFF RECORDS

MOST GAMES AS REFEREE AND LINESMAN:

    149—George Hayes, 1947–1964.

MOST GAMES AS REFEREE:

    105—Bill Chadwick, 1941–1955.

MOST GAMES AS LINESMAN:

    147—George Hayes, 1948–1964.

VII HOCKEY'S MEMORABLE MOMENTS

In the more than half century of the National Hockey League, there have been many memorable moments—individual feats, team performances and rare games. The editors have chosen eleven of these unforgettable happenings on ice.

APRIL 7, 1928 MAROONS VS. RANGERS

The New York Rangers entered the finals of the 1928 Stanley Cup play-offs at a distinct disadvantage. Because of previous commitments, their own arena, Madison Square Garden, was unavailable and the entire series had to be played on the home ice of the Montreal Maroons. Montreal took advantage of the situation and won the first game of the best-of-five series, 2–0.

After a scoreless first period of the second game, the outlook appeared even more grim for the orphaned New Yorkers. A few minutes into the second session, Nels Stewart, the big Maroon center who was the greatest scorer of his time, skated in slowly on the New York goal and let loose a blistering shot that hit the goalie, Lorne Chabot, in the left eye.

Chabot fell unconscious with blood dripping down his cheek. The crowd of 12,000 in Montreal's Forum sat silently as he was carried off on a stretcher.

There was no such thing as a substitute goalie in those days. Lester Patrick, a once-great defenseman who served as manager and coach of the Rangers, had only 10 minutes to find a replacement.

Alex Connell, a big league goalie for Ottawa, was in the stands, but Eddie Gerard, the Maroons' manager, refused to let him play. "If I let you take Connell it could cost me. Suckers were born yesterday and you're talking to the wrong man. I can't hear you," Gerard laughed.

So Patrick returned to his players and told them they would have to finish the game with a goalie from their own squad. It took Frank Boucher, the irrepressible center, to break the gloom. "How about you playing goal?" he asked.

Patrick, 45 years old and long since retired as a player, demurred. "I'm too old," he protested. But he and his players knew that he had had at least some goal-tending experience. Back in hockey's dark ages, goaltenders when penalized had to serve time in the penalty box like any other player. And one of the other members of the team had to take over goal. On the rare occasions when this was necessary. Patrick drew the assignment.

223

Lester Patrick donned the goalie's pads in a memorable Stanley Cup game.
HOCKEY HALL OF FAME

It was an injury to Lorne Chabot which set the stage for the dramatic appearance of Lester Patrick.

Surveying the desperate situation this night of April 7, 1928, Patrick knew he would have to do it again.

Patrick was actually trembling as his players helped him into more elaborate goalie equipment than he had ever worn before, and, on shaky legs, he skated onto the ice to kick out a few of the easy test shots his players made sure he couldn't miss.

Then he announced he was ready and the Rangers went out to play the most inspired game of their lives. They flattened every Montreal player who dared skate near the nets guarded by their white-haired leader and, 30 seconds into the third period, took a 1–0 lead on a goal by Bill Cook. However, with 6 minutes to play, Montreal tied the game on a shot by Stewart and it went into overtime.

Frustrated at being stymied by an old man and with the crowd cheering the visitors, the enraged Maroons mounted attack after attack on the Ranger goal. But, after 7:05 of the overtime, the clever Boucher stole the puck, broke in alone and scored the winner.

Patrick, in tears, was half-dragged and half-carried off the ice by his players to a tremendous ovation from the crowd. With a real goalie, the

Rangers won two of the next three games to clinch the series in which 45-year-old Lester Patrick had provided their finest hour.

MARCH 24–25, 1936 RED WINGS VS. MAROONS

The clock in Montreal's Forum the night of March 24, 1936, showed 8:34 when the referee dropped the puck to start the first-round Stanley Cup playoff series between the Montreal Maroons, champion of the National Hockey League's Canadian Division, and the Detroit Red Wings, titlist in the American Division.

Playoff games, especially in the early going, usually are played close to the vest and nobody was surprised when the first period was scoreless and marked only by three minor penalties.

The second period was more of the same, the only excitement being a mild scuffle that drew 2-minute penalties for Marty Barry of the Wings and the Maroons' Jimmy Ward, whose son, Pete, later would play big league baseball.

However, when the third period also was scoreless with the action being interrupted only by one minor penalty, the fans began to get a little itchy.

The teams skated off the ice for a brief intermission and then they resumed for a 20-minute sudden-death overtime session. And then they played a second overtime period...and a third...and, finally, after nine seconds of the fourth overtime, something happened. Hooley Smith of the Maroons was sent off for a minor penalty and that was all. The fifth overtime was more of the same. The players appeared to be in a weary stupor. They were almost too tired to skate on and off the ice.

But, near the end of the period, there was a flurry of action. Barry, the Detroit center, set up left winger Herb Lewis with a perfect pass. Lewis appeared to have Maroon goalie Lorne Chabot beaten. But his shot hit the post and bounced out.

That flurry finished the action in the fifth overtime, which actually was the eighth 20-minute period of play. After 4:46 of the sixth overtime, history was made. Three years earlier Boston and Toronto had played this long in a Cup playoff before the Bruins scored a 1–0 victory and this was the record.

Club officials had tried to end that game earlier. After about 100 minutes of overtime league president Frank Calder had refused a request that the game be resumed the following night. The teams, and Calder, however, were willing to toss a coin to decide the winner or complete the game without goalies, but both suggestions at the game in 1933 were hooted down by the nearly 15,000 fans in Maple Leaf Gardens.

So tonight, the Red Wings and Maroons knew they were doomed to play to a decision. The break didn't come until 16:30 had elapsed in the sixth overtime, or just short of three full regulation games. Smith repulsed a

Maroon rush with his 90th save and Hec Kilrea headed up ice in a two-man dash with rookie Mud Bruneteau. Bruneteau, who had scored only two goals all season, managed to skate past the weary Maroon defense. As Lionel Conacher lost his footing on the rough ice, Mud took a pass from Kilrea, faked Chabot, who had stopped 66 shots, out of position and poked home the winner into an open net.

At 2:25 A.M. of March 25, five hours and 51 minutes after play had begun, hockey's longest game ended. The defeat seemed to take something out of the Maroons, who lost the next two games and were eliminated from the playoffs while the Red Wings went on to win the Stanley Cup.

MARCH 23, 1944 CANADIENS VS. MAPLE LEAFS

Stanley Cup playoff games usually emphasize defense. The checking is tight and rough. In the short series with a lot at stake, errors can be fatal. The Montreal Canadiens had run away with the regular-season championship of 1943–44. They lost only five games out of 50 on the schedule (with seven ties) and finished 25 points ahead of second-place Detroit.

The Stanley Cup series opened in Montreal with the Canadiens playing third-place Toronto. In a close-checking game, the Maple Leafs won the opener, 3–1. The two teams met again two nights later, March 23, 1944, in Montreal's Forum as the fans wondered how long the Leafs could hold the powerful Canadiens—and their scoring star Maurice Richard—in check.

Bob Davidson, a big, close-checking forward for the Leafs, always drew the assignment of guarding Richard. The Rocket, a 23-year-old French-Canadian, was only in his second season in the National Hockey League but already merited special attention. Davidson and the Leafs were successful through a scoreless first period. But in the second period the home team broke loose.

Taking passes from Toe Blake and defenseman Mike McMahon, Richard wheeled in and beat Leaf goalie Paul Bibeault for the first goal of the game at 1:48. Seventeen seconds later Richard scored again on assists from his famous linemates, Blake and Elmer Lach.

Now that Montreal had a two-goal lead, Toronto had to abandon its conservative checking game. The Leafs needed goals. They got one from Reg Hamilton after 8:50 of the second period, but Richard matched that with his third goal of the night on assists from Lach and Blake at 16:46. The fiery-tempered Richard achieved his hat trick in a single period even though he twice had been set down for two-minute penalties.

The crowd gave its black-eyed idol an ovation as he left the ice after the second period, but there was more to come. The Canadiens were determined not to sit on their two-goal lead. The fabulous Flying Frenchmen came out flying for the final period. After only a minute of play, Richard again was set up by Lach and Blake on the famous Punch Line, and he scored his fourth goal. And, at 8:34 he scored a fifth. The final score of the game was Richard 5, Toronto 1.

After NHL games at the Forum, the three top stars of the contest are honored. This time the crowd of 12,500 was able to give a continuous ovation. Star No. 1, Star No. 2 and Star No. 3—all Maurice Richard!

Richard's show—still the all-time Stanley Cup record—demoralized the Leafs, who lost the next three games as well, the final by an 11–0 score.

"I didn't know until after the game that the five goals set a record," Richard recalled later. "I only had six or seven shots on net all game and each goal was scored in a different way. The funny thing is that when we beat the Leafs 11–0 three games later, I only scored two goals.

"The Leafs always were a close-checking club and they used to put Bob Davidson out to check me every game. Sometimes he stayed so close to me that I got angry and that night, I guess, I took it out on him— and the puck."

APRIL 21, 1951 MAPLE LEAFS VS. CANADIENS

Bill Barilko never really seemed destined for fame. Curly-haired and good-looking, he was a 190-pound defenseman for the Toronto Maple Leafs. Only 19 when the Leafs called him up from the minors at the end of the 1946–47 season, Barilko quickly established himself as a defensive defenseman, the kind who doesn't score goals, doesn't make All-Star teams and doesn't get his picture in the papers very often.

Only among rival players, whom he delighted in belting into the boards, did Barilko gain any real measure of fame and respect. He never scored more than seven goals in a season as a major leaguer and his most out-standing statistic was the 147 minutes in penalties he amassed in 1947–48, his first full year in the NHL. That penalty total led the NHL and for most of his short career he was up among the penalty leaders.

But, while he wasn't a star, Barilko was no slouch, either, and in each of his first three seasons he played an important role as the Maple Leafs won the prestigious Stanley Cup. The Leafs lost in the first round of the 1950 playoffs to Detroit, the eventual winner, and in 1951 Toronto found itself back in the finals against the Montreal Canadiens.

The Maple Leafs won the Cup, four games to one, but the series was not as one-sided as it appeared. Every game was decided in a sudden-death overtime.

Barilko was a key figure in the first game. Near the end of regulation time, Maurice Richard fired what seemed a sure goal at an open Toronto net, only to see Barilko dive full-length to block the shot and preserve the 2–2 tie. Sid Smith then scored the winner for Toronto after 5:51 of

Toronto's Bill Barilko scores the winning goal against Montreal to clinch the Stanley Cup.   WIDE WORLD PHOTOS

Elated Toronto players surround coach Joe Primeau (center) after winning the Cup in 1951. The ill-fated Bill Barilko is on far left.

HOCKEY HALL OF FAME (TUROFSKY)

overtime. The second game went to Montreal, 3–2, after 2:55 of overtime on a goal by Maurice Richard.

The series moved to Montreal for the next two games and Toronto took both. Ted Kennedy won the first game, 2–1, after 4:47 of overtime and Harry Watson the second, 3–2, after 5:15.

The Leafs returned home to a joyous greeting at Maple Leaf Gardens as they prepared to clinch the Cup in the fifth game on April 21, 1951. For once it didn't look as if the game would go into overtime. With a minute to go, Montreal held a 2–1 lead. But Toronto coach Joe Primeau pulled his goalie and, with an extra skater on the ice, the Leafs got a goal from Tod Sloan with 32 seconds left to force the game into overtime.

After only 2:53, it was sudden death for the Canadiens. Barilko, who hadn't recorded a goal or an assist in the series, took a pass from Howie Meeker at mid-ice and in blind desperation fired a shot at the goal as he crossed the blue line. He actually flung himself in the air with the force of his effort and the puck skipped past Montreal goalie Gerry McNeil. The Stanley Cup returned to Toronto.

After the season, Barilko went home to Timmons, a mining town in northern Ontario. For the first time he was a national hero. He didn't get to enjoy it for long. That August, he and a friend, Dr. Henry Hudson, flew into northern Canada on a fishing trip in the doctor's private plane. They were never heard from again.

Some 15 years later, what was believed to be the wreckage of their plane was discovered, reviving briefly memories of the low-scoring but hard-hitting defenseman who once won a Stanley Cup for Toronto.

MARCH 23, 1952 BLACK HAWKS VS. RANGERS

Bill Mosienko, a 30-year-old right winger for the Chicago Black Hawks, and Lorne Anderson, a 20-year-old goalie for the amateur New York Rovers, each had a hope as the 1952 hockey season went into its final dull days before the Stanley Cup playoffs. Mosienko, looking at the NHL record book with some friends, remarked, "Gee, it would be nice to have my name in there with some of the hockey greats." Anderson's wish was more simple, to play in the National Hockey League.

The dream came true for both, but for Anderson it was more like a nightmare.

The Rangers faced their final three games of the season already eliminated from the playoffs. Cincinnati, a minor league team, had owned the rights to Ranger goalie Emile (Cat) Francis, so the NHL regular was shipped down to help that American Hockey League team in its playoff quest. As a result the Rangers called up Anderson to finish the season.

The New Yorkers won Anderson's first game, 6–4, over Boston, but lost the second, 6–3, to Detroit. The final game of the 1952 season was played

Bill Mosienko (8) has just scored his third goal.   WIDE WORLD

Chicago's Bill Mosienko displays his three historic pucks.

HOCKEY HALL OF FAME

on March 23 with the Rangers and Black Hawks performing before a mere 3,254 fans in Madison Square Garden.

This was what is called a "brother-in-law" game. The final placings had long since been decided and nobody wanted to get hurt. With virtually no checking, referee George Gravel did not call a single penalty in the entire 60-minute game.

However, that's not to say there wasn't plenty of action. The Black Hawks' Gus Bodnar scored first with Mosienko getting an assist. Then the Rangers scored three times before the visitors tallied again—and it was still only the first period! The Rangers scored twice more for a 5–2 lead after two periods and expanded this margin to 6–2 in the opening minutes of the third as Ed Slowinski completed the three-goal hat trick.

But then, in a shocking explosion, Mosienko, the speedy 5–6 right winger, made hockey history.

In almost leisurely but precise fashion, the Hawks formed for the attack. Bodnar, the center, passed off to Mosienko and his little winger beat the defenseman to rap home a goal from in front of the net. The time was 6:09 of the third period.

After the goal, there was a face-off at center ice. Bodnar won the draw and hit the streaking Mosienko just as Bill was crossing the blue line. Mosienko took the pass, shot and scored. The time was 6:20 of the third period. Only 11 seconds had elapsed.

Again there was a face-off, again Bodnar controlled the puck, but this time he passed off to George Gee on the left wing. Gee carried over the Ranger blue line, spotted Mosienko breaking toward the net and laid a perfect pass on the right winger's stick. Mosienko fired it past Anderson and, as the red light flashed again, the clock showed 6:30 had elapsed. Mosienko had scored three goals in 21 seconds. No player—or team—had ever scored three times in such a short period of time. Mosienko's dream had come true. He was, indeed in the record book, breaking the old mark by 43 seconds, as the Hawks scored twice more to win, 7–6.

Mosienko went on to play three more full seasons for the Black Hawks and retired at age 32 after the 1954–55 campaign with a career total of 258 goals.

As for the unfortunate Anderson, who had surrendered 17 goals in his brief trial, he never played in another big league game.

DECEMBER 9, 1953 MAPLE LEAFS VS. CANADIENS

Like most wars, hockey's wildest brawl started with a preliminary skirmish. The date was December 9, 1953. The place, Maple Leaf Gardens in Toronto. The opponents, the Maple Leafs and the Montreal Canadiens.

The opening bout involved Ed Mazur of the Canadiens and George

Armstrong of the Leafs. They got into a gloves-off fist-swinging battle on the ice and kept going after they had been sent off to the penalty box. For the latter infraction they were ejected from the game and missed all the action that was to follow. But their penalty minutes were added to what became a record total.

The seeds of the war were sown and cultivated early in the second period when Canadien defenseman Bud MacPherson jabbed Toronto forward Ron Stewart with his stick. Stewart bided his time, waiting for a chance to get even. He got it in the final period at the 18:12 mark.

The real battle started with a shoving match between Stewart and MacPherson. Then Tom Johnson of Montreal entered the hostilities and clamped a headlock on Stewart. Stewart tried to wriggle free to resume his attack on MacPherson, but then decided Johnson was a target of better opportunity. He ducked under the headlock and came up with a straight right to Johnson's face, perhaps the best single blow of the night.

At this point MacPherson and Eric Nesterenko of Toronto went after each other and Stewart took the chance to get even for the stick in the ribs that MacPherson had given him earlier.

Now the battle was fully joined. Both benches emptied and even the goalies got into action, which is most unusual. During most fights the heavily-padded goaltenders take the opportunity for a breather.

For almost 20 minutes the battle raged. Sticks and gloves littered the ice. Several hundred dollars worth of jerseys were ripped and torn. Faces and knuckles were cut and bruised.

And, in the biggest irony of all, Maurice Richard, the most terrible-tempered Canadien of them all, stood almost passively to one side, clutching the jersey of Toronto defenseman Tim Horton as the two paired off away from the major hostilities. "Crazy...crazy...crazy," Richard muttered over and over again.

When the fighters finally collapsed from exhaustion, referee Frank Udvari had to start handing out penalties. Every player on both teams except for Armstrong, Mazur and Canadien defenseman Doug Harvey, who was in the penalty box, had been involved.

With almost two minutes still to play, Udvari sent everybody to the dressing room except for the minimum eight to finish the game. Ted Kennedy, Hugh Bolton, Horton and goalie Harry Lumley remained on ice for Toronto with Butch Bouchard, Goose McCormick, Bert Olmstead and goalie Gerry McNeil for Montreal.

It took the scorekeeper a lot longer to figure out the penalty minutes. And when he finished adding them up it came to 36 penalties for 204 minutes, records that still stand. Montreal received 18 penalties for a one-team record of 106 minutes and Toronto was penalized 18 times for 98 minutes. Twenty-six of the penalties for 184 of the minutes were dealt out in the brawling third period. These records are still in the books, too.

And for the game, Udvari handed out nine misconduct penalties, four major penalties and 17 minors.

Of course, the night's most basic statistic was virtually overlooked. Toronto won the game, 3–0.

MARCH 17, 1955 RED WINGS VS. CANADIENS

"Hockey," as Gordie Howe likes to say, "is a man's game." The history of the National Hockey League abounds with tales of courage. But the finest moment of heroism connected with the game involves not a player, but the president of the league, Clarence S. Campbell.

Campbell, a former hockey referee and an attorney of international stature, had been named president of the NHL in 1946. He had faced many problems in and out of hockey over the years, but nothing like the fierce passions that one of his decisions stirred at the end of the 1955 season.

In the middle was hockey's most exciting and hot-tempered player, Maurice "Rocket" Richard of the Montreal Canadiens. Les Canadiens were rabidly supported by their French-Canadian fans. The Detroit Red Wings had won six straight regular-season NHL championships, almost an insult to the citizens of Montreal who had been accustomed to domination by their own team in the years before that. And Detroit had beaten their beloved Canadiens in the Stanley Cup final just that previous season.

Now, as the season neared its end, Montreal had a slim lead over Detroit and Richard was ahead in the battle for his first scoring title.

On the last Sunday of the regular season, the Canadiens faced Boston. Richard got into a fight with the Bruins' Hal Laycoe and then took a couple of punches at linesman Cliff Thompson when he tried to pull the enraged Rocket away from his opponent.

Campbell quickly heard about the incident and knew he had to make a decision. He called a hearing early in the week in his Montreal office and announced his ruling: Richard was to be suspended for the three remaining games of the season and the Stanley Cup playoffs as well!

The Rocket took the decision calmly enough, but the emotional Montreal fans were enraged. They vowed vengeance on the hated Campbell and their anger grew as they saw Richard losing the scoring title (he was to be second by one point) and their team blowing its chance at the regular-season championship (they ended up two points behind Detroit).

By a horrible scheduling quirk—it would have been ideal if not for the trouble—the Red Wings and Canadiens finished the season with a weekend home-and-home series. Saturday night's next-to-last game in Montreal seemed doomed to violence. Mobs gathered outside the Forum hours before the game, brandishing signs and stirring themselves to hysteria. Calls to the NHL office warned Campbell that he would be killed if he showed up for the game, but the gray-haired executive refused to be intimidated.

As a concession, he agreed to enter the arena after the game had begun, but his arrival midway through the first period was quickly noted. Two hundred police and firemen were unable to keep order. Fans shouted insults at Campbell and pelted him with eggs, peanuts, programs and overshoes. One hoodlum got close enough to slug Campbell twice before being led away. But through it all the league president, a heroic and beleaguered figure, kept his composure.

Detroit took a 4–1 lead in the first period and then, during the intermission, somebody threw a tear gas bomb. The crowd of 14,000 broke for the exits. Before he left, Campbell ordered the game forfeited to Detroit.

As the crowd spilled out onto the streets, rowdy elements began to riot. They threw rocks and bottles at police, tore down overhead trolley lines, broke windows and looted stores. Property damage was estimated at more than $100,000. Police cracked heads and made more than 40 arrests.

It was a shameful episode, but Clarence Campbell emerged with honor and dignity.

NOVEMBER 1, 1959 CANADIENS VS. RANGERS

By 1959 Jacques Plante's reputation as one of the greatest hockey goaltenders of all time was firmly established. He had already won four Vezina Trophies, the award that annually goes to the top goalie in the National Hockey League. And his success as a roving goalie for the Montreal Canadiens had revolutionized the techniques of playing his position.

But, as he skated out on the ice against the Rangers in New York on November 1, 1959, he also had some other souvenirs of his dangerous profession: the scars of 200 stitches in his face, a nose broken four times, a fractured skull and two broken cheekbones.

The fractured cheekbones had come in each of Plante's first two big league seasons. Both times he was hurt in practice from a shot by a teammate. After the second injury he had a plastic mask designed and he wore it in workouts.

The mask was a bit awkward, but during the 1958–59 season, Plante learned that a mask had been developed that would fit snugly against his face. It was just what he wanted, for now the blind spots of the old mask were eliminated. Before the season, Plante asked coach Toe Blake if he could wear the mask during games.

It was not unprecedented. Clint Benedict of the Montreal Maroons had worn one briefly in 1929, but discarded it. Goalies were traditionally barefaced after that and Blake was a traditionalist. He turned down Plante.

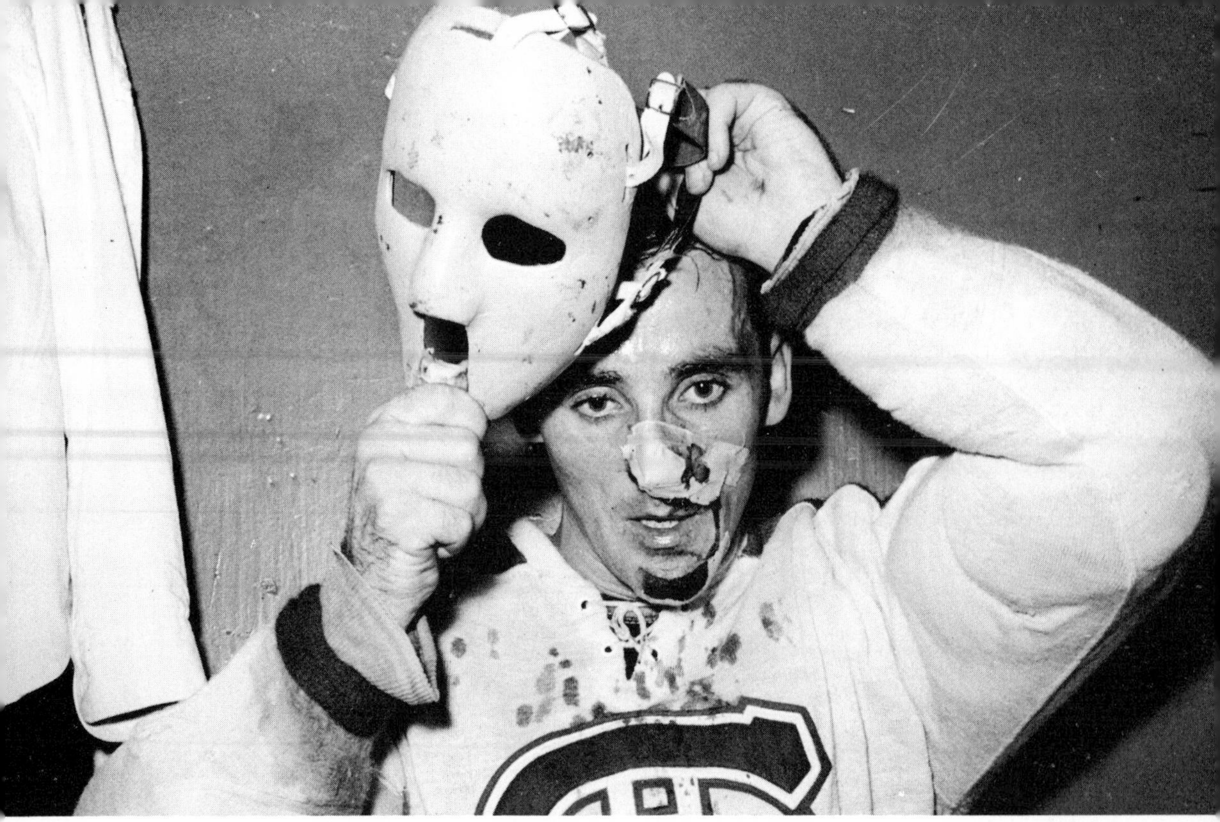

Cut by a shot, Montreal's bloodied Jacques Plante dons the mask.   UPI

Plante returns to the net, wearing his mask for the first time in a game.   UPI

However, in less than two months, tradition was broken. It happened in this game against the Rangers, scoreless for eight minutes until Andy Bathgate, the New Yorkers' hardest shooter, let loose a 25-foot backhander from the left of the net.

Plante, screened by the mass of players, never saw the puck until it smashed into his face, ripping open his cheek and nose. He fell to the ice, blood staining his uniform and the Garden ice. But he recovered enough to walk unassisted to the dressing room with a towel held against his face. It took seven stitches to close the wound.

At that time NHL teams did not carry a spare goalie. It was up to the home club to have someone on hand who could fill in during an emergency. Some teams called on their assistant trainer; others, in Canada especially, would have available the teen-age goalie from their junior team in the same city. The Rangers used a fortyish and pudgy weekend amateur named Joe Schaefer. When Schaefer, a fine fellow, had to play, it really was an emergency.

That was the situation as Plante sat up on the first-aid table. Twenty minutes had elapsed. The game had to resume. Plante looked at Blake. "I won't go back on unless I can wear the mask," he said grimly. Blake, who had fought the new device so stubbornly, had to agree. And hockey history was made.

Fortunately, Plante played well with the mask. The Canadiens beat the Rangers, 3–1, with the losers' only goal coming in the final period. Montreal had arrived at the Garden with an unbeaten streak of seven. They made it eight against the Rangers and finally extended it to 18 before losing to Toronto, 1–0. In the last 11 games of the streak, or all the time he wore the mask, Plante gave up only 13 goals.

The Montreal management reluctantly went along with Plante. "I had to show good results to keep the mask," he later commented, and he did, winning three more Vezina Trophies. Now, all but a few traditionalists in the NHL wear the mask and, as they move on, Plante's mask will become universal.

NOVEMBER 10, 1963 RED WINGS VS. CANADIENS

It was like Babe Ruth's 714 home runs. When Maurice Richard retired from the National Hockey League in 1960 with 544 goals in regular season play, nobody was even close. And nobody, Rocket's French-Canadian fans insisted, would ever approach his scoring record.

But when the 1963–64 campaign began, Gordie Howe, Detroit's durable right winger, was close. He started the season with 540 and it seemed

Detroit's Gordie Howe has just scored his record-breaking 545th goal.   UPI

only a matter of time until he passed the Rocket. Only an injury could stop the husky slope-shouldered Howe from overtaking Richard.

On October 27, 1963, Howe and the Red Wings were playing host to the Canadiens. Gordie had 543 goals and the proud Habitants were determined that Howe would not join the Rocket in the record book at their expense. Toe Blake, coach of the Canadiens, made sure that a line centered by Richard's brother, Henri, was always on ice against Howe's line. It was more than a psychological ploy. When Henri was on the ice, he controlled the puck. And Howe couldn't score without it.

Then Blake assigned Gilles Tremblay, a Montreal winger, to forget about scoring himself and to concentrate on shadowing Howe.

The strategy almost worked. Howe was limited to only two shots all game. But the second was a goal. At 11:04 of the third period Howe got a step on Tremblay and deflected Bruce MacGregor's goal-mouth pass past Montreal net-minder Gump Worsley. It wasn't a picture goal, but it counted and Jean Beliveau, captain of the Canadiens, gravely skated over to shake Howe's hand.

However, the battle was only half over for Howe, then 34 and in his 18th pro season. Now he had to break the record and, game after game, the pressure mounted. Detroit had lost to Montreal, 6–4, the night Howe

238

tied Richard after failing to score in 10 previous games and the whole team suffered as the Red Wings tried to help their captain register No. 545.

But there was nothing coach Sid Abel could do. The Wings lost three of their next five games. Howe's nervous twitch became more pronounced, and newsmen and photographers ran out of clean shirts as they followed Howe from city to city in hope of recording the monumental goal.

Two weeks later, they found themselves back in Detroit's glistening Olympia Stadium. Another sellout crowd of more than 15,000 jammed the building—and again Montreal provided the opposition. The only major change was that instead of Gump Worsley, the Canadiens had little Charlie Hodge in goal.

Again the Canadiens were determined to protect the Rocket's record and again they concentrated solely on stopping Howe. The first period was scoreless but Detroit scored twice in 47 seconds to take a 2–0 lead after 5½ minutes of the second period. At the 13:57 mark, Alex Faulkner of the Wings was penalized five minutes for high-sticking and the redoubtable Howe came along with Billy McNeill to help kill the penalty.

The Canadiens mounted one of their fierce power assaults when McNeill dug out the puck from against the boards deep in the Detroit zone. Howe moved behind him and yelled, "Get going!" The little winger took off down the right wing and swung to the middle of the ice as he crossed into Montreal territory with Howe behind him to the right and defenseman Bill Gadsby on the left wing. As they approached the Canadien goal, McNeill slid the puck to Howe, who, with one motion, swiped a 15-foot shot just off the ice past Hodge and into the cage.

As the red light flashed with 15:06 gone in the period, Hodge slammed his stick against the top of the cage and skated to the sidelines. He knew there would be a prolonged ovation after what McNeill called a "perfect goal."

It was also perfect as Howe passed the Rocket by scoring when his team was short a man. And, unlike the night he tied the record, it came when his team was winning, 3–0, not losing. To Howe, that was as important as any record.

MARCH 12, 1966 BLACK HAWKS VS. RANGERS

Maurice "Rocket" Richard of the Montreal Canadiens became the first player in National Hockey League history to score 50 goals during the 1944–45 season. Then, in 1960–61, Bernie "Boom-Boom" Geoffrion of the same team did it, too. And the following year Bobby Hull of the Chicago Black Hawks also turned the trick in the final game of the season.

Now it was the end of the 1965–66 campaign. Hull, the Golden Jet, had missed five games because of torn knee ligaments but he already had his 50 after 57 games of the 70-game schedule.

Chicago's Bobby Hull poses for the cameramen after tallying his 51st goal.
WIDE WORLD

The sky seemed the limit for Hull, then 27 years old and a handsome, husky, muscular picture athlete. But game 58 passed, and Hull didn't score; then game 59 and game 60 and still the powerful left winger appeared anchored at 50 goals.

On the night of March 12, a Saturday, Hull skated out on the ice of the massive Chicago Stadium as 21,000 fans—4,000 more than listed capacity —watched to see if he could make his 51st goal against the fifth-place New York Rangers.

240

The first period was scoreless and then the Rangers scored twice in the second 20 minutes to take a 2–0 lead as the rest of the Black Hawks seemed to be standing around waiting for Hull to get his record.

As the third period opened, Hull assisted on a goal by teammate Chico Maki and then, with 4:05 gone, Harry Howell of the Rangers was sent off with a two-minute penalty for slashing.

Back on the ice went Hull as perhaps hockey's most explosive point man on the power play. Howell had been in the penalty box almost a minute and a half when the Hawks gathered to start another rush against the under-manned Rangers. Bill Hay and Lou Angotti fed the puck up to Hull and then watched, almost as spectators, as the Golden Jet moved slowly to his left, stopped, crossed the New York blue line and then, as his teammates swooped toward the net, fired a deceptively swift wrist shot at Ranger goalie Cesare Maniago.

Eric Nesterenko, another Black Hawk forward, was near the goal-mouth at the time and he tipped Maniago's stick as the Ranger goalie, who had also given up Geoffrion's 50th goal, tried vainly to make a split save.

As the puck zipped past Maniago and the red light flashed to signify a score, the crowd erupted into what was to be a 7½-minute ovation. But Hull, for a moment, stood still, nerves tingling. If Nesterenko had tipped the puck on its way past Maniago, he, not Hull, would get the goal.

But the official scorer settled all doubts. Hull had his 51st goal after 5:34 of the third period. He skated over to the section where his wife was sitting and whispered to her through the protective glass, "Well, I did it." Then, as he skated around the ice to acknowledge the applause, Hull reached down and put on one of the dozens of hats that frenzied fans had skimmed onto the ice.

It was a glorious moment for Hull. A couple of weeks earlier the normally placid star had exploded into a fist fight with a close-checking rival. He had almost considered quitting because of the pressure of the 51-goal quest. But now the tensions were past. The Hawks went on to win the game, 4–2, and Bobby went on to score three more goals during the rest of the season to put the record at 54. But, as Hull could testify, the first 51 were the hardest.

MARCH 2, 1969 BRUINS VS. PENGUINS

The National Hockey League was founded in 1917 and for more than 50 years no player had ever scored 100 points in a single season.

For awhile, the scoring mark belonged to Dickie Moore, a shifty left wing who totaled 96 points for Montreal in 1958–59. Then, in 1965–66 Chicago's Bobby Hull boosted the mark to 97 and a year later, another Black Hawk player, Stan Mikita, also reached 97.

Mikita's 97 points came in the last year that the NHL operated with just six teams. The next year, six new clubs were added and even though scoring predictably increased, it was spread around more. Mikita repeated as scoring champion but his total fell to 87 points, 10 below the standard he shared with Hull.

That same year, Chicago swapped a center named Phil Esposito to Boston. Espo had been Hull's center in Bobby's 97-point season and was considered a caddy for the great left wing. But he proved to be more than that. Lots more.

Esposito gave Mikita a battle for the scoring crown that year, finishing with 84 points, only three less than the Chicago pivot. The next year, Espo exploded, scoring points at a record-setting pace. It became apparent in February that the NHL's 100-point plateau was going to be broken by the sad-eyed center who set up shop in front of goalies and refused to be moved out of there.

With linemates Ken Hodge on the right and Ron Murphy on the left, Esposito flourished. As the season turned into March, its final month, he had 97 points. On March 1, in a game against the New York Rangers, Esposito cracked the mark with point No. 98. He had been stopped on 10 shots in the first two periods by goalie Ed Giacomin before finally slipping a shorthanded goal past the New York netminder. Later, he assisted on a goal by Bobby Orr for his 99th point.

That set the stage for Pittsburgh's visit to Boston Garden the next night. The Penguins were determined to keep Espo off the scoreboard. He was going to get point No. 100 some place but Pittsburgh didn't want to be the victims.

"Joe Daley was the Pittsburgh goaltender and he did a good job over the first two periods," Esposito would recount. "I had two shots and no goals."

As the Bruins returned to the ice for the game's final 20 minutes, a youngster shouted to Esposito. "Please get that one hundredth point, Phil. I want to be able to say I saw it."

Esposito obliged. With only 17 seconds gone in the period, passes from Ted Green and Hodge sprung Espo, cutting in from the left side. "Daley moved to his right," recalled Esposito, "and hit the ice. I slipped it underneath him."

The fans showered Espo with all kinds of debris including a football helmet, saluting the historic 100th point. Espo added 26 more points that year for the first of four scoring championships in five seasons. In each of those years, he scored past 100 points and in 1970–71, he set an all-time record with 152 points including a record 76 goals.

The 100-point season has become almost routine for Esposito and several other NHL shooters. But it wasn't that way until March 2, 1969, the night the barrier was broken.

VIII THE OFFICIALS

When constabulary duty's to be done,
A policeman's lot is not a happy one.
——Pirates of Penzance, Act II

It is safe to assume that Sir William Gilbert of the operatic composing team of Gilbert and Sullivan never met an ice hockey referee. He was born in Victorian London in 1836 and died in 1911, long before hockey was introduced to his country. If he were living today he presumably would show the same compassion for referees that he did for policemen.

The lot of the hockey referee isn't a happy one either. His constabulary duties consist of bringing discipline and control to 60 minutes of speed and confusion on ice. Players skim along the frozen surface at 20 to 30 miles an hour; there are violent collisions at great speed; sticks are swung like clubs, and pucks whiz over the ice and through the air at upwards of 100 mph.

This is the referee's work day:

He skates between 15 and 20 miles in an average game. He must match the fastest player stride for stride and be on top of every play. The players' bench disgorges fresh skaters as though they were traveling through a revolving door but the harried referee gets no rest, except between periods.

And then there are the hazards of the job. While he is trying to control the game and the players, the referee may be tripped, jammed into the corners, boarded, draped over the protective glass, slashed by a skate, hit by a flying puck or pelted with programs, fruit, vegetables, eggs, overshoes ——or squid.

Squid? "You better believe it," says Bill Chadwick, the only American-born referee to be named to hockey's Hall of Fame. "I was working a Stanley Cup playoff game in Detroit in 1952 when a fan tossed something at me which missed and landed on the ice. I went over to pick it up, but after one look I spun around and skated off in a hurry. I thought at first it was a baby octopus. I found out later it was a squid. But octopus or squid, it sure scared hell out of me."

Chadwick's admission of fear was not uncommon. Fear grips most referees——as it does the policeman on the beat. Men like Bill Chadwick, Red Storey, Cooper Smeaton, Mickey Ion, King Clancy and Mike Rodden were threatened with physical violence while serving as referees in the National Hockey League.

They learned to live with this fear and eventually wound up in hockey's Hall of Fame because they had courage——courage to render a decision and

The man in charge is referee Bill Chadwick, exercising his authority on the Canadiens' Murph Chamberlain.   HOCKEY HALL OF FAME (TUROFSKY)

make it stick in the face of taunts from players, coaches and hostile fans.

Clancy earned his berth in the Hall of Fame as a fighting defenseman. But he is also remembered as a fighting referee, a 150-pound bantam rooster of a man who never allowed himself to be intimidated by a player or coach, a club owner or a fan.

Asked once to explain how he managed to make the shift from player to referee, Clancy said, "I always gave the players a second chance. Maybe that's because I was a player myself. When they skated up to me and said, 'Why you little so-and-so, you couldn't referee a girls' basketball game,' I always gave 'em the same answer. I'd shout right back, 'What did you say?' Hell, they'd never repeat it and the whole thing would end right there."

Clancy never permitted the crowd to sway his decisions. "Hockey fans are the same everywhere," he said. "They all want to see the home team win, and the referee is never right. But I figured a guy paying his way into the rink had a right to boo me. I didn't mind. It just rolled off my thick Irish skin."

In Clancy's mind, Mickey Ion was hockey's most outstanding referee. "When Mickey refereed a game, he was in complete charge," he said. "There's never been anyone to equal him. One night in Boston, Mickey is knocked over the boards and lands in a fan's lap. Boston scores while he is scrambling back over the boards, but Mickey doesn't allow it. He wasn't on the ice and he says nobody is allowed to score unless he's there to see it."

Clancy, who served as a referee for 11 years following his retirement as a player in 1936, will never forget the instructions Ion gave him and Rabbit McVeigh before they worked their first Stanley Cup playoff game in 1938.

"Mickey came into the officials' room and started lecturing us," Clancy said. "He said, 'Crack down on those players right from the start. Don't take anything from anybody. And remember this: There are 15,000 idiots out there, including the players. You two guys are the only sane ones in the building.' And, you know, there were times when I think Mickey was right."

In the early days of pro hockey, referees were picked haphazardly. Retired and active players assisted in the officiating and were not paid. The first referees of the Stanley Cup playoffs were chosen from among the executives of the competing leagues.

Smeaton and Ion got their starts as referees in the days before the first World War. They were paid—sometimes.

"When I was working, we got paid by the game," Smeaton recalled. "But if one of the bosses didn't like your work just once, you didn't come back. And you didn't get paid either."

Mickey Ion (left) and Cooper Smeaton, both members of the Hall of Fame, spell out their occupation.   HOCKEY HALL OF FAME

The referee was the sole official in Smeaton's day. "There were no linesmen to help out," he said. "I had to call the offsides, the penalties, break up the fights and do the arguing. And what fights we had.

"One night in Toronto, Art Ross and Minnie McGiffen were actually arrested for assaulting each other in a game. After the game I was sitting in the referee's room when a fan knocked on the door. He accused me of holding McGiffen while Ross hit him.

"I got peeved and invited the guy into the room. When I got finished with him he didn't feel too good. They had to carry him out. I had to sneak out of the rink by the back door because the crowd and the police were coming after me."

Mike Rodden, one of Smeaton's contemporaries, found this common invasion of the referee's room too much for him one night in Chicago. He had just finished refereeing a game when the Black Hawks' owner, Major Frederic McLaughlin, bolted into the room.

Normally cold and aloof, McLaughlin launched a sarcastic tirade at Rodden which he punctuated with threats of physical harm. It lasted until the referee took off his skates. Then Rodden pointed to the exit and told the astounded major if he didn't get out he would toss him through the door.

Chadwick had similar experiences.

"When I first started refereeing [in 1941], you were more or less at the mercy of the club owners," he said. "You'd have a waiting line outside your door after every period. The owners would be there and the coaches, too. You couldn't keep 'em out. They'd walk in, give you hell and then walk out.

"The referees in those days had nobody to turn to for support. There was no referee-in-chief. All we had was the league president and he was only an intermediary. Then Clarence Campbell took over as president [in 1947] and he backed us up because he knew our problems. He had been a referee."

It was during Red Dutton's reign as NHL president that Chadwick endured his most trying experience with mob violence. He was working a playoff game between the Canadiens and the Black Hawks in Chicago Stadium in 1943. One of his calls infuriated the Chicago fans, who went on a wild rampage, littering the ice with debris while crying for Chadwick's scalp.

The harassed referee ducked for cover, then dispatched a courier to Dutton in his front row box, asking what he should do. Dutton's answer was starkly brief: "You got yourself into this, now get yourself out."

"I needed a police escort to get out of the building that night," Chadwick recalled. "The next game I worked there I was picked up at my hotel by detectives, who escorted me to the stadium and then back to the hotel following the game. Those Chicago fans really gave me a hard time."

Mike Rodden officiated in 1,187 NHL games.   HOCKEY HALL OF FAME

Red Storey refereed from 1951 through 1959.   HOCKEY HALL OF FAME

The Hawks' rooters didn't exactly love King Clancy, either. One female customer in particular used to enjoy sticking a hat pin into his derriere. "Oh, she was a lovely lady," Clancy said. "She occupied a seat close to the ice and every time I would jump onto the sideboards to get out of the way she'd come running and jab me with the hat pin."

Many referees, past and present, readily admit that the job has one other serious drawback. It deals with non-fraternizing. The loneliness of the long distance runner is minor compared to the life of a referee, who is prohibited from mingling with players, club officials or fans.

"Sometimes it gets so lonely you almost go out of your mind," said Bill Friday, one of the best of the current pro referees. "I remember one Christmas eve I had to spend on the road. I walked the streets for several hours, thinking of my wife and children back home in Hamilton [Ontario].

"Know what I finally did? I stopped in a men's wear store and bought myself a shirt. I had it gift wrapped, took it to my hotel room and slipped it under the bed. The next morning, I reached under the bed and took it out and read the card: 'Merry Christmas, Bill,' and then opened the package. I just wanted to be able to open something."

Chadwick claimed it was even tougher when he was officiating. "The referees now have some companionship," he said. "They travel with the

Referee Art Skov turns a deaf ear on the frustrated Canadien, Jean Beliveau.
BARTON SILVERMAN

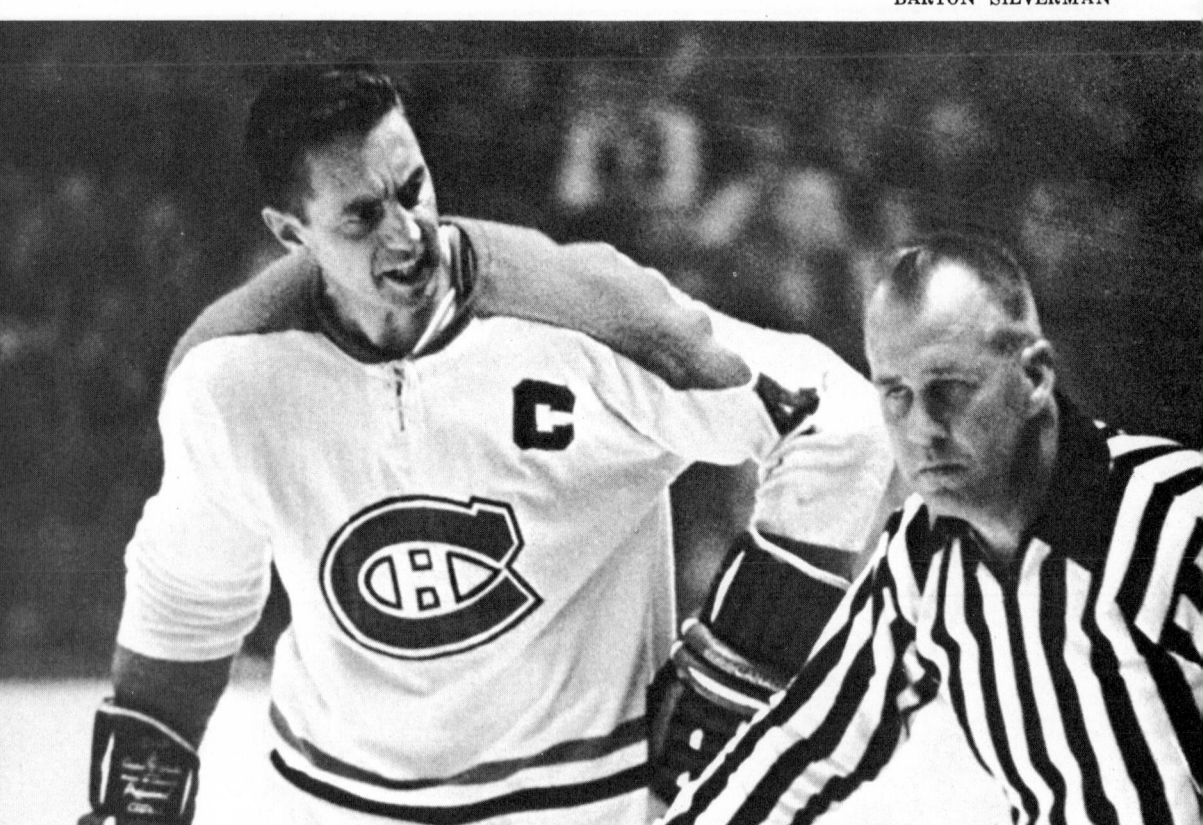

linesmen or arrange to meet them in the various cities. In my day the referee traveled alone and lived alone. I spent half my time in hotel lobbies or movies.

"You couldn't associate with the players, but I always talked to them. I figured if they talked to me off the ice I had a better chance of dealing with them in tight situations on the ice. The big thing is to get the respect of the players."

Chadwick refereed 1,200 regular-season games and 125 playoff games (both records) during his 16 years of service in the NHL. He said he never would have established these longevity records if he hadn't cultivated the respect of the players.

"I never had any real trouble, even with the so-called tough guys," he noted. "My secret was to be consistent but not over-officious. If a referee called everything by the book you'd have nobody on the ice and less people in the stands. You have to use common sense, set a standard and hold it through the entire game.

"The only problem I've noticed among the current referees is a tendency to fluctuate. Some call every infraction at the start of a game and then loosen up or vice versa. A good referee has to be consistent."

Chadwick recalled a wild game between the Bruins and the Maple Leafs in Boston when he was most consistent. He handed out 17 penalties in the opening period, including five against Toronto's Bill Ezinicki. After Ezinicki served his fifth of the period, he complained, "Hey, Bill, what are you trying to do to me?"

"What would you do in my place tonight?" Chadwick countered. Ezinicki thought a moment, smiled and said, "The same darn thing, I guess," and skated away.

When Chadwick, a native New Yorker, broke into the NHL he was paid $75 a game. He was the league's highest-paid official when he retired in 1955, earning approximately $13,000 a year. The top referees now earn close to $30,000 a year.

"It's a good job," said Vern Buffey, referee-in-chief of the WHA. "Sure, the traveling is rough and we still take a lot of abuse. But you get used to it."

Or to paraphrase the words of Sir William Gilbert, the referee's lot still is not a happy one. But at least the pay is good.

Bobby Hull: An All-Star.   KEN REGAN

IX   THE ALL-STAR GAME

A new formula for the National Hockey League's All-Star game was introduced in Montreal on January 21, 1969, when players representing the circuit's East and West Divisions faced off at the start of the 22nd annual classic.

This change was prompted by the expansion of the league from six to 12 teams and from one to two divisions at the start of the 1967–68 season.

The game originated in 1947 when the defending champion Toronto Maple Leafs played a team comprised of the best players of the other five clubs as selected by hockey writers and broadcasters. The vote was based on performance during the 1946–47 campaign.

The Stanley Cup titleholder vs. All-Star team format remained until 1951 when members of the First Team All-Stars of the 1950–51 season opposed the Second Team. In 1953 the league reverted to the original system which lasted through 1968. In that year the Montreal Canadiens, 1966–67 Cup titleholders, opposed the best players of the other 11 teams.

The 1967 game was the first played in mid-season. All the preceding 19 games were played before the start of the regular campaign.

In games against the Cup champions, the All-Stars won nine times, lost seven and tied three. The 1951 and 1952 games between the first and second team All-Stars ended in ties.

Starting with 1969, each member of the winning All-Star team received $500 and the losers $250. Prior to that time, there were no financial rewards for competing players.

In addition, the players are now selected on the basis of performances during the first half of the season in which the game is played, not on those of the previous campaign.

FIRST GAME October 13, 1947 at Toronto
All-Stars 4, Toronto 3

Left wing Doug Bentley of the Chicago Black Hawks broke a 3-3 tie by drilling a shot past goalie Turk Broda in the second minute of the third period and gave the All-Stars a 4–3 victory over the Maple Leafs.

Maurice Richard of Montreal and Syl Apps of the Leafs also starred. Richard assisted on the game-winning goal and scored once himself while Apps collected a goal and an assist.

Bill Mosienko, Chicago right wing, suffered a fractured left ankle when he was checked into the boards early in the second period.

All-Stars: Goal-Durnan (Montreal), Brimsek (Boston). Defense-Bouchard (Montreal), Reardon (Montreal), Stewart (Detroit), Quackenbush (Detroit). Forwards-

M. Bentley (Chicago), D. Bentley (Chicago), Mosienko (Chicago), Warwick (New York), M. Richard (Montreal), Laprade (New York), Lindsay (Detroit), Dumart (Boston), Schmidt (Boston), Bauer (Boston), Leswick (New York). Coach-Dick Irvin (Montreal).

Toronto: Goal-Broda. Defense-Goldham, Stanowski, Mortson, Thomson, Barilko. Forwards-Watson, N. Metz, Poile, Kennedy, Apps, Ezinicki, Lynn, Meeker, Stewart, Klukay, Mackell. Coach-Hap Day.

Referee-King Clancy. Linesmen-Ed Mepham, Jim Primeau.

First Period: 1. Toronto, Watson (Ezinicki) 12:29. Penalties-Mortson, Leswick, Ezinicki 2, Reardon.

Second Period: 2. Toronto, Ezinicki (Apps, Watson) 1:03. 3. All-Stars, M. Bentley (Reardon) 4:39. 4. Toronto, Apps (Watson, Mortson) 5:01. 5. All-Stars, Warwick (Laprade, Reardon) 17:35. Penalties-Lynn, Reardon 2.

Third Period: 6. All-Stars, M. Richard (unassisted) 0:28. 7. All-Stars, D. Bentley (Schmidt, M. Richard) 1:26. Penalties-Mortson 2, Bouchard, Ezinicki, Schmidt.

Attendance-14,138.

SECOND GAME November 3, 1948 at Chicago
All-Stars 3, Toronto 1

Goals by Gaye Stewart, Ted Lindsay and Woody Dumart enabled the All-Stars to defeat the Maple Leafs, 3–1. Dumart accounted for the most spectacular tally when he skated the length of the ice and put the puck past goalie Turk Broda at 3:06 of the second period.

Dumart's goal gave the All-Stars a 2–0 lead. Max Bentley scored for Toronto two minutes later. Stewart, however, added an insurance goal for the visitors with only 28 seconds remaining in the second period. Only eight penalties were handed out by referee Bill Chadwick.

All-Stars: Goal-Brimsek (Boston), Durnan (Montreal). Defense-Stewart (Detroit), Quackenbush (Detroit), N. Colville (New York), Reardon (Montreal), Bouchard (Montreal). Forwards-Lindsay (Detroit), D. Bentley (Chicago), M. Richard (Montreal), Laprade (New York), Howe (Detroit), Stewart (Chicago), Dumart (Boston), Schmidt (Boston), Lach (Montreal), Leswick (New York), Poile (Chicago). Coach-Tommy Ivan (Detroit).

Toronto: Goal-Broda. Defense-Thomson, Mortson, Boesch, Barilko, Mathers, Juzda. Forwards-H. Watson, M. Bentley, Klukay, Kennedy, Meeker, Ezinicki, Lynn, Costello, Mackell, Gardner. Coach-Hap Day.

Referee-Bill Chadwick. Linesmen-Sam Babcock, Mush March.

First Period: No Scoring. Penalties-Ezinicki, Reardon.

Second Period: 1. All-Stars, Lindsay (M. Richard, Lach) 1:35. 2. All-Stars, Dumart (unassisted) 3:06. 3. Toronto, M. Bentley (Costello) 5:13. 4. All-Stars, Stewart (D. Bentley) 19:32. Penalties-Mortson, Howe (major), Stewart, Bouchard, Juzda.

Third Period: No Scoring. Penalty-Bouchard.

Attendance-12,794.

THIRD GAME October 10, 1949 at Toronto
All-Stars 3, Toronto 1

Bob Goldham, a Chicago defenseman, registered the tying goal and assisted on the winner by Paul Ronty as the All-Stars defeated the Maple Leafs, 3–1, for their third straight victory over the Stanley Cup champions.

In the 15th minute of the second period, Goldham, after a rink-long dash, passed neatly to Boston's Ronty, who put the All-Stars ahead, 2–1. Goldham had tied the score with two minutes left in the opening period after Bill Barilko had found the nets for the Leafs three minutes earlier.

All-Stars: Goal-Durnan (Montreal), Rayner (New York). Defense-Stewart (Detroit), Goldham (Chicago), Egan (New York), Quackenbush (Boston), Harmon (Montreal), Reardon (Montreal). Forwards-O'Connor (New York), R. Conacher (Chicago), D. Bentley (Chicago), Mosienko (Chicago), M. Richard (Montreal), Laprade (New York), Abel (Detroit), Howe (Detroit), Lindsay (Detroit), Leswick (New York), Ronty (Boston). Coach-Tommy Ivan (Detroit).

Toronto: Goal-Broda. Defense-Thomson, Boesch, Juzda, Barilko. Forwards-Watson, M. Bentley, Klukay, Meeker, Lynn, Mackell, Kennedy, Gardner, Timgren, Dawes, Smith. Coach-Hap Day.

Referee-Bill Chadwick. Linesmen-Ed Mepham, Jim Primeau.

First Period: 1. Toronto, Barilko (Watson, Gardner) 15:22. 2. All-Stars, Goldham (Laprade) 18:03. Penalties-M. Richard, Meeker, Thomson, Howe.

Second Period: 3. All-Stars, Ronty (Goldham) 14:42. Penalties-Harmon, Thomson, Boesch, Egan, Smith.

Third Period: 4. All-Stars, D. Bentley (Quackenbush) 2:38. Penalties-None. Attendance-13,541.

FOURTH GAME October 8, 1950 at Detroit
Detroit 7, All-Stars 1

Left wing Ted Lindsay scored three goals in leading the Red Wings to a 7–1 triumph over the All-Stars, snapping the Stars' three-year winning streak.

Lindsay beat goalie Chuck Rayner of the Rangers only 19 seconds after the opening face-off. He scored again with three minutes remaining in the first period and registered No. 3 with five minutes left in the game.

Terry Sawchuk, a rookie, also was a standout for the Red Wings. He made 25 saves in goal, several of them spectacular stops.

All-Stars: Goal-Rayner (New York), Broda (Toronto). Defense-Stewart (Chicago), Mortson (Toronto), Thomson (Toronto), Harmon (Montreal), Quackenbush (Boston), Bouchard (Montreal). Forwards-D. Bentley (Chicago), Mosienko (Chicago), M. Richard (Montreal), Laprade (New York), Kennedy (Toronto), Leswick (New York), Ronty (Boston), Smith (Toronto), Peirson (Boston). Coach-Lynn Patrick (Boston).

Detroit: Goal-Sawchuk. Defense-Goldham, Kelly, Reise, Fogolin, Pronovost. Forwards-Lindsay, Gee, Howe, Peters, Stewart, Abel, McFadden, Prystai, Pavelich, Carveth, Black, Couture. Coach-Tommy Ivan.

Referee-George Gravel. Linesmen-George Hayes, Doug Young.

First Period: 1. Detroit, Lindsay (Howe) 0:19. 2. Detroit, Lindsay (Abel) 17:12. Penalties-M. Richard, Leswick 2, Abel, Pronovost, D. Bentley.

Second Period: 3. Detroit, Howe (Lindsay, Kelly) 11:12. 4. Detroit, Peters (Prystai, Kelly) 18:36. 5. Detroit, Pavelich (Prystai, Peters) 19:44. Penalty-Couture.

Third Period: 6. Detroit, Prystai (Pavelich) 7:36. 7. Detroit, Lindsay (unassisted) 14:28. 8. All-Stars, Smith (Peirson) 18:27. Penalties-Peters, Stewart. Attendance-9,166.

FIFTH GAME October 9, 1951 at Toronto
First Team All-Stars 2, Second Team All-Stars 2

Ken Mosdell's goal midway through the third period and two fist fights highlighted a 2–2 tie between the First and Second All-Star teams.

Mosdell, a Montreal forward, forged the deadlock for the Second Team when he converted passes from Tod Sloan and Gus Mortson at 9:25 of the final session.

The fisticuffs involved Detroit's Gordie Howe and Montreal's Maurice Richard in one match and Detroit's Ted Lindsay and Toronto's Ted Kennedy in the other.

First Team: Goal-Sawchuk (Detroit), Lumley (Chicago). Defense-Kelly (Detroit), Quackenbush (Boston), Eddolls (New York), Fogolin (Chicago), Dewsbury (Chicago). Forwards-Schmidt (Boston), Howe (Detroit), Lindsay (Detroit), Raleigh (New York), Peirson (Boston), Sandford (Boston), Sinclair (New York), D. Bentley (Chicago), Stewart (New York), Bodnar (Chicago). Coach-Joe Primeau, Toronto.

Second Team: Goal-Rayner (New York), McNeil (Montreal). Defense-Thomson (Toronto), Reise (Detroit), Bouchard (Montreal), Harvey (Montreal), Mortson (Toronto). Forwards-Kennedy (Toronto), Abel (Detroit), M. Richard (Montreal), Smith (Toronto), M. Bentley (Toronto), Sloan (Toronto), Watson (Toronto), Mosdell (Montreal), Meger (Montreal), Curry (Montreal), Coach-Dick Irvin (Montreal).

Referee-Bill Chadwick. Linesmen-Sam Babcock, Bill Morrison.

First Period: 1. First Team, Howe (Lindsay, Schmidt) 7:59. Penalties-Curry, Eddolls, Sloan.

Second Period: 2. Second Team, Sloan (Watson, M. Bentley) 2:26. 3. First Team, Peirson (Stewart, Raleigh) 16:49. Penalties-Raleigh, Lindsay.

Third Period: 4. Second Team, Mosdell (Sloan, Mortson) 9:25. Penalties-Lindsay, Howe.

Attendance-11,469.

SIXTH GAME October 5, 1952 at Detroit
First Team All-Stars 1, Second Team All-Stars 1

Maurice "Rocket" Richard, taking a neat pass from defenseman Hy Buller, scored at 1:36 of the third period and gave the Second Team All-Stars a 1–1 tie with the First Team.

Marty Pavelich of Detroit had put the First Team in front at 9:57 of the second period after taking passes from Bill Mosienko and Dave Creighton.

After Richard, Montreal's great right wing, tied the score, each team had several scoring opportunities but no success against goalies Terry Sawchuk of Detroit and Gerry McNeil of Montreal.

First Team: Goal-Sawchuk (Detroit). Defense-Kelly (Detroit), Harvey (Montreal), Mortson (Chicago), Quackenbush (Boston), Reise (New York), Goldham (Detroit). Forwards-Lach (Montreal), Howe (Detroit), Lindsay (Detroit), Creighton (Boston), Sandford (Boston), Pavelich (Detroit), Mosienko (Chicago), Leswick (Detroit), Sinclair (Detroit). Coach-Tommy Ivan (Detroit).

Second Team: Goal-Henry (Boston), McNeil (Montreal). Defense-Thomson (Toronto), Buller (New York), Johnson (Montreal), Flaman (Toronto), Bouchard (Montreal). Forwards-Schmidt (Boston), M. Richard (Montreal), Smith (Toronto), Watson (Toronto), Geoffrion (Montreal), Sloan (Toronto), Curry (Montreal), Reay (Montreal), Mosdell (Montreal), Megar (Montreal). Coach-Dick Irvin (Montreal).

Referee-Bill Chadwick. Linesmen-Doug Young, George Hayes.

First Period: No Scoring. Penalties-Buller, Thomson, M. Richard.

Second Period: 1. First Team, Pavelich (Mosienko, Creighton) 9:57. Penalties-Bouchard, Thomson 2.

Third Period: 2. Second Team, M. Richard (Buller) 1:36. Penalty-Lach.

Attendance-10,680.

SEVENTH GAME October 3, 1953 at Montreal
All-Stars 3, Montreal 1

Wally Hergesheimer of the New York Rangers scored two power play goals in the opening period and paced the All-Stars to a 3–1 victory over the Canadiens.

Both of Hergesheimer's tallies came on plays originated by Detroit defenseman Red Kelly. Maurice Richard put Montreal on the scoreboard in the fifth minute of the third period. However, Detroit's Alex Delvecchio put the game out of reach with a goal into an empty net with 33 seconds left to play.

Kelly and Montreal's Bert Olmstead received major penalties for fighting in the third period.

All-Stars: Goal-Sawchuk (Detroit). Defense-Kelly (Detroit), Quackenbush (Boston), Gadsby (Chicago), Thomson (Toronto), Reise (New York), Mortson (Chicago). Forwards-Howe (Detroit), Lindsay (Detroit), Delvecchio (Detroit), Sandford (Boston), Smith (Toronto), Prystai (Detroit), Hergesheimer (New York), Mosienko (Chicago), Ronty (New York), Watson (Toronto). Coach-Lynn Patrick (Boston).

Montreal: Goal-McNeil. Defense-Harvey, St. Laurent, Bouchard, Johnson, MacPherson. Forwards-Moore, Curry, Olmstead, Beliveau, Geoffrion, Gamble, M. Richard, MacKay, Lach, McCormack, Mosdell, Meger, Davis, Mazur. Coach-Dick Irvin.

Referee-Red Storey. Linesmen-Sam Babcock, Doug Davies.

First Period: 1. All-Stars, Hergesheimer (Ronty, Kelly) 4:06. 2. All-Stars, Hergesheimer (Kelly) 5:25. Penalties-Meger, MacPherson, Lindsay.

Second Period-No Scoring. Penalties-Mortson, St. Laurent, Howe, Richard.

Third Period: 3. Montreal, M. Richard (Harvey, Beliveau) 4:30. 4. All-Stars, Delvecchio (unassisted) 19:27. Penalties-Kelly, Olmstead, Smith.

Attendance-14,153.

EIGHTH GAME October 2, 1954 at Detroit
Detroit 2, All-Stars 2

Toronto's Gus Mortson and Boston's Doug Mohns fired second-period goals that enabled the All-Stars to gain a 2–2 deadlock with the Red Wings.

The game was featured by the stellar goaltending of Terry Sawchuk, who played all 60 minutes for the Wings, and Toronto's Harry Lumley and Chicago's Al Rollins, who split the netminding chores for the Stars.

Alex Delvecchio and Gordie Howe collected Detroit's goals, Delvecchio midway in the opening period and Howe 10 minutes later.

All-Stars: Goal-Lumley (Toronto), Rollins (Chicago). Defense-Harvey (Montreal), Mortson (Chicago), Horton (Toronto), Gadsby (Chicago), Howell (New York), Quackenbush (Boston). Forwards-Geoffrion (Montreal), Mackell (Boston), Smith (Toronto), M. Richard (Montreal), Kennedy (Toronto), Beliveau (Montreal), Sandford (Boston), Raleigh (New York), Mosdell (Montreal), Ronty (New York), Mohns (Boston). Coach-King Clancy (Toronto).

Detroit: Goal-Sawchuk. Defense-Goldham, Pronovost, Kelly, Woit, Allen. Forwards-Lindsay, Leswick, Howe, Prystai, Skov, Reibel, Delvecchio, Wilson, Dineen, Poile, Bonin. Coach-Jim Skinner.

Referee-Bill Chadwick. Linesmen-George Hayes, Bill Morrison.

First Period: 1. Detroit, Delvecchio (Lindsay, Reibel) 9:50. 2. Detroit, Howe (Reibel, Kelly) 19:55. Penalties-Mortson, Bonin 2, Mackell, Howell.

Second Period: 3. All-Stars, Mortson (Gadsby, Kennedy) 4:19. 4. All-Stars, Mohns (Beliveau) 13:10. Penalties-Dineen, Bonin, Howell, Sandford, Mohns.

Third Period: No Scoring. Penalties-Lindsay, Mortson, Woit.

Attendance-10,689.

NINTH GAME October 2, 1955 at Detroit
Detroit 3, All-Stars 1

Earl "Dutch" Reibel scored twice as the Red Wings extended their unbeaten streak on home ice to 26 games by downing the All-Stars, 3–1.

The Wings, who finished the 1954–55 season with 19 victories and six ties at the Olympia, took the lead 57 seconds into the second period when Gordie Howe beat Toronto's Harry Lumley. Reibel made it 2–0 five minutes later. Doug Harvey of Montreal scored the Stars' only goal at 16:38 of the third period.

With a minute left in the game, All-Star coach Dick Irvin replaced goalie Terry Sawchuk with an extra forward and Reibel slid a long shot into the empty cage.

All-Stars: Goal-Lumley (Toronto), Sawchuk (Boston). Defense-Harvey (Montreal), Flaman (Boston), Morrison (Toronto), Stanley (Chicago), Martin (Chicago). Forwards-Beliveau (Montreal), M. Richard (Montreal), Smith (Toronto), Mosdell (Montreal), Geoffrion (Montreal), Lewicki (New York), Sullivan (Chicago), Litzenberger (Chicago), Stewart (Toronto), Labine (Boston), Watson (Chicago). Coach-Dick Irvin (Chicago).

Detroit: Goal-Hall. Defense-Goldham, Pronovost, Kelly, Godfrey, Hillman, Hollingworth. Forwards-Lindsay, Reibel, Howe, Delvecchio, Pavelich, Sandford, Chevrefils, Dineen, Toppazzini, Bucyk, Corcoran. Coach-Jim Skinner.

First Period: No Scoring. Penalties-Flaman, Corcoran, Geoffrion, Stewart, Bucyk, Stanley, Morrison.

Second Period: 1. Detroit, Howe (Reibel, Delvecchio) 0:57. 2. Detroit, Reibel (Howe, Lindsay) 5:43. Penalties-Corcoran, Hollingworth.

Third Period: 3. All-Stars, Harvey (Beliveau, Smith) 16:38. 4. Detroit, Reibel (Goldham, Lindsay) 19:33. Penalties-Hollingworth, Harvey.

Attendance-10,111.

TENTH GAME October 9, 1956 at Montreal
Montreal 1, All-Stars 1

The Canadiens and All-Stars played to a 1–1 tie in a game that marked the introduction of the new power play regulation.

Maurice Richard clicked on a power play for Montreal only 33 seconds after the Rangers' Red Sullivan had been penalized for holding in the 15th minute of the second period.

Sullivan came out of the penalty box immediately after Richard's tally. Before the rule change, a player serving a minor penalty had to spend the full two minutes in the penalty box even if his team was scored against while shorthanded.

Detroit's Ted Lindsay evened the score four minutes after Richard's tally.

All-Stars: Goal-Hall (Detroit), Sawchuk (Boston). Defense-Gadsby (New York), Kelly (Detroit), Flaman (Boston), Mortson (Chicago), Morrison (Toronto), Bolton (Toronto). Forwards-Lindsay (Detroit), Sloan (Toronto), Howe (Detroit), Delvecchio (Detroit), Labine (Boston), Duff (Toronto), Armstrong (Toronto), Mickoski (Chicago), Wilson (Chicago), Hergesheimer (Chicago), Creighton (New York), Sullivan (New York). Coach-Jim Skinner (Detroit).

Montreal: Goal-Plante. Defense-Harvey, St. Laurent, Johnson, Turner, Talbot. Forwards-Beliveau, Geoffrion, Olmstead, Curry, Leclair, M. Richard, Moore, H. Richard, Marshall, Provost. Coach-Toe Blake.

Referee-Red Storey. Linesmen-Doug Davies, Bill Roberts.

First Period: No Scoring. Penalties-Flaman, Beliveau 2.

Second Period: 1. Montreal, M. Richard (Olmstead, Harvey) 14:58. 2. All-Stars, Lindsay (Mortson) 18:48. Penalties-Mortson, Sullivan.

Third Period: No Scoring. Penalties-Labine, Mortson.

Attendance-13,095.

ELEVENTH GAME October 5, 1957 at Montreal
All-Stars 5, Montreal 3

Gordie Howe of the Detroit Red Wings and Dean Prentice of the New York Rangers each scored in the third period and gave the All-Stars a 5–3 triumph over the Canadiens.

Howe broke a 3–3 tie at 8:11 and Prentice registered an insurance marker with 3:10 left in the game.

The Canadiens had taken a 3–2 lead in the second period on goals by Bert Olmstead and Stan Smrke, but the Rangers' Andy Bathgate tied it for the Stars at 18:14 of the second period on assists from Prentice and Chicago's Ed Litzenberger.

All-Stars: Goal-Hall (Chicago). Defense-Kelly (Detroit), Flaman (Boston), Gadsby (New York), Morrison (Toronto), M. Pronovost (Detroit), Stanley (Boston). Forwards-Howe (Detroit), Lindsay (Chicago), Litzenberger (Chicago), Chevrefils (Boston), Bathgate (New York), Duff (Toronto), Delvecchio (Detroit), Prentice (New York), Migay (Toronto), Armstrong (Toronto), McKenney (Boston). Coach-Milt Schmidt (Boston).

Montreal: Goal-Plante. Defense-Harvey, St. Laurent, Johnson, Turner, Talbot. Forwards-Beliveau, M. Richard, Curry, Olmstead, Smrke, Moore, Provost, H. Richard, Bonin, Goyette, A. Pronovost, Marshall. Coach-Toe Blake.

Referee-Red Storey. Linesmen-Doug Davies, Bill Morrison.

First Period: 1. All-Stars, Kelly (unassisted) 1:06. 2. Montreal, M. Richard (H. Richard, Moore) 10:53. 3. All-Stars, Stanley (Prentice, Migay) 19:55. Penalties-Migay, Talbot, Howe 2, Harvey.

Second Period: 4. Montreal, Olmstead (Johnson) 0:33. 5. Montreal, Smrke (Bonin) 9:13. 6. All-Stars, Bathgate (Prentice, Litzenberger) 18:14. Penalties-Talbot, Chevrefils, Johnson.

Third Period: 7. All-Stars, Howe (Chevrefils, Morrison) 8:11. 8. All-Stars, Prentice (Bathgate, Litzenberger) 16:50. Penalties-Flaman 2, Olmstead.

Attendance-13,003.

TWELFTH GAME October 4, 1958 at Montreal
Montreal 6, All-Stars 3

Maurice Richard scored Montreal's first and final goals as the Canadiens defeated the All-Stars, 6–3, and ended a three-year non-winning streak for the Stanley Cup champions.

Referee Eddie Powers handed out six minor penalties and four led to goals. Andy Bathgate of the Rangers scored twice for the All-Stars while Bob Pulford of Toronto notched the visitors' other goal.

The Canadiens' Bernie "Boom Boom" Geoffrion suffered pulled neck and chest muscles from a bodycheck by Detroit's Red Kelly.

All-Stars: Goal-Hall (Chicago). Defense-Gadsby (New York), Flaman (Boston), M. Pronovost (Detroit), Mohns (Boston), Kelly (Detroit), St. Laurent (Chicago). Forwards-Howe (Detroit), Bathgate (New York), Henry (New York), Sullivan (New York), Delvecchio (Detroit), Toppazzini (Boston), Harris (Toronto), Duff (Toronto), Litzenberger (Chicago), McKenney (Boston), Pulford (Toronto). Coach-Milt Schmidt (Boston).

Montreal: Goal-Plante. Defense-Harvey, Johnson, Turner, Talbot, Cushenan. Forwards-Beliveau, Geoffrion, Backstrom, M. Richard, Moore, Provost, McDonald, H. Richard, Bonin, Goyette, Marshall, A. Pronovost. Coach-Toe Blake.

Referee-Eddie Powers. Linesmen-George Hayes, Bill Morrison.

First Period: 1. Montreal, M. Richard (Harvey, Moore) 9:19. 2. Montreal, Geoffrion (H. Richard) 16:20. Penalties-Henry, Harvey.

Second Period: 3. Montreal, Marshall (Provost) 2:33. 4. Montreal, H. Richard (Talbot, Moore) 5:08. 5. All-Stars, Pulford (Toppazzini, Harris) 11:39. Penalty-Turner.

Third Period: 6. All-Stars, Bathgate (Litzenberger, Henry) 3:55. 7. Montreal, McDonald (Provost, Marshall) 7:43. 8. All-Stars, Bathgate (Pulford, Sullivan) 13:54. 9. Montreal, M. Richard (Moore, H. Richard) 16:04. Penalties-Mohns, Duff, Provost.

Attendance-13,989.

THIRTEENTH GAME October 3, 1959 at Montreal
Montreal 6, All-Stars 1

Big Jean Beliveau scored twice and defenseman Doug Harvey collected three assists as the Canadiens trounced the All-Stars, 6–1.

The Stars were considerably weakened by the absence of holdouts Bobby Hull, Tod Sloan and Pierre Pilote of Chicago and Bob Pulford, Dick Duff and Tim Horton of Toronto. They had not as yet signed contracts for the season and therefore were ineligible to play.

Leading by only 2–1 going into the third period, Montreal buried the Stars under a four-goal avalanche in the final 20 minutes. The marksmen were Beliveau, Dickie Moore, Henri Richard and Andre Pronovost.

All-Stars: Goal-Sawchuk (Detroit). Defense-M. Pronovost (Detroit), Gadsby (New York), Flaman (Boston), Brewer (Toronto), Mohns (Boston). Forwards-Bathgate (New York), Howe (Detroit), Delvecchio (Detroit), Sullivan (New York), Toppazzini (Boston), Mahovlich (Toronto), Olmstead (Toronto), Litzenberger (Chicago), McKenney (Boston), Armstrong (Toronto). Coach-Punch Imlach (Toronto).

Montreal: Goal-Plante. Defense-Johnson, Harvey, Turner, Langlois, J. C. Tremblay. Forwards-Beliveau, Moore, H. Richard, Geoffrion, Backstrom, Hicke, M. Richard, Provost, McDonald, Bonin, Goyette, Marshall, A. Pronovost. Coach-Toe Blake.

Referee-Frank Udvari. Linesmen-George Hayes, Bob Frampton.

First Period: No Scoring. Penalties-None.

Second Period: 1. Montreal, Beliveau (Hicke, Harvey) 4:25. 2. Montreal, McDonald (Backstrom, Geoffrion) 13:43. 3. All-Stars, McKenney (Litzenberger) 18:30. Penalties-None.

Third Period: 4. Montreal, Moore (H. Richard, Johnson) 7:44. 5. Montreal, H. Richard (Moore, Harvey) 9:31. 6. Montreal, Beliveau (Hicke, Bonin) 11:54. 7. Montreal, Pronovost (Harvey) 15:51. Penalties-Tremblay, Bathgate, Turner.

Attendance-13,818.

FOURTEENTH GAME October 1, 1960 at Montreal
All-Stars 2, Montreal 1

Andy Hebenton took a pass from his New York Ranger teammate, Red Sullivan, and beat goalie Jacques Plante at 15:51 of the second period to give the All-Stars a 2–1 victory over the Canadiens.

Frank Mahovlich of Toronto got the other Stars' goal in the opening minute of the second period and Claude Provost tied the score for the Canadiens 11 minutes later.

This was the first All-Star game in which Maurice Richard, the Canadiens' brilliant right wing, did not participate. He had announced his retirement as a player the previous month.

All-Stars: Goal-Hall (Chicago). Defense-M. Pronovost (Detroit), Stanley (Toronto), Pilote (Chicago), Gadsby (New York), Kelly (Toronto), Armstrong (Boston). Forwards-Howe (Detroit), Hull (Chicago), Horvath (Boston), Stasiuk (Boston), Ullman (Detroit), Bathgate (New York), Hay (Chicago), Hebenton (New York), Sullivan (New York), McKenney (Boston), Mahovlich (Toronto), Pulford (Toronto). Coach-Punch Imlach (Toronto).

Montreal: Goal-Plante. Defense-Harvey, Langlois, Johnson, Turner, Talbot. Forwards-Beliveau, Geoffrion, Bonin, Backstrom, Hicke, Moore, Provost, H. Richard, Marshall, A. Pronovost. Coach-Toe Blake.

Referee-Eddie Powers. Linesmen-George Hayes, Neil Armstrong.

First Period: No Scoring. Penalty-Talbot.

Second Period: 1. All-Stars, Mahovlich (Pilote, Kelly) 0:40. 2. Montreal, Provost (Backstrom, A. Pronovost) 11:40. 3. All-Stars, Hebenton (Sullivan) 15:51. Penalties-Sullivan, Hull, Johnson.

Third Period: No Scoring. Penalties-Hicke, Gadsby, Pilote, Harvey.

Attendance-13,949.

FIFTEENTH GAME October 7, 1961 at Chicago
All-Stars 3, Chicago 1

Teammates Gordie Howe and Alex Delvecchio of the Detroit Red Wings each scored one goal and assisted on another to lead the All-Stars to a 3–1 triumph over the Black Hawks.

Delvecchio opened the scoring in the 12th minute of the opening period and Howe closed it in the 12th minute of the second session. Norm Ullman, another Red Wing, assisted on both tallies.

Eric Nesterenko beat Toronto goalie Johnny Bower for Chicago's only tally at 6:26 of the second period.

All-Stars: Goal-Bower (Toronto), Worsley (New York). Defense-Harvey (New York), Pronovost (Detroit), Boivin (Boston), Stanley (Toronto), Brewer (Toronto), Mohns (Boston). Forwards-Richard (Montreal), McKenney (Boston), Ullman (Detroit), Bathgate (New York), Geoffrion (Montreal), Howe (Detroit), Provost (Montreal), Mahovlich (Toronto), Moore (Montreal), Delvecchio (Detroit), Goyette (Montreal). Coach-Sid Abel (Detroit).

Chicago: Goal-Hall. Defense-Turner, Pilote, Vasko, Evans, Fleming, St. Laurent. Forwards-Hall, Balfour, Horvath, Murphy, Hay, Melnyk, McDonald, Nesterenko, Hull, Wharram, Maki, Mikita. Coach-Rudy Pilous.

Referee-Frank Udvari. Linesmen-George Hayes, Neil Armstrong.

First Period: 1. All-Stars, Delvecchio (Ullman, Howe) 11:37. Penalties-Mahovlich, Hay, Vasko.

Second Period: 2. All-Stars, McKenney (Pronovost, Bathgate) 2:37. 3. Chicago, Nesterenko (Pilote, Hull) 6:26. 4. All-Stars, Howe (Delvecchio, Ullman) 11:38. Penalties-Goyette, Nesterenko 3, McKenney, Mahovlich 2.

Third Period: No Scoring. Penalties-Pilote, Richard, Hull.

Attendance-14,534.

SIXTEENTH GAME October 6, 1962 at Toronto
Toronto 4, All-Stars 1

The Maple Leafs erupted for all their goals in the opening period against Montreal goalie Jacques Plante and went on to defeat the All-Stars, 4–1, for their first victory in the annual classic.

Dick Duff, Bob Pulford, Frank Mahovlich and Eddie Shack beat Plante, who had captured the Vezina Trophy the previous season.

Detroit's Gordie Howe scored the only goal for the Stars. It was his seventh in the competition and enabled him to tie the record held by the retired Maurice Richard.

All-Stars: Goal-Plante (Montreal), Hall (Chicago), Worsley (New York). Defense-Harvey (New York), Talbot (Montreal), Pilote (Chicago), Mohns (Boston), Boivin (Boston). Forwards-McKenney (Boston), Howe (Detroit), Hull (Chicago), Geoffrion (Montreal), Bathgate (New York), Ullman (Detroit), Delvecchio (Detroit), Backstrom (Montreal), Prentice (New York). Coach-Rudy Pilous (Chicago).

Toronto: Goal-Bower. Defense-Brewer, Horton, Douglas, Baun, Hillman, Stanley. Forwards-Kelly, Mahovlich, Nevin, Duff, Armstrong, Stewart, Keon, Harris, Pulford, Shack, MacMillan, Litzenberger. Coach-Punch Imlach.

Referee-Eddie Powers. Linesmen-Matt Pavelich, Ron Wicks.

First Period: 1. Toronto, Duff (Armstrong, Douglas) 5:22. 2. All-Stars, Howe

(Delvecchio, Pilote) 7:26. 3. Toronto, Pulford (Stewart) 10:45. 4. Toronto, Mahovlich (Stanley) 13:03. 5. Toronto, Shack (Keon) 19:32. Penalties-Mohns, Nevin, McKenney, Brewer, Shack, Howe.

Second Period: No Scoring. Penalties-Kelly, Howe, Brewer.

Third Period: No Scoring. Penalties-Baun, Boivin, Shack.

Attendance-14,197.

SEVENTEENTH GAME October 5, 1963 at Toronto
Toronto 3, All-Stars 3

Frank Mahovlich, Toronto's big left wing, scored two goals and collected an assist as the Leafs played a 3–3 tie with the All-Stars.

The Leafs held the lead three times, but each time the Stars rallied for a deadlock. Mahovlich scored his team's first two goals and Ed Litzenberger's tally put Toronto in front, 3–2, at 2:56 of the third period. Just 27 seconds later, Detroit defenseman Marcel Pronovost drilled the puck home from the point.

All-Stars: Goal-Hall (Chicago), Sawchuk (Detroit). Defense-Pilote (Chicago), Vasko (Chicago), Howell (New York), Johnson (Boston), Pronovost (Detroit). Forwards-Howe (Detroit), Richard (Montreal), Bathgate (New York), Hull (Chicago), Delvecchio (Detroit), Ullman (Detroit), Prentice (Boston), Oliver (Boston), Henry (New York), Bucyk (Boston), Geoffrion (Montreal), Provost (Montreal), Beliveau (Montreal). Coach-Sid Abel (Detroit).

Toronto: Goal-Bower, Simmons. Defense-Baun, Horton, Hillman, Douglas, Stanley. Forwards-Mahovlich, Shack, Kelly, Harris, Pulford, Nevin, Keon, Litzenberger, MacMillan, Stewart, Duff, Armstrong. Coach-Punch Imlach.

Referee-Frank Udvari. Linesmen-Matt Pavelich, Neil Armstrong.

First Period: 1. Toronto, Mahovlich (Armstrong, Baun) 2:22. 2. All-Stars, Richard (Henry, Howe) 4:08. 3. Toronto, Mahovlich (Keon, Litzenberger) 12:11. 4. All-Stars, Hull (Geoffrion) 19:27. Penalties-Stanley, Howell, Duff.

Second Period: No Scoring. Penalties-Pronovost, Horton 2, Baun, Hull.

Third Period: 5. Toronto, Litzenberger (Mahovlich, Kelly) 2:56. 6. All-Stars, Pronovost (Bucyk, Oliver) 3:23. Penalty-Stanley.

Attendance-14,003.

EIGHTEENTH GAME October 10, 1964 at Toronto
All-Stars 3, Leafs 2

Montreal's Jean Beliveau scored the tie-breaking goal with six minutes remaining in the second period and led the All-Stars to a 3–2 victory over the Maple Leafs.

Beliveau's goal snapped a 1–1 deadlock. Gordie Howe of Detroit and Bobby Hull of Chicago assisted on the play.

Murray Oliver of Boston put the Stars in front, 3–1, in the seventh minute of the third period, offsetting a Leafs' goal by Jim Pappin later in the session.

All-Stars: Goal-Hall (Chicago), Hodge (Montreal). Defense-Vasko (Chicago), Pilote (Chicago), Laperriere (Montreal), Howell (New York), Boivin (Boston). Forwards-Beliveau (Montreal), Howe (Detroit), B. Hull (Chicago), Delvecchio (Detroit), Gilbert (New York), Oliver (Boston), Henry (New York), Mikita (Chicago), Bucyk (Boston), Provost (Montreal). Coach-Sid Abel (Detroit).

Toronto: Goal-Bower, Sawchuk. Defense-Horton, Douglas, Baun, Brewer, Hillman. Forwards-Pulford, Stewart, Shack, Keon, McKenney, Armstrong, Harris, Ehman, Pappin, Ellis, Bathgate, Mahovlich. Coach-Punch Imlach.

Referee-Frank Udvari. Linesmen-Ron Wicks, Neil Armstrong.

First Period-No Scoring. Penalties-Bathgate, Howell, Baun, Douglas, Oliver.

Second Period: 1. All-Stars, Boivin (Laperriere, Oliver) 10:47. 2. Toronto, Douglas (Bathgate, Mahovlich) 11:45. 3. All-Stars, Beliveau (Hull, Howe) 13:51. Penalties-Laperriere, Mikita, Baun, Howell, Hodge (served by Gilbert).

Third Period: 4. All-Stars, Oliver (Bucyk, Howell) 6:11. 5. Toronto, Pappin (Ehman) 13:35. Penalties-Stewart, Pilote, Douglas, Provost.

Attendance-14,200.

NINETEENTH GAME October 20, 1965 at Montreal
All-Stars 5, Montreal 2

Gordie Howe of Detroit shattered the career All-Star game record for goals by scoring his eighth and ninth while leading the All-Stars to a 5–2 victory over the Canadiens.

The veteran right winger, who also assisted on two other scores, broke the mark of seven goals he shared with the Canadiens' Maurice Richard. Howe broke another All-Star record by lifting his career point total to 16. He played on a line with Norm Ullman, also of Detroit, and Chicago's Bobby Hull.

All-Stars: Goal-Hall (Chicago), Crozier (Detroit), Johnston (Boston). Defense-Gadsby (Detroit), Pilote (Chicago), Howell (New York), Pronovost (Toronto), Green (Boston), Baun (Toronto). Forwards-Ullman (Detroit), Howe (Detroit), Hull (Chicago), Ellis (Toronto), Hadfield (New York), Gilbert (New York), Oliver (Boston), Bucyk (Boston), Mahovlich (Toronto), Nesterenko (Chicago), Delvecchio (Detroit), Mohns (Chicago). Coach-Billy Reay (Chicago).

Montreal: Goal-Hodge, Worsley. Defense-J. C. Tremblay, Harris, Laperriere, Talbot, Harper. Forwards-Beliveau, Rousseau, Duff, Backstrom, Larose, Provost, Richard, Balon, G. Tremblay, Ferguson, Berenson. Coach-Toe Blake.

Referee-Art Skov. Linesmen-Matt Pavelich, Neil Armstrong.

First Period: No Scoring. Penalties-Harris 2, Gadsby, Beliveau, Larose, Pronovost.

Second Period: 1. Montreal, Beliveau (Duff, Rousseau) 6:48. 2. Montreal, Laperriere (Backstrom, Larose) 11:00. 3. All-Stars, Ullman (Hull, Howe) 12:40. 4. All-Stars, Hull (Howe, Oliver) 16:35. 5. All-Stars, Howe (Ullman, Baun) 19:19. Penalty-Balon.

Third Period: 6. All-Stars, Bucyk (Gadsby, Oliver) 10:01. 7. All-Stars, Howe (unassisted) 18:39. Penalties-Ellis, Ferguson, Howell 2.

Attendance-13,351.

TWENTIETH GAME January 18, 1967 at Montreal
Montreal 3, All-Stars 0

John Ferguson, Montreal's aggressive left wing, scored twice as the Canadiens blanked the All-Stars, 3–0, in a dull, listless contest, the first annual All-Star Game played in mid-season.

Speedy Henri Richard put the Canadiens in front at 14:03 of the opening period when he converted passes from Bobby Rousseau and Terry Harper to beat Chicago's Glenn Hall, who was in the Stars' nets.

Ferguson scored less than two minutes later and again with only eight seconds remaining in the game.

All-Stars: Goal-Hall (Chicago), Giacomin (New York). Defense-Stanley (Toronto), Howell (New York), Stapleton (Chicago), Neilson (New York), Pilote (Chicago). Forwards-Ullman (Detroit), Mikita (Chicago), Keon (Toronto), Oliver (Boston), Howe (Detroit), Gilbert (New York), Nevin (New York), B. Hull (Chicago), Mahovlich (Toronto), Bucyk (Boston), Delvecchio (Detroit). Coach-Sid Abel (Detroit).

Montreal: Goal-Hodge, Bauman. Defense-Laperriere, Talbot, Harper, J. C. Tremblay, Harris, Roberts. Forwards-Richard, Beliveau, Backstrom, Balon, Provost, Larose, Cournoyer, Rousseau, Rochefort, Duff, G. Tremblay, Ferguson. Coach-Toe Blake.

Referee-Vern Buffey. Linesmen-Matt Pavelich, Neil Armstrong.

First Period: 1. Montreal, Richard (Rousseau, Harper) 14:03. 2. Montreal, Ferguson (Larose) 15:59. Penalties-None.

Second Period: No Scoring. Penalties-Howell, Richard, Ferguson.

Third Period: 3. Montreal, Ferguson (Richard, Rousseau) 19:52. Penalties-None.

Attendance-14,284.

TWENTY-FIRST GAME January 16, 1968 at Toronto
Toronto 4, All-Stars 3

The Maple Leafs came from behind on second-period goals by Allan Stanley and Pete Stemkowski to defeat the All-Stars, 4–3, before a record All-Star crowd of 15,740.

The Stars took a 2–1 lead on Ken Wharram's goal in the opening minute of the second period. But Stanley, on passes from Stemkowski and Wayne Carleton, tied the score seven minutes later and Stemkowski put the Leafs in front to stay at 16:36.

A moment of silence was observed before the start of the game in tribute to Bill Masterton, the Minnesota forward who died the previous day from a head injury received in a game three days earlier.

All-Stars: Goal-Giacomin (New York), Hall (St. Louis). Defense-Pilote (Chicago), Howell (New York), Orr (Boston), Laperriere (Montreal), Baun (Oakland), J. C. Tremblay (Montreal). Forwards-Mikita (Chicago), B. Hull (Chicago), Beliveau (Montreal), Ullman (Detroit), Howe (Detroit), Bucyk (Boston), Schinkel (Pittsburgh), Rochefort (Philadelphia), Balon (Minnesota), Marshall (New York). Coach-Toe Blake (Montreal).

Toronto: Goal-Gamble, A. Smith. Defense-Rupp, Horton, L. Hillman, Pronovost, Stanley. Forwards-Keon, Mahovlich, Ellis, Armstrong, Oliver, Stemkowski, Walton, Pappin, Pulford, Conacher, Carleton. Coach-Punch Imlach.

Referee-Bill Friday. Linesmen-Brent Castleman and Pat Shetler.

First Period: 1. Toronto, Oliver (Mahovlich, L. Hillman) 5:56. 2. All-Stars, Mikita (Hull, J. C. Tremblay) 19:53. Penalty-Stemkowski.

Second Period: 3. All-Stars, Wharram (Mikita) 0:35. 4. Toronto, Stanley (Stemkowski, Carleton) 7:56. 5. Toronto, Stemkowski (Carleton, Rupp) 16:36. Penalty-Howe.

Third Period: 6. All-Stars, Ellis (Mahovlich, L. Hillman) 3:31. 7. All-Stars, Ullman (Howe, Orr) 8:23. Penalties-Howe, Walton.

Attendance-15,740.

TWENTY-SECOND GAME January 21, 1969 at Montreal
East 3, West 3

For the first time, the All-Star Game pitted a squad from the new NHL West Division against one from the established East Division.

Claude Larose of Minnesota scored a goal with less than three minutes to play to give the underdog West a 3–3 standoff against the powerful East.

East All-Stars: Goal-Giacomin (New York), Cheevers (Boston). Defense-Orr (Boston), J. C. Tremblay (Montreal), Harris (Montreal), Green (Boston), Horton (Toronto), Stapleton (Chicago). Forwards-Beliveau (Montreal), Nevin (New York), Howe (Detroit), D. Hull (Chicago), Esposito (Boston), Ullman (Toronto), Rousseau (Montreal), R. Hull (Chicago), Gilbert (New York), Mikita (Chicago), Mahovlich (Detroit). Coach-Toe Blake (Montreal).

West All-Stars: Goal-Hall (St. Louis), Parent (Philadelphia), Plante (St. Louis). Defense-Van Impe (Philadelphia), Arbour (St. Louis), Harvey (St. Louis), Vasko (Minnesota), Picard (St. Louis), Vadnais (Oakland), White (Los Angeles). Forwards-Berenson (St. Louis), O'Shea (Minnesota), Hicke (Oakland), Hampson (Oakland), Schinkel (Pittsburgh), Roberts (St. Louis), Larose (Minnesota), McDonald (St. Louis), Grant (Minnesota). Coach-Scotty Bowman (St. Louis).

Referee-John Ashley. Linesmen-Neil Armstrong, Matt Pavelich.

First Period: 1. West, Berenson (Harvey, Picard) 4:43. 2. East, Mahovlich (Rousseau, Stapleton) 17:32. Penalty-Vadnais.

Second Period: 3. West, Roberts (Berenson, Picard) 1:53. Penalties-Horton, White.

Third Period: 4. East, Mahovlich (Harris, Gilbert) 3:11. 5. East, Nevin (Ullman) 7:20. 6. West, Larose (Grant, O'Shea) 17:07. Penalties-White, Harvey.

Attendance-16,256.

TWENTY-THIRD GAME January 20, 1970 at St. Louis
East 4, West 1

Chicago's Bobby Hull scored one goal and set up another by Gordie Howe of Detroit as the East All-Stars completely dominated the play and whipped the West, 4–1.

The East set a record with 44 shots on goal including 20 in the last period, all of which were stopped by Jacques Plante of St. Louis. All of the East goals came in the first 30 minutes against Philadelphia's Bernie Parent. The West had just 17 shots, a record low.

Each team scored in the first 37 seconds with Jacques Laperriere hitting for the East and Pittsburgh's Dean Prentice for the West. The two goals were the fastest in All-Star history.

East All-Stars: Goal-Giacomin (New York), T. Esposito (Chicago). Defense-Orr (Boston), Laperriere (Montreal), Neilson (New York), Park (New York), Savard (Montreal), Brewer (Detroit). Forwards-P. Esposito (Boston), Bucyk (Boston), Howe (Detroit), Ratelle (New York), Tkaczuk (New York), Ellis (Toronto), Keon (Toronto), Lemaire (Montreal), B. Hull (Chicago), Gilbert (New York), McKenzie (Boston), Mahovlich (Detroit). Coach-Claude Ruel (Montreal).

West All-Stars: Goal-Hall (St. Louis), Parent (Philadelphia), Plante (St. Louis). Defense- Arbour (St. Louis), White (Los Angeles), Woytowich (Pittsburgh), Howell (Oakland), B. Plager (St. Louis), Vadnais (Oakland). Forwards-Berenson (St. Louis), St. Marseille (St. Louis), Clarke (Philadelphia), Goyette (St. Louis), Parise (Minnesota), Prentice (Pittsburgh), Roberts (St. Louis), O'Shea (Minnesota), Larose (Minnesota), McDonald (St. Louis), Goldsworthy (Minnesota), Grant (Minnesota), Sabourin (St. Louis). Coach-Scotty Bowman (St. Louis).

Referee-Art Skov. Linesmen-Matt Pavelich, Claude Bechard.

First Period: 1. East, Laperriere (unassisted) 0:20. 2. West, Prentice (Berenson, Woytowich) 0:37. 3. East, Howe (B. Hull, Lemaire) 7:20. Penalties-Park, St. Marseille.

Second Period-4. East, B. Hull (Brewer) 3:26. 5. East, Tkaczuk (McKenzie, Bucyk) 9:37. Penalties-Woytowich.

Third Period-None. Penalties-Woytowich.

Attendance-16,587.

TWENTY-FOURTH GAME January 19, 1971 at Boston
West 2, East 1

The Chicago Black Hawks had moved from the East to the West Division at the start of the 1970–71 season and the expansion division reaped an immediate benefit in the All-Star game.

Black Hawk teammates Bobby Hull and Chico Maki scored goals in the first 4½ minutes and that was enough for a 2–1 West victory over the East. Montreal's Yvan Cournoyer got one goal for the East at 6:19 of the first period but the game was scoreless after that.

A crowd of 14,790 paid a record $79,009 to watch that defense-dominated game.

East All-Stars: Goal-Giacomin (New York), Villemure (New York). Defense-Park (New York), Tremblay (Montreal), Orr (Boston), Tallon (Vancouver), Neilson (New York), Smith (Boston). Forwards-Bucyk (Boston), P. Esposito (Boston), Hodge (Boston), Howe (Detroit), Westfall (Boston), Perreault (Buffalo), Cournoyer (Montreal), Keon (Toronto), Balon (New York), Ratelle (New York), P. Mahovlich (Montreal), F. Mahovlich (Montreal). Coach-Harry Sinden (Boston).

West All-Stars: Goal-Wakely (St. Louis), T. Esposito (Chicago). Defense-White (Chicago), Magnuson (Chicago), Harris (Minnesota), Roberts (St. Louis), B. Plager (St. Louis), Stapleton (Chicago). Forwards-Martin (Chicago), Berenson (St. Louis), B. Hull (Chicago), D. Hull (Chicago), Sabourin (St. Louis), Ecclestone (St. Louis), Clarke (Philadelphia), C. Maki (Chicago), Flett (Los Angeles), Grant (Minnesota), Mikita (Chicago), Polis (Pittsburgh). Coach-Scotty Bowman (St. Louis).

Referee-Bill Friday. Linesmen-Neil Armstrong, John D'Amico.

First period: 1. West, C. Maki (unassisted) 0:36. 2. West, R. Hull (Flett) 4:38. 3. East Cournoyer (D. Smith, Balon) 6:19. Penalties-Harris, F. Mahovlich, R. Hull.

Second period: None. Penalties-Bucyk.

Third period-None. Penalties-Stapleton, Magnuson.

Attendance-14,790.

TWENTY-FIFTH GAME January 25, 1972 at Minnesota
East 3, West 2

Behind, 2–0, on West goals by Bobby Hull and Simon Nolet, the East Division All-Stars roared back to tie the score on second period goals by Jean Ratelle and Johnny McKenzie. Then Phil Esposito's third period score gave the East the victory in the silver anniversary game.

A crowd of 15,423 braved sub-zero Minnesota temperatures to watch the clash of the two divisions. Esposito spoiled their fun by scoring his winning goal against Gump Worsley, goaltender for the host Minnesota North Stars.

East All-Stars: Goal-Dryden (Montreal), Villemure (New York). Defense-Park (New York), Tremblay (Montreal), Orr (Boston), Seiling (New York), Smith (Boston). Forwards-Berenson (Detroit), R. Martin (Buffalo), P. Esposito (Boston), Gilbert (New York), Tallon (Vancouver), Perreault (Buffalo), Hadfield (New York), Cournoyer (Montreal), Henderson (Toronto), McKenzie (Boston), Ratelle (New York), F. Mahovlich (Montreal). Coach-Al MacNeil (Montreal).

West All-Stars: Goal-Worsley (Minnesota), T. Esposito (Chicago). Defense-White (Chicago), Magnuson (Chicago), Harris (Minnesota), Vadnais (California), Mohns (Minnesota), Stapleton (Chicago). Forwards-Unger (St. Louis), Goldsworthy (Minnesota), R. Hull (Chicago), D. Hull (Chicago), Lonsberry (Los Angeles), P. Martin

(Chicago), Clarke (Philadelphia), C. Maki (Chicago), Nolet (Philadelphia), Mikita (Chicago), Polis (Pittsburgh). Coach-Billy Reay (Chicago).

Referee-Bruce Hood. Linesmen-Matt Pavelich, Claude Bechard.

First period: 1. West, R. Hull (P. Martin, C. Maki) 17:01. Penalty-Hadfield.

Second period: 2. West, Nolet (D. Hull) 1:11. 3. East, Ratelle (Tremblay, Gilbert) 3:48. 4. East, McKenzie (Park, Seiling) 18:45. Penalty-White.

Third period: 5. East, P. Esposito (Smith, Orr) 1:09. Penalties-White, P. Esposito, Tremblay, Mohns.

Attendance-15,423.

TWENTY-SIXTH GAME January 30, 1973 at New York
East 5, West 4

Greg Polis, who arrived only hours before gametime following the birth of his first child in Pittsburgh, emerged as the star of the game, first ever at New York's Madison Square Garden.

Polis scored two goals for the West and drove off with the car voted to the game's Most Valuable Player. The East, however, drove off with the victory with Bobby Schmautz scoring the decisive goal with only six minutes left to play.

A record All-Star crowd of 17,500 watched the game.

East All-Stars: Goal-Giacomin (New York Rangers), Villemure (New York Rangers). Defense-Savard (Montreal), Park (New York Rangers), G. Bergman (Detroit), Orr (Boston), Lapointe (Montreal), Smith (Boston). Forwards-R. Martin (Buffalo), P. Esposito (Boston), Hodge (Boston), Schmautz (Vancouver), Cournoyer (Montreal), Keon (Toronto), Robert (Buffalo), Westfall (New York Islanders), Ratelle (New York Rangers), Henderson (Toronto), Lemaire (Montreal), F. Mahovlich (Montreal). Coach-Tom Johnson (Boston).

West All-Stars: Goal-T. Esposito (Chicago), Vachon (Los Angeles). Defense-White (Chicago), Harper (Los Angeles), Marotte (Los Angeles), Gibbs (Minnesota), B. Plager (St. Louis), Manery (Atlanta). Forwards-P. Martin (Chicago), Pappin (Chicago), Unger (St. Louis), D. Hull (Chicago), Parise (Minnesota), Dornhoefer (Philadelphia), Clarke (Philadelphia), Berry (Los Angeles), Mikita (Chicago), Polis (Pittsburgh), J. Johnston (California), MacDonald (Pittsburgh).

Referee-Lloyd Gilmour. Linesmen-Neil Armstrong, John D'Amico.

First period: None. Penalties-Orr, Bergman.

Second period: 1. West, Polis (Clarke, MacDonald) 0:55. 2. East, Robert (Park) 3:56. 3. East, F. Mahovlich (unassisted) 16:27. 4. East, Henderson (P. Esposito, Hodge) 19:12. 5. West, P. Martin (D. Hull, Pappin) 19:29. Penalty-Hodge.

Third period: 6. East, Lemaire (F. Mahovlich) 3:19. 7. West, Polis (unassisted) 4:27. 8. West, Harper (Mikita) 9:27. 9. East, Schmautz (Savard) 13:59. Penalty-White.

Attendance-17,500.

ALL-STAR GAME RECORDS

INDIVIDUAL

Most games played—21, Gordie Howe, Detroit.

Most consecutive games played—13, Maurice Richard, Montreal, 1947 through 1959; Gordie Howe, Detroit, 1957 through 1970.

Most goals, lifetime—10, Gordie Howe, Detroit.

Most goals, one game—3, Ted Lindsay, Detroit, 1950.

Most goals, one period—2, Frank Mahovlich, Toronto, first period, 1963; Andy Bathgate, New York, third period, 1958; Wally Hergesheimer, New York, first period, 1953; Ted Lindsay, Detroit, first period, 1950.

Most assists, lifetime—8, Gordie Howe, Detroit.

Most assists, one game—3, Doug Harvey, Montreal, 1959; Dickie Moore, Montreal, 1958.

Most points, lifetime—18, Gordie Howe, Detroit.

Most points, one game—4, Ted Lindsay, Detroit, 1950; Gordie Howe, Detroit, 1965.

Most penalties, lifetime—11, Gordie Howe, Detroit.

Most penalty minutes, lifetime—25, Gordie Howe, Detroit (10 two-minute minors; 1 five-minute major).

Most penalties, one game—3, Eric Nesterenko, Chicago, 1961; Frank Mahovlich, Toronto, 1961; Marcel Bonin, Montreal, 1954; Jim Thomson, Toronto, 1952; Ken Reardon, Montreal, 1947; Bill Ezinicki, Toronto, 1947; Gus Mortson, Toronto, 1947.

Most penalties, one period—3, Eric Nesterenko, Chicago, second period, 1961.

Fastest goal at start of game—19 seconds, Ted Lindsay, Detroit, 1950.

Most games played by a goalie—13, Glenn Hall, Detroit, Chicago, St. Louis.

Most goals against, one game—6, Terry Sawchuk, Detroit, 1959; Glenn Hall, Chicago, 1958.

Most goals against, one period—4, Jacques Plante, Montreal, first period, 1962; Terry Sawchuk, Detroit, third period, 1959.

TEAM

Most goals, both teams, one game—9, Montreal 6, All-Stars 3, 1958.

Most goals, one team, one game—7, Detroit 1950.

Most goals, one team, one period—4. Montreal, third period, 1959; Toronto, first period, 1962.

Most goals, both teams, one period—5, Toronto 4, All-Star 1, first period, 1962; All-Stars 3, Montreal 2, second period, 1965.

Most penalties, both teams, one game—14, All-Stars 8, Detroit 6, 1954; All-Stars 8, Toronto 6, 1964.

Most penalties, one team, one game—8, All-Stars 1954; All-Stars 1964.

Most penalties, both teams, one period—7, All-Stars 4, Chicago 3, second period, 1961; All-Stars 5, Detroit 2, first period, 1955.

Most penalties, one team, one period—5, All-Stars, first period, 1955.

The Hockey Hall of Fame   HOCKEY HALL OF FAME (TUROFSKY)

Inside the Hall of Fame   HOCKEY HALL OF FAME

X THE HALL OF FAME

On Saturday, Aug. 26, 1961, John F. Diefenbaker, then Prime Minister of Canada, stood on a platform in front of a newly-erected building on the grounds of the Canadian National Exhibition in Toronto.

He was flanked by members of the Hockey Hall of Fame Governing Committee, including Clarence S. Campbell, the president of the National Hockey League.

Diefenbaker walked to the microphone and said, "I now officially proclaim the opening of the Hockey Hall of Fame Building."

The development climaxed several years of frustration and negotiation. Kingston, Ontario, had originally been selected as the site of the shrine at which the NHL officials would perpetuate the memories of the sport's founders, long-time club executives, players and referees.

However, the proposed Kingston project ran into difficulties and, in 1960, an agreement was reached by the National Hockey League, the Canadian National Exhibition and the City of Toronto. The contract stipulated that the NHL would pay for the erection of the Hockey Hall of Fame Building over a period of six to eight years.

It normally takes five years after retirement for a player or a referee to be eligible for membership in the Hockey Hall of Fame. However, the Hall's eligibility requirements stipulate that "in exceptional cases, this period may be shortened by the Hockey Hall of Fame Committee."

Members are divided into three categories, players, referees and builders. The latter group includes league and club executives of the National League plus other professional leagues and amateur circuits. The builders' category also may include those who have helped with the development and the promotion of the sport.

Conn Smythe, former president and owner of the Toronto Maple Leafs, is the chairman of the Hall of Fame Governing Committee which elects builders and referees. Players are elected by the Selection Committee of which Frank J. Selke, the retired managing director of the Montreal Canadiens, is the chairman.

The members:

PLAYERS

John James "Jack" Adams: Star forward for the Toronto Arenas, Toronto St. Pats and Ottawa Senators. Later coached and served as general manager of the Detroit Red Wings.

Hobey Baker was a Princeton immortal who made it to the Hall of Fame even though he never played pro hockey.
HOCKEY HALL OF FAME (TUROFSKY)

Ottawa's Clint Benedict posted 10 Stanley Cup shutouts.   HOCKEY HALL OF FAME

Sylvanus "Syl" Apps: A center who was the first winner of the Calder Trophy as the Rookie of the Year for 1936–37. Played entire big league career with Toronto Maple Leafs.

Donald Bain: Never played professional hockey. Was a standout center for the Winnipeg Victorias, an outstanding amateur team, in the late 1890's and early 1900's.

Hobart "Hobey" Baker: Born in Wissahickon, Pa., he captained Princeton's team to two intercollegiate championships. Later played for St. Nicholas amateur team. Also starred in football.

Martin A. "Marty" Barry: A center on the productive Detroit Red Wing line of the mid-1930's which included Larry Aurie and Herbie Lewis. Also played for New York Americans and Boston Bruins.

Jean Beliveau: Scored 507 goals in 18 seasons with Montreal Canadiens as one of the most highly respected players in hockey history. Played on 10 Stanley Cup championship teams.

Clint Benedict: A goalie on five winning Stanley Cup teams, four with Ottawa and one with the Montreal Maroons. Allowed only three goals in a four-game Cup series while with Maroons in 1926–27.

Douglas Wagner "Doug" Bentley: Left wing on crack Chicago Black Hawk line with brother Max Bentley and Bill Mosienko. Played for Hawks from 1939 to 1951.

Maxwell "Max" Bentley: A clever center and a fine stickhandler for the Chicago Black Hawks and Toronto Maple Leafs. Was voted the circuit's Most Valuable Player in 1945–46.

Hector "Toe" Blake: A left wing for the Montreal Maroons and Montreal Canadiens. Was member of great Canadiens' line that included Maurice Richard and Elmer Lach. Later coached Canadiens to eight Stanley Cup crowns.

Richard "Dickie" Boon: Played for amateur teams in the Montreal area in the late 1890's and for the Montreal Wanderers in 1904 and 1905.

Emile "Butch" Bouchard: A Montreal Canadiens' defenseman for 14 years starting in 1941–42. Named to NHL's first All-Star team three times.

Frank Boucher: A center on the famous New York Ranger line that also included the Cook brothers, Bill and Bun. Winner of record seven Lady Byng Trophies. Also, was a Ranger coach and general manager.

George "Buck" Boucher: An older brother of Frank Boucher, he was a leading defenseman for the Ottawa Senators and Montreal Maroons from 1917 to 1929.

Frank Brimsek: A native of Eveleth, Minn., he was nicknamed "Mr. Zero" because he twice had three consecutive shutouts as a goalie for the Boston Bruins. Starred in the late 1930's and early 1940's.

Russell Bowie: Was a rover for the Montreal Victorias for 10 years in the early 1900's. Had career total of 234 goals.

Turk Broda: A champ in the nets and at the dinner table.   ALEXANDRA STUDIO

Harry L. "Punch" Broadbent: As a forward he played for four Stanley Cup winning teams, three as a member of the Ottawa Senators and one with the Montreal Maroons.

Walter "Turk" Broda: Played goal 16 seasons for the Toronto Maple Leafs. Had reputation for excellence in important games.

Harold "Hugh" Harry Cameron: Was famous for rushes up ice while playing defense for the Toronto Arenas and Toronto St. Pats.

Francis "King" Clancy: Was outstanding scoring defenseman for the Ottawa Senators and Toronto Maple Leafs. Also was an NHL referee and a coach for the Leafs and Montreal Maroons.

Aubry "Dit" Clapper: Played right wing and right defense for the Boston Bruins. Spent 20 years as a player in the NHL and also coached the Bruins for two seasons.

Sprague Cleghorn: A defenseman, he played for Ottawa, Toronto, the Montreal Canadiens and Boston Bruins. Played 18 years as a professional and retired in 1928.

Neil Colville: Center on New York Rangers' standout line of late 1930's and 1940's that included brother Mac Colville and Alex Shibicky. Later played as a defenseman for the Rangers.

William "Bill" Cook: A big, strong sharpshooter from the right wing position, he played for 12 years with the New York Rangers. One of original Rangers, who came into NHL in 1926.

Charlie "Chuck" Conacher: A husky, hard-shooting right wing, he played for 10 years for the Toronto Maple Leafs. Was member of standout line of Conacher-Joe Primeau-Harvey Jackson. Also played for Detroit and New York Americans.

Alex Connell: As a goalie for the Ottawa Senators, he once posted a record 446 minutes and 6 seconds without being scored on. The streak included six consecutive shutouts.

Bill Cowley: A clever center, he starred for the Boston Bruins in the late 1930's and early 1940's. Scored 195 goals in 13 NHL seasons.

Samuel Russell "Rusty" Crawford: A fast-skating forward, he played amateur and professional hockey from 1906 through 1929. Ottawa Senators and Toronto Arenas were among his teams.

John Proctor "Jack" Darragh: A clever stickhandler and a speedy skater from the right wing position, he was also noted for possessing an effective backhand shot. Played mostly for the Ottawa Senators.

Allan "Scotty" Davidson: A rugged, powerful defenseman, he starred for Kingston and Toronto before the formation of the NHL. Was shifted to forward toward the end of his career.

Clarence "Happy" Day: A sound, steady defenseman for 10 years with the Toronto Maple Leafs and later with the New York Americans. Was also an NHL referee plus coach and general manager of the Maple Leafs.

Toronto's Happy Day, first a player, later coached Maple Leafs to five Stanley Cups.   HOCKEY HALL OF FAME

Red Dutton, player, coach and manager of the Americans, was the second president of the NHL.

HOCKEY HALL OF FAME

Cyril "Cy" Denneny: A relatively slow-skating left wing, but he possessed one of the most accurate shots among players of his era. Started pro career in 1914 and later played for Ottawa and the Boston Bruins.

Charles Graham Drinkwater: Starred as an amateur player late in the 19th century. Played on championship teams at McGill University in Montreal and for the Montreal Victorias.

William Ronald "Bill" Durnan: Captured the Vezina Trophy six times, including four in succession, while playing for the Montreal Canadiens. Placed five times on NHL's first All-Star team.

Mervyn "Red" Dutton: Starred as defenseman for Calgary of the Western Canadian League, then for Montreal Maroons and New York Americans of NHL. Was also coach of Americans and served as league president from 1943 to 1945.

Arthur Farrell: A stylish player, he was with the Montreal Shamrocks when they won the Stanley Cup in 1898–99 and the championship of the Canadian Amateur League.

Frank Foyston: Standout in Western Canadian League from 1916 to 1926 while with Seattle and Victoria, compiling 186 goals. Later, played two years for the Detroit Cougars.

Frank Fredrickson: An outstanding amateur player and a star in the Pacific Coast, Western Canadian and National Hockey Leagues. As a center, he played in the NHL for Detroit, Boston and Pittsburgh, also coaching and managing Pittsburgh in 1930–31.

Charles "Chuck" Gardiner: A brilliant goalie for the Chicago Black Hawks for seven consecutive seasons starting in 1928. Twice winner of the Vezina Trophy. Also made first All-Star team twice.

Herbert Martin "Herb" Gardiner: Turned pro at 31 years of age with Calgary of the Western Canadian League. He joined the Montreal Canadiens four years later and was named the league's Most Valuable Player.

James Henry "Jimmy" Gardner: Played for the Montreal Shamrocks, Montreal Wanderers and Montreal Canadiens, the latter for two seasons starting in 1913. Also coached the Hamilton, Ont., team of the NHL in 1924–25.

Bernie Geoffrion: Nicknamed "Boom Boom" for the sound his slap shot made as it crashed against the boards. Produced 393 goals in 16 seasons with New York Rangers and Montreal. Coached Rangers for half a season and then named coach of new Atlanta Flames in 1972.

Eddie Gerard: As a defenseman and captain, he led the Ottawa Senators to three Stanley Cup titles. Coached the Montreal Maroons in 1926 and was manager of the New York Americans in 1931.

Hamilton Livingstone "Billy" Gilmour: Played for the Ottawa Silver Seven, winners of three straight Stanley Cup crowns starting in 1902–03.

Frank "Moose" Goheen: A defenseman born in White Bear, Minn., he played for St. Paul in the U.S. Amateur Association and was a member of the 1920 American Olympic team.

Ebenezer R. "Ebbie" Goodfellow: Started out as a center, but was moved to defense by the Detroit Red Wings. Was named the NHL's Most Valuable Player in 1939–40.

Michael "Mike" Grant: Joined the Montreal Victorias in 1894 when they won the Stanley Cup. Later organized exhibition games in the United States.

Wilfred "Shorty" Green: Was player in senior league in Northern Ontario until he turned pro with the Hamilton Tigers of the NHL in 1923. Later played for the New York Americans.

Silas "Si" Griffis: A defenseman known for his speed, he turned pro with the Kenora Thistles in 1907 when they defeated the Montreal Wanderers for the Stanley Cup. He was also a defenseman and captain for the Vancouver Millionaires, who won the Stanley Cup in 1915.

George Hainsworth: Recorded 22 shutouts during 44-game NHL schedule while with the Montreal Canadiens in 1928–29. Won Vezina Trophy three straight years and later was traded to Toronto.

Joseph Henry "Joe" Hall: Noted as a slambang defenseman. Played for Kenora Thistles, Montreal Shamrocks, Quebec Bulldogs and Montreal Canadiens, the latter in 1918–19.

Douglas Norman "Doug" Harvey: Seven-time winner of the James Norris Trophy as NHL's leading defenseman. Named to All-Star team 11 times in 17 seasons. Played the point on Montreal's awesome power play during the 1950s.

George Hay: Was forward in Western Canada with Winnipeg, Regina and Portland until he joined the Chicago Black Hawks in 1926. Later played for Detroit Cougars and Red Wings.

William Milton "Riley" Hern: Mostly a goalie, but played some as a forward. Starred for the Montreal Wanderers when they won the Stanley Cup in 1907, 1908 and 1910.

Harry "Hap" Holmes: Starred in five professional leagues over a 15-year goaltending career. Played on four Stanley Cup champion teams. Memory is perpetuated by trophy carrying his name awarded to leading goalie in American Hockey League each season.

Charles Thomas "Tom" Hooper: Played as forward for Kenora Thistles starting in 1901. Was on Kenora team which won Stanley Cup by defeating the Montreal Wanderers in January, 1907.

G. Reginald "Red" Horner: A 6–2, 202-pound defenseman, he was rough and tough, and accumulated 1,254 penalty minutes during 12 years with the Toronto Maple Leafs starting in 1928.

Dick Irvin played briefly for Chicago and went on to coaching success at Toronto and Montreal.   HOCKEY HALL OF FAME

Gordie Howe: Holds all-time records for goals, assists and points. Played for 25 years with Detroit Red Wings and was named to the All-Star team in 21 of those years. Six-time scoring champion and six-time winner of the Hart Trophy as MVP.

Sydney Harris "Syd" Howe: A forward, he shares the modern record of six goals in a game made with the Detroit Red Wings in 1944. Spent 16 seasons in the NHL.

John Bower "Bouse" Hutton: Goalie for the Ottawa Silver Seven Cup champions of 1903 and 1904. Also was star goalie in lacrosse.

Harry Hyland: A right winger, he turned pro with the Montreal Shamrocks in 1908–09. Joined the Montreal Wanderers the next year and remained with them until 1918 when he became member of Ottawa Senators.

James Dickenson "Dick" Irvin: Played for Regina and Portland of Western Canadian League and for Chicago Black Hawks of NHL as a forward. Also coached Black Hawks, Toronto and Montreal Canadiens, the latter to three Stanley Cup titles.

Harvey "Busher" Jackson: Gained fame on Toronto's "Kid Line" with Charlie Conacher and Joe Primeau in 1930s. Led Leafs to three NHL titles. Named to five All-Star teams and won scoring title in 1932–33. Finished career with New York Americans and Boston Bruins.

Ivan "Ching" Johnson: Was one of the original New York Rangers in 1926–27. A defenseman who relished delivering hard bodychecks, he played in the NHL for 12 years, the last with the New York Americans.

Ernie "Moose" Johnson: Played for Montreal Wanderers until 1910 when moved to New Westminster of Pacific Coast League. Was defenseman throughout most of career, but also played forward.

Aurel Joliat: A 140-pound left wing, he played on a line with the great Howie Morenz for the Montreal Canadiens. Was exceptionally fast and clever. Started 16-year career with Canadiens in 1922.

Gordon "Duke" Keats: A forward, he was a long-time star in the Western Canadian League, mostly with Edmonton. Later played for Boston, Detroit and Chicago of NHL.

Theodore "Ted" Kennedy: As a center, he sparked the Toronto Maple Leafs to five Stanley Cup championships. Also was team captain from 1948 until retirement in 1955.

Elmer James Lach: Was center on line with Maurice Richard in 1944–45 when the Rocket scored a record 50 goals in 50 games. Played for Montreal Canadiens for 14 years, three times being voted to league's first All-Star team.

Edouard "Newsy" Lalonde: Started pro career with Cornwall in 1905 and was one of finest scorers and roughest players of his era. Played with Montreal Canadiens of NHL and with other teams in the National Association and Pacific Coast Leagues.

Jean Baptiste "Jack" Loviolette: Played both as a forward and a defense-man for the Montreal Canadiens from 1909 to 1918. He had outstanding speed. Played on a line with Newsy Lalonde.

Hughie Lehman: A professional goalie for 19 years. Standout in Pacific Coast League for New Westminster and Vancouver. Played for Chicago Black Hawks in 1926–27, their first season in NHL.

Percy LeSueur: Goalie for the Ottawa Senators from 1906 to 1913. Played for Toronto in 1914 and later coached Hamilton team of the NHL.

R.B. Theodore "Ted" Lindsay: Aggressive, combative, productive left wing for Detroit Red Wings. One of the highest career scorers at his position. Emerged from four-year retirement as player in 1964–65 and helped Wings win league title.

Duncan "Mickey" MacKay: Played forward for the Vancouver Millionaires from 1914 to 1926. He joined the Chicago Black Hawks in 1926–27 and later played for Pittsburgh and Boston of the NHL.

Joe Malone: Scored 44 goals during 22-game schedule in 1917–18, his first NHL season with the Montreal Canadiens. Holds NHL record of seven goals in a Stanley Cup game. Starred in several other leagues before joining Canadiens.

Sylvio Mantha: Played defense for the Montreal Canadiens for 13 years starting in 1923–24. Team finished in first place nine times during that period. Was player-coach for Boston Bruins in 1936.

Jack Marshall: Played for the Montreal Wanderers when they won the Stanley Cup in 1906, 1908 and 1910. Was captain of Toronto team which won Cup in 1914.

Fred G. "Steamer" Maxwell: A star amateur who never became a professional, his position was that of rover when each team consisted of seven players. Played senior hockey in Winnipeg starting in 1909. Later became a coach of amateur and professional teams.

Frank McGee: A forward for the Ottawa Silver Seven. In a Stanley Cup game against Dawson City in 1905, he scored 14 goals, including eight in succession during a span of eight minutes and 20 seconds.

William George "Billy" McGimsie: Was a center for 10 years for the Kenora Thistles. Played in several Stanley Cup series against the Montreal Wanderers and Ottawa Silver Seven, the first in 1903.

George McNamara: Helped the Toronto team win the Stanley Cup in 1914 while playing defense. Before that he was with the Montreal Wanderers and with Waterloo of the Trolley League.

Patrick Joseph "Paddy" Moran: A stand-up goalie who used his stick to good advantage, he turned pro with the Quebec Bulldogs in 1902. Played for Haileybury in 1911, but returned to Quebec and helped the Bulldogs win the Stanley Cup in 1912 and 1913.

Howie Morenz: A flashy, dynamic center, he starred for 14 years in the NHL, mostly with the Montreal Canadiens. Montreal traded him to Chicago in 1934 and he moved to the New York Rangers in 1935 before returning to the Canadiens for the 1936–37 campaign.

Boston's Harry Oliver weighed only 155 pounds. HOCKEY HALL OF FAME

William "Bill" Mosienko: Best remembered for scoring three goals in record 21 seconds while playing for Chicago against the New York Rangers on March 23, 1952. Was right wing on line with Bentley brothers, Max and Doug.

Frank Nighbor: A center, he played pro hockey in leagues in Eastern and Western Canada from 1915 to 1929. Starred for Vancouver Millionaires and Ottawa Senators. Scored 41 goals in 20 games in 1916–17.

Reginald "Reg" Noble: Primarily a left wing, but played some defense for Toronto Arenas, Toronto St. Pats, Montreal Maroons and Detroit Cougars. Helped Maroons win Stanley Cup in 1925–26.

Harold "Harry" Oliver: Played as a forward for 11 NHL seasons for the Boston Bruins and New York Americans. Weighed only 155 pounds and rarely was penalized. Helped Bruins win two Stanley Cup crowns.

Lester Patrick: Patriarch of famous hockey family, he was an outstanding player for the Montreal Wanderers and Renfrew Millionaires. He helped form the Pacific Coast League and, in 1926, came East to coach and manage the New York Rangers in their first NHL season. Remained with Rangers until 1946.

Tommy Phillips: Was a hard-shooting, slick stickhandling forward for the Kenora Thistles. In 1906, he scored seven goals in a two-game Stanley Cup series against the Montreal Wanderers.

Didier "Pit" Pitre: Joined the Montreal Canadiens in 1909 and was noted for his blistering shot. A 200-pound forward, he played for the Canadiens until 1923 when he retired.

Walter "Babe" Pratt: A defenseman, he began pro career with New York Rangers in January, 1936, and was traded to Toronto in November, 1942. A standout offensive player for a rearguard.

A. Joseph "Joe" Primeau: Center for famous Kid Line that included Charlie Conacher and Harvey Jackson. A clever stickhandler and play-maker and an excellent penalty killer for the Toronto Maple Leafs.

Harvey Pulford: Played defense for the Ottawa Silver Seven from 1893 to 1908. Was one of the most effective bodycheckers of his era, and had reputation for being a clean player.

Frank Rankin: Played rover position when each team played with seven men. Starred for teams in Stratford, Ont. and Toronto beginning in 1906–07 season.

Claude Earl "Chuck" Rayner: Played 10 seasons in the NHL, all of them in New York. Had 25 career shutouts and was named to All-Star team three times. Named winner of the Hart Trophy as Most Valuable Player in 1949–50, the second goalie ever to win that award.

Kenneth "Ken" Reardon: A rugged, fearless defenseman for the Montreal Canadiens starting in 1940–41. Voted to the NHL All-Star team four times. Later, was a front office executive for the Canadiens.

Maurice "Rocket" Richard: The famed Montreal Canadiens' right wing, whose 544 career goals stood as the record until broken by Detroit's Gordie Howe. Played 18 NHL seasons before retiring after the 1959–60 campaign. Voted into the Hall only nine months after retirement in September, 1960.

George Richardson: Never a professional, but an outstanding amateur from Kingston, Ont. Was with Queen's University team which won the Allan Cup in 1909.

Gordon Roberts: Played for Montreal Wanderers while attending McGill University and studying medicine. When he graduated, he moved west to practice but continued playing hockey. Set an all-time scoring record in Pacific Coast Hockey Association with 43 goals in 23 games.

Arthur Howey "Art" Ross: Turned pro with the Kenora Thistles in 1906. Also played for Haileybury and the Montreal Wanderers. Later was coach and general manager of the Boston Bruins.

Blair Russell: A left wing amateur star for the Montreal Victorias in the early 1900's. On February 23, 1905, he scored six goals in one game.

Ernie Russell: Top scorer for the Montreal Wanderers, for whom he scored 32 goals during a 12-game regular-season schedule in 1910.

J.D. "Jack" Ruttan: A leading amateur player starting in 1905–06 with the Armstrong's Point team of Winnipeg. Also played in the Manitoba University League and the Winnipeg Senior League.

Terry Sawchuk: Considered one of greatest goalies in history. Played more seasons, more games and had more shutouts than any other net-minder. Finished career with 103 shutouts, only goalie ever to reach the century mark.

Bullet Joe Simpson was a New York Americans' defenseman and manager.
HOCKEY HALL OF FAME

Eddie Shore was one of hockey's most dashing figures. HOCKEY HALL OF FAME

Fred Scanlan: A forward for the Montreal Shamrocks, winners of the Stanley Cup in 1898–99 and 1899–1900. Known for his clever play and accurate shot.

Milton Conrad "Milt" Schmidt: A strong skater, smart stickhandler and prolific scorer, he centered Boston's famous Kraut line that also included Bobby Bauer and Woody Dumart.

David "Sweeney" Schriner: A left winger, he starred for the New York Americans and Toronto Maple Leafs. Twice won the NHL's scoring title, in 1935–36 and 1936–37.

Earl Walter Seibert: Was noted for his ability as a rushing defenseman for the New York Rangers, Chicago Black Hawks and Detroit Red Wings. Voted to circuit's first All-Star team four times.

Oliver Levi Seibert: Earl Seibert's father. Was member of the Berlin Rangers, winners of the Western Ontario Association title six straight years from 1900 to 1906. Was a forward during most of his career.

Edward "Eddie" Shore: Generally regarded as the greatest defenseman of all time. Played for the the Boston Bruins for 13½ years, then was traded to the New York Americans for whom he played a half season.

Albert "Babe" Siebert: Was outstanding left wing for Montreal Maroons. Switched to defense in the mid-1930s and continued to star with the New York Rangers, Boston Bruins and Montreal Canadiens.

Harold "Bullet Joe" Simpson: A fast-skating defenseman, he played for teams in Winnipeg and Edmonton before joining the New York Americans in 1925. Was general manager of the Americans from 1932 to 1935.

Alfred E. "Alf" Smith: Was captain of the Ottawa Silver Seven in 1903, 1904 and 1905. Also captained the Pittsburgh Athletic Club in 1909, his final year as a player.

Thomas Smith: An early era star, played for three Stanley Cup champion teams before formation of National Hockey League. Won three scoring titles and twice scored nine goals in a single game. Also had an eight-goal game, a six-goal game and five times scored five goals in a game.

Russell "Barney" Stanley: A forward for the Stanley Cup winning Vancouver Millionaires in the 1914–15 season. Was named general manager-coach of the Chicago Black Hawks in 1927.

John "Black Jack" Stewart: A defense star for the Detroit Red Wings for 10 years starting in 1938–39. Named to the league's first All-Star team three times.

Nelson "Nels" Stewart: A forward, he held the career scoring record of 324 goals until it was broken by Maurice Richard. Starred for the Montreal Maroons, Boston Bruins and New York Americans.

Bruce Stuart: A center, he played for the Portage Lakes team of Houghton, Michigan, in the early 1900's. Later played for the Montreal Wanderers and the Ottawa Silver Seven.

Hod Stuart: A brother of Bruce Stuart, he also played in Houghton, Michigan and for the Montreal Wanderers. Was a defenseman.

Fred "Cyclone" Taylor: A high-scoring forward for teams in Houghton, Michigan, Ottawa, Renfrew and Vancouver. He was a whirlwind on the ice and is reported to have scored a goal once while skating backwards.

Cecil "Tiny" Thompson: Was a goalie in the NHL for 12 seasons, 10 for the Boston Bruins and two for the Detroit Red Wings. Twice was voted to the league's first All-Star team.

Harry Trihey: Starred for McGill University and as a captain for the Montreal Shamrocks when the latter team won two Stanley Cup titles.

Georges Vezina: Turned pro as a goalie with the Montreal Canadiens in 1910 and played with them until November, 1925. Died of tuberculosis the following year. Trophy for the goalies is awarded annually in his memory.

John Phillip "Jack" Walker: Credited with having originated the hook check. Starred mostly on the West Coast for teams in Seattle and Victoria. Also played for Detroit in 1926–27 and 1927–28.

Martin "Marty" Walsh: Played for Ottawa in the Eastern Canada Amateur Association starting in 1908. Was leading scorer of the National Association for three seasons.

Harry Watson: Played all three forward positions on crack amateur teams, including the Toronto Granites. Was with the Granites in 1924 when they represented Canada and won the Olympic title.

Ralph "Cooney" Weiland: Played 11 seasons in NHL. Twice a member of Stanley Cup champions, he coached Boston to another Cup in 1940–41. After leaving pros, launched a long, successful coaching career at Harvard University.

Harry Westwick: Was a rover for the Ottawa Silver Seven when they won three consecutive Stanley Cup titles in the early 1900's.

Fred Whitcroft: A prolific scorer, he played for the Kenora Thistles and Peterborough Colts. Later played for Edmonton where he scored 49 goals in 1908.

Gordon Allan "Phat" Wilson: Ranked among the all-time great amateur players. Was the one of the stars of teams in Port Arthur, Ont., from 1918 to 1933.

REFEREES

William L. "Bill" Chadwick: A native New Yorker, he officiated NHL games for 16 years. Introduced hand signals to explain penalties such as holding and tripping.

Chaucer Elliott: Started refereeing in 1903 and worked in the Ontario Hockey Association for 10 seasons.

Robert W. "Bobby" Hewitson: An NHL referee for almost 10 years until 1934. Later he became secretary and curator of the Hockey Hall of Fame.

Fred J. "Mickey" Ion: Was a leading official in amateur leagues and in the Pacific Coast and National Hockey Leagues until 1943.

Michael J. "Mike" Rodden: Refereed 1,187 NHL games and 1,677 in other leagues.

J. Cooper Smeaton: Was referee-in-chief of the NHL until 1937. Also officiated in amateur leagues and in the National Hockey Association.

Roy A. "Red" Storey: An NHL referee from 1951 until he resigned on April 11, 1959. Worked more than 2,000 games in various circuits.

Frank Udvari: Only the eighth referee elected to the Hall of Fame and the first in nine years when he was named in 1973. Officiated through 1966 and has been a supervisor of officials for league ever since.

BUILDERS

Charles F. Adams: Organizer of the Boston Bruins in 1924, first American team in the National Hockey League. Also negotiated for the erection of the Boston Garden.

Weston W. Adams, Sr.: Longtime president and chairman of the board of both the Boston Bruins and Boston Garden. Was a goalie at Harvard when his father, Charles F. Adams, was awarded Boston franchise, first NHL franchise in United States.

Frank Ahearn: A director, president and owner of the Ottawa Senators. Became president in 1922 and held that position until 1934 when the franchise was transferred to St. Louis.

Sir Montagu Allan: A Montreal financier and sportsman, he presented the Allan Cup for competition in 1908. The trophy is emblematic of the Senior Amateur Championship of Canada.

George V. Brown: A pioneer of hockey in the United States. Organized the Boston Athletic Association hockey team and was the manager of the Boston Arena and Boston Garden.

Walter A. Brown: President of the Boston Bruins and general manager of Boston Garden. Also coached the Boston Olympics to five U.S. national titles between 1930 and 1940.

Frank Calder: First president of the National Hockey League. Served from 1917 until his death in February, 1943. Trophy in his memory is awarded annually to outstanding rookie player.

Angus Daniel Campbell: Played an important part in the development of amateur hockey in Cobalt, Ont., area. Was the first president of the Northern Ontario Association which was formed in 1919.

Clarence S. Campbell: President of the National Hockey League from September, 1946 to the present. Earlier was an NHL referee.

Joseph "Leo" Dandurand: Was among three persons who purchased the Montreal Canadiens in November, 1921. He later coached the Canadiens. Was a delegate to the organizing meeting in 1914 of the Canadian Amateur Hockey Association.

Frank Dilio: A president and secretary of the Junior Amateur Hockey Association. Later, served as registrar and secretary of the Quebec Amateur Hockey Association until 1962.

George Dudley: Was president of the Canadian Amateur Hockey Association, the Ontario Hockey Association and the International Ice Hockey Federation. Headed the hockey section of the 1960 Olympic Games.

Jimmie Dunn: A leading administrator and executive of junior teams and leagues in Western Canada.

Thomas Patrick Gorman: Among the founders of the National Hockey League. Coached or managed seven Stanley Cup winning teams while with the Montreal Canadiens and Maroons, Ottawa Senators and Chicago Black Hawks.

Jim Hendy: President of the United States League and later general manager of the Cleveland Barons of the American League. Published the "Hockey Guide," a leading statistical compendium in the early 1930's.

William Archibald Hewitt: A secretary of the Ontario Hockey Association and a secretary and registrar for the Canadian Amateur Association. Was also a sports editor of the Toronto Star.

Foster William Hewitt: A hockey broadcaster since 1923. Renowned for his exciting descriptions of games involving the Toronto Maple Leafs.

Fred J. Hume: A leading amateur hockey executive in Western Canada. Later, helped develop the New Westminster professional team and the Western Hockey League.

General John Reed Kilpatrick: President of the New York Rangers and Madison Square Garden for 22 years. Also served on the Board of Governors of the NHL.

Thomas F. Lockhart: Organizer and president of the Amateur Hockey Association of the United States and the Eastern Hockey League. Was also a business manager of the New York Rangers.

Paul Loicq: A native of Belgium, he was a president of the International Ice Hockey Federation. Credited with having helped influence the Winter Olympic Games Committee to include hockey on the program.

Major Frederic McLaughlin: Pioneered professional hockey in Chicago. Was an owner and the first president of the Black Hawks and nicknamed the team in honor of the Black Hawk division he commanded during World War I.

Sen. Hartland de Montarville Molson: Former owner of the Montreal Canadiens, elected in the builder's category.

Francis Nelson: A vice-president of the Ontario Hockey Association and an OHA Governor to the Amateur Athletic Union of Canada.

James Norris: He purchased Detroit's NHL franchise in 1933 and changed the name of the team from the Falcons to the Red Wings. He was also an owner of the Detroit Olympia and Chicago Stadium.

James D. Norris: Became a co-owner of the Chicago Black Hawks in 1946 after helping his father, James Norris Sr., with the administrative duties of the Detroit Red Wings.

William M. Northey: President of the Montreal Amateur Athletic Association and a managing director of the Montreal Forum. Was the first trustee of the Allan Cup when it was presented for amateur competition.

John Ambrose O'Brien: Helped with the formation of the National Hockey Association in December, 1909, a five-team league which included the Montreal Canadiens and the Montreal Wanderers.

Frank Patrick: With his brother, Lester Patrick, he played for the famed Renfrew Millionaires. The two later organized the Pacific Coast League. Frank also coached the Boston Bruins and was a general manager of the Montreal Canadiens.

Allan W. Pickard: An executive for several teams and leagues in Western Canada. He was a president of the Saskatchewan Amateur Association and the Canadian Amateur Association.

Lord Stanley of Preston: As Governor General of Canada in 1893, he donated the Stanley Cup to the championship hockey club of the Dominion.

Senator Donat Raymond: A president of the Montreal Maroons and Montreal Canadiens, he headed the Canadian Arena Company which financed the construction of the Montreal Forum in 1924.

John Ross Robertson: A member of the Canadian Parliament, he donated trophies to the winners of the senior, intermediate and junior divisions of the Ontario Hockey Association.

Claude C. Robinson: Was the first secretary of the Canadian Amateur Association and managed the Canadian team in the 1932 Olympic Games.

Frank J. Selke: Worked as coach, manager and front office executive for almost 60 years. Was with the Toronto Maple Leafs in various capacities before becoming managing director of the Montreal Canadiens in 1946.

Frank D. Smith: A founder in 1911 and later secretary-treasurer of the Beaches Hockey League, now known as the Toronto Hockey League.

Conn Smythe: Long-time, fiery president of the Toronto Maple Leafs. Was instrumental in the building of Maple Leaf Gardens which was opened in November, 1931.

Captain James T. Sutherland: An organizer of teams and leagues in the Kingston, Ont., area, he coached the Kingston Junior team and served as president of the Ontario Hockey Association and the Canadian Amateur Hockey Association.

Lloyd Turner: Helped organize the Western Canadian League in 1918. Coached and managed the Fort William, Ont., team and was a founder of teams and leagues in Calgary, Alta.

Fred Waghorne: A native of England, he was among the founders of the Toronto Hockey League. As a referee, he was responsible for introducing a whistle for stopping play during a game. A bell had been used previously.

Arthur M. Wirtz: Got into the hockey business in 1931 when, in partnership with James Norris, Sr., he bought Detroit Red Wings. Switched holdings to native Chicago in 1954 where he rebuilt Black Hawks into one of NHL's most prosperous franchises.

XI NHL RECORDS

(Courtesy of the National Hockey League)

STANDINGS AND SCORING LEADERS
1917-18
FINAL STANDINGS
First Half

	W	L	T	PTS	GF	GA
Montreal Canadiens	10	4	0	20	81	47
Toronto	8	6	0	16	71	75
Ottawa	5	9	0	10	67	79
X–Montreal Wanderers....	1	5	0	2	17	35

X–Forced to withdraw from league after home rink burned down on January 2, 1918.

Second Half

	W	L	T	PTS	GF	GA
Toronto	5	3	0	10	37	34
Ottawa	4	4	0	8	35	35
Montreal C.	3	5	0	6	34	37

Toronto defeated Montreal Canadiens in playoffs and won regular-season championship.

XX–*Leading Scorers*	G
Malone, Mtl. C.	44
Denneny, Ott.	36
Noble, Tor.	28
Lalonde, Mtl. C.	23
Denneny, Tor.	20
Pitre, Mtl. C.	17
Cameron, Tor.	17
Darragh, Ott.	14
Hyland, Mtl. W.-Ott.	14
Gerard, Ott.	13
Skinner, Tor.	13

XX–No records of assists were compiled.

1918-19
FINAL STANDINGS
First Half

	W	L	T	PTS	GF	GA
Montreal	7	3	0	14	57	50
Ottawa	5	5	0	10	39	40
Toronto	3	7	0	6	43	49

Second Half

	W	L	T	PTS	GF	GA
Ottawa	7	1	0	14	32	14
Montreal	3	5	0	6	31	28
Toronto	2	6	0	4	22	43

Montreal defeated Ottawa in playoffs and won regular season championship.

Leading Scorers	G	A	Pts
Lalonde, Mtl.	23	9	32
Cleghorn, Mtl.	23	6	29
Nighbor, Ott.	18	4	22
Denneny, Ott.	18	4	22
Pitre, Mtl.	14	4	18
Skinner, Tor.	12	3	15
Noble, Tor.	11	3	14
Cameron, Tor.-Ott.	11	3	14
Darragh, Ott.	12	1	13
Randall, Tor.	7	6	13

1919–20
FINAL STANDINGS
First Half

	W	L	T	PTS	GF	GA
Ottawa	9	3	0	18	59	23
Montreal	8	4	0	16	62	51
Toronto	5	7	0	10	52	62
Quebec	2	10	0	4	44	81

Second Half

	W	L	T	PTS	GF	GA
Ottawa	10	2	0	20	62	41
Toronto	7	5	0	14	67	44
Montreal	5	7	0	10	67	62
Quebec	2	10	0	4	47	96

Leading Scorers	G	A	Pts
Malone, Que.	39	9	48
Lalonde, Mtl.	36	6	42
Denneny, Tor.	23	12	35
Nighbor, Ott.	26	7	33
Noble, Tor.	24	7	31
Darragh, Ott.	22	5	27
Arbour, Mtl.	22	4	26
Wilson, Tor.	21	5	26
Broadbent, Ott.	19	4	23
Cleghorn, Mtl.	19	3	22
Pitre, Mtl.	15	7	22

1920–21
FINAL STANDINGS
First Half

	W	L	T	PTS	GF	GA
Ottawa	8	2	0	16	49	23
Toronto	5	5	0	10	39	47
Montreal	4	6	0	8	37	51
Hamilton	3	7	0	6	34	38

Second Half

	W	L	T	PTS	GF	GA
Toronto	10	4	0	20	66	53
Montreal	9	5	0	18	75	48
Ottawa	6	8	0	12	48	52
Hamilton	3	11	0	6	58	94

Ottawa defeated Toronto in playoffs and won regular season championship.

Leading Scorers	G	A	Pts
Lalonde, Mtl.	33	8	41
Denneny, Ott.	34	5	39
Dye, Tor.	35	2	37
Malone, Ham.	30	4	34
Cameron, Tor.	18	9	27
Noble, Tor.	20	6	26
Prodgers, Ham.	18	8	26
Denneny, Tor.	17	6	23
Nighbor, Ott.	18	3	21
Berlinquette, Mtl.	12	9	21

1921–22
FINAL STANDINGS

	W	L	T	PTS	GF	GA
Ottawa	14	8	2	30	106	84
Toronto	13	10	1	27	98	97
Montreal C.	12	11	1	25	88	94
Hamilton	7	17	0	14	88	105

Toronto defeated Ottawa in playoffs and won regular season championship.

Leading Scorers	G	A	Pts
Broadbent, Ott.	32	14	46
Denneny, Ott.	27	12	39
Dye, Tor.	30	7	37
Malone, Ham.	25	7	32
Cameron, Tor.	19	8	27
Denneny, Tor.	19	7	26
Noble, Tor.	17	8	25
S. Cleghorn, Mtl. C.	21	3	24
O. Cleghorn, Mtl. C.	17	7	24
Reise, Ham.	9	14	23

1922–23
FINAL STANDINGS

	W	L	T	PTS	GF	GA
Ottawa	14	9	1	29	77	54
Montreal C.	13	9	2	28	73	61
Toronto	13	10	1	27	82	88
Hamilton	6	18	0	12	81	110

Ottawa defeated Montreal Canadiens in playoffs and won regular season championship.

Leading Scorers	G	A	Pts
Dye, Tor.	26	11	37
Denneny, Ott.	21	10	31
Adams, Tor.	19	9	28
B. Boucher, Mtl. C.	23	4	27
O. Cleghorn, Mtl. C.	19	7	26
Roach, Ham.	17	8	25
G. Boucher, Ott.	15	9	24
Joliat, Mtl. C.	13	9	22
Noble, Tor.	12	10	22
Wilson, Ham.	16	3	19

1923–24
FINAL STANDINGS

	W	L	T	PTS	GF	GA
Ottawa	16	8	0	32	74	54
Montreal C.	13	11	0	26	59	48
Toronto	10	14	0	20	59	85
Hamilton	9	15	0	18	63	68

Montreal defeated Ottawa in playoffs and won regular season championship.

Leading Scorers	G	A	Pts
Denneny, Ott.	22	1	23
B. Boucher, Mtl. C.	16	6	22
Joliat, Mtl. C.	15	5	20
Dye, Tor.	17	2	19
G. Boucher, Ott.	14	5	19
Burch, Ham.	16	2	18
Clancy, Ott.	9	8	17
Morenz, Mtl. C.	13	3	16
Adams, Tor.	13	3	16
Noble, Tor.	12	3	15

1924–25
FINAL STANDINGS

	W	L	T	PTS	GF	GA
Hamilton	19	10	1	39	90	60
Toronto	19	11	0	38	90	84
Montreal C.	17	11	2	36	93	56
Ottawa	17	12	1	35	83	66
Montreal M.	9	19	2	20	45	65
Boston	6	24	0	12	49	119

Montreal Canadiens defeated Toronto and Hamilton in playoffs and won the regular season title.

Leading Scorers	G	A	Pts
Dye, Tor.	38	6	44
Denneny, Ott.	27	15	42
Joliat, Mtl. C.	29	11	40
Morenz, Mtl. C.	27	7	34
B. Boucher, Mtl. C.	18	13	31
Adams, Tor.	21	8	29
Burch, Ham.	20	4	24
R. Green, Ham.	19	4	23
Day, Tor.	10	12	22
Herberts, Bos.	17	5	22

1925–26
FINAL STANDINGS

	W	L	T	PTS	GF	GA
Ottawa	24	8	4	52	77	42
Montreal M.	20	11	5	45	91	73
Pittsburgh	19	16	1	39	82	70
Boston	17	15	4	38	92	85
New York A.	12	20	4	28	68	89
Toronto	12	21	3	27	92	114
Montreal C.	11	24	1	23	79	108

Leading Scorers	G	A	Pts
Stewart, Mtl. M.	34	8	42
Denneny, Ott.	24	12	36
Herberts, Bos.	26	5	31
Cooper, Bos.	28	3	31
Morenz, Mtl. C.	23	3	26
Joliat, Mtl. C.	17	9	26
Adams, Tor.	21	5	26
Burch, N.Y.A.	22	3	25
Smith, Ott.	16	9	25
Nighbor, Ott.	12	13	25

1926–27
FINAL STANDINGS
Canadian Division

	W	L	T	PTS	GF	GA
Ottawa	30	10	4	64	86	69
Montreal C.	28	14	2	58	99	67
Montreal M.	20	20	4	44	71	68
New York A.	17	25	2	36	82	91
Toronto	15	24	5	35	79	94

American Division

	W	L	T	PTS	GF	GA
New York R.	25	13	6	56	95	72
Boston	21	20	3	45	97	89
Chicago	19	22	3	41	115	116
Pittsburgh	15	26	3	33	79	108
Detroit	12	28	4	28	76	105

Leading Scorers	G	A	Pts
Bill Cook, N.Y.R.	33	4	37
Irvin, Chi.	18	18	36
Morenz, Mtl. C.	25	7	32
Frederickson, Det-Bos.	18	13	31
Dye, Chi.	25	5	30
Bailey, Tor.	15	13	28
Boucher, N.Y.R.	13	15	28
Burch, N.Y.A.	19	8	27
Oliver, Bos.	18	6	24
Keats, Bos-Det.	16	8	24

1927–28
FINAL STANDINGS
Canadian Division

	W	L	T	PTS	GF	GA
Montreal C.	26	11	7	59	116	48
Montreal M.	24	14	6	54	96	77
Ottawa	20	14	10	50	78	57
Toronto	18	18	8	44	89	88
New York A.	11	27	6	28	63	128

American Division

	W	L	T	PTS	GF	GA
Boston	20	13	11	51	77	70
New York R.	19	16	9	47	94	79
Pittsburgh	19	17	8	46	67	76
Detroit	19	19	6	44	88	79
Chicago	7	34	3	17	68	134

Leading Scorers	G	A	Pts
Morenz, Mtl. C.	33	18	51
Joliat, Mtl. C.	28	11	39
Boucher, N.Y.R.	23	12	35
Hay, Det.	22	13	35
Stewart, Mtl. M.	27	7	34
Gagne, Mtl. C.	20	10	30
Bun Cook, N.Y.R.	14	14	28
Carson, Tor.	20	6	26
Finnigan, Ott.	20	5	25
Bill Cook, N.Y.R.	18	6	24
Keats, Chi.-Det.	14	10	24

1928–29
FINAL STANDINGS
Canadian Division

	W	L	T	PTS	GF	GA
Montreal C.	22	7	15	59	71	43
New York A.	19	13	12	50	53	53
Toronto	21	18	5	47	85	69
Ottawa	14	17	13	41	54	67
Montreal M.	15	20	9	39	67	65

American Division

	W	L	T	PTS	GF	GA
Boston	26	13	5	57	89	52
New York R.	21	13	10	52	72	65
Detroit	19	16	9	47	72	63
Pittsburgh	9	27	8	26	46	80
Chicago	7	29	8	22	33	85

Leading Scorers	G	A	Pts
Bailey, Tor.	22	10	32
Stewart, Mtl. M.	21	8	29
Cooper, Det.	18	9	27
Morenz, Mtl. C.	17	10	27
Blair, Tor.	12	15	27
Boucher, N.Y.R.	10	16	26
Oliver, Bos.	17	6	23
Bill Cook, N.Y.R.	15	8	23
Ward, Mtl. M.	14	8	22
Finnigan, Ott.	15	4	19

1929–30
FINAL STANDINGS
Canadian Division

	W	L	T	PTS	GF	GA
Montreal M.	23	16	5	51	141	114
Montreal C.	21	14	9	51	142	114
Ottawa	21	15	8	50	138	118
Toronto	17	21	6	40	116	124
New York A.	14	25	5	33	113	161

American Division

	W	L	T	PTS	GF	GA
Boston	38	5	1	77	179	98
Chicago	21	18	5	47	117	111
New York R.	17	17	10	44	136	143
Detroit	14	24	6	34	117	133
Pittsburgh	5	36	3	13	102	185

Leading Scorers	G	A	Pts
Weiland, Bos.	43	30	73
Boucher, N.Y.R.	26	36	62
Clapper, Bos.	41	20	61
Bill Cook, N.Y.R.	29	30	59
Kilrea, Ott.	36	22	58
Stewart, Mtl. M.	39	16	55
Morenz, Mtl. C.	40	10	50
Himes, N.Y.A.	28	22	50
Lamb, Ott.	29	20	49
Gainor, Bos.	18	31	49

1930–31
FINAL STANDINGS
Canadian Division

	W	L	T	PTS	GF	GA
Montreal C.	26	10	8	60	129	89
Toronto	22	13	9	53	118	99
Montreal M.	20	18	6	46	105	106
New York A.	18	16	10	46	76	74
Ottawa	10	30	4	24	91	142

American Division

	W	L	T	PTS	GF	GA
Boston	28	10	6	62	143	90
Chicago	24	17	3	51	108	78
New York R.	19	16	9	47	106	87
Detroit	16	21	7	39	102	105
Philadelphia	4	36	4	12	76	184

Leading Scorers	G	A	Pts
Morenz, Mtl. C.	28	23	51
Goodfellow, Det.	25	23	48
Conacher, Tor.	31	12	43
Bill Cook, N.Y.R.	30	12	42
Bailey, Tor.	23	19	42
Primeau, Tor.	9	32	41
Stewart, Mtl. M.	25	14	39
Boucher, N.Y.R.	12	27	39
Weiland, Bos.	25	13	38
Bun Cook, N.Y.R.	18	17	35
Joliat, Mtl. C.	13	22	35

1931–32
FINAL STANDINGS
Canadian Division

	W	L	T	PTS	GF	GA
Montreal C.	25	16	7	57	128	111
Toronto	23	18	7	53	155	127
Montreal	19	22	7	45	142	139
New York A.	16	24	8	40	95	142

American Division

	W	L	T	PTS	GF	GA
New York R.	23	17	8	54	134	112
Chicago	18	19	11	47	86	101
Detroit	18	20	10	46	95	108
Boston	15	21	12	42	122	117

Leading Scorers	G	A	Pts
Jackson, Tor.	28	25	53
Primeau, Tor.	13	37	50
Morenz, Mtl. C.	24	25	49
Bill Cook, N.Y.R.	34	14	48
Conacher, Tor.	34	14	48
Trottier, Mtl. M.	26	18	44
Smith, Mtl. M.	11	33	44
Siebert, Mtl. M.	21	18	39
Clapper, Bos.	17	22	39
Joliat, Mtl. C.	15	24	39

1932–33
FINAL STANDINGS
Canadian Division

	W	L	T	PTS	GF	GA
Toronto	24	18	6	54	119	111
Montreal M.	22	20	6	50	135	119
Montreal C.	18	25	5	41	92	115
New York A.	15	22	11	41	91	118
Ottawa	11	27	10	32	88	131

American Division

	W	L	T	PTS	GF	GA
Boston	25	15	8	58	124	88
Detroit	25	15	8	58	111	93
New York R.	23	17	8	54	135	107
Chicago	16	20	12	44	88	101

Leading Scorers	G	A	Pts
Bill Cook, N.Y.R.	28	22	50
Jackson, Tor.	27	17	44
Northcott, Mtl. M.	22	21	43
Smith, Mtl. M.	20	21	41
Haynes, Mtl. M.	16	25	41
Joliat, Mtl. C.	18	21	39
Barry, Bos.	24	13	37
Bun Cook, N.Y.R.	22	15	37
Stewart, Bos.	18	18	36
Morenz, Mtl. C.	14	21	35

1933–34
FINAL STANDINGS
Canadian Division

	W	L	T	PTS	GF	GA
Toronto	26	13	9	61	174	119
Montreal C.	22	20	6	50	99	101
Montreal M.	19	18	11	49	117	122
New York A.	15	23	10	40	104	132
Ottawa	13	29	6	32	115	143

American Division

	W	L	T	PTS	GF	GA
Detroit	24	14	10	58	113	98
Chicago	20	17	11	51	88	83
New York R.	21	19	8	50	120	113
Boston	18	25	5	41	111	130

Leading Scorers	G	A	Pts
Conacher, Tor.	32	20	52
Primeau, Tor.	14	32	46
Boucher, N.Y.R.	14	30	44
Barry, Bos.	27	12	39
Dillon, N.Y.R.	13	26	39
Stewart, Bos.	21	17	38
Jackson, Tor.	20	18	38
Joliat, Mtl. C.	22	15	37
Smith, Mtl. M.	18	19	37
Thompson, Chi.	20	16	36

1934–35
FINAL STANDINGS

Canadian Division

	W	L	T	PTS	GF	GA
Toronto	30	14	4	64	157	111
Montreal M.	24	19	5	53	123	92
Montreal C.	19	23	6	44	110	145
New York A.	12	27	9	33	100	142
St. Louis	11	31	6	28	86	144

American Division

	W	L	T	PTS	GF	GA
Boston	26	16	6	58	129	112
Chicago	26	17	5	57	118	88
New York R.	22	20	6	50	137	139
Detroit	19	22	7	45	127	114

Leading Scorers	G	A	Pts
Conacher, Tor.	36	21	57
Howe, Det.-St. L.	22	25	47
Aurie, Det.	17	29	46
Boucher, N.Y.R.	13	32	45
Jackson, Tor.	22	22	44
Lewis, Det.	16	27	43
Chapman, N.Y.A.	9	34	43
Barry, Bos.	20	20	40
Schriner, N.Y.A.	18	22	40
Stewart, Bos.	21	18	39
Thompson, Chi.	16	23	39

1935–36
FINAL STANDINGS
Canadian Division

	W	L	T	PTS	GF	GA
Montreal M.	22	16	10	54	114	106
Toronto	23	19	6	52	126	106
New York A.	16	25	7	39	109	122
Montreal C.	11	26	11	33	82	123

American Division

	W	L	T	PTS	GF	GA
Detroit	24	16	8	56	124	103
Boston	22	20	6	50	92	83
Chicago	21	19	8	50	93	92
New York R.	19	17	12	50	91	96

Leading Scorers	G	A	Pts
Schriner, N.Y.A.	19	26	45
Barry, Det.	21	19	40
Thompson, Chi.	17	23	40
Thoms, Tor.	23	15	38
Conacher, Tor.	23	15	38
Smith, Mtl. M.	19	19	38
Romnes, Chi.	13	25	38
Chapman, N.Y.A.	10	28	38
Lewis, Det.	14	23	37
Northcott, Mtl. M.	15	21	36

1936–37
FINAL STANDINGS
Canadian Division

	W	L	T	PTS	GF	GA
Montreal C.	24	18	6	54	115	111
Montreal M.	22	17	9	53	126	110
Toronto	22	21	5	49	119	115
New York A.	15	29	4	34	122	161

American Division

	W	L	T	PTS	GF	GA
Detroit	25	14	9	59	128	102
Boston	23	18	7	53	120	110
New York R.	19	20	9	47	117	106
Chicago	14	27	7	35	99	131

Leading Scorers	G	A	Pts
Schriner, N.Y.A.	21	25	46
Apps, Tor.	16	29	45
Barry, Det.	17	27	44
Aurie, Det.	23	20	43
Jackson, Tor.	21	19	40
Gagnon, Mtl. C.	20	16	36
Gracie, Mtl. M.	11	25	36
Stewart, Bos.-N.Y.A.	23	12	35
Thompson, Chi.	17	18	35
Cowley, Bos.	13	22	35

1937–38

FINAL STANDINGS

Canadian Division

	W	L	T	PTS	GF	GA
Toronto	24	15	9	57	151	127
New York A.	19	18	11	49	110	111
Montreal C.	18	17	13	49	123	128
Montreal M.	12	30	6	30	101	149

American Division

	W	L	T	PTS	GF	GA
Boston	30	11	7	67	142	89
New York R.	27	15	6	60	149	96
Chicago	14	25	9	37	97	139
Detroit	12	25	11	35	99	133

Leading Scorers	G	A	Pts
Drillon, Tor.	26	26	52
Apps, Tor.	21	29	50
Thompson, Chi.	22	22	44
Mantha, Mtl. C.	23	19	42
Dillon, New York R.	21	18	39
Cowley, Bos.	17	22	39
Schriner, N.Y.A.	21	17	38
Thoms, Tor.	14	24	38
Smith, N.Y.R.	14	23	37
Stewart, N.Y.A.	19	17	36
N. Colville, N.Y.R.	17	19	36

1938–39

FINAL STANDINGS

	W	L	T	PTS	GF	GA
Boston	36	10	2	74	156	76
New York R.	26	16	6	58	149	105
Toronto	19	20	9	47	114	107
New York A.	17	21	10	44	119	157
Detroit	18	24	6	42	107	128
Montreal	15	24	9	39	115	146
Chicago	12	28	8	32	91	132

Leading Scorers	G	A	Pts
Blake, Mtl.	24	23	47
Schriner, N.Y.A.	13	31	44
Cowley, Bos.	8	34	42
Smith, N.Y.R.	21	20	41
Barry, Det.	13	28	41
Apps, Tor.	15	25	40
Anderson, N.Y.A.	13	27	40
Gottselig, Chi.	16	23	39
Haynes, Mtl.	5	33	38
Conacher, Bos.	26	11	37
Carr, N.Y.A.	19	18	37
N. Colville, N.Y.R.	18	19	37
Watson, N.Y.R.	15	22	37

1939–40
FINAL STANDINGS

	W	L	T	PTS	GF	GA
Boston	31	12	5	67	170	98
New York R.	27	11	10	64	136	77
Toronto	25	17	6	56	134	110
Chicago	23	19	6	52	112	120
Detroit	16	26	6	38	90	126
New York A.	15	29	4	34	106	140
Montreal	10	33	5	25	90	167

Leading Scorers	G	A	Pts
Schmidt, Bos.	22	30	52
Dumart, Bos.	22	21	43
Bauer, Bos.	17	26	43
Drillon, Tor.	21	19	40
Cowley, Bos.	13	27	40
Hextall, N.Y.R.	24	15	39
N. Colville, N.Y.R.	19	19	38
Howe, Det.	14	23	37
Blake, Mtl.	17	19	36
Armstrong, N.Y.A.	16	20	36

1940–41
FINAL STANDINGS

	W	L	T	PTS	GF	GA
Boston	27	8	13	67	168	102
Toronto	28	14	6	62	145	99
Detroit	21	16	11	53	112	102
New York R.	21	19	8	50	143	125
Chicago	16	25	7	39	112	139
Montreal	16	26	6	38	121	147
New York A.	8	29	11	27	99	186

Leading Scorers	G	A	Pts
Cowley, Bos.	17	45	62
Hextall, N.Y.R.	26	18	44
Drillon, Tor.	23	21	44
Apps, Tor.	20	24	44
L. Patrick, N.Y.R.	20	24	44
Howe, Dte.	20	24	44
N. Colville, N.Y.R.	14	28	42
Wiseman, Bos.	16	24	40
Bauer, Bos.	17	22	39
Schriner, Tor.	24	14	38
R. Conacher, Bos.	24	14	38
Schmidt, Bos.	13	25	38

1941–42
FINAL STANDINGS

	W	L	T	PTS	GF	GA
New York R.	29	17	2	60	177	143
Toronto	27	18	3	57	158	136
Boston	25	17	6	56	160	118
Chicago	22	23	3	47	145	155
Detroit	19	25	4	42	140	147
Montreal	18	27	3	39	134	173
Brooklyn	16	29	3	35	133	175

Leading Scorers	G	A	Pts
Hextall, N.Y.	24	32	56
L. Patrick, N.Y.	32	22	54
Grosso, Det.	23	30	53
Watson, N.Y.	15	37	52
Abel, Det.	18	31	49
Blake, Mtl.	17	28	45
Thoms, Chi.	15	30	45
Drillon, Tor.	23	18	41
Apps, Tor.	18	23	41
Anderson, Bkn.	12	29	41

1942–43
FINAL STANDINGS

	W	L	T	PTS	GF	GA
Detroit	25	14	11	61	169	124
Boston	24	17	9	57	195	176
Toronto	22	19	9	53	198	159
Montreal	19	19	12	50	181	191
Chicago	17	18	15	49	179	180
New York	11	31	8	30	161	253

Leading Scorers	G	A	Pts
D. Bentley, Chi.	33	40	73
Cowley, Bos.	27	45	72
M. Bentley, Chi.	26	44	70
L. Patrick, N.Y.	22	39	61
Carr, Tor.	27	33	60
Taylor, Tor.	18	42	60
Hextall, N.Y.	27	32	59
Blake, Mtl.	23	36	59
Lach, Mtl.	18	40	58
O'Connor, Mtl.	15	43	58

1943-44
FINAL STANDINGS

	W	L	T	PTS	GF	GA
Montreal	38	5	7	83	234	109
Detroit	26	18	6	58	214	177
Toronto	23	23	4	50	214	174
Chicago	22	23	5	49	178	187
Boston	19	26	5	43	223	268
New York	6	39	5	17	162	310

Leading Scorers	G	A	Pts
Cain, Bos.	36	46	82
D. Bentley, Chi.	38	39	77
Carr, Tor.	36	38	74
Liscombe, Det.	36	37	73
Lach, Mtl.	24	48	72
Smith, Chi.	23	49	72
Cowley, Bos.	30	41	71
Mosienko, Chi.	32	38	70
Jackson, Bos.	28	41	69
Bodnar, Tor.	22	40	62

1944-45
FINAL STANDINGS

	W	L	T	PTS	GF	GA
Montreal	38	8	4	80	228	121
Detroit	31	14	5	67	218	161
Toronto	24	22	4	52	183	161
Boston	16	30	4	36	179	219
Chicago	13	30	7	33	141	194
New York	11	29	10	32	154	247

Leading Scorers	G	A	Pts
Lach, Mtl.	26	54	80
Richard, Mtl.	50	23	73
Blake, Mtl.	29	38	67
Cowley, Bos.	25	40	65
Kennedy, Tor.	29	25	54
Mosienko, Chi.	28	26	54
Carveth, Det.	26	28	54
DeMarco, N.Y.	24	30	54
Smith, Chi.	23	31	54
S. Howe, Det.	17	36	53

1945–46
FINAL STANDINGS

	W	L	T	PTS	GF	GA
Montreal	28	17	5	61	172	134
Boston	24	18	8	56	167	156
Chicago	23	20	7	53	200	178
Detroit	20	20	10	50	146	159
Toronto	19	24	7	45	174	185
New York	13	28	9	35	144	191

Leading Scorers	G	A	Pts
M. Bentley, Chi.	31	30	61
Stewart, Tor.	37	15	52
Blake, Mtl.	29	21	50
Smith, Chi.	26	24	50
Richard, Mtl.	27	21	48
Mosienko, Chi.	18	30	48
DeMarco, N.Y.	20	27	47
Lach, Mtl.	13	34	47
Kaleta, Chi.	19	27	46
Taylor, Tor.	23	18	41
Horeck, Chi.	20	21	41

1946–47
FINAL STANDINGS

	W	L	T	PTS	GF	GA
Montreal	34	16	10	78	189	138
Toronto	31	19	10	72	209	172
Boston	26	23	11	63	190	175
Detroit	22	27	11	55	190	193
New York	22	32	6	50	167	186
Chicago	19	37	4	42	193	274

Leading Scorers	G	A	Pts
M. Bentley, Chi.	29	43	72
Richard, Mtl.	45	26	71
Taylor, Det.	17	46	63
Schmidt, Bos.	27	35	62
Kennedy, Tor.	28	32	60
D. Bentley, Chi.	21	34	55
Bauer, Bos.	30	24	54
R. Conacher, Det.	30	24	54
Mosienko, Chi.	25	27	52
Dumart, Bos.	24	28	52

1947–48
FINAL STANDINGS

	W	L	T	PTS	GF	GA
Toronto	32	15	13	77	182	143
Detroit	30	18	12	72	187	148
Boston	23	24	13	59	167	168
New York	21	26	13	55	176	201
Montreal	20	29	11	51	147	169
Chicago	20	34	6	46	195	225

Leading Scorers	G	A	Pts
Lach, Mtl.	30	31	61
O'Connor, N.Y.	24	36	60
D. Bentley, Chi.	20	37	57
Stewart, Tor.-Chi.	27	29	56
M. Bentley, Chi.-Tor.	26	28	54
Poile, Tor.-Chi.	25	29	54
Richard, Mtl.	28	25	53
Apps, Tor.	26	27	53
Lindsay, Det.	33	19	52
R. Conacher, Chi.	22	27	49

1948–49
FINAL STANDINGS

	W	L	T	PTS	GF	GA
Detroit	34	19	7	75	195	145
Boston	29	23	8	66	178	163
Montreal	28	23	9	65	152	126
Toronto	22	25	13	57	147	161
Chicago	21	31	8	50	173	211
New York	18	31	11	47	133	172

Leading Scorers	G	A	Pts
R. Conacher, Chi.	26	42	68
D. Bentley, Chi.	23	43	66
Abel, Det.	28	26	54
Lindsay, Det.	26	28	54
J. Conacher, Det.-Chi.	26	23	49
Ronty, Bos.	20	29	49
Watson, Tor.	26	19	45
Reay, Mtl.	22	23	45
Bodnar, Chi.	19	26	45
Peirson, Bos.	22	21	43

1949–50
FINAL STANDINGS

	W	L	T	PTS	GF	GA
Detroit	37	19	14	88	229	164
Montreal	29	22	19	77	172	150
Toronto	31	27	12	74	176	173
New York	28	31	11	67	170	189
Boston	22	32	16	60	198	228
Chicago	22	38	10	54	203	244

Leading Scorers	G	A	Pts
Lindsay, Det.	23	55	78
Abel, Det.	34	35	69
Howe, Det.	35	33	68
M. Richard, Mtl.	43	22	65
Ronty, Bos.	23	36	59
R. Conacher, Chi.	25	31	56
D. Bentley, Chi.	20	33	53
Peirson, Bos.	27	25	52
Prystai, Chi.	29	22	51
Guidolin, Chi.	17	34	51

1950–51
FINAL STANDINGS

	W	L	T	PTS	GF	GA
Detroit	44	13	13	101	236	139
Toronto	41	16	13	95	212	138
Montreal	25	30	15	65	173	184
Boston	22	30	18	62	178	197
New York	20	29	21	61	169	201
Chicago	13	47	10	36	171	280

Leading Scorers	G	A	Pts
Howe, Det.	43	43	86
M. Richard, Mtl.	42	24	66
M. Bentley, Tor.	21	41	62
Abel, Det.	23	38	61
Schmidt, Bos.	22	39	61
Kennedy, Tor.	18	43	61
Lindsay, Det.	24	35	59
Sloan, Tor.	31	25	56
Kelly, Det.	17	37	54
Smith, Tor.	30	21	51
Gardner, Tor.	23	28	51

1951–52
FINAL STANDINGS

	W	L	T	PTS	GF	GA
Detroit	44	14	12	100	215	133
Montreal	34	26	10	78	195	164
Toronto	29	25	16	74	168	157
Boston	25	29	16	66	162	176
New York	23	34	13	59	192	219
Chicago	17	44	9	43	158	241

Leading Scorers	G	A	Pts
Howe, Det.	47	39	86
Lindsay, Det.	30	39	69
Lach, Mtl.	15	50	65
Raleigh, N.Y.	19	42	61
Smith, Tor.	27	30	57
Geoffrion, Mtl.	30	24	54
Mosienko, Chi.	31	22	53
Abel, Det.	17	36	53
Kennedy, Tor.	19	33	52
Schmidt, Bos.	21	29	50
Peirson, Bos.	20	30	50

1952–53
FINAL STANDINGS

	W	L	T	PTS	GF	GA
Detroit	36	16	18	90	222	133
Montreal	28	23	19	75	155	148
Boston	28	29	13	69	152	172
Chicago	27	28	15	69	169	175
Toronto	27	30	13	67	156	167
New York	17	37	16	50	152	211

Leading Scorers	G	A	Pts
Howe, Det.	49	46	95
Lindsay, Det.	32	39	71
M. Richard, Mtl.	28	33	61
Hergesheimer, N.Y.	30	29	59
Delvecchio, Det.	16	43	59
Ronty, N.Y.	16	38	54
Prystai, Det.	16	34	50
Kelly, Det.	19	27	46
Olmstead, Mtl.	17	28	45
Mackell, Bos.	27	17	44
McFadden, Chi.	23	21	44

1953–54
FINAL STANDINGS

	W	L	T	PTS	GF	GA
Detroit	37	19	14	88	191	132
Montreal	35	24	11	81	195	141
Toronto	32	24	14	78	152	131
Boston	32	28	10	74	177	181
New York	29	31	10	68	161	182
Chicago	12	51	7	31	133	242

Leading Scorers	G	A	Pts
Howe, Det.	33	48	81
M. Richard, Mtl.	37	30	67
Lindsay, Det.	26	36	62
Geoffrion, Mtl.	29	25	54
Olmstead, Mtl.	15	37	52
Kelly, Det.	16	33	49
Reibel, Det.	15	33	48
Sanford, Bos.	16	31	47
Mackell, Bos.	15	32	47
Mosdell, Mtl.	22	24	46
Ronty, N.Y.	13	33	46

1954–55
FINAL STANDINGS

	W	L	T	PTS	GF	GA
Detroit	42	17	11	95	204	134
Montreal	41	18	11	93	228	157
Toronto	24	24	22	70	147	135
Boston	23	26	21	67	169	188
New York	17	35	18	52	150	210
Chicago	13	40	17	43	161	235

Leading Scorers	G	A	Pts
Geoffrion, Mtl.	38	37	75
M. Richard, Mtl.	38	36	74
Beliveau, Mtl.	37	36	73
Reibel, Det.	25	41	66
Howe, Det.	29	33	62
Sullivan, Chi.	19	42	61
Olmstead, Mtl.	10	48	58
Smith, Tor.	33	21	54
Mosdell, Mtl.	22	32	54
Lewicki, N.Y.	29	24	53

1955–56
FINAL STANDINGS

	W	L	T	PTS	GF	GA
Montreal	45	15	10	100	222	131
Detroit	30	24	16	76	183	148
New York	32	28	10	74	204	203
Toronto	24	33	13	61	153	181
Boston	23	34	13	59	147	185
Chicago	19	39	12	50	155	216

Leading Scorers	G	A	Pts
Beliveau, Mtl.	47	41	88
Howe, Det.	38	41	79
M. Richard, Mtl.	38	33	71
Olmstead, Mtl.	14	56	70
Sloan, Tor.	37	29	66
Bathgate, N.Y.	19	47	66
Geoffrion, Mtl.	29	33	62
Reibel, Det.	17	39	56
Delvecchio, Det.	25	26	51
Creighton, N.Y.	20	31	51
Gadsby, N.Y.	9	42	51

1956–57
FINAL STANDINGS

	W	L	T	PTS	GF	GA
Detroit	38	20	12	88	198	157
Montreal	35	23	12	82	210	155
Boston	34	24	12	80	195	174
New York	26	30	14	66	184	227
Toronto	21	34	15	57	174	192
Chicago	16	39	15	47	169	225

Leading Scorers	G	A	Pts
Howe, Det.	44	45	89
Lindsay, Det.	30	55	85
Beliveau, Mtl.	33	51	84
Bathgate, N.Y.	27	50	77
Litzenberger, Chi.	32	32	64
M. Richard, Mtl.	33	29	62
McKenney, Bos.	21	39	60
Moore, Mtl.	29	29	58
H. Richard, Mtl.	18	36	54
Ullman, Det.	16	36	52

1957–58
FINAL STANDINGS

	W	L	T	PTS	GF	GA
Montreal	43	17	10	96	250	158
New York	32	25	13	77	195	188
Detroit	29	29	12	70	176	207
Boston	27	28	15	69	199	194
Chicago	24	39	7	55	163	202
Toronto	21	38	11	53	192	226

Leading Scorers	G	A	Pts
Moore, Mtl.	36	48	84
H. Richard, Mtl.	28	52	80
Bathgate, N.Y.	30	48	78
Howe, Det.	33	44	77
Horvath, Bos.	30	36	66
Litzenberger, Chi.	32	30	62
Mackell, Bos.	20	40	60
Beliveau, Mtl.	27	32	59
Delvecchio, Det.	21	38	59
McKenney, Bos.	28	30	58

1958–59
FINAL STANDINGS

	W	L	T	PTS	GF	GA
Montreal	39	18	13	91	258	158
Boston	32	29	9	73	205	215
Chicago	28	29	13	69	197	208
Toronto	27	32	11	65	189	201
New York	26	32	12	64	201	217
Detroit	25	37	8	58	167	218

Leading Scorers	G	A	Pts
Moore, Mtl.	41	55	96
Beliveau, Mtl.	45	46	91
Bathgate, N.Y.	40	48	88
Howe, Det.	32	46	78
Litzenberger, Chi.	33	44	77
Geoffrion, Mtl.	22	44	66
Sullivan, N.Y.	21	42	63
Hebenton, N.Y.	33	29	62
McKenney, Bos.	32	30	62
Sloan, Chi.	27	35	62

1959-60
FINAL STANDINGS

	W	L	T	PTS	GF	GA
Montreal	40	18	12	92	255	178
Toronto	35	26	9	79	199	195
Chicago	28	29	13	69	191	180
Detroit	26	29	15	67	186	197
Boston	28	34	8	64	220	241
New York	17	38	15	49	187	247

Leading Scorers	G	A	Pts
Hull, Chi.	39	42	81
Horvath, Bos.	39	41	80
Beliveau, Mtl.	34	40	74
Bathgate, N.Y.	26	48	74
H. Richard, Mtl.	30	43	73
Howe, Det.	28	45	73
Geoffrion, Mtl.	30	41	71
McKenney, Bos.	20	49	69
Stasiuk, Bos.	29	39	68
Prentice, N.Y.	32	34	66

1960-61
FINAL STANDINGS

	W	L	T	PTS	GF	GA
Montreal	41	19	10	92	254	188
Toronto	39	19	12	90	234	176
Chicago	29	24	17	75	198	180
Detroit	25	29	16	66	195	215
New York	22	38	10	54	204	248
Boston	15	42	13	43	176	254

Leading Scorers	G	A	Pts
Geoffrion, Mtl.	50	45	95
Beliveau, Mtl.	32	58	90
Mahovlich, Tor.	48	36	84
Bathgate, N.Y.	29	48	77
Howe, Det.	23	49	72
Ullman, Det.	28	42	70
Kelly, Tor.	20	50	70
Moore, Mtl.	35	34	69
H. Richard, Mtl.	24	44	68
Delvecchio, Det.	27	35	62

1961–62
FINAL STANDINGS

	W	L	T	PTS	GF	GA
Montreal	42	14	14	98	259	166
Toronto	37	22	11	85	232	180
Chicago	31	26	13	75	217	186
New York	26	32	12	64	195	207
Detroit	23	33	14	60	184	219
Boston	15	47	8	38	· 177	306

Leading Scorers	G	A	Pts
Hull, Chi.	50	34	84
Bathgate, N.Y.	28	56	84
Howe, Det.	33	44	77
Mikita, Chi.	25	52	77
Mahovlich, Tor.	33	38	71
Delvecchio, Det.	26	43	69
Backstrom, Mtl.	27	38	65
Ullman, Det.	26	38	64
Hay, Chi.	11	52	63
Provost, Mtl.	33	29	62

1962–63
FINAL STANDINGS

	W	L	T	PTS	GF	GA
Toronto	35	23	12	82	221	180
Chicago	32	21	17	81	194	178
Montreal	28	19	23	79	225	183
Detroit	32	25	13	77	200	194
New York	22	36	12	56	211	233
Boston	14	39	17	45	198	281

Leading Scorers	G	A	Pts
Howe, Det.	38	48	86
Bathgate, N.Y.	35	46	81
Mikita, Chi.	31	45	76
Mahovlich, Tor.	36	37	73
Richard, Mtl.	23	50	73
Beliveau, Mtl.	18	49	67
Bucyk, Bos.	27	39	66
Delvecchio, Det.	20	44	64
B. Hull, Chi.	31	31	62
Oliver, Bos.	22	40	62

1963–64
FINAL STANDINGS

	W	L	T	PTS	GF	GA
Montreal	36	21	13	85	209	167
Chicago	36	22	12	84	218	169
Toronto	33	25	12	78	192	172
Detroit	30	29	11	71	191	204
New York	22	38	10	54	186	242
Boston	18	40	12	48	170	212

Leading Scorers	G	A	Pts
Mikita, Chi.	39	50	89
B. Hull, Chi.	43	44	87
Beliveau, Mtl.	28	50	78
Bathgate, NY-Tor.	19	58	77
Howe, Det.	26	47	73
Wharram, Chi.	39	32	71
Oliver, Bos.	24	44	68
Goyette, N.Y.	24	41	65
Gilbert, N.Y.	24	40	64
Keon, Tor.	23	37	60

1964–65
FINAL STANDINGS

	W	L	T	PTS	GF	GA
Detroit	40	23	7	87	224	175
Montreal	36	23	11	83	211	185
Chicago	34	28	8	76	224	176
Toronto	30	26	14	74	204	173
New York	20	38	12	52	179	246
Boston	21	43	6	48	166	253

Leading Scorers	G	A	Pts
Mikita, Chi.	28	59	87
Ullman, Det.	42	41	83
Howe, Det.	29	47	76
B. Hull, Chi.	39	32	71
Delvecchio, Det.	25	42	67
Provost, Mtl.	27	37	64
Gilbert, N.Y.	25	36	61
Pilote, Chi.	14	45	59
Bucyk, Bos.	26	29	55
Backstrom, Mtl.	25	30	55
Esposito, Chi.	23	32	55

1965–66
FINAL STANDINGS

	W	L	T	PTS	GF	GA
Montreal	41	21	8	90	239	173
Chicago	37	25	8	82	240	187
Toronto	34	25	11	79	208	187
Detroit	31	27	12	74	221	194
Boston	21	43	6	48	174	275
New York	18	41	11	47	195	261

Leading Scorers	G	A	Pts
B. Hull, Chi.	54	43	97
Mikita, Chi.	30	48	78
Rousseau, Mtl.	30	48	78
Beliveau, Mtl.	29	48	77
Howe, Det.	29	46	75
Ullman, Det.	31	41	72
Delvecchio, Det.	31	38	69
Nevin, N.Y.	29	33	62
Richard, Mtl.	22	39	61
Oliver, Bos.	18	42	60

1966–67
FINAL STANDINGS

	W	L	T	PTS	GF	GA
Chicago	41	17	12	94	264	170
Montreal	32	25	13	77	202	188
Toronto	32	27	11	75	204	211
New York	30	28	12	72	188	189
Detroit	27	39	4	58	212	241
Boston	17	43	10	44	182	253

Leading Scorers	G	A	Pts
Mikita, Chi.	35	62	97
B. Hull, Chi.	52	28	80
Ullman, Det.	26	44	70
Wharram, Chi.	31	34	65
Howe, Det.	25	40	65
Rousseau, Mtl.	19	44	63
Esposito, Chi.	21	40	61
Goyette, N.Y.	12	49	61
Mohns, Chi.	25	35	60
Richard, Mtl.	21	34	55
Delvecchio, Det.	17	38	55

1967–68
FINAL STANDINGS
East Division

	W	L	T	PTS	GF	GA
Montreal	42	22	10	94	236	167
New York	39	23	12	90	226	183
Boston	37	27	10	84	259	216
Chicago	32	26	16	80	212	222
Toronto	33	31	10	76	209	176
Detroit	27	35	12	66	245	257

West Division

	W	L	T	PTS	GF	GA
Philadelphia	31	32	11	73	173	179
Los Angeles	31	33	10	72	200	224
St. Louis	27	31	16	70	177	191
Minnesota	27	32	15	69	191	226
Pittsburgh	27	34	13	67	195	216
Oakland	15	42	17	47	153	219

Leading Scorers	G	A	Pts
Mikita, Chi.	40	47	87
Esposito, Bos.	35	49	84
Howe, Det.	39	43	82
Ratelle, N.Y.	32	46	78
Gilbert, N.Y.	29	48	77
B. Hull, Chi.	44	31	75
Ullman, Det.-Tor.	35	37	72
Delvecchio, Det.	22	48	70
Bucyk, Bos.	30	39	69
Wharram, Chi.	27	42	69

1968–69
FINAL STANDINGS
East Division

	W	L	T	PTS	GF	GA
Montreal	46	19	11	103	271	202
Boston	42	18	16	100	303	221
New York	41	26	9	91	231	196
Toronto	35	26	15	85	234	217
Detroit	33	31	12	78	239	221
Chicago	34	33	9	77	280	246

West Division

	W	L	T	PTS	GF	GA
St. Louis	37	25	14	88	204	157
Oakland	29	36	11	69	219	251
Philadelphia	20	35	21	61	174	225
Los Angeles	24	42	10	58	185	260
Pittsburgh	20	45	11	51	189	252
Minnesota	18	43	15	51	189	270

Leading Scorers	G	A	Pts
Esposito, Bos.	49	77	126
B. Hull, Chi.	58	49	107
Howe, Det.	44	59	103
Mikita, Chi.	30	67	97
Hodge, Bos.	45	45	90
Cournoyer, Mtl.	43	44	87
Delvecchio, Det.	25	58	83
Berenson, St. L.	35	47	82
Beliveau, Mtl.	33	49	82
Mahovlich, Det.	49	29	78

1969–70
FINAL STANDINGS
East Division

	W	L	T	PTS	GF	GA
Chicago	45	22	9	99	250	170
Boston	40	17	19	99	277	216
Detroit	40	21	15	95	246	199
New York	38	22	16	92	246	189
Montreal	38	22	16	92	244	201
Toronto	29	34	13	71	222	242

West Division

	W	L	T	PTS	GF	GA
St. Louis	37	27	12	86	224	179
Pittsburgh	26	38	12	64	182	238
Minnesota	19	35	22	60	224	257
Oakland	22	40	14	58	169	243
Philadelphia	17	35	24	58	197	225
Los Angeles	14	52	10	38	168	290

Leading Scorers	G	A	Pts
Orr, Bos.	33	87	120
Esposito, Bos.	43	56	99
Mikita, Chi.	39	47	86
Goyette, St. L.	29	49	78
Tkaczuk, N. Y.	27	50	77
Ratelle, N.Y.	32	42	74
Berenson, St. L.	33	39	72
Parise, Minn.	24	48	72
Howe, Det.	31	40	71
Mahovlich, Det.	38	32	70
Balon, N.Y.	33	37	70
McKenzie, Bos.	29	41	70

1970–71
FINAL STANDINGS
East Division

	W	L	T	PTS	GF	GA
Boston	57	14	7	121	399	207
New York	49	18	11	109	259	177
Montreal	42	23	13	97	291	216
Toronto	37	33	8	82	248	211
Buffalo	24	39	15	63	217	291
Vancouver	24	46	8	56	229	296
Detroit	22	45	11	55	209	308

West Division

	W	L	T	PTS	GF	GA
Chicago	49	20	9	107	277	184
St. Louis	34	25	19	87	223	208
Philadelphia	28	33	17	73	207	225
Minnesota	28	34	16	72	191	223
Los Angeles	25	40	13	63	239	303
Pittsburgh	21	37	20	62	221	240
California	20	53	5	45	199	320

Leading Scorers	G	A	Pts
Esposito, Bos.	76	76	152
Orr, Bos.	37	102	139
Bucyk, Bos.	51	65	116
Hodge, Bos.	43	62	105
B. Hull, Chi.	44	52	96
Ullman, Tor.	34	51	85
Cashman, Bos.	21	58	79
McKenzie, Bos.	31	46	77
Keon, Tor.	38	38	76
Beliveau, Mtl.	25	51	76
Stanfield, Bos.	24	52	76

1971–72
FINAL STANDINGS
East Division

	W	L	T	PTS	GF	GA
Boston	54	13	11	119	330	204
New York	48	17	13	109	317	192
Montreal	46	16	16	108	307	205
Toronto	33	31	14	80	209	208
Detroit	33	35	10	76	261	262
Buffalo	16	43	19	51	203	289
Vancouver	20	50	8	48	203	297

West Division

	W	L	T	PTS	GF	GA
Chicago	46	17	15	107	256	166
Minnesota	37	29	12	86	212	191
St. Louis	28	39	11	67	208	247
Pittsburgh	26	38	14	66	220	258
Philadelphia	26	38	14	66	200	236
California	21	39	18	60	216	288
Los Angeles	20	49	9	49	206	305

Leading Scorers	G	A	Pts
Esposito, Bos.	66	67	133
Orr, Bos.	37	80	117
Ratelle, N.Y.	46	63	109
Hadfield, N.Y.	50	56	106
Gilbert, N.Y.	43	54	97
F. Mahovlich, Mtl.	43	53	96
B. Hull, Chi.	50	43	93
Cournoyer, Mtl.	47	36	83
Bucyk, Bos.	32	51	83
Clarke, Phil.	35	46	81
Lemaire, Mtl.	32	49	81

1972–73
FINAL STANDINGS
East Division

	W	L	T	PTS	GF	GA
Montreal	52	10	16	120	329	184
Boston	51	22	5	107	330	235
N.Y. Rangers	47	23	8	102	297	208
Buffalo	37	27	14	88	257	219
Detroit	37	29	12	86	265	243
Toronto	27	41	10	64	247	279
Vancouver	22	47	9	53	233	339
N.Y. Islanders	12	60	6	30	170	347

West Division

	W	L	T	PTS	GF	GA
Chicago	42	27	9	93	284	225
Philadelphia	37	30	11	85	296	256
Minnesota	37	30	11	85	254	230
St. Louis	32	34	12	76	233	251
Pittsburgh	32	37	9	73	257	265
Los Angeles	31	36	11	73	232	245
Atlanta	25	38	15	65	191	239
California	16	46	16	48	213	323

Leading Scorers	G	A	Pts
Esposito, Bos.	55	75	130
Clarke, Phil.	37	67	104
Orr, Bos.	29	72	101
MacLeish, Phil.	50	50	100
Lemaire, Mtl.	44	51	95
Ratelle, N.Y.R.	41	53	94
Redmond, Det.	52	41	93
Bucyk, Bos.	40	53	93
F. Mahovlich, Mtl.	38	55	93
Pappin, Chi.	41	51	92

Hall of Famer Maurice Richard stood supreme.　　　　　LARRY MORRIS

INDIVIDUAL NHL RECORDS

Most seasons played—25, Gordie Howe, Detroit, 1946–47 through 1970–71.

Most games played—1,687, Gordie Howe, Detroit.

Most goals—786, Gordie Howe, Detroit.

Most assists—1,023, Gordie Howe, Detroit.

Most points—1,809, Gordie Howe, Detroit.

Most penalty minutes—1,808, Ted Lindsay, Detroit, Chicago.

Most consecutive games played—630, Andy Hebenton, New York, Boston. Nine 70–game seasons from 1955–56 to 1963–64.

Most consecutive complete games, goalie—502, Glenn Hall, Detroit, Chicago, start of 1955–56 season through first 12 games of 1962–63.

Most career shutouts, goalie—103, Terry Sawchuk, Detroit, Boston, Toronto, Los Angeles, New York.

Most times scoring three or more goals, game—28, Bobby Hull, Chicago (24 three-goal games, 4 four-goal games).

Most goals, season—76, Phil Esposito, Boston, 1970–71.

Most assists, season—102, Bobby Orr, Boston, 1970–71.

Most points, season—152, Phil Esposito, Boston, 1970–71.

Most goals, season by a defenseman—37, Bobby Orr, Boston, 1970–71.

Most assists, season by a defenseman—102, Bobby Orr, Boston, 1970–71.

Most points, season by a defenseman—139, Bobby Orr, 1970–71.

Most power play goals, season—28, Phil Esposito, Boston, 1971–72.

Most goals, season, rookie—44, Richard Martin, Buffalo, 1971–72.

Most assists, season, rookie—52, Jude Drouin, Minnesota, 1970–71.

Most points, season, rookie—77, Marcel Dionne, Detroit, 1971–72.

Most points, season, one line—336, Phil Esposito, center; Ken Hodge, right wing; Wayne Cashman, left wing, 1970–71.

Most penalty minutes, season—291, Keith Magnuson, Chicago, 1970–71.

Most shutouts, season, goalie—22, George Hainsworth, Montreal, 1928–29; modern record: 15, Tony Esposito, Chicago, 1969–70.

Longest consecutive shutout streak, minutes, by goalie—460 minutes, 49 seconds, Alex Connell, Ottawa Senators, 1927–28; modern record, 309 minutes, 21 seconds, Bill Durnan, Montreal, 1948–49.

Longest consecutive goal-scoring streak—16 games, Punch Broadbent, Ottawa Senators, 1921–22; modern record, 10 games, Andy Bathgate, New York, 1962–63; Bobby Hull, Chicago, 1968–69.

Most goals, game—7, Joe Malone, Quebec, January 31, 1920; modern record, 6, Syd Howe, Detroit, February 3, 1944; Gordon (Red) Berenson, St. Louis, November 7, 1968.

Most assists, game—7, Billy Taylor, Detroit, March 16, 1947.

Most points, game—8, Maurice Richard, Montreal, December 28, 1944; Bert Olmstead, Montreal, January 9, 1954.

Most penalties, game—9, Jim Dorey, Toronto, October 16, 1968.

Most penalty minutes, game—48, Jim Dorey, Toronto, October 16, 1968, 4 minors, 2 majors, 2 misconducts, 1 game misconduct.

Most goals, game, defenseman—4, John McKinnon, Pittsburgh, November 19, 1929; Hap Day, Toronto, November 19, 1929.

Most assists, game, defenseman—6, Babe Pratt, Toronto, January 8, 1944; Pat Stapleton, Chicago, March 30, 1969.

Most goals, period—4, Harvey Jackson, Toronto, November 20, 1934; Max Bentley, Chicago, January 28, 1943; Clint Smith, Chicago, March 4, 1945; Gordon (Red) Berenson, St. Louis, November 7, 1968.

Most assists, period—4, Buddy O'Connor, Montreal, November 8, 1942; Doug Bentley, Chicago, January 28, 1943; Joe Carveth, Detroit, January 28, 1944; Phil Watson, Montreal, March 18, 1944; Bill Mosienko, Chicago, March 4, 1945; J. C. Tremblay, Montreal, December 29, 1962; Phil Goyette, New York, October 20, 1963; Jim Wiste, Chicago, November 9, 1969; Cliff Koroll, Chicago, December 16, 1970; Syl Apps, Jr., Pittsburgh, March 24, 1971; Bobby Orr, Boston, February 15, 1972; Jim Pappin, Chicago, March 24, 1973.

Most points, period—5, Les Cunningham, Chicago, January 28, 1940; Max Bentley, Chicago, January 28, 1943; Leo Labine, Boston, November 28, 1954.

Fastest goal, first NHL game—15 seconds, Gus Bodnar, Toronto, October 30, 1943.

Fastest goal, start of game—6 seconds, Henry Boucha, Detroit, January 28, 1973.

Fastest two goals—4 seconds, Nels Stewart, Montreal Maroons, January 3, 1931.

Fastest three goals—21 seconds, Bill Mosienko, Chicago, March 23, 1952.

TEAM

Most points, season—121, Boston Bruins, 1970–71.

Fewest points, season—12, Philadelphia Quakers, 1930–31; modern—30, New York Islanders, 1972–73.

Most victories, season—57, Boston Bruins, 1970–71.

Fewest victories, season—4, Philadelphia Quakers, 1930–31; modern—12, Chicago, 1953–54; New York Islanders, 1972–73.

Most losses, season—60, New York Islanders, 1972–73.

Most ties, season—24, Philadelphia, 1969–70.

Longest consecutive game winning streak—14 games, Boston, December 3, 1929 to January 19, 1930.

Longest unbeaten streak—23 games, Boston, December 22, 1940 to February 25, 1941 (15 victories, 8 ties).

Longest consecutive game winning streak at home—22 games, Boston, December 3, 1929 to November 18, 1930.

Longest unbeaten streak at home—28 games, Montreal, March 13, 1943 to November 2, 1944.

Longest unbeaten streak away from home—15 games, Boston, December 22, 1940 to March 16, 1941; Detroit, October 18, 1951 to December 26, 1951.

Longest consecutive game losing streak—15 games, Philadelphia Quakers, November 29, 1930 to January 10, 1931.

Longest consecutive game winless streak, season—21 games, New York Rangers, January 23, 1944 to March 19, 1944; Chicago, December 17, 1950 to February 1, 1951.

Longest consecutive game streak without being shut out—229 games, Chicago, March 14, 1970 to February 24, 1973.

Most consecutive shutout losses—8, Chicago, 1928–29.

Most shutout victories, season—22, Montreal Canadiens, 1928–29; modern record, 15, Chicago, 1969–70.

Most goals, season—399, Boston, 1970–71.

Fewest goals, season—33, Chicago, 1928–29; modern record, 133, Chicago, 1953–54.

Most goals against, season—347, New York Islanders, 1972–73.

Fewest goals against, season—42, Ottawa Senators, 1925–26; modern record, 131, Toronto, 1953–54; Montreal, 1955–56.

Most assists, season—697, Boston, 1970–71.

Most scoring points, season—1,096, Boston, 1970–71.

Fewest assists, season—45, New York Rangers, 1926–27; modern record, 206, Chicago, 1953–54.

Most penalty minutes, season—1,756, Philadelphia, 1972–73.

Most goals, both teams, game—21, Montreal Canadiens 14, Toronto St. Pats 7, January 10, 1920; modern record, 19, Boston 10, New York Rangers 9, March 4, 1944; Detroit 10, Boston 9, March 16, 1944.

Most goals, one team, game—16, Montreal Canadiens, March 3, 1920.

Most consecutive goals, one team, game—15, Detroit, January 23, 1944, against New York Rangers.

Most points, both teams, game—52, New York Americans 28, Montreal Maroons 24, February 18, 1936; modern record, 46, Boston 25, New York Rangers 21, March 4, 1944.

Most points, one team, game—37, Detroit, January 23, 1944, against New York Rangers; Toronto, March 16, 1957, against New York Rangers.

Most shots on goal, one team, game—83, Boston, March 4, 1941 against Chicago (Sam LoPresti, goalie).

Most penalties and penalty minutes, both teams, game—39 penalties, Los Angeles Kings, Minnesota North Stars at Minnesota, January 10, 1970. Most minutes—204, Montreal at Toronto, December 9, 1953.

Most goals, one team, period—8, Detroit, January 23, 1944.

Most points, one team, period—23, New York, November 21, 1971 on 8 goals and 15 assists.

Most shots on goal, one team, period—37, Boston, March 4, 1941.

Most penalties and penalty minutes, both teams, period—26 penalties, 184 minutes, December 9, 1953. Montreal got 13 penalties and 96 minutes and Toronto got 13 penalties and 88 minutes.

Most penalty minutes, one team, period—96, Montreal, December 9, 1953.

Fastest scoring, both teams—8 goals; 4 minutes and 52 seconds, March 19, 1938, Toronto 5 goals, New York Americans 3.

Fastest five goals, one team—2 minutes and 7 seconds, Pittsburgh, November 22, 1972.

Fastest four goals, one team—1 minute and 20 seconds, Boston, January 21, 1945.

Fastest three goals, one team—20 seconds, Boston, February 5, 1971.

Fastest two goals, one team—4 seconds, Montreal Maroons, January 3, 1931.

THE TROPHIES

HART MEMORIAL TROPHY

Awarded to the league's Most Valuable Player. Selected in a vote of hockey writers and broadcasters in each of the 12 NHL cities. The award was presented by the National Hockey League in 1960 after the original Hart Trophy was retired to the Hockey Hall of Fame. The original Hart Trophy was donated in 1923 by Dr. David A. Hart, father of Cecil Hart, former manager-coach of the Montreal Canadiens.

The winners:

1923–24 Frank Nighbor, Ottawa	1936–37 Babe Siebert, Montreal C.
1924–25 Billy Burch, Hamilton	1937–38 Eddie Shore, Boston
1925–26 Nels Stewart, Montreal M.	1938–39 Toe Blake, Montreal C.
1926–27 Herb Gardiner, Montreal C.	1939–40 Ebbie Goodfellow, Detroit
1927–28 Howie Morenz, Montreal C.	1940–41 Bill Cowley, Boston
1928–29 Roy Worters, New York A.	1941–42 Tommy Anderson, New York A.
1929–30 Nels Stewart, Montreal M.	1942–43 Bill Cowley, Boston
1930–31 Howie Morenz, Montreal C.	1943–44 Babe Pratt, Toronto
1931–32 Howie Morenz, Montreal C.	1944–45 Elmer Lach, Montreal C.
1932–33 Eddie Shore, Boston	1945–46 Max Bentley, Chicago
1933–34 Aurel Joliat, Montreal C.	1946–47 Maurice Richard, Montreal
1934–35 Eddie Shore, Boston	1947–48 Buddy O'Conner, New York
1935–36 Eddie Shore, Boston	1948–49 Sid Abel, Detroit

1949–50	Charlie Rayner, New York	1961–62	Jacques Plante, Montreal
1950–51	Milt Schmidt, Boston	1962–63	Gordie Howe, Detroit
1951–52	Gordie Howe, Detroit	1963–64	Jean Beliveau, Montreal
1952–53	Gordie Howe, Detroit	1964–65	Bobby Hull, Chicago
1953–54	Al Rollins, Chicago	1965–66	Bobby Hull, Chicago
1954–55	Ted Kennedy, Toronto	1966–67	Stan Mikita, Chicago
1955–56	Jean Beliveau, Montreal	1967–68	Stan Mikita, Chicago
1956–57	Gordie Howe, Detroit	1968–69	Phil Esposito, Boston
1957–58	Gordie Howe, Detroit	1969–70	Bobby Orr, Boston
1958–59	Andy Bathgate, New York	1970–71	Bobby Orr, Boston
1959–60	Gordie Howe, Detroit	1971–72	Bobby Orr, Boston
1960–61	Bernie Geoffrion, Montreal	1972–73	Bobby Clarke, Philadelphia

VEZINA TROPHY

Awarded to the goalie or goalies for the team which gives up the **fewest** goals during the regular season. To be eligible, a goalie must play at **least** 25 games.

The trophy was presented to the NHL in 1926–27 by the owners of the Montreal Canadiens in memory of Georges Vezina, former Canadien goalie.

The winners:

1926–27	George Hainsworth, Montreal C.	1931–32	Charlie Gardiner, Chicago
1927–28	George Hainsworth, Montreal C.	1932–33	Tiny Thompson, Boston
1928–29	George Hainsworth, Montreal C.	1933–34	Charlie Gardiner, Chicago
1929–30	Tiny Thompson, Boston	1934–35	Lorne Chabot, Chicago
1930–31	Roy Worters, New York A.	1935–36	Tiny Thompson, Boston

1936–37	Normie Smith, Detroit	1958–59	Jacques Plante, Montreal
1937–38	Tiny Thompson, Boston	1959–60	Jacques Plante, Montreal
1938–39	Frank Brimsek, Boston	1960–61	Johnny Bower, Toronto
1939–40	Davey Kerr, New York	1961–62	Jacques Plante, Montreal
1940–41	Turk Broda, Toronto	1962–63	Glenn Hall, Chicago
1941–42	Frank Brimsek, Boston	1963–64	Charlie Hodge, Montreal
1942–43	Johnny Mowers, Detroit	1964–65	Terry Sawchuk, Toronto
1943–44	Bill Durnan, Montreal		Johnny Bower, Toronto
1944–45	Bill Durnan, Montreal	1965–66	Lorne Worsley, Montreal
1945–46	Bill Durnan, Montreal		Charlie Hodge, Montreal
1946–47	Bill Durnan, Montreal	1966–67	Glenn Hall, Chicago
1947–48	Turk Broda, Toronto		Denis DeJordy, Chicago
1948–49	Bill Durnan, Montreal	1967–68	Lorne Worsley, Montreal
1949–50	Bill Durnan, Montreal		Rogatien Vachon, Montreal
1950–51	Al Rollins, Toronto	1968–69	Glenn Hall, St. Louis
1951–52	Terry Sawchuk, Detroit		Jacques Plante, St. Louis
1952–53	Terry Sawchuk, Detroit	1969–70	Tony Esposito, Chicago
1953–54	Harry Lumley, Toronto	1970–71	Ed Giacomin, New York
1954–55	Terry Sawchuk, Detroit		Gilles Villemure, New York
1955–56	Jacques Plante, Montreal	1971–72	Tony Esposito, Chicago
1956–57	Jacques Plante, Montreal		Gary Smith, Chicago
1957–58	Jacques Plante, Montreal	1972–73	Ken Dryden, Montreal

CLARENCE S. CAMPBELL TROPHY

Awarded to the team finishing in first place in the West Division.

The award was originated in 1967–68 when the circuit expanded from six to 12 teams and from one to two divisions. It is presented in honor of the NHL president.

LADY BYNG TROPHY

Awarded to the player combining the highest type of sportsmanship and gentlemanly conduct plus a high standard of playing ability. Selected by a vote of hockey writers and broadcasters in the 12 NHL cities.

Lady Byng, the wife of the Governor-General of Canada in 1925, presented the Trophy to the NHL during that year.

The winners:

1924–25	Frank Nighbor, Ottawa	1943–44	Clint Smith, Chicago
1925–26	Frank Nighbor, Ottawa	1944–45	Bill Mosienko, Chicago
1926–27	Billy Burch, New York A.	1945–46	Toe Blake, Montreal
1927–28	Frank Boucher, New York R.	1946–47	Bobby Bauer, Boston
1928–29	Frank Boucher, New York R.	1947–48	Buddy O'Connor, New York
1929–30	Frank Boucher, New York R.	1948–49	Bill Quackenbush, Detroit
1930–31	Frank Boucher, New York R.	1949–50	Edgar Laprade, New York
1931–32	Joe Primeau, Toronto	1950–51	Red Kelly, Detroit
1932–33	Frank Boucher, New York R.	1951–52	Sid Smith, Toronto
1933–34	Frank Boucher, New York R.	1952–53	Red Kelly, Detroit
1934–35	Frank Boucher, New York R.	1953–54	Red Kelly, Detroit
1935–36	Doc Romnes, Chicago	1954–55	Sid Smith, Toronto
1936–37	Marty Barry, Detroit	1955–56	Earl Reibel, Detroit
1937–38	Gordie Drillon, Toronto	1956–57	Andy Hebenton, New York
1938–39	Clint Smith, New York R.	1957–58	Camille Henry, New York
1939–40	Bobby Bauer, Boston	1958–59	Alex Delvecchio, Detroit
1940–41	Bobby Bauer, Boston	1959–60	Don McKenney, Boston
1941–42	Syl Apps, Toronto	1960–61	Red Kelly, Toronto
1942–43	Max Bentley, Chicago	1961–62	Dave Keon, Toronto

1962–63 Dave Keon, Toronto	1968–69 Alex Delvecchio, Detroit
1963–64 Ken Wharran, Chicago	1969–70 Phil Goyette, St. Louis
1964–65 Bobby Hull, Chicago	1970–71 Johnny Bucyk, Boston
1965–66 Alex Delvecchio, Detroit	1971–72 Jean Ratelle, New York
1966–67 Stan Mikita, Chicago	1972–73 Gil Perreault, Buffalo
1967–68 Stan Mikita, Chicago	

CALDER MEMORIAL TROPHY

Awarded to the league's outstanding rookie. Selected by a vote of hockey writers and broadcasters in each of the 12 NHL cities. It was originated in 1937 by Frank Calder, first president of the NHL. After his death in 1943, the league presented the Calder Memorial Trophy in his memory.

To be eligible to receive the trophy, a player cannot have participated in more than 20 games in any preceding season or in six or more games in each of any two preceding seasons.

The top rookies (from 1932–33 to 1936–37 they were named but no trophy was presented):

1932–33 Carl Voss, Detroit	1941–42 Grant Warwick, New York R.
1933–34 Russ Blinco, Montreal M.	1942–43 Gaye Stewart, Toronto
1934–35 Dave Schriner, New York A.	1943–44 Gus Bodnar, Toronto
1935–36 Mike Karakas, Chicago	1944–45 Frank McCool, Toronto
1936–37 Syl Apps, Toronto	1945–46 Edgar Laprade, New York
1937–38 Cully Dahlstrom, Chicago	1946–47 Howie Meeker, Toronto
1938–39 Frank Brimsek, Boston	1947–48 Jim McFadden, Detroit
1939–40 Kilby Macdonald, New York R.	1948–49 Pentti Lund, New York
1940–41 Johnny Quilty, Montreal C.	1949–50 Jack Gelineau, Boston

1950–51	Terry Sawchuk, Detroit		1962–63	Kent Douglas, Toronto
1951–52	Bernie Geoffrion, Montreal		1963–64	Jacques Laperriere, Montreal
1952–53	Lorne Worsley, New York		1964–65	Roger Crozier, Detroit
1953–54	Camille Henry, New York		1965–66	Brit Selby, Toronto
1954–55	Ed Litzenberger, Chicago		1966–67	Bobby Orr, Boston
1955–56	Glenn Hall, Detroit		1967–68	Derek Sanderson, Boston
1956–57	Larry Regan, Boston		1968–69	Danny Grant, Minnesota
1957–58	Frank Mahovlich, Toronto		1969–70	Tony Esposito, Chicago
1958–59	Ralph Backstrom, Montreal		1970–71	Gil Perreault, Buffalo
1959–60	Bill Hay, Chicago		1971–72	Ken Dryden, Montreal
1960–61	Dave Keon, Toronto		1972–73	Steve Vickers, New York R.
1961–62	Bobby Rousseau, Montreal			

JAMES NORRIS MEMORIAL TROPHY

Awarded to the league's best defenseman. Selected by a vote of hockey writers and broadcasters in each of the 12 NHL cities.

It was presented in 1953 by the four children of the late James Norris Sr., in memory of the former owner-president of the Detroit Red Wings.

The winners:

1953–54	Red Kelly, Detroit		1959–60	Doug Harvey, Montreal
1954–55	Doug Harvey, Montreal		1960–61	Doug Harvey, Montreal
1955–56	Doug Harvey, Montreal		1961–62	Doug Harvey, New York
1956–57	Doug Harvey, Montreal		1962–63	Pierre Pilote, Chicago
1957–58	Doug Harvey, Montreal		1963–64	Pierre Pilote, Chicago
1958–59	Tom Johnson, Montreal		1964–65	Pierre Pilote, Chicago

1965–66	Jacques Laperriere, Montreal	1969–70	Bobby Orr, Boston
1966–67	Harry Howell, New York	1970–71	Bobby Orr, Boston
1967–68	Bobby Orr, Boston	1971–72	Bobby Orr, Boston
1968–69	Bobby Orr, Boston	1972–73	Bobby Orr, Boston

ART ROSS TROPHY

Awarded to the player who compiles the highest number of scoring points during the regular season.

If players are tied for the lead, the trophy is awarded to the one with the most goals. If still tied, it is given to the player with the fewer number of games played. If these do not break the deadlock, the trophy is presented to the player who scored his first goal of the season at the earliest date.

The trophy was presented by Art Ross, the former manager-coach of the Boston Bruins, to the NHL in 1947.

The scoring champions:

Season	Player and Clubs	Games Played	Goals	Assists	Points
1917–18	Joe Malone, Mtl. Canadiens	20	44	**	44
1918–19	Newsy Lalonde, Mtl. Canadiens	17	23	9	32
1919–20	Joe Malone, Quebec	24	39	9	48
1920–21	Newsy Lalonde, Mtl. Canadiens	24	33	8	41
1921–22	Punch Broadbent, Ottawa	24	32	14	46
1922–23	Babe Dye, Toronto	22	26	11	37

**—number of assists not recorded

Season	Player and Clubs	Games Played	Goals	Assists	Points
1923–24	Cy Denneny, Ottawa	21	22	1	23
1924–25	Babe Dye, Toronto	29	38	6	44
1925–26	Nels Stewart, Montreal	36	34	8	42
1926–27	Bill Cook, N.Y. Rangers	44	33	4	37
1927–28	Howie Morenz, Mtl. Canadiens	43	33	18	51
1928–29	Ace Bailey, Toronto	44	22	10	32
1929–30	Cooney Weiland, Boston	44	43	30	73
1930–31	Howie Morenz, Mtl. Canadiens	39	28	23	51
1931–32	Harvey Jackson, Toronto	48	28	25	53
1932–33	Bill Cook, N.Y. Rangers	48	28	22	50
1933–34	Charlie Conacher, Toronto	42	32	20	52
1934–35	Charlie Conacher, Toronto	48	36	21	57
1935–36	Dave Schriner, N.Y. Americans	48	19	26	45
1936–37	Dave Schriner, N.Y. Americans	48	21	25	46
1937–38	Gordie Drillon, Toronto	48	26	26	52
1938–39	Toe Blake, Mtl. Canadiens	48	24	23	47
1939–40	Milt Schmidt, Boston	48	22	30	52
1940–41	Bill Cowley, Boston	46	17	45	62
1941–42	Bryan Hextall, N.Y. Rangers	48	24	32	56
1942–43	Doug Bentley, Chicago	50	33	40	73
1943–44	Herbie Cain, Boston	48	36	46	82
1944–45	Elmer Lach, Montreal	50	26	54	80
1945–46	Max Bentley, Chicago	47	31	30	61
1946–47	Max Bentley, Chicago	60	29	43	72
1947–48	Elmer Lach, Montreal	60	30	31	61
1948–49	Roy Conacher, Chicago	60	26	42	68
1949–50	Ted Lindsay, Detroit	69	23	55	78
1950–51	Gordie Howe, Detroit	70	43	43	86
1951–52	Gordie Howe, Detroit	70	47	39	86
1952–53	Gordie Howe, Detroit	70	49	46	95
1953–54	Gordie Howe, Detroit	70	33	48	81
1954–55	Bernie Geoffrion, Montreal	70	38	37	75
1955–56	Jean Beliveau, Montreal	70	47	41	88
1956–57	Gordie Howe, Detroit	70	44	45	89
1957–58	Dickie Moore, Montreal	70	36	48	84
1958–59	Dickie Moore, Montreal	70	41	55	96
1959–60	Bobby Hull, Chicago	70	39	42	81
1960–61	Bernie Geoffrion, Montreal	64	50	45	95
1961–62	Bobby Hull, Chicago	70	50	34	84
1962–63	Gordie Howe, Detroit	70	38	48	86
1963–64	Stan Mikita, Chicago	70	39	50	89
1964–65	Stan Mikita, Chicago	70	28	59	87
1965–66	Bobby Hull, Chicago	65	54	43	97
1966–67	Stan Mikita, Chicago	70	35	62	97
1967–68	Stan Mikita, Chicago	72	40	47	87
1968–69	Phil Esposito, Boston	74	49	77	126
1969–70	Bobby Orr, Boston	76	33	87	120
1970–71	Phil Esposito, Boston	78	76	76	152
1971–72	Phil Esposito, Boston	76	66	67	133
1972–73	Phil Esposito, Boston	78	55	75	130

LESTER PATRICK TROPHY

Awarded for outstanding service to hockey in the United States. Eligible recipients are players, officials, coaches, executives and referees.

Selected by a 6-man committee consisting of the President of the NHL, an NHL Governor, a hockey writer for a U.S. national news service, a nationally syndicated sports columnist, an ex-player in the Hockey Hall of Fame and a sports director of a U.S. national radio-television network. Each, except the NHL president, is rotated annually.

Presented by the New York Rangers in 1966 to honor the memory of the long-time general manager and coach of the New York Rangers.

The winners:

1966	Jack Adams		1970	Eddie Shore
1967	Gordie Howe		1971	William Jennings
1968	Tom Lockhart		1972	Clarence Campbell
1969	Bobby Hull		1973	Walter Bush

CONN SMYTHE TROPHY

Awarded to the Most Valuable Player in the Stanley Cup Playoffs. Selected in a vote of the League Governors.

The trophy was presented by Maple Leaf Gardens Ltd. in 1964 to honor the former coach, manager, president and owner of the Toronto Maple Leafs.

The winners:

1964–65	Jean Beliveau, Montreal
1965–66	Roger Crozier, Detroit
1966–67	Dave Keon, Toronto
1967–68	Glenn Hall, St. Louis
1968–69	Serge Savard, Montreal
1969–70	Bobby Orr, Boston
1970–71	Ken Dryden, Montreal
1971–72	Bobby Orr, Boston
1972–73	Yvan Cournoyer, Montreal

PRINCE OF WALES TROPHY

Awarded to the team finishing in first place in the East Division.

The Prince of Wales donated the trophy to the NHL in 1924. From 1927–28 to 1937–38, it was presented to the team finishing first in the American Division of the NHL. From 1938–39 through 1966–67, it was given to the first-place team in the one-division circuit.

NHL COACHES

Atlanta—Bernie Geoffrion 1972–73 to —.

Boston—Art Ross 1924–25 to 1933–34; Frank Patrick 1934–35 to 1935–36; Art Ross 1936–37 to 1938–39; Cooney Weiland 1939–40 to 1940–41; Art Ross 1941–42 to 1944–45; Dit Clapper 1945–46 to 1948–49; George "Buck" Boucher 1949–50; Lynn Patrick 1950–51 to 1954–55; Milt Schmidt 1954–55 to 1960–61; Phil Watson 1961–62; Phil Watson and Milt Schmidt 1962–63; Milt Schmidt 1963–64 to 1965–66; Harry Sinden 1966–67 to 1969–70; Tom Johnson 1970–71 to 1971–72; Tom Johnson and Bep Guidolin 1972–73; Bep Guidolin 1972–73 to —.

Buffalo—Punch Imlach 1970–71; Punch Imlach and Joe Crozier 1971–72; Joe Crozier 1972–73 to —.

Chicago—Pete Muldoon 1926–27; Barney Stanley and Hugh Lehman 1927–28; Herb Gardiner 1928–29; Tom Shaughnessy and Bill Tobin 1929–30; Dick Irvin 1930–31; Dick Irvin and Bill Tobin 1931–32; Godfrey Matheson, Emil Iverson and Tommy Gorman 1932–33; Tommy Gorman 1933–34; Clem Loughlin 1934–35 to 1936–37; Bill Stewart 1937–38; Bill Stewart and Paul Thompson 1938–39; Paul Thompson 1939–40 to 1943–44; Paul Thompson and Johnny Gottselig 1944–45; Johnny Gottselig 1945–46 to 1946–47; Johnny Gottselig and Charlie Conacher 1947–48; Charlie Conacher 1948–49 to 1949–50; Ebbie Goodfellow 1950–51 to 1951–52; Sid Abel 1952–53 to 1953–54; Frank Eddolls 1954–55; Dick Irvin 1955–56; Tommy Ivan 1956–57 to 1957–58; Rudy Pilous 1957–58 to 1962–63; Billy Reay, 1963–64 to —.

Detroit—Art Duncan 1926–27; Jack Adams 1927–28 to 1946–47; Tommy Ivan 1947–48 to 1953–54; Jim Skinner 1954–55 to 1957–58; Sid Abel 1957–58 to 1967–68; Bill Gadsby 1968–69 to 1969–70; Sid Abel 1969–70 to 1970–71; Ned Harkness and Doug Barkley 1970–71; Doug Barkley and Johnny Wilson 1971–72; Johnny Wilson 1972–73; Ted Garvin and Alex Delvecchio 1973–74.

Los Angeles—Red Kelly 1967–68 to 1968–69; Hal Laycoe and Johnny Wilson 1969–70; Larry Regan 1970–71; Larry Regan and Fred Glover 1971–72; Bob Pulford 1972–73 to —.

Minnesota—Wren Blair 1967–68; John Muckler and Wren Blair, 1968–69; Wren Blair and Charlie Burns 1969–70; Jackie Gordon 1970–71 to 1973–74; Jackie Gordon and Parker MacDonald 1973–74.

Montreal—George Kennedy 1917–18 to 1919–20; Leo Dandurand 1920–21 to 1924–25; Cecil Hart 1925–26 to 1931–32; Newsy Lalonde 1932–33 to 1933–34; Newsy Lalonde and Leo Dandurand 1934–35; Sylvio Mantha 1935–36; Cecil Hart 1936–37 to 1937–38; Cecil Hart and Jules Dugal 1938–39; Pit Lepine 1939–40; Dick Irvin 1940–41 to 1954–55; Toe Blake 1955–56 to 1967–68; Claude Ruel 1968–69 to 1969–70; Claude Ruel and Al MacNeil 1970–71; Scotty Bowman 1971–72 to —.

New York—Lester Patrick 1926–27 to 1938–39; Frank Boucher 1939–40 to 1947–48; Frank Boucher and Lynn Patrick 1948–49; Lynn Patrick 1949–50; Neil Colville 1950–51; Neil Colville and Bill Cook 1951–52; Bill Cook 1952–53; Frank Boucher and Murray Patrick 1953–54; Murray Patrick 1954–55; Phil Watson 1955–56 to 1959–60; Alf Pike 1959–60 to 1960–61; Doug Harvey 1961–62; Murray Patrick and Red Sullivan 1962–63; Red Sullivan 1963–64 to 1964–65; Red Sullivan and Emile Francis 1965–66; Emile Francis 1966–67 to 1967–68; Bernie Geoffrion and Emile Francis 1968–69; Emile Francis 1968–69 to 1972–73. Larry Popein and Emile Francis 1973–74.

New York Islanders—Phil Goyette and Earl Ingarfield 1972–73; Al Arbour 1973–74 to —.

California—Rudy Pilous, Bert Olmstead and Gord Fashoway, 1967–68; Fred Glover 1968–69 to 1970–71; Fred Glover and Vic Stasiuk 1971–72; Garry Young and Fred Glover 1972–73; Fred Glover and Marshall Johnston 1973–74.

Philadelphia—Keith Allen 1967–68 to 1968–69; Vic Stasiuk 1969–70 to 1970–71; Fred Shero 1971–72 to —.

Pittsburgh—Red Sullivan 1967–68 to 1968–69; Red Kelly 1969–70 to 1971–72; Red Kelly and Ken Schinkel 1972–73; Ken Schinkel and Marc Boileau 1973–74.

St. Louis—Lynn Patrick and Scotty Bowman, 1967–68; Scotty Bowman 1968–69 to 1969–70; Al Arbour and Scotty Bowman 1970–71; Sid Abel, Bill McCreary and Al Arbour 1971–72; Al Arbour and Jean Guy Talbot 1972–73; Jean Guy Talbot and Lou Angotti 1973–74.

Toronto—Conn Smythe 1927–28 to 1929–30; Conn Smythe and Art Duncan 1930–31; Art Duncan and Dick Irvin 1931–32; Dick Irvin 1932–33 to 1939–40; Hap Day 1940–41 to 1949–50; Joe Primeau 1950–51 to 1952–53; King Clancy 1953–54 to 1955–56; Howie Meeker 1956–57; Billy Reay 1957–58 to 1958–59; Punch Imlach 1958–59 to 1968–69, John McLellan 1969–70 to 1972–73; Red Kelly 1973–74 to —.

Vancouver—Hal Laycoe 1970–71 to 1971–72; Vic Stasiuk 1972–73; Bill McCreary and Phil Maloney 1973–74.

THE ALL-STAR TEAMS

Selected by a vote of hockey writers and broadcasters in the 12 NHL cities at the end of each season. The balloting originated with the 1930–31 campaign.

The teams: 1930–31

First		Second
Gardiner, Chicago	Goal	Thompson, Boston
Shore, Boston	Defense	Mantha, Montreal C.
Clancy, Toronto	Defense	Johnson, New York R.
Morenz, Montreal C.	Center	Boucher, New York R.
Cook, Bill, New York R.	Right Wing	Clapper, Boston
Joliat, Montreal C.	Left Wing	Cook, Bun, New York R.

1931–32

Gardiner, Chicago	Goal	Worters, New York A.
Shore, Boston	Defense	Mantha, Montreal C.
Johnson, New York R.	Defense	Clancy, Toronto
Morenz, Montreal C.	Center	Smith, Montreal M.
Cook, Bill, New York R.	Right Wing	C. Conacher, Toronto
Jackson, Toronto	Left Wing	Joliat, Montreal C.

1932–33

Roach, Detroit	Goal	Gardiner, Chicago
Shore, Boston	Defense	Clancy, Toronto
Johnson, New York R.	Defense	L. Conacher, Montreal M.
Boucher, New York R.	Center	Morenz, Montreal C.
Cook, Bill, New York R.	Right Wing	C. Conacher, Toronto
Northcott, Montreal M.	Left Wing	Jackson, Toronto

1933–34

Gardiner, Chicago	Goal	Worters, New York A.
Clancy, Toronto	Defense	Shore, Boston
L. Conacher, Chi.	Defense	Johnson, New York R.
Boucher, New York R.	Center	Primeau, Toronto
C. Conacher, Toronto	Right Wing	Cook, Bill, New York R.
Jackson, Toronto	Left Wing	Joliat, Montreal C.

1934–35

Chabot, Chicago	Goal	Thompson, Boston
Shore, Boston	Defense	Wentworth, Montreal M.
Seibert, New York R.	Defense	Coulter, Chicago
Boucher, New York R.	Center	Weiland, Detroit
C. Conacher, Toronto	Right Wing	Clapper, Boston
Jackson, Toronto	Left Wing	Joliat, Montreal C.

1935–36

Thompson, Boston	Goal	Cude, Montreal C.
Shore, Boston	Defense	Seibert, Chicago
Sibert, Boston	Defense	Goodfellow, Detroit
Smith, Montreal M.	Center	Thoms, Toronto
C. Conacher, Toronto	Right Wing	Dillon, New York R.
Schriner, New York A.	Left Wing	Thompson, Chicago

1936–37

Smith, Detroit	Goal	Cude, Montreal C.
Siebert, Montreal C.	Defense	Seibert, Chicago
Goodfellow, Detroit	Defense	C. Conacher, Montreal M.
Barry, Detroit	Center	Chapman, New York A.
Aurie, Detroit	Right Wing	Dillon, New York R.
Jackson, Toronto	Left Wing	Schriner, New York A.

1937–38

Thompson, Boston	Goal	Kerr, New York R.
Shore, Boston	Defense	Coulter, New York R.
Siebert, Montreal C.	Defense	Seibert, Chicago
Cowley, Boston	Center	Apps, Toronto
X–Dillon, New York R.	Right Wing	Drillon, Toronto
Thompson, Chicago	Left Wing	Blake, Montreal C.

X–Dillon and Drillon tied for first place in the voting and shared positions on the first and second teams.

1938–39

Brimsek, Boston	Goal	Robertson, New York A.
Shore, Boston	Defense	Seibert, Chicago
Clapper, Boston	Defense	Coulter, New York R.
Apps, Toronto	Center	N. Colville, New York R.
Drillon, Toronto	Right Wing	Bauer, Boston
Blake, Montreal C.	Left Wing	Gottselig, Chicago

1939–40

Kerr, New York R.	Goal	Brimsek, Boston
Clapper, Boston	Defense	Coulter, New York R.
Goodfellow, Detroit	Defense	Seibert, Chicago
Schmidt, Boston	Center	N. Colville, New York R.
Hextall, New York R.	Right Wing	Bauer, Boston
Blake, Montreal C.	Left Wing	Dumart, Boston

1940–41

Broda, Toronto	Goal	Brimsek, Boston
Clapper, Boston	Defense	Seibert, Chicago
Stanowski, Toronto	Defense	Heller, New York R.
Cowley, Boston	Center	Apps, Toronto
Hextall, New York R.	Right Wing	Bauer, Boston
Schriner, Toronto	Left Wing	Dumart, Boston

1941–42

Brimsek, Boston	Goal	Broda, Toronto
Seibert, Chicago	Defense	Egan, New York A.
Anderson, New York A.	Defense	McDonald, Toronto
Apps, Toronto	Center	Watson, New York R.
Hextall, New York R.	Right Wing	Drillon, Toronto
L. Patrick, New York R.	Left Wing	Abel, Detroit

1942–43

Mowers, Detroit	Goal	Brimsek, Boston
Seibert, Chicago	Defense	Crawford, Boston
Stewart, Detroit	Defense	Hollett, Boston
Cowley, Boston	Center	Apps, Toronto
Carr, Toronto	Right Wing	Hextall, New York R.
D. Bentley, Chicago	Left Wing	L. Patrick, New York R.

1943–44

Durnan, Montreal	Goal	Bibeault, Toronto
Seibert, Chicago	Defense	Bouchard, Montreal
Pratt, Toronto	Defense	Clapper, Boston
Cowley, Boston	Center	Lach, Montreal
Carr, Toronto	Right Wing	Richard, Montreal
D. Bentley, Chicago	Left Wing	Cain, Boston

1944–45

Durnan, Montreal	Goal	Karakas, Chicago
Bouchard, Montreal	Defense	Harmon, Montreal
Hollett, Detroit	Defense	Pratt, Toronto
Lach, Montreal	Center	Cowley, Boston
Richard, Montreal	Right Wing	Mosienko, Chicago
Blake, Montreal	Left Wing	S. Howe, Detroit

1945–46

Durnan, Montreal	Goal	Brimsek, Boston
Crawford, Boston	Defense	Reardon, Montreal
Bouchard, Montreal	Defense	Stewart, Detroit
M. Bentley, Chicago	Center	Lach, Montreal
Richard, Montreal	Right Wing	Mosienko, Chicago
Stewart, Toronto	Left Wing	Blake, Montreal

1946–47

Durnan, Montreal	Goal	Brimsek, Boston
Reardon, Montreal	Defense	Stewart, Detroit
Bouchard, Montreal	Defense	Quackenbush, Detroit
Schmidt, Boston	Center	M. Bentley, Chicago
Richard, Montreal	Right Wing	Bauer, Boston
D. Bentley, Chicago	Left Wing	Dumart, Boston

1947–48

Broda, Toronto	Goal	Brimsek, Boston
Quackenbush, Detroit	Defense	Reardon, Montreal
Stewart, Detroit	Defense	N. Colville, New York
Lach, Montreal	Center	O'Connor, New York
Richard, Montreal	Right Wing	Poile, Chicago
Lindsay, Detroit	Left Wing	Stewart, Chicago

1948–49

Durnan, Montreal	Goal	Rayner, New York
Quackenbush, Detroit	Defense	Harmon, Montreal
Stewart, Detroit	Defense	Reardon, Montreal
Abel, Detroit	Center	D. Bentley, Chicago
Richard, Montreal	Right Wing	Howe, Detroit
Conacher, Chicago	Left Wing	Lindsay, Detroit

1949–50

Durnan, Montreal	Goal	Rayner, New York
Mortson, Toronto	Defense	Reise, Detroit
Reardon, Montreal	Defense	Kelly, Detroit
Abel, Detroit	Center	Kennedy, Toronto
Richard, Montreal	Right Wing	Howe, Detroit
Lindsay, Detroit	Left Wing	Leswick, New York

1950–51

Sawchuk, Detroit	Goal	Rayner, New York
Kelly, Detroit	Defense	Thomson, Toronto
Quackenbush, Boston	Defense	Reise, Detroit
Schmidt, Boston	Center	Abel, Detroit
		Kennedy, Toronto
Howe, Detroit	Right Wing	Richard, Montreal
Lindsay, Detroit	Left Wing	Smith, Toronto

1951–52

Sawchuk, Detroit	Goal	Henry, Boston
Kelly, Detroit	Defense	Buller, New York
Harvey, Montreal	Defense	Thomson, Toronto
Lach, Montreal	Center	Schmidt, Boston
Howe, Detroit	Right Wing	Richard, Montreal
Lindsay, Detroit	Left Wing	Smith, Toronto

1952–53

Sawchuk, Detroit	Goal	McNeil, Montreal
Kelly, Detroit	Defense	Quackenbush, Boston
Harvey, Montreal	Defense	Gadsby, Chicago
Mackell, Boston	Center	Delvecchio, Detroit
Howe, Detroit	Right Wing	Richard, Montreal
Lindsay, Detroit	Left Wing	Olmstead, Montreal

1953–54

Lumley, Toronto	Goal	Sawchuk, Detroit
Kelly, Detroit	Defense	Gadsby, Chicago
Harvey, Montreal	Defense	Horton, Toronto
Mosdell, Montreal	Center	Kennedy, Toronto
Howe, Detroit	Right Wing	Richard, Montreal
Lindsay, Detroit	Left Wing	Sandford, Boston

1954–55

Lumley, Toronto	Goal	Sawchuk, Detroit
Harvey, Montreal	Defense	Goldham, Detroit
Kelly, Detroit	Defense	Flaman, Boston
Beliveau, Montreal	Center	Mosdell, Montreal
Richard, Montreal	Right Wing	Geoffrion, Montreal
Smith, Toronto	Left Wing	Lewicki, New York

1955–56

Plante, Montreal	Goal	Hall, Detroit
Harvey, Montreal	Defense	Kelly, Detroit
Gadsby, New York	Defense	Johnson, Montreal
Beliveau, Montreal	Center	Sloan, Toronto
M. Richard, Montreal	Right Wing	Howe, Detroit
Lindsay, Detroit	Left Wing	Olmstead, Montreal

1956–57

Hall, Detroit	Goal	Plante, Montreal
Harvey, Montreal	Defense	Flaman, Boston
Kelly, Detroit	Defense	Gadsby, New York
Beliveau, Montreal	Center	Litzenberger, Chicago
Howe, Detroit	Right Wing	M. Richard, Montreal
Lindsay, Detroit	Left Wing	Chevrefils, Boston

1957–58

Hall, Chicago	Goal	Plante, Montreal
Harvey, Montreal	Defense	Flaman, Boston
Gadsby, New York	Defense	Pronovost, Detroit
H. Richard, Montreal	Center	Beliveau, Montreal
Howe, Detroit	Right Wing	Bathgate, New York
Moore, Montreal	Left Wing	Henry, New York

1958–59

Plante, Montreal	Goal	Sawchuk, Detroit
Johnson, Montreal	Defense	Pronovost, Detroit
Gadsby, New York	Defense	Harvey, Montreal
Beliveau, Montreal	Center	H. Richard, Montreal
Bathgate, New York	Right Wing	Howe, Detroit
Moore, Montreal	Left Wing	Delvecchio, Detroit

1959–60

Hall, Chicago	Goal	Plante, Montreal
Harvey, Montreal	Defense	Stanley, Toronto
Pronovost, Detroit	Defense	Pilote, Chicago
Beliveau, Montreal	Center	Horvath, Boston
Howe, Detroit	Right Wing	Geoffrion, Montreal
Hull, Chicago	Left Wing	Prentice, New York

1960–61

Bower, Toronto	Goal	Hall, Chicago
Harvey, Montreal	Defense	Stanley, Toronto
Pronovost, Detroit	Defense	Pilote, Chicago
Beliveau, Montreal	Center	H. Richard, Montreal
Geoffrion, Montreal	Right Wing	Howe, Detroit
Mahovlich, Toronto	Left Wing	Moore, Montreal

1961–62

Plante, Montreal	Goal	Hall, Chicago
Harvey, New York	Defense	Brewer, Toronto
Talbot, Montreal	Defense	Pilote, Chicago
Mikita, Chicago	Center	Keon, Toronto
Bathgate, New York	Right Wing	Howe, Detroit
Hull, Chicago	Left Wing	Mahovlich, Toronto

1962–63

Hall, Chicago	Goal	Sawchuk, Detroit
Pilote, Chicago	Defense	Horton, Toronto
Brewer, Toronto	Defense	Vasko, Chicago
Mikita, Chicago	Center	Richard, Montreal
Howe, Detroit	Right Wing	Bathgate, New York
Mahovlich, Toronto	Left Wing	Hull, Chicago

1963–64

Hall, Chicago	Goal	Hodge, Montreal
Pilote, Chicago	Defense	Vasko, Chicago
Horton, Toronto	Defense	Laperriere, Montreal
Mikita, Chicago	Center	Beliveau, Montreal
Wharram, Chicago	Right Wing	Howe, Detroit
Hull, Chicago	Left Wing	Mahovlich, Toronto

1964–65

Crozier, Detroit	Goal	Hodge, Montreal
Pilote, Chicago	Defense	Gadsby, Detroit
Laperriere, Montreal	Defense	Brewer, Toronto
Ullman, Detroit	Center	Mikita, Chicago
Provost, Montreal	Right Wing	Howe, Detroit
B. Hull, Chicago	Left Wing	Mahovlich, Toronto

1965–66

Hall, Chicago	Goal	Worsley, Montreal
Laperriere, Montreal	Defense	Stanley, Toronto
Pilote, Chicago	Defense	Stapleton, Chicago
Mikita, Chicago	Center	Beliveau, Montreal
Howe, Detroit	Right Wing	Rousseau, Montreal
B. Hull, Chicago	Left Wing	Mahovlich, Toronto

1966–67

Giacomin, New York	Goal	Hall, Chicago
Pilote, Chicago	Defense	Horton, Toronto
Howell, New York	Defense	Orr, Boston
Mikita, Chicago	Center	Ullman, Detroit
Wharram, Chicago	Right Wing	Howe, Detroit
B. Hull, Chicago	Left Wing	Marshall, New York

1967–68

Worsley, Montreal	Goal	Giacomin, New York
Orr, Boston	Defense	J. C. Tremblay, Montreal
Horton, Toronto	Defense	Neilson, New York
Mikita, Chicago	Center	Esposito, Boston
Howe, Detroit	Right Wing	Gilbert, New York
B. Hull, Chicago	Left Wing	Bucyk, Boston

1968–69

Hall, St. Louis	Goal	Giacomin, New York
Orr, Boston	Defense	Green, Boston
Horton, Toronto	Defense	Harris, Montreal
Esposito, Boston	Center	Beliveau, Montreal
Howe, Detroit	Right Wing	Cournoyer, Montreal
B. Hull, Chicago	Left Wing	F. Mahovlich, Detroit

1969–70

Esposito, Chicago	Goal	Giacomin, New York
Orr, Boston	Defense	Brewer, Detroit
Park, New York	Defense	Laperriere, Montreal
Esposito, Boston	Center	Mikita, Chicago
Howe, Detroit	Right Wing	McKenzie, Boston
B. Hull, Chicago	Left Wing	F. Mahovlich, Detroit

1970–71

Giacomin, New York	Goal	Plante, Toronto
Orr, Boston	Defense	Park, New York
Tremblay, Montreal	Defense	Stapleton, Chicago
Esposito, Boston	Center	Keon, Toronto
Hodge, Boston	Right Wing	Cournoyer, Montreal
Bucyk, Boston	Left Wing	B. Hull, Chicago

1971–72

Esposito, Chicago	Goal	Dryden, Montreal
Orr, Boston	Defense	White, Chicago
Park, New York	Defense	Stapleton, Chicago
Esposito, Boston	Center	Ratelle, New York
Gilbert, New York	Right Wing	Cournoyer, Montreal
B. Hull, Chicago	Left Wing	Hadfield, New York

1972–73

Dryden, Montreal	Goal	Esposito, Chicago
Orr, Boston	Defense	Park, New York
Lapointe, Montreal	Defense	White, Chicago
Esposito, Boston	Center	Clarke, Philadelphia
Redmond, Detroit	Right Wing	Cournoyer, Montreal
F. Mahovlich, Montreal	Left Wing	D. Hull, Chicago

XII WORLD HOCKEY ASSOCIATION

For 55 years, the National Hockey League operated unchallenged as hockey's lone major league. From 1917, when it was organized, until 1972 the NHL varied in size from as few as four teams to as many as 14. But throughout the period it never was faced with any form of competition. Then along came the World Hockey Association.

Formed by Gary Davidson and Dennis Murphy, California attorneys who five years earlier had helped pioneer the American Basketball Association, the WHA announced its intention to begin operations in 1972 with 12 teams playing a 78-game schedule.

The NHL, possibly rushed into action earlier than it wanted to be by the advent of the WHA, added two new teams for 1972, expanding membership to 16. That did not alter WHA plans. The new league held a full scale draft and divided up all of the available player talent, amateur, professional, collegiate and foreign.

The alarming part of the draft, at least to the NHL, was the inclusion of players under contracts to the established league's clubs. The WHA's position was that the controversial reserve clause that binds a player to his team until sold, traded or released, was illegal. Therefore, the new league reasoned, it could draft any player with an expiring contract and ignore the reserve clause. And it did just that.

Using large-sized contracts as bait, the WHA lured some 70 players away from their NHL clubs. The most impressive jumper was Bobby Hull, who left the Chicago Black Hawks to double as player-coach of the Winnipeg Jets. His 10-year contract was for $2.75 million including $1 million up front which Hull received when he signed. The money was put together by all WHA clubs because luring a player of Hull's stature would, of course, be a huge plus not only for Winnipeg, but for the entire league.

Other name players accompanied Hull to the new league. Boston lost goalie Gerry Cheevers to Cleveland, defenseman Ted Green to New England and forwards Johnny McKenzie and Derek Sanderson to Philadelphia, although Sanderson later did a mid-season jump back to the Bruins.

Toronto goalie Bernie Parent turned up with Philadelphia and All-Star defenseman J. C. Tremblay of Montreal skipped off to Quebec.

Almost every NHL club lost some players to the new league. The New York Rangers had only one defection, with defenseman Jim Dorey going to New England. But it cost Madison Square Garden Corporation a considerable amount of money to keep its team intact. Salaries zoomed as five Rangers—Vic Hadfield, Jean Ratelle, Rod Gilbert, Walt Tkaczuk and Brad Park—agreed to multi-year, six-figure contracts.

343

Another NHL team, the newly minted New York Islanders, lost seven of the 20 players it chose in the expansion draft to the new league. That was one-third of the roster—a roster the Islanders paid $11 million to get. It showed. The Islanders lost a record 60 games in their first season.

The NHL initiated several suits to prevent some players from performing with the new league. Legal problems cost Hull 15 games but when he got the green light, he was every bit as exciting as he had been in the NHL. He reached hockey's magic 50-goal plateau for the sixth time in his career and scored 103 points. His linemates, Chris Bordeleau and Norm Beaudin, both soared past 100 points as well, marking the first time in history that all three members of a line had gone over 100.

The scoring championship went to Philadelphia's Andre Lacroix, who totaled 124 points, and the goal-scoring championship went to Danny Lawson of Philadelphia, who notched 61. Lacroix had scored four goals and 11 points and Lawson had 10 goals and 16 points in the NHL in 1971–72.

Hull's Winnipeg team won the West Division championship and New England finished first in the East. The two teams advanced to the final round of the playoff where New England eliminated the Jets in five games.

Hull was a unanimous All-Star selection. Also picked were Lacroix and Lawson, defensemen Tremblay of Quebec and Paul Shmyr of Cleveland and goalie Cheevers of Cleveland.

Hull was also named the Most Valuable Player. Rookie of the Year was New England's Terry Caffery. Tremblay was named the top defenseman and Jack Kelley of New England was the top coach.

1972–73
FINAL STANDINGS
East Division

	W	L	T	PTS	GF	GA
New England	46	30	2	94	318	263
Cleveland	43	32	3	89	287	239
Philadelphia	38	40	0	76	288	305
Ottawa	35	39	4	74	279	301
Quebec	33	40	5	71	276	313
New York	33	43	2	68	303	334

West Division

	W	L	T	PTS	GF	GA
Winnipeg	43	31	4	90	285	249
Houston	39	35	4	82	284	269
Los Angeles	37	35	6	80	259	250
Alberta	38	37	3	79	269	256
Minnesota	38	37	3	79	250	269
Chicago	26	50	2	54	245	295

Leading Scorers	G	A	Pts
Lacroix, Phil	50	74	124
Ward, N.Y.	51	67	118
Lawson, Phil.	61	45	106
Webster, N.E.	53	50	103
Hull, Winn.	51	52	103
Beaudin, Winn.	38	65	103
Bordeleau, Winn.	47	54	101
Gaffery, N.E.	39	61	100
Labossiere, Hou.	36	60	93
Carleton, Ott.	42	49	91

XIII THE RULES

OFFICIAL NATIONAL HOCKEY LEAGUE RULES
(Courtesy of the NHL)
Adopted June 11, 1973

OFFICIAL SIGNALS

HOLDING
Clasping either wrist with the other hand well in front of the chest.

TRIPPING
Strike the right leg with the right hand below the knee keeping both skates on the ice.

HOOKING
A series of tugging motions with both arms, as if pulling something toward the stomach.

HIGH-STICKING
Holding both fists, clenched, one immediately above the other, at the height of the forehead.

INTERFERENCE
Crossed arms stationary in front of chest.

SLASHING
A series of chopping motions with the edge of one hand across the opposite forearm.

346

CHARGING
Rotating clenched fists around one another in front of chest.

DELAYED CALLING OF PENALTY
Referee extends arm and points once to penalized player.

CROSS-CHECKING
A series of forward and backward motions with both fists clenched extending from the chest.

ICING
Arms folded across the chest.

ELBOWING
Tapping either elbow with the opposite hand.

SLOW WHISTLE
Arm, in which whistle is not held, extended above head. If play returns to Neutral Zone without stoppage, arm is drawn down the instant the puck crosses the line.

MISCONDUCT
Placing of both hands on hips several times and pointing to penalized player.

BOARDING
Pounding the closed fist of one hand into the open palm of the other hand.

"WASH-OUT"
Both arms swung laterally across the body with palms down:

1. When used by the Referee it means goal disallowed.

2. When used by Linesmen it means there is no icing or no offside.

SECTION ONE—THE RINK

Rule 1.   Rink

The game of "Ice Hockey" shall be played on an ice surface known as a "RINK."

Rule 2.   Dimensions of Rink

(a)   The official size of the rink shall be two hundred feet long and eighty-five feet wide. The corners shall be rounded in the arc of a circle with radius of twenty-eight feet.

The rink shall be surrounded by a wooden wall or fence known as the "boards" which shall extend not less than forty inches and not more than forty-eight inches above the level of the ice surface. The ideal height of the boards above the ice surface shall be forty-two inches. Except for the official markings provided for in these rules the entire playing surface and the boards shall be white in colour except the kick plate at the bottom of the boards which shall be light blue or light yellow in colour.

Any variations from any of the foregoing dimensions shall require official authorization by the League.

(b)   The boards shall be constructed in such manner that the surface facing the ice shall be smooth and free of any obstruction or any object that could cause injury to players.

All doors giving access to the playing surface must swing away from the ice surface.

All glass, wire or other types of protective screens and gear used to hold them in position shall be mounted on the boards on the side away from the playing surface.

Rule 3.   Goal Posts and Nets

(a)   Ten feet from each end of the rink and in the center of a red line two inches wide, drawn completely across the width of the ice and continued vertically up the side of the boards, regulation goal posts and nets shall be set in such manner as to remain stationary during the progress of a game. The goal posts shall be kept in position by means of metal rods or pipes affixed in the ice or floor and projecting a minimum of eight inches above the ice surface.

Where the length of the playing surface exceeds two hundred feet the goal line and goal posts may be placed not more than fifteen feet from the end of the rink.

(b)   The goal posts shall be of approved design and material, extending vertically four feet above the surface of the ice and set six feet apart measured from the inside of the posts. A crossbar of the same material as the goal posts shall extend from the top of one post to the top of the other.

(NOTE) *For League games the "NHL Official Goal Frame and Net" are approved and adopted. The design and specifications set out in the Plan of Goal printed in this Rule Book are official.*

(c)   There shall be attached to each goal frame a net of approved design made of white nylon cord which shall be draped in such a manner as to prevent the puck coming to rest on the outside of it.

A skirt of heavy white nylon fabric or heavyweight white canvas shall be laced around the "3" base plate of the goal frame in such a way as to protect the net from being cut or broken. This skirt shall not project more than one inch above the base plate.

(NOTE) *The frame of the goal including the small "3" attached to the top crossbar shall be draped with a nylon mesh net so as to completely enclose the back of the frame. The net shall be made of three-ply twisted twine (0.130 inch diameter) or equivalent braided twine of multifilament white nylon with an approximate tensile strength of 700 pounds. The size of the mesh shall be two and one-half inches (inside measurement) from each knot to each diagonal knot when fully stretched. Knotting shall be made so as to ensure no sliding of the twine. The net shall be laced to the frame with medium white nylon cord no smaller in size than # 21.*

(d)   The goal posts, crossbar and the exterior surface of other supporting framework for the goal shall be painted entirely in red. The surface of the base plate inside the goal and supports other than the goal posts shall be painted white.

(e)   The red line, two inches wide, between the goal posts on the ice and extended completely across the rink, shall be known as the "GOAL LINE."

(f)   The Goal area, enclosed by the goal line and the base of the goal, shall be painted white.

Rule 4.   **Goal Crease**

(a)   In front of each goal a "GOAL CREASE" area shall be marked by a red line two inches in width.

(b)   The goal crease shall be laid out as follows: One foot from the outside of each goal post, lines four feet in length and two inches in width shall be drawn at right angles to the goal line and the points of these lines farthest from the goal line shall be joined by another line, two inches in width.

(c)   The goal crease area shall include all the space outlined by the crease lines and extending vertically four feet to the level of the top of the goal frame.

Rule 5.   **Division of Ice Surface**

(a)   The ice area between the two goals shall be divided into three parts by lines, twelve inches in width, and blue in color, drawn sixty feet out from the goal lines, and extended completely across the rink, parallel with the goal lines, and continued vertically up the side of boards.

(b)   That portion of the ice surface in which the goal is situated shall be called the "DEFENDING ZONE" of the team defending that goal; the central portion shall be known as the "NEUTRAL ZONE," and the portion farthest from the defended goal as the "ATTACKING ZONE."

(c)   There shall also be a line, twelve inches in width, and red in color, drawn completely across the rink in center ice, parallel with the goal lines and continued vertically up the side of the boards, known as the "CENTER LINE." This line shall contain at regular intervals markings of a uniform distinctive design which will easily distinguish it from the two blue lines...the outer edges of which must be continuous.

Rule 6.   **Center Ice Spot and Circle**

A circular blue spot, twelve inches in diameter, shall be marked exactly in the center of the rink; and with this spot as a center a circle of fifteen feet radius shall be marked with a blue line two inches in width.

Rule 7.   **Face-off Spots in Neutral Zone**

Two red spots two feet in diameter shall be marked on the ice in the Neutral Zone five feet from each blue line. The spots shall be forty-four feet apart and each shall be a uniform distance from the adjacent boards.

Rule 8.   **End Zone Face-off Spots and Circles**

(a)   In both end zones and on both sides of each goal, red face-off spots and circles shall be marked on the ice. The face-off spots shall be two feet in diameter and the circles shall be two inches wide with a radius of fifteen feet from the center of the face-off spots. Twenty feet from the goal line and parallel to it red lines two feet in length and two inches wide shall be marked on the ice extending from the outer edge of both sides of each face-off circle.

Parallel to the goal line and equidistant from and on opposite sides of the center of each end face-off spot two red lines three feet in length and three inches in width and six feet apart shall be marked on the ice. Perpendicular from the center of these lines and extending away from the center face-off circle is drawn a line three feet long and three inches wide. (The effect of these lines is to produce a 'T' on opposite sides of the center face-off spot.)

(b)   The location of the face-off spots shall be fixed in the following manner:

Along a line twenty feet from each goal line and parallel to it, mark two points twenty-two feet on both sides of the straight line joining the centers of the two goals. Each such point shall be the center of a face-off spot and circle.

Rule 9.   **Players' Bench**

(a)   Each rink shall be provided with seats or benches for the use of players of both teams and the accommodations provided including benches and doors shall be uniform for both teams. Such seats or benches shall have accommodation for at least fourteen persons of each team, and shall be placed immediately alongside the ice, in the neutral zone, as near to the center of the rink as possible with door opening in the Neutral Zone and convenient to the dressing rooms.

The Players' Benches should be on the same side of the playing surface opposite the penalty bench and should be separated by a substantial distance. Each players' bench should be twenty-four feet in length.

Where physically possible each Players' Bench shall have two doors opening in the Neutral Zone and all doors opening to the playing surface shall be constructed so that they swing inward.

(b) None but players in uniform, Manager, Coach and Trainer shall be permitted to occupy the benches so provided.

Rule 10.   **Penalty Bench**

(a) Each rink must be provided with benches or seats to be known as the "PENALTY BENCH." These benches or seats must be capable of accommodating a total of ten persons including the Penalty Timekeepers. Separate penalty benches shall be provided for each team and they shall be situated on opposite sides of the Timekeeper's area. The penalty bench(es) must be situated opposite the Neutral Zone.

(b) On the ice immediately in front of the Penalty Timekeeper's seat there shall be marked in red on the ice a semi-circle of ten feet radius and two inches in width which shall be known as the "REFEREE'S CREASE".

Rule 11.   **Signal and Timing Devices**

(a) Each rink must be provided with a gong, or other suitable sound device, for the use of Timekeepers.

(b) Each rink shall be provided with some form of electrical clock for the purpose of keeping the spectators, players and game officials accurately informed as to all time elements at all stages of the game including the time remaining to be played in any period and the time remaining to be served by at least five penalized players on each team.

Time recording for both game time and penalty time shall show time remaining to be played or served.

(c) Behind each goal electric lights shall be set up for the use of the Goal Judges. A red light will signify the scoring of a goal. Where automatic lights are available, a green light will signify the end of a period or a game.

(NOTE) *A goal cannot be scored when a green light is showing.*

Rule 12.   **Police Protection**

All clubs shall provide adequate police or other protection for all players and officials at all times.

The Referee shall report to the President any failure of this protection observed by him or reported to him with particulars of such failure.

SECTION TWO—TEAMS

Rule 13.   **Composition of Team**

(a) A team shall be composed of six players, who shall be under contract to the club they represent.

(b) Each player and each goalkeeper listed in the line-up of each team shall wear an individual identifying number at least ten inches high on the back of his sweater.

All players of each team shall be dressed uniformly in conformity with approved design and color of their helmets, sweaters, pants, stockings and boots. Any player or goalkeeper not complying with this provision shall not be permitted to participate in the game.

Each Member Club shall design and wear distinctive and contrasting uniforms for their home and road games, no parts of which shall be interchangeable except the pants.

Rule 14.   **Captain of Team**

(a) One Captain shall be appointed by each team, and he alone shall have the privilege of discussing with the Referee any questions relating to interpretation of rules which may arise during the progress of a game. He shall wear the letter "C", approximately three inches in height and in contrasting color, in a conspicuous position on the front of his sweater.

(b) Each team should have a Captain on the ice at all times. If permanent Captain is not on the ice Alternate Captains (not more than three) shall be accorded the privileges of the Captain. Alternate Captains shall wear the letter "A", approximately three inches in height and in contrasting color, in a conspicuous place on the front of their sweaters.

(c) The Referee or Official Scorer shall be advised prior to the start of each game, the name of the Captain of the team, and also the identity of the players who will serve as Alternate Captain when the permanent Captain is off the ice.

(d) No goalkeepers shall be entitled to exercise the privileges of Captain or Alternate Captain on the ice.

(e) Only the Captain or Alternate Captain on the ice at the time of the stoppage of play (but not both) shall have the privilege of discussing with the Referee any point relating to the interpretation of rules. Any Captain, Alternate Captain or player who comes off the bench and makes any protest or intervention with the Referee for any purpose must be awarded a misconduct penalty.

A complaint about a penalty is NOT a matter "relating to the interpretation of the rules" and a misconduct penalty shall be imposed against any Captain, Alternate Captain or other player making such a complaint.

(f) No playing Coach or playing Manager shall be permitted to act as Captain or Alternate Captain.

Rule 15.   **Players in Uniform**

(a) At the beginning of each game the Manager or Coach of each team shall list the players and goalkeepers who shall be eligible to play in the game. Not more than seventeen players, exclusive of goalkeepers, shall be permitted.

In play-offs seventeen players, exclusive of goalkeepers, shall be permitted.

(b) A list of names and numbers of all eligible players and goalkeepers must be handed to the Referee or Official Scorer before the game, and no change shall be permitted in the list or addition thereto shall be permitted after the commencement of the game.

(c) Each team shall be allowed one goalkeeper on the ice at one time. The goalkeeper may be removed and another "player" substituted. Such substitute shall not be permitted the privileges of the goalkeeper.

(d) Each team shall have on its bench, or on a chair immediately beside the bench, a substitute Goalkeeper who shall at all times be fully dressed and equipped ready to play.

Except for the purpose of depending against a penalty shot any substitute goalkeeper entering the game for the first time shall be permitted a warm-up not exceeding two minutes. The Referee shall check the time so permitted.

(e)   Except when both goalkeepers are incapacitated, no player on the playing roster in that game shall be permitted to wear the equipment of the goalkeeper.

(f)   In League Play-off games if both listed Goalkeepers are incapacitated, that team shall be entitled to dress and play any available Goalkeeper who is eligible. No delay shall be permitted in taking his position in the goal, and he shall be permitted the regular two-minute warm-up.

(g)   The Referee shall report to the President for disciplinary action any delay in making a substitution of goalkeepers.

Rule 16.   **Starting Line-Up**

(a)   Prior to the start of the game, at the request of the Referee, the Manager or Coach of the visiting team is required to name the starting lineup to the Referee or the Official Scorer. At any time in the game at the request of the Referee, made to the Captain or Alternate Captain, the visiting team must place a playing lineup on the ice and promptly commence play.

(b)   Prior to the start of the game the Manager or Coach of the home team, having been advised by the Official Scorer or the Referee the names of the starting line-up of the visiting team, shall name the starting line-up of the home team which information shall be conveyed by the Official Scorer or the Referee to the Coach of the visiting team.

(c)   No change in the starting line-up of either team as given to the Referee or Official Scorer, or in the playing line-up on the ice, shall be made until the game is actually in progress. For an infraction of this rule a bench minor penalty shall be imposed upon the offending team, provided such infraction is called to the attention of the Referee before the second face-off in the first period takes place.

(d)   Following the stoppage of play the visiting team shall promptly place a line-up on the ice ready for play and no substitution shall be made from that time until play has been resumed. The home team may then make any desired substitution which does not result in the delay of the game.

(NOTE) *When a substitution has been made under the above rule no additional substitution may be made until play commences.*

Rule 17.   **Equalizing of Teams**
                         D E L E T E D

Rule 18.   **Change of players**

(a)   Players may be changed at any time from the players' bench, provided that the player or players leaving the ice shall always be at the players' bench and out of the play before any change is made.

A goalkeeper may be changed for another player at any time under the conditions set out in this section.

(NOTE 1) *When a goalkeeper leaves his goal area and proceeds to his players' bench for the purpose of substituting another player, the rear Linesman shall be responsible to see that the substitution made is not illegal by reason of the premature departure of the substitute from the bench (before the goalkeeper is within ten feet of the bench). If the substitution is made prematurely, the Linesman shall stop the play immediately by blowing his whistle unless the non-offending team has possession of the puck in which event the stoppage will be delayed until the puck changes hands. There shall be no time penalty to the team making the premature substitution but the resulting face-off will take place on the center "face-off spot."*

(NOTE 2) *If in the course of making a substitution the player entering the game plays the puck with his stick, skates or hands or checks or makes any physical contact with an opposing player while the retiring player is actually on the ice then infraction of "too many men on the ice" will be called.*

If in the course of a substitution either the player entering the play or the player retiring is struck by the puck accidentally the player will not be stopped and no penalty will be called.

(b)   If by reason of insufficient playing time remaining, or by reason of penalties already imposed, a bench minor penalty is imposed for deliberate illegal substitution (too many men on the ice) which cannot be served in its entirety within the legal playing time, a penalty shot shall be awarded against the offending team.

(c)   A player serving a penalty on the penalty bench, who is to be changed after the penalty has been served, must proceed at once by way of the ice and be at his own players' bench before any change can be made.

For any violation of this rule a bench minor penalty shall be imposed.

Rule 19.   **Injured Players**

(a)   When a player, other than a goalkeeper, is injured or compelled to leave the ice during a game, he may retire from the game and be replaced by a substitute, but play must continue without the teams leaving the ice.

(b)   If a goalkeeper sustains an injury or becomes ill he must be ready to resume play immediately or be replaced by a substitute goalkeeper and NO additional time shall be allowed by the referee for the purpose of enabling the injured or ill goalkeeper to resume his position. (See also Section (d).)

(c)   The Referee shall report to the President for disciplinary action any delay in making a goalkeeper substitution.

The substitute goalkeeper shall be subject to the regular rules governing goalkeepers and shall be entitled to the same privileges.

(d)   When a substitution for the regular goalkeeper has been made, such regular goalkeeper shall not resume his position until the first stoppage of play thereafter. When the substitute goalkeeper comes on the ice and starts his warm-up he shall complete it and shall not be allowed any additional warm-up in the same game.

(e)   If a penalized player has been injured he may proceed to the dressing room without the necessity of taking a seat on the penalty bench. If the injured player receives a minor penalty the penalized team shall immediately put a substitute player on the penalty bench who shall serve the penalty without change. If the injured player receives a major penalty the penalized team shall place a substitute player on the penalty bench before the penalty expires and no other replacement for the penalized player shall be permitted to enter the game except from the penalty bench. For violation of this rule a bench minor penalty shall be imposed.

The penalized player who has been injured and been replaced on the penalty bench shall not be eligible to play until his penalty has expired.

(f)   When a player is injured so that he cannot continue play or go to his bench, the play shall not be stopped until the injured player's team has secured possession of the puck; if the player's team is in possession of the puck at the time of injury, play shall be stopped immediately, unless his team is in a scoring position.

(NOTE) *In the case where it is obvious that a player has sustained a serious injury the Referee and/or Linesman may stop the play immediately.*

SECTION THREE—EQUIPMENT

Rule 20.   **Sticks**

(a) The sticks shall be made of wood or other material approved by the Rules Committee, and must not have any projections. Adhesive tape of any colour may be wrapped around the stick at any place for the purpose of reinforcement or to improve control of the puck.

(b) No stick shall exceed fifty-five inches in length from the heel to the end of the shaft nor more than twelve and one-half inches from the heel to the end of the blade.

The blade of the stick shall not be more than three inches in width at any point nor less than two inches. All edges of the blade shall be bevelled. The curvature of the blade of the stick shall be restricted in such a way that the distance of a perpendicular line measured from a straight line drawn from any point at the heel to the end of the blade to the point of maximum curvature shall not exceed one-half inch.

(c) The blade of the goalkeeper's stick shall not exceed three and one-half inches in width at any point except at the heel where it must not exceed four and one-half inches in width; nor shall the goalkeeper's stick exceed fifteen and one-half inches in length from the heel to the end of the blade.

The widened portion of the goalkeeper's stick extending up the shaft from the blade shall not extend more than twenty-four inches from the heel and shall not exceed three and one-half inches in width.

(d) A minor penalty plus a fine of two hundred dollars ($200.00) shall be imposed on any player or goalkeeper who uses a stick not conforming to the provisions of this rule.

(NOTE 1) *When a formal complaint is made by the Captain or Alternate Captain of a team, against the dimensions of any stick, the Referee shall take the stick to the Timekeeper's bench where the necessary measurement shall be made immediately. The result shall be reported to the Penalty Timekeeper who shall record it on the back of the penalty record.*

If the complaint is not sustained a fine of one hundred dollars ($100.00) shall be imposed against the complaining Club by the President.

(NOTE 2) *A player, who participates in the play while taking a replacement stick to his goalkeeper shall incur a minor penalty under this rule but the automatic fine of two hundred dollars ($200.00) shall not be imposed. If his participation causes a foul resulting in a minor or major penalty the referee shall report the incident to the President for disciplinary action.*

(e) A minor penalty plus a ten-minute misconduct penalty shall be imposed on any player who refuses to surrender his stick for measurement when requested to do so by the Referee. In addition this player shall be subject to a $200 fine.

Rule 21.   **Skates**

(a) All hockey skates shall be of a design approved by the Rules Committee. All skates worn by players (but not goalkeepers) and by the Referee and Linesmen shall be equipped with approved safety heel tips.

When the Referee becomes aware that any person is wearing a skate on which the protective heel tip is missing or broken, he shall direct its replacement at the next intermission. If such replacement is not carried out, the Referee shall report the incident to the President for disciplinary action.

(b)   The use of speed skates or fancy skates or any skate so designed that it may cause injury is prohibited.

Rule 22.   **Goalkeeper's Equipment**

(a)   With the exception of skates and stick, all the equipment worn by the goalkeeper must be constructed solely for the purpose of protecting the head or body, and he must not wear any garment or use any contrivance which would give him undue assistance in keeping goal.

(NOTE) *Cages on gloves and abdominal aprons extending down the front of the thighs on the outside of the pants are prohibited. "Cage" shall mean any lacing or webbing or other material in the goalkeeper's glove joining the thumb and index finger which is in excess of the minimum necessary to fill the gap when the goalkeeper's thumb and forefinger in the glove are fully extended and spread and includes any pocket or pouch effect produced by excess lacing or webbing or other material between the thumb and forefinger when fully extended or spread.*

Protective padding attached to the back or forming part of goalkeeper's gloves shall not exceed eight inches in width nor more than sixteen inches in length at any point.

(b)   The leg guards worn by goalkeepers shall not exceed ten inches in extreme width when on the leg of the player.

(NOTE) *At the commencement of each season and prior to play-offs goalkeepers' leg guards shall be checked by League Staff and any violation of this rule shall be reported to the Club involved and to the President of the League.*

(c)   Protective masks of a design approved by the Rules Committee may be worn by goalkeepers.

Rule 23.   **Protective Equipment**

All protective equipment, except gloves, headgear and goalkeeper's leg guards, must be worn under the uniform.

For violation of this rule after warning by the Referee a minor penalty shall be imposed.

(NOTE) *Players including the goalkeeper violating this rule shall not be permitted to participate in game until such equipment has been corrected or removed.*

Rule 24.   **Dangerous Equipment**

(a)   The use of pads or protectors made of metal, or of any other material likely to cause injury to a player, is prohibited.

(b)   A mask or protector of a design approved by the Rules Committee may be worn by a player who has sustained a facial injury involving a bone fracture.

(NOTE) *All elbow pads which do not have a soft protective outer covering of sponge rubber or similar material at least ½ inch thick shall be considered dangerous equipment.*

In the first instance the injured player shall be entitled to wear any protective device prescribed by the Club doctor. If any opposing Club objects to the device it may record its objection with the President who shall promptly poll the Rules Committee for approval or otherwise.

(c)   A glove from which all or part of the palm has been removed or cut to permit the use of the bare hand shall be considered illegal equipment and if any player wears such a glove in play a minor penalty shall be imposed on him.

(NOTE) *The Referee-in-Chief is specifically authorized to make a check of each team's equipment to ensure the compliance with this rule. He shall report his findings to the President for his disciplinary action.*

Rule 25. **Puck**

(a) The puck shall be made of vulcanized rubber, or other approved material, one inch thick and three inches in diameter and shall weigh between five and a half ounces and six ounces. All pucks used in competition must be approved by the Rules Committee.

(b) The home team shall be responsible for providing an adequate supply of official pucks which shall be kept in a frozen condition. This supply of pucks shall be kept at the penalty bench under the control of one of the regular minor officials or a special attendant.

(NOTE) *As of June 10, 1969 pucks manufactured by the Converse Rubber Co. and the Viceroy Manufacturing Co. have been approved by the rules committee.*

(NOTE TO SECTION THREE) *A request for measurement of any equipment covered by this section shall be limited to one request by each Club during the course of any stoppage of play.*

The Referee may, at his own discretion, measure any equipment used for the first time in the game.

SECTION FOUR—PENALTIES

Rule 26. **Penalties**

Penalties shall be actual playing time and shall be divided into the following classes:

(1) Minor Penalties
(2) Bench Minor Penalties
(3) Major Penalties
(4) Misconduct Penalties
(5) Match Penalties
(6) Penalty Shot.

Where coincident penalties are imposed on players of both teams the penalized players of the visiting team shall take their positions on the penalty bench first in the place designated for visiting players.

(NOTE) *When play is not actually in progress and an offense is committed by any player, the same penalty shall apply as though play were actually in progress. Accidental trips occurring simultaneously with, or after, stoppage of play will not be penalized.*

Rule 27. **Minor Penalties**

(a) For a "MINOR PENALTY," any player, other than a goalkeeper, shall be ruled off the ice for two minutes during which time no substitute shall be permitted.

(b) A "BENCH MINOR" penalty involves the removal from the ice of one player of the team against which the penalty is awarded for a period of two minutes. Any player except a goalkeeper of the team may be designated to serve the penalty by the Manager or Coach through the playing Captain and such player shall take his place on the penalty bench promptly and serve the penalty as if it was a minor penalty imposed upon him.

(c) If while a team is "short-handed" by one or more minor or bench minor penalties the opposing team scores a goal, the first of such penalties shall automatically terminate.

(NOTE 1) *"Short-handed" means that the team must be below the numerical strength of its opponents on the ice at the time the goal is scored. The minor or bench minor penalty which terminates automatically is the one which causes the team scored against to be "short-handed" originally (first penalty). Thus coincident minor penalties to both teams do NOT cause either side to be "short-handed."*

This rule shall also apply when a goal is scored on a penalty shot.

When the minor penalties of two players of the same team terminate at the same time the Captain of that team shall designate to the Referee which of such players will return to the ice first and the Referee will instruct the Penalty Timekeeper accordingly.

When a player receives a major penalty and a minor penalty at the same time the major penalty shall be served first by the penalized player except under Rule 28 (c) in which case the minor penalty will be recorded and served first.

(NOTE 2): *This applies to the case where BOTH penalties are imposed on the SAME player.*

See also Note to Rule 33.

Rule 28.   Major Penalties

(a) For the first "MAJOR PENALTY" in any one game, the offender, except the goalkeeper, shall be ruled off the ice for five minutes, during which time no substitute shall be permitted.

An automatic fine of fifty dollars ($50.00) shall also be added when a major penalty is imposed for any foul causing injury to the face or head of an opponent by means of a stick.

(b) For the third major penalty in the same game, to the same player, he shall be ruled off the ice for the balance of the playing time, but a substitute shall be permitted to replace the player so suspended after five minutes shall have elapsed. (Major penalty plus game misconduct penalty with automatic fine of one hundred dollars ($100.00).)

(c) When coincident major penalties or coincident penalties of equal duration, including a major penalty, are imposed against players of both teams, the penalized players shall all take their places on the penalty benches and such penalized players shall not leave the penalty bench until the first stoppage of play following the expiry of their respective penalties. Immediate substitutions shall be made for an equal number of major penalties to each team so penalized and the penalties of the players which substitutions have been made shall not be taken into account for the purpose of the delayed Rule 33.

Where it is required to determine which of the penalized players shall be designated to serve the delayed penalty under Rule 33 the penalized team shall have the right to make such designation not in conflict with Rule 27.

Rule 29.   Misconduct Penalties

(a) "MISCONDUCT" penalties to all players except the goalkeeper, involve removal from the game for a period of ten minutes each. A substitute player is permitted to immediately replace a player serving a misconduct penalty. A player whose misconduct penalty has expired shall remain in the penalty box until the next stoppage of play.

When a player receives a minor penalty and a misconduct penalty at the same time, the penalized team shall immediately put a substitute player on the penalty bench and he shall serve the minor penalty without change.

When a player receives a major penalty and a misconduct penalty at the same time, the penalized team shall place a substitute player on the penalty bench before the major penalty expires and no replacement for the penalized player shall be permitted to enter the game except from the penalty bench. Any violation of this provision shall be treated as an illegal substitution under Rule 18 calling for a bench minor penalty.

(b) A misconduct penalty imposed on any player at any time, shall be accompanied with an automatic fine of fifty dollars ($50.00).

(c) A "GAME MISCONDUCT" penalty involves the suspension of a player for the balance of the game but a substitute is permitted to replace immediately the player so removed. A player incurring a game misconduct penalty shall incur an automatic fine of one hundred dollars ($100.00) and the case shall be reported to the President who shall have full power to impose such further penalties by way of suspension or fine on the penalized player or any other player involved in the altercation.

(NOTE) *For all "Game Misconduct" penalties regardless of when imposed, a total of ten minutes shall be charged in the records against the offending player.*

Rule 30.   **Match Penalties**

(a) A "MATCH" penalty involves the suspension of a player for the balance of the game, and the offender shall be ordered to the dressing room immediately. A substitute player is permitted to replace the penalized player after ten minutes playing time has elapsed when the penalty is imposed under Rule 49, and after five minutes actual playing time has elapsed when the penalty is imposed under Rule 44 or Rule 64.

(NOTE 1) *Regulations regarding additional penalties and substitutes are specifically covered in individual Rules 44, 49 and 64; any additional penalty shall be served by a player to be designated by the Manager or Coach of the offending team through the playing Captain.*

For all "MATCH" penalties, regardless of when imposed, or prescribed additional penalties, a total of ten minutes shall be charged in the records against the offending player.

(NOTE 2) *When coincident match penalties have been imposed under Rule 44 or Rule 64 to a player on both teams Rule 28 (c) and (d) covering coincident major penalties will not be applicable.*

(b) A player incurring a match penalty shall incur an automatic fine of two hundred dollars ($200.00) and the case shall be investigated promptly by the President who shall have full power to impose such further penalty by way of suspension or fine on the penalized player or any other player involved in the altercation.

(NOTE) *The Referee is required to report all match penalties and the surrounding circumstances to the President of the League immediately following the game in which they occur.*

Rule 31.   **Penalty Shot**

(a) Any infraction of the rules which calls for a "Penalty Shot" shall be taken as follows:—

The Referee shall cause to be announced over the public address system the name of the player designated by him or selected by the team entitled to take the shot (as appropriate) and shall then place the puck on the center face-off spot and the player taking the shot will, on the instruction of the Referee, play the puck from there and shall attempt to score on the goalkeeper. The player taking the shot may carry the puck in any part of the Neutral Zone or his own Defending Zone but once the puck has crossed the Attacking Blue Line it must be kept in motion towards the opponent's goal line and once it is shot the play shall be considered complete. No goal can be scored on a rebound of any kind and any time the puck crosses the goal line the shot shall be considered complete.

Only a player designated as a Goalkeeper or Alternate Goalkeeper may defend against the penalty shot.

(b)   The Goalkeeper must remain in his crease until the player taking the penalty shot has touched the puck and in the event of violation of this rule or any foul committed by a goalkeeper the Referee shall allow the shot to be taken and if the shot fails he shall permit the penalty shot to be taken over again.

The goalkeeper may attempt to stop the shot in any manner except by throwing his stick or any object, in which case a goal shall be awarded.

(NOTE) *See Rule 80.*

(c)   In cases where a penalty shot has been awarded under Rule 66 (k)—for illegal entry into the game, under Rule 80 (a)—for throwing a stick and under Rule 83 (b)—for fouling from behind, the Referee shall designate the player who has been fouled as the player who shall take the penalty shot.

In cases where a penalty shot has been awarded under Rule 18 (b)—deliberate illegal substitution with insufficient playing time remaining or Rule 50 (c)—deliberately displacing goal post or Rule 53 (c)—falling on the puck in the crease or Rule 57 (d)—picking up the puck from the crease area—the penalty shot shall be taken by a player selected by the Captain of the non-offending team from the players on the ice at the time when the foul was committed. Such selection shall be reported to the Referee and cannot be changed.

If by reason of injury the player designated by the Referee to take the penalty shot is unable to do so within a reasonable time, the shot may be taken by a player selected by the Captain of the non-offending team from the players on the ice when the foul was committed. Such selection shall be reported to the Referee and cannot be changed.

(d)   Should the player in respect to whom a penalty shot has been awarded himself commit a foul in connection with the same play or circumstances, either before or after the penalty shot penalty has been awarded, be designated to take the shot, he shall first be permitted to do so before being sent to the penalty bench to serve the penalty except when such a penalty is for a game misconduct or match penalty in which case the penalty shot shall be taken by a player selected by the Captain of the non-offending team from the players on the ice at the time when the foul was committed.

If at the time a penalty shot is awarded the goalkeeper of the penalized team has been removed from the ice to substitute another player the goalkeeper shall be permitted to return to the ice before the penalty shot is taken.

(e)   While the penalty shot is being taken, players of both sides shall withdraw to the sides of the rink and beyond the center red line.

(f)   If, while the penalty shot is being taken, any player of the opposing team shall have by some action interfered with or distracted the player taking the shot and because of such action the shot should have failed, a second attempt shall be permitted and the Referee shall impose a misconduct penalty on the player so interfering or distracting.

(g)   If a goal is scored from a penalty shot the puck shall be faced at center ice in the usual way. If a goal is not scored the puck shall be faced at either of the end face-off spots in the zone in which the penalty shot has been tried.

(h) Should a goal be scored from a penalty shot, a further penalty to the offending player shall not be applied unless the offense for which the penalty shot was awarded was such as to incur a major or match penalty, in which case the penalty prescribed for the particular offense shall be imposed.

If the offense for which the penalty shot was awarded was such as would normally incur a minor penalty, then regardless of whether the penalty shot results in a goal or not, no further minor penalty shall be served.

(i) If the foul upon which the penalty shot is based occurs during actual playing time the penalty shot shall be awarded and taken immediately in the usual manner notwithstanding any delay occasioned by a slow whistle by the Referee to permit the play to be completed which delay results in the expiry of the regular playing time in any period.

The time required for the taking of a penalty shot shall not be included in the regular playing time or any overtime.

Rule 32.   **Goalkeeper's Penalties**

(a) A goalkeeper shall not be sent to the penalty bench for an offense which incurs a minor penalty, but instead the minor penalty shall be served by another member of his team who was on the ice when the offense was committed, said player to be designated by the Manager or Coach of the offending team through the playing Captain and such substitute shall not be changed.

(b) Same as 32 (a) above except change "minor" to "major".

(c) Should a goalkeeper incur three major penalties in one game he shall be ruled off the ice for the balance of the playing time and his place will be taken by a member of his own Club, or by a regular substitute goalkeeper who is available. (Major penalty plus game misconduct penalty and automatic fine of one hundred dollars ($100.00).)

(d) Should a goalkeeper on the ice incur a misconduct penalty this penalty shall be served by another member of his team who was on the ice when the offense was committed, said player to be designated by the Manager or Coach of the offending team through the playing Captain and, in addition, the goalkeeper shall be fined fifty dollars ($50.00).

(e) Should a goalkeeper incur a game misconduct penalty, his place then will be taken by a member of his own club, or by a regular substitute goalkeeper who is available, and such player will be allowed the goalkeeper's full equipment. In addition the goalkeeper shall be fined one hundred dollars ($100.00).

(f) Should a goalkeeper incur a match penalty, his place then will be taken by a member of his own club, or by a substitute goalkeeper who is available, and such player will be allowed the goalkeeper's equipment. However, any additional penalties as specifically called for by the individual rules covering match penalties, will apply, and the offending team shall be penalized accordingly; such additional penalty to be served by another member of the team on the ice at the time the offense was committed, said player to be designated by the Manager or Coach of the offending team through the playing Captain. (See Rules 44, 49 and 64.)

(g) A goalkeeper incurring a match penalty shall incur an automatic fine of two hundred dollars ($200.00) and the case shall be investigated promptly by the President who shall have full power to impose such further penalty by way of suspension or fine on the penalized goalkeeper or any other player in the altercation.

(h)   A minor penalty shall be imposed on a goalkeeper who leaves the immediate vicinity of his crease during an altercation. In addition, he shall be subject to a fine of one hundred dollars ($100.00) and this incident shall be reported to the President for such further disciplinary action as may be required.

(NOTE) *All penalties imposed on goalkeeper regardless of who serves penalty or any substitution, shall be charged in the records against the goalkeeper.*

(i)   If a goalkeeper participates in the play in any manner when he is beyond the center red line a minor penalty shall be imposed upon him.

Rule 33.   Delayed Penalties

(a)   If a third player of any team shall be penalized while two players of the same team are serving penalties, the penalty time of the third player shall not commence until the penalty time of one of the two players already penalized shall have elapsed. Nevertheless, the third player penalized must at once proceed to the penalty bench but may be replaced by a substitute until such time as the penalty time of the penalized player shall commence.

(b)   When any team shall have three players serving penalties at the same time and because of the delayed penalty rule, a substitute for the third offender is on the ice, none of the three penalized players on the penalty bench may return to the ice until play has been stopped. When play has been stopped, the player whose full penalty has expired, may return to the play.

Provided however that the Penalty Timekeeper shall permit the return to the ice in the order of expiry of their penalties, of a player or players when by reason of the expiration of their penalties the penalized team is entitled to have more than four players on the ice.

(c)   In the case of delayed penalties, the Referee shall instruct the Penalty Timekeeper that penalized players whose penalties have expired shall only be allowed to return to the ice when there is a stoppage of play.

When the penalties of two players of the same team will expire at the same time the Captain of that team will designate to the Referee which of such players will return to the ice first and the Referee will instruct the Penalty Timekeeper accordingly.

When a major and a minor penalty are imposed at the same time on players of the same team the Penalty Timekeeper shall record the minor as being the first of such penalties.

(NOTE) *This applies to the case where the two penalties are imposed on DIF-FERENT players of the same team. See also Note to Rule 27.*

Rule 34.   Calling of Penalties

(a)   Should an infraction of the rules which would call for a minor, major, misconduct, game misconduct or match penalty be committed by a player of the side in possession of the puck, the Referee shall immediately blow his whistle and give the penalties to the deserving players.

The resulting face-off shall be made at the place where the play was stopped unless the stoppage occurs in the Attacking Zone of the player penalized in which case the face-off shall be made at the nearest face-off spot in the Neutral Zone.

(b)   Should an infraction of the rules which would call for a minor, major, misconduct, game misconduct or match penalty be committed by a player of the team NOT in possession of the puck, the Referee shall signify the calling of a penalty by pointing to the offending player, and on completion of the play by the team in possession, will immediately blow his whistle and give the penalty to the deserving player.

The resulting face-off shall be made at the place where the play was stopped, unless during the period of a delayed whistle due to a foul by a player of the side NOT in possession, the side in possession ices the puck, shoots the puck so that it goes out of bounds or is unplayable then the face-off following the stoppage shall take place in the Neutral Zone near the Defending Blue Line of the team shooting the puck.

If the penalty or penalties to be imposed are minor penalties and a goal is scored on the play by the non-offending side the minor penalty or penalties shall not be imposed but major and match penalties shall be imposed in the normal manner regardless of whether a goal is scored or not.

(NOTE 1) *"Completion of the play by the team in possession" in this rule means that the puck must have come into the possession and control of an opposing player or has been "frozen." This does not mean a rebound off the goalkeeper, the goal or the boards or any accidental contact with the body or equipment of an opposing player.*

(NOTE 2) *If after the Referee has signaled a penalty but before the whistle has been blown the puck shall enter the goal of the non-offending team as the direct result of the action of a player of that team, the goal shall be allowed and the penalty signalled shall be imposed in the normal manner.*

If when a team is "short-handed" by reason of one or more minor or bench minor penalties the Referee signals a further minor penalty or penalties against the "short-handed" team and a goal is scored by the non-offending side before the whistle is blown then the goal shall be allowed, the penalty or penalties signalled shall be washed out and the first of the minor penalties already being served shall automatically terminate under Rule 27 (c).

(c)   Should the same offending player commit other fouls on the same play, either before or after the Referee has blown his whistle, the offending player shall serve such penalties consecutively.

SECTION FIVE—OFFICIALS

Rule 35.   **Appointment of Officials**
(a)   The President shall appoint a Referee, two Linesmen, Game Timekeeper, Penalty Timekeeper, Official Scorer and two Goal Judges for each game.
(b)   The President shall forward to all clubs a list of Referees, and Minor Officials, all of whom must be treated with proper respect at all times during the season by all players and officials of clubs.

Rule 36.   **Referee**
(a)   The REFEREE shall have general supervision of the game, and shall have full control of all game officials and players during the game, including stoppages; and in case of any dispute, his decision shall be final. The Referee shall remain on the ice at the conclusion of each period until all players have proceeded to their dressing rooms.
(b)   All Referees and Linesmen shall be garbed in black trousers and official sweaters.

They shall be equipped with approved whistles and metal tape measures with minimum length of six feet.

(c)   The Referee shall order the teams on the ice at the appointed time for the beginning of a game, and at the commencement of each period. If for any reason there be more than fifteen minutes' delay in the commencement of the game or any undue delay in resuming play after the fifteen minute intervals between periods, the Referee shall state in his report to the President the cause of the delay, and the club or clubs which were at fault.

(d)   It shall be his duty to see to it that all players are properly dressed, and that the approved regulation equipment is in use at all times during the game.

(e)   The Referee shall, before starting the game, see that the appointed Game Time-keeper, Penalty Timekeeper, Official Scorer and Goal Judges are in their respective places, and satisfy himself that the timing and signaling equipment are in order.

(f)   It shall be his duty to impose such penalties as are prescribed by the rules for infractions thereof, and he shall give the final decision in matters of disputed goals. The Referee may consult with the Linesmen or Goal Judge before making his decision.

(g)   The Referee shall announce to the Official Scorer or Penalty Timekeeper all goals legally scored as well as penalties, and for what infractions such penalties are imposed.

The Referee shall cause to be announced over the public address system the reason for not allowing a goal every time the goal signal light is turned on in the course of play. This shall be done at the first stoppage of play regardless of any standard signal given by the Referee when the goal signal light was put on in error.

The Referee shall report to the Official Scorer the name or number of the goal scorer but he shall *not* give any information or advice with respect to assists.

(NOTE) *The name of the scorer and any player entitled to an assist will be announced on the public address system. In the event that the Referee disallows a goal for any violation of the rules, he shall report the reason for disallowance to the Official Scorer who shall announce the Referee's decision correctly over the public address system.*

The infraction of the rules for which each penalty has been imposed will be announced correctly, as reported by the Referee, over the public address system. Where players of both teams are penalized on the same play, the penalty to the visiting player will be announced first.

Where a penalty is imposed by the Referee which calls for a mandatory or automatic fine, only the time portion of the penalty will be reported by the Referee to the Official Scorer and announced on the public address system, and the fine will be collected through the League office.

(h)   The Referee shall see to it that players of opposing teams are separated on the penalty bench to prevent feuding.

(i)   He shall not halt the game for any infractions of the rules concerning off-side play at the blue line, or center lines or any violation of the "Icing the Puck" rule which shall be the function of the Linesman alone, unless the Linesman shall be prevented by some accident from doing so, in which case the duties of the Linesman shall be assumed by the Referee until play is stopped.

(j)   Should a Referee accidentally leave the ice or receive an injury which incapacitates him from discharging his duties while play is in progress the game shall be automatically stopped.

(k) If, through misadventure or sickness, the Referee and Linesmen appointed are prevented from appearing, the Managers or Coaches of the two clubs shall agree on a Referee and Linesman. If they are unable to agree, they shall appoint a player from each side who shall act as Referee and Linesman; the player of the home club acting as Referee, and the player of the visiting club as Linesman.

(l) If the regularly appointed officials appear during the progress of the game, they shall at once replace the temporary officials.

(m) Should a Linesman appointed be unable to act at the last minute or through sickness or accident be unable to finish the game, the Referee shall have the power to appoint another, in his stead, if he deems it necessary, or if required to do so by the Manager or Coach of either of the competing teams.

(n) If, owing to illness or accident, the Referee is unable to continue to officiate, one of the Linesmen shall perform such duties as devolved upon the Referee during the balance of the game, the Linesman to be selected by the Referee.

(o) The Referee shall check Club's rosters and all players in uniform before signing reports of the game.

(p) The Referee shall report to the President promptly and in detail the circumstances of any of the following incidents:—
  (1) When a stick or part thereof is thrown outside the playing area;
  (2) Every obscene gesture made by any person involved in the playing or conduct of the game whether as a participant or as an official of either team or of the League, which gesture he has personally observed or which has been brought to his attention by any game official;
  (3) When any player, trainer, coach or Club executive becomes involved in an altercation with a spectator.
  (4) Every infraction under Rule 77 (c) (slashing).

Rule 37.   Linesman

(a) The duty of the LINESMAN is to determine any infractions of the rules concerning off-side play at the blue line, or center line, or any violation of the "Icing the Puck" rule.

He shall stop the play when the puck goes outside the playing area and when it is interfered with by any ineligible person and when it is struck above the height of the shoulder and when the goal post has been displaced from its normal position. He shall stop the play for off-sides occurring on face-offs circles. He shall stop the play when there has been a premature substitution for a goal-keeper under Rule 18 (a).

(b) He shall face the puck at all times, except at the start of the game, at the beginning of each period and after a goal has been scored.

The Referee may call upon a Linesman to conduct a face-off at any time.

(c) He shall, when requested to do so by the Referee, give his version of any incident that may have taken place during the playing of the game.

(d) He shall not stop the play to impose any penalty except any violation of the Rule 18 (a) & (c)—Change of Players (too many men on the ice) and any violation of Rule 42 (h) (articles thrown on the ice from vicinity of players' or penalty bench) and Rule 46 (c) (stick thrown on ice from players' bench) and he shall report such violation to the Referee who shall impose a bench minor penalty against the offending team.

He shall report immediately to the Referee his version of the circumstances with respect to Rule 50 (c)—Delaying the game by deliberately displacing post from its normal position.

He shall report immediately to the Referee his version of any infraction of the rules constituting a major or match foul or Game Misconduct or any conduct calling for a bench minor penalty or misconduct penalty under these rules.

Rule 38.   **Goal Judge**

(a)   There shall be one GOAL JUDGE at each goal. They shall not be members of either club engaged in a game, nor shall they be replaced during its progress, unless after the commencement of the game it becomes apparent that either Goal Judge, on account of partisanship or any other cause, is guilty of giving unjust decisions, when the Referee may appoint another Goal Judge to act in his stead.

(b)   Goal Judges shall be stationed behind the goals, during the progress of play, in properly screened cages, so that there can be no interference with their activities; and they shall not change goals during the game.

(c)   In the event of a goal being claimed, the Goal Judge of that goal shall decide whether or not the puck has passed between the goal posts and entirely over the goal line, his decision simply being "goal" or "no goal."

Rule 39.   **Penalty Timekeeper**

(a)   The PENALTY TIMEKEEPER shall keep, on the official forms provided, a correct record of all penalties imposed by the officials including the names of the players penalized, the infractions penalized, the duration of each penalty and the time at which each penalty was imposed. He shall report in the Penalty Record each penalty shot awarded, the name of the player taking the shot and the result of the shot.

(b)   The Penalty Timekeeper shall check and ensure that the time served by all penalized players is correct. He shall be responsible for the correct posting of penalties on the scoreboard at all times and shall promptly call to the attention of the Referee any discrepancy between the time recorded on the clock and the official correct time and he shall be responsible for making any adjustments ordered by the Referee.

He shall upon request, give a penalized player correct information as to the unexpired time of his penalty.

(NOTE 1) *The infraction of the rules for which each penalty has been imposed will be announced twice over the public address system as reported by the Referee. Where players of both teams are penalized on the same play, the penalty to the visiting player will be announced first.*

(NOTE 2) *Misconduct penalties and co-incident major penalties should not be recorded on the timing device but such penalized players should be alerted and released at the first stoppage of play following the expiration of their penalties.*

(c)   Upon the completion of each game, the Penalty Timekeeper shall complete and sign three copies of the Penalty Record to be distributed as quickly as possible to the following persons:—

(1) One copy to the Official Scorer for transmission to the League President;

(2) One copy to the visiting Coach or Manager;

(3) One copy to the home Coach or Manager.

(d)   The Referee-in-Chief shall be entitled to inspect, collect, and forward to the League headquarters the actual work sheets used by the Penalty Timekeeper in any game.

Rule 40.   Official Scorer

(a)   Before the start of the game, the Official Scorer shall obtain from the Manager or Coach of both teams a list of all eligible players and the starting line-up of each team which information shall be made known to the opposing team Manager or Coach before the start of play either personally or through the Referee.

The Official Scorer shall secure the names of the Captain and Alternate Captains, from the Manager or Coach at the time the line-ups are collected and will indicate those nominated by placing the letter "C" or "A" opposite their names on the Referee's Report of Match. All of this information shall be presented to the Referee for his signature at the completion of the game.

(b)   The Official Scorer shall keep a record of the goals scored, the scorers, and players to whom assists have been credited, and shall indicate those players on the lists who have actually taken part in the game. He shall also record the time of entry into the game of any substitute goalkeeper. He shall record on the Official Score Sheet a notation where a goal is scored when the goalkeeper has been removed from the ice.

(c)   The Official Scorer shall award the points for goals and assists and his decision shall be final. The awards of points for goals and assists shall be announced twice over the public address system and all changes in such awards shall also be announced in the same manner.

No requests for changes in any award of points shall be considered unless they are made at or before the conclusion of actual play in the game by the team Captain or Alternate Captain.

(d)   At the conclusion of the game the Official Scorer shall complete and sign three copies of the Official Score Sheet for distribution as quickly as possible to the following persons:—

(1) One copy to the League President;

(2) One copy to the visiting Coach or Manager;

(3) One copy to the home Coach or Manager.

(e)   The Official Scorer shall also prepare the Official Report of Match for signature by the Referee and forward it to the League President together with the Official Score Sheet and the Penalty Record.

(f)   The Official Scorer should be in an elevated position, well away from the Players' Benches, with house telephone communication to the Public Address Announcer.

Rule 41.   Game Timekeeper

(a)   The Game Timekeeper shall record the time of starting and finishing of each period in the game and all playing time during the game.

(b)   The Game Timekeeper shall signal the Referee and the competing teams for the start of the game and each succeeding period and the Referee shall start the play promptly in accordance with Rule 81.

To assist in assuring the prompt return to the ice of the teams and the officials the Game Timekeeper shall give a preliminary warning three minutes prior to the resumption of play in each period.

(c)   If the rink is not equipped with an automatic gong or bell or siren or, if such device fails to function, the Game Timekeeper shall signal the end of each period by ringing a gong or bell or by blowing a whistle.

(d)   He shall cause to be announced on the public address system at the nineteenth minute in each period that there is one minute remaining to be played in the period.

(e) In the event of any dispute regarding time, the matter shall be referred to the Referee for adjustment, and his decision shall be final.

Rule 41A.   Statistician

(a) There shall be appointed for duty at every game played in the League a Statistician and such assistants or alternates as may be deemed necessary.

(b) The duty of the Statistician(s) is to correctly record on the official League forms supplied all of the data therein provided for concerning the performances of the individual players and the participating teams.

(c) These records shall be compiled and recorded in strict conformity with the instructions printed on the forms supplied and shall be completed as to totals where required and with such accuracy as to ensure that the data supplied is "in balance."

(d) At the conclusion of each game the Statistician shall sign and distribute three copies of the final and correct Statistician's Report to each of the following persons:—

　　(1) One copy to the League President (through the Official Scorer if possible— otherwise by direct mail);

　　(2) One copy to the visiting Coach or Manager;

　　(3) One copy to the home Coach or Manager.

SECTION SIX—PLAYING RULES

Rule 42.   Abuse of Officials and other Misconduct

　　(NOTE) *In the enforcement of this rule the Referee has, in many instances, the option of imposing a "misconduct penalty" or a "bench minor penalty." In principle the Referee is directed to impose a "bench minor penalty" in respect to the violations which occur on or in the immediate vicinity of the players' bench but off the playing surface, and in all cases affecting non-playing personnel or players. A "misconduct penalty" should be imposed for violations which occur on the playing surface or in the penalty bench area and where the penalized player is readily identifiable.*

(a) A misconduct penalty shall be imposed on any player who uses obscene, profane or abusive language or gestures to any person or who persists in disputing or shows disrespect for the rulings of any official during a game or who intentionally knocks or shoots the puck out of the reach of an official who is retrieving it or who deliberately throws any equipment out of the playing area.

(b) A misconduct penalty shall be imposed on any player or players who bang the boards with their sticks or other instruments any time.

　　In the event that the Coach, Trainer, Manager or Club Executive commits an infraction under this Rule a bench minor penalty shall be imposed.

(c) A misconduct penalty shall be imposed on any penalized player who does not proceed directly and immediately to the penalty box and take his place on the penalty bench.

　　Where coincident penalties are imposed on players of both teams the penalized players of the visiting team shall take their positions on the penalty bench first in the place designated for visiting players, or where there is no special designation then on the bench farthest from the gate.

Any player who (following a fight or other altercation in which he has been involved is broken up, and for which he is penalized) fails to proceed directly and immediately to the penalty bench; or who causes any delay by retrieving his equipment (gloves, sticks, etc. shall be delivered to him at the penalty bench by his teammates); or who persists in continuing or attempting to continue the fight or altercation; or who resists a Linesman in the discharge of his duties shall incur an automatic fine of one hundred dollars ($100.00) in addition to all other penalties or fines incurred.

(d) A misconduct penalty shall be imposed on any player who, after warning by the Referee, persists in any course of conduct (including threatening or abusive language or gestures or similar actions) designed to incite an opponent into incurring a penalty.

(e) In the case of any Club Executive, Manager, Coach or Trainer being guilty of such misconduct, he is to be removed from the bench by order of the Referee, and his case reported to the President for further action.

(f) If any Club Executive, Manager, Coach or Trainer is removed from the bench by order of the Referee, he must not sit near the bench of his club, nor in any way direct or attempt to direct the play of his club.

(g) A bench minor penalty shall be imposed against the offending team if any player, any Club Executive, Manager, Coach or Trainer uses obscene, profane or abusive language or gesture to any person or uses the name of any official coupled with any vociferous remarks.

(h) A bench minor penalty shall be imposed against the offending team if any player, Trainer, Coach, Manager or Club Executive in the vicinity of the players' bench or penalty bench throws anything on the ice during the progress of the game or during stoppage of play.

(NOTE) *The penalty provided under this rule is in addition to any penalty imposed under Rule 46 (c) "Broken Stick."*

(i) A bench minor penalty shall be imposed against the offending team if any player, Trainer, Coach, Manager or Club Executive interferes in any manner with any game official including Referee, Linesman, Timekeepers or Goal Judges in the performance of their duties.

The Referee may assess further penalties under Rule 67 (Molesting Officials) if he deems them to be warranted.

(j) A misconduct penalty shall be imposed on any player or players who, except for the purpose of taking their positions on the penalty bench, enter or remain in the Referee's Crease while he is reporting to or consulting with any game official including Linesmen, Timekeeper, Penalty Timekeeper, Official Scorer or Announcer.

Rule 43.   Adjustment to Clothing and Equipment

(a) Play shall not be stopped, nor the game delayed by reason of adjustments to clothing, equipment, shoes, skates or sticks.

For an infringement of this rule, a minor penalty shall be given.

(b) The onus of maintaining clothing and equipment in proper condition shall be upon the player. If adjustments are required, the player shall retire from the ice and play shall continue uninterruptedly with a substitute.

(c) However a goalkeeper, after a stoppage of play, with the permission of the Referee, may be allowed to make adjustments or repairs to clothing, equipment, shoes or skates.

A goalkeeper may also be permitted by the Referee to replace his mask but no time shall be allowed for repair or fitting of a mask.

For an infraction of the rule by a goalkeeper, a minor penalty shall be imposed.

Rule 44.   **Attempt to Injure**

(a) A match penalty shall be imposed on any player who deliberately attempts to injure an opponent and the circumstances shall be reported to the President for further action. A substitute for the penalized player shall be permitted at the end of the fifth minute.

(b) A Game Misconduct penalty shall be imposed on any player who deliberately attempts to injure an Official, Manager, Coach or Trainer in any manner and the circumstances shall be reported to the President for further action.

Rule 45.   **Board-Checking**

A minor or major penalty, at the discretion of the Referee based upon the degree of violence of the impact with the boards, shall be imposed on any player who body-checks, cross-checks, elbows, charges or trips an opponent in such a manner that causes the opponent to be thrown violently into the boards.

(NOTE) *Any unnecessary contact with a player playing the puck on an obvious "icing" or "off-side" play which results in that player being knocked into the fence is "boarding" and must be penalized as such. In other instances where there is no contact with the fence it should be treated as "charging."*

"Rolling" an opponent (if he is the puck carrier) along the fence where he is endeavouring to go through too small an opening is not boarding. However, if the opponent is not the puck carrier, then such action should be penalized as boarding, charging, interference or if the arms or stick are employed it should be called holding or hooking.

Rule 46.   **Broken Stick**

(a) A player without a stick may participate in the game. A player whose stick is broken may participate in the game provided he drops the broken portion. A minor penalty shall be imposed for an infraction of this rule.

(NOTE) *A broken stick is one which, in the opinion of the Referee, is unfit for normal play.*

(b) A goalkeeper may continue to play with a broken stick until stoppage of play or until he has been legally provided with a stick.

(c) A player whose stick is broken may not receive a stick thrown onto the ice from any part of the rink but must obtain same at his players' bench. A goalkeeper whose stick is broken may not receive a stick thrown onto the ice from any part of the rink but may receive a stick from a teammate without proceeding to his players' bench. A minor penalty plus a misconduct penalty shall be imposed on the player or goalkeeper receiving a stick illegally under this rule.

Rule 47.   **Charging**

(a) A minor or major penalty shall be imposed on a player who runs or jumps into or charges an opponent.

(b)   When a major penalty is imposed under this rule for a foul, resulting in injury to the face or head of an opponent, an automatic fine of fifty dollars ($50.00) shall be imposed.

(c)   A minor or major penalty shall be imposed on a player who charges a goalkeeper while the goalkeeper is within his goal crease.

(NOTE) *If more than two steps or strides are taken it shall be considered a charge.*

A goalkeeper is NOT "fair game" just because he is outside the goal crease area. A penalty for interference or charging (minor or major) should be called in every case where an opposing player makes unnecessary contact with a goalkeeper.

Likewise Referees should be alert to penalize goalkeepers for tripping, slashing or spearing in the vicinity of the goal.

Rule 48.   Cross-Checking and Butt-Ending

(a)   A minor or major penalty, at the discretion of the Referee, shall be imposed on a player who "cross-checks" or "butt-ends" an opponent.

(b)   When a major penalty is imposed under this rule for a foul resulting in injury to the face or head of an opponent, an automatic fine of fifty dollars ($50.00) shall also be imposed.

(NOTE) *Cross-check shall mean a check delivered with both hands on the stick and no part of the stick on the ice.*

Rule 49.   Deliberate Injury of Opponents

(a)   A match penalty shall be imposed on a player who deliberately injures an opponent in any manner.

(b)   In addition to the match penalty, the Referee shall impose a fine of one hundred dollars ($100.00) on any player who deliberately injures another in any manner.

(c)   No substitute shall be permitted to take the place of the penalized player until ten minutes actual playing time shall have elapsed, from the time the penalty was imposed.

(d)   A Game Misconduct penalty shall be imposed on any player who deliberately injures an Official, Manager, Coach or Trainer in any manner and the circumstances shall be reported to the President for further action.

Rule 50.   Delaying the Game

(a)   A minor penalty shall be imposed on any player or goalkeeper who delays the game by deliberately shooting or batting the puck with his stick outside the playing area.

(NOTE) *This penalty shall apply also when a player or goalkeeper deliberately bats or shoots the puck with his stick outside the playing area after a stoppage of play.*

(b)   A minor penalty shall be imposed on any player or goalkeeper who throws or deliberately bats the puck with his hand or stick outside the playing area.

(c)   A minor penalty shall be imposed on any player (including goalkeeper) who delays the game by deliberately displacing a goal post from its normal position. The Referee or linesmen shall stop play immediately when a goal post has been displaced.

If the goal post is deliberately displaced by a goalkeeper or player during the course of a "break-away" a penalty shot will be awarded to the non-offending team, which shot shall be taken by the player last in possession of the puck.

(NOTE) *A player with a "break-away" is defined as a player in control of the puck with no opposition between him and the opposing goal and with a reasonable scoring opportunity.*

If by reason of insufficient time in the regular playing time or by reason of penalties already imposed the minor penalty awarded to a player for displacing his own goal post cannot be served in its entirety within the regular playing time of the game or at any time in overtime, a penalty shot shall be awarded against the offending team.

(d)   A bench minor penalty shall be imposed upon any team which, after warning by the Referee to its Captain or Alternate Captain to place the correct number of players on the ice and commence play, fails to comply with the Referee's direction and thereby causes any delay by making additional substitutions, by persisting in having its players off-side, or in any other manner.

Rule 51.   **Elbowing and Kneeing**

(a)   A minor or major penalty, at the discretion of the Referee, shall be imposed on any player who uses his elbow or knee in such a manner as to in any way foul an opponent.

(b)   When a major penalty is imposed under this rule for a foul resulting in an injury to an opponent an automatic fine of fifty dollars ($50.00) shall also be imposed.

Rule 52.   **Face-Offs**

(a)   The puck shall be "faced-off" by the Referee or the Linesman dropping the puck on the ice between the sticks of the players "facing-off." Players facing-off will stand squarely facing their opponents' end of the rink approximately one stick length apart with the blade of their sticks on the ice.

When the face-off takes place in any of the end face-off circles the players taking part shall take their positions so that they will have one skate on each side and clear of the line running through the face-off spot and with both feet behind and clear of the line parallel to the goal line. The sticks of both players facing-off shall have the full blade on the ice and entirely clear of the spot or place where the puck is to be dropped.

No other player shall be allowed to enter the face-off circle or come within fifteen feet of the players facing-off the puck, and must stand on side on all face-offs.

If a violation of this sub-section of this rule occurs the Referee or Linesman shall re-face the puck.

(NOTE) *If after warning by the Referee or Linesman either of the players fails to take his proper position for the face-off promptly, the official shall be entitled to face-off the puck notwithstanding such default.*

(b)   In the conduct of any face-off anywhere on the playing surface no player facing-off shall make any physical contact with his opponent's body by means of his own body or by his stick except in the course of playing the puck after the face-off has been completed.

For violation of this rule the Referee shall impose a minor penalty or penalties on the player(s) whose action(s) caused the physical contact.

(NOTE) *"Conduct of any face-off" commences when the Referee designates the place of the face-off and he (or the Linesman) takes up his position to drop the puck.*

(c)   If a player facing-off fails to take his proper position immediately when directed by the Official, the Official may order him replaced for that face-off by any teammate then on the ice.

No substitution of players shall be permitted until the face-off has been completed and play has been resumed.

(d)   A second violation of any of the provisions of sub-section (a) hereof by the same team during the same face-off shall be penalized with a minor penalty to the player who commits the second violation of the rule.

(e)   When an infringement of a rule has been committed or a stoppage of play has been caused by any player of the attacking side in the Attacking Zone the ensuing face-off shall be made in the Neutral Zone on the nearest face-off spot.

(NOTE) *This includes stoppage of play caused by player of attacking side shooting the puck on to the back of the defending team's net without any intervening action by the defending team.*

(f)   When an infringement of a rule has been committed by players of both sides in the play resulting in the stoppage, the ensuing face-off will be made at the place of such infringement or at the place where play is stopped.

(g)   When stoppage occurs between the end face-off spots and near end of rink the puck shall be faced-off at the end face-off spot, on the side where the stoppage occurs unless otherwise expressly provided by these rules.

(h)   No face-off shall be made within fifteen feet of the goal or sideboards.

(i)   When a goal is illegally scored as a result of a puck being deflected directly from an official anywhere in the defending zone the resulting face-off shall be made at the end face-off spot in the defending zone.

(j)   When the game is stopped for any reason not specifically covered in the official rules, the puck must be faced-off where it was last played.

(k)   The whistle will not be blown by the official to start play. Playing time will commence from the instant the puck is faced-off and will stop when the whistle is blown.

Rule 53.   Falling on Puck

(a)   A minor penalty shall be imposed on a player other than the goalkeeper who deliberately falls on or gathers a puck into his body.

(NOTE) *Any player who drops to his knees to block shots should not be penalized if the puck is shot under them or becomes lodged in their clothing or equipment but any use of the hands to make the puck unplayable should be penalized promptly.*

(b)   A minor penalty shall be imposed on a goalkeeper who (when his body is entirely outside the boundaries of his own crease area and when the puck is behind the goal line) deliberately falls on or gathers the puck into his body or who holds or places the puck against any part of the goal or against the boards.

(c)   No defending player, except the goalkeeper, will be permitted to fall on the puck or hold the puck or gather a puck into the body or hands when the puck is within the goal crease.

For infringement of this rule, play shall immediately be stopped and a penalty shot shall be ordered against the offending team, but no other penalty shall be given.

(NOTE) *This rule shall be interpreted so that a penalty shot will be awarded only when the puck is in the crease at the instant the offense occurs. However, in cases where the puck is outside the crease, Rule 53 (a) may still apply and a minor penalty may be imposed, even though no penalty shot is awarded.*

Rule 54.   **Fisticuffs**

(a) A major, double minor or minor penalty at the discretion of the Referee, shall be imposed on any player who starts fisticuffs.

(b) A minor penalty shall be imposed on a player who, having been struck, shall retaliate with a blow or attempted blow. However, at the discretion of the Referee a major or a double minor penalty may be imposed if such player continues the altercation.

(NOTE 1) *The Referee is provided very wide latitude in the penalties which he may impose under this rule. This is done intentionally to enable him to differentiate between the obvious degrees of responsibility of the participants either for starting the fighting or persisting in continuing the fighting. The discretion provided should be exercised realistically.*

(NOTE 2) *Referees are directed to employ every means provided by these Rules to stop "brawling" and should use Rule 42 (c) for this purpose.*

(c) A Misconduct or Game Misconduct penalty shall be imposed on any player involved in fisticuffs off the playing surface or with another player who is off the playing surface.

(d) A Game Misconduct penalty shall be imposed on any player or goalkeeper on the ice who is the first to intervene in an altercation then in progress. This penalty is in addition to any other penalty incurred in the same incident.

Rule 55.   **Goals and Assists**

(NOTE) *It is the responsibility of the Official Scorer to award goals and assists, and his decision in this respect is final notwithstanding the report of the Referee or any other game official. Such awards shall be made or withheld strictly in accordance with the provisions of this rule. Therefore, it is essential that the Official Scorer shall be thoroughly familiar with every aspect of this rule, be alert to observe all actions which could affect the making of an award and, above all, the awards must be made or withheld with absolute impartiality.*

In case of an obvious error in awarding a goal or an assist which has been announced, it should be corrected promptly but changes should not be made in the official scoring summary after the Referee has signed the Game Report.

(a) A goal shall be scored when the puck shall have been put between the goal posts by the stick of a player of the attacking side, from in front, and below the cross bar, and entirely across a red line, the width of the diameter of the goal posts drawn on the ice from one goal post to the other.

(b) A goal shall be scored if the puck is put into the goal in any way by a player of the defending side. The player of the attacking side who last played the puck shall be credited with the goal but no assist shall be awarded.

(c) If an attacking player kicks the puck and it is deflected into the net by any player of the defending side except the goalkeeper, the goal shall be allowed. The player who kicked the puck shall be credited with the goal but no assist shall be awarded.

(d) If the puck shall have been deflected into the goal from the shot of an attacking player by striking any part of the person of a player of the same side, a goal shall be allowed. The player who deflected the puck shall be credited with the goal. The goal shall not be allowed if the puck has been kicked, thrown or otherwise deliberately directed into the goal by any means other than a stick.

(e) If a goal is scored as a result of a puck being deflected directly into the net from an official the goal shall not be allowed.

(f)   Should a player legally propel a puck into the goal crease of the opponent club and the puck should become loose and available to another player of the attacking side, a goal scored on the play shall be legal.

(g)   Any goal scored, other than as covered by the official rules, shall not be allowed.

(h)   A "goal" shall be credited in the scoring records to a player who shall have propelled the puck into the opponents' goal. Each "goal" shall count one point in the player's record.

(i)   When a player scores a goal an "assist" shall be credited to the player or players taking part in the play immediately preceding the goal, but not more than two assists can be given on any goal. Each "assist" so credited shall count one point in the player's record.

(j)   Only one point can be credited to any one player on a goal.

Rule 56.   **Gross Misconduct**

(a)   The Referee may suspend from the game and order to the dressing room for the remainder of the game, any player, Manager, Coach, or Trainer guilty of gross misconduct of any kind.

(b)   If a player so dismissed is taking part in the game, he shall be charged with a game misconduct penalty, and a substitute shall be permitted.

(c)   The Referee in charge is to decide on any violation and report the incident to the President of the League for further action.

Rule 57.   **Handling Puck With Hands**

(a)   If a player, except the goalkeeper, closes his hand on the puck the play shall be stopped and a minor penalty shall be imposed on him. A goalkeeper who holds the puck with his hands for longer than three seconds shall be given a minor penalty.

(b)   A goalkeeper must not deliberately hold the puck in any manner which in the opinion of the Referee causes a stoppage of play, nor throw the puck forward towards the opponents' goal, nor deliberately drop the puck into his pads or on to the goal net, nor deliberately pile up snow or obstacles at or near his net, that in the opinion of the Referee would tend to prevent the scoring of a goal.

(NOTE) *The object of this entire rule is to keep the puck in play continuously and any action taken by the goalkeeper which causes an unnecessary stoppage must be penalized without warning.*

(c)   The penalty for infringement of this rule by the goalkeeper shall be a minor penalty.

(NOTE) *In the case of puck thrown forward by the goalkeeper being taken by an opponent, the Referee shall allow the resulting play to be completed, and if a goal is scored by the non-offending team, it shall be allowed and no penalty given; but if a goal is not scored, play shall be stopped and a minor penalty shall be awarded against the goalkeeper.*

(d)   A minor penalty shall be imposed on a player except the goalkeeper who, while play is in progress, picks up the puck off the ice with his hand.

If a player, except the goalkeeper, while play is in progress, picks up the puck with his hand from the ice in the goal crease area the play shall be stopped immediately and a penalty shot shall be awarded to the non-offending team.

(e)   A player shall be permitted to stop or "bat" a puck in the air with his open hand, or push it along the ice with his hand, and the play shall not be stopped unless in the opinion of the Referee he has deliberately directed the puck to a teammate, in which case the play shall be stopped and the puck faced-off at the spot where the offense occurred.

(NOTE) *The object of this rule is to ensure continuous action and the Referee should NOT stop play unless he is satisfied that the directing of the puck to a teammate was in fact DELIBERATE.*

The puck may not be "batted" with the hand directly into the net at any time, but a goal shall be allowed when the puck has been legally "batted" or is deflected into the goal by a defending player except the goalkeeper.

Rule 58.   **High Sticks**

(a) The carrying of sticks above the normal height of the shoulder is prohibited, and a minor penalty may be imposed on any player violating this rule, at the discretion of the Referee.

(b) A goal scored from a stick so carried shall not be allowed, except by a player of the defending team.

(c) When a player carries or holds any part of his stick above the height of his shoulder so that injury to the face or head of an opposing player results, the Referee shall have no alternative but to impose a major penalty on the offending player.

When a major penalty is imposed under this rule for a foul resulting in injury to the face or head of an opponent, an automatic fine of fifty dollars ($50.00) shall be imposed.

(d) Batting the puck above the normal height of the shoulders with the stick is prohibited and when it occurs there shall be a Whistle and ensuing face-off at the spot where the offense occurred unless:

1. the defending player in his own Defending Zone or in the Neutral Zone shall bat the puck to an opponent in which case the play shall continue, or

2. a player of the defending side shall bat the puck into his own goal in which case the goal shall be allowed.

(NOTE) *When player bats the puck to an opponent under sub-section 1 the Referee shall give the "wash-out" signal immediately. Otherwise he will stop the play.*

(e) When either team is below the numerical strength of its opponent and a player of the team of greater numerical strength causes a stoppage of play by striking the puck with his stick above the height of his shoulder, the resulting face-off shall be made at one of the end face-off spots adjacent to the goal of the team causing the stoppage.

Rule 59.   **Holding an Opponent**

A minor penalty shall be imposed on a player who holds an opponent with hands or stick or in any other way.

Rule 60.   **Hooking**

(a) A minor penalty shall be imposed on any player who impedes or seeks to impede the progress of an opponent by "hooking" with his stick.

(b) A major penalty shall be imposed on any player who injures an opponent by "hooking."

When a major penalty is imposed under this rule for a foul resulting in injury to the face or head of an opponent, an automatic fine of fifty dollars ($50.00) shall also be imposed.

(NOTE) *When a player is checking another in such a way that there is only stick-to-stick contact such action is NOT either hooking or holding.*

Rule 61.   **Icing the Puck**

(a) For the purpose of this rule, the center line will divide the ice into halves. Should any player of a team, equal or superior in numerical strength to the opposing team, shoot, bat, or deflect the puck from his own half of the ice, beyond the goal line of the opposing team, play shall be stopped and the puck faced off at the end face-off of the offending team, unless on the play the puck shall have entered the net of the opposing team, in which case the goal shall be allowed.

For the purpose of this rule the point of last contact with the puck by the team in possession shall be used to determine whether icing has occurred or not.

(NOTE 1) *If during the period of a delayed whistle due to a foul by a player of the side NOT in possession, the side in possession "ices" the puck then the face-off following the stoppage of play shall take place in the Neutral zone near the Defending Blue Line of the team "icing" the puck.*

(NOTE 2) *When a team is "Short-handed" as the result of a penalty and the penalty is about to expire, the decision as to whether there has been an "icing" shall be determined at the instant the penalty expires, and if the puck crosses the opponents' goal line after the penalty has expired it is "icing." The action of the penalized player remaining in the penalty box will not alter the ruling.*

(NOTE 3) *For the purpose of interpretation of this rule "Icing the Puck" is completed the instant the puck is touched first by a defending player (other than the goalkeeper) after it has crossed the Goal Line and if ,in the action of so touching the puck it is knocked or deflected into the net it is NO goal.*

(NOTE 4) *When the puck is shot and rebounds from the body or stick of an opponent in his own half of the ice so as to cross the goal line of the player shooting it shall not be considered as "icing."*

(NOTE 5) *Notwithstanding the provisions of this section concerning "batting" the puck in respect to the "icing the puck" rule, the provisions of the final paragraph of Rule 57 (e) apply and NO goal can be scored by batting the puck with the hand into the opponent's goal whether attended or not.*

(NOTE 6) *If while the Linesman has signalled a slow whistle for a clean interception under Rule 71 (c), the player intercepting shoots or bats the puck beyond the opponent's goal line in such a manner as to constitute "icing the puck," the Linesman's "slow whistle" shall be considered exhausted the instant the puck crosses the blue line and "icing" shall be called in the usual manner.*

(b) If a player of the side shooting the puck down the ice who is on-side and eligible to play the puck does so before it is touched by an opposing player, the play shall continue and it shall not be considered a violation of this rule.

(c) If the puck was so shot by a player of a side below the numerical strength of the opposing team, play shall continue and the face-off shall not take place.

(d) If, however, the puck shall go beyond the goal line in the opposite half of the ice directly from either of the players while facing off, it shall not be considered a violation of the rule.

(e) If, in the opinion of the Linesman, a player of the opposing team excepting the goalkeeper is able to play the puck before it passes his goal line, but has not done so, the face-off shall not be allowed and play shall continue. If, in the opinion of the Referee, the defending side intentionally abstains from playing the puck promptly when they are in a position to do so, he shall stop the play and order the resulting face-off on the adjacent corner face-off spot nearest the goal of the team at fault.

(NOTE) *The purpose of this section is to enforce continuous action and both Referee and Linesmen should interpret and apply the rule to produce this result.*

(f)   If the puck shall touch any part of a player of the opposing side or his skates or his stick, or if it passes through any part of the goal crease before it shall have reached his goal line, or shall have touched the goalkeeper or his skates or his stick at any time before or after crossing his goal line it shall not be considered as "icing the puck" and play shall continue.

(NOTE) *If the goaltender takes any action to dislodge the puck from back of the nets the icing shall be washed out.*

(g)   If the Linesman shall have erred in calling an "icing the puck" infraction (regardless of whether either team is short-handed) the puck shall be faced on the center ice face-off spot.

Rule 62.   **Interference**

(a)   A minor penalty shall be imposed on a player who interferes with or impedes the progress of an opponent who is not in possession of the puck, or who deliberately knocks a stick out of an opponent's hand or who prevents a player who has dropped his stick from regaining possession of it or who knocks or shoots any abandoned or broken stick or illegal puck or other debris towards an opposing puck carrier in a manner that could cause him to be distracted.

(NOTE) *The last player to touch the puck—other than a goalkeeper—shall be considered the player in possession. In interpreting this rule the Referee should make sure which of the players is the one creating the interference—Often it is the action and movement of the attacking player which causes the interference since the defending players are entitled to "stand their ground" or "shadow" the attacking players. Players of the side in possession shall not be allowed to "run" deliberate interference for the puck carrier.*

(b)   A minor penalty shall be imposed on any player on the players' bench or on the penalty bench who by means of his stick or his body interferes with the movements of the puck or of any opponent on the ice during the progress of play.

(c)   A minor penalty shall be imposed on a player who, by means of his stick or his body, interferes with or impedes the movements of the goalkeeper by actual physical contact, while he is in his goal crease area unless the puck is already in that area.

(d)   Unless the puck is in the goal crease area, a player of the attacking side not in possession may not stand on the goal crease line or in the goal crease or hold his stick in the goal crease area, and if the puck should enter the net while such condition prevails, a goal shall not be allowed, and the puck shall be faced in the neutral zone at face-off spot nearest the attacking zone of the offending team.

(e)   If a player of the attacking side has been physically interfered with by the action of any defending player so as to cause him to be in the goal crease, and the puck should enter the net while the player so interfered with, is still within the goal crease, the "goal" shall be allowed.

(f)   If when the goalkeeper has been removed from the ice any member of his team (including the goalkeeper) not legally on the ice, including the Manager, Coach or Trainer interferes by means of his body or stick or any other object with the movements of the puck or an opposing player, the Referee shall immediately award a goal to the non-offending team.

(NOTE) *The attention of Referees is directed particularly to three types of offensive interference which should be penalized;*

(1) *When the defending team secures possession of the puck in its own end and the other players of that team run interference for the puck carrier by forming a protective screen against forechecker;*

(2) *When a player facing off obstructs his opposite number after the face-off when the opponent is not in possession of the puck;*

(3) *When the puck carrier makes a drop pass and follows through so as to make bodily contact with an opposing player.*

Defensive interference consists of bodily contact with an opposing player who is not in possession of the puck.

Rule 63.   Interference by Spectators

(a) In the event of a player being held or interfered with by a spectator, the Referee or Linesman shall blow the whistle and play shall be stopped, unless the team of the player interfered with is in possession of the puck at this time when the play shall be allowed to be completed before blowing the whistle, and the puck shall be faced at the spot where last played at time of stoppage.

(NOTE) *The Referee shall report to the President for disciplinary action, all cases in which a player becomes involved in an altercation with a spectator but no penalty should be imposed.*

(b) In the event that objects are thrown on the ice which interfere with the progress of the game the Referee shall blow the whistle and stop the play, and the puck shall be faced-off at the spot play is stopped.

Rule 64.   Kicking Player

A match penalty shall be imposed on any player who kicks or attempts to kick another player, but a substitute shall be permitted at the end of the fifth minute.

(NOTE) *When actual injury results this foul may be penalized also as a deliberate injury under the Rule 49.*

Rule 65.   Kicking Puck

Kicking the puck shall be permitted in all zones, but a goal may not be scored by the kick of an attacking player except if an attacking player kicks the puck and it is deflected into the net by any players of the defending side except the goalkeeper.

Rule 66.   Leaving Players' Bench or Penalty Bench

(a) No player may leave the players' bench or penalty bench at any time during an altercation. Substitutions made prior to the altercation shall be permitted provided the players so substituting do not enter the altercation.

(b) For violation of this rule a Double Minor penalty shall be imposed on the player of the team who was first to leave the players' bench or penalty bench during an altercation. If players of both teams leave their respective benches at the same time, the first identifiable player of each team to do so shall incur a Double Minor penalty, A Game Misconduct penalty shall also be imposed on any player who is penalized under this subsection.

(NOTE) *This automatic fine shall be imposed in addition to the normal penalties imposed for fouls committed by the player after he has left the players' bench.*

(c) Any player (other than those dealt with under subsection (b) hereof) who leaves his players' bench during an altercation and is assessed a minor, major or misconduct penalty for his actions, shall also incur an automatic Game Misconduct penalty.

(d) A player (other than those dealt with under subsection (b) & (c) hereof) who leaves his players' bench during an altercation, shall be subject to an automatic fine of one hundred dollars ($100.00) and the Referee shall report all such infractions to the President who shall have full power to impose such further penalty as he shall deem appropriate.

(NOTE) *For the purpose of determining which player was first to leave his players' bench during an altercation the Referee may consult with the linesmen or Minor Officials.*

(e) In regular League games, any player who incurs a *second* penalty under subsection (b) hereof (for leaving the players' bench first) shall be suspended automatically for the next League game of his team. For each subsequent violation, the automatic suspension shall be increased by one game.

In play-off games, any player who incurs a penalty under subsection (b) hereof (for leaving the players bench first), shall be suspended automatically for the next play-off game of his team. For each subsequent violation, this automatic suspension shall be increased by one game.

The automatic suspensions incurred under this subsection in respect to League games shall have no effect with respect to violations during play-off games.

(f) Except at the end of each period, or on expiration of penalty, no player may at any time leave the penalty bench.

(g) A penalized player who leaves the penalty bench before his penalty has expired, whether play is in progress or not, but does not enter an altercation, shall incur an additional minor penalty, after serving his unexpired penalty.

(h) Any penalized player leaving the penalty bench during stoppage of play and during an altercation shall incur a minor penalty plus a Game Misconduct penalty after serving his unexpired time.

(i) If a player leaves the penalty bench before his penalty is fully served, the Penalty Timekeeper shall note the time and signal the Referee who will immediately stop play.

(j) In the case of a player returning to the ice before his time has expired through an error of the Penalty Timekeeper, he is not to serve an additional penalty, but must serve his unexpired time.

(k) If a player of an attacking side in possession of the puck shall be in such a position as to have no opposition between him and the opposing goalkeeper, and while in such position he shall be interfered with by a player of the opposing side who shall have illegally entered the game, the Referee shall award a penalty shot against the side to which the offending player belongs.

(l) If the opposing goalkeeper has been removed and an attacking player in possession of the puck shall have no player of the defending team to pass and a stick or a part thereof is thrown by an opposing player or the player is fouled from behind thereby being prevented from having a clear shot on an open goal, a goal shall be awarded against the offending team.

If when the opposing goalkeeper has been removed from the ice a player of the side attacking the unattended goal is interfered with by a player who shall have entered the game illegally, the Referee shall immediately award a goal to the non-offending team.

(m) If a Coach or Manager gets on the ice after the start of a period and before that period is ended the Referee shall impose a bench minor penalty against the team and report the incident to the President for disciplinary action.

(n) Any Club Executive or Manager committing the same offense, will be automatically fined two hundred dollars ($200.00).

(o) If a penalized player returns to the ice from the penalty bench before his penalty has expired by his own error or the error of the Penalty Timekeeper, any goal scored by his own team while he is illegally on the ice shall be disallowed, but all penalties imposed on either team shall be served as regular penalties.

(p) If a player shall illegally enter the game from his own players' bench or from the penalty bench, any goal scored by his own team while he is illegally on the ice shall be disallowed, but all penalties imposed against either team shall be served as regular penalties.

Rule 67.   **Molesting Officials**

(a) Any player who touches or holds a Referee, Linesman or any game official with his hand or his stick or trips or body-checks any of such officials, shall automatically receive a ten-minute penalty for misconduct for the first offense, and a game misconduct penalty for a second offense, in the same game. The use of a substitute for the player so suspended shall be permitted.

(b) Any Club Executive, Manager, Coach or Trainer who holds or strikes an official, shall be automatically suspended from the game, ordered to the dressing room, and a substantial fine shall be imposed by the President.

Rule 68.   **Obscene or Profane Language or Gestures**

(a) Players shall not use obscene or profane language or gestures on the ice or anywhere in the rink. For violation of this rule a misconduct penalty shall be imposed except where the violation occurs in the vicinity of the players' bench in which case a bench penalty shall be imposed.

(b) Club Executives, Managers, Coaches and Trainers shall not use obscene or profane language or gestures anywhere in the rink. For violation of this rule a bench minor penalty shall be imposed.

   (NOTE) *It is the responsibility of all game officials and all Club officials to send a confidential report to the President setting out the full details concerning the use of obscene gestures or language by any player, Coach or other official. The President shall take such further disciplinary action as he shall deem appropriate.*

Rule 69.   **Off-Sides**

(a) The position of the player's skates and not that of his stick shall be the determining factor in all instances in deciding an "off-side." A player is off-side when both skates are completely over the outer edge of the determining center line or blue line involved in the play.

   (NOTE 1) *A player is "on-side" when "either" of his skates are in contact with or on his own side of the line at the instant the puck completely crosses the outer edge of that line regardless of the position of his stick.*

   (NOTE 2) *It should be noted that while the position of the player's skates is what determines whether a player is "off-side" nevertheless the question of "off-side" never arises until the puck has completely crossed the outer edge of the line at which time the decision is to be made.*

(b) If in the opinion of the Linesman an intentional off-side play has been made, the puck shall be faced-off at the end face-off spot in the defending zone of the offending team.

   (NOTE 3) *This rule does not apply to a team below the numerical strength of its opponent. In such cases the puck shall be faced-off at the spot from which the pass was made.*

(NOTE 4) *An intentional off-side is one which is made for the purpose of securing a stoppage of play regardless of the reason, or where an off-side play is made under conditions where there is no possibility of completing a legal pass.*

(c)   If the linesmen shall have erred in calling an off-side pass infraction (regardless of whether either team is short-handed) the puck shall be faced-off on the center ice face-off spot.

Rule 70.   Passes

(a)   The puck may be passed by any player to a player of the same side within any one of the three zones into which the ice is divided, but may not be passed forward from a player in one zone to a player of the same side in another zone, except by a player on the defending team, who may make and take forward passes from their own defending zone to the center line without incurring an off-side penalty. This "forward pass" from the Defending Zone must be completed by the pass receiver who is legally on-side at the center line.

(NOTE 1) *The position of the puck (not the player's skates) shall be the determining factor in deciding from which zone the pass was made.*

(NOTE 2) *Passes may be completed legally at the center red line in exactly the same manner as passes at the attacking blue line.*

(b)   Should the puck, having been passed, contact any part of the body, stick or skates of a player of the same side who is legally on-side, the pass shall be considered to have been completed.

(c)   The player last touched by the puck shall be deemed to be in possession.

Rebounds off goalkeeper's pads or other equipment shall not be considered as a change of possession or the completion of the play by the team when applying Rule 34 (b).

(d)   If a player in the Neutral Zone is preceded into the Attacking Zone by the puck passed from the Neutral Zone he shall be eligible to take possession of the puck anywhere in the Attacking Zone except when the "Icing the Puck" rule applies.

(e)   If a player in the same zone from which a pass is made is preceded by the puck into succeeding zones he shall be eligible to take possession of the puck in that zone except where the "Icing the Puck" rule applies.

(f)   If an attacking player passes the puck backward toward his own goal from the Attacking Zone, an opponent may play the puck anywhere regardless of whether he (the opponent) was in the same zone at the time the puck was passed or not. *(No "slow whistle.")*

Rule 71.   Preceding Puck into Attacking Zone

(a)   Players of an attacking team must not precede the puck into the Attacking Zone.

(b)   For violation of this rule, the play is stopped, and puck shall be faced-off in the Neutral Zone at face-off spot nearest the Attacking Zone of the offending team.

(NOTE) *A player actually propelling the puck who shall cross the line ahead of the puck, shall not be considered "off-side."*

(c)   If however, notwithstanding the fact that a member of the attacking team shall have preceded the puck into the Attacking Zone, the puck be cleanly intercepted by a member of the defending team at or near the blue line, and be carried or passed by them into the Neutral Zone the "off-side" shall be ignored and play permitted to continue.

(Officials will carry out this rule by means of the "slow whistle.")

(d) If a player legally carries or passes the puck back into his own Defending Zone while a player of the opposing team is in such Defending Zone, the "off-side" shall be ignored and play permitted to continue.
(No "slow whistle.")

Rule 72.   **Puck Out of Bounds or Unplayable**

(a) When the puck goes outside the playing area at either end, or either side of the rink or strikes any obstacles above the playing surface other than the boards, glass or wire it shall be faced-off from whence it was shot or deflected, unless otherwise expressly provided in these rules.

(b) When the puck becomes lodged in the netting on the outside of either goal so as to make it unplayable, or if it is frozen between players intentionally or otherwise, the Referee shall stop the play and face-off the puck at either of the adjacent face-off spots unless in the opinion of the Referee the stoppage was caused by a player of the attacking team, in which case the resulting face-off shall be conducted in the Neutral Zone.

(NOTE) *This includes stoppage of play caused by player of attacking side shooting the puck onto the back of the defending team's net without any intervening action by the defending team.*

The defending team and/or the attacking team may play the puck off the net at any time. However, should the puck remain on the net for longer than three seconds, play shall be stopped and the face-off shall take place in the end face-off zone except when the stoppage is caused by the attacking team, then the face-off shall take place on a face-off spot in the neutral zone.

(c) A minor penalty shall be imposed on a goalkeeper who deliberately drops the puck on the goal netting to cause a stoppage of play.

(d) If the puck comes to rest on top of the boards surrounding the playing area it shall be considered to be in play and may be played legally by hand or stick.

Rule 73.   **Puck Must Be Kept in Motion**

(a) The puck must at all times be kept in motion.

(b) Except to carry the puck behind its goal once, a side in possession of the puck in its own defense area shall always advance the puck towards the opposing goal, except if it shall be prevented from so doing by players of the opposing side.

For the first infraction of this rule play shall be stopped and a face-off shall be made at either end face-off spot adjacent to the goal of the team causing the stoppage, and the Referee shall warn the Captain or Alternate Captain of the offending team of the reason for the face-off. For a second violation by any player of the same team in the same period a minor penalty shall be imposed on the player violating the rule.

(c) A minor penalty shall be imposed on any player including the goalkeeper who holds, freezes or plays the puck with his stick, skates or body along the boards in such a manner as to cause a stoppage of play unless he is actually being checked by an opponent.

(d) A player beyond his defense area shall not pass nor carry the puck backward into his Defense Zone for the purpose of delaying the game except when his team is below the numerical strength of the opponents on the ice.

(e) For an infringement of this rule, the face-off shall be at the nearest end face-off spot in the Defending Zone of the offending team.

Rule 74.   **Puck Out of Sight and Illegal Puck**

(a)   Should a scramble take place, or a player accidentally fall on the puck, and the puck be out of sight of the Referee, he shall immediately blow his whistle and stop the play. The puck shall then be "faced-off" at the point where the play was stopped, unless otherwise provided for in the rules.

(b)   If, at any time while play is in progress a puck other than the one legally in play shall appear on the playing surface, the play shall not be stopped but shall continue with the legal puck until the play then in progress is completed by change of possession.

Rule 75.   **Puck Striking Official**

Play shall not be stopped if the puck touches an official anywhere on the rink, regardless of whether a team is short-handed or not.

Rule 76.   **Refusing to Start Play**

(a)   If, when both teams are on the ice, one team for any reason shall refuse to play when ordered to do so by the Referee, he shall warn the Captain or Alternate Captain and allow the team so refusing fifteen seconds within which to begin the game or resume play. If at the end of that time the team shall still refuse to play, the Referee shall impose a two-minute penalty on a player of the offending team to be designated by the Manager or Coach of that team, through the playing Captain; and should there be a repetition of the same incident the Referee shall notify the Manager or Coach that he has been fined the sum of two hundred dollars ($200.00), and should there be a recurrence of the same incident, the Referee shall have no alternative but to declare that the game be forfeited to the non-offending club, and the case shall be reported to the President for further action.

(b)   If a team, when ordered to do so by the Referee, through its Club Executive, Manager or Coach, fails to go on the ice, and start play within five minutes, the Club Executive, Manager or Coach shall be fined five hundred dollars ($500.00); the game shall be forfeited, and the case shall be reported to the President for further action.

   (NOTE) *The President of the League shall issue instructions pertaining to records, etc., of a forfeited game.*

Rule 77.   **Slashing**

(a)   A minor or major penalty, at the discretion of the Referee, shall be imposed on any player who impedes or seeks to impede the progress of an opponent by "slashing" with his stick.

(b)   A major penalty shall be imposed on any player who injures an opponent by slashing. When a major penalty is imposed under this rule for a foul resulting in injury to the face or head of an opponent, an automatic fine of fifty dollars ($50.00) shall also be imposed.

   (NOTE) *Referees should penalize as "slashing" any player who swings his stick at any opposing player (whether in or out of range) without actually striking him or where a player on the pretext of playing the puck makes a wild swing at the puck with the object of intimidating an opponent.*

(c)   Any player who swings his stick at another player in the course of any altercation shall be subject to a fine of not less than two hundred dollars ($200.00), with or without suspension, to be imposed by the President.

(NOTE) *The Referee shall impose the normal appropriate penalty provided in the other sections of this rule and shall in addition report promptly to the President all infractions under this section.*

Rule 78. **Spearing**

(a) A minor or major penalty, at the discretion of the Referee, shall be imposed on a player who spears or attempts to spear an opponent. Every penalty under this rule shall include an automatic fine of fifty dollars ($50.00).

(NOTE) *"Attempt to spear" shall include all cases where a spearing gesture is made regardless whether bodily contact is made or not.*

(b) A major penalty shall be imposed on any player who injures an opponent by spearing.

When a major penalty is imposed under this rule for a foul resulting in an injury to an opponent an automatic fine of fifty dollars ($50.00) shall also be imposed.

"Spearing" shall mean stabbing an opponent with the point of the stick blade while the stick is being carried with one hand or both hands.

Spearing may also be treated as a "deliberate attempt to injure" under Rule 44.

Rule 79. **Start of Game and Periods**

(a) The game shall be commenced at the time scheduled by a "face-off" in the center of the rink and shall be renewed promptly at the conclusion of each intermission in the same manner.

No delay shall be permitted by reason of any ceremony, exhibition, demonstration or presentation unless consented to reasonably in advance by the visiting team.

(b) Home clubs shall have the choice of goals to defend at the start of the game except where both players' benches are on the same side of the rink, in which case the home club shall start the game defending the goal nearest to its own bench. The teams shall change ends for each succeeding regular or overtime period.

(c) During the pre-game warm-up (which shall not exceed twenty minutes in duration) and before the commencement of play in any period each team shall confine its activity to its own end of the rink so as to leave clear an area thirty feet wide across the center of the Neutral Zone.

(NOTE 1) *The Game Timekeeper shall be responsible for signalling the commencement and termination of the pre-game warm-up and any violation of this rule by the players shall be reported to the President by the Supervisor when in attendance at game.*

(NOTE 2) *Players shall not be permitted to come on the ice during a stoppage in play or at the end of the first and second periods for the purpose of warming-up. The Referee will report any violation of this rule to the President for disciplinary action.*

(d) Fifteen minutes before the time scheduled for the start of the game both teams shall vacate the ice and proceed to their dressing rooms while the ice is being flooded. Both teams shall be signalled by the Game Timekeeper to return to the ice together in time for the scheduled start of the game.

(e) When a team fails to appear on the ice promptly without proper justification a fine shall be assessed against the offending team. The amount of the fine to be decided by the President.

Rule 80.   **Throwing Stick**

(a)   When any player of the defending side, including the goalkeeper or Manager, Coach or Trainer, deliberately throws his stick or any part thereof or any other object, at the puck in his Defending Zone, the Referee shall allow the play to be completed and if a goal is not scored a penalty shot shall be awarded to the non-offending side, which shot shall be taken by the player designated by the Referee as the player fouled.

If, however, the goal being unattended and the attacking player having no defending player to pass and having a chance to score on an "open net," a stick or part thereof or any other object, be thrown by a defending player thereby preventing a shot on the "open net" a goal shall be awarded to the attacking side.

(NOTE 1) *If the officials are unable to determine the person against whom the offense was made the offended team through the Captain shall designate the player on the ice at the time the offense was committed who will take the shot.*

(NOTE 2) *For the purpose of this rule, an open net is defined as one from which a goaltender has been removed for an additional attacking player.*

(b)   A major penalty shall be imposed on any player *on the ice* who throws his stick or any part thereof or any other object in the direction of the puck carrier in any zone, except when such act has been penalized by the assessment of a penalty shot or the award of a goal.

(NOTE) *When a player discards the broken portion of a stick by tossing it to the side of the ice (and not over the boards) in such a way as will not interfere with play or opposing player, no penalty will be imposed for so doing.*

(c)   The Referee and Linesmen shall report promptly to the President for disciplinary action every case where a stick or any part thereof is thrown outside the playing area.

Rule 81.   **Time of Match**

(a)   The time allowed for a game shall be three twenty-minute periods of actual play with a rest intermission between periods.

Play shall be resumed promptly following each intermission upon the expiry of fifteen minutes from the completion of play in the preceding period. A preliminary warning shall be given by the Game Timekeeper to the officials and to both teams three minutes prior to the resumption of play in each period and the final warning shall be given in sufficient time to enable the teams to resume play promptly.

(NOTE) *For the purpose of keeping the spectators informed as to the time remaining during intermissions the Game Timekeeper will use the electric clock to record length of intermissions.*

(b)   The team scoring the greatest number of goals during the three twenty-minute periods shall be the winner, and shall be credited with two points in the League standing.

(c)   In the intervals between periods, the ice surface shall be flooded unless mutually agreed to the contrary.

(d)   If any unusual delay occurs within five minutes of the end of the first or second periods the Referee may order the next regular intermission to be taken immediately and the balance of the period will be completed on the resumption of play with the teams defending the same goals, after which the teams will change ends and resume play of the ensuing period without delay.

(NOTE) *If a delay takes place with more than five minutes remaining in the first or second period, the Referee will order the next regular intermission to be taken immediately only when requested to do so by the Home Club.*

Rule 82.   **Tied Games**

(a) If, at the end of the three regular twenty-minute periods, the score shall be tied, the game shall be called a "TIE," and each team shall be credited with one point in the League standing.

(b) Special conditions for duration and number of periods of play-off games, shall be arranged by the Board of Governors.

Rule 83.   **Tripping**

(a) A minor penalty shall be imposed on any player who shall place his stick, knee, foot, arm, hand or elbow in such a manner that it shall cause his opponent to trip or fall.

   (NOTE 1) *If in the opinion of the Referee a player is unquestionably hook-checking the puck and obtains possession of it, thereby tripping puck carrier, no penalty shall be imposed.*

(b) When a player, in control of the puck in the opponent's side of the center red line, and having no other opponent to pass than the goalkeeper, is tripped or otherwise fouled from behind thus preventing a reasonable scoring opportunity a penalty shot shall be awarded to the non-offending side. Nevertheless the Referee shall not stop the play until the attacking side has lost possession of the puck to the defending side.

   (NOTE 2) *The intention of this rule is to restore a reasonable scoring opportunity which has been lost by reason of a foul from behind when the foul is committed in the opponent's side of the center red line.*

   By "control of the Puck" is meant the act of propelling the puck with the stick. If while it is being propelled the puck is touched by another player or his equipment or hits the goal or goes free the player shall no longer be considered to be "in control of the puck."

(c) If, when the opposing goalkeeper has been removed from the ice, a player in control of the puck is tripped or otherwise fouled with no opposition between him and the opposing goal, thus preventing a reasonable scoring opportunity, the Referee shall immediately stop the play and award a goal to the attacking team.

Rule 84.   **Unnecessary Roughness**

   At the discretion of the Referee, a minor penalty may be imposed on any player deemed guilty of unnecessary roughness.

Goalie Tony Esposito of the Black Hawks, shown opposing brother Phil of the Bruins, was a college star at Michigan Tech.

DICK RAPHAEL

XIV ANOTHER PART OF THE ICE

The world of ice hockey is by no means limited to the National Hockey League. It has an extensive minor league network which includes the American, Western, International, Central and Eastern Leagues as well as flourishing amateur and collegiate programs in both the United States and Canada.

And as the years go by, more and more players graduate from the Olympic and collegiate ranks into the National Hockey League. Red Berenson, the first super-star of the NHL's expansion West Division, graduated from Michigan and led all collegiate scorers in 1961–62. Tony Esposito, a goal-tender who belongs to the Chicago Black Hawks, was a standout at Michigan Tech. Rod Seiling of the New York Rangers played for Canada's Olympic team in 1964 and veteran pro Tommy Williams was a member of the United States' championship Olympic squad in 1960.

Henry Boucha, captain of the United States silver medal Olympic team in 1972, turned pro with Detroit immediately after those games. Boucha's Olympic teammates, Dick McGlynn, Keith Christiansen, Mike Curran, Kevin Ahearn and Tim Sheehy, all signed professional contracts with the new World Hockey Association.

The National Collegiate Athletic Association started an annual hockey tournament in 1948 and Michigan has dominated the competition, winning the National title seven times. Olympic competition at the Winter Games began in 1920 and a separate World Championship tournament began in 1924. In recent years, the Soviet Union has dominated both competitions.

College Hockey

From somewhat modest beginnings, collegiate hockey in the United States has grown tremendously in recent years. There are highly successful Christmas tournaments in Boston and New York City as well as the climactic NCAA Tournament in March.

U.S. colleges recruit players from Canada and the program is very nearly as extensive as the one the schools follow in tracking down talented football players.

Most collegiate rosters are stocked with a majority of Canadian imports. It is a mutually agreeable arrangement with the athlete getting an education and the school getting a boy who has played hockey all of his life.

For a time there was a feeling among professionals that athletes who played collegiate hockey for three or four years would find the switch to the professional game difficult. This is because there is considerably less body contact in the collegiate game. Checking is allowed only in the defensive zone, while the professional rules allow hitting anywhere on the ice.

The Princeton hockey team of 1902.   CULVER

There are other rule differences as well. All collegiate players must wear helmets; in the pros hockey helmets are optional. And in 1968, the red line was eliminated. Collegiate rinks now have only the two blue lines dividing the ice surface.

Despite the handicaps, a number of collegiate players have successfully moved into professional hockey. And the number appears to be increasing as more youngsters recognize the value of a college education before trying pro hockey.

A list of collegiate champions and runners-up follows:

1948
1. Michigan
2. Dartmouth
1949
1. Boston College
2. Dartmouth
1950
1. Colorado College
2. Boston University

1951
1. Michigan
2. Brown
1952
1. Michigan
2. Colorado College
1953
1. Michigan
2. Minnesota

1954
1. R.P.I.
2. Minnesota
1955
1. Michigan
2. Colorado College
1956
1. Michigan
2. Michigan Tech
1957
1. Colorado College
2. Michigan
1958
1. Denver University
2. North Dakota
1959
1. North Dakota
2. Michigan State
1960
1. Denver University
2. Michigan Tech
1961
1. Denver University
2. St. Lawrence
1962
1. Michigan Tech
2. Clarkson
1963
1. North Dakota
2. Denver University

1964
1. Michigan
2. Denver University
1965
1. Michigan Tech
2. Boston College
1966
1. Michigan State
2. Clarkson
1967
1. Cornell
2. Boston University
1968
1. Denver University
2. North Dakota
1969
1. Denver University
2. Cornell
1970
1. Cornell
2. Clarkson
1971
1. Boston University
2. Minnesota
1972
1. Boston University
2. Cornell
1973
1. Wisconsin
2. Denver University

Olympic Games

When the Winter Olympics began in 1924, hockey was one of the sports on the schedule. It had been added to the Olympic program in 1920 when there was a single competition instead of separate winter and summer Games. Canada dominated at first, winning the championship in each of the first four Olympic competitions. The Canadians won two more titles following World War II before the Soviet Union started a domination which led to three championships in the next four Games.

The one time the Russians missed was in 1960 at Squaw Valley, Calif., when the United States scored one of the major upsets in Olympic history.

The Americans were underdogs in the hockey competition that year. But they were determined to score an upset. "We knew with a couple of breaks, we could upset the odds," recalls goaltender Jack McCartan.

*Action at the 1932 Olympics in Lake Placid, N.Y., as Germany (dark uniforms)
defends against Canada.* **WIDE WORLD**

*Jack McCartan, who would later lead the U.S. to its first Olympic hockey gold
medal, has a tough moment as Sweden scores in 1960 Games at Squaw Valley,
California.* **WIDE WORLD**

Paul Johnson (15) scores winning goal as the U.S. defeats Canada, 2–1, in the 1960 semifinals.   WIDE WORLD

The United States had won five silver medals and one bronze in previous Olympic competition but all would be forgotten after the 1960 team was finished. The Americans moved through the preliminaries, winning several close games. Despite their early successes, they remained the underdogs as the tournament reached its final stages.

Then came the showdown with the Canadian team and most observers expected the American dream to be shattered. "We didn't expect to win," admits McCartan.

But the Americans did win, beating Canada, 2–1, with McCartan making 39 saves, many of them sensational. It was his best game of the Olympics but not the best-remembered. That was because the Russians still stood in the way of the American team.

Two days after they had taken the Canadians, the American team pulled off their second shocking upset. They wiped out a Russian lead and beat the Soviets, 3–2, before a national television audience in the U.S. to win the gold medal.

"It was my biggest thrill in hockey," says McCartan. The sentiment was echoed by Tommy Williams and the rest of his teammates. Both McCartan and Williams turned professional following the Olympics.

American fortunes slipped badly in the next two sets of Olympic Games, but U.S. prestige was restored in 1972 when the lightly-regarded team captured a silver medal.

393

A list of Olympic medal winners follows:

1920
1. Canada
2. USA
3. Czechoslovakia

1924
1. Canada
2. USA
3. Great Britain

1928
1. Canada
2. Sweden
3. Switzerland

1932
1. Canada
2. USA
3. Germany

1936
1. Great Britain
2. Canada
3. USA

No Olympics in 1940 or 1944

1948
1. Canada
2. Czechoslovakia
3. Switzerland

1952
1. Canada
2. USA
3. Sweden

1956
1. Soviet Union
2. USA
3. Canada

1960
1. USA
2. Canada
3. Soviet Union

1964
1. Soviet Union
2. Sweden
3. Czechoslovakia

1968
1. Soviet Union
2. Czechoslovakia
3. Canada

1972
1. Soviet Union
2. USA
3. Czechoslovakia

World Championships

In addition to the Olympics, amateur hockey stages a yearly world championship tournament. The Soviet Union has dominated the competition, winning the crown nine straight years from 1963 through 1971 and ten of eleven years through 1973. Czechoslovakia cracked that domination in 1972, even though the Russians won their third straight Olympic crown that year.

The Russians are acknowledged as the best amateur players in the world, a status they have enjoyed for some time. They proved how good they are in the fall of 1972 when they beat a team of NHL All-Stars three times and tied another contest in an eight-game series that took center stage in the world of hockey.

Soviet dominance in the sport is remarkable when one considers that the Russians didn't even take up hockey until the late 1940s.

"Other people tell stories about how we learned to play ice hockey," noted an official of the USSR Embassy in Ottawa, Ont. "They allege that we employed some eminent foreign specialists, used foreign literature and so on. This is not true.

"When we began to master this game we hadn't seen any foreign ice hockey and we didn't have any literature on this sport," the Russian continued. "We didn't have a single coach who knew the game. The only thing we had was a booklet containing the rules of the game. But the dry paragraphs of the rules did not explain the technical requirements to the players or the tactics of the game. Then we made broad and distinguished use of our game of ball-hockey. That was the birth of our school of hockey. Hockey soon became the favorite sport of our youth and we have emerged on the international level."

The Russian team plays together constantly and their rushes on the ice are machine-like. They are clearly the class of the international amateur teams.

A list of world amateur standings follows:

1924
1. Canada
2. USA
3. Great Britain

1928
1. Canada
2. Sweden
3. Switzerland

1930
1. Canada
2. Germany
3. Switzerland

1931
1. Canada
2. USA
3. Austria

1932
1. Canada
2. USA
3. Germany

1933
1. USA
2. Canada
3. Czechoslovakia

1934
1. Canada
2. USA
3. Germany

1935
1. Canada
2. Switzerland
3. Great Britain

1936
1. Great Britain
2. Canada
3. USA

1937
1. Canada
2. Great Britain
3. Switzerland

1938
1. Canada
2. Great Britain
3. Czechoslovakia

1939
1. Canada
2. USA
3. Switzerland

1940–1946 No Tournament Held

1947
1. Czechoslovakia
2. Sweden
3. Austria

1948
1. Canada
2. Czechoslovakia
3. Switzerland

1949
1. Czechoslovakia
2. Canada
3. USA

1950
1. Canada
2. USA
3. Switzerland

1951
1. Canada
2. Sweden
3. Switzerland
1952
1. Canada
2. USA
3. Sweden
1953
1. Sweden
2. German Federal Republic
3. Switzerland
1954
1. Soviet Union
2. Canada
3. Sweden
1955
1. Canada
2. Soviet Union
3. Czechoslovakia
1956
1. Soviet Union
2. USA
3. Canada
1957
1. Sweden
2. Soviet Union
3. Czechoslovakia
1958
1. Canada
2. Soviet Union
3. Sweden
1959
1. Canada
2. Soviet Union
3. Czechoslovakia
1960
1. USA
2. Canada
3. Soviet Union
1961
1. Canada
2. Czechoslovakia
3. Soviet Union
1962
1. Sweden

2. Canada
3. USA
1963
1. Soviet Union
2. Sweden
3. Czechoslovakia
1964
1. Soviet Union
2. Sweden
3. Czechoslovakia
1965
1. Soviet Union
2. Czechoslovakia
3. Sweden
1966
1. Soviet Union
2. Czechoslovakia
3. Canada
1967
1. Soviet Union
2. Sweden
3. Canada
1968
1. Soviet Union
2. Czechoslovakia
3. Canada
1969
1. Soviet Union
2. Sweden
3. Czechoslovakia
1970
1. Soviet Union
2. Sweden
3. Czechoslovakia
1971
1. Soviet Union
2. Czechoslovakia
3. Sweden
1972
1. Czechoslovakia
2. Soviet Union
3. Sweden
1973
1. Soviet Union
2. Sweden
3. Czechoslovakia

XV ALL-TIME NHL PLAYER REGISTER

The following section includes the record of every player who has ever appeared in a National Hockey League regular-season or playoff game. To the knowledge of the editors, this is the first time these records have appeared in a single volume.

Some of the players listed show only playoff records. This is because in the early years of the NHL, the Stanley Cup playoff series included teams from the Pacific Coast Hockey League (also known as the Pacific Coast Hockey Association). The regular-season records of PCHL players are not listed, but their playoff records against NHL teams are included.

During the middle 1920s and until the late 1930s, the category listing games played was not recorded in official league records. Therefore, in many instances, they do not appear here.

Until the 1966–67 season, the NHL compiled goaltending statistics on the basis of games played divided into goals allowed to produce an average. Now, the NHL uses the number of minutes played instead of games. To keep this record section uniform, it was decided to employ the old method throughout. In most cases the goaltending record has not been affected by more than a fraction.

In the regular season and the playoffs, the goals-against average (AVE) is figured on a per-game basis. In the All-Star games they are figured on a per-period basis (AGP). Goalies who appeared in All-Star games are credited with one game played for each appearance, regardless of the time played.

Where information is missing, it was unavailable.

ALL-TIME LIST OF NATIONAL HOCKEY LEAGUE TEAMS

Atlanta . . . . . . Atlanta Flames	New York A. . . . New York Americans
Boston . . . . . . Boston Bruins	New York I. . . . New York Islanders
Brooklyn A. . . . Brooklyn Americans	New York R. . . . New York Rangers
Buffalo . . . . . . Buffalo Sabres	Ottawa . . . . . . Ottawa Senators
California G.S. . . California Golden Seals	Philadelphia F. . Philadelphia Flyers
Chicago . . . . . Chicago Black Hawks	Philadelphia Q. . Philadelphia Quakers
Detroit C. . . . . Detroit Cougars	Pittsburgh Pe. . . Pittsburgh Penguins
Detroit F. . . . . Detroit Falcons	Pittsburgh Pi. . . Pittsburgh Pirates
Detroit R.W. . . . Detroit Red Wings	Quebec . . . . . Quebec Bulldogs
Hamilton . . . . . Hamilton Tigers	St. Louis B. . . . St. Louis Blues
Los Angeles . . . Los Angeles Kings	St. Louis E. . . . St. Louis Eagles
Minnesota . . . . Minnesota North Stars	Toronto A. . . . . Toronto Arenas
Montreal C. . . . Montreal Canadiens	Toronto M.L. . . Toronto Maple Leafs
Montreal M. . . . Montreal Maroons	Toronto St. P. . . Toronto St. Pats
Montreal W. . . . Montreal Wanderers	Vancouver . . . . Vancouver Canucks

EXPLANATION OF ABBREVIATIONS

A	. . . .	Assists
AVE	. . . .	Average goals-against per game
AGP	. . . .	Average goals-against per period
G	. . . .	Goals scored
GA	. . . .	Goals against
GP	. . . .	Games played
NHL	. . . .	National Hockey League
PCHL	. . . . . .	Pacific Coast Hockey League
Pts	. . . .	Points scored
Sho	. . . .	Shutouts
Per	. . . .	Periods

ABBOT, George *Goalie*

Season	Club	GP	GA	Sho	AVE
1943–44	Boston	1	7	0	7.00

ABBOT, Reginald *Forward*
b. Winnipeg, Man., Feb. 4, 1930

Season	Club	GP	G	A	Pts
1952–53	Montreal C.	3	0	0	0

ABEL, Clarence John (Taffy) *Defenseman*
b. Sault Ste. Marie, Mich., May 28, 1900

Season	Club	GP	G	A	Pts
1926–27	New York R.	44	8	4	12
1927–28	New York R.	22	0	1	1
1928–29	New York R.	33	2	1	3
1929–30	Chicago	--	3	3	6
1930–31	Chicago	--	0	1	1
1931–32	Chicago	--	3	3	6
1932–33	Chicago	--	0	4	4
1933–34	Chicago	--	2	1	3
	Totals	--	18	18	36
Playoffs					
1926–27	New York R.	2	0	1	1
1927–28	New York R.	9	1	0	1
1928–29	New York R.	6	0	0	0
1929–30	Chicago	2	0	0	0
1930–31	Chicago	9	0	0	0
1931–32	Chicago	2	0	0	0
1933–34	Chicago	8	0	0	0
	Totals	38	1	1	2

ABEL, Gerald Scott (Gerry) *Forward*
b. Detroit, Mich., Dec. 25, 1944

Season	Club	GP	G	A	Pts
1966–67	Detroit R.W.	1	0	0	0

ABEL, Sidney Gerald *Forward*
b. Melville, Sask., Feb. 22, 1918

Season	Club	GP	G	A	Pts
1938–39	Detroit R.W.	15	1	1	2
1939–40	Detroit R.W.	24	1	5	6
1940–41	Detroit R.W.	47	11	22	37
1941–42	Detroit R.W.	48	18	31	49
1942–43	Detroit R.W.	49	18	24	42
1945–46	Detroit R.W.	7	0	2	2
1946–47	Detroit R.W.	60	19	29	48
1947–48	Detroit R.W.	60	14	30	44
1948–49	Detroit R.W.	60	28	26	54
1949–50	Detroit R.W.	70	34	35	69
1950–51	Detroit R.W.	69	23	38	61
1951–52	Detroit R.W.	62	17	36	53
1952–53	Chicago	39	5	4	9
	Totals	610	189	283	472
Playoffs					
1938–39	Detroit R.W.	6	1	1	2
1939–40	Detroit R.W.	5	0	3	3
1940–41	Detroit R.W.	9	2	2	4
1941–42	Detroit R.W.	12	4	2	6
1942–43	Detroit R.W.	10	5	8	13
1945–46	Detroit R.W.	3	0	0	0
1946–47	Detroit R.W.	3	1	1	2
1947–48	Detroit R.W.	10	0	3	3
1948–49	Detroit R.W.	11	3	3	6
1949–50	Detroit R.W.	14	6	2	8
1950–51	Detroit R.W.	6	4	3	7
1951–52	Detroit R.W.	7	2	2	4
1952–53	Chicago	1	0	0	0
	Totals	97	28	30	58
All-Star					
1949	NHL All-Stars	1	0	0	0
1950	Detroit	1	0	1	1
1951	NHL 2nd All-Stars	1	0	0	0
	Totals	3	0	1	1

ACHTYMICHUK, Eugene Edward (Gene)
Forward
b. Lamont, Alta., Sept. 7, 1932

Season	Club	GP	G	A	Pts
1956-57	Montreal C.	3	0	0	0
1957-58	Montreal C.	16	3	5	8
1958-59	Detroit R.W.	12	0	0	0
	Totals	31	3	5	8

ACOMB, Douglas *Forward*
b. Toronto, Ont., May 15, 1949

Season	Club	GP	G	A	Pts
1969-70	Toronto M.L.	2	0	1	1

ADAM, Douglas Patrick *Forward*
b. Toronto, Ont., Sept. 7, 1923

Season	Club	GP	G	A	Pts
1949-50	New York R.	4	0	1	1

ADAMS, John *Forward*
b. Calgary, Alta., May 5, 1920

Season	Club	GP	G	A	Pts
1940-41	Montreal C.	--	6	12	18
Playoffs					
1940-41	Montreal C.	3	0	0	0

ADAMS, John J. (Jack) *Forward*
b. Ft. William, Ont., June 14, 1895

Season	Club	GP	G	A	Pts
1917-18	Toronto A.	8	0	0	0
1918-19	Toronto A.	17	3	3	6
1922-23	Toronto St. P.	23	19	9	28
1923-24	Toronto St. P.	22	13	3	16
1924-25	Toronto St. P.	27	21	8	29
1925-26	Toronto St. P.	36	21	5	26
1926-27	Ottawa	--	5	1	6
	Totals	--	82	29	111
Playoffs					
1917-18	Toronto A.	--	2	0	2
1920-21	Vancouver (PCHL)	--	2	1	3
1921-22	Vancouver (PCHL)	--	6	0	6
1924-25	Toronto St. P.	--	1	0	1
1926-27	Ottawa	--	0	0	0
	Totals	--	11	1	12

ADAMS, John Matthew *Goalie*
b. Port Arthur, Ont., July 27, 1946

Season	Club	GP	GA	Sho	AVE
1972-73	Boston	13	39	1	3.00

ADAMS, Stewart *Forward*

Season	Club	GP	G	A	Pts
1929-30	Chicago	--	4	6	10
1930-31	Chicago	--	5	13	18
1931-32	Chicago	--	0	5	5
1932-33	Toronto M.L.	--	0	2	2
	Totals	--	9	26	35
Playoffs					
1929-30	Chicago	--	0	0	0
1930-31	Chicago	--	3	3	6
1931-32	Chicago	--	0	0	0
	Totals	--	3	3	6

AIKEN, John *Goalie*
b. Arlington, Mass., Jan. 1, 1932

Season	Club	GP	GA	Sho	AVE
1957-58	Montreal C.	1	6	0	6.00

AILSBY, Lloyd *Defenseman*
b. Lac Pelletier, Sask., May 11, 1917

Season	Club	GP	G	A	Pts
1951-52	New York R.	3	0	0	0

AITKENHEAD, Andrew *Goalie*
b. Glasgow, Scotland, Mar. 6, 1904

Season	Club	GP	GA	Sho	AVE
1932-33	New York R.	48	107	3	2.23
1933-34	New York R.	48	113	7	2.35
1934-35	New York R.	10	37	1	3.70
	Totals	106	257	11	2.42
Playoffs					
1932-33	New York R.	8	13	2	1.62
1933-34	New York R.	2	2	1	1.00
	Totals	10	15	3	1.50

ALBRIGHT, Clinton Howard *Forward*
b. Winnipeg, Man., Feb. 28, 1926

Season	Club	GP	G	A	Pts
1948-49	New York R.	59	14	5	19

ALDCORN, Gary William *Forward*
b. Shaunavon, Sask., Mar. 7, 1935

Season	Club	GP	G	A	Pts
1956-57	Toronto M.L.	22	5	1	6
1957-58	Toronto M.L.	59	10	14	24
1958-59	Toronto M.L.	5	0	3	3
1959-60	Detroit R.W.	70	22	29	51
1960-61	Det RW-Bos	70	4	9	13
	Totals	226	41	53	94
Playoffs					
1959-60	Detroit R.W.	6	1	2	3

ALEXANDRE, Arthur *Forward*

Season	Club	GP	G	A	Pts
1931-32	Montreal C.	--	0	2	2

ALLEN, Courtney Keith (Bingo) *Defenseman*
b. Saskatoon, Sask., Aug. 21, 1923

Season	Club	GP	G	A	Pts
1953-54	Detroit R.W.	10	0	4	4
1954-55	Detroit R.W.	18	0	0	0
	Totals	28	0	4	4

Playoffs

1953-54	Detroit R.W.	5	0	0	0

All-Star

1954	Detroit R.W.	1	0	0	0

ALLEN, George Trenholme *Defenseman*
b. Bayfield, N.B., July 27, 1914

Season	Club	GP	G	A	Pts
1938-39	New York R.	19	6	6	12
1939-40	Chicago	--	10	12	22
1940-41	Chicago	--	14	17	31
1941-42	Chicago	43	7	13	20
1942-43	Chicago	47	10	14	24
1943-44	Chicago	45	17	24	41
1945-46	Chicago	44	11	15	26
1946-47	Montreal C.	49	7	14	21
	Totals	--	82	115	197

Playoffs

1940-41	Chicago	5	2	2	4
1941-42	Chicago	3	1	1	2
1943-44	Chicago	9	5	4	9
1945-46	Chicago	4	0	0	0
1946-47	Montreal C.	11	1	3	4
	Totals	32	9	10	19

ALLEN, Vivan Mariner (Squee) *Forward*
b. Bayfield, N.B., Sept. 9, 1916

Season	Club	GP	G	A	Pts
1940-41	New York A.	--	0	1	1

ALLUM, William *Defenseman*
b. Winnipeg, Man., Oct. 9, 1916

Season	Club	GP	G	A	Pts
1940-41	New York R.	1	0	1	1

ALMAS, Ralph Clayton (Red) *Goalie*
b. Saskatoon, Sask., April 26, 1924

Season	Club	GP	GA	Sho	AVE
1946-47	Detroit R.W.	1	5	0	5.00
1950-51	Chicago	1	5	0	5.00
1952-53	Detroit R.W.	1	3	0	3.00
	Totals	3	13	0	4.33

ALMAS *(Continued)*

Playoffs	Club	GP	GA	Sho	AVE
1946-47	Detroit R.W.	5	13	0	2.60

AMADIO, David *Defenseman*
b. Glace Bay, N.S., Apr. 23, 1939

Season	Club	GP	G	A	Pts
1957-58	Detroit R.W.	2	0	0	0
1967-68	Los Angeles	58	4	6	10
1968-69	Los Angeles	65	1	5	6
	Totals	125	5	11	16

Playoffs

1967-68	Los Angeles	7	0	2	2
1968-69	Los Angeles	9	1	0	1
	Totals	16	1	2	3

ANDERSON, Dale Norman *Defenseman*
b. Regina, Sask., Mar. 5, 1932

Season	Club	GP	G	A	Pts
1956-57	Detroit R.W.	13	0	0	0

Playoffs

1956-57	Detroit R.W.	2	0	0	0

ANDERSON, James William *Forward*
b. Pembroke, Ont., Dec. 1, 1930

Season	Club	GP	G	A	Pts
1967-68	Los Angeles	7	1	2	3

ANDERSON, Lorne *Goalie*
b. Renfrew, Ont., July 26, 1931

Season	Club	GP	GA	Sho	AVE
1951-52	New York R.	3	18	0	6.00

ANDERSON, Ronald Chester (Goings) *Forward*
b. Red Deer, Alta., July 29, 1945

Season	Club	GP	G	A	Pts
1967-68	Detroit R.W.	18	2	0	2
1968-69	Det RW-LA	63	3	5	8
1969-70	St. Louis B.	59	9	9	18
1970-71	Buffalo	74	14	12	26
1971-72	Buffalo	37	0	4	4
	Totals	251	28	30	58

Playoffs

1968-69	Los Angeles	4	0	0	0
1969-70	St. Louis B.	1	0	0	0
	Totals	5	0	0	0

ANDERSON, Thomas Linton (Cowboy)
Defenseman
b. Edinburgh, Scotland, July 9, 1911

Season	Club	GP	G	A	Pts
1934-35	Detroit R.W.	--	5	2	7
1935-36	New York A.	--	3	2	5

400

ANDERSON (Continued)

Season	Club	GP	G	A	Pts
1936–37	New York A.	--	10	15	25
1937–38	New York A.	--	4	21	25
1938–39	New York A.	--	13	27	40
1939–40	New York A.	--	12	19	31
1940–41	New York A.	--	3	12	15
1941–42	New York A.	48	12	29	41
	Totals	--	62	127	189
Playoffs					
1935–36	New York A.	6	0	0	0
1937–38	New York A.	6	1	4	5
1939–40	New York A.	3	1	3	4
	Totals	15	2	7	9

ANDREA, Paul Lawrence *Forward*
b. North Sydney, N.S., July 31, 1941

Season	Club	GP	G	A	Pts
1965–66	New York R.	4	1	1	2
1967–68	Pittsburgh Pe.	65	11	21	32
1968–69	Pittsburgh Pe.	25	7	6	13
1970–71	Calif–Buff	56	12	21	33
	Totals	150	31	49	80

ANDREWS, Lloyd *Forward*

Season	Club	GP	G	A	Pts
1921–22	Toronto St. P.	11	0	0	0
1922–23	Toronto St. P.	23	5	4	9
1923–24	Toronto St. P.	12	2	1	3
1924–25	Toronto St. P.	7	1	0	1
	Totals	53	8	5	13
Playoffs					
1921–22	Toronto St. P.	--	2	0	2

ANGOTTI, Louis Frederick *Forward*
b. Toronto, Ont., Jan. 16, 1938

Season	Club	GP	G	A	Pts
1964–65	New York R.	70	9	8	17
1965–66	NY R–Chgo	51	6	12	18
1966–67	Chicago	63	6	12	18
1967–68	Philadelphia F.	70	12	37	49
1968–69	Pittsburgh Pe.	71	17	20	37
1969–70	Chicago	70	12	26	38
1970–71	Chicago	65	9	16	25
1971–72	Chicago	65	5	10	15
1972–73	Chicago	77	15	22	37
	Totals	602	91	163	254
Playoffs					
1965–66	Chicago	6	0	0	0
1966–67	Chicago	6	2	1	3
1967–68	Philadelphia F.	7	0	0	0
1969–70	Chicago	8	0	0	0

ANGOTTI (Continued)

Playoffs	Club	GP	G	A	Pts
1970–71	Chicago	16	3	3	6
1971–72	Chicago	6	0	0	0
1972–73	Chicago	16	3	4	7
	Totals	65	8	8	16

ANSLOW, Hubert Wallace *Forward*
b. Pembroke, Ont., Mar. 23, 1926

Season	Club	GP	G	A	Pts
1947–48	New York R.	2	0	0	0

APPS, Joseph Sylvanus *Forward*
b. Paris, Ont., Jan. 18, 1915

Season	Club	GP	G	A	Pts
1936–37	Toronto M.L.	--	16	29	45
1937–38	Toronto M.L.	--	21	29	50
1938–39	Toronto M.L.	--	15	25	40
1939–40	Toronto M.L.	--	13	17	30
1940–41	Toronto M.L.	--	20	24	44
1941–42	Toronto M.L.	38	18	23	41
1942–43	Toronto M.L.	29	23	17	40
1945–46	Toronto M.L.	40	24	16	40
1946–47	Toronto M.L.	54	25	24	49
1947–48	Toronto M.L.	55	26	27	53
	Totals	--	201	231	432
Playoffs					
1936–37	Toronto M.L.	2	0	1	1
1937–38	Toronto M.L.	7	1	4	5
1938–39	Toronto M.L.	10	2	6	8
1939–40	Toronto M.L.	10	5	2	7
1940–41	Toronto M.L.	7	3	2	5
1941–42	Toronto M.L.	13	5	8	13
1946–47	Toronto M.L.	11	5	1	6
1947–48	Toronto M.L.	9	4	4	8
	Totals	69	25	28	53
All-Star					
1947	Toronto M.L.	1	1	1	2

APPS, Sylvanus Marshall (Syl) Jr. *Forward*
b. Toronto, Ont., August 1, 1947

Season	Club	GP	G	A	Pts
1970–71	NY R–Pit Pe	62	10	18	28
1971–72	Pittsburgh Pe.	72	15	44	59
1972–73	Pittsburgh Pe.	77	29	56	85
	Totals	211	54	118	172
Playoffs					
1971–72	Pittsburgh Pe.	4	1	0	1

ARBOUR, Alger (Al) *Defenseman*
b. Sudbury, Ont., Nov. 1, 1932

Season	Club	GP	G	A	Pts
1953-54	Detroit R.W.	36	0	1	1
1956-57	Detroit R.W.	44	1	6	7
1957-58	Detroit R.W.	69	1	6	7
1958-59	Chicago	70	2	10	12
1959-60	Chicago	57	1	5	6
1960-61	Chicago	53	3	2	5
1961-62	Toronto M.L.	52	1	5	6
1962-63	Toronto M.L.	4	1	0	1
1963-64	Toronto M.L.	6	0	1	1
1965-66	Toronto M.L.	4	0	1	1
1967-68	St. Louis B.	74	1	10	11
1968-69	St. Louis B.	67	1	6	7
1969-70	St. Louis B.	68	0	3	3
1970-71	St. Louis B.	22	0	2	2
	Totals	626	12	58	70
Playoffs					
1955-56	Detroit R.W.	4	0	1	1
1956-57	Detroit R.W.	5	0	0	0
1957-58	Detroit R.W.	4	0	1	1
1958-59	Chicago	6	1	2	3
1959-60	Chicago	4	0	0	0
1960-61	Chicago	7	0	0	0
1961-62	Toronto M.L.	8	0	0	0
1963-64	Toronto M.L.	1	0	0	0
1964-65	Toronto M.L.	1	0	0	0
1967-68	St. Louis B.	14	0	3	3
1968-69	St. Louis B.	12	0	0	0
1969-70	St. Louis B.	14	0	1	1
1970-71	St. Louis B.	6	0	0	0
	Totals	86	1	8	9
All-Star					
1969	West All-Stars	1	0	0	0

ARBOUR, Amos *Forward*

Season	Club	GP	G	A	Pts
1918-19	Montreal C.	1	0	0	0
1919-20	Montreal C.	20	22	4	26
1920-21	Montreal C.	22	14	3	17
1921-22	Hamilton	23	8	3	11
1922-23	Hamilton	23	6	1	7
1923-24	Toronto St. P.	20	1	2	3
	Totals	109	51	13	64

ARBOUR, Ernest (Ty) *Forward*

Season	Club	GP	G	A	Pts
1926-27	Pittsburgh Pi.	--	7	8	15
1927-28	Chicago	--	5	5	10
1928-29	Chicago	--	3	4	7
1929-30	Chicago	--	10	8	18
1930-31	Chicago	--	3	3	6
	Totals	--	28	28	56

ARBOUR *(Continued)*

Playoffs	Club	GP	G	A	Pts
1929-20	Chicago	--	1	0	1
1930-31	Chicago	--	1	0	1
	Totals	--	2	0	2

ARBOUR, Jack *Forward*

Season	Club	GP	G	A	Pts
1926-27	Detroit C.	--	4	1	5
1928-29	Toronto M.L.	--	1	0	1
	Totals	--	5	1	6

ARBOUR, John Gilbert (Jack) *Defenseman*
b. Niagara Falls, Ont., Sept. 28, 1945

Season	Club	GP	G	A	Pts
1965-66	Boston	2	0	0	0
1967-68	Boston	4	0	1	1
1968-69	Pittsburgh Pe.	17	0	2	2
1970-71	Vanc-StL B	66	1	6	7
1971-72	St. Louis B.	17	0	0	0
	Totals	106	1	9	10
Playoffs					
1970-71	St. Louis B.	5	0	0	0

ARMSTRONG, George Edward (Chief) *Forward*
b. Skead, Ont., July 6, 1930

Season	Club	GP	G	A	Pts
1949-50	Toronto M.L.	2	0	0	0
1951-52	Toronto M.L.	20	3	3	6
1952-53	Toronto M.L.	52	14	11	25
1953-54	Toronto M.L.	63	17	15	32
1954-55	Toronto M.L.	66	10	18	28
1955-56	Toronto M.L.	67	16	32	48
1956-57	Toronto M.L.	54	18	26	44
1957-58	Toronto M.L.	59	17	25	42
1958-59	Toronto M.L.	59	20	16	36
1959-60	Toronto M.L.	70	23	28	51
1960-61	Toronto M.L.	47	14	19	33
1961-62	Toronto M.L.	70	21	32	53
1962-63	Toronto M.L.	70	19	24	43
1963-64	Toronto M.L.	66	20	17	37
1964-65	Toronto M.L.	59	15	22	37
1965-66	Toronto M.L.	70	16	35	51
1966-67	Toronto M.L.	70	9	24	33
1967-68	Toronto M.L.	62	13	21	34
1968-69	Toronto M.L.	53	11	16	27
1969-70	Toronto M.L.	49	13	15	28
1970-71	Toronto M.L.	59	7	18	25
	Totals	1187	296	417	713
Playoffs					
1951-52	Toronto M.L.	4	0	0	0
1953-54	Toronto M.L.	5	1	0	1
1954-55	Toronto M.L.	4	1	0	1

ARMSTRONG (Continued)

Playoffs

Season	Club	GP	G	A	Pts
1955–56	Toronto M.L.	5	4	2	6
1958–59	Toronto M.L.	12	0	4	4
1959–60	Toronto M.L.	10	1	4	5
1960–61	Toronto M.L.	5	1	1	2
1961–62	Toronto M.L.	12	7	5	12
1962–63	Toronto M.L.	10	3	6	9
1963–64	Toronto M.L.	14	5	8	13
1964–65	Toronto M.L.	6	1	0	1
1965–66	Toronto M.L.	4	0	1	1
1966–67	Toronto M.L.	9	2	1	3
1968–69	Toronto M.L.	4	0	0	0
1970–71	Toronto M.L.	6	0	2	2
	Totals	110	26	34	60

All-Star

1956	NHL All-Stars	1	0	0	0
1957	NHL All-Stars	1	0	0	0
1959	NHL All-Stars	1	0	0	0
1962	Toronto M.L.	1	0	1	1
1963	Toronto M.L.	1	0	1	1
1964	Toronto M.L.	1	0	0	0
1968	Toronto M.L.	1	0	0	0
	Totals	7	0	2	2

ARMSTRONG, Murray Alexander *Forward*
b. Manor, Sask., Jan. 1, 1916

Season	Club	GP	G	A	Pts
1938–39	Toronto M.L.	--	0	1	1
1939–40	New York A.	--	16	20	36
1940–41	New York A.	--	10	14	24
1941–42	New York A.	45	6	22	28
1943–44	Detroit R.W.	28	12	22	34
1944–45	Detroit R.W.	50	15	24	39
1945–46	Detroit R.W.	40	8	18	26
	Totals	--	67	121	188

Playoffs

1939–40	New York A.	3	0	0	0
1943–44	Detroit R.W.	5	0	2	2
1944–45	Detroit R.W.	14	4	2	6
1945–46	Detroit R.W.	5	0	2	2
	Totals	27	4	6	10

ARMSTRONG, Norman (Red) *Defenseman*
b. Owen Sound, Ont., Oct. 17, 1938

Season	Club	GP	G	A	Pts
1962–63	Toronto M.L.	7	1	1	2

ARMSTRONG, Robert Richard *Defenseman*
b. Toronto, Ont., Apr. 7, 1931

Season	Club	GP	G	A	Pts
1950–51	Boston	2	0	0	0
1952–53	Boston	55	0	8	8
1953–54	Boston	64	2	10	12

ARMSTRONG (Continued)

Season	Club	GP	G	A	Pts
1954–55	Boston	57	1	3	4
1955–56	Boston	68	0	12	12
1956–57	Boston	57	1	15	16
1957–58	Boston	47	1	4	5
1958–59	Boston	60	1	9	10
1959–60	Boston	69	5	14	19
1960–61	Boston	54	0	10	10
1961–62	Boston	9	2	1	3
	Totals	542	13	86	99

Playoffs

1951–52	Boston	5	0	0	0
1952–53	Boston	11	1	1	2
1953–54	Boston	4	0	1	1
1954–55	Boston	5	0	0	0
1956–57	Boston	10	0	3	3
1958–59	Boston	7	0	2	2
	Totals	42	1	7	8

All-Star

1960	NHL All-Stars	1	0	0	0

ARNASON, Charles (Chuck) *Forward*
b. Dauphin, Man., July 15, 1951

Season	Club	GP	G	A	Pts
1971–72	Montreal C.	17	3	0	3
1972–73	Montreal C.	19	1	1	2
	Totals	36	4	1	5

ARUNDEL, John O'Gorman *Defenseman*
b. Winnipeg, Man., Nov. 4, 1927

Season	Club	GP	G	A	Pts
1949–50	Toronto M.L.	3	0	0	0

ASHBEE, William Barry *Defenseman*
b. Weston, Ont., July 28, 1939

Season	Club	GP	G	A	Pts
1965–66	Boston	14	0	3	3
1970–71	Philadelphia F.	64	4	23	27
1971–72	Philadelphia F.	73	6	14	20
1972–73	Philadelphia F.	64	1	17	18
	Totals	215	11	57	68

Playoffs

1972–73	Philadelphia F.	11	0	4	4

ASHWORTH, Frank *Forward*
b. Moose Jaw, Sask., Oct. 16, 1927

Season	Club	GP	G	A	Pts
1946–47	Chicago	18	5	4	9

ASMUNDSON, Oscar *Forward*
b. Red Deer, Alta., Nov. 17, 1908

Season	Club	GP	G	A	Pts
1932–33	New York R.	48	5	10	15
1933–34	New York R.	46	2	6	8
1934–35	St. Louis E.	--	4	7	11
	Totals	--	11	23	34

Playoffs

Season	Club	GP	G	A	Pts
1932–33	New York R.	8	0	2	2
1933–34	New York R.	1	0	0	0
	Totals	9	0	2	2

ATANAS, Walter (Ants) *Forward*
b. Hamilton, Ont., Dec. 22, 1922

Season	Club	GP	G	A	Pts
1944–45	New York R.	49	13	8	21

ATKINSON, Steven John (Steve) *Forward*
b. Toronto, Ont., Oct. 16, 1948

Season	Club	GP	G	A	Pts
1968–69	Boston	1	0	0	0
1970–71	Buffalo	57	20	18	38
1971–72	Buffalo	67	14	10	24
1972–73	Buffalo	61	9	9	18
	Totals	186	43	37	80

Playoffs

Season	Club	GP	G	A	Pts
1972–73	Buffalo	1	0	0	0

ATTWELL, Ronald *Forward*
b. Humber Summit, Ont., Feb. 9, 1935

Season	Club	GP	G	A	Pts
1967–68	NY R–StL B	22	1	7	8

AUBUCHON, Oscar *Forward*
b. St. Hyacinthe, Que., Jan. 1, 1917

Season	Club	GP	G	A	Pts
1942–43	Boston	3	3	0	3
1943–44	Bos–NY R	47	16	12	28
	Totals	50	19	12	31

Playoffs

Season	Club	GP	G	A	Pts
1942–43	Boston	6	1	0	1

AURIE, Harry Lawrence *Forward*
b. Sudbury, Ont., Feb. 8, 1905

Season	Club	GP	G	A	Pts
1927–28	Detroit C.	--	13	3	16
1928–29	Detroit C.	--	1	1	2
1929–30	Detroit C.	--	14	5	19
1930–31	Detroit F.	--	12	6	18
1931–32	Detroit F.	--	12	8	20
1932–33	Detroit F.	--	12	11	23
1933–34	Detroit R.W.	--	16	19	35

AURIE *(Continued)*

Season	Club	GP	G	A	Pts
1934–35	Detroit R.W.	--	17	29	46
1935–36	Detroit R.W.	--	16	18	34
1936–37	Detroit R.W.	--	23	20	43
1937–38	Detroit R.W.	--	10	9	19
1938–39	Detroit R.W.	--	1	0	1
	Totals	--	150	129	279

Playoffs

Season	Club	GP	G	A	Pts
1928–29	Detroit C.	--	1	0	1
1931–32	Detroit F.	--	0	0	0
1932–33	Detroit F.	--	1	0	1
1933–34	Detroit R.W.	--	3	7	10
1935–36	Detroit R.W.	--	1	2	3
1936–37	Detroit R.W.	--	0	0	0
	Totals	--	6	9	15

AWREY, Donald William *Defenseman*
b. Kitchener, Ont., July 18, 1943

Season	Club	GP	G	A	Pts
1963–64	Boston	16	1	0	1
1964–65	Boston	47	2	3	5
1965–66	Boston	70	4	3	7
1966–67	Boston	4	1	0	1
1967–68	Boston	74	3	12	15
1968–69	Boston	73	0	13	13
1969–70	Boston	73	3	10	13
1970–71	Boston	74	4	21	25
1971–72	Boston	34	1	8	9
1972–73	Boston	78	2	17	19
	Totals	543	21	87	108

Playoffs

Season	Club	GP	G	A	Pts
1967–68	Boston	4	0	1	1
1968–69	Boston	10	0	1	1
1969–70	Boston	14	0	5	5
1970–71	Boston	7	0	0	0
1971–72	Boston	15	0	4	4
1972–73	Boston	4	0	0	0
	Totals	54	0	11	11

AYERS, Thomas Vernon *Defenseman*
b. Toronto, Ont., Apr. 27, 1909

Season	Club	GP	G	A	Pts
1930–31	New York A.	--	2	1	3
1931–32	New York A.	--	2	4	6
1932–33	New York A.	--	0	3	3
1933–34	Montreal M.	--	0	0	0
1934–35	St. Louis E.	--	2	2	4
1935–36	New York R.	28	0	4	4
	Totals	--	6	14	20

BABANDO, Peter Joseph *Forward*
b. Braeburn, Pa., May 10, 1925

Season	Club	GP	G	A	Pts
1947–48	Boston	60	23	11	34
1948–49	Boston	58	19	14	33
1949–50	Detroit R.W.	55	6	6	12
1950–51	Chicago	70	18	19	37
1951–52	Chicago	49	11	14	25
1952–53	Chgo–NY R	58	9	9	18
	Totals	350	86	73	159
Playoffs					
1947–48	Boston	5	1	1	2
1948–49	Boston	4	0	0	0
1949–50	Detroit R.W.	8	2	2	4
	Totals	17	3	3	6

BACKOR, Peter *Defenseman*
b. Ft. William, Ont., Apr. 29, 1919

Season	Club	GP	G	A	Pts
1944–45	Toronto M.L.	36	4	5	9

BACKSTROM, Ralph *Forward*
b. Kirkland Lake, Ont., Sept. 18, 1937

Season	Club	GP	G	A	Pts
1956–57	Montreal C.	3	0	0	0
1957–58	Montreal C.	2	0	1	1
1958–59	Montreal C.	64	18	22	40
1959–60	Montreal C.	64	13	15	28
1960–61	Montreal C.	69	12	20	32
1961–62	Montreal C.	66	27	38	65
1962–63	Montreal C.	70	23	12	35
1963–64	Montreal C.	70	8	21	29
1964–65	Montreal C.	70	25	30	55
1965–66	Montreal C.	67	22	20	42
1966–67	Montreal C.	69	14	27	41
1967–68	Montreal C.	70	20	25	45
1968–69	Montreal C.	72	13	28	41
1969–70	Montreal C.	72	19	24	43
1970–71	Mtl C–LA	49	15	17	32
1971–72	Los Angeles	76	23	29	52
1972–73	LA–Chicago	79	26	32	58
	Totals	1157	316	407	723
Playoffs					
1958–59	Montreal C.	11	3	5	8
1959–60	Montreal C.	7	0	3	3
1960–61	Montreal C.	5	0	0	0
1961–62	Montreal C.	5	0	1	1
1962–63	Montreal C.	5	0	0	0
1963–64	Montreal C.	7	2	1	3
1964–65	Montreal C.	13	2	3	5
1965–66	Montreal C.	10	3	4	7

BACKSTROM *(Continued)*

Playoffs	Club	GP	G	A	Pts
1966–67	Montreal C.	10	5	2	7
1967–68	Montreal C.	13	4	3	7
1968–69	Montreal C.	14	3	4	7
1972–73	Chicago	16	5	6	11
	Totals	116	27	32	59
All-Star					
1958	Montreal C.	1	0	0	0
1959	Montreal C.	1	0	1	1
1960	Montreal C.	1	0	1	1
1962	NHL All-Stars	1	0	0	0
1965	Montreal C.	1	0	1	1
1967	Montreal C.	1	0	0	0
	Totals	6	0	3	3

BAILEY, Garnet Edward (Ace) *Forward*
b. Lloydminster, Sask., June 13, 1948

Season	Club	GP	G	A	Pts
1968–69	Boston	8	3	3	6
1969–70	Boston	58	11	11	22
1970–71	Boston	36	0	6	6
1971–72	Boston	73	9	13	22
1972–73	Bos–Det RW	70	10	24	34
	Totals	245	33	57	90
Playoffs					
1968–69	Boston	1	0	0	0
1970–71	Boston	1	0	0	0
1971–72	Boston	13	2	4	6
	Totals	15	2	4	6

BAILEY, Irvine Wallace (Ace) *Forward*
b. Bracebridge, Ont., July 3, 1903

Season	Club	GP	G	A	Pts
1926–27	Toronto M.L.	--	15	13	28
1927–28	Toronto M.L.	--	9	3	12
1928–29	Toronto M.L.	--	22	10	32
1929–30	Toronto M.L.	--	22	21	43
1930–31	Toronto M.L.	--	23	19	42
1931–32	Toronto M.L.	--	8	5	13
1932–33	Toronto M.L.	--	10	8	18
1933–34	Toronto M.L.	--	2	3	5
	Totals	--	111	82	193
Playoffs					
1928–29	Toronto M.L.	--	1	2	3
1930–31	Toronto M.L.	--	1	1	2
1931–32	Toronto M.L.	--	1	0	1
1932–33	Toronto M.L.	--	0	1	1
	Totals	--	3	4	7

BAILEY, Robert Allen *Forward*
b. Kenora, Ont., May 29, 1931

Season	Club	GP	G	A	Pts
1953–54	Toronto M.L.	48	2	7	9
1954–55	Toronto M.L.	32	4	2	6
1955–56	Toronto M.L.	6	0	0	0
1957–58	Chgo-Det RW	64	9	12	21
	Totals	150	15	21	36

Playoffs

1953–54	Toronto M.L.	5	0	2	2
1954–55	Toronto M.L.	1	0	0	0
1956–57	Detroit R.W.	5	0	2	2
1957–58	Chicago	4	0	0	0
	Totals	15	0	4	4

BAIRD, Kenneth Stewart (Ken) *Defenseman*
b. Flin Flon, Man., Feb. 1, 1951

Season	Club	GP	G	A	Pts
1971–72	California	10	0	2	2

BALDWIN, Douglas *Defenseman*
b. Winnipeg, Man., Nov. 2, 1922

Season	Club	GP	G	A	Pts
1945–46	Toronto M.L.	15	0	1	1
1946–47	Detroit R.W.	4	0	0	0
1947–48	Chicago	5	0	0	0
	Totals	24	0	1	1

BALFOUR, Earl Frederick *Forward*
b. Toronto, Ont., Jan. 4, 1933

Season	Club	GP	G	A	Pts
1951–52	Toronto M.L.	3	0	0	0
1953–54	Toronto M.L.	17	0	1	1
1955–56	Toronto M.L.	59	14	5	19
1957–58	Toronto M.L.	1	0	0	0
1958–59	Chicago	70	10	8	18
1959–60	Chicago	70	3	5	8
1960–61	Chicago	68	3	3	6
	Totals	288	30	22	52

Playoffs

1951–52	Toronto M.L.	1	0	0	0
1955–56	Toronto M.L.	3	0	1	1
1958–59	Chicago	6	0	2	2
1959–60	Chicago	4	0	0	0
1960–61	Chicago	12	0	0	0
	Totals	26	0	3	3

BALFOUR, Murray *Forward*
b. Regina, Sask., Aug. 24, 1936

Season	Club	GP	G	A	Pts
1956–57	Montreal C.	2	0	0	0
1957–58	Montreal C.	3	1	1	2

BALFOUR *(Continued)*

Season	Club	GP	G	A	Pts
1959–60	Chicago	61	18	12	30
1960–61	Chicago	70	21	27	48
1961–62	Chicago	49	15	15	30
1962–63	Chicago	65	10	23	33
1963–64	Chicago	41	2	10	12
1964–65	Boston	15	0	2	2
	Totals	306	67	90	157

Playoffs

1959–60	Chicago	4	1	0	1
1960–61	Chicago	11	5	5	10
1961–62	Chicago	12	1	1	2
1962–63	Chicago	6	0	2	2
1963–64	Chicago	7	2	2	4
	Totals	40	9	10	19

All-Star

1961	Chicago	1	0	0	0

BALL, Terry James *Defenseman*
b. Selkirk, Man., Nov. 29, 1944

Season	Club	GP	G	A	Pts
1967–68	Philadelphia F.	1	0	0	0
1969–70	Philadelphia F.	61	7	18	25
1970–71	Buffalo	2	0	0	0
1971–72	Buffalo	10	0	1	1
	Totals	74	7	19	26

BALON, David Alexander (Dave) *Forward*
b. Wakaw, Sask., Aug. 2, 1937

Season	Club	GP	G	A	Pts
1959–60	New York R.	3	0	0	0
1960–61	New York R.	13	1	2	3
1961–62	New York R.	30	4	11	15
1962–63	New York R.	70	11	13	24
1963–64	Montreal C.	70	24	18	42
1964–65	Montreal C.	63	18	23	41
1965–66	Montreal C.	45	3	7	10
1966–67	Montreal C.	48	11	8	19
1967–68	Minnesota	73	15	32	47
1968–69	New York R.	75	10	21	31
1969–70	New York R.	76	33	37	70
1970–71	New York R.	78	36	24	60
1971–72	NY R-Vanc	75	23	24	47
1972–73	Vancouver	57	3	2	5
	Totals	776	192	222	414

Playoffs

1961–62	New York R.	6	2	3	5
1963–64	Montreal C.	7	1	1	2
1964–65	Montreal C.	10	0	0	0
1965–66	Montreal C.	9	2	3	5
1966–67	Montreal C.	9	0	2	2
1967–68	Minnesota	14	4	9	13

BALON (Continued)

Playoffs

	Club	GP	G	A	Pts
1968–69	New York R.	4	1	0	1
1969–70	New York R.	6	1	1	2
1970–71	New York R.	13	3	2	5
	Totals	78	14	21	35

All-Star

1965	Montreal C.	1	0	0	0
1966	Montreal C.	1	0	0	0
1971	East All-Stars	1	0	1	1
	Totals	3	0	1	1

BALUIK, Stanley *Forward*
b. Port Arthur, Ont., Oct. 5, 1935

Season	Club	GP	G	A	Pts
1959–60	Boston	7	0	0	0

BARBE, Andre Joseph *Forward*
b. Coniston, Ont., July 27, 1923

Season	Club	GP	G	A	Pts
1950–51	Toronto M.L.	1	0	0	0

BARBER, William (Bill) *Forward*
b. Callander, Ont., July 11, 1952

Season	Club	GP	G	A	Pts
1972–73	Philadelphia F.	69	30	34	64

Playoffs

1972–73	Philadelphia F.	11	3	2	5

BARILKO, William *Defenseman*
b. Timmins, Ont., Mar. 25, 1927

Season	Club	GP	G	A	Pts
1946–47	Toronto M.L.	18	3	7	10
1947–48	Toronto M.L.	57	5	9	14
1948–49	Toronto M.L.	60	5	4	9
1949–50	Toronto M.L.	59	7	10	17
1950–51	Toronto M.L.	58	6	6	12
	Totals	252	26	36	62

Playoffs

1946–47	Toronto M.L.	11	0	3	3
1947–48	Toronto M.L.	9	1	0	1
1948–49	Toronto M.L.	9	0	1	1
1949–50	Toronto M.L.	7	1	1	2
1950–51	Toronto M.L.	11	3	2	5
	Totals	47	5	7	12

All-Star

1947	Toronto M.L.	1	0	0	0
1948	Toronto M.L.	1	0	0	0
1949	Toronto M.L.	1	1	0	1
	Totals	3	1	0	1

BARKLEY, Douglas *Defenseman*
b. Lethbridge, Alta., Jan. 6, 1937

Season	Club	GP	G	A	Pts
1957–58	Chicago	3	0	0	0
1959–60	Chicago	3	0	0	0
1962–63	Detroit R.W.	70	3	24	27
1963–64	Detroit R.W.	67	11	21	32
1964–65	Detroit R.W.	67	5	20	25
1965–66	Detroit R.W.	43	5	15	20
	Totals	253	24	80	104

Playoffs

1962–63	Detroit R.W.	11	0	3	3
1963–64	Detroit R.W.	14	0	5	5
1964–65	Detroit R.W.	5	0	1	1
	Totals	30	0	9	9

BARLOW, Robert George (Bob) *Forward*
b. Hamilton, Ont., June 17, 1935

Season	Club	GP	G	A	Pts
1969–70	Minnesota	70	16	17	33
1970–71	Minnesota	7	0	0	0
	Totals	77	16	17	33

Playoffs

1969–70	Minnesota	6	2	2	4

BARRETT, Frederick William (Fred)
Defenseman
b. Ottawa, Ont., Jan. 26, 1950

Season	Club	GP	G	A	Pts
1970–71	Minnesota	57	0	13	13
1972–73	Minnesota	46	2	4	6
	Totals	103	2	17	19

Playoffs

1972–73	Minnesota	6	0	0	0

BARRIE, Douglas Robert (Doug) *Defenseman*
b. Edmonton, Alta., Oct. 2, 1946

Season	Club	GP	G	A	Pts
1968–69	Pittsburgh Pe.	8	1	1	2
1970–71	Buffalo	75	4	23	27
1971–72	Buff-LA	75	5	18	23
	Totals	158	10	42	52

BARRY, Edward *Forward*
b. Wellesley, Mass., Oct. 9, 1919

Season	Club	GP	G	A	Pts
1946–47	Boston	19	1	3	4

BARRY, Martin J. *Forward*
b. Quebec City, Que., Dec. 8, 1905

Season	Club	GP	G	A	Pts
1927–28	New York A.	--	1	0	1
1929–30	Boston	--	18	15	33

BARRY (Continued)

Season	Club	GP	G	A	Pts
1930-31	Boston	--	20	11	31
1931-32	Boston	--	21	17	38
1932-33	Boston	--	24	13	37
1933-34	Boston	--	27	12	39
1934-35	Boston	--	20	20	40
1935-36	Detroit R.W.	--	21	19	40
1936-37	Detroit R.W.	--	17	27	44
1937-38	Detroit R.W.	--	9	20	29
1938-39	Detroit R.W.	--	13	28	41
1939-40	Montreal C.	--	4	10	14
	Totals	--	**195**	**192**	**387**

Playoffs

Season	Club	GP	G	A	Pts
1929-30	Boston	--	3	3	6
1930-31	Boston	--	1	1	2
1932-33	Boston	--	2	2	4
1934-35	Boston	--	0	0	0
1935-36	Detroit R.W.	--	2	4	6
1936-37	Detroit R.W.	--	4	7	11
1938-39	Detroit R.W.	--	3	1	4
	Totals	--	**15**	**18**	**33**

BARRY, William Raymond (Ray) *Forward*
b. Boston, Mass., Oct. 4, 1928

Season	Club	GP	G	A	Pts
1951-52	Boston	18	1	2	3

BARTLETT, James Baker *Forward*
b. Verdun, Que., May 27, 1932

Season	Club	GP	G	A	Pts
1954-55	Montreal C.	2	0	0	0
1955-56	New York R.	12	0	1	1
1958-59	New York R.	70	11	9	20
1959-60	New York R.	44	8	4	12
1960-61	Boston	63	15	9	24
	Totals	**191**	**34**	**23**	**57**

Playoffs

Season	Club	GP	G	A	Pts
1954-55	Montreal C.	2	0	0	0

BARTON, Cliff J. *Forward*
b. Sault Ste. Marie, Mich., Sept. 3, 1907

Season	Club	GP	G	A	Pts
1929-30	Pittsburgh Pi.	--	4	2	6
1930-31	Philadelphia Q.	--	6	7	13
1939-40	New York R.	3	0	0	0
	Totals	--	**10**	**9**	**19**

BASSEN, Henry (Hank) *Goalie*
b. Calgary, Alta., Dec. 6, 1932

Season	Club	GP	GA	Sho	AVE
1954-55	Chicago	21	63	0	3.00
1955-56	Chicago	12	42	1	3.50
1960-61	Detroit R.W.	34⅓	102	0	2.97

BASSEN (Continued)

Season	Club	GP	GA	Sho	AVE
1961-62	Detroit R.W.	27	76	3	2.81
1962-63	Detroit R.W.	17	53	0	3.18
1963-64	Detroit R.W.	1	4	0	4.00
1965-66	Detroit R.W.	6⅔	17	0	2.55
1966-67	Detroit R.W.	6⅔	22	0	3.30
1967-68	Pittsburgh Pe.	22	62	1	2.82
	Totals	**148⅔**	**441**	**5**	**2.97**

Playoffs

Season	Club	GP	GA	Sho	AVE
1960-61	Detroit R.W.	3⅔	9	0	2.45
1965-66	Detroit R.W.	⅔	2	0	3.00
	Totals	**4⅓**	**11**	**0**	**2.54**

BASTIEN, Aldege (Baz) *Goalie*
b. Timmins, Ont., Aug. 29, 1920

Season	Club	GP	GA	Sho	AVE
1945-46	Toronto M.L.	5	20	0	4.00

BATHGATE, Andrew James (Andy) *Forward*
b. Winnipeg, Man., Aug. 28, 1932

Season	Club	GP	G	A	Pts
1952-53	New York R.	18	0	1	1
1953-54	New York R.	20	2	2	4
1954-55	New York R.	70	20	20	40
1955-56	New York R.	70	19	47	66
1956-57	New York R.	70	27	50	77
1957-58	New York R.	65	30	48	78
1958-59	New York R.	70	40	48	88
1959-60	New York R.	70	26	48	74
1960-61	New York R.	70	29	48	77
1961-62	New York R.	70	28	56	84
1962-63	New York R.	70	35	46	81
1963-64	NY R-Tor ML	71	19	58	77
1964-65	Toronto M.L.	55	16	29	45
1965-66	Detroit R.W.	70	15	32	47
1966-67	Detroit R.W.	60	8	23	31
1967-68	Pittsburgh Pe.	74	20	39	59
1970-71	Pittsburgh Pe.	76	15	29	44
	Totals	**1069**	**349**	**624**	**973**

Playoffs

Season	Club	GP	G	A	Pts
1955-56	New York R.	5	1	2	3
1956-57	New York R.	5	2	0	2
1957-58	New York R.	6	5	3	8
1961-62	New York R.	6	1	2	3
1963-64	Toronto M.L.	14	5	4	9
1964-65	Toronto M.L.	6	1	0	1
1965-66	Detroit R.W.	12	6	3	9
	Totals	**54**	**21**	**14**	**35**

All-Star

Season	Club	GP	G	A	Pts
1957	NHL All-Stars	1	1	1	2
1958	NHL All-Stars	1	2	0	2
1959	NHL All-Stars	1	0	0	0

BATHGATE (Continued)

All-Star	Club	GP	G	A	Pts
1960	NHL All-Stars	1	0	0	0
1961	NHL All-Stars	1	0	1	1
1962	NHL All-Stars	1	0	0	0
1963	NHL All-Stars	1	0	0	0
1964	Toronto M.L.	1	0	1	1
	Totals	8	3	3	6

BATHGATE, Frank Douglas Forward
b. Winnipeg, Man., Feb. 14, 1930

Season	Club	GP	G	A	Pts
1952–53	New York R.	2	0	0	0

BAUER, Robert Theodore Forward
b. Waterloo, Ont., Feb. 16, 1915

Season	Club	GP	G	A	Pts
1936–37	Boston	--	1	0	1
1937–38	Boston	--	20	14	34
1938–39	Boston	--	13	18	31
1939–40	Boston	--	17	26	43
1940–41	Boston	--	17	22	39
1941–42	Boston	36	13	22	35
1945–46	Boston	39	11	10	21
1946–47	Boston	58	30	24	54
1951–52	Boston	1	1	1	2
	Totals	--	123	137	260

Playoffs

1937–38	Boston	3	0	0	0
1938–39	Boston	12	3	2	5
1939–40	Boston	6	1	0	1
1940–41	Boston	11	2	2	4
1945–46	Boston	10	4	3	7
1946–47	Boston	5	1	1	2
	Totals	47	11	8	19

All-Star

1947	NHL All-Stars	1	0	0	0

BAUMAN, Garry Glenwood Goalie
b. Innisfail, Alta., July 21, 1940

Season	Club	GP	GA	Sho	AVE
1966–67	Montreal C.	2	5	0	2.50
1967–68	Minnesota	22	75	0	3.41
1968–69	Minnesota	5	22	0	4.40
	Totals	29	102	0	3.52

All-Star		GP	Per	GA	AGP
1967	Montreal C.	1	1	0	0.00

BAUN, Robert T. (Bob) Defenseman
b. Lanigan, Sask., Sept. 9, 1936

Season	Club	GP	G	A	Pts
1956–57	Toronto M.L.	20	0	5	5
1957–58	Toronto M.L.	67	1	9	10

BAUN (Continued)

Season	Club	GP	G	A	Pts
1958–59	Toronto M.L.	51	1	8	9
1959–60	Toronto M.L.	61	8	9	17
1960–61	Toronto M.L.	70	1	14	15
1961–62	Toronto M.L.	65	4	11	15
1962–63	Toronto M.L.	48	4	8	12
1963–64	Toronto M.L.	52	4	14	18
1964–65	Toronto M.L.	70	0	18	18
1965–66	Toronto M.L.	44	0	6	6
1966–67	Toronto M.L.	54	2	8	10
1967–68	Oakland	67	3	10	13
1968–69	Detroit R.W.	76	4	16	20
1969–70	Detroit R.W.	71	1	18	19
1970–71	Det RW–Tor ML	69	1	20	21
1971–72	Toronto M.L.	74	2	12	14
1972–73	Toronto M.L.	5	1	1	2
	Totals	964	37	187	224

Playoffs

1958–59	Toronto M.L.	12	0	0	0
1959–60	Toronto M.L.	10	1	0	1
1960–61	Toronto M.L.	3	0	0	0
1961–62	Toronto M.L.	12	0	3	3
1962–63	Toronto M.L.	10	0	3	3
1963–64	Toronto M.L.	14	2	3	5
1964–65	Toronto M.L.	6	0	1	1
1965–66	Toronto M.L.	4	0	1	1
1966–67	Toronto M.L.	10	0	0	0
1969–70	Detroit R.W.	4	0	0	0
1970–71	Toronto M.L.	6	0	1	1
1971–72	Toronto M.L.	5	0	0	0
	Totals	96	3	12	15

All-Star

1962	Toronto M.L.	1	0	0	0
1963	Toronto M.L.	1	0	1	1
1964	Toronto M.L.	1	0	0	0
1965	NHL All-Stars	1	0	1	1
1968	NHL All-Stars	1	0	0	0
	Totals	5	0	2	2

BEATTIE, John (Red) Forward
b. Ibstock, England, 1907

Season	Club	GP	G	A	Pts
1930–31	Boston	--	10	11	21
1932–33	Boston	--	8	12	20
1933–34	Boston	--	9	13	22
1934–35	Boston	--	9	19	27
1935–36	Boston	--	14	18	32
1936–37	Boston	--	8	7	15
1937–38	Det RW–NY A	--	4	6	10
1938–39	New York A.	--	0	0	0
	Totals	--	62	85	147

409

BEATTIE (Continued)

Playoffs	Club	GP	G	A	Pts
1932-33	Boston	--	0	0	0
1934-35	Boston	--	1	0	1
1935-36	Boston	--	0	0	0
1936-37	Boston	--	1	0	1
1937-38	New York A.	--	2	2	4
	Totals	--	4	2	6

BEAUDIN, Norman Joseph Andrew (Norm)
Forward
b. Montmartre, Sask., Nov. 28, 1941

Season	Club	GP	G	A	Pts
1967-68	St. Louis B.	13	1	1	2
1970-71	Minnesota	12	0	1	1
	Totals	25	1	2	3

BECKETT, Robert Owen *Forward*
b. Unionville, Ont., Apr. 8, 1936

Season	Club	GP	G	A	Pts
1956-57	Boston	18	0	3	3
1957-58	Boston	9	0	0	0
1961-62	Boston	34	7	2	9
1963-64	Boston	7	0	1	1
	Totals	68	7	6	13

BEHLING, Clarence Roy *Defenseman*
b. Kitchener, Ont., Mar. 16, 1916

Season	Club	GP	G	A	Pts
1942-43	Detroit R.W.	2	1	0	1

BEHLING, Richard *Defenseman*

Season	Club	GP	G	A	Pts
1940-41	Detroit R.W.	--	0	0	0

BEDARD, James Leo *Defenseman*
b. Admiral, Sask., Nov. 19, 1927

Season	Club	GP	G	A	Pts
1949-50	Chicago	6	0	0	0
1950-51	Chicago	17	1	1	2
	Totals	23	1	1	2

BELHUMEUR, Michel *Goalie*
b. Sorel, Que., Sept. 2, 1949

Season	Club	GP	GA	Sho	AVE
1972-73	Philadelphia F.	18⅔	60	0	3.22
Playoffs					
1972-73	Philadelphia F.	⅙	1	0	6.00

BELISLE, Daniel George *Forward*
b. South Porcupine, Ont., May 9, 1937

Season	Club	GP	G	A	Pts
1960-61	New York R.	4	2	0	2

BELIVEAU, Jean *Forward*
b. Three Rivers, Que., Aug. 31, 1931

Season	Club	GP	G	A	Pts
1950-51	Montreal C.	2	1	1	2
1952-53	Montreal C.	3	5	0	5
1953-54	Montreal C.	44	13	21	34
1954-55	Montreal C.	70	37	36	73
1955-56	Montreal C.	70	47	41	88
1958-57	Montreal C.	69	33	51	84
1957-58	Montreal C.	55	27	32	59
1958-59	Montreal C.	64	45	46	91
1959-60	Montreal C.	60	34	40	74
1960-61	Montreal C.	69	32	58	90
1961-62	Montreal C.	43	18	23	41
1962-63	Montreal C.	69	18	49	67
1963-64	Montreal C.	68	28	50	78
1964-65	Montreal C.	58	20	23	43
1965-66	Montreal C.	67	29	48	77
1966-67	Montreal C.	53	12	26	38
1967-68	Montreal C.	59	31	37	68
1968-69	Montreal C.	69	33	49	82
1969-70	Montreal C.	63	19	30	49
1970-71	Montreal C.	70	25	51	76
	Totals	1125	507	712	1219
Playoffs					
1953-54	Montreal C.	10	2	8	10
1954-55	Montreal C.	12	6	7	13
1955-56	Montreal C.	10	12	7	19
1956-57	Montreal C.	10	6	6	12
1957-58	Montreal C.	10	4	8	12
1958-59	Montreal C.	3	1	4	5
1959-60	Montreal C.	8	5	2	7
1960-61	Montreal C.	6	0	5	5
1961-62	Montreal C.	6	2	1	3
1962-63	Montreal C.	5	2	1	3
1963-64	Montreal C.	5	2	0	2
1964-65	Montreal C.	13	8	8	16
1965-66	Montreal C.	10	5	5	10
1966-67	Montreal C.	10	6	5	11
1967-68	Montreal C.	10	7	4	11
1968-69	Montreal C.	14	5	10	15
1970-71	Montreal C.	20	6	16	22
	Totals	162	79	97	176
All-Star					
1953	Montreal C.	1	0	1	1
1954	NHL All-Stars	1	0	1	1
1955	NHL All-Stars	1	0	1	1
1956	Montreal C.	1	0	0	0
1957	Montreal C.	1	0	0	0
1958	Montreal C.	1	0	0	0
1959	Montreal C.	1	2	0	2
1960	Montreal C.	1	0	0	0
1963	NHL All-Stars	1	0	0	0
1964	NHL All-Stars	1	1	0	1

BELIVEAU *(Continued)*

All-Star	Club	GP	G	A	Pts
1965	Montreal C.	1	1	0	1
1968	NHL All-Stars	1	0	0	0
1969	East All-Stars	1	0	0	0
	Totals	13	4	3	7

BELL, Gordon *Goalie*
b. Portage la Prairie, Man., Mar. 13, 1925

Season	Club	GP	GA	Sho	AVE
1945–46	Toronto M.L.	8	31	0	3.87
Playoffs					
1955–56	New York R.	2	9	0	4.50

BELL, Harry *Defenseman*
b. Regina, Sask., Oct. 31, 1925

Season	Club	GP	G	A	Pts
1946–47	New York R.	1	0	1	1

BELL, Joseph Alexander *Forward*
b. Portage la Prairie, Man., Nov. 27, 1923

Season	Club	GP	G	A	Pts
1942–43	New York R.	15	2	5	7
1946–47	New York R.	47	6	4	10
	Totals	62	8	9	17

BELL, William *Defenseman-Forward*
b. Lachine, Que., June 10, 1891

Season	Club	GP	G	A	Pts
1917–18	Mont W&C	8	1	0	1
1918–19	Montreal C.	1	0	0	0
1920–21	Montreal C.	4	0	0	0
1921–22	Mont C-Otta	23	2	1	3
1922–23	Montreal C.	15	0	0	0
1923–24	Montreal C.	10	0	0	0
	Totals	61	3	1	4
Playoffs					
1923–24	Montreal C.	--	0	0	0

BELLEFEUILLE, Peter *Forward*

Season	Club	GP	G	A	Pts
1925–26	Toronto St. P.	36	14	2	16
1926–27	Tor ML-Det C	--	6	0	6
1928–29	Detroit C.	--	1	0	1
1929–30	Detroit C.	--	5	2	7
	Totals	--	26	4	30

BELLEMER, Andrew *Defenseman*
b. Penetang, Ont., July 3, 1904

Season	Club	GP	G	A	Pts
1932–33	Montreal M.	--	0	0	0

BEND, John Linthwaite *Forward*
b. Poplar Point, Man., Dec. 20, 1922

Season	Club	GP	G	A	Pts
1942–43	New York R.	8	3	1	4

BENEDICT, Clinton *Goalie*
b. 1891

Season	Club	GP	GA	Sho	AVE
1917–18	Ottawa	22	114	1	5.18
1918–19	Ottawa	18	53	2	2.94
1919–20	Ottawa	24	68	5	2.67
1920–21	Ottawa	24	75	2	3.13
1921–22	Ottawa	24	84	2	3.50
1922–23	Ottawa	24	54	4	2.25
1923–24	Ottawa	22	45	3	2.04
1924–25	Montreal M.	30	65	2	2.17
1925–26	Montreal M.	36	73	6	2.03
1926–27	Montreal M.	44	68	13	1.54
1927–28	Montreal M.	44	77	6	1.75
1928–29	Montreal M.	37	57	11	1.54
1929–30	Montreal M.	15	41	0	2.73
	Totals	364	874	57	2.37
Playoffs					
1918–19	Ottawa	5	26	0	5.20
1919–20	Ottawa	5	11	1	2.20
1920–21	Ottawa	7	12	2	1.71
1921–22	Ottawa	2	5	1	2.50
1922–23	Ottawa	9	10	3	1.11
1923–24	Ottawa	2	5	0	2.50
1925–26	Montreal M.	8	8	4	1.00
1926–27	Montreal M.	2	2	0	1.00
1927–28	Montreal M.	9	8	4	0.89
	Totals	49	87	15	1.78

BENNETT, Curt Alexander *Forward*
b. Regina, Sask., March 27, 1948

Season	Club	GP	G	A	Pts
1970–71	St. Louis B.	4	2	0	2
1971–72	St. Louis B.	31	3	5	8
1972–73	NY R-Atlanta	68	18	18	36
	Totals	103	23	23	46
Playoffs					
1970–71	St. Louis B.	2	0	0	0
1971–72	St. Louis B.	10	0	0	0
	Totals	12	0	0	0

BENNETT, Frank *Forward*
b. Toronto, Ont.

Season	Club	GP	G	A	Pts
1943–44	Detroit R.W.	7	0	1	1

411

BENNETT, Harvey A. *Goalie*
b. Edington, Sask., July 23, 1925

Season	Club	GP	GA	Sho	AVE
1944-45	Boston	24	103	0	4.29

BENNETT, Max *Forward*
b. Cobalt, Ont., Nov. 4, 1912

Season	Club	GP	G	A	Pts
1935-36	Montreal C.	--	0	0	0

BENOIT, Joseph *Forward*
b. St. Albert, Alta., Feb. 27, 1916

Season	Club	GP	G	A	Pts
1940-41	Montreal C.	--	16	16	32
1941-42	Montreal C.	46	20	16	36
1942-43	Montreal C.	49	30	27	57
1945-46	Montreal C.	39	9	10	19
1946-47	Montreal C.	6	0	0	0
	Totals	--	75	69	144

Playoffs

1942-43	Montreal C.	5	1	3	4

BENSON, Robert *Defenseman*
b. Buffalo, N.Y.

Season	Club	GP	G	A	Pts
1924-25	Boston	8	0	1	1

BENSON, William Lloyd *Forward*
b. Winnipeg, Man., July 29, 1920

Season	Club	GP	G	A	Pts
1940-41	New York A.	--	3	4	7
1941-42	New York A.	45	8	21	29
	Totals	--	11	25	36

BENTLEY, Douglas Wagner *Forward*
b. Delisle, Sask., Sept. 3, 1916

Season	Club	GP	G	A	Pts
1939-40	Chicago	--	12	7	19
1940-41	Chicago	--	8	20	28
1941-42	Chicago	38	12	14	26
1942-43	Chicago	50	33	40	73
1943-44	Chicago	50	38	39	77
1945-46	Chicago	36	19	21	40
1946-47	Chicago	52	21	34	55
1947-48	Chicago	60	20	37	57
1948-49	Chicago	58	23	43	66
1949-50	Chicago	64	20	33	53
1950-51	Chicago	44	9	23	32
1951-52	Chicago	8	2	3	5
1953-54	New York R.	20	2	10	12
	Totals	--	219	324	543

BENTLEY *(Continued)*

Playoffs	Club	GP	G	A	Pts
1939-40	Chicago	2	0	0	0
1940-41	Chicago	5	1	1	2
1941-42	Chicago	3	0	1	1
1943-44	Chicago	9	8	4	12
1945-46	Chicago	4	0	2	2
	Totals	23	9	8	17

All-Star

1947	NHL All-Stars	1	1	0	1
1948	NHL All-Stars	1	0	1	1
1949	NHL All-Stars	1	1	0	1
1950	NHL All-Stars	1	0	0	0
1951	NHL 1st All-Stars	1	0	0	0
	Totals	5	2	1	3

BENTLEY, Maxwell Herbert Lloyd *Forward*
b. Delisle, Sask., Mar. 1, 1920

Season	Club	GP	G	A	Pts
1940-41	Chicago	--	7	10	17
1941-42	Chicago	39	13	17	30
1942-43	Chicago	47	26	44	70
1945-46	Chicago	47	31	30	61
1946-47	Chicago	60	29	43	72
1947-48	Chgo-Tor ML	59	26	28	54
1948-49	Toronto M.L.	60	19	22	41
1949-50	Toronto M.L.	69	23	18	41
1950-51	Toronto M.L.	67	21	41	62
1951-52	Toronto M.L.	69	24	17	41
1952-53	Toronto M.L.	36	12	11	23
1953-54	New York R.	57	14	18	32
	Totals	--	245	299	544

Playoffs

1940-41	Chicago	5	1	3	4
1941-42	Chicago	3	2	0	2
1945-46	Chicago	4	1	0	1
1947-48	Toronto M.L.	9	4	7	11
1948-49	Toronto M.L.	9	4	3	7
1949-50	Toronto M.L.	7	3	3	6
1950-51	Toronto M.L.	11	2	11	13
1951-52	Toronto M.L.	4	1	0	1
	Totals	52	18	27	45

All-Star

1947	NHL All-Stars	1	1	0	1
1948	Toronto M.L.	1	1	0	1
1949	Toronto M.L.	1	0	0	0
1951	NHL 2nd All-Stars	1	0	1	1
	Totals	4	2	1	3

BENTLEY, Reginald *Forward*
b. Delisle, Sask., May 3, 1914

Season	Club	GP	G	A	Pts
1942-43	Chicago	11	1	2	3

BERENSON, Gordon (Red) *Forward*
b. Regina, Sask., Dec. 8, 1939

Season	Club	GP	G	A	Pts
1961–62	Montreal C.	4	1	2	3
1962–63	Montreal C.	37	2	6	8
1963–64	Montreal C.	69	7	9	16
1964–65	Montreal C.	3	1	2	3
1965–66	Montreal C.	23	3	4	7
1966–67	New York R.	30	0	5	5
1967–68	NY R–StL B	74	24	30	54
1968–69	St. Louis B.	76	35	47	82
1969–70	St. Louis B.	67	33	39	72
1970–71	StL B–Det RW	69	21	38	59
1971–72	Detroit R.W.	78	28	41	69
1972–73	Detroit R.W.	78	13	30	43
	Totals	608	168	253	421
Playoffs					
1961–62	Montreal C.	5	2	0	2
1962–63	Montreal C.	5	0	0	0
1963–64	Montreal C.	7	0	0	0
1964–65	Montreal C.	9	0	1	1
1966–67	New York R.	4	0	1	1
1967–68	St. Louis B.	18	5	2	7
1968–69	St. Louis B.	12	7	3	10
1969–70	St. Louis B.	16	7	5	12
	Totals	76	21	12	33
All-Star					
1969	West All-Stars	1	1	1	2
1970	West All-Stars	1	0	1	1
1971	West All-Stars	1	0	0	0
1972	East All-Stars	1	0	0	0
	Totals	4	1	2	3

BERGDINON *Forward*

Season	Club	GP	G	A	Pts
1925–26	Boston	2	0	0	0

BERGMAN, Gary Gunnar *Defenseman*
b. Kenora, Ont., Oct. 7, 1938

Season	Club	GP	G	A	Pts
1964–65	Detroit R.W.	58	4	7	11
1965–66	Detroit R.W.	61	3	16	19
1966–67	Detroit R.W.	70	5	30	35
1967–68	Detroit R.W.	74	13	28	41
1968–69	Detroit R.W.	76	7	30	37
1969–70	Detroit R.W.	69	6	17	23
1970–71	Detroit R.W.	68	8	25	33
1971–72	Detroit R.W.	75	6	31	37
1972–73	Detroit R.W.	68	3	28	31
	Totals	619	55	312	267

BERGMAN *(Continued)*

Playoffs	Club	GP	G	A	Pts
1964–65	Detroit R.W.	5	0	1	1
1965–66	Detroit R.W.	12	0	3	3
1969–70	Detroit R.W.	4	0	1	1
	Totals	21	0	5	5
All-Star					
1973	East All-Stars	1	0	0	0

BERGMAN, Thommie Lars Rudolf *Defenseman*
b. Munkfors, Sweden, Dec. 10, 1947

Season	Club	GP	G	A	Pts
1972–73	Detroit R.W.	75	9	12	21

BERLINQUETTE, Louis *Forward*

Season	Club	GP	G	A	Pts
1917–18	Montreal C.	20	2	0	2
1918–19	Montreal C.	18	5	3	8
1919–20	Montreal C.	24	7	7	14
1920–21	Montreal C.	24	12	9	21
1921–22	Montreal C.	24	12	5	17
1922–23	Montreal C.	24	2	3	5
1924–25	Montreal C.	29	4	2	6
1925–26	Pittsburgh Pi.	30	0	0	0
	Totals	193	44	29	73
Playoffs					
1918–19	Montreal C.	--	1	0	1
1922–23	Montreal C.	--	0	1	1
	Totals	--	1	1	2

BERNIER, Serge Joseph *Forward*
b. Padoue, Que., April 29, 1947

Season	Club	GP	G	A	Pts
1968–69	Philadelphia F.	1	0	0	0
1969–70	Philadelphia F.	1	0	1	1
1970–71	Philadelphia F.	77	23	28	51
1971–72	Phila F–LA	70	23	22	45
1972–73	Los Angeles	75	22	46	68
	Totals	224	68	97	165
Playoffs					
1970–71	Philadelphia F.	4	1	1	2

BERRY, Robert Victor *Forward*
b. Montreal, Que., Nov. 29, 1943

Season	Club	GP	G	A	Pts
1968–69	Montreal C.	2	0	0	0
1970–71	Los Angeles	77	25	38	63
1971–72	Los Angeles	78	17	22	39
1972–73	Los Angeles	78	36	28	64
	Totals	235	78	88	166
All-Star					
1973	West All-Stars	1	0	0	0

BESLER, Phillip Rudolph *Defenseman-Forward*
b. Melville, Sask., Dec. 9, 1913

Season	Club	GP	G	A	Pts
1938–39	Chgo-Det RW	--	1	4	5

BESSONE, Peter *Defenseman*
b. New Bedford, Mass., Jan. 13, 1913

Season	Club	GP	G	A	Pts
1937–38	Detroit R.W.	--	0	1	1

BETTIO, Silvio Angelo *Forward*
b. Copper Cliff, Ont., Dec. 1, 1928

Season	Club	GP	G	A	Pts
1949–50	Boston	44	9	12	21

BEVERIDGE, William S. *Goalie*
b. Ottawa, Ont., July 1, 1909

Season	Club	GP	GA	Sho	AVE
1929–30	Detroit C.	39	114	2	2.92
1930–31	Ottawa	8	32	0	4.00
1932–33	Ottawa	35	95	5	2.71
1933–34	Ottawa	48	143	3	2.98
1934–35	St. Louis E.	48	144	2	3.00
1935–36	Montreal M.	32	71	1	2.22
1936–37	Montreal M.	21	46	1	2.19
1937–38	Montreal M.	48	149	2	3.10
1942–43	New York R.	17	89	1	5.24
	Totals	296	883	17	2.98

Playoffs

1936–37	Montreal M.	5	11	0	2.20

BEVERLEY, Nicholas Gerald (Nick)
Defenseman
b. Toronto, Ont., Apr. 21, 1947

Season	Club	GP	G	A	Pts
1969–70	Boston	2	0	0	0
1971–72	Boston	1	0	0	0
1972–73	Boston	75	1	10	11
	Totals	78	1	10	11

Playoffs

1972–73	Boston	4	0	0	0

BIBEAULT, Paul *Goalie*
b. Montreal, Que., Apr. 13, 1919

Season	Club	GP	GA	Sho	AVE
1940–41	Montreal C.	4	15	0	3.75
1941–42	Montreal C.	38	.131	1	3.47
1942–43	Montreal C.	50	191	1	3.82
1943–44	Toronto M.L.	29	87	5	3.00
1944–45	Boston	26	116	0	4.46
1945–46	Bos–Mont C	26	75	2	2.88
1946–47	Chicago	41	170	1	4.14
	Totals	214	785	10	3.67

BIBEAULT *(Continued)*

Playoffs

	Club	GP	GA	Sho	AVE
1941–42	Montreal C.	3	8	1	2.66
1942–43	Montreal C.	5	15	1	3.00
1943–44	Toronto M.L.	5	23	0	4.60
1944–45	Boston	7	22	0	3.14
	Totals	20	68	2	2.40

BINETTE, Andre *Goalie*
b. Montreal, Que., Dec. 2, 1933

Season	Club	GP	GA	Sho	AVE
1954–55	Montreal C.	1	4	0	4.00

BINKLEY, Leslie John (Les) *Goalie*
b. Owen Sound, Ont., June 6, 1936

Season	Club	GP	GA	Sho	AVE
1967–68	Pittsburgh Pe.	52½	151	6	2.88
1968–69	Pittsburgh Pe.	48	158	0	3.29
1969–70	Pittsburgh Pe.	24½	79	3	3.22
1970–71	Pittsburgh Pe.	30½	89	2	2.85
1971–72	Pittsburgh Pe.	28	98	0	3.51
	Totals	183½	575	11	3.12

Playoffs

1969–70	Pittsburgh Pe.	7	15	0	2.10

BIONDA, Jack Arthur *Defenseman*
b. Huntsville, Ont., Sept. 18, 1933

Season	Club	GP	G	A	Pts
1955–56	Toronto M.L.	13	0	1	1
1956–57	Boston	35	2	3	5
1957–58	Boston	42	1	4	5
1958–59	Boston	3	0	1	1
	Totals	93	3	9	12

Playoffs

1956–57	Boston	10	0	1	1
1958–59	Boston	1	0	0	0
	Totals	11	0	1	1

BITTNER, Richard J. *Goalie*
b. New Haven, Conn., Jan. 12, 1922

Season	Club	GP	GA	Sho	AVE
1949–50	Boston	1	3	0	3.00

BLACK, Stephen *Forward*
b. Ft. William, Ont., Mar. 31, 1927

Season	Club	GP	G	A	Pts
1949–50	Detroit R.W.	69	7	14	21
1950–51	Det RW–Chgo	44	4	6	10
	Totals	113	11	20	31

Playoffs

1949–50	Detroit R.W.	13	0	0	0

All-Star

1950	Detroit R.W.	1	0	0	0

BLACKBURN, John Donald (Don) *Forward*
b. Kirkland Lake, Ont., May 14, 1938

Season	Club	GP	G	A	Pts
1962-63	Boston	6	0	5	5
1967-68	Philadelphia F.	67	9	20	29
1968-69	Philadelphia F.	48	7	9	16
1969-70	New York R.	3	0	0	0
1970-71	New York R.	1	0	0	0
1972-73	NY I-Minn	60	7	10	17
	Totals	185	23	44	67
Playoffs					
1967-68	Philadelphia F.	7	3	0	3
1968-69	Philadelphia F.	4	0	0	0
1969-70	New York R.	1	0	0	0
	Totals	12	3	0	3

BLACKBURN, Robert (Bob) *Defenseman*
b. Rouyn, Que., Feb. 1, 1938

Season	Club	GP	G	A	Pts
1968-69	New York R.	11	0	0	0
1969-70	Pittsburgh Pe.	60	4	7	11
1970-71	Pittsburgh Pe.	64	4	5	9
	Totals	135	8	12	20
Playoffs					
1969-70	Pittsburgh Pe.	6	0	0	0

BLADE, Henry Gordon *Forward*
b. Peterborough, Ont., Apr. 28, 1921

Season	Club	GP	G	A	Pts
1946-47	Chicago	18	1	3	4
1947-48	Chicago	6	1	0	1
	Totals	24	2	3	5

BLADON, Tom *Defenseman*
b. Edmonton, Alta. Dec. 29, 1952

Season	Club	GP	G	A	Pts
1972-73	Philadelphia F.	78	11	31	42
Playoffs					
1972-73	Philadelphia F.	11	0	4	4

BLAINE, Gary James *Forward*
b. St. Boniface, Man., Apr. 19, 1933

Season	Club	GP	G	A	Pts
1954-55	Montreal C.	1	0	0	0

BLAIR, Andrew Dryden *Forward*
b. Winnipeg, Man., Feb. 27, 1908

Season	Club	GP	G	A	Pts
1928-29	Toronto M.L.	--	12	15	27
1929-30	Toronto M.L.	--	11	10	21
1930-31	Toronto M.L.	--	11	8	19
1931-32	Toronto M.L.	--	9	14	23

BLAIR *(Continued)*

Season	Club	GP	G	A	Pts
1932-33	Toronto M.L.	--	6	9	15
1933-34	Toronto M.L.	--	14	9	23
1934-35	Toronto M.L.	--	6	14	20
1935-36	Toronto M.L.	--	5	4	9
1936-37	Chicago	--	0	3	3
	Totals	--	74	86	160
Playoffs					
1928-29	Toronto M.L.	--	3	0	3
1930-31	Toronto M.L.	--	1	0	1
1931-32	Toronto M.L.	--	2	2	4
1932-33	Toronto M.L.	--	0	2	2
1933-34	Toronto M.L.	--	0	2	2
1934-35	Toronto M.L.	--	0	0	0
1935-36	Toronto M.L.	--	0	0	0
	Totals	--	6	6	12

BLAIR, Charles *Forward*
b. Scotland, July 23, 1928

Season	Club	GP	G	A	Pts
1948-49	Toronto M.L.	1	0	0	0

BLAIR, George (Dusty) *Forward*
b. South Porcupine, Ont., Sept. 15, 1929

Season	Club	GP	G	A	Pts
1950-51	Toronto M.L.	2	0	0	0

BLAKE, Francis J. (Mickey) *Defenseman*
b. Barriefield, Ont., Oct. 31, 1912

Season	Club	GP	G	A	Pts
1934-35	St. Louis E.	--	1	1	2
1935-36	Toronto M.L.	--	0	0	0
	Totals	--	1	1	2

BLAKE, Hector (Toe) *Forward*
b. Victoria Mines, Ont., Aug. 21, 1912

Season	Club	GP	G	A	Pts
1934-35	Montreal M.	3	0	0	0
1935-36	Montreal C.	--	1	2	3
1936-37	Montreal C.	--	10	12	22
1937-38	Montreal C.	--	17	16	33
1938-39	Montreal C.	--	24	23	47
1939-40	Montreal C.	--	17	19	36
1940-41	Montreal C.	--	12	20	32
1941-42	Montreal C.	48	17	28	45
1942-43	Montreal C.	48	23	36	59
1943-44	Montreal C.	41	26	33	59
1944-45	Montreal C.	49	29	38	67
1945-46	Montreal C.	50	29	21	50
1946-47	Montreal C.	60	21	29	50
1947-48	Montreal C.	32	9	15	24
	Totals	--	235	292	527

BLAKE (Continued)

Playoffs	Club	GP	G	A	Pts
1936–37	Montreal C.	5	1	0	1
1937–38	Montreal C.	3	3	1	4
1938–39	Montreal C.	3	1	1	2
1940–41	Montreal C.	3	0	3	3
1941–42	Montreal C.	3	0	3	3
1942–43	Montreal C.	5	4	3	7
1943–44	Montreal C.	9	7	11	18
1944–45	Montreal C.	6	0	2	2
1945–46	Montreal C.	9	7	6	13
1946–47	Montreal C.	11	2	7	9
	Totals	57	25	37	62

BLINCO, Russell Percival (Beaver) *Forward*
b. Grand Mere, Que., Mar. 12, 1908

Season	Club	GP	G	A	Pts
1933–34	Montreal M.	--	14	9	23
1934–35	Montreal M.	--	13	14	27
1935–36	Montreal M.	--	13	10	23
1936–37	Montreal M.	--	6	12	18
1937–38	Montreal M.	--	10	9	21
1938–39	Chicago	--	3	12	15
	Totals	--	59	66	125

Playoffs					
1933–34	Montreal M.	--	0	1	1
1934–35	Montreal M.	--	2	2	4
1935–36	Montreal M.	--	0	0	0
1936–37	Montreal M.	--	1	0	1
	Totals	--	3	3	6

BLOCK, Kenneth Ritchard *Defenseman*
b. Grunthal, Man., Mar. 18, 1944

Season	Club	GP	G	A	Pts
1970–71	Vancouver	1	0	0	0

BODDY, Greg Allen *Defenseman*
b. Ponoka, Alta., Mar. 19, 1949

Season	Club	GP	G	A	Pts
1971–72	Vancouver	40	2	5	7
1972–73	Vancouver	74	3	11	14
	Totals	114	5	16	21

BODNAR, August (Gus) *Forward*
b. Ft. William, Ont., Aug. 24, 1925

Season	Club	GP	G	A	Pts
1943–44	Toronto M.L.	50	22	40	62
1944–45	Toronto M.L.	49	8	36	44
1945–46	Toronto M.L.	49	14	23	37
1946–47	Toronto M.L.	39	4	6	10
1947–48	Chicago	46	13	22	35
1948–49	Chicago	59	19	26	45
1949–50	Chicago	70	11	28	39

BODNAR (Continued)

Season	Club	GP	G	A	Pts
1950–51	Chicago	44	8	12	20
1951–52	Chicago	69	14	26	40
1952–53	Chicago	66	16	13	29
1953–54	Chgo-Bos	59	9	18	27
1954–55	Boston	67	4	4	8
	Totals	667	142	254	396

Playoffs					
1943–44	Toronto M.L.	5	0	0	0
1944–45	Toronto M.L.	13	3	1	4
1946–47	Toronto M.L.	1	0	0	0
1952–53	Chicago	7	1	1	2
1953–54	Boston	1	0	0	0
1954–55	Boston	5	0	1	1
	Totals	32	4	3	7

All-Star					
1951	NHL 1st All-Stars	1	0	0	0

BOEHM, Ronald John *Forward*
b. Allan, Sask., Aug. 14, 1943

Season	Club	GP	G	A	Pts
1967–68	Oakland	16	2	1	3

BOESCH, Garth Vernon *Defenseman*
b. Millestone, Sask., Oct. 7, 1920

Season	Club	GP	G	A	Pts
1946–47	Toronto M.L.	35	4	5	9
1947–48	Toronto M.L.	45	2	7	9
1948–49	Toronto M.L.	59	1	10	11
	Totals	139	7	22	29

Playoffs					
1946–47	Toronto M.L.	11	0	2	2
1947–48	Toronto M.L.	8	2	1	3
1948–49	Toronto M.L.	9	0	2	2
	Totals	28	2	5	7

All-Star					
1948	Toronto M.L.	1	0	0	0
1949	Toronto M.L.	1	0	0	0
	Totals	2	0	0	0

BOILEAU, Marc Claude *Forward*
b. Pointe Claire, Que., Sept. 3, 1932

Season	Club	GP	G	A	Pts
1961–62	Detroit R.W.	54	5	6	11

BOILEAU, Rene *Forward*

Season	Club	GP	G	A	Pts
1925–26	New York A.	7	0	0	0

BOISVERT, Gilles *Goalie*
b. Three Rivers, Que., Feb. 15, 1933

Season	Club	GP	GA	Sho	AVE
1959-60	Detroit R.W.	3	9	0	3.00

BOIVIN, Leo Joseph *Defenseman*
b. Prescott, Ont., Aug. 2, 1932

Season	Club	GP	G	A	Pts
1951-52	Toronto M.L.	2	0	1	1
1952-53	Toronto M.L.	70	2	13	15
1953-54	Toronto M.L.	58	1	6	7
1954-55	Tor ML-Bos	66	6	11	17
1955-56	Boston	68	4	16	20
1956-57	Boston	55	2	8	10
1957-58	Boston	33	0	4	4
1958-59	Boston	70	5	16	21
1959-60	Boston	70	4	21	25
1960-61	Boston	57	6	17	23
1961-62	Boston	65	5	18	23
1962-63	Boston	62	2	24	26
1963-64	Boston	65	10	14	24
1964-65	Boston	67	3	10	13
1965-66	Bos-Det RW	62	0	10	10
1966-67	Detroit R.W.	69	4	17	21
1967-68	Pittsburgh Pe.	73	9	13	22
1968-69	Pitts Pe-Minn	69	6	19	25
1969-70	Minnesota	69	3	13	16
	Totals	1150	72	251	323

Playoffs

Season	Club	GP	G	A	Pts
1953-54	Toronto M.L.	5	0	0	0
1954-55	Boston	5	0	1	1
1956-57	Boston	10	2	3	5
1957-58	Boston	12	0	3	3
1958-59	Boston	7	1	2	3
1965-66	Detroit R.W.	12	0	1	1
1969-70	Minnesota	3	0	0	0
	Totals	54	3	10	13

All-Star

1961	NHL All-Stars	1	0	0	0
1962	NHL All-Stars	1	0	0	0
1964	NHL All-Stars	1	1	0	1
	Totals	3	1	0	1

BOLDIREV, Ivan *Forward*
b. Zranjanin, Yugoslavia, Aug. 15, 1949

Season	Club	GP	G	A	Pts
1970-71	Boston	2	0	0	0
1971-72	Bost-Calif	68	16	25	41
1972-73	California	56	11	23	34
	Totals	126	27	48	75

BOLL, Frank Thurman (Buzz) *Forward*
b. Fillmore, Sask., Mar. 6, 1911

Season	Club	GP	G	A	Pts
1933-34	Toronto M.L.	--	12	8	20
1934-35	Toronto M.L.	--	14	4	18
1935-36	Toronto M.L.	--	15	13	28
1936-37	Toronto M.L.	--	6	3	9
1937-38	Toronto M.L.	--	14	11	25
1939-40	New York A.	--	5	10	15
1940-41	New York A.	--	12	14	26
1941-42	New York A.	--	11	15	26
1942-43	Boston	43	25	27	52
1943-44	Boston	39	19	25	44
	Totals	--	133	130	263

Playoffs

Season	Club	GP	G	A	Pts
1933-34	Toronto M.L.	--	0	0	0
1934-35	Toronto M.L.	--	0	0	0
1935-36	Toronto M.L.	--	7	3	10
1936-37	Toronto M.L.	--	0	0	0
1937-38	Toronto M.L.	--	0	0	0
1939-40	New York A.	--	0	0	0
	Totals	--	7	3	10

BOLONCHUK, Larry *Defenseman*
b. Winnipeg, Man., Feb. 26, 1952

Season	Club	GP	G	A	Pts
1972-73	Vancouver	15	0	0	0

BOLTON, Hugh Edward *Defenseman*
b. Toronto, Ont., Apr. 15, 1929

Season	Club	GP	G	A	Pts
1949-50	Toronto M.L.	2	0	0	0
1950-51	Toronto M.L.	13	1	3	4
1951-52	Toronto M.L.	60	3	13	16
1952-53	Toronto M.L.	9	0	0	0
1953-54	Toronto M.L.	9	0	0	0
1954-55	Toronto M.L.	69	2	19	21
1955-56	Toronto M.L.	67	4	16	20
1956-57	Toronto M.L.	6	0	0	0
	Totals	235	10	51	61

Playoffs

Season	Club	GP	G	A	Pts
1951-52	Toronto M.L.	3	0	0	0
1953-54	Toronto M.L.	5	0	1	1
1954-55	Toronto M.L.	4	0	3	3
1955-56	Toronto M.L.	5	0	1	1
	Totals	17	0	5	5

All-Star

1956	NHL All-Stars	1	0	0	0

BONIN, Marcel *Forward*
b. Montreal, Que., Sept. 12, 1932

Season	Club	GP	G	A	Pts
1952-53	Detroit R.W.	37	4	9	13
1953-54	Detroit R.W.	1	0	0	0

BONIN *(Continued)*

Season	Club	GP	G	A	Pts
1954–55	Detroit R.W.	69	16	20	36
1955–56	Boston	67	9	9	18
1957–58	Montreal C.	66	15	24	39
1958–59	Montreal C.	57	13	30	43
1959–60	Montreal C.	59	17	34	51
1960–61	Montreal C.	65	16	35	51
1961–62	Montreal C.	33	7	14	21
	Totals	454	97	175	272

Playoffs

Season	Club	GP	G	A	Pts
1952–53	Detroit R.W.	5	0	1	1
1954–55	Detroit R.W.	11	0	2	2
1957–58	Montreal C.	9	0	1	1
1958–59	Montreal C.	11	10	5	15
1959–60	Montreal C.	8	1	4	5
1960–61	Montreal C.	6	0	1	1
	Totals	50	11	14	25

All-Star

1954	Detroit R.W.	1	0	0	0
1957	Montreal C.	1	0	1	1
1958	Montreal C.	1	0	0	0
1959	Montreal C.	1	0	1	1
1960	Montreal C.	1	0	0	0
	Totals	5	0	2	2

BOONE, Carl George (Buddy) *Forward*
b. Kirkland Lake, Ont., Sept. 11, 1932

Season	Club	GP	G	A	Pts
1957–58	Boston	34	5	3	8

Playoffs

1956–57	Boston	10	1	0	1
1957–58	Boston	12	1	1	2
	Totals	22	2	1	3

BOOTHMAN, George Edward *Forward*
b. Calgary, Alta., Sept. 25, 1916

Season	Club	GP	G	A	Pts
1942–43	Toronto M.L.	9	1	1	2
1943–44	Toronto M.L.	49	16	18	34
	Totals	58	17	19	36

Playoffs

1943–44	Toronto M.L.	5	2	1	3

BORDELEAU, Christian Gerard *Forward*
b. Noranda, Que., Sept. 23, 1947

Season	Club	GP	G	A	Pts
1968–69	Montreal C.	13	1	3	4
1969–70	Montreal C.	48	2	13	15
1970–71	St. Louis B.	78	21	32	53
1971–72	StL B–Chicago	66	14	17	31
	Totals	205	38	65	103

BORDELEAU *(Continued)*

Playoffs

	Club	GP	G	A	Pts
1968–69	Montreal C.	6	1	0	1
1970–71	St. Louis B.	5	0	1	1
1971–72	Chicago	8	3	6	9
	Totals	19	4	7	11

BORDELEAU, Jean-Pierre *Forward*
b. Noranda, Que., June 13, 1949

Season	Club	GP	G	A	Pts
1971–72	Chicago	3	0	2	2
1972–73	Chicago	73	15	15	30
	Totals	76	15	17	32

Playoffs

1969–70	Chicago	1	0	0	0
1972–73	Chicago	14	1	0	1
	Totals	15	1	0	1

BOSTROM, Helge *Defenseman*
b. Winnipeg, Man., Jan. 9, 1894

Season	Club	GP	G	A	Pts
1929–30	Chicago	--	0	1	1
1930–31	Chicago	--	2	2	4
1931–32	Chicago	--	0	0	0
1932–33	Chicago	--	1	0	1
	Totals	--	3	3	6

Playoffs

1923–24	Vancouver (PCHL)	--	1	0	1
1930–31	Chicago	--	0	0	0
	Totals	--	1	0	1

BOUCHA, Henry Charles *Forward*
b. Warroad, Minn., June 1, 1951

Season	Club	GP	G	A	Pts
1971–72	Detroit R.W.	16	1	0	1
1972–73	Detroit R.W.	73	14	14	28
	Totals	89	15	14	29

BOUCHARD, Daniel Hector *Goalie*
b. Val D'Or, Que., Dec. 12, 1950

Season	Club	GP	GA	Sho	AVE
1972–73	Atlanta	32½	100	2	3.09

BOUCHARD, Edmond *Forward*
b. Three Rivers, Que.

Season	Club	GP	G	A	Pts
1921–22	Montreal C.	18	1	4	5
1922–23	Hamilton	24	5	12	17
1923–24	Hmltn–Mont C	24	5	0	5
1924–25	Hamilton	29	2	2	4
1925–26	New York A.	34	3	1	4
1926–27	New York A.	--	2	1	3
1927–28	New York A.	--	1	0	1
1928–29	NY A–Pitts	--	0	0	0
	Totals	--	19	20	39

418

BOUCHARD, Emile Joseph (Butch)

Defenseman

b. Montreal, Que., Sept. 11, 1920

Season	Club	GP	G	A	Pts
1941–42	Montreal C.	44	0	6	6
1942–43	Montreal C.	45	2	16	18
1943–44	Montreal C.	39	5	14	19
1944–45	Montreal C.	50	11	23	34
1945–46	Montreal C.	45	7	10	17
1946–47	Montreal C.	60	5	7	12
1947–48	Montreal C.	60	4	6	10
1948–49	Montreal C.	27	3	3	6
1949–50	Montreal C.	69	1	7	8
1950–51	Montreal C.	52	3	10	13
1951–52	Montreal C.	60	3	9	12
1952–53	Montreal C.	58	2	8	10
1953–54	Montreal C.	70	1	10	11
1954–55	Montreal C.	70	2	15	17
1955–56	Montreal C.	36	0	0	0
Totals		785	49	144	193

Playoffs

Season	Club	GP	G	A	Pts
1941–42	Montreal C.	3	1	1	2
1942–43	Montreal C.	5	0	1	1
1943–44	Montreal C.	9	1	3	4
1944–45	Montreal C.	6	3	4	7
1945–46	Montreal C.	9	2	1	3
1946–47	Montreal C.	11	0	3	3
1948–49	Montreal C.	7	0	0	0
1949–50	Montreal C.	5	0	2	2
1950–51	Montreal C.	11	1	1	2
1951–52	Montreal C.	11	0	2	2
1952–53	Montreal C.	12	1	1	2
1953–54	Montreal C.	11	2	1	3
1954–55	Montreal C.	12	0	1	1
1955–56	Montreal C.	1	0	0	0
Totals		113	11	21	32

All-Star

Season	Club	GP	G	A	Pts
1947	NHL All-Stars	1	0	0	0
1948	NHL All-Stars	1	0	0	0
1950	NHL All-Stars	1	0	0	0
1951	NHL 2nd All-Stars	1	0	0	0
1952	NHL 2nd All-Stars	1	0	0	0
1953	Montreal C.	1	0	0	0
Totals		6	0	0	0

BOUCHARD, Pierre Defenseman

b. Longueuil, Que., Feb. 20, 1948

Season	Club	GP	G	A	Pts
1970–71	Montreal C.	51	0	3	3
1971–72	Montreal C.	60	3	5	8
1972–73	Montreal C.	41	0	7	7
Totals		152	3	15	18

BOUCHARD (Continued)

Playoffs	Club	GP	G	A	Pts
1970–71	Montreal C.	13	0	1	1
1971–72	Montreal C.	1	0	0	0
1972–73	Montreal C.	17	1	3	4
Totals		31	1	4	5

BOUCHARD, Richard Forward

b. Lettelier, Man., Dec. 2, 1934

Season	Club	GP	G	A	Pts
1954–55	New York R.	1	0	0	0

BOUCHER, Frank (Raffles) Forward

b. Ottawa, Ont., Oct. 7, 1901

Season	Club	GP	G	A	Pts
1921–22	Ottawa	24	9	1	10
1926–27	New York R.	44	13	15	28
1927–28	New York R.	44	23	12	35
1928–29	New York R.	44	10	16	26
1929–30	New York R.	42	26	36	62
1930–31	New York R.	44	12	27	39
1931–32	New York R.	48	12	23	35
1932–33	New York R.	46	7	28	35
1933–34	New York R.	48	14	30	44
1934–35	New York R.	48	13	32	45
1935–36	New York R.	48	11	18	29
1936–37	New York R.	44	7	13	20
1937–38	New York R.	18	0	1	1
1943–44	New York R.	15	4	10	14
Totals		557	161	262	423

Playoffs

Season	Club	GP	G	A	Pts
1921–22	Ottawa	2	0	0	0
1922–23	Vancouver (PCHL)	7	2	0	2
1926–27	New York R.	2	0	0	0
1927–28	New York R.	9	7	1	8
1928–29	New York R.	6	1	0	1
1929–30	New York R.	3	1	1	2
1930–31	New York R.	4	0	2	2
1931–32	New York R.	7	3	6	9
1932–33	New York R.	8	2	2	4
1933–34	New York R.	2	0	0	0
1934–35	New York R.	4	0	3	3
1936–37	New York R.	9	2	3	5
Totals		67	18	18	36

BOUCHER, George (Buck) Defenseman

b. Ottawa, Ont., 1896

Season	Club	GP	G	A	Pts
1917–18	Ottawa	22	9	0	9
1918–19	Ottawa	17	5	2	7
1919–20	Ottawa	22	10	4	14
1920–21	Ottawa	23	12	5	17
1921–22	Ottawa	23	12	8	20
1922–23	Ottawa	23	15	9	24
1923–24	Ottawa	21	14	5	19

BOUCHER (Continued)

Season	Club	GP	G	A	Pts
1924–25	Ottawa	28	15	4	19
1925–26	Ottawa	--	8	4	12
1926–27	Ottawa	--	8	3	11
1927–28	Ottawa	--	7	5	12
1928–29	Otta-Mont M	--	4	2	6
1929–30	Montreal M.	--	2	6	8
1930–31	Montreal M.	--	0	0	0
1931–32	Chicago	--	1	5	6
	Totals	--	122	62	184

Playoffs

Season	Club	GP	G	A	Pts
1918–19	Ottawa	--	2	1	3
1919–20	Ottawa	--	2	0	2
1920–21	Ottawa	--	3	0	3
1921–22	Ottawa	--	0	0	0
1922–23	Ottawa	--	2	1	3
1923–24	Ottawa	--	0	1	1
1925–26	Ottawa	--	0	0	0
1926–27	Ottawa	--	0	0	0
1927–28	Ottawa	--	0	0	0
1929–30	Montreal M.	--	0	0	0
1930–31	Montreal M.	--	0	0	0
1931–32	Chicago	--	0	1	1
	Totals	--	9	4	13

BOUCHER, Robert *Forward*
b. Ottawa, Ont.

Season	Club	GP	G	A	Pts
1923–24	Montreal C.	12	0	0	0

BOUCHER, William *Forward*
b. Ottawa, Ont.

Season	Club	GP	G	A	Pts
1921–22	Montreal C.	24	17	5	22
1922–23	Montreal C.	24	23	4	27
1923–24	Montreal C.	23	16	6	22
1924–25	Montreal C.	30	18	13	31
1925–26	Montreal C.	34	8	5	13
1926–27	Mont C-Bos	--	6	0	6
1927–28	New York A.	--	2	1	3
	Totals	--	90	34	124

Playoffs

Season	Club	GP	G	A	Pts
1922–23	Montreal C.	--	1	0	1
1923–24	Montreal C.	--	1	1	2
1924–25	Montreal C.	--	1	0	1
1926–27	Boston	--	0	0	0
	Totals	--	3	1	4

BOUDRIAS, Andre *Forward*
b. Montreal, Que., Sept. 19, 1943

Season	Club	GP	G	A	Pts
1963–64	Montreal C.	4	1	4	5
1964–65	Montreal C.	1	0	0	0

BOUDRIAS (Continued)

Season	Club	GP	G	A	Pts
1966–67	Montreal C.	2	0	1	1
1967–68	Minnesota	74	18	35	53
1968–69	Minn-Chgo	73	8	19	27
1969–70	St. Louis B.	50	3	14	17
1970–71	Vancouver	77	25	41	66
1971–72	Vancouver	78	27	34	61
1972–73	Vancouver	77	30	40	70
	Totals	436	112	188	300

Playoffs

Season	Club	GP	G	A	Pts
1967–68	Minnesota	14	3	6	9
1969–70	St. Louis B.	14	2	4	6
	Totals	28	5	10	15

All-Star

1967	Montreal C.	1	0	0	0

BOUGHNER, Barry Michael *Forward*
b. Delhi, Ont., Jan. 29, 1948

Season	Club	GP	G	A	Pts
1969–70	Oakland	4	0	0	0
1970–71	California	16	0	0	0
	Totals	20	0	0	0

BOURCIER, Conrad *Forward*
b. Montreal, Que., May 28, 1916

Season	Club	GP	G	A	Pts
1935–36	Montreal C.	--	0	0	0

BOURCIER, Jean Louis *Forward*
b. Montreal, Que., Jan. 3, 1912

Season	Club	GP	G	A	Pts
1935–36	Montreal C.	--	0	1	1

BOURGAULT, Leo A. *Defenseman*
b. Sturgeon Falls, Ont., Jan. 17, 1903

Season	Club	GP	G	A	Pts
1926–27	Tor ML-NY R	--	2	1	3
1927–28	New York R.	37	7	0	7
1928–29	New York R.	44	2	3	5
1929–30	New York R.	44	7	6	13
1930–31	NY R-Otta	--	0	5	5
1932–33	Mont C-Chgo	--	2	2	4
1933–34	Montreal C.	--	4	3	7
	Totals	--	24	20	44

Playoffs

Season	Club	GP	G	A	Pts
1926–27	New York R.	2	0	0	0
1927–28	New York R.	9	0	0	0
1928–29	New York R.	6	0	0	0
1929–30	New York R.	3	1	1	2
	Totals	20	1	1	2

420

BOURQUE, Claude Hennessey *Goalie*

b. Oxford, N.S., Mar. 31, 1915

Season	Club	GP	GA	Sho	AVE
1938–39	Montreal C.	25	69	2	2.76
1939–40	Mont C–Det RW	37	123	3	3.32
	Totals	62	192	5	3.10
Playoffs					
1938–39	Montreal C.	3	8	1	2.67

BOUVRETTE, Lionel *Goalie*

b. Hawsbury, Ont., June 10, 1914

Season	Club	GP	GA	Sho	AVE
1942–43	New York R.	1	6	0	6.00

BOWCHER, Clarence *Defenseman*

b. Sudbury, Ont.

Season	Club	GP	G	A	Pts
1926–27	New York A.	--	0	1	1
1927–28	New York A.	--	2	1	3
	Totals	--	2	2	4

BOWER, John William (China Wall) *Goalie*

b. Prince Albert, Sask., Nov. 8, 1924

Season	Club	GP	GA	Sho	AVE
1953–54	New York R.	70	182	5	2.60
1954–55	New York R.	5	13	0	2.60
1956–57	New York R.	2	7	0	3.50
1958–59	Toronto M.L.	39	107	3	2.74
1959–60	Toronto M.L.	66	180	5	2.73
1960–61	Toronto M.L.	58	145	2	2.50
1961–62	Toronto M.L.	59	152	2	2.58
1962–63	Toronto M.L.	42	110	1	2.62
1963–64	Toronto M.L.	50	106	5	2.12
1964–65	Toronto M.L.	34	81	3	2.38
1965–66	Toronto M.L.	33⅓	75	3	2.25
1966–67	Toronto M.L.	24	63	2	2.63
1967–68	Toronto M.L.	37½	84	4	2.24
1968–69	Toronto M.L.	13	37	2	2.85
1969–70	Toronto M.L.	1	5	0	5.00
	Totals	533⅚	1347	37	2.53
Playoffs					
1958–59	Toronto M.L.	12	39	0	3.25
1959–60	Toronto M.L.	10	31	0	3.10
1960–61	Toronto M.L.	3	9	0	3.00
1961–62	Toronto M.L.	10	22	0	2.20
1962–63	Toronto M.L.	10	16	2	1.60
1963–64	Toronto M.L.	14	30	2	2.14
1964–65	Toronto M.L.	5	13	0	2.60
1965–66	Toronto M.L.	2	8	0	4.00
1966–67	Toronto M.L.	2⅔	5	1	1.87
1968–69	Toronto M.L.	2⅗	11	0	4.23
	Totals	71⅓	184	5	2.58

BOWER *(Continued)*

All-Star		GP	Per	GA	AGP
1961	NHL All-Stars	1	1½	1	0.67
1962	Toronto M.L.	1	3	1	0.33
1963	Toronto M.L.	1	2	2	1.00
1964	Toronto M.L.	1	1½	0	0.00
1968	Toronto M.L.	1	2	2	1.00
	Totals	5	10	6	0.60

BOWMAN, Ralph (Scotty) *Defenseman*

b. Winnipeg, Man., Jan. 20, 1911

Season	Club	GP	G	A	Pts
1933–34	Ottawa	--	0	2	2
1934–35	StL E–Det RW	--	3	5	8
1935–36	Detroit R.W.	--	3	2	5
1935–37	Detroit R.W.	--	0	1	1
1937–38	Detroit R.W.	--	0	2	2
1938–39	Detroit R.W.	--	2	3	5
1939–40	Detroit R.W.	--	0	2	2
	Totals	--	8	17	25
Playoffs					
1935–36	Detroit R.W.	--	2	1	3
1936–37	Detroit R.W.	-	0	1	1
1938–39	Detroit R.W.	--	0	0	0
	Totals	--	2	2	4

BOWNASS, John (Jack) *Defenseman*

b. Winnipeg, Man., July 27, 1930

Season	Club	GP	G	A	Pts
1957–58	Montreal C.	4	0	1	1
1958–59	New York R.	35	1	2	3
1959–60	New York R.	37	2	5	7
1961–62	New York R.	4	0	0	0
	Totals	80	3	8	11

BOYD, Irvin (Yank) *Forward*

b. Ardmore, Pa., Nov. 13, 1908

Season	Club	GP	G	A	Pts
1931–32	Boston	--	2	1	3

BOYD, William C. *Forward*

b. Belleville, Ont., May 15, 1898

Season	Club	GP	G	A	Pts
1926–27	New York R.	41	4	1	5
1927–28	New York R.	43	4	0	4
1928–29	New York R.	11	0	0	0
1929–30	New York A.	--	7	6	13
	Totals	--	15	7	22
Playoffs					
1927–28	New York R.	9	0	0	0

BOYER, Walter (Wally) *Forward*
b. Cowan, Man., Sept. 27, 1937

Season	Club	GP	G	A	Pts
1965-66	Toronto M.L.	46	4	17	21
1966-67	Chicago	42	5	6	11
1967-68	Oakland	74	13	20	33
1968-69	Pittsburgh Pe.	62	10	19	29
1969-70	Pittsburgh Pe.	72	11	12	23
1970-71	Pittsburgh Pe.	68	11	30	41
1971-72	Pittsburgh Pe.	1	0	1	1
	Totals	365	54	105	159

Playoffs

1965-66	Toronto M.L.	4	0	1	1
1966-67	Chicago	1	0	0	0
1969-70	Pittsburgh Pe.	10	1	2	3
	Totals	15	1	3	4

BRACKENBOROUGH, John *Forward*

Season	Club	GP	G	A	Pts
1925-26	Boston	7	0	0	0

BRADLEY, Barton William *Forward*
b. Ft. William, Ont., July 29, 1930

Season	Club	GP	G	A	Pts
1949-50	Boston	1	0	0	0

BRANIGAN, Andrew John *Defenseman*
b. Winnipeg, Man., Apr. 11, 1922

Season	Club	GP	G	A	Pts
1940-41	New York A.	--	1	0	1
1941-42	New York A.	21	0	2	2
	Totals	--	1	2	3

BRAYSHAW, Russell Ambrose *Forward*
b. Saskatoon, Sask., Jan. 17, 1918

Season	Club	GP	G	A	Pts
1944-45	Chicago	43	5	9	14

BRENNAN, Douglas R. *Defenseman*
b. Peterborough, Ont., Jan. 10, 1905

Season	Club	GP	G	A	Pts
1931-32	New York R.	38	4	3	7
1932-33	New York R.	48	5	4	9
1933-34	New York R.	37	0	0	0
	Totals	123	9	7	16

Playoffs

1931-32	New York R.	7	1	0	1
1932-33	New York R.	8	0	0	0
1933-34	New York R.	1	0	0	0
	Totals	16	1	0	1

BRENNAN, Thomas *Forward*
b. Philadelphia, Pa., Jan. 2, 1921

Season	Club	GP	G	A	Pts
1943-44	Boston	11	2	1	3
1944-45	Boston	1	0	1	1
	Totals	12	2	2	4

BRENNEMAN, John *Forward*
b. Fort Erie, Ont., Jan. 5, 1943

Season	Club	GP	G	A	Pts
1964-65	Chgo-NY R	39	4	3	7
1965-66	New York R.	11	0	0	0
1966-67	Toronto M.L.	41	6	4	10
1967-68	Det RW-Oakl	40	10	10	20
1968-69	Oakland	21	1	2	3
	Totals	152	21	19	40

BRETTIO, Joseph *Defenseman*
b. Hibbling, Minn., Nov. 29, 1913

Season	Club	GP	G	A	Pts
1944-45	Chicago	3	0	0	0

BREWER, Carl Thomas *Defenseman*
b. Toronto, Ont., Oct. 21, 1938

Season	Club	GP	G	A	Pts
1957-58	Toronto M.L.	2	0	0	0
1958-59	Toronto M.L.	69	3	21	24
1959-60	Toronto M.L.	67	4	19	23
1960-61	Toronto M.L.	51	1	14	15
1961-62	Toronto M.L.	67	1	22	23
1962-63	Toronto M.L.	70	2	23	25
1963-64	Toronto M.L.	57	4	9	13
1964-65	Toronto M.L.	70	4	23	27
1969-70	Detroit R.W.	70	2	37	39
1970-71	St. Louis B.	19	2	9	11
1971-72	St. Louis B.	42	2	16	18
	Totals	584	25	193	218

Playoffs

1958-59	Toronto M.L.	12	0	6	6
1959-60	Toronto M.L.	10	2	3	5
1960-61	Toronto M.L.	5	0	0	0
1961-62	Toronto M.L.	8	0	2	2
1962-63	Toronto M.L.	10	0	1	1
1963-64	Toronto M.L.	12	0	1	1
1964-65	Toronto M.L.	6	1	2	3
1969-70	Detroit R.W.	4	0	0	0
1970-71	St. Louis B.	5	0	2	2
	Totals	72	3	17	20

All-Star

1959	NHL All-Stars	1	0	0	0
1961	NHL All-Stars	1	0	0	0
1962	Toronto M.L.	1	0	0	0
1964	Toronto M.L.	1	0	0	0
1970	East All-Stars	1	0	1	1
	Totals	5	0	1	1

BRIDEN, Archie *Forward*

Season	Club	GP	G	A	Pts
1926-27	Bos-Det C	--	5	2	7
1929-30	Pittsburgh Pi.	--	4	3	7
	Totals	--	9	5	14

BRIERE, Michel *Forward*
b. Shawinigan Falls, Que., Oct. 21, 1949

Season	Club	GP	G	A	Pts
1969-70	Pittsburgh Pe	76	12	32	44
Playoffs					
1969-70	Pittsburgh Pe.	10	5	3	8

BRIMSEK, Francis Charles (Mr. Zero) *Goalie*
b. Eveleth, Minn., Sept. 26, 1915

Season	Club	GP	GA	Sho	AVE
1938-39	Boston	43	69	10	1.60
1939-40	Boston	48	98	6	2.04
1940-41	Boston	48	102	6	2.12
1941-42	Boston	47	112	3	2.38
1942-43	Boston	50	176	1	3.52
1945-46	Boston	34	111	2	3.26
1946-47	Boston	60	175	3	2.91
1947-48	Boston	60	168	3	2.82
1948-49	Boston	54	147	1	2.72
1949-50	Chicago	70	244	5	3.48
	Totals	478	1402	40	2.94
Playoffs					
1938-39	Boston	12	18	1	1.50
1939-40	Boston	6	15	0	2.50
1940-41	Boston	11	23	1	2.09
1941-42	Boston	5	16	0	3.20
1942-43	Boston	9	33	0	3.66
1945-46	Boston	10	29	0	2.90
1946-47	Boston	5	16	0	3.20
1947-48	Boston	5	20	0	4.00
1948-49	Boston	5	16	0	3.20
	Totals	68	186	2	2.74

All-Star		GP	Per	GA	AGP
1947	NHL All-Stars	1	1½	1	0.67

BRINDLEY, Douglas Allen *Forward*
b. Walkerton, Ont., June 8, 1949

Season	Club	GP	G	A	Pts
1970-71	Toronto M.L.	3	0	0	0

BRINK, Milt *Forward*

Season	Club	GP	G	A	Pts
1936-37	Chicago	--	0	0	0

BRISSON, Gerald *Forward*
b. St. Boniface, Man., Sept. 3, 1937

Season	Club	GP	G	A	Pts
1962-63	Montreal C.	4	0	2	2

BROADBENT, Harry (Punch) *Forward*
b. Ottawa, Ont., 1893

Season	Club	GP	G	A	Pts
1918-19	Ottawa	8	4	2	6
1919-20	Ottawa	20	19	4	23
1920-21	Ottawa	9	4	1	5
1921-22	Ottawa	24	32	14	46
1922-23	Ottawa	24	14	0	14
1923-24	Ottawa	22	9	4	13
1924-25	Montreal M.	30	15	4	19
1925-26	Montreal M.	36	12	5	17
1926-27	Montreal M.	--	9	5	14
1927-28	Ottawa	--	3	2	5
1928-29	New York A.	--	1	4	5
	Totals	--	122	45	167
Playoffs					
1918-19	Ottawa	--	2	0	2
1919-20	Ottawa	--	0	0	0
1920-21	Ottawa	--	0	2	2
1921-22	Ottawa	--	0	0	0
1922-23	Ottawa	6	6	1	7
1923-24	Ottawa	--	0	0	0
1925-26	Montreal M.	--	2	0	2
1926-27	Montreal M.	--	0	0	0
1927-28	Ottawa	--	0	0	0
1928-29	New York A.	--	0	0	0
	Totals	--	10	3	13

BRODA, Walter (Turk) *Goalie*
b. Brandon, Man., May 15, 1914

Season	Club	GP	GA	Sho	AVE
1936-37	Toronto M.L.	45	106	3	2.35
1937-38	Toronto M.L.	48	127	6	2.64
1938-39	Toronto M.L.	48	107	8	2.23
1939-40	Toronto M.L.	47	108	4	2.30
1940-41	Toronto M.L.	48	99	4	2.06
1941-42	Toronto M.L.	48	136	6	2.83
1942-43	Toronto M.L.	50	159	1	3.18
1945-46	Toronto M.L.	15	53	0	3.53
1946-47	Toronto M.L.	60	172	4	2.86
1947-48	Toronto M.L.	60	143	5	2.38
1948-49	Toronto M.L.	60	161	5	2.68
1949-50	Toronto M.L.	68	167	9	2.45
1950-51	Toronto M.L.	31	68	6	2.19
1951-52	Toronto M.L.	1	3	0	3.00
	Totals	630	1611	61	2.56
Playoffs					
1936-37	Toronto M.L.	2	5	0	2.50
1937-38	Toronto M.L.	7	13	1	1.85
1938-49	Toronto M.L.	10	20	2	2.00
1939-40	Toronto M.L.	10	19	1	1.90
1940-41	Toronto M.L.	7	15	0	2.14
1941-42	Toronto M.L.	13	31	1	2.38

423

BRODA (Continued)

Playoffs	Club	GP	GA	Sho	AVE
1942–43	Toronto M.L.	6	20	0	3.16
1946–47	Toronto M.L.	11	27	1	2.45
1947–48	Toronto M.L.	9	20	1	2.22
1948–49	Toronto M.L.	9	15	1	1.67
1949–50	Toronto M.L.	7	10	2	1.43
1950–51	Toronto M.L.	8	9	2	1.12
1951–52	Toronto M.L.	2	7	0	3.50
	Totals	101	211	12	2.09

All-Star		GP	Per	GA	AGP
1947	Toronto M.L.	1	3	4	1.33
1948	Toronto M.L.	1	3	3	1.00
1949	Toronto M.L.	1	3	3	1.00
1950	NHL All-Stars	1	1½	5	3.33
	Totals	4	10½	15	1.43

BRODEN, Connell *Forward*
b. Montreal, Que., Apr. 6, 1932

Season	Club	GP	G	A	Pts
1955–56	Montreal C.	3	0	0	0
1957–58	Montreal C.	3	2	1	3
	Totals	6	2	1	3

Playoffs					
1956–57	Montreal C.	6	0	1	1

BRODERICK, Kenneth Lorne *Goalie*
b. Toronto, Ont., Feb. 16, 1942

Season	Club	GP	GA	Sho	AVE
1969–70	Minnesota	6	26	0	4.33

BRODERICK, Len *Goalie*
b. Toronto, Ont., Oct. 11, 1930

Season	Club	GP	GA	Sho	AVE
1957–58	Montreal C.	1	2	0	2.00

BROOKS, Arthur *Goalie*

Season	Club	GP	GA	Sho	AVE
1917–18	Toronto A.	3	18	0	6.00

BROOKS, Donald Ross *Goalie*
b. Toronto, Ont., Oct. 17, 1937

Season	Club	GP	GA	Sho	AVE
1972–73	Boston	15⅙	40	1	2.64

Playoffs					
1972–73	Boston	⅓	3	0	9.00

BROOKS, Gordon John (Gord) *Forward*
b. Cobourg, Ont., Sept. 11, 1950

Season	Club	GP	G	A	Pts
1971–72	St. Louis B.	2	0	0	0

BROPHY, Bernard *Forward*
b. Collingwood, Ont.

Season	Club	GP	G	A	Pts
1925–26	Montreal C.	10	0	0	0
1928–29	Detroit C.	--	2	4	6
1929–30	Detroit C.	--	2	0	2
	Totals	--	4	4	8

Playoffs					
1928–29	Detroit C.	--	0	0	0

BROPHY, Frank *Goalie*

Season	Club	GP	GA	Sho	AVE
1919–20	Quebec	21	151	0	7.18

BROSSART, William (Bill) *Defenseman*
b. Allan, Sask., May 29, 1949

Season	Club	GP	G	A	Pts
1970–71	Philadelphia F.	1	0	0	0
1971–72	Philadelphia F.	42	0	4	4
1972–73	Philadelphia F.	4	0	1	1
	Totals	47	0	5	5

BROWN, Adam *Forward*
b. Johnstone, Scotland, Feb. 4, 1920

Season	Club	GP	G	A	Pts
1941–42	Detroit R.W.	28	6	9	15
1943–44	Detroit R.W.	50	24	18	42
1945–46	Detroit R.W.	48	20	11	31
1946–47	Det RW-Chgo	64	19	30	49
1947–48	Chicago	32	7	10	17
1948–49	Chicago	58	8	12	20
1949–50	Chicago	25	2	2	4
1950–51	Chicago	53	10	12	22
1951–52	Boston	33	8	9	17
	Totals	391	104	113	217

Playoffs					
1941–42	Detroit R.W.	12	0	2	2
1942–43	Detroit R.W.	6	1	1	2
1943–44	Detroit R.W.	5	0	0	0
1945–46	Detroit R.W.	5	1	1	2
	Totals	28	2	4	6

BROWN, Andrew Conrad (Andy) *Goalie*
b. Hamilton, Ont., Feb. 15, 1944

Season	Club	GP	GA	Sho	AVE
1971–72	Detroit R.W.	9⅓	37	0	3.96
1972–73	Det RW-Pitt Pe	14⅓	61	0	4.27
	Totals	23⅔	98	0	4.14

BROWN, Fred *Forward*
b. Kingston, Ont.

Season	Club	GP	G	A	Pts
1927–28	Montreal M.	--	1	0	1

BROWN, George   *Defenseman-Forward*
b. Winnipeg, Man., May 17, 1912

Season	Club	GP	G	A	Pts
1936-37	Montreal C.	--	4	6	10
1937-38	Montreal C.	--	1	7	8
1938-39	Montreal C.	--	1	9	10
	Totals	--	6	22	28
Playoffs					
1937-38	Montreal C.	--	0	0	0

BROWN, Gerald William Joseph   *Forward*
b. Edmonton, Alta., July 7, 1917

Season	Club	GP	G	A	Pts
1941-42	Detroit R.W.	13	4	4	8
1945-46	Detroit R.W.	10	0	1	1
	Totals	23	4	5	9
Playoffs					
1941-42	Detroit R.W.	12	2	1	3

BROWN, Harold Fraser   *Forward*
b. Brandon, Man., Sept. 14, 1920

Season	Club	GP	G	A	Pts
1945-46	New York R.	13	2	1	3

BROWN, Kenneth Murray (Ken)   *Goalie*
b. Port Arthur, Ont., Dec. 19, 1948

Season	Club	GP	GA	Sho	AVE
1970-71	Chicago	⅓	1	0	3.33

BROWN, Larry Wayne   *Defenseman*
b. Brandon, Man., Apr. 14, 1947

Season	Club	GP	G	A	Pts
1969-70	New York R.	15	0	3	3
1970-71	Det RW-NY R	64	2	5	7
1971-72	Philadelphia F.	12	0	0	0
1972-73	Los Angeles	55	0	7	7
	Totals	146	2	15	17
Playoffs					
1970-71	New York R.	11	0	1	1

BROWN, Patrick Cornelius (Conny)   *Forward*
b. Van Kleek Hill, Ont., Jan. 11, 1917

Season	Club	GP	G	A	Pts
1938-39	Detroit R.W.	--	1	0	1
1939-40	Detroit R.W.	--	8	3	11
1940-41	Detroit R.W.	--	1	2	3
1941-42	Detroit R.W.	9	0	3	3
1942-43	Detroit R.W.	23	5	16	21
	Totals	--	15	24	39
Playoffs					
1939-40	Detroit R.W.	5	2	1	3
1940-41	Detroit R.W.	9	0	2	2
	Totals	14	2	3	5

BROWN, Stanley   *Forward*
b. North Bay, Ont., May 9, 1898

Season	Club	GP	G	A	Pts
1926-27	New York R.	24	6	2	8
1927-28	Detroit C.	24	2	0	2
	Totals	48	8	2	10
Playoffs					
1926-27	New York R.	2	0	0	0

BROWN, Stewart Arnold (Arnie)   *Defenseman*
b. Apsley, Ont., Jan. 28, 1942

Season	Club	GP	G	A	Pts
1961-62	Toronto M.L.	2	0	0	0
1963-64	Toronto M.L.	4	0	0	0
1964-65	New York R.	58	1	11	12
1965-66	New York R.	64	1	7	8
1966-67	New York R.	69	2	10	12
1967-68	New York R.	74	1	25	26
1968-69	New York R.	74	10	12	22
1969-70	New York R.	73	15	21	36
1970-71	NY R-Det RW	75	5	18	23
1971-72	Detroit R.W.	77	2	23	25
1972-73	NY I-Atlanta	63	5	8	13
	Totals	633	42	135	177
Playoffs					
1966-67	New York R.	4	0	0	0
1967-68	New York R.	6	0	1	1
1968-69	New York R.	4	0	1	1
1969-70	New York R.	4	0	4	4
	Totals	18	0	6	6

BROWNE, Cecil   *Forward*

Season	Club	GP	G	A	Pts
1927-28	Chicago	--	2	0	2

BRUCE, Arthur Gordon   *Forward*
b. Ottawa, Ont., May 9, 1919

Season	Club	GP	G	A	Pts
1940-41	Boston	--	0	1	1
1941-42	Boston	15	4	8	12
1945-46	Boston	5	0	0	0
	Totals	--	4	9	13
Playoffs					
1940-41	Boston	2	0	0	0
1941-42	Boston	5	2	3	5
	Totals	7	2	3	5

BRUCE, Morley   *Defenseman*

Season	Club	GP	G	A	Pts
1917-18	Ottawa	7	0	0	0
1919-20	Ottawa	21	1	0	1
1920-21	Ottawa	21	3	1	4
1921-22	Ottawa	23	4	0	4
	Totals	72	8	1	9

BRUCE *(Continued)*

Playoffs	Club	GP	G	A	Pts
1920–21	Ottawa	––	0	0	0
1921–22	Ottawa	––	0	0	0
	Totals	––	0	0	0

BRUNETEAU, Edward Ernest Henry *Forward*
b. St. Boniface, Man., Aug. 1, 1919

Season	Club	GP	G	A	Pts
1940–41	Detroit R.W.	12	1	1	2
1943–44	Detroit R.W.	2	0	1	1
1944–45	Detroit R.W.	42	12	13	25
1945–46	Detroit R.W.	46	17	12	29
1946–47	Detroit R.W.	60	9	14	23
1947–48	Detroit R.W.	18	1	1	2
1948–49	Detroit R.W.	1	0	0	0
	Totals	181	40	42	82

Playoffs					
1944–45	Detroit R.W.	14	5	2	7
1945–46	Detroit R.W.	4	1	0	1
1946–47	Detroit R.W.	4	1	4	5
1947–48	Detroit R.W.	6	0	0	0
	Totals	28	7	6	13

BRUNETEAU, Modere (Mud) *Forward*
b. St. Boniface, Man., Nov. 28, 1914

Season	Club	GP	G	A	Pts
1935–36	Detroit R.W.	––	2	0	2
1936–37	Detroit R.W.	––	9	7	16
1937–38	Detroit R.W.	––	3	6	9
1938–39	Detroit R.W.	––	3	7	10
1939–40	Detroit R.W.	––	10	14	24
1940–41	Detroit R.W.	––	11	17	28
1941–42	Detroit R.W.	48	14	19	33
1942–43	Detroit R.W.	50	23	22	45
1943–44	Detroit R.W.	39	35	18	53
1944–45	Detroit R.W.	43	23	24	47
1945–46	Detroit R.W.	28	6	4	10
	Totals	––	139	138	277

Playoffs					
1935–36	Detroit R.W.	7	2	2	4
1936–37	Detroit R.W.	10	2	0	2
1938–39	Detroit R.W.	6	0	0	0
1939–40	Detroit R.W.	5	3	2	5
1940–41	Detroit R.W.	9	2	1	3
1941–42	Detroit R.W.	12	5	1	6
1942–43	Detroit R.W.	10	5	4	9
1943–44	Detroit R.W.	5	1	2	3
1944–45	Detroit R.W.	14	3	2	5
	Totals	78	23	14	27

BRYDGE, William *Defenseman*
b. Renfrew, Ont., 1901

Season	Club	GP	G	A	Pts
1926–27	Toronto M.L.	––	6	3	9
1928–29	Detroit C.	––	2	2	4
1929–30	New York A.	––	2	6	8
1930–31	New York A.	––	2	5	7
1931–32	New York A.	––	2	8	10
1932–33	New York A.	––	4	15	19
1933–34	New York A.	––	6	7	13
1934–35	New York A.	––	2	6	8
1935–36	New York A.	––	0	0	0
	Totals	––	26	52	78

Playoffs					
1928–29	Detroit C.	––	0	0	0

BRYDSON, Glenn *Forward*
b. Swansea, Ont., Nov. 7, 1910

Season	Club	GP	G	A	Pts
1930–31	Montreal M.	––	0	0	0
1931–32	Montreal M.	––	12	13	25
1932–33	Montreal M.	––	11	17	28
1933–34	Montreal M.	––	4	5	9
1934–35	St. Louis E.	––	11	18	29
1935–36	NY R–Chgo	––	10	16	26
1936–37	Chicago	––	7	7	14
1937–38	Chicago	––	1	3	4
	Totals	––	56	79	135

Playoffs					
1930–31	Montreal M.	2	0	0	0
1931–32	Montreal M.	4	0	0	0
1932–33	Montreal M.	2	0	0	0
1935–36	Chicago	2	0	0	0
	Totals	10	0	0	0

BRYDSON, Gordon *Forward*
b. Toronto, Ont.

Season	Club	GP	G	A	Pts
1929–30	Toronto M.L.	––	2	0	2

BUCHANAN, Allaster William *Forward*
b. Winnipeg, Man., May 17, 1927

Season	Club	GP	G	A	Pts
1948–49	Toronto M.L.	3	0	1	1
1949–50	Toronto M.L.	1	0	0	0
	Totals	4	0	1	1

BUCHANAN, Michael *Defenseman*
b. Sault Ste. Marie, Ont., Mar. 1, 1932

Season	Club	GP	G	A	Pts
1951–52	Chicago	1	0	0	0

BUCHANAN, Ralph L. (Bucky) *Forward*
b. Bout de l'Isle, Que., Dec. 28, 1922

Season	Club	GP	G	A	Pts
1948-49	New York R.	2	0	0	0

BUCHANAN, Ronald Leonard *Forward*
b. Montreal, Que., Nov. 15, 1944

Season	Club	GP	G	A	Pts
1966-67	Boston	3	0	0	0
1969-70	St. Louis B.	2	0	0	0
	Totals	5	0	0	0

BUCYK, John Paul *Forward*
b. Edmonton, Alta., May 12, 1935

Season	Club	GP	G	A	Pts
1955-56	Detroit R.W.	38	1	8	9
1956-57	Detroit R.W.	66	10	11	21
1957-58	Boston	68	21	31	52
1958-59	Boston	69	24	36	60
1959-60	Boston	56	16	36	52
1960-61	Boston	70	19	20	39
1961-62	Boston	67	20	40	60
1962-63	Boston	69	27	39	66
1963-64	Boston	62	18	36	54
1964-65	Boston	68	26	29	55
1965-66	Boston	63	27	30	57
1966-67	Boston	59	18	30	48
1967-68	Boston	72	30	39	69
1968-69	Boston	70	24	42	66
1969-70	Boston	76	31	38	69
1970-71	Boston	78	51	65	116
1971-72	Boston	78	32	51	83
1972-73	Boston	78	40	53	93
	Totals	1207	435	634	1069

Playoffs

Season	Club	GP	G	A	Pts
1955-56	Detroit R.W.	10	1	1	2
1956-57	Detroit R.W.	5	0	1	1
1957-58	Boston	12	0	4	4
1958-59	Boston	7	2	4	6
1967-68	Boston	3	0	2	2
1968-69	Boston	10	5	6	11
1969-70	Boston	14	11	8	19
1970-71	Boston	7	2	5	7
1971-72	Boston	15	9	11	20
1972-73	Boston	5	0	2	2
	Totals	88	30	44	74

All-Star

1955	Detroit R.W.	1	0	0	0
1963	NHL All-Stars	1	0	1	1
1964	NHL All-Stars	1	0	1	1
1965	NHL All-Stars	1	1	0	1
1968	NHL All-Stars	1	0	0	0
1970	East All-Stars	1	0	1	1
1971	East All-Stars	1	0	0	0
	Totals	7	1	3	4

BUKOVICH, Anthony John *Forward*
b. Painesdale, Mich., Aug. 30, 1917

Season	Club	GP	G	A	Pts
1943-44	Detroit R.W.	3	0	1	1
1944-45	Detroit R.W.	14	7	2	9
	Totals	17	7	3	10

Playoffs

1944-45	Detroit R.W.	6	0	1	1

BULLER, Hyman *Defenseman*
b. Montreal, Que., Mar. 15, 1926

Season	Club	GP	G	A	Pts
1943-44	Detroit R.W.	7	0	3	3
1944-45	Detroit R.W.	2	0	0	0
1951-52	New York R.	68	12	23	35
1952-53	New York R.	70	7	18	25
1953-54	New York R.	41	3	14	17
	Totals	188	22	58	80

All-Star

1952	NHL 2nd All-Stars	1	0	1	1

BULLOCK, Bruce John *Goalie*
b. Toronto, Ont., May 9, 1949

Season	Club	GP	GA	Sho	AVE
1972-73	Vancouver	14	67	0	4.79

BURCH, William *Defenseman-Forward*
b. Yonkers, N.Y.

Season	Club	GP	G	A	Pts
1922-23	Hamilton	10	6	2	8
1923-24	Hamilton	24	16	2	18
1924-25	Hamilton	27	20	4	24
1925-26	New York A.	36	22	3	25
1926-27	New York A.	--	19	8	27
1927-28	New York A.	--	10	2	12
1928-29	New York A.	--	11	5	16
1929-30	New York A.	--	7	3	10
1930-31	New York A.	--	14	8	22
1931-32	New York A.	--	7	15	22
1932-33	Bos-Chgo	--	5	1	6
	Totals	--	133	53	186

Playoffs

1928-29	New York A.	--	0	0	0

BURCHELL, Frederick (Skippy) *Forward*
b. Montreal, Que., Jan. 9, 1931

Season	Club	GP	G	A	Pts
1950-51	Montreal C.	2	0	0	0
1953-54	Montreal C.	2	0	0	0
	Totals	4	0	0	0

BUREGA, William *Defenseman*
b. Winnipeg, Man., Mar. 13, 1932

Season	Club	GP	G	A	Pts
1955-56	Toronto M.L.	4	0	1	1

BURKE, Edward *Forward*
b. Toronto, Ont., June 3, 1907

Season	Club	GP	G	A	Pts
1931–32	Boston	--	3	0	3
1932–33	New York A.	--	2	0	2
1933–34	New York A.	--	20	10	30
1934–35	New York A.	--	4	10	14
	Totals	--	**29**	**20**	**49**

BURKE, Martin Alphonsos *Defenseman*
b. Toronto, Ont., Jan. 28, 1903

Season	Club	GP	G	A	Pts
1927–28	Pitts Pi-Mont C	--	2	1	3
1928–29	Montreal C.	--	4	2	6
1929–30	Montreal C.	--	2	11	13
1930–31	Montreal C.	--	2	5	7
1931–32	Montreal C.	--	3	6	9
1932–33	Otta-Mont C	--	2	5	7
1933–34	Montreal C.	--	1	4	5
1934–35	Chicago	--	2	2	4
1935–36	Chicago	--	0	3	3
1936–37	Chicago	--	1	3	4
1937–38	Montreal C.	--	0	5	5
	Totals	--	**19**	**47**	**66**

Playoffs

1927–28	Montreal C.	--	1	0	1
1928–29	Montreal C.	--	0	0	0
1929–30	Montreal C.	--	0	1	1
1930–31	Montreal C.	--	1	2	3
1931–32	Montreal C.	--	0	0	0
1933–34	Montreal C.	--	0	1	1
1934–35	Chicago	--	0	0	0
1935–36	Chicago	--	0	0	0
1937–38	Montreal C.	--	0	0	0
	Totals	--	**2**	**4**	**6**

BURMISTER, Roy *Forward*
b. Collingwood, Ont.

Season	Club	GP	G	A	Pts
1929–30	New York A.	--	1	1	2
1931–32	New York A.	--	3	2	5
	Totals	--	**4**	**3**	**7**

BURNETT, James Kelvin (Kelly) *Forward*
b. Lachine, Que., June 16, 1926

Season	Club	GP	G	A	Pts
1952–53	New York R.	3	1	0	1

BURNS, Charles Frederick *Forward*
b. Detroit, Mich., Feb. 14, 1936

Season	Club	GP	G	A	Pts
1958–59	Detroit R.W.	70	9	11	20
1959–60	Boston	62	10	17	27
1960–61	Boston	62	15	26	41

BURNS *(Continued)*

Season	Club	GP	G	A	Pts
1961–62	Boston	70	11	17	28
1962–63	Boston	68	12	10	22
1967–68	Oakland	73	9	26	35
1968–69	Pittsburgh Pe.	76	13	38	51
1969–70	Minnesota	50	3	13	16
1970–71	Minnesota	76	9	19	28
1971–72	Minnesota	77	11	14	25
1972–73	Minnesota	65	4	7	11
	Totals	**749**	**106**	**198**	**304**

Playoffs

1969–70	Minnesota	6	1	0	1
1970–71	Minnesota	12	3	3	6
1971–72	Minnesota	7	1	1	2
1972–73	Minnesota	6	0	0	0
	Totals	**31**	**5**	**4**	**9**

BURNS, Norman *Forward*
b. Youngstown, Alta., Feb. 20, 1918

Season	Club	GP	G	A	Pts
1941–42	New York R.	11	0	4	4

BURNS, Robert *Forward*
b. Gore Bay, Ont., Apr. 4, 1905

Season	Club	GP	G	A	Pts
1928–29	Chicago	--	0	0	0
1929–30	Chicago	--	1	0	1
	Totals	--	**1**	**0**	**1**

BURNS, Robert Arthur (Robin) *Forward*
b. Montreal, Que., Aug. 27, 1946

Season	Club	GP	G	A	Pts
1970–71	Pittsburgh Pe.	10	0	3	3
1971–72	Pittsburgh Pe.	5	0	0	0
1972–73	Pittsburgh Pe.	26	0	2	2
	Totals	**41**	**0**	**5**	**5**

BURROWS, David James (Dave) *Defenseman*
b. Toronto, Ont., Jan. 11, 1949

Season	Club	GP	G	A	Pts
1971–72	Pittsburgh Pe.	77	2	10	12
1972–73	Pittsburgh Pe.	78	3	24	27
	Totals	**155**	**5**	**34**	**39**

BURTON, Cumming Scott *Forward*
b. Sudbury, Ont., May 12, 1936

Season	Club	GP	G	A	Pts
1955–56	Detroit R.W.	3	0	0	0
1957–58	Detroit R.W.	20	0	1	1
1958–59	Detroit R.W.	14	0	1	1
	Totals	**37**	**0**	**2**	**2**

Playoffs

1955–56	Detroit R.W.	3	0	0	0

BUSH, Edward Webster *Defenseman*
b. Collingwood, Ont., July 11, 1918

Season	Club	GP	G	A	Pts
1941–42	Detroit R.W.	18	4	6	10

BUSNIUK, Ronald Edward (Ron) *Forward*
b. Ft. William, Ont., Aug. 13, 1948

Season	Club	GP	G	A	Pts
1972–73	Buffalo	1	0	0	0

BUSWELL, Walter Gerald *Defenseman*
b. Montreal, Que., Nov. 6, 1907

Season	Club	GP	G	A	Pts
1932–33	Detroit F.	--	2	4	6
1933–34	Detroit R.W.	--	1	2	3
1934–35	Detroit R.W.	--	1	3	4
1935-36	Montreal C.	--	0	2	2
1936–37	Montreal C.	--	0	4	4
1937–38	Montreal C.	--	2	15	17
1938–39	Montreal C.	--	3	7	10
1939–40	Montreal C.	--	1	3	4
	Totals	--	10	40	50

Playoffs

Season	Club	GP	G	A	Pts
1932–33	Detroit F.	--	0	0	0
1933–34	Detroit R.W.	--	0	1	1
1936–37	Montreal C.	--	0	0	0
1937–38	Montreal C.	--	0	0	0
1938–39	Montreal C.	--	2	0	2
	Totals	--	2	1	3

BUTLER, Jerome Patrick (Jerry) *Forward*
b. Sarnia, Ont., Feb. 27, 1951

Season	Club	GP	G	A	Pts
1972–73	New York R.	8	1	0	1

BUTLER, John Richard (Dick) *Forward*
b. Delisle, Sask., June 2, 1926

Season	Club	GP	G	A	Pts
1947–48	Chicago	7	2	0	2

BUTTREY, Gordon *Forward*
b. Regina, Sask., Mar. 17, 1926

Season	Club	GP	G	A	Pts
1943–44	Chicago	10	0	0	0

BUZINSKI, Stephen *Goalie*
b. Dunblane, Sask., Oct. 15, 1917

Season	Club	GP	GA	Sho	AVE
1942–43	New York R.	9	55	0	6.11

BYERS, Gordon Charles *Defenseman*
b. Eganville, Ont., Mar. 11, 1930

Season	Club	GP	G	A	Pts
1949–50	Boston	1	0	1	1

BYERS, Jerry *Forward*
b. Kentville, N.S., Mar. 29, 1952

Season	Club	GP	G	A	Pts
1972–73	Minnesota	14	0	2	2

BYERS, Michael Arthur *Forward*
b. Toronto, Ont., Sept. 11, 1946

Season	Club	GP	G	A	Pts
1967–68	Toronto M.L.	10	2	2	4
1968–69	Tor ML–Phila F	10	0	2	2
1970–71	Los Angeles	72	27	18	45
1971–72	LA–Buffalo	74	13	12	25
	Totals	166	42	34	76

Playoffs

Season	Club	GP	G	A	Pts
1968–69	Philadelphia F.	4	0	1	1

CAFFERY, John *Forward*
b. Kingston, Ont., June 30, 1934

Season	Club	GP	G	A	Pts
1954–55	Toronto M.L.	3	0	0	0
1956–57	Boston	47	2	2	4
1957–58	Boston	7	1	0	1
	Totals	57	3	2	5

Playoffs

Season	Club	GP	G	A	Pts
1956–57	Boston	10	1	0	1

CAFFERY, Terrance Michael *Forward*
b. Toronto, Ont., Apr. 1, 1949

Season	Club	GP	G	A	Pts
1969–70	Chicago	6	0	0	0
1970–71	Minnesota	8	0	0	0
	Totals	14	0	0	0

Playoffs

Season	Club	GP	G	A	Pts
1970–71	Minnesota	1	0	0	0

CAHAN, Lawrence Louis (Larry) *Defenseman*
b. Ft. William, Ont., Dec. 25, 1933

Season	Club	GP	G	A	Pts
1954–55	Toronto M.L.	58	0	6	6
1955–56	Toronto M.L.	21	0	2	2
1956–57	New York R.	61	5	4	9
1957–58	New York R.	34	1	1	2
1958–59	New York R.	16	1	0	1
1961–62	New York R.	57	2	7	9
1962–63	New York R.	56	6	14	20
1963–64	New York R.	53	4	8	12
1964–65	New York R.	26	0	5	5
1967–68	Oakland	74	9	15	24
1968–69	Los Angeles	72	3	11	14
1969–70	Los Angeles	70	4	8	12
1970–71	Los Angeles	67	3	11	14
	Totals	665	38	92	130

Playoffs

Season	Club	GP	G	A	Pts
1954–55	Toronto M.L.	4	0	0	0
1956–57	New York R.	3	0	0	0

CAHAN (Continued)

Playoffs	Club	GP	G	A	Pts
1957–58	New York R.	5	0	0	0
1961–62	New York R.	6	0	0	0
1968–69	Los Angeles	11	1	1	2
	Totals	29	1	1	2

CAHILL, Charles *Forward*

Season	Club	GP	G	A	Pts
1925–26	Boston	31	0	1	1

CAIN, Herbert *Forward*
b. Newmarket, Ont., Dec. 24, 1913

Season	Club	GP	G	A	Pts
1933–34	Montreal M.	––	4	5	9
1934–35	Montreal M.	––	20	7	27
1935–36	Montreal M.	––	5	13	18
1936–37	Montreal M.	––	13	17	30
1937–38	Montreal M.	––	11	19	30
1938–39	Montreal C.	––	13	14	27
1939–40	Boston	––	21	10	31
1940–41	Boston	––	8	10	18
1941–42	Boston	35	8	10	18
1942–43	Boston	45	18	18	36
1943–44	Boston	48	36	46	82
1944–45	Boston	50	32	13	45
1945–46	Boston	48	17	12	29
	Totals	––	206	194	400

Playoffs	Club	GP	G	A	Pts
1933–34	Montreal M.	4	0	0	0
1934–35	Montreal M.	4	1	0	1
1935–36	Montreal M.	3	0	1	1
1936–37	Montreal M.	5	1	1	2
1938–39	Montreal C.	3	0	0	0
1939–40	Boston	6	1	3	4
1940–41	Boston	11	3	2	5
1941–42	Boston	5	1	0	1
1942–43	Boston	7	4	2	6
1944–45	Boston	7	5	2	7
1945–46	Boston	9	0	2	2
	Totals	64	16	13	29

CAIN, James F. (Dutch) *Defenseman*
b. Newmarket, Ont.

Season	Club	GP	G	A	Pts
1924–25	Montreal M.	28	4	0	4
1925–26	Toronto St. P.	33	0	0	0
	Totals	61	4	0	4

CALEY, Donald Thomas *Goalie*
b. Dauphin, Man., Oct. 9, 1945

Season	Club	GP	GA	Sho	AVE
1967–68	St. Louis B.	½	3	0	6.00

CALLADINE, Norman *Forward*
b. Peterborough, Ont., 1916

Season	Club	GP	G	A	Pts
1942–43	Boston	3	0	1	1
1943–44	Boston	49	16	27	43
1944–45	Boston	11	3	1	4
	Totals	63	19	29	48

CALLIGHEN, Francis Charles Winslow (Patsy)
Defenseman
b. Toronto, Ont., Feb. 13, 1906

Season	Club	GP	G	A	Pts
1927–28	New York R.	36	0	0	0

Playoffs	Club	GP	G	A	Pts
1927–28	New York R.	9	0	0	0

CAMERON, Angus (Scotty) *Forward*
b. Prince Albert, Sask., Nov. 5, 1921

Season	Club	GP	G	A	Pts
1942–43	New York R.	35	8	11	19

CAMERON, Craig Lauder *Forward*
b. Edmonton, Alta., July 19, 1945

Season	Club	GP	G	A	Pts
1966–67	Detroit R.W.	1	0	0	0
1967–68	St. Louis B.	32	7	2	9
1968–69	St. Louis B.	72	11	5	16
1970–71	St. Louis B.	78	14	6	20
1971–72	Minnesota	64	2	1	3
1972–73	New York I.	72	19	14	33
	Totals	319	53	28	81

Playoffs	Club	GP	G	A	Pts
1967–68	St. Louis B.	14	1	0	1
1968–69	St. Louis B.	2	0	0	0
1970–71	St. Louis B.	6	2	0	2
1971–72	Minnesota	5	0	1	1
	Totals	27	3	1	4

CAMERON, Harry *Defenseman*
b. Pembroke, Ont., 1890

Season	Club	GP	G	A	Pts
1917–18	Toronto M.L.	20	17	0	17
1918–19	Tor A–Otta	14	11	3	14
1919–20	Tor StP–Mont C	23	16	1	17
1920–21	Toronto St. P.	24	18	9	27
1921–22	Toronto St. P.	24	19	8	27
1922–23	Toronto St. P.	22	9	6	15
	Totals	127	90	27	117

Playoffs	Club	GP	G	A	Pts
1917–18	Toronto A.	––	3	0	3
1918–19	Ottawa	––	4	0	4
1920–21	Toronto St. P.	––	0	0	0
1921–22	Toronto St. P.	––	0	0	0
	Totals	––	7	0	7

CAMERON, William Forward
b. Timmins, Ont., 1904

Season	Club	GP	G	A	Pts
1923–24	Montreal C.	18	0	0	0
1925–26	New York A.	21	0	0	0
	Totals	39	0	0	0

CAMPBELL, Bryan Albert Forward
b. Sudbury, Ont., Mar. 27, 1944

Season	Club	GP	G	A	Pts
1967–68	Los Angeles	44	6	15	21
1968–69	Los Angeles	18	2	1	3
1969–70	LA-Chgo	45	5	5	10
1970–71	Chicago	78	17	37	54
1971–72	Chicago	75	5	13	18
	Totals	260	35	71	106

Playoffs

Season	Club	GP	G	A	Pts
1968–69	Los Angeles	6	2	1	3
1969–70	Chicago	8	1	2	3
1970–71	Chicago	4	0	1	1
1971–72	Chicago	4	0	0	0
	Totals	22	3	4	7

CAMPBELL, David Defenseman
b. Lachute, Que., Apr. 27, 1896

Season	Club	GP	G	A	Pts
1920–21	Montreal C.	3	0	0	0

CAMPBELL, Donald Forward
b. Drumheller, Alta., July 12, 1925

Season	Club	GP	G	A	Pts
1943–44	Chicago	17	1	3	4

CAMPBELL, Earl (Spiff) Defenseman

Season	Club	GP	G	A	Pts
1923–24	Ottawa	18	4	1	5
1924–25	Ottawa	30	0	0	0
1925–26	New York A.	29	1	0	1
	Totals	77	5	1	6

Playoffs

Season	Club	GP	G	A	Pts
1923–24	Ottawa	--	0	0	0

CAMPEAU, Jean Claude (Tod) Forward
b. St. Jerome, Que., June 4, 1923

Season	Club	GP	G	A	Pts
1943–44	Montreal C.	2	0	0	0
1947–48	Montreal C.	14	2	2	4
1948–49	Montreal C.	26	3	7	10
	Totals	42	5	9	14

Playoffs

Season	Club	GP	G	A	Pts
1948–49	Montreal C.	1	0	0	0

CARBOL, Leo Defenseman
b. Ottawa, Ont., June 5, 1912

Season	Club	GP	G	A	Pts
1942–43	Chicago	6	0	1	1

CARDIN, Claude Forward
b. Sorel, Que., May 28, 1943

Season	Club	GP	G	A	Pts
1967–68	St. Louis B.	1	0	0	0

CARDWELL, Stephen Michael (Steve) Forward
b. Toronto, Ont., Aug. 13, 1950

Season	Club	GP	G	A	Pts
1970–71	Pittsburgh Pe.	5	0	1	1
1971–72	Pittsburgh Pe.	28	7	8	15
1972–73	Pittsburgh Pe.	20	2	2	4
	Totals	53	9	11	20

Playoffs

Season	Club	GP	G	A	Pts
1971–72	Pittsburgh Pe.	4	0	0	0

CAREY, George Forward

Season	Club	GP	G	A	Pts
1919–20	Quebec	20	11	5	16
1920–21	Hamilton	20	7	1	8
1921–22	Hamilton	23	3	2	5
1922–23	Hamilton	5	1	0	1
1923–24	Toronto St. P.	4	0	0	0
	Totals	72	22	8	30

CARLETON, Kenneth Wayne Forward
b. Sudbury, Ont., Aug. 4, 1946

Season	Club	GP	G	A	Pts
1965–66	Toronto M.L.	2	0	1	1
1966–67	Toronto M.L.	5	1	0	1
1967–68	Toronto M.L.	65	8	11	19
1968–69	Toronto M.L.	12	1	3	4
1969–70	Tor ML-Bos	49	6	20	26
1970–71	Boston	69	22	24	46
1971–72	California	76	17	14	31
	Totals	278	55	73	128

Playoffs

Season	Club	GP	G	A	Pts
1969–70	Boston	14	2	4	6
1970–71	Boston	4	0	0	0
	Totals	18	2	4	6

All-Star

1968	Toronto M.L.	1	0	2	2

CARLIN, Brian John Forward
b. Calgary, Alta. June 13, 1950

Season	Club	GP	G	A	Pts
1971–72	Los Angeles	5	1	0	1

CARON, Alain Luc (Boom-Boom) *Forward*
b. Dolbeau, Que., Apr. 27, 1938

Season	Club	GP	G	A	Pts
1967–68	Oakland	58	9	13	22
1968–69	Montreal C.	2	0	0	0
	Totals	60	9	13	22

CARON, Jacques Joseph *Goalie*
b. Noranda, Que., Apr. 21, 1940

Season	Club	GP	GA	Sho	AVE
1967–68	Los Angeles	1	4	0	4.00
1968–69	Los Angeles	2⅓	9	0	3.86
1971–72	St. Louis B.	27	68	1	2.52
1972–73	St. Louis B.	26	92	1	3.53
	Totals	56⅓	173	2	3.07
Playoffs					
1971–72	St. Louis B.	8⅓	26	0	3.12
1972–73	St. Louis B.	2⅓	8	0	3.43
	Totals	10⅔	34	0	3.19

CARPENTER, Everar Lorne (Eddie)
Defenseman
b. Hartford, Mich.

Season	Club	GP	G	A	Pts
1919–20	Quebec	24	8	3	11
1920–21	Hamilton	20	2	1	3
	Totals	44	10	4	14

CARR, Alfred (Red) *Forward*
b. Winnipeg, Man.

Season	Club	GP	G	A	Pts
1943–44	Toronto M.L.	5	0	1	1

CARR, Eugene William (Gene) *Forward*
b. Nanaimo, B.C., Sept. 17, 1951

Season	Club	GP	G	A	Pts
1971–72	StL B–NY R	74	11	10	21
1972–73	New York R.	50	9	10	19
	Totals	124	20	20	40
Playoffs					
1971–72	New York R.	16	1	3	4
1972–73	New York R.	1	0	1	1
	Totals	17	1	4	5

CARR, Lorne Bell *Forward*
b. Stoughton, Sask., July 2, 1910

Season	Club	GP	G	A	Pts
1933–34	New York R.	14	0	0	0
1934–35	New York A.	--	17	14	31
1935–36	New York A.	--	8	10	18
1936–37	New York A.	--	18	16	34
1937–38	New York A.	--	16	7	23

CARR *(Continued)*

Season	Club	GP	G	A	Pts
1938–39	New York A.	--	19	18	37
1939–40	New York A.	--	8	17	25
1940–41	New York A.	--	13	19	32
1941–42	Toronto M.L.	47	16	17	33
1942–43	Toronto M.L.	50	27	33	60
1943–44	Toronto M.L.	50	36	38	74
1944–45	Toronto M.L.	47	21	25	46
1945–46	Toronto M.L.	42	5	8	13
	Totals	--	204	222	426
Playoffs					
1935–36	New York A.	5	1	1	2
1937–38	New York A.	6	3	1	4
1939–40	New York A.	3	0	0	0
1941–42	Toronto M.L.	13	3	2	5
1942–43	Toronto M.L.	6	1	2	3
1943–44	Toronto M.L.	5	0	1	1
1944–45	Toronto M.L.	13	2	2	4
	Totals	51	10	9	19

CARRIERE, Larry *Defenseman*
b. Montreal, Que., Jan. 30, 1952

Season	Club	GP	G	A	Pts
1972–73	Buffalo	40	2	8	10
Playoffs					
1972–73	Buffalo	6	0	1	1

CARRIGAN, Eugene *Forward*
b. Edmonton, Alta., July 5, 1906

Season	Club	GP	G	A	Pts
1930–31	New York R.	33	2	0	2
1934–35	St. Louis E.	--	0	1	1
	Totals	--	2	1	3

CARROLL, George *Defenseman*

Season	Club	GP	G	A	Pts
1924–25	Mont C–Bos	15	0	0	0

CARRUTHERS, Dwight *Defenseman*
b. Lashburn, Sask., Nov. 7, 1944

Season	Club	GP	G	A	Pts
1965–66	Detroit R.W.	1	0	0	0
1967–68	Philadelphia F.	1	0	0	0
	Totals	2	0	0	0

CARSE, Robert Allison *Forward*
b. Edmonton, Alta., July 19, 1919

Season	Club	GP	G	A	Pts
1939–40	Chicago	--	3	5	8
1940–41	Chicago	--	9	9	18
1941–42	Chicago	33	7	16	23
1942–43	Chicago	47	10	22	32
1947–48	Montreal C.	22	3	3	6
	Totals	--	32	55	87

CARSE *(Continued)*

Playoffs	Club	GP	G	A	Pts
1939-40	Chicago	2	0	0	0
1940-41	Chicago	5	0	0	0
1941-42	Chicago	3	0	2	2
	Totals	10	0	2	2

CARSE, William Alexander *Forward*
b. Edmonton, Alta., May 29, 1914

Season	Club	GP	G	A	Pts
1938-39	New York R.	1	0	1	1
1939-40	Chicago	--	10	13	23
1940-41	Chicago	--	5	15	20
1941-42	Chicago	43	13	14	27
	Totals	--	28	43	71
Playoffs					
1938-39	New York R.	6	1	1	2
1939-40	Chicago	2	1	0	1
1940-41	Chicago	5	0	0	0
1941-42	Chicago	3	1	1	2
	Totals	16	3	2	5

CARSON, Frank *Forward*
b. Parry Sound, Ont., Jan. 12, 1902

Season	Club	GP	G	A	Pts
1925-26	Montreal M.	16	2	1	3
1926-27	Montreal M.	--	2	3	5
1927-28	Montreal M.	--	0	1	1
1930-31	New York A.	--	6	7	13
1931-32	Detroit F.	--	10	14	24
1932-33	Detroit F.	--	12	13	25
1933-34	Detroit R.W.	--	10	9	19
	Totals	--	42	48	90
Playoffs					
1925-26	Montreal M.	--	0	0	0
1926-27	Montreal M.	--	0	0	0
1927-28	Montreal M.	--	0	0	0
1931-32	Detroit F.	--	0	0	0
1932-33	Detroit F.	--	0	1	1
1933-34	Detroit R.W.	--	0	1	1
	Totals	--	0	2	2

CARSON, Gerald (Stub) *Defenseman*
b. Parry Sound, Ont., Oct. 10, 1905

Season	Club	GP	G	A	Pts
1928-29	Mont C-NY R	--	0	0	0
1929-30	Montreal C.	--	1	0	1
1932-33	Montreal C.	--	5	2	7
1933-34	Montreal C.	--	5	1	6
1934-35	Montreal C.	--	0	5	5
1936-37	Montreal M.	--	1	3	4
	Totals	--	12	11	23

CARSON *(Continued)*

Playoffs	Club	GP	G	A	Pts
1928-29	New York R.	5	0	0	0
1929-30	Montreal C.	6	0	0	0
1932-33	Montreal C.	2	0	0	0
1933-34	Montreal C.	2	0	0	0
1934-35	Montreal C.	2	0	0	0
1936-37	Montreal M.	5	0	0	0
	Totals	22	0	0	0

CARSON, William Joseph *Forward*
b. Bracebridge, Ont., Nov. 25, 1900

Season	Club	GP	G	A	Pts
1926-27	Toronto M.L.	--	16	6	22
1927-28	Toronto M.L.	--	20	6	26
1928-29	Tor ML-Bos	--	11	8	19
1929-30	Boston	--	7	4	11
	Totals	--	54	24	78
Playoffs					
1928-29	Boston	--	2	0	2
1929-30	Boston	--	1	0	1
	Totals	--	3	0	3

CARTER, Lyle Dwight *Goalie*
b. Truro, N.S., Apr. 29, 1945

Season	Club	GP	GA	Sho	AVE
1971-72	California	12	50	0	4.16

CARTER, William *Forward*
b. Cornwall, Ont., Dec. 2, 1937

Season	Club	GP	G	A	Pts
1957-58	Montreal C.	1	0	0	0
1960-61	Boston	8	0	0	0
1961-62	Montreal C.	7	0	0	0
	Totals	16	0	0	0

CARVETH, Joseph Gordon *Forward*
b. Regina, Sask., Mar. 21, 1918

Season	Club	GP	G	A	Pts
1940-41	Detroit R.W.	19	2	1	3
1941-42	Detroit R.W.	29	6	11	17
1942-43	Detroit R.W.	43	18	18	36
1943-44	Detroit R.W.	46	21	35	56
1944-45	Detroit R.W.	50	26	28	54
1945-46	Detroit R.W.	48	17	18	35
1946-47	Boston	51	21	15	36
1947-48	Bos-Mont C	57	9	19	28
1948-49	Montreal C.	60	15	22	37
1949-50	Mont C-Det RW	71	14	18	32
1950-51	Detroit R.W.	30	1	4	5
	Totals	504	150	189	339
Playoffs					
1941-42	Detroit R.W.	9	4	0	4
1942-43	Detroit R.W.	10	6	2	8

CARVETH (Continued)

Playoffs	Club	GP	G	A	Pts
1943–44	Detroit R.W.	5	2	1	3
1944–45	Detroit R.W.	14	5	6	11
1945–46	Detroit R.W.	5	0	1	1
1946–47	Boston	5	2	1	3
1948–49	Montreal C.	7	0	1	1
1949–50	Detroit R.W.	14	2	4	6
	Totals	69	21	16	37

All-Star

	Club	GP	G	A	Pts
1950	Detroit R.W.	1	0	0	0

CASHMAN, Wayne John *Forward*
b. Kingston, Ont., June 24, 1945

Season	Club	GP	G	A	Pts
1964–65	Boston	1	0	0	0
1967–68	Boston	12	0	4	4
1968–69	Boston	51	8	23	31
1969–70	Boston	70	9	26	35
1970–71	Boston	77	21	58	79
1971–72	Boston	74	23	29	52
1972–73	Boston	76	29	39	68
	Totals	361	90	179	269

Playoffs					
1967–68	Boston	1	0	0	0
1968–69	Boston	6	0	1	1
1969–70	Boston	14	5	4	9
1970–71	Boston	7	3	2	5
1971–72	Boston	15	4	7	11
1972–73	Boston	5	1	1	2
	Totals	48	13	15	28

CERESINO, Raymond *Forward*
b. Port Arthur, Ont., Apr. 24, 1929

Season	Club	GP	G	A	Pts
1948–49	Toronto M.L.	12	1	1	2

CHABOT, Lorne *Goalie*
b. Montreal, Que., Oct. 5, 1900

Season	Club	GP	GA	Sho	AVE
1926–27	New York R.	36	56	10	1.56
1927–28	New York R.	44	79	11	1.80
1928–29	Toronto M.L.	43	67	12	1.56
1929–30	Toronto M.L.	41	110	6	2.68
1930–31	Toronto M.L.	37	80	6	2.16
1931–32	Toronto M.L.	44	109	4	2.48
1932–33	Toronto M.L.	48	111	5	2.31
1933–34	Montreal C.	47	101	8	2.15
1934–35	Chicago	48	88	8	1.83
1935–36	Montreal M.	16	35	2	2.19
1936–37	New York A.	6	25	1	4.17
	Totals	410	861	73	2.10

CHABOT (Continued)

Playoffs	Club	GP	GA	Sho	AVE
1926–27	New York R.	2	3	1	1.50
1927–28	New York R.	6	8	1	1.50
1928–29	Toronto M.L.	4	5	0	1.25
1930–31	Toronto M.L.	2	4	0	2.00
1931–32	Toronto M.L.	7	15	0	2.14
1932–33	Toronto M.L.	9	18	2	2.00
1933–34	Montreal C.	2	4	0	2.00
1934–35	Chicago	2	1	1	0.50
1935–36	Montreal M.	3	6	0	2.00
	Totals	37	64	5	1.73

CHAD, John *Forward*
b. Provost, Alta., Sept. 16, 1919

Season	Club	GP	G	A	Pts
1939–40	Chicago	--	8	3	11
1940–41	Chicago	--	7	18	25
1945–46	Chicago	13	0	1	1
	Totals	--	15	22	37

Playoffs					
1940–41	Chicago	5	0	0	0
1945–46	Chicago	3	0	1	1
	Totals	8	0	1	1

CHADWICK, Edwin Walter *Goalie*
b. Fergus, Ont., May 8, 1933

Season	Club	GP	GA	Sho	AVE
1955–56	Toronto M.L.	5	3	2	0.60
1956–57	Toronto M.L.	70	192	5	2.74
1957–58	Toronto M.L.	70	226	4	2.23
1958–59	Toronto M.L.	31	93	3	3.00
1959–60	Toronto M.L.	4	15	0	3.75
1961–62	Boston	4	22	0	5.50
	Totals	184	551	14	2.99

CHALMERS, William (Chick) *Forward*
b. Stratford, Ont., Jan. 24, 1934

Season	Club	GP	G	A	Pts
1953–54	New York R.	1	0	0	0

CHAMBERLAIN, Erwin Groves (Murph)
Forward
b. Shawville, Que., Feb. 14, 1915

Season	Club	GP	G	A	Pts
1937–38	Toronto M.L.	--	4	12	16
1938–39	Toronto M.L.	--	10	16	26
1939–40	Toronto M.L.	--	5	17	22
1940–41	Montreal C.	--	10	15	25
1941–42	Mont C-NY A	36	12	12	24
1942–43	Boston	45	9	24	33
1943–44	Montreal C.	47	15	32	47
1944–45	Montreal C.	32	2	12	14
1945–46	Montreal C.	40	12	14	26

CHAMBERLAIN (Continued)

Season	Club	GP	G	A	Pts
1946–47	Montreal C.	49	10	10	20
1947–48	Montreal C.	30	6	3	9
1948–49	Montreal C.	54	5	8	13
	Totals	––	100	175	275

Playoffs

Season	Club	GP	G	A	Pts
1937–38	Toronto M.L.	7	0	0	0
1938–39	Toronto M.L.	10	2	5	7
1939–40	Toronto M.L.	10	0	0	0
1940–41	Montreal C.	3	0	2	2
1942–43	Boston	6	1	1	2
1943–44	Montreal C.	9	5	3	8
1944–45	Montreal C.	6	1	1	2
1945–46	Montreal C.	9	4	2	6
1946–47	Montreal C.	11	1	3	4
1948–49	Montreal C.	4	0	0	0
	Totals	75	14	17	31

CHAMPAGNE, Andre Joseph Orius *Forward*
b. Eastview, Ont., Sept. 19, 1943

Season	Club	GP	G	A	Pts
1962–63	Toronto M.L.	2	0	0	0

CHAPMAN, Arthur V. *Forward*
b. Winnipeg, Man., May 29, 1907

Season	Club	GP	G	A	Pts
1930–31	Boston	––	7	7	14
1931–32	Boston	––	11	14	25
1932–33	Boston	––	3	6	9
1933–34	Bos–NY A	––	5	12	17
1934–35	New York A.	––	9	34	43
1935–36	New York A.	––	10	28	38
1936–37	New York A.	––	8	23	31
1937–38	New York A.	––	2	27	29
1938–39	New York A.	––	3	19	22
1939–40	New York A.	––	4	6	10
	Totals	––	62	176	238

Playoffs

Season	Club	GP	G	A	Pts
1930–31	Boston	–	0	1	1
1932–33	Boston	––	0	0	0
1935–36	New York A.	––	0	3	3
1937–38	New York A.	––	0	1	1
1938–39	New York A.	––	0	0	0
1939–40	New York A.	––	1	0	1
	Totals	––	1	5	6

CHARLEBOIS, Robert Richard (Chuck)
Forward
b. Cornwall, Ont., May 27, 1944

Season	Club	GP	G	A	Pts
1967–68	Minnesota	7	1	0	1

CHARRON, Guy *Forward*
b. Verdun, Que., Jan. 24, 1949

Season	Club	GP	G	A	Pts
1969–70	Montreal C.	5	0	0	0
1970–71	Mtl C–Det RW	39	10	6	16
1971–72	Detroit R.W.	64	9	16	25
1972–73	Detroit R.W.	75	18	18	36
	Totals	183	37	40	77

CHECK, Lude *Forward*
b. Brandon, Man., May 22, 1919

Season	Club	GP	G	A	Pts
1943–44	Detroit R.W.	1	0	0	0
1944–45	Chicago	26	6	2	8
	Totals	27	6	2	8

CHEEVERS, Gerald *Goalie*
b. St. Catherines, Ont., Dec. 2, 1940

Season	Club	GP	GA	Sho	AVE
1961–62	Toronto M.L.	2	7	0	3.50
1965–66	Boston	5⅔	34	0	6.00
1966–67	Boston	17⅓	72	1	3.33
1967–68	Boston	44	125	3	2.84
1968–69	Boston	51¾	145	3	2.80
1969–70	Boston	39¾	108	4	2.72
1970–71	Boston	40	109	3	2.72
1971–72	Boston	40⅓	101	2	2.50
	Totals	240⅔	701	16	2.86

Playoffs

Season	Club	GP	GA	Sho	AVE
1967–68	Boston	4	15	0	3.75
1968–69	Boston	9	16	3	1.68
1969–70	Boston	13	29	0	2.23
1970–71	Boston	6	21	0	3.50
1971–72	Boston	8	21	2	2.61
	Totals	40	102	5	2.51

All-Star

		GP	Per	GA	AGP
1969	East All-Stars	1	1	1	1

CHERNOFF, Michael Terrance *Forward*
b. Yorkton, Sask., May 13, 1946

Season	Club	GP	G	A	Pts
1968–69	Minnesota	1	0	0	0

CHERRY, Richard *Defenseman*
b. Kingston, Ont., Mar. 18, 1937

Season	Club	GP	G	A	Pts
1956–57	Boston	6	0	0	0
1968–69	Philadelphia F.	71	9	6	15
1969–70	Philadelphia F.	68	3	4	7
	Totals	145	12	10	22

Playoffs

Season	Club	GP	G	A	Pts
1968–69	Philadelphia F.	4	1	0	1

CHEVREFILS, Real *Forward*
b. Timmins, Ont., May 2, 1932

Season	Club	GP	G	A	Pts
1951–52	Boston	33	8	17	25
1952–53	Boston	69	19	14	33
1953–54	Boston	14	4	1	5
1954–55	Boston	64	18	22	40
1955–56	Bos-Det RW	63	14	12	26
1956–57	Boston	70	31	17	48
1957–58	Boston	44	9	9	18
1958–59	Boston	30	1	5	6
	Totals	387	104	97	201

Playoffs

Season	Club	GP	G	A	Pts
1951–52	Boston	7	1	1	2
1952–53	Boston	7	0	1	1
1954–55	Boston	5	2	1	3
1956–57	Boston	10	2	1	3
1957–58	Boston	1	0	0	0
	Totals	30	5	4	9

All-Star

Season	Club	GP	G	A	Pts
1955	Detroit R.W.	1	0	0	0
1957	NHL All-Stars	1	0	1	1
	Totals	2	0	1	1

CHISHOLM, Alexander (Lex) *Forward*
b. Galt, Ont., Apr. 1, 1915

Season	Club	GP	G	A	Pts
1939–40	Toronto M.L.	--	6	8	14
1940–41	Toronto M.L.	--	4	0	4
	Totals	--	10	8	18

Playoffs

Season	Club	GP	G	A	Pts
1939–40	Toronto M.L.	--	0	0	0
1940–41	Toronto M.L.	--	1	0	1
	Totals	--	1	0	1

CHISHOLM, Arthur *Forward*

Season	Club	GP	G	A	Pts
1960–61	Boston	3	0	0	0

CHRYSTAL, Robert Harry *Defenseman*
b. Winnipeg, Man., Apr. 30, 1930

Season	Club	GP	G	A	Pts
1953–54	New York R.	64	5	5	10
1954–55	New York R.	68	6	9	15
	Totals	132	11	14	25

CHURCH, John *Defenseman*
b. Kamsack, Sask., May 24, 1915

Season	Club	GP	G	A	Pts
1938–39	Toronto M.L.	--	0	2	2
1939–40	Toronto M.L.	--	1	4	5
1940–41	Toronto M.L.	--	0	1	1

CHURCH *(Continued)*

Season	Club	GP	G	A	Pts
1941–42	Tor ML-NY A	42	1	6	7
1945–46	Boston	43	2	6	8
	Totals	--	4	19	23

Playoffs

Season	Club	GP	G	A	Pts
1939–40	Toronto M.L.	10	1	1	2
1945–46	Boston	9	0	0	0
	Totals	19	1	1	2

CIESLA, Henry Edward (Hank) *Forward*
b. St. Catherine, Ont., Oct. 15, 1934

Season	Club	GP	G	A	Pts
1955–56	Chicago	70	8	23	31
1956–57	Chicago	70	10	8	18
1957–58	New York R.	60	2	6	8
1958–59	New York R.	69	9	14	23
	Totals	269	26	51	77

Playoffs

Season	Club	GP	G	A	Pts
1957–58	New York R.	6	0	2	2

CLANCY, Francis Michael (King) *Defenseman*
b. Ottawa, Ont., Feb. 25, 1903

Season	Club	GP	G	A	Pts
1921–22	Ottawa	24	4	5	9
1922–23	Ottawa	24	3	1	4
1923–24	Ottawa	24	9	8	17
1924–24	Ottawa	29	14	5	19
1925–26	Ottawa	35	8	4	12
1926–27	Ottawa	--	9	10	19
1927–28	Ottawa	--	8	7	15
1928–29	Ottawa	--	13	2	15
1929–30	Ottawa	--	17	23	40
1930–31	Toronto M.L.	--	7	14	21
1931–32	Toronto M.L.	--	10	9	19
1932–33	Toronto M.L.	--	13	12	25
1933–34	Toronto M.L.	--	11	17	28
1934–35	Toronto M.L.	--	5	16	21
1935–36	Toronto M.L.	--	5	10	15
1936–37	Toronto M.L.	--	1	0	1
	Totals	--	137	143	280

Playoffs

Season	Club	GP	G	A	Pts
1921–22	Ottawa	--	0	0	0
1922–23	Ottawa	--	1	0	1
1923–24	Ottawa	--	0	0	0
1925–26	Ottawa	--	1	0	1
1926–27	Ottawa	--	1	1	2
1927–28	Ottawa	--	0	0	0
1929–30	Ottawa	--	0	1	1
1930–31	Toronto M.L.	--	1	0	1
1931–32	Toronto M.L.	--	2	1	3
1932–33	Toronto M.L.	--	0	3	3
1933–34	Toronto M.L.	--	0	0	0

CLANCY (Continued)

Playoffs	Club	GP	G	A	Pts
1934-35	Toronto M.L.	--	1	0	1
1935-36	Toronto M.L.	--	2	2	4
	Totals	--	9	8	17

CLANCY, Terrance John *Forward*
b. Ottawa, Ont., Apr. 2, 1943

Season	Club	GP	G	A	Pts
1967-68	Oakland	7	0	0	0
1968-69	Toronto M.L.	2	0	0	0
1969-70	Toronto M.L.	52	6	5	11
1972-73	Toronto M.L.	32	0	1	1
	Totals	93	6	6	12

CLAPPER, Aubrey Victor (dit)
Defenseman-Forward
b. Newmarket, Ont., Feb. 9, 1907

Season	Club	GP	G	A	Pts
1927-28	Boston	--	4	1	5
1928-29	Boston	--	9	2	11
1929-30	Boston	--	41	20	61
1930-31	Boston	--	22	8	30
1931-32	Boston	--	17	22	39
1932-33	Boston	--	14	14	28
1933-34	Boston	--	10	12	22
1934-35	Boston	--	21	16	37
1935-36	Boston	--	12	13	25
1936-37	Boston	--	17	8	25
1937-38	Boston	--	6	9	15
1938-39	Boston	--	13	13	26
1939-40	Boston	--	10	18	28
1940-41	Boston	--	8	18	26
1941-42	Boston	32	3	12	15
1942-43	Boston	38	5	18	23
1943-44	Boston	50	6	25	31
1944-45	Boston	46	8	14	22
1945-46	Boston	30	2	3	5
1946-47	Boston	6	0	0	0
	Totals	--	228	248	476

Playoffs	Club	GP	G	A	Pts
1927-28	Boston	2	0	0	0
1928-29	Boston	5	1	0	1
1929-30	Boston	6	4	2	6
1930-31	Boston	5	2	4	6
1932-33	Boston	5	1	1	2
1934-35	Boston	4	1	0	1
1935-36	Boston	2	0	1	1
1936-37	Boston	3	2	0	2
1937-38	Boston	3	0	0	0
1938-39	Boston	12	0	1	1
1939-40	Boston	6	0	2	2
1940-41	Boston	11	0	5	5

CLAPPER (Continued)

Playoffs	Club	GP	G	A	Pts
1941-42	Boston	5	0	0	0
1942-43	Boston	9	2	3	5
1944-45	Boston	7	0	0	0
1945-46	Boston	4	0	0	0
	Totals	89	13	19	32

CLARKE, Robert Earle (Bobby) *Forward*
b. Flin Flon, Man., Aug. 13, 1949

Season	Club	GP	G	A	Pts
1969-70	Philadelphia F.	76	15	31	46
1970-71	Philadelphia F.	77	27	36	63
1971-72	Philadelphia F.	78	35	46	81
1972-73	Philadelphia F.	78	37	67	104
	Totals	309	104	180	294

Playoffs		GP	G	A	Pts
1970-71	Philadelphia F.	4	0	0	0
1972-73	Philadelphia F.	11	2	6	8
	Totals	15	2	6	8

All-Star		GP	G	A	Pts
1970	West All-Stars	1	0	0	0
1971	West All-Stars	1	0	0	0
1972	West All-Stars	1	0	0	0
1973	West All-Stars	1	0	1	1
	Totals	4	0	1	1

CLEGHORN, Ogilvie (Odie) *Forward-Goalie*
b. Montreal, Que., 1891

Season	Club	GP	G	A	Pts
1918-19	Montreal C.	17	23	6	29
1919-20	Montreal C.	21	19	3	22
1920-21	Montreal C.	21	5	4	9
1921-22	Montreal C.	23	21	3	24
1922-23	Montreal C.	24	19	7	26
1923-24	Montreal C.	22	3	3	6
1924-25	Montreal C.	30	3	2	5
1925-26	Pittsburgh Pi.	17	3	1	4
1927-28	Pittsburgh Pi.	--	0	0	0
	Totals	--	96	29	125

Season	Goalie Record	GP	GA	Sho	AVE
1925-26	Pittsburgh Pi.	1	2	0	2.00

Playoffs					
1918-19	Montreal C.	5	7	1	8
1922-23	Montreal C.	--	0	0	0
1923-24	Montreal C.	--	0	0	0
1924-25	Montreal C.	--	0	1	1
1925-26	Pittsburgh Pi.	--	0	0	0
1927-28	Pittsburgh Pi.	--	0	0	0
	Totals	--	7	2	9

CLEGHORN, Sprague *Defenseman*
b. Montreal, Que., 1890

Season	Club	GP	G	A	Pts
1918-19	Ottawa	18	6	6	12
1919-20	Ottawa	21	16	5	21
1920-21	Ottawa	16	5	5	10
1921-22	Montreal C.	24	17	7	24
1922-23	Montreal C.	24	9	4	13
1923-24	Montreal C.	23	8	3	11
1924-25	Montreal C.	27	8	1	9
1925-26	Boston	28	6	5	11
1926-27	Boston	--	7	1	8
1927-28	Boston	--	2	2	4
	Totals	--	84	39	123

Playoffs

1918-19	Ottawa	--	2	2	4
1919-20	Ottawa	--	0	1	1
1920-21	Ottawa	--	1	2	3
1922-23	Montreal C.	--	0	0	0
1923-24	Montreal C.	--	2	1	3
1924-25	Montreal C.	--	0	0	0
1926-27	Boston	--	0	1	1
1927-28	Boston	--	0	0	0
	Totals	--	5	7	12

CLEMENT, Bill *Forward*
b. Buckingham, Que., Dec. 20, 1950

Season	Club	GP	G	A	Pts
1971-72	Philadelphia F.	49	9	14	23
1972-73	Philadelphia F.	73	14	14	28
	Totals	122	23	28	51

Playoffs

1972-73	Philadelphia F.	2	0	0	0

CLINE, Bruce *Forward*
b. Massawippi, Que., Nov. 14, 1931

Season	Club	GP	G	A	Pts
1956-57	New York R.	30	2	3	5

CLUNE, Walter James *Defenseman*
b. Toronto, Ont., Feb. 20, 1930

Season	Club	GP	G	A	Pts
1955-56	Montreal C.	5	0	0	0

COFLIN, Hugh Alexander *Defenseman*
b. Blaine Lake, Sask., Dec. 15, 1928

Season	Club	GP	G	A	Pts
1950-51	Chicago	31	0	3	3

COLLINGS, Norman (Dodger) *Forward*
b. Bradford, Ont.

Season	Club	GP	G	A	Pts
1934-35	Montreal C.	--	0	1	1

COLLINS, William Earl (Bill) *Forward*
b. Ottawa, Ont., July 13, 1943

Season	Club	GP	G	A	Pts
1967-68	Minnesota	71	9	11	20
1968-69	Minnesota	75	9	10	19
1969-70	Minnesota	74	29	9	38
1970-71	Mtl C-Det RW	76	11	18	29
1971-72	Detroit R.W.	71	15	25	40
1972-73	Detroit R.W.	78	21	21	42
	Totals	445	94	94	188

Playoffs

1967-68	Minnesota	10	2	4	6
1969-70	Minnesota	6	0	1	1
	Totals	16	2	5	7

COLVILLE, Mathew Lamont (Mac) *Forward*
b. Edmonton, Alta., Jan. 8, 1916

Season	Club	GP	G	A	Pts
1935-36	New York R.	18	1	4	5
1936-37	New York R.	46	7	12	19
1937-38	New York R.	48	14	14	28
1938-39	New York R.	48	7	21	28
1939-40	New York R.	47	7	14	21
1940-41	New York R.	47	14	17	31
1941-42	New York R.	46	14	16	30
1945-46	New York R.	39	7	6	13
1946-47	New York R.	14	0	0	0
	Totals	353	71	104	175

Playoffs

1936-37	New York R.	9	1	2	3
1937-38	New York R.	3	0	2	2
1938-39	New York R.	7	1	2	3
1939-40	New York R.	12	3	2	5
1940-41	New York R.	3	1	1	2
1941-42	New York R.	6	3	1	4
	Totals	40	9	10	19

COLVILLE, Neil Macneil *Defenseman-Forward*
b. Edmonton, Alta., Aug. 4, 1914

Season	Club	GP	G	A	Pts
1935-36	New York R.	1	0	0	0
1936-37	New York R.	45	10	18	28
1937-38	New York R.	45	17	19	36
1938-39	New York R.	47	18	19	37
1939-40	New York R.	48	19	19	38
1940-41	New York R.	48	14	28	42
1941-42	Mtl C-New York RW	48	8	25	33
1944-45	New York R.	4	0	1	1
1945-46	New York R.	49	5	4	9
1946-47	New York R.	60	4	16	20
1947-48	New York R.	55	4	12	16
1948-49	New York R.	14	0	5	5
	Totals	464	99	166	265

COLVILLE (Continued)

Playoffs	Club	GP	G	A	Pts
1936-37	New York R.	9	3	3	6
1937-38	New York R.	3	0	1	1
1938-39	New York R.	7	0	2	2
1939-40	New York R.	12	2	7	9
1940-41	New York R.	3	1	1	2
1941-42	New York R.	6	0	5	5
1947-48	New York R.	6	1	0	1
	Totals	46	7	19	26

All-Star					
1948	NHL All-Stars	1	0	0	0

COLVIN, Les *Goalie*
b. Oshawa, Ont., Feb. 8, 1921

Season	Club	GP	GA	Sho	AVE
1948-49	Boston	1	4	0	4.00

COLWILL, LESLIE John *Forward*
b. Devide, Sask., Jan. 1, 1935

Season	Club	GP	G	A	Pts
1958-59	New York R.	69	7	6	13

COMEAU, Reynald *Forward*
b. Montreal, Que., Oct. 25, 1948

Season	Club	GP	G	A	Pts
1971-72	Montreal C.	4	0	0	0
1972-73	Atlanta	77	21	21	42
	Totals	81	21	21	42

COMIER, Roger *Forward*

Season	Club	GP	G	A	Pts
1925-26	Montreal C.	--	0	0	0

CONACHER, Brian Kennedy *Forward*
b. Toronto, Ont., Aug. 31, 1941

Season	Club	GP	G	A	Pts
1961-62	Toronto M.L.	1	0	0	0
1965-66	Toronto M.L.	2	0	0	0
1966-67	Toronto M.L.	66	14	13	27
1967-68	Toronto M.L.	64	11	14	25
1971-72	Detroit R.W.	22	3	1	4
	Totals	155	28	28	56

Playoffs					
1966-67	Toronto M.L.	12	3	2	5

All-Star					
1968	Toronto M.L.	1	0	0	0

CONACHER, Jr., Charles William (Pete)
Forward
b. Toronto, Ont., July 29, 1932

Season	Club	GP	G	A	Pts
1951-52	Chicago	2	0	1	1
1952-53	Chicago	41	5	6	11

CONACHER (Continued)

Season	Club	GP	G	A	Pts
1953-54	Chicago	70	19	9	28
1954-55	Chgo-NY R	70	12	11	23
1955-56	New York R.	41	11	11	22
	Totals	224	47	38	85

Playoffs					
1952-53	Chicago	2	0	0	0
1955-56	New York R.	5	0	0	0
	Totals	7	0	0	0

CONACHER, Sr., Charles William (Chuck)
Forward
b. Toronto, Ont., Dec. 10, 1909

Season	Club	GP	G	A	Pts
1929-30	Toronto M.L.	--	20	9	29
1930-31	Toronto M.L.	--	31	12	43
1931-32	Toronto M.L.	--	34	14	48
1932-33	Toronto M.L.	--	14	19	33
1933-34	Toronto M.L.	--	32	20	52
1934-35	Toronto M.L.	--	36	21	57
1935-36	Toronto M.L.	--	23	15	38
1936-37	Toronto M.L.	--	3	5	8
1937-38	Toronto M.L.	--	7	9	16
1938-39	Detroit R.W.	--	8	15	23
1939-40	New York A.	--	10	18	28
1940-41	New York A.	--	7	16	23
	Totals	--	225	173	396

Playoffs					
1930-31	Toronto M.L.	--	0	1	1
1931-32	Toronto M.L.	--	6	2	8
1932-33	Toronto M.L.	--	1	1	2
1933-34	Toronto M.L.	--	3	2	5
1934-35	Toronto M.L.	--	1	4	5
1935-36	Toronto M.L.	--	3	2	5
1936-37	Toronto M.L.	--	0	0	0
1938-39	Detroit R.W.	--	2	5	7
1939-40	New York A.	3	1	1	2
	Totals	--	17	18	35

CONACHER, James *Forward*
b. Motherwell, Scotland, May 5, 1921

Season	Club	GP	G	A	Pts
1945-46	Detroit R.W.	20	1	5	6
1946-47	Detroit R.W.	33	16	13	29
1947-48	Detroit R.W.	60	17	23	40
1948-49	Det RW-Chgo	59	26	23	49
1949-50	Chicago	66	13	20	33
1950-51	Chicago	52	10	27	37
1951-52	Chgo-NY R	21	1	2	3
1952-53	New York R.	17	1	4	5
	Totals	338	85	117	202

CONACHER (Continued)

Playoffs	Club	GP	G	A	Pts
1945–46	Detroit R.W.	5	1	1	2
1946–47	Detroit R.W.	5	2	1	3
1947–48	Detroit R.W.	9	2	0	2
	Totals	19	5	2	7

CONACHER, Lionel Pretoria *Defenseman*
b. Toronto, Ont., May 24, 1901

Season	Club	GP	G	A	Pts
1925–26	Pittsburgh Pi.	33	9	4	13
1926–27	Pitts Pi–NY A	--	8	9	17
1927–28	New York A.	--	11	6	17
1928–29	New York A.	--	5	2	7
1929–30	New York A.	--	4	6	10
1930–31	Montreal M.	--	4	3	7
1931–32	Montreal M.	--	7	9	16
1932–33	Montreal M.	--	7	21	28
1933–34	Chicago	--	10	13	23
1934–35	Montreal M.	--	2	6	8
1935–36	Montreal M.	--	7	7	14
1936–37	Montreal M.	--	6	19	25
	Totals	--	80	105	185

Playoffs					
1925–26	Pittsburgh Pi.	--	0	0	0
1928–29	New York A.	--	0	0	0
1930–31	Montreal M.	--	0	0	0
1931–32	Montreal M.	--	0	0	0
1932–33	Montreal M.	--	0	1	1
1933–34	Chicago	--	2	0	2
1934–35	Montreal M.	--	0	0	0
1935–36	Montreal M.	--	0	0	0
1936–37	Montreal M.	--	0	1	1
	Totals	--	2	2	4

CONACHER, Roy Gordon *Forward*
b. Toronto, Ont., Oct. 5, 1916

Season	Club	GP	G	A	Pts
1938–39	Boston	--	26	11	37
1939–40	Boston	--	18	12	30
1940–41	Boston	41	24	14	38
1941–42	Boston	43	24	13	37
1945–46	Boston	4	2	1	3
1946–47	Detroit R.W.	60	30	24	54
1947–48	Chicago	52	22	27	49
1948–49	Chicago	60	26	42	68
1949–50	Chicago	70	25	31	56
1950–51	Chicago	70	26	24	50
1951–52	Chicago	12	3	1	4
	Totals	--	226	200	426

Playoffs					
1938–39	Boston	12	6	4	10
1939–40	Boston	6	2	1	3
1940–41	Boston	11	1	5	6

CONACHER (Continued)

Playoffs	Club	GP	G	A	Pts
1941–42	Boston	5	2	1	3
1945–46	Boston	3	0	0	0
1946–47	Detroit R.W.	5	4	4	8
	Totals	42	15	15	30

All-Star

1949	NHL All-Stars	1	0	0	0

CONN, Maitland (Red) *Forward*
b. Hartley, Man., Oct. 25, 1908

Season	Club	GP	G	A	Pts
1933–34	New York A.	--	4	17	21
1934–35	New York A.	--	5	11	16
	Totals	--	9	28	37

CONNELL, Alex *Goalie*
b. Oshawa, Ont., 1901

Season	Club	GP	GA	Sho	AVE
1924–25	Ottawa	30	66	7	2.20
1925–26	Ottawa	36	39	16	1.08
1926–27	Ottawa	44	69	13	1.57
1927–28	Ottawa	44	57	15	1.30
1928–29	Ottawa	44	68	7	1.55
1929–30	Ottawa	44	118	3	2.68
1930–31	Ottawa	36	110	3	3.06
1931–32	Detroit F.	48	108	6	2.25
1932–33	Ottawa	44	36	1	2.57
1934–35	Montreal M.	48	92	9	1.92
1936–37	Montreal M.	27	64	2	2.37
	Totals	415	827	82	1.99

Playoffs					
1925–26	Ottawa	2	2	0	1.00
1926–27	Ottawa	6	4	2	0.67
1927–28	Ottawa	2	3	0	1.50
1929–30	Ottawa	2	6	0	3.00
1931–32	Detroit F.	2	3	0	1.50
1934–35	Montreal M.	7	8	2	1.14
	Totals	21	26	4	1.24

CONNELLY, Wayne Francis *Forward*
b. Rouyn, Que., Dec. 16, 1939

Season	Club	GP	G	A	Pts
1960–61	Montreal C.	3	0	0	0
1961–62	Boston	61	8	12	20
1962–63	Boston	18	2	6	8
1963–64	Boston	26	2	3	5
1966–67	Boston	64	13	17	30
1967–68	Minnesota	74	35	21	56
1968–69	Minn–Det RW	74	18	25	43
1969–70	Detroit R.W.	76	23	36	59
1970–71	Det RW–StL B	79	13	29	42
1971–72	StL B–Vanc	68	19	25	44
	Totals	543	133	174	307

CONNELLY *(Continued)*

Playoffs	Club	GP	G	A	Pts
1967–68	Minnesota	14	8	3	11
1969–70	Detroit R.W.	4	1	3	4
1970–71	St. Louis B.	6	2	1	3
	Totals	24	11	7	18

CONNOLLY, Albert Patrick (Bert) *Forward*
b. Montreal, Que., Apr. 22, 1909

Season	Club	GP	G	A	Pts
1934–35	New York R.	47	10	11	21
1935–36	New York R.	25	2	2	4
1937–38	Chicago	--	1	2	3
	Totals	--	13	15	28
Playoffs					
1934–35	New York R.	4	1	0	1
1937–38	Chicago	--	0	0	0
	Totals	--	1	0	1

CONNORS, Harry *Forward*
b. Ottawa, Ont.

Season	Club	GP	G	A	Pts
1927–28	Boston	--	9	1	10
1928–29	New York A.	--	6	2	8
1929–30	Otta-Bos	--	1	2	3
1930–31	Ottawa	--	0	0	0
	Totals	--	16	5	21
Playoffs					
1927–28	Boston	--	0	0	0
1928–29	New York A.	--	0	0	0
1929–30	Boston	--	0	0	0
	Totals	--	0	0	0

CONNORS, Robert *Defenseman*

Season	Club	GP	G	A	Pts
1926–27	New York A.	--	1	0	1
1928–29	Detroit C.	--	13	3	16
1929–30	Detroit C.	--	3	7	10
	Totals	--	17	10	27
Playoffs					
1928–29	Detroit C.	--	0	0	0

CONVEY, Edward *Forward*
b. Toronto, Ont.

Season	Club	GP	G	A	Pts
1930–31	New York A.	--	0	0	0
1931–32	New York A.	--	1	0	1
	Totals	--	1	0	1

COOK, Alex (Bud) *Forward*
b. Kingston, Ont., Nov. 15, 1907

Season	Club	GP	G	A	Pts
1931–32	Boston	--	4	4	8
1933–34	Ottawa	--	1	0	1
1934–35	St. Louis E.	--	0	0	0
	Totals	--	5	4	9

COOK, Frederick Joseph (Bun) *Forward*
b. Kingston, Ont., Sept. 18, 1903

Season	Club	GP	G	A	Pts
1926–27	New York R.	44	14	9	23
1927–28	New York R.	44	14	14	28
1928–29	New York R.	43	13	5	18
1929–30	New York R.	43	24	18	42
1930–31	New York R.	44	18	17	35
1931–32	New York R.	45	14	20	34
1932–33	New York R.	48	22	15	37
1933–34	New York R.	48	18	15	33
1934–35	New York R.	48	13	21	34
1935–36	New York R.	26	4	5	9
1936–37	Boston	--	4	5	9
	Totals	--	158	144	302
Playoffs					
1926–27	New York R.	2	0	0	0
1927–28	New York R.	9	2	1	3
1928–29	New York R.	6	1	0	1
1929–30	New York R.	4	2	0	2
1930–31	New York R.	4	0	0	0
1931–32	New York R.	7	6	2	8
1932–33	New York R.	8	2	0	2
1933–34	New York R.	2	0	0	0
1934–35	New York R.	4	2	0	2
	Totals	46	15	3	18

COOK, Lloyd *Defenseman*

Season	Club	GP	G	A	Pts
1924–25	Boston	4	1	0	1
Playoffs					
1917–18	Vancouver (PCHL)	--	2	0	2
1920–21	Vancouver (PCHL)	--	2	1	3
1921–22	Vancouver (PCHL)	--	1	1	2
1922–23	Vancouver (PCHL)	--	0	0	0
1923–24	Vancouver (PCHL)	--	0	0	0
	Totals	--	5	2	7

COOK, Robert Arthur *Forward*
b. Sudbury, Ont., Jan. 6, 1946

Season	Club	GP	G	A	Pts
1970–71	Vancouver	2	0	0	0
1972–73	Det RW–NY I	46	11	7	18
	Totals	48	11	7	18

COOK, Thomas John *Forward*
b. Ft. William, Ont., May 17, 1903

Season	Club	GP	G	A	Pts
1929-30	Chicago	--	14	16	30
1930-31	Chicago	--	15	14	29
1931-32	Chicago	--	12	13	25
1932-33	Chicago	--	12	14	26
1933-34	Chicago	--	5	9	14
1934-35	Chicago	--	13	18	31
1935-36	Chicago	--	4	8	12
1936-37	Chicago	--	0	2	2
1937-38	Montreal M.	--	2	4	6
	Totals	--	77	98	175

Playoffs

Season	Club	GP	G	A	Pts
1929-30	Chicago	--	0	1	1
1930-31	Chicago	--	1	3	4
1931-32	Chicago	--	0	0	0
1933-34	Chicago	--	1	0	1
1934-35	Chicago	--	0	0	0
1935-36	Chicago	--	0	0	0
	Totals	--	2	4	6

COOK, William Osser *Forward*
b. Brantford, Ont., Oct. 9, 1896

Season	Club	GP	G	A	Pts
1926-27	New York R.	44	33	4	37
1927-28	New York R.	43	18	6	24
1928-29	New York R.	43	15	8	23
1929-30	New York R.	44	29	30	59
1930-31	New York R.	44	30	12	42
1931-32	New York R.	48	34	14	48
1932-33	New York R.	48	28	22	50
1933-34	New York R.	48	13	13	26
1934-35	New York R.	48	21	15	36
1935-36	New York R.	44	7	10	17
1936-37	New York R.	21	1	4	5
	Totals	475	229	138	367

Playoffs

Season	Club	GP	G	A	Pts
1926-27	New York R.	2	1	0	1
1927-28	New York R.	9	2	3	5
1928-29	New York R.	6	0	0	0
1929-30	New York R.	4	0	1	1
1930-31	New York R.	4	3	0	3
1931-32	New York R.	7	3	3	6
1932-33	New York R.	8	3	2	5
1933-34	New York R.	2	0	0	0
1934-35	New York R.	4	1	2	3
	Totals	45	13	11	24

COOPER, Carson *Forward*
b. Cornwall, Ont.

Season	Club	GP	G	A	Pts
1924-25	Boston	12	5	3	8
1925-26	Boston	36	28	3	31

COOPER *(Continued)*

Season	Club	GP	G	A	Pts
1926-27	Bos-Mont C	--	9	3	12
1927-28	Detroit C.	--	15	2	17
1928-29	Detroit C.	--	18	9	27
1929-30	Detroit C.	--	18	18	36
1930-31	Detroit F.	--	14	14	28
1931-32	Detroit F.	--	3	5	8
	Totals	--	110	57	167

Playoffs

Season	Club	GP	G	A	Pts
1926-27	Montreal C.	--	0	0	0
1928-29	Detroit C.	2	0	0	0
1931-32	Detroit F.	2	0	0	0
	Totals	--	0	0	0

COOPER, Hal *Forward*
b. New Liskeard, Ont, Aug. 29, 1915

Season	Club	GP	G	A	Pts
1944-45	New York R.	8	0	0	0

COOPER, Joseph *Defenseman*
b. Winnipeg, Man., Dec. 14, 1914

Season	Club	GP	G	A	Pts
1935-36	New York R.	1	0	0	0
1936-37	New York R.	48	0	3	3
1937-38	New York R.	46	3	2	5
1938-39	Chicago	--	3	3	6
1939-40	Chicago	--	4	7	11
1940-41	Chicago	--	5	5	10
1941-42	Chicago	47	6	14	20
1943-44	Chicago	13	1	0	1
1944-45	Chicago	50	4	17	21
1945-46	Chicago	50	2	7	9
1946-47	New York R.	59	2	8	10
	Totals	--	30	66	96

Playoffs

Season	Club	GP	G	A	Pts
1936-37	New York R.	9	1	1	2
1937-38	New York R.	3	0	0	0
1940-41	Chicago	5	1	0	1
1941-42	Chicago	3	0	2	2
1943-44	Chicago	9	1	1	2
1945-46	Chicago	4	0	1	1
	Totals	33	3	5	8

COPP, Robert Alonzo *Defenseman*
b. Port Elgin, N.B., Nov. 15, 1918

Season	Club	GP	G	A	Pts
1942-43	Toronto M.L.	28	3	9	12
1950-51	Toronto M.L.	2	0	0	0
	Totals	30	3	9	12

CORBEAU, Bert *Defenseman*

Season	Club	GP	G	A	Pts
1917–18	Montreal C.	20	8	0	8
1918–19	Montreal C.	16	2	1	3
1919–20	Montreal C.	23	11	5	16
1920–21	Montreal C.	24	12	1	13
1921–22	Montreal C.	22	4	7	11
1922–23	Hamilton	21	10	3	13
1923–24	Toronto St. P.	24	8	6	14
1924–25	Toronto St. P.	30	4	3	7
1925–26	Toronto St. P.	36	5	5	10
1926–27	Toronto M.L.	––	1	2	3
	Totals	––	65	33	98

Playoffs

1917–18	Montreal C.	––	1	0	1
1918–19	Montreal C.	––	1	0	1
1924–25	Toronto St. P.	––	0	0	0
	Totals	––	2	0	2

CORCORAN, Norman *Forward*
b. Toronto, Ont., Aug. 15, 1931

Season	Club	GP	G	A	Pts
1949–50	Boston	1	0	0	0
1952–53	Boston	1	0	0	0
1954–55	Boston	2	0	0	0
1955–56	Det RW-Chgo	25	1	3	4
	Totals	29	1	3	4

Playoffs

1954–55	Boston	4	0	0	0

All-Star

1955	Detroit R.W.	1	0	0	0

CORRIGAN, Charles Hubert Patrick
Defenseman
b. Moosomin, Sask., May 22, 1916

Season	Club	GP	G	A	Pts
1940–41	New York A.	––	2	2	4

CORRIGAN, Michael Douglas *Forward*
b. Ottawa, Ont., Jan. 11, 1946

Season	Club	GP	G	A	Pts
1967–68	Los Angeles	5	0	0	0
1969–70	Los Angeles	36	6	4	10
1970–71	Vancouver	76	21	28	49
1971–72	Vanc-LA	75	15	26	41
1972–73	Los Angeles	78	37	30	67
	Totals	260	79	88	167

CORRIVEAU, Fred Andre *Forward*
b. Grand Mere, Que., May 15, 1928

Season	Club	GP	G	A	Pts
1953–54	Montreal C.	3	0	1	1

COSTELLO, Lester John Thomas *Forward*
b. South Porcupine, Ont., Feb. 16, 1928

Season	Club	GP	G	A	Pts
1948–49	Toronto M.L.	15	2	3	5

Playoffs

1947–48	Toronto M.L.	5	2	2	4
1949–50	Toronto M.L.	1	0	0	0
	Totals	6	2	2	4

All-Star

1948	Toronto M.L.	1	0	1	1

COSTELLO, Murray *Forward*
b. South Porcupine, Ont., Feb. 24, 1934

Season	Club	GP	G	A	Pts
1953–54	Chicago	40	3	2	5
1954–55	Boston	54	4	11	15
1955–56	Bos-Det RW	65	6	6	12
1956–57	Detroit R.W.	3	0	0	0
	Totals	162	13	19	32

Playoffs

1954–55	Boston	1	0	0	0
1955–56	Detroit R.W.	4	0	0	0
	Totals	5	0	0	0

COTCH, Charles *Forward*

Season	Club	GP	G	A	Pts
1924–25	Hamilton	11	1	0	1

COTTON, Harold (Baldy) *Forward*
b. Toronto, Ont., Nov. 5, 1902

Season	Club	GP	G	A	Pts
1925–26	Pittsburgh Pi.	33	7	1	8
1926–27	Pittsburgh Pi.	––	5	0	5
1927–28	Pittsburgh Pi.	––	9	3	12
1928–29	Pitts Pi-Tor ML	––	4	4	8
1929–30	Toronto M.L.	––	21	17	38
1930–31	Toronto M.L.	––	12	17	29
1931–32	Toronto M.L.	––	5	13	18
1932–33	Toronto M.L.	––	10	11	21
1933–34	Toronto M.L.	––	8	14	22
1934–35	Toronto M.L.	––	11	14	25
1935–36	New York A.	––	7	9	16
1936–37	New York A.	––	2	0	2
	Totals	––	101	103	204

Playoffs

1925–26	Pittsburgh Pi.	––	1	0	1
1927–28	Pittsburgh Pi.	––	1	1	2
1928–29	Toronto M.L.	––	0	0	0
1930–31	Toronto M.L.	––	0	0	0
1931–32	Toronto M.L.	––	2	2	4
1932–33	Toronto M.L.	––	0	3	3

COTTON (Continued)

Playoffs	Club	GP	G	A	Pts
1933–34	Toronto M.L.	--	0	2	2
1934–35	Toronto M.L.	--	0	0	0
1935–36	New York A.	--	0	1	1
	Totals	--	4	9	13

COUGHLIN, Jack *Forward*

Season	Club	GP	G	A	Pts
1917–18	Toronto A.	6	2	0	2
1919–20	Que–Mont C	11	0	0	0
1920–21	Hamilton	2	0	0	0
	Totals	19	2	0	2

Playoffs	Club	GP	G	A	Pts
1917–18	Toronto A.	--	0	0	0

COULSON, Darcy *Defenseman*

Season	Club	GP	G	A	Pts
1930–31	Philadelphia Q.	--	0	0	0

COULTER, Arthur Edmund *Defenseman*
b. Winnipeg, Man., May 31, 1909

Season	Club	GP	G	A	Pts
1931–32	Chicago	--	0	1	1
1932–33	Chicago	--	3	2	5
1933–34	Chicago	--	5	2	7
1934–35	Chicago	--	4	8	12
1935–36	Chgo–NY R	--	1	7	8
1936–37	New York R.	47	1	5	6
1937–38	New York R.	43	5	10	15
1938–39	New York R.	44	4	8	12
1939–40	New York R.	48	1	9	10
1940–41	New York R.	35	5	14	19
1941–42	New York R.	47	1	16	17
	Totals	--	30	82	112

Playoffs	Club	GP	G	A	Pts
1931–32	Chicago	2	1	0	1
1933–34	Chicago	8	1	0	1
1934–35	Chicago	2	0	0	0
1936–37	New York R.	9	0	3	3
1938–39	New York R.	7	1	1	2
1939–40	New York R.	12	1	0	1
1940–41	New York R.	3	0	0	0
1941–42	New York R.	6	0	1	1
	Totals	49	4	5	9

COURNOYER, Yvan *Forward*
b. Drummondville, Que., Nov. 22, 1943

Season	Club	GP	G	A	Pts
1963–64	Montreal C.	5	4	0	4
1964–65	Montreal C.	55	7	10	17
1965–66	Montreal C.	65	18	11	29
1966–67	Montreal C.	69	25	15	40

COURNOYER (Continued)

Season	Club	GP	G	A	Pts
1967–68	Montreal C.	64	28	32	60
1968–69	Montreal C.	76	43	44	87
1969–70	Montreal C.	72	27	36	63
1970–71	Montreal C.	65	37	36	73
1971–72	Montreal C.	73	47	36	83
1972–73	Montreal C.	67	40	39	79
	Totals	611	276	259	535

Playoffs	Club	GP	G	A	Pts
1964–65	Montreal C.	12	3	1	4
1965–66	Montreal C.	10	2	3	5
1966–67	Montreal C.	10	2	3	5
1967–68	Montreal C.	13	6	8	14
1968–69	Montreal C.	14	4	7	11
1970–71	Montreal C.	20	10	12	22
1971–72	Montreal C.	6	2	1	3
1972–73	Montreal C.	17	15	10	25
	Totals	102	44	45	89

All-Star	Club	GP	G	A	Pts
1967	Montreal C.	1	0	0	0
1971	East All-Stars	1	1	0	1
1972	East All-Stars	1	0	0	0
1973	East All-Stars	1	0	0	0
	Totals	4	1	0	1

COURTEAU, Maurice Laurent *Goalie*
b. Quebec City, Que., Feb. 18, 1918

Season	Club	GP	GA	Sho	AVE
1943–44	Boston	6	33	0	5.50

COUTU, William *Defenseman*
b. Sault Ste. Marie, Ont.

Season	Club	GP	G	A	Pts
1917–18	Montreal C.	19	2	0	2
1918–19	Montreal C.	15	1	1	2
1919–20	Montreal C.	17	4	0	4
1920–21	Hamilton	24	8	4	12
1921–22	Montreal C.	23	4	3	7
1922–23	Montreal C.	24	5	2	7
1923–24	Montreal C.	16	3	1	4
1924–25	Montreal C.	28	3	2	5
1925–26	Montreal C.	33	2	4	6
1926–27	Boston	--	1	1	2
	Totals	--	33	18	51

Playoffs	Club	GP	G	A	Pts
1922–23	Montreal C.	--	0	0	0
1923–24	Montreal C.	--	0	0	0
1924–25	Montreal C.	--	1	0	1
1926–27	Boston	--	1	0	1
	Totals	--	2	0	2

COUTURE, Gerald Joseph Wilfred Arthur
Forward

b. Saskatoon, Sask., Aug. 6, 1925

Season	Club	GP	G	A	Pts
1945-46	Detroit R.W.	43	3	7	10
1946-47	Detroit R.W.	30	5	10	15
1947-48	Detroit R.W.	19	3	6	9
1948-49	Detroit R.W.	51	19	10	29
1949-50	Detroit R.W.	70	24	7	31
1950-51	Detroit R.W.	53	7	6	13
1951-52	Montreal C.	10	0	1	1
1952-53	Chicago	70	19	18	37
1953-54	Chicago	40	6	5	11
	Totals	356	86	70	156

Playoffs

1944-45	Detroit R.W.	2	0	0	0
1945-46	Detroit R.W.	--	0	2	2
1946-47	Detroit R.W.	1	0	0	0
1948-49	Detroit R.W.	10	2	0	2
1949-50	Detroit R.W.	14	5	4	9
1950-51	Detroit R.W.	6	1	1	2
1952-53	Chicago	7	1	0	1
	Totals	--	9	7	16

All-Star

1950	Detroit R.W.	1	0	0	0

COUTURE, Rosario (Lolo) *Forward*

b. St. Boniface. Man., July 24, 1905

Season	Club	GP	G	A	Pts
1928-29	Chicago	--	1	3	4
1929-30	Chicago	--	8	8	16
1930-31	Chicago	--	8	11	19
1931-32	Chicago	--	9	9	18
1932-33	Chicago	--	10	7	17
1933-34	Chicago	--	5	8	13
1934-35	Chicago	--	7	9	16
1935-36	Montreal C.	--	0	1	1
	Totals	--	48	56	104

Playoffs

1929-30	Chicago	--	0	0	0
1930-31	Chicago	--	0	3	3
1931-32	Chicago	--	0	0	0
1933-34	Chicago	--	1	2	3
1934-35	Chicago	--	0	0	0
	Totals	--	1	5	6

COWLEY, William *Forward*

b. Bristol, Que., June 12, 1912

Season	Club	GP	G	A	Pts
1934-35	St. Louis E.	--	5	7	12
1935-36	Boston	--	11	10	21
1936-37	Boston	--	13	22	35

COWLEY *(Continued)*

Season	Club	GP	G	A	Pts
1937-38	Boston	--	17	22	39
1938-39	Boston	--	8	34	42
1939-40	Boston	--	13	27	40
1940-41	Boston	--	17	45	62
1941-42	Boston	28	4	23	27
1942-43	Boston	48	27	45	72
1943-44	Boston	36	30	41	71
1944-45	Boston	49	25	40	65
1945-46	Boston	26	12	12	24
1946-47	Boston	51	13	25	38
	Totals	--	195	353	548

Playoffs

1935-36	Boston	2	2	1	3
1936-37	Boston	3	0	3	3
1937-38	Boston	3	2	0	2
1938-39	Boston	12	3	11	14
1939-40	Boston	6	0	1	1
1941-42	Boston	5	0	3	3
1942-43	Boston	9	1	7	8
1944-45	Boston	7	3	3	6
1945-46	Boston	10	1	3	4
1946-47	Boston	5	0	2	2
	Totals	62	12	34	46

COX, Abbie *Goalie*

Season	Club	GP	GA	Sho	AVE
1929-30	Montreal M.	1	2	0	2.00
1933-34	Det RW-NY A	2	7	0	3.50
1935-36	Montreal C.	1	1	0	1.00
	Totals	4	10	0	2.50

COX, Daniel Smith *Forward*

b. Little Current, Ont., Oct. 12, 1903

Season	Club	GP	G	A	Pts
1926-27	Toronto M.L.	--	0	1	1
1927-28	Toronto M.L.	41	9	6	15
1928-29	Toronto M.L.	--	12	7	19
1929-30	Tor ML-Otta	--	4	6	10
1930-31	Ottawa	--	9	12	21
1931-32	Detroit F.	--	4	6	10
1932-33	Ottawa	--	4	7	11
1933-34	Otta-NY R	--	5	4	9
	Totals	--	47	49	96

Playoffs

1928-29	Toronto M.L.	4	0	1	1
1931-32	Detroit F.	2	0	0	0
	Totals	6	0	1	1

CRASHLEY, Barton William *Defenseman*
b. Toronto, Ont., June 15, 1946

Season	Club	GP	G	A	Pts
1965–66	Detroit R.W.	1	0	0	0
1966–67	Detroit R.W.	2	0	0	0
1967–68	Detroit R.W.	57	2	14	16
1968–69	Detroit R.W.	1	0	0	0
	Totals	61	2	14	16

CRAWFORD, John Shea (Jack) *Defenseman*
b. Dublin, Ont., Oct. 26, 1916

Season	Club	GP	G	A	Pts
1938–39	Boston	--	4	8	12
1939 40	Boston	--	1	4	5
1940–41	Boston	45	2	8	10
1941–42	Boston	43	2	9	11
1942–43	Boston	49	5	18	23
1943–44	Boston	34	4	16	20
1944–45	Boston	40	5	19	24
1945–46	Boston	48	7	9	16
1946–47	Boston	58	1	17	18
1947–48	Boston	45	3	11	14
1948–49	Boston	55	2	13	15
1949–50	Boston	46	2	8	10
	Totals	--	38	140	178

Playoffs

Season	Club	GP	G	A	Pts
1938–39	Boston	12	1	1	2
1939–40	Boston	6	0	0	0
1940–41	Boston	11	0	2	2
1941–42	Boston	5	0	1	1
1942–43	Boston	6	1	1	2
1944–45	Boston	7	0	5	5
1945–46	Boston	10	1	2	3
1946–47	Boston	2	0	0	0
1947–48	Boston	4	0	1	1
1948–49	Boston	3	0	0	0
	Totals	66	3	13	16

CRAWFORD, Russell (Rusty) *Forward*

Season	Club	GP	G	A	Pts
1917–18	Tor A–Otta	20	3	0	3
1918–19	Toronto A.	18	0	0	0
	Totals	38	3	0	3

Playoffs

Season	Club	GP	G	A	Pts
1917–18	Ottawa	--	2	1	3

CREIGHTON, David Theodore *Forward*
b. Port Arthur, Ont., June 24, 1930

Season	Club	GP	G	A	Pts
1948–49	Boston	12	1	3	4
1949–50	Boston	64	18	13	31
1950–51	Boston	56	5	4	9
1951–52	Boston	49	20	17	37

CREIGHTON *(Continued)*

Season	Club	GP	G	A	Pts
1952–53	Boston	45	8	8	16
1953–54	Boston	69	20	20	40
1954–55	Tor ML–Chgo	63	9	8	17
1955–56	New York R.	70	20	31	51
1956–57	New York R.	70	18	21	39
1957–58	New York R.	70	17	35	52
1958–59	Toronto M.L.	34	3	9	12
1959–60	Toronto M.L.	14	1	5	6
	Totals	616	140	174	314

Playoffs

Season	Club	GP	G	A	Pts
1948–49	Boston	3	0	0	0
1950–51	Boston	5	0	1	1
1951–52	Boston	7	2	1	3
1952–53	Boston	11	4	5	9
1953–54	Boston	4	0	0	0
1955–56	New York R.	5	0	0	0
1956–57	New York R.	5	2	2	4
1957–58	New York R.	6	3	3	6
1958–59	Toronto M.L.	5	0	1	1
	Totals	51	11	13	24

All-Star

Season	Club	GP	G	A	Pts
1952	NHL 1st All-Stars	0	0	1	1
1956	NHL All-Stars	0	0	0	0
	Totals	0	0	1	1

CREIGHTON, Jimmy *Forward*

Season	Club	GP	G	A	Pts
1930–31	Detroit F.	--	1	0	1

CRESSMAN, Glen *Forward*
b. Petersburg, Ont., Aug. 29, 1934

Season	Club	GP	G	A	Pts
1956–57	Montreal C.	4	0	0	0

CRISP, Terrance *Forward*
b. Parry Sound, Ont., May 28, 1943

Season	Club	GP	G	A	Pts
1965–66	Boston	3	0	0	0
1967–68	St. Louis B.	73	9	20	29
1968–69	St. Louis B.	57	6	9	15
1969–70	St. Louis B.	26	5	6	11
1970–71	St. Louis B.	54	5	11	16
1971–72	St. Louis B.	75	13	18	31
1972–73	NY I–Phila F	66	5	21	26
	Totals	354	43	85	128

Playoffs

Season	Club	GP	G	A	Pts
1967–68	St. Louis B.	18	1	5	6
1968–69	St. Louis B.	12	3	4	7
1969–70	St. Louis B.	16	2	3	5

CRISP *(Continued)*

Playoffs	Club	GP	G	A	Pts
1970–71	St. Louis B.	6	1	0	1
1971–72	St. Louis B.	11	1	3	4
1972–73	Philadelphia F.	11	3	2	5
	Totals	**74**	**11**	**17**	**28**

CROGHEN, Maurice *Forward*
b. Montreal, Que., Nov. 19, 1914

Season	Club	GP	G	A	Pts
1937–38	Montreal M.	--	0	0	0

CROSSETT, Stanley *Defenseman*

Season	Club	GP	G	A	Pts
1930–31	Philadelphia Q.	--	0	0	0

CROTEAU, Gary *Forward*
b. Sudbury, Ont., June 20, 1946

Season	Club	GP	G	A	Pts
1968–69	Los Angeles	11	5	1	6
1969–70	LA-Det RW	13	0	2	2
1970–71	California	74	15	28	43
1971–72	California	73	12	12	24
1972–73	California	47	6	15	21
	Totals	**218**	**38**	**58**	**96**
Playoffs					
1968–69	Los Angeles	11	3	2	5

CROZIER, Joseph Richard *Defenseman*
b. Winnipeg, Man., Feb. 19, 1929

Season	Club	GP	G	A	Pts
1959–60	Toronto M.L.	5	0	3	3

CROZIER, Roger Allan *Goalie*
b. Bracebridge, Ont., Mar. 16, 1942

Season	Club	GP	GA	Sho	AVE
1963–64	Detroit R.W.	15	51	2	3.40
1964–65	Detroit R.W.	69½	168	6	2.42
1965–66	Detroit R.W.	62⅓	173	7	2.79
1966–67	Detroit R.W.	54⅓	182	4	3.35
1967–68	Detroit R.W.	28¾	95	1	3.30
1968–69	Detroit R.W.	30⅓	101	0	3.39
1969–70	Detroit R.W.	31⅓	83	0	2.65
1970–71	Buffalo	36⅔	135	1	3.68
1971–72	Buffalo	61	214	2	3.51
1972–73	Buffalo	44	121	3	2.76
	Totals	**433⅓**	**1323**	**26**	**3.02**
Playoffs					
1963–64	Detroit R.W.	1⅔	5	0	3.00
1964–65	Detroit R.W.	7	23	0	3.29
1965–66	Detroit R.W.	11⅓	26	1	2.21
1969–70	Detroit R.W.	½	3	0	5.26
1972–73	Buffalo	4	11	0	2.65
	Totals	**24½**	**68**	**1**	**2.76**

CRUTCHFIELD, Nelson *Defenseman-Forward*
b. Knowlton, Que., July 12, 1911

Season	Club	GP	G	A	Pts
1934–35	Montreal C.	--	5	5	10
Playoffs					
1934–35	Montreal C.	--	0	1	1

CUDE, Wilfred *Goalie*
b. Barry, Wales, July 4, 1910

Season	Club	GP	GA	Sho	AVE
1930–31	Philadelphia Q.	29	127	1	4.38
1931–32	Boston	2	6	1	3.00
1933–34	Det RW-Mont C	30	47	5	1.57
1934–35	Montreal C.	48	145	1	3.02
1935–36	Montreal C.	47	122	6	2.60
1936–37	Montreal C.	44	99	5	2.25
1937–38	Montreal C.	47	126	3	2.68
1938–39	Montreal C.	23	77	2	3.35
1939–40	Montreal C.	7	24	0	3.43
1940–41	Montreal C.	3	13	0	4.33
	Totals	**280**	**786**	**24**	**2.81**
Playoffs					
1933–34	Montreal C.	9	21	1	2.33
1934–35	Montreal C.	2	6	0	3.00
1936–37	Montreal C.	5	13	0	2.60
1937–38	Montreal C.	3	11	0	3.67
	Totals	**19**	**51**	**1**	**2.68**

CULLEN, Brian Joseph *Forward*
b. Ottawa, Ont., Nov. 11, 1933

Season	Club	GP	G	A	Pts
1954–55	Toronto M.L.	27	3	5	8
1955–56	Toronto M.L.	21	2	6	8
1956–57	Toronto M.L.	46	8	12	20
1957–58	Toronto M.L.	67	20	23	43
1958–59	Toronto M.L.	59	4	14	18
1959–60	New York R.	64	8	21	29
1960–61	New York R.	42	11	19	30
	Totals	**326**	**56**	**100**	**156**
Playoffs					
1954–55	Toronto M.L.	4	1	0	1
1955–56	Toronto M.L.	5	1	0	1
1958–59	Toronto M.L.	10	1	0	1
	Totals	**19**	**3**	**0**	**3**

CULLEN, Charles Francis (Barry) *Forward*
b. Ottawa, Ont., June 16, 1935

Season	Club	GP	G	A	Pts
1955–56	Toronto M.L.	3	0	0	0
1956–57	Toronto M.L.	51	6	10	16
1957–58	Toronto M.L.	70	16	25	41
1958–59	Toronto M.L.	40	6	8	14
1959–60	Detroit R.W.	55	4	9	13
	Totals	**219**	**32**	**52**	**84**

CULLEN *(Continued)*

Playoffs	Club	GP	G	A	Pts
1958–59	Toronto M.L.	2	0	0	0
1959–60	Detroit R.W.	4	0	0	0
	Totals	6	0	0	0

CULLEN, Raymond Murray *Forward*
b. Ottawa, Ont., Sept. 20, 1941

Season	Club	GP	G	A	Pts
1965–66	New York R.	8	1	3	4
1966–67	Detroit R.W.	27	8	8	16
1967–68	Minnesota	67	28	25	53
1968–69	Minnesota	67	26	38	64
1969–70	Minnesota	74	17	28	45
1970–71	Vancouver	70	12	21	33
	Totals	313	92	123	215

Playoffs	Club	GP	G	A	Pts
1967–68	Minnesota	14	2	6	8
1969–70	Minnesota	6	1	4	5
	Totals	20	3	10	13

CUNNINGHAM, Leslie Roy *Forward*
b. Calgary, Alta., Oct. 4, 1913

Season	Club	GP	G	A	Pts
1936–37	New York A.	--	1	8	9
1939–40	Chicago	--	6	11	17
	Totals	--	7	19	26

CUNNINGHAM, Robert Gordon *Forward*
b. Welland, Ont., Feb. 26, 1941

Season	Club	GP	G	A	Pts
1960–61	New York R.	3	0	1	1
1961–62	New York R.	1	0	0	0
	Totals	4	0	1	1

CUPOLO, William Donald *Forward*
b. Niagara Falls, Ont., Jan. 8, 1924

Season	Club	GP	G	A	Pts
1944–45	Boston	47	11	13	24
Playoffs					
1944–45	Boston	7	1	2	3

CURRIE, Hugh Roy *Defenseman*
b. Saskatoon, Sask., Oct. 22, 1925

Season	Club	GP	G	A	Pts
1950–51	Montreal C.	1	0	0	0

CURRY, Floyd James (Busher) *Forward*
b. Chapleu, Ont., Aug. 11, 1925

Season	Club	GP	G	A	Pts
1947–48	Montreal C.	31	1	5	6
1949–50	Montreal C.	49	8	8	16
1950–51	Montreal C.	69	13	14	27

CURRY *(Continued)*

Season	Club	GP	G	A	Pts
1951–52	Montreal C.	64	20	18	38
1952–53	Montreal C.	68	16	6	22
1953–54	Montreal C.	70	13	8	21
1954–55	Montreal C.	68	11	10	21
1955–56	Montreal C.	70	14	18	32
1956–57	Montreal C.	70	7	9	16
1957–58	Montreal C.	42	2	3	5
	Totals	601	105	99	204

Playoffs	Club	GP	G	A	Pts
1948–49	Montreal C.	2	0	0	0
1949–50	Montreal C.	5	1	0	1
1950–51	Montreal C.	11	0	2	2
1951–52	Montreal C.	11	4	3	7
1952–53	Montreal C.	12	2	1	3
1953–54	Montreal C.	11	4	0	4
1954–55	Montreal C.	12	8	4	12
1955–56	Montreal C.	10	1	5	6
1956–57	Montreal C.	10	3	2	5
1957–58	Montreal C.	7	0	0	0
	Totals	91	23	17	40

All-Star	Club	GP	G	A	Pts
1951	NHL 2nd All-Stars	1	0	0	0
1952	NHL 2nd All-Stars	1	0	0	0
1953	Montreal C.	1	0	0	0
1956	Montreal C.	1	0	0	0
1957	Montreal C.	1	0	0	0
	Totals	5	0	0	0

CURTIS, Paul Edwin *Defenseman*
b. Peterborough, Ont., Sept. 29, 1947

Season	Club	GP	G	A	Pts
1969–70	Montreal C.	1	0	0	0
1970–71	Los Angeles	64	1	13	14
1971–72	Los Angeles	64	1	12	13
1972–73	LA-StL B	56	1	9	10
	Totals	185	3	34	37

Playoffs	Club	GP	G	A	Pts
1972–73	St. Louis B.	5	0	0	0

CUSHENAN, Ian Robertson *Defenseman*
b. Hamilton, Ont., Nov. 29, 1933

Season	Club	GP	G	A	Pts
1956–57	Chicago	11	0	0	0
1957–58	Chicago	61	2	8	10
1958–59	Montreal C.	35	1	2	3
1959–60	New York R.	17	0	1	1
1963–64	Detroit R.W.	5	0	0	0
	Totals	129	3	11	14

All-Star	Club	GP	G	A	Pts
1958	Montreal C.	1	0	0	0

CUSSON, Jean *Forward*
b. Verdun, Que., Oct. 5, 1942

Season	Club	GP	G	A	Pts
1967–68	Oakland	2	0	0	0

CYR, Claude *Goalie*
b. Montreal, Que., Mar. 27, 1939

Season	Club	GP	GA	Sho	AVE
1958–59	Montreal C.	1	1	0	1.00

DAHLSTROM, Carl (Cully) *Forward*
b. Minneapolis, Minn., July 3, 1913

Season	Club	GP	G	A	Pts
1937–38	Chicago	--	10	9	19
1938–39	Chicago	--	6	14	20
1939–40	Chicago	--	11	19	30
1940–41	Chicago	--	11	14	25
1941–42	Chicago	--	13	14	27
1942–43	Chicago	38	11	13	24
1943–44	Chicago	50	20	22	42
1944–45	Chicago	40	6	13	19
	Totals	--	88	118	206
Playoffs					
1937–38	Chicago	--	3	1	4
1939–40	Chicago	--	0	0	0
1940–41	Chicago	--	3	3	6
1941–42	Chicago	--	0	0	0
1943–44	Chicago	9	0	4	4
	Totals	--	6	8	14

DALEY, Thomas Joseph (Joe) *Goalie*
b. Winnipeg, Man., Feb. 20, 1943

Season	Club	GP	GA	Sho	AVE
1968–69	Pittsburgh Pe.	27	87	2	3.22
1969–70	Pittsburgh Pe.	9	26	0	2.95
1970–71	Buffalo	34⅓	128	1	3.70
1971–72	Detroit R.W.	27	85	--	3.14
	Totals	97⅓	326	3	3.34

DAME, Aurella N. (Bunny) *Forward*
b. Edmonton, Alta.

Season	Club	GP	G	A	Pts
1941–42	Montreal C.	--	2	5	7

DAMORE, Henry *Forward*
b. Niagara Falls, Ont., July 17, 1918

Season	Club	GP	G	A	Pts
1943–44	New York R.	4	1	0	1

DAMORE, Nicholas J. *Goalie*
b. Niagara Falls, Ont., July 10, 1916

Season	Club	GP	GA	Sho	AVE
1941–42	Boston	1	3	0	3.00

DARRAGH, Harold Edward *Forward*
b. Ottawa, Ont., Sept. 13, 1902

Season	Club	GP	G	A	Pts
1925–26	Pittsburgh Pi.	35	10	7	17
1926–27	Pittsburgh Pi.	--	12	3	15
1927–28	Pittsburgh Pi.	--	13	2	15
1928–29	Pittsburgh Pi.	--	9	3	12
1929–30	Pittsburgh Pi.	--	15	17	32
1930–31	Phila Q–Bos	--	3	5	8
1931–32	Toronto M.L.	--	5	10	15
1932–33	Toronto M.L.	--	1	2	3
	Totals	--	68	49	117
Playoffs					
1925–26	Pittsburgh Pi.	--	1	0	1
1927–28	Pittsburgh Pi.	--	0	1	1
1930–31	Boston	--	0	1	1
1931–32	Toronto M.L.	--	0	1	1
	Totals	--	1	3	4

DARRAGH, John Proctor *Forward*
b. Cornwall, Ont., 1891

Season	Club	GP	G	A	Pts
1917–18	Ottawa	18	14	0	14
1918–19	Ottawa	14	12	1	13
1919–20	Ottawa	22	22	5	27
1920–21	Ottawa	24	11	8	19
1922–23	Ottawa	24	7	7	14
1923–24	Ottawa	18	2	0	2
	Totals	120	68	21	89
Playoffs					
1918–19	Ottawa	--	3	0	3
1919–20	Ottawa	--	5	2	7
1920–21	Ottawa	--	0	0	0
1922–23	Ottawa	--	1	0	1
	Totals	--	9	2	11

DAVIDSON, Gordon John *Defenseman*
b. Stratton, Ont., Aug. 5, 1919

Season	Club	GP	G	A	Pts
1942–43	New York R.	35	2	3	5
1943–44	New York R.	16	1	3	4
	Totals	51	3	6	9

DAVIDSON, Robert *Forward*
b. Toronto, Ont., Feb. 10, 1912

Season	Club	GP	G	A	Pts
1934–35	Toronto M.L.	--	0	0	0
1935–36	Toronto M.L.	--	4	4	8
1936–37	Toronto M.L.	--	8	7	15
1937–38	Toronto M.L.	--	3	17	20
1938–39	Toronto M.L.	--	4	10	14
1939–40	Toronto M.L.	--	8	18	26
1940–41	Toronto M.L.	--	3	6	9

DAVIDSON (Continued)

Season	Club	GP	G	A	Pts
1941–42	Toronto M.L.	37	6	20	26
1942–43	Toronto M.L.	50	13	23	36
1943–44	Toronto M.L.	47	19	28	47
1944–45	Toronto M.L.	50	17	18	35
1945–46	Toronto M.L.	41	9	9	18
	Totals	––	94	160	254

Playoffs

Season	Club	GP	G	A	Pts
1935–36	Toronto M.L.	9	1	3	4
1936–37	Toronto M.L.	2	0	0	0
1937–38	Toronto M.L.	7	0	2	2
1938–39	Toronto M.L.	10	1	1	2
1939–40	Toronto M.L.	10	0	3	3
1940–41	Toronto M.L.	7	0	2	2
1941–42	Toronto M.L.	13	1	2	3
1942–43	Toronto M.L.	6	1	2	3
1943–44	Toronto M.L.	5	0	0	0
1944–45	Toronto M.L.	13	1	2	3
	Totals	82	5	17	22

DAVIE, Robert H. (Pinkle) *Defenseman*
b. Beausejour, Man., Sept. 12, 1912

Season	Club	GP	G	A	Pts
1933–1934	Boston	––	0	0	0
1934–35	Boston	––	0	1	1
1935–36	Boston	––	0	0	0
	Totals	––	0	1	1

DAVIS, Lorne Austin *Forward*
b. Regina, Sask., July 20, 1930

Season	Club	GP	G	A	Pts
1951–52	Montreal C.	3	1	1	2
1953–54	Montreal C.	37	6	4	10
1954–55	Chgo–Det RW	30	0	5	5
1955–1956	Boston	15	0	1	1
1959–60	Boston	10	1	1	2
	Totals	95	8	12	20

Playoffs

Season	Club	GP	G	A	Pts
1952–53	Montreal C.	7	1	1	2
1953–54	Montreal C.	11	2	0	2
	Totals	18	3	1	4

All-Star

1953	Montreal C.	1	0	0	0

DAVIS, Robert *Defenseman*
b. Lachine, Que.

Season	Club	GP	G	A	Pts
1932–33	Detroit F.	––	0	0	0

DAVISON, Murray *Defenseman*
b. Brantford, Ont., June 10, 1938

Season	Club	GP	G	A	Pts
1965–66	Boston	1	0	0	0

DAWES, Robert James *Defenseman-Forward*
b. Saskatoon, Sask., Nov. 29, 1924

Season	Club	GP	G	A	Pts
1946–47	Toronto M.L.	1	0	0	0
1948–49	Toronto M.L.	5	1	0	1
1949–50	Toronto M.L.	11	1	2	3
1950–51	Montreal C.	15	0	5	5
	Totals	32	2	7	9

Playoffs

Season	Club	GP	G	A	Pts
1948–49	Toronto M.L.	9	0	0	0
1950–51	Montreal C.	1	0	0	0
	Totals	10	0	0	0

All-Star

1949	Toronto M.L.	1	0	0	0

DAY, Clarence Henry (Happy) *Defenseman*
b. Owen Sound, Ont., June 14, 1901

Season	Club	GP	G	A	Pts
1924–25	Toronto St.P.	26	10	12	22
1925–26	Toronto St.P.	36	14	2	16
1926–27	Toronto M.L.	––	11	5	16
1927–28	Toronto M.L.	––	9	8	17
1928–29	Toronto M.L.	––	6	6	12
1929–30	Toronto M.L.	––	7	14	21
1930–31	Toronto M.L.	––	1	13	14
1931–32	Toronto M.L.	––	7	8	15
1932–33	Toronto M.L.	––	6	14	20
1933–34	Toronto M.L.	––	9	10	19
1934–35	Toronto M.L.	––	2	4	6
1935–36	Toronto M.L.	––	1	13	14
1936–37	Toronto M.L.	––	3	4	7
1937–38	New York A.	––	0	3	3
	Totals	––	86	116	202

Playoffs

Season	Club	GP	G	A	Pts
1924–25	Toronto St.P.	––	0	0	0
1928–29	Toronto M.L.	––	1	0	1
1930–31	Toronto M.L.	––	0	3	3
1931–32	Toronto M.L.	––	3	3	6
1932–33	Toronto M.L.	––	0	1	1
1933–34	Toronto M.L.	––	0	0	0
1934–35	Toronto M.L.	––	0	0	0
1935–36	Toronto M.L.	––	0	0	0
1936–37	Toronto M.L.	––	0	0	0
	Totals	––	4	7	11

DEA, William Fraser *Forward*
b. Edmonton, Alta., Apr. 3, 1933

Season	Club	GP	G	A	Pts
1953–54	New York R.	14	1	1	2
1956–57	Detroit R.W.	69	15	15	30
1957–58	Det RW–Chgo	63	9	12	21
1967–68	Pittsburgh Pe.	73	16	12	28

DEA (Continued)

Season	Club	GP	G	A	Pts
1968–69	Pittsburgh Pe.	66	10	8	18
1969–70	Detroit R.W.	70	10	3	13
1970–71	Detroit R.W.	42	6	3	9
	Totals	397	67	54	121

Playoffs

Season	Club	GP	G	A	Pts
1956–57	Detroit R.W.	5	2	0	2
1969–70	Detroit R.W.	4	0	1	1
	Totals	9	2	1	3

DEACON, Donald *Forward*
b. Regina, Sask., June 2, 1913

Season	Club	GP	G	A	Pts
1936–37	Detroit R.W.	--	0	0	0
1938–39	Detroit R.W.	--	1	3	4
1939–40	Detroit R.W.	--	5	1	6
	Totals	--	6	4	10

Playoffs

Season	Club	GP	G	A	Pts
1938–39	Detroit R.W.	--	2	1	3

DEADMARSH, Ernest Charles (Butch) *Forward*
b. Trail, B.C., Apr. 5, 1950

Season	Club	GP	G	A	Pts
1970–71	Buffalo	10	0	0	0
1971–72	Buffalo	12	1	1	2
1972–73	Buffalo–Atl	53	2	1	3
	Totals	75	3	2	5

DeCOURCY, Robert Philip *Goalie*
b. Toronto, Ont., June 12, 1927

Season	Club	GP	GA	Sho	AVE
1947–48	New York R.	1	6	0	6.00

DeFELICE, Norman *Goalie*
b. Schumacher, Ont., Jan. 19, 1933

Season	Club	GP	GA	Sho	AVE
1956–57	Boston	10	30	0	3.00

DeJORDY, Denis *Goalie*
b. St. Hyacinthe, Que., Nov. 12, 1938

Season	Club	GP	GA	Sho	AVE
1962–63	Chicago	4⅔	12	0	2.57
1963–64	Chicago	5⅔	19	0	3.35
1964–65	Chicago	29⅓	74	3	2.52
1966–67	Chicago	42⅓	104	4	2.46
1967–68	Chicago	47½	128	4	2.69
1968–69	Chicago	50	156	2	3.12
1969–70	Chgo–LA	28⅔	87	0	3.04
1970–71	Los Angeles	56⅓	214	1	3.81
1971–72	LA–Mtl C	10⅓	48	0	4.61
1972–73	Detroit R.W.	22⅙	83	1	3.74
	Totals	297	925	15	3.16

DeJORDY (Continued)

Playoffs

Season	Club	GP	GA	Sho	AVE
1963–64	Chicago	⅓	2	0	6.00
1964–65	Chicago	1⅓	9	0	6.77
1966–67	Chicago	3⅓	10	0	3.00
1967–68	Chicago	11	34	0	3.09
	Totals	16	55	0	3.44

DELMONTE, Armand Romeo (Dutch) *Forward*
b. Timmins, Ont., June 3, 1927

Season	Club	GP	G	A	Pts
1945–46	Boston	1	0	0	0

DeLORY, Valentine Arthur *Forward*
b. Toronto, Ont., Feb. 14, 1927

Season	Club	GP	G	A	Pts
1948–49	New York R.	1	0	0	0

DELVECCHIO, Alexander Peter (Alex) *Forward*
b. Ft. William, Ont., Dec. 4, 1931

Season	Club	GP	G	A	Pts
1950–51	Detroit R.W.	1	0	0	0
1951–52	Detroit R.W.	65	15	22	37
1952–53	Detroit R.W.	70	16	43	59
1953–54	Detroit R.W.	69	11	18	29
1954–55	Detroit R.W.	69	17	31	48
1955–56	Detroit R.W.	70	25	26	51
1956–57	Detroit R.W.	48	16	25	41
1957–58	Detroit R.W.	70	21	38	59
1958–59	Detroit R.W.	70	19	35	54
1959–60	Detroit R.W.	70	19	28	47
1960–61	Detroit R.W.	70	27	35	62
1961–62	Detroit R.W.	70	26	43	69
1962–63	Detroit R.W.	70	20	44	64
1963–64	Detroit R.W.	70	23	30	53
1964–65	Detroit R.W.	68	25	42	67
1965–66	Detroit R.W.	70	31	38	69
1966–67	Detroit R.W.	70	17	38	55
1967–68	Detroit R.W.	74	22	48	70
1968–69	Detroit R.W.	72	25	58	83
1969–70	Detroit R.W.	73	21	47	68
1970–71	Detroit R.W.	77	21	34	55
1971–72	Detroit R.W.	75	20	45	65
1972–73	Detroit R.W.	77	18	53	71
	Totals	1538	455	821	1276

Playoffs

Season	Club	GP	G	A	Pts
1951–52	Detroit R.W.	8	0	3	3
1952–53	Detroit R.W.	6	2	4	6
1953–54	Detroit R.W.	12	2	7	9
1954–55	Detroit R.W.	11	7	8	15
1955–56	Detroit R.W.	10	7	3	10
1956–57	Detroit R.W.	5	3	2	5
1957–58	Detroit R.W.	4	0	1	1
1959–60	Detroit R.W.	6	2	6	8
1960–61	Detroit R.W.	11	4	5	9

DELVECCHIO (Continued)

Playoffs	Club	GP	G	A	Pts
1962-63	Detroit R.W.	11	3	6	9
1963-64	Detroit R.W.	14	3	8	11
1964-65	Detroit R.W.	7	2	3	5
1965-66	Detroit R.W.	12	0	11	11
1969-70	Detroit R.W.	4	0	2	2
	Totals	121	35	69	104

All-Star					
1953	NHL All-Stars	1	1	0	1
1954	Detroit R.W.	1	1	0	1
1955	Detroit R.W.	1	0	1	1
1956	NHL All-Stars	1	0	0	0
1957	NHL All-Stars	1	0	0	0
1958	NHL All-Stars	1	0	0	0
1959	NHL All-Stars	1	0	0	0
1961	NHL All-Stars	1	1	1	2
1962	NHL All-Stars	1	0	1	1
1963	NHL All-Stars	1	0	0	0
1964	NHL All-Stars	1	0	0	0
1965	NHL All-Stars	1	0	0	0
1967	NHL All-Stars	1	0	0	0
	Totals	13	3	3	6

DeMARCO, Albert (Ab) *Forward*
b. North Bay, Ont., May 10, 1916

Season	Club	GP	G	A	Pts
1938-39	Chicago	--	1	0	1
1939-40	Chicago	--	0	5	5
1942-43	Tor ML-Bos	7	4	2	6
1943-44	Bos-NY R	39	14	19	33
1944-45	New York R.	50	24	30	54
1945-46	New York R.	50	20	27	47
1946-47	New York R.	44	9	10	19
	Totals	--	72	93	165

Playoffs					
1939-40	Chicago	2	0	0	0
1942-43	Boston	9	3	0	3
	Totals	11	3	0	3

DeMARCO, Albert Thomas Jr. (Ab)
Defenseman
b. North Bay, Ont., Feb. 27, 1949

Season	Club	GP	G	A	Pts
1969-70	New York R.	3	0	0	0
1970-71	New York R.	2	0	1	1
1971-72	New York R.	48	4	7	11
1972-73	NY R-StL B	65	8	22	30
	Totals	118	12	30	42

Playoffs					
1969-70	New York R.	5	0	0	0
1971-72	New York R.	4	0	1	1
1972-73	St.L. B.	4	1	1	2
	Totals	13	1	2	3

DEMERS, Antonio *Forward*
b. Chambly Bassin, Que., July 22, 1917

Season	Club	GP	G	A	Pts
1939-40	Montreal C.	--	2	3	5
1940-41	Montreal C.	--	13	10	23
1941-42	Montreal C.	7	3	4	7
1942-43	Montreal C.	9	2	5	7
1943-44	New York R.	1	0	0	0
	Totals	--	20	22	42

Playoffs					
1940-41	Montreal C.	3	0	0	0

DENIS, Jean Paul (Johnny) *Forward*
b. Montreal, Que., Feb. 28, 1924

Season	Club	GP	G	A	Pts
1946-47	New York R.	6	0	1	1
1949-50	New York R.	4	0	1	1
	Totals	10	0	2	2

DENIS, Louis Gilbert (Lulu) *Forward*
b. Vonda, Sask., June 7, 1928

Season	Club	GP	G	A	Pts
1949-50	Montreal C.	2	0	1	1
1950-51	Montreal C.	1	0	0	0
	Totals	3	0	1	1

DENNENY, Corbett *Forward*
b. Cornwall, Ont., 1894

Season	Club	GP	G	A	Pts
1917-18	Toronto A.	21	20	0	20
1918-19	Toronto A.	16	7	3	10
1919-20	Toronto St.P.	23	23	12	35
1920-21	Toronto St.P.	20	17	6	23
1921-22	Toronto St.P.	24	19	7	26
1922-23	Ottawa	1	1	0	1
1923-24	Hamilton	23	0	0	0
1926-27	Toronto M.L.	--	7	1	8
1927-28	Chicago	--	5	0	5
	Totals	--	99	29	128

Playoffs					
1917-18	Toronto A.	--	3	2	5
1920-21	Toronto St.P.	--	0	0	0
1921-22	Toronto St.P.	--	3	2	5
	Totals	--	6	4	10

DENNENY, Cyril *Forward*
b. Cornwall, Ont., 1897

Season	Club	GP	G	A	Pts
1917-18	Ottawa	22	36	0	36
1918-19	Ottawa	18	18	4	22
1919-20	Ottawa	22	16	2	18
1920-21	Ottawa	24	34	5	39
1921-22	Ottawa	22	27	12	39

DENNENY (Continued)

Season	Club	GP	G	A	Pts
1922-23	Ottawa	24	21	10	31
1923-24	Ottawa	21	22	1	23
1924-25	Ottawa	28	27	15	42
1925-26	Ottawa	36	24	12	36
1926-27	Ottawa	44	17	6	23
1927-28	Ottawa	--	3	0	3
1928-29	Boston	--	1	2	3
	Totals	--	246	69	315

Playoffs

Season	Club	GP	G	A	Pts
1918-19	Ottawa	5	2	0	2
1919-20	Ottawa	--	0	0	0
1920-21	Ottawa	2	2	0	2
1921-22	Ottawa	2	2	0	2
1922-23	Ottawa	2	2	0	2
1923-24	Ottawa	2	2	0	2
1925-26	Ottawa	2	0	0	0
1926-27	Ottawa	6	5	0	5
1927-28	Ottawa	2	0	0	0
1928-29	Boston	--	0	0	0
	Totals	--	15	0	15

DENNIS, Norman Marshall *Forward*
b. Aurora, Ont., Dec. 10, 1942

Season	Club	GP	G	A	Pts
1968-69	St. Louis B.	2	0	0	0
1969-70	St. Louis B.	5	3	0	3
1970-71	St. Louis B.	4	0	0	0
1971-72	St. Louis B.	1	0	0	0
	Totals	12	3	0	3

Playoffs

Season	Club	GP	G	A	Pts
1969-70	St. Louis B.	2	0	0	0
1970-71	St. Louis B.	3	0	0	0
	Totals	5	0	0	0

DENOIRD, Gerald *Forward*

Season	Club	GP	G	A	Pts
1922-23	Toronto St.P.	15	0	0	0

DESAULNIERS, Gerald *Forward*
b. Shawinigan Falls, Que., Dec. 31, 1928

Season	Club	GP	G	A	Pts
1950-51	Montreal C.	3	0	1	1
1952-53	Montreal C.	2	0	1	1
1953-54	Montreal C.	3	0	0	0
	Totals	8	0	2	2

DESILETS, Joffre Wilfred *Forward*
b. Capreal, Ont., Apr. 16, 1915

Season	Club	GP	G	A	Pts
1935-36	Montreal C.	--	7	6	13
1936-37	Montreal C.	--	7	12	19

DESILETS (Continued)

Season	Club	GP	G	A	Pts
1937-38	Montreal C.	--	6	7	13
1938-39	Chicago	--	11	13	24
1939-40	Chicago	--	6	7	13
	Totals	--	37	45	82

Playoffs

Season	Club	GP	G	A	Pts
1936-37	Montreal C.	5	1	0	1
1937-38	Montreal C.	3	0	0	0
	Totals	18	1	0	1

DESJARDINS, Gerard Ferdinand *Goalie*
b. Sudbury, Ont., July 22, 1944

Season	Club	GP	GA	Sho	AVE
1968-69	Los Angeles	58⅓	190	4	3.26
1969-70	LA-Chicago	47½	167	3	3.52
1970-71	Chicago	20⅓	49	0	2.41
1971-72	Chicago	6	21	0	3.50
1972-73	New York I.	41⅔	195	0	4.69
	Totals	173⅔	622	7	3.58

Playoffs

Season	Club	GP	GA	Sho	AVE
1968-69	Los Angeles	7⅓	28	0	3.90
1971-72	Chicago	1	5	0	5.00
	Totals	8⅓	33	0	4.03

DESJARDINS, Victor A. *Forward*
b. Sault Ste. Marie, Mich., July 4, 1900

Season	Club	GP	G	A	Pts
1930-31	Chicago	--	3	12	15
1931-32	New York R.	48	3	3	6
	Totals	--	6	15	21

Playoffs

Season	Club	GP	G	A	Pts
1930-31	Chicago	9	0	0	0
1931-32	New York R.	6	0	0	0
	Totals	15	0	0	0

DESLAURIERS, Jacques *Defenseman*
b. Montreal, Que., Sept. 3, 1928

Season	Club	GP	G	A	Pts
1955-56	Montreal C.	2	0	0	0

DEWAR, Thomas *Defenseman*
b. Frobisher, Sask., June 10, 1913

Season	Club	GP	G	A	Pts
1943-44	New York R.	9	0	2	2

DEWSBURY, Albert Percy *Defenseman*
b. Goodrich, Ont., Apr. 12, 1926

Season	Club	GP	G	A	Pts
1946-47	Detroit R.W.	23	2	1	3
1949-50	Detroit R.W.	11	2	2	4
1950-51	Chicago	67	5	14	19
1951-52	Chicago	69	7	17	24

DEWSBURY *(Continued)*

Season	Club	GP	G	A	Pts
1952-53	Chicago	69	5	16	21
1953-54	Chicago	69	6	15	21
1954-55	Chicago	2	0	1	1
1955-56	Chicago	37	3	12	15
	Totals	347	30	78	108

Playoffs

Season	Club	GP	G	A	Pts
1946-47	Detroit R.W.	2	0	0	0
1947-48	Detroit R.W.	1	0	0	0
1949-50	Detroit R.W.	4	0	3	3
1952-53	Chicago	7	1	2	3
	Totals	14	1	5	6

All-Star

Season	Club	GP	G	A	Pts
1951	NHL 1st All-Stars	1	0	0	0

DHEERE, Marcel Albert (Ching) *Forward*
b. St. Boniface, Man., Dec. 19, 1920

Season	Club	GP	G	A	Pts
1942-43	Montreal C.	11	1	2	3

Playoffs

Season	Club	GP	G	A	Pts
1942-43	Montreal C.	5	0	0	0

DIACHUK, Edward *Forward*
b. Vegreville, Alta., Aug. 16, 1936

Season	Club	GP	G	A	Pts
1960-61	Detroit R.W.	12	0	0	0

DICK, Harry *Defenseman*
b. Port Colborne, Ont., Nov. 22, 1922

Season	Club	GP	G	A	Pts
1946-47	Chicago	14	0	1	1

DICKENS, Ernest Leslie *Defenseman*
b. Winnipeg, Man., June 25, 1921

Season	Club	GP	G	A	Pts
1941-42	Toronto M.L.	10	2	2	4
1945-46	Toronto M.L.	15	1	3	4
1947-48	Chicago	54	5	15	20
1948-49	Chicago	59	2	3	5
1949-50	Chicago	70	0	13	13
1950-51	Chicago	70	2	8	10
	Totals	278	12	44	56

Playoffs

Season	Club	GP	G	A	Pts
1941-42	Toronto M.L.	13	0	0	0

DICKENSON, John Herbert (Herb) *Forward*
b. Mount Hope, Ont., June 11, 1931

Season	Club	GP	G	A	Pts
1951-52	New York R.	37	14	13	27
1952-53	New York R.	11	4	4	8
	Totals	48	18	17	35

DICKIE, William *Goalie*

Season	Club	GP	GA	Sho	AVE
1941-42	Chicago	1	3	0	3.00

DILL, Robert Edward *Defenseman*
b. St. Paul, Minn., Apr. 25, 1920

Season	Club	GP	G	A	Pts
1943-44	New York R.	28	6	10	16
1944-45	New York R.	48	9	5	14
	Totals	76	15	15	30

DILLABOUGH, Robert Wellington *Forward*
b. Belleville, Ont., Apr. 14, 1941

Season	Club	GP	G	A	Pts
1961-62	Detroit R.W.	5	0	0	0
1964-65	Detroit R.W.	4	0	0	0
1965-66	Boston	53	7	13	20
1966-67	Boston	60	6	12	18
1967-68	Pittsburgh Pe.	47	7	12	19
1968-69	Pitts Pe-Oak	62	7	12	19
1969-70	Oakland	52	5	5	10
	Totals	283	32	54	86

Playoffs

Season	Club	GP	G	A	Pts
1962-63	Detroit R.W.	1	0	0	0
1963-64	Detroit R.W.	1	0	0	0
1964-65	Detroit R.W.	4	0	0	0
1968-69	Oakland	7	3	0	3
1969-70	Oakland	4	0	0	0
	Totals	17	3	0	3

DILLON, Cecil Graham *Forward*
b. Toledo, Ohio, Apr. 26, 1908

Season	Club	GP	G	A	Pts
1930-31	New York R.	25	7	3	10
1931-32	New York R.	48	23	15	38
1932-33	New York R.	48	21	10	31
1933-34	New York R.	48	13	26	39
1934-35	New York R.	48	25	9	34
1935-36	New York R.	48	18	14	32
1936-37	New York R.	48	20	11	31
1937-38	New York R.	48	21	18	39
1938-39	New York R.	48	12	15	27
1939-40	Detroit R.W.	--	7	10	17
	Totals	--	167	131	298

Playoffs

Season	Club	GP	G	A	Pts
1930-31	New York R.	4	0	1	1
1931-32	New York R.	7	2	1	3
1932-33	New York R.	8	8	2	10
1933-34	New York R.	2	0	1	1
1934-35	New York R.	4	2	1	3
1936-37	New York R.	9	0	3	3
1937-38	New York R.	3	1	0	1
1938-39	New York R.	1	0	0	0
1939-40	Detroit R.W.	5	1	0	1
	Totals	43	14	9	23

DINEEN, Gary *Forward*
b. Montreal, Que., Dec. 24, 1943

Season	Club	GP	G	A	Pts
1968-69	Minnesota	4	0	1	1

DINEEN, William Patrick *Forward*
b. Arvida, Que., Sept. 18, 1932

Season	Club	GP	G	A	Pts
1953-54	Detroit R.W.	70	17	8	25
1954-55	Detroit R.W.	69	10	9	19
1955-56	Detroit R.W.	70	12	7	19
1956-57	Detroit R.W.	51	6	7	13
1957-58	Det RW-Chgo	63	6	13	19
	Totals	323	51	44	95

Playoffs

Season	Club	GP	G	A	Pts
1953-54	Detroit R.W.	12	0	0	0
1954-55	Detroit R.W.	11	0	1	1
1955-56	Detroit R.W.	10	1	0	1
1956-57	Detroit R.W.	4	0	0	0
	Totals	37	1	1	2

All-Star

Season	Club	GP	G	A	Pts
1954	Detroit R.W.	1	0	0	0
1955	Detroit R.W.	1	0	0	0
	Totals	2	0	0	0

DINSMORE, Charles (Dinny) *Forward*
b. Toronto, Ont., July 23, 1903

Season	Club	GP	G	A	Pts
1924-25	Montreal M.	30	2	1	3
1925-26	Montreal M.	33	3	1	4
1926-27	Montreal M.	--	1	0	1
	Totals	--	6	2	8

Playoffs

Season	Club	GP	G	A	Pts
1925-26	Montreal M.	--	0	0	0

DION, Conrad *Goalie*
b. St. Remi de Tingwick, Que., Aug. 11, 1918

Season	Club	GP	GA	Sho	AVE
1943-44	Detroit R.W.	26	80	0	3.07
1944-45	Detroit R.W.	12	39	0	3.25
	Totals	38	119	0	3.13

DIONNE, Marcel Elphege *Forward*
b. Drummondville, Que., Aug. 3, 1951

Season	Club	GP	G	A	Pts
1971-72	Detroit R.W.	78	28	49	77
1972-73	Detroit R.W.	77	40	50	90
	Totals	155	68	99	167

DOAK, Gary Walter *Defenseman*
b. Goderich, Ont., Feb. 26, 1946

Season	Club	GP	G	A	Pts
1965-66	Det RW-Bos	24	0	8	8
1966-67	Boston	29	0	1	1

DOAK *(Continued)*

Season	Club	GP	G	A	Pts
1967-68	Boston	59	2	10	12
1968-69	Boston	22	3	3	6
1969-70	Boston	44	1	7	8
1970-71	Vancouver	77	2	10	12
1971-72	NY R-Vanc	55	1	11	12
1972-73	Det RW-Bos	49	0	5	5
	Totals	359	9	55	64

Playoffs

Season	Club	GP	G	A	Pts
1967-68	Boston	4	0	0	0
1969-70	Boston	8	0	0	0
1971-72	New York R.	12	0	0	0
1972-73	Boston	2	0	0	0
	Totals	26	0	0	0

DOHERTY, Fred *Forward*

Season	Club	GP	G	A	Pts
1918-19	Montreal M.	3	0	0	0

DOLSON, Clarence *Goalie*

Season	Club	GP	GA	Sho	AVE
1928-29	Detroit C.	44	63	10	1.43
1929-30	Detroit C.	5	19'	0	3.80
1930-31	Detroit C.	44	105	6	2.39
	Totals	93	187	16	2.01

Playoffs

Season	Club	GP	GA	Sho	AVE
1928-29	Detroit C.	2	7	0	3.50

DONNELLY, Babe *Defenseman*
b. Sault Ste. Marie, Ont., Dec. 22, 1895

Season	Club	GP	G	A	Pts
1926-27	Montreal M.	--	0	1	1

Playoffs

Season	Club	GP	G	A	Pts
1926-27	Montreal M.	--	0	0	0

DORAN, John Michael (Red) *Defenseman*
b. Belleville, Ont., May 24, 1911

Season	Club	GP	G	A	Pts
1933-34	New York A.	--	1	4	5
1935-36	New York A.	--	4	2	6
1936-37	New York A.	--	0	1	1
1937-38	Detroit R.W.	--	0	0	0
1939-40	Montreal C.	--	0	3	3
	Totals	--	5	10	15

Playoffs

Season	Club	GP	G	A	Pts
1935-36	New York A.	--	0	0	0

DORAN, Lloyd George *Forward*
b. South Porcupine, Ont., Jan. 10, 1921

Season	Club	GP	G	A	Pts
1946-47	Detroit R.W.	26	3	2	5

DORATY, Kenneth Edward *Forward*
b. Stittsville, Ont., June 23, 1906

Season	Club	GP	G	A	Pts
1926–27	Chicago	--	0	0	0
1932–33	Toronto M.L.	--	5	11	16
1933–34	Toronto M.L.	--	9	10	19
1934–35	Toronto M.L.	--	1	4	5
1937–38	Detroit R.W.	--	0	1	1
	Totals	--	**15**	**26**	**41**

Playoffs

1932–33	Toronto M.L.	--	5	0	5
1933–34	Toronto M.L.	--	2	2	4
	Totals	--	**7**	**2**	**9**

DOREY, Robert James (Jim) *Defenseman*
b. Kingston, Ont., Aug. 17, 1947

Season	Club	GP	G	A	Pts
1968–69	Toronto M.L.	61	8	22	30
1969–70	Toronto M.L.	46	6	11	17
1970–71	Toronto M.L.	74	7	22	29
1971–72	Tor ML-NY R	51	4	19	23
	Totals	**232**	**25**	**74**	**99**

Playoffs

1968–69	Toronto M.L.	4	0	1	1
1970–71	Toronto M.L.	6	0	1	1
1971–72	New York R.	1	0	0	0
	Totals	**11**	**0**	**2**	**2**

DORNHOEFER, Gerhardt (Gary) *Forward*
b. Kitchener, Ont., Feb. 2, 1943

Season	Club	GP	G	A	Pts
1963–64	Boston	32	12	10	22
1964–65	Boston	20	0	1	1
1965–66	Boston	10	0	1	1
1967–68	Philadelphia F.	65	13	30	43
1968–69	Philadelphia F.	60	8	16	24
1969–70	Philadelphia F.	65	26	29	55
1970–71	Philadelphia F.	57	20	20	40
1971–72	Philadelphia F.	75	17	32	49
1972–73	Philadelphia F.	77	30	49	79
	Totals	**461**	**126**	**188**	**314**

Playoffs

1967–68	Philadelphia F.	3	0	0	0
1968–69	Philadelphia F.	4	0	1	1
1970–71	Philadelphia F.	2	0	0	0
1972–73	Philadelphia F.	11	3	4	7
	Totals	**20**	**3**	**5**	**8**

All-Star

1973	West All-Stars	1	0	0	0

DOROHOY, Edward *Forward*
b. Medicine Hat, Alta., Mar. 13, 1929

Season	Club	GP	G	A	Pts
1948–49	Montreal C.	16	0	0	0

DOUGLAS, Kent Gemmell *Defenseman*
b. Cobalt, Ont., Feb. 6, 1936

Season	Club	GP	G	A	Pts
1962–63	Toronto M.L.	70	7	15	22
1963–64	Toronto M.L.	43	0	1	1
1964–65	Toronto M.L.	67	5	23	28
1965–66	Toronto M.L.	64	6	14	20
1966–67	Toronto M.L.	39	2	12	14
1967–68	Oak-Det RW	76	11	21	32
1968–69	Detroit R.W.	69	2	29	31
	Totals	**428**	**33**	**115**	**148**

Playoffs

1962–63	Toronto M.L.	10	1	1	2
1964–65	Toronto M.L.	5	0	1	1
1965–66	Toronto M.L.	4	0	1	1
	Totals	**19**	**1**	**3**	**4**

All-Star

1962	Toronto M.L.	1	0	1	1
1963	Toronto M.L.	1	0	0	0
1964	Toronto M.L.	1	1	0	1
	Totals	**3**	**1**	**1**	**2**

DOUGLAS, Leslie *Forward*
b. Perth, Ont., Dec. 5, 1918

Season	Club	GP	G	A	Pts
1940–41	Detroit R.W.	18	1	2	3
1942–43	Detroit R.W.	21	5	8	13
1945–46	Detroit R.W.	1	0	0	0
1946–47	Detroit R.W.	12	0	2	2
	Totals	**52**	**6**	**12**	**18**

Playoffs

1942–43	Detroit R.W.	10	3	2	5

DOWNIE, David M. *Forward*
b. Burk's Falls, Ont., Mar. 11, 1909

Season	Club	GP	G	A	Pts
1932–33	Toronto M.L.	--	0	1	1

DRAPER, Bruce *Forward*
b. Toronto, Ont., Oct. 2, 1940

Season	Club	GP	G	A	Pts
1962–63	Toronto M.L.	1	0	0	0

DRILLON, Gordon Arthur *Forward*
b. Moncton, N.B., Oct. 23, 1914

Season	Club	GP	G	A	Pts
1936–37	Toronto M.L.	--	16	17	33
1937–38	Toronto M.L.	--	26	26	52
1938–39	Toronto M.L.	--	18	16	34
1939–40	Toronto M.L.	--	21	19	40
1940–41	Toronto M.L.	--	23	21	44
1941–42	Toronto M.L.	--	23	18	41
1942–43	Montreal C.	49	28	22	50
	Totals	--	**155**	**139**	**294**

DRILLON (Continued)

Playoffs	Club	GP	G	A	Pts
1936-37	Toronto M.L.	--	0	0	0
1937-38	Toronto M.L.	--	7	1	8
1938-39	Toronto M.L.	--	7	6	13
1939-40	Toronto M.L.	--	3	1	4
1940-41	Toronto M.L.	--	3	2	5
1941-42	Toronto M.L.	--	2	3	5
1942-43	Montreal C.	5	4	2	6
	Totals	--	26	15	41

DROUILLARD, Clarence *Forward*
b. Windsor, Ont., Mar. 2, 1914

Season	Club	GP	G	A	Pts
1937-38	Detroit R.W.	--	0	1	1

DROLET, Rene Georges *Forward*
b. Quebec, Que., Nov. 13, 1944

Season	Club	GP	G	A	Pts
1971-72	Philadelphia F.	1	0	0	0

DROUIN, Jude *Forward*
b. Mont-Louis, Que., Oct. 28, 1948

Season	Club	GP	G	A	Pts
1968-69	Montreal C.	9	0	1	1
1969-70	Montreal C.	3	0	0	0
1970-71	Minnesota	75	16	52	68
1971-72	Minnesota	63	13	43	56
1972-73	Minnesota	78	27	46	73
	Totals	228	56	142	198

Playoffs	Club	GP	G	A	Pts
1970-71	Minnesota	12	5	7	12
1971-72	Minnesota	7	4	4	8
1972-73	Minnesota	6	1	3	4
	Totals	25	10	14	24

DROUIN, Paul Emile (Polly) *Forward*
b. Ottawa, Ont., Jan. 1916

Season	Club	GP	G	A	Pts
1935-36	Montreal C.	--	1	8	9
1937-38	Montreal C.	--	7	13	20
1938-39	Montreal C.	--	7	11	18
1939-40	Montreal C.	--	4	11	15
1940-41	Montreal C.	--	4	7	11
	Totals	--	23	50	73

Playoffs	Club	GP	G	A	Pts
1937-38	Montreal C.	--	0	0	0
1938-39	Montreal C.	--	0	1	1
1940-41	Montreal C.	--	0	0	0
	Totals	--	0	1	1

DRUMMOND, James *Defenseman*
b. Toronto, Ont., Oct. 20, 1918

Season	Club	GP	G	A	Pts
1944-45	New York R.	2	0	0	0

DRURY, Herbert *Defenseman-Forward*

Season	Club	GP	G	A	Pts
1925-26	Pittsburgh Pi.	33	6	2	8
1926-27	Pittsburgh Pi.	--	5	1	6
1927-28	Pittsburgh Pi.	--	6	4	10
1928-29	Pittsburgh Pi.	--	5	4	9
1929-30	Pittsburgh Pi.	--	2	0	2
1930-31	Philadelphia Pq.	--	0	2	2
	Totals	--	24	13	37

Playoffs	Club	GP	G	A	Pts
1925-26	Pittsburgh Pi.	--	1	0	1
1927-28	Pittsburgh Pi.	--	0	1	1
	Totals	--	1	1	2

DRYDEN, David Murray *Goalie*
b. Hamilton, Ont., Sept. 5, 1941

Season	Club	GP	GA	Sho	AVE
1961-62	New York R.	⅔	3	0	4.50
1965-66	Chicago	7⅔	23	0	3.00
1967-68	Chicago	21⅓	69	1	3.23
1968-69	Chicago	24⅔	79	3	3.20
1970-71	Buffalo	7	23	1	3.37
1971-72	Buffalo	17	68	0	3.97
1972-73	Buffalo	33⅔	89	3	2.65
	Totals	112	354	8	3.16

Playoffs	Club	GP	GA	Sho	AVE
1965-66	Chicago	⅓	0	0	0.00
1972-73	Buffalo	2	9	0	4.50
	Totals	2⅓	9	0	4.06

DRYDEN, Kenneth Wayne (Ken) *Goalie*
b. Hamilton, Ont., Aug. 8, 1947

Season	Club	GP	GA	Sho	AVE
1970-71	Montreal C.	5½	9	0	1.65
1971-72	Montreal C.	63⅓	142	8	2.24
1972-73	Montreal C.	52⅔	119	6	2.26
	Totals	121½	270	14	2.21

Playoffs	Club	GP	GA	Sho	AVE
1970-71	Montreal C.	20	61	0	3.00
1971-72	Montreal C.	6	17	0	2.83
1972-73	Montreal C.	17	50	1	2.89
	Totals	43	128	1	2.94

All-Star		GP	Per	GA	AGP
1972	East All-Stars	1	1½	2	1.33

DUBE, Joseph Gilles *Forward*
b. Sherbrooke, Que., June 2, 1927

Season	Club	GP	G	A	Pts
1949-50	Montreal C.	12	1	2	3

Playoffs	Club	GP	G	A	Pts
1953-54	Detroit R.W.	2	0	0	0

DUDLEY, Richard Clarence (Rick) *Forward*
b. Toronto, Ont., Jan. 31, 1949

Season	Club	GP	G	A	Pts
1972-73	Buffalo	6	0	1	1

DUFF, Richard *Forward*
b. Kirkland Lake, Ont., Feb. 18, 1936

Season	Club	GP	G	A	Pts
1954-55	Toronto M.L.	3	0	0	0
1955-56	Toronto M.L.	69	18	19	37
1956-57	Toronto M.L.	70	26	14	40
1957-58	Toronto M.L.	65	26	23	49
1958-59	Toronto M.L.	69	29	24	53
1959-60	Toronto M.L.	67	19	22	41
1960-61	Toronto M.L.	67	16	17	33
1961-62	Toronto M.L.	51	17	20	37
1962-63	Toronto M.L.	69	16	19	35
1963-64	Tor ML-NY R	66	11	14	25
1964-65	NY R-Mont C	69	12	16	28
1965-66	Montreal C.	63	21	24	45
1966-67	Montreal C.	51	12	11	23
1967-68	Montreal C.	66	25	21	46
1968-69	Montreal C.	68	19	21	40
1969-70	Mont C-LA	49	6	9	15
1970-71	LA-Buff	60	8	13	21
1971-72	Buffalo	8	2	2	4
	Totals	1030	283	289	572
Playoffs					
1955-56	Toronto M.L.	5	1	4	5
1958-59	Toronto M.L.	12	4	3	7
1959-60	Toronto M.L.	10	2	4	6
1960-61	Toronto M.L.	5	0	1	1
1961-62	Toronto M.L.	12	3	10	13
1962-63	Toronto M.L.	10	4	1	5
1964-65	Montreal C.	13	3	6	9
1965-66	Montreal C.	10	2	5	7
1966-67	Montreal C.	10	2	3	5
1967-68	Montreal C.	13	3	4	7
1968-69	Montreal C.	14	6	8	14
	Totals	114	30	49	79
All-Star					
1956	NHL All-Stars	1	0	0	0
1957	NHL All-Stars	1	0	0	0
1958	NHL All-Stars	1	0	0	0
1962	Toronto M.L.	1	1	0	1
1963	Toronto M.L.	1	0	0	0
1965	Montreal C.	1	0	1	1
1967	Montreal C.	1	0	0	0
	Totals	7	1	1	2

DUFOUR, Marc *Forward*
b. Three Rivers, Que., Sept. 11, 1941

Season	Club	GP	G	A	Pts
1963-64	New York R.	10	1	0	1

DUFOUR (Continued)

Season	Club	GP	G	A	Pts
1964-65	New York R.	2	0	0	0
1968-69	Los Angeles	2	0	0	0
	Totals	14	1	0	1

DUGGAN, Jack *Defenseman*

Season	Club	GP	G	A	Pts
1925-26	Ottawa	27	0	0	0

DUGUID, Lorne Wallace *Forward*
b. Bolton, Ont., Apr. 4, 1910

Season	Club	GP	G	A	Pts
1931-32	Montreal M.	--	0	0	0
1932-33	Montreal M.	--	4	7	11
1933-34	Montreal M.	--	0	1	1
1934-35	Detroit R.W.	--	3	3	6
1935-36	Boston	--	1	4	5
1936-37	Boston	--	1	0	1
	Totals	--	9	15	24
Playoffs					
1932-33	Montreal M.	--	0	0	0
1935-36	Boston	--	1	0	1
	Totals	--	1	0	1

**DUMART, Woodrow Wilson Clarence
(Woody and Porky)** *Forward*
b. Kitchener, Ont., Dec. 23, 1916

Season	Club	GP	G	A	Pts
1936-37	Boston	--	4	4	8
1937-38	Boston	--	13	14	27
1938-39	Boston	--	14	15	29
1939-40	Boston	--	22	21	43
1940-41	Boston	40	18	15	33
1941-42	Boston	35	14	15	29
1945-46	Boston	50	22	12	34
1946-47	Boston	60	24	28	52
1947-48	Boston	59	21	16	37
1948-49	Boston	59	11	12	23
1949-50	Boston	69	14	25	39
1950-51	Boston	70	20	21	41
1951-52	Boston	39	5	8	13
1952-53	Boston	62	5	9	14
1953-54	Boston	69	4	3	7
	Totals	--	211	218	429
Playoffs					
1936-37	Boston	3	0	0	0
1937-38	Boston	3	0	0	0
1938-39	Boston	12	1	3	4
1939-40	Boston	6	1	0	1
1940-41	Boston	11	1	3	4
1945-46	Boston	10	4	3	7
1946-47	Boston	5	1	1	2

DUMART (Continued)

Playoffs	Club	GP	G	A	Pts
1947-48	Boston	5	0	0	0
1948-49	Boston	5	3	0	3
1950-51	Boston	6	1	2	3
1951-52	Boston	7	0	1	1
1952-53	Boston	11	0	2	2
1953-54	Boston	4	0	0	0
	Totals	88	12	15	27

All-Star					
1947	NHL All-Stars	1	0	0	0
1948	NHL All-Stars	1	1	0	1
	Totals	2	1	0	1

DUNCAN, Arthur *Defenseman*

Season	Club	GP	G	A	Pts
1926-27	Detroit C.	--	3	2	5
1927-28	Toronto M.L.	--	7	5	12
1928-29	Toronto M.L.	--	4	4	8
1929-30	Toronto M.L.	--	4	5	9
	Totals	--	18	16	34

Playoffs					
1920-21	Vancouver(PCHL)	--	2	1	3
1921-22	Vancouver(PCHL)	--	0	0	0
1922-23	Vancouver(PCHL)	--	2	2	4
1923-24	Vancouver(PCHL)	--	0	0	0
1928-29	Toronto M.L.	--	0	0	0
	Totals	--	4	3	7

DUNLAP, Frank *Forward*

Season	Club	GP	G	A	Pts
1943-44	Toronto M.L.	5	0	1	1

DUPERE, Denis Gilles *Forward*
b. Jonquiere, Que., June 21, 1948

Season	Club	GP	G	A	Pts
1970-71	Toronto M.L.	20	1	2	3
1971-72	Toronto M.L.	77	7	10	17
1972-73	Toronto M.L.	61	13	23	36
	Totals	158	21	35	56

Playoffs					
1970-71	Toronto M.L.	6	0	0	0
1971-72	Toronto M.L.	5	0	0	0
	Totals	11	0	0	0

DUPONT, Andre *Defenseman*
b. Trois-Rivieres, Que., July 27, 1949

Season	Club	GP	G	A	Pts
1970-71	New York R.	7	1	2	3
1971-72	St. Louis B.	60	3	10	13
1972-73	StL B-Phila F	71	4	26	30
	Totals	138	8	38	46

DUPONT (Continued)

Playoffs	Club	GP	G	A	Pts
1971-72	St. Louis B.	11	1	0	1
1972-73	Philadelphia F.	11	1	2	3
	Totals	22	2	2	4

DURBANO, Harry Steven (Steve) *Defenseman*
b. Toronto, Ont., Dec. 12, 1951

Season	Club	GP	G	A	Pts
1972-73	St. Louis B.	49	3	18	21

Playoffs					
1972-73	St. Louis B.	5	0	2	2

DURNAN, William Ronald *Goalie*
b. Toronto, Ont., Jan. 22, 1915

Season	Club	GP	GA	Sho	AVE
1943-44	Montreal C.	50	109	2	2.18
1944-45	Montreal C.	50	121	1	2.42
1945-46	Montreal C.	40	104	4	2.60
1946-47	Montreal C.	60	138	4	2.30
1947-48	Montreal C.	59	162	5	2.74
1948-49	Montreal C.	60	126	10	2.10
1949-50	Montreal C.	64	141	8	2.20
	Totals	383	901	34	2.35

Playoffs					
1943-44	Montreal C.	9	14	1	1.55
1944-45	Montreal C.	6	15	0	2.50
1945-46	Montreal C.	9	20	0	2.22
1946-47	Montreal C.	11	23	1	2.09
1948-49	Montreal C.	7	17	0	2.43
1949-50	Montreal C.	3	10	0	3.33
	Totals	45	99	2	2.20

All-Star		GP	Per	GA	AGP
1947	NHL All-Stars	1	2	3	1.50
1948	NHL All-Stars	1	2	0	0.00
1949	NHL All-Stars	1	2	1	0.50
	Totals	3	6	4	0.67

DUSSAULT, Joseph Normand (Norm) *Forward*
b. Springfield, Mass., Sept. 26, 1925

Season	Club	GP	G	A	Pts
1947-48	Montreal C.	28	5	10	15
1948-49	Montreal C.	47	9	8	17
1949-50	Montreal C.	67	13	24	37
1950-51	Montreal C.	64	4	20	24
	Totals	206	31	62	93

Playoffs					
1948-49	Montreal C.	2	0	0	0
1949-50	Montreal C.	5	3	1	4
	Totals	7	3	1	4

459

DUTKOWSKI, Laudes (Duke) *Defenseman*
b. Regina, Sask., Aug. 31, 1902

Season	Club	GP	G	A	Pts
1926-27	Chicago	--	3	2	5
1929-30	Chicago	--	7	10	17
1930-31	New York A.	--	2	4	6
1932-33	New York A.	--	4	7	11
1933-34	Chgo-NY A-NY R	--	0	7	7
	Totals	--	16	30	46

Playoffs

1926-27	Chicago	2	0	0	0
1929-30	Chicago	2	0	0	0
1933-34	New York R.	2	0	0	0
	Totals	6	0	0	0

DUTTON, Mervyn (Red) *Defenseman*
b. Russell, Man., July 23, 1898

Season	Club	GP	G	A	Pts
1926-27	Montreal M.	--	4	4	8
1927-28	Montreal M.	--	7	6	13
1928-29	Montreal M.	--	1	3	4
1929-30	Montreal M.	--	3	13	16
1930-31	New York A.	--	1	11	12
1931-32	New York A.	--	3	5	8
1932-33	New York A.	--	0	2	2
1933-34	New York A.	--	2	8	10
1934-35	New York A.	--	3	7	10
1935-36	New York A.	--	5	8	13
	Totals	--	29	67	96

Playoffs

1923-24	Calgary (PCHL)	--	0	0	0
1926-27	Montreal M.	--	0	0	0
1927-28	Montreal M.	--	1	0	1
1929-30	Montreal M.	--	0	0	0
1935-36	New York A.	--	0	0	0
	Totals	--	1	0	1

DYCK, Edward *Goalie*
b. Warman, Sask., Oct. 29, 1950

Season	Club	GP	GA	Sho	AVE
1971-72	Vancouver	9⅔	35	0	3.66
1972-73	Vancouver	21⅔	98	1	4.53
	Totals	31⅓	133	1	4.26

DYCK, Henry Richard *Forward*
b. Saskatoon, Sask., Sept. 5, 1912

Season	Club	GP	G	A	Pts
1943-44	New York R.	1	0	0	0

DYE, Cecil (Babe) *Forward*
b. Hamilton, Ont., May 13, 1898

Season	Club	GP	G	A	Pts
1919-20	Toronto St.P.	21	12	3	15
1920-21	Tor StP-Hmltn	24	35	2	37

DYE *(Continued)*

Season	Club	GP	G	A	Pts
1921-22	Toronto St.P.	24	30	7	37
1922-23	Toronto St.P.	22	26	11	37
1923-24	Toronto St.P.	19	17	2	19
1924-25	Toronto St.P.	29	38	6	44
1925-26	Toronto St.P.	31	18	5	23
1926-27	Chicago	--	25	5	30
1928-29	New York A.	--	1	0	1
	Totals	--	202	41	243

Playoffs

1920-21	Hamilton	--	0	0	0
1921-22	Toronto St.P.	--	9	2	11
1924-25	Toronto St.P.	--	0	0	0
1926-27	Chicago	--	0	0	0
	Totals	--	9	2	11

DYTE, John *Defenseman*
b. Kingston, Ont., Oct. 13, 1918

Season	Club	GP	G	A	Pts
1943-44	Chicago	27	1	0	1

ECCLESTONE, Tim *Forward*
b. Toronto, Ont., Sept. 24, 1947

Season	Club	GP	G	A	Pts
1967-68	St. Louis B.	50	6	8	14
1968-69	St. Louis B.	68	11	23	34
1969-70	St. Louis B.	65	16	21	37
1970-71	StL B-Det RW	74	19	34	53
1971-72	Detroit R.W.	72	18	35	53
1972-73	Detroit R.W.	78	18	30	48
	Totals	407	88	151	239

Playoffs

1967-68	St. Louis B.	12	1	2	3
1968-69	St. Louis B.	12	2	2	4
1969-70	St. Louis B.	16	3	4	7
	Totals	40	6	8	14

All-Star

1971	West All-Stars	1	0	0	0

EDDOLLS, Frank Herbert *Defenseman*
b. Lachine, Que., July 5, 1921

Season	Club	GP	G	A	Pts
1944-45	Montreal C.	43	5	8	13
1945-46	Montreal C.	8	0	1	1
1946-47	Montreal C.	6	0	0	0
1947-48	New York R.	58	6	13	19
1948-49	New York R.	34	4	2	6
1949-50	New York R.	57	2	6	8
1950-51	New York R.	68	3	8	11
1951-52	New York R.	42	3	5	8
	Totals	316	23	43	66

EDDOLLS (Continued)

Playoffs	Club	GP	G	A	Pts
1944–45	Montreal C.	3	0	0	0
1945–46	Montreal C.	8	0	1	1
1946–47	Montreal C.	6	0	0	0
1947–48	New York R.	2	0	0	0
1949–50	New York R.	11	0	1	1
	Totals	30	0	2	2

All-Star

1951	NHL 1st All-Stars	1	0	0	0

EDESTRAND, Darryl *Defenseman*
b. Strathroy, Ont., Nov. 6, 1945

Season	Club	GP	G	A	Pts
1967–68	St. Louis B.	12	0	0	0
1969–70	Philadelphia F.	2	0	0	0
1971–72	Pittsburgh Pe.	77	10	23	33
1972–73	Pittsburgh Pe.	78	15	24	39
	Totals	169	25	47	72

Playoffs	Club	GP	G	A	Pts
1971–72	Pittsburgh Pe.	4	0	2	2

EDMUNDSON, Garry Frank *Forward*
b. Sexsmith, Alta., May 6, 1932

Season	Club	GP	G	A	Pts
1951–52	Montreal C.	1	0	0	0
1959–60	Toronto M.L.	39	4	6	10
1960–61	Toronto M.L.	3	0	0	0
	Totals	43	4	6	10

Playoffs	Club	GP	G	A	Pts
1951–52	Montreal C.	2	0	0	0
1959–60	Toronto M.L.	9	0	1	1
	Totals	11	0	1	1

EDWARDS, Allen Roy *Goalie*
b. Seneca Township, Ont., Mar. 12, 1937

Season	Club	GP	GA	Sho	AVE
1967–68	Detroit R.W.	36½	127	0	3.50
1968–69	Detroit R.W.	35	89	4	2.54
1969–70	Detroit R.W.	44⅔	116	2	2.57
1970–71	Detroit R.W.	35	119	0	3.39
1971–72	Pittsburgh Pe.	14	36	0	2.55
1972–73	Detroit R.W.	50⅓	132	6	2.63
	Totals	215½	619	12	2.88

Playoffs	Club	GP	GA	Sho	AVE
1969–70	Detroit R.W.	3⅓	11	0	3.43

EDWARDS, Gary William *Goalie*
b. Toronto, Ont., Oct. 5, 1947

Season	Club	GP	GA	Sho	AVE
1968–69	St. Louis B.	1/15	0	0	0.00
1969–70	St. Louis B.	1	4	0	4.00
1971–72	Los Angeles	41⅔	150	2	3.59
1972–73	Los Angeles	26	94	1	3.62
	Totals	69	248	3	3.61

EDWARDS, Marvin Wayne *Goalie*
b. St. Catherines, Ont., Aug. 15, 1935

Season	Club	GP	GA	Sho	AVE
1968–69	Pittsburgh Pe.	1	3	0	3.00
1969–70	Toronto M.L.	23⅔	77	1	3.25
1972–73	California	20	87	1	4.32
	Totals	44⅔	167	2	3.78

EGAN, Martin Joseph (Pat) *Defenseman*
b. Blackie, Alta., Apr. 25, 1918

Season	Club	GP	G	A	Pts
1939–40	New York A.	--	4	3	7
1940–41	New York A.	--	4	9	13
1941–42	Brooklyn A.	48	8	20	28
1943–44	Det RW-Bos	48	15	28	43
1944–45	Boston	48	7	15	22
1945–46	Boston	41	8	10	18
1946–47	Boston	60	7	18	25
1947–48	Boston	60	8	11	19
1948–49	Boston	60	6	18	24
1949–50	New York R.	70	5	11	16
1950–51	New York R.	70	5	10	15
	Totals	--	77	153	230

Playoffs	Club	GP	G	A	Pts
1944–45	Boston	7	2	0	2
1945–46	Boston	10	3	0	3
1946–47	Boston	5	0	2	2
1947–48	Boston	5	1	1	2
1948–49	Boston	5	0	0	0
1949–50	New York R.	12	3	1	4
	Totals	44	9	4	13

All-Star

1949	NHL All-Stars	1	0	0	0

EGERS, John Richard (Jack) *Forward*
b. Sudbury, Ont., Jan. 28, 1949

Season	Club	GP	G	A	Pts
1969–70	New York R.	6	3	0	3
1970–71	New York R.	60	7	10	17
1971–72	NY R-StL B	80	23	26	49
1972–73	St.Louis B.	78	24	24	48
	Totals	224	57	60	117

Playoffs	Club	GP	G	A	Pts
1969–70	New York R.	5	3	1	4
1970–71	New York R.	3	0	0	0
1971–72	St. Louis B.	11	1	4	5
1972–73	St. Louis B.	5	0	1	1
	Totals	24	4	6	10

EHMAN, Gerald Joseph *Forward*
b. Cudworth, Sask., Nov. 3, 1932

Season	Club	GP	G	A	Pts
1957–58	Boston	1	1	0	1
1958–59	Det RW-Tor ML	44	12	14	26

EHMAN *(Continued)*

Season	Club	GP	G	A	Pts
1959-60	Toronto M.L.	69	12	16	28
1960-61	Toronto M.L.	14	1	1	2
1963-64	Toronto M.L.	4	1	1	2
1967-68	Oakland	73	19	25	44
1968-69	Oakland	70	21	24	45
1969-70	Oakland	76	11	19	30
1970-71	California	78	18	18	36
	Totals	429	96	118	214

Playoffs

1958-59	Toronto M.L.	12	6	7	13
1959-60	Toronto M.L.	9	0	0	0
1963-64	Toronto M.L.	9	1	0	1
1968-69	Oakland	7	2	2	4
1969-70	Oakland	4	1	1	2
	Totals	41	10	10	20

ELIK, Boris (Bo) *Forward*
b. Geraldton, Ont., Oct. 17, 1929

Season	Club	GP	G	A	Pts
1962-63	Detroit R.W.	3	0	0	0

ELLIOTT, Fred *Forward*

Season	Club	GP	G	A	Pts
1928-29	Ottawa	--	2	0	2

ELLIS, Ronald John Edward (Ron) *Forward*
b. Lindsay, Ont., Jan. 8, 1945

Season	Club	GP	G	A	Pts
1963-64	Toronto M.L.	1	0	0	0
1964-65	Toronto M.L.	62	23	16	39
1965-66	Toronto M.L.	70	19	23	42
1966-67	Toronto M.L.	67	22	23	45
1967-68	Toronto M.L.	74	28	20	48
1968-69	Toronto M.L.	72	25	21	46
1969-70	Toronto M.L.	76	35	19	54
1970-71	Toronto M.L.	78	24	29	53
1971-72	Toronto M.L.	78	23	24	47
1972-73	Toronto M.L.	77	22	29	51
	Totals	655	221	204	425

Playoffs

1964-65	Toronto M.L.	6	3	0	3
1965-66	Toronto M.L.	4	0	0	0
1966-67	Toronto M.L.	12	2	1	3
1968-69	Toronto M.L.	4	2	1	3
1970-71	Toronto M.L.	6	1	1	2
1971-72	Toronto M.L.	5	1	1	2
	Totals	37	9	4	13

All-Star

1964	Toronto M.L.	1	0	0	0
1965	NHL All-Stars	1	0	0	0
1968	Toronto M.L.	1	1	0	1
1970	East All Stars	1	0	0	0
	Totals	4	1	0	1

EMMS, Leighton (Happy) *Defenseman-Forward*
b. Barrie, Ont., Jan. 16, 1905

Season	Club	GP	G	A	Pts
1926-27	Montreal M.	--	0	0	0
1927-28	Montreal M.	--	0	1	1
1930-31	New York A.	--	5	4	9
1931-32	NY A-Det F	--	6	9	15
1932-33	Detroit F.	--	9	13	22
1933-34	Detroit R.W.	--	7	7	14
1934-35	New York A.	--	3	3	6
1935-36	New York A.	--	1	5	6
1936-37	New York A.	--	4	8	12
1937-38	New York A.	--	1	3	4
	Totals	--	36	53	89

Playoffs

1927-28	Montreal M.	--	0	0	0
1931-32	Detroit F.	--	0	0	0
1932-33	Detroit F.	--	0	0	0
1933-34	Detroit R.W.	--	0	0	0
1935-36	New York A.	--	0	0	0
1937-38	New York A.	--	0	0	0
	Totals	--	0	0	0

ERICKSON, Autry Raymond *Defenseman*
b. Lethbridge, Alta., Jan. 25, 1938

Season	Club	GP	G	A	Pts
1959-60	Boston	58	1	6	7
1960-61	Boston	68	2	6	8
1962-63	Chicago	3	0	0	0
1963-64	Chicago	31	0	1	1
1967-68	Oakland	65	4	11	15
1969-70	Oakland	1	0	0	0
	Totals	226	7	24	31

Playoffs

1963-64	Chicago	6	0	0	0
1966-67	Toronto M.L.	1	0	0	0
	Totals	7	0	0	0

ERICKSON, Grant Charles *Forward*
b. Pierceland, Sask., Apr. 28, 1947

Season	Club	GP	G	A	Pts
1968-69	Boston	2	1	0	1
1969-70	Minnesota	4	0	0	0
	Totals	6	1	0	1

ESPOSITO, Anthony James (Tony) *Goalie*
b. Sault Ste. Marie, Ont., Apr. 23, 1943

Season	Club	GP	GA	Sho	AVE
1968-69	Montreal C.	12⅔	34	2	2.68
1969-70	Chicago	62⅔	136	15	2.17
1970-71	Chicago	55⅓	126	6	2.27
1971-72	Chicago	46⅓	82	9	1.76
1972-73	Chicago	55⅔	140	4	2.51
	Totals	232⅔	518	36	2.23

462

ESPOSITO (Continued)

Playoffs	Club	GP	GA	Sho	AVE
1969–70	Chicago	8	27	0	3.37
1970–71	Chicago	18	42	2	2.19
1971–72	Chicago	5	16	0	3.20
1972–73	Chicago	15	46	1	3.08
	Totals	46	131	3	2.85

All-Star	Club	GP	Per	GA	AGP
1970	East All-Stars	1	1½	0	0.00
1971	West All-Stars	1	1½	1	0.67
1972	West All-Stars	1	1½	1	0.67
1973	West All-Stars	1	1½	1	0.67
	Totals	4	6	3	0.50

ESPOSITO, Phillip   *Forward*
b. Sault Ste. Marie, Ont., Feb. 20, 1942

Season	Club	GP	G	A	Pts
1963–64	Chicago	27	3	2	5
1964–65	Chicago	70	23	32	55
1965–66	Chicago	69	27	26	53
1966–67	Chicago	69	21	40	61
1967–68	Boston	74	35	49	84
1968–69	Boston	74	49	77	126
1969–70	Boston	76	43	56	99
1970–71	Boston	78	76	76	152
1971–72	Boston	76	66	67	133
1972–73	Boston	78	55	75	130
	Totals	691	398	500	898

Playoffs	Club	GP	G	A	Pts
1963–64	Chicago	4	0	0	0
1964–65	Chicago	13	3	3	6
1965–66	Chicago	6	1	1	2
1966–67	Chicago	6	0	0	0
1967–68	Boston	4	0	3	3
1968–69	Boston	10	8	10	18
1969–70	Boston	14	13	14	27
1970–71	Boston	7	3	7	10
1971–72	Boston	15	9	15	24
1972–73	Boston	2	0	1	1
	Totals	81	37	54	91

All-Star	Club	GP	G	A	Pts
1969	East All-Stars	1	0	0	0
1970	East All-Stars	1	0	0	0
1971	East All-Stars	1	0	0	0
1972	East All-Stars	1	1	0	1
1973	East All-Stars	1	0	1	1
	Totals	5	1	1	2

EVANS, Christopher Bruce   *Defenseman*
b. Toronto, Ont., Sept. 14, 1946

Season	Club	GP	G	A	Pts
1969–70	Toronto M.L.	2	0	0	0
1971–72	Buff–StL B	63	6	18	24
1972–73	St. Louis B.	77	9	12	21
	Totals	142	15	30	45

EVANS (Continued)

Playoffs	Club	GP	G	A	Pts
1971–72	St. Louis B.	7	1	0	1
1972–73	St. Louis B.	5	0	1	1
	Totals	12	1	1	2

EVANS, Claude   *Goalie*
b. Longueuil, Que., Apr. 28, 1933

Season	Club	GP	GA	Sho	AVE
1954–55	Montreal C.	3	12	0	4.00
1957–58	Boston	1	4	0	4.00
	Totals	4	16	0	4.00

EVANS, Stewart   *Defenseman*
b. Ottawa, Ont., June 19, 1908

Season	Club	GP	G	A	Pts
1930–31	Detroit F.	--	1	4	5
1932–33	Detroit F.	--	2	6	8
1933–34	Det RW–Mont M	--	4	2	6
1934–35	Montreal M.	--	5	7	12
1935–36	Montreal M.	--	3	5	8
1936–37	Montreal M.	--	6	7	13
1937–38	Montreal M.	--	5	11	16
1938–39	Montreal C.	--	2	7	9
	Totals	--	28	49	77

Playoffs	Club	GP	G	A	Pts
1932–33	Detroit F.	--	0	0	0
1933–34	Montreal M.	--	0	0	0
1934–35	Montreal M.	--	0	0	0
1935–36	Montreal M.	--	0	0	0
1936–37	Montreal M.	--	0	0	0
1938–39	Montreal C.	--	0	0	0
	Totals	--	0	0	0

EVANS, William John (Jack and Tex)
Defenseman
b. Garnant, South Wales, Apr. 21, 1928

Season	Club	GP	G	A	Pts
1948–49	New York R.	3	0	0	0
1949–50	New York R.	2	0	0	0
1950–51	New York R.	49	1	0	1
1951–52	New York R.	52	1	6	7
1953–54	New York R.	44	4	4	8
1954–55	New York R.	47	0	5	5
1955–56	New York R.	70	2	9	11
1956–57	New York R.	70	3	6	9
1957–58	New York R.	70	4	8	12
1958–59	Chicago	70	1	8	9
1959–60	Chicago	68	0	4	4
1960–61	Chicago	69	0	8	8
1961–62	Chicago	70	3	14	17
1962–63	Chicago	68	0	8	8
	Totals	752	19	80	99

EVANS *(Continued)*

Playoffs	Club	GP	G	A	Pts
1955-56	New York R.	5	1	0	1
1956-57	New York R.	5	0	1	1
1957-58	New York R.	6	0	0	0
1958-59	Chicago	6	0	0	0
1959-60	Chicago	4	0	0	0
1960-61	Chicago	12	1	1	2
1961-62	Chicago	12	0	0	0
1962-63	Chicago	6	0	0	0
	Totals	56	2	2	4

All-Star

1961	Chicago	1	0	0	0

EZINICKI, William *Forward*
b. Winnipeg, Man., Mar. 11, 1924

Season	Club	GP	G	A	Pts
1944-45	Toronto M.L.	8	1	4	5
1945-46	Toronto M.L.	24	4	8	12
1946-47	Toronto M.L.	60	17	20	37
1947-48	Toronto M.L.	60	11	20	31
1948-49	Toronto M.L.	52	13	15	28
1949-50	Toronto M.L.	67	10	12	22
1950-51	Boston	53	16	19	35
1951-52	Boston	28	5	5	10
1954-55	New York R.	16	2	2	4
	Totals	368	79	105	184

Playoffs

1946-47	Toronto M.L.	11	0	2	2
1947-48	Toronto M.L.	9	3	1	4
1948-49	Toronto M.L.	9	1	4	5
1949-50	Toronto M.L.	5	0	0	0
1950-51	Boston	6	1	1	2
	Totals	40	5	8	13

All-Star

1947	Toronto M.L.	1	1	1	2
1948	Toronto M.L.	1	0	0	0
	Totals	2	1	1	2

FAHEY, John Trevor *Forward*
b. New Waterford, N.S., Jan. 4, 1944

Season	Club	GP	G	A	Pts
1964-65	New York R.	1	0	0	0

FAIRBAIRN, William John (Bill) *Forward*
b. Brandon, Man., Jan. 7, 1947

Season	Club	GP	G	A	Pts
1968-69	New York R.	1	0	0	0
1969-70	New York R.	76	23	33	56
1970-71	New York R.	56	7	23	30
1971-72	New York R.	78	22	37	59
1972-73	New York R.	78	30	33	63
	Totals	289	82	126	208

FAIRBAIRN *(Continued)*

Playoffs	Club	GP	G	A	Pts
1969-70	New York R.	6	0	1	1
1970-71	New York R.	4	0	0	0
1971-72	New York R.	16	5	7	12
1972-73	New York R.	10	1	8	9
	Totals	36	6	16	22

FALKENBERG, Robert Arthur *Defenseman*
b. Stettler, Alta., Jan. 1, 1946

Season	Club	GP	G	A	Pts
1966-67	Detroit R.W.	16	1	1	2
1967-68	Detroit R.W.	20	0	3	3
1968-69	Detroit R.W.	5	0	0	0
1970-71	Detroit R.W.	9	0	1	1
1971-72	Detroit R.W.	4	0	0	0
	Totals	54	1	5	6

FARR, Norman Richard (Rocky) *Goalie*
b. Toronto, Ont., Apr. 7, 1947

Season	Club	GP	GA	Sho	AVE
1972-73	Buffalo	½	3	0	6.00

FARRANT, Walter (Whitey) *Forward*
b. Toronto, Ont., Aug. 12, 1913

Season	Club	GP	G	A	Pts
1943-44	Chicago	1	0	0	0

FASHOWAY, Gordon *Forward*
b. Portage la Prairie, Man., June 16, 1926

Season	Club	GP	G	A	Pts
1950-51	Chicago	13	3	2	5

FAULKNER, Alexander Selm *Forward*
b. Bishops Falls, Nfld., May 21, 1936

Season	Club	GP	G	A	Pts
1961-62	Toronto M.L.	1	0	0	0
1962-63	Detroit R.W.	70	10	10	20
1963-64	Detroit R.W.	30	5	7	12
	Totals	101	15	17	32

Playoffs

1962-63	Detroit R.W.	8	5	0	5
1963-64	Detroit R.W.	4	0	0	0
	Totals	12	5	0	5

FAVELL, Douglas *Goalie*
b. St. Catherines, Ont., Apr. 5, 1945

Season	Club	GP	GA	Sho	AVE
1967-68	Philadelphia F.	37	83	4	2.24
1968-69	Philadelphia F.	20	71	1	3.55
1969-70	Philadelphia F.	13⅔	43	1	3.15
1970-71	Philadelphia F.	40⅔	108	2	2.66
1971-72	Philadelphia F.	50	140	5	2.80
1972-73	Philadelphia F.	40⅓	114	3	2.83
	Totals	201⅔	559	16	2.78

FAVELL (Continued)

Playoffs	Club	GP	GA	Sho	AVE
1967–68	Philadelphia F.	2	8	0	4.00
1968–69	Philadelphia F.	1	5	0	5.00
1970–71	Philadelphia F.	2	8	0	4.00
1972–73	Philadelphia F.	11	29	1	2.60
	Totals	16	50	1	3.12

FEATHERSTONE, Anthony James Forward
b. Toronto, Ont., July 31, 1949

Season	Club	GP	G	A	Pts
1969–70	Oakland	9	0	1	1
1970–71	California	67	8	8	16
	Totals	76	8	9	17

Playoffs	Club	GP	G	A	Pts
1969–70	Oakland	2	0	0	0

FERGUSON, George Forward
b. Trenton, Ont., Aug. 22, 1952

Season	Club	GP	G	A	Pts
1972–73	Toronto M.L.	72	10	13	23

FERGUSON, John Bowie Forward
b. Vancouver, B.C., Sept. 5, 1938

Season	Club	GP	G	A	Pts
1963–64	Montreal C.	59	18	27	45
1964–65	Montreal C.	69	17	27	44
1965–66	Montreal C.	65	11	14	25
1966–67	Montreal C.	67	20	22	42
1967–68	Montreal C.	61	15	18	33
1968–69	Montreal C.	71	29	23	52
1969–70	Montreal C.	48	19	13	32
1970–71	Montreal C.	60	16	14	30
	Totals	500	145	158	303

Playoffs	Club	GP	G	A	Pts
1963–64	Montreal C.	7	0	1	1
1964–65	Montreal C.	13	3	1	4
1965–66	Montreal C.	10	2	0	2
1966–67	Montreal C.	10	4	2	6
1967–68	Montreal C.	13	3	5	8
1968–69	Montreal C.	14	4	3	7
1970–71	Montreal C.	18	4	6	10
	Totals	85	20	18	38

All-Star					
1965	Montreal C.	1	0	0	0
1967	Montreal C.	1	2	0	2
	Totals	2	2	0	2

FERGUSON, Lorne Robert Forward
b. Palmerston, Ont., May 26, 1930

Season	Club	GP	G	A	Pts
1949–50	Boston	3	1	1	2
1950–51	Boston	70	16	17	33
1951–52	Boston	27	3	4	7

FERGUSON (Continued)

Season	Club	GP	G	A	Pts
1954–55	Boston	69	20	14	34
1955–56	Bos-Det RW	63	15	12	27
1956–57	Detroit R.W.	70	13	10	23
1957–58	Det RW–Chgo	53	7	12	19
1958–59	Chicago	67	7	10	17
	Totals	422	82	80	162

Playoffs	Club	GP	G	A	Pts
1950–51	Boston	6	1	0	1
1954–55	Boston	4	1	0	1
1955–56	Detroit R.W.	10	1	2	3
1956–57	Detroit R.W.	5	1	0	1
1958–59	Chicago	6	2	1	3
	Totals	31	6	3	9

FERGUSON, Norman Gerald Forward
b. Sydney, N.S., Oct. 16, 1945

Season	Club	GP	G	A	Pts
1968–69	Oakland	76	34	20	54
1969–70	Oakland	72	11	9	20
1970–71	California	54	14	17	31
1971–72	California	77	14	20	34
	Totals	279	73	66	139

Playoffs	Club	GP	G	A	Pts
1968–69	Oakland	7	1	4	5
1969–70	Oakland	3	0	0	0
	Totals	10	1	4	5

FIELD, Wilfred Spence Defenseman
b. Winnipeg, Man., Apr. 29, 1915

Season	Club	GP	G	A	Pts
1938–39	New York A.	--	1	3	4
1939–40	New York A.	--	1	3	4
1940–41	New York A.	--	5	6	11
1941–42	Brooklyn A.	41	6	9	15
1944–45	Mont C–Chgo	48	4	4	8
	Totals	--	17	25	42

Playoffs	Club	GP	G	A	Pts
1939–40	New York A.	3	0	0	0

FIELDER, Guyle Abner Forward
b. Potlach, Idaho, Nov. 21, 1930

Season	Club	GP	G	A	Pts
1950–51	Chicago	3	0	0	0
1957–58	Detroit R.W.	6	0	0	0
	Totals	9	0	0	0

Playoffs	Club	GP	G	A	Pts
1953–54	Boston	2	0	0	0

FILLION, Marcel Forward
b. Thetford Mines, Que., May 28, 1923

Season	Club	GP	G	A	Pts
1944–45	Boston	1	0	0	0

FILLION, Robert Louis *Forward*
b. Thetford Mines, Que., July 12, 1921

Season	Club	GP	G	A	Pts
1943-44	Montreal C.	41	7	23	30
1944-45	Montreal C.	31	6	8	14
1945-46	Montreal C.	50	10	6	16
1946-47	Montreal C.	57	6	3	9
1947-48	Montreal C.	32	9	9	18
1948-49	Montreal C.	59	3	9	12
	Totals	270	41	58	99
Playoffs					
1943-44	Montreal C.	3	0	0	0
1944-45	Montreal C.	1	3	0	3
1945-46	Montreal C.	9	4	3	7
1946-47	Montreal C.	8	0	0	0
1948-49	Montreal C.	7	0	1	1
	Totals	28	7	4	11

FILMORE, Thomas *Forward*
b. Thamesford, Ont., 1906

Season	Club	GP	G	A	Pts
1930-31	Detroit F.	--	6	2	8
1931-32	Det F-NY A	--	8	6	14
1932-33	New York A.	--	1	4	5
	Totals	--	15	12	27

FINKBEINER, Lloyd *Forward*
b. Guelph, Ont., Mar. 12, 1920

Season	Club	GP	G	A	Pts
1940-41	New York A.	--	0	0	0

FINNEY, Joseph Sidney (Sid) *Forward*
b. Banbridge, Ireland, May 1, 1929

Season	Club	GP	G	A	Pts
1951-52	Chicago	35	6	5	11
1952-53	Chicago	18	4	2	6
1953-54	Chicago	6	0	0	0
	Totals	59	10	7	17
Playoffs					
1952-53	Chicago	7	0	2	2

FINNIGAN, Edward *Forward*
b. Shawville, Que.

Season	Club	GP	G	A	Pts
1934-35	St. Louis E.	--	1	1	2

FINNIGAN, Frank *Forward*
b. Shawville, Que., July 9, 1903

Season	Club	GP	G	A	Pts
1923-24	Ottawa	4	0	0	0
1924-25	Ottawa	29	0	0	0
1925-26	Ottawa	36	2	0	2
1926-27	Ottawa	--	15	1	16

FINNIGAN *(Continued)*

Season	Club	GP	G	A	Pts
1927-28	Ottawa	--	20	5	25
1928-29	Ottawa	--	15	4	19
1929-30	Ottawa	--	21	15	36
1930-31	Ottawa	--	9	8	17
1931-32	Toronto M.L.	--	8	13	21
1932-33	Ottawa	--	4	14	18
1933-34	Ottawa	--	10	10	20
1934-35	StL E-Tor ML	--	7	5	12
1935-36	Toronto M.L.	--	2	6	8
1936-37	Toronto M.L.	--	2	7	9
	Totals	--	115	88	203
Playoffs					
1923-24	Ottawa	--	0	0	0
1925-26	Ottawa	--	0	0	0
1926-27	Ottawa	--	3	0	3
1927-28	Ottawa	--	0	1	1
1929-30	Ottawa	--	0	0	0
1931-32	Toronto M.L.	--	2	3	5
1934-35	Toronto M.L.	--	1	2	3
1935-36	Toronto M.L.	--	0	3	3
1936-37	Toronto M.L.	--	0	0	0
	Totals	--	6	9	15

FISHER, Alvin *Forward*

Season	Club	GP	G	A	Pts
1924-25	Toronto St.P.	9	1	0	1

FISHER, Duncan Robert *Forward*
b. Regina, Sask., Aug. 30, 1927

Season	Club	GP	G	A	Pts
1948-49	New York R.	60	9	16	25
1949-50	New York R.	70	12	21	33
1950-51	NY R-Bos	65	9	20	29
1951-52	Boston	65	15	12	27
1952-53	Boston	7	0	1	1
1958-59	Detroit R.W.	8	0	0	0
	Totals	275	45	70	115
Playoffs					
1947-48	New York R.	1	0	1	1
1949-50	New York R.	12	3	3	6
1950-51	Boston	6	1	0	1
1951-52	Boston	2	0	0	0
	Totals	21	4	4	8

FISHER, Joseph *Forward*
b. Medicine Hat, Alta., July 4, 1916

Season	Club	GP	G	A	Pts
1939-40	Detroit R.W.	--	2	4	6
1940-41	Detroit R.W.	--	5	8	13
1941-42	Detroit R.W.	--	0	0	0
	Totals	--	7	12	19

FISHER (Continued)

Playoffs	Club	GP	G	A	Pts
1939-40	Detroit R.W.	5	1	1	2
1940-41	Detroit R.W.	9	1	0	1
1941-42	Detroit R.W.	--	0	0	0
	Totals	--	2	1	3

FITZPATRICK, Alexander Stewart (Sandy)
Forward
   b. Paisley, Scotland, Dec. 22, 1944

Season	Club	GP	G	A	Pts
1964-65	New York R.	4	0	0	0
1967-68	Minnesota	18	3	6	9
	Totals	22	3	6	9
Playoffs					
1967-68	Minnesota	12	0	0	0

FLAMAN, Ferdinand Charles (Fernie)
Defenseman
   b. Dysart, Sask., Jan. 25, 1927

Season	Club	GP	G	A	Pts
1944-45	Boston	1	0	0	0
1945-46	Boston	1	0	0	0
1946-47	Boston	23	1	4	5
1947-48	Boston	56	4	6	10
1948-49	Boston	60	4	12	16
1949-50	Boston	69	2	5	7
1950-51	Bos-Tor ML	53	3	7	10
1951-52	Toronto M.L.	61	0	7	7
1952-53	Toronto M.L.	66	2	6	8
1953-54	Toronto M.L.	62	0	8	8
1954-55	Boston	70	4	14	18
1955-56	Boston	62	4	17	21
1956-57	Boston	68	6	25	31
1957-58	Boston	66	0	15	15
1958-59	Boston	70	0	21	21
1959-60	Boston	60	2	18	20
1960-61	Boston	62	2	9	11
	Totals	910	34	174	208
Playoffs					
1946-47	Boston	5	0	0	0
1947-48	Boston	5	0	0	0
1948-49	Boston	5	0	1	1
1950-51	Toronto M.L.	9	1	0	1
1951-52	Toronto M.L.	4	0	2	2
1953-54	Toronto M.L.	2	0	0	0
1954-55	Boston	4	1	0	1
1956-57	Boston	10	0	3	3
1957-58	Boston	12	2	2	4
1958-59	Boston	7	0	0	0
	Totals	63	4	8	12
All-Star					
1952	NHL 2nd All-Star	1	0	0	0
1955	NHL All-Stars	1	0	0	0

FLAMAN (Continued)

All-Star	Club	GP	G	A	Pts
1956	NHL All-Stars	1	0	0	0
1957	NHL All-Stars	1	0	0	0
1958	NHL All-Stars	1	0	0	0
1959	NHL All-Stars	1	0	0	0
	Totals	6	0	0	0

FLEMING, Reginald Stephen
Defenseman-Forward
   b. Montreal, Que., Apr. 21, 1936

Season	Club	GP	G	A	Pts
1959-60	Montreal C.	3	0	0	0
1960-61	Chicago	66	4	4	8
1961-62	Chicago	70	7	9	16
1962-63	Chicago	64	7	7	14
1963-64	Chicago	61	3	6	9
1964-65	Boston	67	18	23	41
1965-66	Bos-NY R	69	14	20	34
1966-67	New York R.	61	15	16	31
1967-68	New York R.	73	17	7	24
1968-69	New York R.	72	8	12	20
1969-70	Philadelphia F.	65	9	18	27
1970-71	Buffalo	78	6	10	16
	Totals	749	108	132	240
Playoffs					
1960-61	Chicago	12	1	0	1
1961-62	Chicago	12	2	2	4
1962-63	Chicago	6	0	0	0
1963-64	Chicago	7	0	0	0
1966-67	New York R.	4	0	2	2
1967-68	New York R.	6	0	2	2
1968-69	New York R.	3	0	0	0
	Totals	50	3	6	9
All-Star					
1961	Chicago	1	0	0	0

FLESCH *Forward*

Season	Club	GP	G	A	Pts
1920-21	Hamilton	1	0	0	0

FLETT, William Mayer (Cowboy) *Forward*
   b. Vermillion, Alta., July 21, 1943

Season	Club	GP	G	A	Pts
1967-68	Los Angeles	73	26	20	46
1968-69	Los Angeles	72	24	25	49
1969-70	Los Angeles	69	14	18	32
1970-71	Los Angeles	64	13	24	37
1971-72	LA-Phila F	76	18	22	40
1972-73	Philadelphia F.	69	43	31	74
	Totals	423	138	140	278

FLETT (Continued)

Playoffs

	Club	GP	G	A	Pts
1967–68	Los Angeles	7	1	2	3
1968–69	Los Angeles	10	3	4	7
1972–73	Philadelphia F.	11	3	4	7
	Totals	28	7	10	17

All-Star

1971	West All-Stars	1	0	1	1

FOGOLIN, Lidio John (Lee) *Defenseman*
b. Fort William, Ont., Feb. 27, 1926

Season	Club	GP	G	A	Pts
1948–49	Detroit R.W.	43	1	2	3
1949–50	Detroit R.W.	64	4	8	12
1950–51	Det RW–Chgo	54	3	11	14
1951–52	Chicago	69	0	9	9
1952–53	Chicago	70	2	8	10
1953–54	Chicago	68	0	1	1
1954–55	Chicago	9	0	1	1
1955–56	Chicago	51	0	8	8
	Totals	428	10	48	58

Playoffs

1947–48	Detroit R.W.	2	0	1	1
1948–49	Detroit R.W.	9	0	0	0
1949–50	Detroit R.W.	10	0	0	0
1952–53	Chicago	7	0	1	1
	Totals	28	0	2	2

All-Star

1950	Detroit R.W.	1	0	0	0
1951	NHL 1st All-Stars	1	0	0	0
	Totals	1	0	0	0

FOLEY, Gerald James *Forward*
b. Ware, Mass., Sept. 22, 1932

Season	Club	GP	G	A	Pts
1954–55	Toronto M.L.	4	0	0	0
1956–57	New York R.	69	7	9	16
1957–58	New York R.	68	2	5	7
1968–69	Los Angeles	1	0	0	0
	Totals	142	9	14	23

Playoffs

1956–57	New York R.	3	0	0	0
1957–58	New York R.	6	0	1	1
	Totals	9	0	1	1

FOLEY, Gilbert Anthony (Rick) *Defenseman*
b. Niagara Falls, Ont., Sept. 22, 1945

Season	Club	GP	G	A	Pts
1970–71	Chicago	2	0	1	1
1971–72	Philadelphia F.	58	11	25	36
	Totals	60	11	26	37

Playoffs

1970–71	Chicago	4	0	1	1

FOLK, William Joseph *Defenseman*
b. Regina, Sask., July 11, 1927

Season	Club	GP	G	A	Pts
1951–52	Detroit R.W.	4	0	0	0
1952–53	Detroit R.W.	8	0	0	0
	Totals	12	0	0	0

FONTAINE, Leonard Joseph *Forward*
b. Quebec City, Que., Feb. 25, 1948

Season	Club	GP	G	A	Pts
1972–73	Detroit R.W.	39	8	10	18

FONTEYNE, Valere Ronald *Forward*
b. Wetaskiwin, Alta., Dec. 2, 1933

Season	Club	GP	G	A	Pts
1959–60	Detroit R.W.	69	4	7	11
1960–61	Detroit R.W.	66	6	11	17
1961–62	Detroit R.W.	70	5	5	10
1962–63	Detroit R.W.	67	6	14	20
1963–64	New York R.	69	7	18	25
1964–65	NY R–Det RW	43	2	6	8
1965–66	Detroit R.W.	59	5	10	15
1966–67	Detroit R.W.	28	1	1	2
1967–68	Pittsburgh Pe.	69	6	28	34
1968–69	Pittsburgh Pe.	74	12	17	29
1969–70	Pittsburgh Pe.	68	11	15	26
1970–71	Pittsburgh Pe.	70	4	9	13
1971–72	Pittsburgh Pe.	68	6	13	19
	Totals	820	75	154	229

Playoffs

1959–60	Detroit R.W.	6	0	4	4
1960–61	Detroit R.W.	11	2	3	5
1962–63	Detroit R.W.	11	0	0	0
1964–65	Detroit R.W.	5	0	1	1
1965–66	Detroit R.W.	12	1	0	1
1969–70	Pittsburgh Pe.	10	0	2	2
1971–72	Pittsburgh Pe.	4	0	0	0
	Totals	59	3	10	13

FONTINATO, Louis *Defenseman*
b. Guelph, Ont., Jan. 20, 1932

Season	Club	GP	G	A	Pts
1954–55	New York R.	27	2	2	4
1955–56	New York R.	70	3	15	18
1956–57	New York R.	70	3	12	15
1957–58	New York R.	70	3	8	11
1958–59	New York R.	64	7	6	13
1959–60	New York R.	64	2	11	13
1960–61	New York R.	53	2	3	5
1961–62	Montreal C.	55	2	13	15
1962–63	Montreal C.	63	2	6	8
	Totals	536	26	76	102

Playoffs

1955–56	New York R.	4	0	0	0
1956–57	New York R.	5	0	0	0

FONTINATO (Continued)

	Club	GP	G	A	Pts
1957–58	New York R.	6	0	1	1
1961–62	Montreal C.	6	0	1	1
	Totals	21	0	2	2

FORBES, Vernon (Jake) *Goalie*
b. Toronto, Ont.

Season	Club	GP	GA	Sho	AVE
1919–20	Toronto St.P.	5	21	0	4.20
1920–21	Toronto St.P.	20	78	0	3.90
1922–23	Hamilton	24	110	0	4.58
1923–24	Hamilton	24	70	1	2.92
1924–25	Hamilton	30	61	6	2.03
1925–26	New York A.	36	89	2	2.47
1926–27	New York A.	44	91	8	2.07
1927–28	New York A.	16	51	2	3.19
1928–29	New York A.	1	3	0	3.00
1929–30	New York A.	1	1	0	1.00
1930–31	Philadelphia Q.	2	7	0	3.50
1931–32	New York A.	6	16	0	2.67
1932–33	New York A.	1	2	0	2.00
	Totals	210	600	19	2.86

Playoffs

	Club	GP	GA	Sho	AVE
1920–21	Toronto St.P.	2	7	0	3.50

FORSEY, Jack *Forward*

Season	Club	GP	G	A	Pts
1942–43	Toronto M.L.	19	7	9	16

Playoffs

	Club	GP	G	A	Pts
1942–43	Toronto M.L.	3	0	1	1

FORSLAND, Gus *Forward*
b. Fort William, Ont., Apr. 25, 1908

Season	Club	GP	G	A	Pts
1932–33	Ottawa	--	4	9	13

FORTIER, Charles *Forward*

Season	Club	GP	G	A	Pts
1923–24	Montreal C.	1	0	0	0

FORTIER, David Edward *Defenseman*
b. Sudbury, Ont., June 17, 1951

Season	Club	GP	G	A	Pts
1972–73	Toronto M.L.	23	1	4	5

FORTIN, Raymond *Defenseman*
b. Drummondville, Que., Mar. 11, 1941

Season	Club	GP	G	A	Pts
1967–68	St. Louis B.	24	0	2	2
1968–69	St. Louis B.	11	1	0	1
1969–70	St. Louis B.	57	1	4	5
	Totals	92	2	6	8

FORTIN (Continued)

Playoffs	Club	GP	G	A	Pts
1967–68	St. Louis B.	3	0	0	0
1969–70	St. Louis B.	3	0	0	0
	Totals	6	0	0	0

FOSTER, Harry C. (Yip) *Defenseman*
b. Guelph, Ont., Nov. 25, 1907

Season	Club	GP	G	A	Pts
1929–30	New York R.	31	0	0	0
1931–32	Boston	--	1	2	3
1933–34	Detroit R.W.	--	0	0	0
1934–35	Detroit R.W.	--	2	0	2
	Totals	--	3	2	5

FOSTER, Herbert Stanley *Forward*
b. Brockville, Ont., Aug. 9, 1913

Season	Club	GP	G	A	Pts
1940–41	New York R.	4	1	0	1
1947–48	New York R.	1	0	0	0
	Totals	5	1	0	1

FOWLER, James *Defenseman*
b. Toronto, Ont., Apr. 6, 1915

Season	Club	GP	G	A	Pts
1936–37	Toronto M.L.	--	7	11	18
1937–38	Toronto M.L.	--	10	12	22
1938–39	Toronto M.L.	--	1	6	7
	Totals	--	18	29	47

Playoffs

	Club	GP	G	A	Pts
1936–37	Toronto M.L.	--	0	0	0
1937–38	Toronto M.L.	--	0	2	2
1938–39	Toronto M.L.	--	0	1	1
	Totals	--	0	3	3

FOWLER, Norman (Hec) *Goalie*

Season	Club	GP	GA	Sho	AVE
1924–25	Boston	7	43	0	6.14

FOWLER, Thomas *Forward*
b. Winnipeg, Man., May 18, 1924

Season	Club	GP	G	A	Pts
1946–47	Chicago	24	0	1	1

FOYSTON, Frank *Forward*
b. Minesing, Ont., Feb. 1891

Season	Club	GP	G	A	Pts
1926–27	Detroit C.	--	10	5	15
1927–28	Detroit C.	--	7	2	9
	Totals	--	17	7	24

FOYSTON (Continued)

Playoffs	Club	GP	G	A	Pts
1918–19	Seattle (PCHL)	––	9	0	9
1919–20	Seattle (PCHL)	––	5	2	7
1924–25	Victoria (PCHL)	––	1	0	1
1925–26	Victoria (PCHL)	––	0	0	0
	Totals	––	15	2	17

FRAMPTON, Robert Percy James *Forward*
b. Toronto, Ont., Jan. 20, 1929

Season	Club	GP	G	A	Pts
1949–50	Montreal C.	2	0	0	0

Playoffs					
1949–50	Montreal C.	3	0	0	0

FRANCIS, Emile Percy (Cat) *Goalie*
b. North Battleford, Sask., Sept. 13, 1926

Season	Club	GP	GA	Sho	AVE
1946–47	Chicago	19	104	0	5.47
1947–48	Chicago	54	183	1	3.39
1948–49	New York R.	2	4	0	2.00
1949–50	New York R.	1	8	0	8.00
1950–51	New York R.	5	14	0	2.80
1951–52	New York R.	14	42	0	3.00
	Totals	95	355	1	3.74

FRANKS, James Reginald *Goalie*
b. Melville, Sask., Nov. 8, 1914

Season	Club	GP	GA	Sho	AVE
1937–38	Detroit R.W.	1	3	0	3.00
1942–43	New York R.	23	103	0	4.48
1943–44	Det RW–Bos	18	75	1	4.17
	Totals	42	181	1	4.31

Playoffs					
1936–37	Detroit R.W	1	3	0	3.00

FRASER, Jack *Forward*

Season	Club	GP	G	A	Pts
1923–24	Hamilton	1	0	0	0

FRASER, Archibald McKay *Forward*
b. Souris, Man., Feb. 9, 1914

Season	Club	GP	G	A	Pts
1943–44	New York R.	3	0	1	1

FRASER, Gordon *Defenseman*
b. Pembroke, Ont.

Season	Club	GP	G	A	Pts
1926–27	Chicago	––	14	6	20
1927–28	Detroit C.	––	4	2	6
1928–29	Detroit C.	––	0	0	0
1929–30	Mont C–Pitts Pi	––	6	4	10
1930–31	Philadelphia Q.	––	0	0	0
	Totals	––	24	12	36

FRASER (Continued)

Playoffs	Club	GP	G	A	Pts
1924–25	Victoria (PCHL)	––	2	1	3
1925–26	Victoria (PCHL)	––	0	0	0
1926–27	Chicago	––	1	0	1
	Totals	––	3	1	4

FRASER, Harvey *Forward*
b. Souris, Man., Oct. 14, 1918

Season	Club	GP	G	A	Pts
1944–45	Chicago	21	5	4	9

FREDERICK, Raymond *Goalie*
b. Fort Francis, Ont., July 31, 1929

Season	Club	GP	GA	Sho	AVE
1954–55	Chicago	5	22	0	4.40

FREDERICKSON, Frank *Forward*
b. Winnipeg, Man.

Season	Club	GP	G	A	Pts
1926–27	Det C–Bos	––	18	13	31
1927–28	Boston	––	10	4	14
1928–29	Bos–Pitts Pi	––	6	8	14
1929–30	Pittsburgh Pi.	––	4	7	11
1930–31	Detroit F.	––	1	2	3
	Totals	––	39	34	73

Playoffs					
1924–25	Victoria (PCHL)	––	3	2	5
1925–26	Victoria (PCHL)	––	1	1	2
1926–27	Boston	––	2	4	6
1927–28	Boston	––	0	1	1
	Totals	––	6	8	14

FREW, Irvine *Defenseman*
b. Kilsyth, Scotland, Aug. 16, 1907

Season	Club	GP	G	A	Pts
1933–34	Montreal M.	––	2	1	3
1934–35	St. Louis E.	––	0	2	2
1935–36	Montreal C.	––	0	2	2
	Totals	––	2	5	7

Playoffs					
1933–34	Montreal M.	––	0	0	0

FROST, Harry *Forward*
b. Keer Lake, Ont., Aug. 17, 1914

Season	Club	GP	G	A	Pts
1938–39	Boston	––	0	0	0

FRYDAY, Robert George *Forward*
b. Toronto, Ont., Dec. 5, 1928

Season	Club	GP	G	A	Pts
1951–52	Montreal C.	3	0	0	0

FTOREK, Robert Brian (Robbie) *Forward*
b. Boston, Mass., Jan. 2, 1952

Season	Club	GP	G	A	Pts
1972–73	Detroit R.W.	3	0	0	0

GADSBY, William Alexander *Defenseman*
b. Calgary, Alta., Aug. 8, 1927 .

Season	Club	GP	G	A	Pts
1946–47	Chicago	48	8	10	18
1947–48	Chicago	60	6	10	16
1948–49	Chicago	50	3	10	13
1949–50	Chicago	70	10	24	34
1950–51	Chicago	25	3	7	10
1951–52	Chicago	59	7	15	22
1952–53	Chicago	68	2	20	22
1953–54	Chicago	70	12	29	41
1954–55	Chgo–NY R	70	11	13	24
1955–56	New York R.	70	9	42	51
1956–57	New York R.	70	4	37	41
1957–58	New York R.	65	14	32	46
1958–59	New York R.	70	5	46	51
1959–60	New York R.	65	9	22	31
1960–61	New York R.	65	9	26	35
1961–62	Detroit R.W.	70	7	30	37
1962–63	Detroit R.W.	70	4	24	28
1963–64	Detroit R.W.	64	2	16	18
1964–65	Detroit R.W.	61	0	12	12
1965–66	Detroit R.W.	58	5	12	17
	Totals	1248	130	437	567

Playoffs

Season	Club	GP	G	A	Pts
1952–53	Chicago	7	0	1	1
1955–56	New York R.	5	1	3	4
1956–57	New York R.	5	1	2	3
1957–58	New York R.	6	0	3	3
1962–63	Detroit R.W.	11	1	4	5
1963–64	Detroit R.W.	14	0	4	4
1964–65	Detroit R.W.	7	0	3	3
1965–66	Detroit R.W.	12	1	3	4
	Totals	67	4	23	27

All-Star

Season	Club	GP	G	A	Pts
1953	NHL All-Stars	1	0	0	0
1954	NHL All-Stars	1	0	1	1
1956	NHL All-Stars	1	0	0	0
1957	NHL All-Stars	1	0	0	0
1958	NHL All-Stars	1	0	0	0
1959	NHL All-Stars	1	0	0	0
1960	NHL All-Stars	1	0	0	0
1965	NHL All-Stars	1	0	1	1
	Totals	8	0	2	2

GAGNE, Arthur *Forward*

Season	Club	GP	G	A	Pts
1926–27	Montreal C.	--	14	3	17
1927–28	Montreal C.	--	20	10	30

GAGNE *(Continued)*

Season	Club	GP	G	A	Pts
1928–29	Montreal C.	--	7	3	10
1929–30	Bos-Otta	--	6	5	11
1930–31	Ottawa	--	19	11	30
1931–32	Detroit F.	--	1	1	2
	Totals	--	67	33	100

Playoffs

Season	Club	GP	G	A	Pts
1922–23	Edmonton (PCHL)	--	0	0	0
1926–27	Montreal C.	--	0	0	0
1927–28	Montreal C.	--	1	1	2
1928–29	Montreal C.	--	0	0	0
1929–30	Ottawa	--	1	0	1
	Totals	--	2	1	3

GAGNE, Pierre *Forward*
b. North Bay, Ont., June 5, 1940

Season	Club	GP	G	A	Pts
1959–60	Boston	2	0	0	0

GAGNON, Germain *Forward*
b. Chicoutimi, Que., Dec. 9, 1942

Season	Club	GP	G	A	Pts
1971–72	Montreal C.	4	0	0	0
1972–73	New York I.	63	12	29	41
	Totals	67	12	29	41

GAGNON, John (Black Cat) *Forward*
b. Chicoutimi, Que., June 8, 1905

Season	Club	GP	G	A	Pts
1930–31	Montreal C.	--	18	7	25
1931–32	Montreal C.	--	19	18	37
1932–33	Montreal C.	--	12	23	35
1933–34	Montreal C.	--	9	15	24
1934–35	Bos-Mont C	--	2	6	8
1935–36	Montreal C.	--	7	9	16
1936–37	Montreal C.	--	20	16	36
1937–38	Montreal C.	--	13	17	30
1938–39	Montreal C.	--	12	22	34
1939–40	Mont C-NY R	--	8	8	16
	Totals	--	120	141	261

Playoffs

Season	Club	GP	G	A	Pts
1930–31	Montreal C.	--	6	2	8
1931–32	Montreal C.	--	1	1	2
1932–33	Montreal C.	--	0	2	2
1933–34	Montreal C.	--	1	0	1
1934–35	Montreal C.	--	0	1	1
1936–37	Montreal C.	--	2	1	3
1937–38	Montreal C.	--	1	3	4
1938–39	Montreal C.	--	0	2	2
1939–40	New York R.	--	1	0	1
	Totals	--	12	12	24

GAINOR, Norman (Dutch) *Forward*
b. Calgary, Alta., Apr. 10, 1904

Season	Club	GP	G	A	Pts
1927-28	Boston	41	8	4	12
1928-29	Boston	--	14	5	19
1929-30	Boston	--	18	31	49
1930-31	Boston	--	8	3	11
1931-32	New York R.	46	3	9	12
1934-35	Montreal M.	--	0	4	4
	Totals	--	51	56	107

Playoffs

1927-28	Boston	2	0	0	0
1928-29	Boston	5	2	0	2
1929-30	Boston	6	0	0	0
1930-31	Boston	5	0	1	1
1931-32	New York R.	7	0	0	0
1934-35	Montreal M.	9	0	0	0
	Totals	34	2	1	3

GALBRAITH, Percival (Perk) *Forward*
b. Toronto, Ont., 1899

Season	Club	GP	G	A	Pts
1926-27	Boston	--	9	8	17
1927-28	Boston	--	6	5	11
1928-29	Boston	--	2	1	3
1929-30	Boston	--	7	9	16
1930-31	Boston	--	2	3	5
1931-32	Boston	--	2	1	3
1932-33	Boston	--	1	2	3
1933-34	Boston	--	2	0	2
	Totals	--	31	29	60

Playoffs

1926-27	Boston	--	3	3	6
1927-28	Boston	--	0	1	1
1928-29	Boston	--	0	0	0
1929-30	Boston	--	1	3	4
1930-31	Boston	--	0	0	0
1932-33	Boston	--	0	0	0
	Totals	--	4	7	11

GALLAGHER, John *Defenseman*
b. Kenora, Ont., Jan. 19, 1909

Season	Club	GP	G	A	Pts
1930-31	Montreal M.	--	4	2	6
1931-32	Montreal M.	--	1	0	1
1932-33	Mont M-Det F	--	4	6	10
1936-37	Det RW-NY A	--	1	0	1
1937-38	New York A.	--	3	6	9
1938-39	New York A.	--	1	5	6
	Totals	--	14	19	33

Playoffs

1930-31	Montreal M.	--	0	0	0
1931-32	Montreal M.	--	0	0	0

GALLAGHER *(Continued)*

Playoffs	Club	GP	G	A	Pts
1932-33	Detroit F.	--	1	1	2
1936-37	New York A.	--	1	0	1
1937-38	New York A.	--	0	2	2
1938-39	New York A.	--	0	0	0
	Totals	--	2	3	5

GALLINGER, Donald Calvin *Forward*
b. Port Colborne, Ont., Apr. 10, 1925

Season	Club	GP	G	A	Pts
1942-43	Boston	48	14	20	34
1943-44	Boston	23	13	5	18
1945-46	Boston	50	17	23	40
1946-47	Boston	47	11	19	30
1947-48	Boston	54	10	21	31
	Totals	222	65	88	153

Playoffs

1942-43	Boston	9	3	1	4
1945-46	Boston	10	2	4	6
1946-47	Boston	4	0	0	0
	Totals	23	5	5	10

GAMBLE, Bruce George *Goalie*
b. Port Arthur, Ont., May 24, 1938

Season	Club	GP	GA	Sho	AVE
1958-59	New York R.	2	6	0	3.00
1960-61	Boston	52	195	0	3.75
1961-62	Boston	28	123	1	4.39
1965-66	Toronto M.L.	8⅓	21	4	2.52
1966-67	Toronto M.L.	19⅔	67	0	3.41
1967-68	Toronto M.L.	36⅔	85	5	2.31
1968-69	Toronto M.L.	57⅔	161	3	2.79
1969-70	Toronto M.L.	51	156	5	3.06
1970-71	Tor ML-Phila F	32⅓	120	2	3.78
1971-72	Philadelphia F.	19⅔	58	2	2.94
	Totals	307⅓	992	22	3.23

Playoffs

1968-69	Toronto M.L.	1⅓	13	0	9.09
1970-71	Philadelphia F.	2	12	0	6.00
	Totals	3⅓	25	0	7.29

GAMBLE, Richard Frank *Forward*
b. Moncton, N.B., Nov. 16, 1928

Season	Club	GP	G	A	Pts
1950-51	Montreal C.	1	0	0	0
1951-52	Montreal C.	64	23	17	40
1952-53	Montreal C.	69	11	13	24
1953-54	Montreal C.	32	4	8	12
1954-55	Chgo-Mont C	14	2	0	2
1955-56	Montreal C.	12	0	3	3
1965-66	Toronto M.L.	2	1	0	1
1966-67	Toronto M.L.	1	0	0	0
	Totals	195	41	41	82

472

GAMBLE (Continued)

Playoffs	Club	GP	G	A	Pts
1951–52	Montreal C.	7	0	2	2
1952–53	Montreal C.	5	1	0	1
1954–55	Montreal C.	2	0	0	0
	Totals	14	1	2	3

All-Star

1953	Montreal C.	1	0	0	0

GAMBUCCI, Gary Allan *Forward*
b. Hibbing, Minn., Sept. 27, 1946

Season	Club	GP	G	A	Pts
1971–72	Minnesota	9	1	0	1

GARDINER, Charles Robert (Chuck) *Goalie*
b. Edinburgh, Scotland, Dec. 31 1904

Season	Club	GP	GA	Sho	AVE
1927–28	Chicago	40	114	3	2.85
1928–29	Chicago	44	85	6	1.93
1929–30	Chicago	44	111	3	2.52
1930–31	Chicago	44	78	12	1.77
1931–32	Chicago	48	101	4	2.10
1932–33	Chicago	48	101	5	2.10
1933–34	Chicago	48	83	10	1.73
	Totals	316	673	43	2.13

Playoffs

1929–30	Chicago	2	3	0	1.50
1930–31	Chicago	9	14	2	1.55
1931–32	Chicago	2	6	1	3.00
1933–34	Chicago	8	12	2	1.50
	Totals	21	35	5	1.67

GARDINER, Herbert Martin *Defenseman*
b. Winnipeg, Man., May 1891

Season	Club	GP	G	A	Pts
1926–27	Montreal C.	--	6	6	12
1927–28	Montreal C.	--	4	3	7
	Totals	--	10	9	19

Playoffs

1923–24	Calgary (PCHL)	--	1	0	1
1926–27	Montreal C.	--	0	0	0
1927–28	Montreal C.	--	0	1	1
1928–29	Montreal C.	--	0	0	0
	Totals	--	1	1	2

GARDINER, Wilbert (Bert) *Goalie*
b. Saskatoon, Sask., Mar. 25, 1913

Season	Club	GP	GA	Sho	AVE
1935–36	New York R.	1	1	0	1.00
1940–41	Montreal C.	42	119	2	2.83
1941–42	Montreal C.	10	42	0	4.20
1942–43	Chicago	50	180	1	3.60
1943–44	Boston	41	212	1	5.17
	Totals	144	554	4	3.85

GARDINER (Continued)

Playoffs	Club	GP	GA	Sho	AVE
1938–39	New York R.	6	12	0	2.00
1940–41	Montreal C.	3	8	0	2.67
	Totals	9	20	0	2.22

GARDNER, Calvin Pearly *Forward*
b. Transcona, Man., Oct. 30, 1924

Season	Club	GP	G	A	Pts
1945–46	New York R.	16	8	2	10
1946–47	New York R.	52	13	16	29
1947–48	New York R.	58	7	18	25
1948–49	Toronto M.L.	53	13	22	35
1949–50	Toronto M.L.	30	7	19	26
1950–51	Toronto M.L.	66	23	28	51
1951–52	Toronto M.L.	70	15	26	41
1952–53	Chicago	70	11	24	35
1953–54	Boston	70	14	20	34
1954–55	Boston	70	16	22	38
1955–56	Boston	70	15	21	36
1956–57	Boston	70	12	20	32
	Totals	695	154	238	392

Playoffs

1947–48	New York R.	5	0	0	0
1948–49	Toronto M.L.	9	2	5	7
1949–50	Toronto M.L.	7	1	0	1
1950–51	Toronto M.L.	11	1	1	2
1951–52	Toronto M.L.	3	0	0	0
1952–53	Chicago	7	0	2	2
1953–54	Boston	4	1	1	2
1954–55	Boston	5	0	0	0
1956–57	Boston	10	2	1	3
	Totals	61	7	10	17

All-Star

1948	Toronto M.L.	1	0	0	0
1949	Toronto M.L.	1	0	1	1
	Totals	2	0	1	1

GARDNER, Dave *Forward*
b. Toronto, Ont., Aug. 23, 1952

Season	Club	GP	G	A	Pts
1972–73	Montreal C.	5	1	1	2

GARDNER, George Edward *Goalie*
b. Lachine, Que., Oct. 8, 1942

Season	Club	GP	GA	Sho	AVE
1965–66	Detroit R.W.	1	1	0	1.00
1966–67	Detroit R.W.	9⅓	36	0	3.86
1967–68	Detroit R.W.	9	32	0	3.56
1970–71	Vancouver	15⅓	52	0	3.38
1971–72	Vancouver	20⅔	86	0	4.17
	Totals	55⅓	207	0	3.75

GARIEPY, Raymond *Defenseman*
b. Toronto, Ont., Sept. 4, 1928

Season	Club	GP	G	A	Pts
1953-54	Boston	35	1	6	7
1955-56	Toronto M.L.	1	0	0	0
	Totals	36	1	6	7

GARRETT, Dudley (Red) *Defenseman*
b. Toronto, Ont., July 24, 1924

Season	Club	GP	G	A	Pts
1942-43	New York R.	23	1	1	2

GATHERUM, David L. *Goalie*
b. Fort William, Ont., Mar. 28, 1932

Season	Club	GP	GA	Sho	AVE
1953-54	Detroit R.W.	3	3	1	1.00

GAUDREAULT, Armand Gerard *Forward*
b. Lake St. John, Que., July 14, 1921

Season	Club	GP	G	A	Pts
1944-45	Boston	44	15	9	24
Playoffs					
1944-45	Boston	7	0	2	2

GAUDREAULT, Leo *Forward*
b. Chicoutimi, Que.

Season	Club	GP	G	A	Pts
1927-28	Montreal C.	--	6	2	8
1928-29	Montreal C.	--	0	0	0
1932-33	Montreal C.	--	2	2	4
	Totals	--	8	4	12
Playoffs					
1927-28	Montreal C.	--	0	0	0
1928-29	Montreal C.	--	0	0	0
1932-33	Montreal C.	--	0	0	0
	Totals	--	0	0	0

GAUTHIER, Jean Phillipe *Defenseman*
b. Montreal, Que., Apr. 29, 1937

Season	Club	GP	G	A	Pts
1960-61	Montreal C.	4	0	1	1
1961-62	Montreal C.	12	0	1	1
1962-63	Montreal C.	65	1	17	18
1963-64	Montreal C.	1	0	0	0
1965-66	Montreal C.	2	0	0	0
1966-67	Montreal C.	2	0	0	0
1967-68	Philadelphia F.	65	5	7	12
1968-69	Boston	11	0	2	2
1969-70	Montreal C.	4	0	0	0
	Totals	166	6	28	34
Playoffs					
1962-63	Montreal C.	5	0	0	0
1964-65	Montreal C.	2	0	0	0
1967-68	Philadelphia F.	7	1	3	4
	Totals	14	1	3	4

GAUTHIER, Paul *Goalie*
b. Winnipeg, Man.

Season	Club	GP	GA	Sho	AVE
1937-38	Montreal C.	1	2	0	2.00

GAUTHIER, Rene Fernand (Fern) *Forward*
b. Chicoutimi, Que., Aug. 31, 1919

Season	Club	GP	G	A	Pts
1943-44	New York R.	33	14	10	24
1944-45	Montreal C.	50	18	13	31
1945-46	Detroit R.W.	30	9	8	17
1946-47	Detroit R.W.	40	1	12	13
1947-48	Detroit R.W.	35	1	5	6
1948-49	Detroit R.W.	41	3	2	5
	Totals	229	46	50	96
Playoffs					
1944-45	Montreal C.	4	0	0	0
1945-46	Detroit R.W.	5	3	0	3
1946-47	Detroit R.W.	3	1	0	1
1947-48	Detroit R.W.	10	1	1	2
	Totals	22	5	1	6

GEE, George *Forward*
b. Stratford, Ont., June 28, 1922

Season	Club	GP	G	A	Pts
1945-46	Chicago	35	14	15	29
1946-47	Chicago	60	20	20	40
1947-48	Chicago	60	14	25	39
1948-49	Chgo-Det RW	51	7	14	21
1949-50	Detroit R.W.	69	17	21	38
1950-51	Detroit R.W.	70	17	20	37
1951-52	Chicago	70	18	31	49
1952-53	Chicago	67	18	21	39
1953-54	Chicago	69	10	16	26
	Totals	551	135	183	318
Playoffs					
1945-46	Chicago	4	1	1	2
1948-49	Detroit R.W.	10	1	3	4
1949-50	Detroit R.W.	14	3	6	9
1950-51	Detroit R.W.	6	0	1	1
1952-53	Chicago	7	1	2	3
	Totals	41	6	13	19
All-Star					
1950	Detroit R.W.	1	0	0	0

GELDART, Gary Daniel *Defenseman*
b. Moncton, N.B., June 14, 1950

Season	Club	GP	G	A	Pts
1970-71	Minnesota	4	0	0	0

GELINEAU, John Edward (Jack) *Goalie*
b. Toronto, Ont., Nov. 11, 1924

Season	Club	GP	GA	Sho	AVE
1948-49	Boston	4	12	0	3.00
1949-50	Boston	67	220	3	3.28

GELINEAU (Continued)

Season	Club	GP	GA	Sho	AVE
1950–51	Boston	70	197	4	2.81
1953–54	Chicago	2	18	0	9.00
	Totals	143	447	7	3.13
Playoffs					
1950–51	Boston	4	7	1	1.75

GENDRON, Jean Guy (Smitty) *Forward*
b. Montreal, Que., Aug. 30, 1934

Season	Club	GP	G	A	Pts
1955–56	New York R.	63	5	7	12
1956–57	New York R.	70	9	6	15
1957–58	New York R.	70	10	17	27
1958–59	Boston	60	15	9	24
1959–60	Boston	67	24	11	35
1960–61	Bos-Mont C	66	10	19	29
1961–62	New York R.	69	14	11	25
1962–63	Boston	66	21	22	43
1963–64	Boston	54	5	13	18
1967–68	Philadelphia F.	1	0	1	1
1968–69	Philadelphia F.	74	20	35	55
1969–70	Philadelphia F.	71	23	21	44
1970–71	Philadelphia F.	76	20	16	36
1971–72	Philadelphia F.	56	6	13	19
	Totals	859	182	201	383
Playoffs					
1955–56	New York R.	5	2	1	3
1956–57	New York R.	5	0	1	1
1957–58	New York R.	6	1	0	1
1958–59	Boston	7	1	0	1
1960–61	Montreal C.	5	0	0	0
1961–62	New York R.	6	3	1	4
1968–69	Philadelphia F.	4	0	0	0
1970–71	Philadelphia F.	4	0	1	1
	Totals	42	7	4	11

GEOFFRION, Bernard (Boom-Boom and Boomer) *Forward*
b. Montreal, Que., Feb. 14, 1931

Season	Club	GP	G	A	Pts
1950–51	Montreal C.	18	8	6	14
1951–52	Montreal C.	67	30	24	54
1952–53	Montreal C.	65	22	17	39
1953–54	Montreal C.	54	29	25	54
1954–55	Montreal C.	70	38	37	75
1955–56	Montreal C.	59	29	33	62
1956–57	Montreal C.	41	19	21	40
1957–58	Montreal C.	42	27	23	50
1958–59	Montreal C.	59	22	44	66
1959–60	Montreal C.	59	30	41	71
1960–61	Montreal C.	64	50	45	95
1961–62	Montreal C.	62	23	36	59
1962–63	Montreal C.	51	23	18	41

GEOFFRION (Continued)

Season	Club	GP	G	A	Pts
1963–64	Montreal C.	55	21	18	39
1966–67	New York R.	58	17	25	42
1967–68	New York R.	59	5	16	21
	Totals	883	393	429	822
Playoffs					
1950–51	Montreal C.	11	1	1	2
1951–52	Montreal C.	11	3	1	4
1952–53	Montreal C.	12	6	4	10
1953–54	Montreal C.	11	6	5	11
1954–55	Montreal C.	12	8	5	13
1955–56	Montreal C.	10	5	9	14
1956–57	Montreal C.	10	11	7	18
1957–58	Montreal C.	10	6	5	11
1958–59	Montreal C.	11	5	8	13
1959–60	Montreal C.	8	2	10	12
1960–61	Montreal C.	4	2	1	3
1961–62	Montreal C.	5	0	1	1
1962–63	Montreal C.	5	0	1	1
1963–64	Montreal C.	7	1	1	2
1966–67	New York R.	4	2	0	2
1967–68	New York R.	1	0	1	1
	Totals	132	58	60	118
All-Star					
1952	NHL 2nd All-Stars	1	0	0	0
1953	Montreal C.	1	0	0	0
1954	NHL All-Stars	1	0	0	0
1955	NHL All-Stars	1	0	0	0
1956	Montreal C.	1	0	0	0
1958	Montreal C.	1	1	0	1
1959	Montreal C.	1	0	1	1
1960	Montreal C.	1	0	0	0
1961	NHL All-Stars	1	0	0	0
1962	NHL All-Stars	1	0	0	0
1963	NHL All-Stars	1	0	1	1
	Totals	11	1	2	3

GERAN, George Pierce (Jerry) *Forward*
b. Holyoke, Mass., Aug. 3, 1896

Season	Club	GP	G	A	Pts
1917–18	Montreal W.	4	0	0	0
1925–26	Boston	33	5	1	6
	Totals	37	5	1	6

GERARD, Edward *Defenseman*
b. Ottawa, Ont., 1892

Season	Club	GP	G	A	Pts
1917–18	Ottawa	21	13	0	13
1918–19	Ottawa	18	4	6	10
1919–20	Ottawa	21	9	3	12
1920–21	Ottawa	24	11	4	15
1921–22	Ottawa	21	7	9	16
1922–23	Ottawa	23	6	8	14
	Totals	128	50	30	80

GERARD (Continued)

Playoffs	Club	GP	G	A	Pts
1918–19	Ottawa	--	3	0	3
1919–20	Ottawa	--	2	1	3
1920–21	Ottawa	--	1	0	1
1921–22	Ottawa	--	0	0	0
1922–23	Ottawa	--	1	0	1
	Totals	--	7	1	8

GETLIFFE, Raymond *Forward*
b. Galt, Ont., Apr. 3, 1914

Season	Club	GP	G	A	Pts
1935–36	Boston	--	0	0	0
1936–37	Boston	--	16	15	31
1937–38	Boston	--	11	13	24
1938–39	Boston	--	10	12	22
1939–40	Montreal C.	--	11	12	23
1940–41	Montreal C.	--	15	10	25
1941–42	Montreal C.	--	11	15	26
1942–43	Montreal C.	50	18	28	46
1943–44	Montreal C.	44	28	25	53
1944–45	Montreal C.	41	16	7	23
	Totals	--	136	137	273
Playoffs					
1936–37	Boston	--	2	1	3
1937–38	Boston	--	0	1	1
1938–39	Boston	--	1	1	2
1940–41	Montreal C.	--	1	1	2
1941–42	Montreal C.	--	0	0	0
1942–43	Montreal C.	5	0	1	1
1943–44	Montreal C.	9	5	4	9
1944–45	Montreal C.	6	0	1	1
	Totals	--	9	10	19

GIACOMIN, Edward *Goalie*
b. Sudbury, Ont., June 6, 1939

Season	Club	GP	GA	Sho	AVE
1965–66	New York R.	35	128	0	3.66
1966–67	New York R.	66⅓	173	9	2.61
1967–68	New York R.	65⅔	160	8	2.44
1968–69	New York R.	69	175	7	2.54
1969–70	New York R.	69	163	6	2.35
1970–71	New York R.	44	95	8	2.15
1971–72	New York R.	42½	115	1	2.70
1972–73	New York R.	43	125	4	2.91
	Totals	434½	1134	43	2.63
Playoffs					
1966–67	New York R.	4	14	0	3.50
1967–68	New York R.	6	18	0	3.00
1968–69	New York R.	3	10	0	3.33
1969–70	New York R.	4⅔	19	0	4.13
1970–71	New York R.	12	28	0	2.21
1971–72	New York R.	10	27	0	2.70
1972–73	New York R.	9⅓	23	1	2.56
	Totals	49	139	1	2.82

GIACOMIN (Continued)

All-Star		GP	Per	GA	AGP
1967	NHL All-Stars	1	1	1	1.00
1968	NHL All-Stars	1	1	1	1.00
1969	East All-Stars	1	1½	2	1.33
1970	East All-Stars	1	1½	1	0.67
1971	East All-Stars	1	1½	2	1.33
1973	East All-Stars	1	1½	3	1.50
	Totals	6	8	10	1.25

GIBBS, Barry Paul *Defenseman*
b. Lloydminster, Sask., Sept. 28, 1948

Season	Club	GP	G	A	Pts
1967–68	Boston	16	0	0	0
1968–69	Boston	8	0	0	0
1969–70	Minnesota	56	3	13	16
1970–71	Minnesota	68	5	15	20
1971–72	Minnesota	75	4	20	24
1972–73	Minnesota	63	10	24	34
	Totals	286	22	72	94
Playoffs					
1969–70	Minnesota	6	1	0	1
1970–71	Minnesota	12	0	1	1
1971–72	Minnesota	7	1	1	2
1972–73	Minnesota	6	1	0	1
	Totals	31	3	2	5
All-Star					
1973	West All-Stars	1	0	0	0

GIESEBRECHT, Roy (Gus) *Forward*
b. Petawawa, Ont., Sept. 14, 1918

Season	Club	GP	G	A	Pts
1938–39	Detroit R.W.	--	10	10	20
1939–40	Detroit R.W.	--	4	7	11
1940–41	Detroit R.W.	--	7	18	25
1941–42	Detroit R.W.	34	6	16	22
	Totals	--	27	51	78
Playoffs					
1938–39	Detroit R.W.	6	0	2	2
1940–41	Detroit R.W.	9	2	1	3
	Totals	15	2	3	5

GILBERT, Gilles Joseph *Goalie*
b. St. Esprit, Que., Mar. 31, 1949

Season	Club	GP	GA	Sho	AVE
1969–70	Minnesota	1	6	0	6.00
1970–71	Minnesota	15½	59	0	3.80
1971–72	Minnesota	3⅔	11	0	3.02
1972–73	Minnesota	22	67	2	3.05
	Totals	42⅓	143	2	3.38
Playoffs					
1972–73	Minnesota	1	4	0	4.00

476

GILBERT, Jeannot Elmourt *Forward*
b. Grande Baie, Que., Dec. 29, 1940

Season	Club	GP	G	A	Pts
1962-63	Boston	5	0	0	0
1964-65	Boston	4	0	1	1
	Totals	9	0	1	1

GILBERT, Rodrique Gabriel *Forward*
b. Montreal, Que., July 1, 1941

Season	Club	GP	G	A	Pts
1960-61	New York R.	1	0	1	1
1961-62	New York R.	1	0	0	0
1962-63	New York R.	70	11	20	31
1963-64	New York R.	70	24	40	64
1964-65	New York R.	70	25	36	61
1965-66	New York R.	34	10	15	25
1966-67	New York R.	64	28	18	46
1967-68	New York R.	73	29	48	77
1968-69	New York R.	66	28	49	77
1969-70	New York R.	72	16	37	53
1970-71	New York R.	78	30	31	61
1971-72	New York R.	73	43	54	97
1972-73	New York R.	76	25	59	84
	Totals	748	269	408	677

Playoffs

Season	Club	GP	G	A	Pts
1961-62	New York R.	4	2	3	5
1966-67	New York R.	4	2	2	4
1967-68	New York R.	6	5	0	5
1968-69	New York R.	4	1	0	1
1969-70	New York R.	6	4	5	9
1970-71	New York R.	13	4	6	10
1971-72	New York R.	16	7	8	15
1972-73	New York R.	10	5	1	6
	Totals	63	30	25	55

All-Star

1964	NHL All-Stars	1	0	0	0
1965	NHL All-Stars	1	0	0	0
1967	NHL All-Stars	1	0	0	0
1969	East All-Stars	1	0	1	1
1970	East All-Stars	1	0	0	0
1972	East All-Stars	1	0	1	1
	Totals	6	0	2	2

GILBERTSON, Stan *Forward*
b. Duluth, Minn., Oct. 29, 1944

Season	Club	GP	G	A	Pts
1971-72	California	78	16	16	32
1972-73	California	66	6	15	21
	Totals	144	22	31	53

GILL, Andre *Goalie*
b. Sorel, Que., Sept. 19, 1941

Season	Club	GP	GA	Sho	AVE
1967-68	Boston	5	13	1	2.89

GIRARD, Kenneth *Forward*
b. Toronto, Ont., Dec. 8, 1936

Season	Club	GP	G	A	Pts
1956-57	Toronto M.L.	3	0	1	1
1957-58	Toronto M.L.	3	0	0	0
1959-60	Toronto M.L.	1	0	0	0
	Totals	7	0	1	1

GIROUX, Arthur *Forward*
b. Strathmore, Alta., June 6, 1908

Season	Club	GP	G	A	Pts
1932-33	Montreal C.	--	5	2	7
1934-35	Boston	--	1	0	1
1935-36	Detroit R.W.	--	0	2	2
	Totals	--	6	4	10

Playoffs

Season	Club	GP	G	A	Pts
1932-33	Montreal C.	--	0	0	0

GLADU, Joseph Jean Paul *Forward*
b. St. Hyacinthe, Que., June 20, 1922

Season	Club	GP	G	A	Pts
1944-45	Boston	40	6	14	20

Playoffs

Season	Club	GP	G	A	Pts
1944-45	Boston	7	2	2	4

GLENNIE, Brian Alexander *Defenseman*
b. Toronto, Ont., Aug. 29, 1946

Season	Club	GP	G	A	Pts
1969-70	Toronto M.L.	52	1	14	15
1970-71	Toronto M.L.	54	0	8	8
1971-72	Toronto M.L.	61	2	8	10
1972-73	Toronto M.L.	44	1	10	11
	Totals	211	4	40	44

Playoffs

Season	Club	GP	G	A	Pts
1970-71	Toronto M.L.	3	0	0	0
1971-72	Toronto M.L.	5	0	0	0
	Totals	8	0	0	0

GLOVER, Frederick Austin *Forward*
b. Toronto, Ont., Jan. 5, 1928

Season	Club	GP	G	A	Pts
1949-50	Detroit R.W.	7	0	0	0
1951-52	Detroit R.W.	54	9	9	18
1952-53	Chicago	31	4	2	6
	Totals	92	13	11	24

Playoffs

Season	Club	GP	G	A	Pts
1948-49	Detroit R.W.	2	0	0	0
1950-51	Detroit R.W.	2	0	0	0
	Totals	4	0	0	0

GLOVER, Howard Edward *Forward*
b. Toronto, Ont., Feb. 14, 1935

Season	Club	GP	G	A	Pts
1958–59	Chicago	13	0	1	1
1960–61	Detroit R.W.	66	21	8	29
1961–62	Detroit R.W.	39	7	8	15
1963–64	New York R.	25	1	0	1
1968–69	Montreal C.	1	0	0	0
	Totals	144	29	17	46

Playoffs

1960–61	Detroit R.W.	11	1	2	3

GODFREY, Warren Edward (Rocky)
Defenseman
b. Toronto, Ont., Mar. 23, 1931

Season	Club	GP	G	A	Pts
1952–53	Boston	60	1	13	14
1953–54	Boston	70	5	9	14
1954–55	Boston	62	1	17	18
1955–56	Detroit R.W.	67	2	6	8
1956–57	Detroit R.W.	69	1	8	9
1957–58	Detroit R.W.	67	2	16	18
1958–59	Detroit R.W.	69	6	4	10
1959–60	Detroit R.W.	69	5	9	14
1960–61	Detroit R.W.	63	3	16	19
1961–62	Detroit R.W.	70	4	13	17
1962–63	Boston	66	2	9	11
1963–64	Detroit R.W.	4	0	0	0
1964–65	Detroit R.W.	11	0	0	0
1965–66	Detroit R.W.	26	0	4	4
1966–67	Detroit R.W.	2	0	0	0
1967–68	Detroit R.W.	12	0	1	1
	Totals	787	32	125	157

Playoffs

1952–53	Boston	11	0	1	1
1953–54	Boston	4	0	0	0
1954–55	Boston	3	0	0	0
1956–57	Detroit R.W.	5	0	0	0
1957–58	Detroit R.W.	4	0	0	0
1959–60	Detroit R.W.	6	1	0	1
1960–61	Detroit R.W.	11	0	2	2
1964–65	Detroit R.W.	4	0	1	1
1965–66	Detroit R.W.	4	0	0	0
	Totals	52	1	4	5

All-Star

1955	Detroit R.W.	1	0	0	0

GODIN, Samuel *Forward*
b. Rockland, Ont., Sept. 20, 1909

Season	Club	GP	G	A	Pts
1928–29	Ottawa	--	2	1	3
1933–34	Montreal C.	--	2	2	4
	Totals	--	4	3	7

GOEGAN, Peter John *Defenseman*
b. Fort William, Ont., Mar. 6, 1934

Season	Club	GP	G	A	Pts
1957–58	Detroit R.W.	14	0	2	2
1958–59	Detroit R.W.	67	1	11	12
1959–60	Detroit R.W.	21	3	0	3
1960–61	Detroit R.W.	67	5	29	34
1961–62	Det RW–NY R	46	5	7	12
1962–63	Detroit R.W.	62	1	8	9
1963–64	Detroit R.W.	12	0	0	0
1964–65	Detroit R.W.	4	1	0	1
1965–66	Detroit R.W.	13	0	2	2
1966–67	Detroit R.W.	31	2	6	8
1967–68	Minnesota	46	1	2	3
	Totals	383	19	67	86

Playoffs

1957–58	Detroit R.W.	4	0	0	0
1959–60	Detroit R.W.	6	1	0	1
1960–61	Detroit R.W.	11	0	1	1
1962–63	Detroit R.W.	11	0	2	2
1965–66	Detroit R.W.	1	0	0	0
	Totals	33	1	3	4

GOLDHAM, Robert John *Defenseman*
b. Georgetown, Ont., May 12, 1922

Season	Club	GP	G	A	Pts
1941–42	Toronto M.L.	19	4	7	11
1945–46	Toronto M.L.	49	7	14	21
1946–47	Toronto M.L.	11	1	1	2
1947–48	Chicago	38	2	9	11
1948–49	Chicago	60	1	10	11
1949–50	Chicago	67	2	10	12
1950–51	Detroit R.W.	61	5	18	23
1951–52	Detroit R.W.	69	0	14	14
1952–53	Detroit R.W.	70	1	13	14
1953–54	Detroit R.W.	69	1	15	16
1954–55	Detroit R.W.	69	1	16	17
1955–56	Detroit R.W.	68	3	16	19
	Totals	650	28	143	171

Playoffs

1941–42	Toronto M.L.	13	2	2	4
1950–51	Detroit R.W.	6	0	1	1
1951–52	Detroit R.W.	8	0	1	1
1952–53	Detroit R.W.	6	1	1	2
1953–54	Detroit R.W.	12	0	2	2
1954–55	Detroit R.W.	11	0	4	4
1955–56	Detroit R.W.	10	0	3	3
	Totals	66	3	14	17

All-Star

1947	Toronto M.L.	1	0	0	0
1949	NHL All-Stars	1	1	1	2
1950	Detroit R.W.	1	0	0	0
1952	NHL 1st All-Stars	1	0	0	0

GOLDHAM *(Continued)*

All-Star	Club	GP	G	A	Pts
1954	Detroit R.W.	1	0	0	0
1955	Detroit R.W.	1	0	1	1
	Totals	6	1	2	3

GOLDSWORTHY, Leroy D.
Defenseman-Forward
b. Two Harbors, Minn., Oct. 18, 1908

Season	Club	GP	G	A	Pts
1929-30	New York R.	44	4	1	5
1930-31	Detroit F.	--	1	0	1
1932-33	Detroit F.	--	3	6	9
1933-34	Chicago	--	3	3	6
1934-35	Montreal C.	--	20	9	29
1935-36	Montreal C.	--	15	11	26
1936-37	Boston	--	8	6	14
1937-38	Boston	--	9	10	19
1938-39	New York A.	--	3	11	14
	Totals	--	66	57	123

Playoffs

1929-30	New York R.	4	0	0	0
1932-33	Detroit F.	4	0	0	0
1933-34	Chicago	8	0	0	0
1934-35	Montreal C.	2	1	0	1
1936-37	Boston	3	0	0	0
1937-38	Boston	3	0	0	0
1938-39	New York A.	2	0	0	0
	Totals	26	1	0	1

GOLDSWORTHY, William Alfred *Forward*
b. Waterloo, Ont., Aug. 24, 1944

Season	Club	GP	G	A	Pts
1964-65	Boston	2	0	0	0
1965-66	Boston	13	3	1	4
1966-67	Boston	18	3	5	8
1967-68	Minnesota	68	14	19	33
1968-69	Minnesota	68	14	10	24
1969-70	Minnesota	75	36	29	65
1970-71	Minnesota	77	34	31	65
1971-72	Minnesota	78	31	31	62
1972-73	Minnesota	75	27	33	60
	Totals	474	162	159	321

Playoffs

1967-68	Minnesota	14	8	7	15
1969-70	Minnesota	6	4	3	7
1970-71	Minnesota	7	2	4	6
1971-72	Minnesota	7	2	3	5
1972-73	Minnesota	6	2	2	4
	Totals	40	18	19	37

All-Star

1970	West All-Stars	1	0	0	0
1972	West All-Stars	1	0	0	0
	Totals	2	0	0	0

GOLDUP, Henry (Hank) *Forward*
b. Kingston, Ont., Oct. 29, 1918

Season	Club	GP	G	A	Pts
1939-40	Toronto M.L.	--	6	4	10
1940-41	Toronto M.L.	--	10	5	15
1941-42	Toronto M.L.	44	12	18	30
1942-43	Tor ML-NY R	44	12	27	39
1944-45	New York R.	48	17	25	42
1945-46	New York R.	19	6	1	7
	Totals	--	63	80	143

Playoffs

1939-40	Toronto M.L.	10	5	1	6
1940-41	Toronto M.L.	7	0	0	0
1941-42	Toronto M.L.	13	0	0	0
	Totals	30	5	1	6

GOODEN, William Francis Charles *Forward*
b. Winnipeg, Man., Sept. 8, 1923

Season	Club	GP	G	A	Pts
1942-43	New York R.	12	0	3	3
1943-44	New York R.	41	9	8	17
	Totals	53	9	11	20

GOODFELLOW, Ebenezer Ralston (Ebbie)
Defenseman-Forward
b. Ottawa, Ont., Apr. 9, 1907

Season	Club	GP	G	A	Pts
1929-30	Detroit C.	--	17	17	34
1930-31	Detroit F.	--	25	23	48
1931-32	Detroit F.	--	14	16	30
1932-33	Detroit F.	--	12	8	20
1933-34	Detroit R.W.	--	13	13	26
1934-35	Detroit R.W.	--	12	24	36
1935-36	Detroit R.W.	--	5	18	23
1936-37	Detroit R.W.	--	9	16	25
1937-38	Detroit R.W.	--	0	7	7
1938-39	Detroit R.W.	--	8	8	16
1939-40	Detroit R.W.	--	11	17	28
1940-41	Detroit R.W.	--	5	17	22
1941-42	Detroit R.W.	8	2	2	4
1942-43	Detroit R.W.	11	1	4	5
	Totals	--	134	190	324

Playoffs

1931-32	Detroit F.	--	0	0	0
1932-33	Detroit F.	--	1	0	1
1933-34	Detroit R.W.	--	4	3	7
1935-36	Detroit R.W.	--	1	0	1
1936-37	Detroit R.W.	--	2	2	4
1938-39	Detroit R.W.	--	0	0	0
1939-40	Detroit R.W.	--	0	2	2
1940-41	Detroit R.W.	--	0	1	1
	Totals	--	8	8	16

GOODMAN, Paul *Goalie*
b. Selkirk, Man., Nov. 4, 1909

Season	Club	GP	GA	Sho	AVE
1939–40	Chicago	31	62	4	2.00
1940–41	Chicago	21	55	2	2.61
	Totals	52	117	6	2.25
Playoffs					
1937–38	Chicago	1	5	0	5.00
1939–40	Chicago	2	5	0	2.50
	Totals	3	10	0	3.33

GORDON, Fred *Forward*

Season	Club	GP	G	A	Pts
1926–27	Detroit C.	--	5	5	10
1927–28	Boston	--	3	2	5
	Totals	--	8	7	15
Playoffs					
1927–28	Boston	--	0	0	0

GORDON, John (Jackie) *Forward*
b. Winnipeg, Man., Mar. 3, 1928

Season	Club	GP	G	A	Pts
1948–49	New York R.	31	3	9	12
1949–50	New York R.	1	0	0	0
1950–51	New York R.	4	0	1	1
	Totals	36	3	10	13
Playoffs					
1949–50	New York R.	9	1	1	2

GORING, Robert Thomas (Butch) *Forward*
b. St. Boniface, Man., Oct. 22, 1949

Season	Club	GP	G	A	Pts
1969–70	Los Angeles	59	13	23	36
1970–71	Los Angeles	19	2	5	7
1971–72	Los Angeles	74	21	29	50
1972–73	Los Angeles	67	28	31	59
	Totals	219	64	88	152

GORMAN, Edwin *Defenseman*

Season	Club	GP	G	A	Pts
1924–25	Ottawa	30	1	3	14
1925–26	Ottawa	23	2	1	3
1926–27	Ottawa	--	1	0	1
1927–28	Toronto M.L.	--	0	1	1
	Totals	--	14	5	19
Playoffs					
1925–26	Ottawa	--	0	0	0
1926–27	Ottawa	--	0	0	0
	Totals	--	0	0	0

GOTTSELIG, John P. *Forward*
b. Odessa, Russia, June 24, 1906

Season	Club	GP	G	A	Pts
1928–29	Chicago	--	5	3	8
1929–30	Chicago	--	21	4	25
1930–31	Chicago	--	20	12	32
1931–32	Chicago	--	13	15	28
1932–33	Chicago	--	11	11	22
1933–34	Chicago	--	16	14	30
1934–35	Chicago	--	19	18	37
1935–36	Chicago	--	14	15	29
1936–37	Chicago	--	9	21	30
1937–38	Chicago	--	13	19	32
1938–39	Chicago	--	16	23	39
1939–40	Chicago	--	8	15	23
1940–41	Chicago	--	1	4	5
1942–43	Chicago	10	2	6	8
1943–44	Chicago	45	8	15	23
1944–45	Chicago	1	0	0	0
	Totals	--	176	195	371
Playoffs					
1929–30	Chicago	2	0	0	0
1930–31	Chicago	9	3	3	6
1931–32	Chicago	2	0	0	0
1933–34	Chicago	8	4	3	7
1934–35	Chicago	2	0	0	0
1935–36	Chicago	2	0	2	2
1937–38	Chicago	10	5	4	9
1939–40	Chicago	2	0	1	1
1943–44	Chicago	6	1	1	2
	Totals	43	13	14	27

GOULD, John Milton *Forward*
b. Alliston, Ont., Apr. 11, 1949

Season	Club	GP	G	A	Pts
1971–72	Buffalo	2	1	0	1
1972–73	Buffalo	8	0	1	1
	Totals	10	1	1	2

GOUPILLE, Clifford (Red) *Defenseman*
b. Three Rivers, Que., Sept. 2, 1915

Season	Club	GP	G	A	Pts
1937–38	Montreal C.	--	4	5	9
1938–39	Montreal C.	--	0	2	2
1939–40	Montreal C.	--	2	10	12
1940–41	Montreal C.	--	3	6	9
1941–42	Montreal C.	--	1	5	6
1942–43	Montreal C.	6	2	0	2
	Totals	--	12	28	40
Playoffs					
1937–38	Montreal C.	--	2	0	2
1938–39	Montreal C.	--	0	0	0
1940–41	Montreal C.	--	0	0	0
1941–42	Montreal C.	--	0	0	0
	Totals	--	2	0	2

GOYER, Gerald *Forward*
b. Belleville, Ont., Oct. 20, 1936

Season	Club	GP	G	A	Pts
1967-68	Chicago	40	1	2	3

Playoffs

1967-68	Chicago	3	0	0	0

GOYETTE, Phillipe *Forward*
b. Lachine, Que., Oct. 31, 1933

Season	Club	GP	G	A	Pts
1956-57	Montreal C.	14	3	4	7
1957-58	Montreal C.	70	9	37	46
1958-59	Montreal C.	63	10	18	28
1959-60	Montreal C.	65	21	22	43
1960-61	Montreal C.	62	7	4	11
1961-62	Montreal C.	69	7	27	34
1962-63	Montreal C.	32	5	8	13
1963-64	New York R.	67	24	41	65
1964-65	New York R.	52	12	34	46
1965-66	New York R.	60	11	31	42
1966-67	New York R.	70	12	49	61
1967-68	New York R.	73	25	40	65
1968-69	New York R.	67	13	32	45
1969-70	St. Louis B.	72	29	49	78
1970-71	Buffalo	60	15	46	61
1971-72	Buf-NY R	45	4	25	29
	Totals	941	207	467	674

Playoffs

1956-57	Montreal C.	10	2	1	3
1957-58	Montreal C.	10	4	1	5
1958-59	Montreal C.	10	0	4	4
1959-60	Montreal C.	8	2	1	3
1960-61	Montreal C.	6	3	3	6
1961-62	Montreal C.	6	1	4	5
1962-63	Montreal C.	2	0	0	0
1966-67	New York R.	4	1	0	1
1967-68	New York R.	6	0	1	1
1968-69	New York R.	3	0	0	0
1969-70	St. Louis B.	16	3	11	14
1971-72	New York R.	13	1	3	4
	Totals	94	17	29	46

All-Star

1957	Montreal C.	1	0	0	0
1958	Montreal C.	1	0	0	0
1959	Montreal C.	1	0	0	0
1961	NHL All-Stars	1	0	0	0
	Totals	4	0	0	0

GRABOSKI, Anthony *Defenseman*
b. Timmins, Ont., May 29, 1916

Season	Club	GP	G	A	Pts
1940-41	Montreal C.	--	4	3	7
1941-42	Montreal C.	--	2	5	7
1942-43	Montreal C.	9	0	2	2
	Totals	--	6	10	16

GRABOSKI *(Continued)*

Playoffs	Club	GP	G	A	Pts
1940-41	Montreal C.	--	0	0	0
1941-42	Montreal C.	--	0	0	0
	Totals	--	0	0	0

GRACIE, Robert J. *Forward*
b. North Bay, Ont., Nov. 8, 1911

Season	Club	GP	G	A	Pts
1930-31	Toronto M.L.	--	4	2	6
1931-32	Toronto M.L.	--	13	8	21
1932-33	Toronto M.L.	--	9	13	22
1933-34	Bos-NY A	--	6	12	18
1934-35	NY A-Mont M	--	12	9	21
1935-36	Montreal M.	--	11	14	25
1936-37	Montreal M.	--	11	25	36
1937-38	Montreal M.	--	12	19	31
1938-39	Mont M-Chgo	--	4	7	11
	Totals	--	82	109	191

Playoffs

1930-31	Toronto M.L.	--	0	0	0
1931-32	Toronto M.L.	--	3	1	4
1932-33	Toronto M.L.	--	0	1	1
1934-35	Montreal M.	--	0	2	2
1935-36	Montreal M.	--	0	1	1
1936-37	Montreal M.	--	1	2	3
	Totals	--	4	7	11

GRAHAM, Edward Dixon (Teddy) *Defenseman*
b. Owen Sound, Ont., June 30, 1906

Season	Club	GP	G	A	Pts
1927-28	Chicago	--	1	0	1
1929-30	Chicago	--	1	2	3
1930-31	Chicago	--	0	7	7
1931-32	Chicago	--	0	3	3
1932-33	Chicago	--	3	8	11
1933-34	Mont M-Det RW	--	3	1	4
1934-35	Det RW-StL E	--	0	2	2
1935-36	Boston	--	4	1	5
1936-37	New York A.	--	2	1	3
	Totals	--	14	25	39

Playoffs

1929-30	Chicago	--	0	0	0
1930-31	Chicago	--	0	0	0
1931-32	Chicago	--	0	0	0
1933-34	Detroit R.W.	--	3	1	4
1935-36	Boston	--	0	0	0
	Totals	--	3	1	4

GRAHAM, Leth *Defenseman*

Season	Club	GP	G	A	Pts
1920-21	Ottawa	13	0	0	0
1921-22	Ottawa	2	2	0	2
1922-23	Hamilton	4	1	0	1

GRAHAM (Continued)

Season	Club	GP	G	A	Pts
1923–24	Ottawa	3	0	0	0
1924–25	Ottawa	3	0	0	0
1925–26	Ottawa	1	0	0	0
	Totals	26	3	0	3

GRANT, Benjamin Cameron *Goalie*
b. Owen Sound, Ont., July 14, 1909

Season	Club	GP	GA	Sho	AVE
1928–29	Toronto M.L.	1	2	0	2.00
1929–30	NY A–Tor ML	10	39	0	3.90
1930–31	Toronto M.L.	7	19	2	2.71
1931–32	Toronto M.L.	4	18	0	4.50
1933–34	New York A.	5	18	1	3.60
1943–44	Tor ML–Bos	21	93	0	4.43
	Totals	48	189	3	3.94

GRANT, Daniel Frederick *Forward*
b. Fredericton, N.B., Feb. 21, 1946

Season	Club	GP	G	A	Pts
1965–66	Montreal C.	1	0	0	0
1967–68	Montreal C.	22	3	4	7
1968–69	Minnesota	75	34	31	65
1969–70	Minnesota	76	29	28	57
1970–71	Minnesota	78	34	23	57
1971–72	Minnesota	78	18	25	43
1972–73	Minnesota	78	32	35	67
	Totals	408	150	146	296

Playoffs

Season	Club	GP	G	A	Pts
1967–68	Montreal C.	10	0	3	3
1969–70	Minnesota	6	0	2	2
1970–71	Minnesota	12	5	5	10
1971–72	Minnesota	7	2	1	3
1972–73	Minnesota	6	3	1	4
	Totals	41	10	12	22

All-Star

Season	Club	GP	G	A	Pts
1969	Montreal C.	1	0	1	1
1970	West All-Stars	1	0	0	0
1971	West All-Stars	1	0	0	0
	Totals	3	0	1	1

GRATTON, Normand Lionel (Norm) *Forward*
b. LaSalle, Que., Dec. 22, 1950

Season	Club	GP	G	A	Pts
1971–72	New York R.	3	0	1	1
1972–73	Atl–Buffalo	50	9	11	20
	Totals	53	9	12	21

Playoffs

Season	Club	GP	G	A	Pts
1972–73	Buffalo	6	0	1	1

GRAVELLE, Joseph Gerard Leo *Forward*
b. Aylmer, Que., June 10, 1925

Season	Club	GP	G	A	Pts
1946–47	Montreal C.	53	16	14	30
1947–48	Montreal C.	15	0	0	0
1948–49	Montreal C.	36	4	6	10
1949–50	Montreal C.	70	19	10	29
1950–51	Mont C–Det RW	49	5	4	9
	Totals	223	44	34	78

Playoffs

Season	Club	GP	G	A	Pts
1946–47	Montreal C.	6	2	0	2
1948–49	Montreal C.	7	2	1	3
1949–50	Montreal C.	4	0	0	0
	Totals	17	4	1	5

GRAVES, Hilliard *Forward*
b. Saint John, N.B., Oct. 18, 1950

Season	Club	GP	G	A	Pts
1970–71	California	14	0	0	0
1972–73	California	75	27	25	52
	Totals	89	27	25	52

GRAY, Alexander *Forward*
b. Glasgow, Scotland, June 21, 1899

Season	Club	GP	G	A	Pts
1927–28	New York R.	43	7	0	7
1928–29	Toronto M.L.	--	0	0	0
	Totals	--	7	0	7

Playoffs

Season	Club	GP	G	A	Pts
1927–28	New York R.	9	1	0	1
1928–29	Toronto M.L.	4	0	0	0
	Totals	13	1	0	1

GRAY, Gerald Robert (Gerry) *Goalie*
b. Brantford, Ont., Jan. 28, 1948

Season	Club	GP	GA	Sho	AVE
1970–71	Detroit R.W.	6⅓	30	0	4.73
1972–73	New York I.	1	5	0	5.00
	Totals	7⅓	35	0	4.81

GRAY, Harrison Leroy *Goalie*
b. Calgary, Alta., Sept. 5, 1941

Season	Club	GP	GA	Sho	AVE
1963–64	Detroit R.W.	⅔	5	0	7.50

GRAY, Terence Stanley *Forward*
b. Montreal, Que., Mar. 21, 1938

Season	Club	GP	G	A	Pts
1961–62	Boston	42	8	7	15
1963–64	Montreal C.	4	0	0	0
1967–68	Los Angeles	65	12	16	28

GRAY (Continued)

Season	Club	GP	G	A	Pts
1968-69	St. Louis B.	8	4	0	4
1969-70	St. Louis B.	28	2	5	7
	Totals	147	26	28	54

Playoffs

1967-68	Los Angeles	7	0	2	2
1968-69	St. Louis B.	12	3	2	5
1969-70	St. Louis B.	16	2	1	3
	Totals	35	5	5	10

GREEN, Edward Joseph (Ted) *Defenseman*
b. St. Boniface, Man., Mar. 23, 1940

Season	Club	GP	G	A	Pts
1960-61	Boston	1	0	0	0
1961-62	Boston	66	3	8	11
1962-63	Boston	70	1	11	12
1963-64	Boston	70	4	10	14
1964-65	Boston	70	8	27	35
1965-66	Boston	27	5	13	18
1966-67	Boston	47	6	10	16
1967-68	Boston	72	7	36	43
1968-69	Boston	65	8	38	46
1970-71	Boston	78	5	37	42
1971-72	Boston	54	1	16	17
	Totals	620	48	206	254

Playoffs

1967-68	Boston	4	1	1	2
1968-69	Boston	10	2	7	9
1970-71	Boston	7	1	0	1
1971-72	Boston	10	0	0	0
	Totals	31	4	8	12

All-Star

1969	East All-Stars	1	0	0	0

GREEN, Redvers *Forward*
b. Sudbury, Ont.

Season	Club	GP	G	A	Pts
1923-24	Hamilton	23	11	0	11
1924-25	Hamilton	30	19	4	23
1925-26	New York A.	35	13	4	17
1926-27	New York A.	--	10	4	14
1927-28	New York A.	--	6	1	7
1928-29	Boston	--	0	0	0
	Totals	--	59	13	72

Playoffs

1928-29	Boston	--	0	0	0

GREEN, Wilfred (Shorty) *Forward*
b. Sudbury, Ont.

Season	Club	GP	G	A	Pts
1923-24	Hamilton	22	7	2	9
1924-25	Hamilton	28	18	1	19

GREEN (Continued)

Season	Club	GP	G	A	Pts
1925-26	New York A.	33	6	4	10
1926-27	New York A.	--	2	1	3
	Totals	--	33	8	41

GRENIER, Lucien S.J. *Forward*
b. Malartic, Que., Nov. 3, 1946

Season	Club	GP	G	A	Pts
1969-70	Montreal C.	23	2	3	5
1970-71	Los Angeles	68	9	7	16
1971-72	Los Angeles	60	3	4	7
	Totals	151	14	14	28

Playoffs

1968-69	Montreal C.	2	0	0	0

GRENIER, Richard *Forward*
b. Montreal, Que., Sept. 18, 1952

Season	Club	GP	G	A	Pts
1972-73	New York I.	10	1	1	2

GRIGOR, George *Forward*
b. Edinburgh, Scotland

Season	Club	GP	G	A	Pts
1943-44	Chicago	2	1	0	1

Playoffs

1943-44	Chicago	1	0	0	0

GRISDALE, John Russel *Defenseman*
b. Toronto, Ont., Aug. 23, 1948

Season	Club	GP	G	A	Pts
1972-73	Toronto M.L.	49	1	7	8

GRONSDAHL, Lloyd Gilford *Forward*
b. Norquay, Sask., May 10, 1921

Season	Club	GP	G	A	Pts
1941-42	Boston	10	1	2	3

GROSS, Lloyd *Forward*
b. Kitchener, Ont., Sept. 15, 1907

Season	Club	GP	G	A	Pts
1926-27	Toronto M.L.	--	1	1	2
1933-34	NY A-Bos-Det RW	--	9	4	13
1934-35	Detroit R.W.	--	1	0	1
	Totals	--	11	5	16

GROSSO, Donald (Count) *Forward*
b. Sault Ste. Marie, Ont., Apr. 12, 1915

Season	Club	GP	G	A	Pts
1938-39	Detroit R.W.	--	1	1	2
1939-40	Detroit R.W.	--	2	3	5
1940-41	Detroit R.W.	--	8	7	15
1941-42	Detroit R.W.	48	23	30	53

GROSSO (Continued)

Season	Club	GP	G	A	Pts
1942–43	Detroit R.W.	50	15	17	32
1943–44	Detroit R.W.	42	16	31	47
1944–45	Det RW–Chgo	41	15	16	31
1945–46	Chicago	47	7	10	17
1946–47	Boston	33	0	2	2
	Totals	––	87	117	204

Playoffs

Season	Club	GP	G	A	Pts
1938–39	Detroit R.W.	3	1	2	3
1939–40	Detroit R.W.	5	0	0	0
1940–41	Detroit R.W.	9	1	4	5
1941–42	Detroit R.W.	12	8	6	14
1942–43	Detroit R.W.	10	4	2	6
1943–44	Detroit R.W.	5	1	0	1
1945–46	Chicago	4	0	0	0
	Totals	48	15	14	29

GROSVENAR, Leonard *Forward*
b. Ottawa, Ont.

Season	Club	GP	G	A	Pts
1927–28	Ottawa	––	1	2	3
1928–29	Ottawa	––	3	2	5
1929–30	Ottawa	––	0	3	3
1930–31	Ottawa	––	5	4	9
	Totals	––	9	11	20

Playoffs

Season	Club	GP	G	A	Pts
1927–28	Ottawa	––	0	0	0
1929–30	Ottawa	––	0	0	0
	Totals	––	0	0	0

GRUEN, Danny Patrick *Forward*
b. Thunder Bay, Ont., June 26, 1952

Season	Club	GP	G	A	Pts
1972–73	Detroit R.W.	2	0	0	0

GUEVREMONT, Jocelyn Marcel *Defenseman*
b. Montreal, Que., Mar. 1, 1951

Season	Club	GP	G	A	Pts
1971–72	Vancouver	75	13	38	51
1972–73	Vancouver	78	16	26	42
	Totals	153	29	64	93

GUIDOLIN, Aldo Reno *Defenseman-Forward*
b. Forks of Credit, Ont., June 6, 1932

Season	Club	GP	G	A	Pts
1952–53	New York R.	30	4	4	8
1953–54	New York R.	68	2	6	8
1954–55	New York R.	70	2	5	7
1955–56	New York R.	14	1	0	1
	Totals	182	9	15	24

GUIDOLIN, Armand (Bep) *Forward*
b. Thorold, Ont., Dec. 9, 1925

Season	Club	GP	G	A	Pts
1942–43	Boston	42	7	15	22
1943–44	Boston	47	17	25	42
1945–46	Boston	50	15	17	32
1946–47	Boston	56	10	13	23
1947–48	Detroit R.W.	58	12	10	22
1948–49	Det RW–Chgo	60	4	17	21
1949–50	Chicago	70	17	34	51
1950–51	Chicago	69	12	22	34
1951–52	Chicago	67	13	18	31
	Totals	519	107	171	278

Playoffs

Season	Club	GP	G	A	Pts
1942–43	Boston	9	0	4	4
1945–46	Boston	10	5	2	7
1946–47	Boston	3	0	1	1
1947–48	Detroit R.W.	2	0	0	0
	Totals	24	5	7	12

HADDON, Lloyd Ward *Defenseman*
b. Sarnia, Ont., Aug. 10, 1938

Season	Club	GP	G	A	Pts
1959–60	Detroit R.W.	8	0	0	0

Playoffs

Season	Club	GP	G	A	Pts
1959–60	Detroit R.W.	1	0	0	0

HADFIELD, Victor Edward *Forward*
b. Oakville, Ont., Oct. 4, 1940

Season	Club	GP	G	A	Pts
1961–62	New York R.	44	3	1	4
1962–63	New York R.	36	5	6	11
1963–64	New York R.	69	14	11	25
1964–65	New York R.	70	18	20	38
1965–66	New York R.	67	16	19	35
1966–67	New York R.	69	13	20	33
1967–68	New York R.	59	20	19	39
1968–69	New York R.	73	26	40	66
1969–70	New York R.	71	20	34	54
1970–71	New York R.	63	22	22	44
1971–72	New York R.	78	50	56	106
1972–73	New York R.	63	28	34	62
	Totals	762	235	282	517

Playoffs

Season	Club	GP	G	A	Pts
1961–62	New York R.	4	0	0	0
1966–67	New York R.	4	1	0	1
1967–68	New York R.	6	1	2	3
1968–69	New York R.	4	2	1	3
1970–71	New York R.	12	8	5	13
1971–72	New York R.	16	7	9	16
1972–73	New York R.	9	2	2	4
	Totals	55	21	19	40

HADFIELD (Continued)

All-Star	Club	GP	G	A	Pts
1965	NHL All-Stars	1	0	0	0
1972	East All-Stars	1	0	0	0
	Totals	**2**	**0**	**0**	**0**

HAGGERTY, James *Forward*
b. Port Arthur, Ont., Apr. 14, 1914

Season	Club	GP	G	A	Pts
1941–42	Montreal C.	--	1	1	2

Playoffs

1941–42	Montreal C.	--	2	1	3

HAINSWORTH, George *Goalie*
b. Toronto, Ont., June 26, 1895

Season	Club	GP	GA	Sho	AVE
1926–27	Montreal C.	44	67	14	1.52
1927–28	Montreal C.	44	48	13	1.09
1928–29	Montreal C.	44	43	22	0.98
1929–30	Montreal C.	42	108	4	2.57
1930–31	Montreal C.	44	89	8	2.02
1931–32	Montreal C.	48	111	6	2.31
1932–33	Montreal C.	48	115	7	2.40
1933–34	Toronto M.L.	48	119	3	2.48
1934–35	Toronto M.L.	48	111	6	2.31
1935–36	Toronto M.L.	48	106	8	2.21
1936–37	Tor ML–Mont C	7	21	0	3.00
	Totals	**465**	**938**	**91**	**2.02**

Playoffs

1926–27	Montreal C.	4	6	1	1.50
1927–28	Montreal C.	2	3	0	1.50
1928–29	Montreal C.	3	5	0	1.67
1929–30	Montreal C.	6	6	3	1.00
1930–31	Montreal C.	10	21	2	2.10
1931–32	Montreal C.	4	13	0	3.25
1932–33	Montreal C.	2	8	0	4.00
1933–34	Toronto M.L.	5	11	0	2.20
1934–35	Toronto M.L.	7	12	2	1.71
1935–36	Toronto M.L.	9	27	0	3.00
	Totals	**52**	**112**	**8**	**2.15**

HALDERSON, Harold (Slim) *Forward*
b. Winnipeg, Man., Jan. 6, 1900

Season	Club	GP	G	A	Pts
1926–27	Tor ML–Det C	--	3	2	5

Playoffs

1924–25	Victoria (PCHL)	--	2	1	3
1925–26	Victoria (PCHL)	--	1	0	1
	Totals	**--**	**3**	**1**	**4**

HALE, Larry James *Defenseman*
b. Summerland, B.C., Oct. 9, 1941

Season	Club	GP	G	A	Pts
1968–69	Philadelphia F.	67	3	16	19
1969–70	Philadelphia F.	53	1	9	10

HALE (Continued)

Season	Club	GP	G	A	Pts
1970–71	Philadelphia F.	70	1	11	12
1971–72	Philadelphia F.	6	0	1	1
	Totals	**196**	**5**	**37**	**42**

Playoffs

1968–69	Philadelphia F.	4	0	0	0
1970–71	Philadelphia F.	4	0	0	0
	Totals	**8**	**0**	**0**	**0**

HALEY, Leonard Frank *Forward*
b. Edmonton, Alta., Sept. 15, 1931

Season	Club	GP	G	A	Pts
1959–60	Detroit R.W.	27	1	2	3
1960–61	Detroit R.W.	3	1	0	1
	Totals	**30**	**2**	**2**	**4**

Playoffs

1959–60	Detroit R.W.	6	1	3	4

HALL, Del *Forward*
b. Peterborough, Ont., May 7, 1949

Season	Club	GP	G	A	Pts
1972–73	California	6	0	0	0

HALL, Gary Wayne *Forward*
b. Melita, Man., May 22, 1939

Season	Club	GP	G	A	Pts
1960–61	New York R.	4	0	0	0

HALL, Glenn Henry *Goalie*
b. Humboldt, Sask., Oct. 3, 1931

Season	Club	GP	GA	Sho	AVE
1952–53	Detroit R.W.	6	10	1	1.67
1954–55	Detroit R.W.	2	2	0	1.00
1955–56	Detroit R.W.	70	148	12	2.11
1956–57	Detroit R.W.	70	157	4	2.24
1957–58	Chicago	70	202	7	2.88
1958–59	Chicago	70	208	1	2.97
1959–60	Chicago	70	180	6	2.57
1960–61	Chicago	70	180	6	2.57
1961–62	Chicago	70	186	9	2.65
1962–63	Chicago	65⅓	166	5	2.54
1963–64	Chicago	64⅓	148	7	2.30
1964–65	Chicago	40⅔	99	4	2.43
1965–66	Chicago	62⅓	164	4	2.63
1966–67	Chicago	27⅔	66	2	2.39
1967–68	St. Louis B.	47⅔	118	5	2.48
1968–69	St. Louis B.	39⅓	85	8	2.16
1969–70	St. Louis B.	16⅚	49	1	2.91
1970–71	St. Louis B.	29	71	2	2.41
	Totals	**891⅙**	**2239**	**84**	**2.51**

Playoffs

1955–56	Detroit R.W.	10	28	0	2.80
1956–57	Detroit R.W.	5	15	0	3.00

HALL (Continued)

Playoffs	Club	GP	GA	Sho	AVE
1958–59	Chicago	6	21	0	3.50
1959–60	Chicago	4	14	0	3.50
1960–61	Chicago	12	27	2	2.25
1961–62	Chicago	12	31	2	2.58
1962–63	Chicago	6	25	0	4.17
1963–64	Chicago	6⅔	22	0	3.30
1964–65	Chicago	12⅔	28	1	2.21
1965–66	Chicago	5⅔	22	0	3.88
1966–67	Chicago	3	8	0	2.67
1967–68	St. Louis B.	18	45	1	2.50
1968–69	St. Louis B.	2⅙	5	0	2.31
1969–70	St. Louis B.	7	21	0	3.00
1970–71	St. Louis B.	3	9	0	3.00
	Totals	113⅙	321	6	2.79

All-Star		GP	Per	GA	AGP
1955	Detroit R.W.	1	3	1	0.33
1956	NHL All-Stars	1	1½	0	0.00
1957	NHL All-Stars	1	3	3	1.00
1958	NHL All-Stars	1	3	6	2.00
1960	NHL All-Stars	1	3	1	0.33
1961	Chicago	1	3	3	1.00
1962	NHL All-Stars	1	1	0	0.00
1963	NHL All-Stars	1	1½	2	1.33
1964	NHL All-Stars	1	1½	0	0.00
1965	NHL All-Stars	1	3	2	0.67
1967	NHL All-Stars	1	1½	2	1.33
1968	NHL All-Stars	1	1	1	1.00
1969	West All-Stars	1	1	1	1.00
	Totals	13	27	22	0.81

HALL, Joseph Henry *Defenseman*
b. Stratfordshire, England, 1882

Season	Club	GP	G	A	Pts
1917–18	Montreal C.	20	8	0	8
1918–19	Montreal C.	17	7	1	8
	Totals	37	15	1	16

Playoffs					
1917–18	Montreal C.	--	0	2	2
1918–19	Montreal C.	--	0	0	0
	Totals	--	0	2	2

HALL, Murray Winston *Forward*
b. Kirkland Lake, Ont., Nov. 24, 1940

Season	Club	GP	G	A	Pts
1961–62	Chicago	2	0	0	0
1963–64	Chicago	23	2	0	2
1965–66	Detroit R.W.	1	0	0	0
1966–67	Detroit R.W.	12	4	3	7
1967–68	Minnesota	17	2	1	3
1970–71	Vancouver	77	21	38	59
1971–72	Vancouver	32	6	6	12
	Totals	164	35	48	83

HALL (Continued)

Playoffs	Club	GP	G	A	Pts
1962–63	Chicago	4	0	0	0
1964–65	Detroit R.W.	1	0	0	0
1965–66	Detroit R.W.	1	0	0	0
	Totals	6	0	0	0

All-Star					
1961	Chicago	1	0	0	0

HALL, Robert *Forward*

Season	Club	GP	G	A	Pts
1925–26	New York A.	8	0	0	0

HALLIDAY, Milton *Defenseman-Forward*
b. Ottawa, Ont.

Season	Club	GP	G	A	Pts
1926–27	Ottawa	--	1	0	1
1927–28	Ottawa	--	0	0	0
	Totals	--	1	0	1

Playoffs					
1926–27	Ottawa	--	0	0	0
1927–28	Ottawa	--	0	0	0
	Totals	--	0	0	0

HAMEL, Herbert (Hap) *Forward*

Season	Club	GP	G	A	Pts
1930–31	Toronto M.L.	--	0	0	0

Playoffs					
1930–31	Toronto M.L.	--	0	0	0

HAMEL, Jean *Defenseman*
b. Asbestos, Que., June 6, 1952

Season	Club	GP	G	A	Pts
1972–73	St. Louis B.	55	2	7	9

Playoffs					
1972–73	St. Louis B.	2	0	0	0

HAMILL, Robert George (Red) *Forward*
b. Toronto, Ont., Jan. 11, 1917

Season	Club	GP	G	A	Pts
1937–38	Boston	--	0	1	1
1938–39	Boston	--	0	1	1
1939–40	Boston	--	10	8	18
1940–41	Boston	8	0	1	1
1941–42	Bos-Chgo	43	24	12	36
1942–43	Chicago	50	28	16	44
1945–46	Chicago	38	20	17	37
1946–47	Chicago	60	21	19	40
1947–48	Chicago	60	11	13	24
1948–49	Chicago	57	8	4	12
1949–50	Chicago	59	6	2	8
1950–51	Chicago	2	0	0	0
	Totals	--	128	94	222

HAMILL (Continued)

Playoffs

Playoffs	Club	GP	G	A	Pts
1939–40	Boston	6	0	1	1
1941–42	Chicago	3	0	1	1
1945–46	Chicago	4	1	0	1
	Totals	13	1	2	3

HAMILTON, Allan Guy *Defenseman*
b. Flin Flon, Man., Aug. 20, 1946

Season	Club	GP	G	A	Pts
1965–66	New York R.	4	0	0	0
1967–68	New York R.	2	0	0	0
1968–69	New York R.	16	0	0	0
1969–70	New York R.	59	0	5	5
1970–71	Buffalo	69	2	28	30
1971–72	Buffalo	76	4	30	34
	Totals	226	6	63	69

Playoffs

Playoffs	Club	GP	G	A	Pts
1968–69	New York R.	1	0	0	0
1969–70	New York R.	5	0	0	0
	Totals	6	0	0	0

HAMILTON, Charles (Chuck) *Defenseman*
b. Kirkland Lake, Ont., Jan. 18, 1939

Season	Club	GP	G	A	Pts
1961–62	Montreal C.	1	0	0	0
1972–73	St. Louis B.	3	0	2	2
	Totals	4	0	2	2

HAMILTON, John McIvor (Jackie) *Forward*
b. Trenton, Ont., June 2, 1925

Season	Club	GP	G	A	Pts
1942–43	Toronto M.L.	49	4	22	26
1943–44	Toronto M.L.	49	20	17	37
1945–46	Toronto M.L.	40	7	9	16
	Totals	138	31	48	79

Playoffs

Playoffs	Club	GP	G	A	Pts
1942–43	Toronto M.L.	6	1	1	2
1943–44	Toronto M.L.	5	1	0	1
	Totals	11	2	1	3

HAMILTON, Reginald *Defenseman*
b. Toronto, Ont., Apr. 29, 1914

Season	Club	GP	G	A	Pts
1936–37	Toronto M.L.	--	3	7	10
1937–38	Toronto M.L.	--	1	4	5
1938–39	Toronto M.L.	--	0	7	7
1939–40	Toronto M.L.	--	2	2	4
1940–41	Toronto M.L.	--	3	12	15
1941–42	Toronto M.L.	22	0	4	4
1942–43	Toronto M.L.	11	1	1	2
1943–44	Toronto M.L.	39	4	12	16

HAMILTON (Continued)

Season	Club	GP	G	A	Pts
1944–45	Toronto M.L.	50	3	12	15
1945–46	Chicago	48	1	7	8
1946–47	Chicago	10	0	3	3
	Totals	--	18	71	89

Playoffs

Playoffs	Club	GP	G	A	Pts
1936–37	Toronto M.L.	2	0	1	1
1937–38	Toronto M.L.	7	0	1	1
1938–39	Toronto M.L.	10	0	2	2
1939–40	Toronto M.L.	10	0	0	0
1940–41	Toronto M.L.	8	1	2	3
1943–44	Toronto M.L.	5	1	0	1
1944–45	Toronto M.L.	13	0	0	0
1945–46	Chicago	4	0	1	1
	Totals	59	2	7	9

HAMPSON, Edward George (Ted) *Forward*
b. Togo, Sask., Dec. 11, 1936

Season	Club	GP	G	A	Pts
1959–60	Toronto M.L.	41	2	8	10
1960–61	New York R.	69	6	14	20
1961–62	New York R.	68	4	24	28
1962–63	New York R.	46	4	2	6
1963–64	Detroit R.W.	7	0	1	1
1964–65	Detroit R.W.	1	0	0	0
1966–67	Detroit R.W.	65	13	35	48
1967–68	Det RW–Oak	71	17	37	54
1968–69	Oakland	76	26	49	75
1969–70	Oakland	76	17	35	52
1970–71	Calif–Minn	78	14	26	40
1971–72	Minnesota	78	5	14	19
	Totals	676	108	245	353

Playoffs

Playoffs	Club	GP	G	A	Pts
1961–62	New York R.	6	0	1	1
1968–69	Oakland	7	3	4	7
1969–70	Oakland	4	1	1	2
1970–71	Minnesota	11	3	3	6
1971–72	Minnesota	7	0	1	1
	Totals	35	7	10	17

All-Star

All-Star	Club	GP	G	A	Pts
1969	West All-Stars	1	0	0	0

HANNA, John *Defenseman*
b. Sydney, N.S., Apr. 5, 1935

Season	Club	GP	G	A	Pts
1958–59	New York R.	70	1	10	11
1959–60	New York R.	61	4	8	12
1960–61	New York R.	46	1	8	9
1963–64	Montreal C.	6	0	0	0
1967–68	Philadelphia F.	15	0	0	0
	Totals	198	6	26	32

HANNIGAN, John Gordon *Forward*
b. Schumacher, Ont., Jan. 19, 1929

Season	Club	GP	G	A	Pts
1952-53	Toronto M.L.	65	17	18	35
1953-54	Toronto M.L.	35	4	4	8
1954-55	Toronto M.L.	13	0	2	2
1955-56	Toronto M.L.	48	8	7	15
	Totals	161	29	31	60
Playoffs					
1953-54	Toronto M.L.	5	2	0	2
1955-56	Toronto M.L.	4	0	0	0
	Totals	9	2	0	2

HANNIGAN, Patrick Edward *Forward*
b. Timmins, Ont., Mar. 5, 1936

Season	Club	GP	G	A	Pts
1959-60	Toronto M.L.	1	0	0	0
1960-61	New York R.	53	11	9	20
1961-62	New York R.	56	8	14	22
1967-68	Philadelphia F.	65	11	15	26
1968-69	Philadelphia F.	7	0	1	1
	Totals	182	30	39	69
Playoffs					
1961-62	New York R.	4	0	0	0
1967-68	Philadelphia F.	7	1	2	3
	Totals	11	1	2	3

HANNIGAN, Raymond James *Forward*
b. Schumacher, Ont., July 14, 1927

Season	Club	GP	G	A	Pts
1948-49	Toronto M.L.	3	0	0	0

HANSON, Emil *Defenseman*
b. Centerville, South Dakota, Nov. 18, 1907

Season	Club	GP	G	A	Pts
1932-33	Detroit F.	--	0	0	0

HARBARUK, Mikolaj Nicholas (Nick) *Forward*
b. Drohiczyn, Poland, Aug. 16, 1943

Season	Club	GP	G	A	Pts
1969-70	Pittsburgh Pe.	74	5	17	22
1970-71	Pittsburgh Pe.	78	13	12	25
1971-72	Pittsburgh Pe.	78	12	17	29
1972-73	Pittsburgh Pe.	78	10	15	25
	Totals	308	40	61	101
Playoffs					
1969-70	Pittsburgh Pe.	10	3	0	3
1971-72	Pittsburgh Pe.	4	0	1	1
	Totals	14	3	1	4

HARDY, Jocelyn (Joe) *Forward*
b. Kenogami, Que., Dec. 5, 1945

Season	Club	GP	G	A	Pts
1969-70	Oakland	23	5	4	9
1970-71	California	40	4	10	14
	Totals	63	9	14	23
Playoffs					
1969-70	Oakland	4	0	0	0

HARGREAVES, James *Defenseman*
b. Winnipeg, Man., May 2, 1950

Season	Club	GP	G	A	Pts
1970-71	Vancouver	7	0	1	1
1972-73	Vancouver	59	1	6	7
	Totals	66	1	7	8

HARMON, David Glen *Defenseman*
b. Holland, Man., Jan. 2, 1921

Season	Club	GP	G	A	Pts
1942-43	Montreal C.	27	5	9	14
1943-44	Montreal C.	43	5	16	21
1944-45	Montreal C.	42	5	8	13
1945-46	Montreal C.	49	7	10	17
1946-47	Montreal C.	57	5	9	14
1947-48	Montreal C.	56	10	4	14
1948-49	Montreal C.	59	8	12	20
1949-50	Montreal C.	62	3	16	19
1950-51	Montreal C.	57	2	12	14
	Totals	452	50	96	146
Playoffs					
1942-43	Montreal C.	5	0	1	1
1943-44	Montreal C.	9	1	2	3
1944-45	Montreal C.	6	1	0	1
1945-46	Montreal C.	9	1	4	5
1946-47	Montreal C.	11	1	1	2
1948-49	Montreal C.	7	1	1	2
1949-50	Montreal C.	5	0	1	1
1950-51	Montreal C.	1	0	0	0
	Totals	53	5	10	15
All-Star					
1949	NHL All-Stars	1	0	0	0
1950	NHL All-Stars	1	0	0	0
	Totals	2	0	0	0

HARMS, John *Forward*
b. Saskatoon, Sask., Apr. 29, 1925

Season	Club	GP	G	A	Pts
1943-44	Chicago	1	0	0	0
1944-45	Chicago	43	5	5	10
	Totals	44	5	5	10

HARNOTT, Walter (Happy) *Forward*
b. Montreal, Que., Sept. 24, 1912

Season	Club	GP	G	A	Pts
1933-34	Boston	--	0	0	0

HARPER, Terrance Victor (Terry) *Defenseman*
b. Regina, Sask., Jan. 27, 1940

Season	Club	GP	G	A	Pts
1962-63	Montreal C.	14	1	1	2
1963-64	Montreal C.	70	2	15	17
1964-65	Montreal C.	62	0	7	7
1965-66	Montreal C.	69	1	11	12
1966-67	Montreal C.	56	0	16	16
1967-68	Montreal C.	57	3	8	11
1968-69	Montreal C.	21	0	3	3
1969-70	Montreal C.	75	4	18	22
1970-71	Montreal C.	78	1	21	22
1971-72	Montreal C.	52	2	12	14
1972-73	Los Angeles	77	1	8	9
	Totals	**631**	**15**	**120**	**135**

Playoffs

Season	Club	GP	G	A	Pts
1962-63	Montreal C.	5	1	0	1
1963-64	Montreal C.	7	0	0	0
1964-65	Montreal C.	13	0	0	0
1965-66	Montreal C.	10	2	3	5
1966-67	Montreal C.	10	0	1	1
1967-68	Montreal C.	13	0	1	1
1968-69	Montreal C.	11	0	0	0
1970-71	Montreal C.	20	0	6	6
1971-72	Montreal C.	5	1	1	2
	Totals	**94**	**4**	**12**	**16**

All-Star

Season	Club	GP	G	A	Pts
1965	Montreal C.	1	0	0	0
1967	Montreal C.	1	0	1	1
1973	West All-Stars	1	1	0	1
	Totals	**3**	**1**	**1**	**2**

HARRINGTON, Leland (Hago) *Forward*
b. Melrose, Mass.

Season	Club	GP	G	A	Pts
1925-26	Boston	36	7	2	9
1927-28	Boston	--	1	0	1
1932-33	Montreal C.	--	1	1	2
	Totals	**--**	**9**	**3**	**12**

Playoffs

Season	Club	GP	G	A	Pts
1932-33	Montreal C.	--	1	0	1

HARRIS, Edward Alexander (Ted) *Defenseman*
b. Winnipeg, Man., July 18, 1936

Season	Club	GP	G	A	Pts
1963-64	Montreal C.	4	0	1	1
1964-65	Montreal C.	68	1	14	15
1965-66	Montreal C.	53	0	13	13
1966-67	Montreal C.	65	2	16	18
1967-68	Montreal C.	67	5	16	21
1968-69	Montreal C.	76	7	18	25
1969-70	Montreal C.	74	3	17	20
1970-71	Minnesota	78	2	13	15

HARRIS *(Continued)*

Season	Club	GP	G	A	Pts
1971-72	Minnesota	78	2	15	17
1972-73	Minnesota	78	7	23	30
	Totals	**641**	**29**	**146**	**175**

Playoffs

Season	Club	GP	G	A	Pts
1964-65	Montreal C.	13	0	5	5
1965-66	Montreal C.	10	0	0	0
1966-67	Montreal C.	10	0	1	1
1967-68	Montreal C.	13	0	4	4
1968-69	Montreal C.	14	1	2	3
1970-71	Minnesota	12	0	4	4
1971-72	Minnesota	7	0	1	1
1972-73	Minnesota	5	0	1	1
	Totals	**84**	**1**	**18**	**19**

All-Star

Season	Club	GP	G	A	Pts
1965	Montreal C.	1	0	0	0
1967	Montreal C.	1	0	0	0
1969	East All-Stars	1	0	1	1
1971	West All-Stars	1	0	0	0
1972	West All-Stars	1	0	0	0
	Totals	**5**	**0**	**1**	**1**

HARRIS, Fred *Forward*

Season	Club	GP	G	A	Pts
1924-25	Boston	6	3	1	4

HARRIS, George Francis (Duke) *Forward*
b. Sarnia, Ont., Feb. 25, 1942

Season	Club	GP	G	A	Pts
1967-68	Minn-Tor ML	26	1	4	5

HARRIS, Henry (Smokey) *Forward*

Season	Club	GP	G	A	Pts
1930-31	Boston	--	2	4	6

Playoffs

Season	Club	GP	G	A	Pts
1920-21	Vancouver (PCHL)	--	2	1	3
1921-22	Vancouver (PCHL)	--	0	0	0
1922-23	Vancouver (PCHL)	--	1	1	2
1930-31	Boston	--	0	0	0
	Totals	**--**	**3**	**2**	**5**

HARRIS, Hugh Thomas *Forward*
b. Toronto, Ont., June 7, 1948

Season	Club	GP	G	A	Pts
1972-73	Buffalo	60	12	26	38

Playoffs

Season	Club	GP	G	A	Pts
1972-73	Buffalo	3	0	0	0

HARRIS, Ronald Thomas *Defenseman-Forward*
b. Verdun, Que., June 30, 1942

Season	Club	GP	G	A	Pts
1962-63	Detroit R.W.	1	0	1	1
1963-64	Detroit R.W.	3	0	0	0

HARRIS (Continued)

Season	Club	GP	G	A	Pts
1967-68	Oakland	54	4	6	10
1968-69	Detroit R.W.	73	3	13	16
1969-70	Detroit R.W.	72	2	19	21
1970-71	Detroit R.W.	42	2	8	10
1971-72	Detroit R.W.	61	1	10	11
1972-73	Atl-NY R	70	5	14	19
	Totals	376	17	71	88

Playoffs

Season	Club	GP	G	A	Pts
1969-70	Detroit R.W.	4	0	0	0
1972-73	New York R.	10	0	3	3
	Totals	14	0	3	3

HARRIS, William (Billy) *Forward*
b. Toronto, Ont., Jan. 29, 1952

Season	Club	GP	G	A	Pts
1972-73	New York I.	78	28	22	50

HARRIS, William Edward *Forward*
b. Toronto, Ont., July 29, 1935

Season	Club	GP	G	A	Pts
1955-56	Toronto M.L.	70	9	13	22
1956-57	Toronto M.L.	23	4	6	10
1957-58	Toronto M.L.	68	16	28	44
1958-59	Toronto M.L.	70	22	30	52
1959-60	Toronto M.L.	70	13	25	38
1960-61	Toronto M.L.	66	12	27	39
1961-62	Toronto M.L.	67	15	10	25
1962-63	Toronto M.L.	65	8	24	32
1963-64	Toronto M.L.	63	6	12	18
1964-65	Toronto M.L.	48	1	6	7
1965-66	Detroit R.W.	24	1	4	5
1967-68	Oakland	62	12	17	29
1968-69	Oak-Pitts Pe	73	7	17	24
	Totals	769	126	219	345

Playoffs

Season	Club	GP	G	A	Pts
1955-56	Toronto M.L.	5	1	0	1
1958-59	Toronto M.L.	12	3	4	7
1959-60	Toronto M.L.	9	0	3	3
1960-61	Toronto M.L.	5	1	0	1
1961-62	Toronto M.L.	12	2	1	3
1962-63	Toronto M.L.	10	0	1	1
1963-64	Toronto M.L.	9	1	1	2
	Totals	62	8	10	18

All-Star

1958	NHL All-Stars	1	0	1	1
1962	Toronto M.L.	1	0	0	0
1963	Toronto M.L.	1	0	0	0
	Totals	3	0	1	1

HARRISON, Edward Francis *Forward*
b. Mimico, Ont., July 25, 1927

Season	Club	GP	G	A	Pts
1947-48	Boston	52	6	7	13
1948-49	Boston	59	5	5	10
1949-50	Boston	70	14	12	26
1950-51	Bos-NY R	13	2	0	2
	Totals	194	27	24	51

Playoffs

Season	Club	GP	G	A	Pts
1947-48	Boston	5	1	0	1
1948-49	Boston	4	0	0	0
	Totals	9	1	0	1

HARRISON, James David *Forward*
b. Bonnyville, Alta., July 9, 1947

Season	Club	GP	G	A	Pts
1968-69	Boston	16	1	2	3
1969-70	Bos-Tor ML	54	10	11	21
1970-71	Toronto M.L.	78	13	20	33
1971-72	Toronto M.L.	66	19	17	36
	Totals	214	43	50	93

Playoffs

Season	Club	GP	G	A	Pts
1970-71	Toronto M.L.	6	0	1	1
1971-72	Toronto M.L.	5	1	0	1
	Totals	11	1	1	2

HART, Gerald William *Defenseman*
b. Flin Flon, Man., Jan. 1, 1948

Season	Club	GP	G	A	Pts
1968-69	Detroit R.W.	1	0	0	0
1969-70	Detroit R.W.	3	0	0	0
1970-71	Detroit R.W.	64	2	7	9
1971-72	Detroit R.W.	3	0	0	0
1972-73	New York I.	47	1	11	12
	Totals	118	3	18	21

HART, Harold *Forward*

Season	Club	GP	G	A	Pts
1926-27	Detroit C.	--	0	0	0

HART, Wilfred (Gizzy) *Forward*
b. Weyburn, Sask., June 1, 1902

Season	Club	GP	G	A	Pts
1926-27	Montreal C.	--	3	3	6
1927-28	Montreal C.	--	3	2	5
1932-33	Montreal C.	--	0	3	3
	Totals	--	6	8	14

Playoffs

Season	Club	GP	G	A	Pts
1924-25	Victoria (PCHL)	--	2	1	3
1925-26	Victoria (PCHL)	--	0	0	0
1926-27	Montreal C.	--	0	0	0
1927-28	Montreal C.	--	0	0	0
1932-33	Montreal C.	--	0	1	1
	Totals	--	2	2	4

490

HARVEY, Douglas Norman *Defenseman*
b. Montreal, Que., Dec. 19, 1924

Season	Club	GP	G	A	Pts
1947–48	Montreal C.	35	4	4	8
1948–49	Montreal C.	55	3	13	16
1949–50	Montreal C.	70	4	20	24
1950–51	Montreal C.	70	5	24	29
1951–52	Montreal C.	68	6	23	29
1952–53	Montreal C.	69	4	30	34
1953–54	Montreal C.	68	8	29	37
1954–55	Montreal C.	70	6	43	49
1955–56	Montreal C.	62	5	39	44
1956–57	Montreal C.	70	6	44	50
1957–58	Montreal C.	68	9	32	41
1958–59	Montreal C.	61	4	16	20
1959–60	Montreal C.	66	6	21	27
1960–61	Montreal C.	58	6	33	39
1961–62	New York R.	69	6	24	30
1962–63	New York R.	68	4	35	39
1963–64	New York R.	14	0	2	2
1966–67	Detroit R.W.	2	0	0	0
1968–69	St. Louis B.	70	2	20	22
	Totals	1113	88	452	540

Playoffs

1948–49	Montreal C.	7	0	1	1
1949–50	Montreal C.	5	0	2	2
1950–51	Montreal C.	11	0	5	5
1951–52	Montreal C.	11	0	3	3
1952–53	Montreal C.	12	0	5	5
1953–54	Montreal C.	10	0	2	2
1954–55	Montreal C.	12	0	8	8
1955–56	Montreal C.	10	2	5	7
1956–57	Montreal C.	10	0	7	7
1957–58	Montreal C.	10	2	9	11
1958–59	Montreal C.	11	1	11	12
1959–60	Montreal C.	8	3	0	3
1960–61	Montreal C.	6	0	1	1
1961–62	New York R.	6	0	1	1
1967–68	St. Louis B.	8	0	4	4
	Totals	137	8	64	72

All-Star

1951	NHL 2nd All-Stars	1	0	0	0
1952	NHL 1st All-Stars	1	0	0	0
1953	Montreal C.	1	0	1	1
1954	NHL All-Stars	1	0	0	0
1955	NHL All-Stars	1	1	0	1
1956	Montreal C.	1	0	1	1
1957	Montreal C.	1	0	0	0
1958	Montreal C.	1	0	1	1
1959	Montreal C.	1	0	3	3
1960	Montreal C.	1	0	0	0
1961	NHL All-Stars	1	0	0	0
1962	NHL All-Stars	1	0	0	0
1969	West All-Stars	1	0	1	1
	Totals	13	1	7	8

HARVEY, Frederick John (Buster) *Forward*
b. Fredericton, N.B., Apr. 2, 1950

Season	Club	GP	G	A	Pts
1970–71	Minnesota	59	12	8	20
1972–73	Minnesota	68	21	34	55
	Totals	127	33	42	75

Playoffs

1971–72	Minnesota	1	0	0	0
1972–73	Minnesota	6	0	2	2
	Totals	7	0	2	2

HASSARD, Robert Harry *Forward*
b. Lloydminster, Sask., Mar. 26, 1929

Season	Club	GP	G	A	Pts
1949–50	Toronto M.L.	1	0	0	0
1950–51	Toronto M.L.	12	0	1	1
1952–53	Toronto M.L.	70	8	23	31
1953–54	Toronto M.L.	26	1	4	5
1954–55	Chicago	17	0	0	0
	Totals	126	9	28	37

HATOUM, Edward *Forward*
b. Beirut, Lebanon, Dec. 7, 1947

Season	Club	GP	G	A	Pts
1968–69	Detroit R.W.	16	2	1	3
1969–70	Detroit R.W.	5	0	2	2
1970–71	Vancouver	26	1	3	4
	Totals	47	3	6	9

HAWORTH, Gordon J. *Forward*
b. Drummondville, Que., Feb. 20, 1932

Season	Club	GP	G	A	Pts
1952–53	New York R.	2	0	1	1

HAY, George *Forward*
b. Listowel, Ont., Jan. 1898

Season	Club	GP	G	A	Pts
1926–27	Chicago	--	14	8	22
1927–28	Detroit C.	--	22	13	35
1928–29	Detroit C.	--	11	8	19
1929–30	Detroit C.	--	18	15	33
1930–31	Detroit F.	--	8	10	18
1932–33	Detroit F.	--	1	6	7
	Totals	--	74	60	134

Playoffs

1926–27	Chicago	--	1	2	3
1928–29	Detroit C.	--	1	0	1
1932–33	Detroit F.	--	0	1	1
	Totals	--	2	3	5

HAY, James Alexander (Red-Eye) *Defenseman*
b. Saskatoon, Sask., May 15, 1931

Season	Club	GP	G	A	Pts
1952–53	Detroit R.W.	42	1	4	5
1953–54	Detroit R.W.	12	0	0	0
1954–55	Detroit R.W.	21	0	1	1
	Totals	75	1	5	6
Playoffs					
1952–53	Detroit R.W.	4	0	0	0
1954–55	Detroit R.W.	5	1	0	1
	Totals	9	1	0	1

HAY, William Charles (Red) *Forward*
b. Saskatoon, Sask., Dec. 8, 1935

Season	Club	GP	G	A	Pts
1959–60	Chicago	70	18	37	55
1960–61	Chicago	69	11	48	59
1961–62	Chicago	60	11	52	63
1962–63	Chicago	64	12	33	45
1963–64	Chicago	70	23	33	56
1964–65	Chicago	69	11	26	37
1965–66	Chicago	68	20	31	51
1966–67	Chicago	36	7	13	20
	Totals	506	113	273	386
Playoffs					
1959–60	Chicago	4	1	2	3
1960–61	Chicago	12	2	5	7
1961–62	Chicago	12	3	7	10
1962–63	Chicago	6	3	2	5
1963–64	Chicago	7	3	1	4
1964–65	Chicago	14	3	1	4
1965–66	Chicago	6	0	2	2
1966–67	Chicago	6	0	1	1
	Totals	67	15	21	36
All-Star					
1960	NHL All-Stars	1	0	0	0
1961	Chicago	1	0	0	0
	Totals	2	0	0	0

HAYMES, Paul *Forward*
b. Montreal, Que., Mar. 1, 1910

Season	Club	GP	G	A	Pts
1930–31	Montreal M.	--	1	0	1
1931–32	Montreal M.	--	1	0	1
1932–33	Montreal M.	--	16	25	41
1933–34	Montreal M.	--	5	4	9
1934–35	Mont M-Bos	--	5	5	10
1935–36	Montreal C.	--	5	19	24
1936–37	Montreal C.	--	8	18	26
1937–38	Montreal C.	--	13	22	35
1938–39	Montreal C.	--	5	33	38
1939–40	Montreal C.	--	2	8	10
1940–41	Montreal C.	--	0	0	0
	Totals	--	61	134	195

HAYMES *(Continued)*

Playoffs	Club	GP	G	A	Pts
1930–31	Montreal M.	--	0	0	0
1931–32	Montreal M.	--	0	0	0
1932–33	Montreal M.	--	0	0	0
1933–34	Montreal M.	--	0	1	1
1934–35	Boston	--	0	0	0
1936–37	Montreal C.	--	2	3	5
1937–38	Montreal C.	--	0	4	4
1938–39	Montreal C.	--	0	0	0
	Totals	--	2	8	10

HEAD, Donald Charles *Goalie*
b. Mount Dennis, Ont., June 30, 1933

Season	Club	GP	GA	Sho	AVE
1961–62	Boston	38	161	2	4.24

HEAD, Galen *Forward*
b. Grande Prairie, Alta., Apr. 16, 1947

Season	Club	GP	G	A	Pts
1967–68	Detroit R.W.	1	0	0	0

HEADLEY, Fern *Forward*

Season	Club	GP	G	A	Pts
1924–25	Bos-Mont C	27	1	1	2

HEALEY, Richard Thomas *Defenseman*
b. Vancouver, B.C., Mar. 12, 1938

Season	Club	GP	G	A	Pts
1960–61	Detroit R.W.	1	0	0	0

HEBENTON, Andrew Alex *Forward*
b. Winnipeg, Man., Oct. 3, 1929

Season	Club	GP	G	A	Pts
1955–56	New York R.	70	24	14	38
1956–57	New York R.	70	21	23	44
1957–58	New York R.	70	21	24	45
1958–59	New York R.	70	33	29	62
1959–60	New York R.	70	19	27	46
1960–61	New York R.	70	26	28	54
1961–62	New York R.	70	18	24	42
1962–63	New York R.	70	15	22	37
1963–64	Boston	70	12	11	23
	Totals	630	189	202	391
Playoffs					
1955–56	New York R.	5	1	0	1
1956–57	New York R.	5	2	0	2
1957–58	New York R.	6	2	3	5
1961–62	New York R.	6	1	2	3
	Totals	22	6	5	11
All-Star					
1960	NHL All-Stars	1	1	0	1

HEBERT, Samuel *Goalie*
b. 1894

Season	Club	GP	GA	Sho	AVE
1917–18	Tor A–Otta	2	15	0	7.50
1923–24	Ottawa	2	9	0	4.50
	Totals	4	24	0	6.00

HEFFERNAN, Frank *Forward*

Season	Club	GP	G	A	Pts
1919–20	Toronto St.P.	17	0	0	0

HEFFERNAN, Gerald *Forward*
b. Montreal, Que., July 24, 1916

Season	Club	GP	G	A	Pts
1941–42	Montreal C.	--	5	15	20
1943–44	Montreal C.	43	28	20	48
	Totals	--	33	35	68

Playoffs

1941–42	Montreal C.	--	2	1	3
1942–43	Montreal C.	2	0	0	0
1943–44	Montreal C.	7	1	2	3
	Totals	--	3	3	6

HEINDL, William Wayne (Bill) *Forward*
b. Sherbrooke, Que., May 13, 1946

Season	Club	GP	G	A	Pts
1970–71	Minnesota	12	1	1	2
1971–72	Minnesota	2	0	0	0
1972–73	New York R.	4	1	0	1
	Totals	18	2	1	3

HEINRICH, Lionel Grant *Defenseman-Forward*
b. Churchbridge, Sask., Apr. 20, 1934

Season	Club	GP	G	A	Pts
1955–56	Boston	35	1	1	2

HEISKALA, Earl *Forward*
b. Kirkland Lake, Ont., Nov. 30, 1942

Season	Club	GP	G	A	Pts
1968–69	Philadelphia F.	21	3	3	6
1969–70	Philadelphia F.	65	8	7	15
1970–71	Philadelphia F.	41	2	1	3
	Totals	127	13	11	24

HELLER, Ehrhardt Henry (Ott) *Defenseman*
b. Kitchener, Ont., June 2, 1910

Season	Club	GP	G	A	Pts
1931–32	New York R.	21	2	2	4
1932–33	New York R.	40	5	7	12
1933–34	New York R.	48	2	5	7
1934–35	New York R.	47	3	11	14
1935–36	New York R.	43	2	11	13
1936–37	New York R.	48	5	12	17

HELLER *(Continued)*

Season	Club	GP	G	A	Pts
1937–38	New York R.	48	2	14	16
1938–39	New York R.	48	0	23	23
1939–40	New York R.	47	5	14	19
1940–41	New York R.	48	2	16	18
1941–42	New York R.	35	6	5	11
1942–43	New York R.	45	4	14	18
1943–44	New York R.	50	8	27	35
1944–45	New York R.	45	7	12	19
1945–46	New York R.	34	2	3	5
	Totals	647	55	176	231

Playoffs

1931–32	New York R.	7	3	1	4
1932–33	New York R.	8	3	0	3
1933–34	New York R.	2	0	0	0
1934–35	New York R.	4	0	1	1
1936–37	New York R.	9	0	0	0
1937–38	New York R.	3	0	1	1
1938–39	New York R.	7	0	1	1
1939–40	New York R.	12	0	3	3
1940–41	New York R.	3	0	1	1
1941–42	New York R.	6	0	0	0
	Totals	61	6	8	14

HELMAN, Harry *Defenseman*

Season	Club	GP	G	A	Pts
1922–23	Ottawa	24	0	0	0
1923–24	Ottawa	17	1	0	1
1924–25	Ottawa	1	0	0	0
	Totals	42	1	0	1

HEMMERLING, E.C. (Tony) *Forward*
b. Landis, Sask., May 15, 1914

Season	Club	GP	G	A	Pts
1935–36	New York A.	--	0	0	0
1936–37	New York A.	--	3	3	6
	Totals	--	3	3	6

HENDERSON, John Duncan (Long John)
Goalie
b. Toronto, Ont., Mar. 25, 1933

Season	Club	GP	GA	Sho	AVE
1954–55	Boston	44	109	5	2.40
1955–56	Boston	1	4	0	4.00
	Totals	45	113	5	2.51

Playoffs

1954–55	Boston	2	8	0	4.00

HENDERSON, John Murray (Moe) *Defenseman*
b. Toronto, Ont., Sept. 5, 1921

Season	Club	GP	G	A	Pts
1944–45	Boston	5	0	1	1
1945–46	Boston	48	4	11	15

HENDERSON (Continued)

Season	Club	GP	G	A	Pts
1946–47	Boston	57	5	12	17
1947–48	Boston	49	6	8	14
1948–49	Boston	60	2	9	11
1949–50	Boston	64	3	8	11
1950–51	Boston	66	4	7	11
1951–52	Boston	56	0	6	6
	Totals	405	24	62	86

Playoffs

1944–45	Boston	7	0	1	1
1945–46	Boston	10	1	1	2
1946–47	Boston	4	0	0	0
1947–48	Boston	3	1	0	1
1948–49	Boston	5	0	1	1
1950–51	Boston	5	0	0	0
1951–52	Boston	7	0	0	0
	Totals	41	2	3	5

HENDERSON, Paul Garnet *Forward*
b. Kincardine, Ont., Jan. 28, 1943

Season	Club	GP	G	A	Pts
1962–63	Detroit R.W.	2	0	0	0
1963–64	Detroit R.W.	32	3	3	6
1964–65	Detroit R.W.	70	8	13	21
1965–66	Detroit R.W.	69	22	24	46
1966–67	Detroit R.W.	46	21	19	40
1967–68	Det RW–Tor ML	63	18	23	44
1968–69	Toronto M.L.	74	27	32	59
1969–70	Toronto M.L.	67	20	22	42
1970–71	Toronto M.L.	72	30	30	60
1971–72	Toronto M.L.	73	38	19	57
1972–73	Toronto M.L.	40	18	16	34
	Totals	608	205	204	409

Playoffs

1963–64	Detroit R.W.	14	2	3	5
1964–65	Detroit R.W.	7	0	2	2
1965–66	Detroit R.W.	12	3	3	6
1968–69	Toronto M.L.	4	0	1	1
1970–71	Toronto M.L.	6	5	1	6
1971–72	Toronto M.L.	5	1	2	3
	Totals	48	11	12	13

All-Star

1972	East All-Stars	1	0	0	0
1973	East All-Stars	1	1	0	1
	Totals	2	1	0	1

HENDRICKSON, John Gunnard *Defenseman*
b. Kingston, Ont., Dec. 5, 1936

Season	Club	GP	G	A	Pts
1957–58	Detroit R.W.	1	0	0	0
1958–59	Detroit R.W.	3	0	0	0
1961–62	Detroit R.W.	1	0	0	0
	Totals	5	0	0	0

HENNING, Lorne Edward *Forward*
b. Melfort, Sask., Feb. 22, 1952

Season	Club	GP	G	A	Pts
1972–73	New York I.	63	7	19	26

HENRY, Camille (Eel) *Forward*
b. Quebec City, Que., Jan. 31, 1933

Season	Club	GP	G	A	Pts
1953–54	New York R.	66	24	15	39
1954–55	New York R.	21	5	2	7
1956–57	New York R.	36	14	15	29
1957–58	New York R.	70	32	24	56
1958–59	New York R.	70	23	35	58
1959–60	New York R.	49	12	15	27
1960–61	New York R.	53	28	25	53
1961–62	New York R.	60	23	15	38
1962–63	New York R.	60	37	23	60
1963–64	New York R.	68	29	26	55
1964–65	NY R–Chgo	70	26	18	44
1967–68	New York R.	36	8	12	20
1968–69	St. Louis B.	64	17	22	39
1969–70	St. Louis B.	4	1	2	3
	Totals	817	279	249	528

Playoffs

1956–57	New York R.	5	2	3	5
1957–58	New York R.	6	1	4	5
1961–62	New York R.	5	0	0	0
1964–65	Chicago	14	1	0	1
1967–68	New York R.	6	0	0	0
1968–69	St. Louis B.	12	2	5	7
	Totals	48	6	12	18

All-Star

1958	NHL All-Stars	1	0	1	1
1963	NHL All-Stars	1	0	1	1
1964	NHL All-Stars	1	0	0	0
	Totals	3	0	2	2

HENRY, Gordon David (Red) *Goalie*
b. Owen Sound, Ont., Aug. 17, 1926

Season	Club	GP	GA	Sho	AVE
1948–49	Boston	1	0	1	0.00
1949–50	Boston	2	5	0	2.50
	Totals	3	5	1	1.67

Playoffs

1950–51	Boston	2	10	0	5.00
1952–53	Boston	3	11	0	3.67
	Totals	5	21	0	4.20

HENRY, Samuel James (Sugar Jim) *Goalie*
b. Winnipeg, Man., Oct. 23, 1920

Season	Club	GP	GA	Sho	AVE
1941–42	New York R.	48	143	2	2.98
1945–46	New York R.	11	41	1	3.73

HENRY (Continued)

Season	Club	GP	GA	Sho	AVE
1946–47	New York R.	2	9	0	4.50
1947–48	New York R.	48	153	2	3.19
1948–49	Chicago	60	211	0	3.52
1951–52	Boston	70	176	7	2.51
1952–53	Boston	70	172	8	2.46
1953–54	Boston	70	181	8	2.58
1954–55	Boston	26	79	1	3.00
	Totals	405	1165	29	2.88

Playoffs

Season	Club	GP	GA	Sho	AVE
1941–42	New York R.	6	13	1	2.16
1951–52	Boston	7	18	1	2.57
1952–53	Boston	9	26	0	2.89
1953–54	Boston	4	16	0	4.00
1954–55	Boston	3	8	0	2.67
	Totals	29	81	2	2.79

All-Star		GP	Per	GA	AGP
1952	NHL 2nd All-Stars	1	1½	0	0.00

HERBERTS, James *Defenseman-Forward*

Season	Club	GP	G	A	Pts
1924–25	Boston	30	17	5	22
1925–26	Boston	36	26	5	31
1926–27	Boston	--	15	7	22
1927–28	Bos-Tor ML	--	15	4	19
1928–29	Detroit C.	--	9	5	14
1929–30	Detroit C.	--	1	3	4
	Totals	--	83	29	112

Playoffs

Season	Club	GP	G	A	Pts
1926–27	Boston	--	3	0	3
1928–29	Detroit C.	--	0	0	0
	Totals	--	3	0	3

HERCHENRATTER, Arthur *Forward*
b. Kitchener, Ont., Nov. 24, 1917

Season	Club	GP	G	A	Pts
1940–41	Detroit R.W.	--	1	2	3

HERGERT, Fred *Forward*
b. Calgary, Alta., Jan. 29, 1913

Season	Club	GP	G	A	Pts
1934–35	New York A.	--	1	5	6

HERGESHEIMER, Philip *Forward*
b. Winnipeg, Man., July 9, 1914

Season	Club	GP	G	A	Pts
1939–40	Chicago	--	9	11	20
1940–41	Chicago	--	8	16	24
1941–42	Chgo-Bos	26	3	11	14
1942–43	Chicago	9	1	3	4
	Totals	--	21	41	62

HERGESHEIMER (Continued)

Playoffs	Club	GP	G	A	Pts
1939–40	Chicago	2	0	0	0
1940–41	Chicago	5	0	0	0
	Totals	7	0	0	0

HERGESHEIMER, Walter Edgar *Forward*
b. Winnipeg, Man., Jan. 8, 1927

Season	Club	GP	G	A	Pts
1951–52	New York R.	68	26	12	38
1952–53	New York R.	70	30	29	59
1953–54	New York R.	66	27	16	43
1954–55	New York R.	14	4	2	6
1955–56	New York R.	70	22	18	40
1956–57	Chicago	41	2	8	10
1958–59	New York R.	22	3	0	3
	Totals	351	114	85	199

Playoffs

Season	Club	GP	G	A	Pts
1955–56	New York R.	5	1	0	1

All-Star					
1953	NHL All-Stars	1	2	0	2
1956	NHL All-Stars	1	0	0	0
	Totals	2	2	0	2

HERON, Robert *Forward*
b. Toronto, Ont., Dec. 31, 1917

Season	Club	GP	G	A	Pts
1939–40	Toronto M.L.	--	11	12	23
1940–41	Toronto M.L.	--	9	5	14
1941–42	NY A-Mont C	23	1	2	3
	Totals	--	21	19	40

Playoffs

Season	Club	GP	G	A	Pts
1939–40	Toronto M.L.	10	2	0	2
1940–41	Toronto M.L.	7	0	2	2
	Totals	17	2	2	4

HERRON, Denis *Goalie*
b. Chambly,Que., June 18, 1952

Season	Club	GP	GA	Sho	AVE
1972–73	Pittsburgh Pe.	16	55	2	3.41

HEXIMER, Orville Russell (Obs) *Forward*
b. Niagara Falls, Ont., Feb. 16,1910

Season	Club	GP	G	A	Pts
1929–30	New York R.	19	1	0	1
1932–33	Boston	--	7	5	12
1934–35	New York A.	--	5	2	7
	Totals	--	13	7	20

Playoffs

Season	Club	GP	G	A	Pts
1932–33	Boston	5	0	0	0

HEXTALL, Bryan Aldwyn *Forward*
b. Grenfell, Sask., July 31, 1913

Season	Club	GP	G	A	Pts
1936-37	New York R.	1	0	1	1
1937-38	New York R.	48	17	4	21
1938-39	New York R.	48	20	15	35
1939-40	New York R.	48	24	15	39
1940-41	New York R.	48	26	18	44
1941-42	New York R.	48	24	32	56
1942-43	New York R.	50	27	32	59
1943-44	New York R.	50	21	33	54
1945-46	New York R.	3	0	1	1
1946-47	New York R.	60	21	10	30
1947-48	New York R.	43	8	14	22
	Totals	447	187	175	365

Playoffs

Season	Club	GP	G	A	Pts
1937-38	New York R.	3	2	0	2
1938-39	New York R.	7	0	1	1
1939-40	New York R.	12	4	3	7
1940-41	New York R.	3	0	1	1
1941-42	New York R.	6	1	1	2
1947-48	New York R.	6	1	3	4
	Totals	37	8	9	17

HEXTALL, Bryan Lee *Forward*
b. Winnipeg, Man., May 23, 1941

Season	Club	GP	G	A	Pts
1962-63	New York R.	21	0	2	2
1969-70	Pittsburgh Pe.	66	12	19	31
1970-71	Pittsburgh Pe.	76	16	32	48
1971-72	Pittsburgh Pe.	78	20	24	44
1972-73	Pittsburgh Pe.	78	21	33	54
	Totals	319	69	110	179

Playoffs

Season	Club	GP	G	A	Pts
1969-70	Pittsburgh Pe.	10	0	1	1
1971-72	Pittsburgh Pe.	4	0	2	2
	Totals	14	0	3	3

HEXTALL, Dennis Harold *Forward*
b. Winnipeg, Man., Apr. 17, 1943

Season	Club	GP	G	A	Pts
1968-69	New York R.	13	1	4	5
1969-70	Los Angeles	28	5	7	12
1970-71	California	78	21	31	52
1971-72	Minnesota	33	6	10	16
1972-73	Minnesota	78	30	52	82
	Totals	230	63	104	167

Playoffs

Season	Club	GP	G	A	Pts
1967-68	New York R.	2	0	0	0
1971-72	Minnesota	7	0	2	2
1972-73	Minnesota	6	2	0	2
	Totals	15	2	2	4

HEYLIGER, Victor *Forward*
b. Boston, Mass., Sept. 26, 1911

Season	Club	GP	G	A	Pts
1943-44	Chicago	26	2	3	5

HICKE, Ernest Allen *Forward*
b. Regina, Sask., Nov. 7, 1947

Season	Club	GP	G	A	Pts
1970-71	California	78	22	25	47
1971-72	California	68	11	12	23
1972-73	Atl-NY I	59	14	23	37
	Totals	205	47	60	107

HICKE, William Lawrence *Forward*
b. Regina, Sask., Mar. 31, 1938

Season	Club	GP	G	A	Pts
1959-60	Montreal C.	43	3	10	13
1960-61	Montreal C.	70	18	27	45
1961-62	Montreal C.	70	20	31	51
1962-63	Montreal C.	70	17	22	39
1963-64	Montreal C.	48	11	9	20
1964-65	Mont C-NY R	57	6	12	18
1965-66	New York R.	49	9	18	27
1966-67	New York R.	48	3	4	7
1967-68	Oakland	52	21	19	40
1968-69	Oakland	67	25	36	61
1969-70	Oakland	69	15	29	44
1970-71	California	74	18	17	35
1971-72	Pittsburgh Pe.	12	2	0	2
	Totals	729	168	234	402

Playoffs

Season	Club	GP	G	A	Pts
1958-59	Montreal C.	1	0	0	0
1959-60	Montreal C.	7	1	2	3
1960-61	Montreal C.	5	2	0	2
1961-62	Montreal C.	6	0	2	2
1962-63	Montreal C.	5	0	0	0
1963-64	Montreal C.	7	0	2	2
1968-69	Oakland	7	0	3	3
1969-70	Oakland	4	0	1	1
	Totals	42	3	10	13

All-Star

Season	Club	GP	G	A	Pts
1959	Montreal C.	1	0	2	2
1960	Montreal C.	1	0	0	0
1969	West All-Stars	1	0	0	0
	Totals	3	0	2	2

HICKS, Harold *Defenseman*
b. Ottawa, Ont., Dec. 10, 1900

Season	Club	GP	G	A	Pts
1928-29	Montreal M.	44	2	0	2
1929-30	Detroit C.	44	3	2	5
1930-31	Detroit F.	44	0	0	0
	Totals	132	5	2	7

HICKS, Wayne *Forward*
b. Aberdeen, Wash. Apr. 9, 1937

Season	Club	GP	G	A	Pts
1960–61	Chicago	1	0	0	0
1962–63	Boston	65	7	9	16
1963–64	Montreal C.	2	0	0	0
1967–68	Phila F–Pitts Pe	47	6	14	20
	Totals	115	13	23	36

Playoffs

Season	Club	GP	G	A	Pts
1959–60	Chicago	1	0	1	1
1960–61	Chicago	1	0	0	0
	Totals	2	0	1	1

HIGHTON, Hector Salisbury *Goalie*
b. Medicine Hat, Alta. Dec. 10, 1923

Season	Club	GP	GA	Sho	AVE
1943–44	Chicago	24	108	0	4.50

HILDEBRAND, Issac Bruce (Ike) *Forward*
b. Winnipeg, Man., May 27, 1927

Season	Club	GP	G	A	Pts
1953–54	NY R–Chgo	38	7	11	18
1954–55	Chicago	3	0	0	0
	Totals	41	7	11	18

HILL, John Melvin (Sudden Death) *Forward*
b. Glenboro, Man., Feb. 15, 1914

Season	Club	GP	G	A	Pts
1937–38	Boston	--	2	0	2
1938–39	Boston	--	10	10	20
1939–40	Boston	--	9	11	20
1940–41	Boston	--	5	4	9
1941–42	Brooklyn A.	47	14	23	37
1942–43	Toronto M.L.	49	17	27	44
1943–44	Toronto M.L.	17	9	10	19
1944–45	Toronto M.L.	45	18	17	35
1945–46	Toronto M.L.	35	5	7	12
	Totals	--	89	109	198

Playoffs

Season	Club	GP	G	A	Pts
1938–39	Boston	12	6	3	9
1939–40	Boston	6	0	0	0
1940–41	Boston	11	1	1	2
1942–43	Toronto M.L.	6	3	0	3
1944–45	Toronto M.L.	13	2	3	5
	Totals	48	12	7	19

HILLER, Wilbert Carl (Dutch) *Forward*
b. Kitchener, Ont., May 11, 1915

Season	Club	GP	G	A	Pts
1937–38	New York R.	9	0	1	1
1938–39	New York R.	48	10	19	29
1939–40	New York R.	48	13	19	32

HILLER *(Continued)*

Season	Club	GP	G	A	Pts
1940–41	NY R–Det RW	45	8	10	18
1941–42	Det RW–Bos	50	7	10	17
1942–43	Bos–Mont C	42	8	6	14
1943–44	New York R.	50	18	22	40
1944–45	Montreal C.	48	20	16	36
1945–46	Montreal C.	45	7	11	18
	Totals	385	91	114	205

Playoffs

Season	Club	GP	G	A	Pts
1937–38	New York R.	3	0	0	0
1938–39	New York R.	7	1	0	1
1939–40	New York R.	12	2	4	6
1940–41	Detroit R.W.	9	0	0	0
1941–42	Boston	5	0	1	1
1942–43	Montreal C.	5	1	0	1
1944–45	Montreal C.	6	1	1	2
1945–46	Montreal C.	9	4	2	6
	Totals	56	9	8	17

HILLMAN, Floyd Arthur *Defenseman*
b. Ruthven, Ont., Nov. 19, 1933

Season	Club	GP	G	A	Pts
1956–57	bo	6	0	0	0

HILLMAN, Larry Morley *Defenseman*
b. Kirkland Lake, Ont., Feb. 5, 1937

Season	Club	GP	G	A	Pts
1954–55	Detroit R.W.	6	0	0	0
1955–56	Detroit R.W.	47	0	3	3
1956–57	Detroit R.W.	16	1	2	3
1957–58	Boston	70	3	19	22
1958–59	Boston	55	3	10	13
1959–60	Boston	2	0	1	1
1960–61	Toronto M.L.	62	3	10	13
1961–62	Toronto M.L.	5	0	0	0
1962–63	Toronto M.L.	5	0	0	0
1963–64	Toronto M.L.	33	0	4	4
1964–65	Toronto M.L.	2	0	0	0
1965–66	Toronto M.L.	48	3	25	28
1966–67	Toronto M.L.	55	4	19	23
1967–68	Toronto M.L.	55	3	17	20
1968–69	Minn–Mont C	37	1	10	11
1969–70	Philadelphia F.	76	5	26	31
1970–71	Philadelphia F.	73	3	13	16
1971–72	LA–Buff	65	2	13	15
1972–73	Buffalo	78	5	24	29
	Totals	790	36	196	232

Playoffs

Season	Club	GP	G	A	Pts
1954–55	Detroit R.W.	3	0	0	0
1955–56	Detroit R.W.	10	0	1	1
1957–58	Boston	11	0	2	2
1958–59	Boston	7	0	1	1
1960–61	Toronto M.L.	5	0	0	0

497

HILLMAN *(Continued)*

Playoffs	Club	GP	G	A	Pts
1963-64	Toronto M.L.	11	0	0	0
1965-66	Toronto M.L.	4	1	1	2
1966-67	Toronto M.L.	12	1	2	3
1968-69	Montreal C.	1	0	0	0
1970-71	Philadelphia F.	4	0	2	2
1972-73	Buffalo	6	0	0	0
	Totals	74	2	9	11

All-Star					
1955	Detroit R.W.	1	0	0	0
1962	Toronto M.L.	1	0	0	0
1963	Toronto M.L.	1	0	0	0
1964	Toronto M.L.	1	0	0	0
1968	Toronto M.L.	1	0	2	2
	Totals	5	0	2	2

HILLMAN, Wayne James *Defenseman*
b. Kirkland Lake, Ont., Nov. 13, 1938

Season	Club	GP	G	A	Pts
1961-62	Chicago	19	0	2	2
1962-63	Chicago	67	3	5	8
1963-64	Chicago	59	1	4	5
1964-65	Chgo-NY R	41	1	8	9
1965-66	New York R.	68	3	17	20
1966-67	New York R.	67	2	12	14
1967-68	New York R.	62	0	5	5
1968-69	Minnesota	50	0	8	8
1969-70	Philadelphia F.	68	3	5	8
1970-71	Philadelphia F.	69	5	7	12
1971-72	Philadelphia F.	47	0	3	3
1972-73	Philadelphia F.	74	0	10	10
	Totals	691	18	86	104

Playoffs					
1960-61	Chicago	1	0	0	0
1962-63	Chicago	6	0	2	2
1963-64	Chicago	7	0	1	1
1966-67	New York R.	4	0	0	0
1967-68	New York R.	2	0	0	0
1972-73	Philadelphia F.	8	0	0	0
	Totals	28	0	3	3

HIMES, Norman *Forward*
b. Galt, Ont., Apr. 13, 1903

Season	Club	GP	G	A	Pts
1926-27	New York A.	--	9	2	11
1927-28	New York A.	--	14	5	19
1928-29	New York A.	--	10	0	10
1929-30	New York A.	--	28	22	50
1930-31	New York A.	--	15	9	24
1931-32	New York A.	--	7	21	28
1932-33	New York A.	--	9	25	34
1933-34	New York A.	--	9	16	25
1934-35	New York A.	--	5	13	18
	Totals	--	106	113	219

HIMES *(Continued)*

Playoffs	Club	GP	G	A	Pts
1928-29	New York A.	--	0	0	0

HINSE, Andre *Forward*
b. Trois Riviere, Que., Apr. 19, 1945

Season	Club	GP	G	A	Pts
1967-68	Toronto M.L.	4	0	0	0

HIRSCHFELD, John Albert (Bert) *Forward*
b. Halifax, N.S., Mar. 1, 1929

Season	Club	GP	G	A	Pts
1949-50	Montreal C.	13	1	2	3
1950-51	Montreal C.	20	0	2	2
	Totals	33	1	4	5

Playoffs					
1949-50	Montreal C.	5	1	0	1

HITCHMAN, Lionel *Defenseman*
b. Toronto, Ont., 1903

Season	Club	GP	G	A	Pts
1922-23	Ottawa	3	0	1	1
1923-24	Ottawa	24	2	6	8
1924-25	Otta-Bos	30	3	0	3
1925-26	Boston	36	7	4	11
1926-27	Boston	--	3	6	9
1927-28	Boston	--	5	3	8
1928-29	Boston	--	1	0	1
1929-30	Boston	--	2	7	9
1930-31	Boston	--	0	2	2
1931-32	Boston	--	4	3	7
1932-33	Boston	--	0	1	1
1933-34	Boston	--	1	0	1
	Totals	--	28	33	61

Playoffs					
1922-23	Ottawa	--	1	0	1
1923-24	Ottawa	--	0	0	0
1926-27	Boston	--	1	0	1
1927-28	Boston	--	0	0	0
1928-29	Boston	--	0	1	1
1929-30	Boston	--	1	0	1
1930-31	Boston	--	0	0	0
1932-33	Boston	--	1	0	1
	Totals	--	4	1	5

HODGE, Charles Edward *Goalie*
b. Lachine, Que., July 28, 1933

Season	Club	GP	GA	Sho	AVE
1954-55	Montreal C.	13⅔	31	1	2.27
1957-58	Montreal C.	12	31	1	2.58
1958-59	Montreal C.	2	6	0	3.00
1959-60	Montreal C.	1	3	0	3.00
1960-61	Montreal C.	30	76	4	2.53

HODGE (Continued)

Season	Club	GP	GA	Sho	AVE
1963–64	Montreal C.	62	140	8	2.26
1964–65	Montreal C.	52	135	3	2.60
1965–66	Montreal C.	21⅔	56	1	2.58
1966–67	Montreal C.	34⅓	88	3	2.56
1967–68	Oakland	55⅓	158	3	2.86
1968–69	Oakland	13	48	0	3.69
1969–70	Oakland	12⅓	43	0	3.48
1970–71	Vancouver	32⅔	112	0	3.41
	Totals	342	927	24	2.70

Playoffs

1954–55	Montreal C.	4	6	0	1.50
1963–64	Montreal C.	7	16	1	2.29
1964–65	Montreal C.	5	10	1	2.00
	Totals	16	32	2	2.00

All-Star

		GP	Per	GA	AGP
1964	NHL All-Stars	1	1½	2	1.33
1965	Montreal C.	1	1½	4	2.67
1967	Montreal C.	1	2	0	0.00
	Totals	3	5	6	1.20

HODGE, Kenneth Raymond (Ken) *Forward*
b. Birmingham, England, June 25, l944

Season	Club	GP	G	A	Pts
1964–65	Chicago	1	0	0	0
1965–66	Chicago	63	6	17	23
1966–67	Chicago	69	10	25	35
1967–68	Boston	74	25	31	56
1968–69	Boston	75	45	45	90
1969–70	Boston	72	25	29	54
1970–71	Boston	78	43	62	105
1971–72	Boston	60	16	40	56
1972–73	Boston	73	37	44	81
	Totals	565	207	293	500

Playoffs

1965–66	Chicago	5	0	0	0
1966–67	Chicago	6	0	0	0
1967–68	Boston	4	3	0	3
1968–69	Boston	10	5	7	12
1969–70	Boston	14	3	10	13
1970–71	Boston	7	2	5	7
1971–72	Boston	15	9	8	17
1972–73	Boston	5	1	0	1
	Totals	66	23	30	53

All-Star

1971	East All-Stars	1	0	0	0
1973	East All-Stars	1	0	2	2
	Totals	2	0	2	2

HODGSON, Theodore James *Forward*
b. Hobbema, Alta., June 30, 1945

Season	Club	GP	G	A	Pts
1966–67	Boston	4	0	0	0

HOEKSTRA, Cecil Thomas *Forward*
b. Winnipeg, Man., Apr. 2, 1935

Season	Club	GP	G	A	Pts
1959–60	Montreal C.	4	0	0	0

HOEKSTRA, Edward Adrian *Forward*
b. Winnipeg, Man., Nov. 4, 1937

Season	Club	GP	G	A	Pts
1967–68	Philadelphia F.	70	15	21	36

Playoffs

1967–68	Philadelphia F.	7	0	1	1

HOENE, Phil George *Forward*
b. Duluth, Minn., Mar. 15, 1949

Season	Club	GP	G	A	Pts
1972–73	Los Angeles	4	0	1	1

HOFFINGER, Victor *Defenseman*

Season	Club	GP	G	A	Pts
1927–28	Chicago	--	0	1	1
1928–29	Chicago	--	0	0	0
	Totals	--	0	1	1

HOGABOAM, William Harold (Bill) *Forward*
b. Swift Current, Sask., Sept. 5, 1949

Season	Club	GP	G	A	Pts
1972–73	Atl-Det RW	6	1	0	1

HOGANSON, Dale Gordon (Red) *Defenseman*
b. North Battleford, Sask., July 8, l949

Season	Club	GP	G	A	Pts
1969–70	Los Angeles	49	1	7	8
1970–71	Los Angeles	70	4	10	14
1971–72	LA-Mont C	31	1	2	3
1972–73	Montreal C.	26	0	2	2
	Totals	176	6	21	27

HOGANSON, Paul Edward *Goalie*
b. Toronto, Ont., Nov. 12, 1949

Season	Club	GP	GA	Sho	AVE
1970–71	Pittsburgh Pe.	1	7	0	7.36

HOLBROOK, Terry Eugene *Forward*
b. Petrolia, Ont., July 11, 1950

Season	Club	GP	G	A	Pts
1972–73	Minnesota	21	2	3	5

Playoffs

1972–73	Minnesota	6	0	0	0

HOLLETT, William (Flash)
Defenseman-Forward
b. North Sydney, N.S., Apr. 13, 1912

Season	Club	GP	G	A	Pts
1933–34	Tor ML-Otta	--	7	4	11
1934–35	Toronto M.L.	--	10	16	26
1935–36	Tor ML-Bos	--	2	6	8
1936–37	Boston	--	3	7	10
1937–38	Boston	--	4	10	14
1938–39	Boston	--	10	17	27
1939–40	Boston	--	10	18	28
1940–41	Boston	--	9	15	24
1941–42	Boston	48	19	14	33
1942–43	Boston	50	19	25	44
1943–44	Bos-Det RW	52	15	19	34
1944–45	Detroit R.W.	50	20	21	41
1945–46	Detroit R.W.	38	4	9	13
	Totals	--	132	181	313

Playoffs

1934–35	Toronto M.L.	7	0	0	0
1935–36	Boston	2	0	0	0
1936–37	Boston	3	0	0	0
1937–38	Boston	3	0	1	1
1938–39	Boston	12	1	3	4
1939–40	Boston	6	1	2	3
1940–41	Boston	11	3	4	7
1941–42	Boston	5	0	1	1
1942–43	Boston	9	0	9	9
1943–44	Detroit R.W.	5	0	0	0
1944–45	Detroit R.W.	14	3	4	7
1945–46	Detroit R.W.	5	0	2	2
	Totals	82	8	26	34

HOLLINGWORTH, Gordon (Bucky)
Defenseman
b. Verdun, Que., July 24, 1933

Season	Club	GP	G	A	Pts
1954–55	Chicago	70	3	9	12
1955–56	Detroit R.W.	41	0	2	2
1956–57	Detroit R.W.	25	0	1	1
1957–58	Detroit R.W.	27	1	2	3
	Totals	163	4	14	18

Playoffs

1955–56	Detroit R.W.	3	0	0	0

All-Star

1955	Detroit R.W.	1	0	0	0

HOLMES, Charles Frank *Forward*
b. Edmonton, Alta., Sept. 21, 1934

Season	Club	GP	G	A	Pts
1958–59	Detroit R.W.	15	0	3	3
1961–62	Detroit R.W.	8	1	0	1
	Totals	23	1	3	4

HOLMES, Harold (Hap) *Goalie*
b. 1889

Season	Club	GP	GA	Sho	AVE
1917–18	Toronto A.	16	76	0	4.75
1918–19	Toronto A.	2	9	0	4.50
1926–27	Detroit C.	44	105	6	2.39
1927–28	Detroit C.	44	79	11	1.80
	Totals	106	269	17	2.54

Playoffs

1917–18	Toronto A.	7	28	0	4.00
1918–19	Seattle (PCHL)	4	10	1	2.50
1919–20	Seattle (PCHL)	5	15	0	3.00
1920–21	Vancouver (PCHL)	5	12	0	2.40
1924–25	Victoria (PCHL)	4	8	0	2.00
1925–26	Victoria (PCHL)	4	10	0	2.50
	Totals	29	83	1	2.86

HOLMES, Louis *Forward*
b. Edmonton, Alta., Jan. 29, 1911

Season	Club	GP	G	A	Pts
1931–32	Detroit F.	--	2	4	6
1932–33	Chicago	--	0	0	0
	Totals	--	2	4	6

Playoffs

1931–32	Detroit F.	--	0	0	0

HOLMES, William *Forward*
b. Weyburn, Sask., 1899

Season	Club	GP	G	A	Pts
1925–26	Montreal C.	9	1	0	1
1929–30	New York A.	--	5	4	9
	Totals	--	6	4	10

HOLOTA, John *Forward*
b. Hamilton, Ont., Feb. 25, 1921

Season	Club	GP	G	A	Pts
1942–43	Detroit R.W.	12	2	0	2
1945–46	Detroit R.W.	3	0	0	0
	Totals	15	2	0	2

HOLWEY, Albert R. (Toots) *Defenseman*
b. Toronto, Ont., Sept. 24, 1902

Season	Club	GP	G	A	Pts
1923–24	Toronto St. P.	6	1	0	1
1924–25	Toronto St. P.	25	2	2	4
1925–26	Tor StP-Mont M	29	0	0	0
1926–27	Montreal M.	--	0	0	0
1928–29	Pittsburgh Pi.	--	4	0	4
	Totals	--	7	2	9

Playoffs

1924–25	Toronto St. P.	--	0	0	0
1925–26	Montreal M.	--	0	0	0
	Totals	--	0	0	0

HOMENUKE, Ron *Forward*
b. Hazelton, B.C., Jan. 5, 1952

Season	Club	GP	G	A	Pts
1972-73	Vancouver	1	0	0	0

HORECK, Peter *Forward*
b. Massey, Ont., June 15, 1923

Season	Club	GP	G	A	Pts
1944-45	Chicago	50	20	16	36
1945-46	Chicago	50	20	21	41
1946-47	Chgo-Det RW	56	16	19	35
1947-48	Detroit R.W.	50	12	17	29
1948-49	Detroit R.W.	60	14	16	30
1949-50	Boston	34	5	5	10
1950-51	Boston	66	10	13	23
1951-52	Chicago	60	9	11	20
	Totals	426	106	118	224

Playoffs

1945-46	Chicago	4	0	0	0
1946-47	Detroit R.W.	5	2	0	2
1947-48	Detroit R.W.	10	3	7	10
1948-49	Detroit R.W.	11	1	1	2
1950-51	Boston	4	0	0	0
	Totals	34	6	8	14

HORNE, George (Shorty) *Forward*

Season	Club	GP	G	A	Pts
1925-26	Montreal M.	13	0	0	0
1928-29	Toronto M.L.	--	9	3	12
	Totals	--	9	3	12

Playoffs

1928-29	Toronto M.L.	--	0	0	0

HORNER, George Reginald (Red) *Defenseman*
b. Lynden, Ont., May 29, 1909

Season	Club	GP	G	A	Pts
1928-29	Toronto M.L.	--	0	0	0
1929-30	Toronto M.L.	--	2	7	9
1930-31	Toronto M.L.	--	1	11	12
1931-32	Toronto M.L.	--	7	9	16
1932-33	Toronto M.L.	--	3	8	11
1933-34	Toronto M.L.	--	11	10	21
1934-35	Toronto M.L.	--	4	8	12
1935-36	Toronto M.L.	--	2	9	11
1936-37	Toronto M.L.	--	3	9	12
1937-38	Toronto M.L.	--	4	20	24
1938-39	Toronto M.L.	--	4	10	14
1939-40	Toronto M.L.	--	1	9	10
	Totals	--	42	110	152

Playoffs

1928-29	Toronto M.L.	--	1	0	1
1930-31	Toronto M.L.	--	0	0	0
1931-32	Toronto M.L.	--	2	2	4

HORNER *(Continued)*

Playoffs	Club	GP	G	A	Pts
1932-33	Toronto M.L.	--	1	0	1
1933-34	Toronto M.L.	--	1	0	1
1934-35	Toronto M.L.	--	0	1	1
1935-36	Toronto M.L.	--	1	2	3
1936-37	Toronto M.L.	--	0	0	0
1937-38	Toronto M.L.	--	0	1	1
1938-39	Toronto M.L.	--	1	2	3
1939-40	Toronto M.L.	--	0	2	2
	Totals	--	7	10	17

HORNUNG, Larry John *Defenseman*
b. Gravelbourg, Sask., Nov. 10, 1945

Season	Club	GP	G	A	Pts
1970-71	St. Louis B.	1	0	0	0
1971-72	St. Louis B.	47	2	9	11
	Totals	48	2	9	11

Playoffs

1971-72	St. Louis B.	11	0	2	2

HORTON, Myles Gilbert (Tim)
Defenseman-Forward
b. Cochrane, Ont., Jan. 12, 1930

Season	Club	GP	G	A	Pts
1949-50	Toronto M.L.	1	0	0	0
1951-52	Toronto M.L.	4	0	0	0
1952-53	Toronto M.L.	70	2	14	16
1953-54	Toronto M.L.	70	7	24	31
1954-55	Toronto M.L.	67	5	9	14
1955-56	Toronto M.L.	35	0	5	5
1956-57	Toronto M.L.	66	6	19	25
1957-58	Toronto M.L.	53	6	20	26
1958-59	Toronto M.L.	70	5	21	26
1959-60	Toronto M.L.	70	3	29	32
1960-61	Toronto M.L.	57	6	15	21
1961-62	Toronto M.L.	70	10	28	38
1962-63	Toronto M.L.	70	6	19	25
1963-64	Toronto M.L.	70	9	20	29
1964-65	Toronto M.L.	70	12	16	28
1965-66	Toronto M.L.	70	6	22	28
1966-67	Toronto M.L.	70	8	17	25
1967-68	Toronto M.L.	69	4	23	27
1968-69	Toronto M.L.	74	11	29	40
1969-70	Tor ML-NY R	74	4	24	28
1970-71	New York R.	78	2	18	20
1971-72	Pittsburgh Pe.	44	2	9	11
1972-73	Buffalo	69	1	16	17
	Totals	1391	115	397	512

Playoffs

1949-50	Toronto M.L.	1	0	0	0
1953-54	Toronto M.L.	5	1	1	2
1955-56	Toronto M.L.	2	0	0	0
1958-59	Toronto M.L.	12	0	3	3

HORTON (Continued)

Playoffs	Club	GP	G	A	Pts
1959-60	Toronto M.L.	10	0	1	1
1960-61	Toronto M.L.	5	0	0	0
1961-62	Toronto M.L.	12	3	13	16
1962-63	Toronto M.L.	10	1	3	4
1963-64	Toronto M.L.	14	0	4	4
1964-65	Toronto M.L.	6	0	2	2
1965-66	Toronto M.L.	4	1	0	1
1966-67	Toronto M.L.	12	3	5	8
1968-69	Toronto M.L.	4	0	0	0
1969-70	New York R.	6	1	1	2
1970-71	New York R.	13	1	4	5
1971-72	Pittsburgh Pe.	4	0	1	1
1972-73	Buffalo	6	0	1	1
	Totals	126	11	39	50

All-Star					
1954	NHL All-Stars	1	0	0	0
1962	Toronto M.L.	1	0	0	0
1963	Toronto M.L.	1	0	0	0
1964	Toronto M.L.	1	0	0	0
1968	Toronto M.L.	1	0	0	0
1969	East All-Stars	1	0	0	0
	Totals	6	0	0	0

HORVATH, Bronco Joseph *Forward*
b. Port Colborne, Ont., Mar. 12, 1930

Season	Club	GP	G	A	Pts
1955-56	New York R.	66	12	17	29
1956-57	NY R-Mont C	8	1	2	3
1957-58	Boston	67	30	36	66
1958-59	Boston	45	19	20	39
1959-60	Boston	68	39	41	80
1960-61	Boston	47	15	15	30
1961-62	Chicago	69	17	29	46
1962-63	NY R-Tor ML	50	7	19	26
1967-68	Minnesota	14	1	6	7
	Totals	434	141	185	326

Playoffs					
1955-56	New York R.	5	1	2	3
1957-58	Boston	12	5	3	8
1958-59	Boston	7	2	3	5
1961-62	Chicago	12	4	1	5
	Totals	36	12	9	21

All-Star					
1960	NHL All-Stars	1	0	0	0
1961	Chicago	1	0	0	0
	Totals	2	0	0	0

HOULE, Rejean *Forward*
b. Rouyne, Que., Oct. 25, 1949

Season	Club	GP	G	A	Pts
1969-70	Montreal C.	9	0	1	1
1970-71	Montreal C.	66	10	9	19

HOULE (Continued)

Season	Club	GP	G	A	Pts
1971-72	Montreal C.	77	11	17	28
1972-73	Montreal C.	72	13	35	48
	Totals	224	34	62	96

Playoffs					
1970-71	Montreal C.	20	2	5	7
1971-72	Montreal C.	6	0	0	0
1972-73	Montreal C.	17	3	6	9
	Totals	43	5	11	16

HOWARD, Jack Francis *Defenseman*
b. London, Ont., Oct. 15, 1915

Season	Club	GP	G	A	Pts
1936-37	Toronto M.L.	2	0	0	0

HOWATT, Gary *Forward*
b. Grand Center, Alta., Sept. 26, 1952

Season	Club	GP	G	A	Pts
1972-73	New York I.	8	0	1	1

HOWE, Gordon *Forward*
b. Floral, Sask., Mar. 31, 1928

Season	Club	GP	G	A	Pts
1946-47	Detroit R.W.	58	7	15	22
1947-48	Detroit R.W.	60	16	28	44
1948-49	Detroit R.W.	40	12	25	37
1949-50	Detroit R.W.	70	35	33	68
1950-51	Detroit R.W.	70	43	43	86
1951-52	Detroit R.W.	70	47	39	86
1952-53	Detroit R.W.	70	49	46	95
1953-54	Detroit R.W.	70	33	48	81
1954-55	Detroit R.W.	64	29	33	62
1955-56	Detroit R.W.	70	38	41	79
1956-57	Detroit R.W.	70	44	45	89
1957-58	Detroit R.W.	64	33	44	77
1958-59	Detroit R.W.	70	32	46	78
1959-60	Detroit R.W.	70	28	45	73
1960-61	Detroit R.W.	64	23	49	72
1961-62	Detroit R.W.	70	33	44	77
1962-63	Detroit R.W.	70	38	48	86
1963-64	Detroit R.W.	69	26	47	73
1964-65	Detroit R.W.	70	29	47	76
1965-66	Detroit R.W.	70	29	46	75
1966-67	Detroit R.W.	69	25	40	65
1967-68	Detroit R.W.	74	39	43	82
1968-69	Detroit R.W.	76	44	59	103
1969-70	Detroit R.W.	76	31	40	71
1970-71	Detroit R.W.	63	23	29	52
	Totals	1687	786	1023	1809

Playoffs					
1946-47	Detroit R.W.	5	0	0	0
1947-48	Detroit R.W.	10	1	1	2
1948-49	Detroit R.W.	11	8	3	11

HOWE (Continued)

Playoffs	Club	GP	G	A	Pts
1949-50	Detroit R.W.	1	0	0	0
1950-51	Detroit R.W.	6	4	3	7
1951-52	Detroit R.W.	8	2	5	7
1952-53	Detroit R.W.	6	2	5	7
1953-54	Detroit R.W.	12	4	5	9
1954-55	Detroit R.W.	11	9	11	20
1955-56	Detroit R.W.	10	3	9	12
1956-57	Detroit R.W.	5	2	5	7
1957-58	Detroit R.W.	4	1	1	2
1959-60	Detroit R.W.	6	1	5	6
1960-61	Detroit R.W.	11	4	11	15
1962-63	Detroit R.W.	11	7	9	16
1963-64	Detroit R.W.	14	9	10	19
1964-65	Detroit R.W.	7	4	2	6
1965-66	Detroit R.W.	12	4	6	10
1969-70	Detroit R.W.	4	2	0	2
	Totals	154	67	91	158

All-Star					
1948	NHL All-Stars	1	0	0	0
1949	NHL All-Stars	1	0	0	0
1950	Detroit R.W.	1	1	1	2
1951	NHL 1st All-Stars	1	1	0	1
1952	NHL 1st All-Stars	1	0	0	0
1953	NHL All-Stars	1	0	0	0
1954	Detroit R.W.	1	1	0	1
1955	Detroit R.W.	1	1	1	2
1956	NHL All-Stars	1	0	0	0
1957	NHL All-Stars	1	1	0	1
1958	NHL All-Stars	1	0	0	0
1959	NHL All-Stars	1	0	0	0
1960	NHL All-Stars	1	0	0	0
1961	NHL All-Stars	1	1	1	2
1962	NHL All-Stars	1	1	0	1
1963	NHL All-Stars	1	0	1	1
1964	NHL All-Stars	1	0	1	1
1965	NHL All-Stars	1	2	2	4
1967	NHL All-Stars	1	0	0	0
1968	NHL All-Stars	1	0	1	1
1969	East All-Stars	1	0	0	0
1970	East All-Stars	1	1	0	1
	Totals	22	10	8	18

HOWE, Sydney Harris *Forward*
b. Ottawa, Ont., Sept. 18, 1911

Season	Club	GP	G	A	Pts
1929-30	Ottawa	--	1	1	2
1930-31	Philadelphia Q.	--	9	11	20
1932-33	Ottawa	--	12	12	24
1933-34	Ottawa	--	13	7	20
1934-35	StL E-Det RW	--	22	25	47
1935-36	Detroit R.W.	--	16	14	30
1936-37	Detroit R.W.	--	17	10	27
1937-38	Detroit R.W.	--	8	19	27

HOWE (Continued)

Season	Club	GP	G	A	Pts
1938-39	Detroit R.W.	--	16	20	36
1939-40	Detroit R.W.	--	14	23	37
1940-41	Detroit R.W.	--	20	24	44
1941-42	Detroit R.W.	48	16	19	35
1942-43	Detroit R.W.	50	20	35	55
1943-44	Detroit R.W.	40	32	28	60
1944-45	Detroit R.W.	46	17	36	53
1945-46	Detroit R.W.	26	4	7	11
	Totals	--	237	291	528

Playoffs					
1929-30	Ottawa	--	0	0	0
1935-36	Detroit R.W.	7	3	3	6
1936-37	Detroit R.W.	10	2	5	7
1938-39	Detroit R.W.	6	3	1	4
1939-40	Detroit R.W.	5	2	2	4
1940-41	Detroit R.W.	9	1	7	8
1941-42	Detroit R.W.	12	3	5	8
1942-43	Detroit R.W.	7	1	2	3
1943-44	Detroit R.W.	5	2	2	4
1944-45	Detroit R.W.	7	0	0	0
	Totals	--	17	27	44

HOWE, Victor Stanley *Forward*
b. Saskatoon, Sask., Nov. 2, 1929

Season	Club	GP	G	A	Pts
1950-51	New York R.	3	1	0	1
1953-54	New York R.	1	0	0	0
1954-55	New York R.	29	2	4	6
	Totals	33	3	4	7

HOWELL, Henry Vernon (Harry) *Defenseman*
b. Hamilton, Ont., Dec. 28, 1932

Season	Club	GP	G	A	Pts
1952-53	New York R.	67	3	8	11
1953-54	New York R.	67	7	9	16
1954-55	New York R.	70	2	14	16
1955-56	New York R.	70	3	15	18
1956-57	New York R.	65	2	10	12
1957-58	New York R.	70	4	7	11
1958-59	New York R.	70	4	10	14
1959-60	New York R.	67	7	6	13
1960-61	New York R.	70	7	10	17
1961-62	New York R.	66	6	15	21
1962-63	New York R.	70	5	20	25
1963-64	New York R.	70	5	31	36
1964-65	New York R.	68	2	20	22
1965-66	New York R.	70	4	29	33
1966-67	New York R.	70	12	28	40
1967-68	New York R.	74	5	24	29
1968-69	New York R.	56	4	7	11
1969-70	Oakland	55	4	16	20
1970-71	Calif-LA	46	3	17	20

HOWELL (Continued)

Season	Club	GP	G	A	Pts
1971-72	Los Angeles	77	1	17	18
1972-73	Los Angeles	73	4	11	15
	Totals	1411	94	324	418

Playoffs

Season	Club	GP	G	A	Pts
1955-56	New York R.	5	0	1	1
1956-57	New York R.	5	1	0	1
1957-58	New York R.	6	1	0	1
1961-62	New York R.	6	0	1	1
1966-67	New York R.	4	0	0	0
1967-68	New York R.	6	1	0	1
1968-69	New York R.	2	0	0	0
1969-70	Oakland	4	0	1	1
	Totals	38	3	3	6

All-Star

Season	Club	GP	G	A	Pts
1954	NHL All-Stars	1	0	0	0
1963	NHL All-Stars	1	0	0	0
1964	NHL All-Stars	1	0	1	1
1965	NHL All-Stars	1	0	0	0
1967	NHL All-Stars	1	0	0	0
1968	NHL All-Stars	1	0	0	0
1970	West All-Stars	1	0	0	0
	Totals	7	0	1	1

HOWELL, Ronald *Defenseman-Forward*
b. Hamilton, Ont., Dec. 4, 1935

Season	Club	GP	G	A	Pts
1954-55	New York R.	3	0	0	0
1955-56	New York R.	1	0	0	0
	Totals	4	0	0	0

HRYMNAK, Stephen *Defenseman*
b. Port Arthur, Ont., Mar. 3, 1926

Season	Club	GP	G	A	Pts
1951-52	Chicago	18	2	1	3

HUARD, Roland *Forward*

Season	Club	GP	G	A	Pts
1930-31	Toronto M.L.	--	1	0	1

Playoffs

Season	Club	GP	G	A	Pts
1930-31	Toronto M.L.	--	0	0	0

HUCK, Francis (Fran) *Forward*
b. Regina, Sask., Dec. 4, 1945

Season	Club	GP	G	A	Pts
1969-70	Montreal C.	2	0	0	0
1970-71	Mont C-StL B	34	8	10	18
1972-73	St. Louis B.	58	16	20	36
	Totals	94	24	30	54

Playoffs

Season	Club	GP	G	A	Pts
1970-71	St. Louis B.	6	1	2	3
1972-73	St. Louis B.	5	2	2	4
	Totals	11	3	4	7

HUCUL, Frederick Albert *Defenseman*
b. Tubrose, Sask, Dec. 4, 1931

Season	Club	GP	G	A	Pts
1950-51	Chicago	3	1	0	1
1951-52	Chicago	34	3	7	10
1952-53	Chicago	57	5	7	12
1953-54	Chicago	27	0	3	3
1967-68	St. Louis B.	43	2	13	15
	Totals	164	11	30	41

Playoffs

Season	Club	GP	G	A	Pts
1952-53	Chicago	6	1	0	1

HUDSON, David Richard (Dave) *Forward*
b. St.Thomas, Ont., Dec. 28, 1949

Season	Club	GP	G	A	Pts
1972-73	New York I.	69	12	19	31

HUDSON, Ronald *Forward*
b. Timmins, Ont., Apr. 18, 1914

Season	Club	GP	G	A	Pts
1937-38	Detroit R.W.	--	5	2	7

HUGGINS, Allan *Forward*
b. Toronto, Ont.

Season	Club	GP	G	A	Pts
1930-31	Montreal M.	--	1	1	2

Playoffs

1930-31	Montreal M.	--	0	0	0

HUGHES, Albert *Forward*
b. Collingwood, Ont.

Season	Club	GP	G	A	Pts
1930-31	New York A.	--	5	7	12
1931-32	New York A.	--	1	1	2
	Totals	--	6	8	14

HUGHES, Brenton Alexander *Defenseman*
b. Bowmanville, Ont., June 17, 1943

Season	Club	GP	G	A	Pts
1967-68	Los Angeles	44	4	10	14
1968-69	Los Angeles	72	2	19	21
1969-70	Los Angeles	52	1	7	8
1970-71	Philadelphia F.	30	1	10	11
1971-72	Philadelphia F.	63	2	20	22
1972-73	Phila F-StL B	37	3	12	15
	Totals	298	13	78	91

Playoffs

Season	Club	GP	G	A	Pts
1967-68	Los Angeles	7	0	0	0
1968-69	Los Angeles	11	1	3	4
1970-71	Philadelphia F.	4	0	0	0
	Totals	22	1	3	4

HUGHES, Howard Duncan *Forward*
  b. St. Boniface, Man., Apr. 4, 1939

Season	Club	GP	G	A	Pts
1967-68	Los Angeles	74	9	14	23
1968-69	Los Angeles	73	16	14	30
1969-70	Los Angeles	21	0	4	4
	Totals	168	25	32	57
Playoffs					
1967-68	Los Angeles	7	2	0	2
1968-69	Los Angeles	11	0	1	1
	Totals	18	2	1	3

HUGHES, J. (Rusty) *Defenseman*

Season	Club	GP	G	A	Pts
1929-30	Detroit C.	--	0	1	1

HULL, Dennis William *Forward*
  b. Point Anne, Ont., Nov. 19, 1944

Season	Club	GP	G	A	Pts
1964-65	Chicago	55	10	4	14
1965-66	Chicago	25	1	5	6
1966-67	Chicago	70	25	17	42
1967-68	Chicago	74	18	15	33
1968-69	Chicago	72	30	34	64
1969-70	Chicago	76	17	35	52
1970-71	Chicago	78	40	26	66
1971-72	Chicago	78	30	39	69
1972-73	Chicago	78	39	51	90
	Totals	606	210	226	436
Playoffs					
1964-65	Chicago	6	0	0	0
1965-66	Chicago	3	0	0	0
1966-67	Chicago	6	0	1	1
1967-68	Chicago	11	1	3	4
1969-70	Chicago	8	5	2	7
1970-71	Chicago	18	7	6	13
1971-72	Chicago	8	4	2	6
1972-73	Chicago	16	9	15	24
	Totals	76	26	29	55
All-Star					
1969	East All-Stars	1	0	0	0
1971	West All-Stars	1	0	0	0
1972	West All-Stars	1	0	1	1
1973	West All-Stars	1	0	1	1
	Totals	4	0	2	2

HULL, Robert Marvin *Forward*
  b. Point Anne, Ont., Jan. 3, 1939

Season	Club	GP	G	A	Pts
1957-58	Chicago	70	13	34	47
1958-59	Chicago	70	18	32	50
1959-60	Chicago	70	39	42	81
1960-61	Chicago	67	31	25	56

HULL *(Continued)*

Season	Club	GP	G	A	Pts
1961-62	Chicago	70	50	34	84
1962-63	Chicago	65	31	31	62
1963-64	Chicago	70	43	44	87
1964-65	Chicago	61	39	32	71
1965-66	Chicago	65	54	43	97
1966-67	Chicago	66	52	28	80
1967-68	Chicago	71	44	31	75
1968-69	Chicago	74	58	49	107
1969-70	Chicago	61	38	29	67
1970-71	Chicago	78	44	52	96
1971-72	Chicago	78	50	43	93
	Totals	1036	604	549	1153
Playoffs					
1958-59	Chicago	6	1	1	2
1959-60	Chicago	3	1	0	1
1960-61	Chicago	12	4	10	14
1961-62	Chicago	12	8	5	13
1962-63	Chicago	5	8	2	10
1963-64	Chicago	7	2	5	7
1964-65	Chicago	14	10	7	17
1965-66	Chicago	6	2	2	4
1966-67	Chicago	6	4	2	6
1967-68	Chicago	11	4	6	10
1969-70	Chicago	8	3	8	11
1970-71	Chicago	18	11	14	25
1971-72	Chicago	8	4	4	8
	Totals	116	62	66	128
All-Star					
1960	NHL All-Stars	1	0	0	0
1961	Chicago	1	0	1	1
1962	NHL All-Stars	1	0	0	0
1963	NHL All-Stars	1	1	0	1
1964	NHL All-Stars	1	0	1	1
1965	NHL All-Stars	1	1	1	2
1967	NHL All-Stars	1	0	0	0
1968	NHL All-Stars	1	0	1	1
1969	East All-Stars	1	0	0	0
1970	East All-Stars	1	1	1	2
1971	West All-Stars	1	1	0	1
1972	West All-Stars	1	1	0	1
	Totals	12	5	5	10

HUNT, Frederick Tennyson *Forward*
  b. Brantford, Ont., Jan. 17, 1918

Season	Club	GP	G	A	Pts
1940-41	New York A.	--	2	5	7
1944-45	New York R.	44	13	9	22
	Totals	--	15	14	29

HURLEY, Paul *Defenseman*
  b. Melrose, Mass., July 12, 1946

Season	Club	GP	G	A	Pts
1968-69	Boston	1	0	1	1

HURST, Ronald *Forward*
b. Toronto, Ont., May 18, 1931

Season	Club	GP	G	A	Pts
1955–56	Toronto M.L.	50	7	5	12
1956–57	Toronto M.L.	14	2	2	4
	Totals	64	9	7	16

Playoffs

1955–56	Toronto M.L.	3	0	2	2

HUTCHINSON, Ronald Wayne *Forward*
b. Flin Flon, Man., Oct. 24, 1936

Season	Club	GP	G	A	Pts
1960–61	New York R.	9	0	0	0

HUTTON, William David *Defenseman*
b. Calgary, Alta., Jan. 28, 1910

Season	Club	GP	G	A	Pts
1929–30	Bos-Otta	--	2	1	3
1930–31	Phila Q–Bos	--	1	1	2
	Totals	--	3	2	5

HYLAND, Harry *Forward*
b. Montreal, Que., Jan. 2, 1889

Season	Club	GP	G	A	Pts
1917–18	Mont W–Otta	16	14	0	14

IMLACH, Brent *Forward*
b. Toronto, Ont., Nov. 16, 1946

Season	Club	GP	G	A	Pts
1965–66	Toronto M.L.	2	0	0	0
1966–67	Toronto M.L.	1	0	0	0
	Totals	3	0	0	0

INGARFIELD, Earl Thompson *Forward*
b. Lethbridge, Alta., Oct. 25, 1934

Season	Club	GP	G	A	Pts
1958–59	New York R.	35	1	2	3
1959–60	New York R.	20	1	2	3
1960–61	New York R.	66	13	21	34
1961–62	New York R.	70	26	31	57
1962–63	New York R.	69	19	24	43
1963–64	New York R.	63	15	11	26
1964–65	New York R.	69	15	13	28
1965–66	New York R.	68	20	16	36
1966–67	New York R.	67	12	22	34
1967–68	Pittsburgh Pe.	50	15	22	37
1968–69	Pitts Pe–Oak	66	16	30	46
1969–70	Oakland	54	21	24	45
1970–71	California	49	5	8	13
	Totals	746	179	226	405

Playoffs

1961–62	New York R.	6	3	2	5
1966–67	New York R.	4	1	0	1

INGARFIELD *(Continued)*

Playoffs	Club	GP	G	A	Pts
1968–69	Oakland	7	4	6	10
1969–70	Oakland	4	1	0	1
	Totals	21	9	8	17

INGLIS, William John *Forward*
b. Ottawa, Ont., May 11, 1943

Season	Club	GP	G	A	Pts
1967–68	Los Angeles	12	1	1	2
1968–69	Los Angeles	10	0	1	1
1970–71	Buffalo	14	0	1	1
	Totals	36	1	3	4

Playoffs

1968–69	Los Angeles	11	1	2	3

INGOLSBY, Jack *Defenseman-Forward*
b. Toronto, Ont., June 21, 1924

Season	Club	GP	G	A	Pts
1942–43	Toronto M.L.	8	0	1	1
1943–44	Toronto M.L.	21	5	0	6
	Totals	29	5	1	6

INGRAM, Frank *Forward*
b. Craven, Sask., Sept. 17, 1907

Season	Club	GP	G	A	Pts
1924–25	Boston	1	0	0	0
1929–30	Chicago	--	6	10	16
1930–31	Chicago	--	17	4	21
1931–32	Chicago	--	1	2	3
	Totals	--	24	16	40

Playoffs

1929–30	Chicago	--	0	0	0
1930–31	Chicago	--	0	1	1
	Totals	--	0	1	1

INGRAM, Ronald Walter *Defenseman*
b. Toronto, Ont., July 5, 1933

Season	Club	GP	G	A	Pts
1956–57	Chicago	45	1	6	7
1963–64	Det RW–NY R	66	4	9	13
1964–65	New York R.	3	0	0	0
	Totals	114	5	15	20

Playoffs

1962–63	Chicago	2	0	0	0

IRONS, Robert Richard (Robbie) *Goalie*
b. Toront, Ont., Nov. 19, 1946

Season	Club	GP	GA	Sho	AVE
1968–69	St. Louis B.	1/20	0	0	0.00

IRONSTONE, Joseph *Goalie*

Season	Club	GP	GA	Sho	AVE
1927–28	Toronto M.L.	1	0	1	0.00

506

IRVIN, James Dickinson (Dick) *Forward*
b. Limestone Ridge, Ont., July 19,1892

Season	Club	GP	G	A	Pts
1926-27	Chicago	--	18	18	36
1927-28	Chicago	--	5	4	9
1928-29	Chicago	--	6	1	7
	Totals	--	29	23	52
Playoffs					
1926-27	Chicago	--	2	0	2

IRVINE, Edward Amos (Ted) *Forward*
b. Winnipeg, Man., Dec. 8, 1944

Season	Club	GP	G	A	Pts
1963-64	Boston	1	0	0	0
1967-68	Los Angeles	73	18	22	40
1968-69	Los Angeles	76	15	24	39
1969-70	LA-NY R	75	11	16	27
1970-71	New York R.	76	20	18	38
1971-72	New York R.	78	15	21	36
1972-73	New York R.	53	8	12	20
	Totals	432	87	113	200
Playoffs					
1967-68	Los Angeles	6	1	3	4
1968-69	Los Angeles	11	5	1	6
1969-70	New York R.	6	1	2	3
1970-71	New York R.	12	1	2	3
1971-72	New York R.	16	4	5	9
1972-73	New York R.	10	1	3	4
	Totals	61	13	16	29

IRWIN, Ivan Duane *Defenseman*
b. Chicago, Ill., Mar. 13, 1927

Season	Club	GP	G	A	Pts
1952-53	Montreal C.	4	0	1	1
1953-54	New York R.	56	2	12	14
1954-55	New York R.	60	0	13	13
1955-56	New York R.	34	0	1	1
1957-58	New York R.	1	0	0	0
	Totals	155	2	27	29
Playoffs					
1955-56	New York R.	5	0	0	0

JACKSON, Arthur *Forward*
b. Totonto, Ont., Dec. 15, 1915

Season	Club	GP	G	A	Pts
1934-35	Toronto M.L.	--	1	3	4
1935-36	Toronto M.L.	--	5	15	20
1936-37	Toronto M.L.	--	2	0	2
1937-38	Boston	--	9	3	12
1938-39	New York A.	--	12	13	25
1939-40	Boston	--	7	18	25
1940-41	Boston	--	17	15	32
1941-42	Boston	--	6	18	24

JACKSON *(Continued)*

Season	Club	GP	G	A	Pts
1942-43	Boston	50	22	31	53
1943-44	Boston	49	28	41	69
1944-45	Bos-Tor ML	50	14	21	35
	Totals	--	123	178	301
Playoffs					
1934-35	Toronto M.L.	--	0	0	0
1935-36	Toronto M.L.	--	0	3	3
1937-38	Boston	--	0	0	0
1938-39	New York A.	--	0	0	0
1939-40	Boston	--	1	2	3
1940-41	Boston	--	1	3	4
1941-42	Boston	--	0	1	1
1942-43	Boston	9	6	3	9
1944-45	Toronto M.L.	8	0	0	0
	Totals	--	8	12	20

JACKSON, Douglas *Goalie*
b. Winnipeg, Man,. Dec. 12, 1924

Season	Club	GP	GA	Sho	AVE
1947-48	Chicago	6	42	0	7.00

JACKSON, Harold Russell *Defenseman*
b. Cedar Springs, Ont., Aug. 1, 1918

Season	Club	GP	G	A	Pts
1936-37	Chicago	--	1	3	4
1937-38	Chicago	--	0	0	0
1940-41	Detroit R.W.	--	0	0	0
1942-43	Detroit R.W.	4	0	4	4
1943-44	Detroit R.W.	50	7	12	19
1944-45	Detroit R.W.	50	5	6	11
1945-46	Detroit R.W.	36	3	4	7
1946-47	Detroit R.W.	37	1	5	6
	Totals	--	17	34	51
Playoffs					
1937-38	Chicago	--	0	0	0
1940-41	Detroit R.W.	--	0	0	0
1942-43	Detroit R.W.	6	0	1	1
1943-44	Detroit R.W.	5	0	0	0
1944-45	Detroit R.W.	14	1	1	2
1945-46	Detroit R.W.	5	0	0	0
	Totals	--	1	2	3

JACKSON, Harvey (Busher) *Forward*
b. Toronto, Ont., Jan. 17, 1911

Season	Club	GP	G	A	Pts
1929-30	Toronto M.L.	--	12	6	18
1930-31	Toronto M.L.	--	18	13	31
1931-32	Toronto M.L.	--	28	25	53
1932-33	Toronto M.L.	--	27	17	44
1933-34	Toronto M.L.	--	20	18	38
1934-35	Toronto M.L.	--	22	22	44
1935-36	Toronto M.L.	--	11	11	22
1936-37	Toronto M.L.	--	21	19	40

JACKSON (Continued)

Season	Club	GP	G	A	Pts
1937–38	Toronto M.L.	--	17	17	34
1938–39	Toronto M.L.	--	10	17	27
1939–40	New York A.	--	12	8	20
1940–41	New York A.	--	8	18	26
1941–42	Boston	--	5	7	12
1942–43	Boston	44	19	15	34
1943–44	Boston	42	11	21	32
	Totals	--	241	234	475

Playoffs

Season	Club	GP	G	A	Pts
1930–31	Toronto M.L.	--	0	0	0
1931–32	Toronto M.L.	--	5	2	7
1932–33	Toronto M.L.	--	3	1	4
1933–34	Toronto M.L.	--	1	0	1
1934–35	Toronto M.L.	--	3	2	5
1935–36	Toronto M.L.	--	3	2	5
1936–37	Toronto M.L.	--	1	0	1
1937–38	Toronto M.L.	--	1	0	1
1938–39	Toronto M.L.	--	0	1	1
1939–40	New York A.	--	0	1	1
1941–42	Boston	--	0	1	1
1942–43	Boston	9	1	2	3
	Totals	--	18	12	30

JACKSON, John Alexander *Defenseman*
b. Windson, Ont., May 3, 1925

Season	Club	GP	G	A	Pts
1946–47	Chicago	48	2	5	7

JACKSON, Lloyd *Forward*
b. Ottawa, Ont., Jan. 7, 1912

Season	Club	GP	G	A	Pts
1936–37	New York A.	--	1	1	2

JACKSON, Percy *Goalie*
b. Canmore, Alta., Sept. 21, 1907

Season	Club	GP	GA	Sho	AVE
1931–32	Boston	3	7	0	2.33
1933–34	New York A.	1	9	0	9.00
1934–35	New York R.	1	8	0	8.00
1935–36	Boston	1	1	0	1.00
	Totals	6	25	0	4.17

JACKSON, Stanton *Forward*

Season	Club	GP	G	A	Pts
1921–22	Toronto St. P.	1	0	0	0
1923–24	Toronto St. P.	21	1	1	2
1924–25	Tor StP–Bos	27	5	0	5
1925–26	Boston	28	3	3	6
1926–27	Ottawa	--	0	0	0
	Totals	--	9	4	13

JACKSON, Walter (Red) *Forward*
b. Winnipeg, Man.

Season	Club	GP	G	A	Pts
1932–33	New York A.	--	10	2	12
1933–34	New York A.	--	6	9	15
	Totals	--	16	11	27

JACOBS

Season	Club	GP	G	A	Pts
1918–19	Toronto A.	1	0	0	0

JAMES, Gerald Edwin *Forward*
b. Regina, Sask., Oct. 22, 1934

Season	Club	GP	G	A	Pts
1954–55	Toronto M.L.	1	0	0	0
1955–56	Toronto M.L.	46	3	3	6
1956–57	Toronto M.L.	53	4	12	16
1957–58	Toronto M.L.	15	3	2	5
1959–60	Toronto M.L.	34	4	9	13
	Totals	149	14	26	40

Playoffs

Season	Club	GP	G	A	Pts
1955–56	Toronto M.L.	5	1	0	1
1959–60	Toronto M.L.	10	0	0	0
	Totals	15	1	0	1

JAMIESON, James *Defenseman*
b. Brantford, Ont., Mar. 21, 1922

Season	Club	GP	G	A	Pts
1943–44	New York R.	1	0	1	1

JANKOWSKI, Louis Casimer *Forward*
b. Regina, Sask., June 27, 1931

Season	Club	GP	G	A	Pts
1950–51	Detroit R.W.	1	0	1	1
1952–53	Detroit R.W.	22	1	2	3
1953–54	Chicago	68	15	13	28
1954–55	Chicago	36	3	2	5
	Totals	127	19	18	37

Playoffs

Season	Club	GP	G	A	Pts
1952–53	Detroit R.W.	1	0	0	0

JARRETT, Douglas (Doug) *Defenseman*
b. London, Ont., Apr. 22, 1944

Season	Club	GP	G	A	Pts
1964–65	Chicago	46	2	15	17
1965–66	Chicago	66	4	12	16
1966–67	Chicago	70	5	21	26
1967–68	Chicago	74	4	19	23
1968–69	Chicago	69	0	13	13
1969–70	Chicago	72	4	20	24
1970–71	Chicago	51	1	12	13
1971–72	Chicago	78	6	23	29
1972–73	Chicago	49	2	11	13
	Totals	575	28	146	174

JARRETT (Continued)

Playoffs	Club	GP	G	A	Pts
1964–65	Chicago	11	1	0	1
1965–66	Chicago	5	0	1	1
1966–67	Chicago	6	0	3	3
1967–68	Chicago	11	4	0	4
1969–70	Chicago	8	1	0	1
1970–71	Chicago	18	1	6	7
1971–72	Chicago	8	0	2	2
1972–73	Chicago	15	0	3	3
	Totals	82	7	15	22

JARRETT, Gary Walter *Forward*
b. Toronto, Ont., Sept. 3, 1942

Season	Club	GP	G	A	Pts
1960–61	Toronto M.L.	1	0	0	0
1966–67	Detroit R.W.	4	0	0	0
1967–68	Detroit R.W.	68	18	21	39
1968–69	Oakland	63	22	23	45
1969–70	Oakland	75	12	19	31
1970–71	California	75	15	19	34
1971–72	California	55	5	10	15
	Totals	341	72	92	164

Playoffs	Club	GP	G	A	Pts
1968–69	Oakland	7	2	1	3
1969–70	Oakland	4	1	0	1
	Totals	11	3	1	4

JARRY, Pierre Joseph Reynald *Forward*
b. Montreal, Que., Mar. 30, 1949

Season	Club	GP	G	A	Pts
1971–72	NY R–Tor ML	52	6	7	13
1972–73	Toronto M.L.	74	19	18	37
	Totals	126	25	25	50

Playoffs	Club	GP	G	A	Pts
1971–72	Toronto M.L.	5	0	1	1

JARVIS, James (Bud) *Forward*
b. Fort William, Ont., Dec. 7, 1907

Season	Club	GP	G	A	Pts
1929–30	Pittsburgh Pi.	--	11	8	19
1930–31	Philadelphia Q.	--	5	7	12
1936–37	Toronto M.L.	--	1	0	1
	Totals	--	17	15	32

JEFFREY, Lawrence Joseph (Larry) *Forward*
b. Goderich, Ont., Oct. 12, 1940

Season	Club	GP	G	A	Pts
1961–62	Detroit R.W.	18	5	3	8
1962–63	Detroit R.W.	53	5	11	16
1963–64	Detroit R.W.	58	10	18	28
1964–65	Detroit R.W.	41	4	2	6
1965–66	Toronto M.L.	20	1	1	2

JEFFREY (Continued)

Season	Club	GP	G	A	Pts
1966–67	Toronto M.L.	56	11	17	28
1967–68	New York R.	47	2	4	6
1968–69	New York R.	75	1	6	7
	Totals	368	39	62	101

Playoffs	Club	GP	G	A	Pts
1962–63	Detroit R.W.	9	3	3	6
1963–64	Detroit R.W.	14	1	6	7
1964–65	Detroit R.W.	2	0	0	0
1966–67	Toronto M.L.	6	0	1	1
1967–68	New York R.	3	0	0	0
1968–69	New York R.	4	0	0	0
	Totals	38	4	10	14

JENKINS, Roger *Defenseman*
b. Appleton, Wisc., Nov. 18, 1911

Season	Club	GP	G	A	Pts
1930–31	Chicago	--	0	1	1
1932–33	Chicago	--	3	10	13
1933–34	Chicago	--	2	2	4
1934–35	Montreal C.	--	4	6	10
1935–36	Boston	--	2	6	8
1936–37	Mont C–NY A	--	1	4	5
1937–38	Chicago	--	1	8	9
1938–39	Chgo–NY A	--	2	2	4
	Totals	--	15	39	54

Playoffs	Club	GP	G	A	Pts
1930–31	Chicago	--	0	0	0
1933–34	Chicago	--	0	0	0
1934–35	Montreal C.	--	1	0	1
1935–36	Boston	--	0	1	1
1937–38	Chicago	--	0	6	6
	Totals	--	1	7	8

JENNINGS, Joseph William *Forward*
b. Toronto, Ont., June 28, 1917

Season	Club	GP	G	A	Pts
1940–41	Detroit R.W.	--	1	5	6
1941–42	Detroit R.W.	16	2	1	3
1942–43	Detroit R.W.	8	3	3	6
1943–44	Detroit R.W.	33	6	11	17
1944–45	Boston	39	20	13	33
	Totals	--	32	33	65

Playoffs	Club	GP	G	A	Pts
1940–41	Detroit R.W.	9	2	2	4
1943–44	Detroit R.W.	4	0	0	0
1944–45	Boston	7	2	2	4
	Totals	20	4	4	8

JEREMIAH, Edward *Defenseman-Forward*
b. Worcester, Mass., Nov. 4, 1905

Season	Club	GP	G	A	Pts
1931–32	NY A–Bos	8	0	1	1

JERWA, Frank *Defenseman-Forward*
b. Bankhead, Alta., Feb. 28, 1910

Season	Club	GP	G	A	Pts
1931-32	Boston	--	4	5	9
1932-33	Boston	--	3	4	7
1933-34	Boston	--	0	0	0
	Totals	--	7	9	16

Playoffs

1932-33	Boston	--	0	0	0

JERWA, Joseph *Defenseman*
b. Bankhead, Alta., Jan. 20, 1908

Season	Club	GP	G	A	Pts
1930-31	New York R.	33	4	7	11
1933-34	Boston	--	0	0	0
1935-36	New York A.	--	9	12	21
1936-37	Bos-NY A	--	9	13	22
1937-38	New York A.	--	3	14	17
1938-39	New York A.	--	4	12	16
	Totals	--	29	58	87

Playoffs

1930-31	New York R.	4	0	0	0
1935-36	New York A.	5	2	3	5
1937-38	New York A.	6	0	0	0
1938-39	New York A.	2	0	0	0
	Totals	17	2	3	5

JIRIK, Jaroslav *Forward*
b. Vojnuv, Mestac, Czechoslovakia, Dec. 10, 1939

Season	Club	GP	G	A	Pts
1969-70	St. Louis	3	0	0	0

JOANETTE, Rosario (Kit) *Forward*
b. Valleyfield, Que., Aug. 27, 1915

Season	Club	GP	G	A	Pts
1944-45	Montreal C.	2	0	1	1

JOHNS, Donald Ernest *Defenseman*
b. St. George, Ont., Dec. 13, 1937

Season	Club	GP	G	A	Pts
1960-61	New York R.	63	1	7	8
1962-63	New York R.	6	0	4	4
1963-64	New York R.	57	1	9	10
1964-65	New York R.	22	0	1	1
1965-66	Montreal C.	1	0	0	0
1967-68	Minnesota	4	0	0	0
	Totals	153	2	21	23

JOHNSON, Allan Edmund *Forward*
b. Winnipeg, Man., Mar. 30, 1935

Season	Club	GP	G	A	Pts
1956-57	Montreal C.	2	0	1	1
1960-61	Detroit R.W.	70	16	21	37

JOHNSON *(Continued)*

Season	Club	GP	G	A	Pts
1961-62	Detroit R.W.	31	5	6	11
1962-63	Detroit R.W.	2	0	0	0
	Totals	105	21	28	49

Playoffs

1960-61	Detroit R.W.	11	2	2	4

JOHNSON, Daniel Douglas
b. Winnipegosis, Man., Oct. 1, 1944

Season	Club	GP	G	A	Pts
1969-70	Toronto M.L.	1	0	0	0
1970-71	Vancouver	66	15	11	26
1971-72	Det RW-Vanc	54	3	8	11
	Totals	121	18	19	37

JOHNSON, Earl O. *Forward*
b. Fort Francis, Ont., June 28, 1931

Season	Club	GP	G	A	Pts
1953-54	Detroit R.W.	1	0	0	0

JOHNSON, Ivan Wilfred (Ching) *Defenseman*
b. Winnipeg, Man., Dec. 7, 1897

Season	Club	GP	G	A	Pts
1926-27	New York R.	27	3	2	5
1927-28	New York R.	43	10	6	16
1928-29	New York R.	9	0	0	0
1929-30	New York R.	30	3	3	6
1930-31	New York R.	44	2	6	8
1931-32	New York R.	47	3	10	13
1932-33	New York R.	48	8	9	17
1933-34	New York R.	48	2	6	8
1934-35	New York R.	26	2	3	5
1935-36	New York R.	47	5	3	8
1936-37	New York R.	34	0	0	0
1937-38	New York A.	--	0	0	0
	Totals	--	38	48	86

Playoffs

1926-27	New York R.	2	0	0	0
1927-28	New York R.	9	1	1	2
1928-29	New York R.	6	0	0	0
1929-30	New York R.	4	0	0	0
1930-31	New York R.	4	1	0	1
1931-32	New York R.	7	2	0	2
1932-33	New York R.	8	1	0	1
1933-34	New York R.	2	0	0	0
1934-35	New York R.	3	0	0	0
1936-37	New York R.	9	0	1	1
1937-38	New York A.	6	0	0	0
	Totals	60	5	2	7

JOHNSON, Norman B. *Forward*
b. Moose Jaw, Sask., Nov. 27, 1932

Season	Club	GP	G	A	Pts
1957-58	Boston	15	2	3	5
1958-59	Bos-Chgo	46	3	17	20
	Totals	61	5	20	25

Playoffs

Season	Club	GP	G	A	Pts
1957-58	Boston	12	4	0	4
1959-60	Chicago	2	0	0	0
	Totals	14	4	0	4

JOHNSON, Norman James (Jim) *Forward*
b. Winnipeg, Man., Nov. 7, 1942

Season	Club	GP	G	A	Pts
1964-65	New York R.	1	0	0	0
1965-66	New York R.	5	1	0	1
1966-67	New York R.	2	0	0	0
1967-68	Philadelphia F.	13	2	1	3
1968-69	Philadelphia F.	69	17	27	44
1969-70	Philadelphia F.	72	18	30	48
1970-71	Philadelphia F.	66	16	29	45
1971-72	Phila F-LA	76	21	24	45
	Totals	302	75	111	186

Playoffs

Season	Club	GP	G	A	Pts
1968-69	Philadelphia F.	3	0	0	0
1970-71	Philadelphia F.	4	0	2	2
	Totals	7	0	2	2

JOHNSON, Robert Martin (Bob) *Goalie*
b. Farmington, Mich. Nov. 12, 1948

Season	Club	GP	GA	Sho	AVE
1972-73	St. Louis B.	9⅔	26	0	2.68

JOHNSON, Thomas Christian *Defenseman*
b. Baldur, Man., Feb. 18, 1928

Season	Club	GP	G	A	Pts
1947-48	Montreal C.	1	0	0	0
1950-51	Montreal C.	70	2	8	10
1951-52	Montreal C.	67	0	7	7
1952-53	Montreal C.	70	3	8	11
1953-54	Montreal C.	70	7	11	18
1954-55	Montreal C.	70	6	19	25
1955-56	Montreal C.	64	3	10	13
1956-57	Montreal C.	70	4	11	15
1957-58	Montreal C.	66	8	18	21
1958-59	Montreal C.	70	10	29	39
1959-60	Montreal C.	64	4	25	29
1960-61	Montreal C.	70	1	15	16
1961-62	Montreal C.	62	1	18	19
1962-63	Montreal C.	43	3	5	8
1963-64	Boston	70	4	21	25
1964-65	Boston	51	0	9	9
	Totals	978	51	213	264

JOHNSON *(Continued)*

Playoffs

	Club	GP	G	A	Pts
1949-50	Montreal C.	1	0	0	0
1950-51	Montreal C.	11	0	0	0
1951-52	Montreal C.	11	1	0	1
1952-53	Montreal C.	12	2	3	5
1953-54	Montreal C.	11	1	2	3
1954-55	Montreal C.	12	2	0	2
1955-56	Montreal C.	10	0	2	2
1956-57	Montreal C.	10	0	2	2
1957-58	Montreal C.	2	0	0	0
1958-59	Montreal C.	11	2	3	5
1959-60	Montreal C.	8	0	1	1
1960-61	Montreal C.	6	0	1	1
1961-62	Montreal C.	6	0	1	1
	Totals	111	8	15	23

All-Star

	Club	GP	G	A	Pts
1952	NHL 2nd All-Stars	1	0	0	0
1953	Montreal C.	1	0	0	0
1956	Montreal C.	1	0	0	0
1957	Montreal C.	1	0	1	1
1958	Montreal C.	1	0	0	0
1959	Montreal C.	1	0	1	1
1960	Montreal C.	1	0	0	0
1963	NHL All-Stars	1	0	0	0
	Totals	8	0	2	2

JOHNSON, Virgil *Defenseman*
b. Minneapolis, Minn., Mar 4, 1912

Season	Club	GP	G	A	Pts
1937-38	Chicago	--	1	0	1
1943-44	Chicago	48	1	8	9
1944-45	Chicago	2	0	1	1
	Totals	--	2	9	11

Playoffs

	Club	GP	G	A	Pts
1943-44	Chicago	9	0	3	3

JOHNSON, William *Forward*
b. Winnipeg, Man., Apr. 16, 1928

Season	Club	GP	G	A	Pts
1949-50	Toronto M.L.	1	0	0	0

JOHNSTON, Edward Joseph *Goalie*
b. Montreal, Que., Nov. 23, 1935

Season	Club	GP	GA	Sho	AVE
1962-63	Boston	48⅔	196	1	4.03
1963-64	Boston	70	211	6	3.01
1964-65	Boston	47	163	3	3.47
1965-66	Boston	29	108	1	3.72
1966-67	Boston	31⅓	116	0	3.70
1967-68	Boston	25⅔	73	0	2.84
1968-69	Boston	24	74	2	3.08
1969-70	Boston	36⅕	108	3	2.93
1970-71	Boston	38	96	4	2.52

JOHNSTON (Continued)

Season	Club	GP	GA	Sho	AVE
1971–72	Boston	38	102	2	2.70
1972–73	Boston	42	137	5	3.27
	Totals	430½	1384	27	3.23
Playoffs					
1968–69	Boston	1	4	0	4.00
1969–70	Boston	1	4	0	4.00
1970–71	Boston	1	7	0	7.00
1971–72	Boston	7	13	1	1.86
1972–73	Boston	2⅔	9	0	3.39
	Totals	12⅔	37	1	2.92

JOHNSTON, George Joseph (Wingy) *Forward*
b. St. Charles, Man., July 30, 1920

Season	Club	GP	G	A	Pts
1941–42	Chicago	2	2	0	2
1942–43	Chicago	30	10	7	17
1945–46	Chicago	16	5	4	9
1946–47	Chicago	10	3	1	4
	Totals	58	20	12	32

JOHNSTON, Joseph John (Joey) *Forward*
b. Peterborough, Ont., Mar. 3, 1949

Season	Club	GP	G	A	Pts
1968–69	Minnesota	12	1	0	1
1971–72	California	77	15	17	32
1972–73	California	71	28	21	49
	Totals	160	44	38	82
All-Star					
1973	West All-Stars	1	0	0	0

JOHNSTON, Larry Roy *Defenseman*
b. Kitchener, Ont., July 20, 1943

Season	Club	GP	G	A	Pts
1967–68	Los Angeles	4	0	0	0
1971–72	Detroit R.W.	65	4	20	24
1972–73	Detroit R.W.	73	1	12	13
	Totals	142	5	32	37

JONSTON, Marshall *Forward*
b. Birch Hills, Sask., June 6, 1941

Season	Club	GP	G	A	Pts
1967–68	Minnesota	7	0	0	0
1968–69	Minnesota	13	0	0	0
1969–70	Minnesota	28	0	5	5
1970–71	Minnesota	1	0	0	0
1971–72	California	74	2	11	13
1972–73	California	78	10	20	30
	Totals	201	12	36	48
Playoffs					
1969–70	Minnesota	6	0	0	0

JOHNSTONE, Robert Ross *Defenseman*
b. Montreal, Que., Apr. 7, 1926

Season	Club	GP	G	A	Pts
1943–44	Toronto M.L.	18	2	0	2
1944–45	Toronto M.L.	24	3	4	7
	Totals	42	5	4	9
Playoffs					
1943–44	Toronto M.L.	3	0	0	0

JOLIAT, Aurel *Forward*
b. Ottawa, Ont., Aug. 29, 1901

Season	Club	GP	G	A	Pts
1922–23	Montreal C.	24	13	9	22
1923–24	Montreal C.	24	15	5	20
1924–25	Montreal C.	24	29	11	40
1925–26	Montreal C.	35	17	9	26
1926–27	Montreal C.	--	14	4	18
1927–28	Montreal C.	--	28	11	39
1928–29	Montreal C.	--	12	5	17
1929–30	Montreal C.	--	19	12	31
1930–31	Montreal C.	--	13	22	35
1931–32	Montreal C.	--	15	24	39
1932–33	Montreal C.	--	18	21	39
1933–34	Montreal C.	--	22	15	37
1934–35	Montreal C.	--	17	12	29
1935–36	Montreal C.	--	15	8	23
1936–37	Montreal C.	--	17	15	32
1937–38	Montreal C.	--	6	7	13
	Totals	--	270	190	460
Playoffs					
1922–23	Montreal C.	--	1	1	2
1923–24	Montreal C.	--	3	3	6
1924–25	Montreal C.	--	2	1	3
1926–27	Montreal C.	--	1	0	1
1927–28	Montreal C.	--	0	0	0
1928–29	Montreal C.	--	1	1	2
1929–30	Montreal C.	--	0	2	2
1930–31	Montreal C.	--	0	4	4
1931–32	Montreal C.	--	2	0	2
1932–33	Montreal C.	--	2	1	3
1933–34	Montreal C.	--	0	1	1
1934–35	Montreal M.L.	--	1	0	1
1936–37	Montreal C.	--	0	3	3
1937–38	Montreal C.	--	0	0	0
	Totals	--	13	17	30

JOLIAT, Rene (Bobby) *Forward*

Season	Club	GP	G	A	Pts
1924–25	Montreal C.	1	0	0	0

JONES, Alvin Bernard (Buck) *Defenseman*
b. Owen Sound, Ont., Aug. 17, 1919

Season	Club	GP	G	A	Pts
1938-39	Detroit R.W.	11	0	1	1
1941-42	Detroit R.W.	21	2	1	3
1942-43	Toronto M.L.	16	0	0	0
	Totals	48	2	2	4
Playoffs					
1938-39	Detroit R.W.	6	0	1	1
1942-43	Toronto M.L.	6	0	0	0
	Totals	12	0	1	1

JONES, James William (Jim) *Defenseman*
b. Espanoia, Ont., July 27, 1949

Season	Club	GP	G	A	Pts
1971-72	California	2	0	0	0

JONES, Robert Charles *Forward*
b. Espanola, Ont., Nov. 27, 1945

Season	Club	GP	G	A	Pts
1968-69	New York R.	2	0	0	0

JONES, Ronald Perry (Ron) *Defenseman*
b. Vermillion, Alta., Apr. 11, 1951

Season	Club	GP	G	A	Pts
1971-72	Boston	1	0	0	0
1972-73	Boston	7	0	0	0
	Totals	8	0	0	0

JOYAL, Edward Abel *Forward*
b. Edmonton, Alta., May 8, 1940

Season	Club	GP	G	A	Pts
1962-63	Detroit R.W.	14	2	8	10
1963-64	Detroit R.W.	47	10	7	17
1964-65	Detroit R.W.	46	8	14	22
1965-66	Toronto M.L.	14	0	2	2
1967-68	Los Angeles	74	23	34	57
1968-69	Los Angeles	73	33	19	52
1969-70	Los Angeles	59	18	22	40
1970-71	Los Angeles	69	20	21	41
1971-72	LA–Phila F	70	14	7	21
	Totals	466	128	134	262
Playoffs					
1962-63	Detroit R.W.	11	1	0	1
1963-64	Detroit R.W.	14	2	3	5
1964-65	Detroit R.W.	7	1	1	2
1967-68	Los Angeles	7	4	1	5
1968-69	Los Angeles	11	3	3	6
	Totals	50	11	8	19

JUCKES, Winston Bryan (Bing) *Forward*
b. Hamiota, Man., June 14, 1926

Season	Club	GP	G	A	Pts
1947-48	New York R.	2	0	0	0
1949-50	New York R.	14	2	1	3
	Totals	16	2	1	3

JUNKIN, Joseph *Goalie*
b. Belleville, Ont., Sept. 8, 1946

Season	Club	GP	GA	Sho	AVE
1968-69	Boston	⅖ₗ₅	0	0	0.00

JUZDA, William *Defenseman*
b. Winnipeg, Man., Oct. 29, 1920

Season	Club	GP	G	A	Pts
1940-41	New York R.	5	0	0	0
1941-42	New York R.	45	4	8	12
1945-46	New York R.	32	1	3	4
1946-47	New York R.	45	3	5	8
1947-48	New York R.	60	3	9	12
1948-49	Toronto M.L.	38	1	2	3
1949-50	Toronto M.L.	62	1	14	15
1950-51	Toronto M.L.	65	0	9	9
1951-52	Toronto M.L.	46	1	4	5
	Totals	398	14	54	68
Playoffs					
1941-42	New York R.	6	0	1	1
1947-48	New York R.	6	0	0	0
1948-49	Toronto M.L.	9	0	2	2
1949-50	Toronto M.L.	7	0	0	0
1950-51	Toronto M.L.	11	0	0	0
1951-52	Toronto M.L.	3	0	0	0
	Totals	42	0	3	3
All-Star					
1948	Toronto M.L.	1	0	0	0
1949	Toronto M.L.	1	0	0	0
	Totals	2	0	0	0

KABEL, Robert Gerald *Forward*
b. Dauphin, Man., Nov. 11, 1934

Season	Club	GP	G	A	Pts
1959-60	New York R.	44	5	11	16
1960-61	New York R.	4	0	2	2
	Totals	48	5	13	18

KACHUR, Edward Charles *Forward*
b. Fort William, Ont., Apr. 22, 1934

Season	Club	GP	G	A	Pts
1956-57	Chicago	34	5	7	12
1957-58	Chicago	62	5	7	12
	Totals	96	10	14	24

KAISER, Vernon Charles *Forward*
b. Preston, Ont., Sept. 28, 1925

Season	Club	GP	G	A	Pts
1950–51	Montreal C.	50	7	5	12
Playoffs					
1950–51	Montreal C.	2	0	0	0

KALBFLIESH, Walter (Jeff) *Defenseman*
b. New Hamberg, Ont., Dec. 18, 1911

Season	Club	GP	G	A	Pts
1933–34	Ottawa	--	0	4	4
1934–35	St. Louis E.	--	0	0	0
1935–36	New York A.	--	0	0	0
1936–37	New York A.	--	0	0	0
	Totals	--	0	4	4
Playoffs					
1935–36	New York A.	--	0	0	0

KALETA, Alexander (Killer) *Forward*
b. Canmore, Alta., Nov. 29, 1919

Season	Club	GP	G	A	Pts
1941–42	Chicago	48	7	21	28
1945–46	Chicago	49	19	27	46
1946–47	Chicago	57	24	20	44
1947–48	Chicago	52	10	16	26
1948–49	New York R.	56	12	19	31
1949–50	New York R.	67	17	14	31
1950–51	New York R.	58	3	4	7
	Totals	387	92	121	213
Playoffs					
1941–42	Chicago	3	1	2	3
1945–46	Chicago	4	0	1	1
1949–50	New York R.	10	0	3	3
	Totals	17	1	6	7

KAMINSKY, Max *Forward*
b. Niagara Falls, Ont., Apr. 19, 1913

Season	Club	GP	G	A	Pts
1933–34	Ottawa	--	9	17	26
1934–35	Boston	--	12	15	27
1935–36	Boston	--	1	2	3
	Totals	--	22	34	56
Playoffs					
1934–35	Boston	--	0	0	0
1935–36	Boston	--	0	0	0
	Totals	--	0	0	0

KAMPMAN, Rudolph (Bingo) *Defenseman*
b. Kitchener, Ont., Mar. 12, 1914

Season	Club	GP	G	A	Pts
1937–38	Toronto M.L.	--	1	2	3
1938–39	Toronto M.L.	--	2	8	10

KAMPMAN *(Continued)*

Season	Club	GP	G	A	Pts
1939–40	Toronto M.L.	--	6	9	15
1940–41	Toronto M.L.	--	1	4	5
1941–42	Toronto M.L.	38	4	7	11
	Totals	--	14	30	44
Playoffs					
1937–38	Toronto M.L.	7	0	1	1
1938–39	Toronto M.L.	10	1	1	2
1939–40	Toronto M.L.	10	0	0	0
1940–41	Toronto M.L.	7	0	0	0
1941–42	Toronto M.L.	13	0	2	2
	Totals	47	1	4	5

KANE, Francis Joseph *Defenseman*
b. Stratford, Ont., Jan. 19, 1924

Season	Club	GP	G	A	Pts
1943–44	Detroit R.W.	2	0	0	0

KANNEGIESSER, Gordon Cameron (Gord)
Defenseman
b. North Bay, Ont., Dec. 21, 1945

Season	Club	GP	G	A	Pts
1967–68	St. Louis B.	19	0	1	1
1971–72	St. Louis B.	4	0	0	0
	Totals	23	0	1	1

KANNEGIESSER, Sheldon Bruce *Defenseman*
b. North Bay, Ont., Aug. 15, 1947

Season	Club	GP	G	A	Pts
1970–71	Pittsburgh Pe.	18	0	2	2
1971–72	Pittsburgh Pe.	54	2	4	6
1972–73	Pitt Pe–NY R	6	0	1	1
	Totals	78	2	7	9
Playoffs					
1972–73	New York R.	1	0	0	0

KARAKAS, Michael *Goalie*
b. Aurora, Minn., Dec. 12, 1911

Season	Club	GP	GA	Sho	AVE
1935–36	Chicago	48	92	9	1.91
1936–37	Chicago	48	131	5	2.72
1937–38	Chicago	48	139	1	2.85
1938–39	Chicago	48	132	5	2.75
1939–40	Chgo–Mont M	22	76	0	3.45
1943–44	Chicago	26	79	3	3.03
1944–45	Chicago	48	187	4	3.89
1945–46	Chicago	48	166	1	3.45
	Totals	336	1002	28	2.98
Playoffs					
1935–36	Chicago	2	7	0	3.50
1937–38	Chicago	8	15	2	1.87

KARAKAS *(Continued)*

Playoffs	Club	GP	GA	Sho	AVE
1943–44	Chicago	9	26	1	2.88
1945–46	Chicago	4	26	0	6.50
	Totals	23	74	3	3.22

KARLANDER, Allan David (Al) *Forward*
b. Lac La Hache, B.C., Nov. 5, 1946

Season	Club	GP	G	A	Pts
1969–70	Detroit R.W.	41	5	10	15
1970–71	Detroit R.W.	23	1	4	5
1971–72	Detroit R.W.	71	15	20	35
1972–73	Detroit R.W.	77	15	22	37
	Totals	212	36	56	92
Playoffs					
1969–70	Detroit R.W.	4	0	1	1

KEARNS, Dennis McAleer *Defenseman*
b. Kingston, Ont., Sept. 27, 1945

Season	Club	GP	G	A	Pts
1971–72	Vancouver	73	3	26	29
1972–73	Vancouver	72	4	33	37
	Totals	145	7	59	66

KEATING, John R. (Jack) *Forward*
b. Newcastle, N.B.

Season	Club	GP	G	A	Pts
1931–32	New York A.	--	5	3	8
1932–33	New York A.	--	0	2	2
	Totals	--	5	5	10

KEATING, John Thomas *Forward*
b. Kitchener, Ont., Oct. 9, 1916

Season	Club	GP	G	A	Pts
1938–39	Detroit R.W.	--	1	0	1
1939–40	Detroit R.W.	--	2	0	2
	Totals	--	3	0	3
Playoffs					
1938–39	Detroit R.W.	6	0	0	0

KEATS, Gordon (Duke) *Forward*
b. Montreal, Que., 1895

Season	Club	GP	G	A	Pts
1926–27	Bos-Det C	--	16	8	24
1927–28	Det C-Chgo	--	14	10	24
1928–29	Chicago	--	0	1	1
	Totals	--	30	19	49
Playoffs					
1922–23	Edmonton (PCHL)	--	0	0	0

KEELING, Melville Sidney (Butch) *Forward*
b. Owen Sound, Ont., Aug. 10, 1905

Season	Club	GP	G	A	Pts
1926–27	Toronto M.L.	--	11	2	13
1927–28	Toronto M.L.	41	10	6	16
1928–29	New York R.	43	6	3	9
1929–30	New York R.	44	19	7	26
1930–31	New York R.	44	13	9	22
1931–32	New York R.	48	17	3	20
1932–33	New York R.	47	8	6	14
1933–34	New York R.	48	15	5	20
1934–35	New York R.	47	15	4	19
1935–36	New York R.	47	13	5	18
1936–37	New York R.	48	22	4	26
1937–38	New York R.	39	8	9	17
	Totals	--	157	63	220
Playoffs					
1928–29	New York R.	6	3	0	3
1929–30	New York R.	4	0	3	3
1930–31	New York R.	4	1	1	2
1931–32	New York R.	7	2	1	3
1932–33	New York R.	8	0	2	2
1933–34	New York R.	2	0	0	0
1934–35	New York R.	4	2	1	3
1936–37	New York R.	9	3	2	5
1937–38	New York R.	3	0	1	1
	Totals	47	11	11	22

KEENAN, Donald *Goalie*

Season	Club	GP	GA	Sho	AVE
1958–59	Boston	1	4	0	4.00

KEENAN, Lawrence (Larry) *Forward*
b. North Bay, Ont., Oct. 1, 1940

Season	Club	GP	G	A	Pts
1961–62	Toronto M.L.	2	0	0	0
1967–68	St. Louis B.	40	12	8	20
1968–69	St. Louis B.	47	5	9	14
1969–70	St. Louis B.	56	10	23	33
1970–71	StL B-Buff	61	8	23	31
1971–72	Buff-Phila F	28	3	1	4
	Totals	234	38	64	102
Playoffs					
1967–68	St. Louis B.	18	4	5	9
1968–69	St. Louis B.	12	4	5	9
1969–70	St. Louis B.	16	7	6	13
	Totals	46	15	16	31

KEHOE, Ricky Thomas (Rick) *Forward*
b. Windsor, Ont., July 15, 1951

Season	Club	GP	G	A	Pts
1971–72	Toronto M.L.	38	8	8	16
1972–73	Toronto M.L.	77	33	42	75
	Totals	115	41	50	91

KEHOE (Continued)

Playoffs	Club	GP	G	A	Pts
1971–72	Toronto M.L.	2	0	0	0

KELLER, Ralph *Defenseman*
b. Wilkie, Sask., Feb. 6, 1936

Season	Club	GP	G	A	Pts
1962–63	New York R.	3	1	0	1

KELLY, Leonard Patrick (Red)
Defenseman-Forward
b. Simcoe, Ont., July 9, 1927

Season	Club	GP	G	A	Pts
1947–48	Detroit R.W.	60	6	14	20
1948–49	Detroit R.W.	59	5	11	16
1949–50	Detroit R.W.	70	15	25	40
1950–51	Detroit R.W.	70	17	37	54
1951–52	Detroit R.W.	67	16	31	47
1952–53	Detroit R.W.	70	19	27	46
1953–54	Detroit R.W.	62	16	33	49
1954–55	Detroit R.W.	70	15	30	45
1955–56	Detroit R.W.	70	16	34	50
1956–57	Detroit R.W.	70	10	25	35
1957–58	Detroit R.W.	61	13	18	31
1958–59	Detroit R.W.	67	8	13	21
1959–60	Det RW–Tor ML	68	12	17	29
1960–61	Toronto M.L.	64	20	50	70
1961–62	Toronto M.L.	58	22	27	49
1962–63	Toronto M.L.	66	20	40	60
1963–64	Toronto M.L.	70	11	34	45
1964–65	Toronto M.L.	70	18	28	46
1965–66	Toronto M.L.	63	8	24	32
1966–67	Toronto M.L.	61	14	24	38
	Totals	1316	281	542	823

Playoffs					
1947–48	Detroit R.W.	10	3	2	5
1948–49	Detroit R.W.	11	1	1	2
1949–50	Detroit R.W.	14	1	3	4
1950–51	Detroit R.W.	6	0	1	1
1951–52	Detroit R.W.	5	1	0	1
1952–53	Detroit R.W.	6	0	4	4
1953–54	Detroit R.W.	12	5	1	6
1954–55	Detroit R.W.	11	2	4	6
1955–56	Detroit R.W.	10	2	4	6
1956–57	Detroit R.W.	5	1	0	1
1957–58	Detroit R.W.	4	0	1	1
1959–60	Toronto M.L.	10	3	8	11
1960–61	Toronto M.L.	2	1	0	1
1961–62	Toronto M.L.	12	4	6	10
1962–63	Toronto M.L.	10	2	6	8
1963–64	Toronto M.L.	14	4	9	13
1964–65	Toronto M.L.	6	3	2	5
1965–66	Toronto M.L.	4	0	2	2
1966–67	Toronto M.L.	12	0	5	5
	Totals	164	33	59	92

KELLY (Continued)

All-Star	Club	GP	G	A	Pts
1950	Detroit R.W.	1	0	2	2
1951	NHL 1st All-Stars	1	0	0	0
1952	NHL 1st All-Stars	1	0	0	0
1953	NHL All-Stars	1	0	2	2
1954	Detroit R.W.	1	0	1	1
1955	Detroit R.W.	1	0	0	0
1956	NHL All-Stars	1	0	0	0
1957	NHL All-Stars	1	1	0	1
1958	NHL All-Stars	1	0	0	0
1960	NHL All-Stars	1	0	1	1
1962	Toronto M.L.	1	0	0	0
1963	Toronto M.L.	1	0	1	1
	Totals	12	1	7	8

KELLY, Peter Cameron *Forward*
b. Winnipeg, Man., May 22, 1913

Season	Club	GP	G	A	Pts
1934–35	St. Louis E.	--	3	10	13
1935–36	Detroit R.W.	--	6	8	14
1936–37	Detroit R.W.	--	5	4	9
1937–38	Detroit R.W.	--	0	1	1
1938–39	Detroit R.W.	--	4	9	13
1940–41	New York A.	--	3	5	8
1941–42	Brooklyn A.	--	0	1	1
	Totals	--	21	38	59

Playoffs					
1935–36	Detroit R.W.	--	1	1	2
1936–37	Detroit R.W.	--	2	0	2
1938–39	Detroit R.W.	--	0	0	0
	Totals	--	3	1	4

KELLY, Regis J. (Pep) *Forward*
b. North Bay, Ont., Jan. 17, 1914

Season	Club	GP	G	A	Pts
1934–35	Toronto M.L.	--	11	8	19
1935–36	Toronto M.L.	--	11	8	19
1936–37	Tor ML–Chgo	--	15	4	19
1937–38	Toronto M.L.	--	9	10	19
1938–39	Toronto M.L.	--	11	11	22
1939–40	New York A.	--	11	9	20
1940–41	Chicago	--	5	3	8
1941–42	Brooklyn A.	--	1	0	1
	Totals	--	74	53	127

Playoffs					
1934–35	Toronto M.L.	--	2	0	2
1935–36	Toronto M.L.	--	2	3	5
1937–38	Toronto M.L.	--	2	2	4
1938–39	Toronto M.L.	--	1	0	1
1939–40	New York A.	--	0	1	1
1940–41	Chicago	--	0	0	0
	Totals	--	7	6	13

KELLY, Robert James (Bob) *Forward*
b. Oakville, Ont., Nov. 25, 1950

Season	Club	GP	G	A	Pts
1970–71	Philadelphia F.	76	14	18	32
1971–72	Philadelphia F.	78	14	15	29
1972–73	Philadelphia F.	77	10	11	21
	Totals	231	38	44	82
Playoffs					
1970–71	Philadelphia F.	4	1	0	1
1972–73	Philadelphia F.	11	0	1	1
	Totals	15	1	1	2

KEMP, Stanley *Defenseman*
b. Hamilton, Ont., Mar. 2, 1924

Season	Club	GP	G	A	Pts
1948–49	Toronto M.L.	1	0	0	0

KENDALL, William *Forward*
b. Winnipeg, Man., Apr. 1, 1910

Season	Club	GP	G	A	Pts
1933–34	Chicago	--	3	0	3
1934–35	Chicago	--	6	4	10
1935–36	Chicago	--	2	1	3
1936–37	Chgo–Tor ML	--	5	4	9
1937–38	Chicago	--	0	1	1
	Totals	--	16	10	26
Playoffs					
1934–35	Chicago	--	0	0	0
1936–37	Toronto M.L.	--	0	0	0
	Totals	--	0	0	0

KENNEDY, Forbes Taylor *Forward*
b. Dorchester, N.B., Aug. 18, 1935

Season	Club	GP	G	A	Pts
1956–57	Chicago	69	8	13	21
1957–58	Detroit R.W.	70	11	16	27
1958–59	Detroit R.W.	67	1	4	5
1959–60	Detroit R.W.	17	1	2	3
1961–62	Detroit R.W.	14	1	0	1
1962–63	Boston	49	12	18	30
1963–64	Boston	70	8	17	25
1964–65	Boston	52	6	4	10
1965–66	Boston	50	4	6	10
1967–68	Philadelphia F.	73	10	18	28
1968–69	Phila F–Tor ML	72	8	9	17
	Totals	580	70	107	177
Playoffs					
1957–58	Detroit R.W.	4	1	0	1
1967–68	Philadelphia F.	7	1	4	5
1968–69	Toronto M.L.	1	0	0	0
	Totals	12	2	4	6

KENNEDY, Theodore (Teeder) *Forward*
b. Humberstone, Ont., Dec. 12, 1925

Season	Club	GP	G	A	Pts
1942–43	Toronto M.L.	2	0	1	1
1943–44	Toronto M.L.	49	26	23	49
1944–45	Toronto M.L.	49	29	25	54
1945–46	Toronto M.L.	21	3	2	5
1946–47	Toronto M.L.	60	28	32	60
1947–48	Toronto M.L.	60	25	21	46
1948–49	Toronto M.L.	59	18	21	39
1949–50	Toronto M.L.	53	20	24	44
1950–51	Toronto M.L.	63	18	43	61
1951–52	Toronto M.L.	70	19	33	52
1952–53	Toronto M.L.	43	14	23	37
1953–54	Toronto M.L.	67	15	23	38
1954–55	Toronto M.L.	70	10	42	52
1955–56	Toronto M.L.	30	6	16	22
	Totals	696	231	329	560
Playoffs					
1943–44	Toronto M.L.	5	1	1	2
1944–45	Toronto M.L.	13	7	2	9
1946–47	Toronto M.L.	11	4	5	9
1947–48	Toronto M.L.	9	8	6	14
1948–49	Toronto M.L.	9	2	6	8
1949–50	Toronto M.L.	7	1	2	3
1950–51	Toronto M.L.	11	4	5	9
1951–52	Toronto M.L.	4	0	0	0
1953–54	Toronto M.L.	5	1	1	2
1954–55	Toronto M.L.	4	1	3	4
	Totals	78	29	31	60
All-Star					
1947	Toronto M.L.	1	0	0	0
1948	Toronto M.L.	1	0	0	0
1949	Toronto M.L.	1	0	0	0
1950	NHL All-Stars	1	0	0	0
1951	NHL 2nd All-Stars	1	0	0	0
1954	NHL All-Stars	1	0	1	1
	Totals	6	0	1	1

KENNY, William Ernest *Defenseman*
b. Vermillion, Alta., Aug. 23, 1907

Season	Club	GP	G	A	Pts
1930–31	New York R.	6	0	0	0
1934–35	Chicago	--	0	0	0
	Totals	--	0	0	0

KEON, David Michael (Dave) *Forward*
b. Noranda, Que., Mar. 22, 1940

Season	Club	GP	G	A	Pts
1960–61	Toronto M.L.	70	20	25	45
1961–62	Toronto M.L.	64	26	35	61
1962–63	Toronto M.L.	68	28	28	56
1963–64	Toronto M.L.	70	23	37	60
1964–65	Toronto M.L.	65	21	29	50

KEON (Continued)

Season	Club	GP	G	A	Pts
1965-66	Toronto M.L.	69	24	30	54
1966-67	Toronto M.L.	66	19	33	52
1967-68	Toronto M.L.	67	11	37	48
1968-69	Toronto M.L.	75	27	34	61
1969-70	Toronto M.L.	72	32	30	62
1970-71	Toronto M.L.	76	38	38	76
1971-72	Toronto M.L.	72	18	30	48
1972-73	Toronto M.L.	76	37	36	73
	Totals	910	324	422	746

Playoffs

Season	Club	GP	G	A	Pts
1960-61	Toronto M.L.	5	1	1	2
1961-62	Toronto M.L.	12	5	3	8
1962-63	Toronto M.L.	10	7	5	12
1963-64	Toronto M.L.	14	7	2	9
1964-65	Toronto M.L.	6	2	2	4
1965-66	Toronto M.L.	4	0	2	2
1966-67	Toronto M.L.	12	3	5	8
1968-69	Toronto M.L.	4	1	3	4
1970-71	Toronto M.L.	6	3	2	5
1971-72	Toronto M.L.	5	2	3	5
	Totals	78	31	28	59

All-Star

Season	Club	GP	G	A	Pts
1962	Toronto M.L.	1	0	1	1
1963	Toronto M.L.	1	0	1	1
1964	Toronto M.L.	1	0	0	0
1967	NHL All-Star	1	0	0	0
1968	Toronto M.L.	1	0	0	0
1970	East All-Stars	1	0	0	0
1971	East All-Stars	1	0	0	0
1973	East All-Stars	1	0	0	0
	Totals	8	0	2	2

KERR, David Alexander *Goalie*
b. Toronto, Ont., Jan. 11, 1910

Season	Club	GP	GA	Sho	AVE
1930-31	Montreal M.	30	72	1	2.40
1931-32	New York A.	1	6	0	6.00
1932-33	Montreal M.	25	57	4	2.28
1933-34	Montreal M.	48	122	6	2.54
1934-35	New York R.	37	94	4	2.54
1935-36	New York R.	47	95	8	2.02
1936-37	New York R.	48	106	4	2.21
1937-38	New York R.	48	96	8	2.00
1938-39	New York R.	48	105	6	2.19
1939-40	New York R.	48	77	8	1.60
1940-41	New York R.	48	125	2	2.60
	Totals	428	955	51	2.23

Playoffs

Season	Club	GP	GA	Sho	AVE
1930-31	Montreal M.	2	8	0	4.00
1932-33	Montreal M.	2	5	0	2.50
1933-34	Montreal M.	4	7	1	1.75
1934-35	New York R.	4	10	0	2.50

KERR (Continued)

Playoffs

Club	GP	GA	Sho	AVE
New York R.	9	10	4	1.11
New York R.	3	8	0	2.67
New York R.	1	2	0	2.00
New York R.	12	20	3	1.67
New York R.	3	6	0	2.00
Totals	40	76	8	1.90

(Note: Playoff years 1936-37, 1937-38, 1938-39, 1939-40, 1940-41)

KESSELL, Richard John (Rick) *Forward*
b. Toronto, Ont., July 27, 1949

Season	Club	GP	G	A	Pts
1969-70	Pittsburgh Pe.	8	1	2	3
1970-71	Pittsburgh Pe.	6	0	2	2
1971-72	Pittsburgh Pe.	3	0	1	1
1972-73	Pittsburgh Pe.	66	1	13	14
	Totals	83	2	18	20

KETTER, Kerry Kenneth *Defenseman*
b. Prince George, B.C., Sept. 20, 1947

Season	Club	GP	G	A	Pts
1972-73	Atlanta	41	0	2	2

KILREA, Brian Blair *Forward*
b. Ottawa, Ont., Oct. 21, 1934

Season	Club	GP	G	A	Pts
1957-58	Detroit R.W.	1	0	0	0
1967-68	Los Angeles	25	3	5	8
	Totals	26	3	5	8

KILREA, Hector J. *Forward*
b. Blackburn, Ont., June 11, 1907

Season	Club	GP	G	A	Pts
1925-26	Ottawa	35	5	0	5
1926-27	Ottawa	--	11	7	18
1927-28	Ottawa	--	19	4	23
1928-29	Ottawa	--	5	7	12
1929-30	Ottawa	--	36	22	58
1930-31	Ottawa	--	14	8	22
1931-32	Detroit R.W.	--	13	3	16
1932-33	Ottawa	--	14	8	22
1933-34	Toronto M.L.	--	10	13	23
1934-35	Toronto M.L.	--	11	13	24
1935-36	Detroit R.W.	--	6	17	23
1936-37	Detroit R.W.	--	6	9	15
1937-38	Detroit R.W.	--	9	9	18
1938-39	Detroit R.W.	--	8	9	17
	Totals	--	167	129	296

Playoffs

Season	Club	GP	G	A	Pts
1925-26	Ottawa	--	0	0	0
1926-27	Ottawa	--	1	1	2
1927-28	Ottawa	--	1	0	1
1929-30	Ottawa	--	0	0	0
1931-32	Detroit F.	--	0	0	0

KILREA (Continued)

Playoffs	Club	GP	G	A	Pts
1933–34	Toronto M.L.	--	2	0	2
1934–35	Toronto M.L.	--	0	0	0
1935–36	Detroit R.W.	--	0	3	3
1936–37	Detroit R.W.	--	3	1	4
1938–39	Detroit R.W.	--	1	2	3
	Totals	--	8	7	15

KILREA, Kenneth Armstrong *Forward*
b. Ottawa, Ont., Jan. 16, 1919

Season	Club	GP	G	A	Pts
1938–39	Detroit R.W.	--	0	0	0
1939–40	Detroit R.W.	--	10	8	18
1940–41	Detroit R.W.	--	2	0	2
1941–42	Detroit R.W.	21	3	12	15
1943–44	Detroit R.W.	14	1	3	4
	Totals	--	16	23	39
Playoffs					
1938–39	Detroit R.W.	6	1	1	2
1939–40	Detroit R.W.	5	1	1	2
1943–44	Detroit R.W.	2	0	0	0
	Totals	13	2	2	4

KILREA, Walter Charles *Forward*
b. Ottawa, Ont., Feb. 18, 1909

Season	Club	GP	G	A	Pts
1929–30	Ottawa	--	4	2	6
1930–31	Philadelphia Q.	--	8	12	20
1931–32	New York A.	--	3	8	11
1932–33	Otta-Mont M	--	5	12	17
1933–34	Montreal M.	--	3	1	4
1935–36	Detroit R.W.	--	4	10	14
1936–37	Detroit R.W.	--	8	13	21
1937–38	Detroit R.W.	--	0	0	0
	Totals	--	35	58	93
Playoffs					
1929–30	Ottawa	--	0	0	0
1932–33	Montreal M.	--	0	0	0
1933–34	Montreal M.	--	0	0	0
1935–36	Detroit R.W.	--	2	2	4
1936–37	Detroit R.W.	--	0	2	2
	Totals	--	2	4	6

KINDRACHUK, Orest *Forward*
b. Nanton, Alta., Sept. 14, 1950

Season	Club	GP	G	A	Pts
1972–73	Philadelphia F.	2	0	0	0

KING, Frank Edward *Forward*
b. Toronto, Ont., Mar. 7, 1929

Season	Club	GP	G	A	Pts
1950–51	Montreal C.	10	1	0	1

KINSELLA, Thomas Raymond (Ray) *Forward*
b. Ottawa, Ont., Jan. 27, 1911

Season	Club	GP	G	A	Pts
1930–31	Ottawa	--	0	0	0

KIRK, Robert Hunter *Forward*
b. Belfast, Ireland, Aug. 8, 1910

Season	Club	GP	G	A	Pts
1937–38	New York R.	39	4	8	12

KIRKPATRICK, Robert Drynan *Forward*
b. Regina, Sask., Dec. 1, 1915

Season	Club	GP	G	A	Pts
1942–43	New York R.	49	12	12	24

KITCHEN, Hoble *Defenseman-Forward*
b. Toronto, Ont.

Season	Club	GP	G	A	Pts
1925–26	Montreal M.	30	5	2	7
1926–27	Detroit C.	--	0	2	2
	Totals	--	5	4	9
Playoffs					
1925–26	Montreal M.	--	0	0	0

KLEIN, James Lloyd (Dede) *Forward*
b. Saskatoon, Sask, Jan. 13, 1910

Season	Club	GP	G	A	Pts
1928–29	Boston	--	1	0	1
1931–32	Boston	--	1	0	1
1932–33	New York A.	--	2	2	4
1933–34	New York A.	--	13	9	22
1934–35	New York A.	--	7	3	10
1935–36	New York A.	--	4	8	12
1936–37	New York A.	--	2	1	3
1937–38	New York A.	--	0	1	1
	Totals	--	30	24	54
Playoffs					
1928–29	Boston	--	0	0	0
1935–36	New York A.	--	0	0	0
	Totals	--	0	0	0

KLINGBEIL, Ernest *Forward*

Season	Club	GP	G	A	Pts
1936–37	Chicago	--	1	2	3

KLUKAY, Joseph Francis *Forward*
b. Sault Ste. Marie, Ont., Nov. 6, 1922

Season	Club	GP	G	A	Pts
1946–47	Toronto M.L.	55	9	20	29
1947–48	Toronto M.L.	59	15	15	30
1948–49	Toronto M.L.	45	11	10	21
1949–50	Toronto M.L.	70	15	16	31
1950–51	Toronto M.L.	70	14	16	30

KLUKAY *(Continued)*

Season	Club	GP	G	A	Pts
1951–52	Toronto M.L.	43	4	8	12
1952–53	Boston	70	13	16	29
1953–54	Boston	70	20	17	37
1954–55	Bos–Tor ML	66	8	8	16
1955–56	Toronto M.L.	18	0	1	1
	Totals	566	109	127	236

Playoffs

Season	Club	GP	G	A	Pts
1942–43	Toronto M.L.	1	0	0	0
1946–47	Toronto M.L.	11	1	0	1
1947–48	Toronto M.L.	9	1	1	2
1948–49	Toronto M.L.	9	2	3	5
1949–50	Toronto M.L.	7	3	0	3
1950–51	Toronto M.L.	11	4	3	7
1951–52	Toronto M.L.	4	1	1	2
1952–53	Boston	11	1	2	3
1953–54	Boston	4	0	0	0
1954–55	Toronto M.L.	4	0	0	0
	Totals	71	13	10	23

All-Star

	Club	GP	G	A	Pts
1947	Toronto M.L.	1	0	0	0
1948	Toronto M.L.	1	0	0	0
1949	Toronto M.L.	1	0	0	0
	Totals	3	0	0	0

KLYMKIEW, Julian *Goalie*
b. Winnipeg, Man., July 16, 1933

Season	Club	GP	GA	Sho	AVE
1958–59	New York R.	1	2	0	2.00

KNIBBS, William *Forward*
b. Toronto, Ont., Jan. 24, 1942

Season	Club	GP	G	A	Pts
1964–65	Boston	53	7	10	07

KNOTT, William Earl (Nick)
Defenseman-Forward
b. Kingston, Ont., July 23, 1920

Season	Club	GP	G	A	Pts
1941–42	Brooklyn A.	14	3	1	4

KNOX, Paul *Forward*

Season	Club	GP	G	A	Pts
1954–55	Toronto M.L.	1	0	0	0

KOMADOSKI, Neil *Defenseman*
b. Winnipeg, Man., Nov. 5, 1951

Season	Club	GP	G	A	Pts
1972–73	Los Angeles	62	1	8	9

KONIK, George Samuel *Defenseman-Forward*
b. Flin Flon, Man., May 4, 1938

Season	Club	GP	G	A	Pts
1967–68	Pittsburgh Pe.	52	7	8	15

KOPAK, Russell *Forward*
b. Edmonton, Alta., Apr. 26, 1924

Season	Club	GP	G	A	Pts
1943–44	Boston	24	7	9	16

KORAB, Gerald Joseph (Jerry) *Forward*
b. Sault Ste. Marie, Ont., Sept. 15, 1948

Season	Club	GP	G	A	Pts
1970–71	Chicago	46	4	14	18
1971–72	Chicago	73	9	5	14
1972–73	Chicago	77	12	15	27
	Totals	196	25	34	59

Playoffs

Season	Club	GP	G	A	Pts
1970–71	Chicago	7	1	0	1
1971–72	Chicago	8	0	1	1
1972–73	Chicago	15	0	0	0
	Totals	30	1	1	2

KOROLL, Clifford Eugene (Cliff) *Forward*
b. Canora, Sask., Oct. 1, 1946

Season	Club	GP	G	A	Pts
1969–70	Chicago	73	18	19	37
1970–71	Chicago	72	16	34	50
1971–72	Chicago	76	22	23	45
1972–73	Chicago	77	33	24	57
	Totals	298	89	100	189

Playoffs

Season	Club	GP	G	A	Pts
1969–70	Chicago	8	1	4	5
1970–71	Chicago	18	7	9	16
1971–72	Chicago	8	0	0	0
1972–73	Chicago	16	4	6	10
	Totals	50	12	19	31

KOTANEN, Elno Richard Erwin (Dick)
Defenseman
b. Port Arthur, Ont., Nov. 18, 1925

Season	Club	GP	G	A	Pts
1948–49	New York R.	1	0	1	1
1950–51	New York R.	1	0	0	0
	Totals	2	0	1	1

KOZAK, Donald *Forward*
b. Edmonton, Alb., Feb. 2, 1952

Season	Club	GP	G	A	Pts
1972–73	Los Angeles	72	14	6	20

KOZAK, Lester *Forward*
b. Yorkton, Sask., Oct. 28, 1940

Season	Club	GP	G	A	Pts
1961–62	Toronto M.L.	12	1	0	1

KRAFTCHECK, Stephen S. *Defenseman*
b. Tinturn, Ont., Mar. 3, 1929

Season	Club	GP	G	A	Pts
1950-51	Boston	22	0	0	0
1951-52	New York R.	58	8	9	17
1952-53	New York R.	69	2	9	11
1958-59	Toronto M.L.	8	1	0	1
	Totals	157	11	18	29
Playoffs					
1950-51	Boston	6	0	0	0

KRAKE, Philip Gordon (Skip) *Forward*
b. North Battleford, Sask., Oct. 14, 1943

Season	Club	GP	G	A	Pts
1963-64	Boston	2	0	0	0
1965-66	Boston	2	0	0	0
1966-67	Boston	15	6	2	8
1967-68	Boston	68	5	7	12
1968-69	Los Angeles	30	3	9	12
1969-70	Los Angeles	58	5	17	22
1970-71	Buffalo	74	4	5	9
	Totals	249	23	40	63
Playoffs					
1967-68	Boston	4	0	0	0
1968-69	Los Angeles	6	1	0	1
	Totals	10	1	0	1

KROL, Joseph *Forward*
b. Winnipeg, Man., Aug. 13, 1915

Season	Club	GP	G	A	Pts
1936-37	New York R.	1	0	0	0
1938-39	New York R.	1	1	1	2
1941-42	Brooklyn A.	24	9	3	12
	Totals	26	10	4	14

KRULICKI, James John (Jim) *Forward*
b. Kitchener, Ont., Mar. 9, 1948

Season	Club	GP	G	A	Pts
1970-71	NY R-Det RW	41	0	3	3

KRYSKOW, David Roy (Dave) *Forward*
b. Edmonton, Alta., Dec. 25, 1951

Season	Club	GP	G	A	Pts
1972-73	Chicago	11	1	0	1
Playoffs					
1972-73	Chicago	3	2	0	2

KRYZANOWSKI, Edward Lloyd *Defenseman*
b. Fort Francis, Ont., Nov. 14, 1925

Season	Club	GP	G	A	Pts
1948-49	Boston	36	1	3	4
1949-50	Boston	59	6	10	16

KRYZANOWSKI *(Continued)*

Season	Club	GP	G	A	Pts
1950-51	Boston	69	3	6	9
1951-52	Boston	70	5	3	8
1952-53	Chicago	5	0	0	0
	Totals	239	15	22	37
Playoffs					
1948-49	Boston	5	0	1	1
1950-51	Boston	6	0	0	0
1951-52	Boston	7	0	0	0
	Totals	18	0	1	1

KUHN, Gordon (Doggie) *Forward*
b. Truro, N.S.

Season	Club	GP	G	A	Pts
1932-33	New York A.	--	1	1	2

KUKULOWICZ, Adolph Frank (Aggie) *Forward*
b. Winnipeg, Man., Apr. 2, 1933

Season	Club	GP	G	A	Pts
1952-53	New York R.	3	1	0	1
1953-54	New York R.	1	0	0	0
	Totals	4	1	0	1

KULLMAN, Arnold Edwin *Forward*
b. Winnipeg, Man., Oct. 9, 1927

Season	Club	GP	G	A	Pts
1947-48	Boston	1	0	0	0
1949-50	Boston	12	0	1	1
	Totals	13	0	1	1

KULLMAN, Edward George *Forward*
b. Winnipeg, Man., Dec. 12, 1923

Season	Club	GP	G	A	Pts
1947-48	New York R.	51	15	17	32
1948-49	New York R.	18	4	5	9
1950-51	New York R.	70	14	18	32
1951-52	New York R.	64	11	10	21
1952-53	New York R.	70	8	10	18
1953-54	New York R.	70	4	10	14
	Totals	343	56	70	126
Playoffs					
1947-48	New York R.	6	1	0	1

KUNTZ, Alan Robert *Forward*
b. Toronto, Ont., June 4, 1919

Season	Club	GP	G	A	Pts
1941-42	New York R.	31	10	11	21
1945-46	New York R.	14	0	1	1
	Totals	45	10	12	22
Playoffs					
1941-42	New York R.	6	1	0	1

KURT, Gary David *Goalie*

b. Kitchener, Ont., Mar. 9, 1947

Season	Club	GP	GA	Sho	AVE
1971–72	California	14	60	0	4.29

KURTENBACH, Orland John *Forward*

b. Cudworth, Sask., Sept. 7, 1936

Season	Club	GP	G	A	Pts
1960–61	New York R.	10	0	6	6
1961–62	Boston	8	0	0	0
1963–64	Boston	70	12	25	37
1964–65	Boston	64	6	20	26
1965–66	Toronto M.L.	70	9	6	15
1966–67	New York R.	60	11	25	36
1967–68	New York R.	73	15	20	35
1968–69	New York R.	2	0	0	0
1969–70	New York R.	53	4	10	14
1970–71	Vancouver	52	21	32	53
1971–72	Vancouver	78	24	37	61
1972–73	Vancouver	47	9	19	28
	Totals	587	111	200	311
Playoffs					
1965–66	Toronto M.L.	4	0	0	0
1966–67	New York R.	3	0	2	2
1967–68	New York R.	6	1	0	1
1969–70	New York R.	6	1	2	3
	Totals	19	2	4	6

KWONG, Lawrence (King) *Forward*

b. Vernon, B.C., June 17, 1923

Season	Club	GP	G	A	Pts
1947–48	New York R.	1	0	0	0

KYLE, Walter Lawrence (Gus) *Defenseman*

b. Dysart, Sask., Sept. 11, 1923

Season	Club	GP	G	A	Pts
1949–50	New York R.	70	3	5	8
1950–51	New York R.	64	2	3	5
1951–52	Boston	69	1	12	13
	Totals	203	6	20	26
Playoffs					
1949–50	New York R.	12	1	2	3
1951–52	Boston	2	0	0	0
	Totals	14	1	2	3

KYLE, William *Forward*

b. Dysart, Sask., Dec. 23, 1924

Season	Club	GP	G	A	Pts
1949–50	New York R.	2	0	0	0
1950–51	New York R.	1	0	3	3
	Totals	3	0	3	3

LABADIE, Joseph Gilles Michel (Mike)
Forward

b. St. Francois D'Assisi, Que., Aug. 17, 1932

Season	Club	GP	G	A	Pts
1952–53	New York R.	3	0	0	0

L'ABBE, Maurice Joseph (Moe) *Forward*

b. Montreal, Que., Aug. 12, 1947

Season	Club	GP	G	A	Pts
1972–73	Chicago	5	0	1	1

LABINE, Leo Gerald *Forward*

b. Haileybury, Ont., July 22, 1931

Season	Club	GP	G	A	Pts
1951–52	Boston	15	2	4	6
1952–53	Boston	51	8	15	23
1953–54	Boston	68	16	19	35
1954–55	Boston	67	24	18	42
1955–56	Boston	68	16	18	34
1956–57	Boston	67	18	29	47
1957–58	Boston	62	7	14	21
1958–59	Boston	70	9	23	32
1959–60	Boston	63	16	28	44
1960–61	Bos–Det RW	64	9	21	30
1961–62	Detroit R.W.	47	3	4	7
	Totals	642	128	193	321
Playoffs					
1951–52	Boston	5	0	1	1
1952–53	Boston	7	2	1	3
1953–54	Boston	4	0	1	1
1954–55	Boston	5	2	1	3
1956–57	Boston	10	2	3	5
1957–58	Boston	11	0	2	2
1958–59	Boston	7	2	1	3
1960–61	Detroit R.W.	11	3	2	5
	Totals	60	11	12	23
All-Star					
1955	NHL All-Stars	1	0	0	0
1956	NHL All-Stars	1	0	0	0
	Totals	2	0	0	0

LABOSSIERE, Gordon William *Forward*

b. St. Boniface, Man., Jan. 2, 1940

Season	Club	GP	G	A	Pts
1963–64	New York R.	15	0	0	0
1964–65	New York R.	1	0	0	0
1967–68	Los Angeles	68	13	27	40
1968–69	Los Angeles	48	10	18	28
1970–71	LA–Minn	74	19	14	33
1971–72	Minnesota	9	2	3	5
	Totals	215	44	62	106

LABOSSIERE (Continued)

Playoffs	Club	GP	G	A	Pts
1967–68	Los Angeles	7	2	3	5
1970–71	Minnesota	3	0	0	0
	Totals	10	2	3	5

LABOVITCH, Max *Forward*
b. Winnipeg, Man., Jan. 18, 1924

Season	Club	GP	G	A	Pts
1943–44	New York R.	5	0	0	0

LABRE, Yvon Jules *Defenseman*
b. Sudbury, Ont., Nov. 29, 1949

Season	Club	GP	G	A	Pts
1970–71	Pittsburgh Pe.	21	1	1	2

LABRIE, Guy *Defenseman*
b. St. Charles Bellechase, Que., Aug. 11, 1920

Season	Club	GP	G	A	Pts
1943–44	Boston	15	2	7	9
1944–45	New York R.	27	2	2	4
	Totals	42	4	9	13

LACH, Elmer James *Forward*
b. Nokomis, Sask., Jan. 22, 1918

Season	Club	GP	G	A	Pts
1940–41	Montreal C.	--	7	14	21
1941–42	Montreal C.	1	0	1	1
1942–43	Montreal C.	45	18	40	58
1943–44	Montreal C.	48	24	48	72
1944–45	Montreal C.	50	26	54	80
1945–46	Montreal C.	50	13	34	47
1946–47	Montreal C.	31	14	16	30
1947–48	Montreal C.	60	30	31	61
1948–49	Montreal C.	36	11	18	29
1949–50	Montreal C.	64	15	33	48
1950–51	Montreal C.	65	21	24	45
1951–52	Montreal C.	70	15	50	65
1952–53	Montreal C.	53	16	25	41
1953–54	Montreal C.	48	5	20	25
	Totals	--	215	408	623

Playoffs	Club	GP	G	A	Pts
1940–41	Montreal C.	3	1	0	1
1942–43	Montreal C.	5	2	4	6
1943–44	Montreal C.	9	2	11	13
1944–45	Montreal C.	6	4	4	8
1945–46	Montreal C.	9	5	12	17
1948–49	Montreal C.	1	0	0	0
1949–50	Montreal C.	5	1	2	3
1950–51	Montreal C.	11	2	2	4
1951–52	Montreal C.	11	1	2	3
1952–53	Montreal C.	12	1	6	7
1953–54	Montreal C.	4	0	2	2
	Totals	76	19	45	64

LACH (Continued)

All-Star	Club	GP	G	A	Pts
1948	NHL All-Stars	1	0	1	1
1952	NHL 1st All-Stars	1	0	0	0
1953	Montreal C.	1	0	0	0
	Totals	3	0	1	1

LACOMBE, Francois *Defenseman*
b. Lachine, Que., Feb. 24, 1948

Season	Club	GP	G	A	Pts
1968–69	Oakland	72	2	16	18
1969–70	Oakland	2	0	0	0
1970–71	Buffalo	1	0	1	1
	Totals	75	2	17	19

Playoffs					
1968–69	Oakland	3	1	0	1

LACROIX, Alfonse *Goalie*

Season	Club	GP	GA	Sho	AVE
1925–26	Montreal C.	4	15	0	3.75

LACROIX, Andre *Forward*
b. Lauzon, Que., June 5, 1945

Season	Club	GP	G	A	Pts
1967–68	Philadelphia F.	18	6	8	14
1968–69	Philadelphia F.	75	24	32	56
1969–70	Philadelphia F.	74	22	36	58
1970–71	Philadelphia F.	78	20	22	42
1971–72	Chicago	51	4	7	11
	Totals	296	76	105	181

Playoffs					
1967–68	Philadelphia F.	7	2	3	5
1968–69	Philadelphia F.	4	0	0	0
1970–71	Philadelphia F.	4	0	2	2
1971–72	Chicago	1	0	0	0
	Totals	16	2	5	7

LaFLEUR, Guy Damien *Forward*
b. Thurso, Que., Sept. 20, 1951

Season	Club	GP	G	A	Pts
1971–72	Montreal C.	73	29	35	64
1972–73	Montreal C.	70	28	27	55
	Totals	143	57	62	119

Playoffs					
1971–72	Montreal C.	6	1	4	5
1972–73	Montreal C.	17	3	5	8
	Totals	23	4	9	13

LaFLEUR, Rene *Forward*

Season	Club	GP	G	A	Pts
1924–25	Montreal C.	1	0	0	0

LaFORCE, Ernest *Defenseman*
b. Montreal, Que., June 23, 1916

Season	Club	GP	G	A	Pts
1942–43	Montreal C.	1	0	0	0

LAFORGE, Claude Roger *Forward*
b. Sorel, Que., July 1, 1936

Season	Club	GP	G	A	Pts
1957–58	Montreal C.	5	0	0	0
1958–59	Detroit R.W.	57	2	5	7
1960–61	Detroit R.W.	10	1	0	1
1961–62	Detroit R.W.	38	10	9	19
1963–64	Detroit R.W.	17	2	3	5
1964–65	Detroit R.W.	1	0	0	0
1967–68	Philadelphia F.	63	9	16	25
1968–69	Philadelphia F.	2	0	0	0
	Totals	193	24	33	57

Playoffs

1967–68	Philadelphia F.	5	1	2	3

LAFRAMBOISE, Peter *Forward*
b. Ottawa, Ont., Jan. 18, 1950

Season	Club	GP	G	A	Pts
1971–72	California	5	0	0	0
1972–73	California	77	16	25	41
	Totals	82	16	25	41

LaFRANCE, Adelard *Forward*
b. Chapleau, Ont., Jan. 13, 1912

Season	Club	GP	G	A	Pts
1933–34	Montreal C.	--	0	0	0

LaFRANCE, Leo *Forward*

Season	Club	GP	G	A	Pts
1927–28	Chicago	--	2	0	2

LAFRENIERE, Roger *Forward*
b. Montreal, Que., July 24, 1942

Season	Club	GP	G	A	Pts
1962–63	Detroit R.W.	3	0	0	0
1972–73	St. Louis B.	10	0	0	0
	Totals	13	0	0	0

LAGACE, Jean-Guy *Defenseman*
b. L'Abord a Plouffe, Que., Feb. 5, 1945

Season	Club	GP	G	A	Pts
1968–69	Pittsburgh Pe.	17	0	1	1
1970–71	Buffalo	3	0	0	0
1972–73	Pittsburgh Pe.	31	1	5	6
	Totals	51	1	6	7

LAJEUNESSE, Serge *Defenseman*
b. Montreal, Que., June 11, 1950

Season	Club	GP	G	A	Pts
1970–71	Detroit R.W.	62	1	3	4
1971–72	Detroit R.W.	7	0	0	0
1972–73	Detroit R.W.	28	0	1	1
	Totals	97	1	4	5

LALANDE, Hector *Forward*
b. North Bay, Ont., Nov. 24, 1934

Season	Club	GP	G	A	Pts
1953–54	Chicago	2	0	0	0
1955–56	Chicago	65	8	18	26
1956–57	Chicago	50	11	17	28
1957–58	Chgo-Det RW	34	2	4	6
	Totals	151	21	39	60

LALONDE, Edouard (Newsy)
Defenseman-Forward
b. Cornwall, Ont., Oct. 31, 1887

Season	Club	GP	G	A	Pts
1917–18	Montreal C.	14	23	0	23
1918–19	Montreal C.	17	23	9	32
1919–20	Montreal C.	23	36	6	42
1920–21	Montreal C.	24	33	8	41
1921–22	Montreal C.	20	9	4	13
	Totals	98	124	27	151

Playoffs

1917–18	Montreal C.	--	5	0	5
1918–19	Montreal C.	--	11	1	12
	Totals	--	16	1	17

LALONDE, Robert Patrick (Bobby) *Forward*
b. Montreal, Que., Mar. 27, 1951

Season	Club	GP	G	A	Pts
1971–72	Vancouver	27	1	5	6
1972–73	Vancouver	77	20	27	47
	Totals	104	21	32	53

LALONDE, Ronald *Forward*
b. Toronto, Ont., Oct. 30, 1952

Season	Club	GP	G	A	Pts
1972–73	Pittsburgh Pe.	9	0	0	0

LAMB, Joseph Gordon *Forward*
b. Sussex, N.B., June 18, 1906

Season	Club	GP	G	A	Pts
1927–28	Montreal M.	--	8	5	13
1928–29	Mont M-Otta	--	4	1	5
1929–30	Ottawa	--	29	20	49
1930–31	Ottawa	--	11	14	25
1931–32	New York A.	--	14	11	25

LAMB (Continued)

Season	Club	GP	G	A	Pts
1932-33	Boston	--	11	8	19
1933-34	Boston	--	10	15	25
1934-35	Mont C-StL E	--	14	14	28
1935-36	Montreal M.	--	0	3	3
1936-37	New York A.	--	3	9	12
1937-38	NY A-Det RW	--	4	1	5
	Totals	--	**108**	**101**	**209**

Playoffs

Season	Club	GP	G	A	Pts
1927-28	Montreal M.	--	1	0	1
1929-30	Ottawa	--	0	0	0
1932-33	Boston	--	0	1	1
1935-36	Montreal M.	--	0	0	0
	Totals	--	**1**	**1**	**2**

LAMBERT, Yvon *Forward*
b. Drummondville, Que., May 20, 1950

Season	Club	GP	G	A	Pts
1972-73	Montreal C.	1	0	0	0

LAMIRANCE, Jean Paul *Defenseman*
b. Shawinigan Falls, Que., Aug. 21, 1923

Season	Club	GP	G	A	Pts
1946-47	New York R.	14	1	1	2
1947-48	New York R.	18	0	1	1
1949-50	New York R.	16	4	3	7
1954-55	Montreal C.	1	0	0	0
	Totals	**49**	**5**	**5**	**10**

Playoffs

Season	Club	GP	G	A	Pts
1947-48	New York R.	6	0	0	0
1949-50	New York R.	2	0	0	0
	Totals	**8**	**0**	**0**	**0**

LAMOUREUX, Leo Peter *Defenseman*
b. Espanola, Ont., Oct. 1, 1916

Season	Club	GP	G	A	Pts
1941-42	Montreal C.	1	0	0	0
1942-43	Montreal C.	46	2	16	18
1943-44	Montreal C.	44	8	23	31
1944-45	Montreal C.	49	2	22	24
1945-46	Montreal C.	45	5	7	12
1946-47	Montreal C.	50	2	11	13
	Totals	**235**	**19**	**79**	**98**

Playoffs

Season	Club	GP	G	A	Pts
1943-44	Montreal C.	9	0	3	3
1944-45	Montreal C.	6	1	1	2
1945-46	Montreal C.	9	0	2	2
1946-47	Montreal C.	4	0	0	0
	Totals	**28**	**1**	**6**	**7**

LAMPMAN, Michael (Mike) *Forward*
b. Lakewood, Calif., Apr. 20, 1950

Season	Club	GP	G	A	Pts
1972-73	St. Louis B.	18	2	3	5

LANCIEN, John Gordon (Jack) *Defenseman*
b. Regina, Sask., June 14, 1923

Season	Club	GP	G	A	Pts
1946-47	New York R.	1	0	0	0
1949-50	New York R.	43	0	4	5
1950-51	New York R.	19	0	1	1
	Totals	**63**	**1**	**5**	**6**

Playoffs

Season	Club	GP	G	A	Pts
1947-48	New York R.	2	0	0	0
1949-50	New York R.	4	0	1	1
	Totals	**6**	**0**	**1**	**1**

LANE, Myles J. *Defenseman*
b. Melrose, Mass., Oct. 2, 1905

Season	Club	GP	G	A	Pts
1928-29	New York R.	24	2	0	2
1933-34	Boston	--	2	1	3
	Totals	--	**4**	**1**	**5**

LANGELLE, Peter *Forward*
b. Winnipeg, Man., Nov. 4, 1917

Season	Club	GP	G	A	Pts
1938-39	Toronto M.L.	--	1	0	1
1939-40	Toronto M.L.	--	7	14	21
1940-41	Toronto M.L.	--	4	15	19
1941-42	Toronto M.L.	48	10	22	32
	Totals	--	**22**	**51**	**73**

Playoffs

Season	Club	GP	G	A	Pts
1938-39	Toronto M.L.	11	1	2	3
1939-40	Toronto M.L.	10	0	3	3
1940-41	Toronto M.L.	7	1	1	2
1941-42	Toronto M.L.	13	3	3	6
	Totals	**41**	**5**	**9**	**14**

LANGLOIS, Albert (Junior) *Defenseman*
b. Magog, Que., Nov. 6, 1934

Season	Club	GP	G	A	Pts
1957-58	Montreal C.	1	0	0	0
1958-59	Montreal C.	48	0	3	3
1959-60	Montreal C.	67	1	14	15
1960-61	Montreal C.	61	1	12	13
1961-62	New York R.	69	7	18	25
1962-63	New York R.	60	2	14	16
1963-64	NY R-Det RW	61	5	8	13
1964-65	Detroit R.W.	65	1	12	13
1965-66	Boston	65	4	10	14
	Totals	**497**	**21**	**91**	**112**

LANGLOIS *(Continued)*

Playoffs	Club	GP	G	A	Pts
1957-58	Montreal C.	7	0	1	1
1958-59	Montreal C.	7	0	0	0
1959-60	Montreal C.	8	0	3	3
1960-61	Montreal C.	5	0	0	0
1961-62	New York R.	6	0	1	1
1963-64	Detroit R.W.	14	0	0	0
1964-65	Detroit R.W.	6	1	0	1
	Totals	53	1	5	6
All-Star					
1959	Montreal C.	1	0	0	0
1969	Montreal C.	1	0	0	0
	Totals	2	0	0	0

LANGLOIS, Charles *Defenseman*
b. Lotbiniere, Que., Aug. 25, 1894

Season	Club	GP	G	A	Pts
1924-25	Hamilton	30	6	1	7
1925-26	New York A.	36	9	1	10
1926-27	NY A-Pitts Pi	--	7	1	8
1927-28	Pitts Pi-Mont M	--	0	0	0
	Totals	--	22	3	25
Playoffs					
1927-28	Montreal M.	--	0	0	0

LANYON, Edward George (Ted) *Defenseman*
b. Winnipeg, Man., June 11, 1939

Season	Club	GP	G	A	Pts
1967-68	Pittsburgh Pe.	5	0	0	0

LAPERRIERE, Jacques *Defenseman*
b. Rouyn, Que., Nov. 22, 1941

Season	Club	GP	G	A	Pts
1962-63	Montreal C.	6	0	2	2
1963-64	Montreal C.	65	2	28	30
1964-65	Montreal C.	67	5	22	27
1965-66	Montreal C.	57	6	25	31
1966-67	Montreal C.	61	0	20	20
1967-68	Montreal C.	72	4	21	25
1968-69	Montreal C.	69	5	26	31
1969-70	Montreal C.	73	6	31	37
1970-71	Montreal C.	49	0	16	16
1971-72	Montreal C.	73	3	25	28
1972-73	Montreal C.	57	7	16	23
	Totals	649	38	232	270
Playoffs					
1962-63	Montreal C.	5	0	1	1
1963-64	Montreal C.	7	1	1	2
1964-65	Montreal C.	6	1	1	2
1966-67	Montreal C.	9	0	1	1
1967-68	Montreal C.	13	1	3	4
1968-69	Montreal C.	14	1	3	4

LAPERRIERE *(Continued)*

Playoffs	Club	GP	G	A	Pts
1970-71	Montreal C.	20	4	9	13
1971-72	Montreal C.	4	0	0	0
1972-73	Montreal C.	10	1	3	4
	Totals	88	9	22	41
All-Star					
1964	NHL All-Stars	1	0	1	1
1965	Montreal C.	1	1	0	1
1967	Montreal C.	1	0	0	0
1968	NHL All-Stars	1	0	0	0
1970	East All-Stars	1	1	0	1
	Totals	5	2	1	3

LAPOINTE, Guy Gerard *Defenseman*
b. Montreal, Que., Mar. 18, 1948

Season	Club	GP	G	A	Pts
1968-69	Montreal C.	1	0	0	0
1969-70	Montreal C.	5	0	0	0
1970-71	Montreal C.	78	15	29	44
1971-72	Montreal C.	69	11	38	49
1972-73	Montreal C.	76	19	35	54
	Totals	229	45	102	147
Playoffs					
1970-71	Montreal C.	20	4	5	9
1971-72	Montreal C.	6	0	1	1
1972-73	Montreal C.	17	6	7	13
	Totals	43	10	13	23
All-Star					
1973	East All-Stars	1	0	0	0

LAPRADE, Edgar Louis *Forward*
b. Mine Center, Ont., Oct. 10, 1919

Season	Club	GP	G	A	Pts
1945-46	New York R.	49	15	19	34
1946-47	New York R.	58	15	25	40
1947-48	New York R.	59	13	34	47
1948-49	New York R.	56	18	12	30
1949-50	New York R.	60	22	22	44
1950-51	New York R.	42	10	13	23
1951-52	New York R.	70	9	29	38
1952-53	New York R.	11	2	1	3
1953-54	New York R.	35	1	6	7
1954-55	New York R.	60	3	11	14
	Totals	500	108	172	280
Playoffs					
1947-48	New York R.	6	1	4	5
1949-50	New York R.	12	3	5	8
	Totals	18	4	9	13
All-Star					
1947	NHL All-Stars	1	0	1	1
1948	NHL All-Stars	1	0	0	0

LAPRADE (Continued)

All-Star	Club	GP	G	A	Pts
1949	NHL All-Stars	1	0	1	1
1950	NHL All-Stars	1	0	0	0
	Totals	4	0	2	2

LaPRAIRIE, Ben *Defenseman*

Season	Club	GP	G	A	Pts
1936-37	Chicago	--	0	0	0

LAROCHELLE, Wildor *Forward*
b. Sorel, Que., Sept. 3, 1906

Season	Club	GP	G	A	Pts
1925-26	Montreal C.	33	2	1	3
1926-27	Montreal C.	--	0	1	1
1927-28	Montreal C.	--	3	1	4
1929-30	Montreal C.	--	14	11	15
1930-31	Montreal C.	--	8	5	13
1931-32	Montreal C.	--	18	8	26
1932-33	Montreal C.	--	11	4	15
1933-34	Montreal C.	--	16	11	27
1934-35	Montreal C.	--	9	19	28
1935-36	Mont C-Chgo	--	2	3	5
1935-36	Chicago	--	9	10	19
	Totals	--	92	74	166

Playoffs					
1926-27	Montreal C.	--	0	0	0
1927-28	Montreal C.	--	0	0	0
1929-30	Montreal C.	--	1	0	1
1930-31	Montreal C.	--	1	2	3
1931-32	Montreal C.	--	2	1	3
1932-33	Montreal C.	--	1	0	1
1933-34	Montreal C.	--	1	1	2
1934-35	Montreal C.	--	0	0	0
1935-36	Chicago	--	0	0	0
	Totals	--	6	4	10

LAROSE, Charles *Forward*

Season	Club	GP	G	A	Pts
1925-26	Boston	6	0	0	0

LAROSE, Claude David *Forward*
b. Hearst, Ont., Mar. 2, 1942

Season	Club	GP	G	A	Pts
1962-63	Montreal C.	4	0	0	0
1963-64	Montreal C.	21	1	1	2
1964-65	Montreal C.	68	21	16	37
1965-66	Montreal C.	64	15	18	33
1966-67	Montreal C.	69	19	16	35
1967-68	Montreal C.	42	2	9	11
1968-69	Minnesota	67	25	37	62
1969-70	Minnesota	75	24	23	47
1970-71	Montreal C.	64	10	13	23
1971-72	Montreal C.	77	20	18	38
1972-73	Montreal C.	73	11	23	34
	Totals	624	148	174	322

LAROSE (Continued)

Playoffs	Club	GP	G	A	Pts
1963-64	Montreal C.	2	1	0	1
1964-65	Montreal C.	13	0	1	1
1965-66	Montreal C.	6	0	1	1
1966-67	Montreal C.	10	1	5	6
1967-68	Montreal C.	12	3	2	5
1969-70	Minnesota	6	1	1	2
1970-71	Montreal C.	11	1	0	1
1971-72	Montreal C.	6	2	1	3
1972-73	Montreal C.	17	3	4	7
	Totals	83	12	15	27

All-Star					
1965	Montreal C.	1	0	1	1
1967	Montreal C.	1	0	1	1
1969	West All-Stars	1	1	0	1
1970	West All-Stars	1	0	0	0
	Totals	4	1	2	3

LARSON, Norman Lyle *Forward*
b. Moose Jaw, Sask., Oct., 13, 1920

Season	Club	GP	G	A	Pts
1940-41	New York A.	--	9	9	18
1941-42	New York A.	40	16	9	25
1946-47	New York R.	1	0	0	0
	Totals	--	25	18	43

LATREILLE, Philip *Forward*
b. Montreal, Que., Apr. 22, 1938

Season	Club	GP	G	A	Pts
1960-61	New York R.	4	0	0	0

LAUGHTON, Michael Frederic *Forward*
b. Nelson, B.C., Feb. 21, 1944

Season	Club	GP	G	A	Pts
1967-68	Oakland	35	2	6	8
1968-69	Oakland	53	20	23	43
1969-70	Oakland	76	16	19	35
1970-71	California	25	1	0	1
	Totals	189	39	48	87

Playoffs					
1968-69	Oakland	7	2	3	5
1969-70	Oakland	4	0	1	1
	Totals	11	2	4	6

LAVENDER, Brian James *Forward*
b. Edmonton, Alta., Apr. 20, 1947

Season	Club	GP	G	A	Pts
1971-72	St. Louis B.	46	5	11	16
1972-73	NY I-Det RW	70	8	8	16
	Totals	116	13	19	32

Playoffs					
1971-72	St. Louis B.	3	0	0	0

LAVIOLETTE, Jack *Defenseman-Forward*
b. Belleville, Ont., 1879

Season	Club	GP	G	A	Pts
1917–18	Montreal C.	18	2	0	2

Playoffs

1917–18	Montreal C.	--	0	0	0

LAWSON, Daniel *Forward*
b. Toronto, Ont., Oct. 30, 1947

Season	Club	GP	G	A	Pts
1967–68	Detroit R.W.	1	0	0	0
1968–69	Det RW–Minn	62	8	10	18
1969–70	Minnesota	45	9	8	17
1970–71	Minnesota	33	1	5	6
1971–72	Buffalo	78	10	6	16
	Totals	219	28	29	57

Playoffs

1969–70	Minnesota	6	0	1	1
1970–71	Minnesota	10	0	0	0
	Totals	16	0	1	1

LAYCOE, Harold Richardson *Defenseman*
b. Sutherland, Sask., June 23, 1922

Season	Club	GP	G	A	Pts
1945–46	New York R.	17	0	2	2
1946–47	New York R.	58	1	12	13
1947–48	Montreal C.	14	1	2	3
1948–49	Montreal C.	51	3	5	8
1949–50	Montreal C.	30	0	2	2
1950–51	Mont C–Bos	44	1	3	4
1951–52	Boston	70	5	7	12
1952–53	Boston	54	2	10	12
1953–54	Boston	58	3	16	19
1954–55	Boston	70	4	13	17
1955–56	Boston	65	5	5	10
	Totals	531	25	77	102

Playoffs

1948–49	Montreal C.	7	0	1	1
1949–50	Montreal C.	2	0	0	0
1950–51	Boston	6	0	1	1
1951–52	Boston	7	1	1	2
1952–53	Boston	11	0	2	2
1953–54	Boston	2	0	0	0
1954–55	Boston	5	1	0	1
	Totals	40	2	5	7

LEACH, Lawrence R. *Forward*
b. Humboldt, Sask., June 18, 1936

Season	Club	GP	G	A	Pts
1958–59	Boston	29	4	12	16
1959–60	Boston	69	7	12	19
1961–62	Boston	28	2	5	7
	Totals	126	13	29	42

LEACH *(Continued)*

Playoffs	Club	GP	G	A	Pts
1958–59	Boston	7	1	1	2

LEACH, Reginald Joseph (Reg) *Forward*
b. Riverton, Man., Apr. 23, 1950

Season	Club	GP	G	A	Pts
1970–71	Boston	23	2	4	6
1971–72	Bos–Calif	73	13	20	33
1972–73	California	76	23	12	35
	Totals	172	38	36	74

Playoffs

1970–71	Boston	3	0	0	0

LEBLANC, Jean Paul *Forward*
b. South Durham, Que., Oct. 20, 1946

Season	Club	GP	G	A	Pts
1968–69	Chicago	6	1	2	3

LEBRUN, Albert Ivan *Defenseman*
b. Timmins, Ont., Dec. 1, 1940

Season	Club	GP	G	A	Pts
1960–61	New York R.	4	0	2	2
1965–66	New York R.	2	0	0	0
	Totals	6	0	2	2

LECAINE, William Joseph *Forward*
b. Moose Jaw, Sask., Mar. 11, 1940

Season	Club	GP	G	A	Pts
1968–69	Pittsburgh Pe.	4	0	0	0

LECLAIR, John Louis (Jackie) *Forward*
b. Quebec City, Que., May 30, 1929

Season	Club	GP	G	A	Pts
1954–55	Montreal C.	59	11	22	33
1955–56	Montreal C.	54	6	8	14
1956–57	Montreal C.	47	3	10	13
	Totals	160	20	40	60

Playoffs

1954–55	Montreal C.	12	5	0	5
1955–56	Montreal C.	8	1	1	2
	Totals	20	6	1	7

All-Star

1956	Montreal C.	1	0	0	0

LECLERC, Renald (Rene) *Forward*
b. Ville-de-Vanier, Que., Nov. 12, 1947

Season	Club	GP	G	A	Pts
1968–69	Detroit R.W.	43	2	3	5
1970–71	Detroit R.W.	44	8	8	16
	Totals	87	10	11	21

LEDINGHAM, Walter *Forward*
b. Weyburn, Sask., Oct. 26, 1950

Season	Club	GP	G	A	Pts
1972-73	Chicago	9	0	1	1

LEDUC, Albert (Battleship) *Defenseman*
b. Valleyfield, Que., July 31, 1901

Season	Club	GP	G	A	Pts
1925-26	Montreal C.	32	10	3	13
1926-27	Montreal C.	--	5	2	7
1927-28	Montreal C.	43	8	5	13
1928-29	Montreal C.	--	9	2	11
1929-30	Montreal C.	--	6	8	14
1930-31	Montreal C.	--	8	6	14
1931-32	Montreal C.	--	5	3	8
1932-33	Montreal C.	--	5	3	8
1933-34	NY R-Otta	--	1	3	4
1934-35	Montreal C.	--	0	0	0
	Totals	--	57	35	92

Playoffs

Season	Club	GP	G	A	Pts
1926-27	Montreal C.	4	0	0	0
1927-28	Montreal C.	2	1	0	1
1928-29	Montreal C.	3	1	0	1
1929-30	Montreal C.	6	1	3	4
1930-31	Montreal C.	10	0	2	2
1931-32	Montreal C.	4	1	1	2
1932-33	Montreal C.	2	1	0	1
	Totals	31	5	6	11

LEDUC, Richard Henri (Rich) *Forward*
b. Ile Perrot, Que., Aug. 24, 1951

Season	Club	GP	G	A	Pts
1972-73	Boston	5	1	1	2

LEFLEY, Bryan Andrew *Defenseman*
b. Grosse Isle, Man., Oct. 18, 1948

Season	Club	GP	G	A	Pts
1972-73	New York I.	63	3	7	10

LEFLEY, Charles Thomas (Chuck) *Forward*
b. Winnipeg, Man., Jan. 20, 1950

Season	Club	GP	G	A	Pts
1971-72	Montreal C.	16	0	2	2
1972-73	Montreal C.	65	21	25	46
	Totals	81	21	27	48

Playoffs

Season	Club	GP	G	A	Pts
1970-71	Montreal C.	1	0	0	0
1972-73	Montreal C.	17	3	5	8
	Totals	18	3	5	8

LEGER, Roger *Defenseman*
b. L'Annonciation, Que., Mar. 26, 1919

Season	Club	GP	G	A	Pts
1943-44	New York R.	7	1	2	3
1946-47	Montreal C.	49	4	18	22
1947-48	Montreal C.	48	4	14	18
1948-49	Montreal C.	28	6	7	13
1949-50	Montreal C.	55	3	12	15
	Totals	187	18	53	71

Playoffs

Season	Club	GP	G	A	Pts
1946-47	Montreal C.	11	0	6	6
1948-49	Montreal C.	5	0	1	1
1949-50	Montreal C.	4	0	0	0
	Totals	20	0	7	7

LEGGE, Norman Randall (Randy) *Defenseman*
b. Newmarket, Ont., Dec. 16, 1945

Season	Club	GP	G	A	Pts
1972-73	New York R.	12	0	2	2

LEHMAN, Hugh *Goalie*
b. Pembroke, Ont., 1895

Season	Club	GP	GA	Sho	AVE
1926-27	Chicago	44	116	5	2.64
1927-28	Chicago	4	20	1	5.00
	Totals	48	136	6	2.83

Playoffs

Season	Club	GP	GA	Sho	AVE
1917-18	Vancouver (PCHL)	5	18	0	3.60
1921-22	Vancouver (PCHL)	5	16	1	3.20
1922-23	Vancouver (PCHL)	4	10	0	2.50
1923-24	Vancouver (PCHL)	2	5	0	2.50
1926-27	Chicago	2	10	0	5.00
	Totals	18	59	1	3.28

LEIER, Edward *Forward*
b. Poland, Nov. 3, 1927

Season	Club	GP	G	A	Pts
1949-50	Chicago	5	0	1	1
1950-51	Chicago	11	2	0	2
	Totals	16	2	1	3

LEITER, Robert Edward *Forward*
b. Winnipeg, Man., Mar. 22, 1941

Season	Club	GP	G	A	Pts
1962-63	Boston	51	9	13	22
1963-64	Boston	56	6	13	19
1964-65	Boston	18	3	1	4
1965-66	Boston	9	2	1	3
1968-69	Boston	1	0	0	0
1971-72	Pittsburgh Pe.	78	14	17	31
1972-73	Atlanta	78	26	34	60
	Totals	291	60	79	139

Playoffs

Season	Club	GP	G	A	Pts
1971-72	Pittsburgh Pe.	4	3	0	3

LEMAIRE, Jacques Gerard *Forward*
b. LaSalle, Que., Sept. 7, 1945

Season	Club	GP	G	A	Pts
1967-68	Montreal C.	69	22	20	42
1968-69	Montreal C.	75	29	34	63
1969-70	Montreal C.	69	32	28	60
1970-71	Montreal C.	78	28	28	56
1971-72	Montreal C.	77	32	49	81
1972-73	Montreal C.	77	44	51	95
	Totals	445	187	210	397

Playoffs

1967-68	Montreal C.	13	7	6	13
1968-69	Montreal C.	14	4	2	6
1970-71	Montreal C.	20	9	10	19
1971-72	Montreal C.	6	2	1	3
1972-73	Montreal C.	17	7	13	20
	Totals	70	29	32	61

All-Star

1970	East All-Stars	1	0	1	1
1973	East All-Stars	1	1	0	1
	Totals	2	1	1	2

LEMIEUX, Jacques *Defenseman*
b. Matane, Que., Apr. 8, 1943

Season	Club	GP	G	A	Pts
1967-68	Los Angeles	16	0	3	3
1969-70	Los Angeles	3	0	1	1
	Totals	19	0	4	4

LEMIEUX, Real Gaston *Forward*
b. Victoriaville, Que., Jan. 3, 1945

Season	Club	GP	G	A	Pts
1966-67	Detroit R.W.	1	0	0	0
1967-68	Los Angeles	74	12	23	35
1968-69	Los Angeles	75	11	29	40
1969-70	NY R-LA	73	6	10	16
1970-71	Los Angeles	43	3	6	9
1971-72	Los Angeles	78	13	25	38
1972-73	Los Angeles	74	5	10	15
	Totals	418	50	103	153

Playoffs

1967-68	Los Angeles	7	1	1	2
1968-69	Los Angeles	11	1	3	4
	Totals	18	2	4	6

LEMIEUX, Richard Bernard *Forward*
b. Temiscamingue, Que., Apr. 19, 1951

Season	Club	GP	G	A	Pts
1971-72	Vancouver	42	7	9	16
1972-73	Vancouver	78	17	35	52
	Totals	120	24	44	68

LEMIEUX, Robert *Defenseman*
b. Montreal, Que., Dec. 16, 1944

Season	Club	GP	G	A	Pts
1967-68	Oakland	19	0	1	1

LEPINE, Alfred (Pit) *Forward*
b. St. Anne de Bellevue, Que., July 31, 1901

Season	Club	GP	G	A	Pts
1925-26	Montreal C.	27	9	1	10
1926-27	Montreal C.	--	16	1	17
1927-28	Montreal C.	--	4	1	5
1928-29	Montreal C.	--	6	1	7
1929-30	Montreal C.	--	24	9	33
1930-31	Montreal C.	--	17	7	24
1931-32	Montreal C.	--	19	11	30
1932-33	Montreal C.	--	8	8	16
1933-34	Montreal C.	--	10	8	18
1934-35	Montreal C.	--	12	19	31
1935-36	Montreal C.	--	6	10	16
1936-37	Montreal C.	--	7	8	15
1937-38	Montreal C.	--	5	14	19
	Totals	--	143	98	241

Playoffs

1926-27	Montreal C.	--	0	0	0
1928-29	Montreal C.	--	0	0	0
1929-30	Montreal C.	--	2	2	4
1930-31	Montreal C.	--	4	2	6
1931-32	Montreal C.	-	1	0	1
1932-33	Montreal C.	--	0	0	0
1933-34	Montreal C.	--	0	0	0
1934-35	Montreal C.	--	0	0	0
1936-37	Montreal C.	--	0	1	1
1937-38	Montreal C.	--	0	0	0
	Totals	--	7	5	12

LEPINE, Hector *Forward*

Season	Club	GP	G	A	Pts
1925-26	Montreal C.	33	5	2	7

LESIEUR, Arthur *Defenseman*
b. Fall River, Mass., Sept. 13, 1907

Season	Club	GP	G	A	Pts
1930-31	Montreal C.	--	2	0	2
1931-32	Montreal C.	--	1	2	3
1935-36	Montreal C.	--	1	0	1
	Totals	--	4	2	6

Playoffs

1930-31	Montreal C.	--	0	0	0
1931-32	Montreal C.	--	0	0	0
	Totals	--	0	0	0

LESUK, William Anton (Bill) *Forward*
b. Moose Jaw, Sask., Nov. 1, 1946

Season	Club	GP	G	A	Pts
1968-69	Boston	5	0	1	1
1969-70	Boston	3	0	0	0
1970-71	Philadelphia F.	78	17	19	36
1971-72	Phila F-LA	72	11	16	27
1972-73	Los Angeles	67	6	14	20
	Totals	225	34	50	84
Playoffs					
1968-69	Boston	1	0	0	0
1969-70	Boston	2	0	0	0
1970-71	Philadelphia F.	4	1	0	1
	Totals	7	1	0	1

LESWICK, Anthony Joseph *Forward*
b. Humboldt, Sask., Mar. 17, 1923

Season	Club	GP	G	A	Pts
1945-46	New York R.	50	15	9	24
1946-47	New York R.	59	27	14	41
1947-48	New York R.	60	24	16	40
1948-49	New York R.	60	13	14	27
1949-50	New York R.	69	19	25	44
1950-51	New York R.	70	15	11	26
1951-52	Detroit R.W.	70	9	10	19
1952-53	Detroit R.W.	70	15	12	27
1953-54	Detroit R.W.	70	6	18	24
1954-55	Detroit R.W.	70	10	17	27
1955-56	Chicago	70	11	11	22
1957-58	Detroit R.W.	11	1	2	3
	Totals	729	165	159	324
Playoffs					
1947-48	New York R.	6	3	2	5
1949-50	New York R.	12	2	4	6
1951-52	Detroit R.W.	8	3	1	4
1952-53	Detroit R.W.	6	1	0	1
1953-54	Detroit R.W.	12	3	1	4
1954-55	Detroit R.W.	11	1	2	3
1957-58	Detroit R.W.	4	0	0	0
	Totals	59	13	10	23
All-Star					
1947	NHL All-Stars	1	0	0	0
1948	NHL All-Stars	1	0	0	0
1949	NHL All-Stars	1	0	0	0
1950	NHL All-Stars	1	0	0	0
1952	NHL 1st All-Stars	1	0	0	0
1954	Detroit R.W.	1	0	0	0
	Totals	6	0	0	0

LESWICK, Jack *Forward*

Season	Club	GP	G	A	Pts
1933-34	Chicago	--	1	7	8
Playoffs					
1933-34	Chicago	--	0	0	0

LESWICK, Peter Paul *Forward*
b. Saskatoon, Sask., July 12, 1917

Season	Club	GP	G	A	Pts
1936-37	New York A.	--	1	0	1

LEVANDOSKI, Joseph Thomas *Forward*
b. Cobalt, Ont., Mar. 17, 1922

Season	Club	GP	G	A	Pts
1946-47	New York R.	8	1	1	2

LEVER, Donald *Forward*
b. S. Porcupine, Ont., Nov. 14, 1952

Season	Club	GP	G	A	Pts
1972-73	Vancouver	78	12	26	38

LEVINSKY, Alexander (Mine Boy) *Defenseman*
b. Syracuse, N.Y., Feb. 2, 1910

Season	Club	GP	G	A	Pts
1930-31	Toronto M.L.	--	0	1	1
1931-32	Toronto M.L.	--	5	5	10
1932-33	Toronto M.L.	--	1	4	5
1933-34	Toronto M.L.	--	5	11	16
1934-35	NY R-Chgo	--	3	8	11
1935-36	Chicago	--	1	7	8
1936-37	Chicago	--	0	8	8
1937-38	Chicago	--	3	2	5
1938-39	Chicago	--	1	3	4
	Totals	--	19	49	68
Playoffs					
1930-31	Toronto M.L.	2	0	0	0
1931-32	Toronto M.L.	7	0	0	0
1932-33	Toronto M.L.	9	1	0	1
1933-34	Toronto M.L.	5	0	0	0
1934-35	Chicago	2	0	0	0
1935-36	Chicago	2	0	1	1
1937-38	Chicago	7	1	0	1
	Totals	34	2	1	3

LEWICKI, Daniel *Forward*
b. Fort William, Ont., Mar. 12, 1931

Season	Club	GP	G	A	Pts
1950-51	Toronto M.L.	61	16	18	34
1951-52	Toronto M.L.	51	4	9	13
1952-53	Toronto M.L.	4	1	3	4
1953-54	Toronto M.L.	7	0	1	1
1954-55	New York R.	70	29	24	53
1955-56	New York R.	70	18	27	45
1956-57	New York R.	70	18	20	38
1957-58	New York R.	70	11	19	30
1958-59	Chicago	58	8	14	22
	Totals	461	105	135	240
Playoffs					
1950-51	Toronto M.L.	9	0	0	0
1955-56	New York R.	5	0	3	3

LEWICKI (Continued)

Playoffs

	Club	GP	G	A	Pts
1956–57	New York R.	5	0	1	1
1957–58	New York R.	6	0	0	0
1958–59	Chicago	3	0	0	0
	Totals	28	0	4	4

All-Star

1955	NHL All-Stars	1	0	0	0

LEWIS, Douglas *Forward*
b. Winnipeg, Man., Mar. 3, 1921

Season	Club	GP	G	A	Pts
1946–47	Montreal C.	3	0	0	0

LEWIS, Herbert A. *Forward*
b. Calgary, Alta., Apr. 17, 1906

Season	Club	GP	G	A	Pts
1928–29	Detroit C.	--	9	5	14
1929–30	Detroit C.	--	20	11	31
1930–31	Detroit F.	--	15	6	21
1931–32	Detroit F.	--	5	14	19
1932–33	Detroit F.	--	20	14	34
1933–34	Detroit R.W.	--	16	15	31
1934–35	Detroit R.W.	--	16	27	43
1935–36	Detroit R.W.	--	14	23	37
1936–37	Detroit R.W.	--	14	18	32
1937–38	Detroit R.W.	--	13	18	31
1938–39	Detroit R.W.	--	6	10	16
	Totals	--	148	161	309

Playoffs

	Club	GP	G	A	Pts
1928–29	Detroit C.	--	0	0	0
1931–32	Detroit F.	--	0	0	0
1932–33	Detroit F.	--	1	0	1
1933–34	Detroit R.W.	--	5	2	7
1935–36	Detroit R.W.	--	2	3	5
1936–37	Detroit R.W.	--	4	3	7
1938–39	Detroit R.W.	--	1	2	3
	Totals	--	13	10	23

LEY, Richard Norman (Ricky) *Defenseman*
b. Orillia, Ont., Nov. 2, 1948

Season	Club	GP	G	A	Pts
1968–69	Toronto M.L.	38	1	11	12
1969–70	Toronto M.L.	48	2	13	15
1970–71	Toronto M.L.	76	4	16	20
1971–72	Toronto M.L.	67	1	14	15
	Totals	229	8	54	62

Playoffs

	Club	GP	G	A	Pts
1968–69	Toronto M.L.	3	0	0	0
1970–71	Toronto M.L.	6	0	2	2
1971–72	Toronto M.L.	5	0	0	0
	Totals	14	0	2	2

LIBETT, Lynn Nicholas (Nick) *Forward*
b. Stratford, Ont., Dec. 9, 1945

Season	Club	GP	G	A	Pts
1967–68	Detroit R.W.	22	2	1	3
1968–69	Detroit R.W.	75	10	14	24
1969–70	Detroit R.W.	76	20	20	40
1970–71	Detroit R.W.	78	16	13	29
1971–72	Detroit R.W.	77	31	22	53
1972–73	Detroit R.W.	78	19	34	53
	Totals	406	98	104	202

Playoffs

	Club	GP	G	A	Pts
1969–70	Detroit R.W.	4	2	0	2

LICARI, Anthony *Forward*
b. Ottawa, Ont., Apr. 9, 1921

Season	Club	GP	G	A	Pts
1946–47	Detroit R.W.	9	0	1	1

LIDDINGTON, Robert Allen (Bob) *Forward*
b. Calgary, Alta., Sept. 15, 1948

Season	Club	GP	G	A	Pts
1970–71	Toronto M.L.	11	0	1	1

LINDSAY, Bert *Goalie*

Season	Club	GP	GA	Sho	AVE
1918–19	Toronto A.	16	83	0	5.19

LINDSAY, Robert Blake Theodore (Ted)
Forward
b. Renfrew, Ont., July 29, 1925

Season	Club	GP	G	A	Pts
1944–45	Detroit R.W.	45	17	6	23
1945–46	Detroit R.W.	47	7	10	17
1946–47	Detroit R.W.	59	27	15	42
1947–48	Detroit R.W.	60	33	19	52
1948–49	Detroit R.W.	50	26	28	54
1949–50	Detroit R.W.	69	23	55	78
1950–51	Detroit R.W.	67	24	35	59
1951–52	Detroit R.W.	70	30	39	69
1952–53	Detroit R.W.	70	32	39	71
1953–54	Detroit R.W.	70	26	36	62
1954–55	Detroit R.W.	49	19	19	38
1955–56	Detroit R.W.	67	27	23	50
1956–57	Detroit R.W.	70	30	55	85
1957–58	Chicago	68	15	24	39
1958–59	Chicago	70	22	36	58
1959–60	Chicago	68	7	19	26
1964–65	Detroit R.W.	68	14	14	28
	Totals	1068	379	472	851

Playoffs

	Club	GP	G	A	Pts
1944–45	Detroit R.W.	14	2	0	2
1945–46	Detroit R.W.	5	0	1	1

LINDSAY (Continued)

Playoffs	Club	GP	G	A	Pts
1946–47	Detroit R.W.	5	2	2	4
1947–48	Detroit R.W.	10	3	1	4
1948–49	Detroit R.W.	11	2	6	8
1949–50	Detroit R.W.	13	4	4	8
1950–51	Detroit R.W.	6	0	1	1
1951–52	Detroit R.W.	8	5	2	7
1952–53	Detroit R.W.	6	4	4	8
1953–54	Detroit R.W.	12	4	4	8
1954–55	Detroit R.W.	11	7	12	19
1955–56	Detroit R.W.	10	6	3	9
1956–57	Detroit R.W.	5	2	4	6
1958–59	Chicago	6	2	4	6
1959–60	Chicago	4	1	1	2
1964–65	Detroit R.W.	7	3	0	3
	Totals	133	47	49	96

All-Star					
1947	NHL All-Stars	1	0	0	0
1948	NHL All-Stars	1	1	0	1
1949	NHL All-Stars	1	0	0	0
1950	Detroit R.W.	1	3	1	4
1951	NHL 1st All-Stars	1	0	1	1
1952	NHL 1st All-Stars	1	0	0	0
1953	NHL All-Stars	1	0	0	0
1954	Detroit R.W.	1	0	1	1
1955	Detroit R.W.	1	0	2	2
1956	NHL All-Stars	1	1	0	1
1957	NHL All-Stars	1	0	0	0
	Totals	11	5	5	10

LISCOMBE, Harry Carlyle (Carl) *Forward*
b. Perth, Ont., May 17, 1915

Season	Club	GP	G	A	Pts
1937–38	Detroit R.W.	––	14	10	24
1938–39	Detroit R.W.	––	8	18	26
1939–40	Detroit R.W.	––	2	7	9
1940–41	Detroit R.W.	––	10	10	20
1941–42	Detroit R.W.	47	13	17	30
1942–43	Detroit R.W.	50	19	23	42
1943–44	Detroit R.W.	50	36	37	73
1944–45	Detroit R.W.	42	23	9	32
1945–46	Detroit R.W.	44	12	9	21
	Totals	––	137	140	277

Playoffs	Club	GP	G	A	Pts
1938–39	Detroit R.W.	6	0	0	0
1940–41	Detroit R.W.	8	4	3	7
1941–42	Detroit R.W.	12	6	6	12
1942–43	Detroit R.W.	10	6	8	14
1943–44	Detroit R.W.	5	1	0	1
1944–45	Detroit R.W.	14	4	2	6
1945–46	Detroit R.W.	4	1	0	1
	Totals	59	22	19	41

LITZENBERGER, Edward C. J. *Forward*
b. Neudorf, Sask., July 15, 1932

Season	Club	GP	G	A	Pts
1952–53	Montreal C.	2	1	0	1
1953–54	Montreal C.	3	0	0	0
1954–55	Mont C–Chgo	73	23	28	51
1955–56	Chicago	70	10	29	39
1956–57	Chicago	70	32	32	64
1957–58	Chicago	70	32	30	62
1958–59	Chicago	70	33	44	77
1959–60	Chicago	52	12	18	30
1960–61	Chicago	62	10	22	32
1961–62	Det RW–Tor ML	69	18	22	40
1962–63	Toronto M.L.	58	5	13	18
1963–64	Toronto M.L.	19	2	0	2
	Totals	618	178	238	416

Playoffs	Club	GP	G	A	Pts
1958–59	Chicago	6	3	5	8
1959–60	Chicago	4	0	1	1
1960–61	Chicago	10	1	3	4
1961–62	Toronto M.L.	10	0	2	2
1962–63	Toronto M.L.	9	1	2	3
1963–64	Toronto M.L.	1	0	0	0
	Totals	40	5	13	18

All-Star					
1955	NHL All-Stars	1	0	0	0
1957	NHL All-Stars	1	0	2	2
1958	NHL All-Stars	1	0	1	1
1959	NHL All-Stars	1	0	1	1
1962	Toronto M.L.	1	0	0	0
1963	Toronto M.L.	1	1	1	2
	Totals	6	1	5	6

LOCAS, Jacques *Forward*
b. Pointe aux Trembles, Que., Feb. 12, 1926

Season	Club	GP	G	A	Pts
1947–48	Montreal C.	56	7	8	15
1948–49	Montreal C.	3	0	0	0
	Totals	59	7	8	15

LOCKHART, Howard (Holes) *Goalie*

Season	Club	GP	GA	Sho	AVE
1919–20	Tor StP–Que	6	28	0	4.67
1920–21	Hamilton	24	132	1	5.50
1921–22	Hamilton	24	105	0	4.38
1923–24	Toronto St.P.	1	5	0	5.00
1924–25	Boston	2	11	0	5.50
	Totals	57	281	1	4.93

LOCKING, Norman *Forward*
b. Owen Sound, Ont., May 24, 1911

Season	Club	GP	G	A	Pts
1934-35	Chicago	--	2	5	7
1935-36	Chicago	--	0	1	1
	Totals	--	2	6	8

Playoffs

1934-35	Chicago	--	0	0	0

LONG, Barry Kenneth *Defenseman*
b. Brantford, Ont., Jan. 3, 1949

Season	Club	GP	G	A	Pts
1972-73	Los Angeles	70	2	13	15

LONSBERRY, David Ross *Forward*
b. Humboldt, Sask., Feb. 7, 1947

Season	Club	GP	G	A	Pts
1966-67	Boston	8	0	1	1
1967-68	Boston	19	2	2	4
1968-69	Boston	6	0	0	0
1969-70	Los Angeles	76	20	22	42
1970-71	Los Angeles	76	25	28	53
1971-72	LA-Phila F	82	16	21	37
1972-73	Philadelphia F.	77	21	29	50
	Totals	344	84	103	187

Playoffs

1972-73	Philadelphia F.	11	4	3	7

LO PRESTI, Samuel *Goalie*
b. Eveleth, Minn., Jan. 30, 1917

Season	Club	GP	GA	Sho	AVE
1940-41	Chicago	27	84	1	3.11
1941-42	Chicago	47	152	3	3.23
	Totals	74	236	4	3.19

Playoffs

1940-41	Chicago	5	12	0	2.40
1941-42	Chicago	3	5	1	1.67
	Totals	8	17	1	2.13

LORENTZ, James Peter (Jim) *Forward*
b. Waterloo, Ont., May 1, 1947

Season	Club	GP	G	A	Pts
1968-69	Boston	11	1	3	4
1969-70	Boston	68	7	16	23
1970-71	St. Louis B.	76	19	21	40
1971-72	StL B-NY R-Buff	52	10	15	25
1972-73	Buffalo	78	27	35	62
	Totals	285	64	90	154

Playoffs

1969-70	Boston	11	1	0	1
1970-71	St. Louis B.	6	0	1	1
1972-73	Buffalo	6	0	3	3
	Totals	23	1	4	5

LORRAIN, Rodrique *Forward*
b. Buckingham, Que., July 1915

Season	Club	GP	G	A	Pts
1935-36	Montreal C.	--	0	0	0
1936-37	Montreal C.	--	3	6	9
1937-38	Montreal C.	--	13	19	32
1938-39	Montreal C.	--	10	9	19
1939-40	Montreal C.	--	1	5	6
1941-42	Montreal C.	--	1	0	1
	Totals	--	28	39	67

Playoffs

1936-37	Montreal C.	--	0	0	0
1937-38	Montreal C.	--	0	0	0
1938-39	Montreal C.	--	0	3	3
	Totals	--	0	3	3

LOUGHLIN, Clem *Defenseman*
b. Carroll, Man., 1894

Season	Club	GP	G	A	Pts
1926-27	Detroit C.	--	7	3	10
1927-28	Detroit C.	--	1	2	3
1928-29	Chicago	--	0	1	1
	Totals	-	8	6	14

Playoffs

1925-26	Victoria (PCHL)	--	1	0	1

LOUGHLIN, Wilfred *Defenseman-Forward*

Season	Club	GP	G	A	Pts
1923-24	Toronto St.P.	14	0	0	0

Playoffs

1924-25	Victoria (PCHL)	--	1	0	1

LOW, Ronald Albert (Ron) *Goalie*
b. Birtle, Man., June 21, 1950

Season	Club	GP	GA	Sho	AVE
1972-73	Toronto M.L.	39	152	1	3.89

LOWE, Norman E. (Odie) *Forward*
b. Winnipeg, Man., Apr. 15, 1928

Season	Club	GP	G	A	Pts
1948-49	New York R.	1	0	0	0
1949-50	New York R.	3	1	1	2
	Totals	4	1	1	2

LOWE, Ross Robert *Forward*
b. Oshawa, Ont., Sept. 21, 1928

Season	Club	GP	G	A	Pts
1949-50	Boston	3	0	0	0
1950-51	Bos-Mont C	43	5	3	8
1951-52	Montreal C.	31	1	5	6
	Totals	77	6	8	14

Playoffs

1950-51	Montreal C.	2	0	0	0

LOWERY, Frank *Forward*
b. Ottawa, Ont.

Season	Club	GP	G	A	Pts
1917–18	Ottawa	11	0	0	0
1918–19	Ottawa	10	0	0	0
1920–21	Hamilton	3	0	0	0
1924–25	Montreal M.	28	0	0	0
1925–26	Mont M–Pitts Pi	26	1	0	1
	Totals	78	1	0	1

LOWERY, Gerald *Forward*
b. Ottawa, Ont.

Season	Club	GP	G	A	Pts
1925–26	Pittsburgh Pi.	--	0	0	0
1927–28	Toronto M.L.	--	6	5	11
1928–29	Tor ML–Pitts Pi	--	5	12	17
1929–30	Pittsburgh Pi.	--	16	14	30
1930–31	Philadelphia Q.	--	13	14	27
1931–32	Chicago	--	8	3	11
	Totals	--	48	48	96

Playoffs

Season	Club	GP	G	A	Pts
1925–26	Pittsburgh Pi.	--	0	0	0
1931–32	Chicago	--	1	0	1
	Totals	--	1	0	1

LUCAS, David *Defenseman*
b. Downeyville, Ont., Mar. 22, 1932

Season	Club	GP	G	A	Pts
1962–63	Detroit R.W.	1	0	0	0

LUCE, Donald Harold *Forward*
b. London, Ont., Oct. 2, 1948

Season	Club	GP	G	A	Pts
1969–70	New York R.	12	1	2	3
1970–71	NY R–Det RW	67	3	12	15
1971–72	Buffalo	78	11	8	19
1972–73	Buffalo	78	18	25	43
	Totals	235	33	47	80

Playoffs

Season	Club	GP	G	A	Pts
1969–70	New York R.	5	0	1	1
1972–73	Buffalo	6	1	1	2
	Totals	11	1	2	3

LUMLEY, Harry (Apple Cheeks) *Goalie*
b. Owen Sound, Ont., Nov. 11, 1926

Season	Club	GP	GA	Sho	AVE
1943–44	Det RW–NY R	3	13	0	4.33
1944–45	Detroit R.W.	37	119	1	3.22
1945–46	Detroit R.W.	50	159	2	3.18
1946–47	Detroit R.W.	52	159	3	3.05
1947–48	Detroit R.W.	60	147	7	2.45
1948–49	Detroit R.W.	60	145	6	2.42
1949–50	Detroit R.W.	63	148	7	2.35

LUMLEY *(Continued)*

Season	Club	GP	GA	Sho	AVE
1950–51	Chicago	64	246	3	3.84
1951–52	Chicago	70	241	2	3.44
1952–53	Toronto M.L.	70	167	10	2.38
1953–54	Toronto M.L.	69	128	13	1.85
1954–55	Toronto M.L.	69	134	8	1.94
1955–56	Toronto M.L.	59	159	3	2.69
1957–58	Boston	25	71	3	2.84
1958–59	Boston	11	27	1	2.45
1959–60	Boston	42	147	2	3.50
	Totals	804	2210	71	2.75

Playoffs

Season	Club	GP	GA	Sho	AVE
1944–45	Detroit R.W.	14	31	2	2.21
1945–46	Detroit R.W.	5	16	1	3.20
1947–48	Detroit R.W.	10	30	0	3.00
1948–49	Detroit R.W.	11	26	0	2.36
1949–50	Detroit R.W.	14	28	3	2.00
1953–54	Toronto M.L.	5	15	0	3.00
1954–55	Toronto M.L.	4	14	0	3.50
1955–56	Toronto M.L.	5	14	1	2.80
1957–58	Boston	1	5	0	5.00
1958–59	Boston	7	20	0	2.85
	Totals	76	199	7	2.62

All-Star		GP	Per	GA	AGP
1951	NHL 1st All-Stars	1	1½	1	0.67
1954	NHL All-Stars	1	1½	2	1.33
1955	NHL All-Stars	1	1½	2	1.33
	Totals	3	4½	5	1.11

LUND, Pentti Alexander (Penny) *Forward*
b. Helsinki, Finland, Dec. 6, 1925

Season	Club	GP	G	A	Pts
1948–49	New York R.	59	14	16	30
1949–50	New York R.	64	18	9	27
1950–51	New York R.	59	4	16	20
1951–52	Boston	23	0	5	5
1952–53	Boston	54	8	9	17
	Totals	259	44	55	99

Playoffs

Season	Club	GP	G	A	Pts
1946–47	Boston	1	0	0	0
1947–48	Boston	2	0	0	0
1949–50	New York R.	12	6	5	11
1951–52	Boston	2	1	0	1
1952–53	Boston	2	0	0	0
	Totals	19	7	5	12

LUNDE, Leonard Melvin *Forward*
b. Campbell River, Alta., Nov. 13, 1936

Season	Club	GP	G	A	Pts
1958–59	Detroit R.W.	68	14	12	26
1959–60	Detroit R.W.	66	6	17	23
1960–61	Detroit R.W.	53	6	12	18

LUNDE *(Continued)*

Season	Club	GP	G	A	Pts
1961-62	Detroit R.W.	23	2	9	11
1962-63	Chicago	60	6	22	28
1965-66	Chicago	24	4	7	11
1967-68	Minnesota	7	0	1	1
1970-71	Vancouver	20	1	3	4
	Totals	321	39	83	122

Playoffs

Season	Club	GP	G	A	Pts
1959-60	Detroit R.W.	6	1	2	3
1960-61	Detroit R.W.	10	2	0	2
1962-63	Chicago	4	0	0	0
	Totals	20	3	2	5

LUNDRIGAN, Joseph Roche (Joe) *Defenseman*
b. Corner Brook, Nfld., Sept. 12, 1948

Season	Club	GP	G	A	Pts
1972-73	Toronto M.L.	49	2	7	9

LUNDY, Patrick Anthony *Forward*
b. Saskatoon, Sask., May 31, 1924

Season	Club	GP	G	A	Pts
1945-46	Detroit R.W.	4	3	2	5
1946-47	Detroit R.W.	59	17	17	34
1947-48	Detroit R.W.	11	4	1	5
1948-49	Detroit R.W.	15	4	3	7
1950-51	Chicago	61	9	9	18
	Totals	150	37	32	69

Playoffs

Season	Club	GP	G	A	Pts
1945-46	Detroit R.W.	2	1	0	1
1946-47	Detroit R.W.	5	1	0	1
1947-48	Detroit R.W.	5	1	1	2
1948-49	Detroit R.W.	4	0	0	0
	Totals	16	3	1	4

LYNCH, Jack *Defenseman*
b. Toronto, Ont., May 28, 1952

Season	Club	GP	G	A	Pts
1972-73	Pittsburgh Pe.	47	1	18	19

LYNN, Victor Ivan *Defenseman-Forward*
b. Saskatoon, Sask., Jan. 26, 1925

Season	Club	GP	G	A	Pts
1943-44	Detroit R.W.	3	0	0	0
1945-46	Montreal C.	2	0	0	0
1946-47	Toronto M.L.	31	6	14	20
1947-48	Toronto M.L.	60	12	22	34
1948-49	Toronto M.L.	52	7	9	16
1949-50	Toronto M.L.	70	7	13	20
1950-51	Boston	56	14	6	20
1951-52	Boston	12	2	2	4
1952-53	Chicago	29	0	10	10
1953-54	Chicago	11	1	0	1
	Totals	326	49	76	125

LYNN *(Continued)*

Playoffs

	Club	GP	G	A	Pts
1946-47	Toronto M.L.	11	4	1	5
1947-48	Toronto M.L.	9	2	5	7
1948-49	Toronto M.L.	8	0	1	1
1949-50	Toronto M.L.	7	0	2	2
1950-51	Boston	5	0	0	0
1952-53	Chicago	7	1	1	2
	Totals	47	7	10	17

All-Star

	Club	GP	G	A	Pts
1947	Toronto M.L.	1	0	0	0
1948	Toronto M.L.	1	0	0	0
1949	Toronto M.L.	1	0	0	0
	Totals	3	0	0	0

LYONS, Ronald *Forward*

Season	Club	GP	G	A	Pts
1930-31	Bos-Phila Q	--	2	4	6

MacDONALD, Calvin Parker *Forward*
b. Sydney, N.S., June 14, 1933

Season	Club	GP	G	A	Pts
1952-53	Toronto M.L.	1	0	0	0
1954-55	Toronto M.L.	62	8	3	11
1956-57	New York R.	45	7	8	15
1957-58	New York R.	70	8	10	18
1959-60	New York R.	4	0	0	0
1960-61	Detroit R.W.	70	14	12	26
1961-62	Detroit R.W.	31	5	7	12
1962-63	Detroit R.W.	69	33	28	61
1963-64	Detroit R.W.	68	21	25	46
1964-65	Detroit R.W.	69	13	33	46
1965-66	Bos-Det RW	66	11	16	27
1966-67	Detroit R.W.	16	3	5	8
1967-68	Minnesota	69	19	23	42
1968-69	Minnesota	35	2	9	11
	Totals	675	144	179	323

Playoffs

	Club	GP	G	A	Pts
1954-55	Toronto M.L.	4	0	0	0
1956-57	New York R.	1	1	1	2
1957-58	New York R.	6	1	2	3
1960-61	Detroit R.W.	9	1	0	1
1962-63	Detroit R.W.	11	3	2	5
1963-64	Detroit R.W.	14	3	3	6
1964-65	Detroit R.W.	7	1	1	2
1965-66	Detroit R.W.	9	0	0	0
1967-68	Minnesota	14	4	5	9
	Totals	75	14	14	28

MacDONALD, James Allen Kilby *Forward*
b. Ottawa, Ont., Sept. 6, 1913

Season	Club	GP	G	A	Pts
1939-40	New York R.	44	15	13	28
1940-41	New York R.	47	5	6	11

MacDONALD (Continued)

Season	Club	GP	G	A	Pts
1943–44	New York R.	24	7	9	16
1944–45	New York R.	36	9	6	15
	Totals	151	36	34	70

Playoffs

Season	Club	GP	G	A	Pts
1939–40	New York R.	12	0	2	2
1940–41	New York R.	3	1	0	1
	Totals	15	1	2	3

MacDONALD, Lowell Wilson *Forward*
b. New Glasgow, N.S., Aug. 30, 1941

Season	Club	GP	G	A	Pts
1961–62	Detroit R.W.	1	0	0	0
1962–63	Detroit R.W.	26	2	1	3
1963–64	Detroit R.W.	10	1	4	5
1964–65	Detroit R.W.	9	2	1	3
1967–68	Los Angeles	74	21	24	45
1968–69	Los Angeles	58	14	14	28
1970–71	Pittsburgh Pe.	10	0	1	1
1972–73	Pittsburgh Pe.	78	34	41	75
	Totals	266	74	86	160

Playoffs

Season	Club	GP	G	A	Pts
1962–63	Detroit R.W.	1	0	0	0
1967–68	Los Angeles	7	3	4	7
1968–69	Los Angeles	7	2	3	5
	Totals	15	5	7	12

All-Star

Season	Club	GP	G	A	Pts
1973	West All-Stars	1	0	1	1

MACEY, Hubert *Forward*
b. The Pas, Man., Apr. 13, 1921

Season	Club	GP	G	A	Pts
1941–42	New York R.	9	3	5	8
1942–43	New York R.	9	3	3	6
1946–47	Montreal C.	12	0	1	1
	Totals	30	6	9	15

Playoffs

Season	Club	GP	G	A	Pts
1941–42	New York R.	1	0	0	0
1946–47	Montreal C.	7	0	0	0
	Totals	8	0	0	0

MacFAYDEN, Donald P. *Forward*
b. Grossfield, Alta., Mar. 24, 1907

Season	Club	GP	G	A	Pts
1932–33	Chicago	--	5	9	14
1933–34	Chicago	--	1	3	4
1934–35	Chicago	--	2	5	7
1935–36	Chicago	--	4	16	20
	Totals	--	12	33	45

MacFAYDEN (Continued)

Playoffs

Season	Club	GP	G	A	Pts
1933–34	Chicago	--	2	2	4
1934–35	Chicago	--	0	0	0
1935–36	Chicago	--	0	0	0
	Totals	--	2	2	4

MacGREGOR, Bruce Cameron *Forward*
b. Edmonton, Alta., Apr. 26, 1941

Season	Club	GP	G	A	Pts
1960–61	Detroit R.W.	12	0	1	1
1961–62	Detroit R.W.	65	6	12	18
1962–63	Detroit R.W.	67	11	11	22
1963–64	Detroit R.W.	63	11	21	32
1964–65	Detroit R.W.	66	21	20	41
1965–66	Detroit R.W.	70	20	14	34
1966–67	Detroit R.W.	70	28	19	47
1967–68	Detroit R.W.	71	15	24	39
1968–69	Detroit R.W.	69	18	23	41
1969–70	Detroit R.W.	73	15	23	38
1970–71	Det RW–NY R	74	18	29	47
1971–72	New York R.	75	19	21	40
1972–73	New York R.	52	14	12	26
	Totals	827	196	230	426

Playoffs

Season	Club	GP	G	A	Pts
1960–61	Detroit R.W.	8	1	2	3
1962–63	Detroit R.W.	10	1	4	5
1963–64	Detroit R.W.	14	5	2	7
1964–65	Detroit R.W.	7	0	2	2
1965–66	Detroit R.W.	12	1	4	5
1969–70	Detroit R.W.	4	1	0	1
1970–71	New York R.	13	0	4	4
1971–72	New York R.	16	2	6	8
1972–73	New York R.	10	2	2	4
	Totals	94	13	26	39

MacKAY, Calum (Baldy) *Forward*
b. Toronto, Ont., Jan. 1, 1927

Season	Club	GP	G	A	Pts
1946–47	Detroit R.W.	5	0	0	0
1948–49	Detroit R.W.	1	0	0	0
1949–50	Montreal C.	52	8	10	18
1950–51	Montreal C.	70	18	10	28
1951–52	Montreal C.	12	0	1	1
1953–54	Montreal C.	47	10	13	23
1954–55	Montreal C.	50	14	21	35
	Totals	237	50	55	105

Playoffs

Season	Club	GP	G	A	Pts
1949–50	Montreal C.	5	0	1	1
1950–51	Montreal C.	11	1	0	1
1952–53	Montreal C.	7	1	3	4
1953–54	Montreal C.	3	0	1	1
1954–55	Montreal C.	12	3	8	11
	Totals	38	5	13	18

MacKAY (Continued)

All-Star	Club	GP	G	A	Pts
1953	Montreal C.	1	0	0	0

MacKAY, David *Forward*

Season	Club	GP	G	A	Pts
1940–41	Chicago	--	3	0	3
Playoffs					
1940–41	Chicago	--	0	1	1

MacKAY, Duncan (Mickey) *Forward*
b. 1897

Season	Club	GP	G	A	Pts
1926–27	Chicago	--	14	8	22
1927–28	Chicago	--	17	4	21
1928–29	Pitts Pi-Bos	--	9	2	11
1929–30	Boston	--	4	5	9
	Totals	--	44	19	63
Playoffs					
1921–22	Vancouver (PCHL)	--	1	0	1
1922–23	Vancouver (PCHL)	--	1	0	1
1923–24	Vancouver (PCHL)	--	0	1	1
1926–25	Chicago	--	0	0	0
1928–29	Boston	--	0	0	0
1929–30	Boston	--	0	0	0
	Totals	--	2	1	3

MacKAY, Murdo John *Forward*
b. Fort William, Ont., Aug. 8, 1917

Season	Club	GP	G	A	Pts
1945–46	Montreal C.	5	0	1	1
1947–48	Montreal C.	14	0	2	2
	Totals	19	0	3	3
Playoffs					
1946–47	Montreal C.	9	0	1	1
1948–49	Montreal C.	6	1	1	2
	Totals	15	1	2	3

MACKELL, Fleming David *Forward*
b. Montreal, Que., Apr. 30, 1929

Season	Club	GP	G	A	Pts
1947–48	Toronto M.L.	3	0	0	0
1948–49	Toronto M.L.	11	1	1	2
1949–50	Toronto M.L.	36	7	13	20
1950–51	Toronto M.L.	70	12	13	25
1951–52	Tor ML-Bos	62	3	16	19
1952–53	Boston	65	27	17	44
1953–54	Boston	67	15	32	47
1954–55	Boston	60	11	24	35
1955–56	Boston	52	7	9	16
1956–57	Boston	65	22	17	39
1957–58	Boston	70	20	40	60

MACKELL (Continued)

Season	Club	GP	G	A	Pts
1958–59	Boston	57	17	23	40
1959–60	Boston	47	7	15	22
	Totals	665	149	220	369
Playoffs					
1948–49	Toronto M.L.	9	2	4	6
1949–50	Toronto M.L.	7	1	1	2
1950–51	Toronto M.L.	11	2	3	5
1951–52	Boston	5	2	1	3
1952–53	Boston	11	2	7	9
1953–54	Boston	4	1	1	2
1954–55	Boston	4	0	1	1
1956–57	Boston	10	5	3	8
1957–58	Boston	12	5	14	19
1958–59	Boston	7	2	6	8
	Totals	80	22	41	63
All-Star					
1947	Toronto M.L.	1	0	0	0
1948	Toronto M.L.	1	0	0	0
1949	Toronto M.L.	1	0	0	0
1954	NHL All-Stars	1	0	0	0
	Totals	4	0	0	0

MacKENZIE, Barry *Defenseman*
b. Toronto, Ont., Aug. 16, 1941

Season	Club	GP	G	A	Pts
1968–69	Minnesota	6	0	1	1

MacKENZIE, William Kenneth *Defenseman*
b. Winnipeg, Man., Dec. 12, 1912

Season	Club	GP	G	A	Pts
1932–33	Chicago	--	4	4	8
1933–34	Montreal M.	--	4	3	7
1934–35	New York R.	20	1	0	1
1936–37	Mont M-Mont C	--	4	4	8
1937–38	Mont C-Chgo	--	1	2	3
1938–39	Chicago	--	1	0	1
1939–40	Chicago	--	0	1	1
	Totals	--	15	14	29
Playoffs					
1933–34	Montreal M.	4	0	0	0
1934–35	New York R.	3	0	0	0
1936–37	Montreal C.	5	1	0	1
1937–38	Chicago	7	0	1	1
	Totals	19	1	1	2

MACKEY, Reginald *Defenseman*
b. Ottawa, Ont., May 7, 1900

Season	Club	GP	G	A	Pts
1926–27	New York R.	34	0	0	0
Playoffs					
1926–27	New York R.	1	0	0	0

MACKIE, Howard *Defenseman*
b. Kitchener, Ont., Aug. 30, 1913

Season	Club	GP	G	A	Pts
1936-37	Detroit R.W.	--	1	0	1

MacKINTOSH, Ian Ronald *Forward*
b. Selkirk, Man., June 10, 1927

Season	Club	GP	G	A	Pts
1952-53	New York R.	4	0	0	0

MacLEISH, Richard George (Rick) *Forward*
b. Lindsay, Ont., Jan. 3, 1950

Season	Club	GP	G	A	Pts
1970-71	Philadelphia F.	26	2	4	6
1971-72	Philadelphia F.	17	1	2	3
1972-73	Philadelphia F.	78	50	50	100
	Totals	121	53	56	109

Playoffs

Season	Club	GP	G	A	Pts
1970-71	Philadelphia F.	4	1	0	1
1972-73	Philadelphia F.	10	3	4	7
	Totals	14	4	4	8

MacMILLAN, John *Forward*
b. Lethbridge, Alta., Oct. 25, 1935

Season	Club	GP	G	A	Pts
1960-61	Toronto M.L.	31	3	5	8
1961-62	Toronto M.L.	32	1	0	1
1962-63	Toronto M.L.	6	1	1	2
1963-64	Tor ML-Det RW	33	0	3	3
1964-65	Detroit R.W.	3	0	1	1
	Totals	104	5	10	15

Playoffs

Season	Club	GP	G	A	Pts
1960-61	Toronto M.L.	4	0	0	0
1961-62	Toronto M.L.	3	0	0	0
1962-63	Toronto M.L.	1	0	0	0
1963-64	Detroit R.W.	4	0	1	1
	Totals	12	0	1	1

All-Star

1962	Toronto M.L.	1	0	0	0
1963	Toronto M.L.	1	0	0	0
	Totals	2	0	0	0

MacMILLAN, William Stewart (Billy) *Forward*
b. Charlottetown, P.E.I. Mar. 7, 1943

Season	Club	GP	G	A	Pts
1970-71	Toronto M.L.	76	22	19	41
1971-72	Toronto M.L.	61	10	7	17
1972-73	Atlanta	78	10	15	25
	Totals	215	42	41	83

Playoffs

Season	Club	GP	G	A	Pts
1970-71	Toronto M.L.	6	0	3	3
1971-72	Toronto M.L.	5	0	0	0
	Totals	11	0	3	3

MacNEIL, Allster Wences *Defenseman*
b. Sydney, N.S., Sept. 27, 1935

Season	Club	GP	G	A	Pts
1955-56	Toronto M.L.	1	0	0	0
1956-57	Toronto M.L.	53	4	8	12
1957-58	Toronto M.L.	13	0	0	0
1959-60	Toronto M.L.	4	0	0	0
1961-62	Montreal C.	62	1	7	8
1962-63	Chicago	70	2	19	21
1963-64	Chicago	70	5	19	24
1964-65	Chicago	69	3	7	10
1965-66	Chicago	51	0	1	1
1966-67	New York R.	58	0	4	4
1967-68	Pittsburgh Pe.	74	2	10	12
	Totals	525	17	75	92

Playoffs

Season	Club	GP	G	A	Pts
1961-62	Montreal C.	5	0	0	0
1962-63	Chicago	4	0	1	1
1963-64	Chicago	7	0	2	2
1964-65	Chicago	14	0	1	1
1965-66	Chicago	3	0	0	0
1966-67	New York R.	4	0	0	0
	Totals	37	0	4	4

MacPHERSON, James Albert (Bud)
Defenseman
b. Edmonton, Alta., Mar. 21, 1927

Season	Club	GP	G	A	Pts
1948-49	Montreal C.	3	0	0	0
1950-51	Montreal C.	62	0	16	16
1951-52	Montreal C.	54	2	1	3
1952-53	Montreal C.	59	2	3	5
1953-54	Montreal C.	41	0	5	5
1954-55	Montreal C.	30	1	8	9
1956-57	Montreal C.	10	0	0	0
	Totals	259	5	33	38

Playoffs

Season	Club	GP	G	A	Pts
1950-51	Montreal C.	11	0	2	2
1951-52	Montreal C.	11	0	0	0
1952-53	Montreal C.	4	0	1	1
1953-54	Montreal C.	3	0	0	0
	Totals	29	0	3	3

All-Star

1953	Montreal C.	1	0	0	0

MacSWEYN, Donald Ralph *Defenseman*
b. Hawkesbury, Ont., Sept. 8, 1942

Season	Club	GP	G	A	Pts
1967-68	Philadelphia F.	4	0	0	0
1968-69	Philadelphia F.	24	0	4	4
1969-70	Philadelphia F.	17	0	0	0
1971-72	Philadelphia F.	2	0	1	1
	Totals	47	0	5	5

MacSWEYN (Continued)

Playoffs	Club	GP	G	A	Pts
1968–69	Philadelphia F.	4	0	0	0
1970–71	Philadelphia F.	4	0	0	0
	Totals	8	0	0	0

MADIGAN, Cornelius Dennis (Connie)
Defenseman
b. Port Arthur, Ont., Oct. 4, 1934

Season	Club	GP	G	A	Pts
1972–73	St. Louis B.	20	0	3	3

Playoffs					
1972–73	St. Louis B.	5	0	0	0

MAGGS, Darryl John *Defenseman*
b. Victoria, B.C., Apr. 6, 1949

Season	Club	GP	G	A	Pts
1971–72	Chicago	59	7	4	11
1972–73	Chgo–Calif	71	7	15	22
	Totals	130	14	19	33

Playoffs					
1971–72	Chicago	4	0	0	0

MAGNUSON, Keith Arlen *Defenseman*
b. Saskatoon, Sask., Apr. 27, 1947

Season	Club	GP	G	A	Pts
1969–70	Chicago	76	0	24	24
1970–71	Chicago	76	3	20	23
1971–72	Chicago	74	2	19	21
1972–73	Chicago	77	0	19	19
	Totals	303	5	82	87

Playoffs					
1969–70	Chicago	8	1	2	3
1970–71	Chicago	18	0	2	2
1971–72	Chicago	8	0	1	1
1972–73	Chicago	7	0	2	2
	Totals	41	1	7	8

All-Star					
1971	West All-Stars	1	0	0	0
1972	West All-Stars	1	0	0	0
	Totals	2	0	0	0

MAHAFFY, John *Forward*
b. Montreal, Que., July 18, 1918

Season	Club	GP	G	A	Pts
1942–43	Montreal C.	9	2	5	7
1943–44	Mont C–NY R	28	9	20	29
	Totals	37	11	25	36

Playoffs					
1944–45	Montreal C.	1	0	1	1

MAHOVLICH, Francis William (Frank) *Forward*
b. Timmins, Ont., Jan. 10, 1938

Season	Club	GP	G	A	Pts
1956–57	Toronto M.L.	3	1	0	1
1957–58	Toronto M.L.	67	20	16	36
1958–59	Toronto M.L.	63	22	27	49
1959–60	Toronto M.L.	70	18	21	39
1960–61	Toronto M.L.	70	48	36	84
1961–62	Toronto M.L.	70	33	38	71
1962–63	Toronto M.L.	67	36	37	73
1963–64	Toronto M.L.	70	26	29	55
1964–65	Toronto M.L.	59	23	28	51
1965–66	Toronto M.L.	68	32	24	56
1966–67	Toronto M.L.	63	18	28	46
1967–68	Tor ML–Det RW	63	26	26	52
1968–69	Detroit R.W.	76	49	29	78
1969–70	Detroit R.W.	74	38	32	70
1970–71	Det RW–Mtl C	73	31	42	73
1971–72	Montreal C.	76	43	53	96
1972–73	Montreal C.	78	38	55	93
	Totals	1110	502	521	1023

Playoffs					
1958–59	Toronto M.L.	12	6	5	11
1959–60	Toronto M.L.	10	3	1	4
1960–61	Toronto M.L.	5	1	1	2
1961–62	Toronto M.L.	12	6	6	12
1962–63	Toronto M.L.	9	0	2	2
1963–64	Toronto M.L.	14	4	11	15
1964–65	Toronto M.L.	6	0	3	3
1965–66	Toronto M.L.	4	1	0	1
1966–67	Toronto M.L.	12	3	7	10
1969–70	Detroit R.W.	4	0	0	0
1970–71	Montreal C.	20	14	13	27
1971–72	Montreal C.	6	3	2	5
1972–73	Montreal C.	17	9	14	23
	Totals	131	50	65	115

All-Star					
1959	NHL All-Stars	1	0	0	0
1960	NHL All-Stars	1	1	0	1
1961	NHL All-Stars	1	0	0	0
1962	Toronto M.L.	1	1	0	1
1963	Toronto M.L.	1	2	1	3
1964	Toronto M.L.	1	0	1	1
1965	NHL All-Stars	1	0	0	0
1967	NHL All-Stars	1	0	0	0
1968	Toronto M.L.	1	0	2	2
1969	East All-Stars	1	2	0	2
1970	East All-Stars	1	0	0	0
1971	East All-Stars	1	0	0	0
1972	East All-Stars	1	0	0	0
1973	East All-Stars	1	1	1	2
	Totals	14	7	5	12

MAHOVLICH, Peter Joseph *Forward*
b. Schumacher, Ont., Oct. 10, 1946

Season	Club	GP	G	A	Pts
1965-66	Detroit R.W.	3	0	1	1
1966-67	Detroit R.W.	34	1	3	4
1967-68	Detroit R.W.	15	6	4	10
1968-69	Detroit R.W.	30	2	2	4
1969-70	Montreal C.	36	9	8	17
1970-71	Montreal C.	78	35	26	61
1971-72	Montreal C.	75	35	32	67
1972-73	Montreal C.	61	21	38	59
	Totals	332	109	114	223

Playoffs

1970-71	Montreal C.	20	10	6	16
1971-72	Montreal C.	6	0	2	2
1972-73	Montreal C.	17	4	9	13
	Totals	43	14	17	31

All-Star

1971	East All-Stars	1	0	0	0

MAILLEY, Frank *Forward*

Season	Club	GP	G	A	Pts
1942-43	Montreal C.	1	0	0	0

MAIR, James McKay (Jim) *Defenseman*
b. Schumacher, Ont., May 15, 1946

Season	Club	GP	G	A	Pts
1970-71	Philadelphia F.	2	0	0	0
1971-72	Philadelphia F.	2	0	0	0
1972-73	NY I-Vanc	64	3	11	14
	Totals	68	3	11	14

Playoffs

1970-71	Philadelphia F.	3	1	2	3

MAJEAU, Fern *Forward*
b. Verdun, Que., May 3, 1916

Season	Club	GP	G	A	Pts
1943-44	Montreal C.	44	20	18	38
1944-45	Montreal C.	12	2	6	8
	Totals	56	22	24	46

Playoffs

1943-44	Montreal C.	1	0	0	0

MAKI, Ronald Patrick (Chico) *Forward*
b. Sault Ste. Marie, Ont., Aug. 17, 1939

Season	Club	GP	G	A	Pts
1961-62	Chicago	16	4	6	10
1962-63	Chicago	65	7	17	24
1963-64	Chicago	68	8	14	22
1964-65	Chicago	65	16	24	40
1965-66	Chicago	68	17	31	48
1966-67	Chicago	56	9	29	38
1967-68	Chicago	60	8	16	24

MAKI *(Continued)*

Season	Club	GP	G	A	Pts
1968-69	Chicago	66	7	21	28
1969-70	Chicago	75	10	24	34
1970-71	Chicago	72	22	26	48
1971-72	Chicago	62	13	34	47
1972-73	Chicago	77	13	19	32
	Totals	750	134	261	395

Playoffs

1960-61	Chicago	1	0	0	0
1962-63	Chicago	6	0	1	1
1963-64	Chicago	7	0	0	0
1964-65	Chicago	14	3	9	12
1965-66	Chicago	3	1	1	2
1966-67	Chicago	6	0	0	0
1967-68	Chicago	11	2	5	7
1969-70	Chicago	8	2	2	4
1970-71	Chicago	18	6	5	11
1971-72	Chicago	8	1	4	5
1972-73	Chicago	16	2	8	10
	Totals	98	17	35	52

All-Star

1961	Chicago	1	0	0	0
1971	West All-Stars	1	1	0	1
1972	West All-Stars	1	0	1	1
	Totals	3	1	1	2

MAKI, Wayne *Forward*
b. Sault Ste. Marie, Ont., Nov. 10, 1944

Season	Club	GP	G	A	Pts
1967-68	Chicago	49	5	5	10
1968-69	Chicago	1	0	0	0
1969-70	St. Louis B.	16	2	1	3
1970-71	Vancouver	78	25	38	63
1971-72	Vancouver	76	22	25	47
1972-73	Vancouver	26	3	10	13
	Totals	246	57	79	136

Playoffs

1967-68	Chicago	2	1	0	1

MALONE, Clifford *Forward*
b. Quebec City, Que., Sept. 4, 1925

Season	Club	GP	G	A	Pts
1951-52	Montreal C.	3	0	0	0

MALONE, Joseph *Forward*
b. Quebec City, Que., Feb. 28, 1890

Season	Club	GP	G	A	Pts
1917-18	Montreal C.	20	44	0	44
1918-19	Montreal C.	8	7	1	8
1919-20	Quebec	24	39	6	45
1920-21	Montreal C.	20	30	4	34

541

MALONE (Continued)

Season	Club	GP	G	A	Pts
1921–22	Hamilton	24	25	7	32
1922–23	Montreal C.	20	1	0	1
1923–24	Montreal C.	9	0	0	0
	Totals	125	146	18	164

Playoffs

1918–19	Montreal C.	5	6	1	7

MALONEY, Daniel Charles (Dan) *Forward*
b. Barrie, Ont., Sept. 24, 1950

Season	Club	GP	G	A	Pts
1970–71	Chicago	74	12	14	26
1972–73	Chgo–LA	71	17	24	41
	Totals	145	29	38	67

Playoffs

1970–71	Chicago	10	0	1	1

MALONEY, Philip Francis *Forward*
b. Ottawa, Ont., Oct. 6, 1927

Season	Club	GP	G	A	Pts
1949–50	Boston	70	15	31	46
1950–51	Bos–Tor ML	14	3	0	3
1952–53	Toronto M.L.	29	2	6	8
1958–59	Chicago	24	2	2	4
1959–60	Chicago	21	6	4	10
	Totals	158	28	43	71

Playoffs

1958–59	Chicago	6	0	0	0

MANASTERSKY, Timothy (Tom) *Defenseman*
b. Montreal, Que., Mar. 7, 1929

Season	Club	GP	G	A	Pts
1950–51	Montreal C.	6	0	0	0

MANCUSO, Felix (Gus) *Forward*
b. Niagara Falls, Ont., Apr. 11, 1913

Season	Club	GP	G	A	Pts
1937–38	Montreal C.	--	1	1	2
1939–40	Montreal C.	--	0	0	0
1942–43	New York R.	41	6	8	14
	Totals	--	7	9	16

MANERY, Randy Neal *Defenseman*
b. Leamington, Ont., Jan. 10, 1949

Season	Club	GP	G	A	Pts
1970–71	Detroit R.W.	2	0	0	0
1971–72	Detroit R.W.	1	0	0	0
1972–73	Atlanta	78	5	30	35
	Totals	81	5	30	35

All-Star

1973	Atlanta	1	0	0	0

MANIAGO, Cesare *Goalie*
b. Trail, B.C., Jan. 13, 1939

Season	Club	GP	GA	Sho	AVE
1960–61	Toronto M.L.	7	18	0	2.57
1962–63	Montreal C.	13⅔	42	0	3.07
1965–66	New York R.	27	94	2	3.48
1966–67	New York R.	3⅔	14	0	3.81
1967–68	Minnesota	48	133	6	2.77
1968–69	Minnesota	60	198	1	3.30
1969–70	Minnesota	48⅛	163	2	3.38
1970–71	Minnesota	39⅔	107	5	2.69
1971–72	Minnesota	42½	112	0	2.64
1972–73	Minnesota	45⅔	132	5	2.89
	Totals	335⅓	1013	21	3.02

Playoffs

Season	Club	GP	GA	Sho	AVE
1960–61	Toronto M.L.	2	6	0	3.00
1967–68	Minnesota	14	39	0	2.79
1969–70	Minnesota	3	6	1	2.00
1970–71	Minnesota	8	28	0	3.50
1971–72	Minnesota	2	6	0	3.05
1972–73	Minnesota	5	9	2	1.75
	Totals	34	94	3	2.76

MANN, John Edward Kingsley *Forward*
b. Winnipeg, Man., July 27, 1919

Season	Club	GP	G	A	Pts
1943–44	New York R.	3	0	0	0
1944–45	New York R.	6	3	4	7
	Totals	9	3	4	7

MANN, Norman *Forward*
b. Bradford, England, Mar. 3, 1914

Season	Club	GP	G	A	Pts
1938–39	Toronto M.L.	--	0	0	0
1940–41	Toronto M.L.	--	0	3	3
	Totals	--	3	3	3

MANNERS, Rennison *Forward*

Season	Club	GP	G	A	Pts
1929–30	Pittsburgh Pi.	--	3	2	5

MANSON, Raymond Clifton *Forward*
b. St. Boniface, Man., Dec. 3, 1926

Season	Club	GP	G	A	Pts
1947–48	Boston	1	0	0	0
1948–49	New York R.	1	0	1	1
	Totals	2	0	1	1

MANTHA, Georges *Forward*
b. Lachine, Que., Nov. 29, 1908

Season	Club	GP	G	A	Pts
1928–29	Montreal C.	--	0	0	0
1929–30	Montreal C.	--	5	2	7

MANTHA (Continued)

Season	Club	GP	G	A	Pts
1930–31	Montreal C.	--	11	6	17
1931–32	Montreal C.	--	1	7	8
1932–33	Montreal C.	--	3	6	9
1933–34	Montreal C.	--	6	9	15
1934–35	Montreal C.	--	12	10	22
1935–36	Montreal C.	--	1	12	13
1936–37	Montreal C.	--	13	14	27
1937–38	Montreal C.	--	23	19	42
1938–39	Montreal C.	--	5	5	10
1939–40	Montreal C.	--	9	11	20
1940–41	Montreal C.	--	0	1	1
	Totals	--	89	102	191

Playoffs

1928–29	Montreal C.	--	0	0	0
1929–30	Montreal C.	--	0	0	0
1930–31	Montreal C.	--	5	1	6
1931–32	Montreal C.	--	0	0	0
1932–33	Montreal C.	--	0	0	0
1933–34	Montreal C.	--	0	0	0
1934–35	Montreal C.	--	0	0	0
1936–37	Montreal C.	--	0	0	0
1937–38	Montreal C.	--	1	0	1
1938–39	Montreal C.	--	0	0	0
	Totals	--	6	1	7

MANTHA, Sylvio *Defenseman*
b. Montreal, Que., Apr. 14, 1902

Season	Club	GP	G	A	Pts
1923–24	Montreal C.	24	1	0	1
1924–25	Montreal C.	30	2	0	2
1925–26	Montreal C.	34	2	1	3
1926–27	Montreal C.	--	10	5	15
1927–28	Montreal C.	--	4	11	15
1928–29	Montreal C.	--	9	4	13
1929–30	Montreal C.	--	13	11	24
1930–31	Montreal C.	--	4	7	11
1931–32	Montreal C.	--	5	5	10
1932–33	Montreal C.	--	4	7	11
1933–34	Montreal C.	--	4	6	10
1934–35	Montreal C.	-	3	11	14
1935–36	Montreal C.	--	2	4	6
1936–37	Boston	--	0	0	0
	Totals	--	63	72	135

Playoffs

1924–25	Montreal C.	--	0	0	0
1926–27	Montreal C.	--	1	0	1
1927–28	Montreal C.	--	0	0	0
1928–29	Montreal C.	--	0	0	0
1929–30	Montreal C.	--	2	1	3
1930–31	Montreal C.	--	2	1	3
1931–32	Montreal C.	--	0	1	1

MANTHA (Continued)

Playoffs

	Club	GP	G	A	Pts
1932–33	Montreal C.	--	0	1	1
1933–34	Montreal C.	--	0	0	0
1934–35	Montreal C.	--	0	0	0
	Totals	--	5	4	9

MARACLE, Henry Elmer *Forward*
b. Ayr, Ont., Sept. 8, 1904

Season	Club	GP	G	A	Pts
1930–31	New York R.	11	1	3	4
Playoffs					
1930–31	New York R.	4	0	0	0

MARCETTA, Milan (Mike) *Forward*
b. Cadomin, Alta., Sept. 19, 1936

Season	Club	GP	G	A	Pts
1967–68	Minnesota	36	4	13	17
1968–69	Minnesota	18	3	2	5
	Totals	54	7	15	22

Playoffs

1966–67	Toronto M.L.	3	0	0	0
1967–68	Minnesota	14	7	7	14
	Totals	17	7	7	14

MARCH, Harold C. (Mush) *Forward*
b. Sitton, Sask., Oct. 18, 1908

Season	Club	GP	G	A	Pts
1928–29	Chicago	--	3	3	6
1929–30	Chicago	--	8	7	15
1930–31	Chicago	--	11	6	17
1931–32	Chicago	--	12	10	22
1932–33	Chicago	--	9	11	20
1933–34	Chicago	--	4	13	17
1934–35	Chicago	--	13	17	30
1935–36	Chicago	--	16	19	35
1936–37	Chicago	--	11	6	17
1937–38	Chicago	--	11	17	28
1938–39	Chicago	--	10	11	21
1939–40	Chicago	--	9	14	23
1940–41	Chicago	--	8	9	17
1941–42	Chicago	--	6	26	32
1942–43	Chicago	50	7	29	36
1943–44	Chicago	48	10	27	37
1944–45	Chicago	38	5	5	10
	Totals	--	153	230	383

Playoffs

1929–30	Chicago	--	0	0	0
1930–31	Chicago	--	3	1	4
1931–32	Chicago	--	0	0	0
1933–34	Chicago	--	2	2	4
1934–35	Chicago	--	0	0	0

MARCH (Continued)

Playoffs	Club	GP	G	A	Pts
1935–36	Chicago	--	2	3	5
1937–38	Chicago	--	2	4	6
1939–40	Chicago	--	1	0	1
1940–41	Chicago	--	2	3	5
1941–42	Chicago	--	0	2	2
1943–44	Chicago	--	0	0	0
	Totals	--	12	15	27

MARCHINKO, Brian Nicholas Wayne *Forward*
b. Weyburn, Sask., Aug. 2, 1948

Season	Club	GP	G	A	Pts
1970–71	Toronto M.L.	2	0	0	0
1971–72	Toronto M.L.	3	0	0	0
1972–73	New York I.	36	2	6	8
	Totals	41	2	6	8

MARCON, Louis Angelo *Defenseman*
b. Fort William, Ont., May 28, 1935

Season	Club	GP	G	A	Pts
1958–59	Detroit R.W.	21	0	1	1
1959–60	Detroit R.W.	38	0	3	3
1962–63	Detroit R.W.	1	0	0	0
	Totals	60	0	4	4

MARCOTTE, Donald *Forward*
b. Asbestos, Que., Apr. 15, 1947

Season	Club	GP	G	A	Pts
1965–66	Boston	1	0	0	0
1968–69	Boston	7	1	0	1
1969–70	Boston	35	9	3	12
1970–71	Boston	75	15	13	28
1971–72	Boston	47	6	4	10
1972–73	Boston	78	24	31	55
	Totals	243	55	51	106

Playoffs					
1969–70	Boston	14	2	0	2
1970–71	Boston	4	0	0	0
1971–72	Boston	14	3	0	3
1972–73	Boston	5	1	1	2
	Totals	37	6	1	7

MARIO, Frank George *Forward*
b. Esterhazy, Sask., Feb. 25, 1921

Season	Club	GP	G	A	Pts
1941–42	Boston	9	1	1	2
1944–45	Boston	44	8	18	26
	Totals	53	9	19	28

MARIUCCI, John *Defenseman*
b. Eveleth, Minn., May 8, 1916

Season	Club	GP	G	A	Pts
1940–41	Chicago	23	0	5	5
1941–42	Chicago	47	5	8	13
1945–46	Chicago	50	3	8	11
1946–47	Chicago	52	2	9	11
1947–48	Chicago	51	1	4	5
	Totals	223	11	34	45

Playoffs					
1940–41	Chicago	4	0	2	2
1945–46	Chicago	4	0	1	1
	Totals	8	0	3	3

MARKER, August Solberg (Gus) *Forward*
b. Wetaskewin, Alta., 1, 1907

Season	Club	GP	G	A	Pts
1932–33	Detroit F.	--	1	1	2
1933–34	Detroit R.W.	--	1	0	1
1934–35	Montreal M.	--	11	4	15
1935–36	Montreal M.	--	7	12	19
1936–37	Montreal M.	--	10	12	22
1937–38	Montreal M.	--	9	15	24
1938–39	Toronto M.L.	--	9	6	15
1939–40	Toronto M.L.	--	10	9	19
1940–41	Toronto M.L.	--	4	5	9
1941–42	New York A.	--	2	5	7
	Totals	--	64	69	133

Playoffs					
1933–34	Detroit R.W.	--	0	0	0
1934–35	Montreal M.	--	1	1	2
1935–36	Montreal M.	--	1	0	1
1936–37	Montreal M.	--	0	1	1
1938–39	Toronto M.L.	--	2	2	4
1939–40	Toronto M.L.	--	1	3	4
1940–41	Toronto M.L.	--	0	0	0
	Totals	--	5	7	12

MARKLE, Jack *Forward*
b. Thessalon, Ont, 1909

Season	Club	GP	G	A	Pts
1935–36	Toronto M.L.	--	0	1	1

MARKS, Jack *Forward*

Season	Club	GP	G	A	Pts
1917–18	Mont W-Tor A	6	0	0	0
1919–20	Quebec	1	0	0	0
	Totals	7	0	0	0

MARKS, John Garrison *Defenseman*
b. Hamiota, Man., Mar. 22, 1948

Season	Club	GP	G	A	Pts
1972–73	Chicago	55	3	10	13
Playoffs					
1972–73	Chicago	16	1	2	3

MAROIS, John *Goalie*

Season	Club	GP	GA	Sho	AVE
1953-54	Chicago	2	1	0	5.50

MAROTTE, Jean Gilles *Defenseman-Forward*
b. Montreal, Que., June 7, 1945

Season	Club	GP	G	A	Pts
1965-66	Boston	51	3	17	20
1966-67	Boston	67	7	8	15
1967-68	Chicago	73	0	21	21
1968-69	Chicago	68	5	29	34
1969-70	Chgo-LA	72	5	19	24
1970-71	Los Angeles	78	6	27	33
1971-72	Los Angeles	72	10	24	34
1972-73	Los Angeles	78	6	39	45
	Totals	559	42	184	226

Playoffs

1967-68	Chicago	11	3	1	4

All-Star

1973	West All-Stars	1	0	0	0

MARQUESS, Clarence Emmett (Mark) *Forward*
b. Bassano, Alta., Mar. 26, 1925

Season	Club	GP	G	A	Pts
1946-47	Boston	27	5	4	9

Playoffs

1946-47	Boston	4	0	0	0

MARSH, Gary Arthur *Forward*
b. Toronto, Ont., Mar. 9, 1946

Season	Club	GP	G	A	Pts
1967-68	Detroit R.W.	6	1	3	4
1968-69	Toronto M.L.	1	0	0	0
	Totals	7	1	3	4

MARSHALL, Albert Leroy (Bert) *Defenseman*
b. Kamloops, B.C., Nov. 22, 1943

Season	Club	GP	G	A	Pts
1965-66	Detroit R.W.	61	0	19	19
1966-67	Detroit R.W.	57	0	10	10
1967-68	Det RW-Oak	57	1	9	10
1968-69	Oakland	68	3	15	18
1969-70	Oakland	72	1	15	16
1970-71	California	32	2	6	8
1971-72	California	66	0	14	14
1972-73	Calif-NY R	63	2	6	8
	Totals	476	9	94	103

Playoffs

1965-66	Detroit R.W.	12	1	3	4
1968-69	Oakland	7	0	7	5
1969-70	Oakland	4	0	1	1
1972-73	New York R.	6	0	1	1
	Totals	29	1	12	13

MARSHALL, Donald Robert *Forward*
b. Verdun, Que., Mar. 23, 1932

Season	Club	GP	G	A	Pts
1951-52	Montreal C.	1	0	0	0
1954-55	Montreal C.	39	5	3	8
1955-56	Montreal C.	66	4	1	5
1956-57	Montreal C.	70	12	8	20
1957-58	Montreal C.	68	22	19	41
1958-59	Montreal C.	70	10	22	32
1959-60	Montreal C.	70	16	22	38
1960-61	Montreal C.	70	14	17	31
1961-62	Montreal C.	66	18	28	46
1962-63	Montreal C.	65	13	20	33
1963-64	New York R.	70	11	12	23
1964-65	New York R.	69	20	15	35
1965-66	New York R.	69	26	28	54
1966-67	New York R.	70	24	22	46
1967-68	New York R.	70	19	30	49
1968-69	New York R.	74	20	19	39
1969-70	New York R.	57	9	15	24
1970-71	Buffalo	62	20	29	49
1971-72	Toronto	50	2	14	16
	Totals	1288	265	324	589

Playoffs

1954-55	Montreal C.	12	1	1	2
1955-56	Montreal C.	10	1	0	1
1956-57	Montreal C.	10	1	3	4
1957-58	Montreal C.	10	0	2	2
1958-59	Montreal C.	11	0	2	2
1959-60	Montreal C.	8	2	2	4
1960-61	Montreal C.	6	0	2	2
1961-62	Montreal C.	6	0	1	1
1962-63	Montreal C.	5	0	0	0
1966-67	New York R.	4	0	1	1
1967-68	New York R.	6	2	1	3
1968-69	New York R.	4	1	0	1
1969-70	New York R.	1	0	0	0
1971-72	Toronto M.L.	1	0	0	0
	Totals	94	8	15	23

All-Star

1956	Montreal C.	1	0	0	0
1957	Montreal C.	1	0	0	0
1958	Montreal C.	1	1	1 ,	2
1959	Montreal C.	1	0	0	0
1960	Montreal C.	1	0	0	0
1968	NHL All-Stars	1	0	0	0
	Totals	6	1	1	2

MARSHALL, Willmott Charles (Willie) *Forward*
b. Kirkland Lake, Ont., Dec. 1, 1931

Season	Club	GP	G	A	Pts
1952-53	Toronto M.L.	2	0	0	0
1954-55	Toronto M.L.	16	1	4	5

MARSHALL (Continued)

Season	Club	GP	G	A	Pts
1955-56	Toronto M.L.	6	0	0	0
1958-59	Toronto M.L.	9	0	1	1
	Totals	33	1	5	6

MARTIN, Francis William (Frank) *Defenseman*
b. Cayuga, Ont., May 1, 1933

Season	Club	GP	G	A	Pts
1952-53	Boston	14	0	2	2
1953-54	Boston	68	3	17	20
1954-55	Chicago	66	4	8	12
1955-56	Chicago	61	3	11	14
1956-57	Chicago	70	1	8	9
1957-58	Chicago	3	0	0	0
	Totals	282	11	46	57

Playoffs

Season	Club	GP	G	A	Pts
1952-53	Boston	6	0	1	1
1953-54	Boston	4	0	1	1
	Totals	10	0	2	2

All-Star

1955	NHL All-Stars	1	0	0	0

MARTIN, George Clare *Defenseman*
b. Waterloo, Ont., Feb. 25, 1922

Season	Club	GP	G	A	Pts
1941-42	Boston	13	0	1	1
1946-47	Boston	6	3	0	3
1947-48	Boston	59	5	13	18
1949-50	Detroit R.W.	64	2	5	7
1950-51	Detroit R.W.	50	1	6	7
1951-52	Chgo-NY R	45	1	3	4
	Totals	237	12	28	40

Playoffs

Season	Club	GP	G	A	Pts
1946-47	Boston	5	0	1	1
1947-48	Boston	5	0	0	0
1949-50	Detroit R.W.	10	0	1	1
1950-51	Detroit R.W.	2	0	0	0
	Totals	22	0	2	2

MARTIN, Hubert Jacques (Pit) *Forward*
b. Noranda, Que., Dec. 9, 1943

Season	Club	GP	G	A	Pts
1961-62	Detroit R.W.	1	0	1	1
1963-64	Detroit R.W.	50	9	12	21
1964-65	Detroit R.W.	58	8	9	17
1965-66	Det RW-Bos	51	17	12	29
1966-67	Boston	70	20	22	42
1967-68	Chicago	63	16	19	35
1968-69	Chicago	76	23	38	61
1969-70	Chicago	73	30	33	63
1970-71	Chicago	62	22	33	55

MARTIN (Continued)

Season	Club	GP	G	A	Pts
1971-72	Chicago	78	24	51	75
1972-73	Chicago	78	29	61	90
	Totals	660	198	291	489

Playoffs

Season	Club	GP	G	A	Pts
1963-64	Detroit R.W.	14	1	4	5
1964-65	Detroit R.W.	3	0	1	1
1967-68	Chicago	11	3	6	9
1969-70	Chicago	8	3	3	6
1970-71	Chicago	17	2	7	9
1971-72	Chicago	8	4	2	6
1972-73	Chicago	15	10	6	16
	Totals	76	23	29	52

All-Star

1971	West All-Stars	1	0	0	0
1972	West All-Stars	1	0	1	1
1973	West All-Stars	1	1	0	1
	Totals	3	1	1	2

MARTIN, Jack *Forward*
b. St. Catherines, Ont., Nov. 29, 1940

Season	Club	GP	G	A	Pts
1960-61	Toronto M.L.	1	0	0	0

MARTIN, Richard Lionel *Forward*
b. Verdun, Que., July 26, 1951

Season	Club	GP	G	A	Pts
1971-72	Buffalo	73	44	30	74
1972-73	Buffalo	75	37	36	73
	Totals	148	81	66	147

Playoffs

Season	Club	GP	G	A	Pts
1972-73	Buffalo	6	3	2	5

All-Star

1972	East All-Stars	1	0	0	0
1973	East All-Stars	1	0	0	0
	Totals	2	0	0	0

MARTIN, Ronald *Forward*
b. Calgary, Alta., Aug. 22, 1909

Season	Club	GP	G	A	Pts
1932-33	New York A.	--	5	7	12
1933-34	New York A.	--	8	9	17
	Totals	--	13	16	29

MARTIN, Seth *Goalie*
b. Rossland, B.C., May 4, 1933

Season	Club	GP	GA	Sho	AVE
1967-68	St. Louis B.	25¾	67	1	2.60

Playoffs

1967-68	St. Louis B.	1⅓	5	0	3.77

MARTIN, Thomas *Forward*
  b. Toronto, Ont., Oct. 16, 1947

Season	Club	GP	G	A	Pts
1967–68	Toronto M.L.	3	1	0	1

MASNICK, Paul Andrew *Forward*
  b. Regina, Sask., Apr. 14, 1931

Season	Club	GP	G	A	Pts
1950–51	Montreal C.	43	4	1	5
1951–52	Montreal C.	15	1	2	3
1952–53	Montreal C.	53	5	7	12
1953–54	Montreal C.	50	5	21	26
1954–55	Mont C–Chgo	30	1	1	2
1957–58	Toronto M.L.	41	2	9	11
	Totals	232	18	41	59
Playoffs					
1950–51	Montreal C.	11	2	1	3
1951–52	Montreal C.	6	1	0	1
1952–53	Montreal C.	6	1	0	1
1953–54	Montreal C.	10	0	4	4
	Totals	33	4	5	9

MASON, Charles C. *Forward*
  b. Seaforth, Ont., Feb. 1, 1912

Season	Club	GP	G	A	Pts
1934–35	New York R.	46	5	9	14
1935–36	New York R.	28	1	5	6
1937–38	New York A.	––	0	0	0
1938–39	Chicago	––	1	4	5
	Totals	––	7	18	25
Playoffs					
1934–35	New York R.	4	0	1	1

MASSECAR, George *Forward*
  b. Niagara Falls, Ont.

Season	Club	GP	G	A	Pts
1929–30	New York A.	––	7	3	10
1930–31	New York A.	––	4	7	11
1931–32	New York A.	––	1	1	2
	Totals	––	12	11	23

MASTERTON, William (Bat) *Forward*
  b. Winnipeg, Man., Aug. 16, 1938

Season	Club	GP	G	A	Pts
1967–68	Minnesota	38	4	8	12

MATHERS, Frank Sydney *Defenseman*
  b. Winnipeg, Man., Mar. 29, 1924

Season	Club	GP	G	A	Pts
1948–49	Toronto M.L.	15	1	2	3
1949–50	Toronto M.L.	6	0	1	1
1951–52	Toronto M.L.	2	0	0	0
	Totals	23	1	3	4
All-Star					
1948	Toronto M.L.	1	0	0	0

MATTE, Joseph *Defenseman*
  b. 1893

Season	Club	GP	G	A	Pts
1919–20	Toronto St.P.	16	8	2	10
1920–21	Hamilton	19	7	9	16
1921–22	Hamilton	20	3	3	6
1925–26	Boston	9	0	0	0
	Totals	64	18	14	32
Playoffs					
1923–24	Vancouver (PCHL)	––	1	0	1

MATTE, Joseph *Defenseman*
  b. Ottawa, Ont., Mar. 3, 1909

Season	Club	GP	G	A	Pts
1942–43	Chicago	12	0	2	2

MATTE, Roland *Defenseman*
  b. Bourget, Ont., Mar. 15, 1909

Season	Club	GP	G	A	Pts
1929–30	Detroit C.	––	0	1	1

MATTIUSSI, Richard Arthur *Forward*
  b. Smooth Rock Falls, Ont., May 1, 1938

Season	Club	GP	G	A	Pts
1967–68	Pittsburgh Pe.	32	0	2	2
1968–69	Pitts Pe–Oak	36	1	11	12
1969–70	Oakland	65	4	10	14
1970–71	California	67	3	8	11
	Totals	200	8	31	39
Playoffs					
1968–69	Oakland	7	0	1	1
1969–70	Oakland	1	0	0	0
	Totals	8	0	1	1

MATZ, John *Forward*

Season	Club	GP	G	A	Pts
1924–25	Montreal C.	30	3	2	5
Playoffs					
1924–25	Montreal C.	––	0	0	0

MAXNER, Wayne Douglas *Forward*
  b. Halifax, N.S., Sept. 27, 1942

Season	Club	GP	G	A	Pts
1964–65	Boston	54	7	6	13
1965–66	Boston	8	1	3	4
	Totals	62	8	9	17

MAXWELL, Wally *Forward*
  b. Ottawa, Ont., Aug. 24, 1933

Season	Club	GP	G	A	Pts
1952–53	Toronto M.L.	2	0	0	0

MAYER, Gilles *Goalie*
  b. Ottawa, Ont., Aug. 24, 1930

Season	Club	GP	GA	Sho	AVE
1949-50	Toronto M.L.	1	2	0	2.00
1953-54	Toronto M.L.	1	3	0	3.00
1955-56	Toronto M.L.	6	19	0	3.17
	Totals	8	24	0	3.00

MAYER, Sheppard E. *Forward*
  b. Sturgeon Falls, Ont.

Season	Club	GP	G	A	Pts
1942-43	Toronto M.L.	2	1	2	3

MAZUR, Edward Joseph (Spider) *Forward*
  b. Winnipeg, Man., July 25, 1929

Season	Club	GP	G	A	Pts
1953-54	Montreal C.	67	7	14	21
1954-55	Montreal C.	25	1	5	6
1956-57	Chicago	15	0	1	1
	Totals	107	8	20	28
Playoffs					
1950-51	Montreal C.	2	0	0	0
1951-52	Montreal C.	5	2	0	2
1952-53	Montreal C.	7	2	2	4
1953-54	Montreal C.	11	0	3	3
	Totals	25	4	5	9
All-Star					
1953	Montreal C.	1	0	0	0

McADAM, Samuel *Forward*
  b. Sterling, Scotland, May 31, 1908

Season	Club	GP	G	A	Pts
1930-31	New York R.	4	0	0	0

McANDREW, Hazen *Defenseman*
  b. Mayo, Que., Aug. 7, 1917

Season	Club	GP	G	A	Pts
1941-42	New York A.	7	0	1	1

McANEELEY, Edward (Ted) *Defenseman*
  b. Cranbrook, B.C., Nov. 7, 1950

Season	Club	GP	G	A	Pts
1972-73	California	77	4	13	17

McATEE, Jerome (Jud) *Forward*
  b. Stratford, Ont., May 2, 1920

Season	Club	GP	G	A	Pts
1942-43	Detroit R.W.	--	0	0	0
1943-44	Detroit R.W.	1	0	2	2
1944-45	Detroit R.W.	44	15	11	26
	Totals	--	15	13	28
Playoffs					
1944-45	Detroit R.W.	14	2	1	3

McATEE, Norman Joseph *Forward*
  b. Stratford, Ont., June 28, 1921

Season	Club	GP	G	A	Pts
1946-47	Boston	13	0	1	1

McAULEY, Kenneth Leslie *Goalie*
  b. Edmonton, Alta., Jan. 9, 1921

Season	Club	GP	GA	Sho	AVE
1943-44	New York R.	50	310	0	6.20
1944-45	New York R.	46	227	1	4.94
	Totals	96	537	1	5.61

McBURNEY, James *Forward*
  b. Sault Ste. Marie, Ont., Jan. 3, 1933

Season	Club	GP	G	A	Pts
1952-53	Chicago	1	0	1	1

McCABE, Stanley *Defenseman*
  b. Ottawa, Ont.

Season	Club	GP	G	A	Pts
1929-30	Detroit C.	--	7	3	10
1930-31	Detroit F.	--	2	1	3
1933-34	Montreal M.	--	0	0	0
	Totals	--	9	4	13

McCAFFREY, Bert *Defenseman*
  b. Listowel, Ont.

Season	Club	GP	G	A	Pts
1924-25	Toronto St.P.	30	9	6	15
1925-26	Toronto St.P.	36	14	7	21
1926-27	Toronto M.L.	--	5	5	10
1927-28	Tor ML-Pitts Pi	--	7	4	11
1928-29	Pittsburgh Pi.	--	1	0	1
1929-30	Pitts Pi-Mont C	--	4	7	11
1930-31	Montreal C.	--	2	1	3
	Totals	--	42	30	72
Playoffs					
1924-25	Toronto St.P.	--	1	0	1
1927-28	Pittsburgh Pi.	--	0	0	0
1929-30	Montreal C.	--	1	1	2
	Totals	--	2	1	3

McCAIG, Douglas *Defenseman*
  b. Guelph, Ont., Feb. 24, 1919

Season	Club	GP	G	A	Pts
1941-42	Detroit R.W.	9	0	1	1
1945-46	Detroit R.W.	6	0	1	1
1946-47	Detroit R.W.	47	2	4	6
1947-48	Detroit R.W.	29	3	3	6
1948-49	Det RW-Chgo	56	1	3	4
1949-50	Chicago	64	0	4	4
1950-51	Chicago	53	2	5	7
	Totals	264	8	21	29

McCAIG (Continued)

Playoffs

Season	Club	GP	G	A	Pts
1941–42	Detroit R.W.	12	0	0	0
1946–47	Detroit R.W.	5	0	1	1
	Totals	17	0	1	1

McCALLUM, Duncan Selby *Defenseman*
b. Flin Flon, Man., Mar. 29, 1940

Season	Club	GP	G	A	Pts
1965–66	New York R.	2	0	0	0
1967–68	Pittsburgh Pe.	32	0	2	2
1968–69	Pittsburgh Pe.	62	5	13	18
1969–70	Pittsburgh Pe.	14	0	0	0
1970–71	Pittsburgh Pe.	77	9	20	29
	Totals	187	14	35	49

Playoffs

Season	Club	GP	G	A	Pts
1969–70	Pittsburgh Pe.	10	1	2	3

McCALMON, Edward

Season	Club	GP	G	A	Pts
1927–28	Chicago	--	2	0	2
1930–31	Philadelphia Q.	--	3	0	3
	Totals	--	5	0	5

McCANN, Richard Leo (Rick) *Forward*
b. Hamilton, Ont., May 27, 1944

Season	Club	GP	G	A	Pts
1967–68	Detroit R.W.	3	0	0	0
1968–69	Detroit R.W.	3	0	0	0
1969–70	Detroit R.W.	18	0	1	1
1970–71	Detroit R.W.	5	0	0	0
1971–72	Detroit R.W.	1	0	0	0
	Totals	30	0	1	1

McCARTAN, John William (Jack) *Goalie*
b. St. Paul, Minn., Aug. 5, 1935

Season	Club	GP	GA	Sho	AVE
1959–60	New York R.	4	7	0	1.75
1960–61	New York R.	7⅓	36	1	4.91
	Totals	11⅓	43	1	3.80

McCARTHY, Thomas *Forward*

Season	Club	GP	G	A	Pts
1919–20	Quebec	12	11	2	13
1920–21	Hamilton	22	8	1	9
	Totals	34	19	3	22

McCARTHY, Thomas Patrick Francis *Forward*
b. Toronto, Ont., Sept. 15, 1934

Season	Club	GP	G	A	Pts
1956–57	Detroit R.W.	3	0	0	0
1957–58	Detroit R.W.	18	2	1	3

McCARTHY (Continued)

Season	Club	GP	G	A	Pts
1958–59	Detroit R.W.	15	2	3	5
1960–61	Boston	24	4	5	9
	Totals	60	8	9	17

McCARTNEY, R.

Season	Club	GP	G	A	Pts
1932–33	Montreal C.	--	0	0	0

McCASKILL, Theodore *Forward*
b. Kapuskasing, Ont., Oct. 29, 1936

Season	Club	GP	G	A	Pts
1967–68	Minnesota	4	0	2	2

McCOOL, Frank *Goalie*
b. Calgary, Alta., Oct. 27, 1918

Season	Club	GP	GA	Sho	AVE
1944–45	Toronto M.L.	50	161	4	3.22
1945–46	Toronto M.L.	22	81	0	3.68
	Totals	72	242	4	3.36

Playoffs

Season	Club	GP	GA	Sho	AVE
1944–45	Toronto M.L.	13	30	4	2.30

McCORD, Robert Lomer *Defenseman*
b. Timmins, Ont., Mar. 20, 1934

Season	Club	GP	G	A	Pts
1963–64	Boston	65	1	9	10
1964–65	Boston	43	0	6	6
1965–66	Detroit R.W.	9	0	2	2
1966–67	Detroit R.W.	14	1	2	3
1967–68	Det RW–Minn	73	3	9	12
1968–69	Minnesota	69	4	17	21
1972–73	St. Louis B.	43	1	13	14
	Totals	316	10	58	68

Playoffs

Season	Club	GP	G	A	Pts
1967–68	Minnesota	14	2	5	7

McCORMACK, John Ronald (Goose) *Forward*
b. Edmonton, Alta., Aug. 2, 1925

Season	Club	GP	G	A	Pts
1947–48	Toronto M.L.	3	0	1	1
1948–49	Toronto M.L.	1	0	0	0
1949–50	Toronto M.L.	34	6	5	11
1950–51	Toronto M.L.	46	6	7	13
1951–52	Montreal C.	54	2	10	12
1952–53	Montreal C.	59	1	9	10
1953–54	Montreal C.	51	5	10	15
1954–55	Chicago	63	5	7	12
	Totals	311	25	49	74

McCORMACK *(Continued)*

Playoffs	Club	GP	G	A	Pts
1949–50	Toronto M.L.	6	1	0	1
1952–53	Montreal C.	9	0	0	0
1953–54	Montreal C.	7	0	1	1
	Totals	22	1	1	2

All-Star

1953	Montreal C.	1	0	0	0

McCREARY, Vernon Keith *Forward*
b. Sundridge, Ont., June 19, 1940

Season	Club	GP	G	A	Pts
1964–65	Montreal C.	9	0	3	3
1967–68	Pittsburgh Pe.	70	14	12	26
1968–69	Pittsburgh Pe.	70	25	23	48
1969–70	Pittsburgh Pe.	60	18	8	26
1970–71	Pittsburgh Pe.	59	21	12	33
1971–72	Pittsburgh Pe.	33	4	4	8
1972–73	Atlanta	77	20	21	41
	Totals	378	102	83	185

Playoffs	Club	GP	G	A	Pts
1961–62	Montreal C.	1	0	0	0
1969–70	Pittsburgh Pe.	10	0	4	4
1971–72	Pittsburgh Pe.	1	0	0	0
	Totals	12	0	4	4

McCREARY, William Edward *Forward*
b. Sundridge, Ont., Dec. 2, 1934

Season	Club	GP	G	A	Pts
1953–54	New York R.	2	0	0	0
1954–55	New York R.	8	0	2	2
1957–58	Detroit R.W.	3	1	0	1
1962–63	Montreal C.	14	2	3	5
1967–68	St. Louis B.	70	13	13	26
1968–69	St. Louis B.	71	13	17	30
1969–70	St. Louis B.	73	15	17	32
1970–71	St. Louis B.	68	9	10	19
	Totals	309	53	62	115

Playoffs	Club	GP	G	A	Pts
1967–68	St. Louis B.	15	3	2	5
1968–69	St. Louis B.	12	1	5	6
1969–70	St. Louis B.	15	1	7	8
1970–71	St. Louis B.	6	1	2	3
	Totals	48	6	16	22

McCREAVY, Patrick Joseph *Forward*
b. Owen Sound, Ont., Jan. 16, 1918

Season	Club	GP	G	A	Pts
1939–40	Boston	––	0	0	0
1940–41	Boston	––	0	1	1
1941–42	Bos–Det RW	40	5	9	14
	Totals	––	5	10	15

McCREAVY *(Continued)*

Playoffs	Club	GP	G	A	Pts
1940–41	Boston	––	2	2	4
1941–42	Detroit R.W.	12	1	1	2
	Totals	––	3	3	6

McCREEDY, John *Forward*
b. Winnipeg, Man., May 23, 1917

Season	Club	GP	G	A	Pts
1941–42	Toronto M.L.	––	15	8	23
1944–45	Toronto M.L.	17	2	4	6
	Totals	––	17	12	29

Playoffs	Club	GP	G	A	Pts
1941–42	Toronto M.L.	––	4	3	7
1944–45	Toronto M.L.	8	0	0	0
	Totals	––	4	3	7

McCURRY, Duke *Forward*

Season	Club	GP	G	A	Pts
1925–26	Pittsburgh Pi.	36	13	4	17
1926–27	Pittsburgh Pi.	––	3	3	6
1927–28	Pittsburgh Pi.	––	5	3	8
1928–29	Pittsburgh Pi.	––	0	1	1
	Totals	––	21	11	32

Playoffs	Club	GP	G	A	Pts
1925–26	Pittsburgh Pi.	––	0	2	2
1927–28	Pittsburgh Pi.	––	0	0	0
	Totals	–	0	2	2

McCUSKER, Red

Season	Club	GP	G	A	Pts
1926–27	Chicago	1	0	0	0

McDONAGH, William James *Forward*
b. Rouyn, Que., Apr. 30, 1928

Season	Club	GP	G	A	Pts
1949–50	New York R.	4	0	0	0

McDONALD, Alvin Brian (Ab) *Forward*
b. Winnipeg, Man., Feb. 18, 1936

Season	Club	GP	G	A	Pts
1958–59	Montreal C.	69	13	23	36
1959–60	Montreal C.	68	9	13	22
1960–61	Mont C–Chgo	61	17	16	33
1961–62	Chicago	65	22	18	40
1962–63	Chicago	69	20	41	61
1963–64	Chicago	70	14	32	46
1964–65	Boston	60	9	9	18
1965–66	Detroit R.W.	43	6	16	22
1966–67	Detroit R.W.	12	2	0	2
1967–68	Pittsburgh Pe.	74	22	21	43
1968–69	St. Louis B.	68	21	21	42

McDONALD (Continued)

Season	Club	GP	G	A	Pts
1969-70	St. Louis B.	64	25	30	55
1970-71	St. Louis B.	20	0	5	5
1971-72	Detroit R.W.	19	2	3	5
	Totals	762	182	248	430
Playoffs					
1957-58	Montreal C.	2	0	0	0
1958-59	Montreal C.	11	1	1	2
1960-61	Chicago	8	2	2	4
1961-62	Chicago	12	6	6	12
1962-63	Chicago	6	2	3	5
1963-64	Chicago	7	2	2	4
1965-66	Detroit R.W.	10	1	4	5
1968-69	St. Louis B.	12	2	1	3
1969-70	St. Louis B.	16	5	10	15
	Totals	84	21	29	50
All-Star					
1958	Montreal C.	1	1	0	1
1959	Montreal C.	1	1	0	1
1961	Chicago	1	0	0	0
1969	West All-Stars	1	0	0	0
1970	West All-Stars	1	0	0	0
	Totals	5	2	0	2

McDONALD, Brian Harold *Forward*
b. Toronto, Ont., Mar. 23, 1945

Season	Club	GP	G	A	Pts
1970-71	Buffalo	12	0	0	0
Playoffs					
1967-68	Chicago	8	0	0	0

McDONALD, Byron Russell *Forward*
b. Assiniboia, Sask., Nov. 21, 1917

Season	Club	GP	G	A	Pts
1939-40	Detroit R.W.	--	1	6	7
1944-45	Det RW-Chgo	29	7	14	21
	Totals	--	8	20	28
Playoffs					
1939-40	Detroit R.W.	5	0	2	2

McDONALD, Jack *Forward*

Season	Club	GP	G	A	Pts
1917-18	Mont W-Mont C	12	12	0	12
1918-19	Montreal C.	18	8	4	12
1919-20	Quebec	24	7	6	13
1920-21	Montreal C.	17	0	1	1
1921-22	Montreal C.	2	0	0	0
	Totals	73	27	11	38
Playoffs					
1917-18	Montreal C.	--	1	0	1
1918-19	Montreal C.	--	1	0	1
	Totals	--	2	0	2

McDONALD, John Albert *Forward*
b. Swan River, Man., Nov. 21, 1921

Season	Club	GP	G	A	Pts
1943-44	New York R.	43	10	9	19

McDONALD, Robert *Forward*
b. Toronto, Ont., Jan. 4, 1923

Season	Club	GP	G	A	Pts
1943-44	New York R.	1	0	0	0

McDONALD, Wilfred Kennedy (Bucko)
Defenseman
b. Fergus, Ont., Oct. 31, 1911

Season	Club	GP	G	A	Pts
1934-35	Detroit R.W.	--	1	2	3
1935-36	Detroit R.W.	--	4	6	10
1936-37	Detroit R.W.	--	3	5	8
1937-38	Detroit R.W.	--	3	7	10
1938-39	Det RW-Tor ML	--	3	3	6
1939-40	Toronto M.L.	--	2	5	7
1940-41	Toronto M.L.	--	6	11	17
1941-42	Toronto M.L.	48	2	19	21
1942-43	Toronto M.L.	40	2	11	13
1943-44	Tor ML-NY R	50	7	10	17
1944-45	New York R.	40	2	9	11
	Totals	--	35	88	123
Playoffs					
1935-36	Detroit R.W.	7	3	0	3
1936-37	Detroit R.W.	10	0	0	0
1938-39	Toronto M.L.	10	0	0	0
1939-40	Toronto M.L.	10	0	0	0
1940-41	Toronto M.L.	7	2	0	2
1941-42	Toronto M.L.	13	0	1	1
1942-43	Toronto M.L.	6	1	0	1
	Totals	63	6	1	7

McDONNELL, Moylan *Defenseman*

Season	Club	GP	G	A	Pts
1920-21	Hamilton	20	1	1	2

McDONOUGH, James Allison (Al) *Forward*
b. Hamilton, Ont., June 6, 1950

Season	Club	GP	G	A	Pts
1970-71	Los Angeles	6	2	1	3
1971-72	LA-Pitt Pe	68	10	13	23
1972-73	Pittsburgh Pe.	78	35	41	76
	Totals	152	47	55	102
Playoffs					
1971-72	Pittsburgh Pe.	4	0	1	1

McDUFFE, Peter Arnold *Goalie*
b. Milton, Ont., Feb. 16, 1948

Season	Club	GP	GA	Sho	AVE
1971–72	St. Louis B.	7⅔	29	0	3.72
1972–73	New York R.	1	1	0	1.00
	Totals	8⅔	30	0	3.41
Playoffs					
1971–72	St. Louis B.	1	7	0	7.00

McELMURY, James D. (Jim) *Defenseman*
b. St. Paul, Minn., Oct. 3, 1949

Season	Club	GP	G	A	Pts
1972–73	Minnesota	7	0	1	1

McFADDEN, James Alexander *Forward*
b. Belfast, Ireland, Apr. 15, 1920

Season	Club	GP	G	A	Pts
1947–48	Detroit R.W.	60	24	24	48
1948–49	Detroit R.W.	55	12	20	32
1949–50	Detroit R.W.	68	14	16	30
1950–51	Detroit R.W.	70	14	18	32
1951–52	Chicago	70	10	24	34
1952–53	Chicago	70	23	21	44
1953–54	Chicago	19	3	3	6
	Totals	412	100	126	226
Playoffs					
1946–47	Detroit R.W.	4	0	2	2
1947–48	Detroit R.W.	10	5	3	8
1948–49	Detroit R.W.	8	0	1	1
1949–50	Detroit R.W.	14	2	3	5
1950–51	Detroit R.W.	6	0	0	0
1952–53	Chicago	7	3	0	3
	Totals	49	10	9	19
All-Star					
1950	Detroit R.W.	1	0	0	0

McGIBBON, Irving *Forward*

Season	Club	GP	G	A	Pts
1942–43	Montreal C.	1	0	0	0

McGILL, Jack *Forward*
b. Ottawa, Ont., Nov. 3, 1910

Season	Club	GP	G	A	Pts
1934–35	Montreal C.	--	9	1	10
1935–36	Montreal C.	--	13	7	20
1936–37	Montreal C.	--	5	2	7
	Totals	--	27	10	37
Playoffs					
1934–35	Montreal C.	--	2	0	2
1936–37	Montreal C.	--	0	0	0
	Totals	--	2	0	2

McGILL, John George (Big Jack) *Forward*
b. Edmonton, Alta., Sept. 19, 1921

Season	Club	GP	G	A	Pts
1941–42	Boston	13	8	11	19
1944–45	Boston	14	4	2	6
1945–46	Boston	46	6	14	20
1946–47	Boston	24	5	9	14
	Totals	97	23	36	59
Playoffs					
1941–42	Boston	5	4	1	5
1944–45	Boston	7	3	3	6
1945–46	Boston	10	0	0	0
1946–47	Boston	5	0	0	0
	Totals	27	7	4	11

McGRATTON, Thomas *Goalie*
b. Brantford, Ont., Oct. 19, 1927

Season	Club	GP	GA	Sho	AVE
1947–48	Detroit R.W.	1	1	0	1.00

McGREGOR, Donald Alexander (Sandy)
Forward
b. Toronto, Ont., Mar. 30, 1939

Season	Club	GP	G	A	Pts
1963–64	New York R.	2	0	0	0

McGUIRE, Mickey *Forward*

Season	Club	GP	G	A	Pts
1926–27	Pittsburgh Pi.	--	3	0	3

McINENLY, Bert *Defenseman-Forward*
b. Ottawa, Ont., May 6, 1906

Season	Club	GP	G	A	Pts
1930–31	Detroit F.	--	3	5	8
1931–32	Det F-NY A	--	12	7	19
1932–33	Ottawa	--	2	2	4
1933–34	Boston	--	0	0	0
1934–35	Boston	--	2	1	3
	Totals	--	19	15	34
Playoffs					
1934–35	Boston	--	0	0	0

McINTOSH, Bruce *Defenseman*
b. St. Paul, Minn., Mar. 17, 1949

Season	Club	GP	G	A	Pts
1972–73	Minnesota	2	0	0	0

McINTYRE, John Archibald *Forward*
b. Brussels, Ont., Sept. 8, 1930

Season	Club	GP	G	A	Pts
1949–50	Boston	1	0	1	1
1951–52	Boston	52	12	19	31
1952–53	Boston	70	7	15	22

McINTYRE (Continued)

Season	Club	GP	G	A	Pts
1953-54	Chicago	23	8	3	11
1954-55	Chicago	65	16	13	29
1955-56	Chicago	46	10	5	15
1956-57	Chicago	70	18	14	32
1957-58	Chgo-Det RW	68	15	11	26
1958-59	Detroit R.W.	55	15	14	29
1959-60	Detroit R.W.	49	8	7	15
	Totals	499	109	102	211
Playoffs					
1950-51	Boston	2	0	0	0
1951-52	Boston	7	1	2	3
1952-53	Boston	10	4	2	6
1957-58	Detroit R.W.	4	1	1	2
1959-60	Detroit R.W.	6	1	1	2
	Totals	29	7	6	13

McINTYRE, Lawrence Albert (Larry) *Forward*
b. Moose Jaw, Sask, July 13, 1949

Season	Club	GP	G	A	Pts
1969-70	Toronto M.L.	1	0	0	0
1972-73	Toronto M.L.	40	0	3	3
	Totals	41	0	3	3

McKAY, Raymond Owen *Defenseman*
b. Edmonton, Alta., Aug. 22, 1946

Season	Club	GP	G	A	Pts
1968-69	Chicago	9	0	1	1
1969-70	Chicago	17	0	0	0
1970-71	Chicago	2	0	0	0
1971-72	Buffalo	39	0	3	3
1972-73	Buffalo	1	0	0	0
	Totals	68	0	4	4
Playoffs					
1969-70	Chicago	1	0	0	0

McKECHNIE, Walter *Forward*
b. London, Ont., June 19, 1947

Season	Club	GP	G	A	Pts
1967-68	Minnesota	4	0	0	0
1968-69	Minnesota	58	5	9	14
1969-70	Minnesota	20	1	3	4
1970-71	Minnesota	30	3	1	4
1971-72	California	56	11	20	31
1972-73	California	78	16	38	54
	Totals	246	36	71	107
Playoffs					
1967-68	Minnesota	9	3	2	5

McKELL, Jack *Defenseman*

Season	Club	GP	G	A	Pts
1919-20	Ottawa	21	2	0	2
1920-21	Ottawa	21	2	1	3
	Totals	42	4	1	5
Playoffs					
1919-20	Ottawa	--	0	0	0
1920-21	Ottawa	--	0	0	0
	Totals	--	0	0	0

McKENNEY, Donald Hamilton *Forward*
b. Smith Falls, Ont., Apr. 30, 1934

Season	Club	GP	G	A	Pts
1954-55	Boston	69	22	20	42
1955-56	Boston	65	10	24	34
1956-57	Boston	69	21	39	60
1957-58	Boston	70	28	30	58
1958-59	Boston	70	32	30	62
1959-60	Boston	70	20	49	69
1960-61	Boston	68	26	23	49
1961-62	Boston	70	22	33	55
1962-63	Bos-NY R	62	22	35	57
1963-64	NY R-Tor ML	70	18	23	41
1964-65	Toronto M.L.	52	6	13	19
1965-66	Detroit R.W.	24	1	6	7
1967-68	St. Louis B.	39	9	20	29
	Totals	798	237	345	582
Playoffs					
1954-55	Boston	5	1	2	3
1956-57	Boston	10	1	5	6
1957-58	Boston	12	9	8	17
1958-59	Boston	7	2	5	7
1963-64	Toronto M.L.	12	4	8	12
1964-65	Toronto M.L.	6	0	0	0
1967-68	St. Louis B.	6	1	1	2
	Totals	58	18	29	47
All-Star					
1957	NHL All-Stars	1	0	0	0
1958	NHL All-Stars	1	0	0	0
1959	NHL All-Stars	1	1	0	1
1960	NHL All-Stars	1	0	0	0
1961	NHL All-Stars	1	1	0	1
1962	NHL All-Stars	1	0	0	0
1964	Toronto M.L.	1	0	0	0
	Totals	7	2	0	2

McKENNY, James Claude (Jim) *Defenseman*
b. Ottawa, Ont., Dec. 1, 1946

Season	Club	GP	G	A	Pts
1965-66	Toronto M.L.	2	0	0	0
1966-67	Toronto M.L.	6	1	0	1
1967-68	Toronto M.L.	5	1	0	1
1968-69	Toronto M.L.	7	0	0	0

McKENNY (Continued)

Season	Club	GP	G	A	Pts
1969–70	Toronto M.L.	73	11	33	44
1970–71	Toronto M.L.	68	4	26	30
1971–72	Toronto M.L.	76	5	31	36
1972–73	Toronto M.L.	77	11	41	52
	Totals	314	33	131	164

Playoffs

Season	Club	GP	G	A	Pts
1970–71	Toronto M.L.	6	2	1	3
1971–72	Toronto M.L.	5	3	0	3
	Totals	11	5	1	6

McKENZIE, Brian Stewart *Forward*
b. St. Catharines, Ont., Mar. 16, 1951

Season	Club	GP	G	A	Pts
1971–72	Pittsburgh Pe.	6	1	1	2

McKENZIE, John Albert *Forward*
b. High River, Alta., Dec. 12, 1937

Season	Club	GP	G	A	Pts
1958–59	Chicago	32	3	4	7
1959–60	Detroit R.W.	59	8	12	20
1960–61	Detroit R.W.	16	3	1	4
1963–64	Chicago	45	9	9	18
1964–65	Chicago	51	8	10	18
1965–66	NY R-Bos	71	19	14	33
1966–67	Boston	69	17	19	36
1967–68	Boston	74	28	38	66
1968–69	Boston	60	29	27	56
1969–70	Boston	72	29	41	70
1970–71	Boston	65	31	46	77
1971–72	Boston	77	22	47	69
	Totals	691	206	268	474

Playoffs

Season	Club	GP	G	A	Pts
1958–59	Chicago	2	0	0	0
1959–60	Detroit R.W.	2	0	0	0
1963–64	Chicago	4	0	1	1
1964–65	Chicago	11	0	1	1
1967–68	Boston	4	1	1	2
1968–69	Boston	10	2	2	4
1969–70	Boston	14	5	12	17
1970–71	Boston	7	2	3	5
1971–72	Boston	15	5	12	17
	Totals	69	15	32	47

All-Star

Season	Club	GP	G	A	Pts
1970	East All-Stars	1	0	1	1
1972	East All-Stars	1	1	0	1
	Totals	2	1	1	2

McKINNON, Alexander *Defenseman*
b. Sudbury, Ont.

Season	Club	GP	G	A	Pts
1924–25	Hamilton	30	8	2	10
1925–26	New York A.	35	5	3	8

McKINNON (Continued)

Season	Club	GP	G	A	Pts
1926–27	New York A.	--	2	1	3
1927–28	Pittsburgh Pi.	--	3	1	4
1928–29	Chicago	--	1	1	2
	Totals	--	19	8	27

Playoffs

Season	Club	GP	G	A	Pts
1927–28	Pittsburgh Pi.	--	0	0	0

McKINNON, John *Defenseman*
b. Guysborough, N.S., July 15, 1902

Season	Club	GP	G	A	Pts
1925–26	Montreal C.	2	0	0	0
1926–27	Pittsburgh Pi.	--	13	0	13
1927–28	Pittsburgh Pi.	--	3	3	6
1928–29	Pittsburgh Pi.	--	1	0	1
1929–30	Pittsburgh Pi.	--	10	7	17
1930–31	Philadelphia Q.	--	1	1	2
	Totals	--	28	11	39

Playoffs

Season	Club	GP	G	A	Pts
1927–28	Pittsburgh Pi.	--	0	0	0

McKINNON, Robert *Forward*

Season	Club	GP	G	A	Pts
1928–29	Chicago	--	1	1	2

McLACHLAN, Murray *Goalie*
b. London, Ont., Oct. 20, 1948

Season	Club	GP	GA	Sho	AVE
1970–71	Toronto M.L.	⅓	4	0	9.60

McLEAN *Forward*

Season	Club	GP	G	A	Pts
1919–20	Quebec	7	0	0	0
1920–21	Hamilton	2	0	0	0
	Totals	9	0	0	0

McLEAN, Jack *Forward*
b. Toronto, Ont., Jan. 31, 1923

Season	Club	GP	G	A	Pts
1942–43	Toronto M.L.	27	9	8	17
1943–44	Toronto M.L.	32	3	15	18
1944–45	Toronto M.L.	8	2	1	3
	Totals	67	14	24	38

Playoffs

Season	Club	GP	G	A	Pts
1942–43	Toronto M.L.	6	2	2	4
1943–44	Toronto M.L.	3	0	0	0
1944–45	Toronto M.L.	4	0	0	0
	Totals	13	2	2	4

McLELLAN, Daniel John *Forward*
b. South Porcupine, Ont., Aug. 6, 1928

Season	Club	GP	G	A	Pts
1951–52	Toronto M.L.	2	0	0	0

McLELLAND, David (Dave) *Goalie*
b. Penticton, B.C., Nov. 20, 1952

Season	Club	GP	GA	Sho	AVE
1972–73	Vancouver	2	10	0	5.00

McLENAHAN, Roland Joseph *Defenseman*
b. Fredericton, N.B., Oct. 26, 1921

Season	Club	GP	G	A	Pts
1945–46	Detroit R.W.	9	2	1	3
Playoffs					
1945–46	Detroit R.W.	2	0	0	0

McLEOD, Donald Martin (Don) *Goalie*
b. Trail, B.C., Aug. 24, 1946

Season	Club	GP	GA	Sho	AVE
1970–71	Detroit R.W.	11⅔	60	0	5.15
1971–72	Philadelphia F.	3	14	0	4.64
	Totals	14⅔	74	0	5.05

McLEOD, James Bradley (Jim) *Goalie*
b. Port Arthur, Ont., Apr. 7, 1937

Season	Club	GP	GA	Sho	AVE
1971–72	St. Louis B.	14⅔	44	0	3.00

McLEOD, Robert John (Jackie) *Forward*
b. Regina, Sask., Apr. 30, 1930

Season	Club	GP	G	A	Pts
1949–50	New York R.	38	6	9	15
1950–51	New York R.	41	5	10	15
1951–52	New York R.	13	2	3	5
1952–53	New York R.	3	0	0	0
1954–55	New York R.	11	1	1	2
	Totals	106	14	23	37
Playoffs					
1949–50	New York R.	7	0	0	0

McMAHON, Michael Clarence *Defenseman*
b. Brockville, Ont., Feb. 1, 1917

Season	Club	GP	G	A	Pts
1943–44	Montreal C.	42	7	17	24
1945–46	Mont C-Bos	15	0	1	1
	Totals	57	7	18	25
Playoffs					
1942–43	Montreal C.	5	0	0	0
1943–44	Montreal C.	8	1	2	3
	Totals	13	1	2	3

McMAHON, Michael William *Defenseman*
b. Quebec, Que., Aug. 30, 1941

Season	Club	GP	G	A	Pts
1963–64	New York R.	18	0	1	1
1964–65	New York R.	1	0	0	0
1965–66	New York R.	41	0	12	12
1967–68	Minnesota	74	14	33	47
1968–69	Minn-Chgo	63	0	19	19
1969–70	Det RW-Pitts Pe	14	1	3	4
1970–71	Buffalo	12	0	0	0
1971–72	New York R.	1	0	0	0
	Totals	224	15	68	83
Playoffs					
1967–68	Minnesota	14	3	7	10

McMANUS, Samuel *Forward*
b. Belfast, Ireland, 1909

Season	Club	GP	G	A	Pts
1934–35	Montreal M.	--	0	1	1

McNAB, Maxwell Douglas *Forward*
b. Watson, Sask., June 21, 1924

Season	Club	GP	G	A	Pts
1947–48	Detroit R.W.	12	2	2	4
1948–49	Detroit R.W.	51	10	13	23
1949–50	Detroit R.W.	65	4	4	8
	Totals	128	16	19	35
Playoffs					
1947–48	Detroit R.W.	3	0	0	0
1948–49	Detroit R.W.	10	1	0	1
1949–50	Detroit R.W.	10	0	0	0
1950–51	Detroit R.W.	2	0	0	0
	Totals	25	1	0	1

McNAMARA, Gerald *Goalie*
b. Sturgeon Falls, Ont., Sept. 22, 1934

Season	Club	GP	GA	Sho	AVE
1960–61	Toronto M.L.	5	13	0	2.60
1969–70	Toronto M.L.	⅓	2	0	6.00
	Totals	5⅓	15	0	2.81

McNAMARA, Howard *Defenseman*

Season	Club	GP	G	A	Pts
1919–20	Montreal C.	11	1	0	1

McNAUGHTON, George *Forward*

Season	Club	GP	G	A	Pts
1919–20	Quebec	1	0	0	0

McNEIL, Gerard George *Goalie*
b. Quebec City, Que., Apr. 17, 1926

Season	Club	GP	GA	Sho	AVE
1947–48	Montreal C.	2	7	0	3.50
1949–50	Montreal C.	6	9	1	1.50
1950–51	Montreal C.	70	184	6	2.63
1951–52	Montreal C.	70	164	5	2.34
1952–53	Montreal C.	66	140	10	2.12
1953–54	Montreal C.	53	114	6	2.15
1956–57	Montreal C.	9	32	0	3.55
	Totals	276	650	28	2.36
Playoffs					
1949–50	Montreal C.	2	5	0	2.50
1950–51	Montreal C.	11	25	1	2.27
1951–52	Montreal C.	11	23	1	2.09
1952–53	Montreal C.	8	16	2	2.00
1953–54	Montreal C.	3	3	1	1.00
	Totals	35	72	5	2.06

All-Star		GP	Per	GA	AGP
1951	NHL 2nd All-Stars	1	1½	1	0.67
1952	NHL 2nd All-Stars	1	1½	1	0.67
1953	Montreal C.	1	3	3	1.00
	Totals	3	6	5	0.83

McNEILL, Stuart *Forward*
b. Port Arthur, Ont., Sept. 25, 1938

Season	Club	GP	G	A	Pts
1957–58	Detroit R.W.	2	0	0	0
1959–60	Detroit R.W.	5	0	0	0
	Totals	7	0	0	0

McNEILL, William Ronald *Forward*
b. Edmonton, Alta., Jan. 26, 1936

Season	Club	GP	G	A	Pts
1956–57	Detroit R.W.	64	5	10	15
1957–58	Detroit R.W.	35	5	10	15
1958–59	Detroit R.W.	54	2	5	7
1959–60	Detroit R.W.	47	5	13	18
1962–63	Detroit R.W.	42	3	7	10
1963–64	Detroit R.W.	15	1	1	2
	Totals	257	21	46	67
Playoffs					
1957–58	Detroit R.W.	4	1	1	2

McRAE, Gordon Alexander *Goalie*
b. Sherbrooke, Que., Apr. 12, 1948

Season	Club	GP	GA	Sho	AVE
1972–73	Toronto M.L.	10⅓	39	0	3.77

McSHEFFREY, Bryan *Forward*
b. Ottawa, Ont., Sept. 25, 1952

Season	Club	GP	G	A	Pts
1972–73	Vancouver	33	4	4	8

McVEIGH, Charles (Rabbit) *Forward*
b. Kenora, Ont., Mar. 29, 1898

Season	Club	GP	G	A	Pts
1926–27	Chicago	--	12	4	16
1927–28	Chicago	--	6	7	13
1928–29	New York A.	--	6	2	8
1929–30	New York A.	--	14	14	28
1930–31	New York A.	--	5	11	16
1931–32	New York A.	--	12	15	27
1932–33	New York A.	--	7	12	19
1933–34	New York A.	--	15	12	27
1934–35	New York A.	--	7	11	18
	Totals	--	84	88	172
Playoffs					
1926–27	Chicago	--	0	0	0
1928–29	New York A.	--	0	0	0
	Totals	--	0	0	0

McVICOR, John (Slim) *Defenseman*

Season	Club	GP	G	A	Pts
1930–31	Montreal M.	--	2	4	6
1931–32	Montreal M.	--	0	0	0
	Totals	--	2	4	6
Playoffs					
1930–31	Montreal M.	--	0	0	0
1931–32	Montreal M.	--	0	0	0
	Totals	--	0	0	0

MEEHAN, Gerald Marcus (Gerry) *Forward*
b. Toronto, Ont., Sept. 3, 1946

Season	Club	GP	G	A	Pts
1968–69	Tor ML–Phila F	37	0	5	5
1970–71	Buffalo	77	24	31	55
1971–72	Buffalo	77	19	27	46
1972–73	Buffalo	77	31	29	60
	Totals	268	74	92	166
Playoffs					
1968–69	Philadelphia F.	4	0	0	0
1972–73	Buffalo	6	0	1	1
	Totals	10	0	1	1

MEEKE, Brent *Defenseman*
b. Toronto, Ont., Apr. 10, 1952

Season	Club	GP	G	A	Pts
1972–73	California	3	0	0	0

MEEKER, Howard William *Forward*
b. Kitchener, Ont., Nov. 4, 1924

Season	Club	GP	G	A	Pts
1946–47	Toronto M.L.	55	27	18	45
1947–48	Toronto M.L.	58	14	20	34
1948–49	Toronto M.L.	30	7	7	14
1949–50	Toronto M.L.	70	18	22	40

MEEKER (Continued)

Season	Club	GP	G	A	Pts
1950–51	Toronto M.L.	49	6	14	20
1951–52	Toronto M.L.	54	9	14	23
1952–53	Toronto M.L.	25	1	7	8
1953–54	Toronto M.L.	5	1	0	1
	Totals	346	83	102	185

Playoffs

1946–47	Toronto M.L.	11	3	3	6
1947–48	Toronto M.L.	9	2	4	6
1949–50	Toronto M.L.	7	0	1	1
1950–51	Toronto M.L.	11	1	1	2
1951–52	Toronto M.L.	4	0	0	0
	Totals	42	6	9	15

All-Star

1947	Toronto M.L.	1	0	0	0
1948	Toronto M.L.	1	0	0	0
1949	Toronto M.L.	1	0	0	0
	Totals	3	0	0	0

MEEKING, Harry *Forward*
b. Kitchener, Ont., Nov. 4, 1894

Season	Club	GP	G	A	Pts
1917–18	Toronto A.	20	10	0	10
1918–19	Toronto A.	14	7	3	10
1926–27	Bos-Det C	--	1	0	1
	Totals	--	18	3	21

Playoffs

1917–18	Toronto A.	--	1	2	3
1924–25	Victoria (PCHL)	--	0	2	2
1925–26	Victoria (PCHL)	--	0	0	0
	Totals	--	1	4	5

MEGER, Paul Carl *Forward*
b. Watrous, Sask., Feb. 17, 1929

Season	Club	GP	G	A	Pts
1950–51	Montreal C.	17	2	4	6
1951–52	Montreal C.	69	24	18	42
1952–53	Montreal C.	69	9	17	26
1953–54	Montreal C.	44	4	9	13
1954–55	Montreal C.	13	0	4	4
	Totals	212	39	52	91

Playoffs

1949–50	Montreal C.	2	0	0	0
1950–51	Montreal C.	11	1	3	4
1951–52	Montreal C.	11	0	3	3
1952–53	Montreal C.	5	1	2	3
1953–54	Montreal C.	6	1	0	1
	Totals	35	3	8	11

All-Star

1951	NHL 2nd All-Stars	1	0	0	0
1952	NHL 2nd All-Stars	1	0	0	0
1953	Montreal C.	1	0	0	0
	Totals	3	0	0	0

MEISSNER, Barrie *Forward*
b. Unity, Sask., July 26, 1946

Season	Club	GP	G	A	Pts
1967–68	Minnesota	1	0	0	0
1968–69	Minnesota	5	0	1	1
	Totals	6	0	1	1

MEISSNER, Richard Donald *Forward*
b. Kindersley, Sask., Jan. 6, 1940

Season	Club	GP	G	A	Pts
1959–60	Boston	60	5	6	11
1960–61	Boston	9	0	1	1
1961–62	Boston	66	3	3	6
1963–64	New York R.	35	3	5	8
1964–65	New York R.	1	0	0	0
	Totals	171	11	15	26

MELNYK, Michael Gerald (Gerry) *Forward*
b. Edmonton, Alta., Sept. 16, 1934

Season	Club	GP	G	A	Pts
1959–60	Detroit R.W.	63	10	10	20
1960–61	Detroit R.W.	70	9	16	25
1961–62	Chicago	63	5	16	21
1967–68	St. Louis B.	73	15	35	50
	Totals	269	39	77	116

Playoffs

1955–56	Detroit R.W.	6	0	0	0
1959–60	Detroit R.W.	6	3	0	3
1960–61	Detroit R.W.	11	1	0	1
1961–62	Chicago	7	0	0	0
1964–65	Chicago	6	0	0	0
1967–68	St. Louis B.	17	2	6	8
	Totals	53	6	6	12

All-Star

1961	Chicago	1	0	0	0

MELOCHE, Gilles *Goalie*
b. Montreal, Que., July 12, 1950

Season	Club	GP	GA	Sho	AVE
1970–71	Chicago	2	6	0	3.00
1971–72	California	52	173	4	3.32
1972–73	California	58	235	1	4.06
	Totals	112	414	5	3.69

MENARD, Hillary *Defenseman*
b. Timmins, Ont., Jan. 15, 1934

Season	Club	GP	G	A	Pts
1953–54	Chicago	1	0	0	0

557

MENARD, Howard Hubert *Forward*
b. Timmins, Ont., Apr. 28, 1942

Season	Club	GP	G	A	Pts
1963-64	Detroit R.W.	3	0	0	0
1967-68	Los Angeles	35	9	15	24
1968-69	Los Angeles	56	10	17	27
1969-70	Chgo-Oak	57	4	10	14
	Totals	151	23	42	65
Playoffs					
1967-68	Los Angeles	7	0	5	5
1968-69	Los Angeles	11	3	2	5
1969-70	Oakland	1	0	0	0
	Totals	19	3	7	10

MERONEK, William (Smiley) *Forward*
b. Stony Mountain, Man., Apr. 5, 1917

Season	Club	GP	G	A	Pts
1939-40	Montreal C.	--	2	2	4
1942-43	Montreal C.	12	3	6	9
	Totals	--	5	8	13
Playoffs					
1942-43	Montreal C.	1	0	0	0

MERRICK, Wayne *Forward*
b. Sarnia, Ont., Apr. 23, 1952

Season	Club	GP	G	A	Pts
1972-73	St. Louis B.	50	10	11	21
Playoffs					
1972-73	St. Louis B.	5	0	1	1

MERRILL, Horace *Defenseman*

Season	Club	GP	G	A	Pts
1917-18	Ottawa	4	0	0	0
1919-20	Ottawa	7	0	0	0
	Totals	11	0	0	0

METZ, Donald Maurice *Forward*
b. Wilcox, Sask., Jan. 10, 1916

Season	Club	GP	G	A	Pts
1939-40	Toronto M.L.	--	1	1	2
1940-41	Toronto M.L.	--	4	10	14
1941-42	Toronto M.L.	25	2	3	5
1945-46	Toronto M.L.	7	1	0	1
1946-47	Toronto M.L.	40	4	9	13
1947-48	Toronto M.L.	24	4	6	10
1948-49	Toronto M.L.	33	4	6	10
	Totals	--	20	35	55
Playoffs					
1940-41	Toronto M.L.	6	1	1	2
1941-42	Toronto M.L.	13	4	3	7
1946-47	Toronto M.L.	11	2	3	5
1947-48	Toronto M.L.	2	0	0	0
1948-49	Toronto M.L.	3	0	0	0
	Totals	35	7	7	14

METZ, Nicholas J. *Forward*
b. Wilcox, Sask., Feb. 16, 1914

Season	Club	GP	G	A	Pts
1934-35	Toronto M.L.	--	2	2	4
1935-36	Toronto M.L.	--	14	6	20
1936-37	Toronto M.L.	--	9	11	20
1937-38	Toronto M.L.	--	15	7	22
1938-39	Toronto M.L.	--	11	10	21
1939-40	Toronto M.L.	--	6	5	11
1940-41	Toronto M.L.	--	14	21	35
1941-42	Toronto M.L.	30	11	9	20
1944-45	Toronto M.L.	50	22	13	35
1945-46	Toronto M.L.	41	11	11	22
1946-47	Toronto M.L.	60	12	16	28
1947-48	Toronto M.L.	60	4	8	12
	Totals	--	129	119	248
Playoffs					
1934-35	Toronto M.L.	7	1	1	2
1936-37	Toronto M.L.	--	0	0	0
1937-38	Toronto M.L.	--	0	2	2
1938-39	Toronto M.L.	--	3	3	6
1939-40	Toronto M.L.	--	1	3	4
1940-41	Toronto M.L.	--	3	4	7
1941-42	Toronto M.L.	13	4	4	8
1944-45	Toronto M.L.	7	1	1	2
1946-47	Toronto M.L.	6	4	2	6
1947-48	Toronto M.L.	9	2	0	2
	Totals	--	19	20	39
All-Star					
1947	Toronto M.L.	1	0	0	0

MICHALUK, Arthur *Defenseman*
b. Canmore, Alta., May 4, 1923

Season	Club	GP	G	A	Pts
1947-48	Chicago	5	0	0	0

MICHALUK, John *Forward*
b. Canmore, Alta., Nov. 2, 1928

Season	Club	GP	G	A	Pts
1950-51	Chicago	1	0	0	0

MICKEY, Robert Larry *Forward*
b. Lacombe, Alta., Oct. 21, 1943

Season	Club	GP	G	A	Pts
1964-65	Chicago	1	0	0	0
1965-66	New York R.	7	0	0	0
1966-67	New York R.	8	0	0	0
1967-68	New York R.	4	0	2	2
1968-69	Toronto M.L.	55	8	19	27
1969-70	Montreal C.	21	4	4	8
1970-71	Los Angeles	65	6	12	18
1971-72	Phila F-Buff	18	1	3	4
1972-73	Buffalo	77	15	9	24
	Totals	256	34	49	83

MICKEY *(Continued)*

Playoffs	Club	GP	G	A	Pts
1968-69	Toronto M.L.	3	0	0	0
1972-73	Buffalo	6	1	0	1
	Totals	9	1	0	1

MICKOSKI, Nicholas *Forward*
b. Winnipeg, Man., Dec. 7, 1927

Season	Club	GP	G	A	Pts
1948-49	New York R.	54	13	9	22
1949-50	New York R.	45	10	10	20
1950-51	New York R.	64	20	15	35
1951-52	New York R.	43	7	13	20
1952-53	New York R.	70	19	16	35
1953-54	New York R.	68	19	16	35
1954-55	NY R-Chgo	70	10	33	43
1955-56	Chicago	70	19	20	39
1956-57	Chicago	70	16	20	36
1957-58	Chgo-Det RW	64	13	18	31
1958-59	Detroit R.W.	66	11	15	26
1959-60	Boston	18	1	0	1
	Totals	703	158	185	343

Playoffs	Club	GP	G	A	Pts
1947-48	New York R.	2	0	1	1
1949-50	New York R.	12	1	5	6
1957-58	Detroit R.W.	4	0	0	0
	Totals	18	1	6	7

All-Star

1956	NHL All-Stars	1	0	0	0

MIGAY, Rudolph Joseph *Forward*
b. Fort William, Ont., Nov. 18, 1928

Season	Club	GP	G	A	Pts
1949-50	Toronto M.L.	18	1	5	6
1951-52	Toronto M.L.	19	2	1	3
1952-53	Toronto M.L.	40	5	4	9
1953-54	Toronto M.L.	70	8	15	23
1954-55	Toronto M.L.	67	8	16	24
1955-56	Toronto M.L.	70	12	16	28
1956-57	Toronto M.L.	66	15	20	35
1957-58	Toronto M.L.	48	7	14	21
1958-59	Toronto M.L.	19	1	1	2
1959-60	Toronto M.L.	1	0	0	0
	Totals	418	59	92	151

Playoffs	Club	GP	G	A	Pts
1953-54	Toronto M.L.	5	1	0	1
1954-55	Toronto M.L.	3	0	0	0
1955-56	Toronto M.L.	5	0	0	0
1958-59	Toronto M.L.	2	0	0	0
	Totals	15	1	0	1

All-Star

1957	NHL All-Stars	1	0	1	1

MIKITA, Stanley *Forward*
b. Sokolce, Czechoslovakia, May 20, 1940

Season	Club	GP	G	A	Pts
1958-59	Chicago	3	0	1	1
1959-60	Chicago	67	8	18	26
1960-61	Chicago	66	19	34	53
1961-62	Chicgo	70	25	52	77
1962-63	Chicago	65	31	45	76
1963-64	Chicago	70	39	50	89
1964-65	Chicago	70	28	59	87
1965-66	Chicago	68	30	48	78
1966-67	Chicago	70	35	62	97
1967-68	Chicago	72	40	47	87
1968-69	Chicago	74	30	67	97
1969-70	Chicago	76	39	47	86
1970-71	Chicago	74	24	48	72
1971-72	Chicago	74	26	39	65
1972-73	Chicago	57	27	56	83
	Totals	976	401	673	1074

Playoffs	Club	GP	G	A	Pts
1959-60	Chicago	3	0	1	1
1960-61	Chicago	12	6	5	11
1961-62	Chicago	12	6	15	21
1962-63	Chicago	6	3	2	5
1963-64	Chicago	7	3	6	9
1964-65	Chicago	14	3	7	10
1965-66	Chicago	6	1	2	3
1966-67	Chicago	6	2	2	4
1967-68	Chicago	11	5	7	12
1969-70	Chicago	8	4	6	10
1970-71	Chicago	18	5	13	18
1971-72	Chicago	8	3	1	4
1972-73	Chicago	15	7	13	20
	Totals	126	48	80	128

All-Star

1961	Chicago	1	0	0	0
1964	NHL All-Stars	1	0	0	0
1967	NHL All-Stars	1	0	0	0
1968	NHL All-Stars	1	1	1	2
1969	East All-Stars	1	0	0	0
1971	West All-Stars	1	0	0	0
1972	West All-Stars	1	0	0	0
1973	West All-Stars	1	0	1	1
	Totals	8	1	2	3

MIKKELSON, William Robert (Bill) *Forward*
b. Neepawa, Man., May 21, 1948

Season	Club	GP	G	A	Pts
1971-72	Los Angeles	15	0	1	1
1972-73	New York I.	72	1	10	11
	Totals	87	1	11	12

MIKOL, John Stanley (Jim)
Defenseman-Forward
b. Kitchener, Ont., June 11, 1938

Season	Club	GP	G	A	Pts
1962-63	Toronto M.L.	4	0	1	1
1964-65	New York R.	30	1	3	4
	Totals	34	1	4	5

MILKS, Herbert (Hib) *Defenseman-Forward*
b. Ottawa, Ont., Apr. 1, 1902

Season	Club	GP	G	A	Pts
1925-26	Pittsburgh Pi.	36	14	5	19
1926-27	Pittsburgh Pi.	--	16	6	22
1927-28	Pittsburgh Pi.	44	18	3	21
1928-29	Pittsburgh Pi.	--	9	3	12
1929-30	Pittsburgh Pi.	--	13	11	24
1930-31	Philadelphia Q.	--	17	6	23
1931-32	New York R.	45	0	4	4
1932-33	Ottawa	--	0	3	3
	Totals	--	87	41	128
Playoffs					
1925-26	Pittsburgh Pi.	2	0	0	0
1927-28	Pittsburgh Pi.	2	0	0	0
1931-32	New York R.	6	0	0	0
	Totals	10	0	0	0

MILLAR, Franklin Allan (Al) *Goalie*
b. Winnipeg, Man., Sept. 18, 1929

Season	Club	GP	GA	Sho	AVE
1957-58	Boston	6	25	0	4.17

MILLAR, Hugh Alexander *Defenseman*
b. Edmonton, Alta., Apr. 3, 1921

Season	Club	GP	G	A	Pts
1946-47	Detroit R.W.	4	0	0	0
Playoffs					
1946-47	Detroit R.W.	1	0	0	0

MILLER, Earl *Forward*
b. Regina, Sask.

Season	Club	GP	G	A	Pts
1927-28	Chicago	--	1	1	2
1928-29	Chicago	--	1	1	2
1929-30	Chicago	--	11	5	16
1930-31	Chicago	--	3	4	7
1931-32	Toronto M.L.	--	3	3	6
	Totals	--	19	14	33
Playoffs					
1929-30	Chicago	--	1	0	1
1930-31	Chicago	--	0	0	0
1931-32	Toronto M.L.	--	0	0	0
	Totals	--	1	0	1

MILLER, Jack Leslie *Forward*
b. Delisle, Sask., Sept. 16, 1925

Season	Club	GP	G	A	Pts
1949-50	Chicago	6	0	0	0
1950-51	Chicago	11	0	0	0
	Totals	17	0	0	0

MILLER, Joseph *Goalie*
b. Morrisburg, Ont., Oct. 6, 1900

Season	Club	GP	GA	Sho	AVE
1927-28	NY A-NY R	28	77	5	2.75
1928-29	Pittsburgh Pi.	44	80	11	1.82
1929-30	Pittsburgh Pi.	43	179	0	4.16
1930-31	Philadelphia Q.	14	50	0	3.57
	Totals	129	386	16	2.99
Playoffs					
1927-28	New York R.	3	3	1	1.00

MILLER, Thomas William (Tom) *Forward*
b. Kitchener, Ont., Mar. 31, 1947

Season	Club	GP	G	A	Pts
1970-71	Detroit R.W.	29	1	7	8
1972-73	New York I.	69	13	17	30
	Totals	98	14	24	38

MILLER, William *Forward*
b. Campbellton, N.B., Aug. 1, 1908

Season	Club	GP	G	A	Pts
1934-35	Montreal M.	--	3	0	3
1935-36	Montreal C.	--	1	2	3
1936-37	Montreal C.	--	3	1	4
	Totals	--	7	3	10

MISZUK, John *Defenseman*
b. Naliboki, Poland, Sept. 29, 1940

Season	Club	GP	G	A	Pts
1963-64	Detroit R.W.	42	0	2	2
1965-66	Chicago	2	1	1	2
1966-67	Chicago	3	0	0	0
1967-68	Philadelphia F.	74	5	17	22
1968-69	Philadelphia F.	66	1	13	14
1969-70	Minnesota	50	0	6	6
	Totals	237	7	39	46
Playoffs					
1963-64	Detroit R.W.	3	0	0	0
1965-66	Chicago	3	0	0	0
1966-67	Chicago	2	0	0	0
1967-68	Philadelphia F.	7	0	3	3
1968-69	Philadelphia F.	4	0	0	0
1969-70	Minnesota	0	0	0	0
	Totals	19	0	3	3

MITCHELL, Herbert *Forward*

Season	Club	GP	G	A	Pts
1924-25	Boston	27	3	0	3
1925-26	Boston	26	3	0	3
	Totals	53	6	0	6

MITCHELL, Ivan *Goalie*

Season	Club	GP	GA	Sho	AVE
1919-20	Toronto St. P.	14	68	0	4.86
1920-21	Toronto St. P.	4	22	0	5.50
1921-22	Toronto St. P.	2	6	0	3.00
	Totals	20	96	0	4.80

MITCHELL, William *Defenseman*
b. Toronto, Ont., Sept. 6, 1912

Season	Club	GP	G	A	Pts
1941-42	Chicago	1	0	0	0
1942-43	Chicago	42	1	1	2
1944-45	Chicago	40	3	4	7
	Totals	83	4	5	9

MITCHELL, William Dickie (Red) *Defenseman*
b. Port Dalhousie, Ont., Feb. 22, 1930

Season	Club	GP	G	A	Pts
1963-64	Detroit R.W.	1	0	0	0

MOE, William Carl *Defenseman*
b. Danvers, Mass., Oct. 2, 1916

Season	Club	GP	G	A	Pts
1944-45	New York R.	35	2	4	6
1945-46	New York R.	48	4	4	8
1946-47	New York R.	59	4	10	14
1947-48	New York R.	59	1	15	16
1948-49	New York R.	60	0	9	9
	Totals	261	11	42	53

Playoffs

1947-48	New York R.	1	0	0	0

MOFFAT, Lyle Gordon *Forward*
b. Calgary, Alta., Mar. 19, 1948

Season	Club	GP	G	A	Pts
1972-73	Toronto M.L.	1	0	0	0

MOFFATT, Ronald *Forward*
b. West Hope, N.D.

Season	Club	GP	G	A	Pts
1932-33	Detroit F.	--	1	1	2
1933-34	Detroit R.W.	--	0	0	0
	Totals	--	1	1	2

MOHNS, Douglas Allen *Defenseman-Forward*
b. Capreol, Ont., Dec. 13, 1933

Season	Club	GP	G	A	Pts
1953-54	Boston	70	13	14	27
1954-55	Boston	70	14	18	32
1955-56	Boston	64	10	8	18
1956-57	Boston	68	6	34	40
1957-58	Boston	54	5	16	21
1958-59	Boston	47	6	24	30
1959-60	Boston	65	20	25	45
1960-61	Boston	65	12	21	33
1961-62	Boston	69	16	29	45
1962-63	Boston	68	7	23	30
1963-64	Boston	70	9	17	26
1964-65	Chicago	49	13	20	33
1965-66	Chicago	70	22	27	49
1966-67	Chicago	61	25	35	60
1967-68	Chicago	65	24	29	53
1968-69	Chicago	65	22	19	41
1969-70	Chicago	66	6	27	33
1970-71	Chgo-Minn	56	6	11	17
1971-72	Minnesota	78	6	30	36
1972-73	Minnesota	67	4	13	17
	Totals	1287	246	440	686

Playoffs

1953-54	Boston	4	1	0	1
1954-55	Boston	5	0	0	0
1956-57	Boston	10	2	3	5
1957-58	Boston	12	3	10	13
1958-59	Boston	4	0	2	2
1964-65	Chicago	14	3	4	7
1965-66	Chicago	5	1	0	1
1966-67	Chicago	5	0	5	5
1967-68	Chicago	11	1	5	6
1969-70	Chicago	8	0	2	2
1970-71	Minnesota	6	2	2	4
1971-72	Minnesota	13	2	4	6
1972-73	Minnesota	6	0	1	1
	Totals	103	15	38	53

All-Star

1954	NHL All-Stars	1	1	0	1
1958	NHL All-Stars	1	0	0	0
1959	NHL All-Stars	1	0	0	0
1961	NHL All-Stars	1	0	0	0
1962	NHL All-Stars	1	0	0	0
1965	NHL All-Stars	1	0	0	0
	Totals	6	1	0	1

MOHNS, Lloyd Warren *Defenseman*
b. Petawawa, Ont., July 31, 1921

Season	Club	GP	G	A	Pts
1943-44	New York R.	1	0	0	0

MOLYNEAUX, Laurence S. *Defenseman*
b. West Sutton, Ont., July 8, 1912

Season	Club	GP	G	A	Pts
1937–38	New York R.	2	0	0	0
1938–39	New York R.	43	0	1	1
	Totals	45	0	1	1
Playoffs					
1937–38	New York R.	3	0	0	0
1938–39	New York R.	7	0	0	0
	Totals	10	0	0	0

MONAHAN, Garry Michael *Forward*
b. Barrie, Ont., Oct. 20, 1946

Season	Club	GP	G	A	Pts
1967–68	Montreal C.	11	0	0	0
1968–69	Montreal C.	3	0	0	0
1969–70	Det RW-LA	72	3	7	10
1970–71	Toronto M.L.	78	15	22	37
1971–72	Toronto M.L.	78	14	17	31
1972–73	Toronto M.L.	78	13	18	31
	Totals	320	45	64	109
Playoffs					
1970–71	Toronto M.L.	6	2	0	2
1971–72	Toronto M.L.	5	0	0	0
	Totals	11	2	0	2

MONDOU, Armand *Forward*
b. Yanaska, Que., June 27, 1905

Season	Club	GP	G	A	Pts
1928–29	Montreal C.	--	3	4	7
1929–30	Montreal C.	--	3	5	8
1930–31	Montreal C.	--	5	4	9
1931–32	Montreal C.	--	6	12	18
1932–33	Montreal C.	--	1	3	4
1933–34	Montreal C.	--	5	3	8
1934–35	Montreal C.	--	9	15	24
1935–36	Montreal C.	--	7	11	18
1936–37	Montreal C.	--	1	1	2
1937–38	Montreal C.	--	2	4	6
1938–39	Montreal C.	--	3	7	10
1939–40	Montreal C.	--	2	2	4
	Totals	--	47	71	118
Playoffs					
1928–29	Montreal C.	--	0	0	0
1929–30	Montreal C.	--	1	1	2
1930–31	Montreal C.	--	0	0	0
1931–32	Montreal C.	--	1	2	3
1932–33	Montreal C.	--	0	0	0
1933–34	Montreal C.	--	0	1	1
1934–35	Montreal C.	--	0	1	1
1938–39	Montreal C.	--	1	0	1
	Totals	--	3	5	8

MONTIETH, Henry George (Hank) *Forward*
b. Stratford, Ont., Oct. 2, 1945

Season	Club	GP	G	A	Pts
1968–69	Detroit R.W.	34	1	9	10
1969–70	Detroit R.W.	9	0	0	0
1970–71	Detroit R.W.	34	4	3	7
	Totals	77	5	12	17
Playoffs					
1969–70	Detroit R.W.	4	0	0	0

MOORE, Alfred Ernest (Alfie) *Goalie*
b. Toronto, Ont.

Season	Club	GP	GA	Sho	AVE
1936–37	New York A.	18	64	1	3.56
1938–39	New York A.	2	14	0	7.00
1939–40	Detroit R.W.	1	3	0	3.00
	Totals	21	81	1	3.86
Playoffs					
1937–38	Chicago	1	1	0	1.00
1938–39	New York A.	2	6	0	3.00
	Totals	3	7	0	2.33

MOORE, Richard Winston *Forward*
b. Montreal, Que., Jan. 6, 1931

Season	Club	GP	G	A	Pts
1951–52	Montreal C.	33	18	15	33
1952–53	Montreal C.	18	2	6	8
1953–54	Montreal C.	13	1	4	5
1954–55	Montreal C.	67	16	20	36
1955–56	Montreal C.	70	11	39	50
1956–57	Montreal C.	70	29	29	58
1957–58	Montreal C.	70	36	48	84
1958–59	Montreal C.	70	41	55	96
1959–60	Montreal C.	62	22	42	64
1960–61	Montreal C.	57	35	34	69
1961–62	Montreal C.	57	19	22	41
1962–63	Montreal C.	67	24	26	50
1964–65	Toronto M.L.	38	2	4	6
1967–68	St. Louis B.	27	5	3	8
	Totals	719	261	347	608
Playoffs					
1951–52	Montreal C.	11	1	1	2
1952–53	Montreal C.	12	3	2	5
1953–54	Montreal C.	11	5	8	13
1954–55	Montreal C.	12	1	5	6
1955–56	Montreal C.	10	3	6	9
1956–57	Montreal C.	10	3	7	10
1957–58	Montreal C.	10	4	7	11
1958–59	Montreal C.	11	5	12	17
1959–60	Montreal C.	8	6	4	10
1960–61	Montreal C.	6	3	1	4
1961–62	Montreal C.	6	4	2	6

MOORE *(Continued)*

Playoffs

	Club	GP	G	A	Pts
1962–63	Montreal C.	5	0	1	1
1964–65	Toronto M.L.	5	1	1	2
1967–68	St. Louis B.	18	7	7	14
	Totals	135	46	64	110

All-Star

1953	Montreal C.	1	0	0	0
1956	Montreal C.	1	0	0	0
1957	Montreal C.	1	0	1	1
1958	Montreal C.	1	0	3	3
1959	Montreal C.	1	1	1	2
1960	Montreal C.	1	0	0	0
1961	NHL All-Stars	1	0	0	0
	Totals	7	1	5	6

MORAN, Ambrose *Defenseman*

Season	Club	GP	G	A	Pts
1926–27	Montreal C.	--	0	0	0
1927–28	Chicago	--	1	1	2
	Totals	--	1	1	2

Playoffs

1926–27	Montreal C.	--	0	0	0

MORENZ, Howarth William (Howie) *Forward*
b. Mitchell, Ont., Sept. 21, 1902

Season	Club	GP	G	A	Pts
1923–24	Montreal C.	24	13	3	16
1924–25	Montreal C.	30	27	7	34
1925–26	Montreal C.	31	23	3	26
1926–27	Montreal C.	--	25	7	32
1927–28	Montreal C.	43	33	18	51
1928–29	Montreal C.	--	17	10	27
1929–30	Montreal C.	--	40	10	50
1930–31	Montreal C.	--	28	23	51
1931–32	Montreal C.	--	24	25	49
1932–33	Montreal C.	--	14	21	35
1933–34	Montreal C.	--	8	13	21
1934–35	Chicago	--	8	26	34
1935–36	Chgo–NY R	--	6	15	21
1936–37	Montreal C.	--	4	16	20
	Totals	--	270	197	467

Playoffs

1923–24	Montreal C.	6	7	2	9
1924–25	Montreal C.	6	7	1	8
1926–27	Montreal C.	4	1	0	1
1927–28	Montreal C.	2	0	0	0
1928–29	Montreal C.	3	0	0	0
1929–30	Montreal C.	6	3	0	3
1930–31	Montreal C.	10	1	4	5
1931–32	Montreal C.	4	1	0	1
1932–33	Montreal C.	2	0	3	3

MORENZ *(Continued)*

Playoffs

	Club	GP	G	A	Pts
1933–34	Montreal C.	2	1	1	2
1934–35	Chicago	2	0	0	0
	Totals	47	14	9	23

MORIN, Pete *Forward*
b. Lachine, Que., Dec. 8, 1915

Season	Club	GP	G	A	Pts
1941–42	Montreal C.	--	10	12	22

Playoffs

1941–42	Montreal C.	--	0	0	0

MORISSETTE, Jean Guy *Goalie*
b. Causapscal, Que., Dec. 16, 1937

Season	Club	GP	GA	Sho	AVE
1963–64	Montreal C.	⅔	4	0	6.00

MORRIS, Bernard *Forward*

Season	Club	GP	G	A	Pts
1924–25	Boston	6	2	0	2

Playoffs

1919–20	Seattle (PCHL)	--	0	2	2
1923–24	Calgary (PCHL)	--	0	0	0
	Totals	--	0	0	0

MORRIS, Elwin Gordon (Moe) *Defenseman*
b. Toronto, Ont., Jan. 3, 1921

Season	Club	GP	G	A	Pts
1943–44	Toronto M.L.	50	12	21	33
1944–45	Toronto M.L.	29	0	2	2
1945–46	Toronto M.L.	38	1	5	6
1948–49	New York R.	18	0	1	1
	Totals	137	13	29	42

Playoffs

1943–44	Toronto M.L.	5	1	2	3
1944–45	Toronto M.L.	13	3	0	3
	Totals	18	4	2	6

MORRISON, Donald Macrae *Forward*
b. Saskatoon, Sask., July 14, 1923

Season	Club	GP	G	A	Pts
1947–48	Detroit R.W.	40	10	15	25
1948–49	Detroit R.W.	13	0	1	1
1950–51	Chicago	59	8	12	20
	Totals	112	18	28	46

Playoffs

1947–48	Detroit R.W.	3	0	1	1

563

MORRISON, George Harold *Forward*
b. Toronto, Ont., Dec. 24, 1948

Season	Club	GP	G	A	Pts
1970–71	St. Louis B.	73	15	10	25
1971–72	St. Louis B.	42	2	11	13
	Totals	115	17	21	38
Playoffs					
1970–71	St. Louis B.	3	0	0	0

MORRISON, James Stewart Hunter (Jim)
Defenseman
b. Montreal, Que., Oct. 11, 1931

Season	Club	GP	G	A	Pts
1951–52	Bos–Tor ML	31	0	3	3
1952–53	Toronto M.L.	56	1	8	9
1953–54	Toronto M.L.	60	9	11	20
1954–55	Toronto M.L.	70	5	12	17
1955–56	Toronto M.L.	63	2	17	19
1956–57	Toronto M.L.	63	3	17	20
1957–58	Toronto M.L.	70	3	21	24
1958–59	Boston	70	8	17	25
1959–60	Detroit R.W.	70	3	23	26
1960–61	New York R.	19	1	6	7
1969–70	Pittsburgh Pe.	59	5	15	20
1970–71	Pittsburgh Pe.	73	0	10	10
	Totals	704	40	160	200
Playoffs					
1951–52	Toronto M.L.	2	0	0	0
1953–54	Toronto M.L.	5	0	0	0
1954–55	Toronto M.L.	4	0	1	1
1955–56	Toronto M.L.	5	0	0	0
1958–59	Boston	6	0	6	6
1959–60	Detroit R.W.	6	0	2	2
1969–70	Pittsburgh Pe.	8	0	3	3
	Totals	36	0	12	12
All-Star					
1955	NHL All-Stars	1	0	0	0
1956	NHL All-Stars	1	0	0	0
1957	NHL All-Stars	1	0	1	1
	Totals	3	0	1	1

MORRISON, John (Crutchy) *Forward*

Season	Club	GP	G	A	Pts
1925–26	New York A.	18	0	0	0
Playoffs					
1922–23	Edmonton (PCHL)	--	1	0	1

MORRISON, Lewis *Forward*
b. Gainsborough, Sask., Feb. 11, 1948

Season	Club	GP	G	A	Pts
1969–70	Philadelphia F.	66	9	10	19
1970–71	Philadelphia F.	78	5	7	12

MORRISON *(Continued)*

Season	Club	GP	G	A	Pts
1971–72	Philadelphia F.	58	5	5	10
1972–73	Atlanta	77	6	9	15
	Totals	279	25	31	56
Playoffs					
1970–71	Philadelphia F.	4	0	0	0

MORRISON, Roderick Finlay *Forward*
b. Saskatoon, Sask., Oct. 7, 1925

Season	Club	GP	G	A	Pts
1947–48	Detroit R.W.	34	8	7	15
Playoffs					
1947–48	Detroit R.W.	3	0	0	0

MORTSON, James Angus Gerald (Gus)
Defenseman
b. New Liskeard, Ont., Jan. 24, 1925

Season	Club	GP	G	A	Pts
1946–47	Toronto M.L.	60	5	13	18
1947–48	Toronto M.L.	58	7	11	18
1948–49	Toronto M.L.	60	2	13	15
1949–50	Toronto M.L.	68	3	14	17
1950–51	Toronto M.L.	60	3	10	13
1951–52	Toronto M.L.	65	1	10	11
1952–53	Chicago	68	5	18	23
1953–54	Chicago	68	5	13	18
1954–55	Chicago	65	2	11	13
1955–56	Chicago	52	5	10	15
1956–57	Chicago	70	5	18	23
1957–58	Chicago	67	3	10	13
1958–59	Detroit R.W.	36	0	1	1
	Totals	797	46	152	198
Playoffs					
1946–47	Toronto M.L.	11	1	3	4
1947–48	Toronto M.L.	5	1	2	3
1948–49	Toronto M.L.	9	2	1	3
1949–50	Toronto M.L.	7	0	0	0
1950–51	Toronto M.L.	11	0	1	1
1951–52	Toronto M.L.	4	0	0	0
1952–53	Chicago	7	1	1	2
	Totals	54	5	8	13
All-Star					
1947	Toronto M.L.	1	0	1	1
1948	Toronto M.L.	1	0	0	0
1950	NHL All-Stars	1	0	0	0
1951	NHL 2nd All-Stars	1	0	1	1
1952	NHL 1st All-Stars	1	0	0	0
1953	NHL All-Stars	1	0	0	0
1954	NHL All-Stars	1	1	0	1
1956	NHL All-Stars	1	0	1	1
	Totals	8	1	3	4

MOSDELL, Kenneth Forward
b. Montreal, Que., July 13, 1922

Season	Club	GP	G	A	Pts
1941–42	Brooklyn A.	41	7	9	16
1944–45	Montreal C.	31	12	6	18
1945–46	Montreal C.	13	2	1	3
1946–47	Montreal C.	54	5	10	15
1947–48	Montreal C.	23	1	0	1
1948–49	Montreal C.	60	17	9	26
1949–50	Montreal C.	67	15	12	27
1950–51	Montreal C.	66	13	18	31
1951–52	Montreal C.	44	5	11	16
1952–53	Montreal C.	63	5	14	19
1953–54	Montreal C.	67	22	24	46
1954–55	Montreal C.	70	22	32	54
1955–56	Montreal C.	67	13	17	30
1956–57	Chicago	25	2	4	6
1957–58	Montreal C.	2	0	1	1
	Totals	693	141	168	309

Playoffs

1945–46	Montreal C.	9	4	1	5
1946–47	Montreal C.	4	2	0	2
1948–49	Montreal C.	7	1	1	2
1949–50	Montreal C.	5	0	0	0
1950–51	Montreal C.	11	1	1	2
1951–52	Montreal C.	2	1	0	1
1952–53	Montreal C.	7	3	2	5
1953–54	Montreal C.	11	1	0	1
1954–55	Montreal C.	12	2	7	9
1955–56	Montreal C.	9	1	1	2
1958–59	Montreal C.	2	0	0	0
	Totals	79	16	13	29

All-Star

1951	NHL 2nd All-Stars	1	1	0	1
1952	NHL 2nd All-Stars	1	0	0	0
1953	Montreal C.	1	0	0	0
1954	NHL All-Stars	1	0	0	0
1955	NHL All-Stars	1	0	0	0
	Totals	5	1	0	1

MOSIENKO, William Forward
b. Winnipeg, Man., Nov. 2, 1921

Season	Club	GP	G	A	Pts
1941–42	Chicago	12	6	8	14
1942–43	Chicago	2	2	0	2
1943–44	Chicago	50	32	38	70
1944–45	Chicago	50	28	26	54
1945–46	Chicago	40	18	30	48
1946–47	Chicago	59	25	27	52
1947–48	Chicago	40	16	9	25
1948–49	Chicago	60	17	25	42
1949–50	Chicago	69	18	28	46
1950–51	Chicago	65	21	15	36
1951–52	Chicago	70	31	22	53

MOSIENKO (Continued)

Season	Club	GP	G	A	Pts
1952–53	Chicago	65	17	20	37
1953–54	Chicago	65	15	19	34
1954–55	Chicago	64	12	15	27
	Totals	711	258	282	540

Playoffs

1941–42	Chicago	3	2	0	2
1943–44	Chicago	8	2	2	4
1945–46	Chicago	4	2	0	2
1952–53	Chicago	7	4	2	6
	Totals	22	10	4	14

All-Star

1947	NHL All-Stars	1	0	0	0
1949	NHL All-Stars	1	0	0	0
1950	NHL All-Stars	1	0	0	0
1952	NHL 1st All-Stars	1	0	1	1
1953	NHL All-Stars	1	0	0	0
	Totals	5	0	1	1

MOTT, Morris Forward
b. Creelman, Sask., May 25, 1946

Season	Club	GP	G	A	Pts
1972–73	California	70	6	7	13

MOTTER, Alexander Everett Defenseman
b. Melville, Sask., June 20, 1913

Season	Club	GP	G	A	Pts
1935–36	Boston	--	1	4	5
1937–38	Bos-Det RW	--	5	17	22
1938–39	Detroit R.W.	--	5	11	16
1939–40	Detroit R.W.	--	7	12	19
1940–41	Detroit R.W.	--	13	12	25
1941–42	Detroit R.W.	30	2	4	6
1942–43	Detroit R.W.	50	6	4	10
	Totals	--	39	64	103

Playoffs

1935–36	Boston	--	0	0	0
1938–39	Detroit R.W.	--	0	1	1
1939–40	Detroit R.W.	--	1	1	2
1940–41	Detroit R.W.	--	1	3	4
1941–42	Detroit R.W.	--	1	3	4
1942–43	Detroit R.W.	5	0	1	1
	Totals	--	3	9	12

MOWERS, John Thomas Goalie
b. Niagara Falls, Ont., Oct. 29, 1916

Season	Club	GP	GA	Sho	AVE
1940–41	Detroit R.W.	48	102	4	2.12
1941–42	Detroit R.W.	47	144	5	3.06
1942–43	Detroit R.W.	50	124	6	2.48
1946–47	Detroit R.W.	7	29	0	4.14
	Totals	152	399	15	2.63

565

MOWERS (Continued)

Playoffs	Club	GP	G	A	Pts
1940–41	Detroit R.W.	9	18	0	2.00
1941–42	Detroit R.W.	12	38	0	3.16
1942–43	Detroit R.W.	10	22	2	2.20
1946–47	Detroit R.W.	1	5	0	5.00
	Totals	32	83	2	2.59

MULOIN, John Wayne *Defenseman*
b. Dryden, Ont., Dec. 24, 1941

Season	Club	GP	G	A	Pts
1963–64	Detroit R.W.	3	0	1	1
1969–70	Oakland	71	3	6	9
1970–71	Calif–Minn	73	0	14	14
	Totals	147	3	21	24

Playoffs					
1969–70	Oakland	4	0	0	0
1970–71	Minnesota	7	0	0	0
	Totals	11	0	0	0

MUMMERY, Harry *Defenseman-Goalie*

Season	Club	GP	G	A	Pts
1917–18	Toronto A.	18	3	0	3
1918–19	Toronto A.	13	2	0	2
1919–20	Quebec	24	9	6	15
1920–21	Montreal C.	24	15	5	20
1921–22	Hamilton	20	4	2	6
1922–23	Hamilton	7	0	0	0
	Totals	106	33	13	46

Playoffs	Club	GP	G	A	Pts
1917–18	Toronto A.	--	0	4	4

Season	Goalie Record	GP	GA	Sho	AVE
1919–20	Quebec	2	15	0	7.50

MUNRO, Duncan *Defenseman*
b. Toronto, Ont.

Season	Club	GP	G	A	Pts
1924–25	Montreal M.	27	5	1	6
1925–26	Montreal M.	33	4	6	10
1926–27	Montreal M.	--	6	5	11
1927–28	Montreal M.	--	5	2	7
1929–30	Montreal M.	--	7	2	9
1930–31	Montreal M.	--	0	1	1
1931–32	Montreal C.	--	1	1	2
	Totals	--	28	18	46

Playoffs					
1925–26	Montreal M.	--	1	0	1
1926–27	Montreal M.	--	0	0	0
1927–28	Montreal M.	--	0	2	2
1929–30	Montreal M.	--	2	0	2
1931–32	Montreal C.	--	0	0	0
	Totals	--	3	2	5

MUNRO, Gerald *Defenseman*
b. Sault Ste. Marie, Ont., Nov. 20, 1897

Season	Club	GP	G	A	Pts
1924–25	Montreal M.	29	1	0	1
1925–26	Toronto St.P.	4	0	0	0
	Totals	33	1	0	1

MURDOCH, John Murray *Forward*
b. Lucknow, Ont., May 19, 1904

Season	Club	GP	G	A	Pts
1926–27	New York R.	44	6	4	10
1927–28	New York R.	44	7	3	10
1928–29	New York R.	44	8	6	14
1929–30	New York R.	44	13	13	26
1930–31	New York R.	44	7	7	14
1931–32	New York R.	48	5	16	21
1932–33	New York R.	48	5	11	16
1933–34	New York R.	48	17	10	27
1934–35	New York R.	48	14	15	29
1935–36	New York R.	48	2	9	11
1936–37	New York R.	48	0	14	14
	Totals	508	84	108	192

Playoffs					
1926–27	New York R.	2	0	0	0
1927–28	New York R.	9	2	1	3
1928–29	New York R.	6	0	0	0
1929–30	New York R.	4	3	0	3
1930–31	New York R.	4	0	2	2
1931–32	New York R.	7	0	2	2
1932–33	New York R.	8	3	4	7
1933–34	New York R.	2	0	0	0
1934–35	New York R.	4	0	2	2
1936–37	New York R.	9	1	1	2
	Totals	55	9	12	21

MURDOCH, Robert John (Bob) *Defenseman*
b. Kirkland Lake, Ont., Nov. 20, 1946

Season	Club	GP	G	A	Pts
1970–71	Montreal C.	1	0	2	2
1971–72	Montreal C.	11	1	1	2
1972–73	Montreal C.	69	2	22	24
	Totals	81	3	25	28

Playoffs					
1970–71	Montreal C.	2	0	0	0
1971–72	Montreal C.	1	0	0	0
1972–73	Montreal C.	13	0	3	3
	Totals	16	0	3	3

MURPHY, Hal *Goalie*
b. Montreal, Que., July 6, 1927

Season	Club	GP	GA	Sho	AVE
1952–53	Montreal C.	1	4	0	4.00

MURPHY, Michael John (Mike) *Forward*
b. Toronto, Ont., Sept. 12, 1950

Season	Club	GP	G	A	Pts
1971–72	St. Louis B.	63	20	23	43
1972–73	StL B–NY R	79	22	31	53
	Totals	142	42	54	96

Playoffs

1971–72	St. Louis B.	11	2	3	5
1972–73	New York R.	10	0	0	0
	Totals	21	2	3	5

MURPHY, Robert Ronald (Ron) *Forward*
b. Hamilton, Ont., Apr. 10, 1933

Season	Club	GP	G	A	Pts
1952–53	New York R.	15	3	1	4
1953–54	New York R.	27	1	3	4
1954–55	New York R.	66	14	16	30
1955–56	New York R.	66	16	28	44
1956–57	New York R.	33	7	12	19
1957–58	Chicago	69	11	17	28
1958–59	Chicago	59	17	30	47
1959–60	Chicago	63	15	21	36
1960–61	Chicago	70	21	19	40
1961–62	Chicago	61	12	16	28
1962–63	Chicago	68	18	16	34
1963–64	Chicago	70	11	8	19
1964–65	Detroit R.W.	58	20	19	39
1965–66	Det RW–Bos	34	10	8	18
1966–67	Boston	39	11	16	27
1967–68	Boston	12	0	1	1
1968–69	Boston	60	16	38	54
1969–70	Boston	20	2	5	7
	Totals	890	205	274	479

Playoffs

1955–56	New York R.	5	0	1	1
1956–57	New York R.	5	0	0	0
1959–60	Chicago	4	1	0	1
1960–61	Chicago	12	2	1	3
1962–63	Chicago	1	0	0	0
1963–64	Chicago	7	0	1	1
1964–65	Detroit R.W.	5	0	1	1
1967–68	Boston	4	0	0	0
1968–69	Boston	10	4	5	9
	Totals	53	7	9	16

All-Star

1961	Chicago	1	0	0	0

MURRAY, Allan *Defenseman*
b. Stratford, Ont., Nov. 10, 1908

Season	Club	GP	G	A	Pts
1933–34	New York A.	--	1	1	2
1934–35	New York A.	--	2	1	3
1935–36	New York A.	--	1	0	1

MURRAY *(Continued)*

Season	Club	GP	G	A	Pts
1936–37	New York A.	--	0	2	2
1937–38	New York A.	--	0	1	1
1938–39	New York A.	--	0	0	0
1939–40	New York A.	--	1	4	5
	Totals	--	5	9	14

Playoffs

1935–36	New York A.	--	0	0	0
1937–38	New York A.	--	0	0	0
1939–40	New York A.	--	0	0	0
	Totals	--	0	0	0

MURRAY, James Arnold *Defenseman*
b. Virden, Man., Nov. 25, 1943

Season	Club	GP	G	A	Pts
1967–68	Los Angeles	30	0	2	2

MURRAY, Kenneth R. (Ken) *Defenseman*
b. Toronto, Ont., Jan. 22, 1948

Season	Club	GP	G	A	Pts
1969–70	Toronto M.L.	1	0	1	1
1970–71	Toronto M.L.	4	0	0	0
1972–73	NY I–Det RW	71	1	5	6
	Totals	76	1	6	7

MURRAY, Leo *Forward*
b. Portage La Prairie, Man., Feb. 15, 1902

Season	Club	GP	G	A	Pts
1932–33	Montreal C.	--	0	0	0

MURRAY, Randall (Randy) *Defenseman*
b. Chatham, Ont., Aug. 24, 1945

Season	Club	GP	G	A	Pts
1969–70	Toronto M.L.	1	0	1	1

MURRAY, Terry *Defenseman*
b. Shawville, Que., July 20, 1950

Season	Club	GP	G	A	Pts
1972–73	California	23	0	3	3

MURRAY, Thomas *Goalie*
b. ...

Season	Club	GP	GA	Sho	AVE
1929–30	Montreal C.	1	4	0	4.00

MYERS, Harold Robert (Hap) *Defenseman*
b. Edmonton, Alta., July 28, 1947

Season	Club	GP	G	A	Pts
1970–71	Buffalo	13	0	0	0

MYLES, Victor Robert *Defenseman*
b. Fairlight, Sask., Nov. 12, 1915

Season	Club	GP	G	A	Pts
1942–43	New York R.	45	6	9	15

MYRE, Louis Phillippe (Phil) *Goalie*
b. Ste.-Anne-de-Bellevue, Que., Nov. 1, 1948

Season	Club	GP	GA	Sho	AVE
1969–70	Montreal C.	8⅓	19	0	2.28
1970–71	Montreal C.	28	87	1	3.11
1971–72	Montreal C.	9	32	0	3.63
1972–73	Atlanta	45⅔	138	2	3.03
	Totals	90	276	3	3.06

NANNE, Louis Vincent (Lou) *Defenseman*
b. Sault Ste. Marie, Ont., June 2, 1941

Season	Club	GP	G	A	Pts
1967–68	Minnesota	2	0	1	1
1968–69	Minnesota	41	2	12	14
1969–70	Minnesota	74	3	20	23
1970–71	Minnesota	68	5	11	16
1971–72	Minnesota	78	21	28	49
1972–73	Minnesota	74	15	20	35
	Totals	337	46	92	138
Playoffs					
1969–70	Minnesota	5	0	2	2
1970–71	Minnesota	12	3	6	9
1971–72	Minnesota	7	0	0	0
1972–73	Minnesota	6	1	2	3
	Totals	30	4	10	14

NATTRASS, Ralph William *Defenseman*
b. Gainsboro, Sask., May 26, 1925

Season	Club	GP	G	A	Pts
1946–47	Chicago	35	4	5	9
1947–48	Chicago	60	5	12	17
1948–49	Chicago	60	4	10	14
1949–50	Chicago	69	5	11	16
	Totals	224	18	38	56

NEILSON, James Anthony (Chief) *Defenseman*
b. Big River, Sask., Nov. 28, 1940

Season	Club	GP	G	A	Pts
1962–63	New York R.	69	5	11	16
1963–64	New York R.	69	5	24	29
1964–65	New York R.	62	0	13	13
1965–66	New York R.	65	4	19	23
1966–67	New York R.	61	4	11	15
1967–68	New York R.	67	6	29	35
1968–69	New York R.	76	10	34	44
1969–70	New York R.	62	3	20	23
1970–71	New York R.	77	8	24	32
1971–72	New York R.	78	7	30	37
1972–73	New York R.	52	4	16	20
	Totals	738	56	231	287
Playoffs					
1966–67	New York R.	4	1	0	1
1967–68	New York R.	6	0	2	2

NEILSON *(Continued)*

Playoffs	Club	GP	G	A	Pts
1968–69	New York R.	4	0	3	3
1969–70	New York R.	6	0	1	1
1970–71	New York R.	13	0	3	3
1971–72	New York R.	10	0	3	3
1972–73	New York R.	10	0	4	4
	Totals	53	1	16	17
All-Star					
1967	NHL All-Stars	1	0	0	0
1971	East All-Stars	1	0	0	0
	Totals	2	0	0	0

NELSON, Gordon William *Defenseman*
b. Kinisting, Sask., May 10, 1947

Season	Club	GP	G	A	Pts
1969–70	Toronto M.L.	3	0	0	0

NESTERENKO, Eric Paul *Forward*
b. Flin Flon, Man., Oct. 31, 1933

Season	Club	GP	G	A	Pts
1951–52	Toronto M.L.	1	0	0	0
1952–53	Toronto M.L.	35	10	6	16
1953–54	Toronto M.L.	68	14	9	23
1954–55	Toronto M.L.	62	15	15	30
1955–56	Toronto M.L.	40	4	6	10
1956–57	Chicago	24	8	15	23
1957–58	Chicago	70	20	18	38
1958–59	Chicago	70	16	18	34
1959–60	Chicago	61	13	23	36
1960–61	Chicago	68	19	19	38
1961–62	Chicago	68	15	14	29
1962–63	Chicago	67	12	15	27
1963–64	Chicago	70	7	19	26
1964–65	Chicago	56	14	16	30
1965–66	Chicago	67	15	25	40
1966–67	Chicago	68	14	23	37
1967–68	Chicago	71	11	25	36
1968–69	Chicago	72	15	17	32
1969–70	Chicago	67	16	18	34
1970–71	Chicago	76	8	15	23
1971–72	Chicago	38	4	8	12
	Totals	1219	250	324	574
Playoffs					
1953–54	Toronto M.L.	5	0	1	1
1954–55	Toronto M.L.	4	0	1	1
1958–59	Chicago	6	2	2	4
1959–60	Chicago	4	0	0	0
1960–61	Chicago	11	2	3	5
1961–62	Chicago	12	0	5	5
1962–63	Chicago	6	2	3	5
1963–64	Chicago	7	2	1	3
1964–65	Chicago	14	2	2	4
1965–66	Chicago	6	1	0	1

NESTERENKO (Continued)

Playoffs	Club	GP	G	A	Pts
1966–67	Chicago	6	1	2	3
1967–68	Chicago	10	0	1	1
1969–70	Chicago	7	1	2	3
1970–71	Chicago	18	0	1	1
1971–72	Chicago	8	0	0	0
	Totals	124	13	24	37

All-Star

1961	Chicago	1	1	0	1

NEVILLE, Michael *Forward*
    b. Toronto, Ont.

Season	Club	GP	G	A	Pts
1917–18	Toronto A.	1	1	0	1
1924–25	Toronto St.P.	12	1	0	1
1925–26	Toronto St.P.	33	3	3	6
1930–31	Toronto M.L.	--	1	0	1
	Totals	--	6	3	9

NEVIN, Robert Frank (Bob) *Forward*
    b. South Porcupine, Ont., Mar. 18, 1938

Season	Club	GP	G	A	Pts
1957–58	Toronto M.L.	4	0	0	0
1958–59	Toronto M.L.	2	0	0	0
1960–61	Toronto M.L.	68	21	37	58
1961–62	Toronto M.L.	69	15	30	45
1962–63	Toronto M.L.	58	12	21	33
1963–64	Tor ML–NY R	63	12	16	28
1964–65	New York R.	64	16	14	30
1965–66	New York R.	69	29	33	62
1966–67	New York R.	67	20	24	44
1967–68	New York R.	74	28	30	58
1968–69	New York R.	71	31	25	56
1969–70	New York R.	68	18	19	37
1970–71	New York R.	78	21	25	46
1971–72	Minnesota	72	15	19	34
1972–73	Minnesota	66	5	13	18
	Totals	893	243	306	549

Playoffs	Club	GP	G	A	Pts
1960–61	Toronto M.L.	5	1	0	1
1961–62	Toronto M.L.	12	2	4	6
1962–63	Toronto M.L.	10	3	0	3
1966–67	New York R.	4	0	3	3
1967–68	New York R.	6	0	3	3
1968–69	New York R.	4	0	2	2
1969–70	New York R.	6	1	1	2
1970–71	New York R.	13	5	3	8
1971–72	Minnesota	7	1	1	2
	Totals	67	13	17	30

All-Star

1962	Toronto M.L.	1	0	0	0
1963	Toronto M.L.	1	0	0	0

NEVIN (Continued)

All-Star	Club	GP	G	A	Pts
1967	NHL All-Stars	1	0	0	0
1969	East All-Stars	1	1	0	1
	Totals	4	1	0	1

NEWELL, Gordon Richard (Rick) *Defenseman*
    b. Winnipeg, Man., Feb. 18, 1948

Season	Club	GP	G	A	Pts
1972–73	Detroit R.W.	3	0	0	0

NEWMAN, John

Season	Club	GP	G	A	Pts
1930–31	Detroit F.	--	1	1	2

NEWTON, Cameron Charles (Cam) *Goalie*
    b. Peterborough, Ont., Feb. 25, 1950

Season	Club	GP	GA	Sho	AVE
1970–71	Pittsburgh Pe.	4⅔	16	0	3.41
1972–73	Pittsburgh Pe.	9	35	0	3.94
	Totals	13⅔	51	0	3.75

NICHOLSON, Allan *Forward*
    b. Estevan, Sask., Apr. 26, 1936

Season	Club	GP	G	A	Pts
1955–56	Boston	14	0	0	0
1956–57	Boston	5	0	1	1
	Totals	19	0	1	1

NICHOLSON, Edward George *Defenseman*
    b. Portsmouth, Ont., Sept. 9, 1923

Season	Club	GP	G	A	Pts
1947–48	Detroit R.W.	1	0	0	0

NICHOLSON, John Ivan *Forward*
    b. Charlottetown, P.E.I., Sept. 9, 1914

Season	Club	GP	G	A	Pts
1937–38	Chicago	--	1	0	1

NICHOLSON, Neil *Defenseman*
    b. Saint John, N.B., Sept. 12, 1949

Season	Club	GP	G	A	Pts
1972–73	New York I.	30	3	1	4

Playoffs	Club	GP	G	A	Pts
1969–70	Oakland	2	0	0	0

NIEKAMP, James Lawrence (Jim) *Defenseman*
    b. Detroit, Mich., Mar. 11, 1946

Season	Club	GP	G	A	Pts
1970–71	Detroit R.W.	24	0	2	2
1971–72	Detroit R.W.	5	0	0	0
	Totals	29	0	2	2

NIGHBOR, Frank *Forward*
b. Pembroke Ont., 1893

Season	Club	GP	G	A	Pts
1917–18	Ottawa	9	11	0	11
1918–19	Ottawa	18	18	4	22
1919–20	Ottawa	23	26	7	33
1920–21	Ottawa	24	18	3	21
1921–22	Ottawa	20	8	8	16
1922–23	Ottawa	22	11	5	16
1923–24	Ottawa	20	10	3	13
1924–25	Ottawa	26	5	2	7
1925–26	Ottawa	35	12	13	25
1926–27	Ottawa	--	6	6	12
1927–28	Ottawa	--	8	5	13
1928–29	Ottawa	--	1	4	5
1929–30	Otta–Tor ML	--	2	0	2
	Totals	--	136	60	196

Playoffs

1918–19	Ottawa	--	0	3	3
1919–20	Ottawa	--	6	1	7
1920–21	Ottawa	2	1	2	3
1921–22	Ottawa	2	2	0	2
1922–23	Ottawa	2	0	1	1
1923–24	Ottawa	2	0	1	1
1925–26	Ottawa	--	0	0	0
1926–27	Ottawa	--	1	0	1
1927–28	Ottawa	--	0	0	0
	Totals	--	10	8	18

NOBLE, Reginald *Defenseman-Forward*
b. Collingwood, Ont., June 23, 1895

Season	Club	GP	G	A	Pts
1917–18	Toronto A.	20	28	0	28
1918–19	Toronto A.	17	11	3	14
1919–20	Toronto St.P.	24	24	7	31
1920–21	Toronto St.P.	24	20	6	26
1921–22	Toronto St.P.	24	17	8	25
1922–23	Toronto St.P.	24	12	10	22
1923–24	Toronto St.P.	23	12	3	15
1924–25	Tor StP–Mont M	30	8	6	14
1925–26	Montreal M.	--	9	9	18
1926–27	Montreal M.	--	3	3	6
1927–28	Detroit C.	--	6	8	14
1928–29	Detroit C.	--	6	4	10
1929–30	Detroit C.	--	6	4	10
1930–31	Detroit F.	--	2	5	7
1931–32	Detroit F.	--	3	3	6
1932–33	Montreal M.	--	0	0	0
	Totals	--	167	79	246

Playoffs

1917–18	Toronto A.	--	2	1	3
1920–21	Toronto St.P.	--	0	0	0
1921–22	Toronto St.P.	--	0	2	2
1925–26	Montreal M.	--	0	0	0

NOBLE *(Continued)*

Playoffs	Club	GP	G	A	Pts
1926–27	Montreal M.	--	0	0	0
1928–29	Detroit C.	--	0	0	0
1931–32	Detroit F.	--	0	0	0
1932–33	Montreal M.	--	0	0	0
	Totals	--	2	3	5

NOLAN, Patrick

Season	Club	GP	G	A	Pts
1921–22	Toronto St.P.	2	0	0	0

NOLET, Simon *Forward*
b. St. Odilon, Que., Nov. 23, 1941

Season	Club	GP	G	A	Pts
1967–68	Philadelphia F.	4	0	0	0
1968–69	Philadelphia F.	35	4	10	14
1969–70	Philadelphia F.	56	22	22	44
1970–71	Philadelphia F.	74	9	19	28
1971–72	Philadelphia F.	67	23	20	43
1972–73	Philadelphia F.	70	16	20	36
	Totals	306	74	91	165

Playoffs

1967–68	Philadelphia F.	1	0	0	0
1970–71	Philadelphia F.	4	2	1	3
1972–73	Philadelphia F.	11	3	1	4
	Totals	16	5	2	7

All-Star

1972	West All-Stars	1	1	0	1

NORIS, Joseph S. (Joe) *Defenseman*
b. Denver, Colo., Oct. 26, 1951

Season	Club	GP	G	A	Pts
1971–72	Pittsburgh Pe.	35	2	5	7
1972–73	St. Louis B.	2	0	0	0
	Totals	37	2	5	7

NORRIS, Jack Wayne *Goalie*
b. Saskatoon, Sask., Aug. 5, 1942

Season	Club	GP	GA	Sho	AVE
1964–65	Boston	23	85	1	3.70
1967–68	Chicago	5⅔	22	1	4.00
1968–69	Chicago	1⅔	10	0	6.00
1970–71	Los Angeles	21⅔	85	0	3.90
	Totals	52	203	2	3.89

NORTHCOTT, Laurence (Baldy) *Forward*
b. Calgary, Alta., Sept. 7, 1907

Season	Club	GP	G	A	Pts
1929–30	Montreal M.	--	10	1	11
1930–31	Montreal M.	--	7	3	10
1931–32	Montreal M.	--	19	6	25

NORTHCOTT *(Continued)*

Season	Club	GP	G	A	Pts
1932–33	Montreal M.	--	22	21	43
1933–34	Montreal M.	--	20	13	33
1934–35	Montreal C.	--	9	14	23
1935–36	Montreal M.	--	15	21	36
1936–37	Montreal M.	--	15	14	29
1937–38	Montreal M.	--	11	12	23
1938–39	Chicago	--	5	7	12
	Totals	--	133	112	245

Playoffs

Season	Club	GP	G	A	Pts
1929–30	Montreal M.	--	0	0	0
1930–31	Montreal M.	--	0	1	1
1931–32	Montreal M.	--	1	2	3
1932–33	Montreal M.	--	0	0	0
1933–34	Montreal M.	--	2	0	2
1934–35	Montreal C.	--	4	1	5
1935–36	Montreal M.	--	0	0	0
1936–37	Montreal M.	--	1	1	2
	Totals	--	8	5	13

NYKOLUK, Michael *Forward*
　　b. Toronto, Ont., Dec. 11, 1934

Season	Club	GP	G	A	Pts
1956–57	Toronto M.L.	32	3	1	4

NYSTROM, Robert Thore (Bob) *Forward*
　　b. Kamloops, B.C., Oct. 10, 1952

Season	Club	GP	G	A	Pts
1972–73	New York I.	11	1	1	2

OATMAN, Warren Russell *Forward*
　　b. Tilsonburg, Ont., Feb. 19, 1905

Season	Club	GP	G	A	Pts
1926–27	Det C–Mont M	--	11	4	15
1927–28	Montreal M.	44	7	4	11
1928–29	Mont M–NY R	--	2	1	3
	Totals	--	20	9	29

Playoffs

Season	Club	GP	G	A	Pts
1925–26	Victoria (PCHL)	--	0	0	0
1927–28	Montreal M.	9	1	0	1
1928–29	New York R.	6	0	0	0
	Totals	--	1	0	1

O'BRIEN, Dennis Francis *Defenseman*
　　b. Port Hope, Ont., June 10, 1949

Season	Club	GP	G	A	Pts
1970–71	Minnesota	27	3	2	5
1971–72	Minnesota	70	3	6	9
1972–73	Minnesota	74	3	11	14
	Totals	171	9	19	28

O'BRIEN *(Continued)*

Playoffs

Playoffs	Club	GP	G	A	Pts
1970–71	Minnesota	9	0	0	0
1971–72	Minnesota	3	0	1	1
1972–73	Minnesota	6	1	0	1
	Totals	18	1	1	2

O'BRIEN, Ellard John (Obie)
Defenseman-Forward
　　b. St. Catherines, Ont., May 27, 1930

Season	Club	GP	G	A	Pts
1955–56	Boston	2	0	0	0

O'CONNOR, Herbert William (Buddy) *Forward*
　　b. Montreal, Que., June 21, 1916

Season	Club	GP	G	A	Pts
1941–42	Montreal C.	36	9	16	25
1942–43	Montreal C.	50	15	43	58
1943–44	Montreal C.	44	12	42	54
1944–45	Montreal C.	50	21	23	44
1945–46	Montreal C.	45	11	11	22
1946–47	Montreal C.	46	10	20	30
1947–48	New York R.	60	24	36	60
1948–49	New York R.	46	11	24	35
1949–50	New York R.	66	11	22	33
1950–51	New York R.	66	16	20	36
	Totals	509	140	257	397

Playoffs

	Club	GP	G	A	Pts
1941–42	Montreal C.	3	0	1	1
1942–43	Montreal C.	5	4	5	9
1943–44	Montreal C.	8	1	2	3
1944–45	Montreal C.	2	0	0	0
1945–46	Montreal C.	9	2	3	5
1946–47	Montreal C.	8	3	4	7
1947–48	New York R.	6	1	4	5
1949–50	New York R.	12	4	2	6
	Totals	53	15	21	36

All-Star

		GP	G	A	Pts
1949	NHL All-Stars	1	0	0	0

ODDLEIFSON, Christopher Roy (Chris)
Forward
　　b. Brandon, Man., Sept. 7, 1950

Season	Club	GP	G	A	Pts
1972–73	Boston	6	0	0	0

O'DONNELL, Frederick James (Fred) *Forward*
　　b. Kingston, Ont., Dec. 6, 1949

Season	Club	GP	G	A	Pts
1972–73	Boston	72	10	4	14

Playoffs

	Club	GP	G	A	Pts
1972–73	Boston	5	0	1	1

O'DONOGHUE, Donald Francis (Don) *Forward*
b. Kingston, Ont., Aug. 27, 1949

Season	Club	GP	G	A	Pts
1969-70	Oakland	68	5	6	11
1970-71	California	43	11	9	20
1971-72	California	14	2	2	4
	Totals	125	18	17	35

Playoffs

Season	Club	GP	G	A	Pts
1969-70	Oakland	3	0	0	0

ODROWSKI, Gerald Bernard
Defenseman-Forward
b. Trout Creek, Ont., Oct. 4, 1938

Season	Club	GP	G	A	Pts
1960-61	Detroit R.W.	68	1	4	5
1961-62	Detroit R.W.	69	1	6	7
1962-63	Detroit R.W.	1	0	0	0
1967-68	Oakland	42	4	6	10
1968-69	Oakland	74	5	1	6
1971-72	St. Louis B.	55	1	2	3
	Totals	309	12	19	31

Playoffs

Season	Club	GP	G	A	Pts
1960-61	Detroit R.W.	10	0	0	0
1962-63	Detroit R.W.	2	0	0	0
1968-69	Oakland	7	0	1	1
1971-72	St. Louis B.	11	0	0	0
	Totals	30	0	1	1

O'FLAHERTY, Gerard Joseph *Forward*
b. Pittsburgh, Pa. Aug. 31, 1950

Season	Club	GP	G	A	Pts
1971-72	Toronto M.L.	2	0	0	0
1972-73	Vancouver	78	13	17	30
	Totals	80	13	17	30

O'FLAHERTY, John Benedict (Peanuts)
Forward
b. Toronto, Ont., Apr. 10, 1918

Season	Club	GP	G	A	Pts
1940-41	New York A.	--	4	0	4
1941-42	Brooklyn A.	11	1	1	2
	Totals	--	5	1	6

OGILVIE, Brian *Forward*
b. Stettler, Alta., Jan. 30, 1952

Season	Club	GP	G	A	Pts
1972-73	Chicago	12	1	2	3

O'GRADY, George

Season	Club	GP	G	A	Pts
1917-18	Montreal W.	4	0	0	0

OLESEVICH, Daniel *Goalie*
b. Port Colburne, Ont., Aug. 16, 1937

Season	Club	GP	GA	Sho	AVE
1961-62	New York R.	½	2	0	4.00

OLIVER, Harold (Harry) *Forward*
b. Selkirk, Man., 1899

Season	Club	GP	G	A	Pts
1926-27	Boston	--	18	6	24
1927-28	Boston	--	13	5	18
1928-29	Boston	--	17	6	23
1929-30	Boston	--	16	5	21
1930-31	Boston	--	16	14	30
1931-32	Boston	--	13	7	20
1932-33	Boston	--	11	7	18
1933-34	Boston	--	5	9	14
1934-35	New York A.	--	7	9	16
1935-36	New York A.	--	9	16	25
1936-37	New York A.	--	2	1	3
	Totals	--	127	85	212

Playoffs

Season	Club	GP	G	A	Pts
1926-27	Boston	--	4	2	6
1927-28	Boston	--	2	0	2
1928-29	Boston	--	1	1	2
1929-30	Boston	--	2	1	3
1930-31	Boston	--	0	0	0
1932-33	Boston	--	0	0	0
1935-36	New York A.	--	1	2	3
	Totals	--	10	6	16

OLIVER, Murray Clifford *Forward*
b. Hamilton, Ont., Nov. 14, 1937

Season	Club	GP	G	A	Pts
1957-58	Detroit R.W.	1	0	1	1
1959-60	Detroit R.W.	54	20	19	39
1960-61	Det RW-Bos	70	17	22	39
1961-62	Boston	70	17	29	46
1962-63	Boston	65	22	40	62
1963-64	Boston	70	24	44	68
1964-65	Boston	65	20	23	43
1965-66	Boston	70	18	42	60
1966-67	Boston	65	9	26	35
1967-68	Toronto M.L.	74	16	21	37
1968-69	Toronto M.L.	76	14	36	50
1969-70	Toronto M.L.	76	14	33	47
1970-71	Minnesota	61	9	23	32
1971-72	Minnesota	77	27	29	56
1972-73	Minnesota	75	11	31	42
	Totals	969	238	419	657

Playoffs

Season	Club	GP	G	A	Pts
1959-60	Detroit R.W.	6	1	0	1
1968-69	Toronto M.L.	4	1	2	3
1970-71	Minnesota	12	7	4	11

OLIVER (Continued)

Playoffs	Club	GP	G	A	Pts
1971–72	Minnesota	7	0	6	6
1972–73	Minnesota	6	0	4	4
	Totals	35	9	16	25

All-Star

1963	NHL All-Stars	1	0	1	1
1964	NHL All-Stars	1	1	1	2
1965	NHL All-Stars	1	0	2	2
1967	NHL All-Stars	1	0	0	0
1968	Toronto M.L.	1	1	0	1
	Totals	5	2	4	6

OLMSTEAD, Murray Bert *Forward*
b. Scepter, Sask., Sept. 4, 1926

Season	Club	GP	G	A	Pts
1948–49	Chicago	9	0	2	2
1949–50	Chicago	70	20	29	49
1950–51	Chgo–Mont C	54	18	23	41
1951–52	Montreal C.	69	7	28	35
1952–53	Montreal C.	69	17	28	45
1953–54	Montreal C.	70	15	37	52
1954–55	Montreal C.	70	10	48	58
1955–56	Montreal C.	70	14	56	70
1956–57	Montreal C.	64	15	33	48
1957–58	Montreal C.	57	9	28	37
1958–59	Toronto M.L.	70	10	31	41
1959–60	Toronto M.L.	53	15	21	36
1960–61	Toronto M.L.	67	18	34	52
1961–62	Toronto M.L.	56	13	23	36
	Totals	848	181	421	602

Playoffs

1950–51	Montreal C.	11	2	3	5
1951–52	Montreal C.	11	0	1	1
1952–53	Montreal C.	12	2	2	4
1953–54	Montreal C.	11	0	1	1
1954–55	Montreal C.	12	0	4	4
1955–56	Montreal C.	10	4	10	14
1956–57	Montreal C.	10	0	9	9
1957–58	Montreal C.	9	0	3	3
1958–59	Toronto M.L.	12	4	2	6
1959–60	Toronto M.L.	10	3	4	7
1960–61	Toronto M.L.	3	1	2	3
1961–62	Toronto M.L.	4	0	1	1
	Totals	115	16	42	58

All-Star

1953	Montreal C.	1	0	0	0
1956	Montreal C.	1	0	1	1
1957	Montreal C.	1	1	0	1
1959	NHL All-Stars	1	0	0	0
	Totals	4	1	1	2

OLSON, Dennis *Forward*
b. Kenora, Ont., Nov. 9, 1934

Season	Club	GP	G	A	Pts
1957–58	Detroit R.W.	4	0	0	0

O'NEILL, James Beaton (Peggy) *Forward*
b. Semans, Sask., Apr. 3, 1913

Season	Club	GP	G	A	Pts
1933–34	Boston	--	2	2	4
1934–35	Boston	--	2	11	13
1935–36	Boston	--	2	11	13
1936–37	Boston	--	0	2	2
1940–41	Montreal C.	--	0	3	3
1941–42	Montreal C.	--	0	1	1
	Totals	--	6	30	36

Playoffs

1934–35	Boston	--	0	0	0
1935–36	Boston	--	1	1	2
1940–41	Montreal C.	--	0	0	0
	Totals	--	1	1	2

O'NEILL, Thomas (Windy) *Forward*
b. Deseronto, Ont., Sept. 28, 1923

Season	Club	GP	G	A	Pts
1943–44	Toronto M.L.	33	8	7	15
1944–45	Toronto M.L.	33	2	5	7
	Totals	66	10	12	22

Playoffs

1943–44	Toronto M.L.	4	0	0	0

ORBAN, William *Forward*
b. Regina, Sask., Feb. 20, 1944

Season	Club	GP	G	A	Pts
1967–68	Chicago	39	3	2	5
1968–69	Chgo–Minn	66	5	11	16
1969–70	Minnesota	9	0	2	2
	Totals	114	8	15	23

Playoffs

1967–68	Chicago	3	0	0	0

O'REE, William Eldon *Forward*
b. Fredericton, N.B., Oct. 15, 1935

Season	Club	GP	G	A	Pts
1957–58	Boston	2	0	0	0
1960–61	Boston	43	4	10	14
	Totals	45	4	10	14

O'REILLY, Terry *Forward*
b. Niagara Falls, Ont., June 7, 1951

Season	Club	GP	G	A	Pts
1971–72	Boston	1	1	0	1
1972–73	Boston	72	5	22	27
	Totals	73	6	22	28

Playoffs

1972–73	Boston	5	0	0	0

ORLANDO, James *Defenseman*
b. Montreal, Que., Feb. 27, 1916

Season	Club	GP	G	A	Pts
1936–37	Detroit R.W.	--	0	1	1
1937–38	Detroit R.W.	--	0	0	0
1939–40	Detroit R.W.	--	1	3	4
1940–41	Detroit R.W.	--	1	10	11
1941–42	Detroit R.W.	--	1	7	8
1942–43	Detroit R.W.	40	3	4	7
	Totals	--	6	25	31

Playoffs

1939–40	Detroit R.W.	--	0	0	0
1940–41	Detroit R.W.	--	0	2	2
1941–42	Detroit R.W.	--	0	4	4
1942–43	Detroit R.W.	10	0	3	3
	Totals	--	0	9	9

ORR, Robert Gordon (Bobby) *Defenseman*
b. Parry Sound, Ont., Mar. 20, 1948

Season	Club	GP	G	A	Pts
1966–67	Boston	61	13	28	41
1967–68	Boston	46	11	20	31
1968–69	Boston	67	21	43	64
1969–70	Boston	76	33	87	120
1970–71	Boston	78	37	102	139
1971–72	Boston	76	37	80	117
1972–73	Boston	63	29	72	101
	Totals	467	181	432	613

Playoffs

1967–68	Boston	4	0	2	2
1968–69	Boston	10	1	7	8
1969–70	Boston	14	9	11	20
1970–71	Boston	7	5	7	12
1971–72	Boston	15	5	19	24
1972–73	Boston	5	1	1	2
	Totals	55	21	47	68

All-Star

1968	NHL All-Stars	1	0	1	1
1969	East All-Stars	1	0	0	0
1970	East All-Stars	1	0	0	0
1971	East All-Stars	1	0	0	0
1972	East All-Stars	1	0	1	1
1973	East All-Stars	1	0	0	0
	Totals	6	0	2	2

OSBURN, Randy *Forward*
b. Collingwood, Ont., Nov. 26, 1952

Season	Club	GP	G	A	Pts
1972–73	Toronto M.L.	26	0	2	2

O'SHEA, Daniel Patrick (Danny) *Forward*
b. Toronto, Ont., June 15, 1945

Season	Club	GP	G	A	Pts
1968–69	Minnesota	74	15	34	49
1969–70	Minnesota	75	10	24	34
1970–71	Minn-Chgo	77	18	19	37
1971–72	Chgo-StL B	68	9	12	21
1972–73	St. Louis B.	76	12	26	38
	Totals	370	64	115	179

Playoffs

1969–70	Minnesota	6	1	0	1
1970–71	Minnesota	18	2	5	7
1971–72	St. Louis B.	10	0	2	2
1972–73	St. Louis B.	5	0	0	0
	Totals	39	3	7	10

All-Star

1969	West All-Stars	1	0	1	1
1970	West All-Stars	1	0	0	0
	Totals	2	0	1	1

O'SHEA, Kevin William *Forward*
b. Toronto, Ont., May 28, 1947

Season	Club	GP	G	A	Pts
1970–71	Buffalo	41	4	4	8
1971–72	Buf-StL B	56	6	9	15
1972–73	St. Louis B.	36	3	5	8
	Totals	133	13	18	31

Playoffs

1971–72	St. Louis B.	11	2	1	3
1972–73	St. Louis B.	1	0	0	0
	Totals	12	2	1	3

OUELLETTE, Adeland (Eddie) *Forward*
b. Ottawa, Ont., Mar. 9, 1911

Season	Club	GP	G	A	Pts
1935–36	Chicago	--	3	2	5

Playoffs

1935–36	Chicago	--	0	0	0

OUELLETTE, Gerald Adrian *Forward*
b. Grand Falls, N.B., Nov. 1, 1938

Season	Club	GP	G	A	Pts
1960–61	Boston	34	5	4	9

OUIMET, Edward John (Ted) *Goalie*
b. Noranda, Que., July 6, 1947

Season	Club	GP	GA	Sho	AVE
1969–70	St. Louis B.	1	2	0	2.00

OWEN, George *Defenseman*
b. Hamilton, Ont.

Season	Club	GP	G	A	Pts
1928–29	Boston	--	5	4	9
1929–30	Boston	--	9	4	13
1930–31	Boston	--	12	13	25
1931–32	Boston	--	12	10	22
1932–33	Boston	--	6	2	8
	Totals	--	44	33	77
Playoffs					
1928–29	Boston	--	0	0	0
1929–30	Boston	--	0	2	2
1930–31	Boston	--	2	3	5
1932–33	Boston	--	0	0	0
	Totals	--	2	5	7

PAIEMENT, Rosaire *Forward*
b. Earlton, Ont., Aug. 12, 1945

Season	Club	GP	G	A	Pts
1967–68	Phildelphia F.	7	1	0	1
1968–69	Philadelphia F.	27	2	4	6
1969–70	Philadelphia F.	9	1	1	2
1970–71	Vancouver	78	34	28	62
1971–72	Vancouver	69	10	19	29
	Totals	190	48	52	100
Playoffs					
1967–68	Philadelphia F.	3	3	0	3

PAILLE, Marcel *Goalie*
b. Shawinigan Falls, Que., Dec. 8, 1932

Season	Club	GP	GA	Sho	AVE
1957–58	New York R.	33	102	1	3.10
1958–59	New York R.	1	4	0	4.00
1959–60	New York R.	17	67	1	3.94
1960–61	New York R.	4	16	0	4.00
1961–62	New York R.	10	28	0	2.80
1962–63	New York R.	3	10	0	3.33
1964–65	New York R.	37⅔	135	0	3.58
	Totals	105⅔	362	2	3.43

PALANGIO, Peter *Forward*
b. North Bay, Ont., Sept. 10, 1909

Season	Club	GP	G	A	Pts
1927–28	Detroit C.	--	3	0	3
1936–37	Chicago	--	8	9	17
1937–38	Chicago	--	2	1	3
	Totals	--	13	10	23
Playoffs					
1937–38	Chicago	--	0	0	0

PALAZZARI, Aldo *Forward*
b. Eveleth, Minn., July 25, 1918

Season	Club	GP	G	A	Pts
1943–44	Bos-NY R	35	8	3	11

PANAGABKO, Edwin Arnold *Forward*
b. Norquay, Sask., May 17, 1934

Season	Club	GP	G	A	Pts
1955–56	Boston	28	0	3	3
1956–57	Boston	1	0	0	0
	Totals	29	0	3	3

PAPIKE, Joseph *Forward*
b. Eveleth, Minn., Mar. 28, 1915

Season	Club	GP	G	A	Pts
1940–41	Chicago	--	2	2	4
1941–42	Chicago	--	1	0	1
1944–45	Chicago	2	0	1	1
	Totals	--	3	3	6
Playoffs					
1940–41	Chicago	--	0	2	2

PAPPIN, James Joseph (Jim) *Forward*
b. Copper Cliff, Ont., Sept. 10, 1939

Season	Club	GP	G	A	Pts
1963–64	Toronto M.L.	50	11	8	19
1964–65	Toronto M.L.	44	9	9	18
1965–66	Toronto M.L.	7	0	3	3
1966–67	Toronto M.L.	64	21	11	32
1967–68	Toronto M.L.	58	13	15	28
1968–69	Chicago	75	30	40	70
1969–70	Chicago	66	28	25	53
1970–71	Chicago	58	22	23	45
1971–72	Chicago	64	27	21	48
1972–73	Chicago	76	41	51	92
	Totals	562	201	206	407
Playoffs					
1963–64	Toronto M.L.	11	0	0	0
1966–67	Toronto M.L.	12	7	8	15
1969–70	Chicago	8	3	2	5
1970–71	Chicago	18	10	4	14
1971–72	Chicago	8	2	5	7
1972–73	Chicago	16	8	7	15
	Totals	73	30	26	56
All-Star					
1964	Toronto M.L.	1	1	0	1
1968	Toronto M.L.	1	0	0	0
1973	West All-Stars	1	0	0	0
	Totals	3	1	0	1

PARADISE, Robert H. (Bob) *Defenseman*
b. St. Paul, Minn., Apr. 22, 1944

Season	Club	GP	G	A	Pts
1971–72	Minnesota	6	0	0	0
1972–73	Atlanta	71	1	7	8
	Totals	77	1	7	8

PARENT, Bernard Marcel (Bernie) *Goalie*
b. Montreal, Que., Apr. 3, 1945

Season	Club	GP	GA	Sho	AVE
1965–66	Boston	34⅔	128	1	3.69
1966–67	Boston	17	62	0	3.65
1967–68	Philadelphia F.	37¾	93	4	2.46
1968–69	Philadelphia F.	56	151	1	2.70
1969–70	Philadelphia F.	61⅓	171	3	2.79
1970–71	Phila F–Tor ML	43⅔	119	3	2.71
1971–72	Toronto M.L.	45⅓	116	3	2.56
	Totals	295	840	15	2.84
Playoffs					
1967–68	Philadelphia F.	5	8	0	1.60
1968–69	Philadelphia F.	3	12	0	4.00
1970–71	Toronto M.L.	4	9	0	2.30
1971–72	Toronto M.L.	4	13	0	3.20
	Totals	16	42	0	2.49

All-Star		GP	Per	GA	AGP
1969	West All-Stars	1	1	0	0.00
1970	West All-Stars	1	1½	4	2.67
	Totals	2	2½	4	1.67

PARGETER, George William *Forward*
b. Calgary, Alta., Feb. 24, 1923

Season	Club	GP	G	A	Pts
1946–47	Montreal C.	4	0	0	0

PARISE, Jean Paul (JP) *Forward*
b. Smooth Rock Falls, Ont., Dec. 11, 1941

Season	Club	GP	G	A	Pts
1965–66	Boston	3	0	0	0
1966–67	Boston	18	2	2	4
1967–68	Tor ML–Minn	44	11	17	29
1968–69	Minnesota	76	22	27	49
1969–70	Minnesota	74	24	48	72
1970–71	Minnesota	73	11	23	34
1971–72	Minnesota	71	19	18	37
1972–73	Minnesota	78	27	48	75
	Totals	437	116	183	299
Playoffs					
1967–68	Minnesota	14	2	5	7
1969–70	Minnesota	6	3	2	5
1970–71	Minnesota	12	3	3	6
1971–72	Minnesota	7	3	3	6
1972–73	Minnesota	6	0	0	0
	Totals	45	11	13	24

All-Star		GP	G	A	Pts
1970	West All-Stars	1	0	0	0
1973	West All-Stars	1	0	0	0
	Totals	2	0	0	0

PARIZEAU, Michel Gerard (Mike) *Forward*
b. Montreal, Que., Apr. 9, 1948

Season	Club	GP	G	A	Pts
1971–72	StL B–Phila F	58	3	14	17

PARK, Douglas Bradford (Brad) *Defenseman*
b. Toronto, Ont., July 6, 1948

Season	Club	GP	G	A	Pts
1968–69	New York R.	54	3	23	26
1969–70	New York R.	60	11	26	37
1970–71	New York R.	68	7	37	44
1971–72	New York R.	75	24	49	73
1972–73	New York R.	52	10	43	53
	Totals	309	55	178	233
Playoffs					
1968–69	New York R.	4	0	2	2
1969–70	New York R.	5	1	2	3
1970–71	New York R.	13	0	4	4
1971–72	New York R.	16	4	7	11
1972–73	New York R.	10	2	5	7
	Totals	48	7	20	27
All-Star					
1970	East All-Stars	1	0	0	0
1971	East All-Stars	1	0	0	0
1972	East All-Stars	1	0	1	1
1973	East All-Stars	1	0	1	1
	Totals	4	0	2	2

PARKES, Ernest *Forward*

Season	Club	GP	G	A	Pts
1924–25	Montreal M.	17	0	0	0
Playoffs					
1922–23	Vancouver (PCHL)	--	0	1	1

PARSON, George *Forward*
b. Toronto, Ont., June 28, 1914

Season	Club	GP	G	A	Pts
1937–38	Toronto M.L.	--	5	6	11
1938–39	Toronto M.L.	--	7	7	14
	Totals	--	12	13	25
Playoffs					
1937–38	Toronto M.L.	--	3	2	5
1938–39	Toronto M.L.	--	0	0	0
	Totals	--	3	2	5

PATRICK, Craig *Forward*
b. Detroit, Mich., May 20, 1946

Season	Club	GP	G	A	Pts
1971–72	California	59	8	3	11
1972–73	California	71	20	22	42
	Totals	130	28	25	53

PATRICK, Frederick Murray (Muzz)
Defenseman

b. Victoria, B.C., June 28, 1916

Season	Club	GP	G	A	Pts
1937–38	New York R.	1	0	2	2
1938–39	New York R.	48	1	10	11
1939–40	New York R.	46	2	4	6
1940–41	New York R.	47	2	8	10
1945–46	New York R.	24	0	2	2
	Totals	166	5	26	31
Playoffs					
1937–38	New York R.	3	0	0	0
1938–39	New York R.	7	1	0	1
1939–40	New York R.	12	3	0	3
1940–41	New York R.	3	0	0	0
	Totals	25	4	0	4

PATRICK, Lester *Defenseman-Goalie*

b. Drummondville, Que., Dec. 30, 1883

Season	Club	GP	G	A	Pts
1926–27	New York R.	--	0	0	0
Playoffs					
1926–27	New York R.	--	0	0	0

Playoffs	Goalie Record	GP	GA	Sho	AVE
1927–28	New York R.	1	1	0	1.00

PATRICK, Lynn *Forward*

b. Victoria, B.C., Feb. 3, 1912

Season	Club	GP	G	A	Pts
1934–35	New York R.	48	9	13	22
1935–36	New York R.	48	11	14	25
1936–37	New York R.	45	8	16	24
1937–38	New York R.	48	15	19	34
1938–39	New York R.	35	8	21	29
1939–40	New York R.	48	12	16	28
1940–41	New York R.	48	20	24	44
1941–42	New York R.	47	32	22	54
1942–43	New York R.	50	22	39	61
1945–46	New York R.	38	8	6	14
	Totals	455	145	190	335
Playoffs					
1934–35	New York R.	4	2	2	4
1936–37	New York R.	9	3	0	3
1937–38	New York R.	3	0	1	1
1938–39	New York R.	7	1	1	2
1939–40	New York R.	12	2	2	4
1940–41	New York R.	3	1	0	1
1941–42	New York R.	6	1	0	1
	Totals	44	10	6	16

PATTERSON, George *Forward*
b. Kingston, Ont., May 22, 1906

Season	Club	GP	G	A	Pts
1926–27	Toronto M.L.	--	4	2	6
1927–28	Tor ML–Mont C	--	1	1	2
1928–29	Montreal C.	--	4	5	9
1929–30	New York A.	--	13	4	17
1930–31	New York A.	--	8	6	14
1931–32	New York A.	--	6	0	6
1932–33	New York A.	--	12	7	19
1933–34	NY A–Bos	--	3	1	4
1934–35	Det RW–StL E	--	0	1	1
	Totals	--	51	27	78
Playoffs					
1927–28	Montreal C.	--	0	0	0
1928–29	Montreal C.	--	0	0	0
	Totals	--	0	0	0

PAUL, Arthur Stuart (Butch) *Forward*
b. Rocky Mountain House, Alta., Sept. 11, 1943

Season	Club	GP	G	A	Pts
1964–65	Detroit R.W.	3	0	0	0

PAULHUS, Roland *Defenseman*

Season	Club	GP	G	A	Pts
1925–26	Montreal C.	33	0	0	0

PAVELICH, Martin Nicholas *Forward*
b. Sault Ste. Marie, Ont., Nov. 6, 1927

Season	Club	GP	G	A	Pts
1947–48	Detroit R.W.	41	4	8	12
1948–49	Detroit R.W.	60	10	16	26
1949–50	Detroit R.W.	65	8	15	23
1950–51	Detroit R.W.	67	9	20	29
1951–52	Detroit R.W.	68	17	19	36
1952–53	Detroit R.W.	64	13	20	33
1953–54	Detroit R.W.	65	9	20	29
1954–55	Detroit R.W.	70	15	15	30
1955–56	Detroit R.W.	70	5	13	18
1956–57	Detroit R.W.	64	3	13	16
	Totals	634	93	159	252
Playoffs					
1947–48	Detroit R.W.	10	2	2	4
1948–49	Detroit R.W.	9	0	1	1
1949–50	Detroit R.W.	14	4	2	6
1950–51	Detroit R.W.	6	0	1	1
1951–52	Detroit R.W.	8	2	2	4
1952–53	Detroit R.W.	6	2	1	3
1953–54	Detroit R.W.	12	2	2	4
1954–55	Detroit R.W.	11	1	3	4
1955–56	Detroit R.W.	10	0	1	1
1956–57	Detroit R.W.	5	0	0	0
	Totals	91	13	15	28

PAVELICH (Continued)

All-Star	Club	GP	G	A	Pts
1950	Detroit R.W.	1	1	1	2
1952	NHL 1st All-Stars	1	1	0	1
1954	Detroit R.W.	1	0	0	0
1955	Detroit R.W.	1	0	0	0
	Totals	4	2	1	3

PAYER

Season	Club	GP	G	A	Pts
1917-18	Montreal C.	1	0	0	0

PEARSON, George Alexander Melvin (Mel)
Forward
b. Flin Flon, Man., Apr. 29, 1938

Season	Club	GP	G	A	Pts
1959-60	New York R.	23	1	5	6
1961-62	New York R.	3	0	0	0
1962-63	New York R.	5	1	0	1
1964-65	New York R.	5	0	0	0
1967-68	Pittsburgh Pe.	2	0	1	1
	Totals	38	2	6	8

PIERSON, John Frederick *Forward*
b. Winnipeg, Man., July 21, 1925

Season	Club	GP	G	A	Pts
1946-47	Boston	5	0	0	0
1947-48	Boston	15	4	2	6
1948-49	Boston	59	22	21	43
1949-50	Boston	57	27	25	52
1950-51	Boston	70	19	19	38
1951-52	Boston	68	20	30	50
1952-53	Boston	49	14	15	29
1953-54	Boston	68	21	19	40
1955-56	Boston	33	11	14	25
1956-57	Boston	68	13	26	39
1957-58	Boston	53	2	2	4
	Totals	545	153	173	326
Playoffs					
1947-48	Boston	4	3	2	5
1948-49	Boston	5	3	1	4
1950-51	Boston	2	1	1	2
1951-52	Boston	7	0	2	2
1952-53	Boston	11	3	6	9
1953-54	Boston	4	0	0	0
1956-57	Boston	10	0	3	3
1957-58	Boston	5	0	1	1
	Totals	48	10	16	26
All-Star					
1950	NHL All-Stars	1	0	1	1
1951	NHL 1st All-Stars	1	1	0	1
	Totals	2	1	1	2

PELLETIER, Joseph Georges Roger
Defenseman
b. Montreal, Que., June 22, 1945

Season	Club	GP	G	A	Pts
1967-68	Philadelphia F.	1	0	0	0

PELLETIER, Marcel *Goalie*
b. Drummondville, Que., Dec. 6, 1927

Season	Club	GP	GA	Sho	AVE
1950-51	Chicago	6	29	0	4.83
1962-63	New York R.	2	4	0	2.00
	Totals	8	33	0	4.13

PELYK, Michael *Defenseman*
b. Toronto, Ont., Sept. 29, 1947

Season	Club	GP	G	A	Pts
1967-68	Toronto M.L.	24	0	3	3
1968-69	Toronto M.L.	65	3	9	12
1969-70	Toronto M.L.	36	1	3	4
1970-71	Toronto M.L.	73	5	21	26
1971-72	Toronto M.L.	46	1	4	5
1972-73	Toronto M.L.	72	3	16	19
	Totals	316	13	56	69
Playoffs					
1968-69	Toronto M.L.	4	0	0	0
1970-71	Toronto M.L.	6	0	0	0
1971-72	Toronto M.L.	5	0	0	0
	Totals	15	0	0	0

PENNINGTON, Clifford *Forward*
b. Winnipeg, Man., Apr. 18, 1940

Season	Club	GP	G	A	Pts
1960-61	Montreal C.	4	1	0	1
1961-62	Boston	70	9	32	41
1962-63	Boston	27	7	10	17
	Totals	101	17	42	59

PERREAULT, Fernand *Forward*
b. Chambly Basin, Que., Mar. 31, 1927

Season	Club	GP	G	A	Pts
1947-48	New York R.	2	0	0	0
1949-50	New York R.	1	0	0	0
	Totals	3	0	0	0

PERREAULT, Gilbert *Forward*
b. Victoriaville, Que., Nov. 13, 1950

Season	Club	GP	G	A	Pts
1970-71	Buffalo	78	38	34	72
1971-72	Buffalo	76	26	48	74
1972-73	Buffalo	78	28	60	88
	Totals	232	92	142	234

PERREAULT (Continued)

Playoffs	Club	GP	G	A	Pts
1972–73	Buffalo	6	3	7	10
All-Star					
1971	East All-Stars	1	0	0	0
1972	East All-Stars	1	0	0	0
	Totals	2	0	0	0

PERREAULT, Robert (Miche) *Goalie*
b. Three Rivers, Que., Jan. 28, 1931

Season	Club	GP	GA	Sho	AVE
1955–56	Montreal C.	6	12	1	2.00
1958–59	Detroit R.W.	3	9	1	3.00
1962–63	Boston	21⅓	85	1	3.98
	Totals	30⅓	106	3	3.49

PERRY, Brian *Forward*
b. Aldershot, England, Apr. 6, 1944

Season	Club	GP	G	A	Pts
1968–69	Oakland	61	10	21	31
1969–70	Oakland	34	6	8	14
1970–71	Buffalo	1	0	0	0
	Totals	96	16	29	45
Playoffs					
1968–69	Oakland	6	1	1	2
1969–70	Oakland	2	0	0	0
	Totals	8	1	1	2

PETERS, Frank J. *Defenseman*
b. Rouses Point, N.Y., June 5, 1905

Season	Club	GP	G	A	Pts
1930–31	New York R.	44	0	0	0
Playoffs					
1930–31	New York R.	4	0	0	0

PETERS, Garry Lorne *Forward*
b. Regina, Sask., Oct. 9, 1942

Season	Club	GP	G	A	Pts
1964–65	Montreal C.	13	0	2	2
1965–66	New York R.	63	7	3	10
1966–67	Montreal C.	4	0	1	1
1967–68	Philadelphia F.	31	7	5	12
1968–69	Philadelphia F.	66	8	6	14
1969–70	Philadelphia F.	59	6	10	16
1970–71	Philadelphia F.	73	6	7	13
1971–72	Boston	2	0	0	0
	Totals	311	34	34	68
Playoffs					
1968–69	Philadelphia F.	4	1	1	2
1970–71	Philadelphia F.	4	1	1	2
1971–72	Boston	1	0	0	0
	Totals	9	2	2	4

PETERS, James Meldrum *Forward*
b. Verdun, Que., Oct. 2, 1922

Season	Club	GP	G	A	Pts
1945–46	Montreal C.	47	11	19	30
1946–47	Montreal C.	60	11	13	24
1947–48	Mont C–Bos	59	13	18	31
1948–49	Boston	60	16	15	31
1949–50	Detroit R.W.	70	14	16	30
1950–51	Detroit R.W.	68	17	21	38
1951–52	Chicago	70	15	21	36
1952–53	Chicago	69	22	19	41
1953–54	Chgo–Det RW	71	6	8	14
	Totals	574	125	150	275
Playoffs					
1945–46	Montreal C.	9	3	1	4
1946–47	Montreal C.	11	1	2	3
1947–48	Boston	5	1	2	3
1948–49	Boston	4	0	1	1
1949–50	Detroit R.W.	8	0	2	2
1950–51	Detroit R.W.	6	0	0	0
1952–53	Chicago	7	0	1	1
1953–54	Detroit R.W.	10	0	0	0
	Totals	60	5	9	14
All-Star					
1950	Detroit R.W.	1	1	1	2

PETERS, James Stephen (Jim) *Forward*
b. Montreal, Que., June 20, 1944

Season	Club	GP	G	A	Pts
1964–65	Detroit R.W.	1	0	0	0
1965–66	Detroit R.W.	6	1	1	2
1966–67	Detroit R.W.	2	0	0	0
1967–68	Detroit R.W.	45	5	6	11
1968–69	Los Angeles	76	10	15	25
1969–70	Los Angeles	74	15	9	24
1972–73	Los Angeles	77	4	5	9
	Totals	281	35	36	71
Playoffs					
1968–69	Los Angeles	11	0	2	2

PETTINGER, Eric (Cowboy) *Forward*
b. Regina, Sask.

Season	Club	GP	G	A	Pts
1928–29	Bos–Tor ML	--	3	3	6
1929–30	Toronto M.L.	--	4	9	13
1930–31	Ottawa	--	0	0	0
	Totals	--	7	12	19
Playoffs					
1928–29	Toronto M.L.	--	1	0	1

579

PETTINGER, Gordon Robinson *Forward*
b. Regina, Sask., Nov. 17, 1911

Season	Club	GP	G	A	Pts
1932–33	New York R.	35	1	2	3
1933–34	Detroit R.W.	--	3	14	17
1934–35	Detroit R.W.	--	2	3	5
1935–36	Detroit R.W.	--	8	7	15
1936–37	Detroit R.W.	--	7	15	22
1937–38	Det RW-Bos	--	8	13	21
1938–39	Boston	--	11	14	25
1939–40	Boston	--	2	6	8
	Totals	--	42	74	116
Playoffs					
1932–33	New York R.	8	0	0	0
1933–34	Detroit R.W.	9	1	0	1
1935–36	Detroit R.W.	7	2	2	4
1936–37	Detroit R.W.	10	0	2	2
1937–38	Boston	3	0	0	0
1938–39	Boston	12	1	1	2
	Totals	49	4	5	9

PHILLIPS, Charles *Defenseman*
b. Toronto, Ont., May 19, 1917

Season	Club	GP	G	A	Pts
1942–43	Montreal C.	17	0	0	0

PHILLIPS, Merlyn J. (Bill) *Forward*
b. Toronto, Ont.

Season	Club	GP	G	A	Pts
1925–26	Montreal M.	12	3	1	4
1926–27	Montreal M.	--	15	1	16
1927–28	Montreal M.	--	7	5	12
1928–29	Montreal M.	--	6	5	11
1929–30	Montreal M.	--	13	10	23
1930–31	Montreal M.	--	6	1	7
1931–32	Montreal M.	--	1	1	2
1932–33	New York A.	--	1	7	8
	Totals	--	52	31	83
Playoffs					
1925–26	Montreal M.	--	1	1	2
1926–27	Montreal M.	--	0	0	0
1927–28	Montreal M.	--	2	1	3
1929–30	Montreal M.	--	0	0	0
1930–31	Montreal M.	--	0	0	0
1931–32	Montreal M.	--	0	0	0
	Totals	--	3	2	5

PHILLIPS, W. J. (Batt) *Forward*
b. Carleton Place, Ont.

Season	Club	GP	G	A	Pts
1929–30	Montreal M.	--	1	1	2
Playoffs					
1929–30	Montreal M.	--	0	0	0

PICARD, Jean Noel Yves (Noel) *Defenseman*
b. Montreal, Que., Dec. 25, 1938

Season	Club	GP	G	A	Pts
1964–65	Montreal C.	16	0	7	7
1967–68	St. Louis B.	66	1	10	11
1968–69	St. Louis B.	67	5	19	24
1969–70	St. Louis B.	39	1	4	5
1970–71	St. Louis B.	75	3	8	11
1971–72	St. Louis B.	15	1	5	6
1972–73	StL B-Atl	57	1	10	11
	Totals	335	12	63	75
Playoffs					
1964–65	Montreal C.	3	0	1	1
1967–68	St. Louis B.	13	0	3	3
1968–69	St. Louis B.	12	1	4	5
1969–70	St. Louis B.	16	0	2	2
1970–71	St. Louis B.	6	1	1	2
	Totals	50	2	11	13
All-Star					
1969	West All-Stars	1	0	2	2

PICARD, Roger *Forward*
b. Montreal, Que., Jan. 13, 1933

Season	Club	GP	G	A	Pts
1967–68	St. Louis B.	15	2	2	4

PICKETTS, Fred Harold (Hal) *Forward*
b. Asquith, Sask., Apr. 22, 1909

Season	Club	GP	G	A	Pts
1933–34	New York A.	--	3	1	4

PIDHIRNEY, Harry *Forward*
b. Toronto, Ont., Mar. 5, 1928

Season	Club	GP	G	A	Pts
1957–58	Boston	2	0	0	0

PIKE, Alfred *Forward*
b. Winnipeg, Man., Sept. 15, 1917

Season	Club	GP	G	A	Pts
1939–40	New York R.	47	8	9	17
1940–41	New York R.	48	6	13	19
1941–42	New York R.	34	8	19	27
1942–43	New York R.	41	6	16	22
1945–46	New York R.	33	7	9	16
1946–47	New York R.	31	7	11	18
	Totals	234	42	77	119
Playoffs					
1939–40	New York R.	12	3	1	4
1940–41	New York R.	3	0	1	1
1941–42	New York R.	6	1	0	1
	Totals	21	4	2	6

PILOTE, Pierre Paul *Defenseman*
b. Kenogami, Que., Dec. 11, 1931

Season	Club	GP	G	A	Pts
1955-56	Chicago	20	3	5	8
1956-57	Chicago	70	3	14	17
1957-58	Chicago	70	6	24	30
1958-59	Chicago	70	7	30	37
1959-60	Chicago	70	7	38	45
1960-61	Chicago	70	6	29	35
1961-62	Chicago	59	7	35	42
1962-63	Chicago	59	8	18	26
1963-64	Chicago	70	7	46	53
1964-65	Chicago	68	14	45	59
1965-66	Chicago	51	2	34	36
1966-67	Chicago	70	6	46	52
1967-68	Chicago	74	1	36	37
1968-69	Toronto M.L.	69	3	18	21
	Totals	**890**	**80**	**418**	**498**
Playoffs					
1958-59	Chicago	6	0	2	2
1959-60	Chicago	4	0	1	1
1960-61	Chicago	12	3	12	15
1961-62	Chicago	12	0	7	7
1962-63	Chicago	6	0	8	8
1963-64	Chicago	7	2	6	8
1964-65	Chicago	12	0	7	7
1965-66	Chicago	6	0	2	2
1966-67	Chicago	6	2	4	6
1967-68	Chicago	11	1	3	4
1968-69	Toronto M.L.	4	0	1	1
	Totals	**86**	**8**	**53**	**61**
All-Star					
1960	NHL All-Stars	1	0	1	1
1961	Chicago	1	0	1	1
1962	NHL All-Stars	1	0	1	1
1963	NHL All-Stars	1	0	0	0
1964	NHL All-Stars	1	0	0	0
1965	NHL All-Stars	1	0	0	0
1967	NHL All-Stars	1	0	0	0
1968	NHL All-Stars	1	0	0	0
	Totals	**8**	**0**	**3**	**3**

PINDER, Allen Gerald (Gerry) *Forward*
b. Saskatoon, Sask., Sept. 15, 1948

Season	Club	GP	G	A	Pts
1969-70	Chicago	75	19	20	39
1970-71	Chicago	74	13	18	31
1971-72	California	74	23	31	54
	Totals	**223**	**55**	**69**	**124**
Playoffs					
1969-70	Chicago	8	0	4	4
1970-71	Chicago	9	0	0	0
	Totals	**17**	**0**	**4**	**4**

PITRE, Didler *Forward*
b. Sault Ste. Marie, Ont., 1884

Season	Club	GP	G	A	Pts
1917-18	Montreal C.	19	17	0	17
1918-19	Montreal C.	17	14	4	18
1919-20	Montreal C.	22	15	7	22
1920-21	Montreal C.	23	15	1	16
1921-22	Montreal C.	23	2	3	5
1922-23	Montreal C.	23	1	2	3
	Totals	**127**	**64**	**17**	**81**
Playoffs					
1917-18	Montreal C.	--	0	0	0
1918-19	Montreal C.	--	2	2	4
	Totals	**--**	**2**	**2**	**4**

PLAGER, Barclay Graham *Defenseman*
b. Kirkland Lake, Ont., Mar. 25, 1941

Season	Club	GP	G	A	Pts
1967-68	St. Louis B.	49	5	15	20
1968-69	St. Louis B.	61	4	26	30
1969-70	St. Louis B.	75	6	26	32
1970-71	St. Louis B.	69	4	20	24
1971-72	St. Louis B.	78	7	22	29
1972-73	St. Louis B.	68	8	25	33
	Totals	**400**	**34**	**134**	**168**
Playoffs					
1967-68	St. Louis B.	18	2	5	7
1968-69	St. Louis B.	12	0	4	4
1969-70	St. Louis B.	13	0	2	2
1970-71	St. Louis B.	6	0	3	3
1971-72	St. Louis B.	11	1	4	5
1972-73	St. Louis B.	5	0	1	1
	Totals	**65**	**3**	**19**	**22**
All-Star					
1970	West All-Stars	1	0	0	0
1971	West All-Stars	1	0	0	0
1972	West All-Stars	1	0	0	0
	Totals	**3**	**0**	**0**	**0**

PLAGER, Robert Bryan (Bob) *Defenseman*
b. Kirkland Lake, Ont., Mar. 11, 1943

Season	Club	GP	G	A	Pts
1964-65	New York R.	10	0	0	0
1965-66	New York R.	18	0	5	5
1966-67	New York R.	1	0	0	0
1967-68	St. Louis B.	53	2	5	7
1968-69	St. Louis B.	32	0	7	7
1969-70	St. Louis B.	64	3	11	14
1970-71	St. Louis B.	70	1	19	20
1971-72	St. Louis B.	50	4	7	11
1972-73	St. Louis B.	77	2	31	33
	Totals	**375**	**12**	**85**	**97**

PLAGER (Continued)

Playoffs	Club	GP	G	A	Pts
1967–68	St. Louis B.	18	1	2	3
1968–69	St. Louis B.	9	0	4	4
1969–70	St. Louis B.	16	0	3	3
1970–71	St. Louis B.	6	0	2	2
1971–72	St. Louis B.	11	1	4	5
1972–73	St. Louis B.	5	0	2	2
Totals		65	2	17	19

PLAGER, William Ronald (Bill) *Defenseman*
b. Kirkland Lake, Ont., July 6, 1945

Season	Club	GP	G	A	Pts
1967–68	Minnesota	32	0	2	2
1968–69	St. Louis B.	2	0	0	0
1969–70	St. Louis B.	24	1	4	5
1970–71	St. Louis B.	36	0	3	3
1971–72	St. Louis B.	65	1	11	12
1972–73	Atlanta	76	2	11	13
Totals		235	4	31	35
Playoffs					
1967–68	Minnesota	12	0	2	2
1968–69	St. Louis B.	4	0	0	0
1969–70	St. Louis B.	3	0	0	0
1970–71	St. Louis B.	1	0	0	0
1971–72	St. Louis B.	11	0	0	0
Totals		31	0	2	2

PLAMONDON, Gerard Roger *Forward*
b. Sherbrooke, Que., Jan. 5, 1925

Season	Club	GP	G	A	Pts
1945–46	Montreal C.	6	0	2	2
1947–48	Montreal C.	3	1	1	2
1948–49	Montreal C.	27	5	5	10
1949–50	Montreal C.	37	1	5	6
1950–51	Montreal C.	1	0	0	0
Totals		74	7	13	20
Playoffs					
1945–46	Montreal C.	1	0	0	0
1948–49	Montreal C.	7	5	1	6
1949–50	Montreal C.	3	0	1	1
Totals		11	5	2	7

PLANTE, Jacques (Jake the Snake) *Goalie*
b. Shawinigan Falls, Que., Jan. 17, 1929

Season	Club	GP	GA	Sho	AVE
1952–53	Montreal C.	3	4	0	1.33
1953–54	Montreal C.	17	27	5	1.59
1954–55	Montreal C.	52	110	5	2.11
1955–56	Montreal C.	64	119	7	1.86
1956–57	Montreal C.	61	123	9	2.02
1957–58	Montreal C.	56⅓	119	9	2.11
1958–59	Montreal C.	67	144	9	2.15

PLANTE (Continued)

Season	Club	GP	GA	Sho	AVE
1959–60	Montreal C.	69	175	3	2.54
1960–61	Montreal C.	40	112	2	2.80
1961–62	Montreal C.	70	166	4	2.37
1962–63	Montreal C.	55⅓	138	5	2.49
1963–64	New York R.	65	220	3	3.38
1964–65	New York R.	32⅓	109	2	3.37
1968–69	St. Louis B.	35⅔	70	5	1.96
1969–70	St. Louis B.	30⅔	67	5	2.18
1970–71	Toronto M.L.	38⅔	73	4	1.88
1971–72	Toronto M.L.	32⅔	86	2	2.62
1972–73	Tor ML–Bos	36⅔	103	3	3.08
Totals		825⅓	1965	82	2.38
Playoffs					
1952–53	Montreal C.	4	7	1	1.75
1953–54	Montreal C.	8	15	2	1.87
1954–55	Montreal C.	12	30	0	2.50
1955–56	Montreal C.	10	18	2	1.80
1956–57	Montreal C.	10	18	1	1.80
1957–58	Montreal C.	10	20	1	2.00
1958–59	Montreal C.	11	28	0	2.54
1959–60	Montreal C.	8	11	3	1.37
1960–61	Montreal C.	6	16	0	2.67
1961–62	Montreal C.	6	19	0	3.17
1962–63	Montreal C.	5	14	0	2.80
1968–69	St. Louis B.	9⅚	14	3	1.43
1969–70	St. Louis B.	5⅖	8	1	1.48
1970–71	Toronto M.L.	2	7	0	3.14
1971–72	Toronto M.L.	1	5	0	5.00
1972–73	Boston	2	10	0	5.00
Totals		110¼	240	14	2.14

All-Star		GP	Per	GA	AGP
1956	Montreal C.	1	3	1	0.33
1957	Montreal C.	1	3	5	1.67
1958	Montreal C.	1	3	3	1.00
1959	Montreal C.	1	3	1	0.33
1960	Montreal C.	1	3	2	0.67
1962	NHL All-Stars	1	1	4	4.00
1969	West All-Stars	1	1	2	2.00
1970	West All-Stars	1	1½	0	0.00
Totals		8	8½	18	0.97

PLANTE, Pierre Renald *Forward*
b. Valleyfield, Que., May 14, 1951

Season	Club	GP	G	A	Pts
1971–72	Philadelphia F.	24	1	0	1
1972–73	Phila F–StL B	51	12	16	28
Totals		75	13	16	29
Playoffs					
1972–73	St. Louis B.	5	2	0	2

582

PLASSE, Michel *Goalie*
b. Montreal, Que., June 1, 1948

Season	Club	GP	GA	Sho	AVE
1970-71	St. Louis B.	1	3	0	3.00
1972-73	Montreal C.	15⅔	40	0	2.58
	Totals	16⅔	43	0	2.70

PLAXTON, Hugh *Forward*
b. Barrie, Ont., May 16, 1904

Season	Club	GP	G	A	Pts
1932-33	Montreal M.	--	1	2	3

PLEAU, Lawrence Wilson *Forward*
b. Lynn, Mass., June 29, 1947

Season	Club	GP	G	A	Pts
1969-70	Montreal C.	20	1	0	1
1970-71	Montreal C.	19	1	5	6
1971-72	Montreal C.	55	7	10	17
	Totals	94	9	15	24
Playoffs					
1971-72	Montreal C.	4	0	0	0

PODOLSKY, Nelson *Forward*
b. Winnipeg, Man., Dec. 19, 1925

Season	Club	GP	G	A	Pts
1948-49	Detroit R.W.	1	0	0	0
Playoffs					
1948-49	Detroit R.W.	7	0	0	0

POETA, Anthony Joseph *Forward*
b. North Bay, Ont., Mar. 4, 1933

Season	Club	GP	G	A	Pts
1951-52	Chicago	1	0	0	0

POILE, Donald B. *Forward*
b. Fort William, Ont., June 1, 1932

Season	Club	GP	G	A	Pts
1954-55	Detroit R.W.	4	0	0	0
1957-58	Detroit R.W.	62	7	9	16
	Totals	66	7	9	16
Playoffs					
1957-58	Detroit R.W.	4	0	0	0

POILE, Norman Robert (Bud) *Forward*
b. Fort William, Ont., Feb. 10, 1924

Season	Club	GP	G	A	Pts
1942-43	Toronto M.L.	48	16	19	35
1943-44	Toronto M.L.	11	6	8	14
1945-46	Toronto M.L.	9	1	8	9
1946-47	Toronto M.L.	59	19	17	36
1947-48	Tor ML-Chgo	58	25	29	54
1948-49	Chgo-Det RW	60	21	21	42
1949-50	NY R-Bos	66	19	20	39
	Totals	311	107	122	229

POILE *(Continued)*

Playoffs	Club	GP	G	A	Pts
1942-43	Toronto M.L.	6	2	4	6
1946-47	Toronto M.L.	7	2	0	2
1948-49	Detroit R.W.	10	0	1	1
	Totals	23	4	5	9
All-Star					
1947	Toronto M.L.	1	0	0	0
1948	NHL All-Stars	1	0	0	0
	Totals	2	0	0	0

POIRIER, Gordon *Forward*
b. Maple Creek, Sask., Oct. 27, 1913

Season	Club	GP	G	A	Pts
1939-40	Montreal C.	--	0	1	1

POLANIC, Thomas Joseph *Defenseman*
b. Toronto, Ont., Apr. 2, 1943

Season	Club	GP	G	A	Pts
1969-70	Minnesota	16	0	2	2
1970-71	Minnesota	3	0	0	0
	Totals	19	0	2	2
Playoffs					
1969-70	Minnesota	5	1	1	2

POLICH, John *Forward*
b. Hibbling, Minn., July 8, 1916

Season	Club	GP	G	A	Pts
1939-40	New York R.	1	0	0	0
1940-41	New York R.	2	0	1	1
	Totals	3	0	1	1

POLIS, Gregory Linn (Greg) *Forward*
b. Westlock, Alta., Aug. 8, 1950

Season	Club	GP	G	A	Pts
1970-71	Pittsburgh Pe.	61	18	15	33
1971-72	Pittsburgh Pe.	76	30	19	49
1972-73	Pittsburgh Pe.	78	26	23	49
	Totals	215	74	57	131
Playoffs					
1971-72	Pittsburgh Pe.	4	0	2	2
All-Star					
1971	West All-Stars	1	0	0	0
1972	West All-Stars	1	0	0	0
1973	West All-Stars	1	2	0	0
	Totals	3	2	0	0

POLIZIANI, Daniel *Forward*
b. Sydney, N.S., Jan. 8, 1935

Season	Club	GP	G	A	Pts
1958-59	Boston	1	0	0	0
Playoffs					
1958-59	Boston	3	0	0	0

POPEIN, Lawrence Thomas (Larry) *Forward*
b. Yorkton, Sask., Aug. 11, 1930

Season	Club	GP	G	A	Pts
1954-55	New York R.	70	11	17	28
1955-56	New York R.	64	14	25	39
1956-57	New York R.	67	11	19	30
1957-58	New York R.	70	12	22	34
1958-59	New York R.	61	13	21	34
1959-60	New York R.	66	14	22	36
1960-61	New York R.	4	0	1	1
1967-68	Oakland	47	5	14	19
	Totals	449	80	141	221

Playoffs

1955-56	New York R.	5	0	1	1
1956-57	New York R.	5	0	3	3
1957-58	New York R.	6	1	0	1
	Totals	16	1	4	5

POPIEL, Poul Peter *Defenseman*
b. Sollested, Denmark, Feb. 28, 1943

Season	Club	GP	G	A	Pts
1965-66	Boston	3	0	1	1
1967-68	Los Angeles	1	0	0	0
1968-69	Detroit R.W.	62	2	13	15
1969-70	Detroit R.W.	32	0	4	4
1970-71	Vancouver	78	10	22	32
1971-72	Vancouver	38	1	1	2
	Totals	214	13	41	54

Playoffs

1967-68	Los Angeles	3	1	0	1
1969-70	Detroit R.W.	1	0	0	0
	Totals	4	1	0	1

PORTLAND, John Frederick *Defenseman*
b. Collingwood, Ont., July 30, 1912

Season	Club	GP	G	A	Pts
1933-34	Montreal C.	--	0	2	2
1934-35	Mont C-Bos	--	1	1	2
1936-37	Boston	--	2	4	6
1937-38	Boston	--	0	5	5
1938-39	Boston	--	4	5	9
1939-40	Bos-Chgo	--	1	9	10
1940-41	Chgo-Mont C	--	2	7	9
1941-42	Montreal C.	46	2	9	11
1942-43	Montreal C.	49	3	14	17
	Totals	--	15	56	71

Playoffs

1933-34	Montreal C.	--	0	0	0
1936-37	Boston	3	0	0	0
1937-38	Boston	3	0	0	0
1938-39	Boston	12	0	0	0
1939-40	Chicago	2	0	0	0

PORTLAND *(Continued)*

Playoffs	Club	GP	G	A	Pts
1940-41	Montreal C.	3	0	1	1
1942-43	Montreal C.	5	1	2	3
	Totals	--	1	3	4

POTVIN, Jean Rene *Defenseman*
b. Ottawa, Ont., Mar. 25, 1949

Season	Club	GP	G	A	Pts
1970-71	Los Angeles	4	1	3	4
1971-72	LA-Phila F	68	5	15	20
1972-73	Phila F-NY I	46	3	12	15
	Totals	118	9	30	39

POWELL, Raymond Henry *Forward*
b. Timmins, Ont., Nov. 16, 1925

Season	Club	GP	G	A	Pts
1950-51	Chicago	31	7	15	22

POWIS, Geoffrey *Forward*
b. Winnipeg, Man., June 14, 1945

Season	Club	GP	G	A	Pts
1967-68	Chicago	2	0	0	0

PRATT, Jack *Defenseman*
b. Edinburgh, Scotland

Season	Club	GP	G	A	Pts
1930-31	Boston	--	2	0	2
1931-32	Boston	--	0	0	0
	Totals	--	2	0	2

Playoffs

1930-31	Boston	--	0	0	0

PRATT, Tracy Arnold *Defenseman*
b. New York, N.Y., Mar. 8, 1943

Season	Club	GP	G	A	Pts
1967-68	Oakland	34	0	5	5
1968-69	Pittsburgh Pe.	18	0	5	5
1969-70	Pittsburgh Pe.	65	5	7	12
1970-71	Buffalo	76	1	7	8
1971-72	Buffalo	27	0	10	10
1972-73	Buffalo	74	1	15	16
	Totals	294	7	49	56

Playoffs

1969-70	Pittsburgh Pe.	10	0	1	1
1972-73	Buffalo	6	0	0	0
	Totals	16	0	1	1

PRATT, Walter (Babe) *Defenseman*
b. Stony Mountain, Man., Jan. 7, 1916

Season	Club	GP	G	A	Pts
1935-36	New York R.	17	1	1	2
1936-37	New York R.	47	8	7	15

PRATT (Continued)

Season	Club	GP	G	A	Pts
1937–38	New York R.	47	5	14	19
1938–39	New York R.	48	2	19	21
1939–40	New York R.	48	4	13	17
1940–41	New York R.	47	3	17	20
1941–42	New York R.	47	4	24	28
1942–43	NY R–Tor ML	44	12	27	39
1943–44	Toronto M.L.	50	17	40	57
1944–45	Toronto M.L.	50	18	23	41
1945–46	Toronto M.L.	41	5	20	25
1946–47	Boston	31	4	4	8
	Totals	517	83	209	292

Playoffs

Season	Club	GP	G	A	Pts
1936–37	New York R.	9	3	1	4
1937–38	New York R.	3	0	0	0
1938–39	New York R.	7	1	2	3
1939–40	New York R.	12	3	1	4
1940–41	New York R.	3	1	1	2
1941–42	New York R.	6	1	3	4
1942–43	Toronto M.L.	6	1	2	3
1943–44	Toronto M.L.	5	0	3	3
1945–46	Toronto M.L.	13	2	4	6
	Totals	64	12	17	29

PRENTICE, Dean Sutherland *Forward*
b. Schumacher, Ont., Oct. 5, 1932

Season	Club	GP	G	A	Pts
1952–53	New York R.	55	6	3	9
1953–54	New York R.	52	4	13	17
1954–55	New York R.	70	16	15	31
1955–56	New York R.	70	24	18	42
1956–57	New York R.	68	19	23	42
1957–58	New York R.	38	13	9	22
1958–59	New York R.	70	17	33	50
1959–60	New York R.	70	32	34	66
1960–61	New York R.	56	20	25	45
1961–62	New York R.	68	22	38	60
1962–63	NY R–Bos	68	19	34	53
1963–64	Boston	70	23	16	39
1964–65	Boston	31	14	9	23
1965–66	Bos–Det RW	69	13	31	44
1966–67	Detroit R.W.	68	23	22	45
1967–68	Detroit R.W.	69	17	38	55
1968–69	Detroit R.W.	74	14	20	34
1969–70	Pittsburgh Pe.	75	26	25	51
1970–71	Pittsburgh Pe.	69	21	17	38
1971–72	Minnesota	71	20	27	47
1972–73	Minnesota	73	26	16	42
	Totals	1354	389	466	855

Playoffs

Season	Club	GP	G	A	Pts
1955–56	New York R.	5	1	0	1
1956–57	New York R.	5	0	2	2
1957–58	New York R.	6	1	3	4
1961–62	New York R.	3	0	2	2

PRENTICE (Continued)

Playoffs

Season	Club	GP	G	A	Pts
1965–66	Detroit R.W.	12	5	5	10
1969–70	Pittsburgh Pe.	10	2	5	7
1971–72	Minnesota	7	3	0	3
1972–73	Minnesota	6	1	0	1
	Totals	54	13	17	30

All-Star

Season	Club	GP	G	A	Pts
1957	NHL All-Stars	1	1	2	3
1962	NHL All-Stars	1	0	0	0
1963	NHL All-Stars	1	0	0	0
1970	West All-Stars	1	1	0	1
	Totals	4	2	2	4

PRENTICE, Eric Dayton *Forward*
b. Schumacher, Ont., Aug. 22, 1926

Season	Club	GP	G	A	Pts
1943–44	Toronto M.L.	5	0	0	0

PRICE *Forward*

Season	Club	GP	G	A	Pts
1919–20	Ottawa	1	0	0	0

PRICE, Garry Noel *Defenseman*
b. Brockville, Ont., Dec. 9, 1935

Season	Club	GP	G	A	Pts
1957–58	Toronto M.L.	1	0	0	0
1958–59	Toronto M.L.	28	0	0	0
1959–60	New York R.	6	0	0	0
1960–61	New York R.	1	0	0	0
1961–62	Detroit R.W.	20	0	1	1
1965–66	Montreal C.	15	0	6	6
1966–67	Montreal C.	24	0	3	3
1967–68	Pittsburgh Pe.	70	6	27	33
1968–69	Pittsburgh Pe.	73	2	18	20
1970–71	Los Angeles	62	1	19	20
1972–73	Atlanta	54	1	13	14
	Totals	354	10	87	97

Playoffs

Season	Club	GP	G	A	Pts
1958–59	Toronto M.L.	5	0	0	0
1965–66	Montreal C.	3	0	1	1
	Totals	8	0	1	1

All-Star

Season	Club	GP	G	A	Pts
1967	Montreal C.	1	0	0	0

PRICE, John Rees *Defenseman*
b. Gooderich, Ont., May 8, 1932

Season	Club	GP	G	A	Pts
1951–52	Chicago	1	0	0	0
1952–53	Chicago	10	0	0	0
1953–54	Chicago	46	4	6	10
	Totals	57	4	6	10

Playoffs

Season	Club	GP	G	A	Pts
1952–53	Chicago	4	0	0	0

PRIMEAU, Joseph *Forward*
b. Lindsay, Ont., Jan. 29, 1906

Season	Club	GP	G	A	Pts
1928-29	Toronto M.L.	--	0	1	1
1929-30	Toronto M.L.	--	5	21	26
1930-31	Toronto M.L.	--	9	32	41
1931-32	Toronto M.L.	--	13	37	50
1932-33	Toronto M.L.	--	11	21	32
1933-34	Toronto M.L.	--	14	32	46
1934-35	Toronto M.L.	--	10	20	30
1935-36	Toronto M.L.	--	4	13	17
	Totals	--	66	177	243
Playoffs					
1928-29	Toronto M.L.	--	0	0	0
1930-31	Toronto M.L.	--	0	0	0
1931-32	Toronto M.L.	--	0	6	6
1932-33	Toronto M.L.	--	0	1	1
1933-34	Toronto M.L.	--	2	4	6
1934-35	Toronto M.L.	--	0	3	3
1935-36	Toronto M.L.	--	3	4	7
	Totals	--	5	18	23

PRINGLE, Ellis *Defenseman*
b. Toronto, Ont.

Season	Club	GP	G	A	Pts
1930-31	New York A.	--	0	0	0

PRODGERS, George (Goldie) *Defenseman*
b. 1892

Season	Club	GP	G	A	Pts
1919-20	Toronto St.P.	16	8	6	14
1920-21	Hamilton	23	18	8	26
1921-22	Hamilton	24	15	4	19
1922-23	Hamilton	23	13	3	16
1923-24	Hamilton	23	9	1	10
1924-25	Hamilton	1	0	0	0
1925-26	Montreal C.	--	0	0	0
	Totals	--	63	22	85

PRONOVOST, Claude *Goalie*
b. Shawinigan Falls, Que., July 22, 1935

Season	Club	GP	GA	Sho	AVE
1955-56	Boston	1	0	1	0.00
1958-59	Montreal C.	2	7	0	3.50
	Totals	3	7	1	2.33

PRONOVOST, Joseph Armand Andre *Forward*
b. Shawinigan Falls, Que., July 9, 1936

Season	Club	GP	G	A	Pts
1956-57	Montreal C.	64	10	11	21
1957-58	Montreal C.	66	16	12	28
1958-59	Montreal C.	70	9	14	23
1959-60	Montreal C.	69	12	19	31

PRONOVOST *(Continued)*

Season	Club	GP	G	A	Pts
1960-61	Mont C-Bos	68	12	16	28
1961-62	Boston	70	15	8	23
1962-63	Bos-Det RW	68	13	7	20
1963-64	Detroit R.W.	70	7	16	23
1964-65	Detroit R.W.	3	0	1	1
1967-68	Minnesota	8	0	0	0
	Totals	556	94	104	198
Playoffs					
1956-57	Montreal C.	8	1	0	1
1957-58	Montreal C.	10	2	0	2
1958-59	Montreal C.	11	2	1	3
1959-60	Montreal C.	8	1	2	3
1962-63	Detroit R.W.	11	1	4	5
1963-64	Detroit R.W.	14	4	3	7
1967-68	Minnesota	8	0	1	1
	Totals	70	11	11	22
All-Star					
1957	Montreal C.	1	0	0	0
1958	Montreal C.	1	0	0	0
1959	Montreal C.	1	1	0	1
1960	Montreal C.	1	0	1	1
	Totals	4	1	1	2

PRONOVOST, Joseph Jean Denis *Forward*
b. Shawinigan Falls, Que., Dec. 18, 1945

Season	Club	GP	G	A	Pts
1968-69	Pittsburgh Pe.	76	16	25	41
1969-70	Pittsburgh Pe.	72	20	21	41
1970-71	Pittsburgh Pe.	78	21	24	45
1971-72	Pittsburgh Pe.	68	30	23	53
1972-73	Pittsburgh Pe.	66	21	22	43
	Totals	360	108	115	223
Playoffs					
1969-70	Pittsburgh Pe.	10	3	4	7
1971-72	Pittsburgh Pe.	4	1	1	2
	Totals	14	4	5	9

PRONOVOST, Rene Marcel *Defenseman*
b. Lac la Tortue, Que., June 15, 1930

Season	Club	GP	G	A	Pts
1950-51	Detroit R.W.	37	1	6	7
1951-52	Detroit R.W.	69	7	11	18
1952-53	Detroit R.W.	68	8	19	27
1953-54	Detroit R.W.	57	6	12	18
1954-55	Detroit R.W.	70	9	25	34
1955-56	Detroit R.W.	68	4	13	17
1956-57	Detroit R.W.	70	7	9	16
1957-58	Detroit R.W.	62	2	18	20
1958-59	Detroit R.W.	69	11	21	32
1959-60	Detroit R.W.	69	7	17	24
1960-61	Detroit R.W.	70	6	11	17

PRONOVOST (Continued)

Season	Club	GP	G	A	Pts
1961–62	Detroit R.W.	70	4	14	18
1962–63	Detroit R.W.	69	4	9	13
1963–64	Detroit R.W.	67	3	17	20
1964–65	Detroit R.W.	68	1	15	16
1965–66	Toronto M.L.	54	2	8	10
1966–67	Toronto M.L.	58	2	12	14
1967–68	Toronto M.L.	70	3	17	20
1968–69	Toronto M.L.	34	1	2	3
1969–70	Toronto M.L.	7	0	1	1
	Totals	1206	88	257	345

Playoffs

Season	Club	GP	G	A	Pts
1949–50	Detroit R.W.	9	0	1	1
1950–51	Detroit R.W.	6	0	0	0
1951–52	Detroit R.W.	8	0	1	1
1952–53	Detroit R.W.	6	0	0	0
1953–54	Detroit R.W.	12	2	3	5
1954–55	Detroit R.W.	11	1	2	3
1955–56	Detroit R.W.	10	0	2	2
1956–57	Detroit R.W.	5	0	0	0
1957–58	Detroit R.W.	4	0	1	1
1959–60	Detroit R.W.	6	1	1	2
1960–61	Detroit R.W.	9	2	3	5
1962–63	Detroit R.W.	11	1	4	5
1963–64	Detroit R.W.	14	0	2	2
1964–65	Detroit R.W.	7	0	3	3
1965–66	Toronto M.L.	4	0	0	0
1966–67	Toronto M.L.	12	1	0	1
	Totals	134	8	23	31

All-Star

Season	Club	GP	G	A	Pts
1950	Detroit R.W.	1	0	0	0
1954	Detroit R.W.	1	0	0	0
1955	Detroit R.W.	1	0	0	0
1957	NHL All-Stars	1	0	0	0
1958	NHL All-Stars	1	0	0	0
1959	NHL All-Stars	1	0	0	0
1960	NHL All-Stars	1	0	0	0
1961	NHL All-Stars	1	0	1	1
1963	NHL All-Stars	1	1	0	1
1965	NHL All-Stars	1	0	0	0
1968	Toronto M.L.	1	0	0	0
	Totals	11	1	1	2

PROVOST, Claude *Forward*
b. Montreal, Que., Sept. 17, 1933

Season	Club	GP	G	A	Pts
1955–56	Montreal C.	60	13	16	29
1956–57	Montreal C.	67	16	14	30
1957–58	Montreal C.	70	19	32	51
1958–59	Montreal C.	69	16	22	38
1959–60	Montreal C.	70	17	29	46
1960–61	Montreal C.	49	11	4	15
1961–62	Montreal C.	70	33	29	62

PROVOST (Continued)

Season	Club	GP	G	A	Pts
1962–63	Montreal C.	67	20	30	50
1963–64	Montreal C.	68	15	17	32
1964–65	Montreal C.	70	27	37	64
1965–66	Montreal C.	70	19	36	55
1966–67	Montreal C.	64	11	13	24
1967–68	Montreal C.	73	14	30	44
1968–69	Montreal C.	73	13	15	28
1969–70	Montreal C.	65	10	11	21
	Totals	1005	254	335	589

Playoffs

Season	Club	GP	G	A	Pts
1955–56	Montreal C.	10	3	3	6
1956–57	Montreal C.	10	0	1	1
1957–58	Montreal C.	10	1	3	4
1958–59	Montreal C.	11	6	2	8
1959–60	Montreal C.	8	1	1	2
1960–61	Montreal C.	6	1	3	4
1961–62	Montreal C.	6	2	2	4
1962–63	Montreal C.	5	0	1	1
1963–64	Montreal C.	7	2	2	4
1964–65	Montreal C.	13	2	6	8
1965–66	Montreal C.	10	2	3	5
1966–67	Montreal C.	7	1	1	2
1967–68	Montreal C.	13	2	8	10
1968–69	Montreal C.	10	2	2	4
	Totals	126	25	38	63

All-Star

Season	Club	GP	G	A	Pts
1956	Montreal C.	1	0	0	0
1957	Montreal C.	1	0	0	0
1958	Montreal C.	1	0	2	2
1959	Montreal C.	1	0	0	0
1960	Montreal C.	1	1	0	1
1961	NHL All-Stars	1	0	0	0
1963	NHL All-Stars	1	0	0	0
1964	NHL All-Stars	1	0	0	0
1965	Montreal C.	1	0	0	0
1967	Montreal C.	1	0	0	0
	Totals	10	1	2	3

PRYSTAI, Metro *Forward*
b. Yorkton, Sask., Nov. 7, 1927

Season	Club	GP	G	A	Pts
1947–48	Chicago	54	7	11	18
1948–49	Chicago	59	12	7	19
1949–50	Chicago	65	29	22	51
1950–51	Detroit R.W.	62	20	17	37
1951–52	Detroit R.W.	69	21	22	43
1952–53	Detroit R.W.	70	16	34	50
1953–54	Detroit R.W.	70	12	15	27
1954–55	Det RW–Chgo	69	13	16	29
1955–56	Chgo–Det RW	71	13	19	32
1956–57	Detroit R.W.	70	7	15	22
1957–58	Detroit R.W.	15	1	1	2
	Totals	674	151	179	330

PRYSTAI *(Continued)*

Playoffs	Club	GP	G	A	Pts
1950–51	Detroit R.W.	3	1	0	1
1951–52	Detroit R.W.	8	2	5	7
1952–53	Detroit R.W.	6	4	4	8
1953–54	Detroit R.W.	12	2	3	5
1955–56	Detroit R.W.	9	1	2	3
1956–57	Detroit R.W.	5	2	0	2
	Totals	43	12	14	26

All-Star					
1950	Detroit R.W.	1	1	2	3
1953	NHL All-Stars	1	0	0	0
1954	Detroit R.W.	1	0	0	0
	Totals	3	1	2	3

PULFORD, Robert (Bob) *Forward*
b. Newton Robinson, Ont., Mar. 31, 1936

Season	Club	GP	G	A	Pts
1956–57	Toronto M.L.	65	11	11	22
1957–58	Toronto M.L.	70	14	17	31
1958–59	Toronto M.L.	70	23	14	37
1959–60	Toronto M.L.	70	24	28	52
1960–61	Toronto M.L.	40	11	18	29
1961–62	Toronto M.L.	70	18	21	39
1962–63	Toronto M.L.	70	19	25	44
1963–64	Toronto M.L.	70	18	30	48
1964–65	Toronto M.L.	65	19	20	39
1965–66	Toronto M.L.	70	28	28	56
1966–67	Toronto M.L.	67	17	28	45
1967–68	Toronto M.L.	74	20	30	50
1968–69	Toronto M.L.	72	11	23	34
1969–70	Toronto M.L.	74	18	19	37
1970–71	Los Angeles	59	17	26	43
1971–72	Los Angeles	73	13	24	37
	Totals	1079	281	362	643

Playoffs					
1958–59	Toronto M.L.	12	4	4	8
1959–60	Toronto M.L.	10	4	1	5
1960–61	Toronto M.L.	5	0	0	0
1961–62	Toronto M.L.	12	7	1	8
1962–63	Toronto M.L.	10	2	5	7
1963–64	Toronto M.L.	14	5	3	8
1964–65	Toronto M.L.	6	1	1	2
1965–66	Toronto M.L.	4	1	1	2
1966–67	Toronto M.L.	12	1	10	11
1968–69	Toronto M.L.	4	0	0	0
	Totals	89	25	26	51

All-Star					
1958	NHL All-Stars	1	1	1	2
1960	NHL All-Stars	1	0	0	0
1962	Toronto M.L.	1	1	0	1
1963	Toronto M.L.	1	0	0	0

PULFORD *(Continued)*

All-Star	Club	GP	G	A	Pts
1964	Toronto M.L.	1	0	0	0
1968	Toronto M.L.	1	0	0	0
	Totals	6	2	1	3

PULKKINEN, David Joel John (Dave)
Defenseman
b. Kapuskasing, Ont., May 18, 1949

Season	Club	GP	G	A	Pts
1972–73	New York I.	2	0	0	0

PURPUR, Clifford (Fido) *Forward*
b. Grand Forks, N.D, Sept. 26, 1916

Season	Club	GP	G	A	Pts
1934–35	St. Louis E.	--	2	1	3
1941–42	Chicago	--	0	0	0
1942–43	Chicago	50	13	16	29
1943–44	Chicago	40	9	10	19
1944–45	Chgo–Det RW	21	2	7	9
	Totals	--	26	34	60

Playoffs					
1943–44	Chicago	9	1	1	2
1944–45	Detroit R.W.	7	0	1	1
	Totals	16	1	2	3

PUSIE, Jean *Defenseman*
b. Montreal, Que., Oct. 15, 1910

Season	Club	GP	G	A	Pts
1933–34	New York R.	19	0	2	2
1934–35	Boston	--	1	0	1
1935–36	Montreal C.	--	0	2	2
	Totals	--	1	4	5

Playoffs					
1934–35	Boston	4	0	0	0

QUACKENBUSH, Hubert George (Bill)
Defenseman
b. Toronto, Ont., Mar. 2, 1922

Season	Club	GP	G	A	Pts
1942–43	Detroit R.W.	10	1	1	2
1943–44	Detroit R.W.	43	4	14	18
1944–45	Detroit R.W.	50	7	14	21
1945–46	Detroit R.W.	48	11	10	21
1946–47	Detroit R.W.	44	5	17	22
1947–48	Detroit R.W.	58	6	16	22
1948–49	Detroit R.W.	60	6	17	23
1949–50	Boston	70	8	17	25
1950–51	Boston	70	5	24	29
1951–52	Boston	69	2	17	19
1952–53	Boston	69	2	16	18
1953–54	Boston	45	0	17	17
1954–55	Boston	68	2	20	22
1955–56	Boston	70	3	22	25
	Totals	774	62	222	284

QUACKENBUSH (Continued)

Playoffs	Club	GP	G	A	Pts
1943-44	Detroit R.W.	2	1	0	1
1944-45	Detroit R.W.	14	0	2	2
1945-46	Detroit R.W.	5	0	1	1
1946-47	Detroit R.W.	5	0	0	0
1947-48	Detroit R.W.	10	0	2	2
1948-49	Detroit R.W.	11	1	1	2
1950-51	Boston	6	0	1	1
1951-52	Boston	7	0	3	3
1952-53	Boston	10	0	4	4
1953-54	Boston	4	0	0	0
1954-55	Boston	5	0	5	5
	Totals	79	2	19	21
All-Star					
1947	NHL All-Stars	1	0	0	0
1948	NHL All-Stars	1	0	0	0
1949	NHL All-Stars	1	0	1	1
1950	NHL All-Stars	1	0	0	0
1951	NHL 1st All-Stars	1	0	0	0
1952	NHL 1st All-Stars	1	0	0	0
1953	NHL All-Stars	1	0	0	0
1954	NHL All-Stars	1	0	0	0
	Totals	8	0	1	1

QUACKENBUSH, Maxwell Joseph *Defenseman*
b. Toronto, Ont., Aug. 29, 1928

Season	Club	GP	G	A	Pts
1950-51	Boston	47	4	6	10
1951-52	Chicago	14	0	1	1
	Totals	61	4	7	11
Playoffs					
1950-51	Boston	6	0	0	0

QUENNEVILLE, Leo *Forward*
b. St. Anicet, Que., June 15, 1900

Season	Club	GP	G	A	Pts
1929-30	New York R.	25	0	3	3
Playoffs					
1929-30	New York R.	3	0	0	0

QUILTY, John Francis *Forward*
b. Ottawa, Ont., Jan. 21, 1921

Season	Club	GP	G	A	Pts
1940-41	Montreal C.	--	18	16	34
1941-42	Montreal C.	48	12	12	24
1946-47	Montreal C.	3	1	1	2
1947-48	Mont C-Bos	26	5	5	10
	Totals	--	36	34	70
Playoffs					
1940-41	Montreal C.	3	0	2	2
1941-42	Montreal C.	--	0	1	1
1946-47	Montreal C.	7	3	2	5
	Totals	--	3	5	8

QUINN, John Brian Patrick (Pat) *Defenseman*
b. Hamilton, Ont., Jan. 19, 1943

Season	Club	GP	G	A	Pts
1968-69	Toronto M.L.	40	2	7	9
1969-70	Toronto M.L.	59	0	5	5
1970-71	Vancouver	76	2	11	13
1971-72	Vancouver	57	2	3	5
1972-73	Atlanta	78	2	18	20
	Totals	310	8	44	52
Playoffs					
1968-69	Toronto M.L.	4	0	0	0

RADLEY, Harry John (Yip) *Defenseman*
b. Ottawa, Ont., June 27, 1910

Season	Club	GP	G	A	Pts
1936-37	Montreal M.	--	0	1	1

RAGLAN, Clarence Eldon (Rags) *Defenseman*
b. Pembroke, Ont., Sept. 4, 1927

Season	Club	GP	G	A	Pts
1950-51	Detroit R.W.	33	3	1	4
1951-52	Chicago	35	0	5	5
1952-53	Chicago	32	1	3	4
	Totals	100	4	9	13
Playoffs					
1952-53	Chicago	3	0	0	0

RALEIGH, James Donald (Bones) *Forward*
b. Kenora, Ont., June 27, 1926

Season	Club	GP	G	A	Pts
1943-44	New York R.	15	2	2	4
1947-48	New York R.	52	15	18	33
1948-49	New York R.	41	10	16	26
1949-50	New York R.	70	12	25	37
1950-51	New York R.	64	15	24	39
1951-52	New York R.	70	19	42	61
1952-53	New York R.	55	4	18	22
1953-54	New York R.	70	15	30	45
1954-55	New York R.	69	8	32	40
1955-56	New York R.	29	1	12	13
	Totals	534	101	219	320
Playoffs					
1947-48	New York R.	6	2	0	2
1949-50	New York R.	12	4	5	9
	Totals	18	6	5	11
All-Star					
1951	NHL 1st All-Stars	1	0	1	1
1954	NHL All-Stars	1	0	0	0
	Totals	2	0	1	1

RAMSAY, Craig E. *Forward*
b. Weston, Ont., Mar. 17, 1951

Season	Club	GP	G	A	Pts
1971–72	Buffalo	57	6	10	16
1972–73	Buffalo	76	11	17	28
	Totals	133	17	27	44

Playoffs

1972–73	Buffalo	6	1	1	2

RAMSEY, Beattie *Defenseman*

Season	Club	GP	G	A	Pts
1927–28	Toronto M.L.	--	0	2	2

RAMSEY, Les *Forward*
b. Montreal, Que., July 1, 1920

Season	Club	GP	G	A	Pts
1944–45	Chicago	11	2	2	4

RANDALL, Kenneth *Defenseman*

Season	Club	GP	G	A	Pts
1917–18	Toronto A.	20	12	0	12
1918–19	Toronto A.	14	7	6	13
1919–20	Toronto St.P.	21	10	7	17
1920–21	Toronto St.P.	21	6	1	7
1921–22	Toronto St.P.	24	10	6	16
1922–23	Toronto St.P.	24	3	5	8
1923–24	Hamilton	24	7	1	8
1924–25	Hamilton	30	8	0	8
1925–26	New York A.	34	4	2	6
	Totals	212	67	28	95

Playoffs

1917–18	Toronto A.	--	1	0	1
1920–21	Toronto St.P.	--	0	0	0
1921–22	Toronto St.P.	--	1	0	1
	Totals	--	2	0	2

RANIERI, George Dominic *Forward*
b. Toronto, Ont., Jan. 14, 1936

Season	Club	GP	G	A	Pts
1956–57	Boston	2	0	0	0

RATELLE, Joseph Gilbert Yvon Jean *Forward*
b. Lac St. Jean, Que., Oct. 3, 1940

Season	Club	GP	G	A	Pts
1960–61	New York R.	3	2	1	3
1961–62	New York R.	31	4	8	12
1962–63	New York R.	48	11	9	20
1963–64	New York R.	15	0	7	7
1964–65	New York R.	54	14	21	35
1965–66	New York R.	67	21	30	51
1966–67	New York R.	41	6	5	11
1967–68	New York R.	74	32	46	78
1968–69	New York R.	75	32	46	78

RATELLE *(Continued)*

Season	Club	GP	G	A	Pts
1969–70	New York R.	75	32	42	74
1970–71	New York R.	78	26	46	72
1971–72	New York R.	63	46	63	109
1972–73	New York R.	78	41	53	94
	Totals	702	267	377	644

Playoffs

1966–67	New York R.	4	0	0	0
1967–68	New York R.	6	0	4	4
1968–69	New York R.	4	1	0	1
1969–70	New York R.	6	1	3	4
1970–71	New York R.	13	2	9	11
1971–72	New York R.	6	0	1	1
1972–73	New York R.	10	2	7	9
	Totals	49	6	24	30

All-Star

1970	East All-Stars	1	0	0	0
1971	East All-Stars	1	0	0	0
1972	East All-Stars	1	1	0	1
1973	East All-Stars	1	0	0	0
	Totals	4	1	0	1

RAVLICH, Mathew Joseph *Defenseman*
b. Sault Ste. Marie, Ont., July 12, 1938

Season	Club	GP	G	A	Pts
1962–63	Boston	2	1	0	1
1964–65	Chicago	61	3	16	19
1965–66	Chicago	62	0	16	16
1966–67	Chicago	62	0	3	3
1968–69	Chicago	60	2	12	14
1969–70	Det RW–LA	67	3	13	16
1970–71	Los Angeles	66	3	16	19
1971–72	Boston	25	0	1	1
1972–73	Boston	5	0	1	1
	Totals	410	12	78	90

Playoffs

1964–65	Chicago	14	1	4	5
1965–66	Chicago	6	0	1	1
1967–68	Chicago	4	0	0	0
	Totals	24	1	5	6

RAYMOND, Armand *Defenseman*
b. Mechanicsville, N.Y., Jan. 12, 1913

Season	Club	GP	G	A	Pts
1939–40	Montreal C.	--	0	1	1

RAYMOND, Paul Marcel *Forward*
b. Montreal, Que., Feb. 27, 1913

Season	Club	GP	G	A	Pts
1933–34	Montreal C.	--	1	0	1
1934–35	Montreal C.	--	1	1	2
1937–38	Montreal C.	--	0	2	2
	Totals	--	2	3	5

RAYMOND *(Continued)*

Playoffs	Club	GP	G	A	Pts
1937–38	Montreal C.	--	0	0	0

RAYNER, Claude Earl (Chuck) *Goalie*
    b. Sutherland, Sask., Aug. 11, 1920

Season	Club	GP	GA	Sho	AVE
1940–41	New York A.	12	44	0	3.66
1941–42	Brooklyn A.	36	129	1	3.58
1945–46	New York R.	41	150	1	3.75
1946–47	New York R.	58	177	5	3.05
1947–48	New York R.	12	42	0	3.50
1948–49	New York R.	58	168	7	2.90
1949–50	New York R.	69	181	6	2.62
1950–51	New York R.	66	187	2	2.83
1951–52	New York R.	53	159	2	3.00
1952–53	New York R.	20	58	1	2.90
	Totals	425	1295	25	3.05

Playoffs		GP	GA	Sho	AVE
1947–48	New York R.	6	17	0	2.83
1949–50	New York R.	12	29	1	2.42
	Totals	18	46	1	2.56

All-Star		GP	Per	GA	AGP
1949	NHL All-Stars	1	1½	0	0.00
1950	NHL All-Stars	1	1½	2	1.33
1951	NHL 2nd All-Stars	1	1½	1	0.67
	Totals	3	4½	3	0.67

READ, Melvin Dean (Pee Wee) *Forward*
    b. Montreal, Que., Apr. 10, 1922

Season	Club	GP	G	A	Pts
1946–47	New York R.	6	0	0	0

REARDON, Kenneth Joseph *Defenseman*
    b. Winnipeg, Man., Apr. 1, 1921

Season	Club	GP	G	A	Pts
1940–41	Montreal C	34	2	8	10
1941–42	Montreal C.	41	3	12	15
1945–46	Montreal C.	43	5	4	9
1946–47	Montreal C.	52	5	17	22
1947–48	Montreal C.	58	7	15	22
1948–49	Montreal C.	46	3	13	16
1949–50	Montreal C.	67	1	27	28
	Totals	341	26	96	122

Playoffs		GP	G	A	Pts
1940–41	Montreal C.	3	0	0	0
1941–42	Montreal C.	--	0	0	0
1945–46	Montreal C.	9	1	1	2
1946–47	Montreal C.	7	1	2	3
1948–49	Montreal C.	7	0	0	0
1949–50	Montreal C.	2	0	2	2
	Totals	--	2	5	7

REARDON *(Continued)*

All-Star	Club	GP	G	A	Pts
1947	NHL All-Stars	1	0	2	2
1948	NHL All-Stars	1	0	0	0
1949	NHL All-Stars	1	0	0	0
	Totals	3	0	2	2

REARDON, Terrance George
Defenseman-Forward
    b. Winnipeg, Man., Apr. 6, 1919

Season	Club	GP	G	A	Pts
1939–40	Boston	--	0	0	0
1940–41	Boston	--	6	5	11
1941–42	Montreal C.	33	17	17	34
1942–43	Montreal C.	13	6	6	12
1945–46	Boston	49	12	11	23
1946–47	Boston	60	6	14	20
	Totals	--	47	53	100

Playoffs		GP	G	A	Pts
1939–40	Boston	--	0	1	1
1940–41	Boston	11	2	4	6
1941–42	Montreal C.	--	2	1	3
1945–46	Boston	10	4	0	4
1946–47	Boston	5	0	3	3
	Totals	--	8	9	17

REAUME, Marc Avellin *Defenseman*
    b. Lasalle, Ont., Feb. 7, 1934

Season	Club	GP	G	A	Pts
1954–55	Toronto M.L.	1	0	0	0
1955–56	Toronto M.L.	48	0	12	12
1956–57	Toronto M.L.	63	6	14	20
1957–58	Toronto M.L.	68	1	7	8
1958–59	Toronto M.L.	51	1	5	6
1959–60	Tor ML–Det RW	45	0	2	2
1960–61	Detroit R.W.	38	0	1	1
1963–64	Montreal C.	3	0	0	0
1970–71	Vancouver	27	0	2	2
	Totals	344	8	43	51

Playoffs		GP	G	A	Pts
1954–55	Toronto M.L.	4	0	0	0
1955–56	Toronto M.L.	5	0	2	2
1958–59	Toronto M.L.	10	0	0	0
1959–60	Detroit R.W.	2	0	0	0
	Totals	21	0	2	2

REAY, William *Forward*
    b. Winnipeg, Man., Aug. 21, 1918

Season	Club	GP	G	A	Pts
1943–44	Detroit R.W.	2	2	0	2
1944–45	Detroit R.W.	2	0	0	0
1945–46	Montreal C.	44	17	12	29
1946–47	Montreal C.	59	22	20	42

REAY (Continued)

Season	Club	GP	G	A	Pts
1947-48	Montreal C.	60	6	14	20
1948-49	Montreal C.	60	22	23	45
1949-50	Montreal C.	68	19	26	45
1950-51	Montreal C.	60	6	18	24
1951-52	Montreal C.	68	7	34	41
1952-53	Montreal C.	56	4	15	19
	Totals	479	105	162	267

Playoffs

1945-46	Montreal C.	9	1	2	3
1946-47	Montreal C.	11	6	1	7
1948-49	Montreal C.	7	1	5	6
1949-50	Montreal C.	4	0	1	1
1950-51	Montreal C.	11	3	3	4
1951-52	Montreal C.	10	2	2	4
1952-53	Montreal C.	11	0	2	2
	Totals	63	13	16	29

All-Star

1952	NHL 2nd All-Stars	1	0	0	0

REDAHL, Gordon *Forward*
b. Kinistino, Sask., Aug. 28, 1935

Season	Club	GP	G	A	Pts
1958-59	Boston	18	0	1	1

REDDING, George *Defenseman*

Season	Club	GP	G	A	Pts
1924-25	Boston	27	3	2	5
1925-26	Boston	8	0	0	0
	Totals	35	3	2	5

REDMOND, Michael Edward (Mickey) *Forward*
b. Kirkland Lake, Ont., Dec. 27, 1947

Season	Club	GP	G	A	Pts
1967-68	Montreal C.	41	6	5	11
1968-69	Montreal C.	65	9	15	24
1969-70	Montreal C.	75	27	27	54
1970-71	Mtl C-Det RW	61	20	23	43
1971-72	Detroit R.W.	78	42	29	71
1972-73	Detroit R.W.	76	52	41	93
	Totals	396	156	140	296

Playoffs

1967-68	Montreal C.	2	0	0	0
1968-69	Montreal C.	14	2	3	5
	Totals	16	2	3	5

REDMOND, Richard (Dick) *Defenseman*
b. Kirkland Lake, Ont., Aug. 14, 1949

Season	Club	GP	G	A	Pts
1969-70	Minnesota	7	0	1	1
1970-71	Minn-Calif	20	2	6	8

REDMOND (Continued)

Season	Club	GP	G	A	Pts
1971-72	California	74	10	35	45
1972-73	Calif-Chgo	76	12	32	44
	Totals	177	24	74	98

Playoffs

1972-73	Chicago	13	4	2	6

REGAN, Lawrence Emmett *Forward*
b. North Bay, Ont., Aug. 9, 1930

Season	Club	GP	G	A	Pts
1956-57	Boston	69	14	19	33
1957-58	Boston	59	11	28	39
1958-59	Bos-Tor ML	68	9	27	36
1959-60	Toronto M.L.	47	4	16	20
1960-61	Toronto M.L.	37	3	5	8
	Totals	280	41	95	136

Playoffs

1956-57	Boston	8	0	2	2
1957-58	Boston	12	3	8	11
1958-59	Toronto M.L.	8	1	1	2
1959-60	Toronto M.L.	10	3	3	6
1960-61	Toronto M.L.	4	0	0	0
	Totals	42	7	14	21

REGAN, William Donald *Defenseman*
b. Creighton Mines, Ont., Dec. 11, 1908

Season	Club	GP	G	A	Pts
1929-30	New York R.	10	0	0	0
1930-31	New York R.	42	2	1	3
1932-33	New York A.	--	1	1	2
	Totals	--	3	2	5

Playoffs

1929-30	New York R.	4	0	0	0
1930-31	New York R.	4	0	0	0
	Totals	8	0	0	0

REIBEL, Earl (Dutch) *Forward*
b. Kitchener, Ont., July 21, 1930

Season	Club	GP	G	A	Pts
1953-54	Detroit R.W.	69	15	33	48
1954-55	Detroit R.W.	70	25	41	66
1955-56	Detroit R.W.	68	17	39	56
1956-57	Detroit R.W.	70	13	23	36
1957-58	Det RW-Chgo	69	8	17	25
1958-59	Boston	63	6	8	14
	Totals	409	84	161	245

Playoffs

1953-54	Detroit R.W.	9	1	3	4
1954-55	Detroit R.W.	11	5	7	12
1955-56	Detroit R.W.	10	0	2	2
1956-57	Detroit R.W.	5	0	2	2
1958-59	Boston	4	0	0	0
	Totals	39	6	14	20

REIBEL (Continued)

All-Star	Club	GP	G	A	Pts
1954	Detroit R.W.	1	0	2	2
1955	Detroit R.W.	1	2	1	3
	Totals	2	2	3	5

REID, David *Forward*
b. Toronto, Ont., Jan. 11, 1934

Season	Club	GP	G	A	Pts
1952–53	Toronto M.L.	2	0	0	0
1954–55	Toronto M.L.	1	0	0	0
1955–56	Toronto M.L.	4	0	0	0
	Totals	7	0	0	0

REID, Gordon J. *Defenseman*
b. Mt. Albert, Ont., Feb. 19, 1912

Season	Club	GP	G	A	Pts
1936–37	New York A.	––	0	0	0

REID, Reginald S.

Season	Club	GP	G	A	Pts
1924–25	Toronto St. P.	28	2	0	2
1925–26	Toronto St. P.	12	0	0	0
	Totals	40	2	0	2

REID, Thomas (Tom) *Defenseman*
b. Fort Erie, Ont., June 24, 1946

Season	Club	GP	G	A	Pts
1967–68	Chicago	56	0	4	4
1968–69	Chgo–Minn	48	0	7	7
1969–70	Minnesota	66	1	7	8
1970–71	Minnesota	73	3	14	17
1971–72	Minnesota	78	6	15	21
1972–73	Minnesota	60	1	13	14
	Totals	381	11	60	71

Playoffs

1967–68	Chicago	9	0	0	0
1969–70	Minnesota	6	0	1	1
1970–71	Minnesota	12	0	6	6
1971–72	Minnesota	7	1	4	5
1972–73	Minnesota	6	0	2	2
	Totals	40	1	13	14

REIGLE, Edmond (Rags) *Defenseman*
b. Winnipeg, Man., June 19, 1924

Season	Club	GP	G	A	Pts
1950–51	Boston	17	0	2	2

REINIKKA, Oliver Mathias (Rocco) *Forward*
b. Shuswap, B.C., Aug. 2, 1901

Season	Club	GP	G	A	Pts
1926–27	New York R.	16	0	0	0

REISE, Jr., Leo Charles *Defenseman*
b. Stoney Creek, Ont., June 7, 1922

Season	Club	GP	G	A	Pts
1945–46	Chicago	6	0	0	0
1946–47	Chgo–Det RW	48	4	6	10
1947–48	Detroit R.W.	58	5	4	9
1948–49	Detroit R.W.	59	3	7	10
1949–50	Detroit R.W.	70	4	17	21
1950–51	Detroit R.W.	68	5	16	21
1951–52	Detroit R.W.	54	0	11	11
1952–53	New York R.	61	4	15	19
1953–54	New York R.	70	3	5	8
	Totals	494	28	81	109

Playoffs

1946–47	Detroit R.W.	5	0	1	1
1947–48	Detroit R.W.	10	2	1	3
1948–49	Detroit R.W.	11	1	0	1
1949–50	Detroit R.W.	14	2	0	2
1950–51	Detroit R.W.	6	2	3	5
1951–52	Detroit R.W.	6	1	0	1
	Totals	52	8	5	13

All-Star

1950	Detroit R.W.	1	0	0	0
1951	NHL 2nd All-Stars	1	0	0	0
1952	NHL 1st All-Stars	1	0	0	0
1953	NHL All-Stars	1	0	0	0
	Totals	4	0	0	0

REISE, Sr., Leo Charles *Defenseman*
b. Pembroke, Ont., June 1, 1892

Season	Club	GP	G	A	Pts
1920–21	Hamilton	6	2	0	2
1921–22	Hamilton	24	9	14	23
1922–23	Hamilton	24	6	6	12
1923–24	Hamilton	4	0	0	0
1926–27	New York A.	––	7	6	13
1927–28	New York A.	43	8	1	9
1928–29	New York A.	––	4	1	5
1929–30	New York R.	14	0	1	1
	Totals	––	36	29	65

Playoffs

1928–29	New York A.	2	0	0	0
1929–30	New York R.	4	0	0	0
	Totals	6	0	0	0

RHEAUME, Herbert *Goalie*

Season	Club	GP	GA	Sho	AVE
1925–26	Montreal C.	30	92	0	3.07

RICHARD, Jacques *Forward*
b. Quebec City, Que., Oct. 7, 1952

Season	Club	GP	G	A	Pts
1972–73	Atlanta	74	13	18	31

RICHARD, Joseph Henri *Forward*

b. Montreal, Que., Feb. 29, 1936

Season	Club	GP	G	A	Pts
1955-56	Montreal C.	64	19	21	40
1956-57	Montreal C.	63	18	36	54
1957-58	Montreal C.	67	28	52	80
1958-59	Montreal C.	63	21	30	51
1959-60	Montreal C.	70	30	43	73
1960-61	Montreal C.	70	24	44	68
1961-62	Montreal C.	54	21	29	50
1962-63	Montreal C.	67	23	50	73
1963-64	Montreal C.	66	14	39	53
1964-65	Montreal C.	53	23	29	52
1965-66	Montreal C.	62	22	39	61
1966-67	Montreal C.	65	21	34	55
1967-68	Montreal C.	54	9	19	28
1968-69	Montreal C.	64	15	37	52
1969-70	Montreal C.	62	16	36	52
1970-71	Montreal C.	75	12	37	49
1971-72	Montreal C.	75	12	32	44
1972-73	Montreal C.	71	8	35	43
	Totals	**1165**	**336**	**642**	**978**

Playoffs

Season	Club	GP	G	A	Pts
1955-56	Montreal C.	10	4	4	8
1956-57	Montreal C.	10	2	6	8
1957-58	Montreal C.	10	1	7	8
1958-59	Montreal C.	11	3	8	11
1959-60	Montreal C.	8	3	9	12
1960-61	Montreal C.	6	2	4	6
1962-63	Montreal C.	5	1	1	2
1963-64	Montreal C.	7	1	1	2
1964-65	Montreal C.	13	7	4	11
1965-66	Montreal C.	8	1	4	5
1966-67	Montreal C.	10	4	6	10
1967-68	Montreal C.	13	4	4	8
1968-69	Montreal C.	14	2	4	6
1970-71	Montreal C.	20	5	7	12
1971-72	Montreal C.	6	0	3	3
1972-73	Montreal C.	17	6	4	10
	Totals	**168**	**46**	**76**	**122**

All-Star

Season	Club	GP	G	A	Pts
1956	Montreal C.	1	0	0	0
1957	Montreal C.	1	0	1	1
1958	Montreal C.	1	1	2	3
1959	Montreal C.	1	1	1	2
1960	Montreal C.	1	0	0	0
1961	NHL All-Stars	1	0	0	0
1963	NHL All-Stars	1	1	0	1
1965	Montreal C.	1	0	0	0
1967	Montreal C.	1	1	1	2
	Totals	**9**	**4**	**5**	**9**

RICHARD, Joseph Henri Maurice (Rocket)
Forward

b. Montreal, Que., Aug. 4, 1921

Season	Club	GP	G	A	Pts
1942-43	Montreal C.	16	5	6	11
1943-44	Montreal C.	46	32	22	54
1944-45	Montreal C.	50	50	23	73
1945-46	Montreal C.	50	27	21	48
1946-47	Montreal C.	60	45	26	71
1947-48	Montreal C.	53	28	25	53
1948-49	Montreal C.	59	20	18	38
1949-50	Montreal C.	70	43	22	65
1950-51	Montreal C.	65	42	24	66
1951-52	Montreal C.	48	27	17	44
1952-53	Montreal C.	70	28	33	61
1953-54	Montreal C.	70	37	30	67
1954-55	Montreal C.	67	38	36	74
1955-56	Montreal C.	70	38	33	71
1956-57	Montreal C.	63	33	29	62
1957-58	Montreal C.	28	15	19	34
1958-59	Montreal C.	42	17	21	38
1959-60	Montreal C.	51	19	16	35
	Totals	**978**	**544**	**421**	**965**

Playoffs

Season	Club	GP	G	A	Pts
1943-44	Montreal C.	9	12	5	17
1944-45	Montreal C.	6	6	2	8
1945-46	Montreal C.	9	7	4	11
1946-47	Montreal C.	10	6	5	11
1948-49	Montreal C.	7	2	1	3
1949-50	Montreal C.	5	1	1	2
1950-51	Montreal C.	11	9	4	13
1951-52	Montreal C.	11	4	2	6
1952-53	Montreal C.	12	7	1	8
1953-54	Montreal C.	11	3	0	3
1955-56	Montreal C.	10	5	9	14
1956-57	Montreal C.	10	8	3	11
1957-58	Montreal C.	10	11	4	15
1958-59	Montreal C.	4	0	0	0
1959-60	Montreal C.	8	1	3	4
	Totals	**133**	**82**	**44**	**126**

All-Star

Season	Club	GP	G	A	Pts
1947	NHL All-Stars	1	1	1	2
1948	NHL All-Stars	1	0	1	1
1949	NHL All-Stars	1	0	0	0
1950	NHL All-Stars	1	0	0	0
1951	NHL 2nd All-Stars	1	0	0	0
1952	NHL 2nd All-Stars	1	1	0	1
1953	Montreal C.	1	1	0	1
1954	NHL All-Stars	1	0	0	0
1955	NHL All-Stars	1	0	0	0
1956	Montreal C.	1	1	0	1
1957	Montreal C.	1	1	0	1
1958	Montreal C.	1	2	0	2
1959	Montreal C.	1	0	0	0
	Totals	**13**	**7**	**2**	**9**

RICHARDSON, David George *Forward*
b. St. Boniface, Man., Dec. 11, 1940

Season	Club	GP	G	A	Pts
1963-64	New York R.	34	3	1	4
1964-65	New York R.	7	0	1	1
1965-66	Chicago	3	0	0	0
1967-68	Detroit R.W.	1	0	0	0
	Totals	45	3	2	5

RICHER, Robert (Bob) *Forward*
b. Cowansville, Que., Mar. 5, 1951

Season	Club	GP	G	A	Pts
1972-73	Buffalo	3	0	0	0

RIGGIN, Dennis Melville *Goalie*
b. Kincardine, Ont., Apr. 11, 1936

Season	Club	GP	GA	Sho	AVE
1959-60	Detroit R.W.	9	32	1	3.55
1962-63	Detroit R.W.	9	22	0	2.44
	Totals	18	54	1	3.00

RILEY, Jack *Forward*
b. Berckenia, Ireland, Dec. 29, 1910

Season	Club	GP	G	A	Pts
1933-34	Montreal C.	--	6	11	17
1934-35	Montreal C.	--	4	11	15
	Totals	--	10	22	32
Playoffs					
1933-34	Montreal C.	--	0	1	1
1934-35	Montreal C.	--	0	2	2
	Totals	--	0	3	3

RILEY, James *Defenseman*

Season	Club	GP	G	A	Pts
1926-27	Det RW-Chgo	--	0	2	2
Playoffs					
1919-20	Seattle (PCHL)	--	1	2	3
1926-27	Chicago	--	0	0	0
	Totals	--	1	2	3

RING, Robert *Goalie*

Season	Club	GP	GA	Sho	AVE
1965-66	Boston	½	4	0	8.00

RIOPELLE, Howard Joseph (Rip) *Forward*
b. Ottawa, Ont., Jan. 30, 1922

Season	Club	GP	G	A	Pts
1947-48	Montreal C.	55	5	2	7
1948-49	Montreal C.	48	10	6	16
1949-50	Montreal C.	66	12	8	20
	Totals	169	27	16	43

RIOPELLE *(Continued)*

Playoffs	Club	GP	G	A	Pts
1948-49	Montreal C.	7	1	1	2
1949-50	Montreal C.	1	0	0	0
	Totals	8	1	1	2

RIPLEY, Victor Merrick *Forward*
b. Elgin, Ont., May 30, 1906

Season	Club	GP	G	A	Pts
1928-29	Chicago	--	11	2	13
1929-30	Chicago	--	8	8	16
1930-31	Chicago	--	8	4	12
1931-32	Chicago	--	12	6	18
1932-33	Chgo-Bos	--	4	9	13
1933-34	Bos-NY R	--	7	13	20
1934-35	NY R-StL E	--	1	7	8
	Totals	--	51	49	100
Playoffs					
1929-30	Chicago	2	0	0	0
1930-31	Chicago	9	2	1	3
1931-32	Chicago	2	0	0	0
1932-33	Boston	5	1	0	1
1933-34	New York R.	2	1	0	1
	Totals	20	4	1	5

RITCHIE, David *Defenseman*

Season	Club	GP	G	A	Pts
1917-18	Mont W-Otta	17	9	0	9
1918-19	Toronto A.	4	0	0	0
1919-20	Quebec	21	6	3	9
1920-21	Montreal C.	5	0	0	0
1924-25	Montreal C.	5	0	0	0
1925-26	Montreal C.	2	0	0	0
	Totals	54	15	3	18

RITSON, Alexander Clive *Forward*
b. Peace River, Alta., Mar. 7, 1922

Season	Club	GP	G	A	Pts
1944-45	New York R.	1	0	0	0

RITTINGER, Alan Wilbur *Forward*
b. Regina, Sask., Jan. 28, 1925

Season	Club	GP	G	A	Pts
1943-44	Boston	19	3	7	10

RIVARD, Fernand *Goalie*
b. Grand' Mère, Que., Jan. 18, 1946

Season	Club	GP	GA	Sho	AVE
1968-69	Minnesota	11	48	0	4.36
1969-70	Minnesota	13⅓	42	1	3.15
	Totals	24⅓	90	1	3.70

RIVARD, Joseph Robert (Bob) *Forward*
b. Sherbrooke, Que., Aug. 1, 1939

Season	Club	GP	G	A	Pts
1967-68	Pittsburgh Pe.	27	5	12	17

RIVERS, Gus *Forward*
b. Winnipeg, Man., Nov. 19, 1909

Season	Club	GP	G	A	Pts
1929-30	Montreal C.	--	1	0	1
1930-31	Montreal C.	--	2	5	7
1931-32	Montreal C.	--	1	0	1
	Totals	--	4	5	9
Playoffs					
1929-30	Montreal C.	--	1	0	1
1930-31	Montreal C.	--	1	0	1
1931-32	Montreal C.	--	0	0	0
	Totals	--	2	0	2

RIVERS, John Wayne *Forward*
b. Hamilton, Ont., Feb. 1, 1942

Season	Club	GP	G	A	Pts
1961-62	Detroit R.W.	2	0	0	0
1963-64	Boston	12	2	7	9
1964-65	Boston	58	6	17	23
1965-66	Boston	2	1	1	2
1966-67	Boston	8	2	1	3
1967-68	St. Louis B.	22	4	4	8
1968-69	New York R.	4	0	0	0
	Totals	108	15	30	45

RIZZUTO, Garth Alexander *Forward*
b. Trail, B.C., Sept. 11, 1947

Season	Club	GP	G	A	Pts
1970-71	Vancouver	37	3	4	7

ROACH, John Ross *Goalie*
b. Fort Perry, Ont., June 23, 1900

Season	Club	GP	GA	Sho	AVE
1921-22	Toronto St. P.	22	91	0	4.14
1922-23	Toronto St. P.	24	86	1	3.58
1923-24	Toronto St. P.	23	80	1	3.48
1924-25	Toronto St. P.	30	84	1	2.80
1925-26	Toronto St. P.	36	117	1	3.25
1926-27	Toronto M.L.	44	94	4	2.14
1927-28	Toronto M.L.	43	88	4	2.05
1928-29	New York R.	44	65	13	1.48
1929-30	New York R.	44	143	1	3.25
1930-31	New York R.	44	87	7	1.98
1931-32	New York R.	48	112	9	2.33
1932-33	Detroit F.	48	93	9	1.94
1933-34	Detroit R.W.	18	47	1	2.61
1934-35	Detroit R.W.	23	62	4	2.70
	Totals	491	1249	56	2.54

ROACH *(Continued)*

Playoffs	Club	GP	GA	Sho	AVE
1921-22	Toronto St. P.	7	13	2	1.86
1924-25	Toronto St. P.	2	5	0	2.50
1928-29	New York R.	6	5	3	0.83
1929-30	New York R.	4	7	0	1.75
1930-31	New York R.	4	4	1	1.00
1931-32	New York R.	7	27	1	3.86
1932-33	Detroit F.	4	8	1	2.00
	Totals	34	67	8	1.97

ROACH, Mickey *Forward*
b. Boston, Mass.

Season	Club	GP	G	A	Pts
1919-20	Toronto St. P.	20	10	2	12
1920-21	Tor StP-Hmltn	22	9	7	16
1921-22	Hamilton	24	14	3	17
1922-23	Hamilton	23	17	8	25
1923-24	Hamilton	21	5	3	8
1924-25	Hamilton	30	6	4	10
1925-26	New York A.	25	3	0	3
1926-27	New York A.	--	11	0	11
	Totals	--	75	27	102
Playoffs					
1920-21	Hamilton	--	0	0	0

ROBERT, Claude *Forward*
b. Montreal, Que., Aug. 10, 1928

Season	Club	GP	G	A	Pts
1950-51	Montreal C.	23	1	0	1

ROBERT, Rene Paul *Forward*
b. Trois-Rivieres, Que., Dec. 31, 1948

Season	Club	GP	G	A	Pts
1970-71	Toronto M.L.	5	0	0	0
1971-72	Pitt Pe-Buff	61	13	14	27
1972-73	Buffalo	75	40	43	83
	Totals	141	53	57	110
Playoffs					
1972-73	Buffalo	6	5	3	8
All-Star					
1973	East All-Stars	1	1	0	1

ROBERTO, Philip *Forward*
b. Niagara Falls, Ont., Jan. 1, 1949

Season	Club	GP	G	A	Pts
1969-70	Montreal C.	8	0	1	1
1970-71	Montreal C.	39	14	7	21
1971-72	StL B-Mtl C	76	15	15	30
1972-73	St. Louis B.	77	20	22	42
	Totals	200	49	45	94

ROBERTO *(Continued)*

Playoffs	Club	GP	G	A	Pts
1970–71	Montreal C.	15	0	1	1
1971–72	St. Louis B.	11	7	6	13
1972–73	St. Louis B.	5	2	1	3
	Totals	31	9	8	17

ROBERTS, Douglas William (Doug)
Defenseman
    b. Detroit, Mich., Oct. 28, 1942

Season	Club	GP	G	A	Pts
1965–66	Detroit R.W.	1	0	0	0
1966–67	Detroit R.W.	13	3	1	4
1967–68	Detroit R.W.	37	8	9	17
1968–69	Oakland	76	1	19	20
1969–70	Oakland	76	6	25	31
1970–71	California	78	4	13	17
1971–72	Boston	3	1	0	1
1972–73	Boston	45	4	7	11
	Totals	329	27	74	101
Playoffs					
1968–69	Oakland	7	0	1	1
1969–70	Oakland	4	0	2	2
1972–73	Boston	5	2	0	2
	Totals	16	2	3	5

ROBERTS, James Wilfred (Jim)
Defenseman-Forward
    b. Toronto, Ont., Apr. 9, 1940

Season	Club	GP	G	A	Pts
1963–64	Montreal C.	15	0	1	1
1964–65	Montreal C.	70	3	10	13
1965–66	Montreal C.	70	5	5	10
1966–67	Montreal C.	63	3	0	3
1967–68	St. Louis B.	74	14	23	37
1968–69	St. Louis B.	72	14	19	33
1969–70	St. Louis B.	76	13	17	30
1970–71	St. Louis B.	72	13	18	31
1971–72	StL B–Mtl C	77	12	22	34
1972–73	Montreal C.	77	14	18	32
	Totals	666	91	133	224
Playoffs					
1963–64	Montreal C.	7	0	1	1
1964–65	Montreal C.	13	0	0	0
1965–66	Montreal C.	10	1	1	2
1966–67	Montreal C.	4	1	0	1
1967–68	St. Louis B.	18	4	1	5
1968–69	St. Louis B.	12	1	4	5
1969–70	St. Louis B.	16	2	3	5
1970–71	St. Louis B.	6	2	1	3
1971–72	Montreal C.	6	1	0	1
1972–73	Montreal C.	17	0	2	2
	Totals	109	12	13	25

ROBERTS *(Continued)*

All-Star	Club	GP	G	A	Pts
1965	Montreal C.	1	0	0	0
1969	West All-Stars	1	1	0	1
1970	West All-Stars	1	0	0	0
1971	West All-Stars	1	0	0	0
	Totals	4	1	0	1

ROBERTS, Morris (Moe) *Goalie*
    b. Waterbury, Conn., Dec. 13, 1907

Season	Club	GP	GA	Sho	AVE
1925–26	Boston	1	5	0	5.00
1931–32	New York A.	1	1	0	1.00
1933–34	New York A.	6	25	0	4.17
1951–52	Chicago	⅓	0	0	0.00
	Totals	8⅓	31	0	3.72

ROBERTSON, Earl Cooper *Goalie*
    b. Bingorgh, Sask., Nov. 24, 1911

Season	Club	GP	GA	Sho	AVE
1937–38	New York A.	48	111	6	2.31
1938–39	New York A.	46	98	3	2.13
1939–40	New York A.	48	140	6	2.92
1940–41	New York A.	36	142	1	3.94
1941–42	Brooklyn A.	12	46	0	3.83
	Totals	190	537	16	2.83
Playoffs					
1936–37	Detroit R.W.	6	8	2	1.33
1937–38	New York A.	6	12	0	2.00
1939–40	New York A.	3	9	0	3.00
	Totals	15	29	2	1.93

ROBERTSON, Fred *Defenseman*
    b. Carlisle, England, Oct. 22, 1911

Season	Club	GP	G	A	Pts
1931–32	Toronto M.L.	--	0	0	0
1933–34	Detroit R.W.	--	1	0	1
	Totals	--	1	0	1

ROBERTSON, George Thomas *Forward*
    b. Winnipeg, Man., May 11, 1928

Season	Club	GP	G	A	Pts
1947–48	Montreal C.	1	0	0	0
1948–49	Montreal C.	30	2	5	7
	Totals	31	2	5	7

ROBINSON, Douglas Garnet (Doug) *Forward*
    b. St. Catherines, Ont., Aug. 27, 1940

Season	Club	GP	G	A	Pts
1964–65	Chgo–NY R	61	10	23	33
1965–66	New York R.	51	8	12	20
1966–67	New York R.	1	0	0	0

ROBINSON (Continued)

Season	Club	GP	G	A	Pts
1967-68	Los Angeles	34	9	9	18
1968-69	Los Angeles	31	2	10	12
1970-71	Los Angeles	61	15	13	28
	Totals	239	44	67	111
Playoffs					
1963-64	Chicago	4	0	0	0
1967-68	Los Angeles	7	4	3	7
	Totals	11	4	3	7

ROBINSON, Earle *Forward*
b. Montreal, Que., Mar. 11, 1907

Season	Club	GP	G	A	Pts
1928-29	Montreal M.	--	2	1	3
1929-30	Montreal M.	--	1	2	3
1931-32	Montreal M.	--	0	3	3
1932-33	Montreal M.	--	15	9	24
1933-34	Montreal M.	--	12	16	28
1934-35	Montreal M.	--	17	18	35
1935-36	Montreal M.	--	6	14	20
1936-37	Montreal M.	--	16	18	34
1937-38	Montreal M.	--	4	7	11
1938-39	Chicago	--	9	6	15
1939-40	Montreal C.	--	1	4	5
	Totals	--	83	98	181
Playoffs					
1929-30	Montreal M.	--	0	0	0
1932-33	Montreal M.	--	0	0	0
1933-34	Montreal M.	--	2	0	2
1934-35	Montreal M.	--	2	2	4
1935-36	Montreal M.	--	0	0	0
1936-37	Montreal M.	--	1	2	3
	Totals	--	5	4	9

ROBINSON, Larry *Defenseman*
b. Winchester, Ont., June 2, 1951

Season	Club	GP	G	A	Pts
1972-73	Montreal C.	36	2	4	6
Playoffs					
1972-73	Montreal C.	11	1	4	5

ROBITAILLE, Michael James David (Mike)
Defenseman
b. Midland, Ont., Feb. 12, 1948

Season	Club	GP	G	A	Pts
1969-70	New York R.	4	0	0	0
1970-71	NY R-Det RW	34	5	9	14
1971-72	Buffalo	31	2	10	12
1972-73	Buffalo	65	4	17	21
	Totals	134	11	36	47
Playoffs					
1972-73	Buffalo	6	0	0	0

ROCHE, Desse *Forward*
b. Prescott, Ont., Feb. 1, 1907

Season	Club	GP	G	A	Pts
1930-31	Montreal M.	--	0	1	1
1932-33	Ottawa	--	3	6	9
1933-34	Ottawa	--	14	10	24
1934-35	Detroit R.W.	--	3	1	4
	Totals	--	20	18	38
Playoffs					
1930-31	Montreal M.	--	0	0	0

ROCHE, Earl *Forward*
b. Prescott, Ont., Feb. 22, 1910

Season	Club	GP	G	A	Pts
1930-31	Montreal M.	--	2	0	2
1932-33	Ottawa	--	4	5	9
1933-34	Ottawa	--	13	16	29
1934-35	StL E-Det RW	--	6	6	12
	Totals	--	25	27	52
Playoffs					
1930-31	Montreal M.	--	0	0	0

ROCHE, Ernest Charles *Defenseman*
b. Montreal, Que., Feb. 4, 1930

Season	Club	GP	G	A	Pts
1950-51	Montreal C.	4	0	0	0

ROCHEFORT, David Joseph *Forward*
b. Red Deer, Alta., July 22, 1946

Season	Club	GP	G	A	Pts
1966-67	Detroit R.W.	1	0	0	0

ROCHEFORT, Leon Joseph Fernand *Forward*
b. Cap de la Madelaine, Que., May 4, 1939

Season	Club	GP	G	A	Pts
1960-61	New York R.	1	0	0	0
1962-63	New York R.	23	5	4	9
1963-64	Montreal C.	3	0	0	0
1964-65	Montreal C.	9	2	0	2
1965-66	Montreal C.	1	0	1	1
1966-67	Montreal C.	27	9	7	16
1967-68	Philadelphia F.	74	21	21	42
1968-69	Philadelphia F.	65	14	21	35
1969-70	Los Angeles	76	9	23	32
1970-71	Montreal C.	57	5	10	15
1971-72	Detroit R.W.	64	17	12	29
1972-73	Det RW-Atl	74	11	22	33
	Totals	474	93	121	214
Playoffs					
1965-66	Montreal C.	4	1	1	2
1966-67	Montreal C.	10	1	1	2
1967-68	Philadelphia F.	7	2	0	2

ROCHEFORT *(Continued)*

Playoffs

	Club	GP	G	A	Pts
1968–69	Philadelphia F.	3	0	0	0
1970–71	Montreal C.	10	0	0	0
	Totals	34	4	2	6

All-Star

1968	NHL All-Stars	1	0	0	0

ROCKBURN, Harvey *Defenseman*

Season	Club	GP	G	A	Pts
1929–30	Detroit C.	--	4	0	4
1930–31	Detroit F.	--	0	1	1
1932–33	Ottawa	--	0	1	1
	Totals	--	4	2	6

RODDEN, Edmund Anthony *Forward*
b. Toronto, Ont., Mar. 22, 1901

Season	Club	GP	G	A	Pts
1926–27	Chicago	--	3	3	6
1927–28	Chgo–Tor ML	42	3	8	11
1928–29	Boston	--	0	0	0
1930–31	New York R.	24	0	3	3
	Totals	--	6	14	20

Playoffs

	Club	GP	G	A	Pts
1926–27	Chicago	2	0	1	1
1928–29	Boston	5	0	0	0
	Totals	7	0	1	1

ROLFE, Dale *Defenseman*
b. Timmins, Ont., Apr. 30, 1940

Season	Club	GP	G	A	Pts
1959–60	Boston	3	0	0	0
1967–68	Los Angeles	68	3	13	16
1968–69	Los Angeles	75	3	19	22
1969–70	LA–Det RW	75	3	18	21
1970–71	Det RW–NY R	58	3	16	19
1971–72	New York R.	68	2	14	16
1972–73	New York R.	72	7	25	32
	Totals	419	21	105	126

Playoffs

	Club	GP	G	A	Pts
1967–68	Los Angeles	7	0	1	1
1968–69	Los Angeles	10	0	4	4
1969–70	Detroit R.W.	4	0	2	2
1970–71	New York R.	13	0	1	1
1971–72	New York R.	10	4	3	7
1972–73	New York R.	8	0	5	5
	Totals	52	4	16	20

ROLLINS, Elwin Ira (Al) *Goalie*
b. Vanguard, Sask., Oct. 9, 1926

Season	Club	GP	GA	Sho	AVE
1949–50	Toronto M.L.	2	4	1	2.00
1950–51	Toronto M.L.	40	70	5	1.75

ROLLINS *(Continued)*

Season	Club	GP	GA	Sho	AVE
1951–52	Toronto M.L.	70	154	5	2.20
1952–53	Chicago	70	175	6	2.50
1953–54	Chicago	66	213	5	3.23
1954–55	Chicago	44	150	0	3.41
1955–56	Chicago	58	174	3	3.00
1956–57	Chicago	70	225	3	3.21
1959–60	New York R.	10	31	0	3.10
	Totals	431	1221	28	2.83

Playoffs

	Club	GP	GA	Sho	AVE
1950–51	Toronto M.L.	4	6	0	1.50
1951–52	Toronto M.L.	2	6	0	3.00
1952–53	Chicago	7	18	0	2.57
	Totals	13	30	0	2.30

All-Star

		GP	Per	GA	AGP
1954	NHL All-Stars	1	1½	0	0.00

ROMANCHYCH, Larry Brian *Forward*
b. Vancouver, B.C., Sept. 7, 1949

Season	Club	GP	G	A	Pts
1970–71	Chicago	10	0	2	2
1972–73	Atlanta	70	18	30	48
	Totals	80	18	32	50

ROMBOUGH, Douglas George (Doug) *Forward*
b. Fergus, Ont., July 8, 1950

Season	Club	GP	G	A	Pts
1972–73	Buffalo	5	2	0	2

ROMNES, Elwin N. (Doc) *Forward*
b. White Bear, Minn., Jan. 1, 1909

Season	Club	GP	G	A	Pts
1930–31	Chicago	--	5	7	12
1931–32	Chicago	--	1	0	1
1932–33	Chicago	--	10	12	22
1933–34	Chicago	--	8	21	29
1934–35	Chicago	--	10	14	24
1935–36	Chicago	--	13	25	38
1936–37	Chicago	--	4	14	18
1937–38	Chicago	--	10	22	32
1938–39	Chgo–Tor ML	--	7	20	27
1939–40	New York A.	--	0	1	1
	Totals	--	68	136	204

Playoffs

	Club	GP	G	A	Pts
1930–31	Chicago	--	1	1	2
1931–32	Chicago	--	0	0	0
1933–34	Chicago	--	2	7	9
1934–35	Chicago	--	0	0	0
1935–36	Chicago	--	1	2	3
1937–38	Chicago	--	2	4	6
1938–39	Toronto M.L.	--	1	4	6
	Totals	--	7	18	25

RONAN, Skene *Forward*

Season	Club	GP	G	A	Pts
1918-19	Ottawa	11	0	0	0

RONSON, Leonard Keith *Forward*
b. Brantford, Ont., July 8, 1936

Season	Club	GP	G	A	Pts
1960-61	New York R.	13	2	1	3
1968-69	Oakland	5	0	0	0
	Totals	18	2	1	3

RONTY, Paul *Forward*
b. Toronto, Ont., June 12, 1928

Season	Club	GP	G	A	Pts
1947-48	Boston	24	3	11	14
1948-49	Boston	60	20	29	49
1949-50	Boston	70	23	36	59
1950-51	Boston	71	10	22	32
1951-52	New York R.	65	12	31	43
1952-53	New York R.	70	16	38	54
1953-54	New York R.	70	13	33	46
1954-55	Montreal C.	59	4	11	15
	Totals	488	101	211	312
Playoffs					
1947-48	Boston	5	0	4	4
1948-49	Boston	5	1	2	3
1950-51	Boston	6	0	1	1
1954-55	Montreal C.	5	0	0	0
	Totals	21	1	7	8
All-Star					
1949	NHL All-Stars	1	1	0	1
1950	NHL All-Stars	1	0	0	0
1953	NHL All-Stars	1	0	1	1
1954	NHL All-Stars	1	0	0	0
	Totals	4	1	1	2

ROSS, Arthur Howey *Defenseman*
b. Naughton, Ont., Jan. 13, 1886

Season	Club	GP	G	A	Pts
1917-18	Montreal W.	3	1	0	1

ROSS, James *Defenseman*
b. Edinburgh, Scotland, May 20, 1926

Season	Club	GP	G	A	Pts
1951-52	New York R.	51	2	9	11
1952-53	New York R.	11	0	2	2
	Totals	62	2	11	13

ROSSIGNOL, Roland *Forward*
b. Edmundston, N. B., Oct. 18, 1921

Season	Club	GP	G	A	Pts
1943-44	Detroit R.W.	1	0	1	1
1944-45	Montreal C.	5	2	2	4
1945-46	Detroit R.W.	8	1	2	3
	Totals	14	3	5	8
Playoffs					
1944-45	Montreal C.	1	0	0	0

ROTA, Randy *Forward*
b. Creston, B.C., Aug. 16, 1950

Season	Club	GP	G	A	Pts
1972-73	Montreal C.	2	1	1	2

ROTHSCHILD, Samuel *Forward*
b. Sudbury, Ont., Oct. 16, 1899

Season	Club	GP	G	A	Pts
1924-25	Montreal M.	27	5	4	9
1925-26	Montreal M.	33	2	1	3
1926-27	Montreal M.	--	1	1	2
1927-28	New York A.	--	0	0	0
	Totals	--	8	6	14
Playoffs					
1925-26	Montreal M.	--	0	0	0
1926-27	Montreal M.	--	0	0	0
	Totals	--	0	0	0

ROULSTON, William Orville (Rolly)
Defenseman
b. Toronto, Ont., Apr. 12, 1911

Season	Club	GP	G	A	Pts
1936-37	Detroit R.W.	--	0	5	5
1937-38	Detroit R.W.	--	0	1	1
	Totals	--	0	6	6

ROUSSEAU, Guy *Forward*
b. Montreal, Que., Dec. 21, 1934

Season	Club	GP	G	A	Pts
1954-55	Montreal C.	2	0	1	1
1956-57	Montreal C.	2	0	0	0
	Totals	4	0	1	1

ROUSSEAU, Joseph Jean-Paul Robert (Bobby)
Forward
b. Montreal, Que., July 26, 1940

Season	Club	GP	G	A	Pts
1960-61	Montreal C.	15	1	2	3
1961-62	Montreal C.	70	21	24	45
1962-63	Montreal C.	62	19	18	37
1963-64	Montreal C.	70	25	31	56
1964-65	Montreal C.	66	12	35	47

ROUSSEAU (Continued)

Season	Club	GP	G	A	Pts
1965–66	Montreal C.	70	30	48	78
1966–67	Montreal C.	68	19	44	63
1967–68	Montreal C.	74	19	46	65
1968–69	Montreal C.	76	30	40	70
1969–70	Montreal C.	72	24	34	58
1970–71	Minnesota	63	4	20	24
1971–72	New York R.	78	21	36	57
1972–73	New York R.	78	8	37	45
	Totals	862	233	415	648

Playoffs

Season	Club	GP	G	A	Pts
1961–62	Montreal C.	6	0	2	2
1962–63	Montreal C.	5	0	1	1
1963–64	Montreal C.	7	1	1	2
1964–65	Montreal C.	13	5	8	13
1965–66	Montreal C.	10	4	4	8
1966–67	Montreal C.	10	1	7	8
1967–68	Montreal C.	13	2	4	6
1968–69	Montreal C.	14	3	2	5
1970–71	Minnesota	12	2	6	8
1971–72	New York R.	16	6	11	17
1972–73	New York R.	10	2	3	5
	Totals	116	26	49	75

All-Star

Season	Club	GP	G	A	Pts
1965	Montreal C.	1	0	1	1
1967	Montreal C.	1	0	2	2
1969	East All-Stars	1	0	1	1
	Totals	3	0	4	4

ROUSSEAU, Roland *Defenseman*
b. Montreal, Que., Dec. 1, 1929

Season	Club	GP	G	A	Pts
1952–53	Montreal C.	2	0	0	0

ROWE, Robert *Defenseman*

Season	Club	GP	G	A	Pts
1924–25	Boston	4	1	0	1

Playoffs

Season	Club	GP	G	A	Pts
1918–19	Seattle (PCHL)	--	1	0	1
1919–20	Seattle (PCHL)	--	2	0	2
	Totals	--	3	0	3

ROWE, Ronald Nickolas *Forward*
b. Toronto, Ont., Nov. 30, 1924

Season	Club	GP	G	A	Pts
1947–48	New York R.	5	1	0	1

ROZZINI, Gino *Forward*
b. Shawinigan Falls, Que., Oct. 24, 1918

Season	Club	GP	G	A	Pts
1944–45	Boston	31	5	10	15

Playoffs

Season	Club	GP	G	A	Pts
1944–45	Boston	6	1	2	3

RUELLE, Bernard Edward *Forward*
b. Haughton, Mich., Nov. 23, 1920

Season	Club	GP	G	A	Pts
1943–44	Detroit R.W.	2	1	0	1

RUNGE, Paul *Forward*
b. Edmonton, Alta., Sept. 10, 1909

Season	Club	GP	G	A	Pts
1931–32	Boston	--	0	1	1
1934–35	Montreal C.	--	0	0	0
1935–36	Mont C-Bos	--	8	4	12
1936–37	Mont C-Mont M	--	5	10	15
1937–38	Montreal M.	--	5	7	12
	Totals	--	18	22	40

Playoffs

Season	Club	GP	G	A	Pts
1935–36	Boston	--	0	0	0
1936–37	Montreal M.	--	0	0	0
	Totals	--	0	0	0

RUPP, Duane Edward Franklin *Defenseman*
b. Macnutt, Sask., Mar. 29, 1938

Season	Club	GP	G	A	Pts
1962–63	New York R.	2	0	0	0
1964–65	Toronto M.L.	2	0	0	0
1965–66	Toronto M.L.	2	0	1	1
1966–67	Toronto M.L.	3	0	0	0
1967–68	Toronto M.L.	71	1	8	9
1968–69	Minn-Pitts Pe	59	5	11	16
1969–70	Pittsburgh Pe.	64	2	14	16
1970–71	Pittsburgh Pe.	59	5	28	33
1971–72	Pittsburgh Pe.	34	4	18	22
1972–73	Pittsburgh Pe.	78	7	13	20
	Totals	374	24	93	117

Playoffs

Season	Club	GP	G	A	Pts
1969–70	Pittsburgh Pe.	6	2	2	4
1971–72	Pittsburgh Pe.	4	0	0	0
	Totals	10	2	2	4

All-Star

Season	Club	GP	G	A	Pts
1968	Toronto M.L.	1	0	1	1

RUPP, Patrick Lloyd *Goalie*
b. Detroit, Mich., Aug. 12, 1942

Season	Club	GP	GA	Sho	AVE
1963–64	Detroit R.W.	1	4	0	4.00

RUSSELL, Churchill Davidson *Forward*
b. Winnipeg, Man., Mar. 16, 1923

Season	Club	GP	G	A	Pts
1945–46	New York R.	17	0	5	5
1946–47	New York R.	54	20	8	28
1947–48	New York R.	19	0	3	3
	Totals	90	20	16	36

RUSSELL, Phillip (Phil) *Defenseman*
b. Edmonton, Alta., July 1, 1952

Season	Club	GP	G	A	Pts
1972–73	Chicago	76	6	19	25
Playoffs					
1972–73	Chicago	16	0	3	3

RUTHERFORD, James Earl (Jim) *Goalie*
b. Beeton, Ont., Feb. 17, 1949

Season	Club	GP	GA	Sho	AVE
1970–71	Detroit R.W.	25	94	1	3.76
1971–72	Pittsburgh Pe.	36	116	1	3.22
1972–73	Pittsburgh Pe.	44⅓	129	3	2.91
	Totals	105⅓	339	5	3.23
Playoffs					
1971–72	Pittsburgh Pe.	4	14	0	3.50

RUTLEDGE, Wayne Alvin *Goalie*
b. Barrie, Ont., Jan. 5, 1942

Season	Club	GP	GA	Sho	AVE
1967–68	Los Angeles	40¾	117	2	2.87
1968–69	Los Angeles	15⅓	56	0	3.65
1969–70	Los Angeles	16	68	0	4.25
	Totals	72	241	2	3.35
Playoffs					
1967–68	Los Angeles	2½	8	0	3.23
1968–69	Los Angeles	3⅔	12	0	3.14
	Totals	6⅙	20	0	3.16

SABOURIN, Gary Bruce *Forward*
b. Parry Sound, Ont., Dec. 4, 1943

Season	Club	GP	G	A	Pts
1967–68	St. Louis B.	50	13	10	23
1968–69	St. Louis B.	75	25	23	48
1969–70	St. Louis B.	72	28	14	42
1970–71	St. Louis B.	59	14	17	31
1971–72	St. Louis B.	77	28	17	45
1972–73	St. Louis B.	76	21	27	48
	Totals	409	129	108	237
Playoffs					
1967–68	St. Louis B.	18	4	2	6
1968–69	St. Louis B.	12	6	5	11
1969–70	St. Louis B.	16	5	0	5
1971–72	St. Louis B.	11	3	3	6
1972–73	St. Louis B.	5	1	1	2
	Totals	62	19	11	30
All-Star					
1970	West All-Stars	1	0	0	0
1971	West All-Stars	1	0	0	0
	Totals	2	0	0	0

SABOURIN, Robert *Forward*
b. Sudbury, Ont., Mar. 17, 1933

Season	Club	GP	G	A	Pts
1951–52	Toronto M.L.	1	0	0	0

SACHARUK, Lawrence *Defenseman*
b. Saskatoon, Sask., Oct. 16, 1952

Season	Club	GP	G	A	Pts
1972–73	New York R.	8	1	0	1

ST. LAURENT, Dollard Herve *Defenseman*
b. Verdun, Que., May 12, 1929

Season	Club	GP	G	A	Pts
1950–51	Montreal C.	3	0	0	0
1951–52	Montreal C.	40	3	10	13
1952–53	Montreal C.	54	2	6	8
1953–54	Montreal C.	53	3	12	15
1954–55	Montreal C.	58	3	14	17
1955–56	Montreal C.	46	4	9	13
1956–57	Montreal C.	64	1	11	12
1957–58	Montreal C.	65	3	20	23
1958–59	Chicago	70	4	8	12
1959–60	Chicago	68	4	13	17
1960–61	Chicago	67	2	17	19
1961–62	Chicago	64	0	13	13
	Totals	652	29	133	162
Playoffs					
1951–52	Montreal C.	9	0	3	3
1952–53	Montreal C.	12	0	3	3
1953–54	Montreal C.	10	1	2	3
1954–55	Montreal C.	12	0	5	5
1955–56	Montreal C.	4	0	0	0
1956–57	Montreal C.	7	0	1	1
1957–58	Montreal C.	5	0	0	0
1958–59	Chicago	6	0	1	1
1959–60	Chicago	4	0	1	1
1960–61	Chicago	11	1	2	3
1961–62	Chicago	12	0	4	4
	Totals	92	2	22	24
All-Star					
1953	Montreal C.	1	0	0	0
1956	Montreal C.	1	0	0	0
1957	Montreal C.	1	0	0	0
1958	NHL All-Stars	1	0	0	0
1961	Chicago	1	0	0	0
	Totals	5	0	0	0

ST. MARSEILLE, Francis Leo (Frank) *Forward*
b. Levack, Ont., Dec. 14, 1939

Season	Club	GP	G	A	Pts
1967–68	St. Louis B.	57	16	16	32
1968–69	St. Louis B.	72	12	26	38
1969–70	St. Louis B.	74	16	43	59
1970–71	St. Louis B.	77	19	32	51

ST. MARSEILLE (Continued)

Season	Club	GP	G	A	Pts
1971–72	St. Louis B.	78	16	36	52
1972–73	StL B–LA	74	14	22	36
	Totals	432	93	175	268

Playoffs

Season	Club	GP	G	A	Pts
1967–68	St. Louis B.	18	5	8	13
1968–69	St. Louis B.	12	3	3	6
1969–70	St. Louis B.	15	6	7	13
1970–71	St. Louis B.	6	2	1	3
1971–72	St. Louis B.	11	3	5	8
	Totals	62	19	24	43

All-Star

Season	Club	GP	G	A	Pts
1970	West All-Stars	1	0	0	0

SALESKI, Donald (Don) *Forward*
b. Moose Jaw, Sask., Nov. 10, 1949

Season	Club	GP	G	A	Pts
1971–72	Philadelphia F.	1	0	0	0
1972–73	Philadelphia F.	78	12	9	21
	Totals	79	12	9	21

Playoffs

Season	Club	GP	G	A	Pts
1972–73	Philadelphia F.	11	1	2	3

SAMIS, Philip Lawrence *Defenseman*
b. Edmonton, Alta., Dec. 28, 1927

Season	Club	GP	G	A	Pts
1949–50	Toronto M.L.	2	0	0	0

Playoffs

Season	Club	GP	G	A	Pts
1947–48	Toronto M.L.	5	0	1	1

SANDERSON, Derek Michael *Forward*
b. Niagara Falls, Ont., June 16, 1946

Season	Club	GP	G	A	Pts
1965–66	Boston	2	0	0	0
1966–67	Boston	2	0	0	0
1967–68	Boston	71	24	25	49
1968–69	Boston	61	26	22	48
1969–70	Boston	50	18	23	41
1970–71	Boston	71	29	34	63
1971–72	Boston	78	25	33	58
1972–73	Boston	25	5	10	15
	Totals	360	127	147	274

Playoffs

Season	Club	GP	G	A	Pts
1967–68	Boston	4	0	2	2
1968–69	Boston	9	8	2	10
1969–70	Boston	14	5	4	9
1970–71	Boston	7	2	1	3
1971–72	Boston	11	1	1	2
1972–73	Boston	5	1	2	3
	Totals	50	17	12	29

SANDFORD, Edward Michael *Forward*
b. New Toronto, Ont., Aug. 20, 1928

Season	Club	GP	G	A	Pts
1947–48	Boston	59	10	15	25
1948–49	Boston	56	16	20	36
1949–50	Boston	17	1	4	5
1950–51	Boston	51	10	13	23
1951–52	Boston	65	13	12	25
1952–53	Boston	61	14	21	35
1953–54	Boston	70	16	31	47
1954–55	Boston	60	14	20	34
1955–56	Det RW–Chgo	61	12	9	21
	Totals	500	106	145	251

Playoffs

Season	Club	GP	G	A	Pts
1947–48	Boston	5	1	0	1
1948–49	Boston	5	1	3	4
1950–51	Boston	6	0	1	1
1951–52	Boston	7	2	2	4
1952–53	Boston	11	8	3	11
1953–54	Boston	3	0	1	1
1954–55	Boston	5	1	1	2
	Totals	42	13	11	24

All-Star

Season	Club	GP	G	A	Pts
1951	NHL 1st All-Stars	1	0	0	0
1952	NHL 1st All-Stars	1	0	0	0
1953	NHL All-Stars	1	0	0	0
1954	NHL All-Stars	1	0	0	0
1955	Detroit R.W.	1	0	0	0
	Totals	5	0	0	0

SANDS, Charles Henry *Forward*
b. Fort William, Ont., Mar. 23, 1910

Season	Club	GP	G	A	Pts
1932–33	Toronto M.L.	--	0	3	3
1933–34	Toronto M.L.	--	8	8	16
1934–35	Boston	--	15	12	27
1935–36	Boston	--	6	4	10
1936–37	Boston	--	18	5	23
1937–38	Boston	--	17	12	29
1938–39	Boston	--	7	5	12
1939–40	Montreal C.	--	9	20	29
1940–41	Montreal C.	--	5	13	18
1941–42	Montreal C.	39	11	16	27
1942–43	Montreal C.	31	3	9	12
1943–44	New York R.	9	0	2	2
	Totals	--	99	109	208

Playoffs

Season	Club	GP	G	A	Pts
1932–33	Toronto M.L.	9	2	2	4
1933–34	Toronto M.L.	5	1	0	1
1934–35	Boston	4	0	0	0
1935–36	Boston	2	0	0	0
1936–37	Boston	3	1	2	3
1937–38	Boston	3	1	1	2

SANDS *(Continued)*

Playoffs	Club	GP	G	A	Pts
1938–39	Boston	12	0	0	0
1940–41	Montreal C.	3	1	0	1
1941–42	Montreal C.	3	0	1	1
1942–43	Montreal C.	2	0	0	0
	Totals	46	6	6	12

SARRAZIN, Richard (Dick) *Forward*
b. St. Gabriel de Brandon, Que., Jan. 22, 1946

Season	Club	GP	G	A	Pts
1968–69	Philadelphia F.	54	16	30	46
1969–70	Philadelphia F.	18	1	1	2
1971–72	Philadelphia F.	28	3	4	7
	Totals	100	20	35	55
Playoffs					
1968–69	Philadelphia F.	4	0	0	0

SASKAMOOSE, Fred *Forward*
b. Sandy Lake Reserve, Sask., Dec. 24, 1934

Season	Club	GP	G	A	Pts
1953–54	Chicago	11	0	0	0

SATHER, Glen Cameron *Forward*
b. High River, Alta., Sept. 2, 1943

Season	Club	GP	G	A	Pts
1966–67	Boston	5	0	0	0
1967–68	Boston	65	8	12	20
1968–69	Boston	76	4	11	15
1969–70	Pittsburgh Pe.	76	12	14	26
1970–71	Pitt Pe–NY R	77	10	3	13
1971–72	New York R.	76	5	9	14
1972–73	New York R.	77	11	15	26
	Totals	452	50	64	114
Playoffs					
1967–68	Boston	3	0	0	0
1968–69	Boston	10	0	0	0
1969–70	Pittsburgh Pe.	10	0	2	2
1970–71	New York R.	13	0	1	1
1971–72	New York R.	16	0	1	1
1972–73	New York R.	9	0	0	0
	Totals	61	0	4	4

SAUNDERS, Theodore *Forward*
b. Ottawa, Ont., Aug. 29, 1911

Season	Club	GP	G	A	Pts
1933–34	Ottawa	--	1	3	4

SAVAGE, Gordon (Tony) *Defenseman*
b. Calgary, Alta., July 18, 1906

Season	Club	GP	G	A	Pts
1934–35	Montreal C.	--	1	5	6
Playoffs					
1934–35	Montreal C.	--	0	0	0

SAVARD, Serge *Defenseman*
b. Montreal, Que., Jan. 22, 1946

Season	Club	GP	G	A	Pts
1966–67	Montreal C.	2	0	0	0
1967–68	Montreal C.	67	2	13	15
1968–69	Montreal C.	74	8	23	31
1969–70	Montreal C.	64	12	19	31
1970–71	Montreal C.	37	5	10	15
1971–72	Montreal C.	23	1	8	9
1972–73	Montreal C.	74	7	32	39
	Totals	341	35	105	140
Playoffs					
1967–68	Montreal C.	6	2	0	2
1968–69	Montreal C.	14	4	6	10
1971–72	Montreal C.	6	0	0	0
1972–73	Montreal C.	17	3	8	11
	Totals	43	9	14	23
All-Star					
1970	East All-Stars	1	0	0	0
1973	East All-Stars	1	0	1	1
	Totals	2	0	1	1

SAWCHUK, Terrance Gordon (Terry) *Goalie*
b. Winnipeg, Man., Dec. 28, 1929

Season	Club	GP	GA	Sho	AVE
1949–50	Detroit R.W.	7	16	1	2.28
1950–51	Detroit R.W.	70	139	11	1.98
1951–52	Detroit R.W.	70	133	12	1.94
1952–53	Detroit R.W.	63	120	9	1.90
1953–54	Detroit R.W.	66⅔	129	12	1.93
1954–55	Detroit R.W.	68	132	12	1.94
1955–56	Boston	68	181	9	2.66
1956–57	Boston	34	81	2	2.38
1957–58	Detroit R.W.	70	207	3	2.96
1958–59	Detroit R.W.	67	209	5	3.12
1959–60	Detroit R.W.	58	156	5	2.69
1960–61	Detroit R.W.	35⅔	113	2	3.17
1961–62	Detroit R.W.	43	143	5	3.32
1962–63	Detroit R.W.	48	119	3	2.48
1963–64	Detroit R.W.	52⅓	138	5	2.64
1964–65	Toronto M.L.	36	92	1	2.56
1965–66	Toronto M.L.	25⅓	80	1	3.16
1966–67	Toronto M.L.	23⅓	66	2	2.83
1967–68	Los Angeles	32⅓	99	2	3.06
1968–69	Detroit R.W.	10⅔	28	0	2.62
1969–70	New York R.	6¹³⁄₁₅	20	1	2.91
	Totals	955⅕	2401	103	2.50
Playoffs					
1950–51	Detroit R.W.	6	13	1	2.17
1951–52	Detroit R.W.	8	5	4	0.62
1952–53	Detroit R.W.	6	21	1	3.50
1953–54	Detroit R.W.	12	20	2	1.67
1954–55	Detroit R.W.	11	26	1	2.36

SAWCHUK *(Continued)*

Playoffs	Club	GP	GA	Sho	AVE
1957–58	Detroit R.W.	4	19	0	4.75
1959–60	Detroit R.W.	6	20	0	3.33
1960–61	Detroit R.W.	7⅓	18	1	2.45
1962–63	Detroit R.W.	11	36	0	3.27
1963–64	Detroit R.W.	11⅔	31	1	2.66
1964–65	Toronto M.L.	1	3	0	3.00
1965–66	Toronto M.L.	2	6	0	3.00
1966–67	Toronto M.L.	9⅓	25	0	2.68
1967–68	Los Angeles	4⅔	18	1	3.85
1969–70	New York R.	1⅓	6	0	4.51
	Totals	101⅓	267	12	2.63

All-Star		GP	Per	GA	AGP
1950	Detroit R.W.	1	3	1	0.33
1951	NHL 1st All-Stars	1	1½	1	0.67
1952	NHL 1st All-Stars	1	3	1	0.33
1953	NHL All-Stars	1	3	1	0.33
1954	Detroit R.W.	1	3	2	0.67
1955	NHL All-Stars	1	1½	1	0.67
1956	NHL All-Stars	1	1½	1	0.67
1959	NHL All-Stars	1	3	6	2.00
1963	NHL All-Stars	1	1½	1	0.67
1964	Toronto M.L.	1	1½	2	1.33
1968	NHL All-Stars	1	1	2	2.00
	Totals	11	23½	19	0.81

SCHAEFER, Joseph *Goalie*
b. Long Island City, N.Y., Dec. 21, 1924

Season	Club	GP	GA	Sho	AVE
1959–60	New York R.	⅔	5	0	7.50
1960–61	New York R.	⅚	3	0	3.61
	Totals	1½	8	0	5.33

SCHAEFER, Paul

Season	Club	GP	G	A	Pts
1936–37	Chicago	––	0	0	0

SCHELLA, John Edward *Defenseman*
b. Port Arthur, Ont., May 9, 1947

Season	Club	GP	G	A	Pts
1970–71	Vancouver	38	0	5	5
1971–72	Vancouver	77	2	13	15
	Totals	115	2	18	20

SCHERZA, Charles (Chuck) *Forward*
b. Brandon, Man., Feb. 15, 1923

Season	Club	GP	G	A	Pts
1943–44	Bos–NY R	14	4	3	7
1944–45	New York R.	22	2	3	5
	Totals	36	6	6	12

SCHINKEL, Kenneth C. (Ken) *Forward*
b. Jansen, Sask., Nov. 27, 1932

Season	Club	GP	G	A	Pts
1959–60	New York R.	69	13	16	29
1960–61	New York R.	38	2	6	8
1961–62	New York R.	65	7	21	28
1962–63	New York R.	69	6	9	15
1963–64	New York R.	4	0	0	0
1966–67	New York R.	20	6	3	9
1967–68	Pittsburgh Pe.	57	14	25	39
1968–69	Pittsburgh Pe.	76	18	34	52
1969–70	Pittsburgh Pe.	72	20	25	45
1970–71	Pittsburgh Pe.	50	15	19	34
1971–72	Pittsburgh Pe.	74	15	30	45
1972–73	Pittsburgh Pe.	42	11	10	21
	Totals	636	127	198	325

Playoffs					
1961–62	New York R.	2	1	0	1
1966–67	New York R.	4	0	1	1
1969–70	Pittsburgh Pe.	10	4	1	5
1971–72	Pittsburgh Pe.	3	2	0	2
	Totals	19	7	2	9

All-Star					
1968	NHL All-Stars	1	0	0	0
1969	West All-Stars	1	0	0	0
	Totals	2	0	0	0

SCHMAUTZ, Clifford Harvey (Cliff) *Forward*
b. Saskatoon, Sask., Mar. 17, 1939

Season	Club	GP	G	A	Pts
1970–71	Buff–Phila F	56	13	19	32

SCHMAUTZ, Robert James (Bob) *Forward*
b. Saskatoon, Sask., Mar. 28, 1945

Season	Club	GP	G	A	Pts
1967–68	Chicago	13	3	2	5
1968–69	Chicago	63	9	7	16
1970–71	Vancouver	26	5	5	10
1971–72	Vancouver	60	12	13	25
1972–73	Vancouver	77	38	33	71
	Totals	239	67	60	127

Playoffs					
1967–68	Chicago	11	2	3	5

All-Star					
1973	East All-Stars	1	1	0	1

SCHMIDT, Clarence *Forward*
b. 1923

Season	Club	GP	G	A	Pts
1943–44	Boston	7	1	0	1

SCHMIDT, John *Forward*

b. Odessa, Sask., Nov. 11, 1924

Season	Club	GP	G	A	Pts
1942–43	Boston	45	6	7	13

SCHMIDT, Joseph *Forward*

Season	Club	GP	G	A	Pts
1943–44	Boston	2	0	0	0

SCHMIDT, Milton Conrad *Forward*

b. Kitchener, Ont., Mar. 5, 1918

Season	Club	GP	G	A	Pts
1936–37	Boston	--	2	8	10
1937–38	Boston	--	13	14	27
1938–39	Boston	--	15	17	32
1939–40	Boston	48	22	30	52
1940–41	Boston	45	13	25	38
1941–42	Boston	36	14	21	35
1945–46	Boston	48	13	18	31
1946–47	Boston	59	27	35	62
1947–48	Boston	33	9	17	26
1948–49	Boston	44	10	22	32
1949–50	Boston	68	19	22	41
1950–51	Boston	62	22	39	61
1951–52	Boston	69	21	29	50
1952–53	Boston	68	11	23	34
1953–54	Boston	62	14	18	32
1954–55	Boston	23	4	8	12
	Totals	--	229	346	575

Playoffs

Season	Club	GP	G	A	Pts
1936–37	Boston	3	0	0	0
1937–38	Boston	3	0	0	0
1938–39	Boston	12	3	3	6
1939–40	Boston	6	0	0	0
1940–41	Boston	11	5	6	11
1945–46	Boston	10	3	5	8
1946–47	Boston	5	3	1	4
1947–48	Boston	5	2	5	7
1948–49	Boston	4	0	2	2
1950–51	Boston	6	0	1	1
1951–52	Boston	7	2	1	3
1952–53	Boston	10	5	1	6
1953–54	Boston	4	1	0	1
	Totals	86	24	25	49

All-Star

1947	NHL All-Stars	1	0	1	1
1948	NHL All-Stars	1	0	0	0
1951	NHL 1st All-Stars	1	0	1	1
1952	NHL 2nd All-Stars	1	0	0	0
	Totals	4	0	2	2

SCHNARR, Werner *Forward*

Season	Club	GP	G	A	Pts
1924–25	Boston	24	0	0	0
1925–26	Boston	1	0	0	0
	Totals	25	0	0	0

SCHOCK, Daniel Patrick (Danny) *Forward*

b. Terrace Bay, Ont., Dec. 30, 1948

Season	Club	GP	G	A	Pts
1970–71	Bos–Phila F	20	1	2	3

Playoffs

1969–70	Boston	1	0	0	0

SCHOCK, Ronald Lawrence (Ron) *Forward*

b. Chapleau, Ont., Dec. 19, 1943

Season	Club	GP	G	A	Pts
1963–64	Boston	5	1	2	3
1964–65	Boston	33	4	7	11
1965–66	Boston	24	2	2	4
1966–67	Boston	66	10	20	30
1967–68	St. Louis B.	55	9	9	18
1968–69	St. Louis B.	67	12	27	39
1969–70	Pittsburgh Pe.	76	8	21	29
1970–71	Pittsburgh Pe.	71	14	26	40
1971–72	Pittsburgh Pe.	77	17	29	46
1972–73	Pittsburgh Pe.	78	13	36	49
	Totals	552	90	179	269

Playoffs

Season	Club	GP	G	A	Pts
1967–68	St. Louis B.	12	1	2	3
1968–69	St. Louis B.	12	1	2	3
1969–70	Pittsburgh Pe.	10	1	6	7
1971–72	Pittsburgh Pe.	4	1	0	1
	Totals	38	4	10	14

SCHOENFELD, James (Jim) *Defenseman*

b. Galt, Ont., Sept. 4, 1952

Season	Club	GP	G	A	Pts
1972–73	Buffalo	66	4	15	19

Playoffs

1972–73	Buffalo	6	2	1	3

SCHRINER, David (Sweeney) *Forward*

b. Calgary, Alta., Nov. 30, 1911

Season	Club	GP	G	A	Pts
1934–35	New York A.	--	18	22	40
1935–36	New York A.	--	19	26	45
1936–37	New York A.	--	21	25	46
1937–38	New York A.	--	21	17	38
1938–39	New York A.	--	13	31	44
1939–40	Toronto M.L.	--	11	15	26
1940–41	Toronto M.L.	--	24	14	38
1941–42	Toronto M.L.	47	20	16	36

SCHRINER (Continued)

Season	Club	GP	G	A	Pts
1942–43	Toronto M.L.	37	19	17	36
1944–45	Toronto M.L.	26	27	15	37
1945–46	Toronto M.L.	47	13	6	19
	Totals	--	201	204	405
Playoffs					
1935–36	New York A.	2	3	1	4
1937–38	New York A.	6	1	0	1
1938–39	New York A.	2	0	0	0
1939–40	Toronto M.L.	10	1	3	4
1940–41	Toronto M.L.	7	2	1	3
1941–42	Toronto M.L.	13	6	3	9
1942–43	Toronto M.L.	4	2	2	4
1944–45	Toronto M.L.	13	3	1	4
	Totals	57	18	11	29

SCHULTZ, David (Dave) *Forward*
b. Waldheim, Sask., Oct. 14, 1949

Season	Club	GP	G	A	Pts
1971–72	Philadelphia F.	1	0	0	0
1972–73	Philadelphia F.	76	9	12	21
	Totals	77	9	12	21
Playoffs					
1972–73	Philadelphia F.	11	1	0	1

SCLISIZZI, James Enlo *Forward*
b. Milton, Ont., Aug. 1, 1925

Season	Club	GP	G	A	Pts
1947–48	Detroit R.W.	4	1	0	1
1948–49	Detroit R.W.	50	9	8	17
1949–50	Detroit R.W.	4	0	0	0
1951–52	Detroit R.W.	9	2	1	3
1952–53	Chicago	14	0	2	2
	Totals	81	12	11	23
Playoffs					
1946–47	Detroit R.W.	1	0	0	0
1947–48	Detroit R.W.	6	0	0	0
1948–49	Detroit R.W.	6	0	0	0
	Totals	13	0	0	0

SCOTT, Ganton *Defenseman*

Season	Club	GP	G	A	Pts
1922–23	Toronto St. P.	17	0	0	0
1923–24	Tor StP–Hmltn	8	0	0	0
1924–25	Montreal M.	28	1	1	2
1926–27	Toronto M.L.	1	0	0	0
	Totals	54	1	1	2

SCOTT, Lawrence *Forward*
b. South River, Ont., June 19, 1900

Season	Club	GP	G	A	Pts
1926–27	New York A.	--	6	2	8
1927–28	New York R.	23	0	1	1
	Totals	--	6	3	9

SEGUIN, Daniel G. *Forward*
b. Sudbury, Ont., June 7, 1948

Season	Club	GP	G	A	Pts
1970–71	Minn–Vanc	36	1	6	7

SEIBERT, Earl Walter *Defenseman*
b. Kitchener, Ont., Dec. 7, 1911

Season	Club	GP	G	A	Pts
1931–32	New York R.	44	4	6	10
1932–33	New York R.	45	2	3	5
1933–34	New York R.	48	13	10	23
1934–35	New York R.	48	6	19	25
1935–36	NY R–Chgo	--	5	9	14
1936–37	Chicago	--	9	6	15
1937–38	Chicago	--	8	13	21
1938–39	Chicago	--	4	11	15
1939–40	Chicago	--	3	7	10
1940–41	Chicago	--	3	17	20
1941–42	Chicago	--	7	14	21
1942–43	Chicago	44	5	27	32
1943–44	Chicago	50	8	25	33
1944–45	Chgo–Det RW	47	12	17	29
1945–46	Detroit R.W.	18	0	3	3
	Totals	--	89	187	276
Playoffs					
1931–32	New York R.	7	1	2	3
1932–33	New York R.	8	1	0	1
1933–34	New York R.	2	0	0	0
1934–35	New York R.	4	0	0	0
1935–36	Chicago	2	2	0	2
1937–38	Chicago	10	5	2	7
1939–40	Chicago	2	0	1	1
1940–41	Chicago	5	0	0	0
1941–42	Chicago	3	0	0	0
1943–44	Chicago	9	0	2	2
1944–45	Detroit R.W.	14	2	1	3
	Totals	66	11	8	19

SEILING, Rodney Albert (Rod) *Defenseman*
b. Elmira, Ont., Nov. 14, 1944

Season	Club	GP	G	A	Pts
1962–63	Toronto M.L.	1	0	1	1
1963–64	New York R.	2	0	1	1
1964–65	New York R.	68	4	22	26
1965–66	New York R.	52	5	10	15
1966–67	New York R.	12	1	1	2

SEILING (Continued)

Season	Club	GP	G	A	Pts
1967-68	New York R.	71	5	11	16
1968-69	New York R.	73	4	17	21
1969-70	New York R.	76	5	21	26
1970-71	New York R.	68	5	22	27
1971-72	New York R.	78	5	36	41
1972-73	New York R.	72	9	33	42
	Totals	573	43	175	218

Playoffs

Season	Club	GP	G	A	Pts
1967-68	New York R.	6	1	1	2
1968-69	New York R.	4	1	0	1
1969-70	New York R.	2	0	0	0
1970-71	New York R.	13	1	0	1
1971-72	New York R.	16	1	4	5
	Totals	41	4	5	9

All-Star

1972	East All-Stars	1	0	1	1

SELBY, Robert Briton (Brit) *Forward*
b. Kingston, Ont., Mar. 27, 1945

Season	Club	GP	G	A	Pts
1964-65	Toronto M.L.	3	2	0	2
1965-66	Toronto M.L.	61	14	13	27
1966-67	Toronto M.L.	6	1	1	2
1967-68	Philadelphia F.	56	15	15	30
1968-69	Phila F-Tor ML	77	12	15	27
1969-70	Toronto M.L.	74	10	13	23
1970-71	Tor ML-StL B	67	1	5	6
1971-72	St. Louis B.	6	0	0	0
	Totals	350	55	62	117

Playoffs

Season	Club	GP	G	A	Pts
1965-66	Toronto M.L.	4	0	0	0
1967-68	Philadelphia F.	7	1	1	2
1968-69	Toronto M.L.	4	0	0	0
1970-71	St. Louis B.	1	0	0	0
	Totals	16	1	1	2

SELWOOD, Bradley Wayne (Brad) *Defenseman*
b. Leamington, Ont., Mar. 18, 1948

Season	Club	GP	G	A	Pts
1970-71	Toronto M.L.	28	2	10	12
1971-72	Toronto M.L.	72	4	17	21
	Totals	100	6	27	33

Playoffs

Season	Club	GP	G	A	Pts
1971-72	Toronto M.L.	5	0	0	0

SENICK, George *Forward*
b. Saskatoon, Sask., Sept. 16, 1929

Season	Club	GP	G	A	Pts
1952-53	New York R.	13	2	3	5

SHACK, Edward Steven Phillip (Eddie)
Forward
b. Sudbury, Sask., Sept. 16, 1929

Season	Club	GP	G	A	Pts
1958-59	New York R.	67	7	14	21
1959-60	New York R.	62	8	10	18
1960-61	NY R-Tor ML	67	15	16	31
1961-62	Toronto M.L.	44	7	14	21
1962-63	Toronto M.L.	63	16	9	25
1963-64	Toronto M.L.	64	11	10	21
1964-65	Toronto M.L.	67	5	9	14
1965-66	Toronto M.L.	63	26	17	43
1966-67	Toronto M.L.	63	11	14	25
1967-68	Boston	70	23	19	42
1968-69	Boston	50	11	11	22
1969-70	Los Angeles	73	22	12	34
1970-71	LA-Buff	67	27	19	46
1971-72	Buff-Pitt Pe	68	16	23	39
1972-73	Pittsburgh Pe.	74	25	20	45
	Totals	962	230	217	447

Playoffs

Season	Club	GP	G	A	Pts
1960-61	Toronto M.L.	4	0	0	0
1961-62	Toronto M.L.	9	0	0	0
1962-63	Toronto M.L.	10	2	1	3
1963-64	Toronto M.L.	13	0	1	1
1964-65	Toronto M.L.	5	1	0	1
1965-66	Toronto M.L.	4	2	1	3
1966-67	Toronto M.L.	8	0	0	0
1967-68	Boston	4	0	1	1
1968-69	Boston	9	0	2	2
1971-72	Pittsburgh Pe.	4	0	1	1
	Totals	70	5	7	12

All-Star

1962	Toronto M.L.	1	1	0	1
1963	Toronto M.L.	1	0	0	0
1964	Toronto M.L.	1	0	0	0
	Totals	3	1	0	1

SHACK, Joseph *Forward*
b. Winnipeg, Man., Dec. 8, 1916

Season	Club	GP	G	A	Pts
1942-43	New York R.	20	5	9	14
1944-45	New York R.	50	4	18	22
	Totals	70	9	27	36

SHANNON, Charles Kitchener *Defenseman*
b. Campbellford, Ont., Mar. 22, 1916

Season	Club	GP	G	A	Pts
1936-37	Montreal M.	--	9	7	16
1937-38	Montreal M.	--	0	3	3
1939-40	New York A.	--	0	0	0
	Totals	--	9	10	19

Playoffs

Season	Club	GP	G	A	Pts
1936-37	Montreal M.	--	0	1	1

SHANNON, Gerald *Forward*
b. Campbellford, Ont., Oct. 25, 1910

Season	Club	GP	G	A	Pts
1933-34	Ottawa	--	11	15	26
1934-35	StL E-Bos	--	3	3	6
1935-36	Boston	--	0	1	1
	Totals	--	14	19	33

Playoffs

1934-35	Boston	--	0	0	0

SHAY, Norman *Forward*

Season	Club	GP	G	A	Pts
1924-25	Boston	18	1	1	2
1925-26	Bos-Tor ML	35	4	1	5
	Totals	53	5	2	7

SHEA, Francis (Pat) *Defenseman*
b. Potlach, Idaho, Oct. 29, 1912

Season	Club	GP	G	A	Pts
1931-32	Chicago	--	0	1	1

SHEEHAN, Robert Richard (Bobby) *Forward*
b. Weymouth, Mass., Jan. 11, 1949

Season	Club	GP	G	A	Pts
1969-70	Montreal C.	16	2	1	3
1970-71	Montreal C.	29	6	5	11
1971-72	California	78	20	26	46
	Totals	123	28	32	60

Playoffs

1970-71	Montreal C.	6	0	0	0

SHELTON, Douglas *Forward*
b. Woodstock, Ont., June 27, 1945

Season	Club	GP	G	A	Pts
1967-68	Chicago	5	0	1	1

SHEPPARD, Frank *Forward*
b. Montreal, Que., Oct. 19, 1907

Season	Club	GP	G	A	Pts
1927-28	Detroit C.	--	1	1	2

SHEPPARD, Gregory Wayne (Greg) *Forward*
b. North Battleford, Sask., Apr. 23, 1949

Season	Club	GP	G	A	Pts
1972-73	Boston	64	24	26	50

Playoffs

1972-73	Boston	5	2	1	3

SHEPPARD, Jake O. (Johnny) *Forward*
b. Montreal, Que.

Season	Club	GP	G	A	Pts
1926-27	Detroit C.	--	13	8	21
1927-28	Detroit C.	--	10	10	20

SHEPPARD *(Continued)*

Season	Club	GP	G	A	Pts
1928-29	New York A.	--	5	4	9
1929-30	New York A.	--	14	15	29
1930-31	New York A.	--	5	8	13
1931-32	New York A.	--	1	0	1
1932-33	New York A.	--	17	9	26
1933-34	Bos-Chgo	--	3	4	7
	Totals	--	68	58	126

Playoffs

1928-29	New York A.	--	0	0	0
1933-34	Chicago	--	0	0	0
	Totals	--	0	0	0

SHERF, John *Forward*
b. Calumet, Mich., Apr. 8, 1914

Season	Club	GP	G	A	Pts
1937-38	Det RW-NY A	--	0	0	0
1943-44	Detroit R.W.	8	0	0	0
	Totals	--	0	0	0

Playoffs

1936-37	Detroit R.W.	--	0	1	1
1937-38	New York A.	1	0	0	0
	Totals	--	0	1	1

SHERO, Frederick Alexander *Defenseman*
b. Winnipeg, Man., Oct. 23, 1925

Season	Club	GP	G	A	Pts
1947-48	New York R.	19	1	0	1
1948-49	New York R.	59	3	6	9
1949-50	New York R.	67	2	8	10
	Totals	145	6	14	20

Playoffs

1947-48	New York R.	6	0	1	1
1949-50	New York R.	7	0	1	1
	Totals	13	0	2	2

SHERRITT, Gordon Ephraim *Defenseman*
b. Oakville, Man., Apr. 8, 1922

Season	Club	GP	G	A	Pts
1943-44	Detroit R.W.	8	0	0	0

SHEWCHUK, John Michael *Defenseman*
b. Brantford, Ont., June 19, 1917

Season	Club	GP	G	A	Pts
1938-39	Boston	--	0	0	0
1939-40	Boston	--	2	4	6
1940-41	Boston	--	2	2	4
1941-42	Boston	22	2	0	2
1942-43	Boston	48	2	6	8
1944-45	Boston	47	1	7	8
	Totals	--	9	19	28

SHEWCHUK (Continued)

Playoffs	Club	GP	G	A	Pts
1939–40	Boston	6	0	0	0
1940–41	Boston	--	0	0	0
1941–42	Boston	5	0	1	1
1942–43	Boston	9	0	0	0
	Totals	--	0	1	1

SHIBICKY, Alexis Dimitri *Forward*
b. Winnipeg, Man., May 19, 1914

Season	Club	GP	G	A	Pts
1935–36	New York R.	18	4	2	6
1936–37	New York R.	47	14	8	22
1937–38	New York R.	43	17	18	35
1938–39	New York R.	43	24	9	33
1939–40	New York R.	43	11	21	32
1940–41	New York R.	40	10	14	24
1941–42	New York R.	45	20	14	34
1945–46	New York R.	33	10	5	15
	Totals	322	110	91	201
Playoffs					
1936–37	New York R.	9	1	4	5
1937–38	New York R.	3	2	0	2
1938–39	New York R.	7	3	1	4
1939–40	New York R.	12	2	5	7
1940–41	New York R.	3	1	0	1
1941–42	New York R.	6	3	2	5
	Totals	40	12	12	24

SHIELDS, Allen *Defenseman*
b. Ottawa, Ont., May 10, 1907

Season	Club	GP	G	A	Pts
1927–28	Ottawa	--	0	1	1
1928–29	Ottawa	--	0	1	1
1929–30	Ottawa	--	6	3	9
1930–31	Philadelphia Q.	--	7	3	10
1931–32	New York A.	--	4	1	5
1932–33	Ottawa	--	7	4	11
1933–34	Ottawa	--	4	7	11
1934–35	Montreal M.	--	4	8	12
1935–36	Montreal M.	--	2	7	9
1936–37	NY A–Bos	--	3	4	7
1937–38	Montreal M.	--	5	7	12
	Totals	--	42	46	88
Playoffs					
1927–28	Ottawa	--	0	0	0
1929–30	Ottawa	--	0	0	0
1934–35	Montreal M.	--	0	1	1
1935–36	Montreal M.	--	0	0	0
1936–37	Boston	--	0	0	0
	Totals	--	0	1	1

SHILL, John Walker (Jack) *Forward*
b. Toronto, Ont., Jan. 12, 1913

Season	Club	GP	G	A	Pts
1933–34	Toronto M.L.	--	0	1	1
1934–35	Boston	--	4	4	8
1935–36	Toronto M.L.	--	0	1	1
1936–37	Toronto M.L.	--	4	4	8
1937–38	NY A–Chgo	--	5	6	11
1938–39	Chicago	--	2	4	6
	Totals	--	15	20	35
Playoffs					
1933–34	Toronto M.L.	--	0	0	0
1934–35	Boston	--	0	0	0
1935–36	Toronto M.L.	--	0	3	3
1936–37	Toronto M.L.	--	0	0	0
1937–38	Chicago	--	1	3	4
	Totals	--	1	6	7

SHILL, William Roy *Forward*
b. Toronto, Ont., Mar. 6, 1923

Season	Club	GP	G	A	Pts
1942–43	Boston	7	4	1	5
1945–46	Boston	45	15	12	27
1946–47	Boston	27	2	0	2
	Totals	79	21	13	34
Playoffs					
1945–46	Boston	7	1	2	3

SHIRES, James Arthur (Jim) *Forward*
b. Edmonton, Alta., Nov. 15, 1945

Season	Club	GP	G	A	Pts
1970–71	Detroit R.W.	20	2	1	3
1971–72	St. Louis B.	18	0	3	3
1972–73	Pittsburgh Pe.	18	1	2	3
	Totals	56	3	6	9

SHMYR, Paul *Defenseman*
b. Cudworth, Sask., Jan. 28, 1946

Season	Club	GP	G	A	Pts
1968–69	Chicago	3	1	0	1
1969–70	Chicago	24	0	4	4
1970–71	Chicago	57	1	12	13
1971–72	California	69	6	21	27
	Totals	153	8	37	45
Playoffs					
1969–70	Chicago	7	0	0	0
1970–71	Chicago	9	0	0	0
	Totals	16	0	0	0

610

SHORE, Edward William *Defenseman*
b. St. Qu'Appelle-Cupar, Sask., Nov. 25, 1902

Season	Club	GP	G	A	Pts
1926–27	Boston	--	12	6	18
1927–28	Boston	--	11	6	17
1928–29	Boston	--	12	7	19
1929–30	Boston	--	12	19	31
1930–31	Boston	--	15	16	31
1931–32	Boston	--	9	13	22
1932–33	Boston	--	8	27	35
1933–34	Boston	--	2	10	12
1934–35	Boston	--	7	26	33
1935–36	Boston	--	3	16	19
1936–37	Boston	--	3	1	4
1937–38	Boston	--	3	14	17
1938–39	Boston	--	4	14	18
1939–40	Bos–NY A	--	4	4	8
	Totals	--	105	179	284

Playoffs

Season	Club	GP	G	A	Pts
1926–27	Boston	--	1	1	2
1927–28	Boston	--	0	0	0
1928–29	Boston	--	1	1	2
1929–30	Boston	--	1	0	1
1930–31	Boston	--	2	1	3
1932–33	Boston	--	0	1	1
1934–35	Boston	--	0	1	1
1935–36	Boston	--	1	1	2
1937–38	Boston	--	0	1	1
1938–39	Boston	--	0	4	4
1939–40	New York A.	--	0	2	2
	Totals	--	6	13	19

SHORE, Hamby *Defenseman*
b. Ottawa, Ont., 1886

Season	Club	GP	G	A	Pts
1917–18	Ottawa	18	3	0	3

SHUTT, Steve *Forward*
b. Toronto, Ont., July 1, 1952

Season	Club	GP	G	A	Pts
1972–73	Montreal C.	50	8	8	16

Playoffs

Season	Club	GP	G	A	Pts
1972–73	Montreal C.	1	0	0	0

SIEBERT, Albert Charles (Babe)
Defenseman-Forward
b. Plattsville, Que., Jan. 14, 1904

Season	Club	GP	G	A	Pts
1925–26	Montreal M.	35	16	8	24
1926–27	Montreal M.	--	5	3	8
1927–28	Montreal M.	40	8	9	17
1928–29	Montreal M.	--	3	5	8
1929–30	Montreal M.	--	14	19	33
1930–31	Montreal M.	--	16	12	28
1931–32	Montreal M.	--	21	18	39

SIEBERT *(Continued)*

Season	Club	GP	G	A	Pts
1932–33	New York R.	42	9	10	19
1933–34	NY R–Bos	--	5	7	12
1934–35	Boston	--	6	18	24
1935–36	Boston	--	12	9	21
1936–37	Montreal C.	--	8	20	28
1937–38	Montreal C.	--	8	11	19
1938–39	Montreal C.	--	9	7	16
	Totals	--	140	156	296

Playoffs

Season	Club	GP	G	A	Pts
1925–26	Montreal M.	8	2	2	4
1926–27	Montreal M.	2	1	0	1
1927–28	Montreal M.	9	2	0	2
1929–30	Montreal M.	4	0	0	0
1930–31	Montreal M.	2	0	0	0
1931–32	Montreal M.	4	0	1	1
1932–33	New York R.	8	1	0	1
1934–35	Boston	4	0	0	0
1935–36	Boston	2	0	1	1
1936–37	Montreal C.	5	1	2	3
1937–38	Montreal C.	3	1	1	2
1938–39	Montreal C.	3	0	0	0
	Totals	54	8	7	15

SIMMONS, Donald *Goalie*
b. Port Colborne, Ont., Sept. 13, 1931

Season	Club	GP	GA	Sho	AVE
1956–57	Boston	26	63	4	2.42
1957–58	Boston	37⅓	93	5	2.49
1958–59	Boston	58	184	3	3.17
1959–60	Boston	28	94	2	3.36
1960–61	Boston	18	59	1	3.28
1961–62	Toronto M.L.	9	21	2	2.90
1962–63	Toronto M.L.	28	70	1	2.50
1963–64	Toronto M.L.	20	63	3	3.15
1965–66	New York R.	8	37	0	4.63
1967–68	New York R.	5	13	0	2.60
1968–69	New York R.	3½	8	0	2.40
	Totals	240⅚	705	21	2.93

Playoffs

Season	Club	GP	GA	Sho	AVE
1956–57	Boston	10	29	2	2.90
1957–58	Boston	11	27	1	2.45
1961–62	Toronto M.L.	3	8	0	2.67
	Totals	24	64	3	2.67

All-Star		GP	Per	GA	AGP
1963	Toronto M.L.	1	1	1	1.00

SIMON, John Cullen (Cully) *Defenseman*
b. Brockville, Ont., May 8, 1918

Season	Club	GP	G	A	Pts
1942–43	Detroit R.W.	34	1	1	2
1943–44	Detroit R.W.	46	3	7	10
1944–45	Det RW–Chgo	50	0	3	3
	Totals	130	4	1	15

SIMON (Continued)

Playoffs	Club	GP	G	A	Pts
1942–43	Detroit R.W.	9	1	0	1
1943–44	Detroit R.W.	5	0	0	0
	Totals	14	1	0	1

SIMON, Thain Andrew *Defenseman*
b. Brockville, Ont., Apr. 24, 1922

Season	Club	GP	G	A	Pts
1946–47	Detroit R.W.	3	0	0	0

SIMPSON, Clifford Vernon *Forward*
b. Toronto, Ont., Apr. 4, 1923

Season	Club	GP	G	A	Pts
1946–47	Detroit R.W.	6	0	1	1
Playoffs					
1946–47	Detroit R.W.	1	0	0	0
1947–48	Detroit R.W.	1	0	0	0
	Totals	2	0	0	0

SIMPSON, Joseph (Bullet Joe) *Defenseman*
b. Selkirk, Man.

Season	Club	GP	G	A	Pts
1925–26	New York A.	32	2	2	4
1926–27	New York A.	--	4	2	6
1927–28	New York A.	--	2	0	2
1928–29	New York A.	--	3	2	5
1929–30	New York A.	--	8	13	21
1930–31	New York A.	--	2	0	2
	Totals	--	21	19	40
Playoffs					
1922–23	Edmonton (PCHL)	--	0	1	1
1928–29	New York A.	--	0	0	0
	Totals	--	0	1	1

SINCLAIR, Reginald Alexander *Forward*
b. Lachine, Que., Mar. 6, 1925

Season	Club	GP	G	A	Pts
1950–51	New York R.	70	18	21	39
1951–52	New York R.	69	20	10	30
1952–53	Detroit R.W.	69	11	12	23
	Totals	208	49	43	92
Playoffs					
1952–53	Detroit R.W.	3	1	0	1
All-Star					
1951	NHL 1st All-Stars	1	0	0	0
1952	NHL 1st All-Stars	1	0	0	0
	Totals	2	0	0	0

SINGBUSH, Alexander *Defenseman*
b. Winnipeg, Man., 1915

Season	Club	GP	G	A	Pts
1940–41	Montreal C.	--	0	5	5
Playoffs					
1940–41	Montreal C.	--	0	0	0

SITTLER, Darryl Glen *Forward*
b. Kitchener, Ont., Sept. 18, 1950

Season	Club	GP	G	A	Pts
1970–71	Toronto M.L.	49	10	8	18
1971–72	Toronto M.L.	74	15	17	32
1972–73	Toronto M.L.	78	29	48	77
	Totals	201	54	73	127
Playoffs					
1970–71	Toronto M.L.	6	2	1	3
1971–72	Toronto M.L.	3	0	0	0
	Totals	9	2	1	3

SKILTON, Raymond *Defenseman*

Season	Club	GP	G	A	Pts
1917–18	Montreal W.	1	0	0	0

SKINNER, Alf *Forward*

Season	Club	GP	G	A	Pts
1917–18	Toronto A.	19	13	0	13
1918–19	Toronto A.	17	12	3	15
1924–25	Bos–Mont M	27	1	1	2
1925–26	Pittsburgh Pi.	7	0	0	0
	Totals	60	26	4	30
Playoffs					
1917–18	Toronto A.	--	8	0	8
1920–21	Vancouver (PCHL)	--	4	0	4
1921–22	Vancouver (PCHL)	--	0	0	0
1922–23	Vancouver (PCHL)	--	1	1	2
1923–24	Vancouver (PCHL)	--	0	0	0
	Totals	--	13	1	14

SKOV, Glen Frederick *Forward*
b. Wheatley, Ont., Jan. 26, 1931

Season	Club	GP	G	A	Pts
1949–50	Detroit R.W.	2	0	0	0
1950–51	Detroit R.W.	19	7	6	13
1951–52	Detroit R.W.	70	12	14	26
1952–53	Detroit R.W.	70	12	15	27
1953–54	Detroit R.W.	70	17	10	27
1954–55	Detroit R.W.	70	14	16	30
1955–56	Chicago	70	7	20	27
1956–57	Chicago	67	14	28	42
1957–58	Chicago	70	17	18	35
1958–59	Chicago	70	3	5	8
1959–60	Chicago	69	3	4	7
1960–61	Montreal C.	3	0	0	0
	Totals	650	106	136	242

SKOV (Continued)

Playoffs

Season	Club	GP	G	A	Pts
1950–51	Detroit R.W.	6	0	0	0
1951–52	Detroit R.W.	8	1	4	5
1952–53	Detroit R.W.	6	1	0	1
1953–54	Detroit R.W.	12	1	2	3
1954–55	Detroit R.W.	11	2	0	2
1958–59	Chicago	6	2	1	3
1959–60	Chicago	4	0	0	0
	Totals	53	7	7	14

All-Star

1954	Detroit R.W.	1	0	0	0

SLEAVER, John *Forward*
b. Copper Cliff, Ont., Aug. 18, 1934

Season	Club	GP	G	A	Pts
1953–54	Chicago	1	0	0	0
1956–57	Chicago	12	1	0	1
	Totals	13	1	0	1

SLOAN, Aloysius Martin (Tod) *Forward*
b. Vinton, Que., Nov. 30, 1927

Season	Club	GP	G	A	Pts
1947–48	Toronto M.L.	1	0	0	0
1948–49	Toronto M.L.	29	3	4	7
1950–51	Toronto M.L.	70	31	25	56
1951–52	Toronto M.L.	68	25	23	48
1952–53	Toronto M.L.	70	15	10	25
1953–54	Toronto M.L.	67	11	32	43
1954–55	Toronto M.L.	63	13	15	28
1955–56	Toronto M.L.	70	37	29	66
1956–57	Toronto M.L.	52	14	21	35
1957–58	Toronto M.L.	59	13	25	38
1958–59	Chicago	59	27	35	62
1959–60	Chicago	70	20	20	40
1960–61	Chicago	67	11	23	34
	Totals	745	220	262	482

Playoffs

Season	Club	GP	G	A	Pts
1950–51	Toronto M.L.	11	4	5	9
1951–52	Toronto M.L.	4	0	0	0
1953–54	Toronto M.L.	5	1	1	2
1954–55	Toronto M.L.	4	0	0	0
1955–56	Toronto M.L.	2	0	0	0
1958–59	Chicago	6	3	5	8
1959–60	Chicago	3	0	0	0
1960–61	Chicago	12	1	1	2
	Totals	47	9	12	21

All-Star

1951	NHL 2nd All-Stars	1	1	1	2
1952	NHL 2nd All-Stars	1	0	0	0
1956	NHL All-Stars	1	0	0	0
	Totals	3	1	1	2

SLOBODIAN, Peter Paul *Defenseman*
b. Dauphin, Man., Apr. 24, 1918

Season	Club	GP	G	A	Pts
1940–41	New York A.	--	3	2	5

SLOWINSKI, Edward Stanley *Forward*
b. Winnipeg, Man., Nov. 18, 1922

Season	Club	GP	G	A	Pts
1947–48	Det RW–NY R	38	6	5	11
1948–49	New York R.	20	1	1	2
1949–50	New York R.	63	14	23	37
1950–51	New York R.	69	14	18	32
1951–52	New York R.	64	21	22	43
1952–53	New York R.	37	2	5	7
	Totals	291	58	74	132

Playoffs

1947–48	New York R.	4	0	0	0
1949–50	New York R.	12	2	6	8
	Totals	16	2	6	8

SLY, Darryl Hayward *Defenseman*
b. Collingwood, Ont., Apr. 3, 1939

Season	Club	GP	G	A	Pts
1965–66	Toronto M.L.	2	0	0	0
1967–68	Toronto M.L.	17	0	0	0
1969–70	Minnesota	29	1	0	1
1970–71	Vancouver	31	0	2	2
	Totals	79	1	2	3

SMART, Alexander *Forward*
b. Brandon, Man., May 29, 1918

Season	Club	GP	G	A	Pts
1942–43	Montreal C.	8	5	2	7

SMEDSMO, Dale *Forward*
b. Roseau, Minn., Apr. 23, 1951

Season	Club	GP	G	A	Pts
1972–73	Toronto M.L.	4	0	0	0

SMILLIE, Donald *Forward*

Season	Club	GP	G	A	Pts
1933–34	Boston	--	2	2	4

SMITH, Alexander *Defenseman*
b. Liverpool, England, Apr. 2, 1905

Season	Club	GP	G	A	Pts
1924–25	Ottawa	7	0	0	0
1925–26	Ottawa	36	0	0	0
1926–27	Ottawa	--	4	1	5
1927–28	Ottawa	--	9	4	13
1928–29	Ottawa	--	1	7	8
1929–30	Ottawa	--	2	6	8
1930–31	Ottawa	--	5	6	11

SMITH (Continued)

Season	Club	GP	G	A	Pts
1931–32	Detroit F.	--	6	8	14
1932–33	Otta-Bos	--	7	4	11
1933–34	Boston	--	4	6	10
1934–35	New York A.	--	3	8	11
	Totals	--	41	50	91

Playoffs

Season	Club	GP	G	A	Pts
1925–26	Ottawa	--	0	0	0
1926–27	Ottawa	--	0	0	0
1927–28	Ottawa	--	0	0	0
1929–30	Ottawa	--	0	0	0
1931–32	Detroit F.	--	0	0	0
1932–33	Boston	--	0	2	2
	Totals	--	0	2	2

SMITH, Allan Robert (Al) *Goalie*
b. Toronto, Ont., Nov. 10, 1945

Season	Club	GP	GA	Sho	AVE
1965–66	Toronto M.L.	1⅓	2	0	1.50
1966–67	Toronto M.L.	1	5	0	5.00
1968–69	Toronto M.L.	5⅔	16	0	2.82
1969–70	Pittsburgh Pe.	42	129	2	3.03
1970–71	Pittsburgh Pe.	41⅓	128	2	3.10
1971–72	Detroit R.W.	42⅔	135	4	3.24
	Totals	134	415	8	3.12

Playoffs

Season	Club	GP	GA	Sho	AVE
1969–70	Pittsburgh Pe.	3	10	0	3.33

All-Star		GP	Per	GA	AGP
1968	Toronto M.L.	1	1	1	1.00

SMITH, Arthur

Season	Club	GP	G	A	Pts
1927–28	Toronto M.L.	--	5	3	8
1928–29	Toronto M.L.	--	5	0	5
1929–30	Toronto M.L.	--	3	3	6
1930–31	Ottawa	--	2	4	6
	Totals	--	15	10	25

Playoffs

Season	Club	GP	G	A	Pts
1928–29	Toronto M.L.	--	1	1	2

SMITH, Brian Desmond *Forward*
b. Ottawa, Ont., Sept. 6, 1940

Season	Club	GP	G	A	Pts
1967–68	Los Angeles	58	10	9	19
1968–69	Minnesota	9	0	1	1
	Totals	67	10	10	20

Playoffs

Season	Club	GP	G	A	Pts
1967–68	Los Angeles	7	0	0	0

SMITH, Brain Stuart *Forward*
b. Creighton Mines, Ont., Dec. 6, 1937

Season	Club	GP	G	A	Pts
1957–58	Detroit R.W.	4	0	1	1
1959–60	Detroit R.W.	31	2	5	7
1960–61	Detroit R.W.	26	0	2	2
	Totals	61	2	8	10

Playoffs

Season	Club	GP	G	A	Pts
1959–60	Detroit R.W.	5	0	0	0

SMITH, Carl David *Forward*
b. Cache Bay, Ont., Sept. 18, 1917

Season	Club	GP	G	A	Pts
1943–44	Detroit R.W.	7	1	1	2

SMITH, Clinton James (Snuffy) *Forward*
b. Assiniboia, Sask., Dec. 12, 1913

Season	Club	GP	G	A	Pts
1936–37	New York R.	2	1	0	1
1937–38	New York R.	48	14	23	37
1938–39	New York R.	48	21	20	41
1939–40	New York R.	41	8	16	24
1940–41	New York R.	48	14	11	25
1941–42	New York R.	47	10	24	34
1942–43	New York R.	47	12	21	33
1943–44	Chicago	50	23	49	72
1944–45	Chicago	50	23	31	54
1945–46	Chicago	50	26	24	50
1946–47	Chicago	52	9	17	26
	Totals	483	161	236	397

Playoffs

Season	Club	GP	G	A	Pts
1937–38	New York R.	3	2	0	2
1938–39	New York R.	7	1	2	3
1939–40	New York R.	12	1	3	4
1940–41	New York R.	3	0	0	0
1941–42	New York R.	6	0	0	0
1943–44	Chicago	9	4	8	12
1945–46	Chicago	4	2	1	3
	Totals	44	10	14	24

SMITH, Dallas *Defenseman*
b. Hamiota, Man., Oct. 10, 1941

Season	Club	GP	G	A	Pts
1959–60	Boston	5	1	1	2
1960–61	Boston	70	1	9	10
1961–62	Boston	7	0	0	0
1965–66	Boston	2	0	0	0
1966–67	Boston	33	0	1	1
1967–68	Boston	74	4	23	27
1968–69	Boston	75	4	24	28
1969–70	Boston	75	7	17	24
1970–71	Boston	73	7	38	45
1971–72	Boston	78	8	22	30
1972–73	Boston	78	4	27	31
	Totals	570	36	162	198

SMITH (Continued)

Playoffs	Club	GP	G	A	Pts
1967–68	Boston	4	0	2	2
1968–69	Boston	10	0	3	3
1969–70	Boston	14	0	3	3
1970–71	Boston	7	0	3	3
1971–72	Boston	15	0	4	4
1972–73	Boston	5	0	2	2
	Totals	55	0	17	17

All-Star					
1971	East All-Stars	1	0	1	1
1972	East All-Stars	1	0	1	1
1973	East All-Stars	1	0	0	0
	Totals	3	0	2	2

SMITH, Dalton Joseph *Forward*
b. Cache Bay, Ont., July 26, 1915

Season	Club	GP	G	A	Pts
1943–44	Detroit R.W.	10	1	2	3

SMITH, Desmond Patrick *Defenseman*
b. Ottawa, Ont., Feb. 22, 1914

Season	Club	GP	G	A	Pts
1937–38	Montreal M.	--	3	1	4
1938–39	Montreal C.	--	3	3	6
1939–40	Chgo-Bos	--	3	6	9
1940–41	Boston	--	6	8	14
1941–42	Boston	48	7	7	14
	Totals	--	22	25	47

Playoffs	Club	GP	G	A	Pts
1938–39	Montreal C.	3	0	0	0
1939–40	Boston	6	0	0	0
1940–41	Boston	11	0	2	2
1941–42	Boston	5	1	2	3
	Totals	25	1	4	5

SMITH, Donald *Forward*
b. 1889

Season	Club	GP	G	A	Pts
1919–20	Montreal C.	10	1	0	1

SMITH, Donald Arthur *Forward*
b. Regina, Sask., May 4, 1929

Season	Club	GP	G	A	Pts
1949–50	New York R.	11	1	1	2

Playoffs	Club	GP	G	A	Pts
1949–50	New York R.	1	0	0	0

SMITH, Gary Edward *Goalie*
b. Ottawa, Ont., Feb. 4, 1944

Season	Club	GP	GA	Sho	AVE
1965–66	Toronto M.L.	3	7	0	2.50
1966–67	Toronto M.L.	2	7	0	3.50

SMITH (Continued)

Season	Club	GP	GA	Sho	AVE
1967–68	Oakland	18¾	60	1	3.25
1968–69	Oakland	50	148	4	2.96
1969–70	Oakland	62	195	2	3.11
1970–71	California	66⅓	256	2	3.86
1971–72	Chicago	25⅔	62	5	2.41
1972–73	Chicago	22⅓	79	0	3.54
	Totals	251	814	14	3.28

Playoffs					
1968–69	Oakland	7	23	0	3.29
1969–70	Oakland	4	13	0	3.15
1971–72	Chicago	2	3	1	1.50
1972–73	Chicago	1	5	0	4.62
	Totals	14	44	1	3.14

SMITH, George

Season	Club	GP	G	A	Pts
1921–22	Toronto St. P.	9	0	0	0

SMITH, Glen

Season	Club	GP	G	A	Pts
1950–51	Chicago	2	0	0	0

SMITH, Kenneth Alvin *Forward*
b. Moose Jaw, Sask., May 8, 1924

Season	Club	GP	G	A	Pts
1944–45	Boston	49	20	14	34
1945–46	Boston	23	2	6	8
1946–47	Boston	60	14	7	21
1947–48	Boston	60	11	12	23
1948–49	Boston	59	20	20	40
1949–50	Boston	66	10	31	41
1950–51	Boston	14	1	3	4
	Totals	331	78	93	171

Playoffs					
1944–45	Boston	7	3	4	7
1945–46	Boston	8	0	4	4
1946–47	Boston	5	3	0	3
1947–48	Boston	5	2	3	5
1948–49	Boston	5	0	2	2
	Totals	30	8	13	21

SMITH, Norman *Goalie*
b. Toronto, Ont., Mar. 18, 1908

Season	Club	GP	GA	Sho	AVE
1931–32	Montreal M.	21	68	0	3.24
1934–35	Detroit R.W.	25	52	2	2.09
1935–36	Detroit R.W.	48	103	6	2.15
1936–37	Detroit R.W.	48	102	6	2.13
1937–38	Detroit R.W.	47	130	3	2.77
1938–39	Detroit R.W.	4	12	0	3.00

SMITH *(Continued)*

Season	Club	GP	GA	Sho	AVE
1943–44	Detroit R.W.	5	15	0	3.00
1944–45	Detroit R.W.	1	3	0	3.00
	Totals	199	485	17	2.44
Playoffs					
1935–36	Detroit R.W.	7	12	2	1.71
1936–37	Detroit R.W.	5	6	1	1.20
	Totals	12	18	3	1.50

SMITH, Reginald Joseph (Hooley)
Defenseman-Forward
b. Toronto, Ont., Jan. 7, 1905

Season	Club	GP	G	A	Pts
1924–25	Ottawa	30	10	3	13
1925–26	Ottawa	28	16	9	25
1926–27	Ottawa	--	9	6	15
1927–28	Montreal M.	--	14	5	19
1928–29	Montreal M.	--	10	9	19
1929–30	Montreal M.	--	21	9	30
1930–31	Montreal M.	--	12	14	26
1931–32	Montreal M.	--	11	33	44
1932–33	Montreal M.	--	20	21	41
1933–34	Montreal M.	--	18	19	37
1934–35	Montreal M.	--	5	22	27
1935–36	Montreal M.	--	19	19	38
1936–37	Boston	--	8	10	18
1937–38	New York A.	--	10	10	20
1938–39	New York A.	--	8	11	19
1939–40	New York A.	--	7	8	15
1940–41	New York A.	--	2	7	9
	Totals	--	200	215	415
Playoffs					
1925–26	Ottawa	--	0	0	0
1926–27	Ottawa	--	1	0	1
1927–28	Montreal M.	--	2	1	3
1929–30	Montreal M.	--	1	1	2
1930–31	Montreal M.	--	0	0	0
1931–32	Montreal M.	--	2	1	3
1932–33	Montreal M.	--	2	0	2
1933–34	Montreal M.	--	0	1	1
1934–35	Montreal M.	--	0	0	0
1935–36	Montreal M.	--	0	0	0
1936–37	Boston	--	0	0	0
1937–38	New York A.	--	0	3	3
1938–39	New York A.	--	0	0	0
1939–40	New York A.	--	3	1	4
	Totals	--	11	8	19

SMITH, Richard Allan (Rick) *Defenseman*
b. Kingston, Ont., June 29, 1948

Season	Club	GP	G	A	Pts
1968–69	Boston	48	0	5	5
1969–70	Boston	69	2	8	10

SMITH *(Continued)*

Season	Club	GP	G	A	Pts
1970–71	Boston	67	4	19	23
1971–72	Bos-Calif	78	3	16	19
1972–73	California	64	9	24	33
	Totals	326	18	72	90
Playoffs					
1968–69	Boston	9	0	0	0
1969–70	Boston	14	1	3	4
1970–71	Boston	6	0	0	0
	Totals	29	1	3	4

SMITH, Rodger *Defenseman*

Season	Club	GP	G	A	Pts
1925–26	Pittsburgh Pi.	36	9	1	10
1926–27	Pittsburgh Pi.	--	4	0	4
1927–28	Pittsburgh Pi.	--	1	0	1
1928–29	Pittsburgh Pi.	--	4	2	6
1929–30	Pittsburgh Pi.	--	2	1	3
	Totals	--	20	4	24
Playoffs					
1925–26	Pittsburgh Pi.	--	1	0	1
1927–28	Pittsburgh Pi.	--	2	0	2
	Totals	--	3	0	3

SMITH, Ronald Floyd *Forward*
b. Perth, Ont., May 16, 1935

Season	Club	GP	G	A	Pts
1954–55	Boston	3	0	1	1
1956–57	Boston	23	0	0	0
1960–61	New York R.	29	5	9	14
1962–63	Detroit R.W.	51	9	17	26
1963–64	Detroit R.W.	52	18	13	31
1964–65	Detroit R.W.	67	16	29	45
1965–66	Detroit R.W.	66	21	28	49
1966–67	Detroit R.W.	54	11	14	25
1967–68	Det RW-Tor ML	63	24	22	46
1968–69	Toronto M.L.	64	15	19	34
1969–70	Toronto M.L.	61	4	14	18
1970–71	Buffalo	77	6	11	17
1971–72	Buffalo	6	0	1	1
	Totals	616	129	178	307
Playoffs					
1962–63	Detroit R.W.	11	2	3	5
1963–64	Detroit R.W.	14	4	3	7
1964–65	Detroit R.W.	7	1	3	4
1965–66	Detroit R.W.	12	5	2	7
1968–69	Toronto M.L.	4	0	0	0
	Totals	48	12	11	23

SMITH, Ronald Robert (Ron) *Defenseman*
b. Port Hope, Ont., Nov. 19, 1952

Season	Club	GP	G	A	Pts
1972–73	New York I.	11	1	1	2

SMITH, Sidney James *Forward*
b. Toronto, Ont., July 11, 1925

Season	Club	GP	G	A	Pts
1946-47	Toronto M.L.	14	2	1	3
1947-48	Toronto M.L.	31	7	10	17
1948-49	Toronto M.L.	1	0	0	0
1949-50	Toronto M.L.	68	22	23	45
1950-51	Toronto M.L.	70	30	21	51
1951-52	Toronto M.L.	70	27	30	57
1952-53	Toronto M.L.	70	20	19	39
1953-54	Toronto M.L.	70	22	16	38
1954-55	Toronto M.L.	70	33	21	54
1955-56	Toronto M.L.	55	4	17	21
1956-57	Toronto M.L.	70	17	24	41
1957-58	Toronto M.L.	12	2	1	3
	Totals	601	186	183	369

Playoffs

Season	Club	GP	G	A	Pts
1947-48	Toronto M.L.	2	0	0	0
1948-49	Toronto M.L.	6	5	2	7
1949-50	Toronto M.L.	7	0	3	3
1950-51	Toronto M.L.	11	7	3	10
1951-52	Toronto M.L.	4	0	0	0
1953-54	Toronto M.L.	5	1	1	2
1954-55	Toronto M.L.	4	3	1	4
1955-56	Toronto M.L.	5	1	0	1
	Totals	44	17	10	27

All-Star

Season	Club	GP	G	A	Pts
1949	Toronto M.L.	1	0	0	0
1950	NHL All-Stars	1	1	0	1
1951	NHL 2nd All-Stars	1	0	0	0
1952	NHL 2nd All-Stars	1	0	0	0
1953	NHL All-Stars	1	0	0	0
1954	NHL All-Stars	1	0	0	0
1955	NHL All-Stars	1	0	1	1
	Totals	7	1	1	2

SMITH, Stanford George *Forward*
b. Coal Creek, B.C., Aug. 13, 1917

Season	Club	GP	G	A	Pts
1939-40	New York R.	1	0	0	0
1940-41	New York R.	8	2	1	3
	Totals	9	2	1	3

Playoffs

Season	Club	GP	G	A	Pts
1939-40	New York R.	1	0	0	0

SMITH, Stuart *Forward*

Season	Club	GP	G	A	Pts
1940-41	Montreal C.	--	2	1	3
1941-42	Montreal C.	--	0	1	1
	Totals	--	2	2	4

SMITH, Thomas *Forward*

Season	Club	GP	G	A	Pts
1919-20	Quebec	10	0	0	0

SMITH, Wayne *Defenseman*
b. Kamsack, Sask., Feb. 12, 1943

Season	Club	GP	G	A	Pts
1966-67	Chicago	2	1	1	2

Playoffs

Season	Club	GP	G	A	Pts
1966-67	Chicago	1	0	0	0

SMITH, William John (Billy) *Goalie*
b. Perth, Ont., Dec. 12, 1950

Season	Club	GP	GA	Sho	AVE
1971-72	Los Angeles	5	23	0	4.60
1972-73	New York I.	35⅓	147	0	4.16
	Totals	40⅓	170	0	4.21

SMRKE, Stanley *Forward*
b. Belgrade, Yugoslavia, Sept. 2, 1928

Season	Club	GP	G	A	Pts
1956-57	Montreal C.	4	0	0	0
1957-58	Montreal C.	5	0	3	3
	Totals	9	0	3	3

All-Star

Season	Club	GP	G	A	Pts
1957	Montreal C.	1	1	0	1

SMYLIE, Roderick *Defenseman-Forward*

Season	Club	GP	G	A	Pts
1920-21	Toronto St. P.	23	2	0	2
1921-22	Toronto St. P.	21	0	0	0
1922-23	Toronto St. P.	2	0	0	0
1923-24	Ottawa	14	1	1	2
1924-25	Toronto St. P.	11	0	0	0
1925-26	Toronto St. P.	5	0	0	0
	Totals	76	3	1	4

Playoffs

Season	Club	GP	G	A	Pts
1920-21	Toronto St. P.	--	0	0	0
1921-22	Toronto St. P.	--	1	2	3
1923-24	Ottawa	--	0	0	0
	Totals	--	1	2	3

SNEDDON, Robert Allan (Bob) *Goalie*
b. Montreal, Que., May 31, 1944

Season	Club	GP	GA	Sho	AVE
1970-71	California	3⅔	21	0	5.60

SNELL, Ronald *Forward*
b. Regina, Sask., Aug. 11, 1948

Season	Club	GP	G	A	Pts
1968-69	Pittsburgh Pe.	4	3	1	4
1969-70	Pittsburgh Pe.	3	0	1	1
	Totals	7	3	2	5

SNOW, William Alexander (Sandy) *Forward*
b. Dokin, N. S., Nov. 11, 1946

Season	Club	GP	G	A	Pts
1968-69	Detroit R.W.	3	0	0	0

SOLINGER, Robert Edward *Forward*
b. Star City, Sask., Dec. 23, 1925

Season	Club	GP	G	A	Pts
1951-52	Toronto M.L.	24	5	3	8
1952-53	Toronto M.L.	19	1	1	2
1953-54	Toronto M.L.	39	3	2	5
1954-55	Toronto M.L.	17	1	5	6
	Totals	98	10	11	21

SOMERS, Arthur E. *Forward*
b. Winnipeg, Man., Jan. 17, 1904

Season	Club	GP	G	A	Pts
1929-30	Chicago	--	11	13	24
1930-31	Chicago	--	3	6	9
1931-32	New York R.	48	11	15	26
1932-33	New York R.	48	7	15	22
1933-34	New York R.	8	1	2	3
1934-35	New York R.	41	0	5	5
1949-50	New York R.	55	4	4	8
	Totals	--	37	60	97
Playoffs					
1929-30	Chicago	2	0	0	0
1930-31	Chicago	9	0	0	0
1931-32	New York R.	7	0	1	1
1932-33	New York R.	8	1	4	5
1933-34	New York R.	2	0	0	0
1934-35	New York R.	2	0	0	0
1949-50	New York R.	12	2	5	7
	Totals	42	3	10	13

SONMOR, Glen Robert *Forward*
b. Moose Jaw, Sask., Apr. 22, 1929

Season	Club	GP	G	A	Pts
1953-54	New York R.	15	2	0	2
1954-55	New York R.	13	0	0	0
	Totals	28	2	0	2

SORRELL, John Arthur *Forward*
b. Chesterville, Ont., Jan. 16, 1906

Season	Club	GP	G	A	Pts
1930-31	Detroit F.	--	9	7	16
1931-32	Detroit F.	--	8	5	13
1932-33	Detroit F.	--	14	10	24
1933-34	Detroit R.W.	--	21	10	31
1934-35	Detroit R.W.	--	20	16	36
1935-36	Detroit R.W.	--	13	15	28
1936-37	Detroit R.W.	--	8	16	24
1937-38	Det RW-NY A	--	11	9	20

SORRELL *(Continued)*

Season	Club	GP	G	A	Pts
1938-39	New York A.	--	13	9	22
1939-40	New York A.	--	8	16	24
1940-41	New York A.	--	2	6	8
	Totals	--	127	119	246
Playoffs					
1931-32	Detroit F.	--	1	0	1
1932-33	Detroit F.	--	2	2	4
1933-34	Detroit R.W.	--	0	2	2
1935-36	Detroit R.W.	--	3	4	7
1936-37	Detroit R.W.	--	2	4	6
1937-38	New York A.	--	4	0	4
1938-39	New York A.	--	0	0	0
1939-40	New York A.	--	0	3	3
	Totals	--	12	15	27

SPARROW, Emory *Forward*

Season	Club	GP	G	A	Pts
1924-25	Boston	6	0	0	0

SPECK, Frederick (Fred) *Forward*
b. Thorold, Ont., July 22, 1947

Season	Club	GP	G	A	Pts
1968-69	Detroit R.W.	5	0	0	0
1969-70	Detroit R.W.	5	0	0	0
1971-72	Vancouver	18	1	2	3
	Totals	28	1	2	3

SPEER, Francis William (Bill) *Defenseman*
b. Lindsay, Ont., Mar. 20, 1942

Season	Club	GP	G	A	Pts
1967-68	Pittsburgh Pe.	68	3	13	16
1968-69	Pittsburgh Pe.	34	1	4	5
1969-70	Boston	27	1	3	4
1970-71	Boston	1	0	0	0
	Totals	130	5	20	25
Playoffs					
1969-70	Boston	8	1	0	1

SPENCER, Brian Roy *Forward*
b. Fort St. James, B.C., Sept. 3, 1949

Season	Club	GP	G	A	Pts
1969-70	Toronto M.L.	9	0	0	0
1970-71	Toronto M.L.	50	9	15	24
1971-72	Toronto M.L.	36	1	5	6
1972-73	New York I.	78	14	24	38
	Totals	173	24	44	68
Playoffs					
1970-71	Toronto M.L.	6	0	1	1

SPENCER, Irvin James (Spinner)
Defenseman-Forward
b. Sudbury, Ont., Dec. 4, 1937

Season	Club	GP	G	A	Pts
1959-60	New York R.	32	1	2	3
1960-61	New York R.	56	1	8	9
1961-62	New York R.	43	2	10	12
1962-63	Boston	69	5	17	22
1963-64	Detroit R.W.	25	3	0	3
1967-68	Detroit R.W.	5	0	1	1
	Totals	228	12	38	50

Playoffs

Season	Club	GP	G	A	Pts
1961-62	New York R.	1	0	0	0
1963-64	Detroit R.W.	11	0	0	0
1964-65	Detroit R.W.	1	0	0	0
1965-66	Detroit R.W.	3	0	0	0
	Totals	16	0	0	0

SPEYER, Christopher *Defenseman*
b. Toronto, Ont., June 1906

Season	Club	GP	G	A	Pts
1923-24	Toronto St. P.	3	0	0	0
1924-25	Toronto St. P.	2	0	0	0
	Totals	5	0	0	0

SPOONER (Red) *Goalie*

Season	Club	GP	GA	Sho	AVE
1929-30	Pittsburgh Pi.	1	6	0	6.00

SPRING, Frank *Forward*
b. Cranbrook, B.C., Oct. 19, 1949

Season	Club	GP	G	A	Pts
1969-70	Boston	1	0	0	0

SPRING, Jesse *Defenseman*
b. Toronto, Ont.

Season	Club	GP	G	A	Pts
1923-24	Hamilton	20	3	2	5
1924-25	Hamilton	29	2	0	2
1925-26	Pittsburgh Pi.	32	5	0	5
1928-29	Pittsburgh Pi.	--	0	0	0
1929-30	Pittsburgh Pi.	--	1	0	1
	Totals	--	11	2	13

Playoffs

Season	Club	GP	G	A	Pts
1925-26	Pittsburgh Pi.	--	0	2	2

STACKHOUSE, Ronald Lorne (Ron)
Defenseman
b. Haliburton, Ont., Aug. 26, 1949

Season	Club	GP	G	A	Pts
1970-71	California	78	8	24	32
1971-72	Calif-Det RW	79	6	28	34
1972-73	Detroit R.W.	78	5	29	34
	Totals	235	19	81	100

STACKHOUSE, Theodore *Defenseman*

Season	Club	GP	G	A	Pts
1921-22	Toronto St. P.	12	0	0	0

STALEY, Allan (Red) *Forward*
b. Regina, Sask., Sept. 21, 1928

Season	Club	GP	G	A	Pts
1948-49	New York R.	1	0	1	1

STANDING, George *Forward*
b. Toronto, Ont., Aug. 3, 1941

Season	Club	GP	G	A	Pts
1967-68	Minnesota	2	0	0	0

STANFIELD, Frederic William (Fred) *Forward*
b. Toronto, Ont., May 4. 1944

Season	Club	GP	G	A	Pts
1964-65	Chicago	58	7	10	17
1965-66	Chicago	39	2	2	4
1966-67	Chicago	10	1	0	1
1967-68	Boston	73	20	44	64
1968-69	Boston	71	25	29	54
1969-70	Boston	73	23	35	58
1970-71	Boston	75	24	52	76
1971-72	Boston	78	23	56	79
1972-73	Boston	78	20	58	78
	Totals	555	145	286	431

Playoffs

Season	Club	GP	G	A	Pts
1964-65	Chicago	14	2	1	3
1965-66	Chicago	5	0	0	0
1966-67	Chicago	1	0	0	0
1967-68	Boston	4	0	1	1
1968-69	Boston	10	2	2	4
1969-70	Boston	14	4	12	16
1970-71	Boston	7	3	4	7
1971-72	Boston	15	7	9	16
1972-73	Boston	5	1	1	2
	Totals	75	19	30	49

STANFIELD, James Boviard (Jim) *Forward*
b. Toronto, Ont., Jan. 1, 1947

Season	Club	GP	G	A	Pts
1969-70	Los Angeles	1	0	0	0
1970-71	Los Angeles	2	0	0	0
1971-72	Los Angeles	4	0	1	1
	Totals	7	0	1	1

STANKIEWICZ, Edward *Forward*
b. Kitchener, Ont., Dec. 1, 1929

Season	Club	GP	G	A	Pts
1953-54	Detroit R.W.	1	0	0	0
1955-56	Detroit R.W.	5	0	0	0
	Totals	6	0	0	0

STANKIEWICZ, Myron (Mike) *Forward*
b. Kitchener, Ont., Dec. 4, 1935

Season	Club	GP	G	A	Pts
1968-69	StL B-Phila F	35	0	7	7

STANLEY, Allan Herbert *Defenseman*
b. Timmins, Ont., Mar. 1, 1926

Season	Club	GP	G	A	Pts
1948-49	New York R.	40	2	8	10
1949-50	New York R.	55	4	4	8
1950-51	New York R.	70	7	14	21
1951-52	New York R.	50	5	14	19
1952-53	New York R.	70	5	12	17
1953-54	New York R.	10	0	2	2
1954-55	NY R-Chgo	64	10	16	26
1955-56	Chicago	59	4	14	18
1956-57	Boston	60	6	25	31
1957-58	Boston	69	6	25	31
1958-59	Toronto M.L.	70	1	22	23
1959-60	Toronto M.L.	64	10	23	33
1960-61	Toronto M.L.	68	9	25	34
1961-62	Toronto M.L.	60	9	26	35
1962-63	Toronto M.L.	61	4	15	19
1963-64	Toronto M.L.	70	6	21	27
1964-65	Toronto M.L.	64	2	15	17
1965-66	Toronto M.L.	59	4	14	18
1966-67	Toronto M.L.	53	1	12	13
1967-68	Toronto M.L.	64	1	13	14
1968-69	Philadelphia F.	64	4	13	17
	Totals	1244	100	333	433

Playoffs

Season	Club	GP	G	A	Pts
1949-50	New York R.	12	2	5	7
1957-58	Boston	12	1	3	4
1958-59	Toronto M.L.	12	0	3	3
1959-60	Toronto M.L.	10	2	3	5
1960-61	Toronto M.L.	5	0	3	3
1961-62	Toronto M.L.	12	0	3	3
1962-63	Toronto M.L.	10	1	6	7
1963-64	Toronto M.L.	14	1	6	7
1964-65	Toronto M.L.	6	0	1	1
1965-66	Toronto M.L.	1	0	0	0
1966-67	Toronto M.L.	12	0	2	2
1968-69	Philadelphia F.	4	0	1	1
	Totals	110	7	36	43

All-Star

Season	Club	GP	G	A	Pts
1955	NHL All-Stars	1	0	0	0
1957	NHL All-Stars	1	1	0	1
1960	NHL All-Stars	1	0	0	0
1961	NHL All-Stars	1	0	0	0
1962	Toronto M.L.	1	0	1	1
1963	Toronto M.L.	1	0	0	0
1967	NHL All-Stars	1	0	0	0
1968	Toronto M.L.	1	1	0	1
	Totals	8	2	1	3

STANOWSKI, Walter Peter *Defenseman*
b. Winnipeg, Man., Apr. 28, 1919

Season	Club	GP	G	A	Pts
1939-40	Toronto M.L.	--	2	7	9
1940-41	Toronto M.L.	--	7	14	21
1941-42	Toronto M.L.	24	1	7	8
1944-45	Toronto M.L.	34	2	9	11
1945-46	Toronto M.L.	45	3	10	13
1946-47	Toronto M.L.	51	3	16	19
1947-48	Toronto M.L.	54	2	11	13
1948-49	New York R.	60	1	8	9
1949-50	New York R.	37	1	1	2
1950-51	New York R.	49	1	5	6
	Totals	--	23	88	111

Playoffs

Season	Club	GP	G	A	Pts
1939-40	Toronto M.L.	10	1	0	1
1940-41	Toronto M.L.	7	0	3	3
1941-42	Toronto M.L.	13	2	7	9
1944-45	Toronto M.L.	13	0	1	1
1946-47	Toronto M.L.	8	0	0	0
1947-48	Toronto M.L.	9	0	2	2
	Totals	60	3	13	16

All-Star

Season	Club	GP	G	A	Pts
1947	Toronto M.L.	1	0	0	0

STAPLETON, Patrick James (Pat) *Defenseman*
b. Sarnia, Ont., July 4, 1940

Season	Club	GP	G	A	Pts
1961-62	Boston	69	2	5	7
1962-63	Boston	21	0	3	3
1965-66	Chicago	55	4	30	34
1966-67	Chicago	70	3	31	34
1967-68	Chicago	67	4	34	38
1968-69	Chicago	75	6	50	56
1969-70	Chicago	49	4	38	42
1970-71	Chicago	76	7	44	51
1971-72	Chicago	78	3	38	41
1972-73	Chicago	75	10	21	31
	Totals	635	43	294	337

Playoffs

Season	Club	GP	G	A	Pts
1965-66	Chicago	6	2	3	5
1966-67	Chicago	6	1	1	2
1967-68	Chicago	11	0	4	4
1970-71	Chicago	18	3	14	17
1971-72	Chicago	8	2	2	4
1972-73	Chicago	16	2	15	17
	Totals	65	10	39	49

All-Star

Season	Club	GP	G	A	Pts
1967	NHL All-Stars	1	0	0	0
1969	East All-Stars	1	0	1	1
1971	West All-Stars	1	0	0	0
1972	West All-Stars	1	0	0	0
	Totals	4	0	1	1

STARR, Harold *Defenseman*
b. Ottawa, Ont., July 8, 1905

Season	Club	GP	G	A	Pts
1929-30	Ottawa	--	2	1	3
1930-31	Ottawa	--	2	1	3
1931-32	Montreal M.	--	1	2	3
1932-33	Otta-Mont C	--	0	0	0
1934-35	Det RW-NY R	--	1	1	2
1935-36	New York R.	15	0	0	0
	Totals	--	6	5	11
Playoffs					
1929-30	Ottawa	2	1	0	1
1931-32	Montreal M.	4	0	0	0
1934-35	New York R.	4	0	0	0
	Totals	10	1	0	1

STARR, Wilfred Peter *Forward*
b. Winnipeg, Man., July 22, 1909

Season	Club	GP	G	A	Pts
1932-33	New York A.	--	4	3	7
1933-34	Detroit R.W.	--	2	2	4
1934-35	Detroit R.W.	--	1	1	2
1935-36	Detroit R.W.	--	1	0	1
	Totals	--	8	6	14
Playoffs					
1933-34	Detroit R.W.	--	0	2	2

STASIUK, Victor John *Forward*
b. Lethbridge, Alta., May 23, 1929

Season	Club	GP	G	A	Pts
1949-50	Chicago	17	1	1	2
1950-51	Chgo-Det RW	70	8	13	21
1951-52	Detroit R.W.	58	5	9	14
1952-53	Detroit R.W.	3	0	0	0
1953-54	Detroit R.W.	42	5	2	7
1954-55	Detroit R.W.	59	8	11	19
1955-56	Boston	59	19	18	37
1956-57	Boston	64	24	16	40
1957-58	Boston	70	21	35	56
1958-59	Boston	70	27	33	60
1959-60	Boston	69	29	39	68
1960-61	Bos-Det RW	69	15	38	53
1961-62	Detroit R.W.	59	15	28	43
1962-63	Detroit R.W.	36	6	11	17
	Totals	745	183	254	437
Playoffs					
1951-52	Detroit R.W.	7	0	2	2
1954-55	Detroit R.W.	11	5	3	8
1956-57	Boston	10	2	1	3
1957-58	Boston	12	0	5	5
1958-59	Boston	7	4	2	6
1960-61	Detroit R.W.	11	2	5	7
1962-63	Detroit R.W.	11	3	0	3
	Totals	69	16	18	34

STASIUK *(Continued)*

All-Star	Club	GP	G	A	Pts
1960	NHL All-Stars	1	0	0	0

STEFANIW, Morris Alexander *Forward*
b. North Battleford, Sask., Jan. 10, 1948

Season	Club	GP	G	A	Pts
1972-73	Atlanta	13	1	1	2

STEIN, Philip J. *Goalie*
b. Toronto, Ont., Sept. 13, 1913

Season	Club	GP	GA	Sho	AVE
1939-40	Toronto M.L.	1	2	0	2.00

STEMKOWSKI, Peter David *Forward*
b. Winnipeg, Man., Aug. 25, 1943

Season	Club	GP	G	A	Pts
1963-64	Toronto M.L.	1	0	0	0
1964-65	Toronto M.L.	36	5	15	20
1965-66	Toronto M.L.	56	4	12	16
1966-67	Toronto M.L.	68	13	22	35
1967-68	Tor ML-Det RW	73	10	21	31
1968-69	Detroit R.W.	71	21	31	52
1969-70	Detroit R.W.	76	25	24	49
1970-71	Det RW-NY R	78	18	31	49
1971-72	New York R.	59	11	17	28
1972-73	New York R.	78	22	37	59
	Totals	596	129	210	339
Playoffs					
1964-65	Toronto M.L.	6	0	3	3
1965-66	Toronto M.L.	4	0	0	0
1966-67	Toronto M.L.	12	5	7	12
1969-70	Detroit R.W.	4	1	1	2
1970-71	New York R.	13	3	2	5
1971-72	New York R.	16	4	8	12
1972-73	New York R.	10	4	2	6
	Totals	65	17	23	40
All-Star					
1968	Toronto M.L.	1	1	1	2

STEPHENS, Philip *Defenseman*

Season	Club	GP	G	A	Pts
1917-18	Montreal W.	4	1	0	1
1921-22	Montreal C.	4	0	0	0
	Totals	8	1	0	1

STEPHENSON, Frederick Wayne *Goalie*
b. Fort William, Ont., Jan. 29, 1945

Season	Club	GP	GA	Sho	AVE
1971-72	St. Louis B.	1⅔	9	0	5.40
1972-73	St. Louis B.	42⅓	128	1	3.03
	Totals	44	137	1	3.12
Playoffs					
1972-73	St. Louis B.	2½	14	0	5.25

STERNER, Ulf *Forward*

b. Deje, Sweden, Feb. 11, 1941

Season	Club	GP	G	A	Pts
1964–65	New York R.	4	0	0	0

STEVENS, Paul *Defenseman*

Season	Club	GP	G	A	Pts
1925–26	Boston	17	0	0	0

STEVENSON, Douglas *Goalie*

b. Regina, Sask., Apr. 6, 1924

Season	Club	GP	GA	Sho	AVE
1944–45	NY R–Chgo	6	27	0	4.50
1945–46	Chicago	2	12	0	6.00
	Totals	8	39	0	4.88

STEWART, Charles (Doc) *Goalie*

Season	Club	GP	GA	Sho	AVE
1924–25	Boston	21	64	2	3.05
1925–26	Boston	35	80	6	2.29
1926–27	Boston	--	--	--	--
	Totals	--	--	--	--

STEWART, James Gaye *Forward*

b. Fort William, Ont., June 28, 1923

Season	Club	GP	G	A	Pts
1942–43	Toronto M.L.	48	24	23	47
1945–46	Toronto M.L.	50	37	15	52
1946–47	Toronto M.L.	60	19	14	33
1947–48	Tor ML–Chgo	61	27	29	56
1948–49	Chicago	54	20	18	38
1949–50	Chicago	70	24	19	43
1950–51	Detroit R.W.	67	18	13	31
1951–52	New York R.	69	15	25	40
1952–53	NY R–Mont C	23	1	3	4
	Totals	502	185	159	344
Playoffs					
1941–42	Toronto M.L.	1	0	0	0
1942–43	Toronto M.L.	4	0	2	2
1946–47	Toronto M.L.	11	2	5	7
1950–51	Detroit R.W.	6	0	2	2
	Totals	22	2	9	11
All-Star					
1947	Toronto M.L.	1	0	0	0
1948	NHL All-Stars	1	1	0	1
1950	Detroit R.W.	1	0	0	0
1951	NHL 1st All-Stars	1	0	1	1
	Totals	4	1	1	2

STEWART, John Alexander *Forward*

b. Eriksdale, Man., May 16, 1950

Season	Club	GP	G	A	Pts
1970–71	Pittsburgh Pe.	15	2	1	3
1971–72	Pittsburgh Pe.	25	2	8	10
1972–73	Atlanta	68	17	17	34
	Totals	108	21	26	47

STEWART, John Sherratt (Jack) *Defenseman*

b. Pilot Mound, Man., May 6, 1917

Season	Club	GP	G	A	Pts
1938–39	Detroit R.W.	33	0	1	1
1939–40	Detroit R.W.	47	1	0	1
1940–41	Detroit R.W.	47	2	6	8
1941–42	Detroit R.W.	44	4	7	11
1942–43	Detroit R.W.	44	2	9	11
1945–46	Detroit R.W.	47	4	11	15
1946–47	Detroit R.W.	55	5	9	14
1947–48	Detroit R.W.	60	5	14	19
1948–49	Detroit R.W.	60	4	11	15
1949–50	Detroit R.W.	66	3	11	14
1950–51	Chicago	26	0	2	2
1951–52	Chicago	37	1	3	4
	Totals	566	31	84	115
Playoffs					
1939–40	Detroit R.W.	5	0	0	0
1940–41	Detroit R.W.	9	1	2	3
1941–42	Detroit R.W.	12	0	1	1
1942–43	Detroit R.W.	10	1	2	3
1945–46	Detroit R.W.	5	0	0	0
1946–47	Detroit R.W.	5	0	1	1
1947–48	Detroit R.W.	9	1	3	4
1948–49	Detroit R.W.	11	1	1	2
1949–50	Detroit R.W.	14	1	4	5
	Totals	80	5	14	19
All-Star					
1947	NHL All-Stars	1	0	0	0
1948	NHL All-Stars	1	0	0	0
1949	NHL All-Stars	1	0	0	0
1950	NHL All-Stars	1	0	0	0
	Totals	4	0	0	0

STEWART, Kenneth *Defenseman*

b. Port Arthur, Ont., 1915

Season	Club	GP	G	A	Pts
1941–42	Chicago	--	1	1	2

STEWART, Nelson *Forward*

b. Montreal, Que., Dec. 29, 1902

Season	Club	GP	G	A	Pts
1925–26	Montreal M.	36	34	8	42
1926–27	Montreal M.	--	17	4	21
1927–28	Montreal M.	--	27	7	34
1928–29	Montreal M.	--	21	8	29

STEWART *(Continued)*

Season	Club	GP	G	A	Pts
1929-30	Montreal M.	--	39	16	55
1930-31	Montreal M.	--	25	14	39
1931-32	Montreal M.	--	22	11	33
1932-33	Boston	--	18	18	36
1933-34	Boston	--	21	17	38
1934-35	Boston	--	21	18	39
1935-36	New York A.	--	14	15	29
1936-37	Bos-NY A	--	23	12	35
1937-38	New York A.	--	19	17	36
1938-39	New York A.	--	16	19	35
1939-40	New York A.	--	7	7	14
	Totals	--	324	191	515

Playoffs

Season	Club	GP	G	A	Pts
1925-26	Montreal M.	--	6	1	7
1926-27	Montreal M.	--	0	0	0
1927-28	Montreal M.	--	2	2	4
1929-30	Montreal M.	--	1	1	2
1930-31	Montreal M.	--	1	0	1
1931-32	Montreal M.	--	0	1	1
1932-33	Boston	--	2	0	2
1934-35	Boston	--	0	1	1
1935-36	New York A.	--	1	2	3
1937-38	New York A.	--	2	3	5
1938-39	New York A.	--	0	0	0
1939-40	New York A.	--	0	0	0
	Totals	--	15	11	26

STEWART, Ralph Donald *Forward*
b. Fort William, Ont., Dec. 2, 1948

Season	Club	GP	G	A	Pts
1970-71	Vancouver	3	0	1	1
1972-73	New York I.	31	4	10	14
	Totals	34	4	11	15

STEWART, Robert Harold (Bob) *Defenseman*
b. Charlottetown, P.E.I., Nov. 10, 1950

Season	Club	GP	G	A	Pts
1971-72	Bost-Calif	24	1	2	3
1972-73	California	63	4	17	21
	Totals	87	5	19	24

STEWART, Ronald George (Ron)
Defenseman-Forward
b. Calgary, Alta., July 11, 1932

Season	Club	GP	G	A	Pts
1952-53	Toronto M.L.	70	13	22	35
1953-54	Toronto M.L.	70	14	11	25
1954-55	Toronto M.L.	53	14	5	19
1955-56	Toronto M.L.	69	13	14	27
1956-57	Toronto M.L.	65	15	20	35
1957-58	Toronto M.L.	70	15	24	39

STEWART *(Continued)*

Season	Club	GP	G	A	Pts
1958-59	Toronto M.L.	70	21	13	34
1959-60	Toronto M.L.	67	14	20	34
1960-61	Toronto M.L.	51	13	12	25
1961-62	Toronto M.L.	60	8	9	17
1962-63	Toronto M.L.	63	16	16	32
1963-64	Toronto M.L.	65	14	5	19
1964-65	Toronto M.L.	65	16	11	27
1965-66	Boston	70	20	16	36
1966-67	Boston	56	14	10	24
1967-68	StL B-NY R	74	14	12	26
1968-69	New York R.	75	18	11	29
1969-70	New York R.	76	14	10	24
1970-71	New York R.	76	5	6	11
1971-72	Vanc-NY R	55	3	3	6
1972-73	NY R-NY I	33	2	3	5
	Totals	1353	276	253	529

Playoffs

Season	Club	GP	G	A	Pts
1953-54	Toronto M.L.	5	0	1	1
1954-55	Toronto M.L.	4	0	0	0
1955-56	Toronto M.L.	5	1	1	2
1958-59	Toronto M.L.	12	3	3	6
1959-60	Toronto M.L.	10	0	2	2
1960-61	Toronto M.L.	5	1	0	1
1961-62	Toronto M.L.	11	1	6	7
1962-63	Toronto M.L.	10	4	0	4
1963-64	Toronto M.L.	14	0	4	4
1964-65	Toronto M.L.	6	0	1	1
1967-68	New York R.	6	1	1	2
1968-69	New York R.	4	0	1	1
1969-70	New York R.	6	0	0	0
1970-71	New York R.	13	1	0	1
1971-72	New York R.	8	2	1	3
	Totals	119	14	21	35

All-Star

Season	Club	GP	G	A	Pts
1955	NHL All-Stars	1	0	0	0
1962	Toronto M.L.	1	0	1	1
1963	Toronto M.L.	1	0	0	0
1964	Toronto M.L.	1	0	0	0
	Totals	4	0	1	1

STODDARD, John Edward *Forward*
b. Stony Creek, Ont., Sept. 26, 1926

Season	Club	GP	G	A	Pts
1951-52	New York R.	20	4	2	6
1952-53	New York R.	60	12	13	25
	Totals	80	16	15	31

STRAIN, Neil Gilbert *Forward*
b. Kenora, Ont., Feb. 24, 1926

Season	Club	GP	G	A	Pts
1952-53	New York R.	52	11	13	24

STRATE, Gordon Lynn *Defenseman*
b. Edmonton, Alta., May 28, 1935

Season	Club	GP	G	A	Pts
1956–57	Detroit R.W.	5	0	0	0
1957–58	Detroit R.W.	45	0	0	0
1958–59	Detroit R.W.	11	0	0	0
	Totals	61	0	0	0

STRATTON, Arthur *Forward*
b. Winnipeg, Man., Oct. 8, 1935

Season	Club	GP	G	A	Pts
1959–60	New York R.	18	2	5	7
1963–64	Detroit R.W.	5	0	3	3
1965–66	Chicago	2	0	0	0
1967–68	Pitts Pe–Phila F	70	16	25	41
	Totals	95	18	33	51

Playoffs

1967–68	Philadelphia F.	5	0	0	0

STROBEL, Arthur George *Forward*
b. Regina, Sask., Nov. 28, 1922

Season	Club	GP	G	A	Pts
1943–44	New York R.	7	0	0	0

STUART, William (Red) *Defenseman*

Season	Club	GP	G	A	Pts
1920–21	Toronto St. P.	18	2	1	3
1921–22	Toronto St. P.	24	3	6	9
1922–23	Toronto St. P.	23	7	3	10
1923–24	Toronto St. P.	24	4	3	7
1924–25	Toronto StP–Bos	29	5	2	7
1925–26	Boston	35	6	1	7
1926–27	Boston	--	3	1	4
	Totals	--	30	17	47

Playoffs

1920–21	Toronto St. P.	--	0	0	0
1921–22	Toronto St. P.	--	0	0	0
1926–27	Boston	--	0	0	0
	Totals	--	0	0	0

SULLIVAN, Barry Carter *Forward*
b. Preston, Ont., Sept. 21, 1926

Season	Club	GP	G	A	Pts
1947–48	Detroit R.W.	1	0	0	0

SULLIVAN, Frank Taylor (Sully) *Defenseman*
b. Toronto, Ont., June 16, 1929

Season	Club	GP	G	A	Pts
1949–50	Toronto M.L.	1	0	0	0
1952–53	Toronto M.L.	5	0	0	0
1954–55	Chicago	1	0	0	0
1955–56	Chicago	1	0	0	0
	Totals	8	0	0	0

SULLIVAN, George James (Red) *Forward*
b. Peterborough, Ont., Dec. 24, 1929

Season	Club	GP	G	A	Pts
1949–50	Boston	3	0	1	1
1951–52	Boston	67	12	12	24
1952–53	Boston	32	3	8	11
1954–55	Chicago	70	19	42	61
1955–56	Chicago	63	14	26	40
1956–57	New York R.	42	6	17	23
1957–58	New York R.	70	11	35	46
1958–59	New York R.	70	21	42	63
1959–60	New York R.	70	12	25	37
1960–61	New York R.	70	9	31	40
	Totals	557	107	239	346

Playoffs

1950–51	Boston	2	0	0	0
1951–52	Boston	7	0	0	0
1952–53	Boston	3	0	0	0
1956–57	New York R.	5	1	2	3
1957–58	New York R.	1	0	0	0
	Totals	18	1	2	3

All-Star

1955	NHL All-Stars	1	0	0	0
1956	NHL All-Stars	1	0	0	0
1958	NHL All-Stars	1	0	1	1
1959	NHL All-Stars	1	0	0	0
1960	NHL All-Stars	1	0	1	1
	Totals	5	0	2	2

SUMMERHILL, William Arthur *Forward*
b. Toronto, Ont., July 9, 1915

Season	Club	GP	G	A	Pts
1938–39	Montreal C.	--	6	10	16
1939–40	Montreal C.	--	3	2	5
1941–42	Brooklyn A.	16	5	5	10
	Totals	--	14	17	31

Playoffs

1938–39	Montreal C.	3	0	0	0

SUOMI, Al *Forward*

Season	Club	GP	G	A	Pts
1936–37	Chicago	--	0	0	0

SUTHERLAND, Ronald *Defenseman*
b. Eston, Sask., Feb. 8, 1913

Season	Club	GP	G	A	Pts
1931–32	Boston	--	0	0	0

SUTHERLAND, William Fraser (Bill) *Forward*
b. Regina, Sask., Nov. 10, 1934

Season	Club	GP	G	A	Pts
1967–68	Philadelphia F.	60	20	9	29
1968–69	Tor ML–Phila F	56	14	8	22

SUTHERLAND (Continued)

Season	Club	GP	G	A	Pts
1969–70	Philadelphia F.	51	15	17	32
1970–71	Phila F–StL B	69	19	20	39
1971–72	StL B–Det RW	14	2	4	6
	Totals	250	70	58	128

Playoffs

Season	Club	GP	G	A	Pts
1962–63	Montreal C.	2	0	0	0
1967–68	Philadelphia F.	7	1	3	4
1968–69	Philadelphia F.	4	1	1	2
1970–71	St. Louis B.	1	0	0	0
	Totals	14	2	4	6

SWAIN, Gary Forward
b. WELLAND, Ont., Sept. 11, 1947

Season	Club	GP	G	A	Pts
1968–69	Pittsburgh Pe.	9	1	1	2

SWARBRICK, George Raymond Forward
b. Moose Jaw, Sask., Feb. 16, 1942

Season	Club	GP	G	A	Pts
1967–68	Oakland	49	13	5	18
1968–69	Oak–Pitts Pe	69	4	19	23
1969–70	Pittsburgh Pe.	12	0	1	1
1970–71	Philadelphia F.	2	0	0	0
	Totals	132	17	25	42

SWEENEY, William Forward
b. Guelph, Ont., Jan. 30, 1937

Season	Club	GP	G	A	Pts
1959–60	New York R.	4	1	0	1

SZURA, Joseph Forward
b. Fort William, Ont., Dec. 18, 1938

Season	Club	GP	G	A	Pts
1967–68	Oakland	20	1	3	4
1968–69	Oakland	70	9	12	21
	Totals	90	10	15	25

Playoffs

Season	Club	GP	G	A	Pts
1968–69	Oakland	7	2	3	5

TALBOT, Jean Guy Defenseman
b. Cap de la Madeleine, Que., July 11, 1932

Season	Club	GP	G	A	Pts
1954–55	Montreal C.	3	0	1	1
1955–56	Montreal C.	66	1	13	14
1956–57	Montreal C.	59	0	13	13
1957–58	Montreal C.	55	4	15	19
1958–59	Montreal C.	69	4	17	21
1959–60	Montreal C.	69	1	14	15
1960–61	Montreal C.	70	5	26	31
1961–62	Montreal C.	70	5	42	47
1962–63	Montreal C.	70	3	22	25

TALBOT (Continued)

Season	Club	GP	G	A	Pts
1963–64	Montreal C.	66	1	13	14
1964–65	Montreal C.	67	8	14	22
1965–66	Montreal C.	59	1	14	15
1966–67	Montreal C.	68	3	5	8
1967–68	Minn–Det RW–StL B	59	0	7	7
1968–69	St. Louis B.	69	5	4	9
1969–70	St. Louis B.	75	2	15	17
1970–71	StL B–Buff	62	0	7	7
	Totals	1056	43	242	285

Playoffs

Season	Club	GP	G	A	Pts
1955–56	Montreal C.	9	0	2	2
1956–57	Montreal C.	10	0	2	2
1957–58	Montreal C.	10	0	3	3
1958–59	Montreal C.	11	0	1	1
1959–60	Montreal C.	8	1	1	2
1960–61	Montreal C.	6	1	1	2
1961–62	Montreal C.	6	1	1	2
1962–63	Montreal C.	5	0	0	0
1963–64	Montreal C.	7	0	2	2
1964–65	Montreal C.	13	0	1	1
1965–66	Montreal C.	10	0	2	2
1966–67	Montreal C.	10	0	0	0
1967–68	St. Louis B.	17	0	2	2
1968–69	St. Louis B.	12	0	2	2
1969–70	St. Louis B.	16	1	6	7
	Totals	150	4	26	30

All-Star

Season	Club	GP	G	A	Pts
1956	Montreal C.	1	0	0	0
1957	Montreal C.	1	0	0	0
1958	Montreal C.	1	0	1	1
1960	Montreal C.	1	0	0	0
1962	NHL All-Stars	1	0	0	0
1965	Montreal C.	1	0	0	0
1967	Montreal C.	1	0	0	0
	Totals	7	0	1	1

TALLON, Michael Dale Lee Defenseman
b. Noranda, Que., Oct. 19, 1950

Season	Club	GP	G	A	Pts
1970–71	Vancouver	78	14	42	56
1971–72	Vancouver	69	17	27	44
1972–73	Vancouver	75	13	24	37
	Totals	222	44	93	137

All-Star

Season	Club	GP	G	A	Pts
1971	East All-Stars	1	0	0	0
1972	East All-Stars	1	0	0	0
	Totals	2	0	0	0

TANNAHILL, Donald Andrew (Don) Forward
b. Penetang, Ont., Feb. 21, 1949

Season	Club	GP	G	A	Pts
1972–73	Vancouver	78	22	21	43

TARDIF, Marc *Forward*
b. Granby, Que., June 12, 1949

Season	Club	GP	G	A	Pts
1969-70	Montreal C.	18	3	2	5
1970-71	Montreal C.	76	19	30	49
1971-72	Montreal C.	75	31	22	53
1972-73	Montreal C.	76	25	25	50
	Totals	245	78	79	157
Playoffs					
1970-71	Montreal C.	20	3	1	4
1971-72	Montreal C.	6	2	3	5
1972-73	Montreal C.	14	6	6	12
	Totals	40	11	10	21

TATCHELL, Spencer Harry *Defenseman*
b. Lloydminister, Sask., July 16, 1924

Season	Club	GP	G	A	Pts
1942-43	New York R.	1	0	0	0

TAUGHER, William *Goalie*

Season	Club	GP	GA	Sho	AVE
1925-26	Montreal C.	1	3	0	3.00

TAYLOR, Edward Wray (Ted) *Forward*
b. Brandon, Man., Feb. 25, 1942

Season	Club	GP	G	A	Pts
1964-65	New York R.	4	0	0	0
1965-66	New York R.	4	0	1	1
1966-67	Detroit R.W.	2	0	0	0
1967-68	Minnesota	31	3	5	8
1970-71	Vancouver	56	11	16	27
1971-72	Vancouver	69	9	13	22
	Totals	166	23	35	58

TAYLOR, Harry *Defenseman*
b. St. James, Man., Mar. 28, 1926

Season	Club	GP	G	A	Pts
1946-47	Toronto M.L.	9	0	2	2
1948-49	Toronto M.L.	42	4	7	11
1951-52	Chicago	15	1	1	2
	Totals	66	5	10	15
Playoffs					
1948-49	Toronto M.L.	1	0	0	0

TAYLOR, Ralph F. *Defenseman*
b. Toronto, Ont., Oct. 2, 1905

Season	Club	GP	G	A	Pts
1927-28	Chicago	22	1	1	2
1928-29	Chicago	--	0	0	0
1929-30	Chgo-NY R	--	3	0	3
	Totals	--	4	1	5
Playoffs					
1929-30	New York R.	4	0	0	0

TAYLOR, Robert *Forward*
b. Newton, Mass., Aug. 12, 1904

Season	Club	GP	G	A	Pts
1929-30	Boston	--	0	0	0

TAYLOR, Robert Ian (Bob) *Goalie*
b. Calgary, Alta., Jan. 24, 1945

Season	Club	GP	GA	Sho	AVE
1971-72	Philadelphia F.	5⅓	16	0	3.00
1972-73	Philadelphia F.	19	78	0	4.09
	Totals	24⅓	94	0	3.85

TAYLOR, William Gordon *Forward*
b. Winnipeg, Man., Oct. 14, 1942

Season	Club	GP	G	A	Pts
1964-65	New York R.	2	0	0	0

TAYLOR, William James *Forward*
b. Winnipeg, Man., May 3, 1919

Season	Club	GP	G	A	Pts
1939-40	Toronto M.L.	43	4	6	10
1940-41	Toronto M.L.	48	9	26	35
1941-42	Toronto M.L.	48	12	26	38
1942-43	Toronto M.L.	50	18	42	60
1945-46	Toronto M.L.	48	23	18	41
1946-47	Detroit R.W.	60	17	46	63
1947-48	Bos-NY R	41	4	16	20
	Totals	338	87	180	267
Playoffs					
1939-40	Toronto M.L.	--	1	0	1
1940-41	Toronto M.L.	7	0	3	3
1941-42	Toronto M.L.	13	2	8	10
1942-43	Toronto M.L.	6	2	2	4
1946-47	Detroit R.W.	5	1	5	6
	Totals	--	6	18	24

TEAL, Allen Leslie (Skip) *Forward*
b. Ridgeway, Ont., July 17, 1933

Season	Club	GP	G	A	Pts
1954-55	Boston	1	0	0	0

TENO, Harvey *Goalie*

Season	Club	GP	GA	Sho	AVE
1938-39	Detroit R.W.	5	15	0	3.00

TERBENCHE, Paul *Defenseman-Forward*
b. Cobourg, Ont., Sept. 16, 1945

Season	Club	GP	G	A	Pts
1967-68	Chicago	68	3	7	10
1970-71	Buffalo	3	0	0	0
1971-72	Buffalo	9	0	0	0
1972-73	Buffalo	42	0	7	7
	Totals	122	3	14	17
Playoffs					
1967-68	Chicago	6	0	0	0

TESSIER, Orval Ray *Forward*
b. Cornwall, Ont., June 30, 1933

Season	Club	GP	G	A	Pts
1954–55	Montreal C.	4	0	0	0
1955–56	Boston	23	2	3	5
1960–61	Boston	32	3	4	7
	Totals	59	5	7	12

THIBEAULT, Lawrence Lorrain *Forward*
b. Charletone, Ont., Oct. 2, 1918

Season	Club	GP	G	A	Pts
1944–45	Detroit R.W.	4	0	2	2
1945–46	Montreal C.	1	0	0	0
	Totals	5	0	2	2

THOMAS, Cyril James (Cy) *Forward*
b. Dowlais, Wales, Aug. 5, 1926

Season	Club	GP	G	A	Pts
1947–48	Chgo–Tor ML	14	2	2	4

THOMAS, Robert Wayne *Goalie*
b. Ottawa, Ont., Oct. 9, 1947

Season	Club	GP	GA	Sho	AVE
1972–73	Montreal C.	9⅔	23	1	2.37

THOMPSON, Cecil (Tiny) *Goalie*
b. Sandon, B.C., May 31, 1905

Season	Club	GP	GA	Sho	AVE
1928–29	Boston	44	52	12	1.18
1929–30	Boston	44	98	3	2.23
1930–31	Boston	44	90	3	2.05
1931–32	Boston	43	104	9	2.42
1932–33	Boston	48	88	11	1.83
1933–34	Boston	48	130	5	2.71
1934–35	Boston	48	112	8	2.33
1935–36	Boston	48	82	10	1.71
1936–37	Boston	48	110	6	2.29
1937–38	Boston	48	89	7	1.85
1938–39	Bos–Det RW	44	108	4	2.45
1939–40	Detroit R.W.	46	120	3	2.61
	Totals	553	1183	80	2.14
Playoffs					
1928–29	Boston	5	3	3	0.60
1929–30	Boston	6	12	0	2.00
1930–31	Boston	5	13	0	2.60
1932–33	Boston	5	9	0	1.80
1934–35	Boston	4	7	1	1.75
1935–36	Boston	2	8	1	4.00
1936–37	Boston	3	8	1	2.67
1937–38	Boston	3	6	0	2.00
1938–39	Detroit R.W.	6	15	1	2.50
1939–40	Detroit R.W.	5	12	0	2.40
	Totals	44	73	7	1.66

THOMPSON, Clifford *Defenseman*
b. Winchester, Mass., Dec. 9, 1918

Season	Club	GP	G	A	Pts
1948–49	Boston	10	0	1	1

THOMPSON, Kenneth

Season	Club	GP	G	A	Pts
1917–18	Montreal W.	1	0	0	0

THOMPSON, Loran Errol *Forward*
b. Summerside, P.E.I., May 28, 1950

Season	Club	GP	G	A	Pts
1970–71	Toronto M.L.	1	0	0	0
1972–73	Toronto M.L.	68	13	19	32
	Totals	69	13	19	32

THOMPSON, Paul Ivan *Forward*
b. Calgary, Alta., Nov. 2, 1906

Season	Club	GP	G	A	Pts
1926–27	New York R.	43	7	3	10
1927–28	New York R.	41	4	4	8
1928–29	New York R.	44	10	7	17
1929–30	New York R.	44	7	12	19
1930–31	New York R.	44	7	7	14
1931–32	Chicago	--	8	14	22
1932–33	Chicago	--	13	20	33
1933–34	Chicago	--	20	16	36
1934–35	Chicago	--	16	23	39
1935–36	Chicago	--	17	23	40
1936–37	Chicago	--	17	18	35
1937–38	Chicago	--	22	22	44
1938–39	Chicago	--	5	10	15
	Totals	--	153	179	332
Playoffs					
1926–27	New York R.	2	0	0	0
1927–28	New York R.	8	0	0	0
1928–29	New York R.	6	0	2	2
1929–30	New York R.	4	0	0	0
1930–31	New York R.	4	3	0	3
1931–32	Chicago	2	0	0	0
1933–34	Chicago	8	4	3	7
1934–35	Chicago	2	0	0	0
1935–36	Chicago	2	0	3	3
1937–38	Chicago	10	4	3	7
	Totals	48	11	11	22

THOMS, William D. *Forward*
b. Newmarket, Ont., Mar. 5, 1910

Season	Club	GP	G	A	Pts
1932–33	Toronto M.L.	--	3	9	12
1933–34	Toronto M.L.	--	8	18	26
1934–35	Toronto M.L.	--	9	13	22
1935–36	Toronto M.L.	--	23	15	38
1936–37	Toronto M.L.	--	10	9	19

THOMS (Continued)

Season	Club	GP	G	A	Pts
1937-38	Toronto M.L.	--	14	24	38
1938-39	Tor ML-Chgo	--	7	15	22
1939-40	Chicago	--	9	13	22
1940-41	Chicago	--	13	19	32
1941-42	Chicago	--	15	30	45
1942-43	Chicago	47	15	28	43
1943-44	Chicago	7	3	5	8
1944-45	Chgo-Bos	38	6	8	14
	Totals	--	135	206	341

Playoffs

Season	Club	GP	G	A	Pts
1932-33	Toronto M.L.	--	1	1	2
1933-34	Toronto M.L.	--	0	2	2
1934-35	Toronto M.L.	--	2	0	2
1935-36	Toronto M.L.	--	3	5	8
1936-37	Toronto M.L.	--	0	0	0
1937-38	Toronto M.L.	--	0	1	1
1939-40	Chicago	--	0	0	0
1940-41	Chicago	--	0	0	0
1941-42	Chicago	--	0	1	1
1944-45	Boston	1	0	0	0
	Totals	--	6	10	16

THOMSON, Floyd Harvey *Forward*
b. Sudbury, Ont., June 14, 1949

Season	Club	GP	G	A	Pts
1971-72	St. Louis B.	49	4	6	10
1972-73	St. Louis B.	75	14	20	34
	Totals	124	18	26	44

Playoffs

Season	Club	GP	G	A	Pts
1972-73	St. Louis B.	5	0	1	1

THOMSON, James Richard *Defenseman*
b. Winnipeg, Man., Feb. 23, 1927

Season	Club	GP	G	A	Pts
1945-46	Toronto M.L.	5	0	1	1
1946-47	Toronto M.L.	60	2	14	16
1947-48	Toronto M.L.	59	0	29	29
1948-49	Toronto M.L.	60	4	16	20
1949-50	Toronto M.L.	70	0	13	13
1950-51	Toronto M.L.	69	3	33	36
1951-52	Toronto M.L.	70	0	25	25
1952-53	Toronto M.L.	69	0	22	22
1953-54	Toronto M.L.	61	2	24	26
1954-55	Toronto M.L.	70	4	12	16
1955-56	Toronto M.L.	62	0	7	7
1956-57	Toronto M.L.	62	0	12	12
1957-58	Chicago	70	4	7	11
	Totals	787	19	215	234

Playoffs

Season	Club	GP	G	A	Pts
1946-47	Toronto M.L.	11	0	1	1
1947-48	Toronto M.L.	9	1	1	2

THOMSON (Continued)

Playoffs

Season	Club	GP	G	A	Pts
1948-49	Toronto M.L.	9	1	5	6
1949-50	Toronto M.L.	7	0	2	2
1950-51	Toronto M.L.	11	0	1	1
1951-52	Toronto M.L.	4	0	0	0
1953-54	Toronto M.L.	3	0	0	0
1954-55	Toronto M.L.	4	0	0	0
1955-56	Toronto M.L.	5	0	3	3
	Totals	63	2	13	15

All-Star

Season	Club	GP	G	A	Pts
1947	Toronto M.L.	1	0	0	0
1948	Toronto M.L.	1	0	0	0
1949	Toronto M.L.	1	0	0	0
1950	NHL All-Stars	1	0	0	0
1951	NHL 2nd All-Stars	1	0	0	0
1952	NHL 2nd All-Stars	1	0	0	0
1953	NHL All-Stars	1	0	0	0
	Totals	7	0	0	0

THOMSON, John F. *Defenseman*
b. Bixbridge, England, Jan. 31, 1918

Season	Club	GP	G	A	Pts
1939-40	New York A.	--	1	1	2

THOMSON, Rhys *Defenseman*
b. Toronto, Ont., Aug. 9, 1918

Season	Club	GP	G	A	Pts
1939-40	Montreal C.	--	0	0	0
1941-42	New York A.	--	0	0	0
1942-43	Toronto M.L.	18	0	2	2
	Totals	--	0	2	2

THOMSON, William Ferguson *Forward*
b. Ayrshire, Scotland, Mar. 23, 1914

Season	Club	GP	G	A	Pts
1943-44	Chgo-Det RW	6	2	2	4

Playoffs

Season	Club	GP	G	A	Pts
1943-44	Detroit R.W.	2	0	0	0

THORSTEINSON, Joseph *Forward*
b. Winnipeg, Man.

Season	Club	GP	G	A	Pts
1932-33	New York A.	--	0	0	0

THURIER, Alfred Michael *Forward*
b. Granby, Que., Jan. 11, 1918

Season	Club	GP	G	A	Pts
1940-41	New York A.	--	2	1	3
1941-42	Brooklyn A.	27	7	7	14
1944-45	New York R.	50	16	19	35
	Totals	--	25	27	52

THURLBY, Thomas Newman *Defenseman*
b. Kingston, Ont., Nov. 9, 1938

Season	Club	GP	G	A	Pts
1967-68	Oakland	20	1	1	2

TIMGREN, Raymond Charles *Forward*
b. Windsor, Ont., Sept. 29, 1928

Season	Club	GP	G	A	Pts
1948-49	Toronto M.L.	36	3	12	15
1949-50	Toronto M.L.	68	7	18	25
1950-51	Toronto M.L.	70	1	9	10
1951-52	Toronto M.L.	50	2	4	6
1952-53	Toronto M.L.	12	0	0	0
1954-55	Tor ML-Chgo	15	1	1	2
	Totals	**251**	**14**	**44**	**58**

Playoffs

Season	Club	GP	G	A	Pts
1948-49	Toronto M.L.	9	3	3	6
1949-50	Toronto M.L.	6	0	4	4
1950-51	Toronto M.L.	11	0	1	1
1951-52	Toronto M.L.	4	0	1	1
	Totals	**30**	**3**	**9**	**12**

All-Star

1949	Toronto M.L.	1	0	0	0

TKACZUK, Walter Robert *Forward*
b. Emstedetten, Germany, Sept. 29, 1947

Season	Club	GP	G	A	Pts
1967-68	New York R.	2	0	0	0
1968-69	New York R.	71	12	24	36
1969-70	New York R.	76	27	50	77
1970-71	New York R.	77	26	49	75
1971-72	New York R.	76	24	42	66
1972-73	New York R.	76	27	39	66
	Totals	**378**	**116**	**204**	**320**

Playoffs

Season	Club	GP	G	A	Pts
1968-69	New York R.	4	0	1	1
1969-70	New York R.	6	2	1	3
1970-71	New York R.	13	1	5	6
1971-72	New York R.	16	4	6	10
1972-73	New York R.	10	7	2	9
	Totals	**49**	**14**	**15**	**29**

All-Star

1970	East All-Stars	1	1	0	1

TOPPAZZINI, Gerald *Forward*
b. Copper Cliff, Ont., July 29, 1931

Season	Club	GP	G	A	Pts
1952-53	Boston	69	10	13	23
1953-54	Bos-Chgo	51	5	8	13
1954-55	Chicago	70	9	18	27
1955-56	Det RW-Bos	68	8	14	22
1956-57	Boston	55	15	23	38
1957-58	Boston	64	25	24	49

TOPPAZZINI *(Continued)*

Season	Club	GP	G	A	Pts
1958-59	Boston	70	21	23	44
1959-60	Boston	69	12	33	45
1960-61	Boston	67	15	35	50
1961-62	Boston	70	19	31	50
1962-63	Boston	65	17	18	35
1963-64	Boston	65	7	4	11
	Totals	**783**	**163**	**244**	**407**

Playoffs

Season	Club	GP	G	A	Pts
1952-53	Boston	11	0	3	3
1956-57	Boston	10	0	1	1
1957-58	Boston	12	9	3	12
1958-59	Boston	7	4	2	6
	Totals	**40**	**13**	**9**	**22**

All-Star

1955	Detroit R.W.	1	0	0	0
1958	NHL All-Stars	1	0	1	1
1959	NHL All-Stars	1	0	0	0
	Totals	**3**	**0**	**1**	**1**

TOPPAZZINI, Zellio Peter *Forward*
b. Copper Cliff, Ont., Jan. 5, 1930

Season	Club	GP	G	A	Pts
1948-49	Boston	5	1	1	2
1949-50	Boston	36	5	5	10
1950-51	Bos-NY R	59	14	14	28
1951-52	New York R.	16	1	1	2
1956-57	Chicago	7	0	0	0
	Totals	**123**	**21**	**21**	**42**

Playoffs

1948-49	Boston	2	0	0	0

TOUHEY, William *Forward*
b. Ottawa, Ont., Mar. 23, 1906

Season	Club	GP	G	A	Pts
1927-28	Montreal M.	--	2	0	2
1928-29	Ottawa	--	9	3	12
1929-30	Ottawa	--	10	3	13
1930-31	Ottawa	--	15	15	30
1931-32	Boston	--	5	4	9
1932-33	Ottawa	--	12	7	19
1933-34	Ottawa	--	12	8	20
	Totals	**--**	**65**	**40**	**105**

Playoffs

Season	Club	GP	G	A	Pts
1927-28	Montreal M.	--	0	0	0
1929-30	Ottawa	--	1	0	1
	Totals	**--**	**1**	**0**	**1**

TOUPIN, Jacques *Forward*
b. Three Rivers, Que.

Season	Club	GP	G	A	Pts
1943–44	Chicago	8	1	2	3

Playoffs

Season	Club	GP	G	A	Pts
1943–44	Chicago	4	0	0	0

TOWNSEND, Arthur

Season	Club	GP	G	A	Pts
1926–27	Chicago	1	0	0	0

TRAINOR, Thomas Weston (Wes) *Forward*
b. Charlottetown, P.E.I., Sept. 11, 1922

Season	Club	GP	G	A	Pts
1948–49	New York R.	17	1	2	3

TRAPP, Robert *Defenseman*

Season	Club	GP	G	A	Pts
1926–27	Chicago	--	4	2	6
1927–28	Chicago	--	0	2	2
	Totals	--	4	4	8

Playoffs

Season	Club	GP	G	A	Pts
1922–23	Edmonton (PCHL)	--	0	0	0
1926–27	Chicago	--	0	0	0
	Totals	--	0	0	0

TRAUB, Percy *Defenseman*

Season	Club	GP	G	A	Pts
1926–27	Chicago	--	0	2	2
1927–28	Detroit C.	--	3	1	4
1928–29	Detroit C.	--	0	0	0
	Totals	--	3	3	6

Playoffs

Season	Club	GP	G	A	Pts
1926–37	Chicago	--	0	0	0
1928–29	Detroit C.	--	0	0	0
	Totals	--	0	0	0

TREMBLAY, Gilles *Forward*
b. Montmorency, Que., Dec. 18, 1938

Season	Club	GP	G	A	Pts
1960–61	Montreal C.	45	7	11	18
1961–62	Montreal C.	70	32	22	54
1962–63	Montreal C.	60	25	24	49
1963–64	Montreal C.	61	22	15	37
1964–65	Montreal C.	26	9	7	16
1965–66	Montreal C.	70	27	21	48
1966–67	Montreal C.	62	13	19	32
1967–68	Montreal C.	71	23	28	51
1968–69	Montreal C.	44	10	15	25
	Totals	509	168	162	330

Playoffs

Season	Club	GP	G	A	Pts
1960–61	Montreal C.	6	1	3	4
1961–62	Montreal C.	6	1	0	1

TREMBLAY *(Continued)*

Playoffs

	Club	GP	G	A	Pts
1962–63	Montreal C.	5	2	0	2
1963–64	Montreal C.	2	0	0	0
1965–66	Montreal C.	10	4	5	9
1966–67	Montreal C.	10	0	1	1
1967–68	Montreal C.	9	1	5	6
	Totals	48	9	14	23

All-Star

1965	Montreal C.	1	0	0	0
1967	Montreal C.	1	0	0	0
	Totals	2	0	0	0

TREMBLAY, Jean Claude (J.C.) *Defenseman*
b. Bagotville, Que., Jan. 22, 1939

Season	Club	GP	G	A	Pts
1959–60	Montreal C.	11	0	1	1
1960–61	Montreal C.	29	1	3	4
1961–62	Montreal C.	70	3	17	20
1962–63	Montreal C.	69	1	17	18
1963–64	Montreal C.	70	5	16	21
1964–65	Montreal C.	68	3	17	20
1965–66	Montreal C.	59	6	29	35
1966–67	Montreal C.	60	8	26	34
1967–68	Montreal C.	73	4	26	30
1968–69	Montreal C.	75	7	32	39
1969–70	Montreal C.	58	2	19	21
1970–71	Montreal C.	76	11	52	63
1971–72	Montreal C.	76	6	51	57
	Totals	794	57	306	363

Playoffs

1960–61	Montreal C.	5	0	0	0
1961–62	Montreal C.	6	0	2	2
1962–63	Montreal C.	5	0	0	0
1963–64	Montreal C.	7	2	1	3
1964–65	Montreal C.	13	1	9	10
1965–66	Montreal C.	10	2	9	11
1966–67	Montreal C.	10	2	4	6
1967–68	Montreal C.	13	3	6	9
1968–69	Montreal C.	13	1	4	5
1970–71	Montreal C.	20	3	14	17
1971–72	Montreal C.	6	0	2	2
	Totals	108	14	51	65

All-Star

1959	Montreal C.	1	0	0	0
1965	Montreal C.	1	0	0	0
1967	Montreal C.	1	0	0	0
1968	NHL All-Stars	1	0	1	1
1969	East All-Stars	1	0	0	0
1971	East All-Stars	1	0	0	0
1972	East All-Stars	1	0	1	1
	Totals	7	0	2	2

TREMBLAY, Marcel *Forward*
b. Winnipeg, Man., July 4, 1915

Season	Club	GP	G	A	Pts
1938-39	Montreal C.	--	0	2	2

TREMBLAY, Nils *Forward*
b. Quebec City, Que., July 26, 1923

Season	Club	GP	G	A	Pts
1944-45	Montreal C.	1	0	1	1
1945-46	Montreal C.	2	0	0	0
	Totals	3	0	1	1

Playoffs

1944-45	Montreal C.	2	0	0	0

TROTTIER, David T. *Forward*
b. Pembroke, Ont., June 25, 1906

Season	Club	GP	G	A	Pts
1928-29	Montreal M.	--	2	4	6
1929-30	Montreal M.	--	17	10	27
1930-31	Montreal M.	--	9	8	17
1931-32	Montreal M.	--	26	18	44
1932-33	Montreal M.	--	16	15	31
1933-34	Montreal M.	--	9	17	26
1934-35	Montreal M.	--	10	9	19
1935-36	Montreal M.	--	10	10	20
1936-37	Montreal M.	--	12	11	23
1937-38	Montreal M.	--	9	10	19
1938-39	Detroit R.W.	--	1	1	2
	Totals	--	121	113	234

Playoffs

1929-30	Montreal M.	--	0	2	2
1930-31	Montreal M.	--	0	0	0
1931-32	Montreal M.	--	1	0	1
1932-33	Montreal M.	--	0	0	0
1933-34	Montreal M.	--	0	0	0
1934-35	Montreal M.	--	2	1	3
1935-36	Montreal M.	--	0	0	0
1936-37	Montreal M.	--	1	0	1
	Totals	--	4	3	7

TROTTIER, Guy *Forward*
b. Hull, Que., Apr. 1, 1941

Season	Club	GP	G	A	Pts
1968-69	New York R.	2	0	0	0
1970-71	Toronto M.L.	61	19	5	24
1971-72	Toronto M.L.	52	9	12	21
	Totals	115	28	17	45

Playoffs

1970-71	Toronto M.L.	5	0	0	0
1971-72	Toronto M.L.	4	1	0	1
	Totals	9	1	0	1

TRUDEL, Louis Napoleon *Forward*
b. Salem, Mass., July 21, 1913

Season	Club	GP	G	A	Pts
1933-34	Chicago	--	1	3	4
1934-35	Chicago	--	11	11	22
1935-36	Chicago	--	3	4	7
1936-37	Chicago	--	6	12	18
1937-38	Chicago	--	6	16	22
1938-39	Montreal C.	--	8	13	21
1939-40	Montreal C.	--	12	7	19
1940-41	Montreal C.	--	2	3	5
	Totals	--	49	69	118

Playoffs

1933-34	Chicago	--	0	0	0
1934-35	Chicago	--	0	0	0
1935-36	Chicago	--	0	0	0
1937-38	Chicago	--	0	3	3
1938-39	Montreal C.	--	1	0	1
	Totals	--	1	3	4

TRUDELL, Rene Joseph *Forward*
b. Mariapolis, Man., Jan. 31, 1919

Season	Club	GP	G	A	Pts
1945-46	New York R.	16	3	5	8
1946-47	New York R.	59	8	16	24
1947-48	New York R.	54	13	7	20
	Totals	129	24	28	52

Playoffs

1947-48	New York R.	5	0	0	0

TURLIK, Gordon *Forward*
b. Mickel, B.C., Sept. 17, 1939

Season	Club	GP	G	A	Pts
1959-60	Boston	2	0	0	0

TURNER, Joseph *Goalie*

Season	Club	GP	GA	Sho	AVE
1941-42	Detroit R.W.	1	3	0	3.00

TURNER, Robert George *Defenseman*
b. Regina, Sask., Jan. 31, 1943

Season	Club	GP	G	A	Pts
1955-56	Montreal C.	33	1	4	5
1956-57	Montreal C.	58	1	4	5
1957-58	Montreal C.	68	0	3	3
1958-59	Montreal C.	68	4	24	28
1959-60	Montreal C.	54	0	9	9
1960-61	Montreal C.	60	2	2	4
1961-62	Chicago	69	8	2	10
1962-63	Chicago	70	3	3	6
	Totals	478	19	51	70

Playoffs

1955-56	Montreal C.	10	0	1	1
1956-57	Montreal C.	6	0	1	1

TURNER *(Continued)*

Playoffs	Club	GP	G	A	Pts
1957–58	Montreal C.	10	0	0	0
1958–59	Montreal C.	11	0	2	2
1959–60	Montreal C.	8	0	0	0
1960–61	Montreal C.	5	0	0	0
1961–62	Chicago	12	1	0	1
1962–63	Chicago	6	0	0	0
	Totals	68	1	4	5

All-Star					
1956	Montreal C.	1	0	0	0
1957	Montreal C.	1	0	0	0
1958	Montreal C.	1	0	0	0
1959	Montreal C.	1	0	0	0
1960	Montreal C.	1	0	0	0
1961	Chicago	1	0	0	0
	Totals	6	0	0	0

TUSTIN, Norman Robert *Forward*
b. Regina, Sask., Jan. 3, 1919

Season	Club	GP	G	A	Pts
1941–42	New York R.	18	2	4	6

TUTEN, Audley K. *Defenseman*
b. Enterprise, Alta., Jan. 14, 1915

Season	Club	GP	G	A	Pts
1941–42	Chicago	5	1	1	2
1942–43	Chicago	34	3	7	10
	Totals	39	4	8	12

UBRIACO, Eugene Stephen *Forward*
b. Sault Ste. Marie, Ont., Dec. 26, 1937

Season	Club	GP	G	A	Pts
1967–68	Pittsburgh Pe.	65	18	15	33
1968–69	Pitts Pe-Oak	75	19	18	37
1969–70	Oak-Chgo	37	2	2	4
	Totals	177	39	35	74

Playoffs	Club	GP	G	A	Pts
1968–69	Oakland	7	2	0	2
1969–70	Chicago	4	0	0	0
	Totals	11	2	0	2

ULLMAN, Norman Victor Alexander *Forward*
b. Provost, Alta., Dec. 26, 1935

Season	Club	GP	G	A	Pts
1955–56	Detroit R.W.	66	9	9	18
1956–57	Detroit R.W.	64	16	36	52
1957–58	Detroit R.W.	69	23	28	51
1958–59	Detroit R.W.	69	22	36	58
1959–60	Detroit R.W.	70	24	34	58
1960–61	Detroit R.W.	70	28	42	70
1961–62	Detroit R.W.	70	26	38	64
1962–63	Detroit R.W.	70	26	30	56
1963–64	Detroit R.W.	61	21	30	51

ULLMAN *(Continued)*

Season	Club	GP	G	A	Pts
1964–65	Detroit R.W.	70	42	41	83
1965–66	Detroit R.W.	70	31	41	72
1966–67	Detroit R.W.	68	26	44	70
1967–68	Det RW-Tor ML	71	35	37	72
1968–69	Toronto M.L.	75	35	42	77
1969–70	Toronto M.L.	74	18	42	60
1970–71	Toronto M.L.	73	34	51	85
1971–72	Toronto M.L.	77	23	50	73
1972–73	Toronto M.L.	65	20	35	55
	Totals	1252	459	666	1125

Playoffs	Club	GP	G	A	Pts
1955–56	Detroit R.W.	10	1	3	4
1956–57	Detroit R.W.	5	1	1	2
1957–58	Detroit R.W.	4	0	2	2
1959–60	Detroit R.W.	6	2	2	4
1960–61	Detroit R.W.	11	0	4	4
1962–63	Detroit R.W.	11	4	12	16
1963–64	Detroit R.W.	14	7	10	17
1964–65	Detroit R.W.	7	6	4	10
1965–66	Detroit R.W.	12	6	9	15
1968–69	Toronto M.L.	4	1	0	1
1970–71	Toronto M.L.	6	0	2	2
1971–72	Toronto M.L.	5	1	3	4
	Totals	95	29	52	81

All-Star					
1960	NHL All-Stars	1	0	0	0
1961	NHL All-Stars	1	0	0	0
1962	NHL All-Stars	1	0	0	0
1963	NHL All-Stars	1	0	0	0
1964	NHL All-Stars	1	0	0	0
1965	NHL All-Stars	1	1	1	2
1967	NHL All-Stars	1	0	0	0
1968	NHL All-Stars	1	1	0	1
1969	East All-Stars	1	0	1	1
	Totals	9	2	4	6

UNGER, Garry Douglas *Forward*
b. Edmonton, Alta., Dec. 7, 1947

Season	Club	GP	G	A	Pts
1967–68	Tor ML-Det RW	28	6	11	17
1968–69	Detroit R.W.	76	24	20	44
1969–70	Detroit R.W.	76	42	24	66
1970–71	Det RW-StL B	79	28	28	56
1971–72	St. Louis B.	78	36	34	70
1972–73	St. Louis B.	78	41	39	80
	Totals	415	177	156	333

Playoffs	Club	GP	G	A	Pts
1969–70	Detroit R.W.	4	0	1	1
1970–71	St. Louis B.	6	3	2	5
1971–72	St. Louis B.	11	4	5	9
1972–73	St.Louis	5	1	2	3
	Totals	26	8	10	18

UNGER (Continued)

All-Star	Club	GP	G	A	Pts
1972	West All-Stars	1	0	0	0
1973	West All-Stars	1	0	0	0
	Totals	2	0	0	0

VACHON, Rogatien *Goalie*
b. Palmarolle, Que., Sept. 8, 1945

Season	Club	GP	GA	Sho	AVE
1966-67	Montreal C.	19	47	1	2.47
1967-68	Montreal C.	37⅙	92	4	2.48
1968-69	Montreal C.	34⅓	98	2	2.85
1969-70	Montreal C.	61½	162	4	2.63
1970-71	Montreal C.	44⅔	118	2	2.64
1971-72	Mtl C-LA	26⅔	111	0	4.14
1972-73	Los Angeles	52	148	4	2.85
	Totals	275⅓	776	17	2.81

Playoffs

Season	Club	GP	GA	Sho	AVE
1966-67	Montreal C.	8⅔	22	0	2.54
1967-68	Montreal C.	1⅚	4	0	2.18
1968-69	Montreal C.	7¹⁴⁄₁₅	12	1	1.51
	Totals	18½	38	1	2.04

All-Star		GP	Per	GA	AGP
1973	West All-Stars	1	1½	4	2.67

VADNAIS, Carol *Defenseman-Forward*
b. Montreal, Que., Sept. 25, 1945

Season	Club	GP	G	A	Pts
1966-67	Montreal C.	11	0	3	3
1967-68	Montreal C.	31	1	1	2
1968-69	Oakland	76	15	27	42
1969-70	Oakland	76	24	21	44
1970-71	California	42	10	16	26
1971-72	Calif-Bost	68	18	26	44
1972-73	Boston	78	7	24	31
	Totals	382	75	117	192

Playoffs

Season	Club	GP	G	A	Pts
1966-67	Montreal C.	1	0	0	0
1967-68	Montreal C.	1	0	0	0
1968-69	Oakland	7	1	4	5
1969-70	Oakland	4	2	1	3
1971-72	Boston	15	0	2	2
1972-73	Boston	5	0	0	0
	Totals	33	3	7	10

All-Star

	Club	GP	G	A	Pts
1969	West All-Stars	1	0	0	0
1970	West All-Stars	1	0	0	0
1972	West All-Stars	1	0	0	0
	Totals	3	0	0	0

VAIL, Melville (Sparky) *Defenseman*
b. Meaford, Ont., July 5, 1906

Season	Club	GP	G	A	Pts
1928-29	New York R.	18	3	0	3
1929-30	New York R.	32	1	1	2
	Totals	50	4	1	5

Playoffs

Season	Club	GP	G	A	Pts
1928-29	New York R.	6	0	0	0
1929-30	New York R.	4	0	0	0
	Totals	10	0	0	0

VAN IMPE, Edward Charles *Defenseman*
b. Saskatoon, Sask., May 27, 1940

Season	Club	GP	G	A	Pts
1966-67	Chicago	61	8	11	19
1967-68	Philadelphia F.	67	4	13	17
1968-69	Philadelphia F.	68	7	12	19
1969-70	Philadelphia F.	65	0	10	10
1970-71	Philadelphia F.	77	0	11	11
1971-72	Philadelphia F.	73	4	9	13
1972-73	Philadelphia F.	72	1	11	12
	Totals	483	24	77	101

Playoffs

Season	Club	GP	G	A	Pts
1966-67	Chicago	6	0	0	0
1967-68	Philadelphia F.	7	0	4	4
1968-69	Philadelphia F.	1	0	0	0
1970-71	Philadelphia F.	4	0	1	1
1972-73	Philadelphia F.	11	0	0	0
	Totals	29	0	5	5

All-Star

	Club	GP	G	A	Pts
1969	West All-Stars	1	0	0	0

VASKO, Elmer (Moose) *Defenseman*
b. Duparquet, Que., Dec. 11, 1935

Season	Club	GP	G	A	Pts
1956-57	Chicago	64	3	12	15
1957-58	Chicago	59	6	20	26
1958-59	Chicago	63	6	10	16
1959-60	Chicago	69	3	27	30
1960-61	Chicago	63	4	18	22
1961-62	Chicago	61	2	22	24
1962-63	Chicago	64	4	9	13
1963-64	Chicago	70	2	18	20
1964-65	Chicago	69	1	10	11
1965-66	Chicago	56	1	7	8
1967-68	Minnesota	70	1	6	7
1968-69	Minnesota	72	1	7	8
1969-70	Minnesota	3	0	0	0
	Totals	783	34	166	200

Playoffs

Season	Club	GP	G	A	Pts
1958-59	Chicago	6	0	1	1
1959-60	Chicago	4	0	0	0

VASKO (Continued)

Playoffs	Club	GP	G	A	Pts
1960-61	Chicago	12	1	1	2
1961-62	Chicago	12	0	0	0
1962-63	Chicago	6	0	1	1
1963-64	Chicago	7	0	0	0
1964-65	Chicago	14	1	2	3
1965-66	Chicago	3	0	0	0
1967-68	Minnesota	14	0	2	2
	Totals	78	2	7	9

All-Star					
1961	Chicago	1	0	0	0
1963	NHL All-Stars	1	0	0	0
1964	NHL All-Stars	1	0	0	0
1969	West All-Stars	1	0	0	0
	Totals	4	0	0	0

VENASKY, Victor (Vic) *Forward*
b. Thurnder Bay, Ont., June 3, 1951

Season	Club	GP	G	A	Pts
1972-73	Los Angeles	77	15	19	34

VENERUZZO, Gary Raymond *Forward*
b. Fort William, Ont., June 28, 1943

Season	Club	GP	G	A	Pts
1967-68	St. Louis B.	5	1	1	2
1971-72	St. Louis B.	2	0	0	0
	Totals	7	1	1	2

Playoffs					
1967-68	St. Louis B.	9	0	2	2

VEZINA, Georges *Goalie*
b. Chicoutimi, Que., Jan., 1887

Season	Club	GP	GA	Sho	AVE
1917-18	Montreal C.	21	84	1	4.00
1918-19	Montreal C.	18	78	1	4.33
1919-20	Montreal C.	24	113	0	4.71
1920-21	Montreal C.	24	99	1	4.13
1921-22	Montreal C.	24	94	0	3.91
1922-23	Montreal C.	24	62	2	2.58
1923-24	Montreal C.	24	48	3	2.00
1924-25	Montreal C.	30	56	5	1.87
1925-26	Montreal C.	1	1	0	1.00
	Totals	190	635	13	3.34

Playoffs					
1917-18	Montreal C.	2	10	0	5.00
1918-19	Montreal C.	9	37	0	4.11
1922-23	Montreal C.	2	3	0	1.50
1923-24	Montreal C.	6	6	2	1.00
1924-25	Montreal C.	6	18	1	3.00
	Totals	25	74	3	2.96

VICKERS, Stephen James (Steve) *Forward*
b. Toronto, Ont., Apr. 21, 1951

Season	Club	GP	G	A	Pts
1972-73	New York R.	61	30	23	53

Playoffs					
1972-73	New York R.	10	5	4	9

VILLEMURE, Gilles *Goalie*
b. Three Rivers, Que., May 30, 1940

Season	Club	GP	GA	Sho	AVE
1963-64	New York R.	5	18	0	3.60
1967-68	New York R.	3⅓	8	1	2.40
1968-69	New York R.	4	9	0	2.25
1970-71	New York R.	34	78	4	2.29
1971-72	New York R.	35½	74	3	2.08
1972-73	New York R.	34	78	3	2.29
	Totals	115⅔	265	11	2.29

Playoffs					
1968-69	New York R.	1	4	0	4.00
1970-71	New York R.	1⅓	6	0	4.51
1971-72	New York R.	6	14	0	2.33
1972-73	New York R.	1	2	0	1.97
	Totals	9⅓	26	0	2.78

All-Star		GP	Per	GA	AGP
1971	East All-Stars	1	1½	0	0.00
1972	East All-Stars	1	1½	0	0.00
1973	East All-Stars	1	1½	1	0.67
	Totals	3	4½	1	0.17

VIPOND, Peter *Forward*
b. Oshawa, Ont., Dec. 18, 1949

Season	Club	GP	G	A	Pts
1972-73	California	2	0	0	0

VOLMAR, Douglas Steven (Doug) *Forward*
b. Cleveland, Ohio, Jan. 9, 1945

Season	Club	GP	G	A	Pts
1970-71	Detroit R.W.	2	0	1	1
1971-72	Detroit R.W.	39	9	5	14
1972-73	Los Angeles	21	4	2	6
	Totals	62	13	8	21

Playoffs					
1969-70	Detroit R.W.	2	1	0	1

VOSS, Carl *Forward*
b. Chelsea, Mass., Jan. 6, 1907

Season	Club	GP	G	A	Pts
1932-33	NY R-Det F	--	8	15	23
1933-34	Det RW-Otta	--	7	18	25
1934-35	St. Louis E.	--	13	18	31
1935-36	New York A.	--	3	9	12
1936-37	Montreal M.	--	0	2	2
1937-38	Chicago	--	3	8	11
	Totals	--	34	70	104

VOSS (Continued)

Playoffs	Club	GP	G	A	Pts
1932-33	Detroit F.	4	1	1	2
1935-36	New York A.	5	0	0	0
1936-37	Montreal M.	5	1	0	1
1937-38	Chicago	10	3	2	5
	Totals	24	5	3	8

WAITE, Frank E. (Deacon) *Forward*
b. Qu'Appelle, Sask., Apr. 9, 1906

Season	Club	GP	G	A	Pts
1930-31	New York R.	17	1	3	4

WAKELY, Ernest Alfred Linton (Ernie) *Goalie*
b. Flin Flon, Man., Nov. 27, 1940

Season	Club	GP	GA	Sho	AVE
1962-63	Montreal C.	1	3	0	3.00
1968-69	Montreal C.	1	4	0	4.00
1969-70	St. Louis B.	27½	58	4	2.11
1970-71	St. Louis B.	47⅔	133	3	2.79
1971-72	St. Louis B.	27	92	1	3.42
	Totals	104⅓	290	8	2.79
Playoffs					
1969-70	St. Louis B.	3⅔	17	0	4.72
1970-71	St. Louis B.	3	7	1	2.33
1971-72	St. Louis B.	2	13	0	6.91
	Totals	8⅔	37	1	4.36

All-Star		GP	Per	GA	AGP
1971	West All-Stars	1	1½	0	0.00

WALKER, John Phillip *Forward*
b. Silver Mountain, Ont., 1888

Season	Club	GP	G	A	Pts
1926-27	Detroit C.	--	3	4	7
1927-28	Detroit C.	--	2	4	6
	Totals	--	5	8	13
Playoffs					
1918-19	Seattle (PCHL)	--	3	0	3
1919-20	Seattle (PCHL)	--	1	2	3
1924-25	Victoria (PCHL)	--	4	1	5
	Totals	--	8	3	11

WALL, Robert James Albert (Bob)
Defenseman-Forward
b. Richmond Hill, Ont., Dec. 1, 1942

Season	Club	GP	G	A	Pts
1964-65	Detroit R.W.	1	0	0	0
1965-66	Detroit R.W.	8	1	1	2
1966-67	Detroit R.W.	31	2	2	4
1967-68	Los Angeles	71	5	18	23
1968-69	Los Angeles	71	13	13	26
1969-70	Los Angeles	70	5	13	18

WALL (Continued)

Season	Club	GP	G	A	Pts
1970-71	St. Louis B.	25	2	4	6
1971-72	Detroit R.W.	45	2	4	6
	Totals	322	30	55	85
Playoffs					
1964-65	Detroit R.W.	1	0	0	0
1965-66	Detroit R.W.	6	0	0	0
1967-68	Los Angeles	7	0	1	1
1968-69	Los Angeles	8	0	2	2
	Totals	22	0	3	3

WALSH, James (Flat) *Goalie*
b. Kingston, Ont., Mar. 23, 1897

Season	Club	GP	GA	Sho	AVE
1928-29	NY A-Mont M	11	9	4	0.82
1929-30	Montreal M.	28	71	2	2.54
1930-31	Montreal M.	15	34	2	2.27
1931-32	Montreal M.	27	71	2	2.52
1932-33	Montreal M.	23	62	2	2.70
	Totals	104	247	12	2.38
Playoffs					
1929-30	Montreal M.	4	11	1	2.75
1931-32	Montreal M.	4	5	1	1.25
	Totals	8	16	2	2.00

WALTON, Michael Robert (Mike) *Forward*
b. Kirkland Lake, Ont., Jan. 3. 1945

Season	Club	GP	G	A	Pts
1965-66	Toronto M.L.	6	1	3	4
1966-67	Toronto M.L.	31	7	10	17
1967-68	Toronto M.L.	73	30	29	59
1968-69	Toronto M.L.	66	22	21	43
1969-70	Toronto M.L.	58	21	34	55
1970-71	Tor ML-Bost	45	6	15	21
1971-72	Boston	76	28	28	56
1972-73	Boston	56	25	22	47
	Totals	411	140	162	302
Playoffs					
1966-67	Toronto M.L.	12	4	3	7
1968-69	Toronto M.L.	4	0	0	0
1970-71	Boston	5	2	0	2
1971-72	Boston	15	6	6	12
1972-73	Boston	5	1	1	2
	Totals	41	13	10	23

All-Star		GP	G	A	Pts
1968	Toronto M.L.	1	0	0	0

WALTON, Robert Charles *Forward*
b. Ottawa, Ont., Aug. 5, 1917

Season	Club	GP	G	A	Pts
1943-44	Montreal C.	4	0	0	0

WARD, Donald *Defenseman*
b. Sarnia, Ont., Oct. 19, 1935

Season	Club	GP	G	A	Pts
1957–58	Chicago	3	0	0	0
1959–60	Boston	31	0	1	1
	Totals	34	0	1	1

WARD, James *Forward*
b. Fort William, Ont., Sept. 1, 1906

Season	Club	GP	G	A	Pts
1927–28	Montreal M.	––	10	2	12
1928–29	Montreal M.	––	14	8	22
1929–30	Montreal M.	––	10	7	17
1930–31	Montreal M.	––	14	8	22
1931–32	Montreal M.	––	19	19	38
1932–33	Montreal M.	––	16	17	33
1933–34	Montreal M.	––	14	9	23
1934–35	Montreal M.	––	9	6	15
1935–36	Montreal M.	––	12	19	31
1936–37	Montreal M.	––	14	14	28
1937–38	Montreal M.	––	11	15	26
1938–39	Montreal C.	––	4	3	7
	Totals	––	147	127	274

Playoffs

1927–28	Montreal M.	––	1	1	2
1929–30	Montreal M.	––	0	1	1
1930–31	Montreal M.	––	0	0	0
1931–32	Montreal M.	––	2	1	3
1932–33	Montreal M.	––	0	0	0
1933–34	Montreal M.	––	0	0	0
1934–35	Montreal M.	––	1	1	2
1935–36	Montreal M.	––	0	0	0
1936–37	Montreal M.	––	0	0	0
	Totals	––	4	4	8

WARD, Ronald Leon *Forward*
b. Cornwall, Ont., Sept. 12, 1944

Season	Club	GP	G	A	Pts
1969–70	Toronto M.L.	18	0	1	1
1971–72	Vancouver	71	2	4	6
	Totals	89	2	5	7

WARES, Edward *Forward*
b. Calgary, Alta., Mar. 19, 1915

Season	Club	GP	G	A	Pts
1936–37	New York R.	2	2	0	2
1937–38	Detroit R.W.	––	9	7	16
1938–39	Detroit R.W.	––	8	8	16
1939–40	Detroit R.W.	––	2	6	8
1940–41	Detroit R.W.	––	10	16	26
1941–42	Detroit R.W.	43	9	29	38
1942–43	Detroit R.W.	47	12	18	30
1945–46	Chicago	45	4	11	15
1946–47	Chicago	60	4	7	11
	Totals	––	60	102	162

WARES *(Continued)*

Playoffs	Club	GP	G	A	Pts
1938–39	Detroit R.W.	6	1	0	1
1939–40	Detroit R.W.	5	0	0	0
1940–41	Detroit R.W.	9	0	0	0
1941–42	Detroit R.W.	12	1	3	4
1942–43	Detroit R.W.	10	3	3	6
1945–46	Chicago	3	0	1	1
	Totals	45	5	7	12

WARWICK, Grant David (Knobby) *Forward*
b. Regina, Sask., Oct. 11, 1921

Season	Club	GP	G	A	Pts
1941–42	New York R.	44	16	17	33
1942–43	New York R.	50	17	18	35
1943–44	New York R.	18	8	9	17
1944–45	New York R.	42	20	22	42
1945–46	New York R.	45	19	18	37
1946–47	New York R.	54	20	20	40
1947–48	NY R–Bos	58	23	17	40
1948–49	Boston	58	22	15	37
1949–50	Montreal C.	30	2	6	8
	Totals	399	147	142	289

Playoffs

1941–42	New York R.	6	0	1	1
1947–48	Boston	5	0	3	3
1948–49	Boston	5	2	0	2
	Totals	16	2	4	6

All-Star

1947	NHL All-Stars	1	1	0	1

WARWICK, William Harvey *Forward*
b. Regina, Sask., Nov. 17, 1924

Season	Club	GP	G	A	Pts
1942–43	New York R.	1	0	1	1
1943–44	New York R.	13	3	2	5
	Totals	14	3	3	6

WASNIE, Nicholas *Forward*
b. Winnipeg, Man., Jan. 1, 1904

Season	Club	GP	G	A	Pts
1927–28	Chicago	––	1	0	1
1929–30	Montreal C.	––	12	11	23
1930–31	Montreal C.	––	9	2	11
1931–32	Montreal C.	––	10	2	13
1932–33	New York A.	––	11	12	23
1933–34	Ottawa	––	11	6	17
1934–35	St. Louis E.	––	3	1	4
	Totals	––	57	34	91

Playoffs

1929–30	Montreal C.	––	2	2	4
1930–31	Montreal C.	––	4	1	5
1931–32	Montreal C.	––	0	0	0
	Totals	––	6	3	9

WATSON, Bryan Joseph *Defenseman*
b. Bancroft, Ont., Nov. 14, 1942

Season	Club	GP	G	A	Pts
1963–64	Montreal C.	39	0	2	2
1964–65	Montreal C.	5	0	1	1
1965–66	Detroit R.W.	70	2	7	9
1966–67	Detroit R.W.	48	0	1	1
1967–68	Montreal C.	12	0	1	1
1968–69	Oak-Pitts Pe	68	2	7	9
1969–70	Pittsburgh Pe.	61	1	9	10
1970–71	Pittsburgh Pe.	43	2	6	8
1971–72	Pittsburgh Pe.	75	3	17	20
1972–73	Pittsburgh Pe.	69	1	17	18
	Totals	**490**	**11**	**68**	**79**

Playoffs

Season	Club	GP	G	A	Pts
1963–64	Montreal C.	6	0	0	0
1965–66	Detroit R.W.	12	2	0	2
1969–70	Pittsburgh Pe.	10	0	0	0
1971–72	Pittsburgh Pe.	4	0	0	0
	Totals	**32**	**2**	**0**	**2**

WATSON, Harry Percival *Forward*
b. Saskatoon, Sask., May 6, 1923

Season	Club	GP	G	A	Pts
1941–42	Brooklyn A.	47	10	8	18
1942–43	Detroit R.W.	50	13	18	31
1945–46	Detroit R.W.	44	14	10	24
1946–47	Toronto M.L.	44	19	15	34
1947–48	Toronto M.L.	57	21	20	41
1948–49	Toronto M.L.	60	26	19	45
1949–50	Toronto M.L.	60	19	16	35
1950–51	Toronto M.L.	68	18	19	37
1951–52	Toronto M.L.	70	22	17	39
1952–53	Toronto M.L.	63	16	8	24
1953–54	Toronto M.L.	70	21	7	28
1954–55	Tor ML–Chgo	51	15	17	32
1955–56	Chicago	55	11	14	25
1956–57	Chicago	70	11	19	30
	Totals	**809**	**236**	**207**	**443**

Playoffs

Season	Club	GP	G	A	Pts
1942–43	Detroit R.W.	7	0	0	0
1945–46	Detroit R.W.	5	2	0	2
1946–47	Toronto M.L.	11	3	2	5
1947–48	Toronto M.L.	9	5	2	7
1948–49	Toronto M.L.	9	4	2	6
1949–50	Toronto M.L.	7	0	0	0
1950–51	Toronto M.L.	5	1	2	3
1951–52	Toronto M.L.	4	1	0	1
1953–54	Toronto M.L.	5	0	1	1
	Totals	**62**	**16**	**9**	**25**

All-Star

	Club	GP	G	A	Pts
1947	Toronto M.L.	1	1	2	3
1948	Toronto M.L.	1	0	0	0

WATSON *(Continued)*

All-Star	Club	GP	G	A	Pts
1949	Toronto M.L.	1	0	1	1
1951	NHL 2nd All-Stars	1	0	1	1
1952	NHL 2nd All-Stars	1	0	0	0
1953	NHL All-Stars	1	0	0	0
1955	NHL All-Stars	1	0	0	0
	Totals	**7**	**1**	**4**	**5**

WATSON, James (Jim) *Defenseman*
b. Smithers, B.C., Aug. 19, 1952

Season	Club	GP	G	A	Pts
1972–73	Philadelphia F.	4	0	1	1

Playoffs

1972–73	Philadelphia F.	2	0	0	0

WATSON, James Arthur (Jim) *Defenseman*
b. Malartic, Que., June 28, 1943

Season	Club	GP	G	A	Pts
1963–64	Detroit R.W.	1	0	0	0
1964–65	Detroit R.W.	1	0	0	0
1965–66	Detroit R.W.	2	0	0	0
1967–68	Detroit R.W.	61	0	3	3
1968–69	Detroit R.W.	8	0	1	1
1969–70	Detroit R.W.	4	0	0	0
1970–71	Buffalo	78	2	9	11
1971–72	Buffalo	66	2	6	8
	Totals	**221**	**4**	**19**	**23**

WATSON, Joseph John (Joe) *Defenseman*
b. Smithers, B.C., July 6, 1943

Season	Club	GP	G	A	Pts
1964–65	Boston	4	0	1	1
1966–67	Boston	69	2	13	15
1967–68	Philadelphia F.	73	5	14	19
1968–69	Philadelphia F.	60	2	8	10
1969–70	Philadelphia F.	54	3	11	14
1970–71	Philadelphia F.	57	3	7	10
1971–72	Philadelphia F.	65	3	7	10
1972–73	Philadelphia F.	63	2	24	26
	Totals	**445**	**20**	**85**	**105**

Playoffs

Season	Club	GP	G	A	Pts
1967–68	Philadelphia F.	7	1	1	2
1968–69	Philadelphia F.	4	0	0	0
1970–71	Philadelphia F.	1	0	0	0
1972–73	Philadelphia F.	11	0	2	2
	Totals	**23**	**1**	**3**	**4**

WATSON, Phillipe Henri *Forward*
b. Montreal, Que., Oct. 24, 1914

Season	Club	GP	G	A	Pts
1935–36	New York R.	24	0	2	2
1936–37	New York R.	48	11	17	28

WATSON (Continued)

Season	Club	GP	G	A	Pts
1937–38	New York R.	48	7	25	32
1938–39	New York R.	48	15	22	37
1939–40	New York R.	48	7	28	35
1940–41	New York R.	40	11	25	36
1941–42	New York R.	48	15	37	52
1942–43	New York R.	46	14	28	42
1943–44	Montreal C.	44	17	32	49
1944–45	New York R.	45	11	8	19
1945–46	New York R.	49	12	14	26
1946–47	New York R.	48	6	12	18
1947–48	New York R.	54	18	15	33
	Totals	590	144	265	409

Playoffs

Season	Club	GP	G	A	Pts
1936–37	New York R.	9	0	2	2
1937–38	New York R.	3	0	2	2
1938–39	New York R.	7	1	1	2
1939–40	New York R.	12	3	6	9
1940–41	New York R.	3	0	2	2
1941–42	New York R.	6	1	4	5
1943–44	Montreal C.	9	3	5	8
1947–48	New York R.	5	2	3	5
	Totals	54	10	25	35

WEBSTER, Donald *Forward*
b. Toronto, Ont., July 3, 1924

Season	Club	GP	G	A	Pts
1943–44	Toronto M.L.	27	7	6	13

Playoffs

Season	Club	GP	G	A	Pts
1943–44	Toronto M.L.	5	0	0	0

WEBSTER, John Robert (Chick) *Forward*
b. Toronto, Ont., Nov. 3, 1921

Season	Club	GP	G	A	Pts
1949–50	New York R.	14	0	0	0

WEBSTER, Thomas Ronald (Tom) *Forward*
b. Kirkland Lake, Ont., Oct. 4, 1948

Season	Club	GP	G	A	Pts
1968–69	Boston	9	0	2	2
1969–70	Boston	2	0	1	1
1970–71	Detroit R.W.	78	30	37	67
1971–72	Det RW-Calif	12	3	2	5
	Totals	101	33	42	75

Playoffs

Season	Club	GP	G	A	Pts
1968–69	Boston	1	0	0	0

WEILAND, Ralph (Cooney) *Forward*
b. Egmondville, Ont., Nov. 5, 1904

Season	Club	GP	G	A	Pts
1928–29	Boston	--	11	7	18
1929–30	Boston	--	43	30	73

WEILAND (Continued)

Season	Club	GP	G	A	Pts
1930–31	Boston	--	25	13	38
1931–32	Boston	--	14	12	26
1932–33	Ottawa	--	16	11	27
1933–34	Otta-Det RW	--	13	19	32
1934–35	Detroit R.W.	--	13	25	38
1935–36	Boston	--	14	13	27
1936–37	Boston	--	6	9	15
1937–38	Boston	--	11	12	23
1938–39	Boston	--	7	9	16
	Totals	--	173	160	333

Playoffs

Season	Club	GP	G	A	Pts
1928–29	Boston	--	2	0	2
1929–30	Boston	--	1	5	6
1930–31	Boston	--	6	3	9
1933–34	Detroit R.W.	--	2	2	4
1935–36	Boston	--	1	0	1
1936–37	Boston	--	0	0	0
1937–38	Boston	--	0	0	0
1938–39	Boston	--	0	0	0
	Totals	--	12	10	22

WEIR, Stanley (Stan) *Forward*
b. Ponoka, Alb., Mar. 17, 1952

Season	Club	GP	G	A	Pts
1972–73	California	78	15	24	39

WELLINGTON, Duke *Defenseman*

Season	Club	GP	G	A	Pts
1919–20	Quebec	1	0	0	0

WENTWORTH, Marvin (Cy) *Defenseman*
b. Grimsby, Ont., Jan. 24, 1905

Season	Club	GP	G	A	Pts
1927–28	Chicago	--	5	5	10
1928–29	Chicago	--	2	1	3
1929–30	Chicago	--	3	4	7
1930–31	Chicago	--	4	4	8
1931–32	Chicago	--	3	10	13
1932–33	Montreal M.	--	4	10	14
1933–34	Montreal M.	--	2	5	7
1934–35	Montreal M.	--	4	9	13
1935–36	Montreal M.	--	4	5	9
1936–37	Montreal M.	--	3	4	7
1937–38	Montreal M.	--	4	5	9
1938–39	Montreal C.	--	0	3	3
1939–40	Montreal C.	--	1	3	4
	Totals	--	39	68	107

Playoffs

Season	Club	GP	G	A	Pts
1929–30	Chicago	--	0	0	0
1930–31	Chicago	--	1	1	2
1931–32	Chicago	--	0	0	0
1932–33	Montreal M.	--	0	1	1

WENTWORTH *(Continued)*

Playoffs	Club	GP	G	A	Pts
1933-34	Montreal M.	--	0	2	2
1934-35	Montreal M.	--	3	2	5
1935-36	Montreal M.	--	0	0	0
1936-37	Montreal M.	--	1	0	1
1938-39	Montreal C.	--	0	0	0
	Totals	--	5	6	11

WESTFALL, Edwin Vernon (Ed) *Forward*
b. Belleville, Ont., Sept. 19, 1940

Season	Club	GP	G	A	Pts
1961-62	Boston	63	2	9	11
1962-63	Boston	48	1	11	12
1963-64	Boston	55	1	5	6
1964-65	Boston	68	12	15	27
1965-66	Boston	59	9	21	30
1966-67	Boston	70	12	24	36
1967-68	Boston	73	14	22	36
1968-69	Boston	70	18	24	42
1969-70	Boston	72	14	22	36
1970-71	Boston	78	25	34	59
1971-72	Boston	71	18	26	44
1972-73	New York I.	67	15	31	46
	Totals	794	141	244	385
Playoffs					
1967-68	Boston	4	2	0	2
1968-69	Boston	10	3	7	10
1969-70	Boston	14	3	5	8
1970-71	Boston	7	1	2	3
1971-72	Boston	15	4	3	7
	Totals	50	13	17	30
All-Star					
1971	East All-Stars	1	0	0	0
1973	East All-Stars	1	0	0	0
	Totals	2	0	0	0

WETZEL, Carl David *Goalie*
b. Detroit, Mich., Dec. 12, 1938

Season	Club	GP	GA	Sho	AVE
1964-65	Detroit R.W.	½	4	0	8.00
1967-68	Minnesota	4½	18	0	4.00
	Totals	5	22	0	4.40

WHARRAM, Kenneth Malcolm (Ken) *Forward*
b. Ferris, Ont., July 2, 1933

Season	Club	GP	G	A	Pts
1951-52	Chicago	1	0	0	0
1953-54	Chicago	29	1	7	8
1955-56	Chicago	3	0	0	0
1958-59	Chicago	66	10	9	19
1959-60	Chicago	59	14	11	25

WHARRAM *(Continued)*

Season	Club	GP	G	A	Pts
1960-61	Chicago	64	18	29	45
1961-62	Chicago	62	14	23	37
1962-63	Chicago	55	20	18	38
1963-64	Chicago	70	39	32	71
1964-65	Chicago	68	24	20	44
1965-66	Chicago	69	26	17	43
1966-67	Chicago	70	31	34	65
1967-68	Chicago	74	27	42	69
1968-69	Chicago	76	30	39	69
	Totals	766	252	281	533
Playoffs					
1958-59	Chicago	6	0	2	2
1959-60	Chicago	4	1	1	2
1960-61	Chicago	12	3	5	8
1961-62	Chicago	12	3	4	7
1962-63	Chicago	6	1	5	6
1963-64	Chicago	7	2	2	4
1964-65	Chicago	12	2	3	5
1965-66	Chicago	6	1	0	1
1966-67	Chicago	6	2	2	4
1967-68	Chicago	9	1	3	4
	Totals	80	16	27	43
All-Star					
1961	Chicago	1	0	0	0
1968	NHL All-Stars	1	1	0	1
	Totals	2	1	0	1

WHARTON, Thomas (Len) *Defenseman*
b. Winnipeg, Man., Dec. 13, 1927

Season	Club	GP	G	A	Pts
1944-45	New York R.	1	0	0	0

WHITE, Leonard Arthur (Moe) *Forward*
b. Verdun, Que, July 28, 1919

Season	Club	GP	G	A	Pts
1945-46	Montreal C.	4	0	1	1

WHITE, Sherman *Forward*
b. Amherst, N.S., May 12, 1923

Season	Club	GP	G	A	Pts
1946-47	New York R.	1	0	0	0
1949-50	New York R.	3	0	2	2
	Totals	4	0	2	2

WHITE, Wilfred (Tex) *Forward*

Season	Club	GP	G	A	Pts
1925-26	Pittsburgh Pi.	35	7	1	8
1926-27	Pittsburgh Pi.	--	5	4	9
1927-28	Pittsburgh Pi.	--	5	1	6
1928-29	Pitts Pi-NY A	--	5	5	10
1929-30	Pittsburgh Pi.	--	8	1	9
1930-31	Philadelphia Q.	--	3	0	3
	Totals	--	33	12	45

WHITE (Continued)

Playoffs	Club	GP	G	A	Pts
1925-26	Pittsburgh Pi.	--	0	0	0
1927-28	Pittsburgh Pi.	--	0	0	0
1928-29	New York A.	--	0	0	0
	Totals	--	0	0	0

WHITE, William Earl (Bill) *Defenseman*
b. Toronto, Ont., Aug. 26, 1939

Season	Club	GP	G	A	Pts
1967-68	Los Angeles	74	11	27	38
1968-69	Los Angeles	75	5	28	33
1969-70	LA-Chgo	61	4	16	20
1970-71	Chicago	67	4	21	25
1971-72	Chicago	76	7	22	29
1972-73	Chicago	72	9	38	47
	Totals	425	40	152	192

Playoffs					
1967-68	Los Angeles	7	2	2	4
1968-69	Los Angeles	11	1	4	5
1969-70	Chicago	8	1	2	3
1970-71	Chicago	18	1	4	5
1971-72	Chicago	8	0	3	3
1972-73	Chicago	16	1	6	7
	Totals	68	6	21	27

All-Star					
1969	West All-Stars	1	0	0	0
1970	West All-Stars	1	0	0	0
1971	West All-Stars	1	0	0	0
1972	West All-Stars	1	0	0	0
1973	West All-Stars	1	0	0	0
	Totals	5	0	0	0

WHITELAW, Robert *Defenseman*
b. Motherwell, Scotland, Oct. 5, 1916

Season	Club	GP	G	A	Pts
1940-41	Detroit R.W.	--	0	2	2
1941-42	Detroit R.W.	--	0	0	0
	Totals	--	0	2	2

WHITLOCK, Robert (Bob) *Forward*
b. Charlottetown, P.E.I., July 16, 1949

Season	Club	GP	G	A	Pts
1969-70	Minnesota	1	0	0	0

WIDING, Juha Markku *Forward*
b. Uleaborg, Finland, July 4, 1947

Season	Club	GP	G	A	Pts
1969-70	NY R-LA	48	7	9	16
1970-71	Los Angeles	78	25	40	65
1971-72	Los Angeles	78	27	28	55
1972-73	Los Angeles	77	16	54	70
	Totals	281	75	131	206

WIEBE, Arthur Walter Ronald *Defenseman*
b. Rosthern, Sask, Sept. 28, 1913

Season	Club	GP	G	A	Pts
1934-35	Chicago	--	2	1	3
1935-36	Chicago	--	1	0	1
1936-37	Chicago	--	0	2	2
1937-38	Chicago	--	0	3	3
1938-39	Chicago	--	1	2	3
1939-40	Chicago	--	2	2	4
1940-41	Chicago	--	3	2	5
1941-42	Chicago	--	2	4	6
1942-43	Chicago	33	1	7	8
1943-44	Chicago	21	2	4	6
	Totals	--	14	27	41

Playoffs					
1934-35	Chicago	--	0	0	0
1935-36	Chicago	--	0	0	0
1937-38	Chicago	--	0	1	1
1939-40	Chicago	--	1	0	1
1940-41	Chicago	--	0	0	0
1941-42	Chicago	--	0	0	0
1943-44	Chicago	--	0	2	2
	Totals	--	1	3	4

WILCOX, Archibald *Defenseman*
b. Montreal, Que., May 9, 1903

Season	Club	GP	G	A	Pts
1929-30	Montreal M.	--	3	5	8
1930-31	Montreal M.	--	2	2	4
1931-32	Montreal M.	--	3	3	6
1932-33	Montreal M.	--	0	3	3
1933-34	Mont M-Bos	--	0	1	1
	Totals	--	8	14	22

Playoffs					
1929-30	Montreal M.	--	1	0	1
1930-31	Montreal M.	--	0	0	0
1931-32	Montreal M.	--	0	0	0
1932-33	Montreal M.	--	0	0	0
	Totals	--	1	0	1

WILCOX, Barry *Forward*
b. New Westminster, B.C., Apr. 23, 1948

Season	Club	GP	G	A	Pts
1972-73	Vancouver	31	3	2	5

WILDER, Archibald *Forward*
b. Melville, Sask., Apr. 30, 1917

Season	Club	GP	G	A	Pts
1940-41	Detroit R.W.	--	0	2	2

WILEY, James (Jim) *Forward*
b. Sault St. Marie, Ont., Apr. 28, 1950

Season	Club	GP	G	A	Pts
1972-73	Pittsburgh Pe.	4	0	1	1

WILKENSON, John   *Defenseman*

Season	Club	GP	G	A	Pts
1943-44	Boston	9	0	0	0

WILKINS, Barry James   *Forward*
  b. Toronto, Ont., Feb. 28, 1947

Season	Club	GP	G	A	Pts
1966-67	Boston	1	0	0	0
1968-69	Boston	1	1	0	1
1969-70	Boston	6	0	0	0
1970-71	Vancouver	70	5	18	23
1971-72	Vancouver	45	2	5	7
1972-73	Vancouver	76	11	17	28
	Totals	199	19	40	59

WILLIAMS, Burr   *Defenseman*
  b. Okemah, Okla., Aug. 30, 1909

Season	Club	GP	G	A	Pts
1933-34	Detroit R.W.	--	0	1	1
1934-35	StL E-Bos	--	0	0	0
1936-37	Detroit R.W.	--	0	0	0
	Totals	--	0	1	1

Playoffs

| 1933-34 | Detroit R.W. | -- | 0 | 0 | 0 |

WILLIAMS, Thomas Charles (Tom)   *Forward*
  b. Windsor, Ont., Feb. 7, 1951

Season	Club	GP	G	A	Pts
1971-72	New York R.	3	0	0	0
1972-73	New York R.	10	0	1	1
	Totals	13	0	1	1

WILLIAMS, Thomas Mark (Tom)   *Forward*
  b. Duluth, Minn., Apr. 17, 1940

Season	Club	GP	G	A	Pts
1961-62	Boston	26	6	6	12
1962-63	Boston	69	23	20	43
1963-64	Boston	37	8	15	23
1964-65	Boston	65	13	21	34
1965-66	Boston	70	16	22	38
1966-67	Boston	29	8	13	21
1967-68	Boston	68	18	32	50
1968-69	Boston	26	4	7	11
1969-70	Minnesota	75	15	52	67
1970-71	Minn-Calif	59	17	23	40
1971-72	California	32	3	9	12
	Totals	556	131	220	351

Playoffs

1967-68	Boston	4	1	0	1
1969-70	Minnesota	6	1	5	6
	Totals	10	2	5	7

WILLSON, Donald Arthur   *Forward*
  b. Chatham, Ont., Jan. 1, 1914

Season	Club	GP	G	A	Pts
1937-38	Montreal C.	--	2	7	9

Playoffs

| 1937-38 | Montreal C. | -- | 0 | 0 | 0 |

WILSON, Carol (Cully)   *Forward*
  b. 1893

Season	Club	GP	G	A	Pts
1919-20	Toronto St. P.	23	21	5	26
1920-21	Tor StP-Mont C	17	8	2	10
1921-22	Hamilton	23	7	9	16
1922-23	Hamilton	23	16	3	19
1926-27	Chicago	--	8	4	12
	Totals	--	60	23	83

Playoffs

1918-19	Seattle (PCHL)	--	2	0	2
1923-24	Calgary (PCHL)	--	0	0	0
1926-27	Chicago	--	1	0	1
	Totals	--	3	0	3

WILSON, Duncan Shepherd (Dunc)   *Goalie*
  b. Toronto, Ont., Mar. 22, 1948

Season	Club	GP	GA	Sho	AVE
1969-70	Philadelphia F.	1	3	0	3.00
1970-71	Vancouver	30	128	0	4.28
1971-72	Vancouver	47⅔	173	1	3.61
1972-73	Vancouver	40⅓	159	1	3.94
	Totals	119	463	2	3.98

WILSON, Gerald   *Forward*
  b. Edmonton, Alta., Apr. 10, 1937

Season	Club	GP	G	A	Pts
1956-57	Montreal C.	3	0	0	0

WILSON, John Edward   *Forward*
  b. Kincardine, Ont., June 14, 1929

Season	Club	GP	G	A	Pts
1949-50	Detroit R.W.	1	0	0	0
1951-52	Detroit R.W.	28	4	5	9
1952-53	Detroit R.W.	70	23	19	42
1953-54	Detroit R.W.	70	17	17	34
1954-55	Detroit R.W.	70	12	15	27
1955-56	Chicago	70	24	9	33
1956-57	Chicago	70	18	31	48
1957-58	Detroit R.W.	70	12	27	39
1958-59	Detroit R.W.	70	11	17	28
1959-60	Toronto M.L.	70	15	16	31
1960-61	Tor ML-NY R	59	14	13	27
1961-62	New York R.	40	11	3	14
	Totals	688	161	171	332

WILSON *(Continued)*

Playoffs	Club	GP	G	A	Pts
1949-50	Detroit R.W.	8	0	1	1
1950-51	Detroit R.W.	1	0	0	0
1951-52	Detroit R.W.	8	4	1	5
1952-53	Detroit R.W.	6	2	5	7
1953-54	Detroit R.W.	12	3	0	3
1954-55	Detroit R.W.	11	0	1	1
1957-58	Detroit R.W.	4	2	1	3
1959-60	Toronto M.L.	10	1	2	3
1961-62	New York R.	6	2	2	4
	Totals	66	14	13	27

All-Star					
1954	Detroit R.W.	1	0	0	0
1956	NHL All-Stars	1	0	0	0
	Totals	2	0	0	0

WILSON, Lawrence *Forward*
  b. Kincardine, Ont., Oct. 23, 1930

Season	Club	GP	G	A	Pts
1949-50	Detroit R.W.	1	0	0	0
1951-52	Detroit R.W.	5	0	0	0
1952-53	Detroit R.W.	15	0	4	4
1953-54	Chicago	66	9	33	42
1954-55	Chicago	63	12	11	23
1955-56	Chicago	2	0	0	0
	Totals	152	21	48	69

Playoffs	Club	GP	G	A	Pts
1949-50	Detroit R.W.	4	0	0	0

WILSON, Murray *Forward*
  b. Ottawa, Ont., Aug. 3, 1951

Season	Club	GP	G	A	Pts
1972-73	Montreal C.	52	18	9	27

Playoffs	Club	GP	G	A	Pts
1972-73	Montreal C.	16	2	4	6

WILSON, Robert Wayne *Defenseman*
  b. Sudbury, Ont., Feb. 18, 1934

Season	Club	GP	G	A	Pts
1953-54	Chicago	1	0	0	0

WILSON, Ross Ingram (Lefty) *Goalie*
  b. Toronto, Ont., Oct. 15, 1919

Season	Club	GP	GA	Sho	AVE
1953-54	Detroit R.W.	⅓	0	0	0.00
1955-56	Toronto M.L.	⅓	0	0	0.00
1957-58	Boston	⅝	1	0	1.20
	Totals	1½	1	0	0.67

WILSON, Wallace Lloyd *Forward*
  b. Berwick, N.S., May 25, 1921

Season	Club	GP	G	A	Pts
1947-48	Boston	53	11	8	19

Playoffs					
1947-48	Boston	1	0	0	0

WINKLER, Harold Lang *Goalie*
  b. Gretna, Man., Mar. 20, 1892

Season	Club	GP	GA	Sho	AVE
1926-27	NY R-Bos	--	--	8	--
1927-28	Boston	44	70	15	1.59
	Totals	--	--	23	--

Playoffs					
1922-23	Edmonton (PCHL)	2	3	0	1.50
1926-27	Boston	8	13	2	1.63
1927-28	Boston	2	5	0	2.50
	Totals	12	21	2	1.75

WISEMAN, Edward Randall *Forward*
  b. Newcastle, N.B., Dec. 28, 1912

Season	Club	GP	G	A	Pts
1932-33	Detroit F.	--	8	8	16
1933-34	Detroit R.W.	--	5	9	14
1934-35	Detroit R.W.	--	1	13	24
1935-36	New York A.	--	12	16	28
1936-37	New York A.	--	14	19	33
1937-38	New York A.	--	18	14	32
1938-39	New York A.	--	12	21	33
1939-40	NY A-Bos	--	7	19	26
1940-41	Boston	--	16	24	40
1941-42	Boston	--	12	22	34
	Totals	--	115	165	280

Playoffs					
1932-33	Detroit F.	--	0	0	0
1933-34	Detroit R.W.	--	0	1	1
1935-36	New York A.	--	2	1	3
1937-38	New York A.	--	0	4	4
1938-39	New York A.	--	0	0	0
1939-40	Boston	--	2	1	3
1940-41	Boston	--	6	2	8
1941-42	Boston	--	0	1	1
	Totals	--	10	10	20

WISTE, James (Jim) *Forward*
  b. Moose Jaw, Sask., Feb. 18, 1946

Season	Club	GP	G	A	Pts
1968-69	Chicago	3	0	0	0
1969-70	Chicago	26	0	8	8
1970-71	Vancouver	23	1	2	3
	Totals	59	1	10	11

WITIUK, Stephen *Forward*
b. Winnipeg, Man., Jan. 8, 1929

Season	Club	GP	G	A	Pts
1951-52	Chicago	33	3	8	11

WOCHY, Stephen *Forward*
b. Fort William, Ont., Dec. 25, 1922

Season	Club	GP	G	A	Pts
1944-45	Detroit R.W.	49	19	20	39
1946-47	Detroit R.W.	5	0	0	0
	Totals	54	19	21	39
Playoffs					
1944-45	Detroit R.W.	6	0	1	1

WOIT, Benedict Francis *Defenseman*
b. Fort William, Ont., Jan. 7, 1928

Season	Club	GP	G	A	Pts
1950-51	Detroit R.W.	2	0	0	0
1951-52	Detroit R.W.	58	3	8	11
1952-53	Detroit R.W.	70	1	5	6
1953-54	Detroit R.W.	70	0	2	2
1954-55	Detroit R.W.	62	2	3	5
1955-56	Chicago	63	1	8	9
1956-57	Chicago	9	0	0	0
	Totals	234	7	26	33
Playoffs					
1950-51	Detroit R.W.	4	0	0	0
1951-52	Detroit R.W.	8	1	1	2
1952-53	Detroit R.W.	6	1	3	4
1953-54	Detroit R.W.	12	0	1	1
1954-55	Detroit R.W.	11	0	1	1
	Totals	41	2	6	8
All-Star					
1954	Detroit R.W.	1	0	0	0

WOOD, Robert *Defenseman*
b. Lethbridge, Alta., July 9, 1930

Season	Club	GP	G	A	Pts
1950-51	New York R.	1	0	0	0

WOODS, Alec *Goalie*
b. Falkirk, Scotland

Season	Club	GP	GA	Sho	AVE
1936-37	New York A.	1	3	0	3.00

WORSLEY, Lorne (Gump) *Goalie*
b. Montreal, Que., May 14, 1929

Season	Club	GP	GA	Sho	AVE
1952-53	New York R.	50	153	2	3.06
1954-55	New York R.	65	197	4	3.03
1955-56	New York R.	70	203	4	2.90
1956-57	New York R.	68	220	3	3.23
1957-58	New York R.	37	86	4	2.32

WORSLEY *(Continued)*

Season	Club	GP	GA	Sho	AVE
1958-59	New York R.	66⅓	205	2	3.08
1959-60	New York R.	38⅓	137	0	3.57
1960-61	New York R.	58⅔	193	1	3.29
1961-62	New York R.	58⅔	174	2	2.97
1962-63	New York R.	65⅓	219	2	3.35
1963-64	Montreal C.	7⅓	22	1	3.00
1964-65	Montreal C.	18	50	1	2.78
1965-66	Montreal C.	48⅓	114	2	2.36
1966-67	Montreal C.	14⅔	47	1	3.20
1967-68	Montreal C.	36¾	73	6	1.98
1968-69	Montreal C.	28⅓	64	5	2.26
1969-70	Mont C-Minn	13¹¹/₂₀	34	1	2.51
1970-71	Minnesota	22⅔	57	0	2.49
1971-72	Minnesota	32	68	2	2.12
1972-73	Minnesota	10½	30	0	2.88
	Totals	809½	2346	43	2.89
Playoffs					
1955-56	New York R.	3	15	0	5.00
1956-57	New York R.	5	22	0	4.40
1957-58	New York R.	6	28	0	4.67
1961-62	New York R.	6	22	0	3.67
1964-65	Montreal C.	8	14	2	1.75
1965-66	Montreal C.	10	20	1	2.00
1966-67	Montreal C.	1⅔	2	0	1.20
1967-68	Montreal C.	11	21	1	1.91
1968-69	Montreal C.	6	14	0	2.31
1969-70	Minnesota	3	14	0	4.67
1970-71	Minnesota	4	13	0	3.25
1971-72	Minnesota	3⅓	7	1	2.17
	Totals	67	192	5	2.82

All-Star		GP	Per	GA	AGP
1961	NHL All-Stars	1	1½	0	0.00
1962	NHL All-Stars	1	1	0	0.00
1965	Montreal C.	1	1½	1	0.67
1972	West All-Stars	1	1½	1	0.67
	Totals	4	5½	3	0.75

WORTERS, Roy *Goalie*
b. Toronto, Ont., Oct. 19, 1900

Season	Club	GP	GA	Sho	AVE
1925-26	Pittsburgh Pi.	35	68	7	1.94
1926-27	Pittsburgh Pi.	44	108	4	2.45
1927-28	Pittsburgh Pi.	44	76	11	1.73
1928-29	New York A.	38	46	13	1.21
1929-30	NY A-Mont C	37	137	2	3.70
1930-31	New York A.	44	74	8	1.68
1931-32	New York A.	40	119	5	2.98
1932-33	New York A.	47	116	5	2.47
1933-34	New York A.	36	77	4	2.14
1934-35	New York A.	48	142	3	2.96
1935-36	New York A.	48	122	3	2.54
1936-37	New York A.	23	69	2	3.00
	Totals	484	1154	66	2.38

WORTERS (Continued)

Playoffs	Club	GP	GA	Sho	AVE
1925–26	Pittsburgh Pi.	2	6	0	3.00
1927–28	Pittsburgh Pi.	2	6	0	3.00
1928–29	New York A.	2	1	1	0.50
1935–36	New York A.	5	11	2	2.20
	Totals	11	24	3	2.18

WORTHY, Christopher (Chris) *Goalie*
b. Bristol, England, Oct. 23, 1947

Season	Club	GP	GA	Sho	AVE
1968–69	Oakland	13	54	0	4.15
1969–70	Oakland	1	5	0	5.00
1970–71	California	8	39	0	4.87
	Totals	22	98	0	4.43

WOYTOWICH, Robert Ivan *Defenseman*
b. Winnipeg, Man., Aug. 18, 1941

Season	Club	GP	G	A	Pts
1964–65	Boston	21	2	10	12
1965–66	Boston	68	2	17	19
1966–67	Boston	64	2	7	9
1967–68	Minnesota	66	4	17	21
1968–69	Pittsburgh Pe.	71	9	20	29
1969–70	Pittsburgh Pe.	68	8	25	33
1970–71	Pittsburgh Pe.	78	4	22	26
1971–72	Pitt Pe–LA	67	1	8	9
	Totals	503	32	126	158
Playoffs					
1967–68	Minnesota	14	0	1	1
1969–70	Pittsburgh Pe.	10	1	2	3
	Totals	24	1	3	4
All-Star					
1970	West All-Stars	1	0	1	1

WRIGHT, John *Forward*
b. Toronto, Ont., Nov. 9, 1948

Season	Club	GP	G	A	Pts
1972–73	Vancouver	71	10	27	37

WRIGHT, Keith Edward *Forward*
b. Newmarket, Ont., Apr. 13, 1944

Season	Club	GP	G	A	Pts
1967–68	Philadelphia F.	1	0	0	0

WRIGHT, Larry *Forward*
b. Regina, Sask., Oct. 8, 1951

Season	Club	GP	G	A	Pts
1971–72	Philadelphia F.	27	0	1	1
1972–73	Philadelphia F.	9	0	1	1
	Totals	36	0	2	2

WYCHERLEY, Ralph (Bus) *Forward*
b. Saskatoon, Sask., Feb. 26, 1920

Season	Club	GP	G	A	Pts
1940–41	New York A.	--	4	5	9
1941–42	Brooklyn A.	2	0	2	2
	Totals	--	4	7	11

WYLIE, William Vance (Wiggy) *Forward*
b. Galt, Ont., July 15, 1928

Season	Club	GP	G	A	Pts
1950–51	New York R.	1	0	0	0

WYROZUB, William Randall (Randy) *Forward*
b. Lacombe, Alta., Apr. 8, 1950

Season	Club	GP	G	A	Pts
1970–71	Buffalo	16	2	2	4
1971–72	Buffalo	34	3	4	7
1972–73	Buffalo	45	3	3	6
	Totals	95	8	9	17

YACKEL, Kenneth James *Forward*
b. St. Paul, Minn., Mar. 5, 1932

Season	Club	GP	G	A	Pts
1958–59	Boston	6	0	0	0
Playoffs					
1958–59	Boston	2	0	0	0

YOUNG, Douglas *Defenseman*
b. Medicine Hat, Alta., Oct. 1, 1908

Season	Club	GP	G	A	Pts
1931–32	Detroit F.	--	10	2	12
1932–33	Detroit F.	--	5	6	11
1933–34	Detroit R.W.	--	4	0	4
1934–35	Detroit R.W.	--	4	6	10
1935–36	Detroit R.W.	--	5	12	17
1936–37	Detroit R.W.	--	0	0	0
1937–38	Detroit R.W.	--	3	5	8
1938–39	Detroit R.W.	--	1	5	6
1939–40	Montreal C.	--	3	9	12
1940–41	Montreal C.	--	0	0	0
	Totals	--	35	45	80
Playoffs					
1931–32	Detroit F.	--	0	0	0
1932–33	Detroit F.	--	1	1	2
1933–34	Detroit R.W.	--	0	0	0
1935–36	Detroit R.W.	--	0	2	2
1938–39	Detroit R.W.	--	0	2	2
	Totals	--	1	5	6

YOUNG, Howard John Edward *Defenseman*
b. Toronto, Ont., Aug. 2, 1937

Season	Club	GP	G	A	Pts
1960-61	Detroit R.W.	29	0	8	8
1961-62	Detroit R.W.	31	0	2	2
1962-63	Detroit R.W.	64	4	5	9
1963-64	Chicago	39	0	7	7
1966-67	Detroit R.W.	44	3	14	17
1967-68	Detroit R.W.	62	2	17	19
1968-69	Chicago	57	3	7	10
	Totals	326	12	60	72
Playoffs					
1960-61	Detroit R.W.	11	2	2	4
1962-63	Detroit R.W.	8	0	2	2
	Totals	19	2	4	6

ZAINE, Rodney Carl (Rod) *Forward*
b. Ottawa, Ont., May 18, 1946

Season	Club	GP	G	A	Pts
1970-71	Pittsburgh Pe.	37	8	5	13
1971-72	Buffalo	24	2	1	3
	Totals	61	10	6	16

ZEIDEL, Lawrence *Defenseman*
b. Montreal, Que., June 1, 1928

Season	Club	GP	G	A	Pts
1951-52	Detroit R.W.	19	1	0	1

ZEIDEL *(Continued)*

Season	Club	GP	G	A	Pts
1952-53	Detroit R.W.	9	0	0	0
1953-54	Chicago	64	1	6	7
1967-68	Philadelphia F.	57	1	10	11
1968-69	Philadelphia F.	9	0	0	0
	Totals	158	3	16	18
Playoffs					
1951-52	Detroit R.W.	5	0	0	0
1967-68	Philadelphia F.	7	0	1	1
	Totals	12	0	1	1

ZENIUK, Edward *Defenseman*
b. Landis, Sask., Mar. 8, 1933

Season	Club	GP	G	A	Pts
1954-55	Detroit R.W.	2	0	0	0

ZOBROSKY, Martin

Season	Club	GP	G	A	Pts
1944-45	Chicago	1	0	0	0

ZUNICH, Ralph (Ricky) *Defenseman*
b. Calumet, Mich., Nov. 24, 1910

Season	Club	GP	G	A	Pts
1943-44	Detroit R.W.	2	0	0	0

The following players have appeared in Stanley Cup playoffs only.

AHRENS, Christopher *Defenseman*
b. San Bernadino, Calif., July 31, 1952

Playoffs	Club	GP	G	A	Pts
1972–73	Minnesota	1	0	0	0

ANDERSON, Douglas *Forward*
b. Edmonton, Alta., Oct. 20, 1927

Playoffs	Club	GP	G	A	Pts
1952–53	Montreal C.	2	0	0	0

ANDERSON, Ernest *Forward*

Playoffs	Club	GP	G	A	Pts
1923–24	Calgary (PCHL)	--	0	0	0

ANDERSON, Jocko *Forward*

Playoffs	Club	GP	G	A	Pts
1924–25	Victoria (PCHL)	--	1	0	1

ANDERSON, William *Defenseman*
b. Tillsanberg, Ont., Dec. 13, 1912

Playoffs	Club	GP	G	A	Pts
1942–43	Boston	1	0	0	0

ANDRASCIK, Steve George *Forward*
b. Sherridon, Man., Nov. 6, 1948

Playoffs	Club	GP	G	A	Pts
1971–72	New York R.	1	0	0	0

BROWN, Wayne Hewetson *Forward*
b. Deloro, Ont., Nov. 16, 1930

Playoffs	Club	GP	G	A	Pts
1953–54	Boston	4	0	0	0

CHAMPOUX, Robert *Goalie*
b. St. Helaine, Que., Dec. 2, 1942

Playoffs	Club	GP	GA	Sho	AVE
1963–64	Detroit R.W.	⅔	4	0	6.00

CHERRY, Donald Stewart *Defenseman*
b. Kingston, Ont., Feb. 5, 1934

Playoffs	Club	GP	G	A	Pts
1954–55	Boston	1	0	0	0

COLLINS, Ranleigh Gary *Forward*
b. Toronto, Ont., Sept. 27, 1935

Playoffs	Club	GP	G	A	Pts
1958–59	Toronto M.L.	2	0	0	0

CORBETT, Michael Charles
Defenseman-Forward
b. Toronto, Ont., Oct. 4, 1942

Playoffs	Club	GP	G	A	Pts
1967–68	Los Angeles	2	0	1	1

DAVIES, Kenneth George (Buck) *Forward*
b. Bowmanville, Ont., Aug. 10, 1922

Playoffs	Club	GP	G	A	Pts
1947–48	New York R.	1	0	0	0

EMBERG, Edward *Forward*
b. Montreal, Que., Nov. 18, 1921

Playoffs	Club	GP	G	A	Pts
1944–45	Montreal C.	2	1	0	1

FRIG, Leonard Elroy *Defenseman*
b. Lethridge, Alta., Oct. 30, 1950

Playoffs	Club	GP	G	A	Pts
1972–73	Chicago	4	1	1	2

GRIFFIS, Siles (Si) *Defenseman*
b. Onega, Kan., Sept. 1883

Playoffs	Club	GP	G	A	Pts
1917–18	Vancouver (PCHL)	--	1	0	1

HAIDY, Gordon Adam *Forward*
b. Winnipeg, Man., Apr. 11, 1928

Playoffs	Club	GP	G	A	Pts
1949–50	Detroit R.W.	1	0	0	0

HAYES, Christopher Joseph *Forward*
b. Rouyn, Que., Aug. 24, 1946

Playoffs	Club	GP	G	A	Pts
1971–72	Boston	1	0	0	0

KURYLUK, Mervin *Forward*
b. Yorkton, Sask., Aug. 10, 1937

Playoffs	Club	GP	G	A	Pts
1961–62	Chicago	2	0	0	0

LONG, Stanley Gordon *Defenseman*
b. Owen Sound, Ont., Nov. 6, 1929

Playoffs	Club	GP	G	A	Pts
1951–52	Montreal C.	3	0	0	0

McAVOY, George *Defenseman*
b. Edmonton, Alta., June 21, 1931

Playoffs	Club	GP	G	A	Pts
1954–55	Montreal C.	4	0	0	0

McDONALD, Jack *Forward*

Playoffs	Club	GP	G	A	Pts
1917–18	Vancouver (PCHL) --	2	1	3	
1918–19	Seattle (PCHL) --	1	0	1	
	Totals	--	3	1	4

McKAY, Douglas A. *Forward*
b. Hamilton, Ont., May 28, 1929

Playoffs	Club	GP	G	A	Pts
1949–50	Detroit R.W.	1	0	0	0

McNABNEY, Sidney *Forward*
b. Toronto, Ont., Jan. 15, 1929

Playoffs	Club	GP	G	A	Pts
1950–51	Montreal C.	5	0	1	1

MURRAY, Jack (Muzz)

Playoffs	Club	GP	G	A	Pts
1918–19	Seattle (PCHL) --	2	0	2	
1919–20	Seattle (PCHL) --	0	0	0	
	Totals	--	2	0	2

OATMAN, Edward *Forward*

Playoffs	Club	GP	G	A	Pts
1921–22	Vancouver (PCHL) --	1	1	2	
1923–24	Calgary (PCHL) --	0	1	1	
	Totals	--	1	2	3

REID, Charles *Goalie*

Playoffs	Club	GP	GA	Sho	AVE
1923–24	Calgary (PCHL)	2	9	0	4.50

REID, Gerald Roland *Forward*
b. Owen Sound, Ont., Oct. 13, 1928

Playoffs	Club	GP	G	A	Pts
1948–49	Detroit R.W.	2	0	0	0

RICKEY, Roy *Defenseman*

Playoffs	Club	GP	G	A	Pts
1918–19	Seattle (PCHL) --	1	0	1	
1919–20	Seattle (PCHL) --	2	0	2	
	Totals	--	3	0	3

STAHAN, Frank Ralph (Butch) *Defenseman*
b. Minnedosa, Man., Oct. 29, 1915

Playoffs	Club	GP	G	A	Pts
1944–45	Montreal C.	3	0	1	1

STANFIELD, John Gordon (Jack) *Forward*
b. Toronto, Ont., May 30, 1942

Playoffs	Club	GP	G	A	Pts
1965–66	Chicago	1	0	0	0

STANLEY, Barney *Forward*

Playoffs	Club	GP	G	A	Pts
1917–18	Vancouver (PCHL) --	2	0	2	

TAYLOR, Fred (Cyclone) *Forward*
b. Tara, Ont., 1885

Playoffs	Club	GP	G	A	Pts
1917–18	Vancouver (PCHL) --	9	1	10	
1920–21	Vancouver (PCHL) --	0	1	1	
	Totals	--	9	2	11

THIFFAULT, Leo *Forward*
b. Drummondville, Que., Dec. 16, 1944

Playoffs	Club	GP	G	A	Pts
1967–68	Minnesota	5	0	0	0

WILSON, Gordon Allan *Forward*
b. Port Arthur, Ont., Aug. 13, 1932

Playoffs	Club	GP	G	A	Pts
1954–55	Boston	2	0	0	0

XVI WHA PLAYER REGISTER

This section includes the record of every player who has appeared in a World Hockey Association regular-season or playoff game. This information is based on material supplied by the WHA and its member clubs. It should be noted that the WHA statistics credit goalies with full games regardless of the time played and the goals-against average supplied by the league is figured accordingly.

Where information is missing, it was unavailable.

WORLD HOCKEY ASSOCIATION TEAMS

Chicago Cougars
Cleveland Crusaders
Edmonton Oilers *(formerly Alberta Oilers)*
Houston Aeros
Jersey Knights *(formerly New York Golden Blades, formerly New York Raiders)*
Los Angeles Sharks
Minnesota Fighting Saints
New England Whalers
Quebec Nordiques
Toronto Toros *(formerly Ottawa Nationals)*
Vancouver Blazers *(formerly Philadelphia Blazers)*
Winnipeg Jets

EXPLANATION OF ABBREVIATIONS

A	Assists
AVE	Average goals-against per game
AGP	Average goals-against per period
G	Goals scored
GA	Goals against
GP	Games played
NHL	National Hockey League
PCHL	Pacific Coast Hockey League
Pts	Points scored
Sho	Shutouts
Per	Periods

AHEARN, Kevin *Forward*
b. Boston, Mass., June 20, 1948

Season	Club	GP	G	A	Pts
1972-73	New England	78	20	22	42
Playoffs					
1972-73	New England	14	1	2	3

AMODEO, Mike *Defenseman*
b. Toronto, Ont., June 22, 1952

Season	Club	GP	G	A	Pts
1972-73	Ottawa	61	1	14	15
Playoffs					
1972-73	Ottawa	5	0	1	1

ANDERSON, Ron *Forward*
b. Dryden, Ont., Nov. 15, 1948

Season	Club	GP	G	A	Pts
1972-73	Chicago	73	3	26	29

ANDERSON, Ron C. *Forward*
b. Red Deer, Alberta, July 29, 1945

Season	Club	GP	G	A	Pts
1972-73	Alberta	73	14	15	29

ANDREA, Paul *Forward*
b. North Sydney, N.S., July 31, 1941

Season	Club	GP	G	A	Pts
1972-73	Cleveland	67	21	30	51
Playoffs					
1972-73	Cleveland	9	2	8	10

ANTONOVICH, Mike *Forward*
b. Calumet, Minn., Oct. 18, 1951

Season	Club	GP	G	A	Pts
1972-73	Minnesota	75	20	19	39
Playoffs					
1972-73	Minnesota	5	2	0	2

ARBOUR, John *Defenseman*
b. Niagara Falls, Ont., Sept. 28, 1945

Season	Club	GP	G	A	Pts
1972-73	Minnesota	76	6	27	33
Playoffs					
1972-73	Minnesota	5	0	1	1

ARCHAMBAULT, Michel *Forward*
b. St.-Hyacinthe, Quebec, Sept. 27, 1950

Season	Club	GP	G	A	Pts
1972-73	Quebec	57	12	25	37

ARCHAMBAULT, Yves *Goalie*
b. Montreal, Que., June 22, 1952

Season	Club	GP	GA	Sho	AVE
1972-73	Philadelphia	6	17	0	3.92
Playoffs					
1972-73	Philadelphia	3	11	0	4.31

ASH, Bob *Defenseman*
b. Broadview, Sas., Sept. 29, 1943

Season	Club	GP	G	A	Pts
1972-73	Winnipeg	75	3	14	17
Playoffs					
1972-73	Winnipeg	13	1	3	4

ASMUNDSON, Duke *Defenseman-Forward*
b. Vita, Man., Aug. 17, 1943

Season	Club	GP	G	A	Pts
1972-73	Winnipeg	78	2	14	16
Playoffs					
1972-73	Winnipeg	12	1	2	3

AUBRY, Serge *Goalie*
b. Montreal, Quebec, Jan. 2, 1942

Season	Club	GP	GA	Sho	AVE
1972-73	Quebec	52	182	2	3.59

650

BAIRD, Ken *Defenseman*
b. Flin Flon, Man., Feb. 1, 1951

Season	Club	GP	G	A	Pts
1972-73	Alberta	75	14	15	29

BALL, Terry *Defenseman*
b. Selkirk, Man., Nov. 29, 1944

Season	Club	GP	G	A	Pts
1972-73	Minnesota	78	6	34	40
Playoffs					
1972-73	Minnesota	5	1	2	3

BARBER, Butch *Defenseman*
b. Fairview, Alberta, Aug. 31, 1943

Season	Club	GP	G	A	Pts
1972-73	Chicago	75	4	19	23

BARRIE, Doug *Defenseman*
b. Edmonton, Alberta, Oct. 2, 1946

Season	Club	GP	G	A	Pts
1972-73	Alberta	54	9	22	31

BEAUDIN, Norm *Forward*
b. Montmartre, Sas., Nov. 28, 1941

Season	Club	GP	G	A	Pts
1972-73	Winnipeg	78	38	65	103
Playoffs					
1972-73	Winnipeg	14	13	15	28

BENNETT, John *Forward*
b. Cranston, R.I., Jan. 19, 1950

Season	Club	GP	G	A	Pts
1972-73	Philadelphia	34	4	6	10

BENZELOCK, Jim *Forward*
b. Winnipeg, Man., June 21, 1947

Season	Club	GP	G	A	Pts
1972-73	Alb-Chicago	69	10	13	23

BERGERON, Yves *Forward*
b. Matamic, Abitibi, Quebec, Jan. 11, 1952

Season	Club	GP	G	A	Pts
1972-73	Quebec	65	14	19	33

BINKLEY, Les *Goalie*
b. Owen Sound, Ont., June 6, 1936

Season	Club	GP	GA	Sho	AVE
1972-73	Ottawa	30	106	0	3.72
Playoffs					
1972-73	Ottawa	4	17	0	4.57

BLACK, Milt *Forward*
b. St. Boniface, Man., June 20, 1949

Season	Club	GP	G	A	Pts
1972-73	Winnipeg	78	18	16	34
Playoffs					
1972-73	Winnipeg	14	1	3	4

BLAIN, Jacques *Defenseman*
b. Gatineau, Quebec, July 19, 1947

Season	Club	GP	G	A	Pts
1972-73	Quebec	70	1	10	11

BLANCHETTE, Bernie *Forward*
b. North Battleford, Sas., July 11, 1947

Season	Club	GP	G	A	Pts
1972-73	Chi-Alberta	47	7	7	14

BLOCK, Ken *Defenseman*
b. Steinbach, Man., March 18, 1944

Season	Club	GP	G	A	Pts
1972-73	New York	78	5	53	58

BLUM, Frank *Goalie*
b. Creighton Mines, Ont., June 29, 1952

Season	Club	GP	GA	Sho	AVE
1972-73	Ottawa	2	3	0	6.42

BOLAND, Mike *Forward*
b. Montreal, Que., Dec. 16, 1949

Season	Club	GP	G	A	Pts
1972-73	Ottawa	41	1	15	16
Playoffs					
1972-73	Ottawa	1	0	0	0

BORDELEAU, Chris *Forward*
b. Noranda, Que., Sept. 23, 1947

Season	Club	GP	G	A	Pts
1972-73	Winnipeg	78	47	54	101
Playoffs					
1972-73	Winnipeg	12	5	8	13

BOUDREAU, Michel *Defenseman*

Season	Club	GP	G	A	Pts
1972-73	Philadelphia	33	7	7	14
Playoffs					
1972-73	Philadelphia	2	0	0	0

BOYER, Wally *Forward*
b. Cowan, Man., Aug. 27, 1937

Season	Club	GP	G	A	Pts
1972-73	Winnipeg	70	6	28	34
Playoffs					
1972-73	Winnipeg	14	4	2	6

BRADLEY, Brian *Forward*
b. Sudbury, Ont., Dec. 14, 1944

Season	Club	GP	G	A	Pts
1972-73	New York	78	22	33	55

BRINDLEY, Doug *Forward*
b. Walkerton, Ont., June 8, 1949

Season	Club	GP	G	A	Pts
1972-73	Cleveland	73	15	11	26
Playoffs					
1972-73	Cleveland	9	0	0	0

BRODEUR, Richard *Goalie*
b. Longueuil, Quebec, Sept. 15, 1952

Season	Club	GP	GA	Sho	AVE
1972-73	Quebec	24	102	0	4.75

BROWN, Bob *Defenseman*
b. Toronto, Ont., Dec. 18, 1950

Season	Club	GP	G	A	Pts
1972-73	Phil-NY	21	0	4	4

BROWN, Ken *Goalie*
b. Port Arthur, Ontario, Dec. 19, 1948

Season	Club	GP	GA	Sho	AVE
1972-73	Alberta	20	63	1	3.65

BUCHANAN, Ron *Forward*
b. Montreal, Que., Nov. 15, 1944

Season	Club	GP	G	A	Pts
1972-73	Cleveland	75	37	44	81
Playoffs					
1972-73	Cleveland	9	7	3	10

BURGESS, Don *Forward*
b. Port Edward, Ont., June 8, 1946

Season	Club	GP	G	A	Pts
1972-73	Philadelphia	74	20	22	42
Playoffs					
1972-73	Philadelphia	4	1	0	1

BYERS, Mike *Forward*
b. Toronto, Ont., Sept. 11, 1946

Season	Club	GP	G	A	Pts
1972-73	LA-N. England	75	25	21	46
Playoffs					
1972-73	New England	12	6	5	11

CADLE, Brian *Forward*
b. Vancouver, B.C., Sept. 23, 1947

Season	Club	GP	G	A	Pts
1972-73	Winnipeg	56	4	4	8
Playoffs					
1972-73	Winnipeg	3	0	0	0

CAFFERY, Terry *Forward*
b. Toronto, Ont., April 1, 1949

Season	Club	GP	G	A	Pts
1972-73	New England	74	39	61	100
Playoffs					
1972-73	New England	8	3	7	10

CAHAN, Larry *Defenseman*
b. Fort William, Ont., Dec. 25, 1933

Season	Club	GP	G	A	Pts
1972-73	Chicago	76	1	10	11

CAMPBELL, Bryan *Forward*
b. Sudbury, Ont., March 27, 1944

Season	Club	GP	G	A	Pts
1972-73	Philadelphia	75	25	48	73
Playoffs					
1972-73	Philadelphia	3	0	1	1

CAMPEAU, Rychard *Defenseman*
b. Montreal, Que., April 9, 1952

Season	Club	GP	G	A	Pts
1972-73	Philadelphia	75	1	18	19
Playoffs					
1972-73	Philadelphia	4	1	0	1

CARDIFF, Jim *Defenseman*
b. Dauphin, Man., Aug. 29, 1944

Season	Club	GP	G	A	Pts
1972-73	Philadelphia	78	3	24	27
Playoffs					
1972-73	Philadelphia	4	0	0	0

CARLETON, Wayne *Forward*
b. Sudbury, Ont., Aug. 4, 1946

Season	Club	GP	G	A	Pts
1972-73	Ottawa	76	42	49	91
Playoffs					
1972-73	Ottawa	3	3	3	6

CARLIN, Brian *Forward*
b. Calgary, Alberta, June 13, 1950

Season	Club	GP	G	A	Pts
1972-73	Alberta	64	12	22	34

CARLYLE, Steve *Defenseman*
b. Lacombe, Alberta, March 10, 1950

Season	Club	GP	G	A	Pts
1972-73	Alberta	67	7	10	17

CARON, Alain *Forward*
b. Dolbeau, Quebec, April 27, 1938

Season	Club	GP	G	A	Pts
1972-73	Quebec	68	36	27	63

CARTIER, Jean-Yves *Defenseman*
  b. Verdun, Que.

Season	Club	GP	G	A	Pts
1972-73	Quebec	15	0	3	3

CHARLEBOIS, Bob *Forward*
  b. Cornwall, Ont., May 27, 1944

Season	Club	GP	G	A	Pts
1972-73	Ottawa	78	24	39	63
Playoffs					
1972-73	Ottawa	5	1	1	2

CHARTRE, Claude *Forward*
  b. Grande-Riviere, Gaspe Co., Que., Dec. 21, 1949

Season	Club	GP	G	A	Pts
1972-73	New York	12	2	3	5

CHEEVERS, Gerry *Goalie*
  b. St. Catherines, Ont., Dec. 7, 1940

Season	Club	GP	GA	Sho	AVE
1972-73	Cleveland	52	149	5	2.83
Playoffs					
1972-73	Cleveland	9	22	0	2.40

CHIPCHASE, Jack *Defenseman*
  b. Seaforth, Ont., Apr. 5, 1945

Season	Club	GP	G	A	Pts
1972-73	Philadelphia	3	0	0	0

CHRISTIANSEN, Keith *Forward*
  b. Fort Francis, Ont., April 8, 1947

Season	Club	GP	G	A	Pts
1972-73	Minnesota	64	12	30	42
Playoffs					
1972-73	Minnesota	5	1	0	1

CLEARWATER, Ray *Defenseman*
  b. Winnipeg, Man., Nov. 10, 1942

Season	Club	GP	G	A	Pts
1972-73	Cleveland	78	11	36	47
Playoffs					
1972-73	Cleveland	9	1	2	3

CLIMIE, Ron *Forward*
  b. Hamilton, Ont., March 5, 1950

Season	Club	GP	G	A	Pts
1972-73	Ottawa	31	12	19	31
Playoffs					
1972-73	Ottawa	4	1	0	1

CONACHER, Brian *Forward*
  b. Toronto, Ont., Aug. 31, 1941

Season	Club	GP	G	A	Pts
1972-73	Ottawa	69	8	19	27
Playoffs					
1972-73	Ottawa	5	1	3	4

CONNELLY, Wayne *Forward*
  b. Rouyne, Que., Dec. 16, 1939

Season	Club	GP	G	A	Pts
1972-73	Minnesota	78	40	30	70
Playoffs					
1972-73	Minnesota	5	1	3	4

COTE, Roger *Defenseman*
  b. Belleterre, Quebec, Dec. 22, 1939

Season	Club	GP	G	A	Pts
1972-73	Alberta	60	3	5	8

COTTRINGER, Tom *Goalie*
  b. Niagara Falls, Ont., Dec. 28, 1947

Season	Club	GP	GA	Sho	AVE
1972-73	Philadelphia	2	8	0	3.93

CRASHLEY, Bart *Defenseman*
  b. Toronto, Ont., June 15, 1946

Season	Club	GP	G	A	Pts
1972-73	Los Angeles	70	18	27	45
Playoffs					
1972-73	Los Angeles	6	0	2	2

CUDDIE, Steve *Defenseman*
  b. Toronto, Ont., June 18, 1950

Season	Club	GP	G	A	Pts
1972-73	Winnipeg	77	7	13	20
Playoffs					
1972-73	Winnipeg	12	0	1	1

CUNNIFF, John *Forward*
  b. South Boston, Mass., July 9, 1944

Season	Club	GP	G	A	Pts
1972-73	New England	32	3	5	8
Playoffs					
1972-73	New England	13	1	1	2

CUNNINGHAM, Rick *Defenseman*
  b. Toronto, Ont., March 3, 1951

Season	Club	GP	G	A	Pts
1972-73	Ottawa	78	9	31	40
Playoffs					
1972-73	Ottawa	5	1	1	2

CURRAN, Mike *Goalie*
  b. International Falls, Minn., April 14, 1944

Season	Club	GP	GA	Sho	AVE
1972-73	Minnesota	44	131	4	3.09
Playoffs					
1972-73	Minnesota	2	9	0	5.97

DALEY, Joe *Goalie*
b. East Kildonan, Man., Feb. 20, 1943

Season	Club	GP	GA	Sho	AVE
1972–73	Winnipeg	29	83	2	2.89
Playoffs					
1972–73	Winnipeg	7	25	0	3.55

DANBY, John *Forward*
b. Toronto, Ont., July 20, 1948

Season	Club	GP	G	A	Pts
1972–73	New England	77	14	23	37
Playoffs					
1972–73	New England	8	0	0	0

DESCOTEAUX, Norm *Forward*

Season	Club	GP	G	A	Pts
1972–73	Quebec	2	0	1	1

DESJARDINE, Ken *Defenseman*
b. Toronto, Ontario, Aug. 23, 1947

Season	Club	GP	G	A	Pts
1972–73	Quebec	57	2	6	8

DILLABOUGH, Bob *Forward*
b. Belleville, Ont., April 24, 1941

Season	Club	GP	G	A	Pts
1972–73	Cleveland	72	8	8	16
Playoffs					
1972–73	Cleveland	9	1	0	1

DONNELLY, John *Defenseman*
b. Sept. 28, 1948

Season	Club	GP	G	A	Pts
1972–73	Ottawa	15	1	1	2

DONNELLY, Peter *Goalie*
b. Detroit, Mich., June 14, 1948

Season	Club	GP	GA	Sho	AVE
1972–73	New York	47	155	2	3.56

DOREY, Jim *Defenseman*
b. Kingston, Ont., Aug. 17, 1947

Season	Club	GP	G	A	Pts
1972–73	New England	75	7	56	63
Playoffs					
1972–73	New England	15	3	16	19

DOUGLAS, Kent *Defenseman*
b. Cobalt, Ont., Feb. 6, 1936

Season	Club	GP	G	A	Pts
1972–73	New York	60	3	15	18

DUFOUR, Guy *Forward*
b. Feb. 9, 1946

Season	Club	GP	G	A	Pts
1972–73	Quebec	9	3	2	5

EARL, Tom *Forward*
b. Niagara Falls, Ont., Jan. 27, 1947

Season	Club	GP	G	A	Pts
1972–73	New England	76	10	13	23
Playoffs					
1972–73	New England	15	2	3	5

ERICKSON, Grant *Forward*
b. Pierceland, Sas., April 28, 1947

Season	Club	GP	G	A	Pts
1972–73	Cleveland	77	15	29	44
Playoffs					
1972–73	Cleveland	9	2	1	3

FALKENBERG, Bob *Defenseman*
b. Stettler, Alberta, Jan. 1, 1946

Season	Club	GP	G	A	Pts
1972–73	Alberta	77	6	23	29

FALKMAN, Craig *Forward*
b. St. Paul, Minn., Aug. 1, 1943

Season	Club	GP	G	A	Pts
1972–73	Minnesota	44	1	5	6

FERGUSON, Norm *Forward*
b. Sydney, N.S., Oct. 16, 1945

Season	Club	GP	G	A	Pts
1972–73	New York	56	28	40	68

FISHER, John *Forward*
b. Ayre, Scotland, Dec. 21, 1947

Season	Club	GP	G	A	Pts
1972–73	Alberta	39	0	5	5

FLEMING, Reggie *Forward*
b. Montreal, Que., April 21, 1936

Season	Club	GP	G	A	Pts
1972–73	Chicago	74	23	45	68

FONTEYNE, Val *Forward*
b. Wetaskiwin, Alberta, Dec. 2, 1933

Season	Club	GP	G	A	Pts
1972–73	Alberta	77	7	32	39

FRENCH, John *Forward*
b. Orillia, Ont., Aug. 25, 1950

Season	Club	GP	G	A	Pts
1972–73	New England	74	24	35	59
Playoffs					
1972–73	New England	15	3	11	14

GARDNER, George *Goalie*
b. Lachine, Que., Oct. 8, 1942

Season	Club	GP	GA	Sho	AVE
1972–73	Los Angeles	49	149	1	3.29
Playoffs					
1972–73	Los Angeles	3	11	0	5.67

GAUDETTE, Andre *Forward*
b. Sherbrooke, Quebec, Dec. 16, 1947

Season	Club	GP	G	A	Pts
1972–73	Quebec	76	27	44	71

GAUTHIER, Jean *Defenseman*
b. Montreal, Que., April 29, 1937

Season	Club	GP	G	A	Pts
1972–73	New York	31	2	1	3

GELLARD, Sam *Forward*

Season	Club	GP	G	A	Pts
1972–73	Philadelphia	5	0	0	0

GENDRON, Jean-Guy *Forward*
b. Montreal, Quebec, Aug. 30, 1934

Season	Club	GP	G	A	Pts
1972–73	Quebec	63	18	33	51

GIBBONS, Brian *Defenseman*
b. St. John's, Nfld., July 7, 1947

Season	Club	GP	G	A	Pts
1972–73	Ottawa	73	7	35	42
Playoffs					
1972–73	Ottawa	5	1	2	3

GIBSON, Jack *Forward*
b. Picton, Ont., Aug. 18, 1948

Season	Club	GP	G	A	Pts
1972–73	Ottawa	59	22	12	34
Playoffs					
1972–73	Ottawa	1	1	0	1

GILL, Andre *Goalie*
b. Sorel, Que., Sept. 19, 1941

Season	Club	GP	GA	Sho	AVE
1972–73	Chicago	28	118	0	4.21

GILLOW, Russ *Goalie*
b. Hespeler, Ont., Sept. 2, 1940

Season	Club	GP	GA	Sho	AVE
1972–73	Los Angeles	38	96	2	2.88
Playoffs					
1972–73	Los Angeles	5	12	0	2.91

GILMORE, Tom *Forward*
b. Flin Flon, Man., May 14, 1948

Season	Club	GP	G	A	Pts
1972–73	Los Angeles	70	17	18	35
Playoffs					
1972–73	Los Angeles	5	1	3	4

GIROUX, ReJean *Forward*
b. Quebec City, Sept. 13, 1952

Season	Club	GP	G	A	Pts
1972–73	Quebec	59	10	12	22

GLENWRIGHT, Brian *Forward*
b. Windsor, Ont., Oct. 8, 1949

Season	Club	GP	G	A	Pts
1972–73	Chicago	48	2	5	7

GLOBENSKY, Alan *Forward*
b. Montreal, Que., April 17, 1951

Season	Club	GP	G	A	Pts
1972–73	Quebec	4	0	0	0

GOLEMBROSKY, Frank *Forward*
b. Calgary, Alberta, May 3, 1945

Season	Club	GP	G	A	Pts
1972–73	Phil Quebec	60	8	12	20

GRATTON, Gilles *Goalie*
b. La Salle, Que., July 28, 1952

Season	Club	GP	GA	Sho	AVE
1972–73	Ottawa	51	187	0	3.71
Playoffs					
1972–73	Ottawa	2	7	0	4.84

GRATTON, Jean-Guy *Forward*
b. Ste. Ann Des Plaines, Que., March 8, 1947

Season	Club	GP	G	A	Pts
1972–73	Winnipeg	71	15	12	27
Playoffs					
1972–73	Winnipeg	12	1	1	2

GRAVEL, John *Defenseman*
b. Montreal, Que., Oct. 27, 1943

Season	Club	GP	G	A	Pts
1972–73	Philadelphia	8	1	3	4

GREEN, Ted *Defenseman*
b. Ericksbare, Man., March 23, 1940

Season	Club	GP	G	A	Pts
1972–73	New England	78	16	30	46
Playoffs					
1972–73	New England	12	1	5	6

GRIERSON, Don *Forward*
b. North Bay, Ont., June 18, 1947

Season	Club	GP	G	A	Pts
1972–73	Houston	78	22	22	44
Playoffs					
1972–73	Houston	3	0	0	0

GUINDON, Robert *Forward*
b. Labelle, Quebec, Nov. 19, 1950

Season	Club	GP	G	A	Pts
1972–73	Quebec	71	27	28	55

GUITE, Pierre *Forward*
b. Montreal, Quebec, April 17, 1952

Season	Club	GP	G	A	Pts
1972–73	Quebec	66	10	8	18

HALE, Larry *Defenseman*
b. Summerland, B.C., Oct. 9, 1941

Season	Club	GP	G	A	Pts
1972–73	Houston	68	4	26	30
Playoffs					
1972–73	Houston	10	1	2	3

HALL, Murray *Forward*
b. Kirkland Lake, Ont., Nov. 24, 1940

Season	Club	GP	G	A	Pts
1972–73	Houston	76	28	42	70
Playoffs					
1972–73	Houston	10	4	4	8

HAMILTON, Allan *Defenseman*
b. Flin Flon, Man., Aug. 20, 1946

Season	Club	GP	G	A	Pts
1972–73	Alberta	78	11	49	60

HAMPSON, Ted *Forward*
b. Togo, Sas., Dec. 11, 1936

Season	Club	GP	G	A	Pts
1972–73	Minnesota	76	17	45	62
Playoffs					
1972–73	Minnesota	5	3	1	4

HANEY, Merv *Forward*

Season	Club	GP	G	A	Pts
1972–73	Ottawa	7	0	1	1

HANNA, John *Defenseman*
b. Sydney, N.S., April 5, 1935

Season	Club	GP	G	A	Pts
1972–73	Cleveland	65	6	20	26

HARDY, Joe *Forward*
b. Kenogami, Que., Dec. 5, 1944

Season	Club	GP	G	A	Pts
1972–73	Cleveland	72	17	33	50
Playoffs					
1972–73	Cleveland	7	0	2	2

HARKER, Derek *Defenseman*
b. Edmonton, Alberta, Jan. 7, 1951

Season	Club	GP	G	A	Pts
1972–73	Alberta–Phila	28	0	5	5

HARRIS, Duke *Forward*
b. Sarnia, Ont., Feb. 25, 1942

Season	Club	GP	G	A	Pts
1972–73	Houston	75	30	12	42
Playoffs					
1972–73	Houston	10	1	1	2

HARRISON, Jim *Forward*
b. Glendon, Alberta, July 9, 1947

Season	Club	GP	G	A	Pts
1972–73	Alberta	65	39	48	87

HARVEY, Michel *Forward*
b. Alma, Lac-St.-Jean, Quebec, Jan. 31, 1938

Season	Club	GP	G	A	Pts
1972–73	Quebec	40	6	13	19

HATOUM, Ed *Forward*
b. Beirut, Lebanon, Dec. 7, 1947

Season	Club	GP	G	A	Pts
1972–73	Chicago	16	1	1	2

HEGGEDAL, Howie *Forward*
b. Sept. 15, 1949

Season	Club	GP	G	A	Pts
1972–73	Los Angeles	8	2	1	3
Playoffs					
1972–73	Los Angeles	1	0	0	0

HEISKALA, Earl *Forward*
b. Kirkland Lake, Ont., Nov. 30, 1942

Season	Club	GP	G	A	Pts
1972–73	Los Angeles	70	12	17	29
Playoffs					
1972–73	Los Angeles	5	1	1	2

HENRY, Pierre *Forward*

Season	Club	GP	G	A	Pts
1972–73	Philadelphia	19	2	3	5

HERRIMAN, Don *Forward*
b. Sault Ste. Marie, Ont., Jan. 2, 1946

Season	Club	GP	G	A	Pts
1972–73	Philadelphia	78	24	48	72
Playoffs					
1972–73	Philadelphia	4	1	0	1

HICKE, Bill *Forward*
b. Regina, Sas., March 31, 1938

Season	Club	GP	G	A	Pts
1972–73	Alberta	73	14	24	38

HODGSON, Ted *Forward*
b. Hobbema, Alberta, June 30, 1945

Season	Club	GP	G	A	Pts
1972–73	Cleveland	74	15	23	38
Playoffs					
1972–73	Cleveland	9	1	3	4

HOEKSTRA, Ed *Forward*
b. Winnipeg, Man., Nov. 4, 1937

Season	Club	GP	G	A	Pts
1972–73	Houston	77	11	28	39
Playoffs					
1972–73	Houston	9	1	2	3

HOPIAVOURI, Ralph *Defenseman*
b. Kirkland Lake, Ont., July 15, 1951

Season	Club	GP	G	A	Pts
1972–73	Cleveland	31	4	5	9
Playoffs					
1972–73	Cleveland	8	0	1	1

HORNUNG, Larry *Defenseman*
b. Gravelburg, Sas., Oct. 10, 1945

Season	Club	GP	G	A	Pts
1972–73	Winnipeg	77	13	45	58
Playoffs					
1972–73	Winnipeg	14	2	9	11

HORTON, Bill *Defenseman*
b. Lindsay, Ont., Sept. 5, 1946

Season	Club	GP	G	A	Pts
1972–73	Cleveland	73	2	17	19
Playoffs					
1972–73	Cleveland	9	0	1	1

HUGHES, Bill *Goalie*
b. Kirkland Lake, Ont., Nov. 7, 1947

Season	Club	GP	GA	Sho	AVE
1972–73	Houston	3	11	0	3.88

HUGHES, Frank *Forward*
b. Fernie, B.C., Oct. 1, 1949

Season	Club	GP	G	A	Pts
1972–73	Houston	77	22	19	41
Playoffs					
1972–73	Houston	10	4	4	8

HULL, Bobby *Forward*
b. Pointe Anne, Ont., Jan. 3, 1939

Season	Club	GP	G	A	Pts
1972–73	Winnipeg	63	51	52	103
Playoffs					
1972–73	Winnipeg	14	9	16	25

HURLEY, Paul *Defenseman*
b. Everett, Mass., July 12, 1946

Season	Club	GP	G	A	Pts
1972–73	New England	78	3	15	18
Playoffs					
1972–73	New England	15	0	7	7

HUTCHISON, Dave *Defenseman*
b. May 2, 1952

Season	Club	GP	G	A	Pts
1972–73	Philadelphia	28	0	2	2
Playoffs					
1972–73	Philadelphia	3	0	0	0

HYNDMAN, Mike *Forward*
b. Quebec City, Dec. 8, 1945

Season	Club	GP	G	A	Pts
1972–73	NE–Los Angeles	78	12	21	33
Playoffs					
1972–73	Los Angeles	6	0	3	3

JAKABO, Mike *Defenseman*
b. Sudbury, Ont., July 7, 1947

Season	Club	GP	G	A	Pts
1972–73	Los Angeles	7	0	0	0

JARRETT, Gary *Forward*
b. Toronto, Ont., Sept. 3, 1942

Season	Club	GP	G	A	Pts
1972–73	Cleveland	77	40	38	78
Playoffs					
1972–73	Cleveland	9	8	3	11

JOHNSON, Danny *Forward*
b. Winnipegosis, Man., Oct. 1, 1944

Season	Club	GP	G	A	Pts
1972–73	Winnipeg	77	19	23	42
Playoffs					
1972–73	Winnipeg	14	4	1	5

JOHNSON, Jim *Forward*
b. Winnipeg, Man., Nov. 7, 1942

Season	Club	GP	G	A	Pts
1972-73	Minnesota	33	9	14	23
Playoffs					
1972-73	Minnesota	5	2	1	3

JONES, Bob *Forward*
b. Espanola, Ont., Nov. 27, 1945

Season	Club	GP	G	A	Pts
1972-73	LA-New York	76	13	19	32

JORDAN, Ric *Defenseman*
b. Toronto, Ont., March 31, 1950

Season	Club	GP	G	A	Pts
1972-73	New England	34	1	5	6
Playoffs					
1972-73	New England	4	0	0	0

JOYAL, Ed *Forward*
b. Edmonton, Alberta, May 8, 1940

Season	Club	GP	G	A	Pts
1972-73	Alberta	71	22	16	38

KANNEGIESSER, Gordon *Defenseman*
b. North Bay, Ont., Dec. 21, 1945

Season	Club	GP	G	A	Pts
1972-73	Houston	45	0	10	10
Playoffs					
1972-73	Houston	9	0	1	1

KASSIAN, Dennis *Forward*
b. Vegreville, Alberta, July 14, 1941

Season	Club	GP	G	A	Pts
1972-73	Alberta	50	6	7	13

KENNEDY, Jamie *Forward*
b. Dorchester, N.B., Sept. 7, 1946

Season	Club	GP	G	A	Pts
1972-73	New York	52	4	6	10

KING, Steve *Forward*
b. Toronto, Ont., Sept. 8, 1948

Season	Club	GP	G	A	Pts
1972-73	Ottawa	69	18	34	52
Playoffs					
1972-73	Ottawa	5	0	1	1

KIRK, Gavin *Forward*
b. London, England, Dec. 6, 1951

Season	Club	GP	G	A	Pts
1972-73	Ottawa	78	28	40	68
Playoffs					
1972-73	Ottawa	5	2	3	5

KLATT, Billy *Forward*
b. Minneapolis, Minn., Oct. 16, 1947

Season	Club	GP	G	A	Pts
1972-73	Minnesota	78	36	22	58
Playoffs					
1972-73	Minnesota	5	1	3	4

KNIBBS, Darrel *Forward*
b. Medicine Hat, Alberta, Sept. 21, 1949

Season	Club	GP	G	A	Pts
1972-73	Chicago	41	3	8	11

KONIK, George *Defenseman*
b. Flin Flon, Man., May 4, 1938

Season	Club	GP	G	A	Pts
1972-73	Minnesota	54	4	12	16

KRAKE, Skip *Forward*
b. North Battleford, Sas., Oct. 14, 1943

Season	Club	GP	G	A	Pts
1972-73	Cleveland	28	9	10	19
Playoffs					
1972-73	Cleveland	9	1	2	3

KRUPICKA, Jarda *Forward*
b. Bruno, Czechoslovakia, March 15, 1946

Season	Club	GP	G	A	Pts
1972-73	LA-New York	36	2	2	4

KURT, Gary *Goalie*
b. Kitchener, Ont., March 9, 1947

Season	Club	GP	GA	Sho	AVE
1972-73	New York	36	150	0	4.78

LABOSSIERE, Gordon *Forward*
b. St. Boniface, Man., Jan. 2, 1940

Season	Club	GP	G	A	Pts
1972-73	Houston	77	36	60	96
Playoffs					
1972-73	Houston	6	1	4	5

LACOMBE, Francis *Defenseman*
b. Montreal, Quebec, Feb. 24, 1948

Season	Club	GP	G	A	Pts
1972-73	Quebec	62	10	18	28

LACROIX, Andre *Forward*
b. Lauzon, Que., June 5, 1945

Season	Club	GP	G	A	Pts
1972-73	Philadelphia	78	50	74	124
Playoffs					
1972-73	Philadelphia	4	0	2	2

LANDON, Bruce *Goalie*
b. Kingston, Ont., Oct. 5, 1949

Season	Club	GP	GA	Sho	AVE
1972-73	New England	30	100	1	3.59

LAPIERRE, Camille *Forward*
b. Chicoutimi, Que., Feb. 8, 1951

Season	Club	GP	G	A	Pts
1972-73	Philadelphia	24	5	9	14
Playoffs					
1972-73	Philadelphia	4	0	2	2

LAROSE, Paul *Forward*
b. Noranda, Quebec, Jan. 11, 1950

Season	Club	GP	G	A	Pts
1972-73	Quebec	28	0	7	7

LAROSE, Ray *Defenseman*
b. Quebec City, Que., Nov. 20, 1941

Season	Club	GP	G	A	Pts
1972-73	Houston	68	1	10	11
Playoffs					
1972-73	Houston	8	0	0	0

LAUGHTON, Mike *Forward*
b. Nelson, B.C., Feb. 21, 1944

Season	Club	GP	G	A	Pts
1972-73	New York	67	16	20	36

LAWSON, Danny *Forward*
b. Toronto, Ont., Oct. 30, 1947

Season	Club	GP	G	A	Pts
1972-73	Philadelphia	78	61	45	106
Playoffs					
1972-73	Philadelphia	4	0	1	1

LeBLANC, Jean-Paul *Forward*
b. South Durham, Que., Oct. 20, 1946

Season	Club	GP	G	A	Pts
1972-73	Los Angeles	77	19	50	69
Playoffs					
1972-73	Los Angeles	6	0	5	5

LECLERC, Renald *Forward*
b. Ville de Vanier, Quebec, Nov. 12, 1947

Season	Club	GP	G	A	Pts
1972-73	Quebec	67	24	28	52

LEDUC, Bob *Forward*
b. Sudbury, Ont., May 24, 1944

Season	Club	GP	G	A	Pts
1972-73	Ottawa	78	22	33	55
Playoffs					
1972-73	Ottawa	5	0	2	2

LEMELIN, Jacques *Goalie*
b. Quebec City, Nov. 11, 1949

Season	Club	GP	GA	Sho	AVE
1972-73	Quebec	9	29	0	4.00

LEY, Rick *Defenseman*
b. Orillia, Ont., Nov. 2, 1948

Season	Club	GP	G	A	Pts
1972-73	New England	76	3	27	30
Playoffs					
1972-73	New England	15	3	7	10

LIDDINGTON, Bob *Forward*
b. Calgary, Alberta, Sept. 14, 1948

Season	Club	GP	G	A	Pts
1972-73	Chicago	78	20	11	31

LILYHOLM, Len *Forward*
b. Minneapolis, Minn., April 1, 1941

Season	Club	GP	G	A	Pts
1972-73	Minnesota	77	8	13	21
Playoffs					
1972-73	Minnesota	5	1	0	1

LODBOA, Dan *Forward*
b. Thorold, Ont., Sept. 25, 1946

Season	Club	GP	G	A	Pts
1972-73	Chicago	59	15	18	33

LUND, Larry *Forward*
b. Penticton, B.C., Sept. 9, 1940

Season	Club	GP	G	A	Pts
1972-73	Houston	77	21	45	66
Playoffs					
1972-73	Houston	10	3	7	10

MacMILLAN, Bob *Forward*
b. Charlottetown, P.E.I., Dec. 3, 1952

Season	Club	GP	G	A	Pts
1972-73	Minnesota	75	13	27	40
Playoffs					
1972-73	Minnesota	5	0	3	3

MacNEIL, Bernie *Forward*
b. Sudbury, Ont., March 7, 1950

Season	Club	GP	G	A	Pts
1972-73	Los Angeles	41	4	7	11
Playoffs					
1972-73	Los Angeles	3	0	0	0

MacSWEYN, Ralph *Defenseman*
b. Hawkesbury, Ont., Sept. 8, 1942

Season	Club	GP	G	A	Pts
1972–73	Los Angeles	78	0	23	23
Playoffs					
1972–73	Los Angeles	6	1	2	3

MARTIN, Tom *Forward*
b. Toronto, Ont., Oct. 16, 1947

Season	Club	GP	G	A	Pts
1972–73	Ottawa	74	19	27	46
Playoffs					
1972–73	Ottawa	5	0	5	5

MAVETY, Larry *Defenseman*
b. Woodstock, Ont., May 29, 1942

Season	Club	GP	G	A	Pts
1972–73	LA–Phil–Chicago	73	10	40	50

McANEELEY, Bob *Forward*
b. Prince George, B.C., Nov. 7, 1950

Season	Club	GP	G	A	Pts
1972–73	Alberta	51	5	7	12

MCCALLUM, Dunc *Defenseman*
b. Flin Flon, Man., March 29, 1940

Season	Club	GP	G	A	Pts
1972–73	Houston	69	9	20	29
Playoffs					
1972–73	Houston	10	2	3	5

McCARTAN, Jack *Goalie*
b. St. Paul, Minn., Aug. 5, 1935

Season	Club	GP	GA	Sho	AVE
1972–73	Minnesota	38	129	1	3.58
Playoffs					
1972–73	Minnesota	4	14	0	3.94

McCASKILL, Ted *Forward*
b. Kapuskasing, Ont., Oct. 29, 1936

Season	Club	GP	G	A	Pts
1972–73	Los Angeles	73	11	11	22
Playoffs					
1972–73	Los Angeles	6	2	3	5

McDONALD, Ab *Forward*
b. Winnipeg, Man., Feb. 18, 1936

Season	Club	GP	G	A	Pts
1972–73	Winnipeg	77	17	24	41
Playoffs					
1972–73	Winnipeg	14	2	5	7

McDONALD, Brian *Forward*
b. Toronto, Ont., March 23, 1945

Season	Club	GP	G	A	Pts
1972–73	Houston	71	20	20	40
Playoffs					
1972–73	Houston	10	3	0	3

McGLYNN, Dick *Defenseman*
b. Medford, Mass., July 19, 1948

Season	Club	GP	G	A	Pts
1972–73	Chicago	30	0	0	0

MCKENZIE, John *Forward*
b. High River, Alberta, Dec. 2, 1937

Season	Club	GP	G	A	Pts
1972–73	Philadelphia	60	28	50	78
Playoffs					
1972–73	Philadelphia	4	3	1	4

MCLEOD, Don *Goalie*
b. Trail, B.C., Aug. 24, 1946

Season	Club	GP	GA	Sho	AVE
1972–73	Houston	40	143	1	3.65
Playoffs					
1972–73	Houston	3	8	0	2.69

McLEOD, Jim *Goalie*
b. Arthur, Ont., April 7, 1937

Season	Club	GP	GA	Sho	AVE
1972–73	Chicago	49⅓	166	1	3.36

McMAHON, Mike *Defenseman*
b. Quebec City, Aug. 30, 1941

Season	Club	GP	G	A	Pts
1972–73	Minnesota	75	12	39	51
Playoffs					
1972–73	Minnesota	5	0	5	5

McMASTERS, Jim *Defenseman*
b. Nanton, Alberta, Sept. 20, 1952

Season	Club	GP	G	A	Pts
1972–73	Cleveland	76	1	7	8
Playoffs					
1972–73	Cleveland	9	0	1	1

McNAMARA, Mike *Forward*
b. March 28, 1949

Season	Club	GP	G	A	Pts
1972–73	Quebec	19	0	0	0

MELOCHE, Denis *Forward*

Season	Club	GP	G	A	Pts
1972–73	Philadelphia	4	1	1	2

MELOFF, Chris *Defenseman*
b. Toronto, Ont., May 7, 1952

Season	Club	GP	G	A	Pts
1972-73	Ottawa	28	1	6	7

MENARD, Paul *Goalie*

Season	Club	GP	GA	Sho	AVE
1972-73	Chicago	⅔	5	0	7.50

MIGNEAULT, John *Defenseman*
b. Thompkins, Sas., Feb. 4, 1949

Season	Club	GP	G	A	Pts
1972-73	Philadelphia	55	10	8	18
Playoffs					
1972-73	Philadelphia	4	0	0	0

MORENZ, Brian *Forward*
b. Brampton, Ont., Sept. 28, 1948

Season	Club	GP	G	A	Pts
1972-73	New York	32	7	1	8

MORRIS, Rick *Forward*
b. Hamilton, Ont., July 5, 1946

Season	Club	GP	G	A	Pts
1972-73	Chicago	76	31	17	48

MORRISON, George *Forward*
b. Toronto, Ont., Dec. 24, 1948

Season	Club	GP	G	A	Pts
1972-73	Minnesota	70	16	24	40
Playoffs					
1972-73	Minnesota	5	1	1	2

MORTSON, Keke *Forward*
b. Arntfeld, Que., March 29, 1934

Season	Club	GP	G	A	Pts
1972-73	Houston	69	13	16	29
Playoffs					
1972-73	Houston	10	0	3	3

MOSDELL, Wayne *Defenseman*
b. Dec. 4, 1944

Season	Club	GP	G	A	Pts
1972-73	Philadelphia	9	0	1	1

MOTT, Darwin

Season	Club	GP	G	A	Pts
1972-73	Philadelphia	1	0	0	0

MULOIN, Wayne *Defenseman*
b. Dryden, Ont., Dec. 24, 1941

Season	Club	GP	G	A	Pts
1972-73	Cleveland	67	2	13	15
Playoffs					
1972-73	Cleveland	9	1	3	4

MYERS, Murray *Forward*

Season	Club	GP	G	A	Pts
1972-73	Philadelphia	7	0	0	0
Playoffs					
1972-73	Philadelphia	2	0	0	0

NIEKAMP, Jim *Defenseman*
b. Detroit, Mich., March 11, 1946

Season	Club	GP	G	A	Pts
1972-73	Los Angeles	78	7	22	29
Playoffs					
1972-73	Los Angeles	6	2	1	3

NORRIS, Jack *Goalie*
b. Saskatoon, Sas., Aug. 5, 1942

Season	Club	GP	GA	Sho	AVE
1972-73	Alberta	64	189	1	3.06

O'DONOGHUE, Don *Forward*
b. Kingston, Ont., Aug. 27, 1949

Season	Club	GP	G	A	Pts
1972-73	Philadelphia	74	16	23	39
Playoffs					
1972-73	Philadelphia	4	0	1	1

ODROWSKI, Gerry *Defenseman*
b. Trout Creek, Ont., Oct. 4, 1938

Season	Club	GP	G	A	Pts
1972-73	Los Angeles	78	6	31	37
Playoffs					
1972-73	Los Angeles	6	1	2	3

OLDS, Wally *Defenseman*
b. Warroad, Minn., Aug. 17, 1949

Season	Club	GP	G	A	Pts
1972-73	New York	61	5	7	12

PAIEMENT, Pierre *Forward*

Season	Club	GP	G	A	Pts
1972-73	Philadelphia	8	1	0	1

PAIEMENT, Rosaire *Forward*
b. Earlton, Ont., Aug. 12, 1945

Season	Club	GP	G	A	Pts
1972-73	Chicago	78	33	36	69

PAILLE, Marcel *Goalie*
b. Shawinigan Falls, Que., Dec. 8, 1932

Season	Club	GP	GA	Sho	AVE
1972-73	Philadelphia	15	48	0	4.81
Playoffs					
1972-73	Philadelphia	1	5	0	11.46

PARADISE, Dick *Defenseman*
b. St. Paul, Minn., April 21, 1945

Season	Club	GP	G	A	Pts
1972-73	Minnesota	77	3	15	18
Playoffs					
1972-73	Minnesota	5	0	1	1

PARENT, Bernie *Goalie*
b. Montreal, Que., April 3, 1945

Season	Club	GP	GA	Sho	AVE
1972-73	Philadelphia	63	220	2	3.61
Playoffs					
1972-73	Philadelphia	1	3	0	2.57

PARIZEAU, Michel *Forward*
b. Montreal, Quebec, April 9, 1948

Season	Club	GP	G	A	Pts
1972-73	Quebec	75	25	48	73

PATENAUDE, Rusty *Forward*
b. Williams Lake, B.C., Oct. 17, 1949

Season	Club	GP	G	A	Pts
1972-73	Alberta	78	29	27	56

PAYETTE, Jean *Forward*
b. Cornwall, Ontario, March 29, 1946

Season	Club	GP	G	A	Pts
1972-73	Quebec	71	15	29	44

PEACOSH, Gene *Forward*
b. Sherridon, Man., Sept. 28, 1948

Season	Club	GP	G	A	Pts
1972-73	New York	67	37	34	71

PEARSON, Mel *Forward*
b. Flin Flon, Man., April 29, 1938

Season	Club	GP	G	A	Pts
1972-73	Minnesota	70	8	12	20
Playoffs					
1972-73	Minnesota	5	2	0	2

PERKINS, Ross *Forward*
b. Tisdale, Sas., Nov. 4, 1946

Season	Club	GP	G	A	Pts
1972-73	Alberta	71	21	37	58

PERREAULT, Bob *Goalie*
b. Three Rivers, Que., Jan. 28, 1931

Season	Club	GP	GA	Sho	AVE
1972-73	Los Angeles	1	2	0	2.00

PERRY, Brian *Forward*
b. Aldershort, England, April 6, 1944

Season	Club	GP	G	A	Pts
1972-73	New York	74	13	20	33

PETERS, Garry *Forward*
b. Regina, Sas., Oct. 9, 1942

Season	Club	GP	G	A	Pts
1972-73	New York	23	2	7	9

PINDER, Gerry *Forward*
b. Saskatoon, Sas., Sept. 15, 1948

Season	Club	GP	G	A	Pts
1972-73	Cleveland	78	30	36	66
Playoffs					
1972-73	Cleveland	9	2	9	11

PLANTE, Michel *Forward*
b. Drummondville, Que., Jan. 19, 1952

Season	Club	GP	G	A	Pts
1972-73	Philadelphia	70	13	12	25
Playoffs					
1972-73	Philadelphia	4	0	0	0

PLEAU, Larry *Forward*
b. Boston, Mass., June 29, 1947

Season	Club	GP	G	A	Pts
1972-73	New England	78	39	48	87
Playoffs					
1972-73	New England	15	12	7	19

PLUMB, Ron *Defenseman*
b. Kingston, Ont., July 17, 1950

Season	Club	GP	G	A	Pts
1972-73	Philadelphia	78	10	41	51
Playoffs					
1972-73	Philadelphia	4	0	2	2

POLANO, Nick *Defenseman*
b. Sudbury, Ont., March 25, 1941

Season	Club	GP	G	A	Pts
1972-73	Philadelphia	17	0	3	3

POPIEL, Jan *Forward*
b. Virum, Denmark, Oct. 9, 1947

Season	Club	GP	G	A	Pts
1972-73	Chicago	76	31	34	65

POPIEL, Poul *Defenseman*
  b. Sollested, Denmark, Feb. 28, 1943

Season	Club	GP	G	A	Pts
1972-73	Houston	73	16	48	64
Playoffs					
1972-73	Houston	10	2	9	11

PRENTICE, Bill *Defenseman*
  b. Lindsay, Ont., Aug. 3, 1950

Season	Club	GP	G	A	Pts
1972-73	Houston	3	0	1	1

PROCEVIAT, Dick *Defenseman*
  b. Whitemouth, Man., June 25, 1946

Season	Club	GP	G	A	Pts
1972-73	Chicago	56	4	14	18

PUMPLE, Rich *Forward*
  b. Kirkland Lake, Ont., Nov. 2, 1948

Season	Club	GP	G	A	Pts
1972-73	Cleveland	78	21	20	41
Playoffs					
1972-73	Cleveland	9	3	5	8

REICHMUTH, Craig *Forward*
  b. Russell, Man., Sept. 22, 1947

Season	Club	GP	G	A	Pts
1972-73	New York	73	13	14	27

RILEY, Ron *Forward*
  b. July 20, 1948

Season	Club	GP	G	A	Pts
1972-73	Ottawa	22	0	5	5
Playoffs					
1972-73	Ottawa	2	0	0	0

RIVERS, Wayne *Forward*
  b. Hamilton, Ont., Feb. 1, 1940

Season	Club	GP	G	A	Pts
1972-73	New York	75	37	40	77

RIZZUTO, Garth *Forward*
  b. Trail, B.C., Sept. 11, 1947

Season	Club	GP	G	A	Pts
1972-73	Winnipeg	63	10	10	20
Playoffs					
1972-73	Winnipeg	14	0	1	1

ROULEAU, Michel (Mike) *Forward*
  b. Hull, Quebec, Sept. 28, 1944

Season	Club	GP	G	A	Pts
1972-73	Phil-Quebec	58	7	15	22

ROUSSEAU, Dunc *Forward*
  b. Bissett, Man., Feb. 10, 1945

Season	Club	GP	G	A	Pts
1972-73	Winnipeg	75	16	17	33
Playoffs					
1972-73	Winnipeg	14	3	2	5

ROY, Pierre *Defenseman*
  b. Amos, Abitibi, Quebec, March 12, 1952

Season	Club	GP	G	A	Pts
1972-73	Quebec	64	7	12	19

RUTLEDGE, Wayne *Goalie*
  b. Barrie, Ont., Jan. 5, 1942

Season	Club	GP	GA	Sho	AVE
1972-73	Houston	37	110	0	2.96
Playoffs					
1972-73	Houston	7	20	0	2.83

RYAN, Terry *Forward*
  b. Grand Falls, New., Sept. 10, 1952

Season	Club	GP	G	A	Pts
1972-73	Minnesota	76	13	6	19
Playoffs					
1972-73	Minnesota	5	0	2	2

RYCROFT, Al *Forward*
  b. Beaver Lodge, Alberta, Jan. 1, 1950

Season	Club	GP	G	A	Pts
1972-73	Cleveland	7	0	2	2

RYDMAN, Blaine *Defenseman*
  b. Weyburn, Sas., Dec. 16, 1949

Season	Club	GP	G	A	Pts
1972-73	Minnesota	31	0	1	1
Playoffs					
1972-73	Minnesota	1	0	0	0

SANDERS, Frank *Defenseman*
  b. North St. Paul, Minn., March 8, 1949

Season	Club	GP	G	A	Pts
1972-73	Minnesota	76	8	8	16
Playoffs					
1972-73	Minnesota	4	0	1	1

SARRAZIN, Dick *Forward*
  b. St. Gabriel, Que., Jan. 22, 1946

Season	Club	GP	G	A	Pts
1972-73	N E-Chicago	67	7	15	22

SANDERSON, Derek *Forward*
b. Niagara Falls, Ont., June 16, 1946

Season	Club	GP	G	A	Pts
1972–73	Philadelphia	8	3	3	6

SCHARF, Ted *Forward*
b. Sudbury, Ont., Oct. 3, 1951

Season	Club	GP	G	A	Pts
1972–73	New York	29	2	2	4

SCHELLA, John *Defenseman*
b. Port Arthur, Ont., May 9, 1947

Season	Club	GP	G	A	Pts
1972–73	Houston	77	2	24	26
Playoffs					
1972–73	Houston	10	0	2	2

SELBY, Britt *Forward*
b. Kingston, Ont., March 27, 1945

Season	Club	GP	G	A	Pts
1972–73	Quebec–N E	72	13	30	43
Playoffs					
1972–73	New England	13	3	4	7

SELWOOD, Brad *Defenseman*
b. Learnington, Ont., March 18, 1949

Season	Club	GP	G	A	Pts
1972–73	New England	75	13	21	34
Playoffs					
1972–73	New England	15	3	5	8

SENTES, Rick *Forward*
b. Regina, Sas., Jan. 10, 1947

Season	Club	GP	G	A	Pts
1972–73	Ottawa	74	22	19	41
Playoffs					
1972–73	Ottawa	5	3	1	4

SERVISS, Tom *Forward*
b. Moose Jaw, Sas., May 25, 1948

Season	Club	GP	G	A	Pts
1972–73	Los Angeles	73	11	26	37
Playoffs					
1972–73	Los Angeles	6	0	0	0

SHEEHAN, Bobby *Forward*
b. Weymouth, Mass., Aug. 12, 1949

Season	Club	GP	G	A	Pts
1972–73	New York	75	35	53	88

SHEEHY, Tim *Forward*
b. Ft. Francis, Ont., Sept. 3, 1948

Season	Club	GP	G	A	Pts
1972–73	New England	78	33	38	71
Playoffs					
1972–73	New England	15	9	14	23

SHMYR, John *Defenseman*
b. Cudworth, Sas., Jan. 2, 1945

Season	Club	GP	G	A	Pts
1972–73	Winnipeg	7	0	0	0

SHMYR, Paul *Defenseman*
b. Cudworth, Sas., Jan. 28, 1946

Season	Club	GP	G	A	Pts
1972–73	Cleveland	73	5	44	49
Playoffs					
1972–73	Cleveland	8	1	3	4

SICINSKI, Bobby *Forward*
b. Toronto, Ont., Nov. 13, 1946

Season	Club	GP	G	A	Pts
1972–73	Chicago	77	25	63	88

SIMPSON, Tom *Forward*
b. Oshawa, Ont., Aug. 15, 1952

Season	Club	GP	G	A	Pts
1972–73	Ottawa	57	10	7	17
Playoffs					
1972–73	Ottawa	5	1	0	1

SLATER, Peter *Forward*
b. Renfrew, Ont., Jan. 31, 1948

Season	Club	GP	G	A	Pts
1972–73	Los Angeles	72	12	12	24
Playoffs					
1972–73	Los Angeles	6	0	0	0

SMITH, Al *Goalie*
b. Toronto, Ont., Nov. 10, 1945

Season	Club	GP	GA	Sho	AVE
1972–73	New England	51	162	3	3.17
Playoffs					
1972–73	New England	15	49	0	3.23

SMITH, Brian *Forward*
b. Ottawa, Ont., Sept. 6, 1940

Season	Club	GP	G	A	Pts
1972–73	Houston	48	7	6	13
Playoffs					
1972–73	Houston	10	0	2	2

SMITH, Guy *Forward*
b. Ottawa, Ont., Jan. 2, 1950

Season	Club	GP	G	A	Pts
1972–73	New England	22	3	4	7
Playoffs					
1972–73	New England	11	2	0	2

SPECK, Fred *Forward*
b. Thorold, Ont., July 22, 1947

Season	Club	GP	G	A	Pts
1972–73	Minn–LA	75	16	29	45
Playoffs					
1972–73	Los Angeles	6	3	2	5

SPEER, Bill *Defenseman*
b. Lindsay, Ont., March 20, 1942

Season	Club	GP	G	A	Pts
1972–73	New York	69	3	23	26

SPENCER, Irv *Defenseman*
b. Sudbury, Ont., Dec. 4, 1937

Season	Club	GP	G	A	Pts
1972–73	Philadelphia	54	2	27	29
Playoffs					
1972–73	Philadelphia	4	0	0	0

STANFIELD, Jack *Forward*
b. Toronto, Ont., May 30, 1942

Season	Club	GP	G	A	Pts
1972–73	Houston	71	8	12	20
Playoffs					
1972–73	Houston	9	1	0	1

ST. SAUVEUR, Claude *Forward*

Season	Club	GP	G	A	Pts
1972–73	Philadelphia	2	1	0	1

STEPHANSON, Ken *Defenseman*
b. Nov. 13, 1941

Season	Club	GP	G	A	Pts
1972–73	Ottawa	77	3	16	19
Playoffs					
1972–73	Ottawa	5	1	1	2

SULLIVAN, Danny *Goalie*

Season	Club	GP	GA	Sho	AVE
1972–73	Philadelphia	1	3	0	3.00

SUTHERLAND, Bill *Forward*
b. Regina, Sas., April 16, 1934

Season	Club	GP	G	A	Pts
1972–73	Winnipeg	49	6	16	22
Playoffs					
1972–73	Winnipeg	14	5	9	14

SUTHERLAND, Steve *Forward*
b. Sept. 1, 1946

Season	Club	GP	G	A	Pts
1972–73	Los Angeles	43	11	6	17
Playoffs					
1972–73	Los Angeles	6	0	2	2

SWENSON, Cal *Forward*
b. Watson, Sas., April 16, 1948

Season	Club	GP	G	A	Pts
1972–73	Winnipeg	75	7	21	28
Playoffs					
1972–73	Winnipeg	14	1	5	6

SZURA, Joe *Forward*
b. Fort William, Ont., Dec. 18, 1938

Season	Club	GP	G	A	Pts
1972–73	Los Angeles	73	13	32	45
Playoffs					
1972–73	Los Angeles	2	0	0	0

TAYLOR, Ted *Forward*
b. Oak Leaf, Man., Feb. 25, 1942

Season	Club	GP	G	A	Pts
1972–73	Houston	72	34	42	76
Playoffs					
1972–73	Houston	10	3	1	4

TREMBLAY, Jean Claude (J.C.) *Defenseman*
b. Bagotville, Quebec, Jan. 22, 1939

Season	Club	GP	G	A	Pts
1972–73	Quebec	75	14	75	89

TROOIEN, Jerry *Defenseman*

Season	Club	GP	G	A	Pts
1972–73	Chicago	2	0	0	0

TROTTIER, Guy *Forward*
b. Hull, Que., April 1, 1941

Season	Club	GP	G	A	Pts
1972–73	Ottawa	72	26	32	58
Playoffs					
1972–73	Ottawa	5	1	2	3

TUMILSON, Gordon *Goalie*
b. Winnipeg, Man., July 17, 1951

Season	Club	GP	GA	Sho	AVE
1972–73	Winnipeg	3	10	0	4.34

VIAU, Pierre *Defenseman*
b. Montreal, Que., Jan. 29, 1952

Season	Club	GP	G	A	Pts
1972–73	Chicago	4	0	0	0

WAKELY, Ernie *Goalie*
b. Flin Flon, Man., Nov. 27, 1940

Season	Club	GP	GA	Sho	AVE
1972–73	Winnipeg	49	152	2	3.15
Playoffs					
1972–73	Winnipeg	7	22	2	3.14

WALL, Bob *Defenseman*
b. Richmond Hill, Ont., Dec. 1, 1942

Season	Club	GP	G	A	Pts
1972–73	Alberta	78	16	29	45

WALTERS, Ron *Forward*
b. Castor, Alberta, March 9, 1948

Season	Club	GP	G	A	Pts
1972–73	Alberta	78	28	26	54

WARD, Ron *Forward*
b. Cornwall, Ont., Sept. 12, 1944

Season	Club	GP	G	A	Pts
1972–73	New York	77	51	67	118

WARR, Steve *Defenseman*
b. Peterborough, Ont., Jan. 5, 1951

Season	Club	GP	G	A	Pts
1972–73	Ottawa	72	3	8	11
Playoffs					
1972–73	Ottawa	2	0	0	0

WEBSTER, Tom *Forward*
b. Kirkland, Ont., Oct. 4, 1948

Season	Club	GP	G	A	Pts
1972–73	New England	77	53	50	103
Playoffs					
1972–73	New England	15	12	14	26

WETZEL, Carl *Goalie*
b. Detroit, Mich., Dec. 12, 1948

Season	Club	GP	GA	Sho	AVE
1972–73	Minnesota	1	3	0	3.00

WHIDDEN, Bob *Goalie*
b. Sudbury, Ont., July 27, 1946

Season	Club	GP	GA	Sho	AVE
1972–73	Cleveland	26	88	0	3.28

WHITE, Alton *Forward*
b. Amherst, N.S., May 31, 1945

Season	Club	GP	G	A	Pts
1972–73	NY–Los Ang	70	21	21	42
Playoffs					
1972–73	Los Angeles	6	1	0	1

WHITLOCK, Bob *Forward*
b. Charlottetown, P.E.I., July 16, 1949

Season	Club	GP	G	A	Pts
1972–73	Chicago	75	23	28	51

WILKIE, Ian *Goalie*
b. Edmonton, Alberta, July 20, 1949

Season	Club	GP	GA	Sho	AVE
1972–73	New York	5	27	0	6.40

WILLIAMS, Tom *Forward*
b. Duluth, Minn., April 17, 1940

Season	Club	GP	G	A	Pts
1972–73	New England	69	10	21	31
Playoffs					
1972–73	New England	15	6	11	17

WILLIS, Hal *Defenseman*
b. Liverpool, N.S., June 8, 1946

Season	Club	GP	G	A	Pts
1972–73	New York	74	3	21	24

WINOGRAD, Bob *Defenseman*
b. Winnipeg, Man., June 6, 1950

Season	Club	GP	G	A	Pts
1972–73	New York	52	0	12	12

WISTE, Jim *Forward*
b. Moose Jaw, Sas., Feb. 8, 1946

Season	Club	GP	G	A	Pts
1972–73	Cleveland	70	28	43	71
Playoffs					
1972–73	Cleveland	9	3	8	11

WOYTOWICH, Bob *Defenseman*
b. Winnipeg, Man., Aug. 18, 1941

Season	Club	GP	G	A	Pts
1972–73	Winnipeg	62	2	4	6
Playoffs					
1972–73	Winnipeg	14	1	1	2

VENERUZZO, Gary *Forward*
b. Fort William, Ont., June 28, 1943

Season	Club	GP	G	A	Pts
1972–73	Los Angeles	78	43	30	73
Playoffs					
1972–73	Los Angeles	6	3	0	3

WATSON, Jim *Defenseman*
b. Malartic, Que., June 28, 1943

Season	Club	GP	G	A	Pts
1972–73	Los Angeles	75	5	15	20
Playoffs					
1972–73	Los Angeles	4	0	1	1

YOUNG, Bill *Forward*

b. St. Catharines, Ont., July 5, 1947

Season	Club	GP	G	A	Pts
1972–73	LA–Minn	73	19	18	37

Playoffs

1972–73	Minnesota	5	1	1	2

ZAINE, Rod *Forward*

b. Ottawa, Ont., May 18, 1946

Season	Club	GP	G	A	Pts
1972–73	Chicago	72	3	14	17

ZANUSSI, Joe *Defenseman*

b. Rossland, B.C., Sept. 25, 1947

Season	Club	GP	G	A	Pts
1972–73	Winnipeg	73	4	21	25

Playoffs

1972–73	Winnipeg	14	2	5	7

ZERMIAK, Jerry *Defenseman*

Season	Club	GP	G	A	Pts
1972–73	Los Angeles	1	0	0	0

Playoffs

1972–73	Los Angeles	2	1	0	1

GLOSSARY

Attacking Zone—Area from an opponent's blue line to goal line.

Back Checking—To check an opponent in your defending zone.

Blue Lines—Two lines, one at each end of the rink, 60 feet from the goal line, which define the attacking zone. They are also used to determine off-sides. No attacking player may precede the puck over the defending team's blue line.

Board Checking—To ride or drive an opponent into the dasher boards. Often results in a minor penalty.

Body Check—To use your body to block or hit an opponent. Legal only when the man hit has the puck or was the last player to have touched it.

Charging—If more than three strides are taken before checking an opponent, it is charging. Illegal and calls for a minor penalty.

Checking—Defending against or guarding an opponent. On a line, a right wing checks the other team's left wing and a left wing checks the opposing right wing. Centers check each other. Checking requires harassing an opposing skater with the aim of making him surrender the puck.

Crease—The rectangular area marked off in front of each net. Only a goalie is permitted in the crease and no player may score from there unless he is being pinned in by a defending player.

Cross Checking—To hit an opponent with both hands on the stick and no part of the stick on the ice. Illegal and calls for a penalty.

Curved Stick—A stick with a concave rather than flat blade.

Defending Zone—The area from a team's goal line to its blue line.

Deke—To feint or shift an opponent out of position.

Elbowing—Hitting an opponent with the elbow. Illegal and calls for a minor penalty.

Face-Off—The dropping of the puck between two opposing players to start play. Face-offs follow goals or other stoppages of action and are to hockey what the jump ball is to basketball.

Fore-checking—Checking the opponent in his own zone.

Freezing the Puck—Pinning the puck against the boards with either your skate or stick to force a stoppage of play and a face-off. Sometimes can result in a delay of game penalty if no opposing player is on the puck.

Hat Trick—Three (or more) goals by a single player in a game.

Head-manning—Always advancing the puck to a teammate up ice. Never retreating. This is a favorite maneuver of the Montreal Canadiens.

High Sticking—The carrying of the stick above shoulder level. Always illegal and calls for a minor penalty if one player hits another in this way or a face-off if no other infraction occurs.

Holding—To use your hands on an opponent or his equipment. Illegal and calls for a minor penalty.

Hooking—To impede an opponent with the blade of your stick. Illegal and calls for a minor penalty.

Icing the Puck—Shooting the puck from behind the center red line across an opponent's goal line. Usually done to break up an attack and ease pressure. The puck is brought back and a face-off takes place in the defensive zone of the team that iced the puck. No icing is called against a team that is short-handed because of a penalty.

Interference—Body contact with a man not in possession of the puck or who was not the last man to touch the puck. Also called for knocking an opponent's fallen stick out of his reach. Illegal and calls for a minor penalty.

Kneeing—Using the knee to check an opponent. Illegal and calls for a minor penalty.

Major Penalty—A five minute penalty. (For example, for fighting or spearing.)

Match Penalty—Suspension for the balance of the game.

Minor Penalty—A two-minute penalty. Most penalties are minors.

Misconduct Penalty—A 10-minute penalty against an individual, not a team. A substitute is permitted. Called for various forms of unacceptable behavior or when a player incurs a second major penalty in a game.

Neutral Zone—That area between blue lines. The center ice area.

Off-Sides—Called when an attacking player precedes the puck across the opponent's blue line. Illegal and calls for a face-off.

Off-Sides Pass—Called when the puck is passed to a teammate across two or more lines. Illegal and calls for a face-off from point where the pass originated.

Penalty Killer—A player whose job it is to use up time while a teammate is serving a penalty. The best penalty killers are fast skaters who can break up a power play. Once in possession of the puck, the penalty killer tries to hold onto it and seldom tries to attack. He is content to waste time until his team is at full strength again.

Playmaker—Usually a center whose skating and puck-carrying ability enable him to set up or make a play that can lead to a goal.

Poke Check—The quick thrust of the stick to take a puck away from an opposing player. Usually done best by defensemen rather than forwards. Legal.

Power Play—A manpower advantage resulting from a penalty to the opposing team. Usually four forwards and one defenseman will be used to increase the attacking team's scoring potential.

Puck—The vulcanized rubber disc used in hockey.

Red Line—The line that divides the ice in half. Allows defending teams to clear the puck out of the defensive zone up to mid-ice without incurring an off-sides.

Roughing—Minor fisticuffs or shoving. Illegal and calls for a minor penalty.

Slap Shot—When a player winds and slaps his stick at the puck. Usually a player's strongest shot.

Slashing—To swing stick at an opponent. Illegal and calls for a minor penalty.

Spearing—To use the stick as one would a spear. Illegal and calls for a major penalty.

Stick Handling—The art of carrying the puck with the stick.

Sweep Check—To swing stick along the ice to intercept the puck or hamper an opponent. Legal.

Wash-Out—Disallowing of a goal by a referee; or disallowing of icing or off-sides by a linesman.

INDEX

All persons who appear in the encyclopedia are indexed with the exception of those whose names appear only in the alphabetical National Hockey League Player Register (Chapter XV); the alphabetical World Hockey Association Register (Chapter XVI); the tabular material covering All-Star team members (Chapter IX); trophy winners (Chapter XI); and the 1973–74 Season Roundup which follows this index. **Boldface numerals** denote page references to photo captions.

THE 1973-74 SEASON ROUNDUP

To supplement this revised edition, the 1973–74 season follows in its entirety.

Captain Bobby Clarke says it all for Philadelphia as he quaffs champagne from the Stanley Cup. UPI

NATIONAL HOCKEY LEAGUE

Ever since 1967, when the National Hockey League orchestrated the most ambitious expansion program in the history of sports by doubling in size from six to twelve teams, the magic word has been parity. The Lords of the NHL lived for the day when the expansion infants could compete on an even keel with the established teams. Parity, they called it. They longed to be able to say that on any given night, any team could beat any other team.

For a long time, that just wasn't so. The expansion teams always seemed a stride or two behind the established clubs. And on those rare occasions when a new club rose up to kayo one of its big brothers, the loss was considered a total disaster. The expansion teams were whipping boys. Parity was a dream for the distant future.

Then, in 1973–74, along came the Broad Street Bullies, alias Philadelphia Flyers. The team of tough guys was led by Bobby Clarke, a diabetic center

Bernie Parent, winner of the Conn Smythe Trophy as playoff MVP and the NHL's top netminder, shuts the door on Boston's Phil Esposito, the league's top scorer, and season's MVP. UPI

The head of the Broad Street Bullies was Dave Schultz (hand upraised), who amassed a record 348 minutes in the penalty box. UPI

with a choir-boy expression, and goalie Bernie Parent, who was the first NHL player to jump to the World Hockey Association, and also one of the first to jump back.

The Flyers lived by the coaching creed of scholarly-looking Fred Shero, who often said, "If you can't beat the other team in the alley, you can't beat them on the ice." First Philadelphia would win the alley fight, then repeat on the ice. "We take the most direct route to the puck," philosophized Clarke, captain of the Bullies, "and we arrive in ill humor."

Most of the Flyers were acquired by General Manager Keith Allen through clever trades. In one of his deals, Allen swapped goalie Parent to Toronto to bring a forward named Rick MacLeish to Philadelphia. Parent studied for two seasons under his goaltending idol, Jacques Plante, then fled to the WHA. MacLeish, meanwhile, developed into a 50-goal scorer for the talented young Flyers.

When Parent grew disenchanted with the WHA, he let it be known that he wanted to return to the older league. Allen immediately swung a deal for his rights with Toronto and then signed the goalie to a multi-year contract with Philadelphia.

Back with the Flyers, Parent found some old friends in veteran defensemen Joe Watson and Ed Van Impe, both leftovers from the original Philadelphia expansion team, and some new friends in tough Andre Dupont and Barry Ashbee, acquired through trades, and youngsters Jim Watson and Tom Bladon, draft choices. Together, the defensemen and Parent gave the Flyers the stingiest defense in the NHL. The goalie played in a backbreaking 73 games and compiled a sparkling 1.89 average with 12 shutouts—by far the best individual netminding numbers in the NHL.

The Flyers won the West Division crown by a comfortable seven points over Chicago—the first time the established Black Hawks had missed winning the crown in four seasons in the expansionist West Division. In the East, Boston, led by scoring champion Phil Esposito, finished a fat 14 points ahead of runner-up Montreal. Esposito won his fourth straight scoring title and fifth in the last six years with 145 points.

En route to their division crown, the Flyers led the NHL with a staggering 1,750 penalty minutes, 600 minutes more than the next most penalized team. Of the total, a record 348 minutes belonged to the club's No. 1 hatchetman, Dave Schultz.

In the opening round of the playoffs, Philadelphia wiped out the surprising Atlanta Flames in four straight games and Boston did the same to Toronto. Chicago went five to eliminate Los Angeles while the New York Rangers knocked off the defending Stanley Cup champion Montreal Canadiens in six games.

The semifinals were a struggle. The Bruins eliminated Chicago in six

Buffalo's Rick Martin, eluding Toronto's Pierre Jarry, was the NHL's second-leading goal scorer with 52.   ROBERT SHAVER

games and Philadelphia had to go seven to beat New York. That was a landmark victory. It marked the first time an expansion team had eliminated an established club in the playoffs. Parity, it seemed, was on its way. Two weeks later, it arrived.

Paced by Parent, the Flyers defeated the Bruins in the six-game championship round and brought the Stanley Cup to Philadelphia. The clincher was a 1–0 shutout spun by Parent with the only goal scored, ironically, by MacLeish, the man for whom the goalie once was traded.

Parent, whose airtight goaltending earned him the Conn Smythe Trophy as the Most Valuable Player of the playoffs, and Chicago's Tony Esposito were co-winners of the Vezina Trophy as the netminders with the lowest goals against average during the regular season.

Boston's Phil Esposito won the Hart Trophy as the league's MVP, while teammate Bobby Orr was the winner of the Norris Trophy as the NHL's top defenseman for a record seventh consecutive season.

New York Islander defenseman Denis Potvin was chosen winner of the Calder Memorial Trophy as Rookie of the Year. Boston's John Bucyk was named the Lady Byng Memorial Trophy winner for combined sportsmanship and ability, and Montreal's Henri Richard was the recipient of the Bill Masterton Memorial Trophy for dedication to hockey.

690

1973–74 ALL-STAR TEAM

First		Second
Parent, Philadelphia	Goal	Esposito, Chicago
Orr, Boston	Defense	Ashbee, Philadelphia
Park, New York R.	Defense	White, Chicago
Esposito, Boston	Center	Clarke, Philadelphia
Hodge, Boston	Right Wing	Redmond, Detroit
Martin, Buffalo	Left Wing	Cashman, Boston

1973–74
NHL FINAL STANDINGS

East Division

	W	L	T	PTS	GF	GA
Boston	52	17	9	113	349	221
Montreal	45	24	9	99	293	240
New York Rangers	40	24	14	94	300	251
Toronto	35	27	16	86	274	230
Buffalo	32	34	12	76	242	250
Detroit	29	39	10	68	255	319
Vancouver	24	43	11	59	224	296
New York Islanders	19	41	18	56	182	247

West Division

	W	L	T	PTS	GF	GA
Philadelphia	50	16	12	112	273	164
Chicago	41	14	23	105	272	164
Los Angeles	33	33	12	78	233	231
Atlanta	30	34	14	74	214	238
Pittsburgh	28	41	9	65	242	273
St. Louis	26	40	12	64	206	248
Minnesota	23	38	17	63	235	275
California	13	55	10	36	195	342

Leading Scorers	G	A	Pts
Esposito, Bos.	68	77	145
Orr, Bos.	32	90	122
Hodge, Bos.	50	55	105
Cashman, Bos.	30	59	89
Clarke, Phi.	35	52	87
Martin, Buf.	52	34	86
Apps, Pitt.	24	61	85
Sittler, Tor.	38	46	84
L. MacDonald, Pitt.	43	39	82
Park, N.Y.R.	25	57	82
D. Hextall, Minn.	20	62	82

TWENTY-SEVENTH ALL-STAR GAME January 29, 1974 at Chicago
West 6, East 4

When Montreal teammates Frank Mahovlich and Yvan Cournoyer scored first period goals, it seemed that the established East Division was on its way to another All-Star victory over the expansionist West.

In four previous meetings between the two divisions, the young West had won only once and it looked like an instant replay when the East rushed to the early lead again before a capacity crowd in old Chicago Stadium.

But just as suddenly as the East had burst in front in the opening 20 minutes of the game, did the West strike back in the second period. Goals by Los Angeles' Bob Berry, Atlanta's Al McDonough, and Pittsburgh's Lowell MacDonald gave the West Stars the lead with only one period to go.

The East came out fast in the final period but it was the West that scored. Hometown hero Stan Mikita of Chicago made it 4–2 and then a short-handed goal by St. Louis' Garry Unger increased the West lead to 5–2.

The New York Islanders' Denis Potvin, the only first-year man in the game, connected for the East and then Detroit's Mickey Redmond scored, narrowing the East deficit to one goal. But Chicago's Pit Martin put the game out of reach in the final minute, wrapping up the 6–4 victory.

The 10 goals scored set an All-Star Game record. The stars were rookie Potvin for the East, and veterans Mikita, who had a goal and two assists, and Unger, who scored a goal and an assist for the West. Unger was the game's Most Valuable Player.

East All-Stars: Goal—Gilbert (Boston), D. Dryden (Buffalo). Defense —Smith (Boston), Park (N.Y. Rangers), D. Potvin (N.Y. Islanders), Robinson (Montreal), McKenny (Toronto), Guevremont (Vancouver). Forwards—P. Esposito (Boston), Ullman (Toronto), Martin (Buffalo), Cashman (Boston), Westfall (N.Y. Islanders), F. Mahovlich (Montreal), Hodge (Boston), Cournoyer (Montreal), Schmautz (Vancouver), Redmond (Detroit), Berenson (Detroit), Richard (Montreal). Coach—Scotty Bowman (Montreal).

West All-Stars: Goal—Parent (Philadelphia), T. Esposito (Chicago). Defense—White (Chicago), Burrows (Pittsburgh), Awrey (St. Louis), B. Plager (St. Louis), Van Impe (Philadelphia), Joe Watson (Philadelphia). Forwards—Clarke (Philadelphia), Hextall (Minnesota), Mikita (Chicago), Unger (St. Louis), D. Hull (Chicago), MacDonald (Pittsburgh), Johnston (California), Berry (Los Angeles), Goldsworthy (Minnesota), McDonough (Atlanta), Pappin (Chicago), Martin (Chicago). Coach—Billy Reay (Chicago).

First Period: 1. East, F. Mahovlich (Cournoyer, Ullman) 3:33. 2. East, Cournoyer (Ullman) 16:20. Penalty—Martin.

Second Period: 3. West, Berry (Mikita) 5:59. 4. West, McDonough (Clarke, MacDonald) 13:55. 5. West, MacDonald (B. Plager, Awrey) 19:07. Penalties—Hextall, Berenson.

Third Period: 6. West, Mikita (Unger, White) 2:25. 7. West, Unger (White, Mikita) 7:54. 8. East, D. Potvin (unassisted) 9:55. 9. East, M. Redmond (Berenson) 14:55. 10. West, P. Martin (Pappin) 19:13. Penalty—Plager.

Attendance—17,100.

The New York Islanders' Denis Potvin, who scored a goal in the All-Star Game, won the Calder Cup as Rookie of the Year.   UPI

WORLD HOCKEY ASSOCIATION

On March 31, 1971, Gordie Howe celebrated his 43rd birthday, and a week later, upon the completion of his 25th season in the National Hockey League, the game's greatest all-time scorer announced his retirement.

For the next two years, Gordie Howe stagnated in an office, going through the motions of being a vice-president for the Detroit Red Wings. The job just didn't fit and Howe knew it. Meanwhile, his two sons, Mark and Marty, were developing into first-rate hockey players in the Ontario Hockey Association.

It had been Gordie's lifelong dream to play with his boys. But the dream seemed doomed. The oldest boy, Marty, a defenseman, wouldn't be eligible for the NHL draft until 1974 and brother Mark, a left wing, would have to wait until 1975 to reach the draft age of 20. By then, Gordie would be 47 years old.

Then, along came Jim Smith, president of the Houston Aeros of the World Hockey Association. Smith had an idea and made an offer that the Howes couldn't refuse. He imported the whole Howe family—Pop, the two teen-age sons and even Mrs. Howe—and put them to work for the Aeros. For Gordie, it meant a million-dollar contract and, more important, the chance to play as a teammate with his sons.

The signing coup jolted the NHL, not only over the loss of two promising young players with a magic name, but by the departure of their father, considered one of the very foundations of the older league.

The Howe haul paid immediate dividends for Houston. Playing as if he had never been away from the game, Gordie missed only eight games all season, scored 100 points and was named the league's Most Valuable Player after winning the award six times previously in the NHL. Mark won WHA Rookie of the Year honors, besting Claude St. Sauveur of the Vancouver Blazers and Tom Simpson of the Toronto Toros. He totaled 38 goals and 79 points, ranking him 14th in the league in scoring.

The only players with more points than Gordie were Minnesota's Mike Walton, who won the scoring championship with 57 goals and 117 points, and Andre Lacroix, the 1972–73 scoring champ, who finished second with 111 points.

Led by the three Howes and some stingy goaltending by Don McLeod, Houston won the WHA's Western Division championship, finishing 11 points ahead of runner-up Minnesota. In the East, New England repeated as division champion, a scant four points ahead of Toronto, whose Billy Harris was named Coach of the Year.

In the playoffs, Winnipeg and New England, finalists for the Avco World Trophy a year earlier, both were kayoed in the first round of the playoffs. Even Bobby Hull, who reached the 50-goal plateau for the seventh time in

Gordie Howe (left) and sons Marty (center) and Mark made the Houston Aeros champions of the WHA.   UPI

his 17-year professional career, couldn't prevent Winnipeg from bowing to the Howe-led Aeros in four straight games. Chicago, whose player-coach Pat Stapleton was voted the league's top defenseman, stung New England, Toronto took Cleveland, and Minnesota eliminated Edmonton in other first round action.

In the semifinals, Chicago ousted Toronto in a grueling seven-game series while Houston downed Minnesota in six, winning the last three in a row. Then, the Aeros wiped out Chicago in four straight games for the championship, Houston's first in professional sports since 1961. The score of the final game was 6–2 and on four of Houston's goals an elderly right-winger named Howe picked up assists.

It was the fifth championship team for Gordie Howe and probably the most satisfying because two of his teammates this time were his teen-age sons.

695

Gordie Howe (left) was named the WHA's MVP and Marty Howe (3) was the league's Rookie of the Year.   UPI

1973–74
WHA FINAL STANDINGS
East Division

	W	L	T	PTS	GF	GA
New England	43	31	4	90	291	260
Toronto	41	33	4	86	304	272
Cleveland	37	32	9	83	266	264
Chicago	38	35	5	81	271	273
Quebec	38	36	4	80	306	280
New Jersey	32	42	4	68	268	313

West Division

	W	L	T	PTS	GF	GA
Houston	48	25	5	101	318	219
Minnesota	44	32	2	90	332	275
Edmonton	38	37	3	79	268	269
Winnipeg	34	39	5	73	264	296
Vancouver	27	50	1	55	278	345
Los Angeles	25	53	0	50	239	339

Leading Scorers	G	A	Pts
Walton, Minn.	57	60	117
Lacroix, N.J.	31	80	111
G. Howe, Hous.	31	69	100
Hull, Winn.	53	42	95
Connelly, Minn.	42	53	95
Carleton, Tor.	37	55	92
Lawson, Vanc.	50	38	88
Campbell, Vanc.	27	61	88
Bernier, Que.	37	49	86
Lund, Hous.	33	53	86

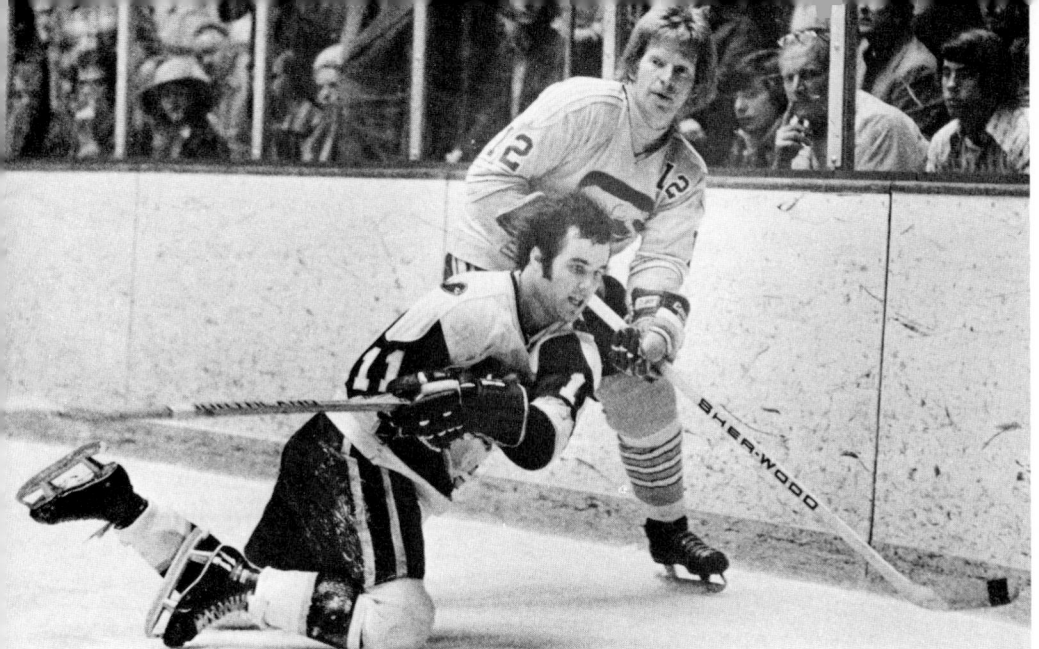

Chicago Cougar coach Pat Stapleton (12), dueling with New England's John French, was the WHA's top backliner. CHICAGO COUGARS

Minnesota's Mike Walton flew past opposing forwards for a 57-goal season and the WHA scoring crown. UPI

SECOND WHA ALL-STAR GAME January 3, 1974 at St. Paul
East 8, West 4

The World Hockey Association played its 1974 All-Star Game in the beautiful St. Paul Civic Center, home of the Minnesota Fighting Saints. The game happened to fall on the 29th birthday of Mike Walton, one of the Saints' top players.

Walton celebrated in fine style, giving himself a birthday gift of three goals. Unfortunately for the West stars, he was the only one celebrating. Walton's hat trick and a goal by Larry Lund of Houston weren't nearly enough to overcome the high-powered East offense.

The East exploded for five goals in the first period by five different shooters. In the first 11 minutes, Quebec's Rejean Houle, Chicago's Ralph Backstrom, and New England's Larry Pleau had staked the East to a comfortable lead. After Walton scored his first goal, Cleveland's Gerry Pinder and Jersey's Andre Lacroix connected for a 5–1 East lead.

The second period belonged to the West, with two goals by Walton and one by Lund sandwiching the lone East goal by Chicago's Rosaire Paiement. Then Lacroix and Pleau each scored his second goal of the game in the final period to secure the East's 8–4 decision.

A crowd of 13,196 packed the St. Paul rink and hometown hero Walton's hat trick earned him selection as the contest's Most Valuable Player. The other stars were the East's Lacroix, with two goals and an assist, and defenseman Pat Stapleton of Chicago.

East All-Stars: Goal—Smith (New England), Cheevers (Cleveland), Gratton (Toronto). Defense—Stapleton (Chicago), Selwood (New England), Ley (New England), Hoganson (Quebec), Tremblay (Quebec), Shmyr (Cleveland). Forwards—Backstrom (Chicago), Bernier (Quebec), Carleton (Toronto), Pleau (New England), Lacroix (Jersey), Jarrett (Cleveland), Harris (New England), Houle (Quebec), Sheehan (Jersey), Webster (New England), Pinder (Cleveland), Paiement (Chicago), Simpson (Toronto). Coach—Jack Kelly (New England).

West All-Stars: Goal—Norris (Edmonton), Garrett (Minnesota), Wakely (Winnipeg). Defense—Hamilton (Edmonton), Hornung (Winnipeg), Smith (Minnesota), Popiel (Houston), Crashley (Los Angeles), Odrowski (Los Angeles), MacSweyn (Vancouver). Forwards—Harrison (Edmonton), B. Hull (Winnipeg), Hughes (Houston), Lawson (Vancouver), G. Howe (Houston), Climie (Edmonton), Tardif (Los Angeles), Walton (Minnesota), Lund (Houston), Huck (Winnipeg), Campbell (Vancouver), Connelly (Minnesota). Coach—Bobby Hull (Winnipeg).

First Period: 1. East, Houle (Bernier, Paiement) 2:11. 2. East, Backstrom (Carleton, Stapleton) 8:02. 3. East, Pleau (Houte, Paiement) 10:39.

4. West, Walton (Lawson) 14:55. 5. East, Pinder (Lacroix, Shmyr) 18:38. 6. East, Lacroix (Jarrett, Pinder) 19:12.

Second Period: 7. West, Walton (Hull, Tardif) 7:27. 8. East, Paiement (Backstrom) 9:15. 9. West, Walton (Hamilton, Climie) 16:04. 10. West, Lund (Hamilton, Hughes) 17:28.

Third Period: 11. East, Lacroix (Jarrett, Pinder) 9:17. 12. East, Pleau (Harris, Webster) 18:59.

Attendance—13,196.

Jersey's Andre Lacroix (right) is congratulated by goalie Gilles Gratton after scoring two goals to power the East to an 8–4 conquest in the WHA All-Star Game.

UPI

A stickless Minnesota goalie Brad Shelstad, stopping Michigan Tech's George Lyle, was voted MVP as the Golden Gophers won the NCAA title. UPI

COLLEGE HOCKEY

Led by the nearly perfect netminding of goalie Brad Shelstad, the University of Minnesota won the National Collegiate Athletic Association championship, upsetting Michigan Tech, 4–2 in the 1974 final game.

Shelstad was selected the tournament's Most Valuable Player after blocking 34 of 36 shots in the title game, and nailing down Minnesota's first NCAA hockey crown.

Coached by Herb Brooks, a member of the United States' 1960 Olympic championship team, the Golden Gophers reached the finals of the tournament by edging Boston University, 5–4 on a shorthanded goal by Mike Polich with only 13 seconds left to play.

Michigan Tech, ranked No. 1 nationally, eliminated Harvard, 6–5 in the tournament's semifinal with Bill Steele's overtime goal deciding the contest.

That set up an all West game for the national crown at Boston Garden. The title game was scoreless for 16 minutes before John Sheridan got Minnesota on the scoreboard. Joe Perpich made it 2–0 early in the second period before George Lyle's goal cut the Gopher lead in half after two periods. Bobby Harris and Papt Phippen gave Shelstad some operating room, building Minnesota's lead to 4–1 before Mike Zuke's last-minute goal for Michigan completed the scoring.

Every player on the championship Minnesota team was an American from the state of Minnesota. That stood in stark contrast to the Michigan Tech team which had only five American players on the 19-man roster.

The championship game summary:

First Period: 1. Minnesota, Sheridan (Miller, Phippen) 15:26.

Second Period: 2. Minnesota, Perpich (Morrow, Polich) 3:24. 3. Michigan Tech, Lyle (D'Alvise) 13:40.

Third Period: 4. Minnesota, R. Harris (Matschke) 4:45. 5. Minnesota, Phippen (Sheridan) 17:17. 6. Michigan Tech, Zuke (Steele, Stemler) 19:12.

Attendance—7,164.

WORLD CHAMPIONSHIPS

In the fall of 1972, Russia's National hockey team played an eight-game series against Team Canada, a squad of the finest players in the National Hockey League. The professionals won that series but the Russians earned enormous respect for their play. They lost that series by the barest of margins, a late goal in the final period of the final game by Paul Henderson. But they had given Team Canada a tremendous scare and proved that their domination of amateur hockey was no accident.

International hockey has been ruled by the Soviets ever since they began studying the game seriously. Russia won 10 consecutive world hockey championships, including three Olympic titles, until the streak was halted by Czechoslovakia in the 1972 world tournament. But the Russians regained their title in 1973 and repeated again in the 1974 tourney held at Helsinki, Finland.

Canada sat out its fourth straight world tournament because of a dispute with the International Hockey Federation over the use of professionals. The United States was eligible only for Group B competition in 1974. That left Czechoslovakia, Finland and Sweden as the top challengers to the Soviet team.

Both Sweden and Finland were forced to forfeit games they had won because of the discovery that some players had used a forbidden stimulant, ephedrine. As the tournament continued, it became obvious that it would come down to a battle between Russia and Czechoslovakia. With two games left to play, the teams were tied for first place and faced each other.

Czechoslovakia took the early lead on a power play goal by Jiri Holik. It stayed 1–0 until midway through the second period when the Russians charged back. The Soviets bunched goals by Boris Mihailov, Aleksander Malchev and Aleksander Yakushev for a 3–1 victory.

Two days later, the Soviets clinched the crown, defeating Sweden, 3–1. Vladimir Shadrin, Valeri Kharlamov, and Malchev scored the goals and the Russians outshot the Swedes, 57–18.

Czechoslovakia finished second in the tournament and Sweden was third.

The Soviets placed Yakushev and defenseman Valeri Vasilyev on the tournament All-Star team.

HALL OF FAME

Seven new members were added to the Hockey Hall of Fame in 1974. The new inductees were Tommy Ivan, Dickie Moore, Carl Voss, Charles Hay, Art Coulter, Tom Dunderdale and Billy Burch.

Ivan coached the Detroit Red Wings to six consecutive National Hockey League championships and three Stanley Cups before moving on to Chicago Black Hawks, where he has been general manager.

Moore won two NHL scoring championships and played on six Stanley Cup championship teams with the Montreal Canadiens. In 1959, he set a scoring record with 96 points.

Hay, former president of Hockey Canada, played a major role in arrangements for the Team Canada-Russia series in 1972.

Voss was NHL Rookie of the Year in 1932–33 with the Detroit Red Wings and was named the NHL's first referee-in-chief in 1950.

Coulter played 10 years in the NHL with Chicago and the New York Rangers. He was named captain of the Rangers in 1935 and helped the team to its last Stanley Cup in 1940.

Burch, who played for the New York Americans, Boston and Chicago, won the Hart Trophy as the NHL's Most Valuable Player in 1925 and the Lady Byng for sportsmanship and effective play two years later.

Dunderdale, a native of Australia, joined the National Hockey Association, predecessor to the NHL, in 1910 and later played four seasons with Victoria of the Pacific Coast Hockey Association where he won the league scoring title in 1913 and 1914.